THE NORTON ANTHOLOGY OF

AMERICAN

LITERATURE

NINTH EDITION

VOLUME E: LITERATURE SINCE 1945

Michael A. Elliott
PROFESSOR OF ENGLISH AND AMERICAN STUDIES
EMORY UNIVERSITY

Sandra M. Gustafson
PROFESSOR OF ENGLISH AND AMERICAN STUDIES
UNIVERSITY OF NOTRE DAME

Amy Hungerford
PROFESSOR OF ENGLISH AND AMERICAN STUDIES
AND DIRECTOR OF THE DIVISION OF THE HUMANITIES
YALE UNIVERSITY

Mary Loeffelholz
PROFESSOR OF ENGLISH
NORTHEASTERN UNIVERSITY

THE NORTON ANTHOLOGY OF

AMERICAN LITERATURE

NINTH EDITION

Robert S. Levine, *General Editor*

PROFESSOR OF ENGLISH AND
DISTINGUISHED UNIVERSITY PROFESSOR AND
DISTINGUISHED SCHOLAR–TEACHER
University of Maryland, College Park

VOLUME E: LITERATURE SINCE 1945

W·W·NORTON & COMPANY

NEW YORK · LONDON

W. W. Norton & Company has been independent since its founding in 1923, when William Warder Norton and Mary D. Herter Norton first published lectures delivered at the People's Institute, the adult education division of New York City's Cooper Union. The firm soon expanded its program beyond the Institute, publishing books by celebrated academics from America and abroad. By midcentury, the two major pillars of Norton's publishing program—trade books and college texts—were firmly established. In the 1950s, the Norton family transferred control of the company to its employees, and today—with a staff of four hundred and a comparable number of trade, college, and professional titles published each year—W. W. Norton & Company stands as the largest and oldest publishing house owned wholly by its employees.

Editor: Julia Reidhead
Managing Editor, College: Marian Johnson
Manuscript Editors: Kurt Wildermuth, Harry Haskell, Michael Fleming, Candace Levy
Assistant Editor: Rachel Taylor
Managing Editor, College Digital Media: Kim Yi
Media Editor: Carly Fraser Doria
Assistant Media Editor: Ava Bramson
Media Project Editor: Kristin Sheerin
Marketing Manager, Literature: Kimberly Bowers
Production Manager: Sean Mintus
Art Director: Debra Morton Hoyt
Text Design: Jo Anne Metsch
Cover Design: Tiani Kennedy
Photo Editor: Cat Abelman
Photo Research: Julie Tesser
Permissions Manager: Megan Jackson Schindel
Permissions Clearing: Margaret Gorenstein
Composition: Westchester Book Group

ISBN: 978-0-393-26450-0

W. W. Norton & Company, Inc., 500 Fifth Avenue, New York, NY 10110
wwnorton.com

W. W. Norton & Company Ltd., 15 Carlisle Street, London W1D 3BS

1 2 3 4 5 6 7 8 9 0

Contents

American Literature since 1945

Preface to the Ninth Edition

The Ninth Edition of *The Norton Anthology of American Literature* is the first for me as General Editor; for the Eighth Edition, I served as Associate General Editor under longstanding General Editor Nina Baym. On the occasion of a new general editorship, we have undertaken one of the most extensive revisions in our long publishing history. Three new section editors have joined the team: Sandra M. Gustafson, Professor of English and Concurrent Professor of American Studies at the University of Notre Dame, who succeeds Wayne Franklin and Philip Gura as editor of "American Literature, Beginnings to 1820"; Michael A. Elliott, Professor of English at Emory University, who succeeds Nina Baym, Robert S. Levine, and Jeanne Campbell Reesman as editor of "American Literature, 1865–1914"; and Amy Hungerford, Professor of English and American Studies at Yale University, who succeeds Jerome Klinkowitz and Patricia B. Wallace as editor of "American Literature since 1945." These editors join Robert S. Levine, editor of "American Literature, 1820–1865," and Mary Loeffelholz, editor of "American Literature, 1914–1945." Each editor, new or continuing, is a well-known expert in the relevant field or period and has ultimate responsibility for his or her section of the anthology, but we have worked closely from first to last to rethink all aspects of this new edition. Volume introductions, author headnotes, thematic clusters, annotations, illustrations, and bibliographies have all been updated and revised. We have also added a number of new authors, selections, and thematic clusters. We are excited about the outcome of our collaboration and anticipate that, like the previous eight editions, this edition of *The Norton Anthology of American Literature* will continue to lead the field.

From the anthology's inception in 1979, the editors have had three main aims: first, to present a rich and substantial enough variety of works to enable teachers to build courses according to their own vision of American literary history (thus, teachers are offered more authors and more selections than they will probably use in any one course); second, to make the anthology self-sufficient by featuring many works in their entirety along with extensive selections for individual authors; third, to balance traditional interests with developing critical concerns in a way that allows for the complex, rigorous, and capacious study of American literary traditions. As early as 1979, we anthologized work by Anne Bradstreet, Mary Rowlandson, Sarah Kemble Knight, Phillis Wheatley, Margaret Fuller, Harriet Beecher Stowe, Frederick Douglass, Sarah Orne Jewett, Kate Chopin, Mary E. Wilkins Freeman, Booker T. Washington, Charles W. Chesnutt, Edith Wharton,

W. E. B. Du Bois, and other writers who were not yet part of a standard canon. Yet we never shortchanged writers—such as Franklin, Emerson, Whitman, Hawthorne, Melville, Dickinson, Hemingway, Fitzgerald, and Faulkner—whose work many students expected to read in their American literature courses, and whom most teachers then and now would not think of doing without.

The so-called canon wars of the 1980s and 1990s usefully initiated a review of our understanding of American literature, a review that has enlarged the number and diversity of authors now recognized as contributors to the totality of American literature. The traditional writers look different in this expanded context, and they also appear different according to which of their works are selected. Teachers and students remain committed to the idea of the literary—that writers strive to produce artifacts that are both intellectually serious and formally skillful—but believe more than ever that writers should be understood in relation to their cultural and historical situations. We address the complex interrelationships between literature and history in the volume introductions, author headnotes, chronologies, and some of the footnotes. As in previous editions, we have worked with detailed suggestions from many teachers on how best to present the authors and selections. We have gained insights as well from the students who use the anthology. Thanks to questionnaires, face-to-face and phone discussions, letters, and email, we have been able to listen to those for whom this book is intended. For the Ninth Edition, we have drawn on the careful commentary of over 240 reviewers and reworked aspects of the anthology accordingly.

Our new materials continue the work of broadening the canon by representing thirteen new writers in depth, without sacrificing widely assigned writers, many of whose selections have been reconsidered, reselected, and expanded. Our aim is always to provide extensive enough selections to do the writers justice, including complete works wherever possible. Our Ninth Edition offers complete longer works, including Hawthorne's *The Scarlet Letter* and Kate Chopin's *The Awakening*, and such new and recently added works as Margaret Fuller's *The Great Lawsuit*, Abraham Cahan's *Yekl: A Tale of the New York Ghetto*, Nella Larsen's *Passing*, Katherine Anne Porter's *Pale Horse, Pale Rider*, Nathanael West's *The Day of the Locust*, and August Wilson's *Fences*. Two complete works—Eugene O'Neill's *Long Day's Journey into Night* and Tennessee Williams's *A Streetcar Named Desire*—are exclusive to *The Norton Anthology of American Literature*. Charles Brockden Brown, Louisa May Alcott, Upton Sinclair, and Junot Díaz are among the writers added to the prior edition, and to this edition we have introduced John Rollin Ridge, Constance Fenimore Woolson, George Saunders, and Natasha Trethewey, among others. We have also expanded and in some cases reconfigured such central figures as Franklin, Hawthorne, Dickinson, Twain, and Hemingway, offering new approaches in the headnotes, along with some new selections. In fact, the headnotes and, in many cases, selections for such frequently assigned authors as William Bradford, Washington Irving, James Fenimore Cooper, William Cullen Bryant, Lydia Maria Child, Henry Wadsworth Longfellow, Ralph Waldo Emerson, Harriet Beecher Stowe, Mark Twain, William Dean Howells, Henry James, Kate Chopin, W. E. B. Du Bois, Edith Wharton, Willa Cather, and William

Faulkner have been revised, updated, and in some cases entirely rewritten in light of recent scholarship. The Ninth Edition further expands its selections of women writers and writers from diverse ethnic, racial, and regional backgrounds—always with attention to the critical acclaim that recognizes their contributions to the American literary record. New and recently added writers such as Samson Occom, Jane Johnston Schoolcraft, John Rollin Ridge, and Sarah Winnemucca, along with the figures represented in "Voices from Native America," enable teachers to bring early Native American writing and oratory into their syllabi, or should they prefer, to focus on these selections as a freestanding unit leading toward the moment after 1945 when Native writers fully entered the mainstream of literary activity.

We are pleased to continue our popular innovation of topical gatherings of short texts that illuminate the cultural, historical, intellectual, and literary concerns of their respective periods. Designed to be taught in a class period or two, or used as background, each of the sixteen clusters consists of brief, carefully excerpted primary and (in one case) secondary texts, about six to ten per cluster, and an introduction. Diverse voices—many new to the anthology—highlight a range of views current when writers of a particular time period were active, and thus allow students better to understand some of the large issues that were being debated at particular historical moments. For example, in "Slavery, Race, and the Making of American Literature," texts by David Walker, William Lloyd Garrison, Angelina Grimké, Sojourner Truth, James M. Whitfield, and Martin R. Delany speak to the great paradox of pre–Civil War America: the contradictory rupture between the realities of slavery and the nation's ideals of freedom.

The Ninth Edition strengthens this feature with eight new and revised clusters attuned to the requests of teachers. To help students address the controversy over race and aesthetics in *Adventures of Huckleberry Finn*, we have revised a cluster in Volume C that shows what some of the leading critics of the past few decades thought was at stake in reading and interpreting slavery and race in Twain's canonical novel. New to Volume A is "American Literature and the Varieties of Religious Expression," which includes selections by Elizabeth Ashbridge, John Woolman, and John Marrant, while Volume B offers "Science and Technology in the Pre–Civil War Nation." Volume C newly features "Becoming American in the Gilded Age," and we continue to include the useful "Modernist Manifestos" in Volume D. We have added to the popular "Creative Nonfiction" in Volume E new selections by David Foster Wallace and Hunter S. Thompson, who join such writers as Jamaica Kincaid and Joan Didion.

The Ninth Edition features an expanded illustration program, both of the black-and-white images, 145 of which are placed throughout the volumes, and of the color plates so popular in the last two editions. In selecting color plates—from Elizabeth Graham's embroidered map of Washington, D.C., at the start of the nineteenth century to Jeff Wall's "After 'Invisible Man'" at the beginning of the twenty-first—the editors aim to provide images relevant to literary works in the anthology while depicting arts and artifacts representative of each era. In addition, graphic works—segments from the colonial children's classic *The New-England Primer* and from Art Spiegelman's canonical graphic novel, *Maus*, and a facsimile page of Emily Dickinson manuscript, along with the many new illustrations—open possibilities for teaching visual texts.

Period-by-Period Revisions

Volume A, Beginnings to 1820. Sandra M. Gustafson, the new editor of Volume A, has substantially revised the volume. Prior editions of Volume A were broken into two historical sections, with two introductions and a dividing line at the year 1700; Gustafson has dropped that artificial divide to tell a more coherent and fluid story (in her new introduction) about the variety of American literatures during this long period. The volume continues to feature narratives by early European explorers of the North American continent as they encountered and attempted to make sense of the diverse cultures they met, and as they sought to justify their aim of claiming the territory for Europeans. These are precisely the issues foregrounded by the revised cluster "First Encounters: Early European Accounts of Native America," which gathers writings by Hernán Cortés, Samuel de Champlain, Robert Juet, and others, including the newly added Thomas Harriot. In addition to the standing material from *The Bay Psalm Book*, we include new material by Roger Williams; additional poems by Annis Boudinot Stockton; Abigail Adams's famous letter urging her husband to "Remember the Ladies"; an additional selection from Olaudah Equiano on his post-emancipation travels; and Charles Brockden Brown's "Memoirs of Carwin the Biloquist" (the complete "prequel" to his first novel, *Wieland*). We continue to offer the complete texts of Rowlandson's enormously influential *A Narrative of the Captivity and Restoration of Mrs. Mary Rowlandson*, Benjamin Franklin's *Autobiography* (which remains one of the most compelling works on the emergence of an "American" self), Royall Tyler's popular play *The Contrast*, and Hannah Foster's novel *The Coquette*, which uses a real-life tragedy to meditate on the proper role of well-bred women in the new republic and testifies to the existence of a female audience for the popular novels of the period. New to this volume is Washington Irving, a writer who looks back to colonial history and forward to Jacksonian America. The inclusion of Irving in both Volumes A and B, with one key overlapping selection, points to continuities and changes between the two volumes.

Five new and revised thematic clusters of texts highlight themes central to Volume A. In addition to "First Encounters," we have included "Native American Oral Literature," "American Literature and the Varieties of Religious Expression," "Ethnographic and Naturalist Writings," and "Native American Eloquence: Negotiation and Resistance." "Native American Oral Literature" features creation stories, trickster tales, oratory, and poetry from a spectrum of traditions, while "Native American Eloquence" collects speeches and accounts by Canassatego and Native American women (both new to the volume), Pontiac, Chief Logan (as cited by Thomas Jefferson), and Tecumseh, which, as a group, illustrate the centuries-long pattern of initial peaceful contact between Native Americans and whites mutating into bitter and violent conflict. This cluster, which focuses on Native Americans' points of view, complements "First Encounters," which focuses on European colonizers' points of view. The Native American presence in the volume is further expanded with increased representation of Samson Occom, which includes an excerpt from his sermon at the execution of Moses Paul, and the inclusion of Sagoyewatha in "American Literature and the Varieties of Religious Expression." Strategically located between the Congregationalist Protestant (or late-Puritan) Jonathan Edwards and the Enlightenment figure Franklin, this cluster brings together works from the perspectives of the major religious groups of the early Americas, including Quakerism (poems by Francis Daniel Pastorius, selections from autographical narratives of Elizabeth Ashbridge and John Woolman), Roman Catholicism (poems by Sor Juana, two Jesuit Relations, with biographical accounts of Father Isaac Jogues and Kateri Tekakwitha), dissenting Protestantism (Marrant), Judaism (Rebecca Samuel), and indigenous beliefs (Sagoyewatha). The new cluster "Ethnographic and Naturalist Writings" includes writings by Sarah Kemble Knight and William Byrd, along with new selections by Alexander Hamilton, William Bartram, and Hendrick Aupaumut. With this cluster, the new cluster on science and technology in Volume B, and a number of new selections and revisions in Volumes C, D, and E, the Ninth Edition pays greater attention to the impact of science on American literary traditions.

Volume B, American Literature, 1820–1865. Under the editorship of Robert S. Levine, this volume over the past several editions has become more diverse. Included here are the complete texts of Emerson's *Nature*, Hawthorne's *Scarlet Letter*, Thoreau's *Walden*, Douglass's *Narrative*, Whitman's *Song of Myself*, Melville's *Benito Cereno* and *Billy Budd*, Rebecca Harding Davis's *Life in the Iron Mills*, and Margaret Fuller's *The Great Lawsuit*. At the same time, aware of the important role of African American writers in the period, and the omnipresence of race and slavery as literary and political themes, we have recently added two major African American writers, William Wells Brown and Frances E. W. Harper, along with Douglass's novella *The Heroic Slave*. Thoreau's "Plea for Captain John Brown," a generous selection from Stowe's *Uncle Tom's Cabin*, and the cluster "Slavery, Race, and the Making of American Literature" also help remind students of how central slavery was to the literary and political life of the nation during this period. "Native Americans: Resistance and Removal" gathers oratory and writings—by Native Americans such as Black Hawk and whites such as Ralph Waldo Emerson—protesting Andrew Jackson's ruthless national policy of Indian removal. Newly added is a selection from *The Life and Adventures of Joaquín Murieta*, by the Native American writer John Rollin Ridge. This potboiler of a novel, set in the new state of California, emerged from the debates that began during the Indian removal period. Through the figure of the legendary Mexican bandit Murieta, who fights back against white expansionists, Ridge responds to the violence encouraged by Jackson and subsequent white leaders as they laid claim to the continent. Political themes, far from diluting the literary imagination of American authors, served to inspire some of the most memorable writing of the pre-Civil War period.

Women writers recently added to Volume B include Lydia Huntley Sigourney, the Native American writer Jane Johnston Schoolcraft, and Louisa May Alcott. Recently added prose fiction includes chapters from Cooper's *The Last of the Mohicans*, Sedgwick's *Hope Leslie*, and Melville's *Moby-Dick*, along with Poe's "The Black Cat" and Hawthorne's "Wakefield."

For the first time, we print Melville's "Hawthorne and His Mosses" as it appeared in the 1850 *Literary World*. Poetry by Emily Dickinson is now presented in the texts established by R. W. Franklin and includes a facsimile page from Fascicle 10. For this edition we have added several poems by Dickinson that were inspired by the Civil War. Other selections added to this edition include Fanny Fern's amusing sketch "Writing 'Compositions,'" the chapter in Frederick Douglass's *My Bondage and My Freedom* on his resistance to the slave-breaker Covey, three poems by Melville ("Dupont's Round Fight," "A Utilitarian View of the Monitor's Fight," and "Art"), and Whitman's "The Sleepers."

Perhaps the most significant addition to Volume B is the cluster "Science and Technology in the Pre–Civil War Nation," with selections by the canonical writers Charles Dickens, Edgar Allan Poe, and Frederick Douglass, by the scientists Jacob Bigelow and Alexander Humboldt, and by the editor-writer Harriet Farley. The cluster calls attention to the strong interest in science and technology throughout this period and should provide a rich context for reconsidering works such as Thoreau's *Walden* and Melville's "The Paradise of Bachelors and the Tartarus of Maids." In an effort to underscore the importance of science and technology to Poe and Hawthorne in particular, we have added two stories that directly address these topics: Poe's "The Facts in the Case of M. Valdemar" and Hawthorne's "The Artist of the Beautiful" (which reads nicely in relation to his "The Birth-Mark" and "Rappaccini's Daughter"). Emerson, Whitman, and Dickinson are among the many other authors in Volume B who had considerable interest in science.

Volume C, American Literature, 1865–1914. Newly edited by Michael A. Elliott, the volume includes expanded selections of key works, as well as new ones that illustrate how many of the struggles of this period prefigure our own. In addition to complete longer works such as Twain's *Adventures of Huckleberry Finn*, Chopin's *The Awakening*, James's *Daisy Miller*, and Stephen Crane's *Maggie: A Girl of the Streets*, the Ninth Edition now includes the complete text of *Yekl: A Tale of the New York Ghetto*, a highly influential novella of immigrant life that depicts the pressures facing newly arrived Jews in the nation's largest metropolis. Also new is a substantial selection from Sarah Orne Jewett's *The Country of the Pointed Firs*, a masterpiece of literary regionalism that portrays a remote seaside community facing change.

Americans are still reflecting on the legacy of the Civil War, and we have added two works approaching that subject from different angles. Constance Fenimore Woolson's "Rodman the Keeper" tells the story of a Union veteran who maintains a cemetery in the South. In "The Private History of a Campaign That Failed," Mark Twain reflects with wit and insight on his own brief experience in the war. In the Eighth Edition, we introduced a section on the critical controversy surrounding race and the conclusion of *Adventures of Huckleberry Finn*. That section remains as important as ever, and new additions incorporate a recent debate about the value of an expurgated edition of the novel.

We have substantially revised clusters designed to give students a sense of the cultural context of the period. New selections in "Realism and Naturalism" demonstrate what was at stake in the debate over realism, among them a feminist response from Charlotte Perkins Gilman. "Becoming

American in the Gilded Age," a new cluster, introduces students to writing about wealth and citizenship at a time when the nation was undergoing transformation. Selections from one of Horatio Alger's popular novels of economic uplift, Andrew Carnegie's "Gospel of Wealth," and Charles W. Chesnutt's "The Future American" together reveal how questions about the composition of the nation both influenced the literature of this period and prefigured contemporary debates on immigration, cultural diversity, and the concentration of wealth.

The turn of the twentieth century was a time of immense literary diversity. "Voices from Native America" brings together a variety of expressive forms—oratory, memoir, ethnography—through which Native Americans sought to represent themselves. It includes new selections by Francis LaFlesche, Zitkala Ša, and Chief Joseph. For the first time, we include the complete text of José Martí's "Our America," in a new translation by Martí biographer Alfred J. López. By instructor request, we have added fiction and nonfiction by African American authors: Charles W. Chesnutt's "Po' Sandy," Pauline Hopkins's "Talma Gordon," and expanded selections from W. E. B. Du Bois's *Souls of Black Folk* and James Weldon Johnson's *Autobiography of an Ex-Colored Man*.

Volume D, American Literature 1914–1945. Edited by Mary Loeffelholz, Volume D offers a number of complete longer works—Eugene O'Neill's *Long Day's Journey into Night* (exclusive to the Norton Anthology), William Faulkner's *As I Lay Dying*, and Willa Cather's *My Ántonia*. To these we have added Nella Larsen's *Passing*, which replaces *Quicksand*, and Nathanael West's *The Day of the Locust*. We added *Passing* in response to numerous requests from instructors and students who regard it as one of the most compelling treatments of racial passing in American literature. The novel also offers rich descriptions of the social and racial geographies of Chicago and New York City. West's darkly comic *The Day of the Locust* similarly offers rich descriptions of the social and racial geography of Los Angeles. West's novel can at times seem bleak and not "politically correct," but in many ways it is the first great American novel about the film industry, and it also has much to say about the growth of California in the early decades of the twentieth century. New selections by Zora Neale Hurston ("Sweat") and John Steinbeck ("The Chrysanthemums") further contribute to the volume's exploration of issues connected with racial and social geographies.

Selections by Ezra Pound, T. S. Eliot, Marianne Moore, Hart Crane, and Langston Hughes encourage students and teachers to contemplate the interrelation of modernist aesthetics with ethnic, regional, and popular writing. In "Modernist Manifestos," F. T. Marinetti, Mina Loy, Ezra Pound, Willa Cather, William Carlos Williams, and Langston Hughes show how the manifesto as a form exerted a powerful influence on international modernism in all the arts. Another illuminating cluster addresses central events of the modern period. In "World War I and Its Aftermath," writings by Ernest Hemingway, Gertrude Stein, Jessie Redmon Fauset, and others explore sharply divided views on the U.S. role in World War I, as well as the radicalizing effect of modern warfare—with 365,000 American casualties—on contemporary writing. We have added to this edition a chapter from Hemingway's first novel, *The Sun Also Rises*, which speaks to the impact of the war on sexuality and gender. Other recent and new additions to Volume D include Faulkner's popular "A Rose for Emily," Katherine Anne Porter's novella *Pale Horse, Pale Rider*, Gertrude Stein's "Objects," Marianne Moore's ambitious longer poem "Marriage," poems by Edgar Lee Masters and Edwin Arlington Robinson, and Jean Toomer's "Blood Burning Moon."

Volume E, American Literature, 1945 to the Present. Amy Hungerford, the new editor of Volume E, has revised the volume to present a wider range of writing in poetry, prose, drama, and nonfiction. As before, the volume offers the complete texts of Tennessee Williams's *A Streetcar Named Desire* (exclusive to this anthology), Arthur Miller's *Death of a Salesman*, Allen Ginsberg's *Howl*, Sam Shepard's *True West*, August Wilson's *Fences*, David Mamet's *Glengarry Glen Ross*, and Louise Glück's long poem *October*. A selection from Art Spiegelman's prize-winning *Maus* opens possibilities for teaching the graphic novel. We also include teachable stand-alone segments from influential novels by Saul Bellow (*The Adventures of Augie March*) and Kurt Vonnegut (*Slaughterhouse-Five*), and, new to this edition, Jack Kerouac (*On the Road*) and Don DeLillo (*White Noise*). The selection from one of DeLillo's most celebrated novels tells what feels like a contemporary story about a nontraditional family navigating an environmental disaster in a climate saturated by mass media. Three newly added stories— Patricia Highsmith's "The Quest for *Blank Claveringi*," Philip K. Dick's "Precious Artifact," and George Saunders's "CivilWarLand in Bad Decline"— reveal the impact of science fiction, fantasy, horror, and (especially in the case of Saunders) mass media on literary fiction. Also appearing for the first time are Edward P. Jones and Lydia Davis, contemporary masters of the short story, who join such short fiction writers as Ann Beattie and Junot Díaz. Recognized literary figures in all genres, ranging from Robert Penn Warren and Elizabeth Bishop to Leslie Marmon Silko and Toni Morrison, continue to be richly represented. In response to instructors' requests, we now include Flannery O'Connor's "A Good Man Is Hard to Find" and James Baldwin's "Sonny's Blues."

One of the most distinctive features of twentieth- and twenty-first-century American literature is a rich vein of African American poetry. This edition adds two contemporary poets from this living tradition: Natasha Trethewey and Tracy K. Smith. Trethewey's selections include personal and historical elegies; Smith draws on cultural materials as diverse as David Bowie's music and the history of the Hubble Space Telescope. These writers join African American poets whose work has long helped define the anthology— Rita Dove, Gwendolyn Brooks, Robert Hayden, Audre Lorde, and others.

This edition gives even greater exposure to literary and social experimentation during the 1960s, 1970s, and beyond. The work of two avant-garde playwrights joins "Postmodern Manifestos" (which pairs nicely with "Modernist Manifestos" in Volume D). Introduced to the anthology through their short, challenging pieces, Charles Ludlam and Richard Foreman cast the mechanics of performance in a new light. Reading their thought pieces in relation to the volume's complete plays helps raise new questions about how the seemingly more traditional dramatic works engage structures of time, plot, feeling, and spectatorship. To our popular cluster "Creative Nonfiction" we have added a new selection by Joan Didion, from "Slouching Towards

Bethlehem," which showcases her revolutionary style of journalism as she comments on experiments with public performance and communal living during the 1960s. A new selection from David Foster Wallace in the same cluster pushes reportage on the Maine Lobster Festival into philosophical inquiry: how can we fairly assess the pain of other creatures? This edition also introduces poet Frank Bidart through his most famous work—*Ellen West*—in which the poet uses experimental forms of verse he pioneered during the 1970s to speak in the voice of a woman battling anorexia. Standing authors in the anthology, notably John Ashbery and Amiri Baraka, fill out the volume's survey of radical change in the forms, and social uses, of literary art.

We are delighted to offer this revised Ninth Edition to teachers and students, and we welcome your comments.

Additional Resources from the Publisher

The Ninth Edition retains the paperback splits format, popular for its flexibility and portability. This format accommodates the many instructors who use the anthology in a two-semester survey, but allows for mixing and matching the five volumes in a variety of courses organized by period or topic, at levels from introductory to advanced. We are also pleased to offer the Ninth Edition in an ebook format. The Digital Anthologies include all the content of the print volumes, with print-corresponding page and line numbers for seamless integration into the print-digital mixed classroom. Annotations are accessible with a click or a tap, encouraging students to use them with minimal interruption to their reading of the text. The e-reading platform facilitates active reading with a powerful annotation tool and allows students to do a full-text search of the anthology and read online or off. The Digital Editions can be accessed from any computer or device with an Internet browser and are available to students at a fraction of the print price at digital.wwnorton.com/americanlit9pre1865 and digital.wwnorton.com/americanlit9post1865. For exam copy access to the Digital Editions and for information on making the Digital Editions available through the campus bookstore or packaging the Digital Editions with the print anthology, instructors should contact their Norton representative.

To give instructors even more flexibility, Norton is making available the full list of 254 Norton Critical Editions. A Norton Critical Edition can be included for free with either package (Volumes A and B; Volumes C, D, E) or any individual split volume. Each Norton Critical Edition gives students an authoritative, carefully annotated text accompanied by rich contextual and critical materials prepared by an expert in the subject. The publisher also offers the much-praised guide *Writing about American Literature*, by Karen Gocsik (University of California–San Diego) and Coleman Hutchison (University of Texas–Austin), free with either package or any individual split volume.

In addition to the Digital Editions, for students using *The Norton Anthology of American Literature*, the publisher provides a wealth of free resources at digital.wwnorton.com/americanlit9pre1865 and digital.wwnorton.com/americanlit9post1865. There students will find more than seventy reading-comprehension quizzes on the period introductions and widely taught works with extensive feedback that points them back to the text. Ideal for self-study or homework assignments, Norton's sophisticated quizzing engine allows instructors to track student results and improvement. For over thirty works in the anthology, the sites also offer Close Reading Workshops that walk students step-by-step through analysis of a literary work. Each workshop prompts students to read, reread, consider contexts, and answer questions along the way, making these perfect assignments to build close-reading skills.

The publisher also provides extensive instructor-support materials. New to the Ninth Edition is an online Interactive Instructor's Guide at iig.wwnorton .com/americanlit9/full. Invaluable for course preparation, this resource provides hundreds of teaching notes, discussion questions, and suggested resources from the much-praised *Teaching with* The Norton Anthology of American Literature: *A Guide for Instructors* by Edward Whitley (Lehigh University). Also at this searchable and sortable site are quizzes, images, and lecture PowerPoints for each introduction, topic cluster, and twenty-five widely taught works. A PDF of *Teaching with NAAL* is available for download at wwnorton.com/instructors.

Finally, Norton Coursepacks bring high-quality digital media into a new or existing online course. The coursepack includes all the reading comprehension quizzes (customizable within the coursepack), the Writing about Literature video series, a bank of essay and exam questions, bulleted summaries of the period introductions, and "Making Connections" discussion or essay prompts to encourage students to draw connections across the anthology's authors and works. Coursepacks are available in a variety of formats, including Blackboard, Canvas, Desire2Learn, and Moodle, at no cost to instructors or students.

Editorial Procedures

As in past editions, editorial features—period introductions, headnotes, annotations, and bibliographies—are designed to be concise yet full and to give students necessary information without imposing a single interpretation. The editors have updated all apparatus in response to new scholarship: period introductions have been entirely or substantially rewritten, as have many headnotes. All selected bibliographies and each period's general-resources bibliographies, categorized by Reference Works, Histories, and Literary Criticism, have been thoroughly updated. The Ninth Edition retains three editorial features that help students place their reading in historical and cultural context—a Texts/Contexts timeline following each period introduction, a map on the front endpaper of each volume, and a chronological chart, on the back endpaper, showing the lifespans of many of the writers anthologized.

Whenever possible, our policy has been to reprint texts as they appeared in their historical moment. There is one exception: we have modernized most spellings and (very sparingly) the punctuation in Volume A on the principle that archaic spellings and typography pose unnecessary problems for beginning students. We have used square brackets to indicate titles supplied by the editors for the convenience of students. Whenever a portion of a text has been omitted, we have indicated that omission with three asterisks.

If the omitted portion is important for following the plot or argument, we give a brief summary within the text or in a footnote. After each work, we cite the date of first publication on the right; in some instances, the latter is followed by the date of a revised edition for which the author was responsible. When the date of composition is known and differs from the date of publication, we cite it on the left.

The editors have benefited from commentary offered by hundreds of teachers throughout the country. Those teachers who prepared detailed critiques, or who offered special help in preparing texts, are listed under Acknowledgments, on a separate page. We also thank the many people at Norton who contributed to the Ninth Edition: Julia Reidhead, who supervised the Ninth Edition; Marian Johnson, managing editor, college; Carly Fraser Doria, media editor; Kurt Wildermuth, Michael Fleming, Harry Haskell, and Candace Levy, manuscript editors; Rachel Taylor and Ava Bramson, assistant editors; Sean Mintus, production manager; Cat Abelman, photo editor; Julie Tesser, photo researcher; Debra Morton Hoyt, art director; Tiani Kennedy, cover designer; Megan Jackson Schindel, permissions manager; and Margaret Gorenstein, who cleared permissions. We also wish to acknowledge our debt to the late George P. Brockway, former president and chairman at Norton, who invented this anthology, and to the late M. H. Abrams, Norton's advisor on English texts. All have helped us create an anthology that, more than ever, testifies to the continuing richness of American literary traditions.

ROBERT S. LEVINE, General Editor

Acknowledgments

Among our many critics, advisors, and friends, the following were of especial help toward the preparation of the Ninth Edition, either with advice or by providing critiques of particular periods of the anthology: Melissa Adams-Campbell (Northern Illinois University); Rolena Adorno (Yale University); Heidi Ajrami (Victoria College); Simone A. James Alexander (Seton Hall University); Brian Anderson (Central Piedmont Community College); Lena Andersson (Fulton-Montgomery Community College); Marilyn Judith Atlas (Ohio University); Sylvia Baer (Gloucester County College); George H. Bailey (Northern Essex Community College); Margarita T. Barceló (MSU Denver); Peter Bellis (University of Alabama–Birmingham); Randall Blankenship (Valencia College); Susanne Bloomfield (University of Nebraska–Kearney); David Bordelon (Ocean County College); Patricia Bostian (Central Piedmont Community College); Maria Brandt (Monroe Community College); Tamara Ponzo Brattoli (Joliet Junior College); Joanna Brooks (San Diego State University); David Brottman (Iowa State University); Arthur Brown (University of Evansville); Martin Brückner (University of Delaware); Judith Budz (Fitchburg State University); Dan Butcher (University of Alabama–Birmingham); Maria J. Cahill (Edison State College); Ann Cameron (Indiana University–Kokomo); Brad Campbell (Cal Poly); Mark Canada (University of North Carolina–Pembroke); Gerry Canavan (Marquette University); Ann Capel (Gadsden State Community College, Ayers Campus); Elisabeth Ceppi (Portland State University); Tom Cerasulo (Elms College); Mark Cirino (University of Evansville); Josh Cohen (Emory University); Matt Cohen (University of Texas–Austin); William Corley (Cal Poly Pomona and U.S. Naval Academy); David Cowart (University of South Carolina); Paul Crumbley (Utah State University); Ryan Cull (New Mexico State University); Sue Currell (University of Sussex); Kathleen Danker (South Dakota State University); Clark Davis (University of Denver); Eve Davis (Virginia Union University); Matthew R. Davis (University of Wisconsin–Stevens Point); Laura Dawkins (Murray State University); Bruce J. Degi (Metropolitan State University of Denver); Jerry DeNuccio (Graceland University); Lisa DeVries (Victoria College); Lorraine C. DiCicco (King's University College); Joshua A. Dickson (SUNY Jefferson); Rick Diguette (Georgia Perimeter College); Raymond F. Dolle (Indiana State University); James Donelan (UC Santa Barbara); Clark Draney (College of Southern Idaho); John Dudley (University of South Dakota); Sara Eaton (North Central College); Julia Eichelberger (College of Charleston); Marilyn Elkins (California State University–Los Angeles); Sharyn Emery (Indiana

University Southeast); Hilary Emmett (University of East Anglia); Terry Engebresten (Idaho State University); Patrick Erben (University of West Georgia); Timothy J. Evans (College of William & Mary); Duncan Faherty (CUNY); Laura Fine (Meredith College); Daniel Fineman (Occidental College); Pat Gantt (Utah State University); Xiongya Gao (Southern University at New Orleans); Becky Jo Gesteland (Weber State University); Paul Gilmore (Rutgers University); Len Gougeon (University of Scranton); Carey Goyette (Clinton Community College); Sarah Graham (University of Leicester); Alan Gravano (Marshall University); James N. Green (Library Company of Philadelphia); Laura Morgan Green (Northeastern University); John Gruesser (Kean University); Bernabe G. Gutierrez (Laredo Community College); Julia Hans (Fitchburg State University); Stephanie Hawkins (University of North Texas); Catherine F. Heath (Victoria College); Roger Hechy (SUNY Oneonta); Terry Heller (Coe College); Carl Herzig (St. Ambrose University); Eric Heyne (University of Alaska–Fairbanks); Thomas Alan Holmes (East Tennessee State University); Greg Horn (Southwest Virginia Community College); Ruth Y. Hsu (University of Hawaii–Manoa); Kate Huber (Temple University); Zach Hutchins (Colorado State University); Thomas Irwin (University of Missouri–St. Louis); Elizabeth Janoski (Lackawanna College); Andrew Jenkins (College of Central Florida); Luke Johnson (Mesabi Range College); Mark Johnson (San Jacinto College); Paul Jones (Ohio University); Roger Walton Jones (Ranger College); Jennifer Jordan-Henley (Roane State Community College); Mark Kamrath (University of Central Florida); Rachel Key (El Centro College); Julie H. Kim (Northeastern Illinois University); Vincent King (Black Hills State University); Denis Kohn (Baldwin Wallace University); Gary Konas (University of Wisconsin–La Crosse); Michael Kowalewski (Carleton College); Michael Lackey (University of Minnesota–Morris); Jennifer Ladino (University of Idaho); Thomas W. LaFleur (Laredo Community College); Andrew Lanham (Yale University); Christopher Leise (Whitman College); Beth Leishman (Northwest MS Community College); Jennifer Levi (Cecil College); Alfred J. López (Purdue University); Paul Madachy (Prince George's Community College); Etta Madden (Missouri State University); Marc Malandra (Biola University); David Malone (Union University); Matt Martin (Wesleyan College); Stephen Mathewson (Central New Mexico Community College); Liz Thompson Mayo (Jackson State Community College); David McCracken (Coker College); Kathleen McDonald (Norwich University); John McGreevy (University of Notre Dame); Dana McMichael (Abilene Christian University); Sandra Measels (Holmes Community College); Eric Mein (Normandale Community College); Christine Mihelich (Marywood University); Deborah M. Mix (Ball State University); Aaron Moe (Washington State University); Joelle Moen (Brigham Young University–Idaho); Lisa Muir (Wilkes Community College); Lori Muntz (Iowa Wesleyan College); Justine Murison (University of Illinois); Jillmarie Murphy (Union College); Harold Nelson (Minot State University); Howard Nelson (Cayuga Community College); Lance Newman (Westminster College); Taryn Okuma (The Catholic University of America); Stanley Orr (University of Hawai'i–West O'ahu); Samuel Otter (University of California–Berkeley); Susan Scott Parrish (University of Michigan); Martha H. Patterson (McKendree University); Michelle Paulsen (Victoria College); Daniel G. Payne (SUNY Oneonta); Ian Peddie (Georgia

Gwinnett College); Aaron Matthew Percich (West Virginia University); Tom Perrin (Huntingdon College); Sandra Petrulionis (Penn State–Altoona); Christopher Phillips (Lafayette College); Maria Pollack (Hudson Valley Community College); Kenneth M. Price (University of Nebraska); Marty G. Price (Mississippi State University); Kieran Quinlan (University of Alabama–Birmingham); Wesley Raabe (Kent State University); Maria Ramos (J. Sargeant Reynolds Community College); Palmer Rampell (Yale University); Rick Randolph (Kauai Community College); Kimberly Reed (Lipscomb University); Joan Reeves (Northeast Alabama Community College); Elizabeth Renker (The Ohio State University); Joseph Rezek (Boston University); Anne Boyd Rioux (University of New Orleans); Marc Robinson (Yale University); Jane Rosecrans (J. Sargeant Reynolds Community College); Phillip Round (University of Iowa); Jeffrey Rubinstein (Hillborough Community College); Maureen Ryan (University of Southern Mississippi); Jamie Sadler (Richmond Community College); Gordon Sayre (University of Oregon); Jennifer Schell (University of Alaska–Fairbanks); Jim Schrantz (Tarrant County College); Joshua Schuster (University of Western Ontario); Marc Seals (University of Wisconsin–Baraboo/Sauk County); Carl Sederholm (Brigham Young University); Larry Severeid (Utah State University–Eastern); Anna Shectman (Yale University); Deborah Sims (USC and UCR); Claudia Slate (Florida Southern College); Brenda R. Smith (Kent State University–Stark); Martha Nell Smith (University of Maryland); Eric Sterling (Auburn University Montgomery); Julia Stern (Northwestern University); Billy J. Stratton (University of Denver); Steve Surryhne (California State University–San Francisco); Timothy Sweet (West Virginia University); David Taylor (University of North Texas); Jan Thompson (University of Nebraska–Kearney); Robin Thompson (Governors State University); Marjory Thrash (Pearl River Community College); Nicole Tonkovich (UC San Diego); Steve Tracy (University of Massachusetts–Amherst); Alan Trusky (Forence-Darlington Tech College); April Van Camp (Indian River State College); Joanne van der Woude (University of Groningen); Abram van Engen (Washington University); Laura Veltman (California Baptist University); Eliza Waggoner (Miami University–Middletown); Catherine Waitinas (Cal Poly State University); Laura Dassow Walls (University of Notre Dame); Raquel Wanzo (Laney College); Bryan Waterman (New York University); Stephanie Wells (Orange Coast College); Jeff Westover (Boise State University); Belinda Wheeler (Paine College); Chris Wheeler (Horry-Georgetown Technical College); Steven J. Whitton (Jacksonville State University); Elizabeth Wiet (Yale University); Jason Williams (Brigham Young University–Idaho); Barbara Williamson (Spokane Falls Community College); Gaye Winter (Mississippi Gulf Coast Community College); Kelly Wisecup (University of North Texas); Aiping Zhang (California State University–Chico).

THE NORTON ANTHOLOGY OF

AMERICAN
LITERATURE

NINTH EDITION

VOLUME E: LITERATURE SINCE 1945

American Literature since 1945

How do we tell the story of American literature in our own time? In one version of that story, we are led into the twenty-first century by an unlikely hero named Oscar Wao, the creation of novelist and short-story writer Junot Díaz in *The Brief Wondrous Life of Oscar Wao* (2008). Oscar is a nerdy, overweight devotee of fantasy fiction and comics, dreaming of becoming the Dominican American J. R. R. Tolkien, author of Oscar's favorite novels, the Lord of the Rings trilogy. Failing at exercise, dating, and the college social scene, Oscar leaves New Jersey for an extended stay with relatives in the Dominican Republic. There he achieves the romantic fulfillment that eluded him at home, but his refugee family's tragic history comes full circle, too, as Oscar's life is changed forever by his unwitting entanglement with the Dominican Republic's brutal political regime. This, Díaz tells us, is *fuku*, a curse that wreaks havoc the world over, anywhere we find those hungry for power crushing the freedom, and the bodies, of the weak.

Díaz's hero and the novel that brings him to life embody what feels truly new in American writing of the twenty-first century. When we read *Oscar Wao*—or virtually any of Díaz's stories, such as "Drown," reprinted in this volume—we plug into an electric, multilingual English renewed by Spanish, African, and Latin American borrowings. What has been called a *mestizo* language was practiced, described, and theorized by the writer Gloria Anzaldúa decades before (see her essay "How to Tame a Wild Tongue," also in this volume). Building on the work of Anzaldúa and others, a writer of Díaz's generation need not justify the hybrid, but can simply inhabit it, using new language to reach new regions of human experience and

Blam, Roy Lichtenstein, 1962. For more information about this painting, see the color insert in this volume.

American culture. Following Díaz's allusions in *Oscar Wao*, readers are led to genre fiction, superhero comics, film, fashion, pop music, arts, religious ritual, modern sexuality, and mass entertainment—a cultural milieu that stretches from New Jersey to Santo Domingo. But Díaz's headlong prose also brings references to more traditionally literary writers such as William Shakespeare, Herman Melville, and the Latin American novelist Gabriel García Márquez, alongside the terms and ideas of literary criticism, history, philosophy, gender theory, and critiques of political power. Twenty-first-century readers have been more than ready to embrace Díaz's capacious literary and cultural vision. They have been willing to wrestle with what is difficult in his writing while they revel in his brilliant, loving use of the lowbrow and the popular. Do readers have to choose between the academic and the popular, between "serious" and "entertaining"? Junot Díaz says no. What do the X-Men comics have to say about theories of dictatorship? *Oscar Wao* explains—in a footnote, no less. Twenty-first-century readers live these intersections daily, code-shifting as they move among family, friends, school, work, nations, and cultures. The fiction of Junot Díaz seems to speak all these languages and more.

Junot Díaz took eleven years to write *The Brief Wondrous Life of Oscar Wao*. He had to invent the hybrid language from which to spin the strands of his story. The Pulitzer Prize committee—known for honoring epic novels that sum up something important about American life—chose *Oscar Wao* for the 2008 prize, marking the arrival in literature of a vision of America already lived by many of its citizens. At the beginning of the twenty-first century, *Oscar Wao* did just what the poet Ezra Pound exhorted ambitious writers to do at the start of the twentieth century: "Make it new." In doing so, of course, Díaz joined a literary tradition even as he broke its molds.

The vitality of contemporary American literature, evident throughout the most recent selections in this volume, is fueled by two great engines, one artistic and one demographic. The artistic urge to experiment galvanized writers inspired by, or reacting against, the influential modernist writers of the first half of the twentieth century who themselves experimented ceaselessly with literary form and with the subjects and stories that could be spoken through poetry, drama, and fiction. At the same time, the demographics of American education and immigration were changing radically, beginning in the middle of the twentieth century. These forces transformed the cast of American high- and middlebrow culture: who participated in American culture, and who was taught the reading and writing skills essential to the creation of modern literature. As an interest in experiment surged through a nation of new readers and writers, the basic elements of literary culture were renewed once more.

NEW READERS, NEW WRITERS, NEW HEROES

Addressing American college students in 1950, the Russian émigré author Vladimir Nabokov gave his audience a multiple-choice quiz: What makes a reader a *good* reader? The options included joining a book club, identifying with characters, and reading a story for what it had to say about society. These were, for Nabokov, trick answers: they were common ways of reading then, as now, but he disparaged them. He wanted readers to take a different approach. The correct answers, he told the students, were owning a dictionary, possessing a good memory, and having imagination. Both the "wrong" answers and the ones Nabokov thought were right tell us a great deal about what the new generation of American readers was looking for when they turned to literature.

These readers—more diverse and better educated than ever before, faced with more choices than ever before—would help to define American and world literature over the next half century. Many of those regularly encountering literary works in the second half of the twentieth century were, or had been, servicemen. Quality paperbacks at low prices were suddenly everywhere, and the format was no longer the province solely of lowbrow "pulp" fiction. Millions of pocket-sized paperbacks had been sent abroad during World War II, given away by publishers through the Armed Services Editions series. Mysteries, Westerns, domestic novels, and works by Charles Dickens and Shakespeare all found their way overseas. *The Great Gatsby*, which had faded from public consciousness by the 1940s, was made popular again by servicemen and their paperbacks. While these books carried aspects of American and British culture into the barracks and bivouacs of soldiers in the theaters of war, those soldiers were also encountering the languages and cultures of Europe, North Africa, India, and Japan in the course of their service, broadening their cultural education in ways not specifically American. Coming back to the United States after 1945, veterans were greeted by an entitlement that dramatically changed American society: the benefits of the GI Bill—the Servicemen's Readjustment Act of 1944—signed into law by President Roosevelt. Under its provisions the government provided money so that veterans could buy homes and attend school, receiving tuition and a

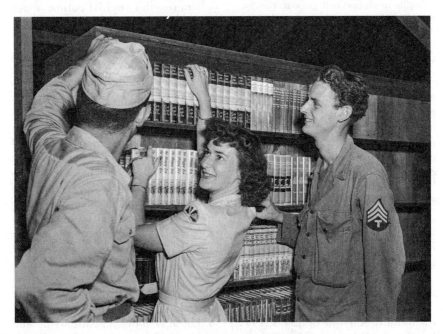

Army Special Services librarian and soldiers in the Philippines, 1946.

The GI Bill (1944), which provided federal subsidies to support college education for returning World War II veterans, democratized American higher education. Shown here, veterans and other students at New York University in January 1945.

stipend for up to four years of college or other professional training. For the first time, men from immigrant, poor, and working-class families, whose parents had little education, were attending college in droves. In 1947, the program's peak year, 49 percent of students admitted to college were veterans. By the time the original version of the law had run its course in 1956, 7.8 million out of the 16 million World War II veterans had benefited from its education and training provisions. Combined with a booming American economy, plentiful jobs, and the widespread urge to start adult lives delayed by military deployment, the entitlement helped to lift millions of individuals and families into the middle class.

That demographic change transformed the demographics of reading and writing for the rest of the century. American readers' increasing sophistication about aesthetic and cultural matters was fueled by their professors' desire to teach the formally complex works promoted by the international modernist writers they admired from the early twentieth century. An influx of writers and scholars fleeing Europe just prior to the outbreak of war had given American intellectuals renewed contact with the literary currents of French, German, and Russian literature. "The New Criticism"—a modernist-inspired method of critical interpretation grounded in reading the text "closely"—was popular in literature classrooms just about everywhere, enshrined in textbooks such as Cleanth Brooks and Robert Penn Warren's *Understanding Poetry* (1938) and *Understanding Fiction* (1943; the writer Flannery O'Connor called *Understanding Fiction* her "Bible"). The method put students from varied backgrounds on an equal footing as readers and helped them to see how literary works were crafted, benefits that explain why students and teachers still practice "close reading" today.

Nabokov's recommended reading practices would serve students well as they encountered complex literary works, European influences, and the challenge of reading closely—and they would serve the future readers of his morally edgy novel *Lolita* (1955), too. *Lolita* is about a gentlemanly and intellectual European pedophile in love with a brash American preteen girl.

Initially banned in the United States, once *Lolita* became available freely to the American public in 1958, it became a best seller even as it tested readers' moral tolerance and aesthetic sophistication. Ironically, then, while Nabokov strove to teach American college students a kind of literary appreciation fostered by his aristocratic European education, the practices he in turn discouraged were too deeply embedded in American history to be set aside by the new college students filling the lecture halls and classrooms where he taught. Literature's capacity to change the culture by encouraging readers to think about their society through the lens of a story had already had significant effects in the nation's history. Nineteenth-century readers identifying with the characters in Harriet Beecher Stowe's *Uncle Tom's Cabin* or turning to Frederick Douglass's autobiography to understand slavery fueled the abolitionist movement that in turn fueled the Civil War. The African American characters that northern white readers identified with or listened to in fiction and autobiography reached them in ways their social lives otherwise prevented.

In the second half of the twentieth century, a new generation read not only for the "aesthetic bliss" Nabokov celebrated and for the formal features of language that "close reading" and an appreciation of international modernism could reveal, but also in order to remake themselves and their society. Those socially engaged acts of reading ensured that writers catering to them would make their mark both on the development of fiction, poetry, and drama as art forms and on politics, commerce, religion, medicine, and domestic life. By the mid-twentieth century, one could already point to a long history of black writers in the United States who used their skills on the page to fight the philosophy, psychology, and policies of white supremacy. The burgeoning civil rights movement and, later, the Black Arts movement, brought many more black writers into publication. While African American members of the armed services were in Europe, James Baldwin—who did not qualify for the service because of the effects of childhood malnutrition—was working in the War Information Office in New York, but he was also honing his craft as a fiction writer, joining a distinguished generation of black writers that included Ralph Ellison, Richard Wright, Langston Hughes, Ann Petry, and others who enjoyed wide audiences in the United States before, during, and after the war. Although James Baldwin left the United States in 1949 and spent most of the rest of his life in Europe, he would become one of the most canny commentators on race to address a mass readership in the postwar period. The essays contained in his well-received 1965 volume, *The Fire Next Time*, are even more direct than the critique to be found in *Black Boy*, the memoir that his mentor Richard Wright had published just twenty years earlier. This was partly due to the genre Baldwin chose: Baldwin's essays were not stories or memoirs, but cultural criticism. He provided a pointed psychological, spiritual, sexual, and practical analysis of racism in America that was as important to the civil rights movement's intellectual evolution as sit-ins and boycotts were to its political success. Baldwin's fiction—such as the story "Sonny's Blues," found in this volume—matched this social analysis with storytelling that could make readers feel the human cost of poverty and addiction in black communities—the outgrowths of the racist society Baldwin's essays lay bare.

"A Man Becomes Invisible." One of a set of images created by photographer Gordon Parks for a photo essay on Ralph Ellison's *Invisible Man*. The essay was published in *Life* magazine on August 25, 1952.

Drawing energy from the newly educated readers and writers of the mid-twentieth century, American fiction and drama in the postwar period frequently celebrated nonconforming outsiders like Baldwin's Sonny: the philosophical character, often a writer or an artist, usually male, who suffers social rejection for his ideals or simply for his identity. The social liberation movements of the second half of the twentieth century—not only the civil rights movement, but also the later Black Power movement, the American Indian Movement (AIM, founded in 1968), the women's liberation movement (which gained momentum in the early 1970s), and the movement for gay rights (which began with a protest at the Stonewall Inn in Greenwich Village, New York City, in 1969, and entered a new phase with the AIDS crisis in the mid-1980s)—inspired content for this infinitely flexible dramatic setup. Notable examples of the outsider character would include the nameless narrator of Ralph Ellison's *Invisible Man* (1952); Augie in Saul Bellow's *The Adventures of Augie March* (1953); the autobiographical narrator of Maxine Hong Kingston's stories in *The Woman Warrior* (1979); Toni Morrison's Milkman Dead and Guitar Bains (*Song of Soloman*, 1979); Don DeLillo's Jack Gladney (*White Noise*, 1985); Sherman Alexie's Junior in his acclaimed young adult novel, *The Absolutely True Diary of a Part-Time Indian* (2007); Junot Díaz's Oscar Wao (*The Brief Wondrous Life of Oscar Wao*, 2007); and Philip Roth's many Jewish protagonists who belong neither in their Jewish communities nor in the Protestant-dominated culture around them, the kind of character central to the story "Defender of the Faith" and embodied perhaps most memorably in Coleman Silk—the contemporary black man who lives out his life as a Jew in Roth's *The Human Stain* (2000). There were limits to American optimism about the prospects for outsiders' lives: like Willy Loman in Arthur Miller's play *Death of a*

Salesman, the outsider trying to reenter society's circle of norms can fail, sometimes spectacularly. These misfit characters can be heroes and antiheroes, weak men or rebels, and their stories can end in tragedy or triumph.

Such outsider characters were related to the rise of a new readership looking for characters with whom they could identify, but they were also inspired by discontent with mass culture in the United States and its perceived insistence on social conformity. That discontent sent young people in the postwar period searching for meaning and identity—beyond the desire for upward mobility, marriage and children, a house in the suburbs, and the sturdy work ethic of their fathers and mothers. The satirical and sometimes simply resistant attitude toward intellectual, cultural, religious, and political authority cultivated among the coterie of so-called beatniks in the late 1940s and 1950s—a group that included Allen Ginsberg, Gary Snyder, Jack Kerouac, and William Burroughs—had become a popular movement among the generation born in the decade after the war. In the 1970s, many important women writers whom readers will find in this anthology—such as Jamaica Kincaid, Anne Sexton, Elizabeth Bishop, Toni Cade Bambara, Toni Morrison, and Leslie Marmon Silko—also resisted conformities of race, education, religion, and gender that they perceived had circumscribed the lives of the women and men around them. Some, like Bishop, found artistic and personal solidarity among artists with whom they shared an aesthetic vision and a common set of cultural touchstones (later in this volume readers can see Bishop among a roomful of male writers at New York's Gotham Book Mart in a group photograph included alongside the selections from poet Randall Jarrell). Others, like Bambara, cultivated a diverse solidarity of women through collective projects and mutual support—as in Bambara's significant gathering of writers in the volume she edited, *The Black Woman: An Anthology* (1970). Toni Morrison spent twenty years as an editor at Random House, the job she held before becoming a full-time writer, where she ensured that black writers received the attention they deserved. And some writers resisted norms by arguing for new ones, as demonstrated in Silko's lifelong advocacy for politically engaged Native American art, which led her to criticize sharply white writers (famously, the poet Gary Snyder) for appropriating Native American sources as well as Native writers (such as fellow fiction writer Louise Erdrich) for being insufficiently committed to Native American

Toni Morrison in 1970 at Random House, where she worked as an editor.

Levittown. Construction and aerial views of housing development in Levittown, PA, built by Levitt & Sons between 1951 and 1957. Levittown was the prototype for similar developments built all over the country in the 1950s and 1960s. They offered largely identical single-family homes for a generation of upwardly mobile middle-class Americans who wanted to move out of cities.

materials. Silko's admonishments to writers regarding the subjects and cultural materials that they should or should not write about suggests how nonconformity with the mainstream could sometimes place different forms of expectation or restraint upon writers. Do writers have to turn to their own heritage for inspiration? Sometimes it has seemed that writers of color are expected to do so, and white writers are free to choose not to. Language itself is a form of conformity and restraint. In the fiction of George Saunders—such as his story "CivilWarLand in Bad Decline," included here—the characters resist (and are sometimes overcome by) the stifling, dystopian worlds of American business where the euphemisms of customer service and "total quality management" jargon make it nearly impossible to describe, or even to perceive, the world beyond capitalist enterprise. Noncomformity had its most theatrical moment in the 1960s youth counterculture, epitomized by LSD advocate Timothy Leary's exhortation to "turn on, tune in, drop out." "Turning on" to the exploration of consciousness through psychedelic drugs such as LSD was meant to expand the mind beyond the limits of conventional thought and perception. For Leary and many in the counterculture, to "tune in" meant that one would seek to be open to the world spiritually, intellectually, and sensually; to "drop out" was to reject social conventions and free the mind of the unconscious limits that accompanied those conventions. The writer Joan Didion turned a critical eye on the counterculture in her essay "Slouching Towards Bethlehem," excerpted below in the "Creative Nonfiction" cluster, but the counterculture was artistically enabling for many, including Didion herself, whose practice of reportage looked little like the conventional journalism of her day. Didion waxed personal in her reporting—breaking the rules of objectivity—as the counterculture around her took to heart the adage that "the personal is political."

"Dropping out" was the 1960s incarnation of an old impulse in American culture, one that can be traced back at least to Henry David Thoreau, alone in his cabin on Walden Pond writing essays about civil disobedience, who was jailed briefly upon his return to town for refusing to pay taxes that supported slavery and the war against Mexico. But this aspect of the counterculture was not as politically engaged as the model of Thoreau might suggest. The ethic of "dropping out" was per-haps most famously embodied by novelist Ken Kesey. Kesey became famous when he pub-lished *One Flew Over the Cuckoo's Nest* (1962), a best-selling novel that told the story of a man sent to a mental institution and, finally, lobotomized, because he would not conform to society's expectations. The money Kesey earned from this book supported him and a group of followers call-

The Merry Pranksters atop their bus, "Further."

ing themselves "The Merry Pranksters," who experimented with drugs, music, art, meditation, macrobiotic diets, and unusual social, sexual, and leadership arrangements. The Pranksters' compound in the redwood groves of La Honda, California, and their converted schoolbus, called "Further" and piloted by Neal Cassady, the model for Jack Kerouac's hero in *On the Road* (1957), became the symbols of the counterculture's ideals and excesses. Kesey's world was described in Thomas Wolfe's book *The Electric Kool-Aid Acid Test* (1968), an early example of a genre that came to be called "cre-ative nonfiction." Like Hunter S. Thompson's "gonzo" journalism—in which the journalist immerses him- or herself in extreme experience in order to report on it vividly—this new genre of writing used literary language (in these cases, the high-energy poetic prose style of the Beat writers) to report on real people and events. Wolfe and Thompson crafted their styles to match—and to make the reader feel that she had somehow experienced—their wild subjects.

Testifying to the broadly shared celebration of the outsider in American prose writing, we can look back to Holden Caulfield in J. D. Salinger's *The Catcher in the Rye* (1951) and to the melancholy, misfit suburbanites of John Cheever's and John Updike's stories to round out the fellowship of noncon-forming heroes. This was a durable narrative and thematic convention that long accompanied protest and cultural transformation but also had its politi-cally quietist side. Nabokov, who told his college student audience they should not identify with characters, would not approve: America's newly expanded and diverse reading public embraced these figures and, yes, *identified* with them as culture heroes and fellow-travelers. That they still speak to readers today—many can be met in the pages of this volume of *The Norton Anthology of American Literature*—reveals how unconventionality itself can become a fertile and endlessly engaging convention.

LITERATURE AND AMERICAN MEDIA

While education, immigration, and political and cultural unrest had an enormous impact on America's readers and writers during the second half of the twentieth century, the medium of writing itself was suddenly surrounded by a rich and shifting context of new media. Many would say that writing—fiction, poetry, and plays especially—had to *compete* with other media in new ways, but that would oversimplify the matter. For the new media that developed after World War II and through into the twenty-first century are closely related to literature and together take up themes and ideas rooted in literature's longer history.

Two major developments dominate our sense of the media landscape of the late twentieth and early twenty-first centuries: first, the rise of television after the Second World War, and second, the invention of the Internet in the 1990s. These two forms of media—and of course, the second is better understood as a whole constellation of media, including text, moving and still images, and sound—fascinated not only their mass publics but also writers and dramatists whose very vocations made them highly aware of the powers and effects of different media. The very first "media theorist" was a trained literary critic, a Canadian-born professor named Marshall McLuhan, whose best-known book, *Understanding Media* (1964), consciously echoed the titles of the much-used literary textbooks of the New Criticism. Famous for his dictum that "the medium is the message," he argued that *how* something is communicated is sometimes the very essence of *what* it communicates. Television shows and print advertising were often the targets of his analyses, but he also wrote lovingly of medieval life, of a time before Gutenberg's printing press, when oral storytelling, music, and traveling dramatic productions constituted the public media of the day. McLuhan's attention to the material medium at the expense of content sometimes seemed absurd to his critics, but his emphasis reflected the public's sense that television in particular was changing American mass culture less because of what was said on television than because of how it delivered a culture of performance into living rooms across the country. The television networks took types of programs already well established in radio and on the vaudeville stage of the early twentieth century—such as the variety show, the interview or advice show, and cowboy and detective stories—and made them come alive every night on screens in American homes. In 1947, about 6,000 sets could be found in those homes; by 1951, the number was over 12 million. McLuhan's prolific writing and speaking about television made him a celebrity. When appointed by Fordham University to hold the prestigious Albert Schweitzer Chair, he was one of the highest paid English professors in the country (with a salary of $100,000 in 1967). He was so well known that Woody Allen gave him an amusing cameo in his film *Annie Hall* (1977): Allen's character pulls McLuhan out from behind a billboard in the lobby of a movie theater in order to refute an annoying man spouting media criticism while waiting in line for tickets. McLuhan lamented the passivity with which viewers received television. Allen makes the scene in which McLuhan appears a commentary on passivity. Allen breaks character and addresses the film's audience: "If life were only like this!" he says to the audience, as McLuhan gives the obnoxious moviegoer an intellectual dressing-down.

Media critic **Marshall McLuhan** (far right) and, addressing the audience, film-maker Woody Allen (center) in *Annie Hall* (1977).

The problem of passivity in the face of spectacle is something that television made urgent and that modern uses of drama highlight in the twentieth and twenty-first centuries. Television made Americans nightly spectators to realities that were far from entertaining. Images of violence against peaceful civil rights protesters and, in the late 1960s and '70s, images of the war in Vietnam—which many term the first "televised war"—galvanized national issues that might otherwise have seemed too local or too far away to engage people throughout the country. Viewers found their passivity challenged: What should they do with the violence or injustice that they saw in front of them on the screen? How did watching something implicate them as participants in what they watched? How did performance in social life constrain them—to norms of gender or race, for example? How might performance free them?

In twentieth- and twenty-first-century drama, playwrights experimented—as Woody Allen does in *Annie Hall*—with the so-called fourth wall, the side of the stage that faces the audience. They explored what would happen when a play broke through that wall, treating the whole theater, including the audience, as its staging area. Even public spaces—parks, streets, and museums—were treated as stages that could include random passersby. The term *fourth wall* comes from the eighteenth-century French playwright Denis Diderot; engaging the audience was routine in Shakespearean drama, and the audience is always crucial to comedy—we have to laugh in order for comedy to work. And in classical Greek drama, the fourth wall is broken whenever the chorus addresses the audience directly and comments on the action. Among the plays included in this volume, for instance, August Wilson's *Fences* (1983) provokes audiences to think about barriers and spheres of action, to consider how enclosures determine human beings' powers of expression. The stage, in every play, fences things in, and, therefore, fences things out. The counterculture experimented with "happenings" that moved performance out to public spaces where the question of what is fenced in or out becomes particularly acute. A description of one such performance appears in the excerpt from Didion's "Slouching Towards Bethlehem" in the Creative Nonfiction cluster in this volume: a performance by the San Francisco Mime Troupe in the section of Golden Gate Park known as the "Panhandle." Disturbingly, the troupe uses the racist tradition of blackface theater to goad people into resisting racist political structures; Didion implicitly asks the reader to consider whether such a performance finally undermines or reinforces racial stereotyping.

Avant-garde theater, as articulated in the "Postmodern Manifestos" by Robert Ludlam and George Foreman included in this volume, invites readers to think of theater as a place where such questions can be explored and where the real-life social roles that people perform can be experimented with. (Ludlam was particularly interested in the performance of gender.) Even realist theater was tending toward this kind of self-conscious meditation on spectatorship. "Reality TV" in the twenty-first century, with its confession booths and "real" people, pushes right through the fourth wall, even as it gives the viewer an uncomfortable voyeuristic feeling as he or she passively consumes, as entertainment, the tears and abuses of the people on the show. What seemed in the early twentieth century like artificiality—the artwork's own acknowledgment that it is fictional— became the ultimate stamp of a certain kind of realism in the twenty-first century.

Poetry was affected, too, by the rising interest in theatricality that the new medium of television stimulated. One of the signal changes in poetic practice, starting with the Beat poets in the middle of the twentieth century, was the growing popularity of public poetry readings. Perhaps the most famous reading of the twentieth century occurred on October 7, 1955, at the Six Gallery in San Francisco—a converted garage with a toilet adjoining the stage area. Jack Kerouac passed the wine jug while Allen Ginsberg read *Howl*, which had not been heard before that night. After using the toilet with the door ajar in front of the audience, Ginsberg pulled up his pants, walked out, and read a tour de force poem that seemed to expose the bodies and the anguish of, as the poem put it, "the best minds of my generation." Joined that night by the poets of what came to be called the "San Francisco Renaissance," Ginsberg's performance reminded the world that poetry was an oral medium, an art of sound—a fact that had faded from view (rightly or wrongly) as readers absorbed the most famous poems of the early twentieth century, including T. S. Eliot's footnoted *The Waste Land* (1922), considered by some the ultimate modernist example of the art form. Readings such as the one at the Six Gallery treated poetry like jazz performance—an experience of musicality, improvisation, and blues-inspired rhythm and

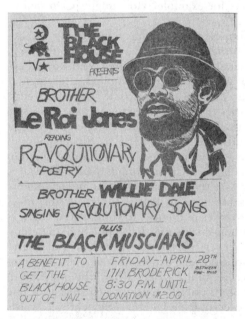

ComCo (Communications Company) poster for a poetry reading by LeRoi Jones (1967). Chester Anderson Papers, Bancroft Library, University of California.

emotion. Robert Lowell explained that part of his own dramatic change of poetic style from formalism to free verse forms in the 1950s came from the realization that his more traditional poems would not make much of a splash at a reading. Sylvia Plath read "Daddy" on BBC radio shortly before her suicide in 1963, her flat, elegant tone playing like a chill wind on the surface of tightly controlled anger. Again and again the poets in this volume turn to music, from Theodore Roethke's "My Papa's Waltz," to the jazz-inspired poetry of Michael Harper, to the dancing figures and film scores in Tracy K. Smith's "Thirst" and "The Universe: Original Motion Picture Soundtrack."

While fiction, like poetry, began to be read onstage regularly during the period covered by this volume, it was not drama or live performance but film that intersected most broadly with narrative: Patricia Highsmith and Philip K. Dick wrote stories that were adapted regularly into popular Hollywood films; film features in Don DeLillo's stories almost as often as television does; and the crosscuts and dialogue of film can be discerned in fictional forms and settings throughout the period. Still-image media such as photography and painting interface with literature, too. Natasha Trethewey's poetry meditates on both these media. For her, they represent the deceptions and the truths of history that the poet must confront. Like Marshall McLuhan, Trethewey reveals messages inherent to different media, such as the oppressive racial spectatorship implicit in much photography, even—or especially—when it is used to reveal the beauty of the downtrodden. What does writing accomplish, then, that television, film, music, photography, and painting cannot quite achieve? Readers will find many answers among the selections here. Writers throughout the period wrestle with, borrow from, and sometimes engulf the media of their times as they reimagine what literature can be and do.

EXPERIMENT AND PLAY IN TWENTIETH- AND TWENTY-FIRST-CENTURY LITERATURE

What is "postmodern"? In contemporary parlance, this is an endlessly useful term that can describe practically anything aesthetically edgy or off-kilter, anything that bends genres or cultural registers, anything that comments on the welter of media in contemporary culture. Students coming to the study of the literature of this period for the first time might well use *postmodern* to define the works that were most influential in the second half of the twentieth century. The "Postmodern Manifestos" in this volume, as well as other examples included here, suggest the variety of ideas and styles that the term can indicate. Don DeLillo's *White Noise* (1985) has been considered one of the best fictional descriptions of life in postmodern America. Postmodern life is imagined by DeLillo as a heap of fragments, a babble of incessant voices flowing from modern media (radio, television, film, and cyberspace) to penetrate our perceptions and thoughts. In DeLillo's America, material consumption and entertainment become the goals of domestic and professional life, and his stories are crammed with cars, stores, fast food, breaking news, tourist attractions, screens, and sports. The human beings caught up in these pursuits, though, always suspect there is something beyond all these glittery attractions. In the face of such a world, the protagonist of *White Noise*, Jack Gladney, seeks genuine transcendence, looking variously to data, psychotropic drugs, mystical sound, and spiritual mantras in his search for meaning. The enchanting words Jack hears muttered by his sleeping daughter turn out to be the name of a car—"*Toyota Celica.*" Is DeLillo suggesting that it is impossible to reclaim the soul in modern, commercial America? Or, rather, is transcendence available to us in all human culture, no matter how banal? Or is Jack's mistake simply funny? This sort of ambiguity and uncertainty, and the way DeLillo shifts between satire and sincerity, suggests what is so inviting to readers in the literature typically called "postmodern." Readers of fiction have found such openness to interpretation especially appealing in the exuberant satires of Thomas Pynchon, George Saunders, Lydia Davis, and Ishmael Reed, to name a few, all found alongside DeLillo in this volume.

In poetry, writers embraced the task of re-enchanting the material, commercial world—a task that poets have been called to since the ancient Greek poet Hesiod celebrated human labor in "Works and Days." In "A Supermarket in California," Allen Ginsberg's speaker, walking and thinking of the nineteenth-century American poet Walt Whitman, looks at the grocery aisles with new wonder: "What peaches and what penumbras!" He catches earthy Walt squeezing the produce and eyeing the handsome grocery boys. Others felt it was poetry's job to probe the material properties of language itself. The poets known as the "L=A=N=G=U=A=G=E" school, and their experimentalist precursor, John Ashbery, questioned the basic expectations of meaning. What can language do and become if it is freed from the requirement that it steadily refer to the world? Perhaps poems should represent the distracted mind as it writes the poem, rather than some object that can discipline the poet's unruly attention. Such poetry can seem difficult—indeed, it *is* difficult to follow meaning and sense if these are not the underlying threads holding a poem together. And yet, like the ambiguous satires of the story writers, postmodern poetry most often wants to play *with* readers, not against them. Ashbery was inspired by mid-century abstract painting—by artists such as Jackson Pollock and Mark Rothko. Readers can take pleasure in the color, texture, feeling, connotations, and shapes of language even if its meanings remain elusive.

Writing in the second half of the twentieth century was not experimental only in matters of form. For many writers, the imperative to create challenging or innovative forms—be they poetic, narrative, or dramatic—paled in significance next to the social changes they, and the world around them, were experiencing. Realism, in whatever genre, could respond to the shocks of contemporary life. When the forms of modernist literature seemed too heady, too abstract, or too intellectual, realism offered a mode suited to the autobiographical and the personal. The poet Robert Lowell lived this transition in his own work: the poems in his first book, *Lord Weary's Castle* (1946), were formally intricate, lyrically beautiful, and concerned with large subjects—the Protestant legacy in commercial life, the spiritual condition of the nation. But in fact these concerns grew from Lowell's own past, from his distinguished, old New England Protestant family, a family from which he dissented when he converted to Catholicism in 1940. *Life Studies* (1959), Lowell's second volume of poetry, changed tack, driving straight for the autobiographical core of his art with freer forms, more direct language, and candid accounts of his ruined loves and his struggles with alcoholism, depression, and mania. Breaking with both social decorum and poetic form, a prose section acknowledges a possibly Jewish ancestor in the poet's white-Anglo-Saxon-Protestant family tree. Alongside work by other poets who used the so-called confessional approach to poetry—including Frank O'Hara, Anne Sexton, Sylvia Plath, Adrienne Rich, and Sharon Olds—Lowell's experiments with subject and form brought newly accessible urgency and emotion to lyric poetry in the decades after World War II. Billy Collins's popular contemporary poetry must be read in this context: the poem "I Chop Some Parsley While Listening to Art Blakey's Version of 'Three Blind Mice'" (1998) uses an immediately personal and ordinary (not to mention humorous) occasion to transcribe the poet's thoughts on the effects of music. This is a different kind of confession—there is no deep trauma remembered here, no scandal or lost love. And the poem doesn't push the boundaries of socially acceptable topics in the manner of confessional poetry. Rather, it pushes the boundaries of poetic relevance—chopping parsley? chopping onions? speculations about the three blind mice of nursery rhyme fame? But the poem's accessible realism and its unapologetic emotion owe a debt to the generation of poets that began with Lowell.

"From the modernism you choose you get the postmodernism you deserve." So declared the critic David Antin in his 1972 essay "Modernism and Postmodernism." Given the wide variety of aesthetic strategies people refer to when they use the word *postmodernism,* Antin is surely correct. While writers who have been called "postmodern" sometimes rejected or reacted against the early-twentieth-century writers and artists who have been called "modernists," their techniques and concerns are often continuous with those of these earlier practitioners. The writers of the early twentieth century took up socially taboo topics, were inspired by other artistic media, and wove high and low culture into their work. They wrestled with profound social changes and with a brutal, seemingly pointless war. And so when late-twentieth-century writers reacted against modernism, they had also decided what the movement meant. From the longer perspective of the twenty-first century, it's clear that the aesthetic epoch reflected in much of this volume could just as well be termed "long modernism." Like their early-twentieth-century precursors, many of the writers included here experiment with literary form and subject as an antidote to what they see as the violent, empty, fragmented, and soul-crushingly conventional forms of modern life.

What is truly *post*modern, then? Writers such as Edward P. Jones, Natasha Trethewey, Patricia Highsmith, George Saunders, and Philip K. Dick turn to personal history, to low-brow visual media, to the new languages of business, and to genres such as horror and science fiction for sources of inspiration and provocation that were not typical for writers of the early twentieth century. Consider, for instance, how a lesbian pulp novel such as *The Fear and the Guilt* (1954), by Wilene Shaw (the pen name of Virginia M. Harrison), sports its genre conventions on its cover: Ruby brings her lover, Christy, to her southern home, where Christy is seduced by Ruby's father (and agrees to marry him). By contrast, Highsmith's carefully crafted realist novel, *The Price of Salt* (1952), upended such pulp conventions. It is a

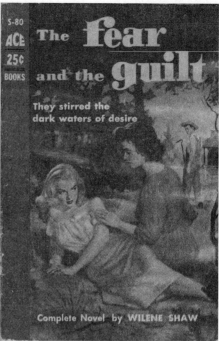

Cover of original 1952 edition of *The Price of Salt*, by Patricia Highsmith, publishing under the pseudonym Claire Morgan. The book's imagery and format placed it in the company of lowbrow erotic genre fiction such as the example on the right, *The Fear and the Guilt* (1954).

love story between two women with an unprecedented happy ending for the couple. Though some critics have noted how its narrative artistry seems to have inspired the cross-country car chase in Nabokov's *Lolita*, and while it is clear that Highsmith learned much from the great modern novelist Henry James, *The Price of Salt* wore a paperback cover and looked as steamy as its pulp sisters. Harkening back to the literature of the nineteenth century, writers understood as postmodern in this sense seek to make readers *feel* something even while they revel in satire and irony, while (for all their confessional force) the writers of "long modernism" can be suspicious of sentiment. Rejecting or reimagining what "elite" literature might look like, writers looking for alternatives to a dominant and elite modernism likewise reimagine their readers and pave the way for the innovations of a writer like Junot Díaz.

LITERATURE NOW

In the United States alone, over 50,000 novels are published each year. Worldwide, the number is well over 200,000. It is cheaper and easier than ever to make written works available to readers. Writing programs have made the professional lives of poets and other writers sustainable, even

Author **Grace Paley** teaching writing at Sarah Lawrence College.

when their work doesn't turn a profit in the publishing market. The Association of Writers and Writing Programs reports that in 1975 there were a total of 79 programs granting creative writing degrees ranging from the associate's degree to the Ph.D. In 2012 that number was 880. The teaching now done by many writers not only allows them to continue writing but also trains new writers, whose work can in turn be found in the ever-increasing numbers of creative writing journals and websites, as well as in the blogs, posts, and Twitter feeds generated daily to keep Web content fresh. If the ranks of readers and writers expanded dramatically in the United States in the wake of World War II, how much more has the audience for writing of all kinds expanded—but also fragmented—in the wake of the Internet? The rise of digital culture and of global publishing has made the ubiquity of writing, and of English, suddenly obvious.

One argument about what literature looks like now is that it is defined by its global audience, massive production, and transnational use of English. The literary critic Rebecca Walkowitz notes that many of the most successful writers now labor with the knowledge that their work will instantly be translated into multiple languages. She argues that this fact has driven a resurgence in literary experimentation with plot and character, elements of fiction that "survive" translation in ways that more material aspects of language—grammar, sound, etymology—cannot. Others point to the way that the migration of literary works to unexpected new contexts changes the interpretation and social meaning of those works. Critics have tracked, for instance, how the southern novelist William Faulkner was received in Japan in the twentieth century, or how the movie *Shrek* has been remade and repurposed by digital film artists in Iran. And Web formats privilege some forms of writing over others: fiction with short (that is, easily scrollable) chapters or sections translates better to online contexts than narratives made up of longer blocks of text. Poetry, by contrast, translates beautifully to the screen. In turn, poetry and fiction appearing in traditional print form sometimes borrow styles from texting, posts, and tweets. Readers should be sure to explore the Poetry Foundation's excellent website, which provides additional poems and readings by virtually every poet in this anthology.

What does all the writing sparked by the rise of the Internet tell us about literature today? Crucially, it reminds us that language itself is a living thing, an artistic medium that changes in the very hands of the writers and speakers who use it. Physical and virtual migrations of people and their writing in the contemporary world are driven by economic, political, religious, and personal forces—forces that call out now, as they always have, for a response in art. As Junot Díaz, Gloria Anzaldúa, Maxine Hong Kingston, Tracy K. Smith, and other writers fold multiple languages into their literary works, they recraft the English we have at our disposal. African immigration, the rise of Spanish as an American language (just as German was in the American West in the nineteenth century), and immigrations yet to come will continually reshape the literary landscape. Today, writing flourishes at the grass roots, much of it thriving apart from major publishers, advertisers, and reviewing venues even as the most admired of the writers in the last half-century become the touchstones of an evolving tradition. While this overabundance has unsettled any shared sense of what merits readers' attention, it also indicates the extraordinary energy and possibility in American literature now. Intrepid readers who go exploring will find as-yet-undiscovered wonders.

AMERICAN LITERATURE SINCE 1945

TEXTS	CONTEXTS
1941 Eudora Welty, **"Petrified Man"**	
1945 Randall Jarrell, **"The Death of the Ball Turret Gunner"**	1945 U.S. drops atomic bombs on Hiroshima and Nagasaki; Japan surrenders, ending World War II • Cold War begins
1947 Tennesse Williams, *A Streetcar Named Desire*	1947 Jackie Robinson becomes the first black Major League ballplayer
1948 Theodore Roethke, *The Lost Son*	
1949 Arthur Miller, *Death of a Salesman*	
1950 Richard Wilbur, **"A World without Objects Is a Sensible Emptiness"** • Charles Olson, **"Projective Verse"**	1950 Senator Joseph McCarthy begins attacks on supposed Communist influence on U.S. government
	1950–53 Korean War
1952 Ralph Ellison, *Invisible Man*	
1953 Saul Bellow, *The Adventures of Augie March*	1953 House Concurrent Resolution 108 dictates government's intention to "terminate" its treaty relations with Native American tribes
	1954 *Brown v. Board of Education* declares segregated schools unconstitutional • Beat Generation poets begin to gather at San Francisco's City Lights Bookshop
1955 Flannery O'Connor, **"Good Country People"**	
1955–68 John Berryman composes *The Dream Songs* (pub. 1964, 1968, 1977)	
1956 Allen Ginsberg, *Howl*	1956 Martin Luther King Jr. leads bus boycott in Montgomery, Alabama
1957 Jack Kerouac, *On the Road*	
1958 Bernard Malamud, **"The Magic Barrel"**	
1959 Philip Roth, **"Defender of the Faith"** • Robert Lowell, *Life Studies* • Frank O'Hara, **"Personism"**	1959 Fidel Castro becomes Communist leader of Cuba
1960 Thomas Pynchon, **"Entropy"** • Gwendolyn Brooks, **"We Real Cool"**	1960 Woolworth lunch counter sit-in in Greensboro, North Carolina, marks beginning of civil rights movement
1961 Denise Levertov, **"The Jacob's Ladder"**	
1962 Robert Hayden, **"Middle Passage"**	1962 United States and Soviet Union come close to war over Russian missiles based in Cuba; missiles withdrawn
1963 James Wright, **"A Blessing"**	1963 Martin Luther King Jr. delivers "I Have a Dream" speech • black church in Birmingham, Alabama, bombed, killing four girls • President John F. Kennedy assassinated

Boldface titles indicate works in the anthology.

TEXTS	CONTEXTS
1964 John Cheever, **"The Swimmer"** • Amiri Baraka (LeRoi Jones), **"An Agony. As Now."** • Frank O'Hara, **"A Step Away from Them"** • Philip K. Dick, **"Precious Artifact"**	
1965 James Baldwin, **"Going to Meet the Man"** • A. R. Ammons, **"Corson's Inlet"**	**1965** Riots break out in Watts section of Los Angeles • Malcolm X assassinated • hippie culture flourishes in San Francisco
	1965–73 Vietnam War
1966 James Merrill, **"The Broken Home"** • Sylvia Plath, *Ariel*	**1966** National Organization for Women (NOW) founded • Hayden and Brooks criticized at Black Writers' Conference, Fisk University, for composing "academic" poetry
1967 A. R. Ammons, **"A Poem Is a Walk"** • W. S. Merwin, **"For a Coming Extinction"** • Patricia Highsmith, **"The Quest for *Blank Claveringi*"**	
1968 Donald Barthelme, **"The Balloon"** • Edward Abbey, *Desert Solitaire* • Joan Didion, **"Slouching Towards Bethlehem"**	**1968** Martin Luther King Jr. assassinated • Senator Robert F. Kennedy assassinated • photo of Earthrise by Apollo 8
1969 N. Scott Momaday, *The Way to Rainy Mountain* • Kurt Vonnegut, *Slaughterhouse-Five* • Galway Kinnell, **"The Porcupine"** • Robert Penn Warren, *Audubon*	**1969** U.S. astronauts land on the moon • Stonewall riots in New York City initiate gay liberation movement • Woodstock Festival held near Bethel, New York
1970 Ishmael Reed, **"Neo-HooDoo Manifesto"**	**1970** National Guard kills four students during antiwar demonstration at Kent State University, Ohio
1971 Audre Lorde, **"Black Mother Woman"**	
1972 Rudolfo Anaya, *Bless Me, Ultima* • Anne Sexton, *The Death of the Fathers*	**1972** Watergate scandal • military draft ends
1973 Alice Walker, **"Everyday Use"** • Adrienne Rich, *Diving into the Wreck*	**1973** *Roe v. Wade* legalizes abortion • American Indian Movement members occupy Wounded Knee, South Dakota
1974 Grace Paley, **"A Conversation with My Father"** • Annie Dillard, *Pilgrim at Tinker Creek*	**1974** President Richard Nixon resigns in wake of Watergate, avoiding impeachment
1975 John Updike, **"Separating"** • John Ashbery, **"Self-Portrait in a Convex Mirror"** • Michael S. Harper, **"Nightmare Begins Responsibility"**	
1976 Elizabeth Bishop, *Geography III* • Maxine Hong Kingston, **"No Name Woman"** • Barry Lopez, *Desert Notes*	**1976** U.S. bicentennial
1977 Audre Lorde, **"Poetry Is Not a Luxury"**	
1978 Ann Beattie, **"Weekend"** • Jamaica Kincaid, **"Girl"**	
1979 Philip Levine, **"Starlight"** • Mary Oliver, **"The Black Snake"**	

TEXTS	CONTEXTS
1980 Toni Cade Bambara, "**Medley**" • Sam Shepard, *True West*	
1981 Leslie Marmon Silko, "**Lullaby**" • James Dickey, "**Falling**" • Simon J. Ortiz, "**From Sand Creek**"	
1982 Raymond Carver, "**Cathedral**" • David Mamet, *Glengarry Glen Ross*	1982 Equal Rights Amendment defeated • antinuclear movement protests manufacture of nuclear weapons • AIDS officially identified in the United States
1983 Toni Morrison, "**Recitatif**" • Joy Harjo, "**Call It Fear**"	
1984 Louise Erdrich, "**Dear John Wayne**"	
1985 Ursula K. Le Guin, "**She Unnames Them**" • Don DeLillo, *White Noise*	1985 Introduction of first desktop publishing software, Aldus pagemaker
1986 Lydia Davis, "**Break It Down**" • Art Spiegelman, *Maus I* • Rita Dove, *Thomas and Beulah* • Li-Young Lee, "**Eating Together**"	
1987 Gloria Anzaldúa, *Borderlands/La Frontera* • Sharon Olds, "**I Go Back to May 1937**"	
1988 Yusef Komunyakaa, "**Facing It**"	
1989 Amy Tan, *The Joy Luck Club*	1989 Soviet Union collapses; Cold War ends • oil tanker *Exxon Valdez* runs aground in Alaska
1990 Robert Pinsky, "**The Want Bone**" • Frank Bidart, "**Ellen West**"	1990 Congress passes Native American Graves Protection and Repatriation Act
1991 Sandra Cisneros, *Woman Hollering Creek*	1991 United States enters Persian Gulf War • World Wide Web introduced
1992 Edward P. Jones, "**The First Day**"	
1993 Gary Snyder, "**Ripples on the Surface**" • A. R. Ammons, *Garbage* • Sherman Alexie, "**This Is What It Means to Say Phoenix, Arizona**"	
	1995 Federal building in Oklahoma City bombed in a terrorist attack
1996 W. S. Merwin, "**Lament for the Makers**" • Sherman Alexie, "**The Exaggeration of Despair**" • Junot Díaz, "**Drown**" • George Saunders, "**CivilWar-Land in Bad Decline**"	
	1997 *Mars Pathfinder* robot explores Mars
1998 Billy Collins, "**I Chop Some Parsley While Listening to Art Blakey's Version of 'Three Blind Mice'**"	

TEXTS	CONTEXTS
1999 Jhumpa Lahiri, **"Sexy"** • Charles Simic, **"Arriving Celebrities"**	
2000 Lucille Clifton, **"Moonchild"**	
	2001 Execution of Timothy McVeigh, convicted of 1995 Oklahoma City bombing • September 11 terrorist attacks on Pentagon and World Trade Center
	2003 United States and Great Britain invade Iraq
2004 Louise Glück, **"October"** • David Foster Wallace, **"Consider the Lobster"**	
2006 Natasha Trethewey, *Native Guard*	
2007 Edwidge Danticat, *Brother, I'm Dying* • Junot Díaz, *The Brief Wondrous Life of Oscar Wao*	**2007** Advent of worst economic recession since the Great Depression.
	2009 Inauguration of Barack Obama as U.S. president
	2010 Massive oil spill in the Gulf of Mexico
2011 Tracy K. Smith, **"My God, It's Full of Stars"**	**2011** Death of terrorist leader Osama bin Laden, architect of 9/11 attacks
	2013 Second inauguration of Barack Obama as U.S. president
	2014 Police shooting of an unarmed black teenager named Michael Brown in Ferguson, Missouri, touches off nationwide protests
	2015 U.S. Supreme Court rules that state bans on same-sex marriage are unconstitutional • hundreds of thousands of migrants from Syria and other areas in the Middle East cross into Europe

ROBERT PENN WARREN
1905–1989

In 1969, with a long, distinguished career as a man of letters already behind him, Robert Penn Warren published his long poem *Audubon: A Vision*. Although Warren wrote many highly regarded poems before the publication of the volume, until the 1960s he was best known for his fiction. In the six books of poetry that followed *Audubon*, Warren developed the claim he had begun earlier in his career to a powerful, distinctive, American voice. The mark of Warren's poetry, from early to late, is a passion directed toward the physical world and toward a knowledge of truth. As a poet he yearns for more than what life usually discloses, yet an intense love for the world accompanies this yearning.

Warren was born in Guthrie in southern Kentucky, and much of his writing reflects his engagement with the lessons of history as they can be read in the experience of the American South. He took this sense of history most immediately from his father, who read history and poetry aloud to the family, and from his maternal grandfather, Gabriel Telemachus Penn. Warren spent his boyhood summers on this grandfather's isolated tobacco farm. There the old man, who had fought on the Confederate side in the Civil War, told Warren tales of war while the two mapped out battles together, or the boy listened while his grandfather recited poetry "by the yard" (as Warren described it), especially Sir Walter Scott and Robert Burns. The memory of an idyllic boyhood spent dreaming amid the natural world informs many of Warren's poems.

The decisive literary moment in Warren's life came when, at the age of sixteen, he enrolled at Vanderbilt University in Nashville. He had wanted to be a naval officer, but an eye injury prevented him from taking up his commission at Annapolis. Vanderbilt was enjoying a feverish interest in poetry at the time. (Even football players, Warren reported, seemed to be writing verse, and Warren remembers that people lined up for the latest issues of the *Dial* and other literary periodicals in which they might find new work by Yeats or Eliot or Hart Crane.) Part of the excitement was due to the presence of the poet John Crowe Ransom, who taught Warren's freshman composition class and soon involved him, even as an undergraduate, with the Fugitives, a group of faculty members and, according to Warren, "bookish, intelligent young businessmen" who met to discuss literature and philosophy. By the time Warren joined it was largely a poetry club at which Ransom and others read and criticized one another's work. Here Warren met Allen Tate, the gifted poet and critic, who found the redheaded undergraduate, five years his junior, "the most gifted person I have ever known." For years to come they constituted a kind of southern axis in American letters, and in 1930 they joined several other southern writers in a political manifesto, *I'll Take My Stand*. The collection of twelve essays envisioned an agrarian South with strong local cultures as the only humane alternative to an increasingly self-destructive industrialism centered in the North.

Warren attended graduate school at the University of California, at Yale, and then as a Rhodes Scholar at Oxford University in England. From 1935 to 1942 he was on the English faculty at Louisiana State University. There, along with Cleanth Brooks and Charles W. Pipkin, he founded the *Southern Review*, which for the seven years of their involvement was the most influential literary quarterly in the country. It was the principal forum for pioneering interpretative essays by "New

Critics" such as Ransom, Kenneth Burke, and R. P. Blackmur. (Brooks and Warren also edited *Understanding Poetry*, the important school anthology and text that introduced students to "close reading" on New Critical principles.) In addition, the *Southern Review* published the best fiction by emerging southern writers such as Katherine Anne Porter and Eudora Welty.

Warren's own fiction brought him wide critical attention in the 1940s. The novel *All the King's Men* (1946), which he conceived as a verse play, won the Pulitzer Prize and later became a film. It portrayed the rise and fall of a southern demagogue who closely resembled Huey Long, the Louisiana governor and senator who was assassinated in the rotunda of the Louisiana statehouse in 1935. Warren's interest was in showing the tangled motives of his protagonist, Willie Stark, a Depression-era governor who led a corrupt regime that was progressive in its social programs. In its focus on violent subjects with historical and psychological resonance, Warren's fiction anticipates his sequence *Audubon: A Vision*. Other novels, like *World Enough and Time* (1950), set in the Kentucky of the 1820s, are based on documents and grow out of his ongoing study of and response to southern history.

From 1944 to 1954 Warren was intensely active in fiction and published almost no poems. In 1952 he married the writer Eleanor Clark, his second wife, and, prompted by the landscapes where they lived in Europe and by the birth of a son and daughter in the mid 1950s, he returned to poetry with a new intimacy and autobiographical intensity. His earlier work, like "Bearded Oaks," had been strongly influenced by the formal control and the elegant, well-mannered rationality of John Crowe Ransom's verse. But beginning with the volume *Promises* (1957), and revealed fully in *Audubon*, Warren's poetic line loosened up, moved with vigor and raw energy. Although the tone of his poems sometimes grows too insistent or rhetorical, his muscular syntax and rhythm forged a "voice-instrument calibrated to experience," in the words of Dave Smith, a poet of a younger generation, indebted to Warren's work.

In *Democracy and Poetry* (1975), his Jefferson Lecture in the Humanities, Warren said, "What poetry most significantly celebrates is the capacity of man to face the deep, dark inwardness of his nature and fate." In *Audubon*, Warren's version of the historical John James Audubon must enter what Yeats once called "the abyss of the self" to create a heroic selfhood at the center of the poetry. Ornithologist and painter of *Birds of America*, Audubon (1785–1851) was artist and scientist, solitary searcher and classifier, consumed by his tasks. Basing part of his poem on Audubon's autobiographical account, Warren imagines a man launched into his true vision after an encounter with violence at the heart of experience: he narrowly escapes being robbed and murdered in the wilderness by a crone and her sons. In this incident Audubon must also confront the violent desire of his own "lust of the eye" and thereby reconcile in himself the need for both passion and reverence toward existence. Passion directs Warren's hero to slay the birds in order to paint them, to put them "In our imagination" (*Audubon* VI, "Love and Knowledge"). But reverence demands the heart's total response to the beauty of existence. This is why Warren commands his hero and himself: "Continue to walk in the world. Yes, love it!" While the most representative figure in Warren's poems is solitary—the individual, like Audubon, confronting versions of the American sublime—Warren also wrote a number of fine poems in other registers, among them some moving love poems. The sense of history that animates so much of his fiction becomes in his poems the persistent struggle of memory to overcome the passage of time, to make *then* into *now*, as reflected in the title of his volume *Now and Then: Poems 1976–1978* (1978). The struggle with time is one aspect of the heroic engagement with existence that was the dramatic center of Warren's work.

Bearded Oaks

The oaks, how subtle and marine,
Bearded, and all the layered light
Above them swims; and thus the scene,
Recessed, awaits the positive night.

So, waiting, we in the grass now lie   5
Beneath the languorous tread of light:
The grasses, kelp-like, satisfy
The nameless motions of the air.

Upon the floor of light, and time,
Unmurmuring, of polyp made,   10
We rest; we are, as light withdraws,
Twin atolls on a shelf of shade.

Ages to our construction went,
Dim architecture, hour by hour:
And violence, forgot now, lent   15
The present stillness all its power.

The storm of noon above us rolled,
Of light the fury, furious gold,
The long drag troubling us, the depth:
Dark is unrocking, unrippling, still.   20

Passion and slaughter, ruth, decay
Descend, minutely whispering down,
Silted down swaying streams, to lay
Foundation for our voicelessness.

All our debate is voiceless here,   25
As all our rage, the rage of stone
If hope is hopeless, then fearless is fear,
And history is thus undone.

Our feet once wrought the hollow street
With echo when the lamps were dead   30
At windows, once our headlight glare
Disturbed the doe that, leaping, fled.

I do not love you less that now
The caged heart makes iron stroke,
Or less that all that light once gave   35
The graduate dark should now revoke.

We live in time so little time
And we learn all so painfully,
That we may spare this hour's term
To practice for eternity.   40

1942

From Audubon[1]

I. Was Not the Lost Dauphin

[A]

Was not the lost dauphin, though handsome was only
Base-born and not even able
To make a decent living, was only
Himself, Jean Jacques, and his passion—what
Is man but his passion?   5

Saw,
Eastward and over the cypress swamp, the dawn,
Redder than meat, break;
And the large bird,
Long neck outthrust, wings crooked to scull air, moved   10
In a slow calligraphy, crank, flat, and black against
The color of God's blood spilt, as though
Pulled by a string.

Saw
It proceed across the inflamed distance.   15

Moccasins set in hoar frost, eyes fixed on the bird,
Thought: "On that sky it is black."
Thought: "In my mind it is white."
Thinking: "*Ardea occidentalis*, heron the great one."

Dawn: his heart shook in the tension of the world.   20

Dawn: and what is your passion?

[B]

October: and the bear,
Daft in the honey-light, yawns.

The bear's tongue, pink as a baby's, out-crisps to the curled tip,
It bleeds the black blood of the blueberry.   25

The teeth are more importantly white
Than has ever been imagined.

The bear feels his own fat
Sweeten, like a drowse, deep to the bone.

Bemused, above the fume of ruined blueberries,   30
The last bee hums.

1. John James Audubon (1785–1851), natural son of French parents (hence "Jean Jacques" in line 4), but later an American citizen. Painter, ornithologist, Kentucky settler, he dedicated his life to the pursuit, classification, and depiction of the *Birds of America* (first published in England, 1827). Among the stories told about his birth was one (false) that he was the Dauphin, the son of the dethroned and executed Louis XVI and Marie Antoinette of France.

The wings, like mica, glint
In the sunlight.

He leans on his gun. Thinks
How thin is the membrane between himself and the world.　　　35

VI. *Love and Knowledge*

Their footless dance
Is of the beautiful liability of their nature.
Their eyes are round, boldly convex, bright as a jewel,
And merciless. They do not know
Compassion, and if they did,　　　5
We should not be worthy of it. They fly
In air that glitters like fluent crystal
And is hard as perfectly transparent iron, they cleave it
With no effort. They cry
In a tongue multitudinous, often like music.　　　10

He slew them, at surprising distances, with his gun.
Over a body held in his hand, his head was bowed low,
But not in grief.

He put them where they are, and there we see them:
In our imagination.　　　15

What is love?

Our name for it is knowledge.

VII. *Tell Me a Story*

[A]

Long ago, in Kentucky, I, a boy, stood
By a dirt road, in first dark, and heard
The great geese hoot northward.

I could not see them, there being no moon
And the stars sparse. I heard them.　　　5

I did not know what was happening in my heart.

It was the season before the elderberry blooms,
Therefore they were going north.

The sound was passing northward.

[B]

Tell me a story.　　　10

In this century, and moment, of mania,
Tell me a story.

Make it a story of great distances, and starlight.

The name of the story will be Time,
But you must not pronounce its name.   15

Tell me a story of deep delight.

                                                              1969

Mortal Limit

I saw the hawk ride updraft in the sunset over Wyoming.
It rose from coniferous darkness, past gray jags
Of mercilessness, past whiteness, into the gloaming
Of dream-spectral light above the last purity of snow-snags.

There—west—were the Tetons.[1] Snow-peaks would soon be   5
In dark profile to break constellations. Beyond what height
Hangs now the black speck? Beyond what range will gold eyes see
New ranges rise to mark a last scrawl of light?

Or, having tasted that atmosphere's thinness, does it
Hang motionless in dying vision before   10
It knows it will accept the mortal limit,
And swing into the great circular downwardness that will restore

The breath of earth? Of rock? Of rot? Of other such
Items, and the darkness of whatever dream we clutch?

                                                              1985

1. High mountain range in northwest Wyoming.

THEODORE ROETHKE
1908–1963

Theodore Roethke had the kind of childhood a poet might have invented. He was born in Saginaw, Michigan, where both his German grandfather and his father kept greenhouses for a living. The greenhouse world, he later said, represented for him "both heaven and hell, a kind of tropics created in the savage climate of Michigan, where austere German Americans turned their love of order and their terrifying efficiency into something truly beautiful." Throughout his life he was haunted both by the ordered, protected world of the greenhouse—the constant activity of growth, the cultivated flowers—and by the desolate landscape of his part of Michigan. "The marsh, thê mire, the Void, is always there, immediate and terrifying. It is a splendid place for schooling the spirit. It is America."

Roethke's poetry often reenacted this "schooling" of the spirit by revisiting the landscapes of his childhood: the nature poems that make up the largest part of his early work try to bridge the distance between a child's consciousness and the adult mysteries presided over by his father. Roethke arranged and rearranged these poems to give the sense of a spiritual autobiography, especially in preparing the volumes *The Lost Son and Other Poems* (1948), *Praise to the End!* (1951), and *The Waking* (1953). In what are known as "the greenhouse poems," the greenhouse world emerged as a "reality harsher than reality," the cultivator's activity pulsating and threatening. Its overseers, like "Frau Bauman, Frau Schmidt, and Frau Schwartze" (the title of one poem) emerge as gods, fates, muses, and witches all in one. By focusing on the minute processes of botanical growth—the rooting, the budding—the poet found a way of participating in the mysteries of this once alien world, whether he was deep in the subterranean root cellar or, as a child, perched high on top of the greenhouse.

In his books *The Lost Son* and *Praise to the End!* Roethke explored the regenerative possibilities of prerational speech (like children's riddles) in which language as sound recaptures nonlogical states of being. In these poems, his most dazzling and original work, Roethke opened up the possibilities of language. The title of one section of the long poem *The Lost Son* is "The Gibber," a pun because the word means both a meaningless utterance and the pouch at the base of a flower's calyx. The pun identifies principles of growth with the possibilities of speech freed from logical meanings, and the sequence as a whole suggests the power of both nature and language to revive the spirit of an adult life: "A lively understandable spirit / Once entertained you. / It will come again. / Be still. / Wait."

If the nature poems of Roethke's first four books explore the anxieties within him since childhood, his later love poems show him in periods of release and momentary pleasure: "And I dance round and round, / A fond and foolish man, / And see and suffer myself / In another being at last." The love poems, many included in *Words for the Wind* (1958) and *The Far Field* (1964), are among the most appealing in modern American verse. His beautiful and tender "Elegy for Jane" should be included in this category. These poems stand in sharp relief to the suffering Roethke experienced in other areas of his personal life—several mental breakdowns and periods of alcoholism—which led to a premature death. *The Far Field*, a posthumous volume, includes fierce, strongly rhymed lyrics in which Roethke tried "bare, even terrible statement," pressing toward the threshold of spiritual insight: "A man goes far to find out what he is— / Death of the self in a long, tearless night, / All natural shapes blazing unnatural light." The nature poems of this last volume, gathered as "The North American Sequence," use extended landscape to find natural analogies for the human passage toward the dark unknown, hoping "in their rhythms to catch the very movement of mind itself."

Roethke is remembered as one of the great teachers of poetry, especially by those young poets and critics who studied with him at the University of Washington from 1948 until the time of his death. James Wright, David Wagoner, and Richard Hugo, among others, attended his classes. He was noted for his mastery of sound and metrics. Although his own poetry was intensely personal, his starting advice to students always deemphasized undisciplined self-expression. "Write like someone else," he instructed beginners. In Roethke's own career, however, this advice had its costs. His apprenticeship to Yeats, in particular, endangered his own poetic voice; in some late poems the echo of this great predecessor makes Roethke all but inaudible.

Roethke was much honored later in his career: a Pulitzer Prize for *The Waking* (1953); a National Book Award and Bollingen Prize for the collected poems, *Words for the Wind* (1958); and a posthumous National Book Award for *The Far Field* (1964).

Cuttings

Sticks-in-a-drowse droop over sugary loam,
Their intricate stem-fur dries;
But still the delicate slips keep coaxing up water;
The small cells bulge;

One nub of growth   5
Nudges a sand-crumb loose,
Pokes through a musty sheath
Its pale tendrilous horn.

1948

Cuttings

(later)

This urge, wrestle, resurrection of dry sticks,
Cut stems struggling to put down feet,
What saint strained so much,
Rose on such lopped limbs to a new life?

I can hear, underground, that sucking and sobbing,   5
In my veins, in my bones I feel it,—
The small waters seeping upward,
The tight grains parting at last.
When sprouts break out,
Slippery as fish   10
I quail, lean to beginnings, sheath-wet.

1948

Root Cellar

Nothing would sleep in that cellar, dank as a ditch,
Bulbs broke out of boxes hunting for chinks in the dark,
Shoots dangled and drooped,
Lolling obscenely from mildewed crates,
Hung down long yellow evil necks, like tropical snakes.   5
And what a congress of stinks!—
Roots ripe as old bait,
Pulpy stems, rank, silo-rich,
Leaf-mold, manure, lime, piled against slippery planks.
Nothing would give up life: 10
Even the dirt kept breathing a small breath.

1948

Big Wind

Where were the greenhouses going,
Lunging into the lashing
Wind driving water
So far down the river
All the faucets stopped?—   5
So we drained the manure-machine
For the steam plant,
Pumping the stale mixture
Into the rusty boilers,
Watching the pressure gauge   10
Waver over to red,
As the seams hissed
And the live steam
Drove to the far
End of the rose-house,   15
Where the worst wind was,
Creaking the cypress window-frames,
Cracking so much thin glass
We stayed all night,
Stuffing the holes with burlap;   20
But she rode it out,
That old rose-house,
She hove into the teeth of it,
The core and pith of that ugly storm,
Ploughing with her stiff prow,   25
Bucking into the wind-waves
That broke over the whole of her,
Flailing her sides with spray,
Flinging long strings of wet across the roof-top,
Finally veering, wearing themselves out, merely   30
Whistling thinly under the wind-vents;
She sailed until the calm morning,
Carrying her full cargo of roses.

1948

Weed Puller

Under the concrete benches,
Hacking at black hairy roots,—
Those lewd monkey-tails hanging from drainholes,—
Digging into the soft rubble underneath,
Webs and weeds,   5
Grubs and snails and sharp sticks,
Or yanking tough fern-shapes,
Coiled green and thick, like dripping smilax,[1]

---

1. A type of fern.

Tugging all day at perverse life:
The indignity of it!—   10
With everything blooming above me,
Lilies, pale-pink cyclamen, roses,
Whole fields lovely and inviolate,—
Me down in that fetor of weeds,
Crawling on all fours,   15
Alive, in a slippery grave.

                                                        1948

Frau Bauman, Frau Schmidt, and Frau Schwartze[1]

Gone the three ancient ladies
Who creaked on the greenhouse ladders,
Reaching up white strings
To wind, to wind
The sweet-pea tendrils, the smilax,[2]   5
Nasturtiums, the climbing
Roses, to straighten
Carnations, red
Chrysanthemums; the stiff
Stems, jointed like corn,   10
They tied and tucked,—
These nurses of nobody else.
Quicker than birds, they dipped
Up and sifted the dirt;
They sprinkled and shook;   15
They stood astride pipes,
Their skirts billowing out wide into tents,
Their hands twinkling with wet;
Like witches they flew along rows
Keeping creation at ease;   20
With a tendril for needle
They sewed up the air with a stem;
They teased out the seed that the cold kept asleep,—
All the coils, loops, and whorls.
They trellised the sun; they plotted for more than themselves. 25

I remember how they picked me up, a spindly kid,
Pinching and poking my thin ribs
Till I lay in their laps, laughing,
Weak as a whiffet;[3]
Now, when I'm alone and cold in my bed,   30
They still hover over me,
These ancient leathery crones,

1. Women who worked in the greenhouse owned
by Roethke's father.
2. A type of fern.

3. A small, young, or unimportant person (probably from *whippet*, a small, delicate-looking racing
dog).

With their bandannas stiffened with sweat,
And their thorn-bitten wrists,
And their snuff-laden breath blowing lightly over me in my first
    sleep.   35

1948

Child on Top of a Greenhouse

The wind billowing out the seat of my britches,
My feet crackling splinters of glass and dried putty,
The half-grown chrysanthemums staring up like accusers,
Up through the streaked glass, flashing with sunlight,
A few white clouds all rushing eastward,   5
A line of elms plunging and tossing like horses,
And everyone, everyone pointing up and shouting!

1948

My Papa's Waltz

The whiskey on your breath
Could make a small boy dizzy;
But I hung on like death:
Such waltzing was not easy.

We romped until the pans   5
Slid from the kitchen shelf;
My mother's countenance
Could not unfrown itself.

The hand that held my wrist
Was battered on one knuckle;   10
At every step you missed
My right ear scraped a buckle.

You beat time on my head
With a palm caked hard by dirt,
Then waltzed me off to bed   15
Still clinging to your shirt.

1948

Dolor

I have known the inexorable sadness of pencils,
Neat in their boxes, dolor of pad and paper-weight,
All the misery of manilla folders and mucilage,

Desolation in immaculate public places,
Lonely reception room, lavatory, switchboard,   5
The unalterable pathos of basin and pitcher,
Ritual of multigraph, paper-clip, comma,
Endless duplication of lives and objects.
And I have seen dust from the walls of institutions,
Finer than flour, alive, more dangerous than silica,   10
Sift, almost invisible, through long afternoons of tedium,
Dropping a fine film on nails and delicate eyebrows,
Glazing the pale hair, the duplicate grey standard faces.

1948

Night Crow

When I saw that clumsy crow
Flap from a wasted tree,
A shape in the mind rose up:
Over the gulfs of dream
Flew a tremendous bird   5
Further and further away
Into a moonless black,
Deep in the brain, far back.

1948

The Lost Son

I. The Flight

At Woodlawn[1] I heard the dead cry:
I was lulled by the slamming of iron,
A slow drip over stones,
Toads brooding wells.
All the leaves stuck out their tongues;   5
I shook the softening chalk of my bones,
Saying,
Snail, snail, glister me forward,
Bird, soft-sigh me home,
Worm, be with me.   10
This is my hard time.

Fished in an old wound,
The soft pond of repose;
Nothing nibbled my line,
Not even the minnows came.   15

Sat in an empty house
Watching shadows crawl,

1. A cemetery.

Scratching.
There was one fly.

Voice, come out of the silence.   20
Say something.
Appear in the form of a spider
Or a moth beating the curtain.

Tell me:
Which is the way I take;   25
Out of what door do I go,
Where and to whom?

Dark hollows said, lee to the wind,
The moon said, back of an eel,
The salt said, look by the sea,   30
Your tears are not enough praise,
You will find no comfort here,
In the kingdom of bang and blab.

Running lightly over spongy ground,
Past the pasture of flat stones,   35
The three elms,
The sheep strewn on a field,
Over a rickety bridge
Toward the quick-water, wrinkling and rippling.

Hunting along the river,   40
Down among the rubbish, the bug-riddled foliage,
By the muddy pond-edge, by the bog-holes,
By the shrunken lake, hunting, in the heat of summer.

The shape of a rat?
It's bigger than that.   45
It's less than a leg
And more than a nose,
Just under the water
It usually goes.

Is it soft like a mouse?   50
Can it wrinkle its nose?
Could it come in the house
On the tips of its toes?

Take the skin of a cat
And the back of an eel,   55
Then roll them in grease,—
That's the way it would feel.

It's sleek as an otter
With wide webby toes
Just under the water   60
It usually goes.

2. *The Pit*

Where do the roots go?
    Look down under the leaves.
Who put the moss there?
    These stones have been here too long.   65
Who stunned the dirt into noise?
    Ask the mole, he knows.
I feel the slime of a wet nest.
    Beware Mother Mildew.
Nibble again, fish nerves.   70

3. *The Gibber*

At the wood's mouth,
By the cave's door,
I listened to something
I had heard before.

Dogs of the groin   75
Barked and howled,
The sun was against me,
The moon would not have me.

The weeds whined,
The snakes cried,   80
The cows and briars
Said to me: Die.

What a small song. What slow clouds. What dark water.
Hath the rain a father? All the caves are ice. Only the snow's here.
I'm cold. I'm cold all over. Rub me in father and mother.   85
Fear was my father, Father Fear.
His look drained the stones.

    What gliding shape
    Beckoning through halls,
    Stood poised on the stair,
    Fell dreamily down?   90

    From the mouths of jugs
    Perched on many shelves,
    I saw substance flowing
    That cold morning.   95

    Like a slither of eels
    That watery cheek
    As my own tongue kissed
    My lips awake.

Is this the storm's heart? The ground is unstilling itself.   100
My veins are running nowhere. Do the bones cast out their fire?

Is the seed leaving the old bed? These buds are live as birds.
Where, where are the tears of the world?
Let the kisses resound, flat like a butcher's palm;
Let the gestures freeze; our doom is already decided.   105
All the windows are burning! What's left of my life?
I want the old rage, the lash of primordial milk!
Goodbye, goodbye, old stones, the time-order is going,
I have married my hands to perpetual agitation,
I run, I run to the whistle of money.   110

    Money money money
    Water water water

    How cool the grass is.
    Has the bird left?
    The stalk still sways.   115
    Has the worm a shadow?
    What do the clouds say?

    These sweeps of light undo me.
    Look, look, the ditch is running white!
    I've more veins than a tree!   120
    Kiss me, ashes, I'm falling through a dark swirl.

4. *The Return*

    The way to the boiler was dark,
    Dark all the way,
    Over slippery cinders
    Through the long greenhouse.   125

    The roses kept breathing in the dark.
    They had many mouths to breathe with.
    My knees made little winds underneath
    Where the weeds slept.

    There was always a single light   130
    Swinging by the fire-pit,
    Where the fireman pulled out roses,
    The big roses, the big bloody clinkers.[2]

    Once I stayed all night.
    The light in the morning came slowly over the white   135
    Snow.
    There were many kinds of cool
    Air.
    Then came steam.

    Pipe-knock.   140

---

2. Large cinders; the residue left in burning coal.

Scurry of warm over small plants.
Ordnung!³ ordnung!
Papa is coming!

    A fine haze moved off the leaves;
    Frost melted on far panes;   145
    The rose, the chrysanthemum turned toward the light.
    Even the hushed forms, the bent yellowy weeds
    Moved in a slow up-sway.

5. "It was beginning winter"

It was beginning winter,
An in-between time,   150
The landscape still partly brown:
The bones of weeds kept swinging in the wind,
Above the blue snow.

It was beginning winter,
The light moved slowly over the frozen field,   155
Over the dry seed-crowns,
The beautiful surviving bones
Swinging in the wind.

Light traveled over the wide field;
Stayed.   160
The weeds stopped swinging.
The mind moved, not alone,
Through the clear air, in the silence.

    Was it light?
    Was it light within?
    Was it light within light?   165
    Stillness becoming alive,
    Yet still?

A lively understandable spirit
Once entertained you.   170
It will come again.
Be still.
Wait.

                                   1948

The Waking

    I wake to sleep, and take my waking slow.
    I feel my fate in what I cannot fear.
    I learn by going where I have to go.

---

3. A call to order (German).

We think by feeling. What is there to know?
I hear my being dance from ear to ear.   5
I wake to sleep, and take my waking slow.

Of those so close beside me, which are you?
God bless the Ground! I shall walk softly there,
And learn by going where I have to go.

Light takes the Tree; but who can tell us how?   10
The lowly worm climbs up a winding stair;
I wake to sleep, and take my waking slow.

Great Nature has another thing to do
To you and me; so take the lively air,
And, lovely, learn by going where to go.   15

This shaking keeps me steady. I should know.
What falls away is always. And is near.
I wake to sleep, and take my waking slow.
I learn by going where I have to go.

                                                    1953

Elegy for Jane

My Student, Thrown by a Horse

I remember the neckcurls, limp and damp as tendrils;
And her quick look, a sidelong pickerel smile;
And how, once startled into talk, the light syllables leaped for her,
And she balanced in the delight of her thought,
A wren, happy, tail into the wind,   5
Her song trembling the twigs and small branches.
The shade sang with her;
The leaves, their whispers turned to kissing;
And the mold sang in the bleached valleys under the rose.

Oh, when she was sad, she cast herself down into such a pure depth,   10
Even a father could not find her:
Scraping her cheek against straw;
Stirring the clearest water.

My sparrow, you are not here,
Waiting like a fern, making a spiny shadow.   15
The sides of wet stones cannot console me,
Nor the moss, wound with the last light.

If only I could nudge you from this sleep,
My maimed darling, my skittery pigeon.
Over this damp grave I speak the words of my love: 20
I, with no rights in this matter,
Neither father nor lover.

                                                    1953

I Knew a Woman

I knew a woman, lovely in her bones,
When small birds sighed, she would sigh back at them;
Ah, when she moved, she moved more ways than one:
The shapes a bright container can contain!
Of her choice virtues only gods should speak,   5
Or English poets who grew up on Greek
(I'd have them sing in chorus, cheek to cheek).

How well her wishes went! She stroked my chin,
She taught me Turn, and Counter-turn, and Stand;[1]
She taught me Touch, that undulant white skin;   10
I nibbled meekly from her proffered hand;
She was the sickle; I, poor I, the rake,
Coming behind her for her pretty sake
(But what prodigious mowing we did make).

Love likes a gander, and adores a goose: 15
Her full lips pursed, the errant note to seize;
She played it quick, she played it light and loose;
My eyes, they dazzled at her flowing knees;
Her several parts could keep a pure repose,
Or one hip quiver with a mobile nose   20
(She moved in circles, and those circles moved).

Let seed be grass, and grass turn into hay:
I'm martyr to a motion not my own;
What's freedom for? To know eternity.
I swear she cast a shadow white as stone.   25
But who would count eternity in days?
These old bones live to learn her wanton ways:
(I measure time by how a body sways).

1958

Wish for a Young Wife

My lizard, my lively writher,
May your limbs never wither,
May the eyes in your face
Survive the green ice
Of envy's mean gaze;   5
May you live out your life
Without hate, without grief,
And your hair ever blaze,

---

1. The triadic parts of a Pindaric ode, a ceremonious poem in the manner of the Greek lyric poet Pindar (c. 522–c. 438 B.C.E.).

In the sun, in the sun,
When I am undone,   10
When I am no one.

1964

In a Dark Time

In a dark time, the eye begins to see,
I meet my shadow in the deepening shade;
I hear my echo in the echoing wood—
A lord of nature weeping to a tree.
I live between the heron and the wren,   5
Beasts of the hill and serpents of the den.

What's madness but nobility of soul
At odds with circumstance? The day's on fire!
I know the purity of pure despair,
My shadow pinned against a sweating wall.   10
That place among the rocks—is it a cave,
Or winding path? The edge is what I have.

A steady storm of correspondences!
A night flowing with birds, a ragged moon,
And in broad day the midnight come again!   15
A man goes far to find out what he is—
Death of the self in a long, tearless night,
All natural shapes blazing unnatural light.

Dark, dark my light, and darker my desire.
My soul, like some heat-maddened summer fly,   20
Keeps buzzing at the sill. Which I is *I*?
A fallen man, I climb out of my fear.
The mind enters itself, and God the mind,
And one is One, free in the tearing wind.

1964

EUDORA WELTY
1909–2001

In her essay "Place in Fiction," Eudora Welty spoke of her work as filled with the spirit of place: "Location is the ground conductor of all the currents of emotion and belief and moral conviction that charge out from the story in its course." Both her outwardly uneventful life and her writing are most intimately connected to the topography and atmosphere, the season and the soil of Mississippi, her lifelong home.

Born in Jackson to parents who came from the North, and raised in comfortable circumstances (her father headed an insurance company), she attended Mississippi State College for Women, then graduated from the University of Wisconsin in 1929. After a course in advertising at the Columbia University School of Business, she returned to Mississippi, working first as a radio writer and newspaper society editor, then for the Depression-era Works Progress Administration, taking photographs of and interviewing local residents. Those travels would be reflected in her fiction and also in a book of her photographs, *One Time and Place*, published in 1971.

She began writing fiction after her return to Mississippi in 1931 and five years later published her first story, "Death of a Traveling Salesman," in a small magazine. Over the next two years six of her stories were published in the *Southern Review*, a serious literary magazine one of whose editors was the poet and novelist Robert Penn Warren. She also received strong support from Katherine Anne Porter, who contributed an introduction to Welty's first book of stories, *A Curtain of Green* (1941). That introduction hailed the arrival of another gifted southern fiction writer, and in fact the volume contained some of the best stories she ever wrote, such as "Petrified Man." Her profusion of metaphor and the difficult surface of her narrative—often oblique and indirect in its effect—were in part a mark of her admiration for modern writers like Virginia Woolf and (as with any young southern writer) William Faulkner. Although Welty's stories were as shapely as those of her mentor, Porter, they were more richly idiomatic and comic in their inclination. A second collection, *The Wide Net*, appeared two years later; and her first novel, *The Robber Bridegroom*, was published in 1942.

In that year and the next she was awarded the O. Henry Memorial Prize for the best piece of short fiction, and from then on she received a steady stream of awards and prizes, including the Pulitzer Prize for her novel *The Optimist's Daughter* (1972). Her most ambitious and longest piece of fiction is *Losing Battles* (1970), in which she aimed to compose a narrative made up almost wholly out of her characters' voices in mainly humorous interplay. Like Robert Frost, Welty loved gossip in all its actuality and intimacy, and if that love failed in the novels to produce compelling, extended sequences, it did result in many lively and entertaining pages. Perhaps her finest single book after *A Curtain of Green* was *The Golden Apples* (1949), a sequence of tales about a fabulous, invented, small Mississippi community named Morgana. Her characters appear and reappear in these related stories and come together most memorably in the brilliant "June Recital," perhaps her masterpiece.

Throughout her fiction Welty's wonderfully sharp sense of humor is strongly evident. Although her characters often consist of involuted southern families, physically handicapped, mentally retarded, or generally unstable kinfolk—and although her narratives are shot through with undercurrents of death, violence, and degradation—Welty transforms everything with an entertaining twist. No matter how desperate a situation may be, she makes us listen to the way a character talks about it; we pay attention to style rather than information. And although her attitude toward human folly is satiric, her satire is devoid of the wish to undermine and mock her characters. Instead, the vivid realizations of her prose give them irresistible life and a memorable expressiveness. Yet she remarked in an essay that "fine story writers seem to be in a sense obstructionists," and Welty's narratives unfold through varied repetitions or reiterations that have, she once claimed, the function of a deliberate double exposure in photography. By making us pay close attention to who is speaking and the implications of that speech, by asking us to imagine the way in which a silent character is responding to that speech, and by making us read behind the deceptively simple response she gives to that character, she makes us active readers, playfully engaged in a typically complicated scene. "Why I Live at the P.O.," "Keela, the Outcast Indian Maiden," "Powerhouse," "June Recital," "Petrified Man," and many others demonstrate the strength and the joy of her art. And although she has been called a "regional" writer, she has noted the condescending nature of that term, which she calls an "outsider's term; it has no meaning for the insider who is doing the writing, because as far as he knows he is simply writing about life" (*On Writing*). So it is with Eudora Welty's fiction.

The text is from *A Curtain of Green* (1941).

Petrified Man

"Reach in my purse and git me a cigarette without no powder in it if you kin, Mrs. Fletcher, honey," said Leota to her ten o'clock shampoo-and-set customer. "I don't like no perfumed cigarettes."

Mrs. Fletcher gladly reached over to the lavender shelf under the lavender-framed mirror, shook a hair net loose from the clasp of the patent-leather bag, and slapped her hand down quickly on a powder puff which burst out when the purse was opened.

"Why, look at the peanuts, Leota!" said Mrs. Fletcher in her marvelling voice.

"Honey, them goobers has been in my purse a week if they's been in it a day. Mrs. Pike bought them peanuts."

"Who's Mrs. Pike?" asked Mrs. Fletcher, settling back. Hidden in this den of curling fluid and henna[1] packs, separated by a lavender swing-door from the other customers, who were being gratified in other booths, she could give her curiosity its freedom. She looked expectantly at the black part in Leota's yellow curls as she bent to light the cigarette.

"Mrs. Pike is this lady from New Orleans," said Leota, puffing, and pressing into Mrs. Fletcher's scalp with strong red-nailed fingers. "A friend, not a customer. You see, like maybe I told you last time, me and Fred and Sal and Joe all had us a fuss, so Sal and Joe up and moved out, so we didn't do a thing but rent out their room. So we rented it to Mrs. Pike. And Mr. Pike." She flicked an ash into the basket of dirty towels. "Mrs. Pike is a very decided blonde. *She* bought me the peanuts."

"She must be cute," said Mrs. Fletcher.

"Honey, 'cute' ain't the word for what she is. I'm tellin' you, Mrs. Pike is attractive. She has her a good time. She's got a sharp eye out, Mrs. Pike has."

She dashed the comb through the air, and paused dramatically as a cloud of Mrs. Fletcher's hennaed hair floated out of the lavender teeth like a small storm-cloud.

"Hair fallin'."

"Aw, Leota."

"Uh-huh, commencin' to fall out," said Leota, combing again, and letting fall another cloud.

"Is it any dandruff in it?" Mrs. Fletcher was frowning, her hair-line eyebrows diving down toward her nose, and her wrinkled, beady-lashed eyelids batting with concentration.

"Nope." She combed again. "Just fallin' out."

"Bet it was that last perm'nent you gave me that did it," Mrs. Fletcher said cruelly. "Remember you cooked me fourteen minutes."

"You had fourteen minutes comin' to you," said Leota with finality.

---

1. Reddish brown dye for tinting hair.

"Bound to be somethin'," persisted Mrs. Fletcher. "Dandruff, dandruff. I couldn't of caught a thing like that from Mr. Fletcher, could I?"

"Well," Leota answered at last, "you know what I heard in here yestiddy, one of Thelma's ladies was settin' over yonder in Thelma's booth gittin' a machineless, and I don't mean to insist or insinuate or anything, Mrs. Fletcher, but Thelma's lady just happ'med to throw out—I forgotten what she was talkin' about at the time—that you was p-r-e-g., and lots of times that'll make your hair do awful funny, fall out and God knows what all. It just ain't our fault, is the way I look at it."

There was a pause. The women stared at each other in the mirror.

"Who was it?" demanded Mrs. Fletcher.

"Honey, I really couldn't say," said Leota. "Not that you look it."

"Where's Thelma? I'll get it out of her," said Mrs. Fletcher.

"Now, honey, I wouldn't go and git mad over a little thing like that," Leota said, combing hastily, as though to hold Mrs. Fletcher down by the hair. "I'm sure it was somebody didn't mean no harm in the world. How far gone are you?"

"Just wait," said Mrs. Fletcher, and shrieked for Thelma, who came in and took a drag from Leota's cigarette.

"Thelma, honey, throw your mind back to yestiddy if you kin," said Leota, drenching Mrs. Fletcher's hair with a thick fluid and catching the overflow in a cold wet towel at her neck.

"Well, I got my lady half wound for a spiral," said Thelma doubtfully.

"This won't take but a minute," said Leota. "Who is it you got in there, old Horse Face? Just cast your mind back and try to remember who your lady was yestiddy who happ'm to mention that my customer was pregnant, that's all. She's dead to know."

Thelma drooped her blood-red lips and looked over Mrs. Fletcher's head into the mirror. "Why, honey, I ain't got the faintest," she breathed. "I really don't recollect the faintest. But I'm sure she meant no harm. I declare, I forgot my hair finally got combed and thought it was a stranger behind me."

"Was it that Mrs. Hutchinson?" Mrs. Fletcher was tensely polite.

"Mrs. Hutchinson? Oh, Mrs. Hutchinson." Thelma batted her eyes. "Naw, precious, she come on Thursday and didn't ev'm mention your name. I doubt if she ev'm knows you're on the way."

"Thelma!" cried Leota staunchly.

"All I know is, whoever it is 'll be sorry some day. Why, I just barely knew it myself!" cried Mrs. Fletcher. "Just let her wait!"

"Why? What're you gonna do to her?"

It was a child's voice, and the women looked down. A little boy was making tents with aluminum wave pinchers[2] on the floor under the sink.

"Billy Boy, hon, mustn't bother nice ladies," Leota smiled. She slapped him brightly and behind her back waved Thelma out of the booth. "Ain't Billy Boy a sight? Only three years old and already just nuts about the beauty-parlor business."

"I never saw him here before," said Mrs. Fletcher, still unmollified.

"He ain't been here before, that's how come," said Leota. "He belongs to Mrs. Pike. She got her a job but it was Fay's Millinery. He oughtn't to try on those ladies' hats, they come down over his eyes like I don't know what.

---

2. Clips used to form and hold (or set) hair curl or wave.

They just git to look ridiculous, that's what, an' of course he's gonna put 'em on: hats. They tole Mrs. Pike they didn't appreciate him hangin' around there. Here, he couldn't hurt a thing."

"Well! I don't like children that much," said Mrs. Fletcher.

"Well!" said Leota moodily.

"Well! I'm almost tempted not to have this one," said Mrs. Fletcher. "That Mrs. Hutchinson! Just looks straight through you when she sees you on the street and then spits at you behind your back."

"Mr. Fletcher would beat you on the head if you didn't have it now," said Leota reasonably. "After going this far."

Mrs. Fletcher sat up straight. "Mr. Fletcher can't do a thing with me."

"He can't!" Leota winked at herself in the mirror.

"No, siree, he can't. If he so much as raises his voice against me, he knows good and well I'll have one of my sick headaches, and then I'm just not fit to live with. And if I really look that pregnant already—"

"Well, now, honey, I just want you to know—I habm't told any of my ladies and I ain't goin' to tell 'em—even that you're losin' your hair. You just get you one of those Stork-a-Lure dresses and stop worryin'. What people don't know don't hurt nobody, as Mrs. Pike says."

"Did you tell Mrs. Pike?" asked Mrs. Fletcher sulkily.

"Well, Mrs. Fletcher, look, you ain't ever goin' to lay eyes on Mrs. Pike or her lay eyes on you, so what diffunce does it make in the long run?"

"I knew it!" Mrs. Fletcher deliberately nodded her head so as to destroy a ringlet Leota was working on behind her ear. "Mrs. Pike!"

Leota sighed. "I reckon I might as well tell you. It wasn't any more Thelma's lady tole me you was pregnant than a bat."

"Not Mrs. Hutchinson?"

"Naw, Lord! It was Mrs. Pike."

"Mrs. Pike!" Mrs. Fletcher could only sputter and let curling fluid roll into her ear. "How could Mrs. Pike possibly know I was pregnant or otherwise, when she doesn't even know me? The nerve of some people!"

"Well, here's how it was. Remember Sunday?"

"Yes," said Mrs. Fletcher.

"Sunday, Mrs. Pike an' me was all by ourself. Mr. Pike and Fred had gone over to Eagle Lake, sayin' they was goin' to catch 'em some fish, but they didn't a course. So we was gettin' in Mrs. Pike's car, it's a 1939 Dodge—"

"1939, eh," said Mrs. Fletcher.

"—An' we was gettin' us a Jax beer apiece—that's the beer that Mrs. Pike says is made right in N.O., so she won't drink no other kind. So I seen you drive up to the drugstore an' run in for just a secont, leavin' I reckon Mr. Fletcher in the car, an' come runnin' out with looked like a perscription. So I says to Mrs. Pike, just to be makin' talk, 'Right yonder's Mrs. Fletcher, and I reckon that's Mr. Fletcher—she's one of my regular customers,' I says."

"I had on a figured print," said Mrs. Fletcher tentatively.

"You sure did," agreed Leota. "So Mrs. Pike, she give you a good look— she's very observant, a good judge of character, cute as a minute, you know— and she says, 'I bet you another Jax that lady's three months on the way.'"

"What gall!" said Mrs. Fletcher. "Mrs. Pike!"

"Mrs. Pike ain't goin' to bite you," said Leota. "Mrs. Pike is a lovely girl, you'd be crazy about her, Mrs. Fletcher. But she can't sit still a minute. We went to the travellin' freak show yestiddy after work. I got through early—nine o'clock. In the vacant store next door. What, you ain't been?"

"No, I despise freaks," declared Mrs. Fletcher.

"Aw. Well, honey, talkin' about bein' pregnant an' all, you ought to see those twins in a bottle, you really owe it to yourself."

"What twins?" asked Mrs. Fletcher out of the side of her mouth.

"Well, honey, they got these two twins in a bottle, see? Born joined plumb together—dead a course." Leota dropped her voice into a soft lyrical hum. "They was about this long—pardon—must of been full time, all right, wouldn't you say?—an' they had these two heads an' two faces an' four arms an' four legs, all kind of joined *here*. See, this face looked this-a-way, and the other face looked that-a-way, over their shoulder, see. Kinda pathetic."

"Glah!" said Mrs. Fletcher disapprovingly.

"Well, ugly? Honey, I mean to tell you—their parents was first cousins and all like that. Billy Boy, git me a fresh towel from off Teeny's stack—this 'n's wringin' wet—an' quit ticklin' my ankles with that curler. I declare! He don't miss nothin'."

"Me and Mr. Fletcher aren't one speck of kin, or he could never of had me," said Mrs. Fletcher placidly.

"Of course not!" protested Leota. "Neither is me an' Fred, not that we know of. Well, honey, what Mrs. Pike liked was the pygmies. They've got these pygmies down there, too, an' Mrs. Pike was just wild about 'em. You know, the teeniniest men in the universe? Well, honey, they can just rest back on their little bohunkus an' roll around an' you can't hardly tell if they're sittin' or standin'. That'll give you some idea. They're about forty-two years old. Just suppose it was your husband!"

"Well, Mr. Fletcher is five foot nine and one half," said Mrs. Fletcher quickly.

"Fred's five foot ten," said Leota, "but I tell him he's still a shrimp, account of I'm so tall." She made a deep wave over Mrs. Fletcher's other temple with the comb. "Well, these pygmies are a kind of a dark brown, Mrs. Fletcher. Not bad lookin' for what they are, you know."

"I wouldn't care for them," said Mrs. Fletcher. "What does that Mrs. Pike see in them?"

"Aw, I don't know," said Leota. "She's just cute, that's all. But they got this man, this petrified man, that ever'thing ever since he was nine years old, when it goes through his digestion, see, somehow Mrs. Pike says it goes to his joints and has been turning to stone."

"How awful!" said Mrs. Fletcher.

"He's forty-two too. That looks like a bad age."

"Who said so, that Mrs. Pike? I bet she's forty-two," said Mrs. Fletcher.

"Naw," said Leota, "Mrs. Pike's thirty-three, born in January, an Aquarian. He could move his head—like this. A course his head and mind ain't a joint, so to speak, and I guess his stomach ain't, either—not yet, anyways. But see—his food, he eats it, and it goes down, see, and then he digests it"—Leota rose on her toes for an instant—"and it goes out to his joints and before you can say 'Jack Robinson,' it's stone—pure stone. He's turning to stone. How'd you liked to be married to a guy like that? All he can do, he can move his head just a quarter of an inch. A course he *looks* just *terrible*."

"I should think he would," said Mrs. Fletcher frostily. "Mr. Fletcher takes bending exercises every night of the world. I make him."

"All Fred does is lay around the house like a rug. I wouldn't be surprised if he woke up some day and couldn't move. The petrified man just sat there moving his quarter of an inch though," said Leota reminiscently.

"Did Mrs. Pike like the petrified man?" asked Mrs. Fletcher.

"Not as much as she did the others," said Leota deprecatingly. "And then she likes a man to be a good dresser, and all that."

"Is Mr. Pike a good dresser?" asked Mrs. Fletcher sceptically.

"Oh, well, yeah," said Leota, "but he's twelve or fourteen years older'n her. She ast Lady Evangeline about him."

"Who's Lady Evangeline?" asked Mrs. Fletcher.

"Well, it's this mind reader they got in the freak show," said Leota. "Was real good. Lady Evangeline is her name, and if I had another dollar I wouldn't do a thing but have my other palm read. She had what Mrs. Pike said was the 'sixth mind' but she had the worst manicure I ever saw on a living person."

"What did she tell Mrs. Pike?" asked Mrs. Fletcher.

"She told her Mr. Pike was as true to her as he could be and besides, would come into some money."

"Humph!" said Mrs. Fletcher. "What does he do?"

"I can't tell," said Leota, "because he don't work. Lady Evangeline didn't tell me enough about my nature or anything. And I would like to go back and find out some more about this boy. Used to go with this boy until he got married to this girl. Oh, shoot, that was about three and a half years ago, when you was still goin' to the Robert E. Lee Beauty Shop in Jackson. He married her for her money. Another fortune-teller tole me that at the time. So I'm not in love with him anymore, anyway, besides being married to Fred, but Mrs. Pike thought, just for the hell of it, see, to ask Lady Evangeline was he happy."

"Does Mrs. Pike know everything about you already?" asked Mrs. Fletcher unbelievingly. "Mercy!"

"Oh, yeah, I tole her ever'thing about ever'thing, from now on back to I don't know when—to when I first started goin' out," said Leota. "So I ast Lady Evangeline for one of my questions, was he happily married, and she says, just like she was glad I ask her, 'Honey,' she says, 'naw, he idn't. You write down this day, March 8, 1941,' she says, 'and mock it down: three years from today him and her won't be occupyin' the same bed.' There it is, up on the wall with them other dates—see, Mrs. Fletcher? And she says, 'Child, you ought to be glad you didn't git him, because he's so mercenary.' So I'm glad I married Fred. He sure ain't mercenary, money don't mean a thing to him. But I sure would like to go back and have my other palm read."

"Did Mrs. Pike believe in what the fortune-teller said?" asked Mrs. Fletcher in a superior tone of voice.

"Lord, yes, she's from New Orleans. Ever'body in New Orleans believes ever'thing spooky. One of 'em in New Orleans before it was raided says to Mrs. Pike one summer she was goin' to go from State to State and meet some grey-headed men, and, sure enough, she says she went on a beautician convention up to Chicago. . . ."

"Oh!" said Mrs. Fletcher. "Oh, is Mrs. Pike a beautician too?"

"Sure she is," protested Leota. "She's a beautician. I'm goin' to git her in here if I can. Before she married. But it don't leave you. She says sure enough, there was three men who was a very large part of making her trip what it was, and they all three had grey in their hair and they went in six States. Got

Christmas cards from 'em. Billy Boy, go see if Thelma's got any dry cotton. Look how Mrs. Fletcher's a-drippin'."

"Where did Mrs. Pike meet Mr. Pike?" asked Mrs. Fletcher primly.

"On another train," said Leota.

"I met Mr. Fletcher, or rather he met me, in a rental library," said Mrs. Fletcher with dignity, as she watched the net come down over her head.

"Honey, me an' Fred, we met in a rumble seat[3] eight months ago and we was practically on what you might call the way to the altar inside of half an hour," said Leota in a guttural voice, and bit a bobby pin open. "Course it don't last. Mrs. Pike says nothin' like that ever lasts."

"Mr. Fletcher and myself are as much in love as the day we married," said Mrs. Fletcher belligerently as Leota stuffed cotton into her ears.

"Mrs. Pike says it don't last," repeated Leota in a louder voice. "Now go git under the dryer. You can turn yourself on, can't you? I'll be back to comb you out. Durin' lunch I promised to give Mrs. Pike a facial. You know— free. Her bein' in the business, so to speak."

"I bet she needs one," said Mrs. Fletcher, letting the swing-door fly back against Leota. "Oh, pardon me."

A week later, on time for her appointment, Mrs. Fletcher sank heavily into Leota's chair after first removing a drug-store rental book, called *Life Is Like That*, from the seat. She stared in a discouraged way into the mirror.

"You can tell it when I'm sitting down, all right," she said.

Leota seemed preoccupied and stood shaking out a lavender cloth. She began to pin it around Mrs. Fletcher's neck in silence.

"I said you sure can tell it when I'm sitting straight on and coming at you this way," Mrs. Fletcher said.

"Why, honey, naw you can't," said Leota gloomily. "Why, I'd never know. If somebody was to come up to me on the street and say, 'Mrs. Fletcher is pregnant!' I'd say, 'Heck, she don't look it to me.'"

"If a certain party hadn't found it out and spread it around, it wouldn't be too late even now," said Mrs. Fletcher frostily, but Leota was almost choking her with the cloth, pinning it so tight, and she couldn't speak clearly. She paddled her hands in the air until Leota wearily loosened her.

"Listen, honey, you're just a virgin compared to Mrs. Montjoy," Leota was going on, still absent-minded. She bent Mrs. Fletcher back in the chair and, sighing, tossed liquid from a teacup on to her head and dug both hands into her scalp. "You know Mrs. Montjoy—her husband's that premature-greyheaded fella?"

"She's in the Trojan Garden Club, is all I know," said Mrs. Fletcher.

"Well, honey," said Leota, but in a weary voice, "she come in here not the week before and not the day before she had her baby—she come in here the very selfsame day, I mean to tell you. Child, we was all plumb scared to death. There she was! Come for her shampoo an' set. Why, Mrs. Fletcher, in an hour an' twenty minutes she was layin' up there in the Babtist Hospital with a seb'm-pound son. It was that close a shave. I declare, if I hadn't been so tired I would of drank up a bottle of gin that night."

"What gall," said Mrs. Fletcher. "I never knew her at all well."

---

3. Folding seat at the rear of an automobile.

"See, her husband was waitin' outside in the car, and her bags was all packed an' in the back seat, an' she was all ready, 'cept she wanted her shampoo an' set. An' havin' one pain right after another. Her husband kep' comin' in here, scared-like, but couldn't do nothin' with her a course. She yelled bloody murder, too, but she always yelled her head off when I give her a perm'nent."

"She must of been crazy," said Mrs. Fletcher. "How did she look?"

"Shoot!" said Leota.

"Well, I can guess," asid Mrs. Fletcher. "Awful."

"Just wanted to look pretty while she was havin' her baby, is all," said Leota airily. "Course, we was glad to give the lady what she was after— that's our motto—but I bet a hour later she wasn't payin' no mind to them little end curls. I bet she wasn't thinkin' about she ought to have on a net. It wouldn't of done her no good if she had."

"No, I don't suppose it would," said Mrs. Fletcher.

"Yeah man! She was a-yellin'. Just like when I give her perm'nent."

"Her husband ought to make her behave. Don't it seem that way to you?" asked Mrs. Fletcher. "He ought to put his foot down."

"Ha," said Leota. "A lot he could do. Maybe some women is soft."

"Oh, you mistake me, I don't mean for her to get soft—far from it! Women have to stand up for themselves, or there's just no telling. But now you take me—I ask Mr. Fletcher's advice now and then, and he appreciates it, espe- cially on something important, like is it time for a permanent—not that I've told him about the baby. He says, 'Why, dear, go ahead!' Just ask their *advice*."

"Huh! If I ever ast Fred's advice we'd be floatin' down the Yazoo River on a houseboat or somethin' by this time," said Leota. "I'm sick of Fred. I told him to go over to Vicksburg."

"Is he going?" demanded Mrs. Fletcher.

"Sure. See, the fortune-teller—I went back and had my other palm read, since we've got to rent the room agin—said my lover was goin' to work in Vicksburg, so I don't know who she could mean, unless she meant Fred. And Fred ain't workin' here—that much is so."

"Is he going to work in Vicksburg?" asked Mrs. Fletcher. "And—"

"Sure. Lady Evangeline said so. Said the future is going to be brighter than the present. He don't want to go, but I ain't gonna put up with nothin' like that. Lays around the house an' bulls—did bull—with that good-for-nothin' Mr. Pike. He says if he goes who'll cook, but I says I never get to eat anyway— not meals. Billy Boy, take Mrs. Grover that *Screen Secrets* and leg it."

Mrs. Fletcher heard stamping feet go out the door.

"Is that that Mrs. Pike's little boy here again?" she asked, sitting up gingerly.

"Yeah, that's still him." Leota stuck out her tongue.

Mrs. Fletcher could hardly believe her eyes. "Well! How's Mrs. Pike, your attractive new friend with the sharp eyes who spreads it around town that perfect strangers are pregnant?" she asked in a sweetened tone.

"Oh, Mizziz Pike." Leota combed Mrs. Fletcher's hair with heavy strokes.

"You act like you're tired," said Mrs. Fletcher.

"Tired? Feel like it's four o'clock in the afternoon already," said Leota. "I ain't told you the awful luck we had, me and Fred? It's the worst thing you ever heard of. Maybe *you* think Mrs. Pike's got sharp eyes. Shoot, there's a limit! Well, you know, we rented out our room to this Mr. and Mrs. Pike from New Orleans when Sal an' Joe Fentress got mad at us 'cause they drank up some home-brew we had in the closet—Sal an' Joe did. So, a week ago Sat'-day Mr. and Mrs. Pike moved in. Well, I kinda fixed up the room, you know—put a sofa pillow on the couch and picked some ragged robbins and put in a vase, but they never did say they appreciated it. Anyway, then I put some old magazines on the table."

"I think that was lovely," said Mrs. Fletcher.

"Wait. So, come night 'fore last, Fred and this Mr. Pike, who Fred just took up with, was back from they said they was fishin', bein' as neither one of 'em has got a job to his name, and we was all settin' around their room. So Mrs. Pike was settin' there, readin' a old *Startling G-Man Tales* that was mine, mind you, I'd bought it myself, and all of a sudden she jumps!—into the air— you'd 'a' thought she'd set on a spider—an' says, 'Canfield'—ain't that silly, that's Mr. Pike—'Canfield, my God A'mighty,' she says, 'honey,' she says, 'we're rich, and you won't have to work.' Not that he turned one hand anyway. Well, me and Fred rushes over to her, and Mr. Pike, too, and there she sets, pointin' her finger at a photo in my copy of *Startling G-Man*. 'See that man?' yells Mrs. Pike. 'Remember him, Canfield?' 'Never forget a face,' says Mr. Pike. 'It's Mr. Petrie, that we stayed with him in the apartment next to ours in Tou- louse Street in N.O. for six weeks. Mr. Petrie.' 'Well,' says Mrs. Pike, like she can't hold out one secont longer, 'Mr. Petrie is wanted for five hundred dollars cash, for rapin' four women in California, and I know where he is.'"

"Mercy!" said Mrs. Fletcher. "Where was he?"

At some time Leota had washed her hair and now she yanked her up by the back locks and sat her up.

"Know where he was?"

"I certainly don't," Mrs. Fletcher said. Her scalp hurt all over.

Leota flung a towel around the top of her customer's head. "Nowhere else but in that freak show! I saw him just as plain as Mrs. Pike. *He* was the petrified man!"

"Who would ever have thought that!" cried Mrs. Fletcher sympathetically.

"So Mr. Pike says, 'Well whatta you know about that', an' he looks real hard at the photo and whistles. And she starts dancin' and singin' about their good luck. She meant our bad luck! I made a point of tellin' that fortune-teller the next time I saw her. I said, 'Listen, that magazine was layin' around the house for a month, and there was the freak show runnin' night an' day, not two steps away from my own beauty parlor, with Mr. Petrie just settin' there waitin'. An' it had to be Mr. and Mrs. Pike, almost perfect strangers.'"

"What gall," said Mrs. Fletcher. She was only sitting there, wrapped in a turban, but she did not mind.

"Fortune-tellers don't care. And Mrs. Pike, she goes around actin' like she thinks she was Mrs. God," said Leota. "So they're goin' to leave tomorrow, Mr. and Mrs. Pike. And in the meantime I got to keep that mean, bad little ole kid here, gettin' under my feet ever' minute of the day an' talkin' back too."

"Have they gotten the five hundred dollars' reward already?" asked Mrs. Fletcher.

"Well," said Leota, "at first Mr. Pike didn't want to do anything about it. Can you feature that? Said he kinda liked that ole bird and said he was real nice to 'em, lent 'em money or somethin'. But Mrs. Pike simply tole him he could just go to hell, and I can see her point. She says, 'You ain't worked a lick in six months, and here I make five hundred dollars in two seconts, and what thanks do I get for it? You go to hell, Canfield,' she says. So," Leota went on in a despondent voice, "they called up the cops and they caught the ole bird, all right, right there in the freak show where I saw him with my own eyes, thinkin' he was petrified. He's the one. Did it under his real name—Mr. Petrie. Four women in California, all in the month of August. So Mrs. Pike gits five hundred dollars. And my magazine, and right next door to my beauty parlor. I cried all night, but Fred said it wasn't a bit of use and to go to sleep, because the whole thing was just a sort of coincidence—you know: can't do nothin' about it. He says it put him clean out of the notion of goin' to Vicksburg for a few days till we rent out the room agin—no tellin' who we'll git this time."

"But can you imagine anybody knowing this old man, that's raped four women?" persisted Mrs. Fletcher, and she shuddered audibly. "Did Mrs. Pike *speak* to him when she met him in the freak show?"

Leota had begun to comb Mrs. Fletcher's hair. "I says to her, I says, 'I didn't notice you fallin' on his neck when he was the petrified man—don't tell me you didn't recognize your fine friend?' And she says, 'I didn't recognize him with that white powder all over his face. He just looked familiar,' Mrs. Pike says, 'and lots of people look familiar.' But she says that ole petrified man did put her in mind of somebody. She wondered who it was! Kep' her awake, which man she'd ever knew it reminded her of. So when she seen the photo, it all come to her. Like a flash. Mr. Petrie. The way he'd turn his head and look at her when she took him in his breakfast."

"Took him in his breakfast!" shrieked Mrs. Fletcher. "Listen—don't tell me. I'd 'a' felt something."

"Four women. I guess those women didn't have the faintest notion at the time they'd be worth a hundred an' twenty-five bucks apiece some day to Mrs. Pike. We ast her how old the fella was then, an's she says he musta had one foot in the grave, at least. Can you beat it?"

"Not really petrified at all, of course," said Mrs. Fletcher meditatively. She drew herself up. "I'd 'a' felt something," she said proudly.

"Shoot! I did feel somethin'," said Leota. "I tole Fred when I got home I felt so funny. I said, 'Fred, that ole petrified man sure did leave me with a funny feelin'.' He says, 'Funny-haha or funny-peculiar?' and I says, 'Funny-peculiar.'" She pointed her comb into the air emphatically.

"I'll bet you did," said Mrs. Fletcher.

They both heard a crackling noise.

Leota screamed, "Billy Boy! What you doin' in my purse?"

"Aw, I'm just eatin' these ole stale peanuts up," said Billy Boy.

"You come here to me!" screamed Leota, recklessly flinging down the comb, which scattered a whole ashtray full of bobby pins and knocked down a row of Coca-Cola bottles. "This is the last straw!"

"I caught him! I caught him!" giggled Mrs. Fletcher. "I'll hold him on my lap. You bad, bad boy, you! I guess I better learn how to spank little old bad boys," she said.

Leota's eleven o'clock customer pushed open the swing-door upon Leota's paddling him heartily with the brush, while he gave angry but belittling screams which penetrated beyond the booth and filled the whole curious beauty parlor. From everywhere ladies began to gather round to watch the paddling. Billy Boy kicked both Leota and Mrs. Fletcher as hard as he could, Mrs. Fletcher with her new fixed smile.

Billy Boy stomped through the group of wild-haired ladies and went out the door, but flung back the words, "If you're so smart, why ain't you rich?"

1941

ELIZABETH BISHOP
1911–1979

"The enormous power of reticence," the poet Octavio Paz said in a tribute, "—that is the great lesson of Elizabeth Bishop." Bishop's reticence originates in a temperament indistinguishable from her style; her remarkable formal gifts allowed her to create ordered and lucid structures that hold strong feelings in place. Chief among these feelings was a powerful sense of loss. Born in Worcester, Massachusetts, she was eight months old when her father died. Her mother suffered a series of breakdowns and was permanently institutionalized when Elizabeth was five. "I've never concealed this," Bishop once wrote, "although I don't like to make too much of it. But of course it is an important fact, to me. I didn't see her again." Her understatement is characteristic. When Bishop wrote about her early life—as she first did in several poems and stories in the 1950s and last did in her extraordinary final book, *Geography III* (1976)—she resisted sentimentality and self-pity. It was as if she could look at the events of her own life with the same unflinching gaze she turned on the landscapes that so consistently compelled her. The deep feeling in her poems rises out of direct and particular description, but Bishop does more than simply observe. Whether writing about her childhood landscape of Nova Scotia or her adopted Brazil, she often opens a poem with long perspectives on time, with landscapes that dwarf the merely human, emphasizing the dignified frailty of a human observer.

Examining her own case, she traces the observer's instinct to early childhood. "In the Waiting Room," a poem written in the early 1970s, probes the sources of her interest in details. Using an incident from when she was seven—a little girl waits for her aunt in the dentist's anteroom—Bishop shows how in the course of the episode she became aware, as if wounded, of the utter strangeness and engulfing power of the world. The spectator in that poem hangs on to details as a kind of life jacket; she observes because she has to.

After her father's death, Bishop and her mother lived with Bishop's maternal grandparents in Great Village, Nova Scotia. She remained there for several years after her mother was institutionalized, until she was removed ("kidnapped," as she says in one of her stories) by her paternal grandparents and taken to live in Worcester, Massachusetts. This experience was followed by a series of illnesses (eczema, bronchitis, and asthma), which plagued her for years. Bishop later lived with an aunt and attended Walnut Hill School, a private high school. In 1934 she graduated from Vassar College, where she had been introduced to Marianne Moore. Moore's meticulous taste for fact was to influence Bishop's poetry, but more immediately Moore's independent life as a poet seemed an alternative to Bishop's vaguer intentions to attend medical school. Bishop lived in New York City and in Key West, Florida; a traveling fellowship took her to Brazil, where she met Lotade Macedo Soares, an architect with whom she lived for sixteen years. Lota committed suicide in 1967, a loss registered in Bishop's late villanelle "One Art" (1976).

Exile and travel were always at the heart of Bishop's poems. The title of her first book, *North & South* (1946), looks backward to the northern seas of Nova Scotia and forward to the tropical worlds of Brazil. Her poems are set among these landscapes, where she can stress the sweep and violence of encircling and eroding geological powers or, in the case of Brazil, a bewildering botanical plenty. *Questions of Travel* (1965), her third volume, constitutes a sequence of poems initiating her, with her botanist-geologist-anthropologist's curiosity, into Brazilian life and the mysteries of what questions a traveler-exile should ask. In this series with its increasing penetration of a new country, a process is at work similar to one Bishop identifies in the great English naturalist Charles Darwin, of whom Bishop once said: "One admires the beautiful solid case being built up out of his endless, heroic observations, almost unconscious or automatic—and then comes a sudden relaxation, a forgetful phrase, and one feels the strangeness of his undertaking, sees the lonely young man, his eyes fixed on facts and minute details, sinking or sliding giddily off into the unknown."

In 1969 Bishop's *Complete Poems* appeared, an ironic title in light of the fact that she continued to publish new poetry. *Geography III* contains some of her best work, poems that, from the perspective of her return to the United States, look back on the appetite for exploration apparent in her earlier verse. The influence of her long friendship with the poet Robert Lowell, and their high regard for one another's work, may be felt in the way *Geography III* explores the memory and autobiography more directly than does her earlier work. Bishop, however, believed that there were limits on the ways in which poems could use the materials of a life. In a well-known 1972 letter to Lowell, she discusses these limits. Having left Brazil, Bishop lived in Boston from 1970 and taught at Harvard University until 1977. She received the Pulitzer Prize for the combined volume *North & South and A Cold Spring* (1955) and the National Book Award for *The Complete Poems*, and in 1976 was the first woman and the first American to receive the Books Abroad Neustadt International Prize for Literature. Since Bishop's death, most of her published work has been gathered in two volumes: *The Complete Poems 1929–1979* and *The Collected Prose*. An edition of her unpublished poems and drafts, *Edgar Allan Poe & The Juke-Box*, was published to some controversy in 2006.

The Man-Moth[1]

Here, above,
cracks in the buildings are filled with battered moonlight.
The whole shadow of Man is only as big as his hat.
It lies at his feet like a circle for a doll to stand on,
and he makes an inverted pin, the point magnetized to the moon.   5
He does not see the moon; he observes only her vast properties,
feeling the queer light on his hands, neither warm nor cold,
of a temperature impossible to record in thermometers.

But when the Man-Moth
pays his rare, although occasional, visits to the surface,   10
the moon looks rather different to him. He emerges
from an opening under the edge of one of the sidewalks

---

1. Newspaper misprint for "mammoth" [Bishop's note]. Bishop explained that when she saw this misprint in the *New York Times* she took it as "an oracle . . . kindly explaining New York City to me, at least for a moment."

and nervously begins to scale the faces of buildings.
He thinks the moon is a small hole at the top of the sky,
proving the sky quite useless for protection.   15
He trembles, but must investigate as high as he can climb.

        Up the façades,
his shadow dragging like a photographer's cloth behind him,
he climbs fearfully, thinking that this time he will manage
to push his small head through that round clean opening   20
and be forced through, as from a tube, in black scrolls on the
      light.
(Man, standing below him, has no such illusions.)
But what the Man-Moth fears most he must do, although
he fails, of course, and falls back scared but quite unhurt.

        Then he returns   25
to the pale subways of cement he calls his home. He flits,
he flutters, and cannot get aboard the silent trains
fast enough to suit him. The doors close swiftly.
The Man-Moth always seats himself facing the wrong way
and the train starts at once at its full, terrible speed,   30
without a shift in gears or a gradation of any sort.
He cannot tell the rate at which he travels backwards.

        Each night he must
be carried through artificial tunnels and dream recurrent dreams.
Just as the ties recur beneath his train, these underlie   35
his rushing brain. He does not dare look out the window,
for the third rail,[2] the unbroken draught of poison,
runs there beside him. He regards it as disease
he has inherited susceptibility to. He has to keep
his hands in pockets, as others must wear mufflers.   40

        If you catch him,
hold up a flashlight to his eye. It's all dark pupil,
an entire night itself, whose haired horizon tightens
as he stares back, and closes up the eye. Then from the lids
one tear, his only possession, like the bee's sting, slips.   45
Slyly he palms it, and if you're not paying attention
he'll swallow it. However, if you watch, he'll hand it over,
cool as from underground springs and pure enough to drink.

        1935

The Fish

    I caught a tremendous fish
    and held him beside the boat
    half out of water, with my hook

2. The exposed electrical conductor of a railway that carries high-voltage power and thus the threat of electrocution.

fast in a corner of his mouth.
He didn't fight.   5
He hadn't fought at all.
He hung a grunting weight,
battered and venerable
and homely. Here and there
his brown skin hung in strips   10
like ancient wallpaper,
and its pattern of darker brown
was like wallpaper:
shapes like full-blown roses
stained and lost through age.   15
He was speckled with barnacles,
fine rosettes of lime,
and infested
with tiny white sea-lice,
and underneath two or three   20
rags of green weed hung down.
While his gills were breathing in
the terrible oxygen
—the frightening gills,
fresh and crisp with blood,   25
that can cut so badly—
I thought of the coarse white flesh
packed in like feathers,
the big bones and the little bones,
the dramatic reds and blacks   30
of his shiny entrails,
and the pink swim-bladder
like a big peony.
I looked into his eyes
which were far larger than mine   35
but shallower, and yellowed,
the irises backed and packed
with tarnished tinfoil
seen through the lenses
of old scratched isinglass.[1]   40
They shifted a little, but not
to return my stare.
—It was more like the tipping
of an object toward the light.
I admired his sullen face,   45
the mechanism of his jaw,
and then I saw
that from his lower lip
—if you could call it a lip—
grim, wet, and weaponlike,   50
hung five old pieces of fish-line,
or four and a wire leader
with the swivel still attached,

---

1. A whitish, semitransparent substance, originally obtained from the swim bladders of some fresh-water fish and occasionally used for windows.

with all their five big hooks
grown firmly in his mouth.   55
A green line, frayed at the end
where he broke it, two heavier lines,
and a fine black thread
still crimped from the strain and snap
when it broke and he got away.   60
Like medals with their ribbons
frayed and wavering,
a five-haired beard of wisdom
trailing from his aching jaw.
I stared and stared   65
and victory filled up
the little rented boat,
from the pool of bilge
where oil had spread a rainbow
around the rusted engine   70
to the bailer rusted orange,
the sun-cracked thwarts,
the oarlocks on their strings,
the gunnels—until everything
was rainbow, rainbow, rainbow!   75
And I let the fish go.

                                                        1946

Over 2,000 Illustrations and a Complete Concordance[1]

Thus should have been our travels:
serious, engravable.
The Seven Wonders of the World are tired
and a touch familiar, but the other scenes,
innumerable, though equally sad and still,   5
are foreign. Often the squatting Arab,
or group of Arabs, plotting, probably,
against our Christian Empire,
while one apart, with outstretched arm and hand
points to the Tomb, the Pit, the Sepulcher.[2]   10
The branches of the date-palms look like files.
The cobbled courtyard, where the Well is dry,
is like a diagram, the brickwork conduits
are vast and obvious, the human figure
far gone in history or theology,   15
gone with its camel or its faithful horse.
Always the silence, the gesture, the specks of birds
suspended on invisible threads above the Site,
or the smoke rising solemnly, pulled by threads.

---

1. Part of the title of an old edition of the Bible described in the opening lines of the poem. A concordance is a guide to occurrences of words and proper names and places in a book.

2. Jesus's burial place, depicted (along with other places associated with his life, such as the Well and the Site) among the "2,000 illustrations" of the title.

Granted a page alone or a page made up   20
of several scenes arranged in cattycornered rectangles
or circles set on stippled gray,
granted a grim lunette,[3]
caught in the toils of an initial letter,
when dwelt upon, they all resolve themselves.   25
The eye drops, weighted, through the lines
the burin[4] made, the lines that move apart
like ripples above sand,
dispersing storms, God's spreading fingerprint,
and painfully, finally, that ignite   30
in watery prismatic white-and-blue.

Entering the Narrows at St. Johns[5]
the touching bleat of goats reached to the ship.
We glimpsed them, reddish, leaping up the cliffs
among the fog-soaked weeds and butter-and-eggs.[6]   35
And at St. Peter's[7] the wind blew and the sun shone madly.
Rapidly, purposefully, the Collegians[8] marched in lines,
crisscrossing the great square with black, like ants.
In Mexico the dead man lay
in a blue arcade; the dead volcanoes   40
glistened like Easter lilies.
The jukebox went on playing "Ay, Jalisco!"
And at Volubilis[9] there were beautiful poppies
splitting the mosaics; the fat old guide made eyes.
In Dingle[1] harbor a golden length of evening   45
the rotting hulks held up their dripping plush.
The Englishwoman poured tea, informing us
that the Duchess was going to have a baby.
And in the brothels of Marrakesh[2]
the little pockmarked prostitutes   50
balanced their tea-trays on their heads
and did their belly-dances; flung themselves
naked and giggling against our knees,
asking for cigarettes. It was somewhere near there
I saw what frightened me most of all: 55
A holy grave, not looking particularly holy,
one of a group under a keyhole-arched stone baldaquin[3]
open to every wind from the pink desert.
An open, gritty, marble trough, carved solid
with exhortation, yellowed   60
as scattered cattle-teeth;
half-filled with dust, not even the dust
of the poor prophet paynim who once lay there.
In a smart burnoose[4] Khadour looked on amused.

3. An oval framing an illustration, often part of an enlarged initial letter.
4. An engraver's tool.
5. In Newfoundland.
6. A plant whose flowers are two shades of yellow.
7. The papal basilica in Rome.
8. Members of constituent orders of the Catholic Church.
9. A ruined Roman city in Morocco.
1. A town in southwest Ireland.
2. A city in Morocco.
3. Architectural canopy.
4. A long cloak with a hood. "Paynim": archaic literary word for pagan, especially Muslim.

Everything only connected by "and" and "and."   65
Open the book. (The gilt rubs off the edges
of the pages and pollinates the fingertips.)
Open the heavy book. Why couldn't we have seen
this old Nativity while we were at it?
—the dark ajar, the rocks breaking with light,   70
an undisturbed, unbreathing flame,
colorless, sparkless, freely fed on straw,
and, lulled within, a family with pets,
—and looked and looked our infant[5] sight away.

                                                      1955

The Bight[1]

On My Birthday

At low tide like this how sheer the water is.
White, crumbling ribs of marl protrude and glare
and the boats are dry, the pilings dry as matches.
Absorbing, rather than being absorbed,
the water in the bight doesn't wet anything,   5
the color of the gas flame turned as low as possible.
One can smell it turning to gas; if one were Baudelaire[2]
one could probably hear it turning to marimba music.
The little ocher dredge at work off the end of the dock
already plays the dry perfectly off-beat claves.   10
The birds are outsize. Pelicans crash
into this peculiar gas unnecessarily hard,
it seems to me, like pickaxes,
rarely coming up with anything to show for it,
and going off with humorous elbowings.   15
Black-and-white man-of-war birds soar
on impalpable drafts
and open their tails like scissors on the curves
or tense them like wishbones, till they tremble.
The frowsy sponge boats keep coming in   20
with the obliging air of retrievers,
bristling with jackstraw gaffs and hooks
and decorated with bobbles of sponges.
There is a fence of chicken wire along the dock
where, glinting like plowshares,   25
the blue-gray shark tails are hung up to dry
for the Chinese-restaurant trade.
Some of the little white boats are still piled up
against each other, or lie on their sides, stove in,
and not yet salvaged, if they ever will be, from the last bad storm,   30

---

5. Its Latin root (*infans*) means "speechless."
1. A bay or an inlet.
2. Charles Baudelaire (1821–1867), French poet

whose theory of correspondences (see line 32) promised links, through poetry, between the physical and spiritual worlds.

like torn-open, unanswered letters.
The bight is littered with old correspondences.
Click. Click. Goes the dredge,
and brings up a dripping jawful of marl.
All the untidy activity continues,   35
awful but cheerful.

1955

At the Fishhouses

Although it is a cold evening,
down by one of the fishhouses
an old man sits netting,
his net, in the gloaming almost invisible
a dark purple-brown,   5
and his shuttle worn and polished.
The air smells so strong of codfish
it makes one's nose run and one's eyes water.
The five fishhouses have steeply peaked roofs
and narrow, cleated gangplanks slant up   10
to storerooms in the gables
for the wheelbarrows to be pushed up and down on.
All is silver: the heavy surface of the sea,
swelling slowly as if considering spilling over,
is opaque, but the silver of the benches,   15
the lobster pots, and masts, scattered
among the wild jagged rocks,
is of an apparent translucence
like the small old buildings with an emerald moss
growing on their shoreward walls.   20
The big fish tubs are completely lined
with layers of beautiful herring scales
and the wheelbarrows are similarly plastered
with creamy iridescent coats of mail,
with small iridescent flies crawling on them.   25
Up on the little slope behind the houses,
set in the sparse bright sprinkle of grass,
is an ancient wooden capstan,[1]
cracked, with two long bleached handles
and some melancholy stains, like dried blood,   30
where the ironwork has rusted.
The old man accepts a Lucky Strike.[2]
He was a friend of my grandfather.
We talk of the decline in the population
and of codfish and herring   35
while he waits for a herring boat to come in.
There are sequins on his vest and on his thumb.

1. Cylindrical drum around which rope is wound,   2. Brand of cigarettes.
used for winching or hoisting the anchor of a ship.

He has scraped the scales, the principal beauty,
from unnumbered fish with that black old knife,
the blade of which is almost worn away.   40

Down at the water's edge, at the place
where they haul up the boats, up the long ramp
descending into the water, thin silver
tree trunks are laid horizontally
across the gray stones, down and down   45
at intervals of four or five feet.

Cold dark deep and absolutely clear,
element bearable to no mortal,
to fish and to seals . . . One seal particularly
I have seen here evening after evening.   50
He was curious about me. He was interested in music;
like me a believer in total immersion,[3]
so I used to sing him Baptist hymns.
I also sang "A Mighty Fortress Is Our God."
He stood up in the water and regarded me   55
steadily, moving his head a little.
Then he would disappear, then suddenly emerge
almost in the same spot, with a sort of shrug
as if it were against his better judgment.
Cold dark deep and absolutely clear,   60
the clear gray icy water . . . Back, behind us,
the dignified tall firs begin.
Bluish, associating with their shadows,
a million Christmas trees stand
waiting for Christmas. The water seems suspended   65
above the rounded gray and blue-gray stones.
I have seen it over and over, the same sea, the same,
slightly, indifferently swinging above the stones,
icily free above the stones,
above the stones and then the world.   70
If you should dip your hand in,
your wrist would ache immediately,
your bones would begin to ache and your hand would burn
as if the water were a transmutation of fire
that feeds on stones and burns with a dark gray flame.   75
If you tasted it, it would first taste bitter,
then briny, then surely burn your tongue.
It is like what we imagine knowledge to be:
dark, salt, clear, moving, utterly free,
drawn from the cold hard mouth   80
of the world, derived from the rocky breasts
forever, flowing and drawn, and since
our knowledge is historical, flowing, and flown.

                                                        1955

3. Form of baptism favored by Baptists.

Questions of Travel

There are too many waterfalls here; the crowded streams
hurry too rapidly down to the sea,
and the pressure of so many clouds on the mountaintops
makes them spill over the sides in soft slow-motion,
turning to waterfalls under our very eyes.   5
—For if those streaks, those mile-long, shiny, tearstains,
aren't waterfalls yet,
in a quick age or so, as ages go here,
they probably will be.
But if the streams and clouds keep travelling, travelling,   10
the mountains look like the hulls of capsized ships,
slime-hung and barnacled.

Think of the long trip home.
Should we have stayed at home and thought of here?
Where should we be today?   15
Is it right to be watching strangers in a play
in this strangest of theatres?
What childishness is it that while there's a breath of life
in our bodies, we are determined to rush
to see the sun the other way around?   20
The tiniest green hummingbird in the world?
To stare at some inexplicable old stonework,
inexplicable and impenetrable,
at any view,
instantly seen and always, always delightful?   25
Oh, must we dream our dreams
and have them, too?
And have we room
for one more folded sunset, still quite warm?

But surely it would have been a pity   30
not to have seen the trees along this road,
really exaggerated in their beauty,
not to have seen them gesturing
like noble pantomimists, robed in pink.
—Not to have had to stop for gas and heard   35
the sad, two-noted, wooden tune
of disparate wooden clogs
carelessly clacking over
a grease-stained filling-station floor.
(In another country the clogs would all be tested.   40
Each pair there would have identical pitch.)
—A pity not to have heard
the other, less primitive music of the fat brown bird
who sings above the broken gasoline pump
in a bamboo church of Jesuit baroque: 45
three towers, five silver crosses.
—Yes, a pity not to have pondered,

blurr'dly and inconclusively,
on what connection can exist for centuries
between the crudest wooden footwear   50
and, careful and finicky,
the whittled fantasies of wooden cages.
—Never to have studied history in
the weak calligraphy of songbirds' cages.
—And never to have had to listen to rain   55
so much like politicians' speeches:
two hours of unrelenting oratory
and then a sudden golden silence
in which the traveller takes a notebook, writes:

"Is it lack of imagination that makes us come   60
to imagined places, not just stay at home?
Or could Pascal[1] have been not entirely right
about just sitting quietly in one's room?

Continent, city, country, society:
the choice is never wide and never free.   65
And here, or there . . . No. Should we have stayed at home,
wherever that may be?"

                                                                      1965

The Armadillo

for Robert Lowell

This is the time of year
when almost every night
the frail, illegal fire balloons appear.
Climbing the mountain height,

rising toward a saint   5
still honored in these parts,
the paper chambers flush and fill with light
that comes and goes, like hearts.

Once up against the sky it's hard
to tell them from the stars—   10
planets, that is—the tinted ones:
Venus going down, or Mars,

or the pale green one. With a wind,
they flare and falter, wobble and toss;
but if it's still they steer between   15
the kite sticks of the Southern Cross,

---

1. French mathematician and philosopher (1623–1662) who said, "Men's misfortunes spring from the single cause that they are unable to stay quietly in one room" (*Pensées*, trans. J. M. Cohen).

receding, dwindling, solemnly
and steadily forsaking us,
or, in the downdraft from a peak,
suddenly turning dangerous.   20

Last night another big one fell.
It splattered like an egg of fire
against the cliff behind the house.
The flame ran down. We saw the pair

of owls who nest there flying up   25
and up, their whirling black-and-white
stained bright pink underneath, until
they shrieked up out of sight.

The ancient owls' nest must have burned.
Hastily, all alone,   30
a glistening armadillo left the scene,
rose-flecked, head down, tail down,

and then a baby rabbit jumped out,
short-eared, to our surprise.
So soft!—a handful of intangible ash   35
with fixed, ignited eyes.

Too pretty, dreamlike mimicry!
O falling fire and piercing cry
and panic, and a weak mailed fist[2]
clenched ignorant against the sky!   40

                                            1965

Sestina[1]

September rain falls on the house.
In the failing light, the old grandmother
sits in the kitchen with the child
beside the Little Marvel Stove,
reading the jokes from the almanac,   5
laughing and talking to hide her tears.

She thinks that her equinoctial tears
and the rain that beats on the roof of the house
were both foretold by the almanac,
but only known to a grandmother.   10
The iron kettle sings on the stove.
She cuts some bread and says to the child,

2. The armadillo, curled tight and protected
against everything but fire.
1. A fixed verse form in which the end words of the
first six-line stanza must be used at the ends of the
lines in the following stanzas in a rotating order;
the final three lines must contain all six words.

It's time for tea now, but the child
is watching the teakettle's small hard tears
dance like mad on the hot black stove,   15
the way the rain must dance on the house.
Tidying up, the old grandmother
hangs up the clever almanac

on its string. Birdlike, the almanac
hovers half open above the child,   20
hovers above the old grandmother
and her teacup full of dark brown tears.
She shivers and says she thinks the house
feels chilly, and puts more wood in the stove.

It was to be, says the Marvel Stove.   25
I know what I know, says the almanac.
With crayons the child draws a rigid house
and a winding pathway. Then the child
puts in a man with buttons like tears
and shows it proudly to the grandmother.   30

But secretly, while the grandmother
busies herself about the stove,
the little moons fall down like tears
from between the pages of the almanac
into the flower bed the child   35
has carefully placed in the front of the house.

Time to plant tears, says the almanac.
The grandmother sings to the marvellous stove
and the child draws another inscrutable house.

1965

In the Waiting Room

In Worcester, Massachusetts,
I went with Aunt Consuelo
to keep her dentist's appointment
and sat and waited for her
in the dentist's waiting room.   5
It was winter. It got dark
early. The waiting room
was full of grown-up people,
arctics and overcoats,
lamps and magazines.   10
My aunt was inside
what seemed like a long time
and while I waited I read
the *National Geographic*

(I could read) and carefully   15
studied the photographs:
the inside of a volcano,
black, and full of ashes;
then it was spilling over
in rivulets of fire.   20
Osa and Martin Johnson[1]
dressed in riding breeches,
laced boots, and pith helmets.
A dead man slung on a pole
—"Long Pig,"[2] the caption said.   25
Babies with pointed heads
wound round and round with string;
black, naked women with necks
wound round and round with wire
like the necks of light bulbs.   30
Their breasts were horrifying.
I read it right straight through.
I was too shy to stop.
And then I looked at the cover:
the yellow margins, the date.   35

Suddenly, from inside,
came an *oh!* of pain
—Aunt Consuelo's voice—
not very loud or long.
I wasn't at all surprised;   40
even then I knew she was
a foolish, timid woman.
I might have been embarrassed,
but wasn't. What took me
completely by surprise   45
was that it was *me*:
my voice, in my mouth.
Without thinking at all
I was my foolish aunt,
I—we—were falling, falling,   50
our eyes glued to the cover
of the *National Geographic*,
February, 1918.

I said to myself: three days
and you'll be seven years old.   55
I was saying it to stop
the sensation of falling off
the round, turning world
into cold, blue-black space.
But I felt: you are an *I*,   60
you are an *Elizabeth*,

---

1. Famous explorers and travel writers.
2. Polynesian cannibals' name for the human carcass.

you are one of *them*.
Why should you be one, too?
I scarcely dared to look.
to see what it was I was.   65
I gave a sidelong glance
—I couldn't look any higher—
at shadowy gray knees,
trousers and skirts and boots
and different pairs of hands   70
lying under the lamps.
I knew that nothing stranger
had ever happened, that nothing
stranger could ever happen.
Why should I be my aunt,   75
or me, or anyone?
What similarities—
boots, hands, the family voice
I felt in my throat, or even
the *National Geographic*   80
and those awful hanging breasts—
held us all together
or made us all just one?
How—I didn't know any
word for it—how "unlikely" . . .   85
How had I come to be here,
like them, and overhear
a cry of pain that could have
got loud and worse but hadn't?

The waiting room was bright   90
and too hot. It was sliding
beneath a big black wave,
another, and another.

Then I was back in it.
The War was on. Outside,   95
in Worcester, Massachusetts,
were night and slush and cold,
and it was still the fifth
of February, 1918.

                                                   1976

The Moose

for Grace Bulmer Bowers

From narrow provinces
of fish and bread and tea,
home of the long tides

where the bay leaves the sea
twice a day and takes   5
the herrings long rides,

where if the river
enters or retreats
in a wall of brown foam
depends on if it meets   10
the bay coming in,
the bay not at home;

where, silted red,
sometimes the sun sets
facing a red sea,   15
and others, veins the flats'
lavender, rich mud
in burning rivulets;

on red, gravelly roads,
down rows of sugar maples,   20
past clapboard farmhouses
and neat, clapboard churches,
bleached, ridged as clamshells,
past twin silver birches,

through late afternoon   25
a bus journeys west,
the windshield flashing pink,
pink glancing off of metal,
brushing the dented flank
of blue, beat-up enamel;   30

down hollows, up rises,
and waits, patient, while
a lone traveller gives
kisses and embraces
to seven relatives   35
and a collie supervises.

Goodbye to the elms,
to the farm, to the dog.
The bus starts. The light
grows richer; the fog,   40
shifting, salty, thin,
comes closing in.

Its cold, round crystals
form and slide and settle
in the white hens' feathers,   45
in gray glazed cabbages,
on the cabbage roses
and lupins like apostles;

the sweet peas cling
to their wet white string
on the whitewashed fences;   50
bumblebees creep
inside the foxgloves,
and evening commences.

One stop at Bass River.   55
Then the Economies—
Lower, Middle, Upper;
Five Islands, Five Houses,[1]
where a woman shakes a tablecloth
out after supper.   60

A pale flickering. Gone.
The Tantramar marshes
and the smell of salt hay.
An iron bridge trembles
and a loose plank rattles   65
but doesn't give way.

On the left, a red light
swims through the dark:
a ship's port lantern.
Two rubber boots show,   70
illuminated, solemn.
A dog gives one bark.

A woman climbs in
with two market bags,
brisk, freckled, elderly.   75
"A grand night. Yes, sir,
all the way to Boston."
She regards us amicably.

Moonlight as we enter
the New Brunswick woods,   80
hairy, scratchy, splintery;
moonlight and mist
caught in them like lamb's wool
on bushes in a pasture.

The passengers lie back.   85
Snores. Some long sighs.
A dreamy divagation
begins in the night,
a gentle, auditory,
slow hallucination. . . .   90

---

1. These are small towns and villages in Nova Scotia, near Halifax.

In the creakings and noises,
an old conversation
—not concerning us,
but recognizable, somewhere,
back in the bus: 95
Grandparents' voices

uninterruptedly
talking, in Eternity:
names being mentioned,
things cleared up finally;   100
what he said, what she said,
who got pensioned;

deaths, deaths and sicknesses;
the year he remarried;
the year (something) happened.   105
She died in childbirth.
That was the son lost
when the schooner foundered.

He took to drink. Yes.
She went to the bad.   110
When Amos began to pray
even in the store and
finally the family had
to put him away.

"Yes . . ." that peculiar   115
affirmative. "Yes . . ."
A sharp, indrawn breath,
half groan, half acceptance,
that means "Life's like that.
We know *it* (also death)."   120

Talking the way they talked
in the old featherbed,
peacefully, on and on,
dim lamplight in the hall,
down in the kitchen, the dog   125
tucked in her shawl.

Now, it's all right now
even to fall asleep
just as on all those nights.
—Suddenly the bus driver   130
stops with a jolt,
turns off his lights.

A moose has come out of
the impenetrable wood
and stands there, looms, rather,   135

in the middle of the road.
It approaches; it sniffs at
the bus's hot hood.

Towering, antlerless,
high as a church,   140
homely as a house
(or, safe as houses).
A man's voice assures us
"Perfectly harmless . . ."

Some of the passengers   145
exclaim in whispers,
childishly, softly,
"Sure are big creatures."
"It's awful plain."
"Look! It's a she!"   150

Taking her time,
she looks the bus over,
grand, otherworldly.
Why, why do we feel
(we all feel) this sweet   155
sensation of joy?

"Curious creatures,"
says our quiet driver,
rolling his *r*'s.
"Look at that, would you."   160
Then he shifts gears.
For a moment longer,

by craning backward,
the moose can be seen
on the moonlit macadam;   165
then there's a dim
smell of moose, an acrid
smell of gasoline.

                                     1976

One Art

The art of losing isn't hard to master;
so many things seem filled with the intent
to be lost that their loss is no disaster.

Lose something every day. Accept the fluster
of lost door keys, the hour badly spent.   5
The art of losing isn't hard to master.

Then practice losing farther, losing faster:
places, and names, and where it was you meant
to travel. None of these will bring disaster.

I lost my mother's watch. And look! my last, or   10
next-to-last, of three loved houses went.
The art of losing isn't hard to master.

I lost two cities, lovely ones. And, vaster,
some realms I owned, two rivers, a continent.
I miss them, but it wasn't a disaster.   15

—Even losing you (the joking voice, a gesture
I love) I shan't have lied. It's evident
the art of losing's not too hard to master
though it may look like (*Write* it!) like disaster.

1976

TENNESSEE WILLIAMS
1911–1983

Speaking of Blanche DuBois, the heroine of *A Streetcar Named Desire*, Tennessee Williams once said, "She was a demonic creature; the size of her feeling was too great for her to contain." In Williams's plays—he wrote and rewrote more than twenty full-length dramas as well as screenplays and shorter works—his characters are driven by the size of their feelings, much as Williams felt driven to write about them.

He was born Thomas Lanier Williams in Columbus, Mississippi. His mother, "Miss Edwina," the daughter of an Episcopalian minister, was repressed and genteel, very much the southern belle in her youth. His father, Cornelius, was a traveling salesman, often away from his family and often violent and drunk when at home. As a child, Williams was sickly and overly protected by his mother; he was closely attached to his sister, Rose, repelled by the roughhouse world of boys, and alienated from his father. The family's move from Mississippi to St. Louis, where Cornelius became a sales manager of the shoe company he had traveled for, was a shock to Mrs. Williams and her young children, used to living in small southern towns where a minister's daughter was an important person. Yet Mrs. Williams could take care of herself; she was a "survivor."

Williams went to the University of Missouri but left after two years; his father then found him a job in the shoe-factory warehouse. He worked there for nearly three years, writing feverishly at night. (His closest friend at the time was a burly coworker, easygoing and attractive to women, named Stanley Kowalski, whose name and characteristics Williams would borrow for *A Streetcar Named Desire*.) Williams found the life so difficult, however, that he succumbed to a nervous breakdown. After recovering at the home of his beloved grandparents, he went on to further studies, finally graduating at the age of twenty-seven. Earlier, Rose had been suffering increasing mental imbalance; the final trauma was apparently brought on by one of Cornelius's alcoholic rages, in which he beat Edwina and, trying to calm Rose, made a gesture that she took to be sexual. Shortly thereafter Edwina signed the papers allowing Rose to be "tragically becalmed" by a prefrontal lobotomy. Rose spent most of her life in sanatoriums, except when Williams brought her out for visits.

The next year, Williams left for New Orleans, the first of many temporary homes; it would provide the setting for *A Streetcar Named Desire*. In New Orleans he changed his name to "Tennessee," later giving—as often when discussing his life—various romantic reasons for doing so. There also he actively entered the homosexual world.

Williams had had plays produced at local theaters and in 1939 he won a prize for a collection of one-act plays, *American Blues*. The next year *Battle of Angels* failed (in 1957 he would rewrite it as *Orpheus Descending*). His first success was *The Glass Menagerie* (1945). Williams called it a "memory play," seen through the recollections of the writer, Tom, who talks to the audience about himself and about the scenes depicting his mother, Amanda, poverty-stricken but genteelly living on memories of her southern youth and her "gentlemen callers"; his crippled sister, Laura, who finds refuge in her "menagerie" of little glass animals; and the traumatic effect of a modern "gentleman caller" on them. While there are similarities between Edwina, Rose, and Tennessee on the one hand, and Amanda, Laura, and Tom on the other, there are also differences: the play is not literally autobiographical.

The financial success of *Menagerie* proved exhilarating, then debilitating. Williams fled to Mexico to work full-time on an earlier play, *The Poker Night*. It had begun as *The Moth*; its first image, as Williams's biographer, Donald Spoto, tells us, was "simply that of a woman, sitting with folded hands near a window, while moonlight streamed in and she awaited in vain the arrival of her boyfriend": named Blanche, she was at first intended as a young Amanda. During rehearsals of *Menagerie*, Williams had asked members of the stage crew to teach him to play poker, and he began to visualize his new play as a series of confrontations between working-class poker players and two refined southern women.

As the focus of his attention changed from Stanley to Blanche, *The Poker Night* turned into *A Streetcar Named Desire*. Upon opening in 1947, it was an even greater success than *The Glass Menagerie*, and it won the Pulitzer Prize. Williams was able to travel and to buy a home in Key West, Florida, where he did much of his ensuing work. At about this time his "transitory heart" found "a home at last" in a young man named Frank Merlo.

For more than a decade thereafter a new Williams play appeared almost every two years. Among the most successful were *The Rose Tattoo* (1950), in which the tempestuous heroine, Serafina, worshiping the memory of her dead husband, finds love again; the Pulitzer Prize–winning *Cat on a Hot Tin Roof* (1955), which portrays the conflict of the dying Big Daddy and his impotent son, Brick, watched and controlled by Brick's wife, "Maggie the Cat"; and *The Night of the Iguana* (1961), which brings a varied group of tormented people together at a rundown hotel on the Mexican coast. His plays were produced widely abroad and also became equally successful films. Yet some of the ones now regarded as the best of this period were commercial failures: *Summer and Smoke* (1948), for example, and the surrealistic and visionary *Camino Real* (1953).

For years Williams had depended on a wide variety of drugs, especially to help him sleep and to keep him awake in the early mornings, when he invariably worked. In the 1960s the drugs began to take a real toll. Other factors contributed to the decline of his later years: Frank Merlo's death, the emergence of younger playwrights of whom he felt blindly jealous, and the violent nature of the 1960s, which seemed both to mirror his inner chaos and to leave him behind.

Yet despite Broadway failures, critical disparagements, and a breakdown for which he was hospitalized, he valiantly kept working. Spoto notes that in Williams's late work, Rose was "the source and inspiration of everything he wrote, either directly—with a surrogate character representing her—or indirectly, in the situation of romanticized mental illness or unvarnished verisimilitude." This observation is

A game of seven-card stud poker continues as the action of *A Streetcar Named Desire* concludes. Original Broadway production, 1947.

certainly true of his last Broadway play, the failed *Clothes for a Summer Hotel* (1980), ostensibly about the ghosts of Scott and Zelda Fitzgerald, and of the play he obsessively wrote and rewrote, *The Two Character Play*, which chronicles the descent of a brother and sister, who are also lovers, into madness and death.

Despite Williams's self-destructiveness, in his writing and in his social life, the work of his great years was now being seriously studied and often revived by regional and community theaters. Critics began to see that he was one of America's best and most dedicated playwrights. And he kept on working. He was collaborating on a film of two stories about Rose when he died, apparently having choked to death on the lid of a pill bottle.

Always reluctant to talk about his work (likening it to a "bird that will be startled away, as by a hawk's shadow"), Williams did not see himself in a tradition of American dramaturgy. He acknowledged the influence of Anton Chekhov, the nineteenth-century Russian writer of dramas with lonely, searching characters; of D. H. Lawrence, the British novelist who emphasized the theme of a sexual life force; and above all of the American Hart Crane, homosexual *poète maudit*, who, he said, "touched fire that burned [himself] alive," adding that "perhaps it is only through self-immolation of such a nature that we living beings can offer to you the entire truth of ourselves." Such a statement indicates the deeply confessional quality of Williams's writing, even in plays not directly autobiographical.

Although he never acknowledged any debt to the American playwright Eugene O'Neill, Williams shared with O'Neill an impatience over the theatrical conventions of realism. *The Glass Menagerie*, for example, uses screened projections, lighting effects, and music to emphasize that it takes place in Tom's memory. *A Streetcar Named Desire* moves in and out of the house on Elysian Fields, while music and lighting reinforce all the major themes. Williams also relies on the effects of language, especially of a vivid and colloquial Southern speech that may be compared with that of William Faulkner, Eudora Welty, or Flannery O'Connor. Rhythms of language become almost a musical indication of character, distinguishing Blanche from other characters. Reading or seeing his plays, we become aware of how symbolic repetitions—in Blanche's and Stanley's turns of phrase, the naked light bulb and the paper lantern, the Mexican woman selling flowers for the dead, the "Varsouviana" waltz and the reverberating voices—produce a heightening of reality: what Williams called "poetic realism."

More than a half century later, does the destruction of Blanche, the "lady," still have the power to move us? Elia Kazan, in his director's notes, calls her "an outdated creature, approaching extinction . . . like a dinosaur." But Blythe Danner, who played Blanche in a 1988 revival, acutely observes that Williams "was attached to the things that were going to destroy him" and that Blanche, similarly, is attracted to and repelled by Stanley: "It's Tennessee fighting, fighting, fighting what he doesn't want to get into, what is very prevalent in his mind. That incredible contradiction in so many people is what he captures better than any other playwright."

Contemporary criticisms of Williams's plays focused on their violence and their obsession with sexuality, which in some of the later work struck some commentators as an almost morbid preoccupation with "perversion"—murder, rape, drugs, incest, nymphomania. The shriller voices making such accusations were attacking Williams for his homosexuality, which could not be publicly spoken of in this country until comparatively recently. These taboo topics, however, figure as instances of Williams's deeper subjects: desire and loneliness. As he said in an interview, "Desire is rooted in a longing for companionship, a release from the loneliness that haunts every individual." Loneliness and desire propel his characters into extreme behavior, no doubt, but such behavior literally dramatizes the plight that Williams saw as universal.

The following text is from *The Theatre of Tennessee Williams*, volume 1 (1971).

A Streetcar Named Desire

And so it was I entered the broken world
To trace the visionary company of love, its voice
An instant in the wind (I know not whither hurled)
But not for long to hold each desperate choice.
        —*"The Broken Tower" by Hart Crane[1]*

THE CHARACTERS

BLANCHE	PABLO
STELLA	A NEGRO WOMAN
STANLEY	A DOCTOR
MITCH	A NURSE
EUNICE	A YOUNG COLLECTOR
STEVE	A MEXICAN WOMAN

Scene One

The exterior of a two-story corner building on a street in New Orleans which is named Elysian Fields and runs between the L & N tracks and the river.[2] The section is poor but, unlike corresponding sections in other American cities, it has a

---

1. American poet (1899–1932).
2. Elysian Fields is a New Orleans street at the northern tip of the French Quarter, between the Louisville & Nashville railroad tracks and the Mississippi River. In Greek mythology the Elysian Fields are the abode of the blessed in the afterlife.

raffish charm. The houses are mostly white frame, weathered grey, with rickety outside stairs and galleries and quaintly ornamented gables. This building contains two flats, upstairs and down. Faded white stairs ascend to the entrances of both.

It is first dark of an evening early in May. The sky that shows around the dim white building is a peculiarly tender blue, almost a turquoise, which invests the scene with a kind of lyricism and gracefully attenuates the atmosphere of decay. You can almost feel the warm breath of the brown river beyond the river warehouses with their faint redolences of bananas and coffee. A corresponding air is evoked by the music of Negro entertainers at a barroom around the corner. In this part of New Orleans you are practically always just around the corner, or a few doors down the street, from a tinny piano being played with the infatuated fluency of brown fingers. This "Blue Piano" expresses the spirit of the life which goes on here.

Two women, one white and one colored, are taking the air on the steps of the building. The white woman is EUNICE, *who occupies the upstairs flat; the colored woman a neighbor, for New Orleans is a cosmopolitan city where there is a relatively warm and easy intermingling of races in the old part of town.*

Above the music of the "Blue Piano" the voices of people on the street can be heard overlapping.

> [*Two men come around the corner,* STANLEY KOWALSKI *and* MITCH. *They are about twenty-eight or thirty years old, roughly dressed in blue denim work clothes.* STANLEY *carries his bowling jacket and a red-stained package from a butcher's. They stop at the foot of the steps.*]

STANLEY [*bellowing*]   Hey there! Stella, baby!

> [STELLA *comes out on the first floor landing, a gentle young woman, about twenty-five, and of a background obviously quite different from her husband's.*]

STELLA [*mildly*]   Don't holler at me like that. Hi, Mitch.

STANLEY   Catch!

STELLA   What?

STANLEY   Meat!

> [*He heaves the package at her. She cries out in protest but manages to catch it: then she laughs breathlessly. Her husband and his companion have already started back around the corner.*]

STELLA [*calling after him*]   Stanley! Where are you going?

STANLEY   Bowling!

STELLA   Can I come watch?

STANLEY   Come on. [*He goes out.*]

STELLA   Be over soon. [*to the white woman*] Hello, Eunice. How are you?

EUNICE   I'm all right. Tell Steve to get him a poor boy's sandwich 'cause nothing's left here.

> [*They all laugh; the colored woman does not stop.* STELLA *goes out.*]

COLORED WOMAN   What was that package he th'ew at 'er? [*She rises from steps, laughing louder.*]

EUNICE   You hush, now!

NEGRO WOMAN   Catch *what!*

> [*She continues to laugh.* BLANCHE *comes around the corner, carrying a valise. She looks at a slip of paper, then at the building, then again at the slip and again at the building. Her expression is one of shocked disbelief. Her appearance is incongruous to this setting. She is daintily dressed in a white suit with a fluffy bodice, necklace and earrings of pearl, white*

gloves and hat, looking as if she were arriving at a summer tea or cocktail party in the garden district. She is about five years older than STELLA. *Her delicate beauty must avoid a strong light. There is something about her uncertain manner, as well as her white clothes, that suggests a moth.*]

EUNICE [*finally*] What's the matter, honey? Are you lost?

BLANCHE [*with faintly hysterical humor*] They told me to take a street-car named Desire, and then transfer to one called Cemeteries[3] and ride six blocks and get off at—Elysian Fields!

EUNICE That's where you are now.

BLANCHE At Elysian Fields?

EUNICE This here is Elysian Fields.

BLANCHE They mustn't have—understood—what number I wanted . . .

EUNICE What number you lookin' for?

[BLANCHE *wearily refers to the slip of paper.*]

BLANCHE Six thirty-two.

EUNICE You don't have to look no further.

BLANCHE [*uncomprehendingly*] I'm looking for my sister, Stella DuBois, I mean—Mrs. Stanley Kowalski.

EUNICE That's the party.—You just did miss her, though.

BLANCHE This—can this be—her home?

EUNICE She's got the downstairs here and I got the up.

BLANCHE Oh. She's—out?

EUNICE You noticed that bowling alley around the corner?

BLANCHE I'm—not sure I did.

EUNICE Well, that's where she's at, watchin' her husband bowl. [*There is a pause.*] You want to leave your suitcase here an' go find her?

BLANCHE No.

NEGRO WOMAN I'll go tell her you come.

BLANCHE Thanks.

NEGRO WOMAN You welcome. [*She goes out.*]

EUNICE She wasn't expecting you?

BLANCHE No. No, not tonight.

EUNICE Well, why don't you just go in and make yourself at home till they get back.

BLANCHE How could I—do that?

EUNICE We own this place so I can let you in.

[*She gets up and opens the downstairs door. A light goes on behind the blind, turning it light blue.* BLANCHE *slowly follows her into the down-stairs flat. The surrounding areas dim out as the interior is lighted. Two rooms can be seen, not too clearly defined. The one first entered is primarily a kitchen but contains a folding bed to be used by* BLANCHE. *The room beyond this is a bedroom. Off this room is a narrow door to a bathroom.*]

EUNICE [*defensively, noticing* BLANCHE's *look*] It's sort of messed up right now but when it's clean it's real sweet.

BLANCHE Is it?

EUNICE Uh-huh, I think so. So you're Stella's sister?

BLANCHE Yes. [*wanting to get rid of her*] Thanks for letting me in.

EUNICE *Por nada,*[4] as the Mexicans say, *por nada*! Stella spoke of you.

3. The end of a streetcar line that stopped at a cemetery. Desire is a New Orleans street. 4. It's nothing (Spanish).

BLANCHE Yes?

EUNICE I think she said you taught school.

BLANCHE Yes.

EUNICE And you're from Mississippi, huh?

BLANCHE Yes.

EUNICE She showed me a picture of your home-place, the plantation.

BLANCHE Belle Reve?[5]

EUNICE A great big place with white columns.

BLANCHE Yes . . .

EUNICE A place like that must be awful hard to keep up.

BLANCHE If you will excuse me, I'm just about to drop.

EUNICE Sure, honey. Why don't you set down?

BLANCHE What I meant was I'd like to be left alone.

EUNICE [*offended*] Aw. I'll make myself scarce, in that case.

BLANCHE I didn't meant to be rude, but—

EUNICE I'll drop by the bowling alley an' hustle her up. [*She goes out the door.*]

> [BLANCHE *sits in a chair very stiffly with her shoulders slightly hunched and her legs pressed close together and her hands tightly clutching her purse as if she were quite cold. After a while the blind look goes out of her eyes and she begins to look slowly around. A cat screeches. She catches her breath with a startled gesture. Suddenly she notices something in a half opened closet. She springs up and crosses to it, and removes a whiskey bottle. She pours a half tumbler of whiskey and tosses it down. She carefully replaces the bottle and washes out the tumbler at the sink. Then she resumes her seat in front of the table.*]

BLANCHE [*faintly to herself*] I've got to keep hold of myself! [STELLA *comes quickly around the corner of the building and runs to the door of the downstairs flat.*]

STELLA [*calling out joyfully*] Blanche!

> [*For a moment they stare at each other. Then* BLANCHE *springs up and runs to her with a wild cry.*]

BLANCHE Stella, oh, Stella, Stella! Stella for Star!

> [*She begins to speak with feverish vivacity as if she feared for either of them to stop and think. They catch each other in a spasmodic embrace.*]

BLANCHE Now, then, let me look at you. But don't you look at me, Stella, no, no, no, not till later, not till I've bathed and rested! And turn that over-light off! Turn that off! I won't be looked at in this merciles glare! [STELLA *laughs and complies.*] Come back here now! Oh, my baby! Stella! Stella for Star! [*She embraces her again.*] I thought you would never come back to this horrible place! What am I saying? I didn't mean to say that. I meant to be nice about it and say—Oh, what a convenient location and such—Ha-a-ha! Precious lamb! You haven't said a *word* to me.

STELLA You haven't given me a chance to, honey! [*She laughs, but her glance at* BLANCHE *is a little anxious.*]

BLANCHE Well, now you talk. Open your pretty mouth and talk while I look around for some liquor! I know you must have some liquor on the place! Where could it be, I wonder? Oh, I spy, I spy!

---

5. Beautiful Dream (French).

[*She rushes to the closet and removes the bottle; she is shaking all over and panting for breath as she tries to laugh. The bottle nearly slips from her grasp.*]

STELLA [*noticing*] Blanche, you sit down and let me pour the drinks. I don't know what we've got to mix with. Maybe a coke's in the icebox. Look'n see, honey, while I'm—

BLANCHE No coke, honey, not with my nerves tonight! Where—where—where is—?

STELLA Stanley? Bowling! He loves it. They're having a—found some soda!—tournament . . .

BLANCHE Just water, baby, to chase it! Now don't get worried, your sister hasn't turned into a drunkard, she's just all shaken up and hot and tired and dirty! You sit down, now, and explain this place to me! What are you doing in a place like this?

STELLA Now, Blanche—

BLANCHE Oh, I'm not going to be hypocritical, I'm going to be honestly critical about it! Never, never, never in my worst dreams could I picture— Only Poe! Only Mr. Edgar Allan Poe!—could do it justice! Out there I suppose is the ghoul-haunted woodland of Weir![6] [*She laughs.*]

STELLA No, honey, those are the L & N tracks.

BLANCHE No, now seriously, putting joking aside. Why didn't you tell me, why didn't you write me, honey, why didn't you let me know?

STELLA [*carefully, pouring herself a drink*] Tell you what, Blanche?

BLANCHE Why, that you had to live in these conditions!

STELLA Aren't you being a little intense about it? It's not that bad at all! New Orleans isn't like other cities.

BLANCHE This has got nothing to do with New Orleans. You might as well say—forgive me, blessed baby! [*She suddenly stops short.*] The subject is closed!

STELLA [*a little drily*] Thanks.

[*During the pause,* BLANCHE *stares at her. She smiles at* BLANCHE.]

BLANCHE [*looking down at her glass, which shakes in her hand*] You're all I've got in the world, and you're not glad to see me!

STELLA [*sincerely*] Why, Blanche, you know that's not true.

BLANCHE No?—I'd forgotten how quiet you were.

STELLA You never did give me a chance to say much, Blanche. So I just got in the habit of being quiet around you.

BLANCHE [*vaguely*] A good habit to get into . . . [*then, abruptly*] You haven't asked me how I happened to get away from the school before the spring term ended.

STELLA Well, I thought you'd volunteer that information—if you wanted to tell me.

BLANCHE You thought I'd been fired?

STELLA No, I—thought you might have—resigned . . .

BLANCHE I was so exhausted by all I'd been through my—nerves broke. [*nervously tamping cigarette*] I was on the verge of—lunacy, almost! So Mr. Graves—Mr. Graves is the high school superintendent—he suggested I take a leave of absence. I couldn't put all of those details into

6. From the refrain of Poe's gothic ballad "Ulalume" (1847).

the wire . . . [*She drinks quickly.*] Oh, this buzzes right through me and feels so *good!*

STELLA   Won't you have another?

BLANCHE   No, one's my limit.

STELLA   Sure?

BLANCHE   You haven't said a word about my appearance.

STELLA   You look just fine.

BLANCHE   God love you for a liar! Daylight never exposed so total a ruin! But you—you've put on some weight, yes, you're just as plump as a little partridge! And it's so becoming to you!

STELLA   Now, Blanche—

BLANCHE   Yes, it is, it is or I wouldn't say it! You just have to watch around the hips a little. Stand up.

STELLA   Not now.

BLANCHE   You hear me? I said stand up! [STELLA *complies reluctantly.*] You messy child, you, you've spilt something on that pretty white lace collar! About your hair—you ought to have it cut in a feather bob with your dainty features. Stella, you have a maid, don't you?

STELLA   No. With only two rooms it's—

BLANCHE   What? *Two* rooms, did you say?

STELLA   This one and— [*She is embarrassed.*]

BLANCHE   The other one? [*She laughs sharply. There is an embarrassed silence.*]

BLANCHE   I am going to take just one little tiny nip more, sort of to put the stopper on, so to speak. . . . Then put the bottle away so I won't be tempted. [*She rises.*] I want you to look at *my* figure! [*She turns around.*] You know I haven't put on one ounce in ten years, Stella? I weigh what I weighed the summer you left Belle Reve. The summer Dad died and you left us . . .

STELLA   [*a little wearily*]   It's just incredible, Blanche, how well you're looking.

BLANCHE   [*They both laugh uncomfortably.*]   But, Stella, there's only two rooms, I don't see where you're going to put me!

STELLA   We're going to put you in here.

BLANCHE   What kind of bed's this—one of those collapsible things? [*She sits on it.*]

STELLA   Does it feel all right?

BLANCHE   [*dubiously*]   Wonderful, honey. I don't like a bed that gives much. But there's no door between the two rooms, and Stanley—will it be decent?

STELLA   Stanley is Polish, you know.

BLANCHE   Oh, yes. They're something like Irish, aren't they?

STELLA   Well—

BLANCHE   Only not so—highbrow? [*They both laugh again in the same way.*] I brought some nice clothes to meet all your lovely friends in.

STELLA   I'm afraid you won't think they are lovely.

BLANCHE   What are they like?

STELLA   They're Stanley's friends.

BLANCHE   Polacks?

STELLA   They're a mixed lot, Blanche.

BLANCHE   Heterogeneous—types?

STELLA   Oh, yes. Yes, types is right!

BLANCHE   Well—anyhow—I brought nice clothes and I'll wear them. I guess you're hoping I'll say I'll put up at a hotel, but I'm not going to put up at a hotel. I want to be *near* you, got to be *with* somebody, I *can't* be *alone*! Because—as you must have noticed—I'm—*not* very *well*. . . . [*Her voice drops and her look is frightened.*]

STELLA   You seem a little bit nervous or overwrought or something.

BLANCHE   Will Stanley like me, or will I be just a visiting in-law, Stella? I couldn't stand that.

STELLA   You'll get along fine together, if you'll just try not to—well— compare him with men that we went out with at home.

BLANCHE   Is he so—different?

STELLA   Yes. A different species.

BLANCHE   In what way; what's he like?

STELLA   Oh, you can't describe someone you're in love with! Here's a picture of him! [*She hands a photograph to* BLANCHE.]

BLANCHE   An officer?

STELLA   A Master Sergeant in the Engineers' Corps. Those are decorations!

BLANCHE   He had those on when you met him?

STELLA   I assure you I wasn't just blinded by all the brass.

BLANCHE   That's not what I—

STELLA   But of course there were things to adjust myself to later on.

BLANCHE   Such as his civilian background! [STELLA *laughs uncertainly.*] How did he take it when you said I was coming?

STELLA   Oh, Stanley doesn't know yet.

BLANCHE [*frightened*]   You—haven't told him?

STELLA   He's on the road a good deal.

BLANCHE   Oh. Travels?

STELLA   Yes.

BLANCHE   Good. I mean—isn't it?

STELLA [*half to herself*]   I can hardly stand it when he is away for a night . . .

BLANCHE   Why, Stella!

STELLA   When he's away for a week I nearly go wild!

BLANCHE   Gracious!

STELLA   And when he comes back I cry on his lap like a baby . . . [*She smiles to herself.*]

BLANCHE   I guess that is what is meant by being in love . . . [STELLA *looks up with a radiant smile.*] Stella—

STELLA   What?

BLANCHE [*in an uneasy rush*]   I haven't asked you the things you probably thought I was going to ask. And so I'll expect you to be understanding about what *I* have to tell *you*.

STELLA   What, Blanche? [*Her face turns anxious.*]

BLANCHE   Well, Stella—you're going to reproach me, I know that you're bound to reproach me—but before you do—take into consideration— you left! I stayed and struggled! You came to New Orleans and looked out for yourself! *I* stayed at *Belle Reve* and tried to hold it together! I'm not meaning this in any reproachful way, but *all* the burden descended on *my* shoulders.

STELLA   The best I could do was make my own living, Blanche.
   [BLANCHE *begins to shake again with intensity.*]
BLANCHE   I know, I know. But you are the one that abandoned Belle
   Reve, not I! I stayed and fought for it, bled for it, almost died for it!
STELLA   Stop this hysterical outburst and tell me what's happened? What
   do you mean fought and bled? What kind of—
BLANCHE   I knew you would, Stella. I knew you would take this attitude
   about it!
STELLA   About—what?—please!
BLANCHE [*slowly*]   The loss—the loss . . .
STELLA   Belle Reve? Lost, is it? No!
BLANCHE   Yes, Stella.
   [*They stare at each other across the yellow-checked linoleum of the table.*
   BLANCHE *slowly nods her head and* STELLA *looks slowly down at her
   hands folded on the table. The music of the "Blue Piano" grows louder.*
   BLANCHE *touches her handkerchief to her forehead.*]
STELLA   But how did it go? What happened?
BLANCHE [*springing up*]   You're a fine one to ask me how it went!
STELLA   Blanche!
BLANCHE   You're a fine one to sit there *accusing me* of it!
STELLA   *Blanche!*
BLANCHE   I, I, *I* took the blows in my face and my body! All of those
   deaths! The long parade to the graveyard! Father, mother! Margaret,
   that dreadful way! So big with it, it couldn't be put in a coffin! But had
   to be burned like rubbish! You just came home in time for the funerals, Stella. And funerals are pretty compared to deaths. Funerals are
   quiet, but deaths—not always. Sometimes their breathing is hoarse,
   and sometimes it rattles, and sometimes they even cry out to you, "Don't
   let me go!" Even the old, sometimes, say, "Don't let me go." As if you
   were able to stop them! But funerals are quiet, with pretty flowers. And,
   oh, what gorgeous boxes they pack them away in! Unless you were there
   at the bed when they cried out, "Hold me!" you'd never suspect there
   was the struggle for breath and bleeding. You didn't dream, but I saw!
   Saw! Saw! And now you sit there telling me with your eyes that I let the
   place go! How in hell do you think all that sickness and dying was paid
   for? Death is expensive, Miss Stella! And old Cousin Jessie's right after
   Margaret's, hers! Why, the Grim Reaper had put up his tent on our
   doorstep! . . . Stella. Belle Reve was his headquarters! Honey—that's
   how it slipped through my fingers! Which of them left us a fortune?
   Which of them left a cent of insurance even? Only poor Jessie—one
   hundred to pay for her coffin. That was all, Stella! And I with my piti-
   ful salary at the school. Yes, accuse me! Sit there and stare at me, think-
   ing I let the place go! *I* let the place go? Where were *you!* In bed with
   your—Polack!
STELLA [*springing*]   Blanche! You be still! That's enough! [*She starts out.*]
BLANCHE   Where are you going?
STELLA   I'm going into the bathroom to wash my face.
BLANCHE   Oh, Stella, Stella, you're crying!
STELLA   Does that surprise you?
BLANCHE   Forgive me—I didn't mean to—

[*The sound of men's voices is heard.* STELLA *goes into the bathroom, closing the door behind her. When the men appear, and* BLANCHE *realizes it must be* STANLEY *returning, she moves uncertainly from the bathroom door to the dressing table, looking apprehensively toward the front door.* STANLEY *enters, followed by* STEVE *and* MITCH. STANLEY *pauses near his door,* STEVE *by the foot of the spiral stair, and* MITCH *is slightly above and to the right of them, about to go out. As the men enter, we hear some of the following dialogue.*]

STANLEY   Is that how he got it?

STEVE   Sure that's how he got it. He hit the old weather-bird for 300 bucks on a six-number-ticket.

MITCH   Don't tell him those things; he'll believe it.
[*Mitch starts out.*]

STANLEY [*restraining Mitch*]   Hey, Mitch—come back here.
[BLANCHE, *at the sound of voices, retires in the bedroom. She picks up* STANLEY's *photo from dressing table, looks at it, puts it down. When* STANLEY *enters the apartment, she darts and hides behind the screen at the head of bed.*]

STEVE [*to* STANLEY *and* MITCH]   Hey, are we playin' poker tomorrow?

STANLEY   Sure—at Mitch's.

MITCH [*hearing this, returns quickly to the stair rail*]   No—not at my place. My mother's still sick!

STANLEY   Okay, at my place . . . [MITCH *starts out again.*] But you bring the beer!
[MITCH *pretends not to hear—calls out "Good night, all," and goes out, singing.* EUNICE's *voice is heard, above.*]

EUNICE   Break it up down there! I made the spaghetti dish and ate it myself.

STEVE [*going upstairs*]   I told you and phoned you we was playing. [*to the men*] Jax beer![7]

EUNICE   You never phoned me once.

STEVE   I told you at breakfast—and phoned you at lunch . . .

EUNICE   Well, never mind about that. You just get yourself home here once in a while.

STEVE   You want it in the papers?
[*More laughter and shouts of parting come from the men.* STANLEY *throws the screen door of the kitchen open and comes in. He is of medium height, about five feet eight or nine, and strongly, compactly built. Animal joy in his being is implicit in all his movements and attitudes. Since earliest manhood the center of his life has been pleasure with women, the giving and taking of it, not with weak indulgence, dependently, but with the power and pride of a richly feathered male bird among hens. Branching out from this complete and satisfying center are all the auxiliary channels of his life, such as his heartiness with men, his appreciation of rough humor, his love of good drink and food and games, his car, his radio, everything that is his, that bears his emblem of the gaudy seed-bearer. He sizes women up at a glance, with sexual classifications, crude images flashing into his mind and determining the way he smiles at them.*]

BLANCHE [*drawing involuntarily back from his stare*]   You must be Stanley. I'm Blanche.

7. A local brand.

STANLEY Stella's sister?

BLANCHE Yes.

STANLEY H'lo. Where's the little woman?

BLANCHE In the bathroom.

STANLEY Oh. Didn't know you were coming in town.

BLANCHE I—uh—

STANLEY Where you from, Blanche?

BLANCHE Why, I—live in Laurel.

[*He has crossed to the closet and removed the whiskey bottle.*]

STANLEY In Laurel, huh? Oh, yeah. Yeah, in Laurel, that's right. Not in my territory. Liquor goes fast in hot weather. [*He holds the bottle to the light to observe its depletion.*] Have a shot?

BLANCHE No, I—rarely touch it.

STANLEY Some people rarely touch it, but it touches them often.

BLANCHE [*faintly*] Ha-ha.

STANLEY My clothes're stickin' to me. Do you mind if I make myself comfortable? [*He starts to remove his shirt.*]

BLANCHE Please, please do.

STANLEY Be comfortable is my motto.

BLANCHE It's mine, too. It's hard to stay looking fresh. I haven't washed or even powdered my face and—here you are!

STANLEY You know you can catch cold sitting around in damp things, especially when you been exercising hard like bowling is. You're a teacher, aren't you?

BLANCHE Yes.

STANLEY What do you teach, Blanche?

BLANCHE English.

STANLEY I never was a very good English student. How long you here for, Blanche?

BLANCHE I—don't know yet.

STANLEY You going to shack up here?

BLANCHE I thought I would if it's not inconvenient for you all.

STANLEY Good.

BLANCHE Traveling wears me out.

STANLEY Well, take it easy.

[*A cat screeches near the window,* BLANCHE *springs up.*]

BLANCHE What's that?

STANLEY Cats . . . Hey, Stella!

STELLA [*faintly, from the bathroom*] Yes, Stanley.

STANLEY Haven't fallen in, have you? [*He grins at* BLANCHE. *She tries unsuccessfully to smile back. There is a silence.*] I'm afraid I'll strike you as being the unrefined type. Stella's spoke of you a good deal. You were married once, weren't you?

[*The music of the polka rises up, faint in the distance.*]

BLANCHE Yes. When I was quite young.

STANLEY What happened?

BLANCHE The boy—the boy died. [*She sinks back down.*] I'm afraid I'm—going to be sick! [*Her head falls on her arms.*]

Scene Two

It is six o'clock the following evening. BLANCHE *is bathing.* STELLA *is completing her toilette.* BLANCHE's *dress, a flowered print, is laid out on* STELLA's *bed.*

STANLEY *enters the kitchen from outside, leaving the door open on the perpetual "Blue Piano" around the corner.*

STANLEY   What's all this monkey doings?

STELLA   Oh, Stan! [*She jumps up and kisses him, which he accepts with lordly composure.*] I'm taking Blanche to Galatoire's[8] for supper and then to a show, because it's your poker night.

STANLEY   How about my supper, huh? I'm not going to no Galatoire's for supper!

STELLA   I put you a cold plate on ice.

STANLEY   Well, isn't that just dandy!

STELLA   I'm going to try to keep Blanche out till the party breaks up because I don't know how she would take it. So we'll go to one of the little places in the Quarter afterward and you'd better give me some money.

STANLEY   Where is she?

STELLA   She's soaking in a hot tub to quiet her nerves. She's terribly upset.

STANLEY   Over what?

STELLA   She's been through such an ordeal.

STANLEY   Yeah?

STELLA   Stan, we've—lost Belle Reve!

STANLEY   The place in the country?

STELLA   Yes.

STANLEY   How?

STELLA [*vaguely*]   Oh, it had to be—sacrificed or something. [*There is a pause while* STANLEY *considers.* STELLA *is changing into her dress.*] When she comes in be sure to say something nice about her appearance. And, oh! Don't mention the baby. I haven't said anything yet, I'm waiting until she gets in a quieter condition.

STANLEY [*ominously*]   So?

STELLA   And try to understand her and be nice to her, Stan.

BLANCHE [*singing in the bathroom*]   "From the land of the sky blue water, They brought a captive maid!"

STELLA   She wasn't expecting to find us in such a small place. You see I'd tried to gloss things over a little in my letters.

STANLEY   So?

STELLA   And admire her dress and tell her she's looking wonderful. That's important with Blanche. Her little weakness!

STANLEY   Yeah. I get the idea. Now let's skip back a little to where you said the country place was disposed of.

STELLA   Oh!—yes . . .

STANLEY   How about that? Let's have a few more details on that subjeck.

STELLA   It's best not to talk much about it until she's calmed down.

STANLEY   So that's the deal, huh? Sister Blanche cannot be annoyed with business details right now!

8. Renowned fancy restaurant with traditional New Orleans cuisine.

STELLA   You saw how she was last night.

STANLEY   Uh-hum, I saw how she was. Now let's have a gander at the bill of sale.

STELLA   I haven't seen any.

STANLEY   She didn't show you no papers, no deed of sale or nothing like that, huh?

STELLA   It seems like it wasn't sold.

STANLEY   Well, what in hell was it then, give away? To charity?

STELLA   Shhh! She'll hear you.

STANLEY   I don't care if she hears me. Let's see the papers!

STELLA   There weren't any papers, she didn't show any papers, I don't care about papers.

STANLEY   Have you ever heard of the Napoleonic code?[9]

STELLA   No, Stanley, I haven't heard of the Napoleonic code and if I have, I don't see what it—

STANLEY   Let me enlighten you on a point or two, baby.

STELLA   Yes?

STANLEY   In the state of Louisiana we have the Napoleonic code according to which what belongs to the wife belongs to the husband and vice versa. For instance if I had a piece of property, or you had a piece of property—

STELLA   My head is swimming!

STANLEY   All right. I'll wait till she gets through soaking in a hot tub and then I'll inquire if *she* is acquainted with the Napoleonic code. It looks to me like you have been swindled, baby, and when you're swindled under the Napoleonic code I'm swindled *too*. And I don't like to be *swindled*.

STELLA   There's plenty of time to ask her questions later but if you do now she'll go to pieces again. I don't understand what happened to Belle Reve but you don't know how ridiculous you are being when you suggest that my sister or I or anyone of our family could have perpetrated a swindle on anyone else.

STANLEY   Then where's the money if the place was sold?

STELLA   Not sold—*lost, lost!*

[He stalks into bedroom, and she follows him.]

Stanley!

[He pulls open the wardrobe trunk standing in middle of room and jerks out an armful of dresses.]

STANLEY   Open your eyes to this stuff! You think she got them out of a teacher's pay?

STELLA   Hush!

STANLEY   Look at these feathers and furs that she come here to preen herself in! What's this here? A solid-gold dress, I believe! And this one! What is these here? Fox-pieces! [He blows on them.] Genuine fox fur-pieces, a half a mile long! Where are your fox-pieces, Stella? Bushy snow-white ones, no less! Where are your white fox-pieces?

STELLA   Those are inexpensive summer furs that Blanche has had a long time.

---

9. This codification of French law (1802), made by Napoleon as emperor, is the basis for Louisiana's civil law.

STANLEY I got an acquaintance who deals in this sort of merchandise. I'll have him in here to appraise it. I'm willing to bet you there's thousands of dollars invested in this stuff here!

STELLA Don't be such an idiot, Stanley!

[*He hurls the furs to the day bed. Then he jerks open a small drawer in the trunk and pulls up a fistful of costume jewelry.*]

STANLEY And what have we here? The treasure chest of a pirate!

STELLA Oh, Stanley!

STANLEY Pearls! Ropes of them! What is this sister of yours, a deep-sea diver? Bracelets of solid gold, too! Where are your pearls and gold bracelets?

STELLA Shhh! Be still, Stanley!

STANLEY And diamonds! A crown for an empress!

STELLA A rhinestone tiara she wore to a costume ball.

STANLEY What's rhinestone?

STELLA Next door to glass.

STANLEY Are you kidding? I have an acquaintance that works in a jewelry store. I'll have him in here to make an appraisal of this. Here's your plantation, or what was left of it, here!

STELLA You have no idea how stupid and horrid you're being! Now close that trunk before she comes out of the bathroom!

[*He kicks the trunk partly closed and sits on the kitchen table.*]

STANLEY The Kowalskis and the DuBoises have different notions.

STELLA [*angrily*] Indeed they have, thank heavens!—*I'm* going outside. [*She snatches up her white hat and gloves and crosses to the outside door.*] You come out with me while Blanche is getting dressed.

STANLEY Since when do you give me orders?

STELLA Are you going to stay here and insult her?

STANLEY You're damn tootin' I'm going to stay here.

[STELLA *goes out to the porch.* BLANCHE *comes out of the bathroom in a red satin robe.*]

BLANCHE [*airily*] Hello, Stanley! Here I am, all freshly bathed and scented, and feeling like a brand new human being!

[*He lights a cigarette.*]

STANLEY That's good.

BLANCHE [*drawing the curtains at the windows*] Excuse me while I slip on my pretty new dress!

STANLEY Go right ahead, Blanche.

[*She closes the drapes between the rooms.*]

BLANCHE I understand there's to be a little card party to which we ladies are cordially *not* invited!

STANLEY [*ominously*] Yeah?

[BLANCHE *throws off her robe and slips into a flowered print dress.*]

BLANCHE Where's Stella?

STANLEY Out on the porch.

BLANCHE I'm going to ask a favor of you in a moment.

STANLEY What could that be, I wonder?

BLANCHE Some buttons in back! You may enter! [*He crosses through drapes with a smoldering look.*] How do I look?

STANLEY You look all right.

BLANCHE   Many thanks! Now the buttons!

STANLEY   I can't do nothing with them.

BLANCHE   You men with your big clumsy fingers. May I have a drag on your cig?

STANLEY   Have one for yourself.

BLANCHE   Why, thanks! . . . It looks like my trunk has exploded.

STANLEY   Me an' Stella were helping you unpack.

BLANCHE   Well, you certainly did a fast and thorough job of it!

STANLEY   It looks like you raided some stylish shops in Paris.

BLANCHE   Ha-ha! Yes—clothes are my passion!

STANLEY   What does it cost for a string of fur-pieces like that?

BLANCHE   Why, those were a tribute from an admirer of mine!

STANLEY   He must have had a lot of—admiration!

BLANCHE   Oh, in my youth I excited some admiration. But look at me now! [*She smiles at him radiantly.*] Would you think it possible that I was once considered to be—attractive?

STANLEY   Your looks are okay.

BLANCHE   I was fishing for a compliment, Stanley.

STANLEY   I don't go in for that stuff.

BLANCHE   What—stuff?

STANLEY   Compliments to women about their looks. I never met a woman that didn't know if she was good-looking or not without being told, and some of them give themselves credit for more than they've got. I once went out with a doll who said to me, "I am the glamorous type, I am the glamorous type!" I said, "So what?"

BLANCHE   And what did she say then?

STANLEY   She didn't say nothing. That shut her up like a clam.

BLANCHE   Did it end the romance?

STANLEY   It ended the conversation—that was all. Some men are took in by this Hollywood glamor stuff and some men are not.

BLANCHE   I'm sure you belong in the second category.

STANLEY   That's right.

BLANCHE   I cannot imagine any witch of a woman casting a spell over you.

STANLEY   That's—right.

BLANCHE   You're simple, straightforward and honest, a little bit on the primitive side I should think. To interest you a woman would have to— [*She pauses with an indefinite gesture.*]

STANLEY [*slowly*]   Lay . . . her cards on the table.

BLANCHE [*smiling*]   Well, I never cared for wishy-washy people. That was why, when you walked in here last night, I said to myself—"My sister has married a man!"—Of course that was all that I could tell about you.

STANLEY [*booming*]   Now let's cut the re-bop![1]

BLANCHE [*pressing hands to her ears*]   Ouuuuu!

STELLA [*calling from the steps*]   Stanley! You come out here and let Blanche finish dressing!

BLANCHE   I'm through dressing, honey.

---

1. Nonsense (from "bebop," a form of jazz).

STELLA Well, you come out, then.

STANLEY Your sister and I are having a little talk.

BLANCHE [*lightly*] Honey, do me a favor. Run to the drugstore and get me a lemon Coke with plenty of chipped ice in it!—Will you do that for me, sweetie?

STELLA [*uncertainly*] Yes. [*She goes around the corner of the building.*]

BLANCHE The poor little thing was out there listening to us, and I have an idea she doesn't understand you as well as I do. . . . All right; now, Mr. Kowalski, let us proceed without any more double-talk. I'm ready to answer all questions. I've nothing to hide. What is it?

STANLEY There is such a thing in this state of Louisiana as the Napoleonic code, according to which whatever belongs to my wife is also mine—and vice versa.

BLANCHE My, but you have an impressive judicial air!
    [*She sprays herself with her atomizer; then playfully sprays him with it. He seizes the atomizer and slams it down on the dresser. She throws back her head and laughs.*]

STANLEY If I didn't know that you was my wife's sister I'd get ideas about you!

BLANCHE Such as what!

STANLEY Don't play so dumb. You know what!

BLANCHE [*she puts the atomizer on the table*] All right. Cards on the table. That suits me. [*She turns to* STANLEY.] I know I fib a good deal. After all, a woman's charm is fifty per cent illusion, but when a thing is important I tell the truth, and this is the truth: I haven't cheated my sister or you or anyone else as long as I have lived.

STANLEY Where's the papers? In the trunk?

BLANCHE Everything that I own is in that trunk.
    [STANLEY *crosses to the trunk, shoves it roughly open and begins to open compartments.*]

BLANCHE What in the name of heaven are you thinking of! What's in the back of that little boy's mind of yours? That I am absconding with some-thing, attempting some kind of treachery on my sister?—Let me do that! It will be faster and simpler . . . [*She crosses to the trunk and takes out a box.*] I keep my papers mostly in this tin box. [*She opens it.*]

STANLEY What's them underneath? [*He indicates another sheaf of paper.*]

BLANCHE These are love-letters, yellowing with antiquity, all from one boy.
    [*He snatches them up. She speaks fiercely.*] Give those back to me!

STANLEY I'll have a look at them first!

BLANCHE The touch of your hands insults them!

STANLEY Don't pull that stuff!
    [*He rips off the ribbon and starts to examine them.* BLANCHE *snatches them from him, and they cascade to the floor.*]

BLANCHE Now that you've touched them I'll burn them!

STANLEY [*staring, baffled*] What in hell are they?

BLANCHE [*on the floor gathering them up*] Poems a dead boy wrote. I hurt him the way that you would like to hurt me, but you can't! I'm not young and vulnerable any more. But my young husband was and I—never mind about that! Just give them back to me!

STANLEY What do you mean by saying you'll have to burn them?

BLANCHE   I'm sorry, I must have lost my head for a moment. Everyone has something he won't let others touch because of their—intimate nature . . .
[*She now seems faint with exhaustion and she sits down with the strong box and puts on a pair of glasses and goes methodically through a large stack of papers.*]
Ambler & Ambler. Hmmmmm. . . . Crabtree. . . . More Ambler & Ambler.

STANLEY   What is Ambler & Ambler?

BLANCHE   A firm that made loans on the place.

STANLEY   Then it *was* lost on a mortgage?

BLANCHE [*touching her forehead*]   That must've been what happened.

STANLEY   I don't want no ifs, ands or buts! What's all the rest of them papers?
[*She hands him the entire box. He carries it to the table and starts to examine the paper.*]

BLANCHE [*picking up a large envelope containing more papers*]   There are thousands of papers, stretching back over hundreds of years, affecting Belle Reve as, piece by piece, our improvident grandfathers and father and uncles and brothers exchanged the land for their epic fornications— to put it plainly! [*She removes her glasses with an exhausted laugh.*] The four-letter word deprived us of our plantation, till finally all that was left—and Stella can verify that!—was the house itself and about twenty acres of ground, including a graveyard, to which now all but Stella and I have retreated. [*She pours the contents of the envelope on the table.*] Here all of them are, all papers! I hereby endow you with them! Take them, peruse them—commit them to memory, even! I think it's wonderfully fitting that Belle Reve should finally be this bunch of old papers in your big, capable hands! . . . I wonder if Stella's come back with my lemon Coke . . . [*She leans back and closes her eyes.*]

STANLEY   I have a lawyer acquaintance who will study these out.

BLANCHE   Present them to him with a box of aspirin tablets.

STANLEY [*becoming somewhat sheepish*]   You see, under the Napoleonic code—a man has to take an interest in his wife's affairs—especially now that she's going to have a baby.
[BLANCHE *opens her eyes. The "Blue Piano" sounds louder.*]

BLANCHE   Stella? Stella going to have a baby? [*dreamily*] I didn't know she was going to have a baby!
[*She gets up and crosses to the outside door.* STELLA *appears around the corner with a carton from the drugstore.* STANLEY *goes into the bedroom with the envelope and the box. The inner rooms fade to darkness and the outside wall of the house is visible,* BLANCHE *meets* STELLA *at the foot of the steps to the sidewalk.*]

BLANCHE   Stella, Stella for star! How lovely to have a baby! It's all right. Everything's all right.

STELLA   I'm sorry he did that to you.

BLANCHE   Oh, I guess he's just not the type that goes for jasmine perfume, but maybe he's what we need to mix with our blood now that we've lost Belle Reve. We thrashed it out. I feel a bit shaky, but I think I handled it nicely, I laughed and treated it all as a joke. [STEVE *and* PABLO *appear, carrying a case of beer.*] I called him a little boy and laughed and flirted. Yes, I was flirting with your husband! [*as the men approach*] The guests

are gathering for the poker party. [*The two men pass between them, and enter the house.*] Which way do we go now, Stella—this way?
STELLA   No, this way. [*She leads* BLANCHE *away.*]
BLANCHE [*laughing*]   The blind are leading the blind!
      [*A tamale* VENDOR *is heard calling.*]
VENDOR'S VOICE   Red-hot!

Scene Three

THE POKER NIGHT[2]

*There is a picture of Van Gogh's[3] of a billiard-parlor at night. The kitchen now suggests that sort of lurid nocturnal brilliance, the raw colors of childhood's spectrum. Over the yellow linoleum of the kitchen table hangs an electric bulb with a vivid green glass shade. The poker players—*STANLEY, STEVE, MITCH *and* PABLO*—wear colored shirts, solid blues, a purple, a red-and-white check, a light green, and they are men at the peak of their physical manhood, as coarse and direct and powerful as the primary colors. There are vivid slices of watermelon on the table, whiskey bottles and glasses. The bedroom is relatively dim with only the light that spills between the portieres and through the wide window on the street.*
      For a moment, there is absorbed silence as a hand is dealt.

STEVE   Anything wild this deal?
PABLO   One-eyed jacks are wild.
STEVE   Give me two cards.
PABLO   You, Mitch?
MITCH   I'm out.
PABLO   One.
MITCH   Anyone want a shot?
STANLEY   Yeah. Me.
PABLO   Why don't somebody go to the Chinaman's and bring back a load of chop suey?
STANLEY   When I'm losing you want to eat! Ante up! Openers? Openers! Get y'r ass off the table, Mitch. Nothing belongs on a poker table but cards, chips and whiskey.
      [*He lurches up and tosses some watermelon rinds to the floor.*]
MITCH   Kind of on your high horse, ain't you?
STANLEY   How many?
STEVE   Give me three.
STANLEY   One.
MITCH   I'm out again. I oughta go home pretty soon.
STANLEY   Shut up.
MITCH   I gotta sick mother. She don't go to sleep until I come in at night.
STANLEY   Then why don't you stay home with her?
MITCH   She says to go out, so I go, but I don't enjoy it. All the while I keep wondering how she is.
STANLEY   Aw, for the sake of Jesus, go home, then!
PABLO   What've you got?

---

2. Williams's first title for *A Streetcar Named Desire* (see headnote).

3. *The Night Café*, by the Dutch Postimpressionist painter Vincent van Gogh (1853–1890).

STEVE   Spade flush.

MITCH   You all are married. But I'll be alone when she goes.—I'm going to the bathroom.

STANLEY   Hurry back and we'll fix you a sugar-tit.

MITCH   Aw, go rut. [*He crosses through the bedroom into the bathroom.*]

STEVE [*dealing a hand*]   Seven card stud.[4] [*telling his joke as he deals*] This ole farmer is out in back of his house sittin' down th'owing corn to the chickens when all at once he hears a loud cackle and this young hen comes lickety split around the side of the house with the rooster right behind her and gaining on her fast.

STANLEY [*impatient with the story*]   Deal!

STEVE   But when the rooster catches sight of the farmer th'owing the corn he puts on the brakes and lets the hen get away and starts pecking corn. And the old farmer says, "Lord God, I hopes I never gits *that* hongry!"

> [STEVE *and* PABLO *laugh. The sisters appear around the corner of the building.*]

STELLA   The game is still going on.

BLANCHE   How do I look?

STELLA   Lovely, Blanche.

BLANCHE   I feel so hot and frazzled. Wait till I powder before you open the door. Do I look done in?

STELLA   Why no. You are as fresh as a daisy.

BLANCHE   One that's been picked a few days.

> [STELLA *opens the door and they enter.*]

STELLA   Well, well, well. I see you boys are still at it?

STANLEY   Where you been?

STELLA   Blanche and I took in a show. Blanche, this is Mr. Gonzales and Mr. Hubbell.

BLANCHE   Please don't get up.

STANLEY   Nobody's going to get up, so don't be worried.

STELLA   How much longer is this game going to continue?

STANLEY   Till we get ready to quit.

BLANCHE   Poker is so fascinating. Could I kibitz?

STANLEY   You could not. Why don't you women go up and sit with Eunice?

STELLA   Because it is nearly two-thirty. [BLANCHE *crosses into the bedroom and partially closes the portieres.*] Couldn't you call it quits after one more hand?

> [*A chair scrapes.* STANLEY *gives a loud whack of his hand on her thigh.*]

STELLA [*sharply*]   That's not fun, Stanley.

> [*The men laugh,* STELLA *goes into the bedroom.*]

STELLA   It makes me so mad when he does that in front of people.

BLANCHE   I think I will bathe.

STELLA   Again?

BLANCHE   My nerves are in knots. Is the bathroom occupied?

STELLA   I don't know.

> [BLANCHE *knocks,* MITCH *opens the door and comes out, still wiping his hands on a towel.*]

---

4. An adventurous and risky variant of poker.

BLANCHE Oh!—good evening.

MITCH Hello. [*He stares at her.*]

STELLA Blanche, this is Harold Mitchell. My sister, Blanche DuBois.

MITCH [*with awkward courtesy*] How do you do, Miss DuBois.

STELLA How is your mother now, Mitch?

MITCH About the same, thanks. She appreciated your sending over that custard.—Excuse me, please.

> [*He crosses slowly back into the kitchen, glancing back at* BLANCHE *and coughing a little shyly. He realizes he still has the towel in his hands and with an embarrassed laugh hands it to* STELLA. BLANCHE *looks after him with a certain interest.*]

BLANCHE That one seems—superior to the others.

STELLA Yes, he is.

BLANCHE I thought he had a sort of sensitive look.

STELLA His mother is sick.

BLANCHE Is he married?

STELLA No.

BLANCHE Is he a wolf?

STELLA Why, Blanche! [BLANCHE *laughs.*] I don't think he would be.

BLANCHE What does—what does he do? [*She is unbuttoning her blouse.*]

STELLA He's on the precision bench in the spare parts department. At the plant Stanley travels for.

BLANCHE Is that something much?

STELLA No. Stanley's the only one of his crowd that's likely to get anywhere.

BLANCHE What makes you think Stanley will?

STELLA Look at him.

BLANCHE I've looked at him.

STELLA Then you should know.

BLANCHE I'm sorry, but I haven't noticed the stamp of genius even on Stanley's forehead.

> [*She takes off the blouse and stands in her pink silk brassiere and white skirt in the light through the portieres. The game has continued in undertones.*]

STELLA It isn't on his forehead and it isn't genius.

BLANCHE Oh. Well, what is it, and where? I would like to know.

STELLA It's a drive that he has. You're standing in the light, Blanche!

BLANCHE Oh, am I!

> [*She moves out of the yellow streak of light.* STELLA *has removed her dress and put on a light blue satin kimona.*]

STELLA [*with girlish laughter*] You ought to see their wives.

BLANCHE [*laughingly*] I can imagine. Big, beefy things, I suppose.

STELLA You know that one upstairs? [*more laughter*] One time [*laughing*] the plaster—[*laughing*] cracked—

STANLEY You hens cut out that conversation in there!

STELLA You can't hear us.

STANLEY Well, you can hear me and I said to hush up!

STELLA This is my house and I'll talk as much as I want to!

BLANCHE Stella, don't start a row.

STELLA He's half drunk!—I'll be out in a minute.

[*She goes into the bathroom,* BLANCHE *rises and crosses leisurely to a small white radio and turns it on.*]

STANLEY   Awright, Mitch, you in?

MITCH   What? Oh!—No, I'm out!

[BLANCHE *moves back into the streak of light. She raises her arms and stretches, as she moves indolently back to the chair. Rhumba music comes over the radio.* MITCH *rises at the table.*]

STANLEY   Who turned that on in there?

BLANCHE   I did. Do you mind?

STANLEY   Turn it off!

STEVE   Aw, let the girls have their music.

PABLO   Sure, that's good, leave it on!

STEVE   Sounds like Xavier Cugat!⁵

[STANLEY *jumps up and, crossing to the radio, turns it off. He stops short at the sight of* BLANCHE *in the chair. She returns his look without flinching. Then he sits again at the poker table. Two of the men have started arguing hotly.*]

STEVE   I didn't hear you name it.

PABLO   Didn't I name it, Mitch?

MITCH   I wasn't listenin'.

PABLO   What were you doing, then?

STANLEY   He was looking through them drapes. [*He jumps up and jerks roughly at curtains to close them.*] Now deal the hand over again and let's play cards or quit. Some people get ants when they win.

[MITCH *rises as* STANLEY *returns to his seat.*]

STANLEY [*yelling*]   Sit down!

MITCH   I'm going to the "head." Deal me out.

PABLO   Sure he's got ants now. Seven five-dollar bills in his pants pocket folded up tight as spitballs.

STEVE   Tomorrow you'll see him at the cashier's window getting them changed into quarters.

STANLEY   And when he goes home he'll deposit them one by one in a piggy bank his mother give him for Christmas. [*dealing*] This game is Spit in the Ocean.⁶

[MITCH *laughs uncomfortably and continues through the portieres. He stops just inside.*]

BLANCHE [*softly*]   Hello! The Little Boys' Room is busy right now.

MITCH   We've—been drinking beer.

BLANCHE   I hate beer.

MITCH   It's—a hot weather drink.

BLANCHE   Oh, I don't think so; it always makes me warmer. Have you got any cigs? [*She has slipped on the dark red satin wrapper.*]

MITCH   Sure.

BLANCHE   What kind are they?

MITCH   Luckies.

BLANCHE   Oh, good. What a pretty case. Silver?

MITCH   Yes. Yes; read the inscription.

---

5. Cuban bandleader (1900–1990), well known for composing and playing rhumbas.   6. Another variant of poker.

BLANCHE Oh, is there an inscription? I can't make it out. [*He strikes a match and moves closer.*] Oh! [*reading with feigned difficulty*] "And if God choose, / I shall but love thee better—after—death!" Why, that's from my favorite sonnet by Mrs. Browning.[7]

MITCH You know it?

BLANCHE Certainly I do!

MITCH There's a story connected with that inscription.

BLANCHE It sounds like a romance.

MITCH A pretty sad one.

BLANCHE Oh?

MITCH The girl's dead now.

BLANCHE [*in a tone of deep sympathy*] Oh!

MITCH She knew she was dying when she give me this. A very strange girl, very sweet—very!

BLANCHE She must have been fond of you. Sick people have such deep, sincere attachments.

MITCH That's right, they certainly do.

BLANCHE Sorrow makes for sincerity, I think.

MITCH It sure brings it out in people.

BLANCHE The little there is belongs to people who have experienced some sorrow.

MITCH I believe you are right about that.

BLANCHE I'm positive that I am. Show me a person who hasn't known any sorrow and I'll show you a shuperficial—Listen to me! My tongue is a little—thick! You boys are responsible for it. The show let out at eleven and we couldn't come home on account of the poker game so we had to go somewhere and drink. I'm not accustomed to having more than one drink. Two is the limit—and *three*! [*She laughs.*] Tonight I had three.

STANLEY Mitch!

MITCH Deal me out. I'm talking to Miss—

BLANCHE DuBois.

MITCH Miss DuBois?

BLANCHE It's a French name. It means woods and Blanche means white, so the two together mean white woods. Like an orchard in spring! You can remember it by that.

MITCH You're French?

BLANCHE We are French by extraction. Our first American ancestors were French Huguenots.

MITCH You are Stella's sister, are you not?

BLANCHE Yes, Stella is my precious little sister. I call her little in spite of the fact she's somewhat older than I. Just slightly. Less than a year. Will you do something for me?

MITCH Sure. What?

BLANCHE I bought this adorable little colored paper lantern at a Chinese shop on Bourbon. Put it over the light bulb! Will you, please?

MITCH Be glad to.

---

7. Elizabeth Barrett Browning (1806–1861), British poet, most famous for her sequence of love poems, *Sonnets from the Portuguese*. The quotation here is from sonnet 43, better known by its first line, "How do I love thee?"

BLANCHE   I can't stand a naked light bulb, any more than I can a rude remark or a vulgar action.

MITCH   [*adjusting the lantern*]   I guess we strike you as being a pretty rough bunch.

BLANCHE   I'm very adaptable—to circumstances.

MITCH   Well, that's a good thing to be. You are visiting Stanley and Stella?

BLANCHE   Stella hasn't been so well lately, and I came down to help her for a while. She's very run down.

MITCH   You're not—?

BLANCHE   Married? No, no. I'm an old maid schoolteacher!

MITCH   You may teach school but you're certainly not an old maid.

BLANCHE   Thank you, sir! I appreciate your gallantry!

MITCH   So you are in the teaching profession?

BLANCHE   Yes. Ah, yes . . .

MITCH   Grade school or high school or—

STANLEY   [*bellowing*]   Mitch!

MITCH   Coming!

BLANCHE   Gracious, what lung-power! . . . I teach high school. In Laurel.

MITCH   What do you teach? What subject?

BLANCHE   Guess!

MITCH   I bet you teach art or music? [BLANCHE *laughs delicately.*] Of course I could be wrong. You might teach arithmetic.

BLANCHE   Never arithmetic, sir; never arithmetic! [*with a laugh*] I don't even know my multiplication tables! No, I have the misfortune of being an English instructor. I attempt to instill a bunch of bobby-soxers and drugstore Romeos with reverence for Hawthorne and Whitman and Poe!

MITCH   I guess that some of them are more interested in other things.

BLANCHE   How very right you are! Their literary heritage is not what most of them treasure above all else! But they're sweet things! And in the spring, it's touching to notice them making their first discovery of love! As if nobody had ever known it before!

> [*The bathroom door opens and* STELLA *comes out.* BLANCHE *continues talking to* MITCH.]

Oh! Have you finished? Wait—I'll turn on the radio.

> [*She turns the knobs on the radio and it begins to play "Wien, Wien, nur du allein."*[8] BLANCHE *waltzes to the music with romantic gestures,* MITCH *is delighted and moves in awkward imitation like a dancing bear.* STANLEY *stalks fiercely through the portieres into the bedroom. He crosses to the small white radio and snatches it off the table. With a shouted oath, he tosses the instrument out the window.*]

STELLA   Drunk—drunk—animal thing, you! [*She rushes through to the poker table.*] All of you—please go home! If any of you have one spark of decency in you—

BLANCHE   [*wildly*]   Stella, watch out, he's—

> [STANLEY *charges after* STELLA.]

MEN   [*feebly*]   Take it easy, Stanley. Easy, fellow.—Let's all—

STELLA   You lay your hands on me and I'll—

> [*She backs out of sight. He advances and disappears. There is the sound of a blow.* STELLA *cries out.* BLANCHE *screams and runs into the kitchen.*

---

8. Vienna, Vienna, you are my only (German); a waltz from an operetta by Franz Lehár (1870–1948).

The men rush forward and there is grappling and cursing. Something is overturned with a crash.]

BLANCHE [*shrilly*] My sister is going to have a baby!

MITCH This is terrible.

BLANCHE Lunacy, absolute lunacy!

MITCH Get him in here, men.

[STANLEY *is forced, pinioned by the two men, into the bedroom. He nearly throws them off. Then all at once he subsides and is limp in their grasp. They speak quietly and lovingly to him and he leans his face on one of their shoulders.*]

STELLA [*in a high, unnatural voice, out of sight*] I want to go away, I want to go away!

MITCH Poker shouldn't be played in a house with women.

[BLANCHE *rushes into the bedroom.*]

BLANCHE I want my sister's clothes! We'll go to that woman's upstairs!

MITCH Where is the clothes?

BLANCHE [*opening the closet*] I've got them! [*She rushes through to* STELLA.] Stella, Stella, precious! Dear, dear little sister, don't be afraid!

[*With her arm around* STELLA, BLANCHE *guides her to the outside door and upstairs.*]

STANLEY [*dully*] What's the matter; what's happened?

MITCH You just blew your top, Stan.

PABLO He's okay, now.

STEVE Sure, my boy's okay!

MITCH Put him on the bed and get a wet towel.

PABLO I think coffee would do him a world of good, now.

STANLEY [*thickly*] I want water.

MITCH Put him under the shower!

[*The men talk quietly as they lead him to the bathroom.*]

STANLEY Let the rut go of me, you sons of bitches!

[*Sounds of blows are heard. The water goes on full tilt.*]

STEVE Let's get quick out of here!

[*They rush to the poker table and sweep up their winnings on their way out.*]

MITCH [*sadly but firmly*] Poker should not be played in a house with women.

[*The door closes on them and the place is still. The Negro entertainers in the bar around the corner play "Paper Doll"*[9] *slow and blue. After a moment* STANLEY *comes out of the bathroom dripping water and still in his clinging wet polka dot drawers.*]

STANLEY Stella! [*There is a pause.*] My baby doll's left me!

[*He breaks into sobs. Then he goes to the phone and dials, still shuddering with sobs.*]

Eunice? I want my baby! [*He waits a moment; then he hangs up and dials again.*] Eunice! I'll keep on ringin' until I talk with my baby!

[*An indistinguishable shrill voice is heard. He hurls phone to floor. Dissonant brass and piano sounds as the rooms dim out to darkness and the outer walls appear in the night light. The "Blue Piano" plays for a brief interval. Finally,* STANLEY *stumbles half-dressed out to the porch and*

9. Popular song of the early 1940s by Johnny Black.

down the wooden steps to the pavement before the building. There he throws back his head like a baying hound and bellows his wife's name: "Stella! Stella, sweetheart! Stella!"]

STANLEY Stell-*lahhhhh!*

EUNICE [*calling down from the door of her upper apartment*] Quit that howling out there an' go back to bed!

STANLEY I want my baby down here. Stella, Stella!

EUNICE She ain't comin' down so you quit! Or you'll git th' law on you!

STANLEY Stella!

EUNICE You can't beat on a woman an' then call 'er back! She won't come! And her goin' t' have a baby! . . . You stinker! You whelp of a Polack, you! I hope they do haul you in and turn the fire hose on you, same as the last time!

STANLEY [*humbly*] Eunice, I want my girl to come down with me!

EUNICE Hah! [*She slams her door.*]

STANLEY [*with heaven-splitting violence*] *STELL-LAHHHHH!*

[*The low-tone clarinet moans. The door upstairs opens again.* STELLA *slips down the rickety stairs in her robe. Her eyes are glistening with tears and her hair loose about her throat and shoulders. They stare at each other. Then they come together with low, animal moans. He falls to his knees on the steps and presses his face to her belly, curving a little with maternity. Her eyes go blind with tenderness as she catches his head and raises him level with her. He snatches the screen door open and lifts her off her feet and bears her into the dark flat.* BLANCHE *comes out the upper landing in her robe and slips fearfully down the steps.*]

BLANCHE Where is my little sister? Stella? Stella?

[*She stops before the dark entrance of her sister's flat. Then catches her breath as if struck. She rushes down to the walk before the house. She looks right and left as if for a sanctuary. The music fades away,* MITCH *appears from around the corner.*]

MITCH Miss DuBois?

BLANCHE Oh!

MITCH All quiet on the Potomac now?

BLANCHE She ran downstairs and went back in there with him.

MITCH Sure she did.

BLANCHE I'm terrified!

MITCH Ho-ho! There's nothing to be scared of. They're crazy about each other.

BLANCHE I'm not used to such—

MITCH Naw, it's a shame this had to happen when you just got here. But don't take it serious.

BLANCHE Violence! Is so—

MITCH Set down on the steps and have a cigarette with me.

BLANCHE I'm not properly dressed.

MITCH That don't make no difference in the Quarter.

BLANCHE Such a pretty silver case.

MITCH I showed you the inscription, didn't I?

BLANCHE Yes. [*During the pause, she looks up at the sky.*] There's so much— so much confusion in the world . . . [*He coughs diffidently.*] Thank you for being so kind! I need kindness now.

Scene Four

It is early the following morning. There is a confusion of street cries like a choral chant.

STELLA is lying down in the bedroom. Her face is serene in the early morning sunlight. One hand rests on her belly, rounding slightly with new maternity. From the other dangles a book of colored comics. Her eyes and lips have that almost narcotized tranquility that is in the faces of Eastern idols.

The table is sloppy with remains of breakfast and the debris of the preceding night, and STANLEY's gaudy pyjamas lie across the threshold of the bathroom. The outside door is slightly ajar on a sky of summer brilliance.

BLANCHE appears at this door. She has spent a sleepless night and her appearance entirely contrasts with STELLA's. She presses her knuckles nervously to her lips as she looks through the door, before entering.

BLANCHE   Stella?

STELLA [*stirring lazily*]   Hmmh?

[BLANCHE *utters a moaning cry and runs into the bedroom, throwing herself down beside* STELLA *in a rush of hysterical tenderness.*]

BLANCHE   Baby, my baby sister!

STELLA [*drawing away from her*]   Blanche, what is the matter with you?

[BLANCHE *straightens up slowly and stands beside the bed looking down at her sister with knuckles pressed to her lips.*]

BLANCHE   He's left?

STELLA   Stan? Yes.

BLANCHE   Will he be back?

STELLA   He's gone to get the car greased. Why?

BLANCHE   Why! I've been half crazy, Stella! When I found out you'd been insane enough to come back in here after what happened—I started to rush in after you!

STELLA   I'm glad you didn't.

BLANCHE   What were you thinking of? [STELLA *makes an indefinite gesture.*] Answer me! What? What?

STELLA   Please, Blanche! Sit down and stop yelling.

BLANCHE   All right, Stella. I will repeat the question quietly now. How could you come back in this place last night? Why, you must have slept with him!

[STELLA *gets up in a calm and leisurely way.*]

STELLA   Blanche, I'd forgotten how excitable you are. You're making much too much fuss about this.

BLANCHE   Am I?

STELLA   Yes, you are, Blanche. I know how it must have seemed to you and I'm awful sorry it had to happen, but it wasn't anything as serious as you seem to take it. In the first place, when men are drinking and playing poker anything can happen. It's always a powder-keg. He didn't know what he was doing. . . . He was as good as a lamb when I came back and he's really very, very ashamed of himself.

BLANCHE   And that—that makes it all right?

STELLA   No, it isn't all right for anybody to make such a terrible row, but—people do sometimes. Stanley's always smashed things. Why, on our wedding night—soon as we came in here—he snatched off one of my slippers and rushed about the place smashing light bulbs with it.

BLANCHE   He did—*what*?

STELLA   He smashed all the light bulbs with the heel of my slipper! [*She laughs.*]

BLANCHE   And you—you *let* him? Didn't *run*, didn't *scream*?

STELLA   I was—sort of—thrilled by it. [*She waits for a moment.*] Eunice and you had breakfast?

BLANCHE   Do you suppose I wanted any breakfast?

STELLA   There's some coffee left on the stove.

BLANCHE   You're so—matter of fact about it, Stella.

STELLA   What other can I be? He's taken the radio to get it fixed. It didn't land on the pavement so only one tube was smashed.

BLANCHE   And you are standing there smiling!

STELLA   What do you want me to do?

BLANCHE   Pull yourself together and face the facts.

STELLA   What are they, in your opinion?

BLANCHE   In my opinion? You're married to a madman!

STELLA   No!

BLANCHE   Yes, you are, your fix is worse than mine is! Only you're not being sensible about it. I'm going to *do* something. Get hold of myself and make myself a new life!

STELLA   Yes?

BLANCHE   But you've given in. And that isn't right, you're not old! You can get out.

STELLA [*slowly and emphatically*]   I'm not in anything I want to get out of.

BLANCHE [*incredulously*]   What—Stella?

STELLA   I said I am not in anything that I have a desire to get out of. Look at the mess in this room! And those empty bottles! They went through two cases last night! He promised this morning that he was going to quit having these poker parties, but you know how long such a promise is going to keep. Oh, well, it's his pleasure, like mine is movies and bridge. People have got to tolerate each other's habits, I guess.

BLANCHE   I don't understand you. [STELLA *turns toward her.*] I don't understand your indifference. Is this a Chinese philosophy you've—cultivated?

STELLA   Is what—what?

BLANCHE   This—shuffling about and mumbling—'One tube smashed—beer bottles—mess in the kitchen!'—as if nothing out of the ordinary has happened! [STELLA *laughs uncertainly and picking up the broom, twirls it in her hands.*]

BLANCHE   Are you deliberately shaking that thing in my face?

STELLA   No.

BLANCHE   Stop it. Let go of that broom. I won't have you cleaning up for him!

STELLA   Then who's going to do it? Are you?

BLANCHE   I? I!

STELLA   No, I didn't think so.

BLANCHE   Oh, let me think, if only my mind would function! We've got to get hold of some money, that's the way out!

STELLA   I guess that money is always nice to get hold of.

BLANCHE Listen to me. I have an idea of some kind. [*Shakily she twists a cigarette into her holder.*] Do you remember Shep Huntleigh? [STELLA *shakes her head.*] Of course you remember Shep Huntleigh. I went out with him at college and wore his pin for a while. Well—

STELLA Well?

BLANCHE I ran into him last winter. You know I went to Miami during the Christmas holidays?

STELLA No.

BLANCHE Well, I did. I took the trip as an investment, thinking I'd meet someone with a million dollars.

STELLA Did you?

BLANCHE Yes. I ran into Shep Huntleigh—I ran into him on Biscayne Boulevard, on Christmas Eve, about dusk . . . getting into his car—Cadillac convertible; must have been a block long!

STELLA I should think it would have been—inconvenient in traffic!

BLANCHE You've heard of oil wells?

STELLA Yes—remotely.

BLANCHE He has them, all over Texas. Texas is literally spouting gold in his pockets.

STELLA My, my.

BLANCHE Y'know how indifferent I am to money. I think of money in terms of what it does for you. But he could do it, he could certainly do it!

STELLA Do what, Blanche?

BLANCHE Why—set us up in a—shop!

STELLA What kind of a shop?

BLANCHE Oh, a—shop of some kind! He could do it with half what his wife throws away at the races.

STELLA He's married?

BLANCHE Honey, would I be here if the man weren't married? [STELLA *laughs a little.* BLANCHE *suddenly springs up and crosses to phone. She speaks shrilly.*] How do I get Western Union?—Operator! Western Union!

STELLA That's a dial phone, honey.

BLANCHE I can't dial, I'm too—

STELLA Just dial O.

BLANCHE O?

STELLA Yes, "O" for Operator! [BLANCHE *considers a moment; then she puts the phone down.*]

BLANCHE Give me a pencil. Where is a slip of paper? I've got to write it down first—the message, I mean . . . [*She goes to the dressing table, and grabs up a sheet of Kleenex and an eyebrow pencil for writing equipment.*] Let me see now . . . [*She bites the pencil.*] 'Darling Shep. Sister and I in desperate situation.'

STELLA I beg your pardon!

BLANCHE 'Sister and I in desperate situation. Will explain details later. Would you be interested in—?' [*She bites the pencil again.*] 'Would you be—interested—in . . .' [*She smashes the pencil on the table and springs up.*] You never get anywhere with direct appeals!

STELLA [*with a laugh*] Don't be so ridiculous, darling!

BLANCHE But I'll think of something, I've *got* to think of—*some*thing! Don't laugh at me, Stella! Please, please don't—I—I want you to look at the contents of my purse! Here's what's in it! [*She snatches her purse open.*] Sixty-five measly cents in coin of the realm!

STELLA [*crossing to bureau*]   Stanley doesn't give me a regular allowance, he likes to pay bills himself, but—this morning he gave me ten dollars to smooth things over. You take five of it, Blanche, and I'll keep the rest.

BLANCHE   Oh, no. No, Stella.

STELLA [*insisting*]   I know how it helps your morale just having a little pocket-money on you.

BLANCHE   No, thank you—I'll take to the streets!

STELLA   Talk sense! How did you happen to get so low on funds?

BLANCHE   Money just goes—it goes places. [*She rubs her forehead.*] Sometime today I've got to get hold of a Bromo!¹

STELLA   I'll fix you one now.

BLANCHE   Not yet—I've got to keep thinking!

STELLA   I wish you'd just let things go, at least for a—while . . .

BLANCHE   Stella, I can't live with him! You can, he's your husband. But how could I stay here with him, after last night, with just those curtains between us?

STELLA   Blanche, you saw him at his worst last night.

BLANCHE   On the contrary, I saw him at his best! What such a man has to offer is animal force and he gave a wonderful exhibition of that! But the only way to live with such a man is to—go to bed with him! And that's your job—not mine!

STELLA   After you've rested a little, you'll see it's going to work out. You don't have to worry about anything while you're here. I mean—expenses . . .

BLANCHE   I have to plan for us both, to get us both—out!

STELLA   You take it for granted that I am in something that I want to get out of.

BLANCHE   I take it for granted that you still have sufficient memory of Belle Reve to find this place and these poker players impossible to live with.

STELLA   Well, you're taking entirely too much for granted.

BLANCHE   I can't believe you're in earnest.

STELLA   No?

BLANCHE   I understand how it happened—a little. You saw him in uniform, an officer, not here but—

STELLA   I'm not sure it would have made any difference where I saw him.

BLANCHE   Now don't say it was one of those mysterious electric things between people! If you do I'll laugh in your face.

STELLA   I am not going to say anything more at all about it!

BLANCHE   All right, then, don't!

STELLA   But there are things that happen between a man and a woman in the dark—that sort of make everything else seem—unimportant. [*Pause.*]

BLANCHE   What you are talking about is brutal desire—just—Desire!— the name of that rattle-trap streetcar that bangs through the Quarter, up one old narrow street and down another . . .

STELLA   Haven't you ever ridden on that streetcar?

---

1. Short for Bromo-Seltzer, a headache and heartburn remedy.

BLANCHE It brought me here.—Where I'm not wanted and where I'm ashamed to be . . .

STELLA Then don't you think your superior attitude is a bit out of place?

BLANCHE I am not being or feeling at all superior, Stella. Believe me I'm not! It's just this. This is how I look at it. A man like that is someone to go out with—once—twice—three times when the devil is in you. But live with? Have a child by?

STELLA I have told you I love him.

BLANCHE Then I *tremble* for you! I just—*tremble* for you. . . .

STELLA I can't help your trembling if you insist on trembling!
[*There is a pause.*]

BLANCHE May I—speak—*plainly?*

STELLA Yes, do. Go ahead. As plainly as you want to.
[*Outside, a train approaches. They are silent till the noise subsides. They are both in the bedroom. Under cover of the train's noise* STANLEY *enters from outside. He stands unseen by the women, holding some packages in his arms, and overhears their following conversation. He wears an undershirt and grease-stained seersucker pants.*]

BLANCHE Well—if you'll forgive me—he's *common!*

STELLA Why, yes, I suppose he is.

BLANCHE Suppose! You can't have forgotten that much of our bringing up, Stella, that you just *suppose* that any part of a gentleman's in his nature! *Not one particle, no!* Oh, if he was just—*ordinary!* Just *plain*—but good and wholesome, but—*no.* There's something downright—*bestial*—about him! You're hating me saying this, aren't you?

STELLA [*coldly*] Go on and say it all, Blanche.

BLANCHE He acts like an animal, has an animal's habits! Eats like one, moves like one, talks like one! There's even something—sub-human—something not quite to the stage of humanity yet! Yes, something—ape-like about him, like one of those pictures I've seen in—anthropological studies! Thousands and thousands of years have passed him right by, and there he is—Stanley Kowalski—survivor of the Stone Age! Bearing the raw meat home from the kill in the jungle! And you—*you* here—*waiting* for him! Maybe he'll strike you or maybe grunt and kiss you! That is, if kisses have been discovered yet! Night falls and the other apes gather! There in the front of the cave, all grunting like him, and swilling and gnawing and hulking! His poker night! you call it—this party of apes! Somebody growls—some creature snatches at something—the fight is on! *God!* Maybe we are a long way from being made in God's image, but Stella—my sister—there has been *some* progress since then! Such things as art—as poetry and music—such kinds of new light have come into the world since then! In some kinds of people some tenderer feelings have had some little beginning! That we have got to make *grow!* And *cling* to, and hold as our flag! In this dark march toward whatever it is we're approaching. . . . *Don't—don't hang back with the brutes!*
[*Another train passes outside.* STANLEY *hesitates, licking his lips. Then suddenly he turns stealthily about and withdraws through front door. The women are still unaware of his presence. When the train has passed he calls through the closed front door.*]

STANLEY Hey! Hey, Stella!

STELLA [*who has listened gravely to* BLANCHE]   Stanley!
BLANCHE   Stell, I—
        [*But* STELLA *has gone to the front door.* STANLEY *enters casually with his packages.*]
STANLEY   Hiyuh, Stella. Blanche back?
STELLA   Yes, she's back.
STANLEY   Hiyuh, Blanche. [*He grins at her.*]
STELLA   You must've got under the car.
STANLEY   Them darn mechanics at Fritz's don't know their ass fr'm—*Hey!*
        [STELLA *has embraced him with both arms, fiercely, and full in the view of* BLANCHE. *He laughs and clasps her head to him. Over her head he grins through the curtains at* BLANCHE. *As the lights fade away, with a lingering brightness on their embrace, the music of the "Blue Piano" and trumpet and drums is heard.*]

Scene Five

BLANCHE *is seated in the bedroom fanning herself with a palm leaf as she reads over a just-completed letter. Suddenly she bursts into a peal of laughter.* STELLA *is dressing in the bedroom.*

STELLA   What are you laughing at, honey?
BLANCHE   Myself, myself, for being such a liar! I'm writing a letter to Shep. [*She picks up the letter.*] "Darling Shep. I am spending the summer on the wing, making flying visits here and there. And who knows, perhaps I shall take a sudden notion to *swoop* down on *Dallas!* How would you feel about that? Ha-ha! [*She laughs nervously and brightly, touching her throat as if actually talking to* SHEP.] Forewarned is forearmed, as they say!"— How does that sound?
STELLA   Uh-huh . . .
BLANCHE [*going on nervously*]   "Most of my sister's friends go north in the summer but some have homes on the Gulf and there has been a continued round of entertainments, teas, cocktails, and luncheons—"
        [*A disturbance is heard upstairs at the Hubbells' apartment.*]
STELLA   Eunice seems to be having some trouble with Steve.
        [EUNICE'S *voice shouts in terrible wrath.*]
EUNICE   I heard about you and that blonde!
STEVE   That's a damn lie!
EUNICE   You ain't pulling the wool over my eyes! I wouldn't mind if you'd stay down at the Four Deuces, but you always going up.
STEVE   Who ever seen me up?
EUNICE   I seen you chasing her 'round the balcony—I'm gonna call the vice squad!
STEVE   Don't you throw that at me!
EUNICE [*shrieking*]   You hit me! I'm gonna call the police!
        [*A clatter of aluminum striking a wall is heard, followed by a man's angry roar, shouts and overturned furniture. There is a crash; then a relative hush.*]
BLANCHE [*brightly*]   Did he *kill* her?
        [EUNICE *appears on the steps in daemonic disorder.*]

STELLA   No! She's coming downstairs.

EUNICE   Call the police, I'm going to call the police! [*She rushes around the corner.*]

[*They laugh lightly.* STANLEY *comes around the corner in his green and scarlet silk bowling shirt. He trots up the steps and bangs into the kitchen.* BLANCHE *registers his entrance with nervous gestures.*]

STANLEY   What's a matter with Eun-uss?

STELLA   She and Steve had a row. Has she got the police?

STANLEY   Naw. She's gettin' a drink.

STELLA   That's much more practical!

[STEVE *comes down nursing a bruise on his forehead and looks in the door.*]

STEVE   She here?

STANLEY   Naw, naw. At the Four Deuces.

STEVE   That rutting hunk! [*He looks around the corner a bit timidly, then turns with affected boldness and runs after her.*]

BLANCHE   I must jot that down in my notebook. Ha-ha! I'm compiling a notebook of quaint little words and phrases I've picked up here.

STANLEY   You won't pick up nothing here you ain't heard before.

BLANCHE   Can I count on that?

STANLEY   You can count on it up to five hundred.

BLANCHE   That's a mighty high number. [*He jerks open the bureau drawer, slams it shut and throws shoes in a corner. At each noise* BLANCHE *winces slightly. Finally she speaks.*] What sign were you born under?

STANLEY   [*while he is dressing*]   Sign?

BLANCHE   Astrological sign. I bet you were born under Aries. Aries people are forceful and dynamic. They dote on noise! They love to bang things around! You must have had lots of banging around in the army and now that you're out, you make up for it by treating inanimate objects with such a fury!

[STELLA *has been going in and out of closet during this scene. Now she pops her head out of the closet.*]

STELLA   Stanley was born just five minutes after Christmas.

BLANCHE   Capricorn—the Goat!

STANLEY   What sign were *you* born under?

BLANCHE   Oh, my birthday's next month, the fifteenth of September; that's under Virgo.

STANLEY   What's Virgo?

BLANCHE   Virgo is the Virgin.

STANLEY   [*contemptuously*]   Hah! [*He advances a little as he knots his tie.*] Say, do you happen to know somebody named Shaw?

[*Her face expresses a faint shock. She reaches for the cologne bottle and dampens her handkerchief as she answers carefully.*]

BLANCHE   Why, everybody knows somebody named Shaw!

STANLEY   Well, this somebody named Shaw is under the impression he met you in Laurel, but I figure he must have got you mixed up with some other party because this other party is someone he met at a hotel called the Flamingo.

[BLANCHE *laughs breathlessly as she touches the cologne-dampened handkerchief to her temples.*]

BLANCHE   I'm afraid he does have me mixed up with this "other party."
The Hotel Flamingo is not the sort of establishment I would dare to be
seen in!

STANLEY   You know of it?

BLANCHE   Yes, I've seen it and smelled it.

STANLEY   You must've got pretty close if you could smell it.

BLANCHE   The odor of cheap perfume is penetrating.

STANLEY   That stuff you use is expensive?

BLANCHE   Twenty-five dollars an ounce! I'm nearly out. That's just a hint
if you want to remember my birthday! [*She speaks lightly but her voice
has a note of fear.*]

STANLEY   Shaw must've got you mixed up. He goes in and out of Laurel
all the time so he can check on it and clear up any mistake.

   [*He turns away and crosses to the portieres.* BLANCHE *closes her eyes as if
   faint. Her hand trembles as she lifts the handkerchief again to her forehead.* STEVE *and* EUNICE *come around corner.* STEVE'S *arm is around
   EUNICE'S shoulder and she is sobbing luxuriously and he is cooing love-
   words. There is a murmur of thunder as they go slowly upstairs in a tight
   embrace.*]

STANLEY [*to* STELLA]   I'll wait for you at the Four Deuces!

STELLA   Hey! Don't I rate one kiss?

STANLEY   Not in front of your sister.

   [*He goes out.* BLANCHE *rises from her chair. She seems faint; looks
   about her with an expression of almost panic.*]

BLANCHE   Stella! What have you heard about me?

STELLA   Huh?

BLANCHE   What have people been telling you about me?

STELLA   Telling?

BLANCHE   You haven't heard any—unkind—gossip about me?

STELLA   Why, no, Blanche, of course not!

BLANCHE   Honey, there was—a good deal of talk in Laurel.

STELLA   About *you,* Blanche?

BLANCHE   I wasn't so good the last two years or so, after Belle Reve had
started to slip through my fingers.

STELLA   All of us do things we—

BLANCHE   I never was hard or self-sufficient enough. When people are
soft—soft people have got to shimmer and glow—they've got to put on
soft colors, the colors of butterfly wings, and put a—paper lantern over
the light. . . . It isn't enough to be soft. You've got to be soft *and attractive.* And I—I'm fading now! I don't know how much longer I can turn
the trick.

   [*The afternoon has faded to dusk.* STELLA *goes into the bedroom and
   turns on the light under the paper lantern. She holds a bottled soft
   drink in her hand.*]

BLANCHE   Have you been listening to me?

STELLA   I don't listen to you when you are being morbid! [*She advances
with the bottled Coke.*]

BLANCHE [*with abrupt change to gaiety*]   Is that Coke for me?

STELLA   Not for anyone else!

BLANCHE   Why, you precious thing, you! Is it just Coke?

STELLA [*turning*] You mean you want a shot in it!

BLANCHE Well, honey, a shot never does a Coke any harm! Let me! You mustn't wait on me!

STELLA I like to wait on you, Blanche. It makes it seem more like home. [*She goes into the kitchen, finds a glass and pours a shot of whiskey into it.*]

BLANCHE I have to admit I love to be waited on . . .
[*She rushes into the bedroom.* STELLA *goes to her with the glass.* BLANCHE *suddenly clutches* STELLA's *free hand with a moaning sound and presses the hand to her lips.* STELLA *is embarrassed by her show of emotion.* BLANCHE *speaks in a choked voice.*]
You're—you're—so *good* to me! And I—

STELLA Blanche.

BLANCHE I know, I won't! You hate me to talk sentimental! But honey, *believe* I feel things more than I *tell* you! I *won't* stay long! I won't, I *promise* I—

STELLA Blanche!

BLANCHE [*hysterically*] I won't, I promise, *I'll* go! Go *soon*! I will *really*! I *won't* hang around until he—throws me out . . .

STELLA Now will you stop talking foolish?

BLANCHE Yes, honey. Watch how you pour—that fizzy stuff foams over!
[BLANCHE *laughs shrilly and grabs the glass, but her hand shakes so it almost slips from her grasp.* STELLA *pours the Coke into the glass. It foams over and spills.* BLANCHE *gives a piercing cry.*]

STELLA [*shocked by the cry*] Heavens!

BLANCHE Right on my pretty white skirt!

STELLA Oh . . . Use my hanky. Blot gently.

BLANCHE [*slowly recovering*] I know—gently—gently . . .

STELLA Did it stain?

BLANCHE Not a bit. Ha-ha! Isn't that lucky? [*She sits down shakily, taking a grateful drink. She holds the glass in both hands and continues to laugh a little.*]

STELLA Why did you scream like that?

BLANCHE I don't know why I screamed! [*continuing nervously*] Mitch—Mitch is coming at seven. I guess I am just feeling nervous about our relations. [*She begins to talk rapidly and breathlessly.*] He hasn't gotten a thing but a good-night kiss, that's all I have given him, Stella. I want his respect. And men don't want anything they get too easy. But on the other hand men lose interest quickly. Especially when the girl is over—thirty. They think a girl over thirty ought to—the vulgar term is—"put out." . . . And I—I'm not "putting out." Of course he—he doesn't know—I mean I haven't informed him—of my real age!

STELLA Why are you sensitive about your age?

BLANCHE Because of hard knocks my vanity's been given. What I mean is—he thinks I'm sort of—prim and proper, you know! [*She laughs out sharply.*] I want to *deceive* him enough to make him—want me . . .

STELLA Blanche, do you want *him*?

BLANCHE I want to *rest*! I want to breathe quietly again! Yes—I *want* Mitch . . . *very badly*! Just think! If it happens! I can leave here and not be anyone's problem . . .

[STANLEY *comes around the corner with a drink under his belt.*]

STANLEY [*bawling*]   Hey, Steve! Hey, Eunice! Hey, Stella!

[*There are joyous calls from above. Trumpet and drums are heard from around the corner.*]

STELLA [*kissing* BLANCHE *impulsively*]   It *will* happen!

BLANCHE [*doubtfully*]   It will?

STELLA   It *will*! [*She goes across into the kitchen, looking back at* BLANCHE.] It will, honey, *it will.* . . . But don't take another drink! [*Her voice catches as she goes out the door to meet her husband.*]

[BLANCHE *sinks faintly back in her chair with her drink.* EUNICE *shrieks with laughter and runs down the steps.* STEVE *bounds after her with goatlike screeches and chases her around corner.* STANLEY *and* STELLA *twine arms as they follow, laughing. Dusk settles deeper. The music from the Four Deuces is slow and blue.*]

BLANCHE   Ah, me, ah, me, ah, me . . .

[*Her eyes fall shut and the palm leaf fan drops from her fingers. She slaps her hand on the chair arm a couple of times. There is a little glimmer of lightning about the building.* A YOUNG MAN *comes along the street and rings the bell.*]

BLANCHE   Come in.

[*The* YOUNG MAN *appears through the portieres. She regards him with interest.*]

BLANCHE   Well, well! What can I do for *you*?

YOUNG MAN   I'm collecting for *The Evening Star.*

BLANCHE   I didn't know that stars took up collections.

YOUNG MAN   It's the paper.

BLANCHE   I know, I was joking—feebly! Will you—have a drink?

YOUNG MAN   No, ma'am. No, thank you. I can't drink on the job.

BLANCHE   Oh, well, now, let's see. . . . No, I don't have a dime! I'm not the lady of the house. I'm her sister from Mississippi. I'm one of those poor relations you've heard about.

YOUNG MAN   That's all right. I'll drop by later. [*He starts to go out. She approaches a little.*]

BLANCHE   Hey! [*He turns back shyly. She puts a cigarette in a long holder.*] Could you give me a light? [*She crosses toward him. They meet at the door between the two rooms.*]

YOUNG MAN   Sure. [*He takes out a lighter.*] This doesn't always work.

BLANCHE   It's temperamental? [*It flares.*] Ah!—thank you. [*He starts away again.*] Hey! [*He turns again, still more uncertainly. She goes close to him.*] Uh—what time is it?

YOUNG MAN   Fifteen of seven, ma'am.

BLANCHE   So late? Don't you just love these long rainy afternoons in New Orleans when an hour isn't just an hour—but a little piece of eternity dropped into your hands—and who knows what to do with it? [*She touches his shoulders.*] You—uh—didn't get wet in the rain?

YOUNG MAN   No, ma'am. I stepped inside.

BLANCHE   In a drugstore? And had a soda?

YOUNG MAN   Uh-huh.

BLANCHE   Chocolate?

YOUNG MAN   No, ma'am. Cherry.

BLANCHE [*laughing*]   Cherry!

YOUNG MAN   A cherry soda.

BLANCHE   You make my mouth water. [*She touches his cheek lightly, and smiles. Then she goes to the trunk.*]

YOUNG MAN   Well, I'd better be going—

BLANCHE [*stopping him*]   Young man!

[*He turns. She takes a large, gossamer scarf from the trunk and drapes it about her shoulders. In the ensuing pause, the "Blue Piano" is heard. It continues through the rest of this scene and the opening of the next. The young man clears his throat and looks yearningly at the door.*]

Young man! Young, young, young man! Has anyone ever told you that you look like a young Prince out of the Arabian Nights?

[*The* YOUNG MAN *laughs uncomfortably and stands like a bashful kid.* BLANCHE *speaks softly to him.*]

Well, you do, honey lamb! Come here. I want to kiss you, just once, softly and sweetly on your mouth!

[*Without waiting for him to accept, she crosses quickly to him and presses her lips to his.*]

Now run along, now, quickly! It would be nice to keep you, but I've got to be good—and keep my hands off children.

[*He stares at her a moment. She opens the door for him and blows a kiss at him as he goes down the steps with a dazed look. She stands there a little dreamily after he has disappeared. Then* MITCH *appears around the corner with a bunch of roses.*]

BLANCHE [*gaily*]   Look who's coming! My Rosenkavalier! Bow to me first . . . now present them! *Ahhhh—Merciiii!*[2]

[*She looks at him over them, coquettishly pressing them to her lips. He beams at her self-consciously.*]

Scene Six

It is about two A.M on the same evening. The outer wall of the building is visible. BLANCHE *and* MITCH *come in. The utter exhaustion which only a neurasthenic personality can know is evident in* BLANCHE'*s voice and manner.* MITCH *is stolid but depressed. They have probably been out to the amusement park on Lake Pontchartrain, for* MITCH *is bearing, upside down, a plaster statuette of Mae West, the sort of prize won at shooting galleries and carnival games of chance.*

BLANCHE [*stopping lifelessly at the steps*]   Well— [MITCH *laughs uneasily.*] Well . . .

MITCH   I guess it must be pretty late—and you're tired.

BLANCHE   Even the hot tamale man has deserted the street, and he hangs on till the end. [MITCH *laughs uneasily again.*] How will you get home?

MITCH   I'll walk over to Bourbon and catch an owl-car.

BLANCHE [*laughing grimly*]   Is that streetcar named Desire still grinding along the tracks at this hour?

MITCH [*heavily*]   I'm afraid you haven't gotten much fun out of this evening, Blanche.

BLANCHE   I spoiled it for *you*.

2. "Merci": thank you (French). "My Rosenkavalier": Knight of the Rose (German); title of a romantic opera (1911) by Richard Strauss.

MITCH   No, you didn't, but I felt all the time that I wasn't giving you much—entertainment.

BLANCHE   I simply couldn't rise to the occasion. That was all. I don't think I've ever tried so hard to be gay and made such a dismal mess of it. I get ten points for trying!—I *did* try.

MITCH   Why did you try if you didn't feel like it, Blanche?

BLANCHE   I was just obeying the law of nature.

MITCH   Which law is that?

BLANCHE   The one that says the lady must entertain the gentleman—or no dice! See if you can locate my door key in this purse. When I'm so tired my fingers are all thumbs!

MITCH   [*rooting in her purse*]   This it?

BLANCHE   No, honey, that's the key to my trunk which I must soon be packing.

MITCH   You mean you are leaving here soon?

BLANCHE   I've outstayed my welcome.

MITCH   This it?
      [*The music fades away.*]

BLANCHE   Eureka! Honey, you open the door while I take a last look at the sky. [*She leans on the porch rail. He opens the door and stands awkwardly behind her.*] I'm looking for the Pleiades, the Seven Sisters, but these girls are not out tonight. Oh, yes they are, there they are! God bless them! All in a bunch going home from their little bridge party. . . . Y' get the door open? Good boy! I guess you—want to go now . . .
      [*He shuffles and coughs a little.*]

MITCH   Can I—uh—kiss you—good night?

BLANCHE   Why do you always ask me if you may?

MITCH   I don't know whether you want me to or not.

BLANCHE   Why should you be so doubtful?

MITCH   That night when we parked by the lake and I kissed you, you—

BLANCHE   Honey, it wasn't the kiss I objected to. I liked the kiss very much. It was the other little—familiarity—that I—felt obliged to—discourage. . . . I didn't resent it! Not a bit in the world! In fact, I was somewhat flattered that you—desired me! But, honey, you know as well as I do that a single girl, a girl alone in the world, has got to keep a firm hold on her emotions or she'll be lost!

MITCH   [*solemnly*]   Lost?

BLANCHE   I guess you are used to girls that like to be lost. The kind that get lost immediately, on the first date!

MITCH   I like you to be exactly the way that you are, because in all my—experience—I have never known anyone like you.
      [BLANCHE *looks at him gravely; then she bursts into laughter and then claps a hand to her mouth.*]

MITCH   Are you laughing at me?

BLANCHE   No, honey. The lord and lady of the house have not yet returned, so come in. We'll have a nightcap. Let's leave the lights off. Shall we?

MITCH   You just—do what you want to.
      [BLANCHE *precedes him into the kitchen. The outer wall of the building disappears and the interiors of the two rooms can be dimly seen.*]

BLANCHE [*remaining in the first room*] The other room's more comfortable—go on in. This crashing around in the dark is my search for some liquor.

MITCH You want a drink?

BLANCHE I want *you* to have a drink! You have been so anxious and solemn all evening, and so have I; we have both been anxious and solemn and now for these few last remaining moments of our lives together—I want to create—*joie de vivre*! I'm lighting a candle.

MITCH That's good.

BLANCHE We are going to be very Bohemian. We are going to pretend that we are sitting in a little artists' cafe on the Left Bank in Paris! [*She lights a candle stub and puts it in a bottle.*] *Je suis la Dame aux Camellias! Vous êtes—Armand!*[3] Understand French?

MITCH [*heavily*] Naw. Naw, I—

BLANCHE *Voulez-vous couchez avec moi ce soir? Vous ne comprenez pas? Ah, quelle dommage!*[4]—I mean it's a damned good thing. . . . I've found some liquor! Just enough for two shots without any dividends, honey . . .

MITCH [*heavily*] That's—good.

[*She enters the bedroom with the drinks and the candle.*]

BLANCHE Sit down! Why don't you take off your coat and loosen your collar?

MITCH I better leave it on.

BLANCHE No. I want you to be comfortable.

MITCH I am ashamed of the way I perspire. My shirt is sticking to me.

BLANCHE Perspiration is healthy. If people didn't perspire they would die in five minutes. [*She takes his coat from him.*] This is a nice coat. What kind of material is it?

MITCH They call that stuff alpaca.

BLANCHE Oh. Alpaca.

MITCH It's very light-weight alpaca.

BLANCHE Oh. Light-weight alpaca.

MITCH I don't like to wear a wash-coat even in summer because I sweat through it.

BLANCHE Oh.

MITCH And it don't look neat on me. A man with a heavy build has got to be careful of what he puts on him so he don't look too clumsy.

BLANCHE You are not too heavy.

MITCH You don't think I am?

BLANCHE You are not the delicate type. You have a massive bone-structure and a very imposing physique.

MITCH Thank you. Last Christmas I was given a membership to the New Orleans Athletic Club.

BLANCHE Oh, good.

MITCH It was the finest present I ever was given. I work out there with the weights and I swim and I keep myself fit. When I started there, I was

---

3. I am the Lady of the Camellias! You are— Armand! (French). Both are characters in the popular romantic play *La Dame aux Camélias* (1852), by the French author Alexandre Dumas *fils*; she is a courtesan who gives up her true love, Armand.
4. Would you like to sleep with me this evening? You don't understand? Ah, what a pity! (French).

getting soft in the belly but now my belly is hard. It is so hard now that a man can punch me in the belly and it don't hurt me. Punch me! Go on! See?

    [*She pokes lightly at him.*]

BLANCHE   Gracious. [*Her hand touches her chest.*]

MITCH   Guess how much I weigh, Blanche?

BLANCHE   Oh, I'd say in the vicinity of—one hundred and eighty?

MITCH   Guess again.

BLANCHE   Not that much?

MITCH   No. More.

BLANCHE   <u>Well, you're a tall man and you</u> can carry a good deal of weight without looking awkward.

MITCH   I weigh two hundred and seven pounds and I'm six feet one and one half inches tall in my bare feet—without shoes on. And that is what I weigh stripped.

BLANCHE   Oh, my goodness, me! It's awe-inspiring.

MITCH [*embarrassed*]   My weight is not a very interesting subject to talk about. [*He hesitates for a moment.*] What's yours?

BLANCHE   <u>My weight?</u>

MITCH   Yes.

BLANCHE   Guess!

MITCH   Let me lift you.

BLANCHE   Samson![5] Go on, lift me. [*He comes behind her and puts his hands on her waist and raises her lightly off the ground.*] Well?

MITCH   You are light as a feather.

BLANCHE   Ha-ha! [*He lowers her but keeps his hands on her waist.* BLANCHE *speaks with an affectation of demureness.*] You may release me now.

MITCH   Huh?

BLANCHE [*gaily*]   I said unhand me, sir. [*He fumblingly embraces her. Her voice sounds gently reproving.*] Now, Mitch. Just because Stanley and Stella aren't at home is no reason why you shouldn't behave like a gentleman.

MITCH   Just give me a slap whenever I step out of bounds.

BLANCHE   That won't be necessary. You're a natural gentleman, one of the very few that are left in the world. I don't want you to think that I am severe and old maid school-teacherish or anything like that. It's just— well—

MITCH   Huh?

BLANCHE   I guess it is just that I have—old-fashioned ideals! [*She rolls her eyes, knowing he cannot see her face.* MITCH *goes to the front door. There is a considerable silence between them.* BLANCHE *sighs and* MITCH *coughs self-consciously.*]

MITCH [*finally*]   Where's Stanley and Stella tonight?

BLANCHE   They have gone out. With Mr. and Mrs. Hubbell upstairs.

MITCH   Where did they go?

BLANCHE   I think they were planning to go to a midnight prevue at Loew's State.

MITCH   We should all go out together some night.

---

5. Legendary strong man in the Bible's Book of Judges; he is captured by the Philistines after he reveals the secret of his strength, his long hair, to the temptress Delilah.

BLANCHE   No. That wouldn't be a good plan.

MITCH   Why not?

BLANCHE   You are an old friend of Stanley's?

MITCH   We was together in the Two-Forty-First.[6]

BLANCHE   I guess he talks to you frankly?

MITCH   Sure.

BLANCHE   Has he talked to you about me?

BLANCHE   Oh—not very much.

BLANCHE   The way you say that, I suspect that he has.

MITCH   No, he hasn't said much.

BLANCHE   But what he *has* said. What would you say his attitude toward me was?

MITCH   Why do you want to ask that?

BLANCHE   Well—

MITCH   Don't you get along with him?

BLANCHE   What do you think?

MITCH   I don't think he understands you.

BLANCHE   That is putting it mildly. If it weren't for Stella about to have a baby, I wouldn't be able to endure things here.

MITCH   He isn't—nice to you?

BLANCHE   He is insufferably rude. Goes out of his way to offend me.

MITCH   In what way, Blanche?

BLANCHE   Why, in every conceivable way.

MITCH   I'm surprised to hear that.

BLANCHE   Are you?

MITCH   Well, I—don't see how anybody could be rude to you.

BLANCHE   It's really a pretty frightful situation. You see, there's no privacy here. There's just these portieres between the two rooms at night. He stalks through the rooms in his underwear at night. And I have to ask him to close the bathroom door. That sort of commonness isn't necessary. You probably wonder why I don't move out. Well, I'll tell you frankly. A teacher's salary is barely sufficient for her living expenses. I didn't save a penny last year and so I had to come here for the summer. That's why I have to put up with my sister's husband. And he has to put up with me, apparently so much against his wishes. . . . Surely he must have told you how much he hates me!

MITCH   I don't think he hates you.

BLANCHE   He hates me. Or why would he insult me? The first time I laid eyes on him I thought to myself, that man is my executioner! That man will destroy me, unless——

MITCH   Blanche—

BLANCHE   Yes, honey?

MITCH   Can I ask you a question?

BLANCHE   Yes. What?

MITCH   How old are you?

[*She makes a nervous gesture.*]

BLANCHE   Why do you want to know?

---

6. Engineering battalion in World War II.

MITCH   I talked to my mother about you and she said, "How old is Blanche?"
And I wasn't able to tell her. [*There is another pause.*]

BLANCHE   You talked to your mother about me?

MITCH   Yes.

BLANCHE   Why?

MITCH   I told my mother how nice you were, and I liked you.

BLANCHE   Were you sincere about that?

MITCH   You know I was.

BLANCHE   Why did your mother want to know my age?

MITCH   Mother is sick.

BLANCHE   I'm sorry to hear it. Badly?

MITCH   She won't live long. Maybe just a few months.

BLANCHE   Oh.

MITCH   She worries because I'm not settled.

BLANCHE   Oh.

MITCH   She wants me to be settled down before she— [*His voice is hoarse
and he clears his throat twice, shuffling nervously around with his hands
in and out of his pockets.*]

BLANCHE   You love her very much, don't you?

MITCH   Yes.

BLANCHE   I think you have a great capacity for devotion. You will be
lonely when she passes on, won't you? [MITCH *clears his throat and nods.*]
I understand what that is.

MITCH   To be lonely?

BLANCHE   I loved someone, too, and the person I loved I lost.

MITCH   Dead? [*She crosses to the window and sits on the sill, looking out.
She pours herself another drink.*] A man?

BLANCHE   He was a boy, just a boy, when I was a very young girl. When I
was sixteen, I made the discovery—love. All at once and much, much too
completely. It was like you suddenly turned a blinding light on something that had always been half in shadow, that's how it struck the world
for me. But I was unlucky. Deluded. There was something different
about the boy, a nervousness, a softness and tenderness which wasn't like
a man's, although he wasn't the least bit effeminate looking—still—that
thing was there. . . . He came to me for help. I didn't know that. I didn't
find out anything till after our marriage when we'd run away and come
back and all I knew was I'd failed him in some mysterious way and wasn't
able to give the help he needed but couldn't speak of! He was in the
quicksands and clutching at me—but I wasn't holding him out, I was slipping in with him! I didn't know that. I didn't know anything except I loved
him unendurably but without being able to help him or help myself. Then
I found out. In the worst of all possible ways. By coming suddenly into a
room that I thought was empty—which wasn't empty, but had two people
in it . . . the boy I had married and an older man who had been his friend
for years . . .

[*A locomotive is heard approaching outside. She claps her hands to her
ears and crouches over. The headlight of the locomotive glares into the
room as it thunders past. As the noise recedes she straightens slowly and
continues speaking.*]

Afterward we pretended that nothing had been discovered. Yes, the three of us drove out to Moon Lake Casino, very drunk and laughing all the way.

[*Polka music sounds, in a minor key faint with distance.*]

We danced the Varsouviana![7] Suddenly in the middle of the dance the boy I had married broke away from me and ran out of the casino. A few moments later—a shot!

[*The polka stops abruptly.* BLANCHE *rises stiffly. Then, the polka resumes in a major key.*]

I ran out—all did!—all ran and gathered about the terrible thing at the edge of the lake! I couldn't get near for the crowding. Then somebody caught my arm. "Don't go any closer! Come back! You don't want to see!" See? See what! Then I heard voices say—Allan! Allan! The Grey boy! He'd stuck the revolver into his mouth, and fired—so that the back of his head had been—blown away!

[*She sways and covers her face.*]

It was because—on the dance floor—unable to stop myself—I'd suddenly said—"I saw! I know! You disgust me . . ." And then the searchlight which had been turned on the world was turned off again and never for one moment since has there been any light that's stronger than this—kitchen—candle . . .

[MITCH *gets up awkwardly and moves toward her a little. The polka music increases.* MITCH *stands beside her.*]

MITCH [*drawing her slowly into his arms*]   You need somebody. And I need somebody, too. Could it be—you and me, Blanche?

[*She stares at him vacantly for a moment. Then with a soft cry huddles in his embrace. She makes a sobbing effort to speak but the words won't come. He kisses her forehead and her eyes and finally her lips. The Polka tune fades out. Her breath is drawn and released in long, grateful sobs.*]

BLANCHE   Sometimes—there's God—so quickly!

Scene Seven

It is late afternoon in mid-September.

The portieres are open and a table is set for a birthday supper, with cake and flowers.

STELLA is completing the decorations as STANLEY comes in.

STANLEY   What's all this stuff for?
STELLA   Honey, it's Blanche's birthday.
STANLEY   She here?
STELLA   In the bathroom.
STANLEY [*mimicking*]   "Washing out some things"?
STELLA   I reckon so.
STANLEY   How long she been in there?
STELLA   All afternoon.
STANLEY [*mimicking*]   "Soaking in a hot tub"?
STELLA   Yes.
STANLEY   Temperature 100 on the nose, and she soaks herself in a hot tub.

---

7. Fast Polish waltz, similar to the polka.

STELLA   She says it cools her off for the evening.

STANLEY   And you run out an' get her cokes, I suppose? And serve 'em to Her Majesty in the tub? [STELLA *shrugs*.] Set down here a minute.

STELLA   Stanley, I've got things to do.

STANLEY   Set down! I've got th' dope on your big sister, Stella.

STELLA   Stanley, stop picking on Blanche.

STANLEY   That girl calls *me* common!

STELLA   Lately you been doing all you can think of to rub her the wrong way, Stanley, and Blanche is sensitive and you've got to realize that Blanche and I grew up under very different circumstances than you did.

STANLEY   So I been told. And told and told and told! You know she's been feeding us a pack of lies here?

STELLA   No, I don't, and—

STANLEY   Well, she has, however. But now the cat's out of the bag! I found out some things!

STELLA   What—things?

STANLEY   Things I already suspected. But now I got proof from the most reliable sources—which I have checked on!

[BLANCHE *is singing in the bathroom a saccharine popular ballad which is used contrapuntally with* STANLEY'S *speech*.]

STELLA [*to* STANLEY]   Lower your voice!

STANLEY   Some canary bird, huh!

STELLA   Now please tell me quietly what you think you've found out about my sister.

STANLEY   Lie Number One: All this squeamishness she puts on! You should just know the line she's been feeding to Mitch. He thought she had never been more than kissed by a fellow! But Sister Blanche is no lily! Ha-ha! Some lily she is!

STELLA   What have you heard and who from?

STANLEY   Our supply-man down at the plant has been going through Laurel for years and he knows all about her and everybody else in the town of Laurel knows all about her. She is as famous in Laurel as if she was the President of the United States, only she is not respected by any party! This supply-man stops at a hotel called the Flamingo.

BLANCHE [*singing blithely*]   "Say, it's only a paper moon, Sailing over a cardboard sea—But it wouldn't be make-believe If you believed in me!"[8]

STELLA   What about the—Flamingo?

STANLEY   She stayed there, too.

STELLA   My sister lived at Belle Reve.

STANLEY   This is after the home-place had slipped through her lily-white fingers! She moved to the Flamingo! A second-class hotel which has the advantage of not interfering in the private social life of the personalities there! The Flamingo is used to all kinds of goings-on. But even the management of the Flamingo was impressed by Dame Blanche! In fact they was so impressed by Dame Blanche that they requested her to turn in her room key—for permanently! This happened a couple of weeks before she showed here.

---

8. From "It's Only a Paper Moon" (1933), a popular song by Harold Arlen.

BLANCHE [*singing*]   "It's a Barnum and Bailey world, Just as phony as it can be—But it wouldn't be make-believe If you believed in me!"

STELLA   What—contemptible—lies!

STANLEY   Sure, I can see how you would be upset by this. She pulled the wool over your eyes as much as Mitch's!

STELLA   It's pure invention! There's not a word of truth in it and if I were a man and this creature had dared to invent such things in my presence—

BLANCHE [*singing*]   "Without your love, It's a honky-tonk parade! Without your love, It's a melody played In a penny arcade . . ."

STANLEY   Honey, I told you I thoroughly checked on these stories! Now wait till I finished. The trouble with Dame Blanche was that she couldn't put on her act any more in Laurel! They got wised up after two or three dates with her and then they quit, and she goes on to another, the same old line, same old act, same old hooey! But the town was too small for this to go on forever! And as time went by she became a town character. Regarded as not just different but downright loco—nuts. [STELLA *draws back*.] And for the last year or two she has been washed up like poison. That's why she's here this summer, visiting royalty, putting on all this act—because she's practically told by the mayor to get out of town! Yes, did you know there was an army camp near Laurel and your sister's was one of the places called "Out-of-Bounds"?

BLANCHE   "It's only a paper moon, Just as phony as it can be—But it wouldn't be make-believe If you believed in me!"

STANLEY   Well, so much for her being such a refined and particular type of girl. Which brings us to Lie Number Two.

STELLA   I don't want to hear any more!

STANLEY   She's not going back to teach school! In fact I am willing to bet you that she never had no idea of returning to Laurel! She didn't resign temporarily from the high school because of her nerves! No, siree, Bob! She didn't. They kicked her out of that high school before the spring term ended—and I hate to tell you the reason that step was taken! A seventeen-year-old boy—she'd gotten mixed up with!

BLANCHE   "It's a Barnum and Bailey world, Just as phony as it can be—"
   [*In the bathroom the water goes on loud; little breathless cries and peals of laughter are heard as if a child were frolicking in the tub.*]

STELLA   This is making me—sick!

STANLEY   The boy's dad learned about it and got in touch with the high school superintendent. Boy, oh, boy, I'd like to have been in that office when Dame Blanche was called on the carpet! I'd like to have seen her trying to squirm out of that one! But they had her on the hook good and proper that time and she knew that the jig was all up! They told her she better move on to some fresh territory. Yep, it was practickly a town ordinance passed against her!
   [*The bathroom door is opened and* BLANCHE *thrusts her head out, holding a towel about her hair.*]

BLANCHE   Stella!

STELLA [*faintly*]   Yes, Blanche?

BLANCHE   Give me another bath-towel to dry my hair with. I've just washed it.

STELLA   Yes, Blanche. [*She crosses in a dazed way from the kitchen to the bathroom door with a towel.*]

BLANCHE   What's the matter, honey?

STELLA   Matter? Why?

BLANCHE   You have such a strange expression on your face!

STELLA   Oh— [*she tries to laugh*] I guess I'm a little tired!

BLANCHE   Why don't you bathe, too, soon as I get out?

STANLEY [*calling from the kitchen*]   How soon is that going to be?

BLANCHE   Not so terribly long! Possess your soul in patience!

STANLEY   It's not my soul, it's my kidneys I'm worried about!

[BLANCHE *slams the door.* STANLEY *laughs harshly.* STELLA *comes slowly back into the kitchen.*]

STANLEY   Well, what do you think of it?

STELLA   I don't believe all of those stories and I think your supply-man was mean and rotten to tell them. It's possible that some of the things he said are partly true. There are things about my sister I don't approve of—things that caused sorrow at home. She was always—flighty!

STANLEY   Flighty!

STELLA   But when she was young, very young, she married a boy who wrote poetry. . . . He was extremely good-looking. I think Blanche didn't just love him but worshipped the ground he walked on! Adored him and thought him almost too fine to be human! But then she found out—

STANLEY   What?

STELLA   This beautiful and talented young man was a degenerate. Didn't your supply-man give you that information?

STANLEY   All we discussed was recent history. That must have been a pretty long time ago.

STELLA   Yes, it was—a pretty long time ago . . .

[STANLEY *comes up and takes her by the shoulders rather gently. She gently withdraws from him. Automatically she starts sticking little pink candles in the birthday cake.*]

STANLEY   How many candles you putting in that cake?

STELLA   I'll stop at twenty-five.

STANLEY   Is company expected?

STELLA   We asked Mitch to come over for cake and ice-cream.

[STANLEY *looks a little uncomfortable. He lights a cigarette from the one he has just finished.*]

STANLEY   I wouldn't be expecting Mitch over tonight.

[STELLA *pauses in her occupation with candles and looks slowly around at* STANLEY.]

STELLA   Why?

STANLEY   Mitch is a buddy of mine. We were in the same outfit together— Two-forty-first Engineers. We work in the same plant and now on the same bowling team. You think I could face him if—

STELLA   Stanley Kowalski, did you—did you repeat what that—?

STANLEY   You're goddam right I told him! I'd have that on my conscience the rest of my life if I knew all that stuff and let my best friend get caught!

STELLA   Is Mitch through with her?

STANLEY   Wouldn't you be if—?

STELLA   I said, *Is Mitch through with her?*

[BLANCHE's *voice is lifted again, serenely as a bell. She sings* "But it wouldn't be make-believe If you believed in me."]

STANLEY   No, I don't think he's necessarily through with her—just wised up!

STELLA   Stanley, she thought Mitch was—going to—going to marry her. I was hoping so, too.

STANLEY   Well, he's not going to marry her. Maybe he *was*, but he's not going to jump in a tank with a school of sharks—now! [*He rises.*] Blanche! Oh, Blanche! Can I please get in my bathroom? [*There is a pause.*]

BLANCHE   Yes, indeed, sir! Can you wait one second while I dry?

STANLEY   Having waited one hour I guess one second ought to pass in a hurry.

STELLA   And she hasn't got her job? Well, what will she do!

STANLEY   She's not stayin' here after Tuesday. You know that, don't you? Just to make sure I bought her ticket myself. A bus ticket.

STELLA   In the first place, Blanche wouldn't go on a bus.

STANLEY   She'll go on a bus and like it.

STELLA   No, she won't, no, she won't, Stanley!

STANLEY   *She'll go!* Period. P.S. She'll go *Tuesday!*

STELLA [*slowly*]   What'll—she—do? What on earth will she—*do!*

STANLEY   Her future is mapped out for her.

STELLA   What do you mean?
          [BLANCHE *sings.*]

STANLEY   Hey, canary bird! Toots! Get *OUT* of the *BATHROOM!*
          [*The bathroom door flies open and* BLANCHE *emerges with a gay peal of laughter, but as* STANLEY *crosses past her, a frightened look appears in her face, almost a look of panic. He doesn't look at her but slams the bathroom door shut as he goes in.*]

BLANCHE [*snatching up a hairbrush*]   Oh, I feel so good after my long, hot bath, I feel so good and cool and—rested!

STELLA [*sadly and doubtfully from the kitchen*]   Do you, Blanche?

BLANCHE [*snatching up a hairbrush*]   Yes, I do, so refreshed! [*She tinkles her highball glass.*] A hot bath and a long, cold drink always give me a brand new outlook on life! [*She looks through the portieres at* STELLA, *standing between them, and slowly stops brushing.*] Something has happened!—What is it?

STELLA [*turning away quickly*]   Why, nothing has happened, Blanche.

BLANCHE   You're lying! Something has!
          [*She stares fearfully at* STELLA, *who pretends to be busy at the table. The distant piano goes into a hectic breakdown.*]

Scene Eight

Three quarters of an hour later.

The view through the big windows is fading gradually into a still-golden dusk. A torch of sunlight blazes on the side of a big water-tank or oil-drum across the empty lot toward the business district which is now pierced by pinpoints of lighted windows or windows reflecting the sunset.

The three people are completing a dismal birthday supper. STANLEY *looks sullen.* STELLA *is embarrassed and sad.*

BLANCHE *has a tight, artificial smile on her drawn face. There is a fourth place at the table which is left vacant.*

BLANCHE [*suddenly*]   Stanley, tell us a joke, tell us a funny story to make us all laugh. I don't know what's the matter, we're all so solemn. Is it because I've been stood up by my beau?
[STELLA *laughs feebly.*]
It's the first time in my entire experience with men, and I've had a good deal of all sorts, that I've actually been stood up by anybody! Ha-ha! I don't know how to take it. . . . Tell us a funny little story, Stanley! Something to help us out.

STANLEY   I didn't think you liked my stories, Blanche.

BLANCHE   I like them when they're amusing but not indecent.

STANLEY   I don't know any refined enough for your taste.

BLANCHE   Then let me tell one.

STELLA   Yes, you tell one, Blanche. You used to know lots of good stories.
[*The music fades.*]

BLANCHE   Let me see, now. . . . I must run through my repertoire! Oh, yes—I love parrot stories! Do you all like parrot stories? Well, this one's about the old maid and the parrot. This old maid, she had a parrot that cursed a blue streak and knew more vulgar expressions than Mr. Kowalski!

STANLEY   Huh.

BLANCHE   And the only way to hush the parrot up was to put the cover back on its cage so it would think it was night and go back to sleep. Well, one morning the old maid had just uncovered the parrot for the day—when who should she see coming up the front walk but the preacher! Well, she rushed back to the parrot and slipped the cover back on the cage and then she let in the preacher. And the parrot was perfectly still, just as quiet as a mouse, but just as she was asking the preacher how much sugar he wanted in his coffee—the parrot broke the silence with a loud—[*She whistles.*]—and said—"God *damn*, but that was a short day!"
[*She throws back her head and laughs.* STELLA *also makes an ineffectual effort to seem amused.* STANLEY *pays no attention to the story but reaches way over the table to spear his fork into the remaining chop which he eats with his fingers.*]

BLANCHE   Apparently Mr. Kowalski was not amused.

STELLA   Mr. Kowalski is too busy making a pig of himself to think of anything else!

STANLEY   That's right, baby.

STELLA   Your face and your fingers are disgustingly greasy. Go and wash up and then help me clear the table.
[*He hurls a plate to the floor.*]

STANLEY   That's how I'll clear the table! [*He seizes her arm.*] Don't ever talk that way to me! "Pig—Polack—disgusting—vulgar—greasy!"—them kind of words have been on your tongue and your sister's too much around here! What do you two think you are? A pair of queens? Remember what Huey Long[9] said—"Every Man is a King!" And I am the king

---

9. Demagogic Louisiana political leader, governor, and senator (1893–1935).

around here, so don't forget it! [*He hurls a cup and saucer to the floor.*] My place is cleared! You want me to clear your places?

[STELLA *begins to cry weakly.* STANLEY *stalks out on the porch and lights a cigarette. The Negro entertainers around the corner are heard.*]

BLANCHE   What happened while I was bathing? What did he tell you, Stella?

STELLA   Nothing, nothing, nothing!

BLANCHE   I think he told you something about Mitch and me! You know why Mitch didn't come but you won't tell me! [STELLA *shakes her head helplessly.*] I'm going to call him!

STELLA   I wouldn't call him, Blanche.

BLANCHE   I am, I'm going to call him on the phone.

STELLA [*miserably*]   I wish you wouldn't.

BLANCHE   I intend to be given some explanation from someone!

[*She rushes to the phone in the bedroom.* STELLA *goes out on the porch and stares reproachfully at her husband. He grunts and turns away from her.*]

STELLA   I hope you're pleased with your doings. I never had so much trouble swallowing food in my life, looking at that girl's face and the empty chair! [*She cries quietly.*]

BLANCHE [*at the phone*]   Hello. Mr. Mitchell, please. . . . Oh. . . . I would like to leave a number if I may. Magnolia 9047. And say it's important to call. . . . Yes, very important. . . . Thank you.

[*She remains by the phone with a lost, frightened look.* STANLEY *turns slowly back toward his wife and takes her clumsily in his arms.*]

STANLEY   Stell, it's gonna be all right after she goes and after you've had the baby. It's gonna be all right again between you and me the way that it was. You remember the way that it was? Them nights we had together? God, honey, it's gonna be sweet when we can make noise in the night the way that we used to and get the colored lights going with nobody's sister behind the curtains to hear us!

[*Their upstairs neighbors are heard in bellowing laughter at something.* STANLEY *chuckles.*]

Steve an' Eunice . . .

STELLA   Come on back in. [*She returns to the kitchen and starts lighting the candles on the white cake.*] Blanche?

BLANCHE   Yes. [*She returns from the bedroom to the table in the kitchen.*] Oh, those pretty, pretty little candles! Oh, don't burn them, Stella.

STELLA   I certainly will.

[STANLEY *comes back in.*]

BLANCHE   You ought to save them for baby's birthdays. Oh, I hope candles are going to glow in his life and I hope that his eyes are going to be like candles, like two blue candles lighted in a white cake!

STANLEY [*sitting down*]   What poetry!

BLANCHE [*she pauses reflectively for a moment*]   I shouldn't have called him.

STELLA   There's lots of things could have happened.

BLANCHE   There's no excuse for it, Stella. I don't have to put up with insults. I won't be taken for granted.

STANLEY   Goddamn, it's hot in here with the steam from the bathroom.

BLANCHE I've said I was sorry three times. [*The piano fades out.*] I take hot baths for my nerves. Hydrotherapy, they call it. You healthy Polack, without a nerve in your body, of course you don't know what anxiety feels like!

STANLEY I am not a Polack. People from Poland are Poles, not Polacks. But what I am is a one-hundred-per-cent American, born and raised in the greatest country on earth and proud as hell of it, so don't ever call me a Polack.

[*The phone rings.* BLANCHE *rises expectantly.*]

BLANCHE Oh, that's for me, I'm sure.

STANLEY *I'm* not sure. Keep your seat. [*He crosses leisurely to phone.*] H'lo. Aw, yeh, hello, Mac.

[*He leans against wall, staring insultingly in at* BLANCHE. *She sinks back in her chair with a frightened look.* STELLA *leans over and touches her shoulder.*]

BLANCHE Oh, keep your hands off me, Stella. What is the matter with you? Why do you look at me with that pitying look?

STANLEY [*bawling*] QUIET IN THERE!—We've got a noisy woman on the place.—Go on, Mac. At Riley's? No, I don't wanta bowl at Riley's. I had a little trouble with Riley last week. I'm the team captain, ain't I? All right, then, we're not gonna bowl at Riley's, we're gonna bowl at the West Side or the Gala! All right, Mac. See you!

[*He hangs up and returns to the table.* BLANCHE *fiercely controls herself, drinking quickly from her tumbler of water. He doesn't look at her but reaches in a pocket. Then he speaks slowly and with false amiability.*]

Sister Blanche, I've got a little birthday remembrance for you.

BLANCHE Oh, have you, Stanley? I wasn't expecting any, I—I don't know why Stella wants to observe my birthday! I'd much rather forget it—when you—reach twenty-seven! Well—age is a subject that you'd prefer to—ignore!

STANLEY Twenty-seven?

BLANCHE [*quickly*] What is it? Is it for *me*?

[*He is holding a little envelope toward her.*]

STANLEY Yes, I hope you like it!

BLANCHE Why, why—Why, it's a—

STANLEY Ticket! Back to Laurel! On the Greyhound! Tuesday!

[*The Varsouviana music steals in softly and continues playing.* STELLA *rises abruptly and turns her back.* BLANCHE *tries to smile. Then she tries to laugh. Then she gives both up and springs from the table and runs into the next room. She clutches her throat and then runs into the bathroom. Coughing, gagging sounds are heard.*]

Well!

STELLA You didn't need to do that.

STANLEY Don't forget all that I took off her.

STELLA You needn't have been so cruel to someone alone as she is.

STANLEY Delicate piece she is.

STELLA She is. She was. You didn't know Blanche as a girl. Nobody, nobody, was tender and trusting as she was. But people like you abused her, and forced her to change.

[*He crosses into the bedroom, ripping off his shirt, and changes into a brilliant silk bowling shirt. She follows him.*]

Do you think you're going bowling now?

STANLEY Sure.

STELLA You're not going bowling. [*She catches hold of his shirt.*] Why did you do this to her?

STANLEY I done nothing to no one. Let go of my shirt. You've torn it.

STELLA I want to know why. Tell me why.

STANLEY When we first met, me and you, you thought I was common. How right you was, baby. I was common as dirt. You showed me the snapshot of the place with the columns. I pulled you down off them columns and how you loved it, having them colored lights going! And wasn't we happy together, wasn't it all okay till she showed here?

> [STELLA *makes a slight movement. Her look goes suddenly inward as if some interior voice had called her name. She begins a slow, shuffling progress from the bedroom to the kitchen, leaning and resting on the back of the chair and then on the edge of a table with a blind look and listening expression.* STANLEY, *finishing with his shirt, is unaware of her reaction.*]

And wasn't we happy together? Wasn't it all okay? Till she showed here. Hoity-Toity, describing me as an ape. [*He suddenly notices the change in* STELLA.] Hey, what is it, Stel? [*He crosses to her.*]

STELLA [*quietly*] Take me to the hospital.

> [*He is with her now, supporting her with his arm, murmuring indistinguishably as they go outside.*]

Scene Nine

A while later that evening. BLANCHE *is seated in a tense hunched position in a bedroom chair that she has recovered with diagonal green and white stripes. She has on her scarlet satin robe. On the table beside chair is a bottle of liquor and a glass. The rapid, feverish polka tune, the "Varsouviana," is heard. The music is in her mind; she is drinking to escape it and the sense of disaster closing in on her, and she seems to whisper the words of the song. An electric fan is turning back and forth across her.*

MITCH *comes around the corner in work clothes: blue denim shirt and pants. He is unshaven. He climbs the steps to the door and rings.* BLANCHE *is startled.*

BLANCHE Who is it, please?

MITCH [*hoarsely*] Me. Mitch.

> [*The polka tune stops.*]

BLANCHE Mitch!—Just a minute.

> [*She rushes about frantically, hiding the bottle in a closet, crouching at the mirror and dabbing her face with cologne and powder. She is so excited that her breath is audible as she dashes about. At last she rushes to the door in the kitchen and lets him in.*]

Mitch!—Y'know, I really shouldn't let you in after the treatment I have received from you this evening! So utterly uncavalier! But hello, beautiful!

> [*She offers him her lips. He ignores it and pushes past her into the flat. She looks fearfully after him as he stalks into the bedroom.*]

My, my, what a cold shoulder! And such uncouth apparel! Why, you haven't even shaved! The unforgivable insult to a lady! But I forgive you. I forgive you because it's such a relief to see you. You've stopped that

polka tune that I had caught in my head. Have you ever had anythin
caught in your head? No, of course you haven't, you dumb angel-puss
you'd never get anything awful caught in your head!

> [*He stares at her while she follows him while she talks. It is obvious that
> he has had a few drinks on the way over.*]

MITCH   Do we have to have that fan on?

BLANCHE   No!

MITCH   I don't like fans.

BLANCHE   Then let's turn it off, honey. I'm not partial to them!

> [*She presses the switch and the fan nods slowly off. She clears her throat
> uneasily as* MITCH *plumps himself down on the bed in the bedroom and
> lights a cigarette.*]

I don't know what there is to drink. I—haven't investigated.

MITCH   I don't want Stan's liquor.

BLANCHE   It isn't Stan's. Everything here isn't Stan's. Some things on the
premises are actually mine! How is your mother? Isn't your mother well?

MITCH   Why?

BLANCHE   Something's the matter tonight, but never mind. I won't cross-
examine the witness. I'll just—[*She touches her forehead vaguely. The
polka tune starts up again.*]—pretend I don't notice anything different
about you! That—music again . . .

MITCH   What music?

BLANCHE   The "Varsourviana"! The polka tune they were playing when
Allan—Wait!

> [*A distant revolver shot is heard.* BLANCHE *seems relieved.*]

There now, the shot! It always stops after that.

> [*The polka music dies out again.*]

Yes, now it's stopped.

MITCH   Are you boxed out of your mind?

BLANCHE   I'll go and see what I can find in the way of— [*She crosses into
the closet, pretending to search for the bottle.*] Oh, by the way, excuse me
for not being dressed. But I'd practically given you up! Had you forgotten your invitation to supper?

MITCH   I wasn't going to see you any more.

BLANCHE   Wait a minute. I can't hear what you're saying and you talk so
little that when you do say something, I don't want to miss a single syllable of it. . . . What am I looking around here for? Oh, yes—liquor!
We've had so much excitement around here this evening that I *am* boxed
out of my mind! [*She pretends suddenly to find the bottle. He draws his foot
up on the bed and stares at her contemptuously.*] Here's something. Southern Comfort! What is that, I wonder?

MITCH   If you don't know, it must belong to Stan.

BLANCHE   Take your foot off the bed. It has a light cover on it. Of course
you boys don't notice things like that. I've done so much with this place
since I've been here.

MITCH   I bet you have.

BLANCHE   You saw it before I came. Well, look at it now! This room is
almost—dainty! I want to keep it that way. I wonder if this stuff ought
to be mixed with something? Ummm, it's sweet, so sweet! It's terribly,

terribly sweet! Why, it's a *liqueur*, I believe! Yes, that's what it *is*, a liqueur! [MITCH *grunts.*] I'm afraid you won't like it, but try it, and maybe you will.

MITCH   I told you already I don't want none of his liquor and I mean it. You ought to lay off his liquor. He says you been lapping it up all summer like a wild cat!

BLANCHE   What a fantastic statement! Fantastic of him to say it, fantastic of you to repeat it! I won't descend to the level of such cheap accusations to answer them, even!

MITCH   Huh.

BLANCHE   What's in your mind? I see something in your eyes!

MITCH   [*getting up*]   It's dark in here.

BLANCHE   I like it dark. The dark is comforting to me.

MITCH   I don't think I ever seen you in the light. [BLANCHE *laughs breathlessly.*] That's a fact!

BLANCHE   Is it?

MITCH   I've never seen you in the afternoon.

BLANCHE   Whose fault is that?

MITCH   You never want to go out in the afternoon.

BLANCHE   Why, Mitch, you're at the plant in the afternoon!

MITCH   Not Sunday afternoon. I've asked you to go out with me sometimes on Sundays but you always make an excuse. You never want to go out till after six and then it's always some place that's not lighted much.

BLANCHE   There is some obscure meaning in this but I fail to catch it.

MITCH   What it means is I've never had a real good look at you, Blanche. Let's turn the light on here.

BLANCHE   [*fearfully*]   Light? Which light? What for?

MITCH   This one with the paper thing on it. [*He tears the paper lantern off the light bulb. She utters a frightened gasp.*]

BLANCHE   What did you do that for?

MITCH   So I can take a look at you good and plain!

BLANCHE   Of course you don't really mean to be insulting!

MITCH   No, just realistic.

BLANCHE   I don't want realism. I want magic! [MITCH *laughs.*] Yes, yes, magic! I try to give that to people. I misrepresent things to them. I don't tell truth, I tell what *ought* to be truth. And if that is sinful, then let me be damned for it!—*Don't turn the light on!*
  [MITCH *crosses to the switch. He turns the light on and stares at her. She cries out and covers her face. He turns the lights off again.*]

MITCH   [*slowly and bitterly*]   I don't mind you being older than what I thought. But all the rest of it—Christ! That pitch about your ideals being so old-fashioned and all the malarkey that you've dished out all summer. Oh, I knew you weren't sixteen any more. But I was a fool enough to believe you was straight.

BLANCHE   Who told you I wasn't—"straight"? My loving brother-in-law. And you believed him.

MITCH   I called him a liar at first. And then I checked on the story. First I asked our supply-man who travels through Laurel. And then I talked directly over long-distance to this merchant.

BLANCHE   Who is this merchant?

MITCH Kiefaber.

BLANCHE The merchant Kiefaber of Laurel! I know the man. He whistled at me. I put him in his place. So now for revenge he makes up stories about me.

MITCH Three people, Kiefaber, Stanley and Shaw, swore to them!

BLANCHE Rub-a-dub-dub, three men in a tub! And such a filthy tub!

MITCH Didn't you stay at a hotel called The Flamingo?

BLANCHE Flamingo? No! Tarantula was the name of it! I stayed at a hotel called The Tarantula Arms!

MITCH [*stupidly*] Tarantula?

BLANCHE Yes, a big spider! That's where I brought my victims. [*She pours herself another drink.*] Yes, I had many intimacies with strangers. After the death of Allan—intimacies with strangers was all I seemed able to fill my empty heart with. . . . I think it was panic, just panic, that drove me from one to another, hunting for some protection—here and there, in the most—unlikely places—even, at last, in a seventeen-year-old boy but—somebody wrote the superintendent about it—"This woman is morally unfit for her position!"

[*She throws back her head with convulsive, sobbing laughter. Then she repeats the statement, gasps, and drinks.*]

True? Yes, I suppose—unfit somehow—anyway. . . . So I came here. There was nowhere else I could go. I was played out. You know what played out is? My youth was suddenly gone up the water-spout, and—I met you. You said you needed somebody. Well, I needed somebody, too. I thanked God for you, because you seemed to be gentle—a cleft in the rock of the world that I could hide in! But I guess I was asking, hoping—too much! Kiefaber, Stanley and Shaw have tied an old tin can to the tail of the kite.

[*There is a pause.* MITCH *stares at her dumbly.*]

MITCH You lied to me, Blanche.

BLANCHE Don't say I lied to you.

MITCH Lies, lies, inside and out, all lies.

BLANCHE Never inside, I didn't lie in my heart . . .

[*A* VENDOR *comes around the corner. She is a blind* MEXICAN WOMAN *in a dark shawl, carrying bunches of those gaudy tin flowers that lower-class Mexicans display at funerals and other festive occasions. She is calling barely audibly. Her figure is only faintly visible outside the building.*]

MEXICAN WOMAN Flores. Flores, Flores para los muertos.[1] Flores. Flores.

BLANCHE What? Oh! Somebody outside . . . [*She goes to the door, opens it and stares at the* MEXICAN WOMAN.]

MEXICAN WOMAN [*she is at the door and offers* BLANCHE *some of her flowers*] Flores? Flores para los muertos?

BLANCHE [*frightened*] No, no! Not now! Not now!

[*She darts back into the apartment, slamming the door.*]

MEXICAN WOMAN [*she turns away and starts to move down the street*] Flores para los muertos.

[*The polka tune fades in.*]

BLANCHE [*as if to herself*] Crumble and fade and—regrets—recriminations . . . "If you'd done this, it wouldn't've cost me that!"

---

1. Flowers for the dead (Spanish).

MEXICAN WOMAN   Corones para los muertos.[2] Corones . . .

BLANCHE   Legacies! Huh. . . . And other things such as bloodstained pillow-slips—"Her linen needs changing"—"Yes, Mother. But couldn't we get a colored girl to do it?" No, we couldn't of course. Everything gone but the—

MEXICAN WOMAN   Flores.

BLANCHE   Death—I used to sit here and she used to sit over there and death was as close as you are. . . . We didn't dare even admit we had ever heard of it!

MEXICAN WOMAN   Flores para los muertos, flores—flores . . .

BLANCHE   The opposite is desire. So do you wonder? How could you possibly wonder! Not far from Belle Reve, before we had lost Belle Reve, was a camp where they trained young soldiers. On Sunday nights they would go in town to get drunk—

MEXICAN WOMAN [softly]   Corones . . .

BLANCHE   —and on the way back they would stagger onto my lawn and call—"Blanche! Blanche!"—the deaf old lady remaining suspected nothing. But sometimes I slipped outside to answer their calls. . . . Later the paddy-wagon would gather them up like daisies . . . the long way home . . .

[The MEXICAN WOMAN turns slowly and drifts back off with her soft mournful cries. BLANCHE goes to the dresser and leans forward on it. After a moment, MITCH rises and follows her purposefully. The polka music fades away. He places his hands on her waist and tries to turn her about.]

BLANCHE   What do you want?

MITCH [fumbling to embrace her]   What I been missing all summer.

BLANCHE   Then marry me, Mitch!

MITCH   I don't think I want to marry you anymore.

BLANCHE   No?

MITCH [dropping his hands from her waist]   You're not clean enough to bring in the house with my mother.

BLANCHE   Go away, then. [He stares at her.] Get out of here quick before I start screaming fire! [Her throat is tightening with hysteria.] Get out of here quick before I start screaming fire.

[He still remains staring. She suddenly rushes to the big window with its pale blue square of the soft summer light and cries wildly.]

Fire! Fire! Fire!

[With a startled gasp, MITCH turns and goes out the outer door, clatters awkwardly down the steps and around the corner of the building. BLANCHE staggers back from the window and falls to her knees. The distant piano is slow and blue.]

Scene Ten

It is a few hours later that night.

BLANCHE has been drinking fairly steadily since MITCH left. She has dragged her wardrobe trunk into the center of the bedroom. It hangs open with flowery dresses thrown across it. As the drinking and packing went on, a mood of hysterical exhilaration came into her and she has decked herself out in a somewhat

---

2. Wreaths for the dead (Spanish).

soiled and crumpled white satin evening gown and a pair of scuffed silver slippers with brilliants set in their heels.

Now she is placing the rhinestone tiara on her head before the mirror of the dressing-table and murmuring excitedly as if to a group of spectral admirers.

BLANCHE   How about taking a swim, a moonlight swim at the old rock-quarry? If anyone's sober enough to drive a car! Ha-ha! Best way in the world to stop your head buzzing! Only you've got to be careful to dive where the deep pool is—if you hit a rock you don't come up till tomorrow . . .

> [*Tremblingly she lifts the hand mirror for a closer inspection. She catches her breath and slams the mirror face down with such violence that the glass cracks. She moans a little and attempts to rise.* STANLEY *appears around the corner of the building. He still has on the vivid green silk bowling shirt. As he rounds the corner the honky-tonk music is heard. It continues softly throughout the scene. He enters the kitchen, slamming the door. As he peers in at* BLANCHE *he gives a low whistle. He has had a few drinks on the way and has brought some quart beer bottles home with him.*]

BLANCHE   How is my sister?

STANLEY   She is doing okay.

BLANCHE   And how is the baby?

STANLEY [*grinning amiably*]   The baby won't come before morning so they told me to go home and get a little shut-eye.

BLANCHE   Does that mean we are to be alone in here?

STANLEY   Yep. Just me and you, Blanche. Unless you got somebody hid under the bed. What've you got on those fine feathers for?

BLANCHE   Oh, that's right. You left before my wire came.

STANLEY   You got a wire?

BLANCHE   I received a telegram from an old admirer of mine.

STANLEY   Anything good?

BLANCHE   I think so. An invitation.

STANLEY   What to? A fireman's ball?

BLANCHE [*throwing back her head*]   A cruise of the Caribbean on a yacht!

STANLEY   Well, well. What do you know?

BLANCHE   I have never been so surprised in my life.

STANLEY   I guess not.

BLANCHE   It came like a bolt from the blue!

STANLEY   Who did you say it was from?

BLANCHE   An old beau of mine.

STANLEY   The one that give you the white fox-pieces?

BLANCHE   Mr. Shep Huntleigh. I wore his ATO pin my last year at college. I hadn't seen him again until last Christmas. I ran in to him on Biscayne Boulevard. Then—just now—this wire—inviting me on a cruise of the Caribbean! The problem is clothes. I tore into my trunk to see what I have that's suitable for the tropics!

STANLEY   And come up with that—gorgeous—diamond—tiara?

BLANCHE   This old relic? Ha-ha! It's only rhinestones.

STANLEY   Gosh. I thought it was Tiffany diamonds. [*He unbuttons his shirt.*]

BLANCHE   Well, anyhow, I shall be entertained in style.

STANLEY   Uh-huh. It goes to show, you never know what is coming.

BLANCHE Just when I thought my luck had begun to fail me—

STANLEY Into the picture pops this Miami millionaire.

BLANCHE This man is not from Miami. This man is from Dallas.

STANLEY This man is from Dallas?

BLANCHE Yes, this man is from Dallas where gold spouts out of the ground!

STANLEY Well, just so he's from somewhere! [*He starts removing his shirt.*]

BLANCHE Close the curtains before you undress any further.

STANLEY [*amiably*] This is all I'm going to undress right now. [*He rips the sack off a quart beer bottle*] Seen a bottle-opener?
>   [*She moves slowly toward the dresser, where she stands with her hands knotted together.*]

I used to have a cousin who could open a beer bottle with his teeth. [*pounding the bottle cap on the corner of table*] That was his only accomplishment, all he could do—he was just a human bottle-opener. And then one time, at a wedding party, he broke his front teeth off! After that he was so ashamed of himself he used t' sneak out of the house when company came . . .
>   [*The bottle cap pops off and a geyser of foam shoots up. Stanley laughs happily, holding up the bottle over his head.*]

Ha-ha! Rain from heaven! [*He extends the bottle toward her*] Shall we bury the hatchet and make it a loving-cup? Huh?

BLANCHE No, thank you.

STANLEY Well, it's a red-letter night for us both. You having an oil millionaire and me having a baby.
>   [*He goes to the bureau in the bedroom and crouches to remove something from the bottom drawer.*]

BLANCHE [*drawing back*] What are you doing in here?

STANLEY Here's something I always break out on special occasions like this. The silk pyjamas I wore on my wedding night!

BLANCHE Oh.

STANLEY When the telephone rings and they say, "You've got a son!" I'll tear this off and wave it like a flag! [*He shakes out a brilliant pyjama coat.*] I guess we are both entitled to put on the dog. [*He goes back to the kitchen with the coat over his arm.*]

BLANCHE When I think of how divine it is going to be to have such a thing as privacy once more—I could weep with joy!

STANLEY This millionaire from Dallas is not going to interfere with your privacy any?

BLANCHE It won't be the sort of thing you have in mind. This man is a gentleman and he respects me. [*improvising feverishly*] What he wants is my companionship. Having great wealth sometimes makes people lonely! A cultivated woman, a woman of intelligence and breeding, can enrich a man's life—immeasurably! I have those things to offer, and this doesn't take them away. Physical beauty is passing. A transitory possession. But beauty of the mind and richness of the spirit and tenderness of the heart—and I have all of those things—aren't taken away, but grow! Increase with the years! How strange that I should be called a destitute woman! When I have all of these treasures locked in my heart. [*A choked sob comes from her.*] I think of myself as a very, very rich woman! But I have been foolish—casting my pearls before swine!

STANLEY Swine, huh?

BLANCHE Yes, swine! Swine! And I'm thinking not only of you but of your friend, Mr. Mitchell. He came to see me tonight. He dared to come here in his work clothes! And to repeat slander to me, vicious stories that he had gotten from you! I gave him his walking papers . . .

STANLEY You did, huh?

BLANCHE But then he came back. He returned with a box of roses to beg my forgiveness! He implored my forgiveness. But some things are not forgivable. Deliberate cruelty is not forgivable. It is the one unforgivable thing in my opinion and it is the one thing of which I have never, never been guilty. And so I told him, I said to him, "Thank you," but it was foolish of me to think that we could ever adapt ourselves to each other. Our ways of life are too different. Our attitudes and our backgrounds are incompatible. We have to be realistic about such things. So farewell, my friend! And let there be no hard feelings . . .

STANLEY Was this before or after the telegram came from the Texas oil millionaire?

BLANCHE What telegram? No! No, after! As a matter of fact, the wire came just as—

STANLEY As a matter of fact there wasn't no wire at all!

BLANCHE Oh, oh!

STANLEY There isn't no millionaire! And Mitch didn't come back with roses 'cause I know where he is—

BLANCHE Oh!

STANLEY There isn't a goddam thing but imagination!

BLANCHE Oh!

STANLEY And lies and conceit and tricks!

BLANCHE Oh!

STANLEY And look at yourself! Take a look at yourself in that worn-out Mardi Gras outfit, rented for fifty cents from some rag-picker! And with the crazy crown on! What queen do you think you are?

BLANCHE Oh—God . . .

STANLEY I've been on to you from the start! Not once did you pull any wool over this boy's eyes! You come in here and sprinkle the place with powder and spray perfume and cover the light-bulb with a paper lantern, and lo and behold the place has turned into Egypt and you are the Queen of the Nile! Sitting on your throne and swilling down my liquor! I say—Ha!—Ha! Do you hear me? Ha—ha—ha! [He walks into the bedroom.]

BLANCHE Don't come in here!

[Lurid reflections appear on the walls around BLANCHE. The shadows are of a grotesque and menacing form. She catches her breath, crosses to the phone and jiggles the hook. STANLEY goes into the bathroom and closes the door.]

Operator, operator! Give me long-distance, please. . . . I want to get in touch with Mr. Shep Huntleigh of Dallas. He's so well known he doesn't require any address. Just ask anybody who—Wait!!—No, I couldn't find it right now. . . . Please understand, I—No! No, wait!. . . . One moment! Someone is—Nothing! Hold on, please!

[She sets the phone down and crosses warily into the kitchen. The night is filled with inhuman voices like cries in a jungle. The shadows and

[*lurid reflections move sinuously as flames along the wall spaces. Through the back wall of the rooms, which have become transparent, can be seen the sidewalk. A prostitute has rolled a drunkard. He pursues her along the walk, overtakes her and there is a struggle. A policeman's whistle breaks it up. The figures disappear. Some moments later the Negro Woman appears around the corner with a sequined bag which the prostitute had dropped on the walk. She is rooting excitedly through it.* BLANCHE *presses her knuckles to her lips and returns slowly to the phone. She speaks in a hoarse whisper.*]

BLANCHE   Operator! Operator! Never mind long-distance. Get Western Union. There isn't time to be—Western—Western Union!

[*She waits anxiously.*]

Western Union? Yes! I—want to—Take down this message! "In desperate, desperate circumstances! Help me! Caught in a trap. Caught in—" Oh!

[*The bathroom door is thrown open and* STANLEY *comes out in the brilliant silk pyjamas. He grins at her as he knots the tasseled sash about his waist. She gasps and backs away from the phone. He stares at her for a count of ten. Then a clicking becomes audible from the telephone, steady and rasping.*]

STANLEY   You left th' phone off th' hook.

[*He crosses to it deliberately and sets it back on the hook. After he has replaced it, he stares at her again, his mouth slowly curving into a grin, as he weaves between* BLANCHE *and the outer door. The barely audible "Blue Piano" begins to drum up louder. The sound of it turns into the roar of an approaching locomotive.* BLANCHE *crouches, pressing her fists to her ears until it has gone by.*]

BLANCHE [*finally straightening*]   Let me—let me get by you!

STANLEY   Get by me? Sure. Go ahead. [*He moves back a pace in the doorway.*]

BLANCHE   You—you stand over there! [*She indicates a further position.*]

STANLEY [*grinning*]   You got plenty of room to walk by me now.

BLANCHE   Not with you there! But I've got to get out somehow!

STANLEY   You think I'll interfere with you? Ha-ha!

[*The "Blue Piano" goes softly. She turns confusedly and makes a faint gesture. The inhuman jungle voices rise up. He takes a step toward her, biting his tongue which protrudes between his lips.*]

STANLEY [*softly*]   Come to think of it—maybe you wouldn't be bad to—interfere with . . .

[BLANCHE *moves backward through the door into the bedroom.*]

BLANCHE   Stay back! Don't you come toward me another step or I'll—

STANLEY   What?

BLANCHE   Some awful thing will happen! It will!

STANLEY   What are you putting on now?

[*They are now both inside the bedroom.*]

BLANCHE   I warn you, don't, I'm in danger!

[*He takes another step. She smashes a bottle on the table and faces him, clutching the broken top.*]

STANLEY   What did you do that for?

BLANCHE   So I could twist the broken end in your face!

STANLEY   I bet you would do that!

BLANCHE   I would! I will if you—

STANLEY   Oh! So you want some roughhouse! All right, let's have some roughhouse!

> [*He springs toward her, overturning the table. She cries out and strikes at him with the bottle top but he catches her wrist.*]

Tiger—tiger! Drop the bottle-top! Drop it! We've had this date with each other from the beginning!

> [*She moans. The bottle-top falls. She sinks to her knees: He picks up her inert figure and carries her to the bed. The hot trumpet and drums from the Four Deuces sound loudly.*]

Scene Eleven

It is some weeks later. STELLA *is packing* BLANCHE's *things. Sounds of water can be heard running in the bathroom.*

*The portieres are partly open on the poker players—*STANLEY, STEVE, MITCH *and* PABLO—*who sit around the table in the kitchen. The atmosphere of the kitchen is now the same raw, lurid one of the disastrous poker night.*

The building is framed by the sky of turquoise. STELLA *has been crying as she arranges the flowery dresses in the open trunk.*

EUNICE *comes down the steps from her flat above and enters the kitchen. There is an outburst from the poker table.*

STANLEY   Drew to an inside straight and made it, by God.

PABLO   *Maldita sea tu suerto!*

STANLEY   Put it in English, greaseball.

PABLO   I am cursing your rutting luck.

STANLEY [*prodigiously elated*]   You know what luck is? Luck is believing you're lucky. Take at Salerno.[3] I believed I was lucky. I figured that 4 out of 5 would not come through but I would . . . and I did. I put that down as a rule. To hold front position in this rat-race you've got to believe you are lucky.

MITCH   You . . . you . . . you . . . Brag . . . brag . . . bull . . . bull.

> [STELLA *goes into the bedroom and starts folding a dress.*]

STANLEY   What's the matter with him?

EUNICE [*walking past the table*]   I always did say that men are callous things with no feelings, but this does beat anything. Making pigs of yourselves. [*She comes through the portieres into the bedroom.*]

STANLEY   What's the matter with her?

STELLA   How is my baby?

EUNICE   Sleeping like a little angel. Brought you some grapes. [*She puts them on a stool and lowers her voice.*] Blanche?

STELLA   Bathing.

EUNICE   How is she?

STELLA   She wouldn't eat anything but asked for a drink.

EUNICE   What did you tell her?

STELLA   I—just told her that—we'd made arrangements for her to rest in the country. She's got it mixed in her mind with Shep Huntleigh.

> [BLANCHE *opens the bathroom door slightly.*]

BLANCHE   Stella.

---

3. Important beachhead in the Allied invasion of Italy in World War II.

STELLA Yes, Blanche.

BLANCHE If anyone calls while I'm bathing take the number and tell them I'll call right back.

STELLA Yes.

BLANCHE That cool yellow silk—the bouclé. See if it's crushed. If it's not too crushed I'll wear it and on the lapel that silver and turquoise pin in the shape of a seahorse. You will find them in the heart-shaped box I keep my accessories in. And Stella . . . Try and locate a bunch of artificial violets in that box, too, to pin with the seahorse on the lapel of the jacket.

[*She closes the door.* STELLA *turns to* EUNICE.]

STELLA I don't know if I did the right thing.

EUNICE What else could you do?

STELLA I couldn't believe her story and go on living with Stanley.

EUNICE Don't ever believe it. Life has got to go on. No matter what happens, you've got to keep on going.

[*The bathroom door opens a little.*]

BLANCHE [*looking out*] Is the coast clear?

STELLA Yes, Blanche. [*to* EUNICE] Tell her how well she's looking.

BLANCHE Please close the curtains before I come out.

STELLA They're closed.

STANLEY —How many for you?

PABLO Two.

STEVE Three.

[BLANCHE *appears in the amber light of the door. She has a tragic radiance in her red satin robe following the sculptural lines of her body. The "Varsouviana" rises audibly as* BLANCHE *enters the bedroom.*]

BLANCHE [*with faintly hysterical vivacity*] I have just washed my hair.

STELLA Did you?

BLANCHE I'm not sure I got the soap out.

EUNICE Such fine hair!

BLANCHE [*accepting the compliment*] It's a problem. Didn't I get a call?

STELLA Who from, Blanche?

BLANCHE Shep Huntleigh . . .

STELLA Why, not yet, honey!

BLANCHE How strange! I—

[*At the sound of* BLANCHE's *voice* MITCH's *arm supporting his cards has sagged and his gaze is dissolved into space.* STANLEY *slaps him on the shoulder.*]

STANLEY Hey, Mitch, come to!

[*The sound of this new voice shocks* BLANCHE. *She makes a shocked gesture, forming his name with her lips.* STELLA *nods and looks quickly away.* BLANCHE *stands quite still for some moments—the silver-backed mirror in her hand and a look of sorrowful perplexity as though all human experience shows on her face.* BLANCHE *finally speaks but with sudden hysteria.*]

BLANCHE What's going on here?

[*She turns from* STELLA *to* EUNICE *and back to* STELLA. *Her rising voice penetrates the concentration of the game.* MITCH *ducks his head lower but* STANLEY *shoves back his chair as if to rise.* STEVE *places a restraining hand on his arm.*]

BLANCHE [*continuing*]   What's happened here? I want an explanation of what's happened here.

STELLA [*agonizingly*]   Hush! Hush!

EUNICE   Hush! Hush! Honey.

STELLA   Please, Blanche.

BLANCHE   Why are you looking at me like that? Is something wrong with me?

EUNICE   You look wonderful, Blanche. Don't she look wonderful?

STELLA   Yes.

EUNICE   I understand you are going on a trip.

STELLA   Yes, Blanche *is*. She's going on a vacation.

EUNICE   I'm green with envy.

BLANCHE   Help me, help me get dressed!

STELLA [*handing her dress*]   Is this what you—

BLANCHE   Yes, it will do! I'm anxious to get out of here—this place is a trap!

EUNICE   What a pretty blue jacket.

STELLA   It's lilac colored.

BLANCHE   You're both mistaken. It's Della Robbia blue.[4] The blue of the robe in the old Madonna pictures. Are these grapes washed?
   [*She fingers the bunch of grapes which* EUNICE *had brought in.*]

EUNICE   Huh?

BLANCHE   Washed, I said. Are they washed?

EUNICE   They're from the French Market.

BLANCHE   That doesn't mean they've been washed. [*The cathedral bells chime.*] Those cathedral bells—they're the only clean thing in the Quarter. Well, I'm going now. I'm ready to go.

EUNICE [*whispering*]   She's going to walk out before they get here.

STELLA   Wait, Blanche.

BLANCHE   I don't want to pass in front of those men.

EUNICE   Then wait'll the game breaks up.

STELLA   Sit down and . . .
   [BLANCHE *turns weakly, hesitantly about. She lets them push her into a chair.*]

BLANCHE   I can smell the sea air. The rest of my time I'm going to spend on the sea. And when I die, I'm going to die on the sea. You know what I shall die of [*She plucks a grape.*] I shall die of eating an unwashed grape one day out on the ocean. I will die—with my hand in the hand of some nice-looking ship's doctor, a very young one with a small blond mustache and a big silver watch. "Poor lady," they'll say, "the quinine did her no good. That unwashed grape has transported her soul to heaven." [*The cathedral chimes are heard.*] And I'll be buried at sea sewn up in a clean white sack and dropped overboard—at noon—in the blaze of summer— and into an ocean as blue as [*chimes again*] my first lover's eyes!
   [*A* DOCTOR *and a* MATRON *have appeared around the corner of the building and climbed the steps to the porch. The gravity of their profession is exaggerated—the unmistakable aura of the state institution with its cynical detachment. The* DOCTOR *rings the doorbell. The murmur of the game is interrupted.*]

---

4. A shade of light blue seen in terra cottas made by the Della Robbia family during the Italian Renaissance.

EUNICE [*whispering to* STELLA]   That must be them.
> [STELLA *presses her fists to her lips.*]

BLANCHE [*rising slowly*]   What is it?

EUNICE [*affectedly casual*]   Excuse me while I see who's at the door.

STELLA   Yes.
> [EUNICE *goes into the kitchen.*]

BLANCHE [*tensely*]   I wonder if it's for me.
> [*A whispered colloquy takes place at the door.*]

EUNICE [*returning, brightly*]   Someone is calling for Blanche.

BLANCHE   It *is* for me, then! [*She looks fearfully from one to the other and then to the portieres. The "Varsouviana" faintly plays.*] Is it the gentleman I was expecting from Dallas?

EUNICE   I think it is, Blanche.

BLANCHE   I'm not quite ready.

STELLA   Ask him to wait outside.

BLANCHE   I . . .
> [EUNICE *goes back to the portieres. Drums sound very softly.*]

STELLA   Everything packed?

BLANCHE   My silver toilet articles are still out.

STELLA   Ah!

EUNICE [*returning*]   They're waiting in front of the house.

BLANCHE   They! Who's "they"?

EUNICE   There's a lady with him.

BLANCHE   I cannot imagine who this "lady" could be! How is she dressed?

EUNICE   Just—just a sort of a—plain-tailored outfit.

BLANCHE   Possibly she's— [*Her voice dies out nervously.*]

STELLA   Shall we go, Blanche?

BLANCHE   Must we go through that room?

STELLA   I will go with you.

BLANCHE   How do I look?

STELLA   Lovely.

EUNICE [*echoing*]   Lovely.
> [BLANCHE *moves fearfully to the portieres.* EUNICE *draws them open for her.* BLANCHE *goes into the kitchen.*]

BLANCHE [*to the men*]   Please don't get up. I'm only passing through.
> [*She crosses quickly to outside door.* STELLA *and* EUNICE *follow. The poker players stand awkwardly at the table—all except* MITCH *who remains seated, looking down at the table.* BLANCHE *steps out on a small porch at the side of the door. She stops short and catches her breath.*]

DOCTOR   How do you do?

BLANCHE   You are not the gentleman I was expecting. [*She suddenly gasps and starts back up the steps. She stops by* STELLA, *who stands just outside the door, and speaks in a frightening whisper.*] That man isn't Shep Huntleigh.
> [*The "Varsouviana" is playing distantly.* STELLA *stares back at* BLANCHE. EUNICE *is holding* STELLA'S *arm. There is a moment of silence—no sound but that of* STANLEY *steadily shuffling the cards.* BLANCHE *catches her breath again and slips back into the flat. She enters the flat with a peculiar smile, her eyes wide and brilliant. As soon as her sister goes past her,* STELLA *closes her eyes and clenches her hands.* EUNICE *throws her arms comfortingly about her. Then she starts up to her flat.* BLANCHE *stops just*

inside the door. MITCH *keeps staring down at his hands on the table, but the other men look at her curiously. At last she starts around the table toward the bedroom. As she does,* STANLEY *suddenly pushes back his chair and rises as if to block her way. The* MATRON *follows her into the flat.*]

STANLEY   Did you forget something?

BLANCHE [*shrilly*]   Yes! Yes, I forgot something!
   [*She rushes past him into the bedroom. Lurid reflections appear on the walls in odd, sinuous shapes. The "Varsouviana" is filtered into a weird distortion, accompanied by the cries and noises of the jungle.* BLANCHE *seizes the back of a chair as if to defend herself.*]

STANLEY [*sotto voce*][5]   Doc, you better go in.

DOCTOR [*sotto voce, motioning to the* MATRON]   Nurse, bring her out.
   [*The* MATRON *advances on one side,* STANLEY *on the other. Divested of all the softer properties of womanhood, the* MATRON *is a peculiarly sinister figure in her severe dress. Her voice is bold and toneless as a firebell.*]

MATRON   Hello, Blanche.
   [*The greeting is echoed and re-echoed by other mysterious voices behind the walls, as if reverberated through a canyon of rock.*]

STANLEY   She says that she forgot something.
   [*The echo sounds in threatening whispers.*]

MATRON   That's all right.

STANLEY   What did you forget, Blanche?

BLANCHE   I—I—

MATRON   It don't matter. We can pick it up later.

STANLEY   Sure. We can send it along with the trunk.

BLANCHE [*retreating in panic*]   I don't know you—I don't know you. I want to be—left alone—please!

MATRON   Now, Blanche!

ECHOES [*rising and falling*]   Now, Blanche—now, Blanche—now, Blanche!

STANLEY   You left nothing here but spilt talcum and old empty perfume bottles—unless it's the paper lantern you want to take with you. You want the lantern?
   [*He crosses to dressing table and seizes the paper lantern, tearing it off the light bulb, and extends it toward her. She cries out as if the lantern was herself. The* MATRON *steps boldly toward her. She screams and tries to break past the* MATRON. *All the men spring to their feet.* STELLA *runs out to the porch, with* EUNICE *following to comfort her, simultaneously with the confused voices of the men in the kitchen.* STELLA *rushes into* EUNICE'S *embrace on the porch.*]

STELLA   Oh, my God, Eunice help me! Don't let them do that to her, don't let them hurt her! Oh, God, oh, please God, don't hurt her! What are they doing to her? What are they doing? [*She tries to break from* EUNICE'S *arms.*]

EUNICE   No, honey, no, no, honey. Stay here. Don't go back in there. Stay with me and don't look.

STELLA   What have I done to my sister? Oh, God, what have I done to my sister?

EUNICE   You done the right thing, the only thing you could do. She couldn't stay here; there wasn't no other place for her to go.

---

5. In an undertone [Italian].

[*While* STELLA *and* EUNICE *are speaking on the porch the voices of the men in the kitchen overlap them.* MITCH *has started toward the bedroom.* STANLEY *crosses to block him.* STANLEY *pushes him aside.* MITCH *lunges and strikes at* STANLEY. STANLEY *pushes* MITCH *back.* MITCH *collapses at the table, sobbing. During the preceding scenes, the* MATRON *catches hold of* BLANCHE'S *arm and prevents her flight.* BLANCHE *turns wildly and scratches at the* MATRON. *The heavy woman pinions her arms.* BLANCHE *cries out hoarsely and slips to her knees.*]

MATRON   These fingernails have to be trimmed. [*The* DOCTOR *comes into the room and she looks at him.*] Jacket, Doctor?

DOCTOR   Not unless necessary.

[*He takes off his hat and now he becomes personalized. The unhuman quality goes. His voice is gentle and reassuring as he crosses to* BLANCHE *and crouches in front of her. As he speaks her name, her terror subsides a little. The lurid reflections fade from the walls, the inhuman cries and noises die out and her own hoarse crying is calmed.*]

DOCTOR   Miss DuBois.

[*She turns her face to him and stares at him with desperate pleading. He smiles; then he speaks to the* MATRON.]

It won't be necessary.

BLANCHE [*faintly*]   Ask her to let go of me.

DOCTOR [*to the* MATRON]   Let go.

[*The* MATRON *releases her.* BLANCHE *extends her hands toward the* DOCTOR. *He draws her up gently and supports her with his arm and leads her through the portieres.*]

BLANCHE [*holding tight to his arm*]   Whoever you are—I have always depended on the kindness of strangers.

[*The poker players stand back as* BLANCHE *and the* DOCTOR *cross the kitchen to the front door. She allows him to lead her as if she were blind. As they go out on the porch,* STELLA *cries out her sister's name from where she is crouched a few steps up on the stairs.*]

STELLA   Blanche! Blanche, Blanche!

[BLANCHE *walks on without turning, followed by the* DOCTOR *and the* MATRON. *They go around the corner of the building.* EUNICE *descends to* STELLA *and places the child in her arms. It is wrapped in a pale blue blanket.* STELLA *accepts the child, sobbingly.* EUNICE *continues downstairs and enters the kitchen where the men, except for* STANLEY, *are returning silently to their places about the table.* STANLEY *has gone out on the porch and stands at the foot of the steps looking at* STELLA.]

STANLEY [*a bit uncertainly*]   Stella?

[*She sobs with inhuman abandon. There is something luxurious in her complete surrender to crying now that her sister is gone.*]

STANLEY [*voluptuously, soothingly*]   Now, honey. Now, love. Now, now, love. [*He kneels beside her and his fingers find the opening of her blouse.*] Now, now, love. Now, love. . . .

[*The luxurious sobbing, the sensual murmur fade away under the swelling music of the "Blue Piano" and the muted trumpet.*]

STEVE   This game is seven-card stud.

CURTAIN

1947

JOHN CHEEVER
1912–1982

" I t seems to me that man's inclination toward light, toward brightness, is very
nearly botanical—and I mean spiritual light. One not only needs it, one struggles for it." These sentences from an interview with John Cheever, conducted by the
novelist John Hersey, at first glance look strange coming from a "*New Yorker* writer"
of entertaining stories in which harried, well-to-do, white middle-class suburbanites
conduct their lives. "Our Chekhov of the exurbs," he was dubbed by the reviewer
John Leonard, with reference to the mythical community of Shady Hill (which
Cheever created along the lines of existing ones in Fairfield, Connecticut, or Westchester County, New York). Yet Chekhov's own characters, living in darkness, aspire
toward "spiritual light," with a similarly "botanical" inclination. Trapped in their
beautifully appointed houses and neighborhoods but carried along by the cool,
effortless prose of their creator, Cheever's characters are viewed with a sympathetic
irony, well-seasoned by sadness.

Cheever's early years were not notably idyllic, and he displays little nostalgia for
a lost childhood. Born in Quincy, Massachusetts, he grew up in what he describes
as shabby gentility, with his father departing the family when his son was fifteen.
(Cheever had an older brother, Fred, with whom he formed a strong but troubled
relationship.) Two years later his father lost the family's money in the crash of 1929,
and by that time Cheever had been expelled from Thayer Academy, in Braintree.
The expulsion marked the end of his formal education and the beginning of his
career as a writer; for, remarkably, he wrote a short story about the experience,
titled it "Expelled," and sent it to the *New Republic*, where Malcolm Cowley (who
would become a lifelong friend) published it.

During the 1930s Cheever lived in New York City, in impoverished circumstances,
taking odd jobs to support himself and winning a fellowship to the writer's colony at
Yaddo, in Saratoga Springs, New York. His New York life would provide the material
for many of his early stories, whose protagonists are rather frequently in desperate
economic situations. With the coming of World War II, Cheever joined the armed
forces and served in the Pacific theater but saw no combat. In 1941 he married Mary
Winternitz. About the marriage, which produced three children and lasted through
four decades, Cheever said, "That two people—both of us tempermental, quarrelsome, and intensely ambitious—could have gotten along for such a vast period of
time is for me a very good example of the boundlessness of human nature." Meanwhile, with the help of Malcolm Cowley, he began to publish in the *New Yorker*, and
in 1943, while he was serving in the military, his first book of stories (*The Way Some
People Live*) was published to favorable reviews. Over the decades to follow the stories continued to appear, largely in the *New Yorker*, where he became—along with
J. D. Salinger and John Updike—a recurrent phenomenon. Five further volumes of
short fiction were published, and in 1978 *The Stories of John Cheever* gathered those
he wished to be remembered for.

Although he is praised for his skill as a realist depictor of suburban manners and
morals, Cheever's art cannot be adequately understood in such terms alone. As Stephen
C. Moore has pointed out, "His best stories move from a base in a mimetic presentation of surface reality—the *scenery* of apparently successful American middle
class life—to fables of heroism." Cheever's embattled heroes express themselves in
taking up challenges that are essentially fabulous, and foolhardy: swimming home

across the backyard pools of Westchester ("The Swimmer," printed here); performing feats of physical daredeviltry in suburban living rooms ("O Youth and Beauty"); or dealing with the myriad demands and temptations that beset the hero who, having escaped death in an airplane, returns home to more severe trials ("The Country Husband"). Whatever the specific narrative, we are always aware of the storyteller's art, shaping ordinary life into the odder, more willful figures of fantasy and romance.

While Cheever will be remembered primarily as a short-story writer, his output includes a respectable number of novels. In 1957 he won a National Book Award for his first one, *The Wapshot Chronicle* (it was followed by *The Wapshot Scandal*, in 1964), notable for its New England seacoast setting and domestic flavor, if less so for a continuously engaging narrative line. Perhaps his most gripping novel is *Bullet Park* (1969), which, like the best of the stories, is both realistic and fabulous. The suburban milieu, seen from the 5:42 train from New York, has never been depicted more accurately, even lovingly, by Cheever. And as is to be expected, his protagonist's carefully built, pious suburban existence turns out to be a mess. The novel provoked interesting disagreement about its merits (some critics felt the narrative manipulations both ruthless and sentimental), but there was no disagreement about the vivid quality of its represented life, on the commuter train or at the cocktail party. In the years just previous to his death, and after a bout with alcohol and drug addiction, Cheever published his two final novels, *Falconer* (1978) and *Oh What a Paradise It Seems* (1980), the former receiving much praise for its harrowing rendering of prison life. (Farragut, the novel's hero, is sent to Falconer Prison for killing his brother; Cheever lived in Ossining, New York, home of Sing Sing Prison, during his later years.)

From the beginning to the end of his career he was and remained a thoroughly professional writer, wary of pronouncing on the world at large (there is a noticeable absence of politics and ideology in his work) or on the meaning and significance of his own art. As one sees from his *Journals* (1991), he agonized over the disruptive facts of his alcoholism and his homosexuality. But he remained a private man, seemingly untouched by experiments—or fads—in fiction writing. Whether or not, as T. S. Eliot said about Henry James, he had a mind so fine that no idea could violate it, Cheever remained firmly resistant to ideas of all sorts. This insular tendency is probably a reason why his work makes less than a "major" claim on us, but it is also the condition responsible for his devoted and scrupulous attention to the particularities of middle-class life at the far edge of its promised dream.

This text of "The Swimmer" is from *The Brigadier and the Golf Widow* (1964).

The Swimmer

It was one of those midsummer Sundays when everyone sits around saying: "I *drank* too much last night." You might have heard it whispered by the parishioners leaving church, heard it from the lips of the priest himself, struggling with his cassock in the *vestiarium*,[1] heard it from the golf links and the tennis courts, heard it from the wildlife preserve where the leader of the Audubon group was suffering from a terrible hangover. "I *drank* too much," said Donald Westerhazy. "We all *drank* too much," said Lucinda Merrill. "It must have been the wine," said Helen Westerhazy. "I *drank* too much of that claret."

This was at the edge of the Westerhazys' pool. The pool, fed by an artesian well with a high iron content, was a pale shade of green. It was a fine

---

1. Cloakroom for religious vestments adjacent to a church's sanctuary.

day. In the west there was a massive stand of cumulus cloud so like a city seen from a distance—from the bow of an approaching ship—that it might have had a name. Lisbon. Hackensack.[2] The sun was hot. Neddy Merrill sat by the green water, one hand in it, one around a glass of gin. He was a slender man—he seemed to have the especial slenderness of youth—and while he was far from young he had slid down his banister that morning and given the bronze backside of Aphrodite[3] on the hall table a smack, as he jogged toward the smell of coffee in his dining room. He might have been compared to a summer's day, particularly the last hours of one, and while he lacked a tennis racket or a sail bag the impression was definitely one of youth, sport, and clement weather. He had been swimming and now he was breathing deeply, stertorously as if he could gulp into his lungs the components of that moment, the heat of the sun, the intenseness of his pleasure. It all seemed to flow into his chest. His own house stood in Bullet Park,[4] eight miles to the south, where his four beautiful daughters would have had their lunch and might be playing tennis. Then it occurred to him that by taking a dogleg to the south-west he could reach his home by water.

His life was not confining and the delight he took in this observation could not be explained by its suggestion of escape. He seemed to see, with a cartographer's eye, that string of swimming pools, that quasi-subterranean stream that curved across the county. He had made a discovery, a contribution to modern geography; he would name the stream Lucinda after his wife. He was not a practical joker nor was he a fool but he was determinedly original and had a vague and modest idea of himself as a legendary figure. The day was beautiful and it seemed to him that a long swim might enlarge and celebrate its beauty.

He took off a sweater that was hung over his shoulders and dove in. He had an inexplicable contempt for men who did not hurl themselves into pools. He swam a choppy crawl, breathing either with every stroke or every fourth stroke and counting somewhere well in the back of his mind the one-two one-two of a flutter kick. It was not a serviceable stroke for long distances but the domestication of swimming had saddled the sport with some customs and in his part of the world a crawl was customary. To be embraced and sustained by the light green water was less a pleasure, it seemed, than the resumption of a natural condition, and he would have liked to swim without trunks, but this was not possible, considering his project. He hoisted himself up on the far curb—he never used the ladder—and started across the lawn. When Lucinda asked where he was going he said he was going to swim home.

The only maps and charts he had to go by were remembered or imaginary but these were clear enough. First there were the Grahams, the Hammers, the Lears, the Howlands, and the Crosscups. He would cross Ditmar Street to the Bunkers and come, after a short portage, to the Levys, the Welchers, and the public pool in Lancaster. Then there were the Hallorans, the Sachses, the Biswangers, Shirley Adams, the Gilmartins, and the Clydes. The day was lovely, and that he lived in a world so generously supplied with water seemed like a clemency, a beneficence. His heart was high and he ran across the grass. Making his way home by an uncommon route gave him

2. A town in New Jersey. Lisbon is the capital of Portugal.
3. Greek goddess of love and beauty.
4. Fictive suburb used as a location for many of Cheever's stories and novels.

the feeling that he was a pilgrim, an explorer, a man with a destiny, and he knew that he would find friends all along the way; friends would line the banks of the Lucinda River.

He went through a hedge that separated the Westerhazys' land from the Grahams', walked under some flowering apple trees, passed the shed that housed their pump and filter, and came out at the Grahams' pool. "Why, Neddy," Mrs. Graham said, "what a marvelous surprise. I've been trying to get you on the phone all morning. Here, let me get you a drink." He saw then, like any explorer, that the hospitable customs and traditions of the natives would have to be handled with diplomacy if he was ever going to reach his destination. He did not want to mystify or seem rude to the Grahams nor did he have the time to linger there. He swam the length of their pool and joined them in the sun and was rescued, a few minutes later, by the arrival of two carloads of friends from Connecticut. During the uproarious reunions he was able to slip away. He went down by the front of the Grahams' house, stepped over a thorny hedge, and crossed a vacant lot to the Hammers'. Mrs. Hammer, looking up from her roses, saw him swim by although she wasn't quite sure who it was. The Lears heard him splashing past the open windows of their living room. The Howlands and the Crosscups were away. After leaving the Howlands' he crossed Ditmar Street and started for the Bunkers', where he could hear, even at that distance, the noise of a party.

The water refracted the sound of voices and laughter and seemed to suspend it in midair. The Bunkers' pool was on a rise and he climbed some stairs to a terrace where twenty-five or thirty men and women were drinking. The only person in the water was Rusty Towers, who floated there on a rubber raft. Oh how bonny and lush were the banks of the Lucinda River! Prosperous men and women gathered by the sapphire-colored waters while caterer's men in white coats passed them cold gin. Overhead a red de Haviland trainer was circling around and around and around in the sky with something like the glee of a child in a swing. Ned felt a passing affection for the scene, a tenderness for the gathering, as if it was something he might touch. In the distance he heard thunder. As soon as Enid Bunker saw him she began to scream: "Oh look who's here! What a marvelous surprise! When Lucinda said that you couldn't come I thought I'd *die.*" She made her way to him through the crowd, and when they had finished kissing she led him to the bar, a progress that was slowed by the fact that he stopped to kiss eight or ten other women and shake the hands of as many men. A smiling bartender he had seen at a hundred parties gave him a gin and tonic and he stood by the bar for a moment, anxious not to get stuck in any conversation that would delay his voyage. When he seemed about to be surrounded he dove in and swam close to the side to avoid colliding with Rusty's raft. At the far end of the pool he bypassed the Tomlinsons with a broad smile and jogged up the garden path. The gravel cut his feet but this was the only unpleasantness. The party was confined to the pool, and as he went toward the house he heard the brilliant, watery sound of voices fade, heard the noise of a radio from the Bunkers' kitchen, where someone was listening to a ballgame. Sunday afternoon. He made his way through the parked cars and down the grassy border of their driveway to Alewives' Lane. He did not want to be seen on the road in his bathing trunks but there was no traffic and he made the short distance to the Levys' driveway, marked with a private property sign and a green tube for the *New York Times.* All the doors and windows of the big house were open but there were no signs of life; not even a dog barked. He went around the side of the house to the pool and saw that the Levys had only recently left. Glasses and bottles and dishes of nuts were on a table at the deep end, where there was a bathhouse or gazebo, hung with Japanese lanterns. After swimming the pool he got himself a glass and poured a drink. It was his fourth or fifth drink and he had swum nearly half the length of the Lucinda River. He felt tired, clean, and pleased at that moment to be alone; pleased with everything.

It would storm. The stand of cumulus cloud—that city—had risen and darkened, and while he sat there he heard the percussiveness of thunder again. The de Haviland trainer was still circling overhead and it seemed to Ned that he could almost hear the pilot laugh with pleasure in the afternoon; but when there was another peal of thunder he took off for home. A train whistle blew and he wondered what time it had gotten to be. Four? Five? He thought of the provincial station at that hour, where a waiter, his tuxedo concealed by a raincoat, a dwarf with some flowers wrapped in newspaper, and a woman who had been crying would be waiting for the local. It was suddenly growing dark; it was that moment when the pin-headed birds seem to organize their song into some acute and knowledgeable recognition of the storm's approach. Then there was a fine noise of rushing water from the crown of an oak at his back, as if a spigot there had been turned. Then the noise of fountains came from the crowns of all the tall trees. Why did he love storms, what was the meaning of his excitement when the door sprang open and the rain wind fled rudely up the stairs, why had the simple task of shutting the windows of an old house seemed fitting and urgent, why did the first watery notes of a storm wind have for him the unmistakable sound of good news, cheer, glad tidings? Then there was an explosion, a smell of cordite, and rain lashed the Japanese lanterns that Mrs. Levy had bought in Kyoto the year before last, or was it the year before that?

He stayed in the Levys' gazebo until the storm had passed. The rain had cooled the air and he shivered. The force of the wind had stripped a maple of its red and yellow leaves and scattered them over the grass and the water. Since it was midsummer the tree must be blighted, and yet he felt a peculiar sadness at this sign of autumn. He braced his shoulders, emptied his glass, and started for the Welchers' pool. This meant crossing the Lindleys' riding ring and he was surprised to find it overgrown with grass and all the jumps dismantled. He wondered if the Lindleys had sold their horses or gone away for the summer and put them out to board. He seemed to remember having heard something about the Lindleys and their horses but the memory was unclear. On he went, barefoot through the wet grass, to the Welchers', where he found their pool was dry.

This breach in his chain of water disappointed him absurdly, and he felt like some explorer who seeks a torrential headwater and finds a dead stream. He was disappointed and mystified. It was common enough to go away for the summer but no one ever drained his pool. The Welchers had definitely gone away. The pool furniture was folded, stacked, and covered with a tarpaulin. The bathhouse was locked. All the windows of the house were shut, and when he went around to the driveway in front he saw a for-sale sign nailed to a tree. When had he last heard from the Welchers—when, that is, had he and Lucinda last regretted an invitation to dine with them? It seemed only a week or so ago. Was his memory failing or had he so disciplined it in the repression of unpleasant facts that he had damaged his sense of the truth? Then in the distance he heard the sound of a tennis game. This cheered him, cleared away all his apprehensions and let him regard the overcast sky and the cold air with indifference. This was the day that Neddy Merrill swam across the county. That was the day! He started off then for his most difficult portage.

Had you gone for a Sunday afternoon ride that day you might have seen him, close to naked, standing on the shoulders of route 424, waiting for a chance to cross. You might have wondered if he was the victim of foul play, had his car broken down, or was he merely a fool. Standing barefoot in the deposits of the highway—beer cans, rags, and blowout patches—exposed to all kinds of ridicule, he seemed pitiful. He had known when he started that this was a part of his journey—it had been on his maps—but confronted with the lines of traffic, worming through the summery light, he found himself unprepared. He was laughed at, jeered at, a beer can was thrown at him, and he had no dignity or humor to bring to the situation. He could have gone back, back to the Westerhazys', where Lucinda would still be sitting in the sun. He had signed nothing, vowed nothing, pledged nothing, not even to himself. Why, believing as he did, that all human obduracy was susceptible to common sense, was he unable to turn back? Why was he determined to complete his journey even if it meant putting his life in danger? At what point had this prank, this joke, this piece of horseplay become serious? He could not go back, he could not even recall with any clearness the green water at the Wester-hazys', the sense of inhaling the day's components, the friendly and relaxed voices saying that they had *drunk* too much. In the space of an hour, more or less, he had covered a distance that made his return impossible.

An old man, tooling down the highway at fifteen miles an hour, let him get to the middle of the road, where there was a grass divider. Here he was exposed to the ridicule of the northbound traffic, but after ten or fifteen minutes he was able to cross. From here he had only a short walk to the Recreation Center at the edge of the Village of Lancaster, where there were some handball courts and a public pool.

The effect of the water on voices, the illusion of brilliance and suspense, was the same here as it had been at the Bunkers' but the sounds here were louder, harsher, and more shrill, and as soon as he entered the crowded enclosure he was confronted with regimentation. "ALL SWIMMERS MUST TAKE A SHOWER BEFORE USING THE POOL. ALL SWIMMERS MUST USE THE FOOTBATH. ALL SWIMMERS MUST WEAR THEIR IDENTIFICATION DISKS." He took a shower, washed his feet in a cloudy and bitter solution and made his way to the edge of the water. It stank of chlorine and looked to him like a sink. A pair of life-guards in a pair of towers blew police whistles at what seemed to be regular intervals and abused the swimmers through a public address system. Neddy remembered the sapphire water at the Bunkers' with longing and thought that he might contaminate himself—damage his own prosperousness and charm—by swimming in this murk, but he reminded himself that he was an explorer, a pilgrim, and that this was merely a stagnant bend in the Lucinda River. He dove, scowling with distaste, into the chlorine and had to swim with his head above water to avoid collisions, but even so he was bumped into, splashed and jostled. When he got to the shallow end both lifeguards were shouting at him: "Hey, you, you without the identification disk, get outa the water." He did, but they had no way of pursuing him and he went through the reek of suntan oil and chlorine out through the hurricane fence and passed the handball courts. By crossing the road he entered the wooded part of the Halloran estate. The woods were not cleared and the footing was treacherous and difficult until he reached the lawn and the clipped beech hedge that encircled their pool.

The Hallorans were friends, an elderly couple of enormous wealth who seemed to bask in the suspicion that they might be Communists. They were zealous reformers but they were not Communists, and yet when they were accused, as they sometimes were, of subversion, it seemed to gratify and excite them. Their beech hedge was yellow and he guessed this had been blighted like the Levys' maple. He called hullo, hullo, to warn the Hallorans of his approach, to palliate his invasion of their privacy. The Hallorans, for reasons that had never been explained to him, did not wear bathing suits. No explanations were in order, really. Their nakedness was a detail in their uncompromising zeal for reform and he stepped politely out of his trunks before he went through the opening in the hedge.

Mrs. Halloran, a stout woman with white hair and a serene face, was reading the *Times*. Mr. Halloran was taking beech leaves out of the water with a scoop. They seemed not surprised or displeased to see him. Their pool was perhaps the oldest in the county, a fieldstone rectangle, fed by a brook. It had no filter or pump and its waters were the opaque gold of the stream.

"I'm swimming across the county," Ned said.

"Why, I didn't know one could," exclaimed Mrs. Halloran.

"Well, I've made it from the Westerhazys'," Ned said. "That must be about four miles."

He left his trunks at the deep end, walked to the shallow end, and swam this stretch. As he was pulling himself out of the water he heard Mrs. Halloran say: "We've been *terribly* sorry to hear about all your misfortunes, Neddy."

"My misfortunes?" Ned asked. "I don't know what you mean."

"Why, we heard that you'd sold the house and that your poor children . . ."

"I don't recall having sold the house," Ned said, "and the girls are at home."

"Yes," Mrs. Halloran sighed. "Yes . . ." Her voice filled the air with an unseasonable melancholy and Ned spoke briskly. "Thank you for the swim."

"Well, have a nice trip," said Mrs. Halloran.

Beyond the hedge he pulled on his trunks and fastened them. They were loose and he wondered if, during the space of an afternoon, he could have lost some weight. He was cold and he was tired and the naked Hallorans and their dark water had depressed him. The swim was too much for his strength but how could he have guessed this, sliding down the banister that morning and sitting in the Westerhazys' sun? His arms were lame. His legs felt rubbery and ached at the joints. The worst of it was the cold in his bones and the feeling that he might never be warm again. Leaves were falling down around him and he smelled woodsmoke on the wind. Who would be burning wood at this time of year?

He needed a drink. Whiskey would warm him, pick him up, carry him through the last of his journey, refresh his feeling that it was original and valorous to swim across the county. Channel swimmers took brandy. He needed a stimulant. He crossed the lawn in front of the Hallorans' house and went down a little path to where they had built a house for their only daughter Helen and her husband Eric Sachs. The Sachses' pool was small and he found Helen and her husband there.

"Oh, *Neddy*," Helen said. "Did you lunch at Mother's?"

"Not *really*," Ned said. "I *did* stop to see your parents." This seemed to be explanation enough. "I'm terribly sorry to break in on you like this but I've taken a chill and I wonder if you'd give me a drink."

"Why, I'd *love* to," Helen said, "but there hasn't been anything in this house to drink since Eric's operation. That was three years ago."

Was he losing his memory, had his gift for concealing painful facts let him forget that he had sold his house, that his children were in trouble, and that his friend had been ill? His eyes slipped from Eric's face to his abdomen, where he saw three pale, sutured scars, two of them at least a foot long. Gone was his navel, and what, Neddy thought, would the roving hand, bed-checking one's gifts at 3 A.M. make of a belly with no navel, no link to birth, this breach in the succession?

"I'm sure you can get a drink at the Biswangers'," Helen said. "They're having an enormous do. You can hear it from here. Listen!"

She raised her head and from across the road, the lawns, the gardens, the woods, the fields, he heard again the brilliant noise of voices over water. "Well, I'll get wet," he said, still feeling that he had no freedom of choice about his means of travel. He dove into the Sachses' cold water and, gasping, close to drowning, made his way from one end of the pool to the other. "Lucinda and I want *terribly* to see you," he said over his shoulder, his face set toward the Biswangers'. "We're sorry it's been so long and we'll call you *very* soon."

He crossed some fields to the Biswangers' and the sounds of revelry there. They would be honored to give him a drink, they would be happy to give him a drink, they would in fact be lucky to give him a drink. The Biswangers invited him and Lucinda for dinner four times a year, six weeks in advance. They were always rebuffed and yet they continued to send out their invitations, unwilling to comprehend the rigid and undemocratic realities of their society. They were the sort of people who discussed the price of things at cocktails, exchanged market tips during dinner, and after dinner told dirty stories to mixed company. They did not belong to Neddy's set—they were not even on Lucinda's Christmas card list. He went toward their pool with feelings of indifference, charity, and some unease, since it seemed to be getting dark and these were the longest days of the year. The party when he joined it was noisy and large. Grace Biswanger was the kind of hostess who asked the optometrist, the veterinarian, the real-estate dealer and the dentist. No one was swimming and the twilight, reflected on the water of the pool, had a wintry gleam. There was a bar and he started for this. When Grace Biswanger saw him she came toward him, not affectionately as he had every right to expect, but bellicosely.

"Why, this party has everything," she said loudly, "including a gate crasher."

She could not deal him a social blow—there was no question about this and he did not flinch. "As a gate crasher," he asked politely, "do I rate a drink?"

"Suit yourself," she said. "You don't seem to pay much attention to invitations."

She turned her back on him and joined some guests, and he went to the bar and ordered a whiskey. The bartender served him but he served him rudely. His was a world in which the caterer's men kept the social score, and to be rebuffed by a part-time barkeep meant that he had suffered some loss of social esteem. Or perhaps the man was new and uninformed. Then he heard Grace at his back say: "They went for broke overnight—nothing but income— and he showed up drunk one Sunday and asked us to loan him five thousand dollars. . . ." She was always talking about money. It was worse than eating your peas off a knife. He dove into the pool, swam its length and went away.

The next pool on his list, the last but two, belonged to his old mistress, Shirley Adams. If he had suffered any injuries at the Biswangers' they would be cured here. Love—sexual roughhouse in fact—was the supreme elixir, the painkiller, the brightly colored pill that would put the spring back into his step, the joy of life in his heart. They had had an affair last week, last month, last year. He couldn't remember. It was he who had broken it off, his was the upper hand, and he stepped through the gate of the wall that surrounded her pool with nothing so considered as self-confidence. It seemed in a way to be his pool as the lover, particularly the illicit lover, enjoys the possessions of his mistress with an authority unknown to holy matrimony. She was there, her hair the color of brass, but her figure, at the edge of the lighted, cerulean water, excited in him no profound memories. It had been, he thought, a light-hearted affair, although she had wept when he broke it off. She seemed confused to see him and he wondered if she was still wounded. Would she, God forbid, weep again?

"What do you want?" she asked.

"I'm swimming across the county."

"Good Christ. Will you ever grow up?"

"What's the matter?"

"If you've come here for money," she said, "I won't give you another cent."

"You could give me a drink."

"I could but I won't. I'm not alone."

"Well, I'm on my way."

He dove in and swam the pool, but when he tried to haul himself up onto the curb he found that the strength in his arms and his shoulders had gone, and he paddled to the ladder and climbed out. Looking over his shoulder he saw, in the lighted bathhouse, a young man. Going out onto the dark lawn he smelled chrysanthemums or marigolds—some stubborn autumnal fragrance—on the night air, strong as gas. Looking overhead he saw that the stars had come out, but why should he seem to see Andromeda, Cepheus, and Cassiopeia? What had become of the constellations of midsummer? He began to cry.

It was probably the first time in his adult life that he had ever cried, certainly the first time in his life that he had ever felt so miserable, cold, tired, and bewildered. He could not understand the rudeness of the caterer's barkeep or the rudeness of a mistress who had come to him on her knees and showered his trousers with tears. He had swum too long, he had been immersed too long, and his nose and his throat were sore from the water. What he needed then was a drink, some company, and some clean dry clothes, and while he could have cut directly across the road to his home he went on to the Gilmartins' pool. Here, for the first time in his life, he did not dive but went down the steps into the icy water and swam a hobbled side stroke that he might have learned as a youth. He staggered with fatigue on his way to the Clydes' and paddled the length of their pool, stopping again and again with his hand on the curb to rest. He climbed up the ladder and wondered if he had the strength to get home. He had done what he wanted, he had swum the county, but he was so stupefied with exhaustion that his triumph seemed vague. Stooped, holding onto the gateposts for support, he turned up the driveway of his house.

The place was dark. Was it so late that they had all gone to bed? Had Lucinda stayed at the Westerhazys' for supper? Had the girls joined her there or gone someplace else? Hadn't they agreed, as they usually did on Sunday, to regret all their invitations and stay at home? He tried the garage doors to see what cars were in but the doors were locked and rust came off the handles onto his hands. Going toward the house, he saw that the force of the thunderstorm had knocked one of the rain gutters loose. It hung down over the front door like an umbrella rib, but it could be fixed in the morning. The house was locked, and he thought that the stupid cook or the stupid maid must have locked the place up until he remembered that it had been some time since they had employed a maid or a cook. He shouted, pounded on the door, tried to force it with his shoulder, and then, looking in at the windows, saw that the place was empty.

1964

ROBERT HAYDEN
1913–1980

"Hayden is by far the best chronicler and rememberer of the African American heritage in these Americas that I know of," the poet Michael Harper, whose own sense of history is indebted to Robert Hayden's work, has said. Hayden's poems save what has vanished, what has been lost to standard histories, like a 1920s prizefighter from the Midwest ("Free Fantasia: Tiger Flowers") or a miner trapped in Crystal Cave ("Beginnings, V"). He records the loss of what others never noticed as missing, and in their recovery he discovers a significance in the passing moment, the passed-over figure, the inarticulate gesture, which lasts through time. Always, in his words, "opposed to the chauvinistic and the doctrinaire" in art, he cherished the freedom of the poet to write about whatever seized the imagination. But his imagination was in its nature elegiac and historical. As he remembers and re-creates the African American heritage, he speaks to the struggles of the individual spirit for freedom and to painful self-divisions known to the people of many times and places. But if the circumstances he confronts in his poems are often harsh, his work captures the energy and joyfulness that make survival possible.

Born in Detroit, Michigan, Hayden grew up in a poor neighborhood called by its inhabitants, with affectionate irony, "Paradise Valley." His powerful sequence *Elegies for Paradise Valley* (1978) resurrects the neighborhood in its racial and ethnic mix. Memory for Hayden is an act of love that leads to self-awareness; in this sequence and in poems like "Those Winter Sundays," he writes about his own past, confronts its pain, and preserves its sustaining moments of happiness.

Hayden had a deep understanding of the conflicts that divide the self. His family history gave him an early acquaintance with such self-division: his parents' marriage ended when he was young, and his mother left him in the care of foster parents (whose surname he adopted) when she left Detroit to look for work. He remained with the Haydens even after his mother returned to Detroit when he was a teenager and lived for a period with his foster family until conflict arose between her and his foster mother. "I lived in the midst of so much turmoil all the time I didn't know if I loved or hated," he once said. As an African American and as a poet Hayden also lived between worlds. He courageously maintained his sense of vocation through years of critical neglect and amid the demands of full-time teaching at Fisk University from 1946 to 1968. He published his first book, *Heart-Shape in the Dust*, in 1940, but his mature work did not appear in quantity until his volume *Ballad of Remembrance* (1962). At the same time his belief that the poet should not be restricted by any set of themes, racial or otherwise, and the highly formal quality of his work led to criticism by some young African American writers in the 1960s. But Hayden never abandoned his belief in the power of art to speak universally. In a 1974 interview he told Dennis Gendron of rereading Yeats's poem "Easter 1916" in the wake of the riots in Detroit— "that is the kind of poetry I want to write," he said, in admiration of the ways Yeats conceived a particular historical and political moment so that it speaks across time and place.

In fact, Hayden did himself write that kind of poetry. His most famous poem, "Middle Passage," demonstrates his transfiguring imagination and the knowledge of historical documents, which began early in his career. In 1936, after leaving college because of increasingly difficult economic conditions, Hayden joined the Federal Writers Project of the Works Progress Administration, and for two years he researched the history of abolition movements and the Underground Railroad in Michigan. "Middle Passage" is a collage of accounts of the slave ships that transported men and women from Africa into slavery in the New World. Through the multiple voices in the poem, Hayden lets the accounts of those who participated in (and profited from) the slave trade reveal the evidence of their own damnation. The blindness that attacks one of the ships becomes a symbol of the devastating suffering of those transported into slavery and of the moral blindness everywhere evident in the traders' accounts. The collage technique allows Hayden to suggest the fragmentation of the story; the silences in the poem evoke the missing voices of those who suffered and died on the voyages or in the intolerable conditions of slavery. At the heart of the poem is the account of a rebellion led by one of the slaves (Cinquez) on the ship *Amistad*. Cinquez is one of several figures in Hayden's poems who dramatize "The deep immortal human wish / the timeless will" ("Middle Passage") that for Hayden is the indomitable yearning for freedom. This "timeless will" and struggle also appear in his poems about Harriet Tubman ("Runagate Runagate"), Nat Turner, Frederick Douglass, Phillis Wheatley, and the later figures Paul Robeson and Bessie Smith.

Hayden's experiment with collage technique in "Middle Passage" connects him to modernist poets like T. S. Eliot and William Carlos Williams and to an African American tradition acutely aware of the power of voice. He continued to experiment with poetic form and with the creation of different voices, always testing the possibilities of craft and forging a language to express what he knew and felt. His sequences *Beginnings* and *Elegies for Paradise Valley* demonstrate his formal originality, as does his late poem "American Journal," with its long lines and its approximation to prose. Hayden loved language and was unafraid to be lushly descriptive as well as to be precisely imagistic. His work summons us to notice the world as we had not before and offers us candor, clearsightedness, and a transforming gaiety.

From 1968 until his death, Hayden was professor of English at the University of Michigan at Ann Arbor. In 1976 he became the first African American to be appointed poetry consultant to the Library of Congress, the position now known as poet laureate of the United States.

Middle Passage[1]

I

Jesús, Estrella, Esperanza, Mercy[2]

    Sails flashing to the wind like weapons,
    sharks following the moans the fever and the dying;
    horror the corposant and compass rose.[3]

Middle Passage:
        voyage through death   5
                to life upon these shores.

    "10 April 1800—
    Blacks rebellious. Crew uneasy. Our linguist says
    their moaning is a prayer for death,   10
    ours and their own. Some try to starve themselves.
    Lost three this morning leaped with crazy laughter
    to the waiting sharks, sang as they went under."

Desire, Adventure, Tartar, Ann:

    Standing to America, bringing home   15
    black gold, black ivory, black seed.

        Deep in the festering hold thy father lies,
        of his bones New England pews are made,
        those are altar lights that were his eyes.[4]

Jesus   Saviour   Pilot   Me   20
Over   Life's   Tempestuous   Sea[5]

We pray that Thou wilt grant, O Lord,
safe passage to our vessels bringing
heathen souls unto Thy chastening.

1. Main route for the slave trade in the Atlantic between Africa and the West Indies.
2. Names of slave ships. (*Estrella* and *Esperanza* are Spanish for "Star" and "Hope," respectively.)
3. Circle printed on a map showing compass directions. "Corposant": a fiery luminousness that can appear on the decks of ships during electrical storms.
4. "Full fathom five thy father lies; / Of his bones are coral made; / Those are pearls that were his eyes" (Shakespeare's *Tempest* 1.2.400–402). The sprite Ariel is singing about the supposed death by drowning of the king of Naples.
5. Words from a Protestant hymn.

Jesus   Saviour   25

    "8 bells. I cannot sleep, for I am sick
    with fear, but writing eases fear a little
    since still my eyes can see these words take shape
    upon the page & so I write, as one
    would turn to exorcism. 4 days scudding,   30
    but now the sea is calm again. Misfortune
    follows in our wake like sharks (our grinning
    tutelary gods). Which one of us
    has killed an albatross?[6] A plague among
    our blacks—Ophthalmia: blindness—& we   35
    have jettisoned the blind to no avail.
    It spreads, the terrifying sickness spreads.
    Its claws have scratched sight from the Capt.'s eyes
    & there is blindness in the fo'c'sle[7]
    & we must sail 3 weeks before we come   40
    to port."

        What port awaits us, Davy Jones'
        or home? I've heard of slavers drifting, drifting,
        playthings of wind and storm and chance, their crews
        gone blind, the jungle hatred   45
        crawling up on deck.

Thou   Who   Walked   On   Galilee

    "Deponent further sayeth *The Bella J*
    left the Guinea Coast
    with cargo of five hundred blacks and odd   50
    for the barracoons[8] of Florida:

    "That there was hardly room 'tween-decks for half
    the sweltering cattle stowed spoon-fashion there;
    that some went mad of thirst and tore their flesh
    and sucked the blood: 55

    "That Crew and Captain lusted with the comeliest
    of the savage girls kept naked in the cabins;
    that there was one they called The Guinea Rose
    and they cast lots and fought to lie with her:

    "That when the Bo's'n piped all hands,[9] the flames   60
    spreading from starboard already were beyond
    control, the negroes howling and their chains
    entangled with the flames:

---

6. A bird of good omen; to kill one is an unlucky and impious act (as in Samuel Taylor Coleridge's *Rime of the Ancient Mariner*).
7. Short for forecastle, the place in a ship where sailors are quartered.
8. Barracks or enclosures for slaves.
9. I.e., when the boatswain (petty officer aboard a ship) signaled to summon all the crew on deck.

"That the burning blacks could not be reached,
that the Crew abandoned ship,   65
leaving their shrieking negresses behind,
that the Captain perished drunken with the wenches:

"Further Deponent sayeth not."

Pilot   Oh   Pilot   Me

II

Aye, lad, and I have seen those factories,   70
Gambia, Rio Pongo, Calabar;[1]
have watched the artful mongos[2] baiting traps
of war wherein the victor and the vanquished

Were caught as prizes for our barracoons.
Have seen the nigger kings whose vanity   75
and greed turned wild black hides of Fellatah,
Mandingo, Ibo, Kru[3] to gold for us.

And there was one—King Anthracite we named him—
fetish face beneath French parasols
of brass and orange velvet, impudent mouth   80
whose cups were carven skulls of enemies:

He'd honor us with drum and feast and conjo[4]
and palm-oil-glistening wenches deft in love,
and for tin crowns that shone with paste,
red calico and German-silver trinkets   85

Would have the drums talk war and send
his warriors to burn the sleeping villages
and kill the sick and old and lead the young
in coffles[5] to our factories.

Twenty years a trader, twenty years,   90
for there was wealth aplenty to be harvested
from those black fields, and I'd be trading still
but for the fevers melting down my bones.

III

Shuttles in the rocking loom of history,
the dark ships move, the dark ships move,   95
their bright ironical names
like jests of kindness on a murderer's mouth;

---

1. A city in southeast Nigeria. Gambia is a river
and nation in West Africa. Rio Pongo is a water-
course, dry for most of the year, in East Africa.
2. I.e., Africans.

3. African tribes.
4. Dance.
5. Train of slaves fastened together.

plough through thrashing glister toward
fata morgana's lucent melting shore,
weave toward New World littorals[6] that are   100
mirage and myth and actual shore.

Voyage through death,
                voyage whose chartings are unlove.

A charnel stench, effluvium of living death
spreads outward from the hold,   105
where the living and the dead, the horribly dying,
lie interlocked, lie foul with blood and excrement.

> *Deep in the festering hold thy father lies,*
> *the corpse of mercy rots with him,*
> *rats eat love's rotten gelid eyes.*   110

But, oh, the living look at you
with human eyes whose suffering accuses you,
whose hatred reaches through the swill of dark
to strike you like a leper's claw.

You cannot stare that hatred down   115
or chain the fear that stalks the watches
and breathes on you its fetid scorching breath;
cannot kill the deep immortal human wish,
the timeless will.

> "But for the storm that flung up barriers   120
> of wind and wave, *The Amistad*,[7] señores,
> would have reached the port of Príncipe in two,
> three days at most; but for the storm we should
> have been prepared for what befell.
> Swift as the puma's leap it came. There was   125
> that interval of moonless calm filled only
> with the water's and the rigging's usual sounds,
> then sudden movement, blows and snarling cries
> and they had fallen on us with machete
> and marlinspike. It was as though the very   130
> air, the night itself were striking us.
> Exhausted by the rigors of the storm,
> we were no match for them. Our men went down
> before the murderous Africans. Our loyal
> Celestino ran from below with gun   135
> and lantern and I saw, before the cane-
> knife's wounding flash, Cinquez,
> that surly brute who calls himself a prince,

6. Coastal regions. "Fata morgana": mirage.
7. A Spanish ship—the name means "Friendship"—that carried fifty-three illegally obtained slaves out of Havana, Cuba, in July 1839. The slaves revolted and seized the ship.

directing, urging on the ghastly work.[8]
He hacked the poor mulatto down, and then   140
he turned on me. The decks were slippery
when daylight finally came. It sickens me
to think of what I saw, of how these apes
threw overboard the butchered bodies of
our men, true Christians all, like so much jetsam.   145
Enough, enough. The rest is quickly told:
Cinquez was forced to spare the two of us
you see to steer the ship to Africa,
and we like phantoms doomed to rove the sea
voyaged east by day and west by night,   150
deceiving them, hoping for rescue,
prisoners on our own vessel, till
at length we drifted to the shores of this
your land, America, where we were freed
from our unspeakable misery. Now we   155
demand, good sirs, the extradition of
Cinquez and his accomplices to La
Havana.[9] And it distresses us to know
there are so many here who seem inclined
to justify the mutiny of these blacks.   160
We find it paradoxical indeed
that you whose wealth, whose tree of liberty
are rooted in the labor of your slaves
should suffer the august John Quincy Adams
to speak with so much passion of the right   165
of chattel slaves to kill their lawful masters
and with his Roman rhetoric weave a hero's
garland for Cinquez.[1] I tell you that
we are determined to return to Cuba
with our slaves and there see justice done. Cinquez—   170
or let us say 'the Prince'—Cinquez shall die."

The deep immortal human wish,
the timeless will:

Cinquez its deathless primaveral image,
life that transfigures many lives.   175

Voyage through death
          to life upon these shores.

                                                    1962

---

8. During the mutiny the Africans, led by a man called Cinqué, or Cinquez, killed the captain, his slave Celestino, and the mate, but spared the two slave owners.
9. After two months the *Amistad* reached Long Island Sound, where it was detained by the American ship *Washington*, the slaves were imprisoned, and the owners were freed. The owners began litigation to return the slaves to Havana to be tried for murder.
1. The case reached the Supreme Court in 1841; the Africans were defended by former president John Quincy Adams, and the court released the thirty-seven survivors to return to Africa.

Homage to the Empress of the Blues[1]

Because there was a man somewhere in a candystripe silk shirt,
gracile and dangerous as a jaguar and because a woman moaned for him
in sixty-watt gloom and mourned him Faithless Love
Twotiming Love Oh Love Oh Careless Aggravating Love,

    She came out on the stage in yards of pearls, emerging like   5
    a favorite scenic view, flashed her golden smile and sang.

Because grey laths began somewhere to show from underneath
torn hurdygurdy[2] lithographs of dollfaced heaven;
and because there were those who feared alarming fists of snow
on the door and those who feared the riot-squad of statistics,   10

    She came out on the stage in ostrich feathers, beaded satin,
    and shone that smile on us and sang.

                    1962

Those Winter Sundays

    Sundays too my father got up early
    and put his clothes on in the blueblack cold,
    then with cracked hands that ached
    from labor in the weekday weather made
    banked fires blaze. No one ever thanked him.   5

    I'd wake and hear the cold splintering, breaking.
    When the rooms were warm, he'd call,
    and slowly I would rise and dress,
    fearing the chronic angers of that house,

    Speaking indifferently to him,   10
    who had driven out the cold
    and polished my good shoes as well.
    What did I know, what did I know
    of love's austere and lonely offices?

                    1962

1. Bessie Smith (1895–1937), one of the greatest American blues singers. Her flamboyant style, which grew out of the black vaudeville tradition, made her popular in the 1920s.

2. A disreputable kind of dance hall, so called because of the hurdy-gurdies (barrel organs) that provided the music for dancing. "Laths": the strips of wood that form a backing for wall plaster.

Free Fantasia: Tiger Flowers[1]

for Michael

The sporting people
along St. Antoine—[2]
that scufflers'
paradise of ironies—
            bet salty money   5
on his righteous
            hook and jab.

I was a boy then, running
(unbeknownst to Pa)
errands for Miss Jackie   10
and Stack-o'-Diamonds' Eula Mae.
. . . Their perfumes,
rouged Egyptian faces.
            Their pianolas jazzing.

O Creole babies,   15
Dixie odalisques,[3]
speeding through cutglass
dark to see the macho angel
            trick you'd never
turn, his bluesteel prowess   20
            in the ring.

Hardshell believers
amen'd the wreck
as God A'mighty's
will. I'd thought   25
            such gaiety could not
die. Nor could our
            elegant avenger.

The Virgin Forest
by Rousseau[4]—   30
its psychedelic flowers
towering, its deathless
            dark dream figure
death the leopard
            claws—I choose it   35
now as elegy
            for Tiger Flowers.

                                                    1975

---

1. A midwestern boxer (1895–1927) who in 1926 became the first African American middleweight champion.
2. Street in Detroit, Michigan.
3. Female slaves or concubines in a harem.
4. Henri Rousseau (1844–1910), French painter known for jungle scenes and exotic colors.

RANDALL JARRELL
1914–1965

"Monstrously knowing and monstrously innocent. . . . A Wordsworth with the obsession of a Lewis Carroll"—so Robert Lowell once described his friend and fellow poet Randall Jarrell. Jarrell was a teacher and a critic as well as a poet, and for many writers of his generation—Lowell, Delmore Schwartz, and John Berryman among them—he was the critic whose taste was most unerring, who seemed to know instantly what was genuine and what was not. An extraordinary teacher, he loved the activity of teaching, both in and out of the classroom; "the gods who had taken away the poet's audience had given him students," he once said. The novelist Peter Taylor recalls that when he came to Vanderbilt University as a freshman in the mid-1930s, Jarrell, then a graduate student, had already turned the literary students into disciples; he held court discussing Chekhov on the sidelines of touch football games. For all his brilliance Jarrell was, at heart, democratic. Believing that poetry belongs to every life, his teaching, his literary criticism, and his poetry aimed to recapture and reeducate a general audience lost to poetry in an age of specialization. Jarrell's interests were democratic as well, and he had a lifelong fascination with popular culture. Witty and incisive, Jarrell could be intimidating; at the same time he remained deeply in touch with childhood's mystery and enchantment. It was as if, his close friend the philosopher Hannah Arendt once said, he "had emerged from the enchanted forests." He loved fairy tales, translated a number of them, and wrote several books for children, among them *The Bat-Poet* (1964). The childlike quality of the person informs Jarrell's poems as well; he is unembarrassed by the adult heart still in thrall to childhood's wishes.

Jarrell was born in Nashville, Tennessee, but spent much of his childhood in Long Beach, California. After his parents divorced when he was eleven, he remained for a year with his grandparents in Hollywood, then returned to live with his mother in Nashville. He majored in psychology at Vanderbilt and stayed on there to do graduate work in English. In 1937 he left Nashville to teach at Kenyon College (Gambier, Ohio) at the invitation of his old Vanderbilt professor John Crowe Ransom, the New Critic and Fugitive poet. From that time on Jarrell almost always had some connection with a university: after Kenyon, the University of Texas, Sarah Lawrence College, and from 1947 until his death, the Women's College of the University of North Carolina at Greensboro. But, as suggested by his novel *Pictures from an Institution* (1954) with its mixed satiric and tender views of academic life, he was never satisfied with a cloistered education. As poetry editor of *The Nation* (1946), and then in a series of essays and reviews collected as *Poetry and the Age* (1953), he introduced readers to the work of his contemporaries—Elizabeth Bishop, Robert Lowell, John Berryman, the William Carlos Williams of *Paterson*—and influentially reassessed the reputations of Walt Whitman and Robert Frost.

Among the poets who emerged after World War II, Jarrell stands out for his colloquial plainness. While others—Richard Wilbur and the early Robert Lowell, for example—were writing highly structured poems with complicated imagery, Jarrell's work feels and sounds close to what he calls in one poem the "dailiness of life" ("Well Water"). He is master of the everyday heartbreak and identifies with ordinary forms of loneliness. Jarrell's gift of imaginative sympathy appears in the treatment of soldiers in his war poems, the strongest to come out of World War II. He had been trained as an Army Air Force pilot and after that as a control operator,

The Gotham Book Mart. This midtown Manhattan store was famous for its literary eminences. A December 1948 party drew a roomful of midcentury writers, including, clockwise, W. H. Auden on the ladder, Elizabeth Bishop, Delmore Schwartz, Randall Jarrell, Charles Henri Ford, William Rose Benét, Stephen Spender, Marya Zaturenska, Horace Gregory, Tennessee Williams, Richard Eberhart, Gore Vidal, and José Garcia Villa.

and he had a sense of the war's special casualties. With their understanding of soldiers as both destructive and innocent at the same time, these poems make his volumes *Little Friend, Little Friend* (1945) and *Losses* (1948) powerful and moving. Jarrell also empathized with the dreams, loneliness, and disappointments of women, whose perspective he often adopted, as in the title poem of his collection *The Woman at the Washington Zoo* (1960) and his poem "Next Day."

Against the blasted or unrealized possibilities of adult life Jarrell often poised the rich mysteries of childhood. The title poem of his last book, *The Lost World* (1965), looks back to his Los Angeles playtime, the movie sets and plaster dinosaurs and pterodactyls against whose eternal lighthearted presence he measures his own aging. The poem has Jarrell's characteristic sense of loss but also his capacity for a mysterious happiness, which animates the poem even as he holds "nothing" in his hands.

Jarrell suffered a nervous breakdown in February 1965, but returned to teaching that fall. In October he was struck by a car and died. His *Complete Poems* were published posthumously (1969), as were a translation of Goethe's *Faust*, Part I, in preparation at his death, and two books of essays, *The Third Book of Criticism* (1969) and *Kipling, Auden & Co.* (1980).

90 North[1]

At home, in my flannel gown, like a bear to its floe,
I clambered to bed; up the globe's impossible sides
I sailed all night—till at last, with my black beard,
My furs and my dogs, I stood at the northern pole.

There in the childish night my companions lay frozen,   5
The stiff furs knocked at my starveling throat,
And I gave my great sigh: the flakes came huddling,
Were they really my end? In the darkness I turned to my rest.

—Here, the flag snaps in the glare and silence
Of the unbroken ice. I stand here,   10
The dogs bark, my beard is black, and I stare
At the North Pole . . .
                    And now what? Why, go back.

Turn as I please, my step is to the south.
The world—my world spins on this final point
Of cold and wretchedness: all lines, all winds   15
End in this whirlpool I at last discover.

And it is meaningless. In the child's bed
After the night's voyage, in that warm world
Where people work and suffer for the end
That crowns the pain—in that Cloud-Cuckoo-Land[2]   20

I reached my North and it had meaning.
Here at the actual pole of my existence,
Where all that I have done is meaningless,
Where I die or live by accident alone—

Where, living or dying, I am still alone;   25
Here where North, the night, the berg of death
Crowd me out of the ignorant darkness,
I see at last that all the knowledge

I wrung from the darkness—that the darkness flung me—
Is worthless as ignorance: nothing comes from nothing,   30
The darkness from the darkness. Pain comes from the darkness
And we call it wisdom. It is pain.

                                                    1942

1. The latitude of the North Pole.
2. A fantasy world; in Aristophanes' comedy *The* *Birds* (414 B.C.E.), an imaginary city the cuckoos build in the sky.

The Death of the Ball Turret Gunner[1]

From my mother's sleep I fell into the State,
And I hunched in its belly till my wet fur froze.
Six miles from earth, loosed from its dream of life,
I woke to black flak[2] and the nightmare fighters.
When I died they washed me out of the turret with a hose.   5

1945

Second Air Force

Far off, above the plain the summer dries,
The great loops of the hangars sway like hills.
Buses and weariness and loss, the nodding soldiers
Are wire, the bare frame building, and a pass
To what was hers; her head hides his square patch   5
And she thinks heavily: My son is grown.
She sees a world: sand roads, tar-paper barracks,
The bubbling asphalt of the runways, sage,
The dunes rising to the interminable ranges,
The dim flights moving over clouds like clouds.   10
The armorers in their patched faded green,
Sweat-stiffened, banded with brass cartridges,
Walk to the line; their Fortresses,[1] all tail,
Stand wrong and flimsy on their skinny legs,
And the crews climb to them clumsily as bears.   15
The head withdraws into its hatch (a boy's),
The engines rise to their blind laboring roar,
And the green, made beasts run home to air.
Now in each aspect death is pure.
(At twilight they wink over men like stars   20
And hour by hour, through the night, some see
The great lights floating in—from Mars, from Mars.)
How emptily the watchers see them gone.

They go, there is silence; the woman and her son
Stand in the forest of the shadows, and the light   25
Washes them like water. In the long-sunken city
Of evening, the sunlight stills like sleep
The faint wonder of the drowned; in the evening,
In the last dreaming light, so fresh, so old,

---

1. A ball turret was a plexiglass sphere set into the belly of a B-17 or B-24 [bomber], and inhabited by two .50 caliber machine-guns and one man, a short, small man. When this gunner tracked with his machine-guns a fighter attacking his bomber from below, he revolved with the turret; hunched upside-down in his little sphere, he looked like the foetus in the womb. The fighters which attacked him were armed with cannon firing explosive shells. The hose was a steam hose [Jarrell's note].
2. Antiaircraft fire.
1. B-17 Flying Fortresses, an American bomber in World War II.

The soldiers pass like beasts, unquestioning, 30
And the watcher for an instant understands
What there is then no need to understand;
But she wakes from her knowledge, and her stare,
A shadow now, moves emptily among
The shadows learning in their shadowy fields 35
The empty missions.
                              Remembering,
She hears the bomber calling, *Little Friend!*[2]
To the fighter hanging in the hostile sky,
And sees the ragged flame eat, rib by rib, 40
Along the metal of the wing into her heart:
The lives stream out, blossom, and float steadily
To the flames of the earth, the flames
That burn like stars above the lands of men.

She saves from the twilight that takes everything 45
A squadron shipping, in its last parade—
Its dogs run by it, barking at the band—
A gunner walking to his barracks, half-asleep,
Starting at something, stumbling (above, invisible,
The crews in the steady winter of the sky 50
Tremble in their wired fur); and feels for them
The love of life for life. The hopeful cells
Heavy with someone else's death, cold carriers
Of someone else's victory, grope past their lives
Into her own bewilderment: The years meant *this*? 55

But for them the bombers answer everything.

                                                        1945

Next Day

Moving from Cheer to Joy, from Joy to All,
I take a box
And add it to my wild rice, my Cornish game hens.
The slacked or shorted, basketed, identical
Food-gathering flocks 5
Are selves I overlook. Wisdom, said William James,[1]

Is learning what to overlook. And I am wise
If that is wisdom.
Yet somehow, as I buy All from these shelves

---

2. In "Second Air Force" the woman visiting her son remembers what she has read on the front page of her newspaper the week before, a conversation between a bomber, in flames over Germany, and one of the fighters protecting it: "Then I heard the bomber call me in: 'Little Friend, Little Friend, I got two engines on fire. Can you see me, Little Friend?' I said, 'I'm crossing right over you. Let's go home'" [Jarrell's note].
1. From *The Principles of Psychology*, by the American philosopher William James (1842–1910).

And the boy takes it to my station wagon,　　　　　　　　10
What I've become
Troubles me even if I shut my eyes.

When I was young and miserable and pretty
And poor, I'd wish
What all girls wish: to have a husband,　　　　　　　　15
A house and children. Now that I'm old, my wish
Is womanish:
That the boy putting groceries in my car

See me. It bewilders me he doesn't see me.
For so many years　　　　　　　　20
I was good enough to eat: the world looked at me
And its mouth watered. How often they have undressed me,
The eyes of strangers!
And, holding their flesh within my flesh, their vile

Imaginings within my imagining,　　　　　　　　25
I too have taken
The chance of life. Now the boy pats my dog
And we start home. Now I am good.
The last mistaken,
Ecstatic, accidental bliss, the blind　　　　　　　　30

Happiness that, bursting, leaves upon the palm
Some soap and water—
It was so long ago, back in some Gay
Twenties, Nineties, I don't know . . . Today I miss
My lovely daughter　　　　　　　　35
Away at school, my sons away at school,

My husband away at work—I wish for them.
The dog, the maid,
And I go through the sure unvarying days
At home in them. As I look at my life,　　　　　　　　40
I am afraid
Only that it will change, as I am changing:

I am afraid, this morning, of my face.
It looks at me
From the rear-view mirror, with the eyes I hate,　　　　　　　　45
The smile I hate. Its plain, lined look
Of gray discovery
Repeats to me: "You're old." That's all, I'm old.

And yet I'm afraid, as I was at the funeral
I went to yesterday.　　　　　　　　50
My friend's cold made-up face, granite among its flowers,
Her undressed, operated-on, dressed body
Were my face and body.
As I think of her I hear her telling me

How young I seem; I *am* exceptional;   55
I think of all I have.
But really no one is exceptional,
No one has anything, I'm anybody,
I stand beside my grave
Confused with my life, that is commonplace and solitary.   60

                                                            1965

Well Water

What a girl called "the dailiness of life"
(Adding an errand to your errand. Saying,
"Since you're up . . ." Making you a means to
A means to a means to) is well water
Pumped from an old well at the bottom of the world.   5
The pump you pump the water from is rusty
And hard to move and absurd, a squirrel-wheel
A sick squirrel turns slowly, through the sunny
Inexorable hours. And yet sometimes
The wheel turns of its own weight, the rusty   10
Pump pumps over your sweating face the clear
Water, cold, so cold! you cup your hands
And gulp from them the dailiness of life.

                                                            1965

Thinking of the Lost World

This spoonful of chocolate tapioca
Tastes like—like peanut butter, like the vanilla
Extract Mama told me not to drink.
Swallowing the spoonful, I have already traveled
Through time to my childhood. It puzzles me   5
That age is like it.
                    Come back to that calm country
Through which the stream of my life first meandered,
My wife, our cat, and I sit here and see
Squirrels quarreling in the feeder, a mockingbird   10
Copying our chipmunk, as our end copies
Its beginning.
            Back in Los Angeles, we missed
Los Angeles. The sunshine of the Land
Of Sunshine is a gray mist now, the atmosphere   15
Of some factory planet: when you stand and look
You see a block or two, and your eyes water.
The orange groves are all cut down . . . My bow
Is lost, all my arrows are lost or broken,
My knife is sunk in the eucalyptus tree   20

Too far for even Pop to get it out,
And the tree's sawed down. It and the stair-sticks
And the planks of the tree house are all firewood
Burned long ago; its gray smoke smells of Vicks.[1]

Twenty Years After, thirty-five years after,   25
Is as good as ever—better than ever,
Now that D'Artagnan[2] is no longer old—
Except that it is unbelievable.
I say to my old self: "I believe. Help thou
Mine unbelief."   30
                    I believe the dinosaur
Or pterodactyl's married the pink sphinx
And lives with those Indians in the undiscovered
Country between California and Arizona
That the mad girl told me she was princess of—   35
Looking at me with the eyes of a lion,
Big, golden, without human understanding,
As she threw paper-wads from the back seat
Of the car in which I drove her with her mother
From the jail in Waycross to the hospital   40
In Daytona. If I took my eyes from the road
And looked back into her eyes, the car would—I'd be—

Or if only I could find a crystal set[3]
Sometimes, surely, I could still hear their chief
Reading to them from Dumas or *Amazing Stories*;   45
If I could find in some Museum of Cars
Mama's dark blue Buick, Lucky's electric,
Couldn't I be driven there? Hold out to them,
The paraffin half picked out, Tawny's dewclaw—
And have walk to me from among their wigwams   50
My tall brown aunt, to whisper to me: "Dead?
They told you I was dead?"
                              As if you could die!
If I never saw you, never again
Wrote to you, even, after a few years,   55
How often you've visited me, having put on,
As a mermaid puts on her sealskin, another face
And voice, that don't fool me for a minute—
That are yours for good . . . All of them are gone
Except for me; and for me nothing is gone—   60
The chicken's body is still going round
And round in widening circles, a satellite
From which, as the sun sets, the scientist bends
A look of evil on the unsuspecting earth.
Mama and Pop and Dandeen are still there   65
In the Gay Twenties.
                    The Gay Twenties! You say

---

1. A remedy for colds.
2. Hero of *The Three Musketeers* (1844), by Alexandre Dumas *père*; its sequel was *Twenty Years*

After (1845).
3. Old-fashioned radio receiver, often built by children in the 1920s and '30s.

The Gay Nineties . . . But it's all right: they *were* gay,
O so gay! A certain number of years after,
Any time is Gay, to the new ones who ask: 70
"Was that the first World War or the second?"
Moving between the first world and the second,
I hear a boy call, now that my beard's gray:
"Santa Claus! Hi, Santa Claus!" It *is* miraculous
To have the children call you Santa Claus.   75
I wave back. When my hand drops to the wheel,
It is brown and spotted, and its nails are ridged
Like Mama's. Where's my own hand? My smooth
White bitten-fingernailed one? I seem to see
A shape in tennis shoes and khaki riding-pants   80
Standing there empty-handed; I reach out to it
Empty-handed, my hand comes back empty,
And yet my emptiness is traded for its emptiness,
I have found that Lost World in the Lost and Found
Columns whose gray illegible advertisements   85
My soul has memorized world after world:
LOST—NOTHING. STRAYED FROM NOWHERE. NO REWARD.
I hold in my own hands, in happiness,
Nothing: the nothing for which there's no reward.

1965

JOHN BERRYMAN
1914–1972

From a generation whose ideal poem was short, self-contained, and ironic, John Berryman emerged as the author of two extended and passionate works: "Homage to Mistress Bradstreet" and the lyric sequence *The Dream Songs*. It was as if Berryman needed more space than the single lyric provided—a larger theater in which to play out an unrelenting psychic drama. He had written shorter poems—songs and sonnets—but his discovery of large-scale dramatic situations and strange new voices astonished his contemporaries.

Berryman seemed fated to intense suffering and self-preoccupation. His father, a banker, shot himself outside his son's window when the boy was twelve. The suicide haunted Berryman to the end of his own life, which also came by suicide. Berryman, who was born John Smith, took a new name from his stepfather, also a banker. His childhood was a series of displacements: ten years near McAlester, Oklahoma, then Tampa, Florida, and after his father's suicide, Gloucester, Massachusetts, and New York City. His mother's second marriage ended in divorce, but his stepfather sent him to private school in Connecticut. Berryman graduated from Columbia College in 1936 and won a fellowship to Clare College, Cambridge, England.

He was later to say of himself, "I masquerade as a writer. Actually I am a scholar." However misleading this may be about his poetry, it reminds us that throughout his life Berryman drew nourishment from teaching—at Wayne State, at Harvard

(1940–43), then off and on at Princeton, and from 1955 until his death, at the University of Minnesota. He chose to teach not creative writing but literature and the "history of civilization," and he claimed that such teaching forced him into areas in which he would not otherwise have done detailed work. A mixture of bookishness and wildness characterizes all his writing: five years of research lay behind the intensities of "Homage to Mistress Bradstreet," while an important constituent of "huffy Henry's" personality in *The Dream Songs* is his professorial awkwardness and exhibitionism.

Berryman seemed drawn to borrowing identities in his poetry. In his first important volume, *The Dispossessed* (1948), he had experimented with various dramatic voices in the short poems "Nervous Songs: The Song of the Demented Priest," "A Professor's Song," "The Song of the Tortured Girl," and "The Song of the Man Forsaken and Obsessed." The *dispossession* of the book's title had two opposite and urgent meanings for him: "the miserable, *put out of one's own*, and the relieved, saved, undevilled, de-spelled." Taking on such roles was for Berryman both a revelation of his cast-out, fatherless state and an exorcism of it. It was perhaps in that spirit that he entered into an imaginary dialogue with what he felt as the kindred nature of the Puritan poet Anne Bradstreet. "Both of our worlds unhanded us." What started out to be a poem of fifty lines emerged as the fifty-seven stanzas of "Homage to Mistress Bradstreet" (1956), a work so absorbing that after completing it Berryman claimed to be "a ruin for two years." It was not Bradstreet's poetry that engaged him. Quite the contrary: he was fascinated by the contrast between her "bald abstract rime" and her life of passionate suffering. The poem explores the kinship between Bradstreet and Berryman as figures of turbulence and rebellion.

Berryman took literary encouragement from another American poet of the past, Stephen Crane, about whom he wrote a book-length critical study in 1950. Crane's poems, he said, have "the character of a 'dream,' something seen naively in a new relation." Berryman's attraction to a poetry that accommodated the nightmare antics of the dream world became apparent in his own long work, *The Dream Songs*. It was modeled, he claimed, on "the greatest American poem," Whitman's "Song of Myself," in which the speaker assumes a fluid, ever-changing persona. *77 Dream Songs* was published in 1964. Additional poems, to a total of 385, appeared in *His Toy, His Dream, His Rest* (1968). (Some uncollected dream songs were published posthumously in *Henry's Fate*, 1977, and drafts of others remained in manuscript.) Obvious links exist between Berryman and other so-called confessional writers such as Robert Lowell, Sylvia Plath, and Anne Sexton. But the special autobiographical flavor of *The Dream Songs* is that of a psychic vaudeville; as in dreams, the poet represents himself through a fluid series of alter egos, whose voices often flow into one another in single poems. One of these voices is that of a blackface minstrel, and Berryman's appropriation of this dialect prompted Michael Harper's poem "Tongue-Tied in Black and White," written both as homage to Berryman and as part of Harper's quarrel with the use of "that needful black idiom offending me" ("Tongue-Tied in Black and White"). Despite the suffering that these poems enact, Berryman seemed to find a secret strength through the staginess, variety, resourcefulness, and renewals of these poems.

The Dream Songs brought Berryman a success that was not entirely beneficial. The collection *Love and Fame* (1970) shows him beguiled by his own celebrity and wrestling with some of its temptations. In an unfinished, posthumously published novel, *Recovery*, he portrays himself as increasingly prey to alcoholism. Berryman had been married twice before, and his hospitalization for drinking and for periods of insanity had put a strain on his third marriage. He came to distrust his poetry as a form of exhibitionism, and in his use of the discipline of prose and in the prayers that crowd his last two volumes of poetry (*Delusions, Etc.* appeared posthumously), he was clearly in search of some new and humbling style. Having been raised a strict Catholic and fallen away from the church, he tried to return to it in his last years, speaking of his need for a "God of rescue." On January 7, 1972, Berryman committed suicide by leaping from a Minneapolis bridge.

Homage to Mistress Bradstreet

Anne Bradstreet ("Born 1612 Anne Dudley, married at 16 Simon Bradstreet, a Cambridge man, steward to the Countess of Warwick and protege of her father Thomas Dudley secretary to the Earl of Lincoln. Crossed in the *Arbella*, 1630, under Governor Winthrop" [Berryman's note]) came to the Massachusetts Bay Colony when she was eighteen years old. She was one of the first poets on American soil. Of this poem, Berryman says:

> An American historian somewhere observes that all colonial settlements are intensely conservative, *except* in the initial break-off point (whether religious, political, legal, or whatever). Trying to do justice to both parts of this obvious truth—which I came upon only after the poem was finished—I concentrated upon the second and the poem laid itself out in a series of rebellions. I had her rebel first against the new environment and above all against her barrenness (which in fact lasted for years), then against her marriage (which in fact seems to have been brilliantly happy), and finally against her continuing life of illness, loss, and age. These are the three large sections of the poem; they are preceded and followed by an exordium and coda, of four stanzas each, spoken by the "I" of the twentieth-century poet, which modulates into her voice, who speaks most of the poem. Such is the plan. Each rebellion, of course, is succeeded by submission, although even in the moment of the poem's supreme triumph—the presentment, too long to quote now, of the birth of her first child—rebellion survives.

Berryman wrote two stanzas of the poem and found himself stalled for five years, during which he gathered material, until he discovered the strategy of dialogue and inserted himself in the poem. "Homage to Mistress Bradstreet" was first published in *Partisan Review* in 1953, but did not appear as a book until 1956.

In his exordium (stanzas 1–4), the poet makes an intense identification between himself and Bradstreet, both of them alienated by hardship or circumstance from those around them: "We are on each other's hands / who care. Both of our worlds unhanded us." The identification is so complete that in the subsequent stanzas he hears her voice recounting the tribulations of life in a new country, her yearnings for the England she left behind, her lonely dedication to her poetry, and the personal suffering in her early barrenness and miscarriages. Stanza 17 continues in Bradstreet's voice.

From Homage to Mistress Bradstreet

*   *   *

17

The winters close, Springs open, no child stirs
under my withering heart, O seasoned heart   130
God grudged his aid.
All things else soil like a shirt.
Simon is much away. My executive[1] stales.
The town came through for the cartway by the pales,[2]
but my patience is short,   135
I revolt from, I am like, these savage foresters

---

1. Power to act.   2. Stockade fence.

18

whose passionless dicker in the shade, whose glance
impassive & scant, belie their murderous cries
when quarry seems to show.
Again I must have been wrong, twice.[3]   140
Unwell in a new way. Can that begin?
God brandishes. O love, O I love. Kin,
gather. My world is strange
and merciful, ingrown months, blessing a swelling trance.[4]

19

So squeezed, wince you I scream? I love you & hate   145
off with you. Ages! *Useless.* Below my waist
he has me in Hell's vise.
Stalling. He let go. Come back: brace
me somewhere. No. No. Yes! everything down
hardens I press with horrible joy down   150
my back cracks like a wrist
shame I am voiding oh behind it is too late

20

hide me forever I work thrust I must free
now I all muscles & bones concentrate
what is living from dying?   155
Simon I must leave you so untidy
Monster you are killing me Be sure
I'll have you later Women do endure
I can *can* no longer
and it passes the wretched trap whelming and I am me   160

21

drencht & powerful, I did it with my body!
One proud tug greens Heaven. Marvellous,
unforbidding Majesty.
Swell, imperious bells. I fly.
Mountainous, woman not breaks and will bend: 165
sways God nearby: anguish comes to an end.
Blossomed Sarah,[5] and I
blossom. Is that thing alive? I hear a famisht howl.

22

Beloved household, I am Simon's wife,
and the mother of Samuel—whom greedy yet I miss   170
out of his kicking place.

---

3. One of the several allusions to her failure to
become pregnant.
4. Her first child was not born until about 1633

[Berryman's note].
5. Wife of Abraham, barren until old age, when
she gave birth to Isaac (Genesis 17.19).

More in some ways I feel at a loss,
freer. Cantabanks & mummers,[6] nears
longing for you. Our chopping[7] scores my ears,
our costume bores my eyes.   175
St. George[8] to the good sword, rise! chop-logic's rife

23

& fever & Satan & Satan's ancient fere.[9]
Pioneering is not feeling well,
not Indians, beasts.
Not all their riddling can forestall   180
one leaving. Sam, your uncle has had to
go from us to live with God. 'Then Aunt went too?'
Dear, she does wait still.
Stricken: 'Oh. Then he takes us one by one.' My dear.

24

Forswearing it otherwise, they starch their minds.   185
Folkmoots, & blether, blether. John Cotton rakes[1]
to the synod of Cambridge.[2]
Down from my body my legs flow,
out from it arms wave, on it my head shakes.
Now Mistress Hutchinson rings forth a call—   190
should she? many creep out a broken wall—
affirming the Holy Ghost
dwells in one justified. Factioning passion blinds

25

all to all her good, all—can she be exiled?
Bitter sister, victim! I miss you.   195
—I miss you, Anne,[3]
day or night weak as a child,
tender & empty, doomed, quick to no tryst.
—I hear you. Be kind, you who leaguer[4]
my image in the mist.   200
—Be kind you, to one unchained eager far & wild

---

6. Ballad singers and mimes.
7. *Chopping*: disputing, snapping, haggling;
axing [Berryman's note].
8. Patron saint of England; the slayer of dragons.
9. *Fere*: his friend Death [Berryman's note].
1. "*Rakes*: inclines, as a mast; bows" [Berryman's note]. "Folkmoots": a town assembly for debate. "Blether": nonsense.
2. In the first synod (a body for religious debate), Cotton agreed to the condemnation and banishment of his follower Anne Hutchinson. Her heresies included a deemphasis of perfect moral conduct as evidence of the justification for Christian salvation.

3. One might say: He [the poet] is enabled to speak, at last, in the fortune of an echo of her—and when she is loneliest (her former spiritual adviser [John Cotton] having deserted Anne Hutchinson, and this her [Bradstreet's] closest friend banished), as if she had summoned him; and only thus, perhaps, is she enabled to hear him. This second section of the poem is a dialogue, his voice however ceasing well before it ends at [line] 307, and hers continuing for the whole third part until the coda ([stanzas] 54–57) [Berryman's note].
4. Beleaguer, besiege.

26

and if, O my love, my heart is breaking, please
neglect my cries and I will spare you. Deep
in Time's grave, Love's, you lie still.
Lie still.—Now? That happy shape   205
my forehead had under my most long, rare,
ravendark, hidden, soft bodiless hair
you award me still.
You must not love me, but I do not bid you cease.

27

Veiled my eyes, attending. How can it be I?   210
Moist, with parted lips, I listen, wicked.
I shake in the morning & retch.
Brood I do on myself naked.
A fading world I dust, with fingers new.
—I have earned the right to be alone with you.   215
—What right can that be?
Convulsing, if you love, enough, like a sweet lie.

28

Not that, I know, you can. This cratered skin,
like the crabs & shells of my Palissy[5] ewer, touch!
Oh, you do, you do?   220
Falls on me what I like a witch,
for lawless holds, annihilations of law
which Time and he and man abhor, foresaw:
sharper than what my Friend[6]
brought me for my revolt when I moved smooth & thin,   225

29

faintings black, rigour, chilling, brown
parching, back, brain burning, the grey pocks
itch, a manic stench
of pustules snapping, pain floods the palm,
sleepless, or a red shaft with a dreadful start   230
rides at the chapel, like a slipping heart.
My soul strains in one qualm
ah but *this* is not to save me but to throw me down.

30

And out of this I lull. It lessens. Kiss me.
That once. As sings out up in sparkling dark   235
a trail of a star & dies,
while the breath flutters, sounding, mark,

5. Bernard Palissy (1510–1590), French Protestant ceramicist noted for special glazes and highly
ornamented pieces.

6. Allusion to the punishments of God visited on
those who rebel against him (cf. Isaiah 1.6).

so shorn ought such caresses to us be
who, deserving nothing, flush and flee
the darkness of that light,   240
a lurching frozen from a warm dream. Talk to me.

31[7]

—It is Spring's New England. Pussy willows wedge
up in the wet. Milky crestings, fringed
yellow, in heaven, eyed
by the melting hand-in-hand or mere   245
desirers single, heavy-footed, rapt,
make surge poor human hearts. Venus is trapt—
the hefty pike shifts, sheer[8]—
in Orion blazing. Warblings, odours, nudge to an edge—

32

—Ravishing, ha, what crouches outside ought,   250
flamboyant, ill, angelic. Often, now,
I am afraid of you.
I am a sobersides; I know.
I *want* to take you for my lover.—Do.
—I hear a madness. Harmless I to you   255
am not, not I?—No.
—I cannot but be. Sing a concord of our thought.

33

—Wan dolls in indigo on gold:[9] refrain
my western lust. I am drowning in this past.
I lose sight of you   260
who mistress me from air. Unbraced
in delirium of the grand depths,[1] giving away
haunters what kept me, I breathe solid spray.
—I am losing you!
Straiten me on.[2]—I suffered living like a stain: 265

34

I trundle the bodies, on the iron bars,
over that fire backward & forth; they burn;

7. Berryman (in *Poets on Poetry*) called this speech of the poet to Bradstreet "an only half-subdued aria-stanza."
8. Lines 246–47 are opposed images of the bottom of the sea against the summit of the sky, as imaged by the planet Venus and the constellation Orion. "Sheer" in the sense of "invisible" (quoted from comments by Berryman in the Italian translation of "Mistress Bradstreet" by Sergio Perosa).
9. Cf., on Byzantine icons [here, the impassive Madonnas painted against gold backgrounds in medieval altarpieces of the Eastern Church], Frederick Rolfe ("Baron Corvo"): "Who ever dreams of praying (with expectation of response)

for the prayer of a Tintoretto or a Titian, or a Bellini, or a Botticelli? But who can refrain from crying 'O Mother!' to these unruffleable wan dolls in indigo on gold?" (quoted from *The Desire and Pursuit of the Whole* by Graham Greene in *The Last Childhood*) [Berryman's note].
1. "Délires des grandes profoundeurs," described by [the twentieth-century French marine explorer Jacques-Yves] Cousteau and others; a euphoria, sometimes fatal, in which the hallucinated diver offers passing fish his line, helmet, anything [Berryman's note; he translates the French phrase in line 262].
2. I.e., tighten your embrace.

bits fall. I wonder if
I killed them. Women serve my turn.
—Dreams! You are good.—No.—Dense with hardihood   270
the wicked are dislodged, and lodged the good.
In green space we are safe.
God awaits us (but I am yielding) who Hell wars.

35

—I cannot feel myself God waits. He flies
nearer a kindly world; or he is flown.   275
One Saturday's rescue[3]
won't show. Man is entirely alone
may be. I am a man of griefs & fits
trying to be my friend. And the brown smock splits,
down the pale flesh a gash   280
broadens and Time holds up your heart against my eyes.

36

—Hard and divided heaven! creases me. Shame
is failing. My breath is scented, and I throw
hostile glances towards God.
Crumpling plunge of a pestle, bray:[4]   285
sin cross & opposite, wherein I survive
nightmares of Eden. Reaches foul & live
he for me, this soul
to crunch, a minute tangle of eternal flame.

37

I fear Hell's hammer-wind. But fear does wane.   290
Death's blossoms grain my hair; I cannot live.
A black joy clashes
joy, in twilight. The Devil said
'I will deal toward her softly, and her enchanting cries
will fool the horns of Adam.'[5] Father of lies,   295
a male great pestle smashes
small women swarming towards the mortar's rim in vain.

38

I see the cruel spread Wings black with saints!
Silky my breasts not his, mine, mine to withhold
or tender, tender.   300
I am sifting, nervous, and bold.
The light is changing. Surrender this loveliness

---

3. As of cliffhangers, movie serials wherein each week's episode ends with a train bearing down on the strapped heroine or with the hero dangling over an abyss into which Indians above him peer with satisfaction before they hatchet the rope; *rescue*: forcible recovery (by the owner) of goods distrained [Berryman's note].

4. Punning (according to Berryman's notes) on (1) the pulverizing action of a mortar and pestle and (2) the strident noise of a donkey.

5. Referring to Satan's temptation of Eve, who was to eat the apple from the Tree of Knowledge and then convince Adam to do so (cf. Genesis 3).

you cannot make me do. *But* I will. Yes.
What horror, down stormy air,
warps towards me? My threatening promise faints   305

39[6]

torture me, Father, lest not I be thine!
Tribunal terrible & pure, my God,
mercy for him and me.
Faces half-fanged, Christ drives abroad,
and though the crop hopes, Jane[7] is so slipshod   310
I cry. Evil dissolves, & love, like foam;
that love. Prattle of children powers me home,
my heart claps like the swan's
under a frenzy of *who* love me & who shine.[8]

⁂   ⁂   ⁂

1953, 1956

From The Dream Songs[1]

1

Huffy Henry hid   the day,
unappeasable Henry sulked.
I see his point,—a trying to put things over.
It was the thought that they thought
they could *do* it made Henry wicked & away.   5
But he should have come out and talked.

All the world like a woolen lover
once did seem on Henry's side.
Then came a departure.
Thereafter nothing fell out as it might or ought.   10
I don't see how Henry, pried
open for all the world to see, survived.

6. The stanza is unsettled, like [stanza] 24, by a middle line, signaling a broad transition [Berryman's note].
7. A servant.
8. The final stanzas present Bradstreet's intensified vision of death and damnation and include the death of her father, blaspheming. But in the last four stanzas the poem modulates back into the poet's voice and his vow to keep Bradstreet alive in his loving memory and in his writing. "Hover, utter, still, a sourcing whom my lost candle like the firefly loves."
1. These poems were written over a period of thirteen years. (77 *Dream Songs* was published in 1964, and the remaining poems appeared in *His Toy, His Dream, His Rest* in 1968. Some uncol-lected dream songs were included in the volume *Henry's Fate*, which appeared five years after Berryman committed suicide in 1972.) Berryman placed an introductory note at the head of *His Toy, His Dream, His Rest*: "The poem then, whatever its wide cast of characters, is essentially about an imaginary character (not the poet, not me) named Henry, a white American in early middle age sometimes in blackface, who has suffered an irreversible loss and talks about himself sometimes in the first person, sometimes in the third, sometimes even in the second; he has a friend, never named, who addresses him as Mr. Bones and variants thereof. Requiescant in pace." (The final sentence here is Latin for "Rest in peace.")

What he has now to say is a long
wonder the world can bear & be.
Once in a sycamore I was glad   15
all at the top, and I sang.
Hard on the land wears the strong sea
and empty grows every bed.

14

Life, friends, is boring. We must not say so.
After all, the sky flashes, the great sea yearns,
we ourselves flash and yearn,
and moreover my mother told me as a boy
(repeatingly) 'Ever to confess you're bored   5
means you have no

Inner Resources.' I conclude now I have no
inner resources, because I am heavy bored.
Peoples bore me,
literature bores me, especially great literature,   10
Henry bores me, with his plights & gripes
as bad as achilles,[2]

who loves people and valiant art, which bores me.
And the tranquil hills, & gin, look like a drag
and somehow a dog   15
has taken itself & its tail considerably away
into mountains or sea or sky, leaving
behind: me, wag.

29

There sat down, once, a thing on Henry's heart
so heavy, if he had a hundred years
& more, & weeping, sleepless, in all them time
Henry could not make good.
Starts again always in Henry's ears   5
the little cough somewhere, an odour, a chime.

And there is another thing he has in mind
like a grave Sienese face[3] a thousand years
would fail to blur the still profiled reproach of. Ghastly,
with open eyes, he attends, blind.
All the bells say: too late. This is not for tears;   10
thinking.

2. Greek hero of Homer's *Iliad*, who, angry at
slights against his honor, sulked in his tent and
refused to fight against the Trojans.

3. Allusion to the somber, austere mosaiclike religious portraits by the Italian painters who worked
in Siena during the 13th and 14th centuries.

But never did Henry, as he thought he did,
end anyone and hacks her body up
and hide the pieces, where they may be found.   15
He knows: he went over everyone, & nobody's missing.
Often he reckons, in the dawn, them up.
Nobody is ever missing.

40

I'm scared a lonely. Never see my son,
easy be not to see anyone,
combers[4] out to sea
know they're goin somewhere but not me.
Got a little poison, got a little gun.   5
I'm scared a lonely.

I'm scared a only one thing, which is me,
from othering I don't take nothin, see,
for any hound dog's sake.
But this is where I livin, where I rake   10
my leaves and cop my promise,[5] this' where we
cry oursel's awake.

Wishin was dyin but I gotta make
it all this way to that bed on these feet
where peoples said to meet.   15
Maybe but even if I see my son
forever never, get back on the take,
free, black & forty-one.[6]

384

The marker slants, flowerless, day's almost done,
I stand above my father's grave with rage,
often, often before
I've made this awful pilgrimage to one
who cannot visit me, who tore his page   5
out: I come back for more,

I spit upon this dreadful banker's grave
who shot his heart out in a Florida dawn
O ho alas alas
When will indifference come, I moan & rave   10

4. Waves that roll over and break with a foamy
crest.
5. Slang for "pile up potential."

6. Playing on "free, white, and twenty-one," colloquial expression for legally independent.

I'd like to scrabble till I got right down
away down under the grass

and ax the casket open ha to see
just how he's taking it, which he sought so hard
we'll tear apart   15
the mouldering grave clothes ha & then Henry
will heft the ax once more, his final card,
and fell it on the start.

1968

BERNARD MALAMUD
1914–1986

Bernard Malamud began late as a writer, publishing his first novel at age thirty-eight and reaching a wider audience about a decade later. It is his second novel (*The Assistant*, 1957) that most readers, rightly, consider his best. Malamud knew well the urban life he wrote about in that book. He was born in Brooklyn, graduated from Erasmus Hall High School in Brooklyn and the City College of New York, then earned a master's degree at Columbia. During the 1940s he taught evening classes at Erasmus Hall and Harlem Evening High School, while writing short stories that by 1950 had begun to appear in such magazines as *Partisan Review* and *Commentary*. Along with Saul Bellow, he was an important member of the group of Jewish novelists who flourished in the 1950s and beyond, but unlike Bellow, his stories were usually notable for the way they captured the speech and manners of working-class, recently immigrant Jews.

That urban Jewish milieu was absent from his first novel, *The Natural* (1952), which tells of an injured Major League pitcher reborn into a splendid outfielder. (Malamud may have been influenced by John R. Tunis's popular boy's book, *The Kid from Tompkinsville*, 1939.) The book contains much allegorical play with the Grail legend and other myths, but it held at arm's length Malamud's deeper concerns, which came to full expression in *The Assistant*, with its vivid but depressing rendering of a grocer's day-to-day existence. Rejecting the frenetic verbal energy of his first novel, Malamud wrote *The Assistant* in a low-key, rather toneless style, just right for catching the drab solemnities of his characters' lives. Like Bellow's *The Victim*, published a few years previously, the novel is about human responsibility and the possibilities for conversion, seen through the conflict between Jew and Gentile. This conflict is given life through faithfully rendered speech and the patient yet always surprising turns of event with which the story unfolds. If the allegorical twist at its end is too ingenious for belief, still *The Assistant* remains unforgettable.

In subsequent novels Malamud extended and relaxed his style. The comic *A New Life* (1962) is about a hapless college professor at a West Coast university (Malamud taught at Oregon State for a time). *The Fixer* (1966) is a parable-history of the ritual murder of a Christian child. *The Tenants* (1971) attempted, in eventually violent, sensationalistic terms, to portray one minority's experience confronting another's—

Jew against African American. *Dubin's Lives* (1979) is a somewhat conventional tale of a writer of biographies who is suddenly overtaken by life, in the form of a desirable young woman (the novel is set in Vermont, where Malamud lived for years, teaching at Bennington College from 1961 until he retired). *God's Grace* (1982), by contrast, is a parable or fable, set in a post-thermonuclear future.

While these later novels seem sometimes abstract and didactic, *The Assistant* and Malamud's short fiction present memorable portraits of embattled Jews in grotesque circumstances. At times these figures resemble heroes of folklore; at other times they threaten to collapse into caricatures. In a story such as "The Lady in the Lake," the pathetic-comic hero becomes both. At his best, in that story or ones such as "The Magic Barrel" (printed here), "Idiots First," and "The Last Mohican," Malamud imagines, intensely and purely, his lonely questers for perfection as they become entangled in the imperfections of a social world. Such occasions of tragicomic humiliation sound the deeper note that was Malamud's trademark.

The following text is from the short-story collection *The Magic Barrel* (1958).

The Magic Barrel

Not long ago there lived in uptown New York, in a small, almost meager room, though crowded with books, Leo Finkle, a rabbinical student at the Yeshiva University.[1] Finkle, after six years of study, was to be ordained in June and had been advised by an acquaintance that he might find it easier to win himself a congregation if he were married. Since he had no present prospects of marriage, after two tormented days of turning it over in his mind, he called in Pinye Salzman, a marriage broker whose two-line advertisement he had read in the *Forward*.[2]

The matchmaker appeared one night out of the dark fourth-floor hallway of the graystone rooming house where Finkle lived, grasping a black, strapped portfolio that had been worn thin with use. Salzman, who had been long in the business, was of slight but dignified build, wearing an old hat, and an overcoat too short and tight for him. He smelled frankly of fish, which he loved to eat, and although he was missing a few teeth, his presence was not displeasing, because of an amiable manner curiously contrasted with mournful eyes. His voice, his lips, his wisp of beard, his bony fingers were animated, but give him a moment of repose and his mild blue eyes revealed a depth of sadness, a characteristic that put Leo a little at ease although the situation, for him, was inherently tense.

He at once informed Salzman why he had asked him to come, explaining that his home was in Cleveland, and that but for his parents, who had married comparatively late in life, he was alone in the world. He had for six years devoted himself almost entirely to his studies, as a result of which, understandably, he had found himself without time for a social life and the company of young women. Therefore he thought it the better part of trial and error—of embarrassing fumbling—to call in an experienced person to advise him on these matters. He remarked in passing that the function of the marriage broker was ancient and honorable, highly approved in the Jewish

---

1. In New York City; it offers courses in theological as well as secular disciplines. Generically, "yeshiva" is a term for a Jewish seminary.

2. *The Jewish Daily Forward*, a Yiddish-language daily newspaper published in New York City.

community, because it made practical the necessary without hindering joy. Moreover, his own parents had been brought together by a matchmaker. They had made, if not a financially profitable marriage—since neither had possessed any worldly goods to speak of—at least a successful one in the sense of their everlasting devotion to each other. Salzman listened in embarrassed surprise, sensing a sort of apology. Later, however, he experienced a glow of pride in his work, an emotion that had left him years ago, and he heartily approved of Finkle.

The two went to their business. Leo had led Salzman to the only clear place in the room, a table near a window that overlooked the lamp-lit city. He seated himself at the matchmaker's side but facing him, attempting by an act of will to suppress the unpleasant tickle in his throat. Salzman eagerly unstrapped his portfolio and removed a loose rubber band from a thin packet of much-handled cards. As he flipped through them, a gesture and sound that physically hurt Leo, the student pretended not to see and gazed steadfastly out the window. Although it was still February, winter was on its last legs, signs of which he had for the first time in years begun to notice. He now observed the round white moon, moving high in the sky through a cloud menagerie, and watched with half-open mouth as it penetrated a huge hen, and dropped out of her like an egg laying itself. Salzman, though pretending through eyeglasses he had just slipped on, to be engaged in scanning the writing on the cards, stole occasional glances at the young man's distinguished face, noting with pleasure the long, severe scholar's nose, brown eyes heavy with learning, sensitive yet ascetic lips, and a certain, almost hollow quality of the dark cheeks. He gazed around at shelves upon shelves of books and let out a soft, contented sigh.

When Leo's eyes fell upon the cards, he counted six spread out in Salzman's hand.

"So few?" he asked in disappointment.

"You wouldn't believe me how much cards I got in my office," Salzman replied. "The drawers are already filled to the top, so I keep them now in a barrel, but is every girl good for a new rabbi?"

Leo blushed at this, regretting all he had revealed of himself in a curriculum vitae he had sent to Salzman. He had thought it best to acquaint him with his strict standards and specifications, but in having done so, he felt he had told the marriage broker more than was absolutely necessary.

He hesitantly inquired, "Do you keep photographs of your clients on file?"

"First comes family, amount of dowry, also what kind promises," Salzman replied, unbuttoning his tight coat and settling himself in the chair. "After come pictures, rabbi."

"Call me Mr. Finkle. I'm not yet a rabbi."

Salzman said he would, but instead called him doctor, which he changed to rabbi when Leo was not listening too attentively.

Salzman adjusted his horn-rimmed spectacles, gently cleared his throat and read in an eager voice the contents of the top card:

"Sophie P. Twenty four years. Widow one year. No children. Educated high school and two years college. Father promises eight thousand dollars. Has wonderful wholesale business. Also real estate. On the mother's side comes teachers, also one actor. Well known on Second Avenue."

Leo gazed up in surprise. "Did you say a widow?"

"A widow don't mean spoiled, rabbi. She lived with her husband maybe four months. He was a sick boy she made a mistake to marry him."

"Marrying a widow has never entered my mind."

"This is because you have no experience. A widow, especially if she is young and healthy like this girl, is a wonderful person to marry. She will be thankful to you the rest of her life. Believe me, if I was looking now for a bride, I would marry a widow."

Leo reflected, then shook his head.

Salzman hunched his shoulders in an almost imperceptible gesture of disappointment. He placed the card down on the wooden table and began to read another:

"Lily H. High school teacher. Regular. Not a substitute. Has savings and new Dodge car. Lived in Paris one year. Father is successful dentist thirty-five years. Interested in professional man. Well Americanized family. Wonderful opportunity."

"I knew her personally," said Salzman. "I wish you could see this girl. She is a doll. Also very intelligent. All day you could talk to her about books and theater and what not. She also knows current events."

"I don't believe you mentioned her age?"

"Her age?" Salzman said, raising his brows. "Her age is thirty-two years."

Leo said after a while, "I'm afraid that seems a little too old."

Salzman let out a laugh. "So how old are you, rabbi?"

"Twenty-seven."

"So what is the difference, tell me, between twenty-seven and thirty-two? My own wife is seven years older than me. So what did I suffer?—Nothing. If Rothschild's[3] daughter wants to marry you, would you say on account her age, no?"

"Yes," Leo said dryly.

Salzman shook off the no in the yes. "Five years don't mean a thing. I give you my word that when you will live with her for one week you will forget her age. What does it mean five years—that she lived more and knows more than somebody who is younger? On this girl, God bless her, years are not wasted. Each one that it comes makes better the bargain."

"What subjects does she teach in high school?"

"Languages. If you heard the way she speaks French, you will think it is music. I am in the business twenty-five years, and I recommend her with my whole heart. Believe me, I know what I'm talking, rabbi."

"What's on the next card?" Leo said abruptly.

Salzman reluctantly turned up the third card:

"Ruth K. Nineteen years. Honor student. Father offers thirteen thousand cash to the right bridegroom. He is a medical doctor. Stomach specialist with marvelous practice. Brother in law owns own garment business. Particular people."

Salzman looked as if he had read his trump card.

"Did you say nineteen?" Leo asked with interest.

"On the dot."

"Is she attractive?" He blushed. "Pretty?"

3. Once prominent, enormously wealthy family of Jewish international bankers and business leaders.

Salzman kissed his finger tips. "A little doll. On this I give you my word. Let me call the father tonight and you will see what means pretty."

But Leo was troubled. "You're sure she's that young?"

"This I am positive. The father will show you the birth certificate."

"Are you positive there isn't something wrong with her?" Leo insisted.

"Who says there is wrong?"

"I don't understand why an American girl her age should go to a marriage broker."

A smile spread over Salzman's face.

"So for the same reason you went, she comes."

Leo flushed. "I am pressed for time."

Salzman, realizing he had been tactless, quickly explained. "The father came, not her. He wants she should have the best, so he looks around himself. When we will locate the right boy he will introduce him and encourage. This makes a better marriage than if a young girl without experience takes for herself. I don't have to tell you this."

"But don't you think this young girl believes in love?" Leo spoke uneasily.

Salzman was about to guffaw but caught himself and said soberly, "Love comes with the right person, not before."

Leo parted dry lips but did not speak. Noticing that Salzman had snatched a glance at the next card, he cleverly asked, "How is her health?"

"Perfect," Salzman said, breathing with difficulty. "Of course, she is a little lame on her right foot from an auto accident that it happened to her when she was twelve years, but nobody notices on account she is so brilliant and also beautiful."

Leo got up heavily and went to the window. He felt curiously bitter and upbraided himself for having called in the marriage broker. Finally, he shook his head.

"Why not?" Salzman persisted, the pitch of his voice rising.

"Because I detest stomach specialists."

"So what do you care what is his business? After you marry her do you need him? Who says he must come every Friday night in your house?"

Ashamed of the way the talk was going, Leo dismissed Salzman, who went home with heavy, melancholy eyes.

Though he had felt only relief at the marriage broker's departure, Leo was in low spirits the next day. He explained it as arising from Salzman's failure to produce a suitable bride for him. He did not care for his type of clientele. But when Leo found himself hesitating whether to seek out another matchmaker, one more polished than Pinye, he wondered if it could be—his protestations to the contrary, and although he honored his father and mother—that he did not, in essence, care for the matchmaking institution? This thought he quickly put out of mind yet found himself still upset. All day he ran around in the woods—missed an important appointment, forgot to give out his laundry, walked out of a Broadway cafeteria without paying and had to run back with the ticket in his hand; had even not recognized his landlady in the street when she passed with a friend and courteously called out, "A good evening to you, Doctor Finkle." By nightfall, however, he had regained sufficient calm to sink his nose into a book and there found peace from his thoughts.

Almost at once there came a knock on the door. Before Leo could say enter, Salzman, commercial cupid, was standing in the room. His face was gray and meager, his expression hungry, and he looked as if he would expire on his feet. Yet the marriage broker managed, by some trick of the muscles, to display a broad smile.

"So good evening. I am invited?"

Leo nodded, disturbed to see him again, yet unwilling to ask the man to leave.

Beaming still, Salzman laid his portfolio on the table. "Rabbi, I got for you tonight good news."

"I've asked you not to call me rabbi. I'm still a student."

"Your worries are finished. I have for you a first-class bride."

"Leave me in peace concerning this subject," Leo pretended lack of interest.

"The world will dance at your wedding."

"Please, Mr. Salzman, no more."

"But first must come back my strength," Salzman said weakly. He fumbled with the portfolio straps and took out of the leather case an oily paper bag, from which he extracted a hard, seeded roll and a small, smoked white fish. With a quick motion of his hand he stripped the fish out of its skin and began ravenously to chew. "All day in a rush," he muttered.

Leo watched him eat.

"A sliced tomato you have maybe?" Salzman hesitantly inquired.

"No."

The marriage broker shut his eyes and ate. When he had finished he carefully cleaned up the crumbs and rolled up the remains of the fish, in the paper bag. His spectacled eyes roamed the room until he discovered, amid some piles of books, a one-burner gas stove. Lifting his hat he humbly asked, "A glass tea you got, rabbi?"

Conscience-stricken, Leo rose and brewed the tea. He served it with a chunk of lemon and two cubes of lump sugar, delighting Salzman.

After he had drunk his tea, Salzman's strength and good spirits were restored.

"So tell me, rabbi," he said amiably, "you considered some more the three clients I mentioned yesterday?"

"There was no need to consider."

"Why not?"

"None of them suits me."

"What then suits you?"

Leo let it pass because he could give only a confused answer.

Without waiting for a reply, Salzman asked, "You remember this girl I talked to you—the high school teacher?"

"Age thirty-two?"

But, surprisingly, Salzman's face lit in a smile. "Age twenty-nine."

Leo shot him a look. "Reduced from thirty-two?"

"A mistake," Salzman avowed. "I talked today with the dentist. He took me to his safety deposit box and showed me the birth certificate. She was twenty-nine years last August. They made her a party in the mountains where she went for her vacation. When her father spoke to me the first time I forgot to write the age and I told you thirty-two, but now I remember this was a different client, a widow."

"The same one you told me about? I thought she was twenty-four?"

"A different. Am I responsible that the world is filled with widows?"

"No, but I'm not interested in them, nor for that matter, in school teachers."

Salzman pulled his clasped hands to his breast. Looking at the ceiling he devoutly exclaimed, "Yiddishe kinder,[4] what can I say to somebody that he is not interested in high school teachers? So what then you are interested?"

Leo flushed but controlled himself.

"In what else will you be interested," Salzman went on, "if you not interested in this fine girl that she speaks four languages and has personally in the bank ten thousand dollars? Also her father guarantees further twelve thousand. Also she has a new car, wonderful clothes, talks on all subjects, and she will give you a first-class home and children. How near do we come in our life to paradise?"

"If she's so wonderful, why wasn't she married ten years ago?"

"Why?" said Salzman with a heavy laugh. "—Why? Because she is *partikiler*.[5] This is why. She wants the *best*."

Leo was silent, amused at how he had entangled himself. But Salzman had aroused his interest in Lily H., and he began seriously to consider calling on her. When the marriage broker observed how intently Leo's mind was at work on the facts he had supplied, he felt certain they would soon come to an agreement.

Late Saturday afternoon, conscious of Salzman, Leo Finkle walked with Lily Hirschorn along Riverside Drive. He walked briskly and erectly, wearing with distinction the black fedora he had that morning taken with trepidation out of the dusty hat box on his closet shelf, and the heavy black Saturday coat he had thoroughly whisked clean. Leo also owned a walking stick, a present from a distant relative, but quickly put temptation aside and did not use it. Lily, petite and not unpretty, had on something signifying the approach of spring. She was au courant,[6] animatedly, with all sorts of subjects, and he weighed her words and found her surprisingly sound—score another for Salzman, whom he uneasily sensed to be somewhere around, hiding perhaps high in a tree along the street, flashing the lady signals with a pocket mirror; or perhaps a cloven-hoofed Pan,[7] piping nuptial ditties as he danced his invisible way before them, strewing wild buds on the walk and purple grapes in their path, symbolizing fruit of a union, though there was of course still none.

Lily startled Leo by remarking, "I was thinking of Mr. Salzman, a curious figure, wouldn't you say?"

Not certain what to answer, he nodded.

She bravely went on, blushing, "I for one am grateful for his introducing us. Aren't you?"

He courteously replied, "I am."

"I mean," she said with a little laugh—and it was all in good taste, or at least gave the effect of being not in bad—"do you mind that we came together so?"

He was not displeased with her honesty, recognizing that she meant to set the relationship aright, and understanding that it took a certain amount of experience in life, and courage, to want to do it quite that way. One had to have some sort of past to make that kind of beginning.

---

4. Jewish children (Yiddish); the sense is, what do these children know of the world as their parents knew it.
5. Yiddish corruption of "particular."

6. In keeping with the times (French).
7. Ancient Greek rural deity, part man and part goat, who presided over shepherds and flocks.

He said that he did not mind. Salzman's function was traditional and honorable—valuable for what it might achieve, which, he pointed out, was frequently nothing.

Lily agreed with a sigh. They walked on for a while and she said after a long silence, again with a nervous laugh, "Would you mind if I asked you something a little bit personal? Frankly, I find the subject fascinating." Although Leo shrugged, she went on half embarrassedly, "How was it that you came to your calling? I mean was it a sudden passionate inspiration?"

Leo, after a time, slowly replied, "I was always interested in the Law."[8]

"You saw revealed in it the presence of the Highest?"

He nodded and changed the subject. "I understand that you spent a little time in Paris, Miss Hirschorn?"

"Oh, did Mr. Salzman tell you, Rabbi Finkle?" Leo winced but she went on, "It was ages ago and almost forgotten. I remember I had to return for my sister's wedding."

And Lily would not be put off. "When," she asked in a trembly voice, "did you become enamored of God?"

He stared at her. Then it came to him that she was talking not about Leo Finkle, but of a total stranger, some mystical figure, perhaps even passionate prophet that Salzman had dreamed up for her—no relation to the living or dead. Leo trembled with rage and weakness. The trickster had obviously sold her a bill of goods, just as he had him, who'd expected to become acquainted with a young lady of twenty-nine, only to behold, the moment he laid eyes upon her strained and anxious face, a woman past thirty-five and aging rapidly. Only his self control had kept him this long in her presence.

"I am not," he said gravely, "a talented religious person," and in seeking words to go on, found himself possessed by shame and fear. "I think," he said in a strained manner, "that I came to God not because I loved Him, but because I did not."

This confession he spoke harshly because its unexpectedness shook him.

Lily wilted. Leo saw a profusion of loaves of bread go flying like ducks high over his head, not unlike the winged loaves by which he had counted himself to sleep last night. Mercifully, then, it snowed, which he would not put past Salzman's machinations.

He was infuriated with the marriage broker and swore he would throw him out of the room the minute he reappeared. But Salzman did not come that night, and when Leo's anger had subsided, an unaccountable despair grew in its place. At first he thought this was caused by his disappointment in Lily, but before long it became evident that he had involved himself with Salzman without a true knowledge of his own intent. He gradually realized—with an emptiness that seized him with six hands—that he had called in the broker to find him a bride because he was incapable of doing it himself. This terrifying insight he had derived as a result of his meeting and conversation with Lily Hirschorn. Her probing questions had somehow irritated him into revealing—to himself more than her—the true nature of his relationship to God, and from that it had come upon him, with shocking force, that apart from his

---

8. The "Law," or Torah, consists of Genesis, Exodus, Leviticus, Numbers, and Deuteronomy—that part of Old Testament Scripture called the Pentateuch (Five Books of Moses).

parents, he had never loved anyone. Or perhaps it went the other way, that he did not love God so well as he might, because he had not loved man. It seemed to Leo that his whole life stood starkly revealed and he saw himself for the first time as he truly was—unloved and loveless. This bitter but somehow not fully unexpected revelation brought him to a point of panic, controlled only by extraordinary effort. He covered his face with his hands and cried.

The week that followed was the worst of his life. He did not eat and lost weight. His beard darkened and grew ragged. He stopped attending seminars and almost never opened a book. He seriously considered leaving the Yeshiva, although he was deeply troubled at the thought of the loss of all his years of study—saw them like pages torn from a book, strewn over the city—and at the devastating effect of this decision upon his parents. But he had lived without knowledge of himself, and never in the Five Books and all the Commentaries—mea culpa[9]—had the truth been revealed to him. He did not know where to turn, and in all this desolating loneliness there was no *to whom*, although he often thought of Lily but not once could bring himself to go downstairs and make the call. He became touchy and irritable, especially with his landlady, who asked him all manner of personal questions; on the other hand, sensing his own disagreeableness, he waylaid her on the stairs and apologized abjectly, until mortified, she ran from him. Out of this, however, he drew the consolation that he was a Jew and that a Jew suffered. But gradually, as the long and terrible week drew to a close, he regained his composure and some idea of purpose in life: to go on as planned. Although he was imperfect, the ideal was not. As for his quest of a bride, the thought of continuing afflicted him with anxiety and heartburn, yet perhaps with this new knowledge of himself he would be more successful than in the past. Perhaps love would now come to him and a bride to that love. And for this sanctified seeking who needed a Salzman?

The marriage broker, a skeleton with haunted eyes, returned that very night. He looked, withal, the picture of frustrated expectancy—as if he had steadfastly waited the week at Miss Lily Hirschorn's side for a telephone call that never came.

Casually coughing, Salzman came immediately to the point: "So how did you like her?"

Leo's anger rose and he could not refrain from chiding the matchmaker: "Why did you lie to me, Salzman?"

Salzman's pale face went dead white, the world had snowed on him.

"Did you not state that she was twenty-nine?" Leo insisted.

"I gave you my word—"

"She was thirty-five, if a day. *At least* thirty-five."

"Of this don't be too sure. Her father told me—"

"Never mind. The worst of it was that you lied to her."

"How did I lie to her, tell me?"

"You told her things about me that weren't true. You made me out to be more, consequently less than I am. She had in mind a totally different person, a sort of semimystical Wonder Rabbi."

"All I said, you was a religious man."

---

9. Literally, "through my fault" (Latin), an admission of error. "Commentaries": explanatory commentaries on the Pentateuch.

"I can imagine."

Salzman sighed. "This is my weakness that I have," he confessed. "My wife says to me I shouldn't be a salesman, but when I have two fine people that they would be wonderful to be married, I am so happy that I talk too much." He smiled wanly. "This is why Salzman is a poor man."

Leo's anger left him. "Well, Salzman, I'm afraid that's all."

The marriage broker fastened hungry eyes on him.

"You don't want anymore a bride?"

"I do," said Leo, "but I have decided to seek her in a different way. I am no longer interested in an arranged marriage. To be frank, I now admit the necessity of premarital love. That is, I want to be in love with the one I marry."

"Love?" said Salzman, astounded. After a moment he remarked, "For us, our love is our life, not for the ladies. In the ghetto they—"

"I know, I know," said Leo. "I've thought of it often. Love, I have said to myself, should be a by-product of living and worship rather than its own end. Yet for myself I find it necessary to establish the level of my need and fulfill it."

Salzman shrugged but answered, "Listen, rabbi, if you want love, this I can find for you also. I have such beautiful clients that you will love them the minute your eyes will see them."

Leo smiled unhappily. "I'm afraid you don't understand."

But Salzman hastily unstrapped his portfolio and withdrew a manila packet from it.

"Pictures," he said, quickly laying the envelope on the table.

Leo called after him to take the pictures away, but as if on the wings of the wind, Salzman had disappeared.

March came. Leo had returned to his regular routine. Although he felt not quite himself yet—lacked energy—he was making plans for a more active social life. Of course it would cost something, but he was an expert in cutting corners; and when there were no corners left he would make circles rounder. All the while Salzman's pictures had lain on the table, gathering dust. Occasionally as Leo sat studying, or enjoying a cup of tea, his eyes fell on the manila envelope, but he never opened it.

The days went by and no social life to speak of developed with a member of the opposite sex—it was difficult, given the circumstances of his situation. One morning Leo toiled up the stairs to his room and stared out the window at the city. Although the day was bright his view of it was dark. For some time he watched people in the street below hurrying along and then turned with a heavy heart to his little room. On the table was the packet. With a sudden relentless gesture he tore it open. For a half-hour he stood by the table in a state of excitement, examining the photographs of the ladies Salzman had included. Finally, with a deep sigh he put them down. There were six, of varying degrees of attractiveness, but look at them long enough and they all became Lily Hirschorn: all past their prime, all starved behind bright smiles, not a true personality in the lot. Life, despite their frantic yoohooings, had passed them by; they were pictures in a brief case that stank of fish. After a while, however, as Leo attempted to return the photographs into the envelope, he found in it another, a snapshot of the type taken by a machine for a quarter. He gazed at it a moment and let out a cry.

Her face deeply moved him. Why, he could at first not say. It gave him the impression of youth—spring flowers, yet age—a sense of having been used to the bone, wasted; this came from the eyes, which were hauntingly familiar, yet absolutely strange. He had a vivid impression that he had met her before, but try as he might he could not place her although he could almost recall her name, as if he had read it in her own handwriting. No, this couldn't be; he would have remembered her. It was not, he affirmed, that she had an extraordinary beauty—no, though her face was attractive enough; it was that *something* about her moved him. Feature for feature, even some of the ladies of the photographs could do better; but she leaped forth to his heart—had *lived*, or wanted to—more than just wanted, perhaps regretted how she had lived—had somehow deeply suffered: it could be seen in the depths of those reluctant eyes, and from the way the light enclosed and shone from her, and within her, opening realms of possibility: this was her own. Her he desired. His head ached and eyes narrowed with the intensity of his gazing, then as if an obscure fog had blown up in the mind, he experienced fear of her and was aware that he had received an impression, somehow, of evil. He shuddered, saying softly, it is thus with us all. Leo brewed some tea in a small pot and sat sipping it without sugar, to calm himself. But before he had finished drinking, again with excitement he examined the face and found it good: good for Leo Finkle. Only such a one could understand him and help him seek whatever he was seeking. She might, perhaps, love him. How she had happened to be among the discards in Salzman's barrel he could never guess, but he knew he must urgently go find her.

Leo rushed downstairs, grabbed up the Bronx telephone book, and searched for Salzman's home address. He was not listed, nor was his office. Neither was he in the Manhattan book. But Leo remembered having written down the address on a slip of paper after he had read Salzman's advertisement in the "personals" column of the *Forward*. He ran up to his room and tore through his papers, without luck. It was exasperating. Just when he needed the matchmaker he was nowhere to be found. Fortunately Leo remembered to look in his wallet. There on a card he found his name written and a Bronx address. No phone number was listed, the reason—Leo now recalled—he had originally communicated with Salzman by letter. He got on his coat, put a hat on over his skull cap and hurried to the subway station. All the way to the far end of the Bronx he sat on the edge of his seat. He was more than once tempted to take out the picture and see if the girl's face was as he remembered it, but he refrained, allowing the snapshot to remain in his inside coat pocket, content to have her so close. When the train pulled into the station he was waiting at the door and bolted out. He quickly located the street Salzman had advertised.

The building he sought was less than a block from the subway, but it was not an office building, nor even a loft, nor a store in which one could rent office space. It was a very old tenement house. Leo found Salzman's name in pencil on a soiled tag under the bell and climbed three dark flights to his apartment. When he knocked, the door was opened by a thin, asthmatic, gray-haired woman, in felt slippers.

"Yes?" she said, expecting nothing. She listened without listening. He could have sworn he had seen her, too, before but knew it was an illusion.

"Salzman—does he live here? Pinye Salzman," he said, "the matchmaker?"

She stared at him a long minute. "Of course."

He felt embarrassed. "Is he in?"

"No." Her mouth, though left open, offered nothing more.

"The matter is urgent. Can you tell me where his office is?"

"In the air." She pointed upward.

"You mean he has no office?" Leo asked.

"In his socks."

He peered into the apartment. It was sunless and dingy, one large room divided by a half-open curtain, beyond which he could see a sagging metal bed. The near side of a room was crowded with rickety chairs, old bureaus, a three-legged table, racks of cooking utensils, and all the apparatus of a kitchen. But there was no sign of Salzman or his magic barrel, probably also a figment of the imagination. An odor of frying fish made Leo weak to the knees.

"Where is he?" he insisted. "I've got to see your husband."

At length she answered, "So who knows where he is? Every time he thinks a new thought he runs to a different place. Go home, he will find you."

"Tell him Leo Finkle."

She gave no sign she had heard.

He walked downstairs, depressed.

But Salzman, breathless, stood waiting at his door.

Leo was astounded and overjoyed. "How did you get here before me?"

"I rushed."

"Come inside."

They entered. Leo fixed tea, and a sardine sandwich for Salzman. As they were drinking he reached behind him for the packet of pictures and handed them to the marriage broker.

Salzman put down his glass and said expectantly, "You found somebody you like?"

"Not among these."

The marriage broker turned away.

"Here is the one I want." Leo held forth the snapshot.

Salzman slipped on his glasses and took the picture into his trembling hand. He turned ghastly and let out a groan.

"What's the matter?" cried Leo.

"Excuse me. Was an accident this picture. She isn't for you."

Salzman frantically shoved the manila packet into his portfolio. He thrust the snapshot into his pocket and fled down the stairs.

Leo, after momentary paralysis, gave chase and cornered the marriage broker in the vestibule. The landlady made hysterical outcries but neither of them listened.

"Give me back the picture, Salzman."

"No." The pain in his eyes was terrible.

"Tell me who she is then."

"This I can't tell you. Excuse me."

He made to depart, but Leo, forgetting himself, seized the matchmaker by his tight coat and shook him frenziedly.

"Please," sighed Salzman. "*Please*."

Leo ashamedly let him go. "Tell me who she is," he begged. "It's very important for me to know."

"She is not for you. She is a wild one—wild, without shame. This is not a bride for a rabbi."

"What do you mean wild?"

"Like an animal. Like a dog. For her to be poor was a sin. This is why to me she is dead now."

"In God's name, what do you mean?"

"Her I can't introduce to you," Salzman said.

"Why are you so excited?"

"Why, he asks," Salzman said, bursting into tears. "This is my baby, my Stella, she should burn in hell."

Leo hurried up to bed and hid under the covers. Under the covers he thought his life through. Although he soon fell asleep he could not sleep her out of his mind. He woke, beating his breast. Though he prayed to be rid of her, his prayers went unanswered. Through days of torment he endlessly struggled not to love her; fearing success, he escaped it. He then concluded to convert her to goodness, himself to God. The idea alternately nauseated and exalted him.

He perhaps did not know that he had come to a final decision until he encountered Salzman in a Broadway cafeteria. He was sitting alone at a rear table, sucking the bony remains of a fish. The marriage broker appeared haggard, and transparent to the point of vanishing.

Salzman looked up at first without recognizing him. Leo had grown a pointed beard and his eyes were weighted with wisdom.

"Salzman," he said, "love has at last come to my heart."

"Who can love from a picture?" mocked the marriage broker.

"It is not impossible."

"If you can love her, then you can love anybody. Let me show you some new clients that they just sent me their photographs. One is a little doll."

"Just her I want," Leo murmured.

"Don't be a fool, doctor. Don't bother with her."

"Put me in touch with her, Salzman," Leo said humbly. "Perhaps I can be of service."

Salzman had stopped eating and Leo understood with emotion that it was now arranged.

Leaving the cafeteria, he was, however, afflicted by a tormenting suspicion that Salzman had planned it all to happen this way.

Leo was informed by letter that she would meet him on a certain corner, and she was there one spring night, waiting under a street lamp. He appeared, carrying a small bouquet of violets and rosebuds. Stella stood by the lamp post, smoking. She wore white with red shoes, which fitted his expectations, although in a troubled moment he had imagined the dress red, and only the shoes white. She waited uneasily and shyly. From afar he saw that her eyes—clearly her father's—were filled with desperate innocence. He pictured, in her, his own redemption. Violins and lit candles revolved in the sky. Leo ran forward with flowers outthrust.

Around the corner, Salzman, leaning against a wall, chanted prayers for the dead.

1958

RALPH ELLISON
1914-1994

When Ralph Waldo Ellison began writing what would become *Invisible Man* (1952), American readers and critics were skeptical that black experience could rise to the level of "universal" significance that defined high literary ambition at the time. Asked in 1953 whether he thought "the Negro writer" could "escape provincialism when his literature is concerned with a minority," Ellison stressed the universality of the individual human being. Ellison was true to the experience, thoughts, imagination, and inner truth of the individual in his fiction. He consciously departed from the model of his mentor, Richard Wright, setting aside the social realism perfected by Wright—and thereafter expected of black writers—in favor of the styles and techniques of Modernism. Inspired by Melville, Hemingway, Joyce, and others, he stepped away from realism to reconsider humanity through the eyes of an unnamed black narrator described only as "invisible."

Ellison was born and raised in Oklahoma, won a state scholarship, and attended the Tuskegee Institute, where he was a music major, his instrument the trumpet. He embraced both the Western classical repertoire and the world of Kansas City jazz then just reaching its heyday. Befriending the blues singer Jimmy Rushing and other members of what would be the great Count Basie band of the 1930s, Ellison saw in this "deep, rowdy stream of jazz" the power and control that constituted art. His abiding love of music is found in some of the essays in his collection *Shadow and Act* (1964). Ellison also immersed himself in the visual arts, admiring the African American sculptor Richmond Barthé, with whom he studied for a short time after he arrived in New York City in the early 1940s. He invoked Picasso as a master artist who could transform folk content into universal form, and he was inspired by the photography in Richard Wright's *Twelve Million Black Voices* (1941). Ellison collected art throughout his life, and readers of his fiction have noted that visual elements such as framing, color, shape, pigment, and the image of the canvas recur in his work as often as the more commonly noted elements of sound and music.

Ellison created *Invisible Man* through an arduous, seven-year process of planning and revision, inspired by his Modernist literary models and informed by his knowledge of music and the visual arts. When the novel was published in 1952, he was criticized for being less political than he should be as a black writer. The most prominent of these critics, Irving Howe, took the author to task for not following Wright's lead and devoting his fiction to the "Negro cause". Howe believed that African Americans should write social protest novels about the tragedy of black ghetto life. But Ellison's intellectual sphere was much broader, and in his life he crossed and recrossed what W. E. B. Du Bois called "the color line." He married a white woman at a time when this was against the law in several states, and he enjoyed an artistic circle that included not only the artists, writers, and musicians of the Harlem Renaissance but also the thriving Yiddish language writers in New York (an acquaintance reported that he was nearly fluent in Yiddish). Ellison wrote parts of *Invisible Man* at the office of a Jewish friend on Fifth Avenue, and in a letter he noted that white people at Radio City Music Hall looking through his windows as he typed seemed to think he was doing something obscene. For a short time he lived in the Hudson Valley with Saul Bellow, also featured in this volume, who was the son of Russian Jewish parents. Both Bellow and Ellison aspired to be great *American* writers.

"I wasn't, and am not, *primarily* concerned with injustice, but with art," Ellison declared. And yet he saw the novel as a driver of social change. "Serious literature" engaged what Ellison described as the "moral core" of a society; for Ellison, this meant the values of democracy and equality. Ellison called *Invisible Man* an "attempt to return to the mood of personal moral responsibility for democracy which typified the best of our nineteenth-century fiction." Readers may note that the narrator is told by a wealthy trustee to read Ralph Waldo Emerson (Ellison's namesake); the speech in "Battle Royal" sounds Emersonian, and references to Emerson and Melville can be found throughout the narrative. Ellison believed that in devoting himself to the novel as an art form, he took on "the responsibilities inherited by those who practice the craft in the U.S."—those of "describing for all that fragment of the huge diverse American experience which I know best" and of "shaping . . . the culture as I should like it to be." "The American novel," Ellison explained, "is in this sense a conquest of the frontier; as it describes our experience, it creates it."

Invisible Man won the National Book Award, and Ellison subsequently received a number of awards and lectureships. He taught at the Salzburg Seminar, Bard College, and the University of Chicago. In 1970 he was named Albert Schweitzer Professor of the Humanities at New York University, where he taught until his retirement. Always humble, Ellison called *Invisible Man* "an attempt" at a great novel, and he wondered whether it would "be around in 20 years." Ellison's self-critical habits of mind kept him from completing another book after *Invisible Man*; when he died in 1994 he left a mass of notes and manuscript material meant for several novels. Editors assembled the late novel *Juneteenth* (1999) from over 2,000 manuscript pages. A version of the novel Ellison worked on right after *Invisible Man*, titled *Three Days Before the Shooting . . .* , was similarly pieced together and published in 2010.

"Battle Royal," the excerpt from *Invisible Man* reprinted here, was originally published as a stand-alone story called "Invisible Man" in a 1947 issue of Cyril Connolly's *Horizon*, a leading British art and literature journal. It appeared in a special double issue titled "Art on the American *Horizon*," alongside contributions from the American poets Wallace Stevens, Marianne Moore, and e.e. cummings; art critic Clement Greenberg; and media critic Marshall McLuhan. It was republished in the United States in 1948 as "Battle Royal" in *'48: The Magazine of the Year*. Because many readers assumed that black writers drew only from personal experience, the story was received as if it were fact. Ellison had to insist that the story was "an imaginative re-creation of certain aspects of our American life and the effect these have upon our personality. As such," he advised, "it is to be read as a near allegory or an extended metaphor. . . . The facts themselves are of no moment, are, for me, even amusing."

From Invisible Man

Prologue[1]

I am an invisible man. No, I am not a spook like those who haunted Edgar Allan Poe; nor am I one of your Hollywood-movie ectoplasms. I am a man of substance, of flesh and bone, fiber and liquids—and I might even be said to possess a mind. I am invisible, understand, simply because people refuse to see me. Like the bodiless heads you see sometimes in circus sideshows, it is as though I have been surrounded by mirrors of hard, distorting glass.

---

1. Ras the Destroyer, Rinehart, and Brother Jack, mentioned in the prologue, are characters who will appear later in the novel.

When they approach me they see only my surroundings, themselves, or figments of their imagination—indeed, everything and anything except me.

Nor is my invisibility exactly a matter of a bio-chemical accident to my epidermis. That invisibility to which I refer occurs because of a peculiar disposition in the eyes of those with whom I come in contact. A matter of the construction of their *inner* eyes, those eyes with which they look through their physical eyes upon reality. I am not complaining, nor am I protesting either. It is sometimes advantageous to be unseen, although it is most often rather wearing on the nerves. Then too, you're constantly being bumped against by those of poor vision. Or again, you often doubt if you really exist. You wonder whether you aren't simply a phantom in other people's minds. Say, a figure in a nightmare which the sleeper tries with all his strength to destroy. It's when you feel like this that, out of resentment, you begin to bump people back. And, let me confess, you feel that way most of the time. You ache with the need to convince yourself that you do exist in the real world, that you're a part of all the sound and anguish, and you strike out with your fists, you curse and you swear to make them recognize you. And, alas, it's seldom successful.

One night I accidentally bumped into a man, and perhaps because of the near darkness he saw me and called me an insulting name. I sprang at him, seized his coat lapels and demanded that he apologize. He was a tall blond man, and as my face came close to his he looked insolently out of his blue eyes and cursed me, his breath hot in my face as he struggled. I pulled his chin down sharp upon the crown of my head, butting him as I had seen the West Indians do, and felt his flesh tear and the blood gush out, and I yelled, "Apologize! Apologize!" But he continued to curse and struggle, and I butted him again and again until he went down heavily, on his knees, profusely bleeding. I kicked him repeatedly, in a frenzy because he still uttered insults though his lips were frothy with blood. Oh yes, I kicked him! And in my outrage I got out my knife and prepared to slit his throat, right there beneath the lamplight in the deserted street, holding him in the collar with one hand, and opening the knife with my teeth—when it occurred to me that the man had not *seen* me, actually; that he, as far as he knew, was in the midst of a walking nightmare! And I stopped the blade, slicing the air as I pushed him away, letting him fall back to the street. I stared at him hard as the lights of a car stabbed through the darkness. He lay there, moaning on the asphalt; a man almost killed by a phantom. It unnerved me. I was both disgusted and ashamed. I was like a drunken man myself, wavering about on weakened legs. Then I was amused: Something in this man's thick head had sprung out and beaten him within an inch of his life. I began to laugh at this crazy discovery. Would he have awakened at the point of death? Would Death himself have freed him for wakeful living? But I didn't linger. I ran away into the dark, laughing so hard I feared I might rupture myself. The next day I saw his picture in the *Daily News*, beneath a caption stating that he had been "mugged." Poor fool, poor blind fool, I thought with sincere compassion, mugged by an invisible man!

Most of the time (although I do not choose as I once did to deny the violence of my days by ignoring it) I am not so overtly violent. I remember that I am invisible and walk softly so as not to awaken the sleeping ones. Sometimes it is best not to awaken them; there are few things in the world as dangerous as sleepwalkers. I learned in time though that it is possible to carry on a fight against them without their realizing it. For instance, I have been carrying on a fight with Monopolated Light & Power for some time now. I use their service and pay them nothing at all, and they don't know it. Oh, they suspect that power is being drained off, but they don't know where. All they know is that according to the master meter back there in their power station a hell of a lot of free current is disappearing somewhere into the jungle of Harlem. The joke, of course, is that I don't live in Harlem but in a border area. Several years ago (before I discovered the advantages of being invisible) I went through the routine process of buying service and paying their outrageous rates. But no more. I gave up all that, along with my apartment, and my old way of life: That way based upon the fallacious assumption that I, like other men, was visible. Now, aware of my invisibility, I live rent-free in a building rented strictly to whites, in a section of the basement that was shut off and forgotten during the nineteenth century, which I discovered when I was trying to escape in the night from Ras the Destroyer. But that's getting too far ahead of the story, almost to the end, although the end is in the beginning and lies far ahead.

The point now is that I found a home—or a hole in the ground, as you will. Now don't jump to the conclusion that because I call my home a "hole" it is damp and cold like a grave; there are cold holes and warm holes. Mine is a warm hole. And remember, a bear retires to his hole for the winter and lives until spring; then he comes strolling out like the Easter chick breaking from its shell. I say all this to assure you that it is incorrect to assume that, because I'm invisible and live in a hole, I am dead. I am neither dead nor in a state of suspended animation. Call me Jack-the-Bear,[2] for I am in a state of hibernation.

My hole is warm and full of light. Yes, *full* of light. I doubt if there is a brighter spot in all New York than this hole of mine, and I do not exclude Broadway. Or the Empire State Building on a photographer's dream night. But that is taking advantage of you. Those two spots are among the darkest of our whole civilization—pardon me, our whole *culture* (an important distinction, I've heard)—which might sound like a hoax, or a contradiction, but that (by contradiction, I mean) is how the world moves: Not like an arrow, but a boomerang. (Beware of those who speak of the *spiral* of history; they are preparing a boomerang. Keep a steel helmet handy.) I know; I have been boomeranged across my head so much that I now can see the darkness of lightness. And I love light. Perhaps you'll think it strange that an invisible man should need light, desire light, love light. But maybe it is exactly because I *am* invisible. Light confirms my reality, gives birth to my form. A beautiful girl once told me of a recurring nightmare in which she lay in the center of a large dark room and felt her face expand until it filled the whole room, becoming a formless mass while her eyes ran in bilious jelly up the chimney. And so it is with me. Without light I am not only invisible, but formless as well; and to be unaware of one's form is to live a death. I myself, after existing some twenty years, did not become alive until I discovered my invisibility.

That is why I fight my battle with Monopolated Light & Power. The deeper reason, I mean: It allows me to feel my vital aliveness. I also fight them for taking so much of my money before I learned to protect myself. In my hole in

2. Also the title of a 1940 jazz recording by Duke Ellington and his orchestra.

the basement there are exactly 1,369 lights. I've wired the entire ceiling, every inch of it. And not with fluorescent bulbs, but with the older, more-expensive-to-operate kind, the filament type. An act of sabotage, you know. I've already begun to wire the wall. A junk man I know, a man of vision, has supplied me with wire and sockets. Nothing, storm or flood, must get in the way of our need for light and ever more and brighter light. The truth is the light and light is the truth. When I finish all four walls, then I'll start on the floor. Just how that will go, I don't know. Yet when you have lived invisible as long as I have you develop a certain ingenuity. I'll solve the problem. And maybe I'll invent a gadget to place my coffee pot on the fire while I lie in bed, and even invent a gadget to warm my bed—like the fellow I saw in one of the picture magazines who made himself a gadget to warm his shoes! Though invisible, I am in the great American tradition of tinkers. That makes me kin to Ford, Edison and Franklin. Call me, since I have a theory and a concept, a "thinker-tinker." Yes, I'll warm my shoes; they need it, they're usually full of holes. I'll do that and more.

Now I have one radio-phonograph; I plan to have five. There is a certain acoustical deadness in my hole, and when I have music I want to *feel* its vibration, not only with my ear but with my whole body. I'd like to hear five recordings of Louis Armstrong playing and singing "What Did I Do to Be So Black and Blue"—all at the same time. Sometimes now I listen to Louis while I have my favorite dessert of vanilla ice cream and sloe gin. I pour the red liquid over the white mound, watching it glisten and the vapor rising as Louis bends that military instrument into a beam of lyrical sound. Perhaps I like Louis Armstrong because he's made poetry out of being invisible. I think it must be because he's unaware that he *is* invisible. And my own grasp of invisibility aids me to understand his music. Once when I asked for a cigarette, some jokers gave me a reefer, which I lighted when I got home and sat listening to my phonograph. It was a strange evening. Invisibility, let me explain, gives one a slightly different sense of time, you're never quite on the beat. Sometimes you're ahead and sometimes behind. Instead of the swift and imperceptible flowing of time, you are aware of its nodes, those points where time stands still or from which it leaps ahead. And you slip into the breaks and look around. That's what you hear vaguely in Louis' music.

Once I saw a prizefighter boxing a yokel. The fighter was swift and amazingly scientific. His body was one violent flow of rapid rhythmic action. He hit the yokel a hundred times when the yokel held up his arms in stunned surprise. But suddenly the yokel, rolling about in the gale of boxing gloves, struck one blow and knocked science, speed and footwork as cold as a well-digger's posterior. The smart money hit the canvas. The long shot got the nod. The yokel had simply stepped inside of his opponent's sense of time. So under the spell of the reefer I discovered a new analytical way of listening to music. The unheard sounds came through, and each melodic line existed of itself, stood out clearly from all the rest, said its piece, and waited patiently for the other voices to speak. That night I found myself hearing not only in time, but in space as well. I not only entered the music but descended, like Dante, into its depths. *And beneath the swiftness of the hot tempo there was a slower tempo and a cave and I entered it and looked around and heard an old woman singing a spiritual as full of Weltschmerz as flamenco, and beneath that lay a still lower level on which I saw a beautiful girl the color of ivory pleading in a voice like my mother's as she stood before a group of slaveowners who bid for her naked body, and below that I found a lower level and a more rapid tempo and I heard someone shout:*

"Brothers and sisters, my text this morning is the 'Blackness of Blackness.'"

And a congregation of voices answered: "That blackness is most black, brother, most black . . ."

"In the beginning . . ."

"At the very start," they cried.

". . . there was blackness . . ."

"Preach it . . ."

". . . and the sun . . ."

"The sun, Lawd . . ."

". . . was blood red . . ."

"Red . . ."

"Now black is . . ." the preacher shouted.

"Bloody . . ."

"I said black is . . ."

"Preach it, brother . . ."

". . . an' black ain't . . ."

"Red, Lawd, red: He said it's red!"

"Amen, brother . . ."

"Black will git you . . ."

"Yes, it will . . ."

". . . an' black won't . . ."

"Now, it won't!"

"It do . . ."

"It do, Lawd . . ."

". . . an' it don't."

"Halleluiah . . ."

". . . It'll put you, glory, glory, Oh my Lawd, in the WHALE'S BELLY."

"Preach it, dear brother . . ."

". . . an' make you tempt . . ."

"Good God a-mighty!"

"Old Aunt Nelly!"

"Black will make you . . ."

"Black . . ."

". . . or black will un-make you."

"Ain't it the truth, Lawd?"

And at that point a voice of trombone timbre screamed at me, "Git out of here, you fool! Is you ready to commit treason?"

And I tore myself away, hearing the old singer of spirituals moaning, "Go curse your God, boy, and die."

I stopped and questioned her, asked her what was wrong.

"I dearly loved my master, son," she said.

"You should have hated him," I said.

"He gave me several sons," she said, "and because I loved my sons I learned to love their father though I hated him too."

"I too have become acquainted with ambivalence," I said. "That's why I'm here."

"What's that?"

"Nothing, a word that doesn't explain it. Why do you moan?"

"I moan this way 'cause he's dead," she said.

"Then tell me, who is that laughing upstairs?"

"Them's my sons. They glad."

"Yes, I can understand that too," I said.

"I laughs too, but I moans too. He promised to set us free but he never could bring hisself to do it. Still I loved him . . ."

"Loved him? You mean . . . ?"

"Oh, yes, but I loved something else even more."

"What more?"

"Freedom."

"Freedom," I said. "Maybe freedom lies in hating."

"Naw, son, it's in loving. I loved him and give him the poison and he withered away like a frost-bit apple. Them boys woulda tore him to pieces with they homemade knives."

"A mistake was made somewhere," I said, "I'm confused." And I wished to say other things, but the laughter upstairs became too loud and moan-like for me and I tried to break out of it, but I couldn't. Just as I was leaving I felt an urgent desire to ask her what freedom was and went back. She sat with her head in her hands, moaning softly; her leather-brown face was filled with sadness.

"Old woman, what is this freedom you love so well?" I asked around a corner of my mind.

She looked surprised, then thoughtful, then baffled. "I done forgot, son. It's all mixed up. First I think it's one thing, then I think it's another. It gits my head to spinning. I guess now it ain't nothing but knowing how to say what I got up in my head. But it's a hard job, son. Too much is done happen to me in too short a time. Hit's like I have a fever. Ever'time I starts to walk my head gits to swirling and I falls down. Or if it ain't that, it's the boys; they gits to laughing and wants to kill up the white folks. They's bitter, that's what they is . . ."

"But what about freedom?"

"Leave me 'lone, boy; my head aches!"

I left her, feeling dizzy myself. I didn't get far.

Suddenly one of the sons, a big fellow six feet tall, appeared out of nowhere and struck me with his fist.

"What's the matter, man?" I cried.

"You made Ma cry!"

"But how?" I said, dodging a blow.

"Askin' her them questions, that's how. Git outa here and stay, and next time you got questions like that, ask yourself!"

He held me in a grip like cold stone, his fingers fastening upon my windpipe until I thought I would suffocate before he finally allowed me to go. I stumbled about dazed, the music beating hysterically in my ears. It was dark. My head cleared and I wandered down a dark narrow passage, thinking I heard his footsteps hurrying behind me. I was sore, and into my being had come a profound craving for tranquillity, for peace and quiet, a state I felt I could never achieve. For one thing, the trumpet was blaring and the rhythm was too hectic. A tom-tom beating like heart-thuds began drowning out the trumpet, filling my ears. I longed for water and I heard it rushing through the cold mains my fingers touched as I felt my way, but I couldn't stop to search because of the footsteps behind me.

"Hey, Ras," I called. "Is it you, Destroyer? Rinehart?"

No answer, only the rhythmic footsteps behind me. Once I tried crossing the road, but a speeding machine struck me, scraping the skin from my leg as it roared past.

Then somehow I came out of it, ascending hastily from this underworld of sound to hear Louis Armstrong innocently asking,

> *What did I do*
> *To be so black*
> *And blue?*

At first I was afraid; this familiar music had demanded action, the kind of which I was incapable, and yet had I lingered there beneath the surface I might have attempted to act. Nevertheless, I know now that few really listen to this music. I sat on the chair's edge in a soaking sweat, as though each of my 1,369 bulbs had everyone become a klieg light[3] in an individual setting for a third degree with Ras and Rinehart in charge. It was exhausting—as though I had held my breath continuously for an hour under the terrifying serenity that comes from days of intense hunger. And yet, it was a strangely satisfying experience for an invisible man to hear the silence of sound. I had discovered unrecognized compulsions of my being—even though I could not answer "yes" to their promptings. I haven't smoked a reefer since, however; not because they're illegal, but because to *see* around corners is enough (that is not unusual when you are invisible). But to hear around them is too much; it inhibits action. And despite Brother Jack and all that sad, lost period of the Brotherhood, I believe in nothing if not in action.

Please, a definition: A hibernation is a covert preparation for a more overt action.

Besides, the drug destroys one's sense of time completely. If that happened, I might forget to dodge some bright morning and some cluck would run me down with an orange and yellow street car, or a bilious bus! Or I might forget to leave my hole when the moment for action presents itself.

Meanwhile I enjoy my life with the compliments of Monopolated Light & Power. Since you never recognize me even when in closest contact with me, and since, no doubt, you'll hardly believe that I exist, it won't matter if you know that I tapped a power line leading into the building and ran it into my hole in the ground. Before that I lived in the darkness into which I was chased, but now I see. I've illuminated the blackness of my invisibility—and vice versa. And so I play the invisible music of my isolation. The last statement doesn't seem just right, does it? But it is; you hear this music simply because music is heard and seldom seen, except by musicians. Could this compulsion to put invisibility down in black and white be thus an urge to make music of invisibility? But I am an orator, a rabble rouser—Am? I *was,* and perhaps shall be again. Who knows? All sickness is not unto death, neither is invisibility.

I can hear you say, "What a horrible, irresponsible bastard!" And you're right. I leap to agree with you. I am one of the most irresponsible beings that ever lived. Irresponsibility is part of my invisibility; any way you face it, it is a denial. But to whom can I be responsible, and why should I be, when

---

3. Powerful arc light used in making movies.

you refuse to see me? And wait until I reveal how truly irresponsible I am. Responsibility rests upon recognition, and recognition is a form of agreement. Take the man whom I almost killed: Who was responsible for that near murder—I? I don't think so, and I refuse it. I won't buy it. You can't give it to me. *He* bumped *me*, *he* insulted *me*. Shouldn't he, for his own personal safety, have recognized my hysteria, my "danger potential"? He, let us say, was lost in a dream world. But didn't *he* control that dream world—which, alas, is only too real!—and didn't *he* rule me out of it? And if he had yelled for a policeman, wouldn't *I* have been taken for the offending one? Yes, yes, yes! Let me agree with you, I was the irresponsible one; for I should have used my knife to protect the higher interests of society. Some day that kind of foolishness will cause us tragic trouble. All dreamers and sleepwalkers must pay the price, and even the invisible victim is responsible for the fate of all. But I shirked that responsibility; I became too snarled in the incompatible notions that buzzed within my brain. I was a coward . . .

But what did *I* do to be so blue? Bear with me.

Chapter I

[BATTLE ROYAL]

It goes a long way back, some twenty years. All my life I had been looking for something, and everywhere I turned someone tried to tell me what it was. I accepted their answers too, though they were often in contradiction and even self-contradictory. I was naïve. I was looking for myself and asking everyone except myself questions which I, and only I, could answer. It took me a long time and much painful boomeranging of my expectations to achieve a realization everyone else appears to have been born with: That I am nobody but myself. But first I had to discover that I am an invisible man!

And yet I am no freak of nature, nor of history. I was in the cards, other things having been equal (or unequal) eighty-five years ago. I am not ashamed of my grandparents for having been slaves. I am only ashamed of myself for having at one time been ashamed. About eighty-five years ago they were told that they were free, united with others of our country in everything pertaining to the common good, and, in everything social, separate like the fingers of the hand. And they believed it. They exulted in it. They stayed in their place, worked hard, and brought up my father to do the same. But my grandfather is the one. He was an odd old guy, my grandfather, and I am told I take after him. It was he who caused the trouble. On his deathbed he called my father to him and said, "Son, after I'm gone I want you to keep up the good fight. I never told you, but our life is a war and I have been a traitor all my born days, a spy in the enemy's country ever since I give up my gun back in the Reconstruction. Live with your head in the lion's mouth. I want you to overcome 'em with yeses, undermine 'em with grins, agree 'em to death and destruction, let 'em swoller you till they vomit or bust wide open." They thought the old man had gone out of his mind. He had been the meekest of men. The younger children were rushed from the room, the shades drawn and the flame of the lamp turned so low that it sputtered on the wick like the old man's breathing. "Learn it to the younguns," he whispered fiercely; then he died.

But my folks were more alarmed over his last words than over his dying. It was as though he had not died at all, his words caused so much anxiety. I was warned emphatically to forget what he had said and, indeed, this is the first time it has been mentioned outside the family circle. It had a tremendous effect upon me, however. I could never be sure of what he meant. Grandfather had been a quiet old man who never made any trouble, yet on his deathbed he had called himself a traitor and a spy, and he had spoken of his meekness as a dangerous activity. It became a constant puzzle which lay unanswered in the back of my mind. And whenever things went well for me I remembered my grandfather and felt guilty and uncomfortable. It was as though I was carrying out his advice in spite of myself. And to make it worse, everyone loved me for it. I was praised by the most lily-white men of the town. I was considered an example of desirable conduct—just as my grandfather had been. And what puzzled me was that the old man had defined it as *treachery*. When I was praised for my conduct I felt a guilt that in some way I was doing something that was really against the wishes of the white folks, that if they had understood they would have desired me to act just the opposite, that I should have been sulky and mean, and that that really would have been what they wanted, even though they were fooled and thought they wanted me to act as I did. It made me afraid that some day they would look upon me as a traitor and I would be lost. Still I was more afraid to act any other way because they didn't like that at all. The old man's words were like a curse. On my graduation day I delivered an oration in which I showed that humility was the secret, indeed, the very essence of progress. (Not that I believed this—how could I, remembering my grandfather?—I only believed that it worked.) It was a great success. Everyone praised me and I was invited to give the speech at a gathering of the town's leading white citizens. It was a triumph for our whole community.

It was in the main ballroom of the leading hotel. When I got there I discovered that it was on the occasion of a smoker, and I was told that since I was to be there anyway I might as well take part in the battle royal to be fought by some of my schoolmates as part of the entertainment. The battle royal came first.

All of the town's big shots were there in their tuxedoes, wolfing down the buffet foods, drinking beer and whiskey and smoking black cigars. It was a large room with a high ceiling. Chairs were arranged in neat rows around three sides of a portable boxing ring. The fourth side was clear, revealing a gleaming space of polished floor. I had some misgivings over the battle royal, by the way. Not from a distaste for fighting, but because I didn't care too much for the other fellows who were to take part. They were tough guys who seemed to have no grandfather's curse worrying their minds. No one could mistake their toughness. And besides, I suspected that fighting a battle royal might detract from the dignity of my speech. In those pre-invisible days I visualized myself as a potential Booker T. Washington.[4] But the other fellows didn't care too much for me either, and there were nine of them. I felt superior to them in my way, and I didn't like the manner in which we were all crowded together into the servants' elevator. Nor did they like my being there. In fact, as the warmly lighted floors flashed past the elevator

4. African American author and educator (1856–1915).

we had words over the fact that I, by taking part in the fight, had knocked one of their friends out of a night's work.

We were led out of the elevator through a rococo hall into an anteroom and told to get into our fighting togs. Each of us was issued a pair of boxing gloves and ushered out into the big mirrored hall, which we entered looking cautiously about us and whispering, lest we might accidentally be heard above the noise of the room. It was foggy with cigar smoke. And already the whiskey was taking effect. I was shocked to see some of the most important men of the town quite tipsy. They were all there—bankers, lawyers, judges, doctors, fire chiefs, teachers, merchants. Even one of the more fashionable pastors. Something we could not see was going on up front. A clarinet was vibrating sensuously and the men were standing up and moving eagerly forward. We were a small tight group, clustered together, our bare upper bodies touching and shining with anticipatory sweat; while up front the big shots were becoming increasingly excited over something we still could not see. Suddenly I heard the school superintendent, who had told me to come, yell, "Bring up the shines, gentlemen! Bring up the little shines!"

We were rushed up to the front of the ballroom, where it smelled even more strongly of tobacco and whiskey. Then we were pushed into place. I almost wet my pants. A sea of faces, some hostile, some amused, ringed around us, and in the center, facing us, stood a magnificent blonde—stark naked. There was dead silence. I felt a blast of cold air chill me. I tried to back away, but they were behind me and around me. Some of the boys stood with lowered heads, trembling. I felt a wave of irrational guilt and fear. My teeth chattered, my skin turned to goose flesh, my knees knocked. Yet I was strongly attracted and looked in spite of myself. Had the price of looking been blindness, I would have looked. The hair was yellow like that of a circus kewpie doll, the face heavily powdered and rouged, as though to form an abstract mask, the eyes hollow and smeared a cool blue, the color of a baboon's butt. I felt a desire to spit upon her as my eyes brushed slowly over her body. Her breasts were firm and round as the domes of East Indian temples, and I stood so close as to see the fine skin texture and beads of pearly perspiration glistening like dew around the pink and erected buds of her nipples. I wanted at one and the same time to run from the room, to sink through the floor, or go to her and cover her from my eyes and the eyes of the others with my body; to feel the soft thighs, to caress her and destroy her, to love her and murder her, to hide from her, and yet to stroke where below the small American flag tattooed upon her belly her thighs formed a capital V. I had a notion that of all in the room she saw only me with her impersonal eyes.

And then she began to dance, a slow sensuous movement; the smoke of a hundred cigars clinging to her like the thinnest of veils. She seemed like a fair bird-girl girdled in veils calling to me from the angry surface of some gray and threatening sea. I was transported. Then I became aware of the clarinet playing and the big shots yelling at us. Some threatened us if we looked and others if we did not. On my right I saw one boy faint. And now a man grabbed a silver pitcher from a table and stepped close as he dashed ice water upon him and stood him up and forced two of us to support him as his head hung and moans issued from his thick bluish lips. Another boy began to plead to go home. He was the largest of the group, wearing dark red fighting trunks much too small to conceal the erection which projected from him as though in answer to the insinuating low-registered moaning of the clarinet. He tried to hide himself with his boxing gloves.

And all the while the blonde continued dancing, smiling faintly at the big shots who watched her with fascination, and faintly smiling at our fear. I noticed a certain merchant who followed her hungrily, his lips loose and drooling. He was a large man who wore diamond studs in a shirtfront which swelled with the ample paunch underneath, and each time the blonde swayed her undulating hips he ran his hand through the thin hair of his bald head and, with his arms upheld, his posture clumsy like that of an intoxicated panda, wound his belly in a slow and obscene grind. This creature was completely hypnotized. The music had quickened. As the dancer flung herself about with a detached expression on her face, the men began reaching out to touch her. I could see their beefy fingers sink into the soft flesh. Some of the others tried to stop them and she began to move around the floor in graceful circles, as they gave chase, slipping and sliding over the polished floor. It was mad. Chairs went crashing, drinks were spilt, as they ran laughing and howling after her. They caught her just as she reached a door, raised her from the floor, and tossed her as college boys are tossed at a hazing, and above her red, fixed-smiling lips I saw the terror and disgust in her eyes, almost like my own terror and that which I saw in some of the other boys. As I watched, they tossed her twice and her soft breasts seem to flatten against the air and her legs flung wildly as she spun. Some of the more sober ones helped her to escape. And I started off the floor, heading for the anteroom with the rest of the boys.

Some were still crying and in hysteria. But as we tried to leave we were stopped and ordered to get into the ring. There was nothing to do but what we were told. All ten of us climbed under the ropes and allowed ourselves to be blindfolded with broad bands of white cloth. One of the men seemed to feel a bit sympathetic and tried to cheer us up as we stood with our backs against the ropes. Some of us tried to grin. "See that boy over there?" one of the men said. "I want you to run across at the bell and give it to him right in the belly. If you don't get him, I'm going to get you. I don't like his looks." Each of us was told the same. The blindfolds were put on. Yet even then I had been going over my speech. In my mind each word was as bright as flame. I felt the cloth pressed into place, and frowned so that it would be loosened when I relaxed.

But now I felt a sudden fit of blind terror. I was unused to darkness. It was as though I had suddenly found myself in a dark room filled with poisonous cottonmouths. I could hear the bleary voices yelling insistently for the battle royal to begin.

"Get going in there!"

"Let me at that big nigger!"

I strained to pick up the school superintendent's voice, as though to squeeze some security out of that slightly more familiar sound.

"Let me at those black sonsabitches!" someone yelled.

"No, Jackson, no!" another voice yelled. "Here, somebody, help me hold Jack."

"I want to get at that ginger-colored nigger. Tear him limb from limb," the first voice yelled.

I stood against the ropes trembling. For in those days I was what they called ginger-colored, and he sounded as though he might crunch me between his teeth like a crisp ginger cookie.

Quite a struggle was going on. Chairs were being kicked about and I could hear voices grunting as with a terrific effort. I wanted to see, to see more desperately than ever before. But the blindfold was tight as a thick skin-puckering scab and when I raised my gloved hands to push the layers of white aside a voice yelled, "Oh, no you don't, black bastard! Leave that alone!"

"Ring the bell before Jackson kills him a coon!" someone boomed in the sudden silence. And I heard the bell clang and the sound of the feet scuffling forward.

A glove smacked against my head. I pivoted, striking out stiffly as someone went past, and felt the jar ripple along the length of my arm to my shoulder. Then it seemed as though all nine of the boys had turned upon me at once. Blows pounded me from all sides while I struck out as best I could. So many blows landed upon me that I wondered if I were not the only blindfolded fighter in the ring, or if the man called Jackson hadn't succeeded in getting me after all.

Blindfolded, I could no longer control my motions. I had no dignity. I stumbled about like a baby or a drunken man. The smoke had become thicker and with each new blow it seemed to sear and further restrict my lungs. My saliva became like hot bitter glue. A glove connected with my head, filling my mouth with warm blood. It was everywhere. I could not tell if the moisture I felt upon my body was sweat or blood. A blow landed hard against the nape of my neck. I felt myself going over, my head hitting the floor. Streaks of blue light filled the black world behind the blindfold. I lay prone, pretending that I was knocked out, but felt myself seized by hands and yanked to my feet. "Get going, black boy! Mix it up!" My arms were like lead, my head smarting from blows. I managed to feel my way to the ropes and held on, trying to catch my breath. A glove landed in my mid-section and I went over again, feeling as though the smoke had become a knife jabbed into my guts. Pushed this way and that by the legs milling around me, I finally pulled erect and discovered that I could see the black, sweat-washed forms weaving in the smoky-blue atmosphere like drunken dancers weaving to the rapid drum-like thuds of blows.

Everyone fought hysterically. It was complete anarchy. Everybody fought everybody else. No group fought together for long. Two, three, four, fought one, then turned to fight each other, were themselves attacked. Blows landed below the belt and in the kidney, with the gloves open as well as closed, and with my eye partly opened now there was not so much terror. I moved carefully, avoiding blows, although not too many to attract attention, fighting from group to group. The boys groped about like blind, cautious crabs crouching to protect their mid-sections, their heads pulled in short against their shoulders, their arms stretched nervously before them, with their fists testing the smoke-filled air like the knobbed feelers of hypersensitive snails. In one corner I glimpsed a boy violently punching the air and heard him scream in pain as he smashed his hand against a ring post. For a second I saw him bent over holding his hand, then going down as a blow caught his unprotected head. I played one group against the other, slipping in and throwing a punch then stepping out of range while pushing the others into the melee to take the blows blindly aimed at me. The smoke was agonizing and there were no rounds, no bells at three minute intervals to relieve our exhaustion. The room spun around me, a swirl of lights, smoke, sweating bodies surrounded by tense white faces. I bled from both nose and mouth, the blood spattering upon my chest.

The men kept yelling, "Slug him, black boy! Knock his guts out!"

"Uppercut him! Kill him! Kill that big boy!"

Taking a fake fall, I saw a boy going down heavily beside me as though we were felled by a single blow, saw a sneaker-clad foot shoot into his groin as the two who had knocked him down stumbled upon him. I rolled out of range, feeling a twinge of nausea.

The harder we fought the more threatening the men became. And yet, I had begun to worry about my speech again. How would it go? Would they recognize my ability? What would they give me?

I was fighting automatically when suddenly I noticed that one after another of the boys was leaving the ring. I was surprised, filled with panic, as though I had been left alone with an unknown danger. Then I understood. The boys had arranged it among themselves. It was the custom for the two men left in the ring to slug it out for the winner's prize. I discovered this too late. When the bell sounded two men in tuxedoes leaped into the ring and removed the blindfold. I found myself facing Tatlock, the biggest of the gang. I felt sick at my stomach. Hardly had the bell stopped ringing in my ears than it clanged again and I saw him moving swiftly toward me. Thinking of nothing else to do I hit him smash on the nose. He kept coming, bringing the rank sharp violence of stale sweat. His face was a black blank of a face, only his eyes alive—with hate of me and aglow with a feverish terror from what had happened to us all. I became anxious. I wanted to deliver my speech and he came at me as though he meant to beat it out of me. I smashed him again and again, taking his blows as they came. Then on a sudden impulse I struck him lightly and as we clinched, I whispered, "Fake like I knocked you out, you can have the prize."

"I'll break your behind," he whispered hoarsely.

"For *them?*"

"For *me*, sonofabitch!"

They were yelling for us to break it up and Tatlock spun me half around with a blow, and as a joggled camera sweeps in a reeling scene, I saw the howling red faces crouching tense beneath the cloud of blue-gray smoke. For a moment the world wavered, unraveled, flowed, then my head cleared and Tatlock bounced before me. That fluttering shadow before my eyes was his jabbing left hand. Then falling forward, my head against his damp shoulder, I whispered,

"I'll make it five dollars more."

"Go to hell!"

But his muscles relaxed a trifle beneath my pressure and I breathed, "Seven?"

"Give it to your ma," he said, ripping me beneath the heart.

And while I still held him I butted him and moved away. I felt myself bombarded with punches. I fought back with hopeless desperation. I wanted to deliver my speech more than anything else in the world, because I felt that only these men could judge truly my ability, and now this stupid clown was ruining my chances. I began fighting carefully now, moving in to punch him and out again with my greater speed. A lucky blow to his chin and I had him going too—until I heard a loud voice yell, "I got my money on the big boy."

Hearing this, I almost dropped my guard. I was confused: Should I try to win against the voice out there? Would not this go against my speech, and was not this a moment for humility, for nonresistance? A blow to my head as I danced about sent my right eye popping like a jack-in-the-box and settled my dilemma. The room went red as I fell. It was a dream fall, my body languid and fastidious as to where to land, until the floor became impatient and smashed up to meet me. A moment later I came to. An hypnotic voice said FIVE emphatically. And I lay there, hazily watching a dark red spot of my own blood shaping itself into a butterfly, glistening and soaking into the soiled gray world of the canvas.

When the voice drawled TEN I was lifted up and dragged to a chair. I sat dazed. My eye pained and swelled with each throb of my pounding heart and I wondered if now I would be allowed to speak. I was wringing wet, my mouth still bleeding. We were grouped along the wall now. The other boys ignored me as they congratulated Tatlock and speculated as to how much they would be paid. One boy whimpered over his smashed hand. Looking up front, I saw attendants in white jackets rolling the portable ring away and placing a small square rug in the vacant space surrounded by chairs. Perhaps, I thought, I will stand on the rug to deliver my speech.

Then the M.C. called to us, "Come on up here boys and get your money."

We ran forward to where the men laughed and talked in their chairs, waiting. Everyone seemed friendly now.

"There it is on the rug," the man said. I saw the rug covered with coins of all dimensions and a few crumpled bills. But what excited me, scattered here and there, were the gold pieces.

"Boys, it's all yours," the man said. "You get all you grab."

"That's right, Sambo," a blond man said, winking at me confidentially.

I trembled with excitement, forgetting my pain. I would get the gold and the bills, I thought. I would use both hands. I would throw my body against the boys nearest me to block them from the gold.

"Get down around the rug now," the man commanded, "and don't anyone touch it until I give the signal."

"This ought to be good," I heard.

As told, we got around the square rug on our knees. Slowly the man raised his freckled hand as we followed it upward with our eyes.

I heard, "These niggers look like they're about to pray!"

Then, "Ready," the man said. "Go!"

I lunged for a yellow coin lying on the blue design of the carpet, touching it and sending a surprised shriek to join those rising around me. I tried frantically to remove my hand but could not let go. A hot, violent force tore through my body, shaking me like a wet rat. The rug was electrified. The hair bristled up on my head as I shook myself free. My muscles jumped, my nerves jangled, writhed. But I saw that this was not stopping the other boys. Laughing in fear and embarrassment, some were holding back and scooping up the coins knocked off by the painful contortions of the others. The men roared above us as we struggled.

"Pick it up, goddamnit, pick it up!" someone called like a bass-voiced parrot. "Go on, get it!"

I crawled rapidly around the floor, picking up the coins, trying to avoid the coppers and to get greenbacks and the gold. Ignoring the shock by laughing, as I brushed the coins off quickly, I discovered that I could contain the electricity—a contradiction, but it works. Then the men began to push us onto the rug. Laughing embarrassedly, we struggled out of their hands and kept after the coins. We were all wet and slippery and hard to hold. Suddenly I saw a boy lifted into the air, glistening with sweat like a circus seal, and dropped, his wet back landing flush upon the charged rug, heard him yell and saw him literally dance upon his back, his elbows beating a frenzied tattoo upon the floor, his muscles twitching like the flesh of a horse stung by many flies. When he finally rolled off, his face was gray and no one stopped him when he ran from the floor amid booming laughter.

"Get the money," the M.C. called. "That's good hard American cash!"

And we snatched and grabbed, snatched and grabbed. I was careful not to come too close to the rug now, and when I felt the hot whiskey breath descend upon me like a cloud of foul air I reached out and grabbed the leg of a chair. It was occupied and I held on desperately.

"Leggo, nigger! Leggo!"

The huge face wavered down to mine as he tried to push me free. But my body was slippery and he was too drunk. It was Mr. Colcord, who owned a chain of movie houses and "entertainment palaces." Each time he grabbed me I slipped out of his hands. It became a real struggle. I feared the rug more than I did the drunk, so I held on, surprising myself for a moment by trying to topple *him* upon the rug. It was such an enormous idea that I found myself actually carrying it out. I tried not to be obvious, yet when I grabbed his leg, trying to tumble him out of the chair, he raised up roaring with laughter, and, looking at me with soberness dead in the eye, kicked me viciously in the chest. The chair leg flew out of my hand and I felt myself going and rolled. It was as though I had rolled through a bed of hot coals. It seemed a whole century would pass before I would roll free, a century in which I was seared through the deepest levels of my body to the fearful breath within me and the breath seared and heated to the point of explosion. It'll all be over in a flash, I thought as I rolled clear. It'll all be over in a flash.

But not yet, the men on the other side were waiting, red faces swollen as though from apoplexy as they bent forward in their chairs. Seeing their fingers coming toward me I rolled away as a fumbled football rolls off the receiver's fingertips, back into the coals. That time I luckily sent the rug sliding out of place and heard the coins ringing against the floor and the boys scuffling to pick them up and the M.C. calling, "All right, boys, that's all. Go get dressed and get your money."

I was limp as a dish rag. My back felt as though it had been beaten with wires.

When we had dressed the M.C. came in and gave us each five dollars, except Tatlock, who got ten for being last in the ring. Then he told us to leave. I was not to get a chance to deliver my speech, I thought. I was going out into the dim alley in despair when I was stopped and told to go back. I returned to the ballroom, where the men were pushing back their chairs and gathering in groups to talk.

The M.C. knocked on a table for quiet. "Gentlemen," he said, "we almost forgot an important part of the program. A most serious part, gentlemen. This boy was brought here to deliver a speech which he made at his graduation yesterday . . ."

"Bravo!"

"I'm told that he is the smartest boy we've got out there in Greenwood. I'm told that he knows more big words than a pocket-sized dictionary."

Much applause and laughter.

"So now, gentlemen, I want you to give him your attention."

There was still laughter as I faced them, my mouth dry, my eye throbbing. I began slowly, but evidently my throat was tense, because they began shouting, "Louder! Louder!"

"We of the younger generation extol the wisdom of that great leader and educator," I shouted, "who first spoke these flaming words of wisdom: 'A ship lost at sea for many days suddenly sighted a friendly vessel. From the mast of the unfortunate vessel was seen a signal: "Water, water; we die of thirst!" The answer from the friendly vessel came back: "Cast down your bucket where you are." The captain of the distressed vessel, at last heeding the injunction, cast down his bucket, and it came up full of fresh sparkling water from the mouth of the Amazon River.' And like him I say, and in his words, 'To those of my race who depend upon bettering their condition in a foreign land, or who underestimate the importance of cultivating friendly relations with the Southern white man, who is his next-door neighbor, I would say: "Cast down your bucket where you are"—cast it down in making friends in every manly way of the people of all races by whom we are surrounded . . .'"

I spoke automatically and with such fervor that I did not realize that the men were still talking and laughing until my dry mouth, filling up with blood from the cut, almost strangled me. I coughed, wanting to stop and go to one of the tall brass, sand-filled spittoons to relieve myself, but a few of the men, especially the superintendent, were listening and I was afraid. So I gulped it down, blood, saliva and all, and continued. (What powers of endurance I had during those days! What enthusiasm! What a belief in the lightness of things!) I spoke even louder in spite of the pain. But still they talked and still they laughed, as though deaf with cotton in dirty ears. So I spoke with greater emotional emphasis. I closed my ears and swallowed blood until I was nauseated. The speech seemed a hundred times as long as before, but I could not leave out a single word. All had to be said, each memorized nuance considered, rendered. Nor was that all. Whenever I uttered a word of three or more syllables a group of voices would yell for me to repeat it. I used the phrase "social responsibility," and they yelled:

"What's that word you say, boy?"

"Social responsibility," I said.

"What?"

"Social . . ."

"Louder."

". . . responsibility."

"More!"

"Respon—"

"Repeat!"

"—sibility."

The room filled with the uproar of laughter until, no doubt, distracted by having to gulp down my blood, I made a mistake and yelled a phrase I had often seen denounced in newspaper editorials, heard debated in private.

"Social . . ."

"What?" they yelled.

". . . equality—"

The laughter hung smokelike in the sudden stillness. I opened my eyes, puzzled. Sounds of displeasure filled the room. The M.C. rushed forward. They shouted hostile phrases at me. But I did not understand.

A small dry mustached man in the front row blared out, "Say that slowly, son!"

"What, sir?"

"What you just said!"

"Social responsibility, sir," I said.

"You weren't being smart, were you, boy?" he said, not unkindly.

"No, sir!"

"You sure that about 'equality' was a mistake?"

"Oh, yes, sir," I said. "I was swallowing blood."

"Well, you had better speak more slowly so we can understand. We mean to do right by you, but you've got to know your place at all times. All right, now, go on with your speech."

I was afraid. I wanted to leave but I wanted also to speak and I was afraid they'd snatch me down.

"Thank you, sir," I said, beginning where I had left off, and having them ignore me as before.

Yet when I finished there was a thunderous applause. I was surprised to see the superintendent come forth with a package wrapped in white tissue paper, and, gesturing for quiet, address the men.

"Gentlemen, you see that I did not overpraise the boy. He makes a good speech and some day he'll lead his people in the proper paths. And I don't have to tell you that that is important in these days and times. This is a good, smart boy, and so to encourage him in the right direction, in the name of the Board of Education I wish to present him a prize in the form of this . . ."

He paused, removing the tissue paper and revealing a gleaming calfskin brief case.

". . . in the form of this first-class article from Shad Whitmore's shop."

"Boy," he said, addressing me, "take this prize and keep it well. Consider it a badge of office. Prize it. Keep developing as you are and some day it will be filled with important papers that will help shape the destiny of your people."

I was so moved that I could hardly express my thanks. A rope of bloody saliva forming a shape like an undiscovered continent drooled upon the leather and I wiped it quickly away. I felt an importance that I had never dreamed.

"Open it and see what's inside," I was told.

My fingers a-tremble, I complied, smelling the fresh leather and finding an official-looking document inside. It was a scholarship to the state college for Negroes. My eyes filled with tears and I ran awkwardly off the floor.

I was overjoyed; I did not even mind when I discovered that the gold pieces I had scrambled for were brass pocket tokens advertising a certain make of automobile.

When I reached home everyone was excited. Next day the neighbors came to congratulate me. I even felt safe from grandfather, whose deathbed curse usually spoiled my triumphs. I stood beneath his photograph with my brief case in hand and smiled triumphantly into his stolid black peasant's face. It was a face that fascinated me. The eyes seemed to follow everywhere I went.

That night I dreamed I was at a circus with him and that he refused to laugh at the clowns no matter what they did. Then later he told me to open my brief case and read what was inside and I did, finding an official envelope stamped with the state seal; and inside the envelope I found another and another, endlessly, and I thought I would fall of weariness. "Them's years," he said. "Now open that one." And I did and in it I found an engraved document containing a short message in letters of gold. "Read it," my grandfather said. "Out loud!"

"To Whom It May Concern," I intoned. "Keep This Nigger-Boy Running."

I awoke with the old man's laughter ringing in my ears.

(It was a dream I was to remember and dream again for many years after. But at that time I had no insight into its meaning. First I had to attend college.)

1952

SAUL BELLOW
1915–2005

Winner of the Nobel Prize in Literature in 1976, Saul Bellow distinguished himself through a writing career that spanned nearly two-thirds of a century. Bellow, the child of Russian Jewish immigrants, was born in Lachine, Quebec, a suburb of Montreal, and spent nine years there before moving with his family to Chicago. While relishing the style of big-city life typical of the 1920s and 1930s, he pursued an increasingly intellectual track through Tuley High School, the University of Chicago, and Northwestern University. Literature was always Bellow's great love, but as his biographer James Atlas explains, the antisemitic establishment was unreceptive to his ambitions. "In search of career advice," Atlas notes, Bellow sought counsel from the chair of Northwestern's English Department, William Frank Bryan, who warned him against postgraduate study in the field, because "no Jew could really grasp the tradition of English literature. . . . No Jew would ever have the right *feeling* for it." Bellow therefore began work toward a master's degree in sociology and anthropology at the University of Wisconsin. Discouraged by the technical work required and chided by his new advisor for being too literary, he dropped out after just one semester, returning to Chicago and a lifelong career in literature that involved teaching (initially at a downtown teachers college, later most prestigiously as a member of the University of Chicago's Committee on Social Thought), editing (first for the *Encyclopaedia Britannica*, then for his own journal, *The Noble Savage*), and writing fiction. Except for brief service in the bureaucracy of the merchant marine during World War II, a Guggenheim Fellowship year in Paris (1948–49), and some time living in New York City and the New England countryside, Bellow made Chicago his primary residence and the setting for his most characteristic work, most famously *The Adventures of Augie March* (1953). In finding a voice for the protagonist of this novel Bellow discovered his own style, a mix of the urban colloquial and the erudite.

Bellow's first novel, *Dangling Man*, was not published until he was nearly thirty. It is a short series of elegantly morose meditations, told through the journal of a young man waiting to be inducted into the army and with the "freedom" of having nothing to do but wait. Eventually he is drafted: "Long live regimentation," he sardonically exults. Bellow's second novel, *The Victim* (1947), continues the investigation of ways people strive to be relieved of self-determination. This book concerns a week in the life of Asa Leventhal, alone in New York City while his wife visits a relative; he is suddenly confronted by a figure from the past (Kirby Allbee, a Gentile) who succeeds in implicating Leventhal with the past and its present manifestations. *The Victim* is Bellow's most somberly naturalistic depiction of a man brought up against forces larger than himself, yet from the opening sentence ("On some nights New York is as hot as Bangkok") a poetic dimension appears and helps create the sense of mystery and disturbance felt by both the main character and the reader.

Dangling Man and *The Victim* are highly wrought, mainly humorless books; in two long novels published in the 1950s Bellow opened up into new ranges of aspiration and situational zaniness, which brought him respectful admiration from many critics. *The Adventures of Augie March* and *Henderson the Rain King* (1959) are each narrated by an "I" who, like Mark Twain's Huck Finn, is good at lighting out for the territory ahead of whoever means to tie him down. The hero's adventures, whether occurring in Chicago, Mexico, or Africa, are exuberantly delivered in an always stimulating and sometimes overactive prose. *Augie* is filled with sights and sounds, colors and surfaces; its tone is self-involved, affectionate, and affirmative; *Henderson*, Bellow's most extravagant narrative, has the even more fabulous air of a quest-romance, in which the hero returns home from Africa at peace with the world he had been warring against.

The ironic motto for Bellow's novels of the 1950s may well be "Seize the Day," as in the title of perhaps his most sharply defined piece of fiction. This short novel (1956) is both painful and exhilarating because it so fully exposes its hero (Tommy Wilhelm, an aging out-of-work ex-actor) to the insults of other people who don't understand him, to a city (New York, particularly its Upper West Side) impervious to his needs, and to a narrative prose that mixes ridicule and affection so thoroughly as to make them scarcely distinguishable. *Seize the Day* combines, within Tommy's monologues, a wildness and pathos of bitter comedy that was a powerful new element in Bellow's work.

In "Where Do We Go from Here? The Future of Fiction," an essay published in 1965, Bellow pointed out that nineteenth-century American literature—Emerson, Thoreau, Whitman, Melville—was highly didactic in its efforts to "instruct a young and raw nation." Bellow sees himself in this instructive tradition and in the international company of "didactic" novelists like Dostoyevsky, D. H. Lawrence, and Joseph Conrad; he believes also that "the imagination is looking for new ways to express virtue . . . we have barely begun to comprehend what a human being is." These concerns animate the novels Bellow wrote in the years since *Henderson*. In *Herzog* (1964) the hero is another down-and-outer, a professor-intellectual, a student of Romanticism and of the glorification of Self, which Herzog believes both modern life and modernist literature have been undercutting. At the same time he is a comic and pathetic victim of marital disorder; like all Bellow's heroes (and Bellow himself),

Herzog has a terrible time with women, yet cannot live without them. In *Mr. Sammler's Planet* (1970), written out of the disorders of the late 1960s, the atmosphere is grimmer. Sammler, an aging Jew living (again) on New York's Upper West Side, analyzes and judges but cannot understand the young or blacks, or the mass of people gathered at Broadway and Ninety-Sixth Street. He sees about him everywhere "poverty of soul" but admits that he too has "a touch of the same disease—the disease of the single self explaining what was what and who was who."

These novels, as well as *Humboldt's Gift* (1975), have been accused of parading too single-handedly attitudes toward which their author is sympathetic, whereas *The Dean's December* (1982) was criticized by John Updike, in a review, for being too much *"about* Saul Bellow," even though indirectly. Subsequently, a collection of shorter fiction, *Him with His Foot in His Mouth* (1984); the novels *More Die of Heartbreak* (1987) and *Ravelstein* (2000); three novellas, *The Bellarosa Connection* (1989), *A Theft* (1989), and *The Actual* (1997); and three stories collected as *Something to Remember Me By* (1991) exhibit various talky, informal protagonists and narrators with a lot on their minds. Matters of form and plot in these works seem less important than the ideas and active energy struck off by human beings in turmoil—usually comic turmoil. What Bellow finds moving in Theodore Dreiser's work, "his balkiness and sullenness, and then his allegiance to life," is still found in his own: complaint and weariness, fault-finding, accusation of self and others—these gestures directed at "life" also make up the stuff of life and the "allegiance" out of which Bellow's heroes are made. We read him for this range of interest; for flexibility and diversity of style and idiom; and for the eloquences of nostalgia, invective, and lamentation that make up his intensely imagined world.

Married five times, he ended his academic career with a brief residency at Boston University, afterward retiring to rural Vermont, where he died two months short of his ninetieth birthday and five years after publishing *Ravelstein*, his nineteenth book and a work indicative of the conservative, traditionalist posture of his later career.

From The Adventures of Augie March

Chapter 1

I am an American, Chicago born—Chicago, that somber city—and go at things as I have taught myself, free-style, and will make the record in my own way: first to knock, first admitted; sometimes an innocent knock, sometimes a not so innocent. But a man's character is his fate, says Heraclitus,[1] and in the end there isn't any way to disguise the nature of the knocks by acoustical work on the door or gloving the knuckles.

Everybody knows there is no fineness or accuracy of suppression; if you hold down one thing you hold down the adjoining.

My own parents were not much to me, though I cared for my mother. She was simple-minded, and what I learned from her was not what she taught, but on the order of object lessons. She didn't have much to teach, poor woman. My brothers and I loved her. I speak for them both; for the elder it is safe enough; for the younger one, Georgie, I have to answer—he was born an idiot—but I'm in no need to guess, for he had a song he sang as he ran drag-footed with his stiff idiot's trot, up and down along the curl-wired fence in the backyard:

---

1. Early Greek philosopher (fl. c. 480 B.C.E.) famous for his cryptic aphorisms and for positing the existence of the human soul.

> Georgie Mahchy, Augie, Simey
> Winnie Mahchy, evwy, evwy love Mama.

He was right about everyone save Winnie, Grandma Lausch's poodle, a pursy old overfed dog. Mama was Winnie's servant, as she was Grandma Lausch's. Loud-breathing and wind-breaking, she lay near the old lady's stool on a cushion embroidered with a Berber[2] aiming a rifle at a lion. She was personally Grandma's, belonged to her suite; the rest of us were the governed, and especially Mama. Mama passed the dog's dish to Grandma, and Winnie received her food at the old lady's feet from the old lady's hands. These hands and feet were small; she wore a shriveled sort of lisle on her legs and her slippers were gray—ah, the gray of that felt, the gray despotic to souls—with pink ribbons. Mama, however, had large feet, and around the house she wore men's shoes, usually without strings, and a dusting or mobcap like somebody's fanciful cotton effigy of the form of the brain. She was meek and long, round-eyed like Georgie—gentle green round eyes and a gentle freshness of color in her long face. Her hands were work-reddened, she had very few of her teeth left—to heed the knocks as they come—and she and Simon wore the same ravelly coat-sweaters. Besides having round eyes, Mama had circular glasses that I went with her to the free dispensary on Harrison Street[3] to get. Coached by Grandma Lausch, I went to do the lying. Now I know it wasn't so necessary to lie, but then everyone thought so, and Grandma Lausch especially, who was one of those Machiavellis of small street and neighborhood that my young years were full of. So Grandma, who had it all ready before we left the house and must have put in hours plotting it out in thought and phrase, lying small in her chilly small room under the featherbed, gave it to me at breakfast. The idea was that Mama wasn't keen enough to do it right. That maybe one didn't need to be keen didn't occur to us; it was a contest. The dispensary would want to know why the Charities didn't pay for the glasses. So you must say nothing about the Charities, but that sometimes money from my father came and sometimes it didn't, and that Mama took boarders. This was, in a delicate and choosy way, by ignoring and omitting certain large facts, true. It was true enough for *them*, and at the age of nine I could appreciate this perfectly. Better than my brother Simon, who was too blunt for this kind of maneuver and, anyway, from books, had gotten hold of some English schoolboy notions of honor. *Tom Brown's Schooldays*[4] for many years had an influence we were not in a position to afford.

Simon was a blond boy with big cheekbones and wide gray eyes and had the arms of a cricketer—I go by the illustrations; we never played anything but softball. Opposed to his British style was his patriotic anger at George III.[5] The mayor was at that time ordering the schoolboard to get history books that dealt more harshly with the king, and Simon was very hot at Cornwallis.[6] I admired this patriotic flash, his terrific personal wrath at the general, and his satisfaction over his surrender at Yorktown,[7] which would

2. Non-Arab North African tribesman.
3. Downtown location of Chicago's social welfare agency.
4. Novel (1857) based on experiences at Rugby School, by the English jurist and religious reformer Thomas Hughes (1822–1896).
5. King (1738–1820) of England, Scotland, and Ireland during a period (r. 1760–1820) that included the American Revolution.
6. Charles Cornwallis (1738–1805), British general who made the final surrender in the American Revolution.
7. Village in southeast Virginia where in 1781 British forces surrendered to George Washington's Continental Army, effectively ending the American Revolution.

often come over him at lunch while we ate our bologna sandwiches. Grandma had a piece of boiled chicken at noon, and sometimes there was the gizzard for bristle-headed little Georgie, who loved it and blew at the ridgy thing more to cherish than to cool it. But this martial true-blood pride of Simon's disqualified him for the crafty task to be done at the dispensary; he was too disdainful to lie and might denounce everybody instead. I could be counted on to do the job, because I enjoyed it. I loved a piece of strategy. I had enthusiasms too; I had Simon's, though there was never much meat in Cornwallis for me, and I had Grandma Lausch's as well. As for the truth of these statements I was instructed to make—well, it was a fact that we had a boarder. Grandma Lausch was our boarder, not a relation at all. She was supported by two sons, one from Cincinnati and one from Racine, Wisconsin. The daughters-in-law did not want her, and she, the widow of a powerful Odessa[8] businessman—a divinity over us, bald, whiskery, with a fat nose, greatly armored in a cutaway, a double-breasted vest, powerfully buttoned (his blue photo, enlarged and retouched by Mr. Lulov, hung in the parlor, doubled back between the portico columns of the full-length mirror, the dome of the stove beginning where his trunk ended)—she preferred to live with us, because for so many years she was used to direct a house, to command, to govern, to manage, scheme, devise, and intrigue in all her languages. She boasted French and German besides Russian, Polish, and Yiddish; and who but Mr. Lulov, the retouch artist from Division Street,[9] could have tested her claim to French? And he was a serene bogus too, that triple-backboned gallant tea-drinker. Except that he had been a hackie in Paris, once, and if he told the truth about that might have known French among other things, like playing tunes on his teeth with a pencil or singing and keeping time with a handful of coins that he rattled by jigging his thumb along the table, and how to play chess.

Grandma Lausch played like Timur, whether chess or klabyasch,[1] with palatal catty harshness and sharp gold in her eyes. Klabyasch she played with Mr. Kreindl, a neighbor of ours who had taught her the game. A powerful stub-handed man with a large belly, he swatted the table with those hard hands of his, flinging down his cards and shouting "*Shtoch! Yasch! Menél! Klabyasch!*"[2] Grandma looked sardonically at him. She often said, after he left, "If you've got a Hungarian friend you don't need an enemy." But there was nothing of the enemy about Mr. Kreindl. He merely, sometimes, sounded menacing because of his drill-sergeant's bark. He was an old-time Austro-Hungarian[3] conscript, and there was something soldierly about him: a neck that had strained with pushing artillery wheels, a campaigner's red in the face, a powerful bite in his jaw and gold-crowned teeth, green cockeyes and soft short hair, altogether Napoleonic.[4] His feet slanted out on the ideal of

8. City in the Ukraine on the Black Sea, departure point for many Russian Jews who emigrated to North America in the late 19th and early 20th centuries.

9. Commercial and shopping street on Chicago's North Side.

1. Card game taking its name from the Yiddish verb for "to gather." "Timur": also known as Tamerlane, Mongol warrior (1336–1405) whose conquests

stretched from the Ukraine to northern India.

2. Successive winning tricks.

3. The dual monarchy of Austria and Hungary (1867–1918) encompassed Austria, Hungary, Bohemia, and parts of Poland, Romania, Italy, and the Balkans.

4. Era and style of Napoléon Bonaparte's (1769–1821) rule as Napoléon I, emperor of the French (1804–15).

Frederick the Great,[5] but he was about a foot under the required height for guardsmen. He had a masterly look of independence. He and his wife—a woman quiet and modest to the neighbors and violently quarrelsome at home—and his son, a dental student, lived in what was called the English basement at the front of the house. The son, Kotzie, worked evenings in the corner drugstore and went to school in the neighborhood of County Hospital, and it was he who told Grandma about the free dispensary. Or rather, the old woman sent for him to find out what one could get from those state and county places. She was always sending for people, the butcher, the grocer, the fruit peddler, and received them in the kitchen to explain that the Marches had to have discounts. Mama usually had to stand by. The old woman would tell them, "You see how it is—do I have to say more? There's no man in the house and children to bring up." This was her most frequent argument. When Lubin, the caseworker, came around and sat in the kitchen, familiar, bald-headed, in his gold glasses, his weight comfortable, his mouth patient, she shot it at him: "How do you expect children to be brought up?" While he listened, trying to remain comfortable but gradually becoming like a man determined not to let a grasshopper escape from his hand. "Well, my dear, Mrs. March could raise your rent," he said. She must often have answered—for there were times when she sent us all out to be alone with him—"Do you know what things would be like without me? You ought to be grateful for the way I hold them together." I'm sure she even said, "And when I die, Mr. Lubin, you'll see what you've got on your hands." I'm one hundred per cent sure of it. To us nothing was ever said that might weaken her rule by suggesting it would ever end. Besides, it would have shocked us to hear it, and she, in her miraculous knowledge of us, able to be extremely close to our thoughts—she was one sovereign who knew exactly the proportions of love, respect, and fear of power in her subjects—understood how we would have been shocked. But to Lubin, for reasons of policy and also because she had to express feelings she certainly had, she must have said it. He had a harassed patience with her of "deliver me from such clients," though he tried to appear master of the situation. He held his derby between his thighs (his suits, always too scanty in the pants, exposed white socks and bulldog shoes, crinkled, black, and bulging with toes), and he looked into the hat as though debating whether it was wise to release his grasshopper on the lining for a while.

"I pay as much as I can afford," she would say.

She took her cigarette case out from under her shawl, she cut a Murad[6] in half with her sewing scissors and picked up the holder. This was still at a time when women did not smoke. Save the intelligentsia—the term she applied to herself. With the holder in her dark little gums between which all her guile, malice, and command issued, she had her best inspirations of strategy. She was as wrinkled as an old paper bag, an autocrat, hard-shelled and jesuitical,[7]

5. Frederick II (1712–1786), called "the Great," king of Prussia (r. 1740–86), patron of the arts and philosophy.
6. A Turkish cigarette, named for the Murad River.

7. Reference to the Society of Jesus, commonly called Jesuits, a Catholic religious order famous for its intellectual rigor, founded in 1540 by the Spanish priest Ignatius of Loyola (1491–1556).

a pouncy old hawk of a Bolshevik,[8] her small ribboned gray feet immobile on the shoekit and stool Simon had made in the manual-training class, dingy old wool Winnie whose bad smell filled the flat on the cushion beside her. If wit and discontent don't necessarily go together, it wasn't from the old woman that I learned it. She was impossible to satisfy. Kreindl, for example, on whom we could depend, Kreindl who carried up the coal when Mama was sick and who instructed Kotzie to make up our prescriptions for nothing, she called "that trashy Hungarian," or "Hungarian pig." She called Kotzie "the baked apple"; she called Mrs. Kreindl "the secret goose," Lubin "the shoemaker's son," the dentist "the butcher," the butcher "the timid swindler." She detested the dentist, who had several times unsuccessfully tried to fit her with false teeth. She accused him of burning her gums when taking the impressions. But then she tried to pull his hands away from her mouth. I saw that happen: the stolid, square-framed Dr. Wernick, whose compact forearms could have held off a bear, painfully careful with her, determined, concerned at her choked screams, and enduring her scratches. To see her struggle like that was no easy thing for me, and Dr. Wernick was sorry to see me there too, I know, but either Simon or I had to squire her wherever she went. Here particularly she needed a witness to Wernick's cruelty and clumsiness as well as a shoulder to lean on when she went weakly home. Already at ten I was only a little shorter than she and big enough to hold her small weight.

"You saw how he put his paws over my face so I couldn't breathe?" she said. "God made him to be a butcher. Why did he become a dentist? His hands are too heavy. The touch is everything to a dentist. If his hands aren't right he shouldn't be let practice. But his wife worked hard to send him through school and make a dentist of him. And I must go to him and be burned because of it."

The rest of us had to go to the dispensary—which was like the dream of a multitude of dentists' chairs, hundreds of them in a space as enormous as an armory, and green bowls with designs of glass grapes, drills lifted zigzag as insects' legs, and gas flames on the porcelain swivel trays—a thundery gloom in Harrison Street of limestone county buildings and cumbersome red streetcars with metal grillwork on their windows and monarchical iron whiskers of cowcatchers front and rear. They lumbered and clanged, and their brake tanks panted in the slushy brown of a winter afternoon or the bare stone brown of a summer's, salted with ash, smoke, and prairie dust, with long stops at the clinics to let off dumpers, cripples, hunchbacks, brace-legs, crutch-wielders, tooth and eye sufferers, and all the rest.

So before going with my mother for the glasses I was always instructed by the old woman and had to sit and listen with profound care. My mother too had to be present, for there must be no slip-up. She must be coached to say nothing. "Remember, Rebecca," Grandma would rerepeat, "let him answer everything." To which Mama was too obedient even to say yes, but only sat and kept her long hands folded on the bottle-fly iridescence of the dress the old woman had picked for her to wear. Very healthy and smooth, her color; none of us inherited this high a color from her, or the form of her nose with nostrils turned back and showing a little of the partition. "You keep out of it. If they ask you something, you look at Augie like this." And she illustrated

8. Left-wing political party allied with other Communist forces in the Russian Revolution (1917).

how Mama was to turn to me, terribly exact, if she had only been able to drop her habitual grandeur. "Don't tell anything. Only answer questions," she said to me. My mother was anxious that I should be worthy and faithful. Simon and I were her miracles or accidents; Georgie was her own true work in which she returned to her fate after blessed and undeserved success. "Augie, listen to Grandma. Hear what she says," was all she ever dared when the old woman unfolded her plan.

"When they ask you, 'Where is your father?' you say, 'I don't know where, miss.' No matter how old she is, you shouldn't forget to say 'miss.' If she wants to know where he was the last time you heard from him, you must tell her that the last time he sent a money order was about two years ago from Buffalo, New York. Never say a word about the Charity. The Charity you should never mention, you hear that? Never. When she asks you how much the rent is, tell her eighteen dollars. When she asks where the money comes from, say you have boarders. How many? Two boarders. Now, say to me, how much rent?"

"Eighteen dollars."

"And how many boarders?"

"Two."

"And how much do they pay?"

"How much should I say?"

"Eight dollars each a week."

"Eight dollars."

"So you can't go to a private doctor, if you get sixty-four dollars a month. The eyedrops alone cost me five when I went, and he scalded my eyes. And these specs"—she tapped the case—"cost ten dollars the frames and fifteen the glasses."

Never but at such times, by necessity, was my father mentioned. I claimed to remember him; Simon denied that I did, and Simon was right. I liked to imagine it.

"He wore a uniform," I said. "Sure I remember. He was a soldier."

"Like hell he was. You don't know anything about it."

"Maybe a sailor."

"Like hell. He drove a truck for Hall Brothers laundry on Marshfield,[9] that's what he did. *I* said he used to wear a uniform. Monkey sees, monkey does; monkey hears, monkey says." Monkey was the basis of much thought with us. On the sideboard, on the Turkestan runner, with their eyes, ears, and mouth covered, we had see-no-evil, speak-no-evil, hear-no-evil, a lower trinity of the house. The advantage of lesser gods is that you can take their names any way you like. "Silence in the courthouse, monkey wants to speak; speak, monkey, speak." "The monkey and the bamboo were playing in the grass . . ." Still the monkeys could be potent, and awesome besides, and deep social critics when the old woman, like a great lama—for she is Eastern to me, in the end—would point to the squatting brown three, whose mouths and nostrils were drawn in sharp blood-red, and with profound wit, her unkindness finally touching greatness, say, "Nobody asks you to love the whole world, only to be honest, *ehrlich*.[1] Don't have a loud mouth. The more you love people the more they'll mix you up. A child loves, a person respects.

---

9. Commercial avenue on Chicago's North Side.   1. Sincere (German).

Respect is better than love. And that's respect, the middle monkey." It never occurred to us that she sinned mischievously herself against that convulsed speak-no-evil who hugged his lips with his hands; but no criticism of her came near our minds at any time, much less when the resonance of a great principle filled the whole kitchen.

She used to read us lessons off poor Georgie's head. He would kiss the dog. This bickering handmaiden of the old lady, at one time. Now a dozy, long-sighing crank and proper object of respect for her years of right-minded but not exactly lovable busyness. But Georgie loved her—and Grandma, whom he would kiss on the sleeve, on the knee, taking knee or arm in both hands and putting his underlip forward, chaste, lummoxy, caressing, gentle and diligent when he bent his narrow back, blouse bagging all over it, whitish hair pointy and close as a burr or sunflower when the seeds have been picked out of it. The old lady let him embrace her and spoke to him in the following way: "Hey, you, boy, clever *junge*,[2] you like the old Grandma, my minister, my *cavalyer*?[3] That's-a-boy. You know who's good to you, who gives you gizzards and necks? Who? Who makes noodles for you? Yes. Noodles are slippery, hard to pick up with a fork and hard to pick up with the fingers. You see how the little bird pulls the worm? The little worm wants to stay in the ground. The little worm doesn't want to come out. Enough, you're making my dress wet." And she'd sharply push his forehead off with her old prim hand, having fired off for Simon and me, mindful always of her duty to wise us up, one more animadversion on the trustful, loving, and simple surrounded by the cunning-hearted and tough, a fighting nature of birds and worms, and a desperate mankind without feelings. Illustrated by Georgie. But the principal illustration was not Georgie but Mama, in her love-originated servitude, simpleminded, abandoned with three children. This was what old lady Lausch was driving at, now, in the later wisdom of her life, that she had a second family to lead.

And what must Mama have thought when in any necessary connection my father was brought into the conversation? She sat docile. I conceive that she thought of some detail about him—a dish he liked, perhaps meat and potatoes, perhaps cabbage or cranberry sauce; perhaps that he disliked a starched collar, or a soft collar; that he brought home the *Evening American* or the *Journal*.[4] She thought this because her thoughts were always simple; but she felt abandonment, and greater pains than conscious mental ones put a dark streak to her simplicity. I don't know how she made out before, when we were alone after the desertion, but Grandma came and put a regulating hand on the family life. Mama surrendered powers to her that maybe she had never known she had and took her punishment in drudgery; occupied a place, I suppose, among women conquered by a superior force of love, like those women whom Zeus got the better of in animal form and who next had to take cover from his furious wife. Not that I can see my big, gentle, dilapidated, scrubbing, and lugging mother as a fugitive of immense beauty from such classy wrath, or our father as a marble-legged Olympian. She had sewed buttonholes in a coat factory in a Wells Street[5] loft and he was a laundry

2. Young man (German).
3. Yiddish borrowing from the German *kava-lier* (gentleman) and Polish *kawaler* (bachelor, gallant).

4. Chicago newpapers of the era.
5. Light-industrial street immediately north of Chicago's downtown area.

driver—there wasn't even so much as a picture of him left when he blew. But she does have a place among such women by the deeper right of continual payment. And as for vengeance from a woman, Grandma Lausch was there to administer the penalties under the standards of legitimacy, representing the main body of married womankind.

Still the old lady had a heart. I don't mean to say she didn't. She was tyrannical and a snob about her Odessa luster and her servants and governesses, but though she had been a success herself she knew what it was to fall through susceptibility. I began to realize this when I afterward read some of the novels she used to send me to the library for. She taught me the Russian alphabet so that I could make out the titles. Once a year she read *Anna Karenina* and *Eugene Onegin*.[6] Occasionally I got into hot water by bringing a book she didn't want. "How many times do I have to tell you if it doesn't say *roman* I don't want it? You didn't look inside. Are your fingers too weak to open the book? Then they should be too weak to play ball or pick your nose. For that you've got strength! *Bozhe moy!*[7] God in Heaven! You haven't got the brains of a cat, to walk two miles and bring me a book about religion because it says Tolstoi on the cover."

The old *grande dame*, I don't want to be misrepresenting her. She was suspicious of what could have been, given one wrong stitch of heredity, a family vice by which we could have been exploited. She didn't want to read Tolstoi on religion. She didn't trust him as a family man because the countess had had such trouble with him. But although she never went to the synagogue, ate bread on Passover, sent Mama to the pork butcher where meat was cheaper, loved canned lobster and other forbidden food, she was not an atheist and free-thinker. Mr. Anticol, the old junky she called (search me why) "Rameses"—after the city named with Pithom in the Scriptures maybe;[8] no telling what her inspirations were—was that. A real rebel to God. Icy and canny, she would listen to what he had to say and wouldn't declare herself. He was ruddy, and gloomy; his leathery serge cap made him flat-headed, and his alley calls for rags, old iron—"recks aline," he sung it—made him gravel-voiced and gruff. He had tough hair and brows and despising brown eyes; he was a studious, shaggy, meaty old man. Grandma bought a set of the *Encyclopedia Americana*—edition of 1892, I think—from him and saw to it that Simon and I read it; and he too, whenever he met us, asked, "How's the set?" believing, I reckon, that it taught irreverence to religion. What had made him an atheist was a massacre of Jews in his town. From the cellar where he was hidden he saw a laborer pissing on the body of his wife's younger brother, just killed. "So don't talk to me about God," he said. But it was he that talked about God, all the time. And while Mrs. Anticol stayed pious, it was his idea of grand apostasy to drive to the reform synagogue on the high holidays and park his pink-eye nag among the luxurious, whirl-wired touring cars of the rich Jews who bared their heads inside as if they were attending a theater, a kind of abjectness in them that gave him grim entertainment to the end of his life. He caught a cold in the rain and died of pneumonia.

---

6. Verse narrative (1823–31) by the Russian poet Aleksandr Pushkin (1799–1837). "*Anna Karenina*": novel (1875–77) by the Russian novelist Leo Tolstoy (1828–1910).
7. My God! (Russian).

8. Exodus 1.11: "Therefore they set taskmasters over them to afflict them with heavy burdens; and they built for Pharoah store-cities, Pithom and Raamses."

Grandma, all the same, burned a candle on the anniversary of Mr. Lausch's death, threw a lump of dough on the coals when she was baking, as a kind of offering, had incantations over baby teeth and stunts against the evil eye. It was kitchen religion and had nothing to do with the giant God of the Creation who turned back the waters and exploded Gomorrah, but it was on the side of religion at that. And while we're on that side I'll mention the Poles—we were just a handful of Jews among them in the neighborhood— and the swollen, bleeding hearts on every kitchen wall, the pictures of saints, baskets of death flowers tied at the door, communions, Easters, and Christmases. And sometimes we were chased, stoned, bitten, and beat up for Christ-killers, all of us, even Georgie, articled, whether we liked it or not, to this mysterious trade. But I never had any special grief from it, or brooded, being by and large too larky and boisterous to take it to heart, and looked at it as needing no more special explanation than the stone-and-bat wars of the street gangs or the swarming on a fall evening of parish punks to rip up fences, screech and bawl at girls, and beat up strangers. It wasn't in my nature to fatigue myself with worry over being born to this occult work, even though some of my friends and playmates would turn up in the middle of these mobs to trap you between houses from both ends of a passageway. Simon had less truck with them. School absorbed him more, and he had his sentiments anyway, a mixed extract from Natty Bumppo, Quentin Durward, Tom Brown, Clark at Kaskaskia, the messenger who brought the good news from Ratisbon,[9] and so on, that kept him more to himself. I was just a slow understudy to this, just as he never got me to put in hours on his Sandow muscle builder[1] and the gimmick for developing the sinews of the wrist. I was an easy touch for friendships, and most of the time they were cut short by older loyalties. I was pals longest with Stashu Kopecs, whose mother was a midwife graduated from the Aesculapian School of Midwifery on Milwaukee Avenue.[2] Well to do, the Kopecses had an electric player piano and linoleums in all the rooms, but Stashu was a thief, and to run with him I stole too: coal off the cars, clothes from the lines, rubber balls from the dime store, and pennies off the newsstands. Mostly for the satisfaction of dexterity, though Stashu invented the game of stripping in the cellar and putting on girls' things swiped from the clotheslines. Then he too showed up in a gang that caught me one cold afternoon of very little snow while I was sitting on a crate frozen into the mud, eating Nabisco[3] wafers, my throat full of the sweet dust. Foremost, there was a thug of a kid, about thirteen but undersized, hard and grieved-looking. He came up to accuse me, and big Moonya Staplanski, just out of the St. Charles Reformatory[4] and headed next for the one at Pontiac,[5] backed him up.

"You little Jew bastard, you hit my brother," Moonya said.

9. The French name for the German city of Regensburg, which was captured by Napoleon's armies in 1809. "Natty Bumppo": protagonist of the Leatherstocking novels by the American novelist James Fenimore Cooper (1789–1851). "Quentin Durward": eponymous hero in the novel (1823) by the Scottish poet and novelist Sir Walter Scott (1771–1832). "Tom Brown": see n. 4, p. 211. "Clark at Kaskaskia": the American military leader George Rogers Clark (1752–1818) captured the British frontier fort at Kaskaskia, Illinois, in 1778.

1. Device named after Eugen Sandow (1867–1925), American physical culturist born in Germany, famous for his performances as a bodybuilder and for advocacy of physical education.
2. Commercial and shopping street on Chicago's North Side, at this time a Polish-American neighborhood.
3. Brand name of the National Biscuit Company.
4. Site of the Illinois State Reformatory for Boys.
5. Site of the Illinois Correctional Center.

"I never did. I never even saw him before."

"You took away a nickel from him. How did you buy them biscuits else, you?"

"I got them at home."

Then I caught sight of Stashu, hayheaded and jeering, pleased to sickness with his deceit and his new-revealed brotherhood with the others, and I said, "Hey, you lousy bed-wetter, Stashu, you know Moon ain't even got a brother."

Here the kid hit me and the gang jumped me, Stashu with the rest, tearing the buckles from my sheepskin coat and bloodying my nose.

"Who is to blame?" said Grandma Lausch when I came home. "You know who? You are, Augie, because that's all the brains you have to go with that piss-in-bed *accoucherka's*[6] son. Does Simon hang around with them? Not Simon. He has too much sense." I thanked God she didn't know about the stealing. And in a way, because that was her schooling temperament, I suspect she was pleased that I should see where it led to give your affections too easily. But Mama, the prime example of this weakness, was horrified. Against the old lady's authority she didn't dare to introduce her feelings during the hearing, but when she took me into the kitchen to put a compress on me she nearsightedly pored over my scratches, whispering and sighing to me, while Georgie tottered around behind her, long and white, and Winnie lapped water under the sink.

1953

6. Yiddish borrowing from the Polish *akuszerka* (midwife).

ARTHUR MILLER
1915–2005

For much modern American drama the family is the central subject, as the anthology selections show. In *Long Day's Journey into Night* Eugene O'Neill studied his own family through the Tyrones; in Tennessee Williams's *A Streetcar Named Desire* the Kowalskis are one family, which Blanche invades, while Blanche and Stella, as sisters, are another. Most of Arthur Miller's plays, as well, concentrate on the family and envision an ideal world as, perhaps, an enlarged family. Often the protagonist's sense of family draws him into conflict with—and eventual doom in—the outside world. Yet Miller recognized that an ideal is sometimes a rationalization. Joe Keller insists in *All My Sons* (1947) that during the war he shipped damaged airplane parts to support his family, but a desire for commercial success was part of his motive. Eddie Carbone in *A View from the Bridge* (1955) accepts death because of his sense of responsibility to his niece, but married man though he is, he may also be in love with that same niece. In *Death of a Salesman* (1949) Willy Loman's delusions and self-deceptions derive from, and return to, his image of himself as family provider, an image he cannot live up to; driven by his desire to be "well liked," a successful social personality, he fails to connect with either of his sons and neglects his wife. Thus Miller's treatment of the family leads to a treatment both of personal ideals and of the society within which families have to operate.

Miller was born into a German Jewish family in Manhattan; his father was a well-to-do but almost illiterate clothing manufacturer, his mother an avid reader. When his father's business collapsed after the stock market crash in 1929, the family moved to Brooklyn, where Miller graduated from high school. His subsequent two years of work in an automobile-parts warehouse to earn money for college tuition are warmly recalled in his play *A Memory of Two Mondays* (1955). At the University of Michigan he enrolled as a journalism student. These were the years of the Spanish Civil War, the rise of fascism, and the attraction of Marxism as a way out of the Depression, and here Miller formed his political views. He also began to write plays, which won prizes at the university and in New York. He then went to work for the Federal Theater Project, wrote radio plays, toured army camps to gather material for a film, and married Mary Slattery, the first of his three wives.

In 1947 Miller enjoyed his first Broadway success, *All My Sons*. (*The Man Who Had All the Luck* had failed in 1944.) This strongly realistic portrayal of a family divided because of the father's insistence on business as usual during World War II drew the attention of audiences and theater critics. *Death of a Salesman*, his masterpiece, was produced two years later and won the Pulitzer Prize. An adaptation of Ibsen's *An Enemy of the People* followed in 1951. It was suggested to him by the actors Fredric March and Florence Eldridge, but Miller was clearly drawn by Ibsen's hero, Dr. Stockmann, who leads a fight against pollution with strong but confused idealism.

In the early 1950s, the hysterical search for supposed Communist infiltration of American life reached its height as Senator Joseph McCarthy summoned suspect after suspect to hearings in Washington. Miller later said that at this time he was reading a book about the Salem witch trials and saw that "the main point of the hearings, precisely as in seventeenth-century Salem, was that the accused make public confession, damn his confederates as well as his Devil master, and guarantee his sterling new allegiance by breaking disgusting old vows—whereupon he was let loose to rejoin the society of extremely decent people." Out of this insight came *The Crucible* (1953), in which the hero, John Proctor, allows himself to be executed rather than sign away his name and his children's respect. Hysteria touched Miller personally when he was denied a passport and in 1957 was convicted of contempt of Congress for refusing to name suspected Communists (this conviction was unanimously overturned by the Supreme Court the following year).

Miller had long been looking for a way to dramatize what he had earlier learned about mob control of the Brooklyn waterfront and finally did so in the one-act play *A View from the Bridge*, produced with *A Memory of Two Mondays* in 1955; later he would rework *View* into a full-length play. Meanwhile, he had met the glamorous movie actress Marilyn Monroe; they married in 1956, after he divorced his first wife. He wrote the screenplay *The Misfits* for Monroe, but in their private life, their complex natures were ill-sorted. The marriage ended in divorce in 1961, and a year later he married the photographer Ingeborg Morath, with whom he collaborated on several books of photographs and essays.

In 1964 two plays opened: *After the Fall* (in which the protagonist is a thinly disguised Miller investigating his family, his responsibilities, and his wives) and *Incident at Vichy* (about Jews and Nazis in Vichy, France). While these were by no means as successful as *Salesman*, they returned him seriously to the stage. Among later plays are *The Price* (1968), *The Creation of the World and Other Business* (1972), *The Archbishop's Ceiling* (1977), and two one-act plays under the title *Danger: Memory!* (1986). These last fared poorly in New York, but found successful productions elsewhere in the world.

Actor Lee J. Cobb as Willy Loman being restrained by actors Arthur
Kennedy (left) and Cameron Mitchell (right) as his sons Biff and Hap,
respectively, in the 1949 original Broadway production of **Death of a
Salesman**.

Miller in his later years was something of an activist. In the late 1960s he was
asked to become president of PEN (Poets, Essayists, Novelists), the international
writers' group. By opening this organization to writers in what were then Iron Curtain countries and speaking out for those repressed by totalitarian regimes, he
became a respected champion of human rights.

Like his contemporary Tennessee Williams, Miller rejected the influence of
"mawkish twenties slang" and "deadly repetitiveness." Again like Williams, Miller
was impatient with prosy dialogue and well-made structures. As he explained, the
success of *A Streetcar Named Desire* in 1947 helped him write *Death of a Salesman*:

> With *Streetcar*, Tennessee had printed a license to speak at full throat, and it
> helped strengthen me as I turned to Willy Loman, a salesman always full of
> words, and better yet, a man who could never cease trying, like Adam, to name

himself and the world's wonders. I had known all along that this play could not be encompassed by conventional realism, and for one integral reason: in Willy the past was as alive as what was happening at the moment, sometimes even crashing in to completely overwhelm his mind. I wanted precisely the same fluidity of form.

In *Salesman* the action moves effortlessly from the present—the last twenty-four hours of Willy's life—into moments in his memory, symbolized in the stage setting by the idyllic leaves around his house that, in these past moments, block out the threatening apartment houses. The successful realization of this fluidity on the stage was greatly aided by Miller's director, Elia Kazan, and his stage designer, Jo Mielziner, both of whom had worked with Williams two years earlier on *Streetcar*. A striking difference between Williams and Miller, however, is the latter's overt moralizing, which adds a didactic element to his plays not to be found in those of Williams.

The text is from *Arthur Miller's Collected Plays* (1957).

Death of a Salesman

Certain Private Conversations in Two Acts and a Requiem

THE CHARACTERS

WILLY LOMAN	THE WOMAN	JENNY
LINDA	CHARLEY	STANLEY
BIFF	UNCLE BEN	MISS FORSYTHE
HAPPY	HOWARD WAGNER	LETTA
BERNARD		

The action takes place in WILLY LOMAN's *house and yard and in various places he visits in the New York and Boston of today.*

Act One

A melody is heard, playing upon a flute. It is small and fine, telling of grass and trees and the horizon. The curtain rises.

Before us is the Salesman's house. We are aware of towering, angular shapes behind it, surrounding it on all sides. Only the blue light of the sky falls upon the house and forestage; the surrounding area shows an angry flow of orange. As more light appears, we see a solid vault of apartment houses around the small, fragile-seeming home. An air of the dream clings to the place, a dream rising out of reality. The kitchen at center seems actual enough, for there is a kitchen table with three chairs, and a refrigerator. But no other fixtures are seen. At the back of the kitchen there is a draped entrance, which leads to the living-room. To the right of the kitchen, on a level raised two feet, is a bedroom furnished only with a brass bedstead and a straight chair. On a shelf over the bed a silver athletic trophy stands. A window opens onto the apartment house at the side.

Behind the kitchen, on a level raised six and a half feet, is the boys' bedroom, at present barely visible. Two beds are dimly seen, and at the back of the room a dormer window. (This bedroom is above the unseen living-room.) At the left a stairway curves up to it from the kitchen.

The entire setting is wholly or, in some places, partially transparent. The roofline of the house is one-dimensional; under and over it we see the apartment buildings. Before the house lies an apron, curving beyond the forestage into the orchestra. This forward area serves as the back yard as well as the locale of all WILLY'S *imaginings and of his city scenes. Whenever the action is in the present the actors observe the imaginary wall-lines, entering the house only through its door at the left. But in the scenes of the past these boundaries are broken, and characters enter or leave a room by stepping "through" a wall onto the forestage.*

From the right, WILLY LOMAN, *the Salesman, enters, carrying two large sample cases. The flute plays on. He hears but is not aware of it. He is past sixty years of age, dressed quietly. Even as he crosses the stage to the doorway of the house, his exhaustion is apparent. He unlocks the door, comes into the kitchen, and thankfully lets his burden down, feeling the soreness of his palms. A word-sigh escapes his lips—it might be "Oh, boy, oh, boy." He closes the door, then carries his cases out into the living-room, through the draped kitchen doorway.*

LINDA, *his wife, has stirred in her bed at the right. She gets out and puts on a robe, listening. Most often jovial, she has developed an iron repression of her exceptions to* WILLY'S *behavior—she more than loves him, she admires him, as though his mercurial nature, his temper, his massive dreams and little cruelties, served her only as sharp reminders of the turbulent longings within him, longings which she shares but lacks the temperament to utter and follow to their end.*

LINDA [*hearing* WILLY *outside the bedroom, calls with some trepidation*] Willy!

WILLY   It's all right. I came back.

LINDA   Why? What happened? [*slight pause*] Did something happen, Willy?

WILLY   No, nothing happened.

LINDA   You didn't smash the car, did you?

WILLY [*with casual irritation*]   I said nothing happened. Didn't you hear me?

LINDA   Don't you feel well?

WILLY   I'm tired to the death. [*The flute has faded away. He sits on the bed beside her, a little numb.*] I couldn't make it. I just couldn't make it, Linda.

LINDA [*very carefully, delicately*]   Where were you all day? You look terrible.

WILLY   I got as far as a little above Yonkers. I stopped for a cup of coffee. Maybe it was the coffee.

LINDA   What?

WILLY [*after a pause*]   I suddenly couldn't drive any more. The car kept going off onto the shoulder, y'know?

LINDA [*helpfully*]   Oh. Maybe it was the steering again. I don't think Angelo knows the Studebaker.

WILLY   No, it's me, it's me. Suddenly I realize I'm goin' sixty miles an hour and I don't remember the last five minutes. I'm—I can't seem to—keep my mind to it.

LINDA   Maybe it's your glasses. You never went for your new glasses.

WILLY   No, I see everything. I came back ten miles an hour. It took me nearly four hours from Yonkers.

LINDA [*resigned*]   Well, you'll just have to take a rest, Willy, you can't continue this way.

WILLY   I just got back from Florida.

LINDA   But you didn't rest your mind. Your mind is overactive, and the mind is what counts, dear.

WILLY   I'll start out in the morning. Maybe I'll feel better in the morning. [*She is taking off his shoes.*] These goddam arch supports are killing me.

LINDA   Take an aspirin. Should I get you an aspirin? It'll soothe you.

WILLY [*with wonder*]   I was driving along, you understand? And I was fine. I was even observing the scenery. You can imagine, me looking at scenery, on the road every week of my life. But it's so beautiful up there, Linda, the trees are so thick, and the sun is warm. I opened the windshield and just let the warm air bathe over me. And then all of a sudden I'm goin' off the road! I'm tellin' ya, I absolutely forgot I was driving. If I'd've gone the other way over the white line I might've killed somebody. So I went on again—and five minutes later I'm dreamin' again, and I nearly— [*He presses two fingers against his eyes.*] I have such thoughts, I have such strange thoughts.

LINDA   Willy, dear. Talk to them again. There's no reason why you can't work in New York.

WILLY   They don't need me in New York. I'm the New England man. I'm vital in New England.

LINDA   But you're sixty years old. They can't expect you to keep traveling every week.

WILLY   I'll have to send a wire to Portland. I'm supposed to see Brown and Morrison tomorrow morning at ten o'clock to show the line. Goddammit, I could sell them! [*He starts putting on his jacket.*]

LINDA [*taking the jacket from him*]   Why don't you go down to the place tomorrow and tell Howard you've simply got to work in New York? You're too accommodating, dear.

WILLY   If old man Wagner was alive I'd a been in charge of New York now! That man was a prince, he was a masterful man. But that boy of his, that Howard, he don't appreciate. When I went north the first time, the Wagner Company didn't know where New England was!

LINDA   Why don't you tell those things to Howard, dear?

WILLY [*encouraged*]   I will, I definitely will. Is there any cheese?

LINDA   I'll make you a sandwich.

WILLY   No, go to sleep. I'll take some milk. I'll be up right away. The boys in?

LINDA   They're sleeping. Happy took Biff on a date tonight.

WILLY [*interested*]   That so?

LINDA   It was so nice to see them shaving together, one behind the other, in the bathroom. And going out together. You notice? The whole house smells of shaving lotion.

WILLY   Figure it out. Work a lifetime to pay off a house. You finally own it, and there's nobody to live in it.

LINDA   Well, dear, life is a casting off. It's always that way.

WILLY   No, no, some people—some people accomplish something. Did Biff say anything after I went this morning?

LINDA   You shouldn't have criticized him, Willy, especially after he just got off the train. You mustn't lose your temper with him.

WILLY   When the hell did I lose my temper? I simply asked him if he was making any money. Is that a criticism?

LINDA   But, dear, how could he make any money?

WILLY [*worried and angered*] There's such an undercurrent in him. He became a moody man. Did he apologize when I left this morning?

LINDA He was crestfallen, Willy. You know how he admires you. I think if he finds himself, then you'll both be happier and not fight any more.

WILLY How can he find himself on a farm? Is that a life? A farmhand? In the beginning, when he was young, I thought, well, a young man, it's good for him to tramp around, take a lot of different jobs. But it's more than ten years now and he has yet to make thirty-five dollars a week?

LINDA He's finding himself, Willy.

WILLY Not finding yourself at the age of thirty-four is a disgrace!

LINDA Shh!

WILLY The trouble is he's lazy, goddammit!

LINDA Willy, please!

WILLY Biff is a lazy bum!

LINDA They're sleeping. Get something to eat. Go on down.

WILLY Why did he come home? I would like to know what brought him home.

LINDA I don't know. I think he's still lost, Willy. I think he's very lost.

WILLY Biff Loman is lost. In the greatest country in the world a young man with such—personal attractiveness, gets lost. And such a hard worker. There's one thing about Biff—he's not lazy.

LINDA Never.

WILLY [*with pity and resolve*] I'll see him in the morning; I'll have a nice talk with him. I'll get him a job selling. He could be big in no time. My God! Remember how they used to follow him around in high school? When he smiled at one of them their faces lit up. When he walked down the street . . . [*He loses himself in reminiscences.*]

LINDA [*trying to bring him out of it*] Willy, dear, I got a new kind of American-type cheese today. It's whipped.

WILLY Why do you get American when I like Swiss?

LINDA I just thought you'd like a change—

WILLY I don't want a change! I want Swiss cheese. Why am I always being contradicted?

LINDA [*with a covering laugh*] I thought it would be a surprise.

WILLY Why don't you open a window in here, for God's sake?

LINDA [*with infinite patience*] They're all open, dear.

WILLY The way they boxed us in here. Bricks and windows, windows and bricks.

LINDA We should've bought the land next door.

WILLY The street is lined with cars. There's not a breath of fresh air in the neighborhood. The grass don't grow any more, you can't raise a carrot in the back yard. They should've had a law against apartment houses. Remember those two beautiful elm trees out there? When I and Biff hung the swing between them?

LINDA Yeah, like being a million miles from the city.

WILLY They should've arrested the builder for cutting those down. They massacred the neighborhood. [*lost*] More and more I think of those days, Linda. This time of year it was lilac and wisteria. And then the peonies would come out, and the daffodils. What fragrance in this room!

LINDA Well, after all, people had to move somewhere.

WILLY   No, there's more people now.

LINDA   I don't think there's more people. I think—

WILLY   There's more people! That's what's ruining this country! Population is getting out of control. The competition is maddening! Smell the stink from that apartment house! And another one on the other side . . . How can they whip cheese?

>[*On* WILLY's *last line,* BIFF *and* HAPPY *raise themselves up in their beds, listening.*]

LINDA   Go down, try it. And be quiet.

WILLY   [*turning to* LINDA, *guiltily*] You're not worried about me, are you, sweetheart?

BIFF   What's the matter?

HAPPY   Listen!

LINDA   You've got too much on the ball to worry about.

WILLY   You're my foundation and my support, Linda.

LINDA   Just try to relax, dear. You make mountains out of molehills.

WILLY   I won't fight with him any more. If he wants to go back to Texas, let him go.

LINDA   He'll find his way.

WILLY   Sure. Certain men just don't get started till later in life. Like Thomas Edison, I think. Or B. F. Goodrich. One of them was deaf. [*He starts for the bedroom doorway.*] I'll put my money on Biff.

LINDA   And Willy—if it's warm Sunday we'll drive in the country. And we'll open the windshield, and take lunch.

WILLY   No, the windshields don't open on the new cars.

LINDA   But you opened it today.

WILLY   Me? I didn't. [*He stops.*] Now isn't that peculiar! Isn't that a remarkable—[*He breaks off in amazement and fright as the flute is heard distantly.*]

LINDA   What, darling?

WILLY   That is the most remarkable thing.

LINDA   What, dear?

WILLY   I was thinking of the Chevvy. [*slight pause*] Nineteen twenty-eight . . . when I had that red Chevvy—[*breaks off*] That funny? I coulda sworn I was driving that Chevvy today.

LINDA   Well, that's nothing. Something must've reminded you.

WILLY   Remarkable. Ts. Remember those days? The way Biff used to simonize that car? The dealer refused to believe there was eighty thousand miles on it. [*He shakes his head.*] Heh! [*to* LINDA] Close your eyes, I'll be right up. [*He walks out of the bedroom.*]

HAPPY   [*to* BIFF] Jesus, maybe he smashed up the car again!

LINDA   [*calling after* WILLY] Be careful on the stairs, dear! The cheese is on the middle shelf! [*She turns, goes over to the bed, takes his jacket, and goes out of the bedroom.*]

>[*Light has risen on the boys' room. Unseen,* WILLY *is heard talking to himself, "Eighty thousand miles," and a little laugh.* BIFF *gets out of bed, comes downstage a bit, and stands attentively.* BIFF *is two years older than his brother* HAPPY, *well built, but in these days bears a worn air and seems less self-assured. He has succeeded less, and his dreams are stronger and less acceptable than* HAPPY's. HAPPY *is tall, powerfully made.*]

Sexuality is like a visible color on him, or a scent that many women have discovered. He, like his brother, is lost, but in a different way, for he has never allowed himself to turn his face toward defeat and is thus more confused and hard-skinned, although seemingly more content.]

HAPPY [*getting out of bed*]   He's going to get his license taken away if he keeps that up. I'm getting nervous about him, y'know, Biff?

BIFF   His eyes are going.

HAPPY   No, I've driven with him. He sees all right. He just doesn't keep his mind on it. I drove into the city with him last week. He stops at a green light and then it turns red and he goes. [*He laughs.*]

BIFF   Maybe he's color-blind.

HAPPY   Pop? Why he's got the finest eye for color in the business. You know that.

BIFF [*sitting down on his bed*]   I'm going to sleep.

HAPPY   You're not still sour on Dad, are you Biff?

BIFF   He's all right, I guess.

WILLY [*underneath them, in the living-room*]   Yes, sir, eighty thousand miles—eighty-two thousand!

BIFF   You smoking?

HAPPY [*holding out a pack of cigarettes*]   Want one?

BIFF [*taking a cigarette*]   I can never sleep when I smell it.

WILLY   What a simonizing job, heh!

HAPPY [*with deep sentiment*]   Funny, Biff, y'know? Us sleeping in here again? The old beds. [*He pats his bed affectionately.*] All the talk that went across those two beds, huh? Our whole lives.

BIFF   Yeah. Lotta dreams and plans.

HAPPY [*with a deep and masculine laugh*]   About five hundred women would like to know what was said in this room.
[*They share a soft laugh.*]

BIFF   Remember that big Betsy something—what the hell was her name— over on Bushwick Avenue?

HAPPY [*combing his hair*]   With the collie dog!

BIFF   That's the one. I got you in there, remember?

HAPPY   Yeah, that was my first time—I think. Boy, there was a pig! [*They laugh, almost crudely.*] You taught me everything I know about women. Don't forget that.

BIFF   I bet you forgot how bashful you used to be. Especially with girls.

HAPPY   Oh, I still am, Biff.

BIFF   Oh, go on.

HAPPY   I just control it, that's all. I think I got less bashful and you got more so. What happened, Biff? Where's the old humor, the old confidence? [*He shakes* BIFF's *knee.* BIFF *gets up and moves restlessly about the room.*] What's the matter?

BIFF   Why does Dad mock me all the time?

HAPPY   He's not mocking you, he—

BIFF   Everything I say there's a twist of mockery on his face. I can't get near him.

HAPPY   He just wants you to make good, that's all. I wanted to talk to you about Dad for a long time, Biff. Something's—happening to him. He— talks to himself.

BIFF I noticed that this morning. But he always mumbled.

HAPPY But not so noticeable. It got so embarrassing I sent him to Florida. And you know something? Most of the time he's talking to you.

BIFF What's he say about me?

HAPPY I can't make it out.

BIFF What's he say about me?

HAPPY I think the fact that you're not settled, that you're still kind of up in the air . . .

BIFF There's one or two other things depressing him, Happy.

HAPPY What do you mean?

BIFF Never mind. Just don't lay it all to me.

HAPPY But I think if you just got started—I mean—is there any future for you out there?

BIFF I tell ya, Hap, I don't know what the future is. I don't know—what I'm supposed to want.

HAPPY What do you mean?

BIFF Well, I spent six or seven years after high school trying to work myself up. Shipping clerk, salesman, business of one kind or another. And it's a measly manner of existence. To get on that subway on the hot mornings in summer. To devote your whole life to keeping stock, or making phone calls, or selling or buying. To suffer fifty weeks of the year for the sake of a two-week vacation, when all you really desire is to be outdoors, with your shirt off. And always to have to get ahead of the next fella. And still—that's how you build a future.

HAPPY Well, you really enjoy it on a farm? Are you content out there?

BIFF [*with rising agitation*] Hap, I've had twenty or thirty different kinds of jobs since I left home before the war, and it always turns out the same. I just realized it lately. In Nebraska when I herded cattle, and the Dakotas, and Arizona, and now in Texas. It's why I came home now, I guess, because I realized it. This farm I work on, it's spring there now, see? And they've got about fifteen new colts. There's nothing more inspiring or— beautiful than the sight of a mare and a new colt. And it's cool there now, see? Texas is cool now, and it's spring. And whenever spring comes to where I am, I suddenly get the feeling, my God, I'm not gettin' anywhere! What the hell am I doing, playing around with horses, twenty-eight dollars a week! I'm thirty-four years old. I oughta be makin' my future. That's when I come running home. And now, I get here, and I don't know what to do with myself. [*after a pause*] I've always made a point of not wasting my life, and everytime I come back here I know that all I've done is to waste my life.

HAPPY You're a poet, you know that, Biff? You're a—you're an idealist!

BIFF No, I'm mixed up very bad. Maybe I oughta get married. Maybe I oughta get stuck into something. Maybe that's my trouble. I'm like a boy. I'm not married. I'm not in business, I just—I'm like a boy. Are you content, Hap? You're a success, aren't you? Are you content?

HAPPY Hell, no!

BIFF Why? You're making money, aren't you?

HAPPY [*moving about with energy, expressiveness*] All I can do now is wait for the merchandise manager to die. And suppose I get to be merchandise manager? He's a good friend of mine, and he just built a terrific estate on

Long Island. And he lived there about two months and sold it, and now he's building another one. He can't enjoy it once it's finished. And I know that's just what I would do. I don't know what the hell I'm workin' for. Sometimes I sit in my apartment—all alone. And I think of the rent I'm paying. And it's crazy. But then, it's what I always wanted. My own apartment, a car, and plenty of women. And still, goddammit, I'm lonely.

BIFF [with enthusiasm]   Listen why don't you come out West with me?

HAPPY   You and I, heh?

BIFF   Sure, maybe we could buy a ranch. Raise cattle, use our muscles. Men built like we are should be working out in the open.

HAPPY [avidly]   The Loman Brothers, heh?

BIFF [with vast affection]   Sure, we'd be known all over the counties!

HAPPY [enthralled]   That's what I dream about, Biff. Sometimes I want to just rip my clothes off in the middle of the store and outbox that goddam merchandise manager. I mean I can outbox, outrun, and outlift anybody in that store, and I have to take orders from those common, petty sons-of-bitches till I can't stand it any more.

BIFF   I'm tellin' you, kid, if you were with me I'd be happy out there.

HAPPY [enthused]   See, Biff, everybody around me is so false that I'm constantly lowering my ideals . . .

BIFF   Baby, together we'd stand up for one another, we'd have someone to trust.

HAPPY   If I were around you—

BIFF   Hap, the trouble is we weren't brought up to grub for money. I don't know how to do it.

HAPPY   Neither can I!

BIFF   Then let's go!

HAPPY   The only thing is—what can you make out there?

BIFF   But look at your friend. Builds an estate and then hasn't the peace of mind to live in it.

HAPPY   Yeah, but when he walks into the store the waves part in front of him. That's fifty-two thousand dollars a year coming through the revolving door, and I got more in my pinky finger than he's got his head.

BIFF   Yeah, but you just said—

HAPPY   I gotta show some of those pompous, self-important executives over there that Hap Loman can make the grade. I want to walk into the store the way he walks in. Then I'll go with you, Biff. We'll be together yet, I swear. But take those two we had tonight. Now weren't they gorgeous creatures?

BIFF   Yeah, yeah, most gorgeous I've had in years.

HAPPY   I get that any time I want, Biff. Whenever I feel disgusted. The only trouble is, it gets like bowling or something. I just keep knockin' them over and it doesn't mean anything. You still run around a lot?

BIFF   Naa. I'd like to find a girl—steady, somebody with substance.

HAPPY   That's what I long for.

BIFF   Go on! You'd never come home.

HAPPY   I would! Somebody with character, with resistance! Like Mom, y'know? You're gonna call me a bastard when I tell you this. That girl Charlotte I was with tonight is engaged to be married in five weeks. [He tries on his new hat.]

BIFF   No kiddin'!

HAPPY   Sure, the guy's in line for the vice-presidency of the store. I don't know what gets into me, maybe I just have an overdeveloped sense of competition or something, but I went and ruined her, and furthermore I can't get rid of her. And he's the third executive I've done that to. Isn't that a crummy characteristic? And to top it all, I go to their weddings! [*indignantly, but laughing*] Like I'm not supposed to take bribes. Manufacturers offer me a hundred-dollar bill now and then to throw an order their way. You know how honest I am, but it's like this girl, see. I hate myself for it. Because I don't want the girl, and, still, I take it and—I love it!

BIFF   Let's go to sleep.

HAPPY   I guess we didn't settle anything, heh?

BIFF   I just got one idea that I think I'm going to try.

HAPPY   What's that?

BIFF   Remember Bill Oliver?

HAPPY   Sure, Oliver is very big now. You want to work for him again?

BIFF   No, but when I quit he said something to me. He put his arm on my shoulder, and he said, "Biff, if you ever need anything, come to me."

HAPPY   I remember that. That sounds good.

BIFF   I think I'll go to see him. If I could get ten thousand or even seven or eight thousand dollars I could buy a beautiful ranch.

HAPPY   I bet he'd back you. 'Cause he thought highly of you, Biff. I mean, they all do. You're well liked, Biff. That's why I say to come back here, and we both have the apartment. And I'm tellin' you, Biff, any babe you want . . .

BIFF   No, with a ranch I could do the work I like and still be something. I just wonder though. I wonder if Oliver still thinks I stole that carton of basketballs.

HAPPY   Oh, he probably forgot that long ago. It's almost ten years. You're too sensitive. Anyway, he didn't really fire you.

BIFF   Well, I think he was going to. I think that's why I quit. I was never sure whether he knew or not. I know he thought the world of me, though. I was the only one he'd let lock up the place.

WILLY [*below*]   You gonna wash the engine, Biff?

HAPPY   Shh!

[BIFF *looks at* HAPPY, *who is gazing down, listening.* WILLY *is mumbling in the parlor.*]

HAPPY   You hear that?

[*They listen.* WILLY *laughs warmly.*]

BIFF [*growing angry*]   Doesn't he know Mom can hear that?

WILLY   Don't get your sweater dirty, Biff!

[*A look of pain crosses* BIFF's *face.*]

HAPPY   Isn't that terrible? Don't leave again, will you? You'll find a job here. You gotta stick around. I don't know what to do about him, it's getting embarrassing.

WILLY   What a simonizing job!

BIFF   Mom's hearing that!

WILLY   No kiddin', Biff, you got a date? Wonderful!

HAPPY   Go on to sleep. But talk to him in the morning, will you?

BIFF [*reluctantly getting into bed*] With her in the house. Brother!

HAPPY [*getting into bed*] I wish you'd have a good talk with him.

[*The light on their room begins to fade.*]

BIFF [*to himself in bed*] That selfish, stupid . . .

HAPPY Sh . . . Sleep, Biff.

[*Their light is out. Well before they have finished speaking,* WILLY's *form is dimly seen below in the darkened kitchen. He opens the refrigerator, searches in there, and takes out a bottle of milk. The apartment houses are fading out, and the entire house and surroundings become covered with leaves. Music insinuates itself as the leaves appear.*]

WILLY Just wanna be careful with those girls, Biff, that's all. Don't make any promises. No promises of any kind. Because a girl, y'know, they always believe what you tell 'em, and you're very young, Biff, you're too young to be talking seriously to girls.

[*Light rises on the kitchen.* WILLY, *talking, shuts the refrigerator door and comes downstage to the kitchen table. He pours milk into a glass. He is totally immersed in himself, smiling faintly.*]

WILLY Too young entirely, Biff. You want to watch your schooling first. Then when you're all set, there'll be plenty of girls for a boy like you. [*He smiles broadly at a kitchen chair.*] That so? The girls pay for you? [*He laughs.*] Boy, you must really be makin' a hit.

[WILLY *is gradually addressing—physically—a point offstage, speaking through the wall of the kitchen, and his voice has been rising in volume to that of a normal conversation.*]

WILLY I been wondering why you polish the car so careful. Ha! Don't leave the hubcaps, boys. Get the chamois to the hubcaps. Happy, use newspaper on the windows, it's the easiest thing. Show him how to do it, Biff! You see, Happy? Pad it up, use it like a pad. That's it, that's it, good work. You're doin' all right, Hap. [*He pauses, then nods in approbation for a few seconds, then looks upward.*] Biff, first thing we gotta do when we get time is clip that big branch over the house. Afraid it's gonna fall in a storm and hit the roof. Tell you what. We get a rope and sling her around, and then we climb up there with a couple of saws and take her down. Soon as you finish the car, boys, I wanna see ya. I got a surprise for you, boys.

BIFF [*offstage*] Whatta ya got, Dad?

WILLY No, you finish first. Never leave a job till you're finished— remember that, [*looking toward the "big trees"*] Biff, up in Albany I saw a beautiful hammock. I think I'll buy it next trip, and we'll hang it right between those two elms. Wouldn't that be something? Just swingin' there under those branches. Boy, that would be . . .

[YOUNG BIFF *and* YOUNG HAPPY *appear from the direction* WILLY *was addressing.* HAPPY *carries rags and a pail of water.* BIFF, *wearing a sweater with a block "S," carries a football.*]

BIFF [*pointing in the direction of the car offstage*] How's that, Pop, professional?

WILLY Terrific. Terrific job, boys. Good work, Biff.

HAPPY Where's the surprise, Pop?

WILLY In the back seat of the car.

HAPPY Boy! [*He runs off.*]

BIFF What is it, Dad? Tell me, what'd you buy?

WILLY [*laughing, cuffs him*] Never mind, something I want you to have.

BIFF [*turns and starts off*]   What is it, Hap?

HAPPY [*offstage*]   It's a punching bag!

BIFF   Oh, Pop!

WILLY   It's got Gene Tunney's[1] signature on it!

[HAPPY *runs onstage with a punching bag.*]

BIFF   Gee, how'd you know we wanted a punching bag?

WILLY   Well, it's the finest thing for the timing.

HAPPY [*lies down on his back and pedals with his feet*]   I'm losing weight, you notice, Pop?

WILLY [*to* HAPPY]   Jumping rope is good too.

BIFF   Did you see the new football I got?

WILLY [*examining the ball*]   Where'd you get a new ball?

BIFF   The coach told me to practice my passing.

WILLY   That so? And he gave you the ball, heh?

BIFF   Well, I borrowed it from the locker room. [*He laughs confidentially.*]

WILLY [*laughing with him at the left*]   I want you to return that.

HAPPY   I told you he wouldn't like it!

BIFF [*angrily*]   Well, I'm bringing it back!

WILLY [*stopping the incipient argument, to* HAPPY]   Sure, he's gotta practice with a regulation ball, doesn't he? [*to* BIFF] Coach'll probably congratulate you on your initiative!

BIFF   Oh, he keeps congratulating my initiative all the time, Pop.

WILLY   That's because he likes you. If somebody else took that ball there'd be an uproar. So what's the report, boys, what's the report?

BIFF   Where'd you go this time, Dad? Gee we were lonesome for you.

WILLY [*pleased, puts an arm around each boy and they come down to the apron*]   Lonesome, heh?

BIFF   Missed you every minute.

WILLY   Don't say? Tell you a secret, boys. Don't breathe it to a soul. Someday I'll have my own business, and I'll never have to leave home any more.

HAPPY   Like Uncle Charley, heh?

WILLY   Bigger than Uncle Charley! Because Charley is not—liked. He's liked, but he's not—well liked.

BIFF   Where'd you go this time, Dad?

WILLY   Well, I got on the road, and I went north to Providence. Met the Mayor.

BIFF   The Mayor of Providence!

WILLY   He was sitting in the hotel lobby.

BIFF   What'd he say?

WILLY   He said, "Morning!" And I said, "You got a fine city here, Mayor." And then he had coffee with me. And then I went to Waterbury. Waterbury is a fine city. Big clock city, the famous Waterbury clock. Sold a nice bill there. And then Boston—Boston is the cradle of the Revolution. A fine city. And a couple of other towns in Mass., and on to Portland and Bangor and straight home!

BIFF   Gee, I'd love to go with you sometime, Dad.

WILLY   Soon as summer comes.

HAPPY   Promise?

---

1. World heavyweight boxing champion from 1926 to 1928.

WILLY   You and Hap and I, and I'll show you all the towns. America is full of beautiful towns and fine, upstanding people. And they know me, boys, they know me up and down New England. The finest people. And when I bring you fellas up, there'll be open sesame for all of us, 'cause one thing, boys: I have friends. I can park my car in any street in New England, and the cops protect it like their own. This summer, heh?

BIFF and HAPPY [*together*]   Yeah! You bet!

WILLY   We'll take our bathing suits.

HAPPY   We'll carry your bags, Pop!

WILLY   Oh, won't that be something! Me comin' into the Boston stores with you boys carryin' my bags. What a sensation!

[BIFF *is prancing around, practicing passing the ball.*]

WILLY   You nervous, Biff, about the game?

BIFF   Not if you're gonna be there.

WILLY   What do they say about you in school, now that they made you captain?

HAPPY   There's a crowd of girls behind him everytime the classes change.

BIFF [*taking* WILLY's *hand*]   This Saturday, Pop, this Saturday—just for you, I'm going to break through for a touchdown.

HAPPY   You're supposed to pass.

BIFF   I'm takin' one play for Pop. You watch me, Pop, and when I take off my helmet, that means I'm breakin' out. Then you watch me crash through that line!

WILLY [*kisses* BIFF]   Oh, wait'll I tell this in Boston!

[BERNARD *enters in knickers. He is younger than* BIFF, *earnest and loyal, a worried boy.*]

BERNARD   Biff, where are you? You're supposed to study with me today.

WILLY   Hey, looka Bernard. What're you lookin' so anemic about, Bernard?

BERNARD   He's gotta study, Uncle Willy. He's got Regents[2] next week.

HAPPY [*tauntingly, spinning* BERNARD *around*]   Let's box, Bernard!

BERNARD   Biff! [*He gets away from* HAPPY.] Listen, Biff, I heard Mr. Birnbaum say that if you don't start studyin' math he's gonna flunk you, and you won't graduate. I heard him!

WILLY   You better study with him, Biff. Go ahead now.

BERNARD   I heard him!

BIFF   Oh, Pop, you didn't see my sneakers! [*He holds up a foot for* WILLY *to look at.*]

WILLY   Hey, that's a beautiful job of printing!

BERNARD [*wiping his glasses*]   Just because he printed University of Virginia on his sneakers doesn't mean they've got to graduate him, Uncle Willy!

WILLY [*angrily*]   What're you talking about? With scholarships to three universities they're gonna flunk him?

BERNARD   But I heard Mr. Birnbaum say—

WILLY   Don't be a pest, Bernard! [*to his boys*] What an anemic!

BERNARD   Okay, I'm waiting for you in my house, Biff.

[BERNARD *goes off. The Lomans laugh.*]

WILLY   Bernard is not well liked, is he?

BIFF   He's liked, but he's not well liked.

---

2. Compulsory statewide high school examinations in New York.

HAPPY   That's right, Pop.

WILLY   That's just what I mean. Bernard can get the best marks in school, y'understand, but when he gets out in the business world, y'understand, you are going to be five times ahead of him. That's why I thank Almighty God you're both built like Adonises.[3] Because the man who makes an appearance in the business world, the man who creates personal interest, is the man who gets ahead. Be liked and you will never want. You take me, for instance. I never have to wait in line to see a buyer. "Willy Loman is here!" That's all they have to know, and I go right through.

BIFF   Did you knock them dead, Pop?

WILLY   Knocked 'em cold in Providence, slaughtered 'em in Boston.

HAPPY   [on his back, pedaling again]   I'm losing weight, you notice, Pop?
    [LINDA enters, as of old, a ribbon in her hair, carrying a basket of washing.]

LINDA   [with youthful energy]   Hello, dear!

WILLY   Sweetheart!

LINDA   How'd the Chevvy run?

WILLY   Chevrolet, Linda, is the greatest car ever built. [to the boys] Since when do you let your mother carry wash up the stairs?

BIFF   Grab hold there, boy!

HAPPY   Where to, Mom?

LINDA   Hang them up on the line. And you better go down to your friends, Biff. The cellar is full of boys. They don't know what to do with themselves.

BIFF   Ah, when Pop comes home they can wait!

WILLY   [laughs appreciatively]   You better go down and tell them what to do, Biff.

BIFF   I think I'll have them sweep out the furnace room.

WILLY   Good work, Biff.

BIFF   [goes through wall-line of kitchen to doorway at back and calls down] Fellas! Everybody sweep out the furnace room! I'll be right down!

VOICES   All right! Okay, Biff.

BIFF   George and Sam and Frank, come out back! We're hangin' up the wash! Come on, Hap, on the double!
    [He and HAPPY carry out the basket.]

LINDA   The way they obey him!

WILLY   Well, that training, the training. I'm tellin' you, I was sellin' thousands and thousands, but I had to come home.

LINDA   Oh, the whole block'll be at that game. Did you sell anything?

WILLY   I did five hundred gross in Providence and seven hundred gross in Boston.

LINDA   No! Wait a minute, I've got a pencil. [She pulls pencil and paper out of her apron pocket.] That makes your commission . . . Two hundred— my God! Two hundred and twelve dollars!

WILLY   Well, I didn't figure it yet, but . . .

LINDA   How much did you do?

WILLY   Well, I—I did—about a hundred and eighty gross in Providence. Well, no—it came to—roughly two hundred gross on the whole trip.

LINDA   [without hesitation]   Two hundred gross. That's . . . [She figures.]

---

3. In Greek mythology Adonis was a beautiful youth favored by Aphrodite, the goddess of love.

WILLY   The trouble was that three of the stores were half closed for inventory in Boston. Otherwise I woulda broke records.

LINDA   Well, it makes seventy dollars and some pennies. That's very good.

WILLY   What do we owe?

LINDA   Well, on the first there's sixteen dollars on the refrigerator—

WILLY   Why sixteen?

LINDA   Well, the fan belt broke, so it was a dollar eighty.

WILLY   But it's brand new.

LINDA   Well, the man said that's the way it is. Till they work themselves in, y'know.

[*They move through the wall-line into the kitchen.*]

WILLY   I hope we didn't get stuck on that machine.

LINDA   They got the biggest ads of any of them!

WILLY   I know, it's a fine machine. What else?

LINDA   Well, there's nine-sixty for the washing machine. And for the vacuum cleaner there's three and a half due on the fifteenth. Then the roof, you got twenty-one dollars remaining.

WILLY   It don't leak, does it?

LINDA   No, they did a wonderful job. Then you owe Frank for the carburetor.

WILLY   I'm not going to pay that man! That goddam Chevrolet, they ought to prohibit the manufacture of that car!

LINDA   Well, you owe him three and a half. And odds and ends, comes to around a hundred and twenty dollars by the fifteenth.

WILLY   A hundred and twenty dollars! My God, if business don't pick up I don't know what I'm gonna do!

LINDA   Well, next week you'll do better.

WILLY   Oh, I'll knock 'em dead next week. I'll go to Hartford. I'm very well liked in Hartford. You know, the trouble is, Linda, people don't seem to take to me.

[*They move onto the forestage.*]

LINDA   Oh, don't be foolish.

WILLY   I know it when I walk in. They seem to laugh at me.

LINDA   Why? Why would they laugh at you? Don't talk that way, Willy.

[WILLY *moves to the edge of the stage.* LINDA *goes into the kitchen and starts to darn stockings.*]

WILLY   I don't know the reason for it, but they just pass me by. I'm not noticed.

LINDA   But you're doing wonderful, dear. You're making seventy to a hundred dollars a week.

WILLY   But I gotta be at it ten, twelve hours a day. Other men—I don't know—they do it easier. I don't know why—I can't stop myself—I talk too much. A man oughta come in with a few words. One thing about Charley. He's a man of few words, and they respect him.

LINDA   You don't talk too much, you're just lively.

WILLY [*smiling*]   Well, I figure, what the hell, life is short, a couple of jokes. [*to himself*] I joke too much! [*The smiles goes.*]

LINDA   Why? You're—

WILLY   I'm fat. I'm very—foolish to look at, Linda. I didn't tell you, but Christmas time I happened to be calling on F. H. Stewarts, and a salesman I know, as I was going in to see the buyer I heard him say something about—walrus. And I—I cracked him right across the face. I won't take that. I simply will not take that. But they do laugh at me. I know that.

LINDA   Darling . . .

WILLY   I gotta overcome it. I know I gotta overcome it. I'm not dressing to advantage, maybe.

LINDA   Willy, darling, you're the handsomest man in the world—

WILLY   Oh, no, Linda.

LINDA   To me you are. [*slight pause*] The handsomest.

[*From the darkness is heard the laughter of a woman.* WILLY *doesn't turn to it, but it continues through* LINDA's *lines.*]

LINDA   And the boys, Willy. Few men are idolized by their children the way you are.

[*Music is heard as behind a scrim,*[4] *to the left of the house,* THE WOMAN, *dimly seen, is dressing.*]

WILLY [*with great feeling*]   You're the best there is, Linda, you're a pal, you know that? On the road—on the road I want to grab you sometimes and just kiss the life outa you.

[*The laughter is loud now, and he moves into a brightening area at the left, where* THE WOMAN *has come from behind the scrim and is standing, putting on her hat, looking into a "mirror" and laughing.*]

WILLY   'Cause I get so lonely—especially when business is bad and there's nobody to talk to. I get the feeling that I'll never sell anything again, that I won't make a living for you, or a business, a business for the boys. [*He talks through* THE WOMAN's *subsiding laughter;* THE WOMAN *primps at the "mirror."*] There's so much I want to make for—

THE WOMAN   Me? You didn't make me, Willy. I picked you.

WILLY [*pleased*]   You picked me?

THE WOMAN [*who is quite proper-looking,* WILLY's *age*]   I did. I've been sitting at that desk watching all the salesmen go by, day in, day out. But you've got such a sense of humor, and we do have such a good time together, don't we?

WILLY   Sure, sure. [*He takes her in his arms.*] Why do you have to go now?

THE WOMAN   It's two o'clock . . .

WILLY   No, come on in! [*He pulls her.*]

THE WOMAN   . . . my sisters'll be scandalized. When'll you be back?

WILLY   Oh, two weeks about. Will you come up again?

THE WOMAN   Sure thing. You do make me laugh. It's good for me. [*She squeezes his arm, kisses him.*] And I think you're a wonderful man.

WILLY   You picked me, heh?

THE WOMAN   Sure. Because you're so sweet. And such a kidder.

WILLY   Well, I'll see you next time I'm in Boston.

THE WOMAN   I'll put you right through to the buyers.

WILLY [*slapping her bottom*]   Right. Well, bottoms up!

THE WOMAN [*slaps him gently and laughs*]   You just kill me, Willy. [*He suddenly grabs her and kisses her roughly.*] You kill me. And thanks for the stockings. I love a lot of stockings. Well, good night.

---

4. Part of a stage set; a painted gauze curtain that becomes transparent when lighted from the back.

WILLY   Good night. And keep your pores open!

THE WOMAN   Oh, Willy!

[THE WOMAN *bursts out laughing, and* LINDA's *laughter blends in.* THE WOMAN *disappears into the dark. Now the area at the kitchen table brightens.* LINDA *is sitting where she was at the kitchen table, but now is mending a pair of her silk stockings.*]

LINDA   You are, Willy. The handsomest man. You've got no reason to feel that—

WILLY   [*coming out of* THE WOMAN's *dimming area and going over to* LINDA] I'll make it all up to you, Linda. I'll—

LINDA   There's nothing to make up, dear. You're doing fine, better than—

WILLY   [*noticing her mending*]   What's that?

LINDA   Just mending my stockings. They're so expensive—

WILLY   [*angrily, taking them from her*]   I won't have you mending stockings in this house! Now throw them out!

[LINDA *puts the stockings in her pocket.*]

BERNARD   [*entering on the run*]   Where is he? If he doesn't study!

WILLY   [*moving to the forestage, with great agitation*]   You'll give him the answers!

BERNARD   I do, but I can't on a Regents! That's a state exam! They're liable to arrest me!

WILLY   Where is he? I'll whip him, I'll whip him!

LINDA   And he'd better give back that football, Willy, it's not nice.

WILLY   Biff! Where is he? Why is he taking everything?

LINDA   He's too rough with the girls, Willy. All the mothers are afraid of him!

WILLY   I'll whip him!

BERNARD   He's driving the car without a license!

[THE WOMAN's *laugh is heard.*]

WILLY   Shut up!

LINDA   All the mothers—

WILLY   Shut up!

BERNARD   [*backing quietly away and out*]   Mr. Birnbaum says he's stuck up.

WILLY   Get outa here!

BERNARD   If he doesn't buckle down he'll flunk math! [*He goes off.*]

LINDA   He's right, Willy, you've gotta—

WILLY   [*exploding at her*]   There's nothing the matter with him! You want him to be a worm like Bernard? He's got spirit, personality . . .

[*As he speaks,* LINDA, *almost in tears, exits into the living-room.* WILLY *is alone in the kitchen, wilting and staring. The leaves are gone. It is night again, and the apartment houses look down from behind.*]

WILLY   Loaded with it. Loaded! What is he stealing? He's giving it back, isn't he? Why is he stealing? What did I tell him? I never in my life told him anything but decent things.

[HAPPY *in pajamas has come down the stairs;* WILLY *suddenly becomes aware of* HAPPY's *presence.*]

HAPPY   Let's go now, come on.

WILLY   [*sitting down at the kitchen table*]   Huh! Why did she have to wax the floors herself? Everytime she waxes the floors she keels over. She knows that!

HAPPY Shh! Take it easy. What brought you back tonight?

WILLY I got an awful scare. Nearly hit a kid in Yonkers. God! Why didn't I go to Alaska with my brother Ben that time! Ben! That man was a genius, that man was success incarnate! What a mistake! He begged me to go.

HAPPY Well, there's no use in—

WILLY You guys! There was a man started with the clothes on his back and ended up with diamond mines!

HAPPY Boy, someday I'd like to know how he did it.

WILLY What's the mystery? The man knew what he wanted and went out and got it! Walked into a jungle, and comes out, the age of twenty-one, and he's rich! The world is an oyster, but you don't crack it open on a mattress!

HAPPY Pop, I told you I'm gonna retire you for life.

WILLY You'll retire me for life on seventy goddam dollars a week? And your women and your car and your apartment, and you'll retire me for life! Christ's sake, I couldn't get past Yonkers today! Where are you guys, where are you? The woods are burning! I can't drive a car!

[CHARLEY *has appeared in the doorway. He is a large man, slow of speech, laconic, immovable. In all he says, despite what he says, there is pity, and, now, trepidation. He has a robe over pajamas, slippers on his feet. He enters the kitchen.*]

CHARLEY Everything all right?

HAPPY Yeah, Charley, everything's . . .

WILLY What's the matter?

CHARLEY I heard some noise. I thought something happened. Can't we do something about the walls? You sneeze in here, and in my house hats blow off.

HAPPY Let's go to bed, Dad. Come on.

[CHARLEY *signals to* HAPPY *to go.*]

WILLY You go ahead, I'm not tired at the moment.

HAPPY [*to* WILLY] Take it easy, huh? [*He exits.*]

WILLY What're you doin' up?

CHARLEY [*sitting down at the kitchen table opposite* WILLY] Couldn't sleep good. I had a heartburn.

WILLY Well, you don't know how to eat.

CHARLEY I eat with my mouth.

WILLY No, you're ignorant. You gotta know about vitamins and things like that.

CHARLEY Come on, let's shoot. Tire you out a little.

WILLY [*hesitantly*] All right. You got cards?

CHARLEY [*taking a deck from his pocket*] Yeah, I got them. Someplace. What is it with those vitamins?

WILLY [*dealing*] They build up your bones. Chemistry.

CHARLEY Yeah, but there's no bones in a heartburn.

WILLY What are you talkin' about? Do you know the first thing about it?

CHARLEY Don't get insulted.

WILLY Don't talk about something you don't know anything about.

[*They are playing. Pause.*]

CHARLEY What're you doin' home?

WILLY   A little trouble with the car.

CHARLEY   Oh. [*pause*] I'd like to take a trip to California.

WILLY   Don't say.

CHARLEY   You want a job?

WILLY   I got a job, I told you that. [*after a slight pause*] What the hell are you offering me a job for?

CHARLEY   Don't get insulted.

WILLY   Don't insult me.

CHARLEY   I don't see no sense in it. You don't have to go on this way.

WILLY   I got a good job. [*slight pause*] What do you keep comin' in here for?

CHARLEY   You want me to go?

WILLY [*after a pause, withering*]   I can't understand it. He's going back to Texas again. What the hell is that?

CHARLEY   Let him go.

WILLY   I got nothin' to give him, Charley, I'm clean, I'm clean.

CHARLEY   He won't starve. None a them starve. Forget about him.

WILLY   Then what have I got to remember?

CHARLEY   You take it too hard. To hell with it. When a deposit bottle is broken you don't get your nickel back.

WILLY   That's easy enough for you to say.

CHARLEY   That ain't easy for me to say.

WILLY   Did you see the ceiling I put up in the living-room?

CHARLEY   Yeah, that's a piece of work. To put up a ceiling is a mystery to me. How do you do it?

WILLY   What's the difference?

CHARLEY   Well, talk about it.

WILLY   You gonna put up a ceiling?

CHARLEY   How could I put up a ceiling?

WILLY   Then what the hell are you bothering me for?

CHARLEY   You're insulted again.

WILLY   A man who can't handle tools is not a man. You're disgusting.

CHARLEY   Don't call me disgusting, Willy.

[UNCLE BEN, *carrying a valise and an umbrella, enters the forestage from around the right corner of the house. He is a stolid man, in his sixties, with a mustache and an authoritative air. He is utterly certain of his destiny, and there is an aura of far places about him. He enters exactly as* WILLY *speaks.*]

WILLY   I'm getting awfully tired, Ben.

[BEN's *music is heard.* BEN *looks around at everything.*]

CHARLEY   Good, keep playing; you'll sleep better. Did you call me Ben?

[BEN *looks at his watch.*]

WILLY   That's funny. For a second there you reminded me of my brother Ben.

BEN   I only have a few minutes. [*He strolls, inspecting the place.* WILLY *and* CHARLEY *continue playing.*]

CHARLEY   You never heard from him again, heh? Since that time?

WILLY   Didn't Linda tell you? Couple of weeks ago we got a letter from his wife in Africa. He died.

CHARLEY   That so.

BEN [*chuckling*]   So this is Brooklyn, eh?

CHARLEY   Maybe you're in for some of his money.

WILLY   Naa, he had seven sons. There's just one opportunity I had with that man . . .

BEN   I must make a train, William. There are several properties I'm looking at in Alaska.

WILLY   Sure, sure! If I'd gone with him to Alaska that time, everything would've been totally different.

CHARLEY   Go on, you'd froze to death up there.

WILLY   What're you talking about?

BEN   Opportunity is tremendous in Alaska, William. Surprised you're not up there.

WILLY   Sure, tremendous.

CHARLEY   Heh?

WILLY   There was the only man I ever met who knew the answers.

CHARLEY   Who?

BEN   How are you all?

WILLY [*taking a pot, smiling*]   Fine, fine.

CHARLEY   Pretty sharp tonight.

BEN   Is Mother living with you?

WILLY   No, she died a long time ago.

CHARLEY   Who?

BEN   That's too bad. Fine specimen of a lady, Mother.

WILLY [*to* CHARLEY]   Heh?

BEN   I'd hoped to see the old girl.

CHARLEY   Who died?

BEN   Heard anything from Father, have you?

WILLY [*unnerved*]   What do you mean, who died?

CHARLEY [*taking a pot*]   What're you talkin' about?

BEN [*looking at his watch*]   William, it's half-past eight!

WILLY [*as though to dispel his confusion he angrily stops* CHARLEY'*s hand*]   That's my build!

CHARLEY   I put the ace—

WILLY   If you don't know how to play the game I'm not gonna throw my money away on you!

CHARLEY [*rising*]   It was my ace, for God's sake!

WILLY   I'm through, I'm through!

BEN   When did Mother die?

WILLY   Long ago. Since the beginning you never knew how to play cards.

CHARLEY [*picks up the cards and goes to the door*]   All right! Next time I'll bring a deck with five aces.

WILLY   I don't play that kind of game!

CHARLEY [*turning to him*]   You ought to be ashamed of yourself!

WILLY   Yeah?

CHARLEY   Yeah! [*He goes out.*]

WILLY [*slamming the door after him*]   Ignoramus!

BEN [*as* WILLY *comes toward him through the wall-line of the kitchen*]   So you're William.

WILLY [*shaking* BEN'*s hand*]   Ben! I've been waiting for you so long! What's the answer? How did you do it?

BEN   Oh, there's a story in that.
     [LINDA *enters the forestage, as of old, carrying the wash basket.*]
LINDA   Is this Ben?
BEN [*gallantly*]   How do you do, my dear.
LINDA   Where've you been all these years? Willy's always wondered why
     you—
WILLY [*pulling BEN away from her impatiently*]   Where is Dad? Didn't you
     follow him? How did you get started?
BEN   Well, I don't know how much you remember.
WILLY   Well, I was just a baby, of course, only three or four years old—
BEN   Three years and eleven months.
WILLY   What a memory, Ben!
BEN   I have many enterprises, William, and I have never kept books.
WILLY   I remember I was sitting under the wagon in—was it Nebraska?
BEN   It was South Dakota, and I gave you a bunch of wild flowers.
WILLY   I remember you walking away down some open road.
BEN [*laughing*]   I was going to find Father in Alaska.
WILLY   Where is he?
BEN   At that age I had a very faulty view of geography, William. I discov-
     ered after a few days that I was heading due south, so instead of Alaska,
     I ended up in Africa.
LINDA   Africa!
WILLY   The Gold Coast!
BEN   Principally diamond mines.
LINDA   Diamond mines!
BEN   Yes, my dear. But I've only a few minutes—
WILLY   No! Boys! Boys! [YOUNG BIFF *and* HAPPY *appear.*] Listen to this.
     This is your Uncle Ben, a great man! Tell my boys, Ben!
BEN   Why, boys, when I was seventeen I walked into the jungle, and when
     I was twenty-one I walked out. [*He laughs.*] And by God I was rich.
WILLY [*to the boys*]   You see what I been talking about? The greatest things
     can happen!
BEN [*glancing at his watch*]   I have an appointment in Ketchikan Tuesday
     week.
WILLY   No, Ben! Please tell about Dad. I want my boys to hear. I want them
     to know the kind of stock they spring from. All I remember is a man with
     a big beard, and I was in Mamma's lap, sitting around a fire, and some
     kind of high music.
BEN   His flute. He played the flute.
WILLY   Sure, the flute, that's right!
     [*New music is heard, a high, rollicking tune.*]
BEN   Father was a very great and a very wild-hearted man. We would start
     in Boston, and he'd toss the whole family into the wagon, and then he'd
     drive the team right across the country; through Ohio, and Indiana,
     Michigan, Illinois, and all the Western states. And we'd stop in the towns
     and sell the flutes that he'd made on the way. Great inventor, Father.
     With one gadget he made more in a week than a man like you could make
     in a lifetime.
WILLY   That's just the way I'm bringing them up, Ben—rugged, well liked,
     all-around.

BEN Yeah? [*to* BIFF] Hit that, boy—hard as you can. [*He pounds his stomach.*]

BIFF Oh, no, sir!

BEN [*taking boxing stance*] Come on, get to me! [*He laughs.*]

WILLY Go to it, Biff! Go ahead, show him!

BIFF Okay! [*He cocks his fist and starts in.*]

LINDA [*to* WILLY] Why must he fight, dear?

BEN [*sparring with* BIFF] Good boy! Good boy!

WILLY How's that, Ben, heh?

HAPPY Give him the left, Biff!

LINDA Why are you fighting?

BEN Good boy! [*Suddenly comes in, trips* BIFF, *and stands over him, the point of his umbrella poised over* BIFF's *eye.*]

LINDA Look out, Biff!

BIFF Gee!

BEN [*patting* BIFF's *knee*] Never fight fair with a stranger, boy. You'll never get out of the jungle that way. [*taking* LINDA's *hand and bowing*] It was an honor and a pleasure to meet you, Linda.

LINDA [*withdrawing her hand coldly, frightened*] Have a nice—trip.

BEN [*to* WILLY] And good luck with your—what do you do?

WILLY Selling.

BEN Yes. Well . . . [*He raises his hand in farewell to all.*]

WILLY No, Ben, I don't want you to think . . . [*He takes* BEN's *arm to show him.*] It's Brooklyn, I know, but we hunt too.

BEN Really, now.

WILLY Oh, sure, there's snakes and rabbits and—that's why I moved out here. Why, Biff can fell any one of these trees in no time! Boys! Go right over to where they're building the apartment house and get some sand. We're gonna rebuild the entire front stoop right now! Watch this, Ben!

BIFF Yes, sir! On the double, Hap!

HAPPY [*as he and* BIFF *run off*] I lost weight, Pop, you notice?
    [CHARLEY *enters in knickers, even before the boys are gone.*]

CHARLEY Listen, if they steal any more from that building the watchman'll put the cops on them!

LINDA [*to* WILLY] Don't let Biff . . .
    [BEN *laughs lustily.*]

WILLY You shoulda seen the lumber they brought home last week. At least a dozen six-by-tens worth all kinds a money.

CHARLEY Listen, if that watchman—

WILLY I gave them hell, understand. But I got a couple of fearless characters there.

CHARLEY Willy, the jails are full of fearless characters.

BEN [*clapping* WILLY *on the back, with a laugh at* CHARLEY] And the stock exchange, friend!

WILLY [*joining in* BEN's *laughter*] Where are the rest of your pants?

CHARLEY My wife bought them.

WILLY Now all you need is a golf club and you can go upstairs and go to sleep. [*to* BEN] Great athlete! Between him and his son Bernard they can't hammer a nail!

BERNARD [*rushing in*]   The watchman's chasing Biff!

WILLY [*angrily*]   Shut up! He's not stealing anything!

LINDA [*alarmed, hurrying off left*]   Where is he? Biff, dear! [*She exits.*]

WILLY [*moving toward the left, away from* BEN]   There's nothing wrong. What's the matter with you?

BEN   Nervy boy. Good!

WILLY [*laughing*]   Oh, nerves of iron, that Biff!

CHARLEY   Don't know what it is. My New England man comes back and he's bleedin', they murdered him up there.

WILLY   It's contacts, Charley, I got important contacts!

CHARLEY [*sarcastically*]   Glad to hear it, Willy. Come in later, we'll shoot a little casino. I'll take some of your Portland money. [*He laughs at* WILLY *and exits.*]

WILLY [*turning to* BEN]   Business is bad, it's murderous. But not for me, of course.

BEN   I'll stop by on my way back to Africa.

WILLY [*longingly*]   Can't you stay a few days? You're just what I need, Ben, because I—I have a fine position here, but I—well, Dad left when I was such a baby and I never had a chance to talk to him and I still feel— kind of temporary about myself.

BEN   I'll be late for my train.

[*They are at opposite ends of the stage.*]

WILLY   Ben, my boys—can't we talk? They'd go into the jaws of hell for me, see, but I—

BEN   William, you're being first-rate with your boys. Outstanding, manly chaps!

WILLY [*hanging on to his words*]   Oh, Ben, that's good to hear! Because sometimes I'm afraid that I'm not teaching them the right kind of—Ben, how should I teach them?

BEN [*giving great weight to each word, and with a certain vicious audacity*] William, when I walked into the jungle, I was seventeen. When I walked out I was twenty-one. And, by God, I was rich! [*He goes off into darkness around the right corner of the house.*]

WILLY   . . . was rich! That's just the spirit I want to imbue them with! To walk into a jungle! I was right! I was right! I was right!

[BEN *is gone, but* WILLY *is still speaking to him as* LINDA, *in nightgown and robe, enters the kitchen, glances around for* WILLY, *then goes to the door of the house, looks out and sees him. Comes down to his left. He looks at her.*]

LINDA   Willy, dear? Willy?

WILLY   I was right!

LINDA   Did you have some cheese? [*He can't answer.*] It's very late, darling. Come to bed, heh?

WILLY [*looking straight up*]   Gotta break your neck to see a star in this yard.

LINDA   You coming in?

WILLY   Whatever happened to that diamond watch fob? Remember? When Ben came from Africa that time? Didn't he give me a watch fob with a diamond in it?

LINDA   You pawned it, dear. Twelve, thirteen years ago. For Biff's radio correspondence course.

WILLY   Gee, that was a beautiful thing. I'll take a walk.

LINDA   But you're in your slippers.

WILLY [*starting to go around the house at the left*]   I was right! I was! [*half to* LINDA, *as he goes, shaking his head*] What a man! There was a man worth talking to. I was right!

LINDA [*calling after* WILLY]   But in your slippers, Willy!

[WILLY *is almost gone when* BIFF, *in his pajamas, comes down the stairs and enters the kitchen.*]

BIFF   What is he doing out there?

LINDA   Sh!

BIFF   God Almighty, Mom, how long has he been doing this?

LINDA   Don't, he'll hear you.

BIFF   What the hell is the matter with him?

LINDA   It'll pass by morning.

BIFF   Shouldn't we do anything?

LINDA   Oh, my dear, you should do a lot of things, but there's nothing to do so go to sleep.

[HAPPY *comes down the stairs and sits on the steps.*]

HAPPY   I never heard him so loud, Mom.

LINDA   Well, come around more often; you'll hear him. [*She sits down at the table and mends the lining of* WILLY's *jacket.*]

BIFF   Why didn't you ever write me about this, Mom?

LINDA   How would I write to you? For over three months you had no address.

BIFF   I was on the move. But you know I thought of you all the time. You know that, don't you, pal?

LINDA   I know, dear, I know. But he likes to have a letter. Just to know that there's still a possibility for better things.

BIFF   He's not like this all the time, is he?

LINDA   It's when you come home he's always the worst.

BIFF   When I come home?

LINDA   When you write you're coming, he's all smiles, and talks about the future, and—he's just wonderful. And then the closer you seem to come, the more shaky he gets, and then, by the time you get here, he's arguing, and he seems angry at you. I think it's just that maybe he can't bring himself to—to open up to you. Why are you so hateful to each other? Why is that?

BIFF [*evasively*]   I'm not hateful, Mom.

LINDA   But you no sooner come in the door than you're fighting!

BIFF   I don't know why. I mean to change. I'm tryin', Mom, you understand?

LINDA   Are you home to stay now?

BIFF   I don't know. I want to look around, see what's doin'.

LINDA   Biff, you can't look around all your life, can you?

BIFF   I just can't take hold, Mom. I can't take hold of some kind of a life.

LINDA   Biff, a man is not a bird, to come and go with the springtime.

BIFF   Your hair . . . [*He touches her hair.*] Your hair got so gray.

LINDA   Oh, it's been gray since you were in high school. I just stopped dyeing it, that's all.

BIFF   Dye it again, will ya? I don't want my pal looking old. [*He smiles.*]

LINDA   You're such a boy! You think you can go away for a year and . . . You've got to get it into your head now that one day you'll knock on this door and there'll be strange people here—

BIFF   What are you talking about? You're not even sixty, Mom.

LINDA   But what about your father?

BIFF [*lamely*]   Well, I meant him too.

HAPPY   He admires Pop.

LINDA   Biff, dear, if you don't have any feeling for him, then you can't have any feeling for me.

BIFF   Sure I can, Mom.

LINDA   No. You can't just come to see me, because I love him. [*with a threat, but only a threat, of tears*] He's the dearest man in the world to me, and I won't have anyone making him feel unwanted and low and blue. You've got to make up your mind now, darling, there's no leeway any more. Either he's your father and you pay him that respect, or else you're not to come here. I know he's not easy to get along with—nobody knows that better than me—but . . .

WILLY [*from the left, with a laugh*]   Hey, hey, Biffo!

BIFF [*starting to go out after* WILLY]   What the hell is the matter with him? [HAPPY *stops him.*]

LINDA   Don't—don't go near him!

BIFF   Stop making excuses for him! He always, always wiped the floor with you. Never had an ounce of respect for you.

HAPPY   He's always had respect for—

BIFF   What the hell do you know about it?

HAPPY [*surlily*]   Just don't call him crazy!

BIFF   He's got no character—Charley wouldn't do this. Not in his own house—spewing out that vomit from his mind.

HAPPY   Charley never had to cope with what he's got to.

BIFF   People are worse off than Willy Loman. Believe me, I've seen them!

LINDA   Then make Charley your father, Biff. You can't do that, can you? I don't say he's a great man. Willy Loman never made a lot of money. His name was never in the paper. He's not the finest character that ever lived. But he's a human being, and a terrible thing is happening to him. So attention must be paid. He's not to be allowed to fall into his grave like an old dog. Attention, attention must be finally paid to such a person. You called him crazy—

BIFF   I didn't mean—

LINDA   No, a lot of people think he's lost his—balance. But you don't have to be very smart to know what his trouble is. The man is exhausted.

HAPPY   Sure!

LINDA   A small man can be just as exhausted as a great man. He works for a company thirty-six years this March, opens up unheard-of territories to their trademark, and now in his old age they take his salary away.

HAPPY [*indignantly*]   I didn't know that, Mom.

LINDA   You never asked, my dear! Now that you get your spending money someplace else you don't trouble your mind with him.

HAPPY   But I gave you money last—

LINDA Christmas time, fifty dollars! To fix the hot water it cost ninety-seven fifty! For five weeks he's been on straight commission, like a beginner, an unknown!

BIFF Those ungrateful bastards!

LINDA Are they any worse than his sons? When he brought them business, when he was young, they were glad to see him. But now his old friends, the old buyers that loved him so and always found some order to hand him in a pinch—they're all dead, retired. He used to be able to make six, seven calls a day in Boston. Now he takes his valises out of the car and puts them back and takes them out again and he's exhausted. Instead of walking he talks now. He drives seven hundred miles, and when he gets there no one knows him any more, no one welcomes him. And what goes through a man's mind, driving seven hundred miles home without having earned a cent? Why shouldn't he talk to himself? Why? When he has to go to Charley and borrow fifty dollars a week and pretend to me that it's his pay? How long can that go on? How long? You see what I'm sitting here and waiting for? And you tell me he has no character? The man who never worked a day but for your benefit? When does he get the medal for that? Is this his reward—to turn around at the age of sixty-three and find his sons, who he loved better than his life, one a philandering bum—

HAPPY Mom!

LINDA That's all you are, my baby! [to BIFF] And you! What happened to the love you had for him? You were such pals! How you used to talk to him on the phone every night! How lonely he was till he could come home to you!

BIFF All right, Mom. I'll live here in my room, and I'll get a job. I'll keep away from him, that's all.

LINDA No, Biff. You can't stay here and fight all the time.

BIFF He threw me out of this house, remember that.

LINDA Why did he do that? I never knew why.

BIFF Because I know he's a fake and he doesn't like anybody around who knows!

LINDA Why a fake? In what way? What do you mean?

BIFF Just don't lay it all at my feet. It's between me and him—that's all I have to say. I'll chip in from now on. He'll settle for half my pay check. He'll be all right. I'm going to bed. [He starts for the stairs.]

LINDA He won't be all right.

BIFF [turning on the stairs, furiously] I hate this city and I'll stay here. Now what do you want?

LINDA He's dying, Biff.
[HAPPY turns quickly to her, shocked.]

BIFF [after a pause] Why is he dying?

LINDA He's been trying to kill himself.

BIFF [with great horror] How?

LINDA I live from day to day.

BIFF What're you talking about?

LINDA Remember I wrote you that he smashed up the car again? In February?

BIFF   Well?

LINDA   The insurance inspector came. He said that they have evidence. That all these accidents in the last year—weren't—weren't—accidents.

HAPPY   How can they tell that? That's a lie.

LINDA   It seems there's a woman . . . [*she takes a breath as*]

{ BIFF [*sharply but contained*]   What woman?
{ LINDA [*simultaneously*]   . . . and this woman . . .

LINDA   What?

BIFF   Nothing. Go ahead.

LINDA   What did you say?

BIFF   Nothing. I just said what woman?

HAPPY   What about her?

LINDA   Well, it seems she was walking down the road and saw his car. She says that he wasn't driving fast at all, and that he didn't skid. She says he came to that little bridge, and then deliberately smashed into the railing, and it was only the shallowness of the water that saved him.

BIFF   Oh, no, he probably just fell asleep again.

LINDA   I don't think he fell asleep.

BIFF   Why not?

LINDA   Last month . . . [*with great difficulty*] Oh, boys, it's so hard to say a thing like this! He's just a big stupid man to you, but I tell you there's more good in him than in many other people. [*She chokes, wipes her eyes.*] I was looking for a fuse. The lights blew out, and I went down the cellar. And behind the fuse box—it happened to fall out—was a length of rubber pipe—just short.

HAPPY   No kidding?

LINDA   There's a little attachment on the end of it. I knew right away. And sure enough, on the bottom of the water heater there's a new little nipple on the gas pipe.

HAPPY [*angrily*]   That—jerk.

BIFF   Did you have it taken off?

LINDA   I'm—I'm ashamed to. How can I mention it to him? Every day I go down and take away that little rubber pipe. But, when he comes home, I put it back where it was. How can I insult him that way? I don't know what to do. I live from day to day, boys. I tell you, I know every thought in his mind. It sounds so old-fashioned and silly, but I tell you he put his whole life into you and you've turned your backs on him. [*She is bent over in the chair, weeping, her face in her hands.*] Biff, I swear to God! Biff, his life is in your hands!

HAPPY [*to* BIFF]   How do you like that damned fool!

BIFF [*kissing her*]   All right, pal, all right. It's all settled now. I've been remiss. I know that, Mom. But now I'll stay, and I swear to you, I'll apply myself. [*kneeling in front of her, in a fever of self-reproach*] It's just—you see, Mom, I don't fit in business. Not that I won't try. I'll try, and I'll make good.

HAPPY   Sure you will. The trouble with you in business was you never tried to please people.

BIFF   I know, I—

HAPPY   Like when you worked for Harrison's. Bob Harrison said you were
tops, and then you go and do some damn fool thing like whistling whole
songs in the elevator like a comedian.

BIFF [*against* HAPPY]   So what? I like to whistle sometimes.

HAPPY   You don't raise a guy to a responsible job who whistles in the elevator!

LINDA   Well, don't argue about it now.

HAPPY   Like when you'd go off and swim in the middle of the day instead
of taking the line around.

BIFF [*his resentment rising*]   Well, don't you run off? You take off sometimes, don't you? On a nice summer day?

HAPPY   Yeah, but I cover myself!

LINDA   Boys!

HAPPY   If I'm going to take a fade the boss can call any number where I'm
supposed to be and they'll swear to him that I just left. I'll tell you something that I hate to say, Biff, but in the business world some of them think
you're crazy.

BIFF [*angered*]   Screw the business world!

HAPPY   All right, screw it! Great, but cover yourself!

LINDA   Hap, Hap!

BIFF   I don't care what they think! They've laughed at Dad for years, and
you know why? Because we don't belong in this nuthouse of a city! We
should be mixing cement on some open plain, or—or carpenters. A carpenter is allowed to whistle!

   [WILLY *walks in from the entrance of the house, at left.*]

WILLY   Even your grandfather was better than a carpenter. [*Pause. They
watch him.*] You never grew up. Bernard does not whistle in the elevator, I assure you.

BIFF [*as though to laugh* WILLY *out of it*]   Yeah, but you do, Pop.

WILLY   I never in my life whistled in an elevator! And who in the business
world thinks I'm crazy?

BIFF   I didn't mean it like that, Pop. Now don't make a whole thing out of
it, will ya?

WILLY   Go back to the West! Be a carpenter, a cowboy, enjoy yourself!

LINDA   Willy, he was just saying—

WILLY   I heard what he said!

HAPPY [*trying to quiet* WILLY]   Hey, Pop, come on now . . .

WILLY [*continuing over* HAPPY'*s line*]   They laugh at me, heh? Go to Filene's,
go to the Hub, go to Slattery's, Boston. Call out the name Willy Loman
and see what happens! Big Shot!

BIFF   All right, Pop.

WILLY   Big!

BIFF   All right!

WILLY   Why do you always insult me?

BIFF   I didn't say a word. [*to* LINDA] Did I say a word?

LINDA   He didn't say anything, Willy.

WILLY [*going to the doorway of the living-room*]   All right, good night,
good night.

LINDA   Willy, dear, he just decided . . .

WILLY [*to* BIFF] If you get tired hanging around tomorrow, paint the ceiling I put up in the living-room.

BIFF I'm leaving early tomorrow.

HAPPY He's going to see Bill Oliver, Pop.

WILLY [*interestedly*] Oliver? For what?

BIFF [*with reserve, but trying, trying*] He always said he'd stake me. I'd like to go into business, so maybe I can take him up on it.

LINDA Isn't that wonderful?

WILLY Don't interrupt. What's wonderful about it? There's fifty men in the City of New York who'd stake him. [*to* BIFF] Sporting goods?

BIFF I guess so. I know something about it and—

WILLY He knows something about it! You know sporting goods better than Spalding, for God's sake! How much is he giving you?

BIFF I don't know, I didn't even see him yet, but—

WILLY Then what're you talkin' about?

BIFF [*getting angry*] Well, all I said was I'm gonna see him, that's all!

WILLY [*turning away*] Ah, you're counting your chickens again.

BIFF [*starting left for the stairs*] Oh, Jesus, I'm going to sleep!

WILLY [*calling after him*] Don't curse in this house!

BIFF [*turning*] Since when did you get so clean?

HAPPY [*trying to stop them*] Wait a . . .

WILLY Don't use that language to me! I won't have it!

HAPPY [*grabbing* BIFF, *shouts*] Wait a minute! I got an idea. I got a feasible idea. Come here, Biff, let's talk this over now, let's talk some sense here. When I was down in Florida last time, I thought of a great idea to sell sporting goods. It just came back to me. You and I, Biff—we have a line, the Loman Line. We train a couple of weeks, and put on a couple of exhibitions, see?

WILLY That's an idea!

HAPPY Wait! We form two basketball teams, see? Two water-polo teams. We play each other. It's a million dollars' worth of publicity. Two brothers, see? The Loman Brothers. Displays in the Royal Palms—all the hotels. And banners over the ring and the basketball court: "Loman Brothers." Baby, we could sell sporting goods!

WILLY That is a one-million-dollar idea!

LINDA Marvelous!

BIFF I'm in great shape as far as that's concerned.

HAPPY And the beauty of it is, Biff, it wouldn't be like a business. We'd be out playin' ball again . . .

BIFF [*enthused*] Yeah, that's . . .

WILLY Million-dollar . . .

HAPPY And you wouldn't get fed up with it, Biff. It'd be the family again. There'd be the old honor, and comradeship, and if you wanted to go off for a swim or somethin'—well, you'd do it! Without some smart cooky gettin' up ahead of you!

WILLY Lick the world! You guys together could absolutely lick the civilized world.

BIFF I'll see Oliver tomorrow. Hap, if we could work that out . . .

LINDA Maybe things are beginning to—

WILLY [*wildly enthused, to* LINDA]   Stop interrupting! [*to* BIFF] But don't wear sport jacket and slacks when you see Oliver.

BIFF   No, I'll—

WILLY   A business suit, and talk as little as possible, and don't crack any jokes.

BIFF   He did like me. Always liked me.

LINDA   He loved you!

WILLY [*to* LINDA]   Will you stop! [*to* BIFF] Walk in very serious. You are not applying for a boy's job. Money is to pass. Be quiet, fine, and serious. Everybody likes a kidder, but nobody lends him money.

HAPPY   I'll try to get some myself, Biff. I'm sure I can.

WILLY   I see great things for you kids, I think your troubles are over. But remember, start big and you'll end big. Ask for fifteen. How much you gonna ask for?

BIFF   Gee, I don't know—

WILLY   And don't say "Gee." "Gee" is a boy's word. A man walking in for fifteen thousand dollars does not say "Gee!"

BIFF   Ten, I think, would be top though.

WILLY   Don't be so modest. You always started too low. Walk in with a big laugh. Don't look worried. Start off with a couple of your good stories to lighten things up. It's not what you say, it's how you say it—because personality always wins the day.

LINDA   Oliver always thought the highest of him—

WILLY   Will you let me talk?

BIFF   Don't yell at her, Pop, will ya?

WILLY [*angrily*]   I was talking, wasn't I?

BIFF   I don't like you yelling at her all the time, and I'm tellin' you, that's all.

WILLY   What're you, takin' over this house?

LINDA   Willy—

WILLY [*turning on her*]   Don't take his side all the time, goddammit!

BIFF [*furiously*]   Stop yelling at her!

WILLY [*suddenly pulling on his cheek, beaten down, guilt ridden*]   Give my best to Bill Oliver—he may remember me. [*He exits through the living-room doorway.*]

LINDA [*her voice subdued*]   What'd you have to start that for? [BIFF *turns away.*] You see how sweet he was as soon as you talked hopefully? [*She goes over to* BIFF.] Come up and say good night to him. Don't let him go to bed that way.

HAPPY   Come on, Biff, let's buck him up.

LINDA   Please, dear. Just say good night. It takes so little to make him happy. Come. [*She goes through the living-room doorway, calling upstairs from within the living-room*] Your pajamas are hanging in the bathroom, Willy!

HAPPY [*looking toward where* LINDA *went out*]   What a woman! They broke the mold when they made her. You know that, Biff?

BIFF   He's off salary. My God, working on commission!

HAPPY   Well, let's face it: he's no hot-shot selling man. Except that sometimes, you have to admit, he's a sweet personality.

BIFF [*deciding*]   Lend me ten bucks, will ya? I want to buy some new ties.

HAPPY I'll take you to a place I know. Beautiful stuff. Wear one of my striped shirts tomorrow.

BIFF She got gray. Mom got awful old. Gee, I'm gonna go in to Oliver tomorrow and knock him for a—

HAPPY Come on up. Tell that to Dad. Let's give him a whirl. Come on.

BIFF [*steamed up*] You know, with ten thousand bucks, boy!

HAPPY [*as they go into the living-room*] That's the talk, Biff, that's the first time I've heard the old confidence out of you! [*from within the living-room, fading off*] You're gonna live with me, kid, and any babe you want just say the word . . . [*The last lines are hardly heard. They are mounting the stairs to their parents' bedroom.*]

LINDA [*entering her bedroom and addressing* WILLY, *who is in the bathroom. She is straightening the bed for him.*] Can you do anything about the shower? It drips.

WILLY [*from the bathroom*] All of a sudden everything falls to pieces! Goddam plumbing, oughta be sued, those people. I hardly finished putting it in and the thing . . . [*His words rumble off.*]

LINDA I'm just wondering if Oliver will remember him. You think he might?

WILLY [*coming out of the bathroom in his pajamas*] Remember him? What's the matter with you, you crazy? If he'd've stayed with Oliver he'd be on top by now! Wait'll Oliver gets a look at him. You don't know the average caliber any more. The average young man today—[*he is getting into bed*]—is got a caliber of zero. Greatest thing in the world for him was to bum around.

[BIFF *and* HAPPY *enter the bedroom. Slight pause.*]

WILLY [*stops short, looking at* BIFF] Glad to hear it, boy.

HAPPY He wanted to say good night to you, sport.

WILLY [*to* BIFF] Yeah. Knock him dead, boy. What'd you want to tell me?

BIFF Just take it easy, Pop. Good night. [*He turns to go.*]

WILLY [*unable to resist*] And if anything falls off the desk while you're talking to him—like a package or something—don't you pick it up. They have office boys for that.

LINDA I'll make a big breakfast—

WILLY Will you let me finish? [*to* BIFF] Tell him you were in the business in the West. Not farm work.

BIFF All right, Dad.

LINDA I think everything—

WILLY [*going right through her speech*] And don't undersell yourself. No less than fifteen thousand dollars.

BIFF [*unable to bear him*] Okay. Good night, Mom. [*He starts moving.*]

WILLY Because you got a greatness in you, Biff, remember that. You got all kinds a greatness . . . [*He lies back, exhausted.* BIFF *walks out.*]

LINDA [*calling after* BIFF] Sleep well, darling!

HAPPY I'm gonna get married, Mom. I wanted to tell you.

LINDA Go to sleep, dear.

HAPPY [*going*] I just wanted to tell you.

WILLY Keep up the good work. [HAPPY *exits.*] God . . . remember that Ebbets Field[5] game? The championship of the city?

5. Brooklyn sports stadium.

LINDA Just rest. Should I sing to you?

WILLY Yeah. Sing to me. [LINDA *hums a soft lullaby.*] When tha
out—he was the tallest, remember?

LINDA Oh, yes. And in gold.
[BIFF *enters the darkened kitchen, takes a cigarette, and lea*
He comes downstage into a golden pool of light. He smokes, staring at the
night.]

WILLY Like a young god. Hercules[6]—something like that. And the sun,
the sun all around him. Remember how he waved to me? Right up from
the field, with the representatives of three colleges standing by? And the
buyers I brought, and the cheers when he came out—Loman, Loman,
Loman! God Almighty, he'll be great yet. A star like that, magnificent,
can never really fade away!
[*The light on* WILLY *is fading. The gas heater begins to glow through the*
kitchen wall, near the stairs, a blue flame beneath red coils.]

LINDA [*timidly*] Willy dear, what has he got against you?

WILLY I'm so tired. Don't talk any more.
[BIFF *slowly returns to the kitchen. He stops, stares toward the heater.*]

LINDA Will you ask Howard to let you work in New York?

WILLY First thing in the morning. Everything'll be all right.
[BIFF *reaches behind the heater and draws out a length of rubber tub-*
ing. He is horrified and turns his head toward WILLY's *room, still dimly*
lit, from which the strains of LINDA's *desperate but monotonous hum-*
ming rise.]

WILLY [*staring through the window into the moonlight*] Gee, look at the
moon moving between the buildings!
[BIFF *wraps the tubing around his hand and quickly goes up the stairs.*]

CURTAIN

Act Two

Music is heard, gay and bright. The curtain rises as the music fades away. WILLY,
in shirt sleeves, is sitting at the kitchen table, sipping coffee, his hat in his lap.
LINDA *is filling his cup when she can.*

WILLY Wonderful coffee. Meal in itself.

LINDA Can I make you some eggs?

WILLY No. Take a breath.

LINDA You look so rested, dear.

WILLY I slept like a dead one. First time in months. Imagine, sleeping till
ten on a Tuesday morning. Boys left nice and early, heh?

LINDA They were out of here by eight o'clock.

WILLY Good work!

LINDA It was so thrilling to see them leaving together. I can't get over the
shaving lotion in this house!

WILLY [*smiling*] Mmm—

LINDA Biff was very changed this morning. His whole attitude seemed to
be hopeful. He couldn't wait to get downtown to see Oliver.

6. In Greek and Roman mythology the son of the chief god (Zeus, Jupiter), famous for his great
strength.

WILLY   He's heading for a change. There's no question, there simply are certain men that take longer to get—solidified. How did he dress?

LINDA   His blue suit. He's so handsome in that suit. He could be a—anything in that suit!

[WILLY *gets up from the table.* LINDA *holds his jacket for him.*]

WILLY   There's no question, no question at all. Gee, on the way home tonight I'd like to buy some seeds.

LINDA   [*laughing*]   That'd be wonderful. But not enough sun gets back there. Nothing'll grow any more.

WILLY   You wait, kid, before it's all over we're gonna get a little place out in the country, and I'll raise some vegetables, a couple of chickens . . .

LINDA   You'll do it yet, dear.

[WILLY *walks out of his jacket.* LINDA *follows him.*]

WILLY   And they'll get married, and come for a weekend. I'd build a little guest house. 'Cause I got so many fine tools, all I'd need would be a little lumber and some peace of mind.

LINDA   [*joyfully*]   I sewed the lining . . .

WILLY   I could build two guest houses, so they'd both come. Did he decide how much he's going to ask Oliver for?

LINDA   [*getting him into the jacket*]   He didn't mention it, but I imagine ten or fifteen thousand. You going to talk to Howard today?

WILLY   Yeah. I'll put it to him straight and simple. He'll just have to take me off the road.

LINDA   And Willy, don't forget to ask for a little advance, because we've got the insurance premium. It's the grace period now.

WILLY   That's a hundred . . . ?

LINDA   A hundred and eight, sixty-eight. Because we're a little short again.

WILLY   Why are we short?

LINDA   Well, you had the motor job on the car . . .

WILLY   That goddam Studebaker!

LINDA   And you got one more payment on the refrigerator . . .

WILLY   But it just broke again!

LINDA   Well, it's old, dear.

WILLY   I told you we should've bought a well-advertised machine. Charley bought a General Electric and it's twenty years old and it's still good, that son-of-a-bitch.

LINDA   But, Willy—

WILLY   Whoever heard of a Hastings refrigerator? Once in my life I would like to own something outright before it's broken! I'm always in a race with the junkyard! I just finished paying for the car and it's on its last legs. The refrigerator consumes belts like a goddam maniac. They time those things. They time them so when you finally paid for them, they're used up.

LINDA   [*buttoning up his jacket as he unbuttons it*]   All told, about two hundred dollars would carry us, dear. But that includes the last payment on the mortgage. After this payment, Willy, the house belongs to us.

WILLY   It's twenty-five years!

LINDA   Biff was nine years old when we bought it.

WILLY   Well, that's a great thing. To weather a twenty-five year mortgage is—

LINDA   It's an accomplishment.

WILLY   All the cement, the lumber, the reconstruction I put in this house! There ain't a crack to be found in it anymore.

LINDA   Well, it served its purpose.

WILLY   What purpose? Some stranger'll come along, move in, and that's that. If only Biff would take this house, and raise a family . . . [*He starts to go.*] Good-by, I'm late.

LINDA [*suddenly remembering*]   Oh, I forgot! You're supposed to meet them for dinner.

WILLY   Me?

LINDA   At Frank's Chop House on Forty-eighth near Sixth Avenue.

WILLY   Is that so! How about you?

LINDA   No, just the three of you. They're gonna blow you to a big meal!

WILLY   Don't say! Who thought of that?

LINDA   Biff came to me this morning, Willy, and he said, "Tell Dad, we want to blow him to a big meal." Be there six o'clock. You and your two boys are going to have dinner.

WILLY   Gee whiz! That's really somethin'. I'm gonna knock Howard for a loop, kid. I'll get an advance, and I'll come home with a New York job. Goddammit, now I'm gonna do it!

LINDA   Oh, that's the spirit, Willy!

WILLY   I will never get behind a wheel the rest of my life!

LINDA   It's changing, Willy, I can feel it changing!

WILLY   Beyond a question. G'by, I'm late. [*He starts to go again.*]

LINDA [*calling after him as she runs to the kitchen table for a handkerchief*] You got your glasses?

WILLY [*feels for them, then comes back in*]   Yeah, yeah, got my glasses.

LINDA [*giving him the handkerchief*]   And a handkerchief.

WILLY   Yeah, handkerchief.

LINDA   And your saccharine?

WILLY   Yeah, my saccharine.

LINDA   Be careful on the subway stairs.
   [*She kisses him, and a silk stocking is seen hanging from her hand.* WILLY *notices it.*]

WILLY   Will you stop mending stockings? At least while I'm in the house. It gets me nervous. I can't tell you. Please.
   [LINDA *hides the stocking in her hand as she follows* WILLY *across the forestage in front of the house.*]

LINDA   Remember, Frank's Chop House.

WILLY [*passing the apron*]   Maybe beets would grow out there.

LINDA [*laughing*]   But you tried so many times.

WILLY   Yeah. Well, don't work hard today. [*He disappears around the right corner of the house.*]

LINDA   Be careful!
   [*As* WILLY *vanishes,* LINDA *waves to him. Suddenly the phone rings. She runs across the stage and into the kitchen and lifts it.*]

LINDA   Hello? Oh, Biff! I'm so glad you called, I just . . . Yes, sure, I just told him. Yes, he'll be there for dinner at six o'clock, I didn't forget. Listen, I was just dying to tell you. You know that little rubber pipe I told you about? That he connected to the gas heater? I finally decided to go down the cellar this morning and take it away and destroy it. But it's gone! Imagine? He took it away himself, it isn't there! [*She listens.*] When? Oh, then you took it. Oh—nothing, it's just that I'd hoped he'd taken it away himself. Oh, I'm not worried, darling, because this morning he left in such high spirits, it was like the old days! I'm not afraid any more. Did Mr. Oliver see you? . . . Well, you wait there then. And make a nice impression on him, darling. Just don't perspire too much before you see him. And have a nice time with Dad. He may have big news too! . . . That's right, a New York job. And be sweet to him tonight, dear. Be loving to him. Because he's only a little boat looking for a harbor. [*She is trembling with sorrow and joy.*] Oh, that's wonderful, Biff, you'll save his life. Thanks, darling. Just put your arm around him when he comes into the restaurant. Give him a smile. That's the boy . . . Good-by, dear. . . . You got your comb? . . . That's fine. Good-by, Biff dear.

> [*In the middle of her speech,* HOWARD WAGNER, *thirty-six, wheels in a small typewriter table on which is a wire-recording machine and proceeds to plug it in. This is on the left forestage. Light slowly fades on* LINDA *as it rises on* HOWARD. HOWARD *is intent on threading the machine and only glances over his shoulder as* WILLY *appears.*]

WILLY   Pst! Pst!

HOWARD   Hello, Willy, come in.

WILLY   Like to have a little talk with you, Howard.

HOWARD   Sorry to keep you waiting. I'll be with you in a minute.

WILLY   What's that, Howard?

HOWARD   Didn't you ever see one of these? Wire recorder.

WILLY   Oh. Can we talk a minute?

HOWARD   Records things. Just got delivery yesterday. Been driving me crazy, the most terrific machine I ever saw in my life. I was up all night with it.

WILLY   What do you do with it?

HOWARD   I bought it for dictation, but you can do anything with it. Listen to this. I had it home last night. Listen to what I picked up. The first one is my daughter. Get this. [*He flicks the switch and "Roll out the Barrel" is heard being whistled.*] Listen to that kid whistle.

WILLY   That is lifelike, isn't it?

HOWARD   Seven years old. Get that tone.

WILLY   Ts, ts. Like to ask a little favor if you . . .

> [*The whistling breaks off, and the voice of* HOWARD's *daughter is heard.*]

HIS DAUGHTER   "Now you, Daddy."

HOWARD   She's crazy for me! [*Again the same song is whistled.*] That's me! Ha! [*He winks.*]

WILLY   You're very good!

> [*The whistling breaks off again. The machine runs silent for a moment.*]

HOWARD   Sh! Get this now, this is my son.

HIS SON   "The capital of Alabama is Montgomery; the capital of Arizona is Phoenix; the capital of Arkansas is Little Rock; the capital of California is Sacramento . . ." [*and on, and on*]

HOWARD   [*holding up five fingers*]   Five years old, Willy!

WILLY   He'll make an announcer some day!

HIS SON [*continuing*]   "The capital . . ."

HOWARD   Get that—alphabetical order! [*The machine breaks off suddenly.*] Wait a minute. The maid kicked the plug out.

WILLY   It certainly is a—

HOWARD   Sh, for God's sake!

HIS SON   "It's nine o'clock, Bulova watch time. So I have to go to sleep."

WILLY   That really is—

HOWARD   Wait a minute! The next is my wife.
   [*They wait.*]

HOWARD'S VOICE   "Go on, say something." [*pause*] "Well, you gonna talk?"

HIS WIFE   "I can't think of anything."

HOWARD'S VOICE   "Well, talk—it's turning."

HIS WIFE [*shyly, beaten*]   "Hello." [*silence*] "Oh, Howard, I can't talk into this . . ."

HOWARD [*snapping the machine off*]   That was my wife.

WILLY   That is a wonderful machine. Can we—

HOWARD   I tell you, Willy, I'm gonna take my camera, and my handsaw, and all my hobbies, and out they go. This is the most fascinating relaxation I ever found.

WILLY   I think I'll get one myself.

HOWARD   Sure, they're only a hundred and a half. You can't do without it. Supposing you wanna hear Jack Benny,[7] see? But you can't be at home at that hour. So you tell the maid to turn the radio on when Jack Benny comes on, and this automatically goes on with the radio . . .

WILLY   And when you come home you . . .

HOWARD   You can come home twelve o'clock, one o'clock, any time you like, and you get yourself a Coke and sit yourself down, throw the switch, and there's Jack Benny's program in the middle of the night!

WILLY   I'm definitely going to get one. Because lots of time I'm on the road, and I think to myself, what I must be missing on the radio!

HOWARD   Don't you have a radio in the car?

WILLY   Well, yeah, but who ever thinks of turning it on?

HOWARD   Say, aren't you supposed to be in Boston?

WILLY   That's what I want to talk to you about, Howard. You got a minute? [*He draws a chair in from the wing.*]

HOWARD   What happened? What're you doing here?

WILLY   Well . . .

HOWARD   You didn't crack up again, did you?

WILLY   Oh, no. No . . .

HOWARD   Geez, you had me worried there for a minute. What's the trouble?

WILLY   Well, tell you the truth, Howard. I've come to the decision that I'd rather not travel any more.

HOWARD   Not travel! Well, what'll you do?

WILLY   Remember, Christmas time, when you had the party here? You said you'd try to think of some spot for me here in town.

HOWARD   With us?

WILLY   Well, sure.

7. Vastly popular radio comedian of the 1930s and 1940s.

HOWARD   Oh, yeah, yeah. I remember. Well, I couldn't think of anything for you, Willy.

WILLY   I tell ya, Howard. The kids are all grown up, y'know. I don't need much any more. If I could take home—well, sixty-five dollars a week, I could swing it.

HOWARD   Yeah, but Willy, see I—

WILLY   I tell ya why, Howard. Speaking frankly and between the two of us, y'know—I'm just a little tired.

HOWARD   Oh, I could understand that, Willy. But you're a road man, Willy, and we do a road business. We've only got a half-dozen salesmen on the floor here.

WILLY   God knows, Howard, I never asked a favor of any man. But I was with the firm when your father used to carry you in here in his arms.

HOWARD   I know that, Willy, but—

WILLY   Your father came to me the day you were born and asked me what I thought of the name of Howard, may he rest in peace.

HOWARD   I appreciate that, Willy, but there just is no spot here for you. If I had a spot I'd slam you right in, but I just don't have a single solitary spot.

   [*He looks for his lighter.* WILLY *has picked it up and gives it to him. Pause.*]

WILLY   [*with increasing anger*]   Howard, all I need to set my table is fifty dollars a week.

HOWARD   But where am I going to put you, kid?

WILLY   Look, it isn't a question of whether I can sell merchandise, is it?

HOWARD   No, but it's a business, kid, and everybody's gotta pull his own weight.

WILLY   [*desperately*]   Just let me tell you a story, Howard—

HOWARD   'Cause you gotta admit, business is business.

WILLY   [*angrily*]   Business is definitely business, but just listen for a minute. You don't understand this. When I was a boy—eighteen, nineteen—I was already on the road. And there was a question in my mind as to whether selling had a future for me. Because in those days I had a yearning to go to Alaska. See, there were three gold strikes in one month in Alaska, and I felt like going out. Just for the ride, you might say.

HOWARD   [*barely interested*]   Don't say.

WILLY   Oh, yeah, my father lived many years in Alaska. He was an adventurous man. We've got quite a little streak of self-reliance in our family. I thought I'd go out with my older brother and try to locate him, and maybe settle in the North with the old man. And I was almost decided to go, when I met a salesman in the Parker House. His name was Dave Singleman. And he was eighty-four years old, and he'd drummed merchandise in thirty-one states. And old Dave, he'd go up to his room, y'understand, put on his green velvet slippers—I'll never forget—and pick up his phone and call the buyers, and without ever leaving his room, at the age of eighty-four, he made a living. And when I saw that, I realized that selling was the greatest career a man could want. 'Cause what could be more satisfying than to be able to go, at the age of eighty-four, into twenty or thirty different cities, and pick up a phone, and be remembered and loved and helped by so many different people? Do you know? when he died—and by the way he died the death of a salesman, in his green velvet slippers in the smoker of the New York, New Haven and Hartford, going into Boston—when he died, hundreds of salesmen and buyers were at his funeral. Things were sad on a lotta trains for months after that. [*He stands up.* HOWARD *has not looked at him.*] In those days there was personality in it, Howard. There was respect, and comradeship, and gratitude in it. Today, it's all cut and dried, and there's no chance for bringing friendship to bear—or personality. You see what I mean? They don't know me anymore.

HOWARD [*moving away, toward the right*]   That's just the thing, Willy.

WILLY   If I had forty dollars a week—that's all I'd need. Forty dollars, Howard.

HOWARD   Kid, I can't take blood from a stone, I—

WILLY [*desperation is on him now*]   Howard, the year Al Smith[8] was nominated, your father came to me and—

HOWARD [*starting to go off*]   I've got to see some people, kid.

WILLY [*stopping him*]   I'm talking about your father! There were promises made across this desk! You mustn't tell me you've got people to see—I put thirty-four years into this firm, Howard, and now I can't pay my insurance! You can't eat the orange and throw the peel away—a man is not a piece of fruit! [*after a pause*] Now pay attention. Your father—in 1928 I had a big year. I averaged a hundred and seventy dollars a week in commissions.

HOWARD [*impatiently*]   Now, Willy, you never averaged—

WILLY [*banging his hand on the desk*]   I averaged a hundred and seventy dollars a week in the year of 1928! And your father came to me—or rather, I was in the office here—it was right over this desk—and he put his hand on my shoulder—

HOWARD [*getting up*]   You'll have to excuse me, Willy, I gotta see some people. Pull yourself together. [*going out*] I'll be back in a little while.

[*On* HOWARD's *exit, the light on his chair grows very bright and strange.*]

WILLY   Pull myself together! What the hell did I say to him? My God, I was yelling at him! How could I! [WILLY *breaks off, staring at the light, which occupies the chair, animating it. He approaches this chair, standing across the desk from it.*] Frank, Frank, don't you remember what you told me that time? How you put your hand on my shoulder, and Frank . . . [*He leans on the desk and as he speaks the dead man's name he accidentally switches on the recorder, and instantly*]

HOWARD's SON   ". . . of New York is Albany. The capital of Ohio is Cincinnati, the capital of Rhode Island is . . ." [*The recitation continues.*]

WILLY [*leaping away with fright, shouting*]   Ha! Howard! Howard! Howard!

HOWARD [*rushing in*]   What happened?

WILLY [*pointing at the machine, which continues nasally, childishly, with the capital cities*]   Shut it off! Shut it off!

HOWARD [*pulling the plug out*]   Look, Willy . . .

WILLY [*pressing his hands to his eyes*]   I gotta get myself some coffee. I'll get some coffee . . .

[WILLY *starts to walk out.* HOWARD *stops him.*]

---

8. Democratic candidate for president in 1928.

HOWARD [*rolling up the cord*]   Willy, look . . .

WILLY   I'll go to Boston.

HOWARD   Willy, you can't go to Boston for us.

WILLY   Why can't I go?

HOWARD   I don't want you to represent us. I've been meaning to tell you for a long time now.

WILLY   Howard, are you firing me?

HOWARD   I think you need a good long rest, Willy.

WILLY   Howard—

HOWARD   And when you feel better, come back, and we'll see if we can work something out.

WILLY   But I gotta earn money, Howard. I'm in no position to—

HOWARD   Where are your sons? Why don't your sons give you a hand?

WILLY   They're working on a very big deal.

HOWARD   This is no time for false pride, Willy. You go to your sons and you tell them that you're tired. You've got two great boys, haven't you?

WILLY   Oh, no question, no question, but in the meantime . . .

HOWARD   Then that's that, heh?

WILLY   All right, I'll go to Boston tomorrow.

HOWARD   No, no.

WILLY   I can't throw myself on my sons. I'm not a cripple!

HOWARD   Look, kid, I'm busy, I'm busy this morning.

WILLY [*grasping* HOWARD's *arm*]   Howard, you've got to let me go to Boston!

HOWARD [*hard, keeping himself under control*]   I've got a line of people to see this morning. Sit down, take five minutes, and pull yourself together, and then go home, will ya? I need the office, Willy. [*He starts to go, turns, remembering the recorder, starts to push off the table holding the recorder.*] Oh, yeah. Whenever you can this week, stop by and drop off the samples. You'll feel better, Willy, and then come back and we'll talk. Pull yourself together, kid, there's people outside.

> [HOWARD *exits, pushing the table off left.* WILLY *stares into space, exhausted. Now the music is heard—*BEN's *music—first distantly, then closer, closer. As* WILLY *speaks,* BEN *enters from the right. He carries valise and umbrella.*]

WILLY   Oh, Ben, how did you do it? What is the answer? Did you wind up the Alaska deal already?

BEN   Doesn't take much time if you know what you're doing. Just a short business trip. Boarding ship in an hour. Wanted to say good-by.

WILLY   Ben, I've got to talk to you.

BEN [*glancing at his watch*]   Haven't the time, William.

WILLY [*crossing the apron to* BEN]   Ben, nothing's working out. I don't know what to do.

BEN   Now, look here, William. I've bought timberland in Alaska and I need a man to look after things for me.

WILLY   God, timberland! Me and my boys in those grand outdoors!

BEN   You've a new continent at your doorstep, William. Get out of these cities, they're full of talk and time payments and courts of law. Screw on your fists and you can fight for a fortune up there.

WILLY   Yes, yes! Linda, Linda!

[LINDA *enters as of old, with the wash.*]

LINDA   Oh, you're back?

BEN   I haven't much time.

WILLY   No, wait! Linda, he's got a proposition for me in Alaska.

LINDA   But you've got— [*to* BEN] He's got a beautiful job here.

WILLY   But in Alaska, kid, I could—

LINDA   You're doing well enough, Willy!

BEN [*to* LINDA]   Enough for what, my dear?

LINDA [*frightened of* BEN *and angry at him*]   Don't say those things to him!
Enough to be happy right here, right now. [*to* WILLY, *while* BEN *laughs*]
Why must everybody conquer the world? You're well liked, and the boys
love you, and someday—[*to* BEN]—why, old man Wagner told him just the
other day that if he keeps it up he'll be a member of the firm, didn't he,
Willy?

WILLY   Sure, sure. I am building something with this firm, Ben, and if a
man is building something he must be on the right track, mustn't he?

BEN   What are you building? Lay your hand on it. Where is it?

WILLY [*hesitantly*]   That's true, Linda, there's nothing.

LINDA   Why? [*to* BEN] There's a man eighty-four years old—

WILLY   That's right, Ben, that's right. When I look at that man I say, what
is there to worry about?

BEN   Bah!

WILLY   It's true, Ben. All he has to do is go into any city, pick up the phone,
and he's making his living and you know why?

BEN [*picking up his valise*]   I've got to go.

WILLY [*holding* BEN *back*]   Look at this boy!

[BIFF, *in his high school sweater, enters carrying suitcase.* HAPPY *carries*
BIFF's *shoulder guards, gold helmet, and football pants.*]

WILLY   Without a penny to his name, three great universities are begging
for him, and from there the sky's the limit, because it's not what you do,
Ben. It's who you know and the smile on your face! It's contacts, Ben,
contacts! The whole wealth of Alaska passes over the lunch table at the
Commodore Hotel, and that's the wonder, the wonder of this country,
that a man can end with diamonds here on the basis of being liked! [*He
turns to* BIFF.] And that's why when you get out on that field today it's
important. Because thousands of people will be rooting for you and loving you. [*to* BEN, *who has again begun to leave*] And Ben! when he walks
into a business office his name will sound out like a bell and all the
doors will open to him! I've seen it, Ben, I've seen it a thousand times!
You can't feel it with your hand like timber, but it's there!

BEN   Good-by, William.

WILLY   Ben, am I right? Don't you think I'm right? I value your advice.

BEN   There's a new continent at your doorstep, William. You could walk
out rich. Rich! [*He is gone.*]

WILLY   We'll do it here, Ben! You hear me? We're gonna do it here!
[*Young* BERNARD *rushes in. The gay music of the Boys is heard.*]

BERNARD   Oh, gee, I was afraid you left already!

WILLY   Why? What time is it?

BERNARD   It's half-past one!

WILLY Well, come on, everybody! Ebbets Field next stop! Where's the pennants? [*He rushes through the wall-line of the kitchen and out into the living-room.*]

LINDA [*to* BIFF] Did you pack fresh underwear?

BIFF [*who has been limbering up*] I want to go!

BERNARD Biff, I'm carrying your helmet, ain't I?

HAPPY No, I'm carrying the helmet.

BERNARD Oh, Biff, you promised me.

HAPPY I'm carrying the helmet.

BERNARD How am I going to get in the locker room?

LINDA Let him carry the shoulder guards. [*She puts her coat and hat on in the kitchen.*]

BERNARD Can I, Biff? 'Cause I told everybody I'm going to be in the locker room.

HAPPY In Ebbets Field it's the clubhouse.

BERNARD I meant the clubhouse. Biff!

HAPPY Biff!

BIFF [*grandly, after a slight pause*] Let him carry the shoulder guards.

HAPPY [*as he gives* BERNARD *the shoulder guards*] Stay close to us now.
        [WILLY *rushes in with the pennants.*]

WILLY [*handing them out*] Everybody wave when Biff comes out on the field. [HAPPY *and* BERNARD *run off.*] You set now, boy?
        [*The music has died away.*]

BIFF Ready to go, Pop. Every muscle is ready.

WILLY [*at the edge of the apron*] You realize what this means?

BIFF That's right, Pop.

WILLY [*feeling* BIFF'S *muscles*] You're comin' home this afternoon captain of the All-Scholastic Championship Team of the City of New York.

BIFF I got it, Pop. And remember, pal, when I take off my helmet, that touchdown is for you.

WILLY Let's go! [*He is starting out, with his arm around* BIFF, *when* CHAR-LEY *enters, as of old, in knickers.*] I got no room for you, Charley.

CHARLEY Room? For what?

WILLY In the car.

CHARLEY You goin' for a ride? I wanted to shoot some casino.

WILLY [*furiously*] Casino! [*incredulously*] Don't you realize what today is?

LINDA Oh, he knows, Willy. He's just kidding you.

WILLY That's nothing to kid about!

CHARLEY No, Linda, what's goin' on?

LINDA He's playing in Ebbets Field.

CHARLEY Baseball in this weather?

WILLY Don't talk to him. Come on, come on! [*He is pushing them out.*]

CHARLEY Wait a minute, didn't you hear the news?

WILLY What?

CHARLEY Don't you listen to the radio? Ebbets Field just blew up.

WILLY You go to hell! [CHARLEY *laughs. Pushing them out*] Come on, come on! We're late.

CHARLEY [*as they go*] Knock a homer, Biff, knock a homer!

WILLY [*the last to leave, turning to* CHARLEY] I don't think that was funny, Charley. This is the greatest day of his life.

CHARLEY   Willy, when are you going to grow up?

WILLY   Yeah, heh? When this game is over, Charley, you'll be laughing out of the other side of your face. They'll be calling him another Red Grange.[9] Twenty-five thousand a year.

CHARLEY [*kidding*]   Is that so?

WILLY   Yeah, that's so.

CHARLEY   Well, then, I'm sorry, Willy. But tell me something.

WILLY   What?

CHARLEY   Who is Red Grange?

WILLY   Put up your hands. Goddam you, put up your hands!

[CHARLEY, *chuckling, shakes his head and walks away, around the left corner of the stage.* WILLY *follows him. The music rises to a mocking frenzy.*]

WILLY   Who the hell do you think you are, better than everybody else? You don't know everything, you big, ignorant, stupid . . . Put up your hands!

[*Light rises, on the right side of the forestage, on a small table in the reception room of* CHARLEY's *office. Traffic sounds are heard.* BERNARD, *now mature, sits whistling to himself. A pair of tennis rackets and an overnight bag are on the floor beside him.*]

WILLY [*offstage*]   What are you walking away for? Don't walk away! If you're going to say something say it to my face! I know you laugh at me behind my back. You'll laugh out of the other side of your goddam face after this game. Touchdown! Touchdown! Eighty thousand people! Touchdown! Right between the goal posts.

[BERNARD *is a quiet, earnest, but self-assured young man.* WILLY's *voice is coming from right upstage now.* BERNARD *lowers his feet off the table and listens.* JENNY, *his father's secretary, enters.*]

JENNY [*distressed*]   Say, Bernard, will you go out in the hall?

BERNARD   What is that noise? Who is it?

JENNY   Mr. Loman. He just got off the elevator.

BERNARD [*getting up*]   Who's he arguing with?

JENNY   Nobody. There's nobody with him. I can't deal with him any more, and your father gets all upset everytime he comes. I've got a lot of typing to do, and your father's waiting to sign it. Will you see him?

WILLY [*entering*]   Touchdown! Touch— [*He sees* JENNY.] Jenny, Jenny, good to see you. How're ya? Workin'? Or still honest?

JENNY   Fine. How've you been feeling?

WILLY   Not much any more, Jenny. Ha, ha! [*He is surprised to see the rackets.*]

BERNARD   Hello, Uncle Willy.

WILLY [*almost shocked*]   Bernard! Well, look who's here! [*He comes quickly, guiltily to* BERNARD *and warmly shakes his hand.*]

BERNARD   How are you? Good to see you.

WILLY   What are you doing here?

BERNARD   Oh, just stopped by to see Pop. Get off my feet till my train leaves. I'm going to Washington in a few minutes.

WILLY   Is he in?

---

9. Harold Edward Grange (1903–1991), all-American halfback at the University of Illinois from 1923 to 1925, who then played professionally for the Chicago Bears.

BERNARD Yes, he's in his office with the accountant. Sit down.

WILLY [*sitting down*] What're you going to do in Washington?

BERNARD Oh, just a case I've got there, Willy.

WILLY That so? [*indicating the rackets*] You going to play tennis there?

BERNARD I'm staying with a friend who's got a court.

WILLY Don't say. His own tennis court. Must be fine people, I bet.

BERNARD They are, very nice. Dad tells me Biff's in town.

WILLY [*with a big smile*] Yeah, Biff's in. Working on a very big deal, Bernard.

BERNARD What's Biff doing?

WILLY Well, he's been doing very big things in the West. But he decided to establish himself here. Very big. We're having dinner. Did I hear your wife had a boy?

BERNARD That's right. Our second.

WILLY Two boys! What do you know!

BERNARD What kind of a deal has Biff got?

WILLY Well, Bill Oliver—very big sporting-goods man—he wants Biff very badly. Called him in from the West. Long distance, carte blanche, special deliveries. Your friends have their own private tennis court?

BERNARD You still with the old firm, Willy?

WILLY [*after a pause*] I'm—I'm overjoyed to see how you made the grade, Bernard, overjoyed. It's an encouraging thing to see a young man really—really—Looks very good for Biff—very—[*He breaks off, then*] Bernard—[*He is so full of emotion, he breaks off again.*]

BERNARD What is it, Willy?

WILLY [*small and alone*] What—what's the secret?

BERNARD What secret?

WILLY How—how did you? Why didn't he ever catch on?

BERNARD I wouldn't know that, Willy.

WILLY [*confidentially, desperately*] You were his friend, his boyhood friend. There's something I don't understand about it. His life ended after that Ebbets Field game. From the age of seventeen nothing good ever happened to him.

BERNARD He never trained himself for anything.

WILLY But he did, he did. After high school he took so many correspondence courses. Radio mechanics; television; God knows what, and never made the slightest mark.

BERNARD [*taking off his glasses*] Willy, do you want to talk candidly?

WILLY [*rising, faces* BERNARD] I regard you as a very brilliant man, Bernard. I value your advice.

BERNARD Oh, the hell with the advice, Willy. I couldn't advise you. There's just one thing I've always wanted to ask you. When he was supposed to graduate, and the math teacher flunked him—

WILLY Oh, that son-of-a-bitch ruined his life.

BERNARD Yeah, but, Willy, all he had to do was go to summer school and make up that subject.

WILLY That's right, that's right.

BERNARD Did you tell him not to go to summer school?

WILLY Me? I begged him to go. I ordered him to go!

BERNARD Then why wouldn't he go?

WILLY   Why? Why! Bernard, that question has been trailing me like a ghost for the last fifteen years. He flunked the subject, and laid down and died like a hammer hit him!

BERNARD   Take it easy, kid.

WILLY   Let me talk to you—I got nobody to talk to. Bernard, Bernard, was it my fault? Y'see? It keeps going around in my mind, maybe I did something to him. I got nothing to give him.

BERNARD   Don't take it so hard.

WILLY   Why did he lay down? What is the story there? You were his friend!

BERNARD   Willy, I remember, it was June, and our grades came out. And he'd flunked math.

WILLY   That son-of-a-bitch!

BERNARD   No, it wasn't right then. Biff just got very angry, I remember, and he was ready to enroll in summer school.

WILLY [surprised]   He was?

BERNARD   He wasn't beaten by it at all. But then, Willy, he disappeared from the block for almost a month. And I got the idea that he'd gone up to New England to see you. Did he have a talk with you then?

   [WILLY stares in silence.]

BERNARD   Willy?

WILLY [with a strong edge of resentment in his voice]   Yeah, he came to Boston. What about it?

BERNARD   Well, just that when he came back—I'll never forget this, it always mystifies me. Because I'd thought so well of Biff, even though he'd always taken advantage of me. I loved him, Willy, y'know? And he came back after that month and took his sneakers—remember those sneakers with "University of Virginia" printed on them? He was so proud of those, wore them every day. And he took them down in the cellar, and burned them up in the furnace. We had a fist fight. It lasted at least half an hour. Just the two of us, punching each other down the cellar, and crying right through it. I've often thought of how strange it was that I knew he'd given up his life. What happened in Boston, Willy?

   [WILLY looks at him as at an intruder.]

BERNARD   I just bring it up because you asked me.

WILLY [angrily]   Nothing. What do you mean, "What happened?" What's that got to do with anything?

BERNARD   Well, don't get sore.

WILLY   What are you trying to do, blame it on me? If a boy lays down is that my fault?

BERNARD   Now, Willy, don't get—

WILLY   Well, don't—don't talk to me that way! What does that mean, "What happened?"

   [CHARLEY enters. He is in his vest, and he carries a bottle of bourbon.]

CHARLEY   Hey, you're going to miss that train. [He waves the bottle.]

BERNARD   Yeah, I'm going. [He takes the bottle.] Thanks, Pop. [He picks up his rackets and bag.] Good-by, Willy, and don't worry about it. You know, "If at first you don't succeed . . ."

WILLY   Yes, I believe in that.

BERNARD   But sometimes, Willy, it's better for a man just to walk away.

WILLY   Walk away?

BERNARD   That's right.

WILLY   But if you can't walk away?

BERNARD [*after a slight pause*]   I guess that's when it's tough. [*extending his hand*] Good-by, Willy.

WILLY [*shaking* BERNARD'*s hand*]   Good-by, boy.

CHARLEY [*an arm on* BERNARD'*s shoulder*]   How do you like this kid? Gonna argue a case in front of the Supreme Court.

BERNARD [*protesting*]   Pop!

WILLY [*genuinely shocked, pained, and happy*]   No! The Supreme Court!

BERNARD   I gotta run. 'By, Dad!

CHARLEY   Knock 'em dead, Bernard!

   [BERNARD *goes off.*]

WILLY [*as* CHARLEY *takes out his wallet*]   The Supreme Court! And he didn't even mention it!

CHARLEY [*counting out money on the desk*]   He don't have to—he's gonna do it.

WILLY   And you never told him what to do, did you? You never took any interest in him.

CHARLEY   My salvation is that I never took any interest in anything. There's some money—fifty dollars. I got an accountant inside.

WILLY   Charley, look . . . [*with difficulty*] I got my insurance to pay. If you can manage it—I need a hundred and ten dollars.

   [CHARLEY *doesn't reply for a moment; merely stops moving.*]

WILLY   I'd draw it from my bank but Linda would know, and I . . .

CHARLEY   Sit down, Willy.

WILLY [*moving toward the chair*]   I'm keeping an account of everything, remember. I'll pay every penny back. [*He sits.*]

CHARLEY   Now listen to me, Willy.

WILLY   I want you to know I appreciate . . .

CHARLEY [*sitting down on the table*]   Willy, what're you doin'? What the hell is goin' on in your head?

WILLY   Why? I'm simply . . .

CHARLEY   I offered you a job. You can make fifty dollars a week. And I won't send you on the road.

WILLY   I've got a job.

CHARLEY   Without pay? What kind of job is a job without pay? [*He rises.*] Now, look kid, enough is enough. I'm no genius but I know when I'm being insulted.

WILLY   Insulted!

CHARLEY   Why don't you want to work for me?

WILLY   What's the matter with you? I've got a job.

CHARLEY   Then what're you walkin' in here every week for?

WILLY [*getting up*]   Well, if you don't want me to walk in here—

CHARLEY   I am offering you a job!

WILLY   I don't want your goddam job!

CHARLEY   When the hell are you going to grow up?

WILLY [*furiously*]   You big ignoramus, if you say that to me again I'll rap you one! I don't care how big you are! [*He's ready to fight. Pause.*]

CHARLEY [*kindly, going to him*]   How much do you need, Willy?

WILLY   Charley, I'm strapped, I'm strapped. I don't know what to do. I was just fired.

CHARLEY   Howard fired you?

WILLY   That snotnose. Imagine that? I named him. I named him Howard.

CHARLEY   Willy, when're you gonna realize that them things don't mean anything? You named him Howard, but you can't sell that. The only thing you got in this world is what you can sell. And the funny thing is that you're a salesman, and you don't know that.

WILLY   I've always tried to think otherwise. I guess. I always felt that if a man was impressive, and well liked, that nothing—

CHARLEY   Why must everybody like you? Who liked J. P. Morgan?¹ Was he impressive? In a Turkish bath he'd look like a butcher. But with his pockets on he was very well liked. Now listen, Willy, I know you don't like me, and nobody can say I'm in love with you, but I'll give you a job because—just for the hell of it, put it that way. Now what do you say?

WILLY   I—I just can't work for you, Charley.

CHARLEY   What're you, jealous of me?

WILLY   I can't work for you, that's all, don't ask me why.

CHARLEY   [angered, takes out more bills]   You been jealous of me all your life, you damned fool! Here, pay your insurance. [He puts the money in WILLY's hand.]

WILLY   I'm keeping strict accounts.

CHARLEY   I've got some work to do. Take care of yourself. And pay your insurance.

WILLY   [moving to the right]   Funny, y'know? After all the highways, and the trains, and the appointments, and the years, you end up worth more dead than alive.

CHARLEY   Willy, nobody's worth nothin' dead. [after a slight pause] Did you hear what I said?
   [WILLY stands still, dreaming.]

CHARLEY   Willy!

WILLY   Apologize to Bernard for me when you see him. I didn't mean to argue with him. He's a fine boy. They're all fine boys, and they'll end up big—all of them. Someday they'll all play tennis together. Wish me luck, Charley. He saw Bill Oliver today.

CHARLEY   Good luck.

WILLY   [on the verge of tears]   Charley, you're the only friend I got. Isn't that a remarkable thing? [He goes out.]

CHARLEY   Jesus!
   [CHARLEY stares after him a moment and follows. All light blacks out. Suddenly raucous music is heard, and a red glow rises behind the screen at right. STANLEY, a young waiter, appears, carrying a table, followed by HAPPY, who is carrying two chairs.]

STANLEY   [putting the table down]   That's all right, Mr. Loman, I can handle it myself. [He turns and takes the chairs from HAPPY and places them at the table.]

HAPPY   [glancing around]   Oh, this is better.

---

1. John Pierpont Morgan (1837–1913), American banker and philanthropist famed for his enormous wealth.

STANLEY   Sure, in the front there you're in the middle of all kinds a noise. Whenever you got a party. Mr. Loman, you just tell me and I'll put you back here. Y'know, there's a lotta people they don't like it private, because when they go out they like to see a lotta action around them because they're sick and tired to stay in the house by theirself. But I know you, you ain't from Hackensack. You know what I mean?

HAPPY [sitting down]   So how's it coming, Stanley?

STANLEY   Ah, it's a dog life. I only wish during the war they'd a took me in the Army. I coulda been dead by now.

HAPPY   My brother's back, Stanley.

STANLEY   Oh, he come back, heh? From the Far West.

HAPPY   Yeah, big cattle man, my brother, so treat him right. And my father's coming too.

STANLEY   Oh, your father too!

HAPPY   You got a couple of nice lobsters?

STANLEY   Hundred per cent, big.

HAPPY   I want them with the claws.

STANLEY   Don't worry, I don't give you no mice. [HAPPY laughs.] How about some wine? It'll put a head on the meal.

HAPPY   No. You remember, Stanley, that recipe I brought you from overseas? With the champagne in it?

STANLEY   Oh, yeah, sure. I still got it tacked up yet in the kitchen. But that'll have to cost a buck apiece anyways.

HAPPY   That's all right.

STANLEY   What'd you, hit a number or somethin'?

HAPPY   No, it's a little celebration. My brother is—I think he pulled off a big deal today. I think we're going into business together.

STANLEY   Great! That's the best for you. Because a family business, you know what I mean?—that's the best.

HAPPY   That's what I think.

STANLEY   'Cause what's the difference? Somebody steals? It's in the family. Know what I mean? [sotto voce]² Like this bartender here. The boss is goin' crazy what kinda leak he's got in the cash register. You put it in but it don't come out.

HAPPY [raising his head]   Sh!

STANLEY   What?

HAPPY   You notice I wasn't lookin' right or left, was I?

STANLEY   No.

HAPPY   And my eyes are closed.

STANLEY   So what's the—?

HAPPY   Strudel's comin'.

STANLEY [catching on, looks around]   Ah, no, there's no—
[He breaks off as a furred, lavishly dressed girl enters and sits at the next table. Both follow her with their eyes.]

STANLEY   Geez, how'd ya know?

HAPPY   I got radar or something. [staring directly at her profile] Oooooooo . . . Stanley.

STANLEY   I think that's for you, Mr. Loman.

---

2. In an undertone [Italian].

HAPPY   Look at that mouth. Oh, God. And the binoculars.

STANLEY   Geez, you got a life, Mr. Loman.

HAPPY   Wait on her.

STANLEY [*going to the girl's table*]   Would you like a menu, ma'am?

GIRL   I'm expecting someone, but I'd like a—

HAPPY   Why don't you bring her—excuse me, miss, do you mind? I sell champagne, and I'd like you to try my brand. Bring her a champagne, Stanley.

GIRL   That's awfully nice of you.

HAPPY   Don't mention it. It's all company money. [*He laughs.*]

GIRL   That's a charming product to be selling, isn't it?

HAPPY   Oh, gets to be like everything else. Selling is selling, y'know.

GIRL   I suppose.

HAPPY   You don't happen to sell, do you?

GIRL   No, I don't sell.

HAPPY   Would you object to a compliment from a stranger? You ought to be on a magazine cover.

GIRL [*looking at him a little archly*]   I have been.
        [STANLEY *comes in with a glass of champagne.*]

HAPPY   What'd I say before, Stanley? You see? She's a cover girl.

STANLEY   Oh, I could see, I could see.

HAPPY [*to the* GIRL]   What magazine?

GIRL   Oh, a lot of them. [*She takes the drink.*] Thank you.

HAPPY   You know what they say in France, don't you? "Champagne is the drink of the complexion"—Hya, Biff!
        [BIFF *has entered and sits with* HAPPY.]

BIFF   Hello, kid. Sorry I'm late.

HAPPY   I just got here. Uh, Miss—?

GIRL   Forsythe.

HAPPY   Miss Forsythe, this is my brother.

BIFF   Is Dad here?

HAPPY   His name is Biff. You might've heard of him. Great football player.

GIRL   Really? What team?

HAPPY   Are you familiar with football?

GIRL   No, I'm afraid I'm not.

HAPPY   Biff is quarterback with the New York Giants.

GIRL   Well, that's nice, isn't it? [*She drinks.*]

HAPPY   Good health.

GIRL   I'm happy to meet you.

HAPPY   That's my name. Hap. It's really Harold, but at West Point they called me Happy.

GIRL [*now really impressed*]   Oh, I see. How do you do? [*She turns her profile.*]

BIFF   Isn't Dad coming?

HAPPY   You want her?

BIFF   Oh, I could never make that.

HAPPY   I remember the time that idea would never come into your head. Where's the old confidence, Biff?

BIFF   I just saw Oliver—

HAPPY Wait a minute. I've got to see that old confidence again. Do you want her? She's on call.

BIFF Oh, no. [*He turns to look at the* GIRL.]

HAPPY I'm telling you. Watch this. [*turning to the* GIRL] Honey? [*She turns to him.*] Are you busy?

GIRL Well, I am . . . but I could make a phone call.

HAPPY Do that, will you, honey? And see if you can get a friend. We'll be here for a while. Biff is one of the greatest football players in the country.

GIRL [*standing up*] Well, I'm certainly happy to meet you.

HAPPY Come back soon.

GIRL I'll try.

HAPPY Don't try, honey, try hard.

[*The* GIRL *exits.* STANLEY *follows, shaking his head in bewildered admiration.*]

HAPPY Isn't that a shame now? A beautiful girl like that? That's why I can't get married. There's not a good woman in a thousand. New York is loaded with them, kid!

BIFF Hap, look—

HAPPY I told you she was on call!

BIFF [*strangely unnerved*] Cut it out, will ya? I want to say something to you.

HAPPY Did you see Oliver?

BIFF I saw him all right. Now look, I want to tell Dad a couple of things and I want you to help me.

HAPPY What? Is he going to back you?

BIFF Are you crazy? You're out of your goddam head, you know that?

HAPPY Why? What happened?

BIFF [*breathlessly*] I did a terrible thing today, Hap. It's been the strangest day I ever went through. I'm all numb, I swear.

HAPPY You mean he wouldn't see you?

BIFF Well, I waited six hours for him, see? All day. Kept sending my name in. Even tried to date his secretary so she'd get me to him, but no soap.

HAPPY Because you're not showin' the old confidence, Biff. He remembered you, didn't he?

BIFF [*stopping* HAPPY *with a gesture*] Finally, about five o'clock, he comes out. Didn't remember who I was or anything. I felt like such an idiot, Hap.

HAPPY Did you tell him my Florida idea?

BIFF He walked away. I saw him for one minute. I got so mad I could've torn the walls down! How the hell did I ever get the idea I was a salesman there? I even believed myself that I'd been a salesman for him! And then he gave me one look and—I realized what a ridiculous lie my whole life has been! We've been talking in a dream for fifteen years. I was a shipping clerk.

HAPPY What'd you do?

BIFF [*with great tension and wonder*] Well, he left, see. And the secretary went out. I was all alone in the waiting-room. I don't know what came over me, Hap. The next thing I know I'm in his office—paneled walls, everything. I can't explain it. I—Hap, I took his fountain pen.

HAPPY   Geez, did he catch you?

BIFF   I ran out. I ran down all eleven flights. I ran and ran and ran.

HAPPY   That was an awful dumb—what'd you do that for?

BIFF   [*agonized*]   I don't know, I just—wanted to take something, I don't know. You gotta help me, Hap, I'm gonna tell Pop.

HAPPY   You crazy? What for?

BIFF   Hap, he's got to understand that I'm not the man somebody lends that kind of money to. He thinks I've been spiting him all these years and it's eating him up.

HAPPY   That's just it. You tell him something nice.

BIFF   I can't.

HAPPY   Say you got a lunch date with Oliver tomorrow.

BIFF   So what do I do tomorrow?

HAPPY   You leave the house tomorrow and come back at night and say Oliver is thinking it over. And he thinks it over for a couple of weeks, and gradually it fades away and nobody's the worse.

BIFF   But it'll go on forever!

HAPPY   Dad is never so happy as when he's looking forward to something! [WILLY *enters.*]

HAPPY   Hello, scout!

WILLY   Gee, I haven't been here in years!
[STANLEY *has followed* WILLY *in and sets a chair for him.* STANLEY *starts off but* HAPPY *stops him.*]

HAPPY   Stanley!
[STANLEY *stands by, waiting for an order.*]

BIFF   [*going to* WILLY *with guilt, as to an invalid*]   Sit down, Pop. You want a drink?

WILLY   Sure, I don't mind.

BIFF   Let's get a load on.

WILLY   You look worried.

BIFF   N-no. [*to* STANLEY] Scotch all around. Make it doubles.

STANLEY   Doubles, right. [*He goes.*]

WILLY   You had a couple already, didn't you?

BIFF   Just a couple, yeah.

WILLY   Well, what happened, boy? [*nodding affirmatively, with a smile*] Everything go all right?

BIFF   [*takes a breath, then reaches out and grasps* WILLY'S *hand*] Pal . . . [*He is smiling bravely, and* WILLY *is smiling too.*] I had an experience today.

HAPPY   Terrific, Pop.

WILLY   That so? What happened?

BIFF   [*high, slightly alcoholic, above the earth*]   I'm going to tell you everything from first to last. It's been a strange day. [*Silence. He looks around, composes himself as best he can, but his breath keeps breaking the rhythm of his voice.*] I had to wait quite a while for him, and—

WILLY   Oliver?

BIFF   Yeah, Oliver. All day, as a matter of cold fact. And a lot of—instances—facts, Pop, facts about my life came back to me. Who was it, Pop? Who ever said I was a salesman with Oliver?

WILLY   Well, you were.

BIFF   No, Dad, I was a shipping clerk.

WILLY   But you were practically—

BIFF [*with determination*]   Dad, I don't know who said it first, but I was never a salesman for Bill Oliver.

WILLY   What're you talking about?

BIFF   Let's hold on to the facts tonight, Pop. We're not going to get anywhere bullin' around. I was a shipping clerk.

WILLY [*angrily*]   All right, now listen to me—

BIFF   Why don't you let me finish?

WILLY   I'm not interested in stories about the past or any crap of that kind because the woods are burning, boys, you understand? There's a big blaze going on all around. I was fired today.

BIFF [*shocked*]   How could you be?

WILLY   I was fired, and I'm looking for a little good news to tell your mother, because the woman has waited and the woman has suffered. The gist of it is that I haven't got a story left in my head, Biff. So don't give me a lecture about facts and aspects. I am not interested. Now what've you got to say to me?

   [STANLEY *enters with three drinks. They wait until he leaves.*]

WILLY   Did you see Oliver?

BIFF   Jesus, Dad!

WILLY   You mean you didn't go up there?

HAPPY   Sure he went up there.

BIFF   I did. I—saw him. How could they fire you?

WILLY [*on the edge of his chair*]   What kind of a welcome did he give you?

BIFF   He won't even let you work on commission?

WILLY   I'm out! [*driving*] So tell me, he gave you a warm welcome?

HAPPY   Sure, Pop, sure!

BIFF [*driven*]   Well, it was kind of—

WILLY   I was wondering if he'd remember you. [*to* HAPPY] Imagine, man doesn't see him for ten, twelve years and gives him that kind of a welcome!

HAPPY   Damn right!

BIFF [*trying to return to the offensive*]   Pop, look—

WILLY   You know why he remembered you, don't you? Because you impressed him in those days.

BIFF   Let's talk quietly and get this down to the facts, huh?

WILLY [*as though* BIFF *had been interrupting*]   Well, what happened? It's great news, Biff. Did he take you into his office or'd you talk in the waiting-room?

BIFF   Well, he came in, see, and—

WILLY [*with a big smile*]   What'd he say? Betcha he threw his arm around you.

BIFF   Well, he kinda—

WILLY   He's a fine man. [*to* HAPPY] Very hard man to see, y'know.

HAPPY [*agreeing*]   Oh, I know.

WILLY [*to* BIFF]   Is that where you had the drinks?

BIFF   Yeah, he gave me a couple of—no, no!

HAPPY [*cutting in*]   He told him my Florida idea.

WILLY   Don't interrupt. [*to* BIFF] How'd he react to the Florida idea?

BIFF   Dad, will you give me a minute to explain?

WILLY   I've been waiting for you to explain since I sat down here! What happened? He took you into his office and what?

BIFF   Well—I talked. And—he listened, see.

WILLY   Famous for the way he listens, y'know. What was his answer?

BIFF   His answer was— [*He breaks off, suddenly angry.*] Dad, you're not letting me tell you what I want to tell you!

WILLY [*accusing, angered*]   You didn't see him, did you?

BIFF   I did see him!

WILLY   What'd you insult him or something? You insulted him, didn't you?

BIFF   Listen, will you let me out of it, will you just let me out of it!

HAPPY   What the hell!

WILLY   Tell me what happened!

BIFF [*to* HAPPY]   I can't talk to him!
[*A single trumpet note jars the ear. The light of green leaves stains the house, which holds the air of night and a dream.* YOUNG BERNARD *enters and knocks on the door of the house.*]

YOUNG BERNARD [*frantically*]   Mrs. Loman, Mrs. Loman!

HAPPY   Tell him what happened!

BIFF [*to* HAPPY]   Shut up and leave me alone!

WILLY   No, no. You had to go and flunk math!

BIFF   What math? What're you talking about?

YOUNG BERNARD   Mrs. Loman, Mrs. Loman!
[LINDA *appears in the house, as of old.*]

WILLY [*wildly*]   Math, math, math!

BIFF   Take it easy, Pop!

YOUNG BERNARD   Mrs. Loman!

WILLY [*furiously*]   If you hadn't flunked you'd've been set by now!

BIFF   Now, look, I'm gonna tell you what happened, and you're going to listen to me.

YOUNG BERNARD   Mrs. Loman!

BIFF   I waited six hours—

HAPPY   What the hell are you saying?

BIFF   I kept sending in my name but he wouldn't see me. So finally he . . . [*He continues unheard as light fades low on the restaurant.*]

YOUNG BERNARD   Biff flunked math!

LINDA   No!

YOUNG BERNARD   Birnbaum flunked him! They won't graduate him!

LINDA   But they have to. He's gotta go to the university. Where is he? Biff! Biff!

YOUNG BERNARD   No, he left. He went to Grand Central.

LINDA   Grand—You mean he went to Boston!

YOUNG BERNARD   Is Uncle Willy in Boston?

LINDA   Oh, maybe Willy can talk to the teacher. Oh, the poor, poor boy!
[*Light on house area snaps out.*]

BIFF [*at the table, now audible, holding up a gold fountain pen*]   . . . so I'm washed up with Oliver, you understand? Are you listening to me?

WILLY [*at a loss*]   Yeah, sure. If you hadn't flunked—

BIFF   Flunked what? What're you talking about?

WILLY   Don't blame everything on me! I didn't flunk math—you did! What pen?

HAPPY   That was awful dumb, Biff, a pen like that is worth—

WILLY [*seeing the pen for the first time*]   You took Oliver's pen?

BIFF [*weakening*]   Dad, I just explained it to you.

WILLY   You stole Bill Oliver's fountain pen!

BIFF   I didn't exactly steal it! That's just what I've been explaining to you!

HAPPY   He had it in his hand and just then Oliver walked in, so he got nervous and stuck it in his pocket!

WILLY   My God, Biff!

BIFF   I never intended to do it, Dad!

OPERATOR'S VOICE   Standish Arms, good evening!

WILLY [*shouting*]   I'm not in my room!

BIFF [*frightened*]   Dad, what's the matter? [*He and* HAPPY *stand up.*]

OPERATOR   Ringing Mr. Loman for you!

WILLY   I'm not there, stop it!

BIFF [*horrified, gets down on one knee before* WILLY]   Dad, I'll make good, I'll make good. [WILLY *tries to get to his feet.* BIFF *holds him down.*] Sit down now.

WILLY   No, you're no good, you're no good for anything.

BIFF   I am, Dad, I'll find something else, you understand? Now don't worry about anything. [*He holds up* WILLY'*s face.*] Talk to me, Dad.

OPERATOR   Mr. Loman does not answer. Shall I page him?

WILLY [*attempting to stand, as though to rush and silence the* OPERATOR] No, no, no!

HAPPY   He'll strike something, Pop.

WILLY   No, no . . .

BIFF [*desperately, standing over* WILLY]   Pop, listen! Listen to me! I'm telling you something good. Oliver talked to his partner about the Florida idea. You listening? He—he talked to his partner, and he came to me . . . I'm going to be all right, you hear? Dad, listen to me, he said it was just a question of the amount!

WILLY   Then you . . . got it?

HAPPY   He's gonna be terrific, Pop!

WILLY [*trying to stand*]   Then you got it, haven't you? You got it! You got it!

BIFF [*agonized, holds* WILLY *down*]   No, no. Look, Pop. I'm supposed to have lunch with them tomorrow. I'm just telling you this so you'll know that I can still make an impression, Pop. And I'll make good somewhere, but I can't go tomorrow, see?

WILLY   Why not? You simply—

BIFF   But the pen, Pop!

WILLY   You give it to him and tell him it was an oversight!

HAPPY   Sure, have lunch tomorrow!

BIFF   I can't say that—

WILLY   You were doing a crossword puzzle and accidentally used his pen!

BIFF   Listen, kid, I took those balls years ago, now I walk in with his fountain pen? That clinches it, don't you see? I can't face him like that! I'll try elsewhere.

PAGE'S VOICE   Paging Mr. Loman!

WILLY   Don't you want to be anything?

BIFF   Pop, how can I go back?

WILLY   You don't want to be anything, is that what's behind it?

BIFF [*now angry at* WILLY *for not crediting his sympathy*]   Don't take it that way! You think it was easy walking into that office after what I'd done to him? A team of horses couldn't have dragged me back to Bill Oliver!

WILLY   Then why'd you go?

BIFF   Why did I go? Why did I go! Look at you! Look at what's become of you!

[*Off left,* THE WOMAN *laughs.*]

WILLY   Biff, you're going to go to that lunch tomorrow, or—

BIFF   I can't go. I've got no appointment!

HAPPY   Biff for . . . !

WILLY   Are you spiting me?

BIFF   Don't take it that way! Goddammit!

WILLY [*strikes* BIFF *and falters away from the table*]   You rotten little louse! Are you spiting me?

THE WOMAN   Someone's at the door, Willy!

BIFF   I'm no good, can't you see what I am?

HAPPY [*separating them*]   Hey, you're in a restaurant! Now cut it out, both of you? [*The girls enter.*] Hello, girls, sit down.

[THE WOMAN *laughs, off left.*]

MISS FORSYTHE   I guess we might as well. This is Letta.

THE WOMAN   Willy, are you going to wake up?

BIFF [*ignoring* WILLY]   How're ya, miss, sit down. What do you drink?

MISS FORSYTHE   Letta might not be able to stay long.

LETTA   I gotta get up early tomorrow. I got jury duty. I'm so excited! Were you fellows ever on a jury?

BIFF   No, but I been in front of them! [*The girls laugh.*] This is my father.

LETTA   Isn't he cute? Sit down with us, Pop.

HAPPY   Sit him down, Biff!

BIFF [*going to him*]   Come on, slugger, drink us under the table. To hell with it! Come on, sit down, pal.

[*On* BIFF's *last insistence,* WILLY *is about to sit.*]

THE WOMAN [*now urgently*]   Willy, are you going to answer the door!

[THE WOMAN's *call pulls* WILLY *back. He starts right, befuddled.*]

BIFF   Hey, where are you going?

WILLY   Open the door.

BIFF   The door?

WILLY   The washroom . . . the door . . . where's the door?

BIFF [*leading* WILLY *to the left*]   Just go straight down.

[WILLY *moves left.*]

THE WOMAN   Willy, Willy, are you going to get up, get up, get up, get up?

[WILLY *exits left.*]

LETTA   I think it's sweet you bring your daddy along.

MISS FORSYTHE   Oh, he isn't really your father!

BIFF [*at left, turning to her resentfully*]   Miss Forsythe, you've just seen a prince walk by. A fine, troubled prince. A hard-working, unappreciated prince. A pal, you understand? A good companion. Always for his boys.

LETTA   That's so sweet.

HAPPY   Well, girls, what's the program? We're wasting time. Come on, Biff. Gather round. Where would you like to go?

BIFF   Why don't you do something for him?

HAPPY   Me!

BIFF   Don't you give a damn for him, Hap?

HAPPY   What're you talking about? I'm the one who—

BIFF   I sense it, you don't give a good goddam about him. [*He takes the rolled-up hose from his pocket and puts it on the table in front of* HAPPY.] Look what I found in the cellar, for Christ's sake. How can you bear to let it go on?

HAPPY   Me? Who goes away? Who runs off and—

BIFF   Yeah, but he doesn't mean anything to you. You could help him—I can't! Don't you understand what I'm talking about? He's going to kill himself, don't you know that?

HAPPY   Don't I know it! Me!

BIFF   Hap, help him! Jesus . . . help him . . . Help me, help me, I can't bear to look at his face! [*Ready to weep, he hurries out, up right.*]

HAPPY [*starting after him*]   Where are you going?

MISS FORSYTHE   What's he so mad about?

HAPPY   Come on, girls, we'll catch up with him.

MISS FORSYTHE [*as* HAPPY *pushes her out*]   Say, I don't like that temper of his!

HAPPY   He's just a little overstrung, he'll be all right!

WILLY [*off left, as* THE WOMAN *laughs*]   Don't answer! Don't answer!

LETTA   Don't you want to tell your father—

HAPPY   No, that's not my father. He's just a guy. Come on, we'll catch Biff, and, honey, we're going to paint this town! Stanley, where's the check! Hey, Stanley!

[*They exit.* STANLEY *looks toward left.*]

STANLEY [*calling to* HAPPY *indignantly*]   Mr. Loman! Mr. Loman!

[STANLEY *picks up a chair and follows them off. Knocking is heard off left.* THE WOMAN *enters, laughing.* WILLY *follows her. She is in a black slip; he is buttoning his shirt. Raw, sensuous music accompanies their speech.*]

WILLY   Will you stop laughing? Will you stop?

THE WOMAN   Aren't you going to answer the door? He'll wake the whole hotel.

WILLY   I'm not expecting anybody.

THE WOMAN   Whyn't you have another drink, honey, and stop being so damn self-centered?

WILLY   I'm so lonely.

THE WOMAN   You know you ruined me, Willy? From now on, whenever you come to the office, I'll see that you go right through to the buyers. No waiting at my desk any more, Willy. You ruined me.

WILLY   That's nice of you to say that.

THE WOMAN   Gee, you are self-centered! Why so sad? You are the saddest, self-centeredest soul I ever did see-saw. [*She laughs. He kisses her.*] Come on inside, drummer boy. It's silly to be dressing in the middle of the night. [*As knocking is heard*] Aren't you going to answer the door?

WILLY   They're knocking on the wrong door.

THE WOMAN   But I felt the knocking. And he heard us talking in here. Maybe the hotel's on fire!

WILLY [*his terror rising*]   It's a mistake.

THE WOMAN   Then tell them to go away!

WILLY   There's nobody there.

THE WOMAN   It's getting on my nerves, Willy. There's somebody standing out there and it's getting on my nerves!

WILLY [*pushing her away from him*]   All right, stay in the bathroom here, and don't come out. I think there's a law in Massachusetts about it, so don't come out. It may be that new room clerk. He looked very mean. So don't come out. It's a mistake, there's no fire.

   [*The knocking is heard again. He takes a few steps away from her, and she vanishes into the wing. The light follows him, and now he is facing* YOUNG BIFF, *who carries a suitcase.* BIFF *steps toward him. The music is gone.*]

BIFF   Why didn't you answer?

WILLY   Biff! What are you doing in Boston?

BIFF   Why didn't you answer? I've been knocking for five minutes, I called you on the phone—

WILLY   I just heard you. I was in the bathroom and had the door shut. Did anything happen home?

BIFF   Dad—I let you down.

WILLY   What do you mean?

BIFF   Dad . . .

WILLY   Biffo, what's this about? [*putting his arm around* BIFF] Come on, let's go downstairs and get you a malted.

BIFF   Dad, I flunked math.

WILLY   Not for the term?

BIFF   The term. I haven't got enough credits to graduate.

WILLY   You mean to say Bernard wouldn't give you the answers?

BIFF   He did, he tried, but I only got a sixty-one.

WILLY   And they wouldn't give you four points?

BIFF   Birnbaum refused absolutely. I begged him, Pop, but he won't give me those points. You gotta talk to him before they close the school. Because if he saw the kind of man you are, and you just talked to him in your way, I'm sure he'd come through for me. The class came right before practice, see, and I didn't go enough. Would you talk to him? He'd like you, Pop. You know the way you could talk.

WILLY   You're on. We'll drive right back.

BIFF   Oh, Dad, good work! I'm sure he'll change for you!

WILLY   Go downstairs and tell the clerk I'm checkin' out. Go right down.

BIFF   Yes, sir! See, the reason he hates me, Pop—one day he was late for class so I got up at the blackboard and imitated him. I crossed my eyes and talked with a lithp.

WILLY [*laughing*]   You did? The kids like it?

BIFF   They nearly died laughing!

WILLY   Yeah? What'd you do?

BIFF   The thquare root of thixthy twee is . . . [WILLY *bursts out laughing;* BIFF *joins him.*] And in the middle of it he walked in!

   [WILLY *laughs and* THE WOMAN *joins in offstage.*]

WILLY [*without hesitation*]   Hurry downstairs and—

BIFF   Somebody in there?

WILLY   No, that was next door.

[THE WOMAN *laughs offstage.*]

BIFF Somebody got in your bathroom!

WILLY No, it's the next room, there's a party—

THE WOMAN [*enters laughing. She lisps this*] Can I come in? There's something in the bathtub, Willy, and it's moving!

[WILLY *looks at* BIFF, *who is staring open-mouthed and horrified at* THE WOMAN.]

WILLY Ah—you better go back to your room. They must be finished painting by now. They're painting her room so I let her take a shower here. Go back, go back . . . [*He pushes her.*]

THE WOMAN [*resisting*] But I've got to get dressed, Willy, I can't—

WILLY Get out of here! Go back, go back . . . [*suddenly striving for the ordinary*] This is Miss Francis, Biff, she's a buyer. They're painting her room. Go back, Miss Francis, go back . . .

THE WOMAN But my clothes, I can't go out naked in the hall!

WILLY [*pushing her offstage*] Get outa here! Go back, go back!

[BIFF *slowly sits down on his suitcase as the argument continues offstage.*]

THE WOMAN Where's my stockings? You promised me stockings, Willy!

WILLY I have no stockings here!

THE WOMAN You had two boxes of size nine sheers for me, and I want them!

WILLY Here, for God's sake, will you get outa here!

THE WOMAN [*enters holding a box of stockings*] I just hope there's nobody in the hall. That's all I hope. [*to* BIFF] Are you football or baseball?

BIFF Football.

THE WOMAN [*angry, humiliated*] That's me too. G'night. [*She snatches her clothes from* WILLY, *and walks out.*]

WILLY [*after a pause*] Well, better get going. I want to get to the school first thing in the morning. Get my suits out of the closet. I'll get my valise. [BIFF *doesn't move.*] What's the matter? [BIFF *remains motionless, tears falling.*] She's a buyer. Buys for J. H. Simmons. She lives down the hall—they're painting. You don't imagine— [*He breaks off. After a pause*] Now listen, pal, she's just a buyer. She sees merchandise in her room and they have to keep it looking just so . . . [*Pause. Assuming command*] All right, get my suits. [BIFF *doesn't move.*] Now stop crying and do as I say. I gave you an order. Biff, I gave you an order! Is that what you do when I give you an order? How dare you cry! [*putting his arm around* BIFF] Now look, Biff, when you grow up you'll understand about these things. You mustn't—you mustn't overemphasize a thing like this. I'll see Birnbaum first thing in the morning.

BIFF Never mind.

WILLY [*getting down beside* BIFF] Never mind! He's going to give you those points. I'll see to it.

BIFF He wouldn't listen to you.

WILLY He certainly will listen to me. You need those points for the U. of Virginia.

BIFF I'm not going there.

WILLY Heh? If I can't get him to change that mark you'll make it up in summer school. You've got all summer to—

BIFF [*his weeping breaking from him*] Dad . . .

WILLY [*infected by it*]   Oh, my boy . . .

BIFF   Dad . . .

WILLY   She's nothing to me, Biff. I was lonely, I was terribly lonely.

BIFF   You—you gave her Mama's stockings! [*His tears break through and he rises to go.*]

WILLY [*grabbing for* BIFF]   I gave you an order!

BIFF   Don't touch me, you—liar!

WILLY   Apologize for that!

BIFF   You fake! You phony little fake! You fake! [*Overcome, he turns quickly and weeping fully goes out with his suitcase,* WILLY *is left on the floor on his knees.*]

WILLY   I gave you an order! Biff, come back here or I'll beat you! Come back here! I'll whip you!

[STANLEY *comes quickly in from the right and stands in front of* WILLY.]

WILLY [*shouts at* STANLEY]   I gave you an order . . .

STANLEY   Hey, let's pick it up, pick it up, Mr. Loman. [*He helps* WILLY *to his feet.*] Your boys left with the chippies. They said they'll see you home.

[*A second waiter watches some distance away.*]

WILLY   But we were supposed to have dinner together.

[*Music is heard,* WILLY's *theme.*]

STANLEY   Can you make it?

WILLY   I'll—sure, I can make it. [*suddenly concerned about his clothes*] Do I—I look all right?

STANLEY   Sure, you look all right. [*He flicks a speck off* WILLY's *lapel.*]

WILLY   Here—here's a dollar.

STANLEY   Oh, your son paid me. It's all right.

WILLY [*putting it in* STANLEY's *hand*]   No, take it. You're a good boy.

STANLEY   Oh, no, you don't have to . . .

WILLY   Here—here's some more, I don't need it any more. [*after a slight pause*] Tell me—is there a seed store in the neighborhood?

STANLEY   Seeds? You mean like to plant?

[*As* WILLY *turns,* STANLEY *slips the money back into his jacket pocket.*]

WILLY   Yes. Carrots, peas . . .

STANLEY   Well, there's hardware stores on Sixth Avenue, but it may be too late now.

WILLY [*anxiously*]   Oh, I'd better hurry. I've got to get some seeds. [*He starts off to the right.*] I've got to get some seeds, right away. Nothing's planted. I don't have a thing in the ground.

[WILLY *hurries out as the light goes down.* STANLEY *moves over to the right after him, watches him off. The other waiter has been staring at* WILLY.]

STANLEY [*to the waiter*]   Well, whatta you looking at?

[*The waiter picks up the chairs and moves off right.* STANLEY *takes the table and follows him. The light fades on this area. There is a long pause, the sound of the flute coming over. The light gradually rises on the kitchen, which is empty.* HAPPY *appears at the door of the house, followed by* BIFF. HAPPY *is carrying a large bunch of long-stemmed roses. He enters the kitchen, looks around for* LINDA. *Not seeing her, he turns to* BIFF, *who is just outside the house door, and makes a gesture with his hands, indicating "Not here, I guess." He looks into the living-room and freezes. Inside,* LINDA, *unseen, is seated,* WILLY's *coat on her lap. She rises ominously and quietly and moves toward* HAPPY, *who backs up into the kitchen, afraid.*]

HAPPY   Hey, what're you doing up? [LINDA *says nothing but moves toward him implacably.*] Where's Pop? [*He keeps backing to the right, and now* LINDA *is in full view in the doorway to the living-room.*] Is he sleeping?

LINDA   Where were you?

HAPPY [*trying to laugh it off*]   We met two girls, Mom, very fine types. Here, we brought you some flowers. [*offering them to her*] Put them in your room, Ma.

[*She knocks them to the floor at* BIFF's *feet. He has now come inside and closed the door behind him. She stares at* BIFF, *silent.*]

HAPPY   Now what'd you do that for? Mom, I want you to have some flowers—

LINDA [*cutting* HAPPY *off, violently to* BIFF]   Don't you care whether he lives or dies?

HAPPY [*going to the stairs*]   Come upstairs, Biff.

BIFF [*with a flare of disgust, to* HAPPY]   Go away from me! [*to* LINDA] What do you mean, lives or dies? Nobody's dying around here, pal.

LINDA   Get out of my sight! Get out of here!

BIFF   I wanna see the boss.

LINDA   You're not going near him!

BIFF   Where is he? [*He moves into the living-room and* LINDA *follows.*]

LINDA [*shouting after* BIFF]   You invite him for dinner. He looks forward to it all day—[BIFF *appears in his parents' bedroom, looks around and exits*]—and then you desert him there. There's no stranger you'd do that to!

HAPPY   Why? He had a swell time with us. Listen, when I—[LINDA *comes back into the kitchen*]—desert him I hope I don't outlive the day!

LINDA   Get out of here!

HAPPY   Now look, Mom . . .

LINDA   Did you have to go to women tonight? You and your lousy rotten whores!

[BIFF *re-enters the kitchen.*]

HAPPY   Mom, all we did was follow Biff around trying to cheer him up! [*to* BIFF] Boy, what a night you gave me!

LINDA   Get out of here, both of you, and don't come back! I don't want you tormenting him any more. Go on now, get your things together! [*to* BIFF] You can sleep in his apartment. [*She starts to pick up the flowers and stops herself.*] Pick up this stuff, I'm not your maid any more. Pick it up, you bum, you!

[HAPPY *turns his back to her in refusal.* BIFF *slowly moves over and gets down on his knees, picking up the flowers.*]

LINDA   You're a pair of animals! Not one, not another living soul would have had the cruelty to walk out on that man in a restaurant!

BIFF [*not looking at her*]   Is that what he said?

LINDA   He didn't have to say anything. He was so humiliated he nearly limped when he came in.

HAPPY   But, Mom, he had a great time with us—

BIFF [*cutting him off violently*]   Shut up!

[*Without another word,* HAPPY *goes upstairs.*]

LINDA   You! You didn't even go in to see if he was all right!

BIFF [*still on the floor in front of* LINDA, *the flowers in his hand; with self-loathing*]   No. Didn't. Didn't do a damned thing. How do you like that, heh? Left him babbling in a toilet.

LINDA   You louse. You . . .

BIFF   Now you hit it on the nose! [*He gets up, throws the flowers in the waste-basket.*] The scum of the earth, and you're looking at him!

LINDA   Get out of here!

BIFF   I gotta talk to the boss, Mom. Where is he?

LINDA   You're not going near him. Get out of this house!

BIFF [*with absolute assurance, determination*]   No. We're gonna have an abrupt conversation, him and me.

LINDA   You're not talking to him!
　　　　[*Hammering is heard from outside the house, off right.* BIFF *turns toward the noise.*]

LINDA [*suddenly pleading*]   Will you please leave him alone?

BIFF   What's he doing out there?

LINDA   He's planting the garden!

BIFF [*quietly*]   Now? Oh, my God!
　　　　[BIFF *moves outside,* LINDA *following. The light dies down on them and comes up on the center of the apron as* WILLY *walks into it. He is carrying a flashlight, a hoe, and a handful of seed packets. He raps the top of the hoe sharply to fix it firmly, and then moves to the left, measuring off the distance with his foot. He holds the flashlight to look at the seed packets, reading off the instructions. He is in the blue of night.*]

WILLY   Carrots . . . quarter-inch apart. Rows . . . one-foot rows. [*He measures it off.*] One foot. [*He puts down a package and measures off.*] Beets. [*He puts down another package and measures again.*] Lettuce. [*He reads the package, puts it down.*] One foot— [*He breaks off as* BEN *appears at the right and moves slowly down to him.*] What a proposition, ts, ts. Terrific, terrific. 'Cause she's suffered, Ben, the woman has suffered. You understand me? A man can't go out the way he came in, Ben, a man has got to add up to something. You can't, you can't— [BEN *moves toward him as though to interrupt.*] You gotta consider, now. Don't answer so quick. Remember, it's a guaranteed twenty-thousand-dollar proposition. Now look, Ben, I want you to go through the ins and outs of this thing with me. I've got nobody to talk to, Ben, and the woman has suffered, you hear me?

BEN [*standing still, considering*]   What's the proposition?

WILLY   It's twenty thousand dollars on the barrelhead. Guaranteed, gilt-edged, you understand?

BEN   You don't want to make a fool of yourself. They might not honor the policy.

WILLY   How can they dare refuse? Didn't I work like a coolie to meet every premium on the nose? And now they don't pay off! Impossible!

BEN   It's called a cowardly thing, William.

WILLY   Why? Does it take more guts to stand here the rest of my life ringing up a zero?

BEN [*yielding*]   That's a point, William. [*He moves, thinking, turns.*] And twenty thousand—that *is* something one can feel with the hand, it is there.

WILLY [*now assured, with rising power*]   Oh, Ben, that's the whole beauty of it! I see it like a diamond, shining in the dark, hard and rough, that I can pick up and touch in my hand. Not like—like an appointment! This would not be another damned-fool appointment, Ben, and it changes all the aspects. Because he thinks I'm nothing, see, and so he spites me. But the funeral— [*straightening up*] Ben, that funeral will be massive! They'll come from Maine, Massachusetts, Vermont, New Hampshire! All the old-timers with the strange license plates—that boy will be thunder-struck, Ben, because he never realized—I am known! Rhode Island, New York, New Jersey—I am known, Ben, and he'll see it with his eyes once and for all. He'll see what I am, Ben! He's in for a shock, that boy!

BEN [*coming down to the edge of the garden*]   He'll call you a coward.

WILLY [*suddenly fearful*]   No, that would be terrible.

BEN   Yes. And a damned fool.

WILLY   No, no, he mustn't, I won't have that! [*He is broken and desperate.*]

BEN   He'll hate you, William.

     [*The gay music of the Boys is heard.*]

WILLY   Oh, Ben, how do we get back to all the great times? Used to be so full of light, and comradeship, the sleigh-riding in winter, and the rud-diness on his cheeks. And always some kind of good news coming up, always something nice coming up ahead. And never even let me carry the valises in the house, and simonizing, simonizing that little red car! Why, why can't I give him something and not have him hate me?

BEN   Let me think about it. [*He glances at his watch.*] I still have a little time. Remarkable proposition, but you've got to be sure you're not mak-ing a fool of yourself.

     [BEN *drifts off upstage and goes out of sight.* BIFF *comes down from the left.*]

WILLY [*suddenly conscious of* BIFF, *turns and looks up at him, then begins picking up the packages of seeds in confusion*]   Where the hell is that seed? [*indignantly*] You can't see nothing out here! They boxed in the whole goddam neighborhood!

BIFF   There are people all around here. Don't you realize that?

WILLY   I'm busy. Don't bother me.

BIFF [*taking the hoe from* WILLY]   I'm saying good-by to you, Pop. [WILLY *looks at him, silent, unable to move.*] I'm not coming back any more.

WILLY   You're not going to see Oliver tomorrow?

BIFF   I've got no appointment, Dad.

WILLY   He put his arm around you, and you've got no appointment?

BIFF   Pop, get this now, will you? Everytime I've left it's been a fight that sent me out of here. Today I realized something about myself and I tried to explain it to you and I—I think I'm just not smart enough to make any sense out of it for you. To hell with whose fault it is or anything like that. [*He takes* WILLY's *arm.*] Let's just wrap it up, heh? Come on in, we'll tell Mom. [*He gently tries to pull* WILLY *to left.*]

WILLY [*frozen, immobile, with guilt in his voice*]   No, I don't want to see her.

BIFF   Come on! [*He pulls again, and* WILLY *tries to pull away.*]

WILLY [*highly nervous*]   No, no, I don't want to see her.

BIFF [*tries to look into* WILLY's *face, as if to find the answer there*]   Why don't you want to see her?

WILLY [*more harshly now*]   Don't bother me, will you?

BIFF   What do you mean, you don't want to see her? You don't want them calling you yellow, do you? This isn't your fault; it's me, I'm a bum. Now come inside! [WILLY *strains to get away.*] Did you hear what I said to you?

[WILLY *pulls away and quickly goes by himself into the house.* BIFF *follows.*]

LINDA [*to* WILLY]   Did you plant, dear?

BIFF [*at the door, to* LINDA]   All right, we had it out. I'm going and I'm not writing any more.

LINDA [*going to* WILLY *in the kitchen*]   I think that's the best way, dear. 'Cause there's no use drawing it out, you'll just never get along.

[WILLY *doesn't respond.*]

BIFF   People ask where I am and what I'm doing, you don't know, and you don't care. That way it'll be off your mind and you can start brightening up again. All right? That clears it, doesn't it? [WILLY *is silent, and* BIFF *goes to him.*] You gonna wish me luck, scout? [*He extends his hand.*] What do you say?

LINDA   Shake his hand, Willy.

WILLY [*turning to her, seething with hurt*]   There's no necessity to mention the pen at all, y'know.

BIFF [*gently*]   I've got no appointment, Dad.

WILLY [*erupting fiercely*]   He put his arm around . . . ?

BIFF   Dad, you're never going to see what I am, so what's the use of arguing? If I strike oil I'll send you a check. Meantime forget I'm alive.

WILLY [*to* LINDA]   Spite, see?

BIFF   Shake hands, Dad.

WILLY   Not my hand.

BIFF   I was hoping not to go this way.

WILLY   Well, this is the way you're going. Good-by.

[BIFF *looks at him a moment, then turns sharply and goes to the stairs.*]

WILLY [*stops him with*]   May you rot in hell if you leave this house!

BIFF [*turning*]   Exactly what is it that you want from me?

WILLY   I want you to know, on the train, in the mountains, in the valleys, wherever you go, that you cut down your life for spite!

BIFF   No, no.

WILLY   Spite, spite, is the word of your undoing! And when you're down and out, remember what did it. When you're rotting somewhere beside the railroad tracks, remember, and don't you dare blame it on me!

BIFF   I'm not blaming it on you!

WILLY   I won't take the rap for this, you hear?

[HAPPY *comes down the stairs and stands on the bottom step, watching.*]

BIFF   That's just what I'm telling you!

WILLY [*sinking into a chair at the table, with full accusation*]   You're trying to put a knife in me—don't think I don't know what you're doing!

BIFF   All right, phony! Then let's lay it on the line. [*He whips the rubber tube out of his pocket and puts it on the table.*]

HAPPY   You crazy—

LINDA   Biff! [*She moves to grab the hose, but* BIFF *holds it down with his hand.*]

BIFF   Leave it there! Don't move it!

WILLY [*not looking at it*]   What is that?

BIFF   You know goddam well what that is.

WILLY [*caged, wanting to escape*]   I never saw that.

BIFF   You saw it. The mice didn't bring it into the cellar! What is this supposed to do, make a hero out of you? This supposed to make me sorry for you?

WILLY   Never heard of it.

BIFF   There'll be no pity for you, you hear it? No pity!

WILLY [*to* LINDA]   You hear the spite!

BIFF   No, you're going to hear the truth—what you are and what I am!

LINDA   Stop it!

WILLY   Spite!

HAPPY [*coming down toward* BIFF]   You cut it now!

BIFF [*to* HAPPY]   The man don't know who we are! The man is gonna know! [*to* WILLY] We never told the truth for ten minutes in this house!

HAPPY   We always told the truth!

BIFF [*turning on him*]   You big blow, are you the assistant buyer? You're one of the two assistants to the assistant, aren't you?

HAPPY   Well, I'm practically—

BIFF   You're practically full of it! We all are! And I'm through with it. [*to* WILLY] Now hear this, Willy, this is me.

WILLY   I know you!

BIFF   You know why I had no address for three months? I stole a suit in Kansas City and I was in jail. [*to* LINDA, who is sobbing] Stop crying. I'm through with it.

[LINDA *turns away from them, her hands covering her face.*]

WILLY   I suppose that's my fault!

BIFF   I stole myself out of every good job since high school!

WILLY   And whose fault is that?

BIFF   And I never got anywhere because you blew me so full of hot air I could never stand taking orders from anybody! That's whose fault it is!

WILLY   I hear that!

LINDA   Don't, Biff!

BIFF   It's goddam time you heard that! I had to be boss big shot in two weeks, and I'm through with it!

WILLY   Then hang yourself! For spite, hang yourself!

BIFF   No! Nobody's hanging himself, Willy! I ran down eleven flights with a pen in my hand today. And suddenly I stopped, you hear me? And in the middle of that office building, do you hear this? I stopped in the middle of that building and I saw—the sky. I saw the things that I love in this world. The work and the food and time to sit and smoke. And I looked at the pen and said to myself, what the hell am I grabbing this for? Why am I trying to become what I don't want to be? What am I doing in an office, making a contemptuous, begging fool of myself, when all I want is out there, waiting for me the minute I say I know who I am! Why can't I say that, Willy? [*He tries to make* WILLY *face him, but* WILLY *pulls away and moves to the left.*]

WILLY [*with hatred, threateningly*]   The door of your life is wide open!

BIFF   Pop! I'm a dime a dozen, and so are you!

WILLY [*turning on him now in an uncontrolled outburst*]   I am not a dime a dozen! I am Willy Loman, and you are Biff Loman!

[BIFF *starts for* WILLY, *but is blocked by* HAPPY. *In his fury,* BIFF *seems on the verge of attacking his father.*]

BIFF   I am not a leader of men, Willy, and neither are you. You were never anything but a hard-working drummer who landed in the ash can like all the rest of them! I'm one dollar an hour, Willy! I tried seven states and couldn't raise it. A buck an hour! Do you gather my meaning? I'm not bringing home any prizes any more, and you're going to stop waiting for me to bring them home!

WILLY [*directly to* BIFF]   You vengeful, spiteful mut!

[BIFF *breaks from* HAPPY. WILLY, *in fright, starts up the stairs.* BIFF *grabs him.*]

BIFF [*at the peak of his fury*]   Pop, I'm nothing! I'm nothing, Pop. Can't you understand that? There's no spite in it any more. I'm just what I am, that's all.

[BIFF's *fury has spent itself, and he breaks down, sobbing, holding on to* WILLY, *who dumbly fumbles for* BIFF's *face.*]

WILLY [*astonished*]   What're you doing? What're you doing? [*to* LINDA] Why is he crying?

BIFF [*crying, broken*]   Will you let me go, for Christ's sake? Will you take that phony dream and burn it before something happens? [*Struggling to contain himself, he pulls away and moves to the stairs.*] I'll go in the morning. Put him—put him to bed. [*Exhausted,* BIFF *moves up the stairs to his room.*]

WILLY [*after a long pause, astonished, elevated*]   Isn't that—isn't that remarkable? Biff—he likes me!

LINDA   He loves you, Willy!

HAPPY [*deeply moved*]   Always did, Pop.

WILLY   Oh, Biff! [*staring wildly*] He cried! Cried to me. [*He is choking with his love, and now cries out his promise.*] That boy—that boy is going to be magnificent!

[BEN *appears in the light just outside the kitchen.*]

BEN   Yes, outstanding, with twenty thousand behind him.

LINDA [*sensing the racing of his mind, fearfully, carefully*]   Now come to bed, Willy. It's all settled now.

WILLY [*finding it difficult not to rush out of the house*]   Yes, we'll sleep. Come on. Go to sleep, Hap.

BEN   And it does take a great kind of a man to crack the jungle.

[*In accents of dread,* BEN's *idyllic music starts up.*]

HAPPY [*his arm around* LINDA]   I'm getting married, Pop, don't forget it. I'm changing everything. I'm gonna run that department before the year is up. You'll see, Mom. [*He kisses her.*]

BEN   The jungle is dark but full of diamonds, Willy.

[WILLY *turns, moves, listening to* BEN.]

LINDA   Be good. You're both good boys, just act that way, that's all.

HAPPY   'Night, Pop. [*He goes upstairs.*]

LINDA [*to* WILLY]   Come, dear.

BEN [*with greater force*]   One must go in to fetch a diamond out.

WILLY [*to* LINDA, *as he moves slowly along the edge of the kitchen, toward the door*]   I just want to get settled down, Linda. Let me sit alone for a little.

LINDA [*almost uttering her fear*]   I want you upstairs.

WILLY [*taking her in his arms*]   In a few minutes, Linda. I couldn't sleep right now. Go on, you look awful tired. [*He kisses her.*]

BEN   Not like an appointment at all. A diamond is rough and hard to the touch.

WILLY   Go on now. I'll be right up.

LINDA   I think this is the only way, Willy.

WILLY   Sure, it's the best thing.

BEN   Best thing!

WILLY   The only way. Everything is gonna be—go on, kid, get to bed. You look so tired.

LINDA   Come right up.

WILLY   Two minutes.

[LINDA *goes into the living-room, then reappears in her bedroom.* WILLY *moves just outside the kitchen door.*]

WILLY   Loves me. [*wonderingly*] Always loved me. Isn't that a remarkable thing? Ben, he'll worship me for it!

BEN [*with promise*]   It's dark there, but full of diamonds.

WILLY   Can you imagine that magnificence with twenty thousand dollars in his pocket?

LINDA [*calling from her room*]   Willy! Come up!

WILLY [*calling into the kitchen*]   Yes! Yes. Coming! It's very smart, you realize that, don't you, sweetheart? Even Ben sees it. I gotta go, baby. 'By! 'By! [*going over to* BEN, *almost dancing*] Imagine? When the mail comes he'll be ahead of Bernard again!

BEN   A perfect proposition all around.

WILLY   Did you see how he cried to me? Oh, if I could kiss him, Ben!

BEN   Time, William, time!

WILLY   Oh, Ben, I always knew one way or another we were gonna make it, Biff and I!

BEN [*looking at his watch*]   The boat. We'll be late. [*He moves slowly off into the darkness.*]

WILLY [*elegiacally, turning to the house*]   Now when you kick off, boy, I want a seventy-yard boot, and get right down the field under the ball, and when you hit, hit low and hit hard, because it's important, boy. [*He swings around and faces the audience.*] There's all kinds of important people in the stands, and the first thing you know . . . [*suddenly realizing he is alone*] Ben! Ben, where do I . . . ? [*He makes a sudden movement of search.*] Ben, how do I . . . ?

LINDA [*calling*]   Willy, you coming up?

WILLY [*uttering a gasp of fear, whirling about as if to quiet her*]   Sh! [*He turns around as if to find his way; sounds, faces, voices, seem to be swarming in upon him and he flicks at them, crying,*] Sh! Sh! [*Suddenly music, faint and high, stops him. It rises in intensity, almost to an unbearable scream. He goes up and down on his toes, and rushes off around the house.*] Shhh!

LINDA   Willy?

[*There is no answer.* LINDA *waits.* BIFF *gets up off his bed. He is still in his clothes.* HAPPY *sits up.* BIFF *stands listening.*]

LINDA [*with real fear*]   Willy, answer me! Willy!

[*There is the sound of a car starting and moving away at full speed.*]

LINDA No!

BIFF [*rushing down the stairs*] Pop!

> [*As the car speeds off, the music crashes down in a frenzy of sound, which becomes the soft pulsation of a single cello string.* BIFF *slowly returns to his bedroom. He and* HAPPY *gravely don their jackets.* LINDA *slowly walks out of her room. The music has developed into a dead march. The leaves of day are appearing over everything.* CHARLEY *and* BERNARD *somberly dressed, appear and knock on the kitchen door.* BIFF *and* HAPPY *slowly descend the stairs to the kitchen as* CHARLEY *and* BERNARD *enter. All stop a moment when* LINDA, *in clothes of mourning, bearing a little bunch of roses, comes through the draped doorway into the kitchen. She goes to* CHARLEY *and takes his arm. Now all move toward the audience, through the wall-line of the kitchen. At the limit of the apron,* LINDA *lays down the flowers, kneels, and sits back on her heels. All stare down at the grave.*]

Requiem

CHARLEY It's getting dark, Linda.

> [LINDA *doesn't react. She stares at the grave.*]

BIFF How about it, Mom? Better get some rest, heh? They'll be closing the gate soon.

> [LINDA *makes no move. Pause.*]

HAPPY [*deeply angered*] He had no right to do that. There was no necessity for it. We would've helped him.

CHARLEY [*grunting*] Hmmm.

BIFF Come along, Mom.

LINDA Why didn't anybody come?

CHARLEY It was a very nice funeral.

LINDA But where are all the people he knew? Maybe they blame him.

CHARLEY Naa. It's a rough world, Linda. They wouldn't blame him.

LINDA I can't understand it. At this time especially. First time in thirty-five years we were just about free and clear. He only needed a little salary. He was even finished with the dentist.

CHARLEY No man only needs a little salary.

LINDA I can't understand it.

BIFF There were a lot of nice days. When he'd come home from a trip; or on Sundays, making the stoop; finishing the cellar; putting on the new porch; when he built the extra bathroom; and put up the garage. You know something, Charley, there's more of him in that front stoop than in all the sales he ever made.

CHARLEY Yeah. He was a happy man with a batch of cement.

LINDA He was so wonderful with his hands.

BIFF He had the wrong dreams. All, all, wrong.

HAPPY [*almost ready to fight* BIFF] Don't say that!

BIFF He never knew who he was.

CHARLEY [*stopping* HAPPY's *movement and reply. To* BIFF] Nobody dast blame this man. You don't understand: Willy was a salesman. And for a salesman, there is no rock bottom to the life. He don't put a bolt to a nut, he don't tell you the law or give you medicine. He's a man way out there in the blue, riding on a smile and a shoeshine. And when they start not smiling back—that's an earthquake. And then you get yourself a couple of spots on your hat, and you're finished. Nobody dast blame this man. A salesman is got to dream, boy. It comes with the territory.

BIFF   Charley, the man didn't know who he was.

HAPPY [*infuriated*]   Don't say that!

BIFF   Why don't you come with me, Happy?

HAPPY   I'm not licked that easily. I'm staying right in this city, and I'm gonna beat this racket! [*He looks at* BIFF, *his chin set.*] The Loman Brothers!

BIFF   I know who I am, kid.

HAPPY   All right, boy. I'm gonna show you and everybody else that Willy Loman did not die in vain. He had a good dream. It's the only dream you can have—to come out number-one man. He fought it out here, and this is where I'm gonna win it for him.

BIFF [*with a hopeless glance at* HAPPY, *bends toward his mother*]   Let's go, Mom.

LINDA   I'll be with you in a minute. Go on, Charley. [*He hesitates.*] I want to, just for a minute. I never had a chance to say good-by.

[CHARLEY *moves away, followed by* HAPPY. BIFF *remains a slight distance up and left of* LINDA. *She sits there, summoning herself. The flute begins, not far away, playing behind her speech.*]

LINDA   Forgive me, dear. I can't cry. I don't know what it is, but I can't cry. I don't understand it. Why did you ever do that? Help me, Willy, I can't cry. It seems to me that you're just on another trip. I keep expecting you. Willy, dear, I can't cry. Why did you do it? I search and search and I search, and I can't understand it, Willy. I made the last payment on the house today. Today, dear. And there'll be nobody home. [*A sob rises in her throat.*] We're free and clear. [*Sobbing more fully, released*] We're free. [BIFF *comes slowly toward her.*] We're free . . . We're free . . .

[BIFF *lifts her to her feet and moves out up right with her in his arms.* LINDA *sobs quietly.* BERNARD *and* CHARLEY *come together and follow them, followed by* HAPPY. *Only the music of the flute is left on the darkening stage as over the house the hard towers of the apartment buildings rise into sharp focus, and*]

CURTAIN

1949

ROBERT LOWELL
1917–1977

I n "North Haven," her poem in memory of Robert Lowell, Elizabeth Bishop translates the birdsong as Lowell seemed to hear it: "repeat, repeat, repeat, revise, revise, revise." Repeatedly, even obsessively, Lowell returned to certain subjects in his poems. Each return confirmed an existing pattern even as it opened the possibility for revision. In fact, Lowell's life was full of revision. Descended from Protestant New Englanders, he converted to Catholicism, then fell away from it; he married three times; and he changed his poetic style more than once. In the later part of his career Lowell revised even his published poems and did so repeatedly. "Revision is inspiration," he once said, "no reading of the finished work as exciting as writing-in the last changes." Revision allowed for Lowell's love of stray events, his attraction to the fluidity of life (in this, he resembles Wallace Stevens). But Lowell also wanted to organize life into formal patterns, to locate the random moment in the design of an epic history (his Catholicism can be seen, in part, as an expression of this desire). History offered plot and repetition: just as patterns of his childhood recurred in adult life, the sins of his New England ancestors were reenacted by contemporary America. Lowell's vision of history leaned toward apocalypse, toward the revelation of a prior meaning that the poet agonized to determine, and yet he cherished the freedom of "human chances," with all their indeterminacy. His poems had to accommodate these opposing impulses. Concerning the sequence of poems in *Notebook 1967–1968*, begun as a poetic diary, he said: "Accident threw up the subject and the plot swallowed them—famished for human chances." If Lowell often swallowed up the casual, the random, the ordinary, and the domestic into the forms of his poems, his best plots have a spontaneity whose meanings cannot be fixed.

The burden of family history was substantial for Lowell, whose ancestors included members of Boston's patrician families. His grandfather was a well-known Episcopal minister and head of the fashionable St. Mark's School, which the poet was later to attend. His great-granduncle James Russell Lowell had been a poet and the ambassador to England. The family's light note was provided by the poet Amy Lowell, "big and a scandal, as if Mae West were a cousin." In the context of this history Lowell's father, who fared badly in business after his retirement from service as a naval officer, appeared as a diminished figure.

Lowell's first act of revising family history was to leave New England after two years at Harvard (1935–37) in order to study at Ohio's Kenyon College with John Crowe Ransom, the poet and critic. The move brought him in closer touch with the New Criticism and its predilections for "formal difficult poems," the wit and irony of English Metaphysical writers such as John Donne. He also, through Ransom and the poet Allen Tate, came into contact with (although he never formally joined) the Fugitive movement, whose members were southern agrarians opposed to what they regarded as the corrupting values of northern industrialism.

Two of the acts that most decisively separated Lowell from family history were his conversion to Roman Catholicism (1940) and his resistance to American policies in World War II. Although he tried to enlist in the navy, he refused to be drafted into the army. He opposed the saturation bombing of Hamburg and the Allied policy of unconditional surrender and was as a result sentenced to a year's confinement in New York City's West Street jail. The presiding judge at his hearing admonished him for "marring" his family traditions. In his first book, *Lord Weary's Castle* (1946), his Catholicism provided a set of symbols and a distanced platform from which to express his violent antagonism to Protestant mercantile Boston. The stunning, apocalyptic conclusions of these early poems ("the Lord survives the rainbow of his will" or "The blue kingfisher dives on you in fire") render the devastating judgment of the eternal on the fallen history of the individual and the nation.

Alongside these poems drawing on Old Testament anger in *Lord Weary's Castle* were poems, such as "Mr. Edwards and the Spider," that explored from within the nervous intensity that underlay Puritan revivalism. Later dramatic narratives with modern settings, such as "The Mills of the Kavanaghs" and "Falling Asleep over the Aeneid," reveal his psychological interest in and obsession with ruined New England families.

In *Life Studies* (1959) Lowell changed his style dramatically. His subjects became explicitly autobiographical, his language more open and direct. In 1957 he gave readings in California, where Allen Ginsberg and the other Beats had just made their strongest impact in San Francisco. In contrast to their candid, breezy writing, Lowell felt his own seemed "distant, symbol-ridden, and willfully difficult. . . . I felt my old poems hid what they were really about, and many times offered a stiff, humorless, and even impenetrable surface." Although more controlled and severe than Beat writers, he was stimulated by Ginsberg's self-revelations to write more openly than he had about his parents and grandparents, about the mental breakdowns he suffered in the 1950s, and about the difficulties of marriage. (Lowell divorced his first wife, the novelist Jean Stafford, and married the critic Elizabeth Hardwick in 1949.)

Life Studies, by and large, records his ambivalence toward the New England where he resettled after the war, on Boston's "hardly passionate Marlborough Street." Revising his stance toward New England and family history, he no longer denounces the city of his fathers as if he were a privileged outsider. In complicated psychological portraits of his childhood and his relation to his parents and his wives, he assumes a portion of the weakness and vulnerability for himself.

In 1960 Lowell left Boston to live in New York City. *For the Union Dead* (1964), the book that followed, continued the autobiographical vein of *Life Studies*. Lowell called it a book about "witheredness . . . lemony, soured and dry, the drouth I had touched with my own hands." These poems seem more carefully controlled than his earlier *Life Studies*. Often they organize key images from the past into a pattern that illuminates the present. The book includes a number of poems that fuse private and public themes, such as "Fall 1961" and the volume's title poem.

In 1969 Lowell published *Notebook 1967–1968* and then revised these poems for a second, augmented edition, called simply *Notebook* (1970). In 1973, in a characteristic act, he once more revised, rearranged, and expanded *Notebook*'s poems and published them in two separate books. The more personal poems, recording the breakup of his second marriage and his separation from his wife and daughter, were published as *For Lizzie and Harriet*. Those dealing more with public subjects, past and present, were published as *History*. These two books show Lowell once again engaged with the relations between the random event, or the moment in a personal life, and an epic design. In these unrhymed, loosely blank-verse revisions of the sonnet, Lowell responded to the books he was reading, to the events of his personal life, and to the Vietnam War, of which he was an outspoken critic. "Things I felt or saw, or read were drift in the whirlpool."

At the same time a new collection of sonnets, *The Dolphin* (1973), appeared, recording his marriage to Lady Caroline Blackwood. (Lowell's friend the poet Elizabeth Bishop objected to his use of Blackwood's letters in the volume.) He divided his time between Blackwood's home in England and periods of teaching writing and literature at Harvard—a familiar pattern for him, in which the old tensions between New England and "elsewhere" were being constantly explored and renewed. His last book, *Day by Day* (1977), records those stresses as well as new marital difficulties. It also contains some of his most powerful poems about his childhood.

For those who cherish the work of the early Lowell, with its manic, rhythmic energy and its enjambed lines building to fierce power, or those who admire the passionate engagement of *Life Studies* or *For the Union Dead*, the poems of his last four books can be disappointing. At times flat and dispirited, they can seem worked up rather than fully imagined. Yet the later Lowell demonstrates his substantial gifts in a quieter mode.

Lowell's career included an interest in the theater, for which he wrote a version of *Prometheus Bound*, a translation of Racine's *Phaedra*, and adaptations of Melville and Hawthorne stories gathered as *The Old Glory*. He also translated from modern European poetry and the classics, often freely as "imitations," which brought important poetic voices into English currency. His *Selected Poems* (his own choices) appeared in

1976. When he died suddenly at the age of sixty, he was the dominant and most honored poet of his generation—not only for his ten volumes of verse but for his broad activity as a man of letters. He took upon himself the role of poet as public figure, sometimes at great personal cost. He was with the group of writers who led Vietnam War protesters against the Pentagon in 1967, where Norman Mailer, a fellow protester, observed that "Lowell gave off at times the unwilling haunted saintliness of a man who was repaying the moral debts of ten generations of ancestors."

Colloquy in Black Rock[1]

Here the jack-hammer jabs into the ocean;
My heart, you race and stagger and demand
More blood-gangs for your nigger-brass percussions,
Till I, the stunned machine of your devotion,
Clanging upon this cymbal of a hand,   5
Am rattled screw and footloose. All discussions

End in the mud-flat detritus of death.
My heart, beat faster, faster. In Black Mud[2]
Hungarian workmen give their blood
For the martyre Stephen,[3] who was stoned to death.   10

Black Mud, a name to conjure with: O mud
For watermelons gutted to the crust,
Mud for the mole-tide[4] harbor, mud for mouse,
Mud for the armored Diesel fishing tubs that thud
A year and a day[5] to wind and tide; the dust   15
Is on this skipping heart that shakes my house,

House of our Savior who was hanged till death.
My heart, beat faster, faster. In Black Mud
Stephen the martyre was broken down to blood:
Our ransom is the rubble of his death.   20
Christ walks on the black water. In Black Mud
Darts the kingfisher. On Corpus Christi, heart,
Over the drum-beat of St. Stephen's choir
I hear him, *Stupor Mundi*,[6] and the mud
Flies from his hunching wings and beak—my heart,   25
The blue kingfisher dives on you in fire.

1946

1. A section of Bridgeport, Connecticut, where Lowell went to live in 1944 after serving his jail term as a conscientious objector. It had a large Hungarian population.
2. The speaker's name for mud flats near Black Rock.
3. A reference to the wartime blood donations of the workers; the patron saint of Hungary, King Stephen I (977–1038); and St. Stephen Promartyr, the first Christian to be killed for his faith.
4. Special currents produced by a mole (breakwater).
5. Perhaps the "year and a day" of Lowell's prison sentence.
6. Marvel of the world. "Kingfisher": a short-tailed bird that dives for fish; associated in the poem's last line with Christ, the "fisher of men." "Corpus Christi": a Catholic feast day, celebrating the transformation of the communion wafer into the body of Christ.

The Quaker Graveyard in Nantucket

[*For Warren Winslow,*[1] *Dead at Sea*]

Let man have dominion over the fishes of the sea and the fowls of
the air and the beasts of the whole earth, and every creeping creature that moveth upon the earth.[2]

I

A brackish reach of shoal off Madaket[3]—
The sea was still breaking violently and night
Had steamed into our North Atlantic Fleet,
When the drowned sailor clutched the drag-net. Light
Flashed from his matted head and marble feet,   5
He grappled at the net
With the coiled, hurdling muscles of his thighs:
The corpse was bloodless, a botch of reds and whites,
Its open, staring eyes
Were lustreless dead-lights[4]   10
Or cabin-windows on a stranded hulk
Heavy with sand. We weight the body, close
Its eyes and heave it seaward whence it came,
Where the heel-headed dogfish barks its nose
On Ahab's[5] void and forehead; and the name   15
Is blocked in yellow chalk.
Sailors, who pitch this portent at the sea
Where dreadnaughts shall confess
Its hell-bent deity,
When you are powerless   20
To sand-bag this Atlantic bulwark, faced
By the earth-shaker, green, unwearied, chaste
In his steel scales: ask for no Orphean lute
To pluck life back.[6] The guns of the steeled fleet
Recoil and then repeat   25
The hoarse salute.

II

Whenever winds are moving and their breath
Heaves at the roped-in bulwarks of this pier,
The terns and sea-gulls tremble at your death
In these home waters. Sailor, can you hear   30
The Pequod's[7] sea wings, beating landward, fall
Headlong and break on our Atlantic wall

1. A cousin of Lowell's who died in the sinking
of a naval vessel during World War II.
2. From Genesis 1.26, the account of the creation of humankind.
3. On Nantucket Island.
4. Shutters over portholes to keep out water in a
storm. The images in lines 4–11 come from "The
Shipwreck," the opening chapter of *Cape Cod*,
by Henry David Thoreau (1817–1862).
5. Protagonist of the novel *Moby-Dick*, by Herman Melville (1819–1891); he drowns as the culmination of his obsessive hunt for the white
whale. Melville uses Ahab's forehead as an
emblem of his monomaniac passion.
6. In Greek mythology Orpheus, through his
music, tried to win the freedom of his bride,
Eurydice, from the Underworld. "Earth-shaker":
an epithet for Poseidon, the Greek god of the
oceans and of earthquakes.
7. Ahab's ship, destroyed by Moby-Dick.

Off 'Sconset, where the yawing S-boats[8] splash
The bellbuoy, with ballooning spinnakers,
As the entangled, screeching mainsheet clears   35
The blocks: off Madaket, where lubbers[9] lash
The heavy surf and throw their long lead squids
For blue-fish? Sea-gulls blink their heavy lids
Seaward. The winds' wings beat upon the stones,
Cousin, and scream for you and the claws rush   40
At the sea's throat and wring it in the slush
Of this old Quaker graveyard where the bones
Cry out in the long night for the hurt beast
Bobbing by Ahab's whaleboats in the East.

III

All you recovered from Poseidon died   45
With you, my cousin, and the harrowed brine
Is fruitless on the blue beard of the god,
Stretching beyond us to the castles in Spain,
Nantucket's westward haven. To Cape Cod
Guns, cradled on the tide,   50
Blast the eelgrass about a waterclock
Of bilge and backwash, roil the salt and sand
Lashing earth's scaffold, rock
Our warships in the hand
Of the great God, where time's contrition blues   55
Whatever it was these Quaker[1] sailors lost
In the mad scramble of their lives. They died
When time was open-eyed,
Wooden and childish; only bones abide
There, in the nowhere, where their boats were tossed   60
Sky-high, where mariners had fabled news
Of IS,[2] the whited monster. What it cost
Them is their secret. In the sperm-whale's slick
I see the Quakers drown and hear their cry:
"If God himself had not been on our side,   65
If God himself had not been on our side,
When the Atlantic rose against us, why,
Then it had swallowed us up quick."

IV

This is the end of the whaleroad[3] and the whale
Who spewed Nantucket bones on the thrashed swell   70
And stirred the troubled waters to whirlpools
To send the Pequod packing off to hell:
This is the end of them, three-quarters fools,
Snatching at straws to sail

---

8. Type of large racing sailboats. "Yawing": steering wildly in heavy seas.
9. Sailor's term for clumsy crew members.
1. The whaling population of Nantucket
included many Quakers.
2. The white whale is here imagined as a force
like the God of Exodus 3.14, who, when asked his
name by Moses, replies, "I AM THAT I AM." Also an
abbreviation of Iesu Salvator, Latin for Jesus, savior of men.
3. An Anglo-Saxon epithet for the sea.

Seaward and seaward on the turntail whale,   75
Spouting out blood and water as it rolls,
Sick as a dog to these Atlantic shoals:
Clamavimus,[4] O depths. Let the sea-gulls wail

For water, for the deep where the high tide
Mutters to its hurt self, mutters and ebbs.   80
Waves wallow in their wash, go out and out,
Leave only the death-rattle of the crabs,
The beach increasing, its enormous snout
Sucking the ocean's side.
This is the end of running on the waves;   85
We are poured out like water. Who will dance
The mast-lashed master of Leviathans
Up from this field of Quakers in their unstoned graves?

V

When the whale's viscera go and the roll
Of its corruption overruns this world   90
Beyond tree-swept Nantucket and Woods Hole[5]
And Martha's Vineyard, Sailor, will your sword
Whistle and fall and sink into the fat?
In the great ash-pit of Jehoshaphat[6]
The bones cry for the blood of the white whale,   95
The fat flukes arch and whack about its ears,
The death-lance churns into the sanctuary, tears
The gun-blue swingle,[7] heaving like a flail,
And hacks the coiling life out: it works and drags
And rips the sperm-whale's midriff into rags,   100
Gobbets of blubber spill to wind and weather,
Sailor, and gulls go round the stoven timbers
Where the morning stars sing out together
And thunder shakes the white surf and dismembers
The red flag hammered in the mast-head.[8] Hide,   105
Our steel, Jonas Messias, in Thy side.[9]

VI. OUR LADY OF WALSINGHAM[1]

There once the penitents took off their shoes
And then walked barefoot the remaining mile;
And the small trees, a stream and hedgerows file
Slowly along the munching English lane,   110
Like cows to the old shrine, until you lose

4. We have called (Latin), adapting the opening
of Psalm 130: "Out of the depths have I cried unto
thee, O Lord."
5. On the coast of Massachusetts, near the
island of Martha's Vineyard.
6. "The day of judgment. The world, according to
some prophets, will end in fire" [Lowell's note]. In
Joel 3, the Last Judgment takes place in the valley
of Jehoshaphat.
7. Knifelike wooden instrument for beating flax
(into fiber for spinning).

8. At the end of Moby-Dick, the arm of the American Indian Tashtego appears from the waves and
nails Ahab's flag to the sinking mast.
9. Because he emerged alive from the belly of a
whale, the prophet Jonah is often linked with the
messiah as a figure of salvation.
1. Lowell took these details from E. I. Watkin's
Catholic Art and Culture (1942), which includes
a description of the medieval shrine of the Virgin
at Walsingham.

Track of your dragging pain.
The stream flows down under the druid tree,
Shiloah's[2] whirlpools gurgle and make glad
The castle of God. Sailor, you were glad   115
And whistled Sion by that stream. But see:

Our Lady, too small for her canopy,
Sits near the altar. There's no comeliness
At all or charm in that expressionless
Face with its heavy eyelids. As before,   120
This face, for centuries a memory,
Non est species, neque decor,[3]
Expressionless, expresses God: it goes
Past castled Sion. She knows what God knows,
Not Calvary's Cross nor crib at Bethlehem   125
Now, and the world shall come to Walsingham.

VII

The empty winds are creaking and the oak
Splatters and splatters on the cenotaph,
The boughs are trembling and a gaff
Bobs on the untimely stroke   130
Of the greased wash exploding on a shoal-bell
In the old mouth of the Atlantic. It's well;
Atlantic, you are fouled with the blue sailors,
Sea-monsters, upward angel, downward fish:
Unmarried and corroding, spare of flesh   135
Mart once of supercilious, wing'd clippers,
Atlantic, where your bell-trap guts its spoil
You could cut the brackish winds with a knife
Here in Nantucket, and cast up the time
When the Lord God formed man from the sea's slime   140
And breathed into his face the breath of life,
And blue-lung'd combers lumbered to the kill.
The Lord survives the rainbow[4] of His will.

1946

Mr. Edwards and the Spider[1]

I saw the spiders marching through the air,
Swimming from tree to tree that mildewed day
In latter August when the hay
Came creaking to the barn. But where

2. The stream that flows past God's Temple on Mount Sion (Isaiah 8.6). In Isaiah 51.11 the redeemed come "singing into Zion."
3. There is no ostentation or elegance (Latin).
4. Alluding to God's covenant with Noah after the Flood. The rainbow symbolized the fact that humanity would never again be destroyed by flood (Genesis 9.11).

1. Jonathan Edwards (1703–1758), Puritan preacher and theologian. Lowell quotes his writings throughout. The details of the first stanza come from his youthful essay "Of Insects" ("The Habits of Spiders").

The wind is westerly,   5
Where gnarled November makes the spiders fly
Into the apparitions of the sky,
They purpose nothing but their ease and die
Urgently beating east to sunrise and the sea;

What are we in the hands of the great God?   10
It was in vain you set up thorn and briar
    In battle array against the fire
    And treason crackling in your blood;
        For the wild thorns grow tame
And will do nothing to oppose the flame;   15
Your lacerations tell the losing game
You play against a sickness past your cure.
How will the hands be strong? How will the heart endure?[2]

A very little thing, a little worm,
Or hourglass-blazoned spider,[3] it is said,   20
    Can kill a tiger. Will the dead
    Hold up his mirror and affirm
        To the four winds the smell
And flash of his authority? It's well
If God who holds you to the pit of hell,   25
Much as one holds a spider, will destroy,
Baffle and dissipate your soul. As a small boy

On Windsor Marsh,[4] I saw the spider die
When thrown into the bowels of fierce fire:
    There's no long struggle, no desire   30
    To get up on its feet and fly—
        It stretches out its feet
And dies. This is the sinner's last retreat;
Yes, and no strength exerted on the heat
Then sinews the abolished will, when sick   35
And full of burning, it will whistle on a brick.

But who can plumb the sinking of that soul?
Josiah Hawley,[5] picture yourself cast
    Into a brick-kiln where the blast
    Fans your quick vitals to a coal—   40
        If measured by a glass,
How long would it seem burning! Let there pass
A minute, ten, ten trillion; but the blaze
Is infinite, eternal: this is death,
To die and know it. This is the Black Widow, death.   45

                                        1946

---

2. This stanza draws on Edwards's sermon "Sinners in the Hands of an Angry God," whose point
of departure is Ezekiel 22.14: "Can thine heart
endure or can thine hands be strong in the days
that I shall deal with thee?" (cf. line 18).
3. The poisonous black widow spider has, on the
underside of its abdomen, a red marking that
resembles an hourglass.
4. East Windsor, Connecticut, Edwards's childhood home.
5. Edwards's uncle, Joseph Hawley.

My Last Afternoon with Uncle Devereux Winslow

1922: the stone porch of my grandfather's summer house

I

"I won't go with you. I want to stay with Grandpa!"
That's how I threw cold water
on my Mother and Father's
watery martini pipe dreams at Sunday dinner.
. . . Fontainebleau, Mattapoisett, Puget Sound. . . .[1]   5
Nowhere was anywhere after a summer
at my Grandfather's farm.
Diamond-pointed, athirst and Norman,[2]
its alley of poplars
paraded from Grandmother's rose garden   10
to a scary stand of virgin pine,
scrub, and paths forever pioneering.

One afternoon in 1922,
I sat on the stone porch, looking through
screens as black-grained as drifting coal.   15
Tockytock, tockytock
clumped our Alpine, Edwardian cuckoo clock,
slung with strangled, wooden game.
Our farmer was cementing a root-house[3] under the hill.
One of my hands was cool on a pile   20
of black earth, the other warm
on a pile of lime. All about me
were the works of my Grandfather's hands:
snapshots of his *Liberty Bell* silver mine;
his high school at *Stuttgart am Neckar,*[4]   25
stogie-brown beams; fools'-gold nuggets;
octagonal red tiles,
sweaty with a secret dank, crummy with ant-stale;
a Rocky Mountain chaise longue,
its legs, shellacked saplings.   30
A pastel-pale Huckleberry Finn
fished with a broom straw in a basin
hollowed out of a millstone.
Like my Grandfather, the décor
was manly, comfortable,   35
overbearing, disproportioned.

What were those sunflowers? Pumpkins floating shoulder-high?
It was sunset, Sadie and Nellie
bearing pitchers of ice-tea,

---

1. Sound connected to the Pacific Ocean via the Strait of Juan de Fuca, in the Pacific Northwest. "Fontainebleau": rich pastoral suburb of Paris, site of one of the royal châteaux. "Mattapoisett": town in Plymouth County, Massachusetts, first settled in the 1750s.

2. A stage of Romanesque architecture developed in the French province of Normandy.
3. For storing bulbs, root vegetables, etc.
4. City in Germany, on the Neckar River. "*Liberty Bell* silver mine": located near Telluride, Colorado; it boomed in the 1890s.

oranges, lemons, mint, and peppermints,   40
and the jug of shandygaff,
which Grandpa made by blending half and half
yeasty, wheezing homemade sarsaparilla with beer.
The farm, entitled *Char-de-sa*
in the Social Register,   45
was named for my Grandfather's children:
Charlotte, Devereux, and Sarah.
No one had died there in my lifetime . . .
Only Cinder, our Scottie puppy
paralyzed from gobbling toads.   50
I sat mixing black earth and lime.

                          II

I was five and a half.
My formal pearl gray shorts
had been worn for three minutes.
My perfection was the Olympian   55
poise of my models in the imperishable autumn
display windows
of Rogers Peet's boys' store below the State House
in Boston. Distorting drops of water
pinpricked my face in the basin's mirror.   60
I was a stuffed toucan
with a bibulous, multicolored beak.

                          III

Up in the air
by the lakeview window in the billards-room,
lurid in the doldrums of the sunset hour,   65
my Great Aunt Sarah
was learning *Samson and Delilah*.[5]
She thundered on the keyboard of her dummy piano,
with gauze curtains like a boudoir table,
accordionlike yet soundless.   70
It had been bought to spare the nerves
of my Grandmother,
tone-deaf, quick as a cricket,
now needing a fourth for "Auction,"[6]
and casting a thirsty eye   75
on Aunt Sarah, risen like the phoenix
from her bed of troublesome snacks and Tauchnitz classics.[7]

Forty years earlier,
twenty, auburn headed,
grasshopper notes of genius!   80
Family gossip says Aunt Sarah

5. A piano version of the opera by Camille Saint-
Saëns (1835–1921).
6. Auction bridge, a card game.

7. German paperback editions that included standard English and American works (in English).

tilted her archaic Athenian nose
and jilted an Astor.[8]
Each morning she practiced
on the grand piano at Symphony Hall,   85
deathlike in the off-season summer—
its naked Greek statues draped with purple
like the saints in Holy Week. . . .
On the recital day, she failed to appear.

IV

I picked with a clean finger nail at the blue anchor   90
on my sailor blouse washed white as a spinnaker.
What in the world was I wishing?
. . . A sail-colored horse browsing in the bullrushes . . .
A fluff of the west wind puffing
my blouse, kiting me over our seven chimneys,   95
troubling the waters. . . .
As small as sapphires were the ponds: *Quittacus, Snippituit,*
and *Assawompses,* halved by "the Island,"
where my Uncle's duck blind
floated in a barrage of smoke-clouds.   100
Double-barreled shotguns
stuck out like bundles of baby crow-bars.
A single sculler in a camouflaged kayak
was quacking to the decoys. . . .

At the cabin between the waters,   105
the nearest windows were already boarded.
Uncle Devereux was closing camp for the winter.
As if posed for "the engagement photograph,"
he was wearing his severe
war-uniform of a volunteer Canadian officer.   110
Daylight from the doorway riddled his student posters,
tacked helter-skelter on walls as raw as a boardwalk.
Mr. Punch,[9] a water melon in hockey tights,
was tossing off a decanter of Scotch.
La Belle France in a red, white and blue toga   115
was accepting the arm of her "protector,"
the ingenu and porcine Edward VII.[1]
The pre-war music hall belles
had goose necks, glorious signatures, beauty-moles,
and coils of hair like rooster tails.   120
The finest poster was two or three young men in khaki kilts
being bushwhacked on the veldt[2]—
They were almost life-size. . . .

8. A member of the wealthiest family in the United States during the 19th century.
9. A plump cartoon-figure emblem of the English humor magazine *Punch*, founded in 1841.
1. Edward VII (1841–1910), king of England, famous as a ladies' man, is depicted with his arm around the female emblem of France in a poster celebrating the Entente Cordiale, a rapprochement between England and France.
2. Open country in South Africa. The Boer War (1899–1902) was fought by the English against the Boers, descendants of Dutch settlers there.

My Uncle was dying at twenty-nine.
"You are behaving like children,"   125
said my Grandfather,
when my Uncle and Aunt left their three baby daughters,
and sailed for Europe on a last honeymoon . . .
I cowered in terror.
I wasn't a child at all—   130
unseen and all-seeing, I was Agrippina[3]
in the Golden House of Nero. . . .
Near me was the white measuring-door
my Grandfather had penciled with my Uncle's heights.
In 1911, he had stopped growing at just six feet.   135
While I sat on the tiles,
and dug at the anchor on my sailor blouse,
Uncle Devereux stood behind me.
He was as brushed as Bayard, our riding horse.
His face was putty.   140
His blue coat and white trousers
grew sharper and straighter.
His coat was a blue jay's tail,
his trousers were solid cream from the top of the bottle.
He was animated, hierarchical,   145
like a ginger snap man in a clothes-press.
He was dying of the incurable Hodgkin's disease. . . .
My hands were warm, then cool, on the piles
of earth and lime,
a black pile and a white pile. . . .   150
Come winter,
Uncle Devereux would blend to the one color.

                                                                    1959

Home after Three Months Away[1]

Gone now the baby's nurse,
a lioness who ruled the roost
and made the Mother cry.
She used to tie
gobbets of porkrind[2] in bowknots of gauze—   5
three months they hung like soggy toast
on our eight foot magnolia tree,
and helped the English sparrows
weather a Boston winter.

---

3. Mother of the Roman emperor Nero. Involved in court intrigue and affairs of state, she poisoned her second husband and was later murdered by her son.

1. This poem was written following one of Lowell's hospitalizations at McLean Psychiatric Hospital in Belmont, Massachusetts.
2. Small chunks of fried or roasted skin of a pig.

Three months, three months!   10
Is Richard now himself again?[3]
Dimpled with exaltation,
my daughter holds her levee in the tub.
Our noses rub,
each of us pats a stringy lock of hair—   15
they tell me nothing's gone.
Though I am forty-one,
not forty now, the time I put away
was child's-play. After thirteen weeks
my child still dabs her cheeks   20
to start me shaving. When
we dress her in her sky-blue corduroy,
she changes to a boy,
and floats my shaving brush
and washcloth in the flush. . . .   25
Dearest, I cannot loiter here
in lather like a polar bear.

Recuperating, I neither spin nor toil.[4]
Three stories down below,
a choreman tends our coffin's length of soil,   30
and seven horizontal tulips blow.
Just twelve months ago,
these flowers were pedigreed
imported Dutchmen; now no one need
distinguish them from weed.   35
Bushed by the late spring snow,
they cannot meet
another year's snowballing enervation.

I keep no rank nor station.
Cured, I am frizzled, stale and small.   40

                                         1958

Memories of West Street and Lepke[1]

Only teaching on Tuesdays, book-worming
in pajamas fresh from the washer each morning,
I hog a whole house on Boston's
"hardly passionate Marlborough Street,"[2]

---

3. Variation of "Richard's himself again," a line spoken by Richard III before the battle of Bosworth in a 1700 adaptation of Shakespeare's *Richard III* (1591?) by English actor-manager and playwright Colley Cibber (1671–1757).
4. Allusion to Matthew 6.28: "Consider the lilies of the field, how they grow: they neither toil nor spin."
1. In 1943 Lowell was sentenced to a year in New York City's West Street jail for his refusal to serve in the armed forces. Among the prisoners was Lepke Buchalter, head of the organized crime syndicate Murder Incorporated, who had been convicted of murder.
2. William James's phrase for a street in the elegant Back Bay section of Boston, where Lowell lived in the 1950s.

where even the man   5
scavenging filth in the back alley trash cans,
has two children, a beach wagon, a helpmate,
and is a "young Republican."
I have a nine months' daughter,
young enough to be my granddaughter.   10
Like the sun she rises in her flame-flamingo infants' wear.

These are the tranquillized *Fifties*,
and I am forty. Ought I to regret my seedtime?
I was a fire-breathing Catholic C.O.,[3]
and made my manic statement,   15
telling off the state and president, and then
sat waiting sentence in the bull pen
beside a Negro boy with curlicues
of marijuana in his hair.

Given a year.   20
I walked on the roof of the West Street Jail, a short
enclosure like my school soccer court,
and saw the Hudson River once a day
through sooty clothesline entanglements
and bleaching khaki tenements.   25
Strolling, I yammered metaphysics with Abramowitz,
a jaundice-yellow ("it's really tan")
and fly-weight pacifist,
so vegetarian,
he wore rope shoes and preferred fallen fruit.   30
He tried to convert Bioff and Brown,
the Hollywood pimps, to his diet.
Hairy, muscular, suburban,
wearing chocolate double-breasted suits,
they blew their tops and beat him black and blue.   35

I was so out of things, I'd never heard
of the Jehovah's Witnesses.[4]
"Are you a C.O.?" I asked a fellow jailbird.
"No," he answered, "I'm a J.W."
He taught me the "hospital tuck,"[5]   40
and pointed out the T-shirted back
of *Murder Incorporated*'s Czar Lepke,
there piling towels on a rack,
or dawdling off to his little segregated cell full
of things forbidden the common man: 45
a portable radio, a dresser, two toy American
flags tied together with a ribbon of Easter palm.
Flabby, bald, lobotomized,
he drifted in a sheepish calm,
where no agonizing reappraisal   50

3. Conscientious objector (to war).   of conscience.
4. A Christian revivalist sect that strongly opposes   5. The authorized, efficient way of making beds
war and denies the power of the state in matters   in a hospital.

jarred his concentration on the electric chair—
hanging like an oasis in his air
of lost connections. . . .

1959

Skunk Hour

for Elizabeth Bishop

Nautilus Island's[1] hermit
heiress still lives through winter in her Spartan cottage;
her sheep still graze above the sea.
Her son's a bishop. Her farmer
is first selectman in our village;   5
she's in her dotage.

Thirsting for
the hierarchic privacy
of Queen Victoria's century,
she buys up all   10
the eyesores facing her shore,
and lets them fall.

The season's ill—
we've lost our summer millionaire,
who seemed to leap from an L. L. Bean   15
catalogue.[2] His nine-knot yawl
was auctioned off to lobstermen.
A red fox stain covers Blue Hill.

And now our fairy
decorator brightens his shop for fall;   20
his fishnet's filled with orange cork,
orange, his cobbler's bench and awl;
there is no money in his work,
he'd rather marry.

One dark night,   25
my Tudor Ford climbed the hill's skull;
I watched for love-cars. Lights turned down,
they lay together, hull to hull,
where the graveyard shelves on the town. . . .
My mind's not right.   30

A car radio bleats,
"Love, O careless Love. . . ." I hear

1. The poem is set in Castine, Maine, where
Lowell had a summer house.
2. From a mail-order house in Maine that primarily sells sporting goods and clothing to the
wealthy and upper middle class.

my ill-spirit sob in each blood cell,
as if my hand were at its throat. . . .
I myself am hell;[3]   35
nobody's here—

only skunks, that search
in the moonlight for a bite to eat.
They march on their soles up Main Street:
white stripes, moonstruck eyes' red fire   40
under the chalk-dry and spar spire
of the Trinitarian Church.

I stand on top
of our back steps and breathe the rich air—
a mother skunk with her column of kittens swills the garbage pail.   45
She jabs her wedge-head in a cup
of sour cream, drops her ostrich tail,
and will not scare.

                                                                        1959

Night Sweat

Work-table, litter, books and standing lamp,
plain things, my stalled equipment, the old broom—
but I am living in a tidied room,
for ten nights now I've felt the creeping damp
float over my pajamas' wilted white . . .   5
Sweet salt embalms me and my head is wet,
everything streams and tells me this is right;
my life's fever is soaking in night sweat—
one life, one writing! But the downward glide
and bias of existing wrings us dry—   10
always inside me is the child who died,
always inside me is his will to die—
one universe, one body . . . in this urn
the animal night sweats of the spirit burn.
Behind me! You! Again I feel the light   15
lighten my leaded eyelids, while the gray
skulled horses whinny for the soot of night.
I dabble in the dapple of the day,
a heap of wet clothes, seamy, shivering,
I see my flesh and bedding washed with light,   20
my child exploding into dynamite,
my wife . . . your lightness alters everything,
and tears the black web from the spider's sack,
as your heart hops and flutters like a hare.
Poor turtle, tortoise, if I cannot clear   25

3. "Which way I fly is Hell, myself am Hell" (Satan in Milton's *Paradise Lost* 4.75).

the surface of these troubled waters here,
absolve me, help me, Dear Heart, as you bear
this world's dead weight and cycle on your back.

1964

For the Union Dead[1]

"Relinquunt Omnia Servare Rem Publicam."[2]

The old South Boston Aquarium stands
in a Sahara of snow now. Its broken windows are boarded.
The bronze weathervane cod has lost half its scales.
The airy tanks are dry.

Once my nose crawled like a snail on the glass;   5
my hand tingled
to burst the bubbles
drifting from the noses of the cowed, compliant fish.

My hand draws back. I often sigh still
for the dark downward and vegetating kingdom   10
of the fish and reptile. One morning last March,
I pressed against the new barbed and galvanized

fence on the Boston Common. Behind their cage,
yellow dinosaur steamshovels were grunting
as they cropped up tons of mush and grass   15
to gouge their underworld garage.

Parking spaces luxuriate like civic
sandpiles in the heart of Boston.
A girdle of orange, Puritan-pumpkin colored girders
braces the tingling Statehouse,   20

shaking over the excavations, as it faces Colonel Shaw
and his bell-cheeked Negro infantry
on St. Gaudens' shaking Civil War relief,
propped by a plank splint against the garage's earthquake.

Two months after marching through Boston,   25
half the regiment was dead;

---

1. First published as "Colonel Shaw and the Massachusetts' 54th" in a paperback edition of *Life Studies* (1960). It became the title poem of *For the Union Dead* (1964).
2. Robert Gould Shaw (1837–1863) led the first all–African American regiment in the Union army during the Civil War. He was killed in the attack against Fort Wagner, South Carolina. A bronze relief by the sculptor Augustus Saint-Gaudens (1848–1897), dedicated in 1897, standing opposite the Massachusetts State House on Boston Common, commemorates the deaths. A Latin inscription on the monument reads *Omnia Reliquit Servare Rem Publicam* ("He leaves all behind to save the Republic"). Lowell's epigraph alters the inscription slightly, changing the third-person singular (*he*) to the third-person plural: "*They* give up everything to save the Republic."

at the dedication
William James[3] could almost hear the bronze Negroes breathe.

Their monument sticks like a fishbone
in the city's throat.   30
Its Colonel is as lean
as a compass-needle.

He has an angry wrenlike vigilance,
a greyhound's gentle tautness;
he seems to wince at pleasure,   35
and suffocate for privacy.

He is out of bounds now. He rejoices in man's lovely,
peculiar power to choose life and die—
when he leads his black soldiers to death,
he cannot bend his back.   40

On a thousand small town New England greens,
the old white churches hold their air
of sparse, sincere rebellion; frayed flags
quilt the graveyards of the Grand Army of the Republic.

The stone statues of the abstract Union Soldier   45
grow slimmer and younger each year—
wasp-waisted, they doze over muskets
and muse through their sideburns . . .

Shaw's father wanted no monument
except the ditch,   50
where his son's body was thrown[4]
and lost with his "niggers."

The ditch is nearer.
There are no statues for the last war[5] here;
on Boylston Street,[6] a commercial photograph   55
shows Hiroshima boiling[7]

over a Mosler Safe, the "Rock of Ages"[8]
that survived the blast. Space is nearer.
When I crouch to my television set,
the drained faces of Negro school-children rise like balloons.[9]   60

Colonel Shaw
is riding on his bubble,
he waits
for the blessed break.

3. Philosopher and psychologist (1842–1910) who taught at Harvard.
4. By the Confederate soldiers at Fort Wagner.
5. World War II.
6. In Boston, where the poem is set.
7. On August 6, 1945, the United States dropped an atomic bomb on this Japanese city.

8. Biblical reference to an indestructible and supernatural rock, the foundation of an everlasting kingdom. Used as an advertising slogan by Mosler Safes.
9. Probably news photographs connected with contemporary civil rights demonstrations to secure desegregation of schools in the South.

The Aquarium is gone. Everywhere,   65
giant finned cars nose forward like fish;
a savage servility
slides by on grease.

                                                    1960, 1964

GWENDOLYN BROOKS
1917–2000

" If there was ever a born poet," the writer Alice Walker once said in an interview, "I think it is Brooks." A passionate sense of language and an often daring use of formal structures are hallmarks of Gwendolyn Brooks's poetry. She used these gifts in a career characterized by dramatic evolution, a career that linked two very different generations of African American poets. "Until 1967," Brooks said, "my own Blackness did not confront me with a shrill spelling of itself." She then grouped herself with militant black writers and defined her work as belonging primarily to the African American community. In her earlier work, however, Brooks followed the example of the older writers of the Harlem Renaissance, Langston Hughes and Countee Cullen among them, who honored the ideal of an integrated society. In that period her work received support largely from white audiences. But Brooks's changing sense of her commitments should not obscure her persistent, underlying concerns. She never lacked political awareness, and in remarkably versatile poems, both early and late, she wrote about black experience and black rage, with a particular awareness of the complex lives of black women.

Brooks was born in Topeka, Kansas; she grew up in Chicago and is closely identified with the energies and problems of its black community. She went to Chicago's Englewood High School and graduated from Wilson Junior College. Brooks remembered writing poetry from the time she was seven and keeping poetry notebooks from the time she was eleven. She got her education in the moderns—poets such as Pound and Eliot—under the guidance of a rich Chicago socialite, Inez Cunningham Stark, who was a reader for *Poetry* magazine and taught a poetry class at the Southside Community Art Center. Her first book, *A Street in Bronzeville* (1945), took its title from the name journalists gave to Chicago's black ghetto. Her poems portrayed the waste and loss that are the inevitable result of what Langston Hughes called the "dream deferred." With her second book of poems, *Annie Allen* (1949), Brooks became the first African American to receive the Pulitzer Prize for poetry.

In *Annie Allen* and in her Bronzeville poems (*Bronzeville Boys and Girls*, 1956, continued the work begun in *A Street in Bronzeville*), Brooks concentrated on portraits of what Hughes called "the ordinary aspects of black life," stressing the vitality and the often subversive morality of ghetto figures. She portrayed the good girls who want to be bad; the bored children of hardworking, pious mothers; the laments of women, some of them mothers, abandoned by their men. Brooks's diction was a combination of street talk, the florid biblical speech of black Protestant preachers, and the traditional vocabulary of English and American verse. She wrote vigorous, strongly accented, and strongly rhymed lines with a great deal of alliteration.

She also cultivated traditional lyric forms; for example, she was one of the few modern poets to write extensively in the sonnet form.

A great change in Brooks's life came at Fisk University in 1967 with the Second Black Writers' Conference, in whose charged activist atmosphere she encountered many of the new young black poets. After this, Brooks tested the possibility of writing poetry exclusively for black audiences. She drew closer to militant political groups as a result of conducting poetry workshops for some members of the Blackstone Rangers, a teenage gang in Chicago. In autobiographical writings such as her prose *Report from Part One* (1972), Brooks became more self-conscious about her own potential role as a leader of black feminists. She left her New York publisher to have her work printed by African American publishers, especially the Broadside Press. Brooks's poetry, too, changed, in both its focus and its technique. Her subjects tended to be more explicitly political and to deal with questions of revolutionary violence and issues of African American identity. Stylistically, her work evolved out of the concentrated imagery and narratives of her earlier writing, with its often formal diction, and moved toward an increased use of the energetic, improvisatory rhythms of jazz, the combinations of African chants, and an emphatically spoken language. The resulting poetry constantly revises itself and its sense of the world, open to change but evoking history. "How does one convey the influence Gwendolyn Brooks has had on generations—not only writers but people from all walks of life?" the poet Rita Dove has remarked, remembering how, as a young woman, she was "struck by these poems . . . that weren't afraid to take language and swamp it, twist it, and engage it so that it shimmered and dashed and lingered."

FROM A STREET IN BRONZEVILLE

to David and Keziah Brooks

kitchenette building

We are things of dry hours and the involuntary plan,
Grayed in, and gray. "Dream" makes a giddy sound, not strong
Like "rent," "feeding a wife," "satisfying a man."

But could a dream send up through onion fumes
Its white and violet, fight with fried potatoes   5
And yesterday's garbage ripening in the hall,
Flutter, or sing an aria down these rooms

Even if we were willing to let it in,
Had time to warm it, keep it very clean,
Anticipate a message, let it begin?   10

We wonder. But not well! not for a minute!
Since Number Five is out of the bathroom now,
We think of lukewarm water, hope to get in it.

1945

the mother

Abortions will not let you forget.
You remember the children you got that you did not get,
The damp small pulps with a little or with no hair,
The singers and workers that never handled the air.
You will never neglect or beat   5
Them, or silence or buy with a sweet.
You will never wind up the sucking-thumb
Or scuttle off ghosts that come.
You will never leave them, controlling your luscious sigh,
Return for a snack of them, with gobbling mother-eye.   10

I have heard in the voices of the wind the voices of my dim
      killed children.
I have contracted. I have eased
My dim dears at the breasts they could never suck.
I have said, Sweets, if I sinned, if I seized
Your luck   15
And your lives from your unfinished reach,
If I stole your births and your names,
Your straight baby tears and your games,
Your stilted or lovely loves, your tumults, your marriages, aches,
      and your deaths,
If I poisoned the beginnings of your breaths,   20
Believe that even in my deliberateness I was not deliberate.
Though why should I whine,
Whine that the crime was other than mine?—
Since anyhow you are dead.
Or rather, or instead,   25
You were never made.

But that too, I am afraid,
Is faulty: oh, what shall I say, how is the truth to be said?
You were born, you had body, you died.
It is just that you never giggled or planned or cried.   30

Believe me, I loved you all.
Believe me, I knew you, though faintly, and I loved, I loved you
All.

                                                                               1945

a song in the front yard

   I've stayed in the front yard all my life.
   I want a peek at the back
   Where it's rough and untended and hungry weed grows.
   A girl gets sick of a rose.

   I want to go in the back yard now   5
   And maybe down the alley,

To where the charity children play.
I want a good time today.

They do some wonderful things.
They have some wonderful fun.   10
My mother sneers, but I say it's fine
How they don't have to go in at quarter to nine.
My mother, she tells me that Johnnie Mae
Will grow up to be a bad woman.
That George'll be taken to Jail soon or late   15
(On account of last winter he sold our back gate.)

But I say it's fine. Honest, I do.
And I'd like to be a bad woman, too,
And wear the brave stockings of night-black lace
And strut down the streets with paint on my face.   20

                                                                    1945

the white troops had their orders but the Negroes looked like men

They had supposed their formula was fixed.
They had obeyed instructions to devise
A type of cold, a type of hooded gaze.
But when the Negroes came they were perplexed.
These Negroes looked like men. Besides, it taxed   5
Time and the temper to remember those
Congenital iniquities that cause
Disfavor of the darkness. Such as boxed
Their feelings properly, complete to tags—
A box for dark men and a box for Other—   10
Would often find the contents had been scrambled.
Or even switched. Who really gave two figs?
Neither the earth nor heaven ever trembled.
And there was nothing startling in the weather.

                                                                    1945

———————

From The Womanhood

The Children of the Poor

II

What shall I give my children? who are poor,
Who are adjudged the leastwise of the land,
Who are my sweetest lepers, who demand

No velvet and no velvety velour;
But who have begged me for a brisk contour,   5
Crying that they are quasi, contraband
Because unfinished, graven by a hand
Less than angelic, admirable or sure.
My hand is stuffed with mode, design, device.
But I lack access to my proper stone.   10
And plenitude of plan shall not suffice
Nor grief nor love shall be enough alone
To ratify my little halves who bear
Across an autumn freezing everywhere.

1949

We Real Cool

THE POOL PLAYERS.
SEVEN AT THE GOLDEN SHOVEL.

We real cool. We
Left school. We

Lurk late. We
Strike straight. We

Sing sin. We   5
Thin gin. We

Jazz June. We
Die soon.

1960

The Bean Eaters

They eat beans mostly, this old yellow pair.
Dinner is a casual affair.
Plain chipware on a plain and creaking wood,
Tin flatware.

Two who are Mostly Good.   5
Two who have lived their day,
But keep on putting on their clothes
And putting things away.

And remembering . . .
Remembering, with twinklings and twinges,   10
As they lean over the beans in their rented back room that is full of beads
    and receipts and dolls and cloths, tobacco crumbs, vases and fringes.

1960

A Bronzeville Mother Loiters in Mississippi. Meanwhile a Mississippi Mother Burns Bacon

From the first it had been like a
Ballad. It had the beat inevitable. It had the blood.
A wildness cut up, and tied in little bunches,
Like the four-line stanzas of the ballads she had never quite
Understood—the ballads they had set her to, in school.   5

Herself: the milk-white maid, the "maid mild"
Of the ballad. Pursued
By the Dark Villain. Rescued by the Fine Prince.
The Happiness-Ever-After.
That was worth anything.   10
It was good to be a "maid mild."
That made the breath go fast.

Her bacon burned. She
Hastened to hide it in the step-on can, and
Drew more strips from the meat case. The eggs and sour-milk biscuits   15
Did well. She set out a jar
Of her new quince preserve.

. . . But there was a something about the matter of the Dark Villain.
He should have been older, perhaps.
The hacking down of a villain was more fun to think about   20
When his menace possessed undisputed breadth, undisputed height,
And a harsh kind of vice.
And best of all, when his history was cluttered
With the bones of many eaten knights and princesses.

The fun was disturbed, then all but nullified   25
When the Dark Villain was a blackish child
Of fourteen, with eyes still too young to be dirty,
And a mouth too young to have lost every reminder
Of its infant softness.

That boy must have been surprised! For   30
These were grown-ups. Grown-ups were supposed to be wise.
And the Fine Prince—and that other—so tall, so broad, so
Grown! Perhaps the boy had never guessed
That the trouble with grown-ups was that under the magnificent shell of
    adulthood, just under,
Waited the baby full of tantrums.   35

It occurred to her that there may have been something
Ridiculous in the picture of the Fine Prince
Rushing (rich with the breadth and height and
Mature solidness whose lack, in the Dark Villain, was impressing her,
Confronting her more and more as this first day after the trial   40
And acquittal wore on) rushing

With his heavy companion to hack down (unhorsed)
That little foe.
So much had happened, she could not remember now what that foe had done
Against her, or if anything had been done.   45
The one thing in the world that she did know and knew
With terrifying clarity was that her composition
Had disintegrated. That, although the pattern prevailed,
The breaks were everywhere. That she could think
Of no thread capable of the necessary   50
Sew-work.

She made the babies sit in their places at the table.
Then, before calling Him, she hurried
To the mirror with her comb and lipstick. It was necessary
To be more beautiful than ever.   55
The beautiful wife.
For sometimes she fancied he looked at her as though
Measuring her. As if he considered, Had she been worth It?

Had *she* been worth the blood, the cramped cries, the little stuttering
    bravado,
The gradual dulling of those Negro eyes,   60
The sudden, overwhelming *little-boyness* in that barn?
Whatever she might feel or half-feel, the lipstick necessity was something
    apart. He must never conclude
That she had not been worth It.

He sat down, the Fine Prince, and
Began buttering a biscuit. He looked at his hands.   65
He twisted in his chair, he scratched his nose.
He glanced again, almost secretly, at his hands.
More papers were in from the North, he mumbled. More meddling
    headlines.
With their pepper-words, "bestiality," and "barbarism," and
"Shocking."   70
The half-sneers he had mastered for the trial worked across
His sweet and pretty face.

What he'd like to do, he explained, was kill them all.
The time lost. The unwanted fame.
Still, it had been fun to show those intruders   75
A thing or two. To show that snappy-eyed mother,
That sassy, Northern, brown-black——

Nothing could stop Mississippi.
He knew that. Big Fella
Knew that.   80
And, what was so good, Mississippi knew that.
Nothing and nothing could stop Mississippi.
They could send in their petitions, and scar
Their newspapers with bleeding headlines. Their governors
Could appeal to Washington. . . .   85

"What I want," the older baby said, "is 'lasses on my jam."
Whereupon the younger baby
Picked up the molasses pitcher and threw
The molasses in his brother's face. Instantly
The Fine Prince leaned across the table and slapped   90
The small and smiling criminal.

She did not speak. When the Hand
Came down and away, and she could look at her child,
At her baby-child,
She could think only of blood.   95
Surely her baby's cheek
Had disappeared, and in its place, surely,
Hung a heaviness, a lengthening red, a red that had no end.
She shook her head. It was not true, of course.
It was not true at all. The   100
Child's face was as always, the
Color of the paste in her paste-jar.

She left the table, to the tune of the children's lamentations, which were
     shriller
Than ever. She
Looked out of a window. She said not a word. *That*   105
Was one of the new Somethings—
The fear,
Tying her as with iron.

Suddenly she felt his hands upon her. He had followed her
To the window. The children were whimpering now.   110
Such bits of tots. And she, their mother,
Could not protect them. She looked at her shoulders, still
Gripped in the claim of his hands. She tried, but could not resist the idea
That a red ooze was seeping, spreading darkly, thickly, slowly,
Over her white shoulders, her own shoulders,   115
And over all of Earth and Mars.

He whispered something to her, did the Fine Prince, something
About love, something about love and night and intention.

She heard no hoof-beat of the horse and saw no flash of the shining steel.
He pulled her face around to meet   120
His, and there it was, close close,
For the first time in all those days and nights,
His mouth, wet and red,
So very, very, very red,
Closed over hers.   125

Then a sickness heaved within her. The courtroom Coca-Cola,
The courtroom beer and hate and sweat and drone,
Pushed like a wall against her. She wanted to bear it.
But his mouth would not go away and neither would the
Decapitated exclamation points in that Other Woman's eyes.   130

She did not scream.
She stood there.
But a hatred for him burst into glorious flower,
And its perfume enclasped them—big,
Bigger than all magnolias.   135

The last bleak news of the ballad.
The rest of the rugged music.
The last quatrain.

                                                                    1960

The Last Quatrain of the Ballad of Emmett Till[1]

> after the murder,
> after the burial

Emmett's mother is a pretty-faced thing;
      the tint of pulled taffy.
She sits in a red room,   5
      drinking black coffee.
She kisses her killed boy.
      And she is sorry.
Chaos in windy grays
      through a red prairie.   10

                                                                    1960

The Blackstone Rangers[1]

I. As Seen by Disciplines[2]

There they are.
Thirty at the corner.
Black, raw, ready.
Sores in the city
that do not want to heal.   5

II. The Leaders

Jeff. Gene. Geronimo. And Bop.
They cancel, cure and curry.
Hardly the dupes of the downtown thing
the cold bonbon,
the rhinestone thing. And hardly   10
in a hurry.

1. A fourteen-year-old African American boy lynched in Mississippi in 1955 for allegedly "leering" at a white woman.

1. A tough Chicago street gang. Blackstone Street is the eastern boundary of Chicago's black ghetto.
2. I.e., law enforcers.

Hardly Belafonte, King,
Black Jesus, Stokely, Malcolm X or Rap.[3]
Bungled trophies.
Their country is a Nation on no map.   15

Jeff, Gene, Geronimo and Bop
in the passionate noon,
in bewitching night
are the detailed men, the copious men.
They curry, cure,   20
they cancel, cancelled images whose Concerts
are not divine, vivacious; the different tins
are intense last entries; pagan argument;
translations of the night.

The Blackstone bitter bureaus   25
(bureaucracy is footloose) edit, fuse
unfashionable damnations and descent;
and exulting, monstrous hand on monstrous hand,
construct, strangely, a monstrous pearl or grace.

III. Gang Girls

A RANGERETTE

Gang Girls are sweet exotics.   30
Mary Ann
uses the nutrients of her orient,
but sometimes sighs for Cities of blue and jewel
beyond her Ranger rim of Cottage Grove.[4]
(Bowery Boys, Disciples, Whip-Birds will   35
dissolve no margins, stop no savory sanctities.)

Mary is
a rose in a whiskey glass.

Mary's
Februaries shudder and are gone. Aprils   40
fret frankly, lilac hurries on.
Summer is a hard irregular ridge.
October looks away.
And that's the Year!

3. "Belafonte": Harold George Belafonte (b. 1927), Jamaican American musician, actor, and social activist, who popularized the Caribbean musical style and has advocated for civil rights and humanitarian causes throughout his career. "King": Martin Luther King Jr. (1929–1968), Baptist pastor, one of the most prominent civil rights activists of the 1950s and 1960s. He followed a philosophy of nonviolence and led nonviolent demonstrations against segregation and injustice. He was also a gifted and eloquent orator on the subject of civil rights. "Black Jesus": one representation of Jesus, generally accepted by the black Christian community in Africa. "Stokely":

Stokely Carmichael (1941–1998), Trinidadian American black activist, leader of the Student Nonviolent Coordinating Committee (SNCC) and the Black Panthers. He urged African Americans to form and lead their own organizations and to reject the values and cultural mores of American society. "Malcolm X": born Malcolm Little (1925–1965), also known as Malik El-Shabazz, a Black Muslim minister, a national spokesman for the Nation of Islam, and one of the most prominent black nationalist leaders in the United States. He advocated black pride, economic self-reliance, and identity politics.
4. Street of overcrowded tenements in the ghetto.

    Save for her bugle-love.   45
Save for the bleat of not-obese devotion.
Save for Somebody Terribly Dying, under
the philanthropy of robins. Save for her Ranger
bringing
an amount of rainbow in a string-drawn bag.   50
"Where did you get the diamond?" Do not ask:
but swallow, straight, the spirals of his flask
and assist him at your zipper; pet his lips
and help him clutch you.

Love's another departure.   55
Will there be any arrivals, confirmations?
Will there be gleaning?

Mary, the Shakedancer's child
from the rooming-flat, pants carefully, peers at
her laboring lover. . . .   60
    Mary! Mary Ann!
Settle for sandwiches! settle for stocking caps!
for sudden blood, aborted carnival,
the props and niceties of non-loneliness—
the rhymes of Leaning.   65

                1968

To the Diaspora[1]

you did not know you were Afrika

When you set out for Afrika
you did not know you were going.
Because
you did not know you were Afrika.
You did not know the Black continent   5
that had to be reached
was you.

I could not have told you then that some sun
would come,
somewhere over the road,   10
would come evoking the diamonds
of you, the Black continent—
somewhere over the road.
You would not have believed my mouth.

When I told you, meeting you somewhere close   15
to the heat and youth of the road,
liking my loyalty, liking belief,
you smiled and you thanked me but very little believed me.

---

1. People settled far from their ancestral homelands.

Here is some sun. Some.
Now off into the places rough to reach.   20
Though dry, though drowsy, all unwillingly a-wobble,
into the dissonant and dangerous crescendo.
Your work, that was done, to be done to be done to be done.

1981

PATRICIA HIGHSMITH
1921–1995

Patricia Highsmith's career is connected to the most popular entertainments of the late twentieth century. Born in 1921 in Fort Worth, Texas, Highsmith worked in a comic book studio during World War II, writing heroic, jingoistic comic books with titles like "The Destroyer" and "The Fighting Yank." The influences of comics, crime and detective fiction, science fiction, horror, and Hollywood film are all palpable in her work, even as she consistently invoked such canonical European writers as Fyodor Dostoyevsky and André Gide when discussing her primary influences. The premise of one of her most famous novels, *The Talented Mr. Ripley* (1955), was inspired by Henry James's great novel *The Ambassadors* (1903), which features a naïve American man sent to retrieve the scion of a wealthy American family who has fallen prey to the seductions of Europe. Highsmith won prizes for detective and crime fiction throughout her life, in both Europe and America, but more traditional literary honors were elusive.

Highsmith's blend of the popular and the highbrow, of the visceral and the intellectual, distinguishes her work and has startled readers for over half a century. She died in 1995, just days before the publication of her thirtieth work of fiction. She had also written, in 1966, a handbook for writing suspense stories, and two additional story collections were published in the years following her death. Because Highsmith deftly combined the suspense plots of genre fiction with knotty philosophical questions and unforgettable characters, her work found a natural outlet in the movies. Her first novel, *Strangers on a Train* (1950), was adapted by Alfred Hitchcock in 1951. Later film adaptations of *The Talented Mr. Ripley* (in France in 1960 and in the United States in 1999) and *The Price of Salt* (1952; adapted as *Carol* in 2015) have helped to keep Highsmith's fiction steadily in front of audiences.

Highsmith's most famous work—the five-novel Ripley series that began with *The Talented Mr. Ripley* and ended with *Ripley Under Water* (1991)—dared readers to sympathize with Tom Ripley, murderer of his rich friend, Dickie Greenleaf. Tom impersonates Greenleaf for a time after the murder, eventually taking over Dickie's clothes, possessions, relationships, and trust fund. Inheriting Dickie's money, Tom reverts to his own identity and goes on to lead a life of wealth and intrigue in subsequent novels. Readers found themselves rooting for Tom to succeed as Highsmith skillfully drew on class resentments, the dynamics of homophobia and homoerotic attraction, and the American tradition of the self-made man to craft her unlikely hero. As recent criticism points out, readers could understand Ripley as deviating from a 1950s repressive society, but in his materialism and upper-class strivings, they could also think of him as a model American citizen. Highsmith so identified with Tom Ripley that she would sign letters "Pat H, alias Ripley," and said that she often had the feeling that Ripley was writing the novels and she was "merely typing" them.

Murder and eroticism were linked in Highsmith's mind: "Murder is a kind of making love, a kind of possessing," she wrote in her journal, reflecting upon a woman she became attracted to while working at Bloomingdale's. That attraction inspired Highsmith's other major literary accomplishment: the novel *The Price of Salt*, published under the pseudonym Claire Morgan. The novel is widely regarded as the first lesbian love story with a happy ending. In it, the young protagonist, Therese, a set designer, meets Carol, a beautiful and married older woman. The experienced Carol seduces Therese, Therese subsequently leaves her fiancé, and the two women set out on a road trip, followed by a private detective hired by Carol's husband. Carol faces the agonizing choice of abandoning Therese or giving up her child in divorce proceedings. Carol eventually chooses Therese, and they live happily together in an apartment in New York City.

In her short fiction, Highsmith explored human relationships with animals, a theme that drives "The Quest for *Blank Claveringi*," the story reprinted here, in which an aging scientist seeks to crown his life's work by documenting and then naming after himself a species of giant snails. The story is typical Highsmith in that she was particularly attracted to animals that were not usual human companions. In the 1960s, she kept a collection of over 300 beloved snails, pets she would bring out at dinner parties to slither around the table. In many stories, especially those contained in *The Animal-Lover's Book of Beastly Murder* (1975), she imagined animals of all kinds taking violent revenge on human beings for acts of abuse. Highsmith's ability—and willingness—to enter into the minds of creatures operating far from human social norms (whether those creatures were mammal, reptile, human, or otherwise) makes her fiction both daring and strange, reminding us of the work of writers such as Franz Kafka, who famously imagined a man transformed into a dung beetle, or the playwright Eugene Ionesco, who in 1959 staged a play in which the inhabitants of a French town turn into rhinoceroses.

Highsmith moved to Europe permanently in 1963 to be near women who were romantically important to her; her work has been much appreciated there. Late in her life, her fiction reflected the topics of her times—including the Israeli-Arab conflict, fundamentalist Christianity, and the AIDS crisis. She became increasingly and publicly anti-Semitic as she aged, losing some of her public admiration as a consequence. Today her reputation stands on the unique qualities and literary strength of her first two decades as a writer. Her fiction brings news of humanity's darkest, strangest, and most fundamental elements.

The Quest for *Blank Claveringi*

Avery Clavering, a professor of zoology at a California university, heard of the giant snails of Kuwa in a footnote of a book on molluscs. His sabbatical had been coming up in three months when he read the few lines:

> It is said by Matusas Islands natives that snails even larger than this exist on the uninhabited island of Kuwa, twenty-five miles distant from the Matusas. The Matusans claim that these snails have a shell diameter of twenty feet and that they are man-eating. Dr. Wm. J. Stead, now living in the Matusas, visited Kuwa in 1949 without finding any snails at all, but the legend persists.

The item aroused Professor Clavering's interest, because he very much wanted to discover some animal, bird, reptile or even mollusc to which he could give his name. *Something-or-other Claveringi.*[1] The professor was forty-eight. His time, perhaps, was not growing short, but he had achieved no particular renown. The discovery of a new species would win him immortality in his field.

The Matusas, the professor saw on a map, were three small islands arranged like the points of an isosceles triangle not far from Hawaii. He wrote a letter to Dr. Stead and received the following reply, written on an abominable typewriter, so many words pale, he could scarcely read it:

> April 8th, 19—
>
> Dear Professor Clavering:
> I have long heard of the giant snails of Kuwa, but before you make a trip of such length, I must tell you that the natives here assure me a group of them went about twenty years ago to Kuwa to exterminate these so-called man-eating snails which they imagined could swim the ocean between Kuwa and the Matusas and do some damage to the latter islands. They claim to have killed off the whole community of them except for one old fellow they could not kill. This is typical of native stories—there's always one that got away. I haven't much doubt the snails were no bigger than three feet across and that they were not * * * * (here a word was illegible, due both to the pale ribbon and a squashed insect). You say you read of my effort in 1949 to find the giant snails. What the footnote did not say is that I have made several trips since to find them. I retired to the Matusas, in fact, for that purpose. I now believe the snails to be mere folklore, a figment of the natives' imagination. If I were you, I would not waste time or money on an expedition.
>
> Yours sincerely,
> Wm. J. Stead, M.D.

Professor Clavering had the money and the time. He detected a sourness in Dr. Stead's letter. Maybe Dr. Stead had just had bad luck. By post, Professor Clavering hired a thirty-foot sailboat with an auxiliary motor from Hawaii. He wanted to make the trip alone from the Matusas. *Blank Claveringi.* Regardless of the size, the snail was apt to be different from any known snail, because of its isolation—if it existed. He planned to go one month ahead of his wife and to join her and their twenty-year-old daughter Wanda in Hawaii for a more orthodox holiday after he had visited Kuwa. A month would give him plenty of time to find the snail, even if there were only one, to take photographs, and make notes.

It was late June when Professor Clavering, equipped with water tanks, tinned beef, soup and milk, biscuits, writing materials, camera, knife,

1. In scientific naming (called "binomial nomenclature"), each species of animal is given two Latin names, designating first the genus, or group, to which an animal belongs, and, second, the animal's particular species. Species may be named after the person who first records the animal's existence in modern scientific classification. In this case, the person's name is given a Latin ending. Prof. Clavering does not know the genus to which a giant snail may belong ("*Something-or-other*"), but he plans to name the species after himself, "*Claveringi.*"

hatchet, and a Winchester .22² which he hardly knew how to use, set forth from one of the Matusas bound for Kuwa. Dr. Stead, who had been his host for a few days, saw him off. Dr. Stead was seventy-five, he said, but he looked older, due perhaps to the ravages of drink and the apparently aimless life he led now. He had not looked for the giant snail in two years, he said.

"I've given the last third of my life to looking for this snail, you might say," Dr Stead added. "But that's man's fate, I suppose, the pursuit of the non-existent. Well—good luck to you, Professor Clavering!" He waved his old American straw hat as the *Samantha* left the dock under motor power.

Professor Clavering had made out to Stead that if he did find snails, he would come back at once, get some natives to accompany him, and return to Kuwa with materials to make crates for the snails. Stead had expressed doubt whether he could persuade any natives to accompany him, if the snail or snails were really large. But then, Dr. Stead had been negative about everything pertaining to Professor Clavering's quest. Professor Clavering was glad to get away from him.

After about an hour, Professor Clavering cut the motor and tentatively hoisted some sail. The wind was favorable, but he knew little about sails, and he paid close attention to his compass. At last, Kuwa came into view, a tan hump on a sea of blue. He was quite close before he saw any greenery, and this was only the tops of some trees. Already, he was looking for anything resembling a giant snail, and regretting he had not brought binoculars, but the island was only three miles long and one mile broad. He decided to aim for a small beach. He dropped anchor, two of them, in water so clear he could see the sand under it. He stood for a few minutes on the deck.

The only life he saw was a few birds in the tops of trees, brightly colored, crested birds, making cries he had never heard before. There was no low-lying vegetation whatsoever, none of the grass and reeds that might have been expected on an island such as this—much like the Matusas in soil color—and this augured well of the presence of snails that might have devoured everything green within their reach. It was only a quarter to two. Professor Clavering ate part of a papaya, two boiled eggs, and brewed coffee on his alcohol burner, as he had had nothing to eat since 6 a.m. Then with his hunting knife and hatchet in the belt of his khaki shorts, and his camera around his neck, he lowered himself into the water. The *Samantha* carried no rowboat.

He sank up to his neck, but he could walk on the bottom. He held the camera high. He emerged panting, as he was some twenty pounds over-weight. Professor Clavering was to regret every one of those pounds before the day was over, but as he got his breath and looked around him, and felt himself drying off in the warm sunlight, he was happy. He wiped his hatchet and knife with dry sand, then walked inland, alert for the rounded form of a snail's shell, moving or stationary, anywhere. But as snails were more or less noctur-nal, he thought any snails might well be sleeping in some cave or crevice with no idea of emerging until nightfall.

He decided to cross the island first, then follow the coast to right or left and circle the island. He had not gone a quarter of a mile, when his heart

2. A small-bore rifle used largely for target shooting and small game.

gave a leap. Ten yards before him, he saw three bent saplings with their top leaves chewed off. The young trees were four inches in diameter at their bases. It would have taken a considerable weight to bend them down, something like a hundred pounds. The professor looked on the trees and the ground for the glaze left by snails, but found none. But rain could have washed it away. A snail whose shell was three feet in diameter would not weigh enough to bend such a tree, so Professor Clavering now hoped for something bigger. He pushed on.

He arrived at the other side of the island. The sea had eaten a notch into the shore, forming a mostly dry gulley of a hundred yards' length and a depth of thirty feet. The land here was sandy but moist, and there was, he saw, a little vegetation in the form of patchy grass. But here, the lower branches of all the trees had been divested of their leaves, and so long ago that the branches had dried and fallen off. All this bespoke the presence of land snails. Professor Clavering stooped and looked down into the gulley. He saw, just over the edge of his side of the crevice, the pink-tan curve of something that was neither rock nor sand. If it was a snail, it was monstrous. Involuntarily, he took a step backward, scattering pebbles down the gulley.

The professor ran round the gulley to have a better look. It was a snail, and its shell was about fifteen feet high. He had a view of its left side, the side without the spiral. It resembled a peach-colored sail filled with wind, and the sunlight made nacreous,[3] silvery patches gleam and twinkle as the great thing stirred. The little rain of pebbles had aroused it, the professor realized. If the shell was fifteen or eighteen feet in diameter, he reckoned that the snail's body or foot would be something like six yards long when extended. Rooted to the spot, the professor stood, thrilled as much by the (as yet) empty phrase *Blank Claveringi* which throbbed in his head as by the fact he was looking upon something no man had seen before, or at least no scientist. The crate would have to be bigger than he had thought, but the *Samantha* would be capable of taking it on her forward deck.

The snail was backing to pull its head from the narrow part of the gulley. The moist body, the color of tea with milk, came into view with the slowness of an enormous snake awakening from slumber. All was silent, except for pebbles dropping from the snail's underside as it lifted its head, except for the professor's constrained breathing. The snail's head, facing inland, rose higher and higher, and its antennae, with which it saw, began to extend. Professor Clavering realized he had disturbed it from its diurnal sleep, and a brief terror caused him to retreat again, sending more pebbles down the slope.

The snail heard this, and slowly turned its enormous head toward him.

The professor felt paralyzed. A gigantic face regarded him, a face with drooping, scalloped cheeks or lips, with antennae six feet long now, the eyes on the ends of them scrutinizing him at his own level and scarcely ten feet away, with the disdain of a Herculean lorgnette,[4] with the unknown potency of a pair of oversized telescopes. The snail reared so high, it had to arch its

---

3. Resembling the iridescent coating from which pearls are formed and that lines the inside of shells.
4. Of the size of the Greek hero, Hercules, renowned for his strength. A lorgnette is a pair of glasses or opera glasses held in front of the eyes by a long side handle.

antennae to keep him in view. Six yards long? It would be more like eight or ten yards. The snail turned itself to move toward him.

Still, the professor did not budge. He knew about snails' teeth, the twenty-odd thousand pairs of them even in a small garden snail, set in comblike structures, the upper front teeth visible, moving up and down constantly just under transparent flesh. A snail of this size, with proportionate teeth, could chew through a tree as quickly as a woodsman's axe, the professor thought. The snail was advancing up the bank with monumental confidence. He had to stand still for a few seconds simply to admire it. *His* snail! The professor opened his camera and took a picture, just as the snail was hauling its shell over the edge of the quarry.

"You are magnificent!" Professor Clavering said in a soft and awestruck voice. Then he took a few steps backward.

It was pleasant to think he could skip nimbly about, comparatively speaking, observing the snail from all angles, while the snail could only creep toward him at what seemed the rate of one yard in ten seconds. The professor thought to watch the snail for an hour or so, then go back to the *Samantha* and write some notes. He would sleep aboard the boat, take some more photographs tomorrow morning, then start under engine power back to the Matusas. He trotted for twenty yards, then turned to watch the snail approach.

The snail travelled with its head lifted three feet above the ground, keeping the professor in the focus of its eyes. It was moving faster. Professor Clavering retreated sooner than he intended, and before he could get another picture.

Now Professor Clavering looked around for a mate of the snail. He was rather glad not to see another snail, but he cautioned himself not to rule out the possibility of a mate. It wouldn't be pleasant to be cornered by two snails, yet the idea excited him. Impossible to think of a situation in which he could not escape from two slow, lumbering creatures like the—the what? *Amygdalus Persica* (his mind stuck on peaches, because of the beautiful color of the shell) *Carnivora*[5] (perhaps) *Claveringi*. That could be improved upon, the professor thought as he walked backward, watching.

A little grove of trees gave him an idea. If he stood in the grove, the snail could not reach him, and he would also have a close view. The professor took a stand amid twelve or fifteen trees, all about twenty feet high. The snail did not slacken its speed, but began to circle the grove, still watching the professor. Finding no opening big enough between two trees, the snail raised its head higher, fifteen feet high, and began to creep up on the trees. Branches cracked, and one tree snapped.

Professor Clavering ducked and retreated. He had a glimpse of a great belly gliding unhurt over a jagged tree trunk, of a circular mouth two feet across, open and showing the still wider upper band of teeth like shark's teeth, munching automatically up and down. The snail cruised gently down over the tree tops, some of which sprang back into position as the snail's weight left them.

Click! went the professor's camera.

5. The genus comprising carnivores, or meat-eaters. *"Amygdalus Persica"*: scientific name for the peach tree.

What a sight that had been! Something like a slow hurdle. He imagined entertaining friends with an account of it, substantiated by the photograph, once he got back to California. Old Professor McIlroy of the biology department had laughed at him for spending seven thousand dollars on an effort he predicted would be futile!

Professor Clavering was tiring, so he cut directly for the *Samantha*. He noticed that the snail veered also in a direction that would intercept him, if they kept on at their steady though different speeds, and the professor chuckled and trotted for a bit. The snail also picked up speed, and the professor remembered the wide, upward rippling of the snail's body as it had hurdled the trees. It would be interesting to see how fast the snail could go on a straight course. Such a test would have to wait for America.

He reached the water and saw his beach a few yards away to his right, but no ship was there. He'd made a mistake, he thought, and his beach was on the other side of the island. Then he caught sight of the *Samantha* half a mile out on the ocean, drifting away.

'Damn!' Professor Clavering said aloud. He'd done something wrong with the anchors. Did he dare try to swim to it? The distance frightened him, and it was growing wider every moment.

A rattle of pebbles behind him made him turn. The snail was hardly twenty feet away.

The professor trotted down toward the beach. There was bound to be some slit on the coast, a cave however small, where he could be out of reach of the snail. He wanted to rest for a while. What really annoyed him now was the prospect of a chilly night without blankets or food. The Matusas natives had been right: there was nothing to eat on Kuwa.

Professor Clavering stopped dead, his shoes sliding on sand and pebbles. Before him, not fifty feet away on the beach, was another snail as big as the one following him, and somewhat lighter in colour. Its tail was in the sea, and its muzzle dripped water as it reared itself to get a look at him.

It was this snail, the professor realized, that had chewed through the hemp ropes and let the boat go free. Was there something about new hemp ropes that appealed to snails? This question he put out of his mind for the nonce. He had a snail before and behind him. The professor trotted on along the shore. The only crevice of shelter he was sure existed was the gulley on the other side of the island. He forced himself to walk at a moderate pace for a while, to breathe normally, then he sat down and treated himself to a rest.

The first snail was the first to appear, and as it had lost sight of him, it lifted its head and looked slowly to right and left, though without slackening its progress. The professor sat motionless, bare head lowered, hoping the snail would not see him. But he was not that lucky. The snail saw him and altered its course to a straight line for him. Behind it came the second snail—its wife? its husband?—the professor could not tell and there was no way of telling.

Professor Clavering had to leave his resting place. The weight of his hatchet reminded him that he at least had a weapon. A good scare, he thought, a minor wound might discourage them. He knew they were hungry, that their teeth could tear his flesh more easily than they tore trees, and that alive or dead, he would be eaten by these snails if he permitted it to happen. He drew his hatchet and faced them, conscious that he cut a not very formidable figure with his slight paunch, his pale, skinny legs, his height of five feet seven, about a third the snails' height, but his brows above his glasses were set with a determination to defend his life.

The first snail reared when it was ten feet away. The professor advanced and swung the hatchet at the projecting mantle on the snail's left side. He had not dared get close enough, his aim was inches short, and the weight of the hatchet pulled the professor off balance. He staggered and fell under the raised muzzle, and had just time to roll himself from under the descending mouth before it touched the ground where he had been. Angry now, he circled the snail and swung a blow at the nacreous shell, which turned the blade. The hatchet took an inch-deep chip, but nothing more. The professor swung again, higher this time and in the center of the shell's posterior, trying for the lung valve beneath, but the valve was still higher, he knew, ten feet from the ground, and once more his hatchet took only a chip. The snail began to turn itself to face him.

The professor then confronted the second snail, rushed at it and swung the hatchet, cutting it in the cheek. The hatchet sank up to its wooden handle, and he had to tug to get it out, and then had to run a few yards, as the snail put on speed and reared its head for a biting attack. Glancing back, the professor saw that no liquid (he had not, of course, expected blood) came from the cut in the snail's cheek, and in fact he couldn't see the cut. And the blow had certainly been no discouragement to the snail's advance.

Professor Clavering began to walk at a sensible pace straight for the snails' lair on the other side of the island. By the time he scrambled down the side of the gulley, he was winded and his legs hurt. But he saw to his relief that the gulley narrowed to a sharp V. Wedged in that, he would be safe. Professor Clavering started into the V, which had an overhanging top rather like a cave, when he saw that what he had taken for some rounded rocks were moving—at least some of them were. They were baby snails! They were larger than good-sized beach balls. And the professor saw, from the way a couple of them were devouring grass blades, that they were hungry.

A snail's head appeared high on his left. The giant parent snail began to descend the gulley. A crepitation,[6] a pair of antennae against the sky on his right, heralded the arrival of the second snail. He had nowhere to turn except the sea, which was not a bad idea, he thought, as these were land snails. The professor waded out and turned left, walking waist-deep in water. It was slow going, and a snail was coming after him. He got closer to the land and ran in thigh-deep water.

The first snail, the darker one, entered the water boldly and crept along in a depth of several inches, showing signs of being willing to go into deeper water when it got abreast of Professor Clavering. The professor hoped the other snail, maybe the mother, had stayed with the young. But it hadn't. It was following along the land, and accelerating. The professor plunged wildly for the shore where he would be able to move faster.

Now, thank goodness, he saw rocks. Great igneous masses of rocks covered a sloping hill down to the sea. There was bound to be a niche, some place there where he could take shelter. The sun was sinking into the ocean,

6. A crackling sound.

it would be dark soon, and there was no moon, he knew. The professor was thirsty. When he reached the rocks, he flung himself like a corpse into a trough made by four or five scratchy boulders, which caused him to lie in a curve. The rocks rose two feet above his body, and the trough was hardly a foot wide. A snail couldn't, he reasoned, stick its head down here and bite him.

The peachy curves of the snails' shells appeared, and one, the second, drew closer.

'I'll strike it with my hatchet if it comes!' the professor swore to himself. 'I'll cut its face to ribbons with my knife!' He was now reconciled to killing both adults, because he could take back a pair of the young ones, and in fact more easily because they were smaller.

The snail seemed to sniff like a dog, though inaudibly, as its muzzle hovered over the professor's hiding place. Then with majestic calm it came down on the rocks between which the professor lay. Its slimy foot covered the aperture and within seconds had blocked out almost all the light.

Professor Clavering drew his hunting knife in anger and panic, and plunged it several times into the snail's soft flesh. The snail seemed not even to wince. A few seconds later, it stopped moving, though the professor knew that it was not only not dead, as the stabs hadn't touched any vital organs, but that it had fastened itself over his trench in the firmest possible way. No slit of light showed. The professor was only grateful that the irregularity of the rocks must afford a supply of air. Now he pressed frantically with his palms against the snail's body, and felt his hands slip and scrape against rock. The firmness of the snail, his inability to budge it, made him feel slightly sick for a moment.

An hour passed. The professor almost slept, but the experience was more like a prolonged hallucination. He dreamed, or feared, that he was being chewed by twenty thousand pairs of teeth into a heap of mince,[7] which the two giant snails shared with their offspring. To add to his misery, he was cold and hungry. The snail's body gave no warmth, and was even cool.

Some hours later, the professor awoke and saw stars above him. The snail had departed. It was pitch dark. He stood up cautiously, trying not to make a sound, and stepped out of the crevice. He was free! On a sandy stretch of beach a few yards away, Professor Clavering lay down, pressed against a vertical face of rock. Here he slept the remaining hours until dawn.

He awakened just in time, and perhaps not the dawn but a sixth sense had awakened him. The first snail was coming toward him and was only ten feet away. The professor got up on trembling legs, and trotted inland, up a slope. An idea came to him: if he could push a boulder of, say, five hundred pounds— possible with a lever—onto an adult snail in the gulley, and smash the spot below which its lung lay, then he could kill it. Otherwise, he could think of no other means at his disposal that could inflict a fatal injury. His gun might, but the gun was on the *Samantha*. He had already estimated that it might be a week, or never, that help would come from the Matusas. The *Samantha* would not necessarily float back to the Matusas, would not necessarily be seen by any other ship for days, and even if it was seen, would it be apparent she was drifting? And if so, would the spotters make a beeline for the Matusas to

7. Ground food, especially meat.

report it? Not necessarily. The professor bent quickly and licked some dew from a leaf. The snails were twenty yards behind him now.

The trouble is, I'm becoming exhausted, he said to himself.

He was even more tired at noon. Only one snail pursued him, but the professor imagined the other resting or eating a tree top, in order to be fresh later. The professor could trot a hundred yards, find a spot to rest in, but he dared not shut his eyes for long, lest he sleep. And he was definitely weak from lack of food.

So the day passed. His idea of dropping a rock down the gulley was thwarted by two factors: the second snail was guarding the gulley now, at the top of its V, and there was no such rock as he needed within a hundred yards.

When dusk came, the professor could not find the hill where the igneous rocks were. Both snails had him in their sight now. His watch said a quarter to seven. Professor Clavering took a deep breath and faced the fact that he must make an attempt to kill one or both snails before dark. Almost without thinking, or planning—he was too spent for that—he chopped down a slender tree and hacked off its branches. The leaves of these branches were devoured by the two snails five minutes after the branches had fallen to the ground. The professor dragged his tree several yards inland, and sharpened one end of it with the hatchet. It was too heavy a weapon for one hand to wield, but in two hands, it made a kind of battering ram, or giant spear.

At once, Professor Clavering turned and attacked, running with the spear pointed slightly upward. He aimed for the first snail's mouth, but struck too low, and the tree end penetrated about four inches into the snail's chest—or the area below its face. No vital organ here, except the long, straight esophagus, which in these giant snails would be set deeper than four inches. He had nothing for his trouble but lacerated hands. His spear hung for a few seconds in the snail's flesh, then fell out onto the ground. The professor retreated, pulling his hatchet from his belt. The second snail, coming up abreast of the other, paused to chew off a few inches of the tree stump, then joined its mate in giving attention to Professor Clavering. There was something contemptuous, something absolutely assured, about the snails' slow progress toward him, as if they were thinking, "Escape us a hundred, a thousand times, we shall finally reach you and devour every trace of you."

The professor advanced once more, circled the snail he had just hit with the tree spear, and swung his hatchet at the rear of its shell. Desperately, he attacked the same spot with five or six direct hits, for now he had a plan. His hacking operation had to be halted, because the second snail was coming up behind him. Its snout and an antenna even brushed the professor's legs moistly and staggered him, before he could step out of its way. Two more hatchet blows the professor got in, and then he stopped, because his right arm hurt. He had by no means gone through the shell, but he had no strength for more effort with the hatchet. He went back for his spear. His target was a small one, but he ran toward it with desperate purpose.

The blow landed. It even broke through.

The professor's hands were further torn, but he was oblivious of them. His success made him as joyous as if he had killed both his enemies, as if a rescue ship with food, water, and a bed were even then sailing into Kuwa's beach.

The snail was twisting and rearing up with pain.

Professor Clavering ran forward, lifted the drooping spear and pushed it with all his might farther into the snail, pointing it upward to go as close as possible to the lung. Whether the snail died soon or not, it was hors de combat,[8] the professor saw. And he himself experienced something like physical collapse an instant after seeing the snail's condition. He was quite incapable of taking on the other snail in the same manner, and the other snail was coming after him. The professor tried to walk in a straight line away from both snails, but he weaved with fatigue and faintness. He looked behind him. The unhurt snail was thirty feet away. The wounded snail faced him, but was motionless, half in and half out of its shell, suffering in silence some agony of asphyxiation. Professor Clavering walked on.

Quite by accident, just as it was growing dark, he came upon his field of rocks. Among them he took shelter for the second time. The snail's snout probed the trench in which he lay, but could not quite reach him. Would it not be better to remain in the trench tomorrow, to hope for rain for water? He fell asleep before he could come to any decision.

Again, when the professor awakened at dawn, the snail had departed. His hands throbbed. Their palms were encrusted with dried blood and sand. He thought it wise to go to the sea and wash them in salt water.

The giant snail lay between him and the sea, and at his approach, the snail very slowly began to creep toward him. Professor Clavering made a wobbling detour and continued on his way toward the water. He dipped his hands and moved them rapidly back and forth, at last lifted water to his face, longed to wet his dry mouth, warned himself that he should not, and yielded anyway, spitting out the water almost at once. Land snails hated salt and could be killed by salt crystals. The professor angrily flung handfuls of water at the snail's face. The snail only lifted its head higher, out of the professor's range. Its form was slender now, and it had, oddly, the grace of a horned gazelle, of some animal of the deer family. The snail lowered its snout, and the professor trudged away, but not quickly enough: the snail came down on his shoulder and the suctorial[9] mouth clamped.

The professor screamed. *My God*, he thought, as a piece of his shirt, a piece of flesh and possibly bone was torn from his left shoulder, *why was I such an ass as to linger?* The snail's weight pushed him under, but it was shallow here, and he struggled to his feet and walked toward the land. Blood streamed hotly down his side. He could not bear to look at his shoulder to see what had happened, and would not have been surprised if his left arm had dropped off in the next instant. The professor walked on aimlessly in shallow water near the land. He was still going faster than the snail.

Then he lifted his eyes to the empty horizon, and saw a dark spot in the water in the mid-distance. He stopped, wondering if it were real or a trick of his eyes: but now he made out the double body of a catamaran,[1] and he thought he saw Dr. Stead's straw hat. They had come from the Matusas!

"Hello!" The professor was shocked at the hoarseness, the feebleness of his voice. Not a chance that he had been heard.

But with hope now, the professor's strength increased. He headed for a little beach—not his beach, a smaller one—and when he got there he stood

---

8. "Out of action" because of injury in battle (French).

9. Adapted for sucking.

1. A boat with two hulls.

in its center, his good arm raised, and shouted, "Dr. *Stead*! This way!—On the beach!" He could definitely see Dr. Stead's hat and four dark heads.

There was no answering shout. Professor Clavering could not tell if they had heard him or not. And the accursed snail was only thirty feet away now! He'd lost his hatchet, he realized. And the camera that had been under water with him was now ruined, and so were the two pictures in it. No matter. He would live.

"*Here!*" he shouted, again lifting his arm.

The natives heard this. Suddenly all heads in the catamaran turned to him.

Dr. Stead pointed to him and gesticulated, and dimly Professor Clavering heard the good doctor urging the boatman to make for the shore. He saw Dr. Stead half stand up in the catamaran.

The natives gave a whoop—at first Professor Clavering thought it a whoop of joy, or of recognition, but almost at once a wild swing of the sail, a splash of a couple of oars, told him that the natives were trying to change their course.

Pebbles crackled. The snail was near. And this of course was what the natives had seen—the giant snail.

"*Please—Here!*" the professor screamed. He plunged again into the water. "*Please!*"

Dr. Stead was trying, that the professor could see. But the natives were rowing, paddling with hands even, and their sail was carrying them obliquely away.

The snail made a splash as it entered the sea. To drown or to be eaten alive? the professor wondered. He was waist-deep when he stumbled, waist-deep but head under when the snail crashed down upon him, and he realized as the thousands of pairs of teeth began to gnaw at his back, that his fate was both to drown and to be chewed to death.

1967, 1970

RICHARD WILBUR
b. 1921

Richard Wilbur was born in New York City and grew up in the country in New Jersey. His father was a painter, and his mother came from a family prominent in journalism. He was educated at Amherst College, where Robert Frost was a frequent guest and teacher, and Wilbur's remarkable gifts as a prosodist often remind us of the older poet. Of the effects of his college years Wilbur says: "Most American poets of my generation were taught to admire the English metaphysical poets of the seventeenth century and such contemporary masters of irony as John Crowe Ransom. We were led by our teachers and by the critics whom we read to feel that the most adequate and convincing poetry is that which accommodates mixed feelings, clashing ideas, and incongruous images." Nevertheless, over his long and varied career he has written in a wide range of forms, including the dramatic monologue.

After graduation and service in the infantry in Italy and France (1943–45), Wilbur returned to study for an M.A. at Harvard, with a firm notion of what he expected to get out of poetry. "My first poems were written in answer to the inner and outer disorders of the Second World War and they helped me . . . to take ahold of raw events and convert them, provisionally, into experience." He reasserted the balance of mind against instinct and violence: "The praiseful, graceful soldier / Shouldn't be fired by his gun." The poised lyrics in *The Beautiful Changes* (1947), including the lovely title poem of that volume, and *Ceremony* (1950) also reclaimed the value of pleasure, defined as an interplay of intelligence with sensuous enjoyment. Whether looking at a real French landscape, as in "Grasse: The Olive Trees," or a French landscape painting, as in "Ceremony," the point was to show the witty shaping power of the mind in nature.

Wilbur prefers strict stanzaic forms and meters; "limitation makes for power: the strength of the genie comes of his being confined in a bottle." In individual lines and the structure of an entire poem, his emphasis is on a civilized balancing of perceptions. "A World without Objects Is a Sensible Emptiness" begins with the "tall camels of the spirit" but qualifies our views of lonely spiritual impulses. The poem summons us back to find visionary truth grasped through sensual experience. "All shining things need to be shaped and borne." Wilbur favors what he has called "a spirituality which is not abstracted, not dissociated and world-renouncing," as is clear from "Love Calls Us to the Things of This World," a hymn of praise to clothes hanging on a laundry line ("Oh, let there be nothing on earth but laundry"). "A good part of my work could, I suppose, be understood as a public quarrel with the aesthetics of Edgar Allan Poe"—presumably with Poe's notion that poetry provided *indefinite* sensations and aspired to the abstract condition of music.

Wilbur was among the first of the younger postwar poets to adopt a style of living and working different from the masters of an earlier generation—from Eliot, an ironic priestlike modernist who lived as a publisher-poet in England, or William Carlos Williams, a doctor in New Jersey, or Wallace Stevens, a remote insurance executive in Connecticut. Wilbur was a teacher-poet and gave frequent readings. Instead of thinking of himself as an alienated artist, he came to characterize himself as a "poet-citizen," part of what he judged a widening community of poets addressing themselves to an audience increasingly responsive to poetry. Wilbur's taste for civilized wit and his metrical skill made him an ideal translator of the seventeenth-century satirical comedies of Molière, *The Misanthrope* (1955) and *Tartuffe* (1963). They are frequently staged, as is the musical version of Voltaire's *Candide* for which Wilbur was one of the collaborating lyricists. Wilbur received the Pulitzer Prize for his volume *Things of This World* (1956) and served as the second poet laureate of the United States in 1987–88. In 1989 he won his second Pulitzer Prize, for his *New and Collected Poems*. Wilbur's *Collected Poems, 1943–2004* appeared in 2004.

The Beautiful Changes

One wading a Fall meadow finds on all sides
The Queen Anne's Lace lying like lilies
On water; it glides
So from the walker, it turns
Dry grass to a lake, as the slightest shade of you   5
Valleys my mind in fabulous blue Lucernes.[1]

1. Lakes having the quality of Switzerland's Lake Lucerne, known for its beauty.

The beautiful changes as a forest is changed
By a chameleon's tuning his skin to it;
As a mantis, arranged
On a green leaf, grows   10
Into it, makes the leaf leafier, and proves
Any greenness is deeper than anyone knows.

Your hands hold roses always in a way that says
They are not only yours; the beautiful changes
In such kind ways,   15
Wishing ever to sunder
Things and things' selves for a second finding, to lose
For a moment all that it touches back to wonder.

                                                        1947

The Death of a Toad

A toad the power mower caught,
Chewed and clipped of a leg, with a hobbling hop has got
To the garden verge, and sanctuaried him
Under the cineraria leaves, in the shade
Of the ashen heartshaped leaves, in a dim,   5
Low, and a final glade.

The rare original heartsblood goes,
Spends on the earthen hide, in the folds and wizenings, flows
In the gutters of the banked and staring eyes. He lies
As still as if he would return to stone,   10
And soundlessly attending, dies
Toward some deep monotone,

Toward misted and ebullient seas
And cooling shores, toward lost Amphibia's emperies.[1]
Day dwindles, drowning, and at length is gone   15
In the wide and antique eyes, which still appear
To watch, across the castrate lawn,
The haggard daylight steer.

                                                        1950

"A World without Objects Is a Sensible Emptiness"[1]

The tall camels of the spirit
Steer for their deserts, passing the last groves loud

---

1. Archaic for "empires." "Amphibia" refers to "double life" and animals who live on water or land.
1. From "Meditation 65," by the English Meta-physical poet Thomas Traherne (c. 1638–1674): "Life without objects is sensible emptiness, and that is a greater misery than death or nothing." ("Sensible" = "palpable to the senses.")

With the sawmill shrill of the locust, to the whole honey of the arid
    Sun. They are slow, proud,

    And move with a stilted stride   5
  To the land of sheer horizon, hunting Traherne's
Sensible emptiness, there where the brain's lantern-slide
    Revels in vast returns.

    O connoisseurs of thirst,
  Beasts of my soul who long to learn to drink   10
Of pure mirage, those prosperous islands are accurst
    That shimmer on the brink

    Of absence; auras, lustres,
  And all shinings need to be shaped and borne.
Think of those painted saints, capped by the early masters   15
    With bright, jauntily-worn

    Aureate plates, or even
  Merry-go-round rings. Turn, O turn
From the fine sleights of the sand, from the long empty oven
    Where flames in flamings burn   20

    Back to the trees arrayed
  In bursts of glare, to the halo-dialing run
Of the country creeks, and the hills' bracken tiaras made
    Gold in the sunken sun,

    Wisely watch for the sight   25
  Of the supernova[2] burgeoning over the barn,
Lampshine blurred in the stream of beasts, the spirit's right
    Oasis, light incarnate.

                                          1950

Love Calls Us to the Things of This World

    The eyes open to a cry of pulleys,
  And spirited from sleep, the astounded soul
  Hangs for a moment bodiless and simple
  As false dawn.
               Outside the open window   5
  The morning air is all awash with angels.

    Some are in bed-sheets, some are in blouses,
  Some are in smocks: but truly there they are.
  Now they are rising together in calm swells

---

2. A scientific term for an exploding star, here associated with the Star of Bethlehem.

Of halcyon[1] feeling, filling whatever they wear 10
With the deep joy of their impersonal breathing;

    Now they are flying in place, conveying
The terrible speed of their omnipresence, moving
And staying like white water; and now of a sudden
They swoon down into so rapt a quiet 15
That nobody seems to be there.
                   The soul shrinks

    From all that it is about to remember,
From the punctual rape of every blessèd day,
And cries, 20
        "Oh, let there be nothing on earth but laundry,
Nothing but rosy hands in the rising steam
And clear dances done in the sight of heaven."

    Yet, as the sun acknowledges
With a warm look the world's hunks and colors, 25
The soul descends once more in bitter love
To accept the waking body, saying now
In a changed voice as the man yawns and rises,

    "Bring them down from their ruddy gallows;
Let there be clean linen for the backs of thieves; 30
Let lovers go fresh and sweet to be undone,
And the heaviest nuns walk in a pure floating
Of dark habits,
            keeping their difficult balance."

                             1956

1. Calm, peaceful. The word originated as the name of a mythological bird anciently fabled to breed at about the time of the winter solstice in a nest floating on the sea, and then to charm the wind and waves so that the sea became especially calm.

JACK KEROUAC
1922–1969

Like many trailblazing writers, Jack Kerouac led a life filled with contradictions. Regarded as a liberator of prose and champion of idiomatic American expression, he did not start learning English until grade school and did not feel comfortable speaking it until he finished high school (his parents were French Canadian, and French was the family's language at home in Lowell, Massachusetts; his given name was "Jean-Louis"). Having won a football scholarship to Columbia University, he rejected the athletic crowd to join the literary innovators gathering at the college neighborhood's popular West End Bar, among them Allen Ginsberg and William S. Burroughs, who would achieve fame as a poet and a novelist, respectively. Not famous himself until the late 1950s, when a wave of interest in the Beat Movement installed him as its unwilling leader, Kerouac rode the crest of the counterculture's growing fascination with Eastern religions, most notably Zen Buddhism, while never rejecting the Catholicism of his childhood. Even adulatory responses to his work risked contradiction. Critics praised his most famous novel, *On the Road* (1957), for its seeming embrace of expansive westward energies reminiscent of America's Manifest Destiny myth, even though the book in fact moves from the West Coast to the East. The final chapter is set in New York City.

Kerouac's ambitions were monumental, but his heavy drinking killed him by age forty-seven. His several marriages, until the last one, ended in annulment, desertion, or divorce. His greatest loyalty as an adult was to his widowed mother, in later years an invalid, for whom he cared until his death. Wartime service in the merchant marine had given Kerouac skills useful during the wanderings that characterized his life; railroad brakeman and forest-fire lookout were among the jobs he took during the late 1940s and early 1950s. Once royalties from *On the Road* could sustain the transient life he preferred, he spent his time visiting friends and writing as inspiration struck. "Home" was a series of addresses in Massachusetts, New York (on Long Island), and Florida, most of them chosen for his mother's convenience.

Kerouac is known for a writing practice he called "spontaneous prose," reminiscent of jazz improvisation in its emphasis on rhythms, inflections, and freewheeling references. A rejection of what he and other Beat writers saw as the overly formal and elite style of the Modernist literary works that then dominated the high-cultural landscape, the practice of spontaneous prose sought to eliminate the gap between thought and word, between experience and voice, between life and art. Asked by his friends Ginsberg and Burroughs in 1953 to explain how he wrote his novel *The Subterraneans* in three days flat, he composed a manifesto called "The Essentials of Spontaneous Prose," which he then taped above his desk. (It was published in the *Black Mountain Review* in 1957.) Among its tenets are these: "No time for poetry but exactly what is"; "Remove literary grammatical and syntactical inhibition"; "Bookmovie is the movie in words, the visual American form." He advocated "not 'selectivity' of expression but following free deviation (association) of mind into limitless blow-on-subject seas of thought, swimming in sea of English with no discipline other than rhythms of rhetorical exhalation and expostulated statement, like a fist coming down on a table with each complete utterance, bang!" After his first book, *The Town and the City* (1950), a social novel in a realistic mode, he composed all his novels in the exuberant form of prose he perfected.

"My work comprises one vast book like [Marcel] Proust's except that my remembrances are written on the run instead of afterwards in a sick bed," Kerouac observes at the start of his novel *Big Sur* (1962), comparing his project to the French modernist Proust's seven-volume *Remembrance of Things Past* (1913–27). Though Kerouac's canon consists of more than a dozen novels published during his lifetime and others recovered from manuscript and issued after his death, the author had seen them as one grand project, the parts of which he intended to revise, integrate, and present to readers as a single massive narrative. Neither writing nor publishing them in the order in which he had conceived their action, Kerouac did not live long enough to begin his intended synthesis. But he named the project "the Duluoz Legend," from the name of his protagonist in *Big Sur* and other works. Central to the legend is Kerouac's close friendship with legendary counterculture and Beat figure Neal Cassady (fictionalized as Dean Moriarity in *On the Road* and as Cody Pomeray in *Visions of Cody*, 1972). Their relationship had been the motivation for both the author's wanderings and his impulsive, sometimes explosive manner of writing.

On the Road, the first and last chapters of which are reprinted here, was written in 1951, though by then Kerouac had been thinking about writing a road novel for several

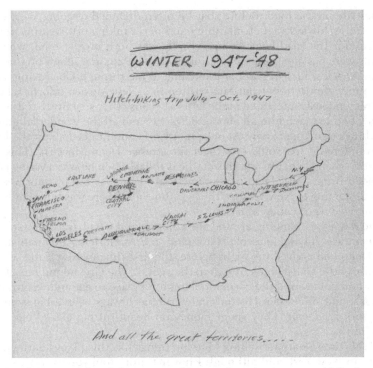

Jack Kerouac's hand-drawn map of his travels in the summer and fall of 1947.

years. He composed much of it on a single scroll of typing paper in a three-week rush fueled by wine, coffee, and Benzedrine. In the opening chapter, the Kerouac figure and narrator, Sal Paradise, describes Dean Moriarty's kinetic speech and the foundations of their remarkable friendship. Readers meet "Carlo Marx," based on Allen Ginsberg; "Old Bull Lee" and "Jane," based on William and Jane Burroughs; and "Elmer Hassel," based on Kerouac's friend from his Columbia days, Herbert Huncke. In the book's final chapter, Sal has returned to New York disillusioned after Dean abandoned him in Mexico, where Sal was broke and suffering from a fever. Dean's too-little, too-late show of friendship—traveling cross-country by bus and hitching rides, apparently just to see Sal for a day or two and meet Sal's new girlfriend—confounds Sal. But for Kerouac, Dean's return leads to the book's famous final sentence, honoring Dean as the muse for a new, ecstatic prose.

From On the Road

Part One

I

I first met Dean not long after my wife and I split up. I had just gotten over a serious illness that I won't bother to talk about, except that it had something to do with the miserably weary split-up and my feeling that everything was dead. With the coming of Dean Moriarty began the part of my life you could call my life on the road. Before that I'd often dreamed of going West to see the country, always vaguely planning and never taking off. Dean is the perfect guy for the road because he actually was born on the road, when his parents were passing through Salt Lake City in 1926, in a jalopy, on their way to Los Angeles. First reports of him came to me through Chad King, who'd shown me a few letters from him written in a New Mexico reform school. I was tremendously interested in the letters because they so naïvely and sweetly asked Chad to teach him all about Nietzsche[1] and all the wonderful intellectual things that Chad knew. At one point Carlo and I talked about the letters and wondered if we would ever meet the strange Dean Moriarty. This is all far back, when Dean was not the way he is today, when he was a young jailkid shrouded in mystery. Then news came that Dean was out of reform school and was coming to New York for the first time; also there was talk that he had just married a girl called Marylou.

One day I was hanging around the campus and Chad and Tim Gray told me Dean was staying in a cold-water pad[2] in East Harlem, the Spanish Harlem. Dean had arrived the night before, the first time in New York, with his beautiful little sharp chick Marylou; they got off the Greyhound bus at 50th Street and cut around the corner looking for a place to eat and went right in Hector's, and since then Hector's cafeteria has always been a big symbol of New York for Dean. They spent money on beautiful big glazed cakes and creampuffs.

All this time Dean was telling Marylou things like this: "Now, darling, here we are in New York and although I haven't quite told you everything that I was thinking about when we crossed Missouri and especially at the point when we passed the Boonville reformatory which reminded me of my jail problem, it is absolutely necessary now to postpone all those leftover things concerning our personal lovethings and at once begin thinking of specific worklife plans . . ." and so on in the way that he had in those early days.

I went to the cold-water flat with the boys, and Dean came to the door in his shorts. Marylou was jumping off the couch; Dean had dispatched the occupant of the apartment to the kitchen, probably to make coffee, while he proceeded with his love-problems, for to him sex was the one and only holy and important thing in life, although he had to sweat and curse to make a living and so on. You saw that in the way he stood bobbing his head, always looking down, nodding, like a young boxer to instructions, to make you think he was listening to every word, throwing in a thousand "Yeses" and "That's rights." My first impression of Dean was of a young Gene Autry[3]—trim, thin-hipped, blue-eyed, with a real Oklahoma accent—a sideburned hero of the snowy West. In fact he'd just been working on a ranch, Ed Wall's in Colorado, before marrying Marylou and coming East. Marylou was a pretty blonde with immense ringlets of hair like a sea of golden tresses; she sat there on the edge of the couch with her hands hanging in her lap and her smoky blue country eyes fixed in a wide stare because she was in an evil gray New York pad that she'd heard about back West, and waiting like a

1. Friedrich Nietzsche (1844–1900), German philosopher.
2. A cheap apartment with no running hot water.

3. American actor and singer (1907–1998), known for his cowboy roles in popular Westerns.

longbodied emaciated Modigliani[4] surrealist woman in a serious room. But, outside of being a sweet little girl, she was awfully dumb and capable of doing horrible things. That night we all drank beer and pulled wrists and talked till dawn, and in the morning, while we sat around dumbly smoking butts from ashtrays in the gray light of a gloomy day, Dean got up nervously, paced around, thinking, and decided the thing to do was to have Marylou make breakfast and sweep the floor. "In other words we've got to get on the ball, darling, what I'm saying, otherwise it'll be fluctuating and lack of true knowledge or crystallization of our plans." Then I went away.

During the following week he confided in Chad King that he absolutely had to learn how to write from him; Chad said I was a writer and he should come to me for advice. Meanwhile Dean had gotten a job in a parking lot, had a fight with Marylou in their Hoboken apartment—God knows why they went there—and she was so mad and so down deep vindictive that she reported to the police some false trumped-up hysterical crazy charge, and Dean had to lam[5] from Hoboken. So he had no place to live. He came right out to Paterson, New Jersey, where I was living with my aunt, and one night while I was studying there was a knock on the door, and there was Dean, bowing, shuffling obsequiously in the dark of the hall, and saying, "Hel-lo, you remember me—Dean Moriarty? I've come to ask you to show me how to write."

"And where's Marylou?" I asked, and Dean said she'd apparently whored a few dollars together and gone back to Denver—"the whore!" So we went out to have a few beers because we couldn't talk like we wanted to talk in front of my aunt, who sat in the living room reading her paper. She took one look at Dean and decided that he was a madman.

In the bar I told Dean, "Hell, man, I know very well you didn't come to me only to want to become a writer, and after all what do I really know about it except you've got to stick to it with the energy of a benny addict."[6] And he said, "Yes, of course, I know exactly what you mean and in fact all those problems have occurred to me, but the thing that I want is the realization of those factors that should one depend on Schopenhauer's[7] dichotomy for any inwardly realized . . ." and so on in that way, things I understood not a bit and he himself didn't. In those days he really didn't know what he was talking about; that is to say, he was a young jailkid all hung-up on the wonderful possibilities of becoming a real intellectual, and he liked to talk in the tone and using the words, but in a jumbled way, that he had heard from "real intellectuals"—although, mind you, he wasn't so naïve as that in all other things, and it took him just a few months with Carlo Marx to become completely *in there* with all the terms and jargon. Nonetheless we understood each other on other levels of madness, and I agreed that he could stay at my house till he found a job and furthermore we agreed to go out West sometime. That was the winter of 1947.

One night when Dean ate supper at my house—he already had the parking-lot job in New York—he leaned over my shoulder as I typed rapidly away and said, "Come on man, those girls won't wait, make it fast."

4. Amedeo Modigliani (1884–1920), modernist Italian painter and sculptor, known for his elongated human forms, lived and worked in Paris after 1906.
5. To escape or live on the run, usually to evade legal troubles.
6. Benzedrine, a form of amphetamine, typically makes its users hyperactive.
7. Artur Schopenhauer (1788–1860), German Romantic philosopher.

I said, "Hold on just a minute, I'll be right with you soon as I finish this chapter," and it was one of the best chapters in the book. Then I dressed and off we flew to New York to meet some girls. As we rode in the bus in the weird phosphorescent void of the Lincoln Tunnel we leaned on each other with fingers waving and yelled and talked excitedly, and I was beginning to get the bug like Dean. He was simply a youth tremendously excited with life, and though he was a con-man, he was only conning because he wanted so much to live and to get involved with people who would otherwise pay no attention to him. He was conning me and I knew it (for room and board and "how-to-write," etc.), and he knew I knew (this has been the basis of our relationship), but I didn't care and we got along fine—no pestering, no cater-ing; we tiptoed around each other like heartbreaking new friends. I began to learn from him as much as he probably learned from me. As far as my work was concerned he said, "Go ahead, everything you do is great." He watched over my shoulder as I wrote stories, yelling, "Yes! That's right! Wow! Man!" and "Phew!" and wiped his face with his handkerchief. "Man, wow, there's so many things to do, so many things to write! How to even *begin* to get it all down and without modified restraints and all hung-up on like literary inhibi-tions and grammatical fears . . ."

"That's right, man, now you're talking." And a kind of holy lightning I saw flashing from his excitement and his visions, which he described so torren-tially that people in buses looked around to see the "overexcited nut." In the West he'd spent a third of his time in the poolhall, a third in jail, and a third in the public library. They'd seen him rushing eagerly down the win-ter streets, bareheaded, carrying books to the poolhall, or climbing trees to get into the attics of buddies where he spent days reading or hiding from the law.

We went to New York—I forget what the situation was, two colored girls—there were no girls there; they were supposed to meet him in a diner and didn't show up. We went to his parking lot where he had a few things to do—change his clothes in the shack in back and spruce up a bit in front of a cracked mirror and so on, and then we took off. And that was the night Dean met Carlo Marx. A tremendous thing happened when Dean met Carlo Marx. Two keen minds that they are, they took to each other at the drop of a hat. Two piercing eyes glanced into two piercing eyes—the holy con-man with the shining mind, and the sorrowful poetic con-man with the dark mind that is Carlo Marx. From that moment on I saw very little of Dean, and I was a little sorry too. Their energies met head-on, I was a lout compared, I couldn't keep up with them. The whole mad swirl of everything that was to come began then; it would mix up all my friends and all I had left of my family in a big dust cloud over the American Night. Carlo told him of Old Bull Lee, Elmer Hassel, Jane: Lee in Texas growing weed, Hassel on Riker's Island, Jane wandering on Times Square in a benzedrine hallucination, with her baby girl in her arms and ending up in Bellevue.[8] And Dean told Carlo of unknown people in the West like Tommy Snark, the clubfooted poolhall rotation shark and cardplayer and queer saint. He told him of Roy Johnson, Big Ed Dunkel, his boyhood

8. New York City's Bellevue Hospital Center, America's oldest public hospital, has a famous psychiatric treatment facility. "Riker's Island": island in the East River between Queens and the Bronx; it is the site of New York City's main jail complex. "Times Square": busy hub of Manhat-tan's entertainment district.

buddies, his street buddies, his innumerable girls and sex-parties and pornographic pictures, his heroes, heroines, adventures. They rushed down the street together, digging everything in the early way they had, which later became so much sadder and perceptive and blank. But then they danced down the streets like dingledodies,[9] and I shambled after as I've been doing all my life after people who interest me, because the only people for me are the mad ones, the ones who are mad to live, mad to talk, mad to be saved, desirous of everything at the same time, the ones who never yawn or say a commonplace thing, but burn, burn, burn like fabulous yellow roman candles exploding like spiders across the stars and in the middle you see the blue centerlight pop and everybody goes "Awww!" What did they call such young people in Goethe's[1] Germany? Wanting dearly to learn how to write like Carlo, the first thing you know, Dean was attacking him with a great amorous soul such as only a con-man can have. "Now, Carlo, let *me* speak—here's what *I'm* saying . . ." I didn't see them for about two weeks, during which time they cemented their relationship to fiendish allday-allnight-talk proportions.

Then came spring, the great time of traveling, and everybody in the scattered gang was getting ready to take one trip or another. I was busily at work on my novel and when I came to the halfway mark, after a trip down South with my aunt to visit my brother Rocco, I got ready to travel West for the very first time.

Dean had already left. Carlo and I saw him off at the 34th Street Greyhound station. Upstairs they had a place where you could make pictures for a quarter. Carlo took off his glasses and looked sinister. Dean made a profile shot and looked coyly around. I took a straight picture that made me look like a thirty-year-old Italian who'd kill anybody who said anything against his mother. This picture Carlo and Dean neatly cut down the middle with a razor and saved a half each in their wallets. Dean was wearing a real Western business suit for his big trip back to Denver; he'd finished his first fling in New York. I say fling, but he only worked like a dog in parking lots. The most fantastic parking-lot attendant in the world, he can back a car forty miles an hour into a tight squeeze and stop at the wall, jump out, race among fenders, leap into another car, circle it fifty miles an hour in a narrow space, back swiftly into tight spot, *hump*, snap the car with the emergency so that you see it bounce as he flies out; then clear to the ticket shack, sprinting like a track star, hand a ticket, leap into a newly arrived car before the owner's half out, leap literally under him as he steps out, start the car with the door flapping, and roar off to the next available spot, arc, pop in, brake, out, run; working like that without pause eight hours a night, evening rush hours and after-theater rush hours, in greasy wino pants with a frayed fur-lined jacket and beat[2] shoes that flap. Now he'd bought a new suit to go back in; blue with pencil stripes, vest and all—eleven dollars on Third Avenue, with a watch and watch chain, and a portable typewriter with which he was going to start writing in a Denver rooming house as soon as he got a job there. We had a farewell meal of franks and beans in a Seventh Avenue Riker's,[3] and

9. Kerouac's neologism: a wild, free-spirited person.
1. Johann Wolfgang von Geothe (1749–1832), German Romantic writer of novels, poetry, drama, and memoirs.
2. Worn, beaten-down; Kerouac adopted this usage of *beat* to describe his postwar generation of disaffected writers, artists, and intellectuals.
3. Popular chain of New York City cafeterias. (The name is unrelated to that of the Riker's Island jail complex.)

then Dean got on the bus that said Chicago and roared off into the night. There went our wrangler. I promised myself to go the same way when spring really bloomed and opened up the land.

And this was really the way that my whole road experience began, and the things that were to come are too fantastic not to tell.

Yes, and it wasn't only because I was a writer and needed new experiences that I wanted to know Dean more, and because my life hanging around the campus had reached the completion of its cycle and was stultified, but because, somehow in spite of our difference in character, he reminded me of some long-lost brother; the sight of his suffering bony face with the long sideburns and his straining muscular sweating neck made me remember my boyhood in those dye-dumps and swim-holes and riversides of Paterson and the Passaic.[4] His dirty workclothes clung to him so gracefully, as though you couldn't buy a better fit from a custom tailor but only earn it from the Natural Tailor of Natural Joy, as Dean had, in his stresses. And in his excited way of speaking I heard again the voices of old companions and brothers under the bridge, among the motorcycles, along the wash-lined neighborhood and drowsy doorsteps of afternoon where boys played guitars while their older brothers worked in the mills. All my other current friends were "intellectuals"—Chad the Nietzschean anthropologist, Carlo Marx and his nutty surrealist low-voiced serious staring talk, Old Bull Lee and his critical anti-everything drawl—or else they were slinking criminals like Elmer Hassel, with that hip sneer; Jane Lee the same, sprawled on the Oriental cover of her couch, sniffing at the *New Yorker*. But Dean's intelligence was every bit as formal and shining and complete, without the tedious intellectualness. And his "criminality" was not something that sulked and sneered; it was a wild yea-saying overburst of American joy; it was Western, the west wind, an ode from the Plains, something new, long prophesied, long a-coming (he only stole cars for joy rides). Besides, all my New York friends were in the negative, nightmare position of putting down society and giving their tired bookish or political or psychoanalytical reasons, but Dean just raced in society, eager for bread and love; he didn't care one way or the other, "so long's I can get that lil ole gal with that lil sumpin down there tween her legs, boy," and "so long's we can *eat*, son, y'ear me? I'm *hungry*, I'm *starving*, let's *eat right now!*"—and off we'd rush to *eat*, whereof, as saith Ecclesiastes,[5] "It is your portion under the sun."

A western kinsman of the sun, Dean. Although my aunt warned me that he would get me in trouble, I could hear a new call and see a new horizon, and believe it at my young age; and a little bit of trouble or even Dean's eventual rejection of me as a buddy, putting me down, as he would later, on starving sidewalks and sickbeds—what did it matter? I was a young writer and I wanted to take off.

Somewhere along the line I knew there'd be girls, visions, everything; somewhere along the line the pearl would be handed to me.

---

4. Paterson is a city in northern New Jersey; the Passaic River runs through the region.

5. One of the 24 books of the Hebrew Bible, Ecclesiastes meditates on life's transitory nature.

Part Five

Dean drove from Mexico City and saw Victor again in Gregoria and pushed that old car all the way to Lake Charles, Louisiana, before the rear end finally dropped on the road as he had always known it would. So he wired Inez for airplane fare and flew the rest of the way. When he arrived in New York with the divorce papers in his hands, he and Inez immediately went to Newark and got married; and that night, telling her everything was all right and not to worry, and making logics where there was nothing but inestimable sorrowful sweats, he jumped on a bus and roared off again across the awful continent to San Francisco to rejoin Camille and the two baby girls. So now he was three times married, twice divorced, and living with his second wife.[6]

In the fall I myself started back home from Mexico City and one night just over Laredo border in Dilley, Texas, I was standing on the hot road underneath an arc-lamp with the summer moths smashing into it when I heard the sound of footsteps from the darkness beyond, and lo, a tall old man with flowing white hair came clomping by with a pack on his back, and when he saw me as he passed, he said, "Go moan for man," and clomped on back to his dark. Did this mean that I should at last go on my pilgrimage on foot on the dark roads around America? I struggled and hurried to New York, and one night I was standing in a dark street in Manhattan and called up to the window of a loft where I thought my friends were having a party. But a pretty girl stuck her head out the window and said, "Yes? Who is it?"

"Sal Paradise," I said, and heard my name resound in the sad and empty street.

"Come on up," she called. "I'm making hot chocolate." So I went up and there she was, the girl with the pure and innocent dear eyes that I had always searched for and for so long. We agreed to love each other madly. In the winter we planned to migrate to San Francisco, bringing all our beat furniture and broken belongings with us in a jalopy panel truck. I wrote to Dean and told him. He wrote back a huge letter eighteen thousand words long, all about his young years in Denver, and said he was coming to get me and personally select the old truck himself and drive us home. We had six weeks to save up the money for the truck and began working and counting every cent. And suddenly Dean arrived anyway, five and a half weeks in advance, and nobody had any money to go through with the plan.

I was taking a walk in the middle of the night and came back to my girl to tell her what I thought about during my walk. She stood in the dark little pad with a strange smile. I told her a number of things and suddenly I noticed the hush in the room and looked around and saw a battered book on the radio. I knew it was Dean's high-eternity-in-the-afternoon Proust.[7] As in a dream I saw him tiptoe in from the dark hall in his stocking feet. He

6. Dean is shuttling between coasts and women. Camille, who lives in San Francisco, is Dean's second wife and mother of his two children; though they are in the process of divorcing, Dean remains attached to her. Inez, who lives in Newark, New Jersey, becomes Dean's third wife. Sal and Dean had last been together in Mexico City, where Dean had abandoned Sal while Sal was sick.

7. Marcel Proust (1871–1922), French novelist, author of the dreamy, semi-autobiographical seven-volume novel, *À la recherche du temps perdu* (translated as *Remembrance of Things Past* or *In Search of Lost Time*).

couldn't talk any more. He hopped and laughed, he stuttered and fluttered his hands and said, "Ah—ah—you must listen to hear." We listened, all ears. But he forgot what he wanted to say. "Really listen—ahem. Look, dear Sal—sweet Laura—I've come—I'm gone—but wait—ah yes." And he stared with rocky sorrow into his hands. "Can't talk no more—do you understand that it is—or might be—But listen!" We all listened. He was listening to sounds in the night. "Yes!" he whispered with awe. "But you see—no need to talk any more—and further."

"But why did you come so soon, Dean?"

"Ah," he said, looking at me as if for the first time, "so soon, yes. We— we'll know—that is, I don't know. I came on the railroad pass—cabooses— old hard-bench coaches—Texas—played flute and wooden sweet potato[8] all the way." He took out his new wooden flute. He played a few squeaky notes on it and jumped up and down in his stocking feet. "See?" he said. "But of course, Sal, I can talk as soon as ever and have many things to say to you in fact with my own little bangtail mind I've been reading and reading this gone[9] Proust all the way across the country and digging a great number of things I'll never have TIME to tell you about and we STILL haven't talked of Mexico and our parting there in fever—but no need to talk. Absolutely, now, yes?"

"All right, we won't talk." And he started telling the story of what he did in LA on the way over in every possible detail, how he visited a family, had dinner, talked to the father, the sons, the sisters—what they looked like, what they ate, their furnishings, their thoughts, their interests, their very souls; it took him three hours of detailed elucidation, and having concluded this he said, "Ah, but you see what I wanted to REALLY tell you—much later—Arkansas, crossing on train—playing flute—play cards with boys, my dirty deck—won money, blew sweet-potato solo—for sailors. Long long awful trip five days and five nights just to SEE you, Sal."

"What about Camille?"

"Gave permission of course—waiting for me. Camille and I all straight forever-and-ever . . ."

"And Inez?"

"I—I—I want her to come back to Frisco with me live other side of town— don't you think? Don't know why I came." Later he said in a sudden moment of gaping wonder, "Well and yes, of course, I wanted to see your sweet girl and you—glad of you—love you as ever." He stayed in New York three days and hastily made preparations to get back on the train with his railroad passes and again recross the continent, five days and five nights in dusty coaches and hard-bench crummies, and of course we had no money for a truck and couldn't go back with him. With Inez he spent one night explaining and sweating and fighting, and she threw him out. A letter came for him, care of me. I saw it. It was from Camille. "My heart broke when I saw you go across the tracks with your bag. I pray and pray you get back safe. . . . I do want Sal and his friend to come and live on the same street. . . . I know you'll make it but I can't help worrying—now that we've decided every-thing. . . . Dear Dean, it's the end of the first half of the century. Welcome

---

8. A kind of ocarina, a hollow wooden wind instrument shaped like a sweet potato.   9. Slang for "great" or "fine."

with love and kisses to spend the other half with us. We all wait for you. [Signed] Camille, Amy, and Little Joanie." So Dean's life was settled with his most constant, most embittered, and best-knowing wife Camille, and I thanked God for him.

The last time I saw him it was under sad and strange circumstances. Remi Boncœur had arrived in New York after having gone around the world several times in ships. I wanted him to meet and know Dean. They did meet, but Dean couldn't talk any more and said nothing, and Remi turned away. Remi had gotten tickets for the Duke Ellington[1] concert at the Metropolitan Opera and insisted Laura and I come with him and his girl. Remi was fat and sad now but still the eager and formal gentleman, and he wanted to do things the *right way*, as he emphasized. So he got his bookie to drive us to the concert in a Cadillac. It was a cold winter night. The Cadillac was parked and ready to go. Dean stood outside the windows with his bag, ready to go to Penn Station and on across the land.

"Good-by, Dean," I said. "I sure wish I didn't have to go to the concert."

"D'you think I can ride to Fortieth Street with you?" he whispered. "Want to be with you as much as possible, m'boy, and besides it's so durned cold in this here New Yawk . . ." I whispered to Remi. No, he wouldn't have it, he liked me but he didn't like my idiot friends. I wasn't going to start all over again ruining his planned evenings as I had done at Alfred's in San Francisco in 1947 with Roland Major.

"Absolutely out of the question, Sal!" Poor Remi, he had a special necktie made for this evening; on it was painted a replica of the concert tickets, and the names Sal and Laura and Remi and Vicki, the girl, together with a series of sad jokes and some of his favorite sayings such as "You can't teach the old maestro a new tune."

So Dean couldn't ride uptown with us and the only thing I could do was sit in the back of the Cadillac and wave at him. The bookie at the wheel also wanted nothing to do with Dean. Dean, ragged in a motheaten overcoat he brought specially for the freezing temperatures of the East, walked off alone, and the last I saw of him he rounded the corner of Seventh Avenue, eyes on the street ahead, and bent to it again. Poor little Laura, my baby, to whom I'd told everything about Dean, began almost to cry.

"Oh, we shouldn't let him go like this. What'll we do?"

Old Dean's gone, I thought, and out loud I said, "He'll be all right." And off we went to the sad and disinclined concert for which I had no stomach whatever and all the time I was thinking of Dean and how he got back on the train and rode over three thousand miles over that awful land and never knew why he had come anyway, except to see me.

So in America when the sun goes down and I sit on the old broken-down river pier watching the long, long skies over New Jersey and sense all that raw land that rolls in one unbelievable huge bulge over to the West Coast, and all that road going, all the people dreaming in the immensity of it, and in Iowa I know by now the children must be crying in the land where they let the children cry, and tonight the stars'll be out, and don't you know that God is

---

1. Edward Kennedy "Duke" Ellington (1899–1974), leading American jazz composer, pianist, and band leader.

Pooh Bear? the evening star must be drooping and shedding her sparkler dims on the prairie, which is just before the coming of complete night that blesses the earth, darkens all rivers, cups the peaks and folds the final shore in, and nobody, nobody knows what's going to happen to anybody besides the forlorn rags of growing old, I think of Dean Moriarty, I even think of Old Dean Moriarty the father we never found, I think of Dean Moriarty.

1957

KURT VONNEGUT
1922–2007

As a counterculture hero of the turbulent 1960s and a best-selling author among readers of popular fiction in the four decades afterward, Kurt Vonnegut was at once more traditional and more complicated than his enthusiasts might believe. To a generation of young people who felt their country had forsaken them, he offered examples of common decency and cultural idealism as basic as a grade-school civics lesson. For a broader readership who felt conventional fiction was inadequate to express the way their lives had been disrupted by the era's radical social changes, he wrote novels structured in more pertinently contemporary terms, bereft of such unifying devices as conclusive characterization and chronologically organized plots. His most famous novel, *Slaughterhouse-Five* (1969), takes as its organizing incident the Allied firebombing of the German city of Dresden late in World War II, as witnessed by the American prisoner of war Billy Pilgrim. Yet despite its origins in the 1940s, the manner of its telling is much more akin to the writing of Americans of the 1960s, who were coming to terms with the Vietnam War. Like the war in Southeast Asia, *Slaughterhouse-Five* abjured the certainties of an identifiable beginning, middle, and end; both presented a mesmerizing sense of confused, apparently directionless present, with no sense of completion or conclusion. Together, this World War II novel and the later war during which it was written speak for the unsettling nature of the American 1960s; the assassination of presidential candidate Robert F. Kennedy figures in the book's concluding chapter. Yet this unconventional structure is paired with the language of American vernacular (much in the manner of Vonnegut's hero, Mark Twain). Where more elevated speech would obscure his point, this author speaks plainly and simply, drawing his words, phrases, and inflections from the American middle class and its common experiences of life.

Vonnegut was born in Indianapolis, Indiana, to a family prominent in business and the arts. During the Great Depression of the 1930s, the sensitive, well-read teenager saw his mother's inherited wealth dissipate, his father's career as an architect crumble for lack of work, and his extended family scatter around the country in search of new careers. Service as a World War II infantryman taught him not only how politics reshapes the world but also how science (Vonnegut had been studying biochemistry in college before enlistment) could be used to create effects as destructive to humankind as the Dresden firestorm, which Vonnegut himself endured as a prisoner of war. Working as a publicist for the General Electric Corporation after the war, the author learned firsthand about the strategies for managing the lifestyles

At left, **Dresden in 1945,** following the Allied firebombing. At right, **Senator Robert F. Kennedy** lies mortally wounded by an assassin's bullet on June 4, 1968. These two events bookend Vonnegut's *Slaughterhouse-Five.*

of millions. In short, before writing his first story in 1950 Kurt Vonnegut had shared many formative experiences of his generation. Reworking those experiences would yield fictions and a public stance that helped his fellow Americans adjust to a reinvented postwar world.

Vonnegut's advice, like Mark Twain's, would be unapologetically lowbrow. Part of each writer's appeal is that he pokes holes in the pseudo-sophistications of supposedly more serious approaches. In a 1982 lecture, "Fates Worse Than Death," Vonnegut noted that the self-consciously highbrow *New Yorker* magazine had never published his work. Indeed, he wrote his short stories of the 1950s for the immensely more general readership of *Collier's* and the *Saturday Evening Post.* These stories (collected in 1968 as *Welcome to the Monkey House*) deflate the pretentions of wealth, expertise, and influence with demonstrations of middle-class values and common sense. At the same time Vonnegut was writing novels in formats borrowed from popular subgenres: science fiction dystopia for *Player Piano* (1952), space opera for *The Sirens of Titan* (1959), spy thriller for *Mother Night* (1961), scientific apocalypse and intrigue for *Cat's Cradle* (1963), and prince-and-the-pauper critique of riches for *God Bless You, Mr. Rosewater* (1965). Each work challenges the technical and thematic conventions of the novel, yet each time within the familiarity of a popular form.

In the middle 1960s, with his family-magazine markets having gone out of business, Vonnegut began writing essays for popular magazines such as *Esquire, McCall's,* and the *Ladies Home Journal.* Reviewing *The Random House Dictionary* for the *New York Times Book Review* (October 30, 1966), he contrasted the assignment's linguistic complexity with his own shuffling, hands-in-pockets approach; as lexicographers debated theories like prescriptive versus descriptive standards of language, Vonnegut could just shrug and say that the former, "as nearly as I could tell, was like an honest cop, while descriptive was like a boozed-up war buddy from Mobile, Alabama." In other essays the author's similarly self-effacing humor undermined positions that used intellectual pretentions to support their points. To the overenthusiasts for science fiction who try to include writers like Leo Tolstoy and Franz Kafka in their brotherhood, he objects that "it is as though I were to claim everybody of note belonged fundamentally to Delta Upsilon, my own lodge, incidentally, whether he knew it or not. Kafka would have made a desperately unhappy D.U."

With the success of *Slaughterhouse-Five* and the widespread appreciation of his essays and personal appearances, Kurt Vonnegut became much more publically outspoken about major issues. From his new home in New York City (where he moved in 1970 following nearly two decades of writing in obscurity on Cape Cod, Massachusetts) the author wrote novels such as *Galápagos* (1985), *Hocus Pocus* (1990), and *Timequake* (1997), works treating such topics as the evolution and possible devolution of humankind and America's economic and social role at the end of the twentieth century. Vonnegut's challenges to the conventions of traditional fiction make him as innovative as any of the literary disruptionists of the postmodern era, yet he trusts in the honesty of plain and accurate statement. His last book was a series of sociopolitical essays collected as *A Man without a Country* (2005). Two years before his death, the author found himself once more embraced by a new young audience seeking an explanation for their era's woes. Hence his advice in "How to Write with Style," from his 1981 collection, *Palm Sunday*: "I myself find that I trust my writing most, and others seem to trust it most, when I sound like a person from Indianapolis, which I am."

From Slaughterhouse-Five

Chapter 1[1]

All this happened, more or less. The war parts, anyway, are pretty much true. One guy I knew really *was* shot in Dresden[2] for taking a teapot that wasn't his. Another guy I knew really *did* threaten to have his personal enemies killed by hired gunmen after the war. And so on. I've changed all the names.

I really *did* go back to Dresden with Guggenheim money[3] (God love it) in 1967. It looked a lot like Dayton, Ohio, more open spaces than Dayton has. There must be tons of human bone meal in the ground.

I went back there with an old war buddy, Bernard V. O'Hare, and we made friends with a cab driver, who took us to the slaughterhouse where we had been locked up at night as prisoners of war. His name was Gerhard Müller. He told us that he was a prisoner of the Americans for a while. We asked him how it was to live under Communism, and he said that it was terrible at first, because everybody had to work so hard, and because there wasn't much shelter or food or clothing. But things were much better now. He had a pleasant little apartment, and his daughter was getting an excellent education. His mother was incinerated in the Dresden fire-storm. So it goes.

He sent O'Hare a postcard at Christmastime, and here is what it said:

---

1. In conventional terms an autobiographical preface. Vonnegut's innovation is to format it as indistinguishable from the eight chapters of fictive narrative that follow (in which he identifies himself as a participant three times), before a final chapter that in conventional terms would be an autobiographical epilogue.
2. City in southeastern Germany destroyed in a bombing raid by the British Royal Air Force on the night of February 13–14, 1945.
3. Fellowship funded by the Guggenheim Foundation, New York City.

"I wish you and your family also as to your friend Merry Christmas and a happy New Year and I hope that we'll meet again in a world of peace and freedom in the taxi cab if the accident will."

I like that very much: "If the accident will."

I would hate to tell you what this lousy little book cost me in money and anxiety and time. When I got home from the Second World War twenty-three years ago, I thought it would be easy for me to write about the destruction of Dresden, since all I would have to do would be to report what I had seen. And I thought, too, that it would be a masterpiece or at least make me a lot of money, since the subject was so big.

But not many words about Dresden came from my mind then—not enough of them to make a book, anyway. And not many words come now, either, when I have become an old fart with his memories and his Pall Malls,[4] with his sons full grown.

I think of how useless the Dresden part of my memory has been, and yet how tempting Dresden has been to write about, and I am reminded of the famous limerick:

> There was a young man from Stamboul,
> Who soliloquized thus to his tool:
> "You took all my wealth
> And you ruined my health,
> And now you won't *pee*, you old fool."

And I'm reminded, too, of the song that goes:

> My name is Yon Yonson,
> I work in Wisconsin,
> I work in a lumbermill there.
> The people I meet when I walk down the street,
>
> They say, "What's your name?"
> And I say,
> "My name is Yon Yonson,
> I work in Wisconsin . . ."

And so on to infinity.

Over the years, people I've met have often asked me what I'm working on, and I've usually replied that the main thing was a book about Dresden.

I said that to Harrison Starr,[5] the movie-maker, one time, and he raised his eyebrows and inquired, "Is it an anti-war book?"

"Yes," I said. "I guess."

"You know what I say to people when I hear they're writing anti-war books?"

"No. What *do* you say, Harrison Starr?"

"I say, 'Why don't you write an anti-*glacier* book instead?'"

What he meant, of course, was that there would always be wars, that they were as easy to stop as glaciers. I believe that, too.

---

4. Popular brand of cigarettes.   5. American filmmaker (b. 1937).

And, even if wars didn't keep coming like glaciers, there would still be plain old death.

When I was somewhat younger, working on my famous Dresden book, I asked an old war buddy named Bernard V. O'Hare if I could come to see him. He was a district attorney in Pennsylvania. I was a writer on Cape Cod.[6] We had been privates in the war, infantry scouts. We had never expected to make any money after the war, but we were doing quite well.

I had the Bell Telephone Company find him for me. They are wonderful that way. I have this disease late at night sometimes, involving alcohol and the telephone. I get drunk, and I drive my wife away with a breath like mustard gas and roses. And then, speaking gravely and elegantly into the telephone, I ask the telephone operators to connect me with this friend or that one, from whom I have not heard in years.

I got O'Hare on the line in this way. He is short and I am tall. We were Mutt and Jeff in the war. We were captured together in the war. I told him who I was on the telephone. He had no trouble believing it. He was up. He was reading. Everybody else in his house was asleep.

"Listen—" I said, "I'm writing this book about Dresden. I'd like some help remembering stuff. I wonder if I could come down and see you, and we could drink and talk and remember."

He was unenthusiastic. He said he couldn't remember much. He told me, though, to come ahead.

"I think the climax of the book will be the execution of poor old Edgar Derby," I said. "The irony is *so* great. A whole city gets burned down, and thousands and thousands of people are killed. And then this one American foot soldier is arrested in the ruins for taking a teapot. And he's given a regular trial, and then he's shot by a firing squad."

"Um," said O'Hare.

"Don't you think that's really where the climax should come?"

"I don't know anything about it," he said. "That's your trade, not mine."

As a trafficker in climaxes and thrills and characterization and wonderful dialogue and suspense and confrontations, I had outlined the Dresden story many times. The best outline I ever made, or anyway the prettiest one, was on the back of a roll of wallpaper.

I used my daughter's crayons, a different color for each main character. One end of the wallpaper was the beginning of the story, and the other end was the end, and then there was all that middle part, which was the middle. And the blue line met the red line and then the yellow line, and the yellow line stopped because the character represented by the yellow line was dead. And so on. The destruction of Dresden was represented by a vertical band of orange cross-hatching, and all the lines that were still alive passed through it, came out the other side.

The end, where all the lines stopped, was a beetfield on the Elbe, outside of Halle.[7] The rain was coming down. The war in Europe had been over for a

6. Peninsula in eastern Massachusetts; Vonnegut's residence from 1952 to 1970.
7. The River Elbe flows through Germany; Halle is a German city located on the River Saale, a tributary of the Elbe.

couple of weeks. We were formed in ranks, with Russian soldiers guarding us—Englishmen, Americans, Dutchmen, Belgians, Frenchmen, Canadians, South Africans, New Zealanders, Australians, thousands of us about to stop being prisoners of war.

And on the other side of the field were thousands of Russians and Poles and Yugoslavians and so on guarded by American soldiers. An exchange was made there in the rain—one for one. O'Hare and I climbed into the back of an American truck with a lot of others. O'Hare didn't have any souvenirs. Almost everybody else did. I had a ceremonial Luftwaffe[8] saber, still do. The rabid little American I call Paul Lazzaro in this book had about a quart of diamonds and emeralds and rubies and so on. He had taken these from dead people in the cellars of Dresden. So it goes.

An idiotic Englishman, who had lost all his teeth somewhere, had his souvenir in a canvas bag. The bag was resting on my insteps. He would peek into the bag every now and then, and he would roll his eyes and swivel his scrawny neck, trying to catch people looking covetously at his bag. And he would bounce the bag on my insteps.

I thought this bouncing was accidental. But I was mistaken. He *had* to show somebody what was in the bag, and he had decided he could trust me. He caught my eye, winked, opened the bag. There was a plaster model of the Eiffel Tower in there. It was painted gold. It had a clock in it.

"There's a smashin' thing," he said.

And we were flown to a rest camp in France, where we were fed chocolate malted milkshakes and other rich foods until we were all covered with baby fat. Then we were sent home, and I married a pretty girl who was covered with baby fat, too.

And we had babies.

And they're all grown up now, and I'm an old fart with his memories and his Pall Malls. My name is Yon Yonson, I work in Wisconsin, I work in a lumbermill there.

Sometimes I try to call up old girl friends on the telephone late at night, after my wife has gone to bed. "Operator, I wonder if you could give me the number of a Mrs. So-and-So. I think she lives at such-and-such."

"I'm sorry, sir. There is no such listing."

"Thanks, Operator. Thanks just the same."

And I let the dog out, or I let him in, and we talk some. I let him know I like him, and he lets me know he likes me. He doesn't mind the smell of mustard gas and roses.

"You're all right, Sandy," I'll say to the dog. "You know that, Sandy? You're O.K."

Sometimes I'll turn on the radio and listen to a talk program from Boston or New York. I can't stand recorded music if I've been drinking a good deal.

Sooner or later I go to bed, and my wife asks me what time it is. She always has to know the time. Sometimes I don't know, and I say, "Search *me*."

I think about my education sometimes. I went to the University of Chicago for a while after the Second World War. I was a student in the Depart-

8. German Air Force.

ment of Anthropology. At that time, they were teaching that there was absolutely no difference between anybody. They may be teaching that still.

Another thing they taught was that nobody was ridiculous or bad or disgusting. Shortly before my father died, he said to me, "You know—you never wrote a story with a villain in it."

I told him that was one of the things I learned in college after the war.

While I was studying to be an anthropologist, I was also working as a police reporter for the famous Chicago City News Bureau for twenty-eight dollars a week. One time they switched me from the night shift to the day shift, so I worked sixteen hours straight. We were supported by all the newspapers in town, and the AP and the UP[9] and all that. And we would cover the courts and the police stations and the Fire Department and the Coast Guard out on Lake Michigan and all that. We were connected to the institutions that supported us by means of pneumatic tubes which ran under the streets of Chicago.

Reporters would telephone in stories to writers wearing headphones, and the writers would stencil the stories on mimeograph sheets. The stories were mimeographed and stuffed into the brass and velvet cartridges which the pneumatic tubes ate. The very toughest reporters and writers were women who had taken over the jobs of men who'd gone to war.

And the first story I covered I had to dictate over the telephone to one of those beastly girls. It was about a young veteran who had taken a job running an old-fashioned elevator in an office building. The elevator door on the first floor was ornamental iron lace. Iron ivy snaked in and out of the holes. There was an iron twig with two iron lovebirds perched upon it.

This veteran decided to take his car into the basement, and he closed the door and started down, but his wedding ring was caught in all the ornaments. So he was hoisted into the air and the floor of the car went down, dropped out from under him, and the top of the car squashed him. So it goes.

So I phoned this in, and the woman who was going to cut the stencil asked me, "What did his wife say?"

"She doesn't know yet," I said. "It just happened."

"Call her up and get a statement."

"What?"

"Tell her you're Captain Finn of the Police Department. Say you have some sad news. Give her the news, and see what she says."

So I did. She said about what you would expect her to say. There was a baby. And so on.

When I got back to the office, the woman writer asked me, just for her own information, what the squashed guy had looked like when he was squashed.

I told her.

"Did it bother you?" she said. She was eating a Three Musketeers Candy Bar.

"Heck no, Nancy," I said. "I've seen lots worse than that in the war."

Even then I was supposedly writing a book about Dresden. It wasn't a famous air raid back then in America. Not many Americans knew how much worse

---

9. Associated Press and United Press, rival wire news services subscribed to by various newspapers.

it had been than Hiroshima,[1] for instance. I didn't know that, either. There hadn't been much publicity.

I happened to tell a University of Chicago professor at a cocktail party about the raid as I had seen it, about the book I would write. He was a member of a thing called The Committee on Social Thought.[2] And he told me about the concentration camps, and about how the Germans had made soap and candles out of the fat of dead Jews and so on.

All I could say was, "I know, I know. I *know*."

World War Two had certainly made everybody very tough. And I became a public relations man for General Electric in Schenectady, New York, and a volunteer fireman in the village of Alplaus, where I bought my first home. My boss there was one of the toughest guys I ever hope to meet. He had been a lieutenant colonel in public relations in Baltimore. While I was in Schenectady he joined the Dutch Reformed Church, which is a very tough church, indeed.

He used to ask me sneeringly sometimes why I hadn't been an officer, as though I'd done something wrong.

My wife and I had lost our baby fat. Those were our scrawny years. We had a lot of scrawny veterans and their scrawny wives for friends. The nicest veterans in Schenectady, I thought, the kindest and funniest ones, the ones who hated war the most, were the ones who'd really fought.

I wrote the Air Force back then, asking for details about the raid on Dresden, who ordered it, how many planes did it, why they did it, what desirable results there had been and so on. I was answered by a man who, like myself, was in public relations. He said that he was sorry, but that the information was top secret still.

I read the letter out loud to my wife, and I said, "Secret? My God—from *whom?*"

We were United World Federalists back then. I don't know what we are now. Telephoners, I guess. We telephone a lot—or *I* do, anyway, late at night.

A couple of weeks after I telephoned my old war buddy, Bernard V. O'Hare, I really *did* go to see him. That must have been in 1964 or so—whatever the last year was for the New York World's Fair.[3] *Eheu, fugaces labuntur anni.*[4] My name is Yon Yonson. There was a young man from Stamboul.

I took two little girls with me, my daughter, Nanny, and her best friend, Allison Mitchell. They had never been off Cape Cod before. When we saw a river, we had to stop so they could stand by it and think about it for a while. They had never seen water in that long and narrow, unsalted form before. The river was the Hudson. There were carp in there and we saw them. They were as big as atomic submarines.

---

1. City in southwestern Japan destroyed on August 6, 1945, in the first atomic bombing, by the United States Army Air Force.
2. Prestigious interdisciplinary committee that includes the University of Chicago's most eminent professors.
3. The 1964 World's Fair was held at Flushing Meadows, Queens, New York City, from April 22, 1964, to October 18, 1964, and again from April 21, 1965, to October 17, 1965.
4. Alas, the fleeting years are slipping by (Latin); from Ode 2.14 by the Roman poet Horace (65–8 B.C.E.).

We saw waterfalls, too, streams jumping off cliffs into the valley of the Delaware. There were lots of things to stop and see—and then it was time to go, always time to go. The little girls were wearing white party dresses and black party shoes, so strangers would know at once how nice they were. "Time to go, girls," I'd say. And we would go.

And the sun went down, and we had supper in an Italian place, and then I knocked on the front door of the beautiful stone house of Bernard V. O'Hare. I was carrying a bottle of Irish whiskey like a dinner bell.

I met his nice wife, Mary, to whom I dedicate this book. I dedicate it to Gerhard Müller, the Dresden taxi driver, too. Mary O'Hare is a trained nurse, which is a lovely thing for a woman to be.

Mary admired the two little girls I'd brought, mixed them in with her own children, sent them all upstairs to play games and watch television. It was only after the children were gone that I sensed that Mary didn't like me or didn't like *something* about the night. She was polite but chilly.

"It's a nice cozy house you have here," I said, and it really was.

"I've fixed up a place where you can talk and not be bothered," she said.

"Good," I said, and I imagined two leather chairs near a fire in a paneled room, where two old soldiers could drink and talk. But she took us into the kitchen. She had put two straight-backed chairs at a kitchen table with a white porcelain top. That table top was screaming with reflected light from a two-hundred-watt bulb overhead. Mary had prepared an operating room. She put only one glass on it, which was for me. She explained that O'Hare couldn't drink the hard stuff since the war.

So we sat down. O'Hare was embarrassed, but he wouldn't tell me what was wrong. I couldn't imagine what it was about me that could burn up Mary so. I was a family man. I'd been married only once. I wasn't a drunk. I hadn't done her husband any dirt in the war.

She fixed herself a Coca-Cola, made a lot of noise banging the ice-cube tray in the stainless steel sink. Then she went into another part of the house. But she wouldn't sit still. She was moving all over the house, opening and shutting doors, even moving furniture around to work off anger.

I asked O'Hare what I'd said or done to make her act that way.

"It's all right," he said. "Don't worry about it. It doesn't have anything to do with you." That was kind of him. He was lying. It had everything to do with me.

So we tried to ignore Mary and remember the war. I took a couple of belts of the booze I'd brought. We would chuckle or grin sometimes, as though war stories were coming back, but neither one of us could remember anything good. O'Hare remembered one guy who got into a lot of wine in Dresden, before it was bombed, and we had to take him home in a wheelbarrow. It wasn't much to write a book about. I remembered two Russian soldiers who had looted a clock factory. They had a horse-drawn wagon full of clocks. They were happy and drunk. They were smoking huge cigarettes they had rolled in newspaper.

That was about *it* for memories, and Mary was still making noise. She finally came out in the kitchen again for another Coke. She took another tray of ice cubes from the refrigerator, banged it in the sink, even though there was already plenty of ice out.

Then she turned to me, let me see how angry she was, and that the anger was for me. She had been talking to herself, so what she said was a fragment of a much larger conversation. "You were just *babies* then!" she said.

"What?" I said.

"You were just babies in the war—like the ones upstairs!"

I nodded that this was true. We *had* been foolish virgins in the war, right at the end of childhood.

"But you're not going to write it that way, are you." This wasn't a question. It was an accusation.

"I—I don't know," I said.

"Well, *I* know," she said. "You'll pretend you were men instead of babies, and you'll be played in the movies by Frank Sinatra and John Wayne or some of those other glamorous, war-loving, dirty old men. And war will look just wonderful, so we'll have a lot more of them. And they'll be fought by babies like the babies upstairs."

So then I understood. It was war that made her so angry. She didn't want her babies or anybody else's babies killed in wars. And she thought wars were partly encouraged by books and movies.

So I held up my right hand and I made her a promise: "Mary," I said, "I don't think this book of mine is ever going to be finished. I must have written five thousand pages by now, and thrown them all away. If I ever do finish it, though, I give you my word of honor: there won't be a part for Frank Sinatra or John Wayne.

"I tell you what," I said, "I'll call it 'The Children's Crusade.'"

She was my friend after that.

O'Hare and I gave up on remembering, went into the living room, talked about other things. We became curious about the real Children's Crusade, so O'Hare looked it up in a book he had, *Extraordinary Popular Delusions and the Madness of Crowds*, by Charles Mackay, LL.D.[5] It was first published in London in 1841.

Mackay had a low opinion of *all* Crusades. The Children's Crusade struck him as only slightly more sordid than the ten Crusades for grown-ups. O'Hare read this handsome passage out loud:

History in her solemn page informs us that the crusaders were but ignorant and savage men, that their motives were those of bigotry unmitigated, and that their pathway was one of blood and tears. Romance, on the other hand, dilates upon their piety and heroism, and portrays, in her most glowing and impassioned hues, their virtue and magnanimity, the imperishable honor they acquired for themselves, and the great services they rendered to Christianity.

And then O'Hare read this: *Now what was the grand result of all these struggles? Europe expended millions of her treasures, and the blood of two million of her people; and a handful of quarrelsome knights retained possession of Palestine for about one hundred years!*

Mackay told us that the Children's Crusade started in 1213, when two monks got the idea of raising armies of children in Germany and France,

5. British poet (1814–1889), journalist, and editor (most famously of the *Glasgow Argus* from 1844 to 1848).

and selling them in North Africa as slaves. Thirty thousand children volunteered, thinking they were going to Palestine. *They were no doubt idle and deserted children who generally swarm in great cities, nurtured on vice and daring,* said Mackay, *and ready for anything.*

Pope Innocent the Third[6] thought they were going to Palestine, too, and he was thrilled. "These children are awake while we are asleep!" he said.

Most of the children were shipped out of Marseilles,[7] and about half of them drowned in shipwrecks. The other half got to North Africa where they were sold.

Through a misunderstanding, some children reported for duty at Genoa,[8] where no slave ships were waiting. They were fed and sheltered and questioned kindly by good people there—then given a little money and a lot of advice and sent back home.

"Hooray for the good people of Genoa," said Mary O'Hare.

I slept that night in one of the children's bedrooms. O'Hare had put a book for me on the bedside table. It was *Dresden, History, Stage and Gallery,* by Mary Endell.[9] It was published in 1908, and its introduction began:

It is hoped that this little book will make itself useful. It attempts to give to an English-reading public a bird's-eye view of how Dresden came to look as it does, architecturally; of how it expanded musically, through the genius of a few men, to its present bloom; and it calls attention to certain permanent landmarks in art that make its Gallery the resort of those seeking lasting impressions.

I read some history further on:

Now, in 1760, Dresden underwent siege by the Prussians.[1] On the fifteenth of July began the cannonade. The Picture-Gallery took fire. Many of the paintings had been transported to the Königstein,[2] but some were seriously injured by splinters of bombshells,—notably Francia's "Baptism of Christ."[3] Furthermore, the stately Kreuzkirche[4] tower, from which the enemy's movements had been watched day and night, stood in flames. It later succumbed. In sturdy contrast with the pitiful fate of the Kreuzkirche, stood the Frauenkirche,[5] from the curves of whose stone dome the Prussian bombs rebounded like rain. Friederich[6] was obliged finally to give up the siege, because he learned of the fall of Glatz,[7] the critical point of his new conquests. "We must be off to Silesia, so that we do not lose everything."

The devastation of Dresden was boundless. When Goethe[8] as a young student visited the city, he still found sad ruins: "Von der Kuppel der Frauenkirche sah ich diese leidigen Trümmer zwischen die schöne städtische Ordnung hineingesät, da rühmte mir der Küster die Kunst des Baumeisters, welcher Kirche und Kuppel auf einen so unerwünschten Fall schon eingerichtet und

6. Born Lotario dei Conti di Segni (c. 1160–1216); as Pope Innocent III, he organized the Fourth Crusade (which included the Children's Crusade) in order to capture Muslim-controlled Jerusalem for Christendom.
7. Seaport in southern France.
8. Seaport in northwest Italy.
9. Dates and nationality unknown; writer of the introduction to this book, by the German illustrator Fritz August Gottfried Endell (1873–1955).
1. The Seven Years' War (1756–63), in which England and Prussia defeated Austria, France, Russia, Sweden, and Saxony.

2. Fortress overlooking the town of the same name, on the Elbe's left bank.
3. Painting (1509) by the Italian artist Francesco Raibolini (c. 1450–1517).
4. Church of the Cross (German).
5. Church of Our Lady (German).
6. Frederick II (1712–1786), known as the Great, ruler of Prussia (1740–86).
7. German name for the Polish city Kłodzko in Lower Silesia, the southwestern region of today's Poland.
8. Johann Wolfgang von Goethe (1749–1832), German poet and dramatist.

*bombenfest erbaut hatte. Der gute Sakristan deutete mir alsdann auf Ruinene
nach allen Seiten und sagte bedenklich lakonisch: Das hat der Feind gethan!"*[9]

The two little girls and I crossed the Delaware River where George Washington had crossed it,[1] the next morning. We went to the New York World's
Fair, saw what the past had been like, according to the Ford Motor Car
Company and Walt Disney, saw what the future would be like, according to
General Motors.

And I asked myself about the present: how wide it was, how deep it was,
how much was mine to keep.

I taught creative writing in the famous Writers Workshop at the University
of Iowa[2] for a couple of years after that. I got into some perfectly beautiful
trouble, got out of it again. I taught in the afternoons. In the mornings I wrote.
I was not to be disturbed. I was working on my famous book about Dresden.

And somewhere in there a nice man named Seymour Lawrence[3] gave me
a three-book contract, and I said, "O.K., the first of the three will be my
famous book about Dresden."

The friends of Seymour Lawrence call him "Sam." And I say to Sam now:
"Sam—here's the book."

It is so short and jumbled and jangled, Sam, because there is nothing intelligent to say about a massacre. Everybody is supposed to be dead, to never say
anything or want anything ever again. Everything is supposed to be very
quiet after a massacre, and it always is, except for the birds.

And what do the birds say? All there is to say about a massacre, things like
"Poo-tee-weet?"

I have told my sons that they are not under any circumstances to take
part in massacres, and that the news of massacres of enemies is not to fill
them with satisfaction or glee.

I have also told them not to work for companies which make massacre
machinery, and to express contempt for people who think we need machinery
like that.

As I've said: I recently went back to Dresden with my friend O'Hare. We
had a million laughs in Hamburg and West Berlin and East Berlin and Vienna
and Salzburg and Helsinki, and in Leningrad, too. It was very good for me,
because I saw a lot of authentic backgrounds for made-up stories which I
will write later on. One of them will be "Russian Baroque" and another will

---

9. From the dome of the Church of Our Lady I
saw those sad ruins strewn amidst the city's lovely
orderliness; at that point the sacristan praised the
skill of the architect, who had seen to it that
church and dome would withstand bombing
should such an unfortunate situation occur. Then
the good sacristan pointed out ruins in all directions and said in a pensive and laconic way: "The
enemy did this!" (German).
1. Commanding the Continental Army during
the American Revolution, George Washington

(1732–1799) crossed the Delaware River with his
troops on December 25, 1776, an event depicted
by the German-born American artist Emanuel
Gottlieb Leutze (1816–1868) in his painting
George Washington Crossing the Delaware (1851).
2. Creative writing program founded in 1936;
the Famous Writers School of Greenwich, Connecticut, was a mail-order school in the 1960s.
3. American publisher (1926–1994) whose
imprint was with the Delacorte Press.

be "No Kissing" and another will be "Dollar Bar" and another will be "If the Accident Will," and so on.

And so on.

There was a Lufthansa[4] plane that was supposed to fly from Philadelphia to Boston to Frankfurt. O'Hare was supposed to get on in Philadelphia and I was supposed to get on in Boston, and off we'd go. But Boston was socked in, so the plane flew straight to Frankfurt from Philadelphia. And I became a non-person in the Boston fog, and Lufthansa put me in a limousine with some other non-persons and sent us to a motel for a non-night.

The time would not pass. Somebody was playing with the clocks, and not only with the electric clocks, but the wind-up kind, too. The second hand on my watch would twitch once, and a year would pass, and then it would twitch again.

There was nothing I could do about it. As an Earthling, I had to believe whatever clocks said—and calendars.

I had two books with me, which I'd meant to read on the plane. One was *Words for the Wind*, by Theodore Roethke,[5] and this is what I found in there:

> *I wake to sleep, and take my waking slow.*
> *I feel my fate in what I cannot fear.*
> *I learn by going where I have to go.*[6]

My other book was Erika Ostrovsky's *Céline and His Vision*.[7] Céline was a brave French soldier in the First World War—until his skull was cracked. After that he couldn't sleep, and there were noises in his head. He became a doctor, and he treated poor people in the daytime, and he wrote grotesque novels all night. No art is possible without a dance with death, he wrote.

The truth is death, he wrote. *I've fought nicely against it as long as I could . . . danced with it, festooned it, waltzed it around . . . decorated it with streamers, titillated it . . .*

Time obsessed him. Miss Ostrovsky reminded me of the amazing scene in *Death on the Installment Plan*[8] where Céline wants to stop the bustling of a street crowd. He screams on paper, *Make them stop . . . don't let them move anymore at all . . . There, make them freeze . . . once and for all! . . . So that they won't disappear anymore!*

I looked through the Gideon Bible in my motel room[9] for tales of great destruction. *The sun was risen upon the Earth when Lot entered into Zo-ar*, I read. *Then the Lord rained upon Sodom and upon Gomorrah brimstone and fire from the Lord out of Heaven; and He overthrew those cities, and all the plain, and all the inhabitants of the cities, and that which grew upon the ground.*

4. German national airline.
5. A 1957 collection by the American poet (1908–1963).
6. From Roethke's 1953 poem "The Waking" (see p. 40).
7. A 1967 study, by the Austrian-born American critic (b. c. 1927) of modern French literature, of Louis-Ferdinand Destouches (1894–1961), French novelist writing under the pen name Louis-Ferdinand Céline.
8. Published in 1936.
9. The Gideons are a Christian traveling men's association established in 1899 and active since 1908 in publishing Bibles and placing them in all hotel and motel rooms.

So it goes.

Those were vile people in both those cities, as is well known. The world was better off without them.

And Lot's wife, of course, was told not to look back where all those people and their homes had been. But she *did* look back, and I love her for that, because it was so human.

So she was turned to a pillar of salt. So it goes.

People aren't supposed to look back. I'm certainly not going to do it anymore.
I've finished my war book now. The next one I write is going to be fun.
This one is a failure, and had to be, since it was written by a pillar of salt. It begins like this:
Listen:
Billy Pilgrim has come unstuck in time.
It ends like this:
Poo-tee-weet?

1969

GRACE PALEY
1922–2007

" A Conversation with My Father" is not Grace Paley's only story about a daughter's visit with an elderly, terminally ill father. Like other repeated situations in her work, such visits enable Paley to explore nontraditional matters through traditional means, such as dialogue. Unlike her contemporaries whose concern with fiction making overshadows the situations their stories would otherwise convey, Paley directs her imaginative explanations to realistic events, in which larger social and moral issues reinforce her literary innovations. Her ability to adapt nontraditional techniques into realistic short stories makes her accessible to a readership otherwise unfriendly to the aesthetic solipsism of self-exploratory fiction (or "metafiction" as it has come to be called).

That Paley's protagonist talks with her father rather than simply writing about him indicates an important characteristic: in such narratives the author wishes not to present a lecture (though figures in her stories sometimes give them) but rather to achieve an understanding through dialogue. This dialectic quality is evident in the stories in her first collection, *The Little Disturbances of Man* (1959), some of which draw on situations first encountered when adapting to marriage and family life in the difficult circumstances of an army camp. By the time of *Enormous Changes at the Last Minute* (1974) Paley had developed her most noteworthy theme, that of women (often single mothers) building satisfactory relationships with the world around them by talking with each other (and sometimes to themselves). The title story from this second collection also shows Paley expanding her language to include an almost poetic phraseology whose facility with metaphors and similes makes much of her narrative action happen directly on the page. Here a father, the same father, is recalled as a child first seeing the American flag, then as a young immigrant taking advantage of what that symbol represents: "Under its protection and working like a horse, he'd read Dickens, gone to medical school, and shot like a surface-to-air missile right into the middle class." By making a comparison to current military technology erupt from the sentence's quainter, almost century-old references, Paley startles her reader and employs a kind of alternative narrative action.

Grace Paley was born in New York City, the child of Russian Jewish immigrants from Ukraine. She attended Hunter College, but graduated from the Merchants and Bankers Business and Secretarial School. Married during college, she had two children and was later divorced, not remarrying until 1972. During the 1950s she became an activist for social issues, first working to close Washington Square (in her Greenwich Village neighborhood) to traffic, later protesting the Vietnam War; in 1978 she was arrested on the White House lawn in a demonstration against nuclear weapons. The success of *Enormous Changes at the Last Minute* drew the attention of other writers to her, and throughout the 1970s and 1980s she was a regular participant on literary panels with innovative fictionalists such as Donald Barthelme and William H. Gass. Her third collection, *Later the Same Day* (1985), continued her method of using metafictive techniques for writing otherwise realistic short stories. In the front matter of *Enormous Changes at the Last Minute*, where a disclaimer about correspondences between fact and fiction would customarily appear, she posted this warning: "Everyone in this book is imagined into life except the father. No matter what story he has to live in, he's my father, I. Goodside, M.D., artist, and storyteller."

Paley also published several volumes of poetry; like her short stories, Paley's poems are marked by their humor, observations of life, and humanity of voice. "Here" is a late, lovely example of her gifts as a poet. In addition, Paley wrote direct social commentary. Especially noteworthy was her essay in the September 1975 issue of *Ms.* magazine, "Other People's Children," objecting to the massive and hurried evacuation of South Vietnamese children during the Vietnam War's last days on the grounds that mothers' rights and interests were grossly violated.

The text below is from *Enormous Changes at the Last Minute* (1974).

A Conversation with My Father

My father is eighty-six years old and in bed. His heart, that bloody motor, is equally old and will not do certain jobs any more. It still floods his head with brainy light. But it won't let his legs carry the weight of his body around the house. Despite my metaphors, his muscle failure is not due to his old heart, he says, but to a potassium shortage. Sitting on one pillow, leaning on three, he offers last-minute advice and makes a request.

"I would like you to write a simple story just once more," he says, "the kind de Maupassant wrote, or Chekhov,[1] the kind you used to write. Just recognizable people and then write down what happened to them next."

I say, "Yes, why not? That's possible." I want to please him, though I don't remember writing that way. I *would* like to try to tell such a story, if he means the kind that begins: "There was a woman . . ." followed by plot, the absolute line between two points which I've always despised. Not for literary reasons, but because it takes all hope away. Everyone, real or invented, deserves the open destiny of life.

---

1. Anton Chekhov (1860–1904), Russian dramatist and story writer, whose characters often discuss moral nuances at length. Guy de Maupassant (1850–1893), French author of well-made sentimental stories and novels.

Finally I thought of a story that had been happening for a couple of years right across the street. I wrote it down, then read it aloud. "Pa," I said, "how about this? Do you mean something like this?"

> Once in my time there was a woman and she had a son. They lived nicely, in a small apartment in Manhattan. This boy at about fifteen became a junkie, which is not unusual in our neighborhood. In order to maintain her close friendship with him, she became a junkie too. She said it was part of the youth culture, with which she felt very much at home. After a while, for a number of reasons, the boy gave it all up and left the city and his mother in disgust. Hopeless and alone, she grieved. We all visit her.

"O.K., Pa, that's it," I said, "an unadorned and miserable tale."

"But that's not what I mean," my father said. "You misunderstood me on purpose. You know there's a lot more to it. You know that. You left everything out. Turgenev[2] wouldn't do that. Chekhov wouldn't do that. There are in fact Russian writers you never heard of, you don't have an inkling of, as good as anyone, who can write a plain ordinary story, who would not leave out what you have left out. I object not to facts but to people sitting in trees talking senselessly, voices from who knows where . . ."

"Forget that one, Pa, what have I left out now? In this one?"

"Her looks, for instance."

"Oh. Quite handsome, I think. Yes."

"Her hair?"

"Dark, with heavy braids, as though she were a girl or a foreigner."

"What were her parents like, her stock? That she became such a person. It's interesting, you know."

"From out of town. Professional people. The first to be divorced in their county. How's that? Enough?" I asked.

"With you, it's all a joke," he said. "What about the boy's father? Why didn't you mention him? Who was he? Or was the boy born out of wedlock?"

"Yes," I said. "He was born out of wedlock."

"For Godsakes, doesn't anyone in your stories get married? Doesn't anyone have the time to run down to City Hall before they jump into bed?"

"No," I said. "In real life, yes. But in my stories, no."

"Why do you answer me like that?"

"Oh, Pa, this is a simple story about a smart woman who came to N.Y.C. full of interest love trust excitement very up to date, and about her son, what a hard time she had in this world. Married or not, it's of small consequence."

"It is of great consequence," he said.

"O.K.," I said.

"O.K. O.K. yourself," he said, "but listen. I believe you that she's good-looking, but I don't think she was so smart."

"That's true," I said. "Actually that's the trouble with stories. People start out fantastic. You think they are extraordinary, but it turns out as the work goes along, they're just average with a good education. Sometimes the other

2. Ivan Turgenev (1818–1883), Russian novelist noted for his tragic vision.

way around, the person's a kind of dumb innocent, but he outwits you and you can't even think of an ending good enough."

"What do you do then?" he asked. He had been a doctor for a couple of decades and then an artist for a couple of decades and he's still interested in details, craft, technique.

"Well, you just have to let the story lie around till some agreement can be reached between you and the stubborn hero."

"Aren't you talking silly, now?" he asked. "Start again," he said. "It so happens I'm not going out this evening. Tell the story again. See what you can do this time."

"O.K.," I said. "But it's not a five-minute job." Second attempt:

Once, across the street from us, there was a fine handsome woman, our neighbor. She had a son whom she loved because she'd known him since birth (in helpless chubby infancy, and in the wrestling, hugging ages, seven to ten, as well as earlier and later). This boy, when he fell into the fist of adolescence, became a junkie. He was not a hopeless one. He was in fact hopeful, an ideologue and successful converter. With his busy brilliance, he wrote persuasive articles for his high-school newspaper. Seeking a wider audience, using important connections, he drummed into Lower Manhattan newsstand distribution a periodical called *Oh! Golden Horse!*[3]

In order to keep him from feeling guilty (because guilt is the stony heart of nine tenths of all clinically diagnosed cancers in America today, she said), and because she had always believed in giving bad habits room at home where one could keep an eye on them, she too became a junkie. Her kitchen was famous for a while—a center for intellectual addicts who knew what they were doing. A few felt artistic like Coleridge and others were scientific and revolutionary like Leary.[4] Although she was often high herself, certain good mothering reflexes remained, and she saw to it that there was lots of orange juice around and honey and milk and vitamin pills. However, she never cooked anything but chili, and that no more than once a week. She explained, when we talked to her, seriously, with neighborly concern, that it was her part in the youth culture and she would rather be with the young, it was an honor, than with her own generation.

One week, while nodding through an Antonioni film,[5] this boy was severely jabbed by the elbow of a stern and proselytizing girl, sitting beside him. She offered immediate apricots and nuts for his sugar level, spoke to him sharply, and took him home.

She had heard of him and his work and she herself published, edited, and wrote a competitive journal called *Man Does Live By Bread Alone*. In the organic heat of her continuous presence he could not help but become interested once more in his muscles, his arteries, and nerve

3. "Horse" is slang for heroin.
4. Timothy Leary (1920–1996), American psychologist who in the 1960s encouraged experimentation with hallucinogenic drugs. Samuel Taylor Coleridge (1772–1834), English poet who wrote "Kubla Khan" under the influence of opium.
5. Michelangelo Antonioni (1912–2007), Italian filmmaker known for his intellectual style. The boy could be "nodding" in response to the film or the heroin.

connections. In fact he began to love them, treasure them, praise them with funny little songs in *Man Does Live . . .*

> *the fingers of my flesh transcend*
> *my transcendental soul*
> *the tightness in my shoulders end*
> *my teeth have made me whole*

To the mouth of his head (that glory of will and determination) he brought hard apples, nuts, wheat germ, and soybean oil. He said to his old friends, from now on, I guess I'll keep my wits about me. I'm going on the natch. He said he was about to begin a spiritual deep-breathing journey. How about you too, Mom? he asked kindly.

His conversion was so radiant, splendid, that neighborhood kids his age began to say that he had never been a real addict at all, only a journalist along for the smell of the story. The mother tried several times to give up what had become without her son and his friends a lonely habit. This effort only brought it to supportable levels. The boy and his girl took their electronic mimeograph and moved to the bushy edge of another borough. They were very strict. They said they would not see her again until she had been off drugs for sixty days.

At home alone in the evening, weeping, the mother read and reread the seven issues of *Oh! Golden Horse!* They seemed to her as truthful as ever. We often crossed the street to visit and console. But if we mentioned any of our children who were at college or in the hospital or dropouts at home, she would cry out, My baby! My baby! and burst into terrible, face-scarring, time-consuming tears. The End.

First my father was silent, then he said, "Number One: You have a nice sense of humor. Number Two: I see you can't tell a plain story. So don't waste time." Then he said sadly, "Number Three: I suppose that means she was alone, she was left like that, his mother. Alone. Probably sick?"

I said, "Yes."

"Poor woman. Poor girl, to be born in a time of fools to live among fools. The end. The end. You were right to put that down. The end."

I didn't want to argue, but I had to say, "Well, it is not necessarily the end, Pa."

"Yes," he said, "what a tragedy. The end of a person."

"No, Pa," I begged him. "It doesn't have to be. She's only about forty. She could be a hundred different things in this world as time goes on. A teacher or a social worker. An ex-junkie! Sometimes it's better than having a master's in education."

"Jokes," he said. "As a writer that's your main trouble. You don't want to recognize it. Tragedy! Plain tragedy! Historical tragedy! No hope. The end."

"Oh, Pa," I said. "She could change."

"In your own life, too, you have to look it in the face."

He took a couple of nitroglycerin. "Turn to five," he said, pointing to the dial on the oxygen tank. He inserted the tubes into his nostrils and breathed deep. He closed his eyes and said, "No."

I had promised the family to always let him have the last word when arguing, but in this case I had a different responsibility. That woman lives across the street. She's my knowledge and my invention. I'm sorry for her. I'm not going to leave her there in that house crying. (Actually neither would Life, which unlike me has no pity.)

Therefore: She did change. Of course her son never came home again. But right now, she's the receptionist in a storefront community clinic in the East Village.[6] Most of the customers are young people, some old friends. The head doctor has said to her, "If we only had three people in this clinic with your experiences . . ."

"The doctor said that?" My father took the oxygen tubes out of his nostrils and said, "Jokes. Jokes again."

"No, Pa, it could really happen that way, it's a funny world nowadays."

"No," he said. "Truth first. She will slide back. A person must have character. She does not."

"No, Pa," I said. "That's it. She's got a job. Forget it. She's in that storefront working."

"How long will it be?" he asked. "Tragedy! You too. When will you look it in the face?"

1974

Here

Here I am in the garden laughing
an old woman with heavy breasts
and a nicely mapped face

how did this happen
well that's who I wanted to be   5

at last   a woman
in the old style   sitting
stout thighs apart under
a big skirt   grandchild sliding
on   off my lap   a pleasant   10
summer perspiration

that's my old man across the yard
he's talking to the meter reader[1]
he's telling him the world's sad story
how electricity is oil or uranium   15
and so forth   I tell my grandson

---

6. Immigrant neighborhood east of Greenwich Village in lower Manhattan that in the 1960s became home to an antiestablishment youth counterculture.

1. A utilities worker who reads electric, gas, water, or steam consumption meters and records the volume used.

run over to your grandpa   ask him
to sit beside me for a minute   I
am suddenly exhausted by my desire
to kiss his sweet explaining lips   20

2000

JAMES DICKEY
1923–1997

James Dickey was born in Atlanta, Georgia, and grew up in one of its suburbs, where he was a high school football star and a self-professed "wild motorcycle rider." After a year (1942) at Clemson College in South Carolina, he enlisted in the army air force. As a young man he had admired the English Romantic poet Byron, largely for what he symbolized: bold, masculine swagger and a love of martial and sexual adventure. During off-hours from combat missions in the South Pacific, Dickey began to frequent wartime libraries, where he read writers like Herman Melville and James Agee and explored anthologies of modern poetry. After the war, at Vanderbilt University and through the encouragement of one of his professors, Dickey began seriously writing poetry.

His first published poem appeared in *Sewanee Review* while he was still a college senior; his first book of verse, *Into the Stone*, appeared in 1960. From that time Dickey consistently regarded poetry as the center of his career, although he was at different periods an advertising man for Coca-Cola in New York and Atlanta, a college teacher, a training officer for pilots during the Korean War, a best-selling novelist (*Deliverance*, 1970), and a screenwriter (adapting *Deliverance* for Hollywood).

Dickey's work examines the heroic and sometimes excessive figure of the self in moments of crisis or danger. It shows a desire to ascend beyond the human world, to resist the downward pull of mortality in ways that may remind us of the modern American poet Hart Crane. In the title poem of his volume *Drowning with Others* (1962), for example, the speaker imagines the moment when a man feels "my own wingblades spring," and finds himself "rising and singing / With my last breath," free of the "down-soaring dead." *Helmets* (1964) includes a powerful group of war poems in which Dickey struggles for a vision that will allow him to transcend death. In other earlier work he often explores the instinctual and unconscious aspect of experience and sometimes identifies with totemic animals, as in "The Heaven of Animals," where he envisions a world in which "Their instincts wholly bloom / And they rise. / The soft eyes open."

In Dickey's earlier poems the speaker was primarily an observer, describing as if from outside these states of animal and instinctual grace. The poet tended to write in short lines—three accents or beats per line. With *Buckdancer's Choice* (1965) Dickey became interested in longer "split lines," which he used from then on. The line of verse is splintered into phrases, each group of words separated from the next by spaces designed to take the place of punctuation. The purpose is to approximate the way the mind "associates in bursts of words, in jumps." Instead of being spoken by a distanced observer, the poem is placed within the mind of someone caught in a moment of crisis or excitement.

One of his most central later poems written in the longer line is "Falling," with its rendering of the consciousness of a stewardess who falls from an airplane into space. Like the earlier "Drowning with Others," this poem confirms the importance in Dickey's work of flight, that figure for the self's transcendence of mortality. In "Falling" he gives us the woman's "superhuman act" as she drifts above the tiny human world and possesses, for those moments, a godlike vision. Yet even as Dickey's poem suspends the moment of falling, it admits the pull of gravity that brings the woman closer and closer to the ground and to her death. "Falling" expresses Dickey's enduring interest in danger and in the immortal longings of the titanic self.

Dickey's interest in violence and power as subjects is suggested by the apocalyptic title of his 1970 volume *The Eye Beaters, Blood, Victory, Madness, Buckhead and Mercy*, and many of his later poems are designed to administer shocks to the reader's system. Dickey enjoyed cutting a flamboyant public figure with a reputation for hard drinking and fast motorcycles. He also enjoyed being a publicist for the life of the poet, as if he were a latter-day Byron, sometimes situating himself in a paradoxical cross between serious literary criticism and advertisements for himself. He published the series *Self-Interviews* as well as a penetrating collection of reviews of other poets, *Babel to Byzantium* (1968). In 1966–68 he was consultant in poetry at the Library of Congress, the position later known as poet laureate of the United States.

Drowning with Others

There are moments a man turns from us
Whom we have all known until now.
Upgathered, we watch him grow,
Unshipping his shoulder bones

Like human, everyday wings   5
That he has not ever used,
Releasing his hair from his brain,
A kingfisher's crest, confused

By the God-tilted light of Heaven.
His deep, window-watching smile   10
Comes closely upon us in waves,
And spreads, and now we are

At last within it, dancing.
Slowly we turn and shine
Upon what is holding us,   15
As under our feet he soars,

Struck dumb as the angel of Eden,[1]
In wide, eye-opening rings.
Yet the hand on my shoulder fears
To feel my own wingblades spring,   20

1. Probably the cherub who guards the entrance to the Garden of Eden after Adam and Eve have been banished (Genesis 3.24).

To feel me sink slowly away
In my hair turned loose like a thought
Of a fisherbird dying in flight.
If I opened my arms, I could hear

Every shell in the sea find the word   25
It has tried to put into my mouth.
Broad flight would become of my dancing,
And I would obsess the whole sea,

But I keep rising and singing
With my last breath. Upon my back,   30
With his hand on my unborn wing,
A man rests easy as sunlight

Who has kept himself free of the forms
Of the deaf, down-soaring dead,
And me laid out and alive   35
For nothing at all, in his arms.

                                            1962

The Heaven of Animals

Here they are. The soft eyes open.
If they have lived in a wood
It is a wood.
If they have lived on plains
It is grass rolling   5
Under their feet forever.

Having no souls, they have come,
Anyway, beyond their knowing.
Their instincts wholly bloom
And they rise.   10
The soft eyes open.

To match them, the landscape flowers,
Outdoing, desperately
Outdoing what is required:
The richest wood,   15
The deepest field.

For some of these,
It could not be the place
It is, without blood.
These hunt, as they have done,   20
But with claws and teeth grown perfect,

More deadly than they can believe.
They stalk more silently,

And crouch on the limbs of trees,
And their descent   25
Upon the bright backs of their prey

May take years
In a sovereign floating of joy.
And those that are hunted
Know this as their life,   30
Their reward: to walk

Under such trees in full knowledge
Of what is in glory above them,
And to feel no fear,
But acceptance, compliance.   35
Fulfilling themselves without pain

At the cycle's center,
They tremble, they walk
Under the tree,
They fall, they are torn,   40
They rise, they walk again.

                                                                              1962

Falling

"A 29-year-old stewardess fell . . . to her death tonight when she
was swept through an emergency door that suddenly sprang
open. . . . The body . . . was found . . . three hours after the accident."

                                                        —*New York Times*

The states when they black out and lie there rolling   when they turn
To something transcontinental   move by   drawing moonlight out of the
      great
One-sided stone hung off the starboard wingtip   some sleeper next to
An engine is groaning for coffee   and there is faintly coming in
Somewhere the vast beast-whistle of space. In the galley with its racks   5
Of trays   she rummages for a blanket   and moves in her slim tailored
Uniform to pin it over the cry at the top of the door. As though she blew

The door down with a silent blast from her lungs   frozen   she is black
Out finding herself   with the plane nowhere and her body taking by the
      throat
The undying cry of the void   falling   living   beginning to be
      something   10
That no one has ever been and lived through   screaming without enough air
Still neat   lipsticked   stockinged   girdled by regulation   her hat
Still on   her arms and legs in no world   and yet spaced also strangely
With utter placid rightness on thin air   taking her time   she holds it
In many places   and now, still thousands of feet from her death she seems   15
To slow   she develops interest   she turns in her maneuverable body

To watch it. She is hung high up in the overwhelming middle of things in
    her
Self   in low body-whistling wrapped intensely   in all her dark dance-
    weight
Coming down from a marvelous leap   with the delaying, dumfounding
    ease
Of a dream of being drawn   like endless moonlight to the harvest soil   20
Of a central state of one's country   with a great gradual warmth coming
Over her   floating   finding more and more breath in what she has been
    using
For breath   as the levels become more human   seeing clouds placed
    honestly
Below her left and right   riding slowly toward them   she clasps it all
To her and can hang her hands and feet in it in peculiar ways   and   25
Her eyes opened wide by wind, can open her mouth as wide   wider and
    suck
All the heat from the cornfields   can go down on her back with a feeling
Of stupendous pillows stacked under her   and can turn   turn as to
    someone
In bed   smile, understood in darkness   can go away   slant   slide
Off tumbling   into the emblem of a bird with its wings half-spread   30
Or whirl madly on herself   in endless gymnastics in the growing
    warmth
Of wheatfields rising toward the harvest moon.   There is time to live
In superhuman health   seeing mortal unreachable lights far down seeing
An ultimate highway with one late priceless car probing it   arriving
In a square town   and off her starboard arm the glitter of water catches 35
The moon by its own shaken side   scaled, roaming silver   My God it is
    good
And evil   lying in one after another of all the positions for love
Making   dancing   sleeping   and now cloud wisps at her no
Raincoat   no matter   all small towns brokenly brighter from inside
Cloud   she walks over them like rain   bursts out to behold a Greyhound 40
Bus shooting light through its sides   it is the signal to go straight
Down like a glorious diver   then feet first   her skirt stripped beautifully
Up   her face in fear-scented cloths   her legs deliriously bare   then
Arms out   she slow-rolls over   steadies out   waits for something great
To take control of her   trembles near feathers   planes head-down   45
The quick movements of bird-necks turning her head   gold eyes the
    insight-
eyesight of owls blazing into the hencoops   a taste for chicken
    overwhelming
Her   the long-range vision of hawks enlarging all human lights of cars
Freight trains   looped bridges   enlarging the moon racing slowly
Through all the curves of a river   all the darks of the midwest blazing 50
From above. A rabbit in a bush turns white   the smothering chickens
Huddle   for over them there is still time for something to live
With the streaming half-idea of a long stoop   a hurtling   a fall
That is controlled   that plummets as it wills   turns gravity
Into a new condition, showing its other side like a moon   shining   55
New Powers   there is still time to live on a breath made of nothing
But the whole night   time for her to remember to arrange her skirt

Like a diagram of a bat   tightly it guides her   she has this flying-skin
Made of garments   and there are also those sky-divers on TV   sailing
In sunlight   smiling under their goggles   swapping batons back and
    forth   60
And He who jumped without a chute and was handed one by a diving
Buddy. She looks for her grinning companion   white teeth   nowhere
She is screaming   singing hymns   her thin human wings spread out
From her neat shoulders   the air beast-crooning to her   warbling
And she can no longer behold the huge partial form of the world   now   65
She is watching her country lose its evoked master shape   watching it lose
And gain   get back its houses and peoples   watching it bring up
Its local lights   single homes   lamps on barn roofs   if she fell
Into water she might live   like a diver   cleaving   perfect   plunge

Into another   heavy silver   unbreathable   slowing   saving   70
Element: there is water   there is time to perfect all the fine
Points of diving   feet together   toes pointed   hands shaped right
To insert her into water like a needle   to come out healthily dripping
And be handed a Coca-Cola   there they are   there are the waters
Of life   the moon packed and coiled in a reservoir   so let me begin   75
To plane across the night air of Kansas   opening my eyes superhumanly
Bright   to the damned moon   opening the natural wings of my jacket
By Don Loper[1]   moving like a hunting owl toward the glitter of water
One cannot just *fall   just tumble screaming all that time   one must* use
It   she is now through with all   through all   clouds   damp   hair   80
Straightened   the last wisp of fog pulled apart on her face like wool
    revealing
New darks   new progressions of headlights along dirt roads from chaos

And night   a gradual warming   a new-made, inevitable world of one's
    own
Country   a great stone of light in its waiting waters   hold   hold out
For water: who knows when what correct young woman must take up her
    body   85
And fly   and head for the moon-crazed inner eye of midwest imprisoned
Water   stored up for her for years   the arms of her jacket slipping
Air up her sleeves to go   all over her? What final things can be said
Of one who starts out sheerly in her body in the high middle of night
Air   to track down water like a rabbit where it lies like life itself   90
Off to the right in Kansas? She goes toward   the blazing-bare lake
Her skirts neat   her hands and face warmed more and more by the air
Rising from pastures of beans   and under her   under chenille bedspreads
The farm girls are feeling the goddess in them struggle and rise brooding
On the scratch-shining posts of the bed   dreaming of female signs   95
Of the moon   male blood like iron   of what is really said by the moan
Of airliners passing over them at dead of midwest midnight   passing
Over brush fires   burning out in silence on little hills   and will wake
To see the woman they should be   struggling on the rooftree to become
Stars: for her the ground is closer   water is nearer   she passes   100

---

1. Hollywood costume and clothing designer (1906–1972).

It   then banks   turns   her sleeves fluttering differently as she rolls
Out to face the east, where the sun shall come up from wheatfields she
        must
Do something with water   fly to it   fall in it   drink it   rise
From it   but there is none left upon earth   the clouds have drunk it back
The plants have sucked it down   there are standing toward her only   105
The common fields of death   she comes back from flying to falling
Returns to a powerful cry   the silent scream with which she blew down
The coupled door of the airliner   nearly   nearly losing hold
Of what she has done   remembers   remembers the shape at the heart
Of cloud   fashionably swirling   remembers she still has time to die   110
Beyond explanation. Let her now take off her hat in summer air the
        coutour
Of cornfields   and have enough time to kick off her one remaining
Shoe with the toes   of the other foot   to unhook her stockings
With calm fingers, noting how fatally easy it is to undress in midair
Near death   when the body will assume without effort any position   115
Except the one that will sustain it   enable it to rise   live
Not die   nine farms hover close   widen   eight of them separate, leaving
One in the middle   then the fields of that farm do the same   there is no
Way to back off   from her chosen ground   but she sheds the jacket
With its silver sad impotent wings   sheds the bat's guiding tailpiece   120
Of her skirt   the lightning-charged clinging of her blouse   the intimate
Inner flying-garment of her slip in which she rides like the holy ghost
Of a virgin   sheds the long windsocks of her stockings   absurd
Brassiere   then feels the girdle required by regulations squirming
Off her: no longer monobuttocked   she feels the girdle flutter   shake   125
In her hand   and float   upward   her clothes rising off her ascending
Into cloud   and fights away from her head the last sharp dangerous shoe
Like a dumb bird   and now will drop in   SOON   now will drop

In like this   the greatest thing that ever came to Kansas   down from all
Heights   all levels of American breath   layered in the lungs from the
        frail   130
Chill of space to the loam where extinction slumbers in corn tassels thickly
And breathes like rich farmers counting: will come among them after
Her last superhuman act   the last slow careful passing of her hands
All over her unharmed body   desired by every sleeper in his dream:
Boys finding for the first time their loins filled with heart's blood   135
Widowed farmers whose hands float under light covers to find themselves
Arisen at sunrise   the splendid position of blood unearthly drawn
Toward clouds   all feel something   pass over them as she passes
Her palms over *her* long legs   *her* small breasts   and deeply between
Her thighs   her hair shot loose from all pins   streaming in the wind   140
Of her body   let her come openly   trying at the last second to land
On her back   This is it   THIS
                        All those who find her impressed
In the soft loam   gone down   driven well into the image of her body
The furrows for miles flowing in upon her where she lies very deep   145
In her mortal outline   in the earth as it is in cloud   can tell nothing
But that she is there   inexplicable   unquestionable   and remember
That something broke in them as well   and began to live and die more

When they walked for no reason into their fields to where the whole earth
Caught her   interrupted her maiden flight   told her how to lie   she
    cannot   150
Turn   go away   cannot move   cannot slide off it and assume another
Position   no sky-diver with any grin could save her   hold her in his arms
Plummet with her   unfold above her his wedding silks   she can no longer
Mark the rain with whirling women that take the place of a dead wife
Or the goddess in Norwegian farm girls   or all the back-breaking whores   155
Of Wichita. All the known air above her is not giving up quite one
Breath   it is all gone   and yet not dead   not anywhere else
Quite   lying still in the field on her back   sensing the smells
Of incessant growth try to lift her   a little sight left in the corner
Of one eye   fading   seeing something wave   lies believing   160
That she could have made it   at the best part of her brief goddess
State   to water   gone in headfirst   come out smiling   invulnerable
Girl in a bathing-suit ad   but she is lying like a sunbather at the last
Of moonlight   half-buried in her impact on the earth   not far
From a railroad trestle   a water tank   she could see if she could   165
Raise her head from her modest hole   with her clothes beginning
To come down all over Kansas   into bushes   on the dewy sixth green
Of a golf course   one shoe   her girdle coming down fantastically
On a clothesline, where it belongs   her blouse on a lightning rod:

Lies in the fields   in *this* field   on her broken back as though on   170
A cloud she cannot drop through   while farmers sleepwalk without
Their women from houses   a walk like falling toward the far waters
Of life   in moonlight   toward the dreamed eternal meaning of their farms
Toward the flowering of the harvest in their hands   that tragic cost
Feels herself go   go toward   go outward   breathes at last fully   175
Not   and tries   less   once   tries   tries   AH, GOD—

                                                    1981

Postmodern Manifestos

The manifesto speaks in the voice of the true believer. But as the selections in this cluster show, manifestos do not always take themselves completely seriously even while—or we might say, especially *because*—they seek to overturn ideas that many hold dear. Whether these are prevailing ideas about art and what it should do, about people and how they might relate to each other, or about the very essence of a human being, sometimes the would-be reformer has to make fun first, just to loosen things up. Ranging, then, from the earnest to the jokey, and always driven by the energy of change, the genre of the literary manifesto is itself a literary form. All the examples of the genre here are written by literary artists experienced in the craft of writing and, for the dramatists, in the craft of creating performances.

In the twentieth century, the manifesto was an especially popular form in the early years (the 1910s and '20s) and in the 1960s and '70s. At each moment, writers felt that the forms of art had become, for one reason or another, constraining. Despite this feeling of constraint, in each case the artistic vanguard believed that existing forms of art contained the ingredients for a new artistic era. Taken together, the pieces gathered here look to four aspects of literary form for the engine of change: the process of *making* that the medium requires; the *conceptual* aspects of the medium; the *social* aspects of the medium; and perhaps most important, the *material* aspects of the medium (which means words and the physical acts and things that may be combined with words—including breathing and moving, staging and props, and, of course, paper). The writers in this cluster suggest how writers might tap into these aspects of their art to create a new vision of what art can be and do.

Feeling stifled under modernist formalism and the mainstream culture of the 1950s, many poets sought a return to the "unstructured places of being" that A. R. Ammons has called poetry's true source. After several decades in which impersonality and objectivity were the key values in poetry criticism, poets shifted the focus from the poem as artifact (the "well-wrought urn," in the critic Cleanth Brooks's phrase) to the poem as open-ended process, an activity, as Ammons suggests, that is like the physical act of walking or, for the poet Charles Olson, that is rooted in the acts of breathing and voicing. The unconscious began to take up a larger place in poetry, and accident and chance became, at times, structuring principles, as we see in some of Ammons's poems. A similar emphasis on process informed the work of the abstract expressionist painters, avant-garde theater companies, and improvisatory groups of jazz musicians. The jazz trumpeter Charlie "Bird" Parker, known for his kinetic musical explorations, became for many writers a model of artistic activity. When Olson, in his manifesto "Projective Verse," described poetry as a "transfer of energy" he revealed the implicit physiology underlying this new paradigm; the shift from artifact to process relocated poetry in the body, with its breath, movement, and changes. For some poets and dramatists—like Audre Lorde or Charles Ludlam—a focus on the body as an element of artistic process allowed the artist to explore experiences that had been silenced or made taboo. In many cases tapping into the energy of the body led directly to the erotic, as is clear in Frank O'Hara's remark that the appeal of poetic measure is like buying a "pair of pants . . . tight enough so everyone will want to go to bed with you."

The rejection of traditional form—that "well-wrought urn"—did not mean, however, that form was rejected wholesale in favor of process during this period. The very physicality of process extended to a new awareness of form's physicality. When Ronald Sukenick says that the novel "must make maximum expressive use of all

369

elements of the printed page, including the relation of print to blank space," he is resisting the ease of realist fiction that invites the reader to forget that what he or she is reading is made of words. William Gass imagines "concepts" as the specific stuff out of which fiction is made, but treats concepts as a special kind of materiality—a materiality that "stains the fingers" like paint, even while concepts aspire to the abstract purity of mathematics. Richard Foreman seeks to explore the materiality of both objects and bodies on the stage, and similarly rejects the traditional sorts of emotional immersion that drive both plays and novels. He calls for an "engine" for drama that is somehow internal to the material form itself and to the spectator's physical, material, and sensory experience of it.

Art is for other human beings, and it speaks to our human experience of life. This fact drives the charming sociality of O'Hara's "personism"—which began as a joke between friends—and the urgent seriousness of Lorde's desire to make language new so that experience shut out of language could be made visible and sayable between persons. Ludlam's manifesto, like his theatrical practice, looks toward the interaction between audience and performance for that electric energy that can unsettle settled ideas. The manifesto is meant to be *usable*, something that can be activated, its fresh ideas entering the social world through speaking, thinking, writing, breathing bodies as they make and share art.

RONALD SUKENICK

R onald Sukenick (1932–2004) was an innovative fictionist, beginning with his novel *Up* (1968). As the title of his collection *The Death of the Novel and Other Stories* (1969) suggests, he viewed critical theory about fiction as just one more story, with neither more nor less credibility than any other work of the imagination. As he argues in the text reprinted here, adapted from a publicity release he prepared for his second novel, *Out* (1973), and collected in his *In Form: Digressions on the Act of Fiction* (1985), fictive narrative is not *about* something but *is* something— not a representation of the world but something added to that world as another object to be encountered. This approach not only stands traditional mimesis on its head but argues that representation in fiction is fundamentally dishonest—a fraudulent totalization that misrepresents reality. What is reality? For Sukenick, in his story collections and novels that reached through the 1980s and 1990s to conclude with the posthumously published *Last Fall* (2005), fiction was above all an activity, a self-conscious act of creating a literary work with no illusions about the nature of its making. All aspects of his career focused on this purpose, including his teaching of creative writing (at the University of Colorado), his encouragement of independent publishing through the Coordinating Council of Literary Magazines, and his founding of the *American Book Review* in 1977 as an alternative to establishment journalism.

Innovative Fiction / Innovative Criteria

It seems strange to have to talk about innovation in fiction, but the American novel until the end of the sixties was so static that we have not yet fully understood how parochial and narrow the accepted literary norm for fiction had become.

Properly speaking, there is no such thing as "innovative fiction." The novel *is* innovation—it is not called the "novel" for nothing. Fiction is the most fluid and changing of literary forms, the one that most immediately reflects the changes in our collective consciousness, and in fact that is one of its great virtues. As soon as fiction gets frozen into one particular model, it loses that responsiveness to our immediate experience that is its hallmark. It becomes literary. It seems to me that this is one of the major factors contributing to the recent decline in the popularity of fiction: people no longer believe in the novel as a medium that gets at the truth of their lives.

The form of fiction that comes down to us through Jane Austen, George Eliot, and Hemingway[1] is no longer adequate to capture our experience. Either the novel will change, or it will die. Today's money-making novels are those that sell to the movies—in other words, they are essentially written for another medium. No one takes novels seriously until they become movies, which is to say that no one takes novels seriously.

Perhaps I exaggerate slightly, but not much. If we are going to have a wide and serious audience for fiction again we are going to have to re-examine the source of the novel's power beyond the particular forms of fiction that have become so dull to so many.

And first of all we will have to make a fundamental distinction between fiction and data. The great advantage of fiction over history, journalism, or any other supposedly "factual" kind of writing is that it is an expressive medium. It transmits feeling, energy, excitement. Television can give us the news, but fiction can best express our response to the news. No other medium—especially not film—can so well deal with our strongest and often most intimate responses to the large and small facts of our daily lives. No other medium, in other words, can so well keep track of the reality of our experience. But to do this successfully the novel must continually reinvent itself to remain in touch with the texture of our lives. It must make maximum expressive use of all elements of the printed page, including the relation of print to blank space. It must break through the literary formulas when necessary while at the same time preserving what is essential to fiction: incident, feeling, power, scope, and the sense of consciousness struggling with circumstance.

There is not one new fiction, but many. Novelists today have an unprecedented number of stylistic options, a range of choice involving not so much a struggle of an old form with a new, but an opening out, a broader awareness of the possibilities of the medium. Perhaps the most sensible working definition for what is new in fiction is simply what is not old, what lies outside the literary clichés of the formula of plot, character, and social realism. But this situation also creates problems of judgment: novelty does not guarantee quality, and it becomes crucial to distinguish the superficial from the substantial, regardless of form. To make such distinctions we must go back to the sources of fiction, stripped of inessentials and historical trappings, so that we can recognize the fundamental virtues of the novel though they

---

1. Ernest Hemingway (1899–1961), American novelist and short-story writer. Jane Austen (1775–1817), English novelist. George Eliot, pen name of Mary Ann Evans (1819–1880), English novelist and essayist.

may appear in odd recombinations and unaccustomed forms. New fiction requires new criteria, but such criteria will be rooted in the essentials of the medium: not plot, but ongoing incident; not characterization, but consciousness struggling with circumstance; not social realism, but a sense of situation; and so on. Innovative fiction, when successful by these criteria, is not "experimental" but represents the progressive struggle of art to rescue the truth of our experience.

1974

WILLIAM H. GASS

William H. Gass (b. 1924) earned a Ph.D. in philosophy and taught the subject for his full academic career, beginning at Purdue University and continuing at Washington University in St. Louis, Missouri. Yet his major interests have been literary. His early work, the novel *Omensetter's Luck* (1966) and the story collection *In the Heart of the Heart of the Country* (1968), identified him as a proponent of serious fiction, but it was his novella, *Willie Masters' Lonesome Wife* (1968), and his first book of essays, *Fiction and the Figures of Life* (1970, from which the piece reprinted here is taken), that established his credentials as a radical innovator. The novella is as anti-illusionistic as anything Ronald Sukenick might conceive: printed in several different typefaces on four different colors of paper with various graphic devices coursing through the text, including coffee-cup stains and a cascade of footnotes that at one point chase the narrative off the page, it speaks boldly for a fiction that seeks to be nothing more than its own obvious self. In his one other novel, *The Tunnel* (1995), Gass examines historical ideas in a similarly self-conscious manner. His most frequent venues, however, have been books of essays, in which he uses philosophical principles as argumentative support for innovative fiction. Gass's essays, like his literary debates with the realist John Gardner, make eloquent arguments for the worth of such fiction, on ethical and aesthetic grounds.

The Medium of Fiction

It seems a country-headed thing to say: that literature is language, that stories and the places and the people in them[1] are merely made of words as chairs are made of smoothed sticks and sometimes of cloth or metal tubes. Still, we cannot be too simple at the start, since the obvious is often the unobserved. Occasionally we should allow the trite to tease us into thought, for such old friends, the clichés in our life, are the only strangers we can know. It seems incredible, the ease with which we sink through books quite out of sight,[2] pass clamorous pages into soundless dreams. That novels should be made of words, and merely words, is shocking, really. It's as

1. For the people, see "The Concept of Character in Fiction" [Gass's note; this essay appears later in his collection].
2. This, as well as the comparison with mathe-

matics, is returned to in "In Terms of the Toenail: Fiction and the Figures of Life" [Gass's note; this essay appears later in his collection].

though you had discovered that your wife were made of rubber: the bliss of all those years, the fears . . . from sponge.

Like the mathematician, like the philosopher, the novelist makes things out of concepts. Concepts, consequently, must be his critical concern: not the defects of his person, the crimes on his conscience, other men's morals, or their kindness or cruelty. The painter squeezes space through his pigments. Paint stains his fingers. How can he forget the color he has loaded on his brush or that blank canvas audience before him? Yet the novelist frequently behaves as if his work were all heart, character, and story; he professes to hate abstraction, mathematics, and the pure works of mind. Of course, unlike poetry, and despite its distinguished figures, for a long time now the novel has been an amateur's affair, an open field for anybody's running, and it has drawn the idle, sick, and gossipaceous, the vaguely artistic—prophets, teachers, muckrakers—all the fanatical explainers, those dreamily scientific, and those anally pedantic.

Paint stains the fingers; the sculptor's hair is white with dust; but concepts have no physical properties; they do not permit smell or reflect light; they do not fill space or contain it; they do not age. "Five" is no wider, older, or fatter than "four"; "apple" isn't sweeter than "quince," rounder than "pear," smoother than "peach." To say, then, that literature is language is to say that literature is made of meanings, concepts, ideas, forms (please yourself with the term), and that these are so static and eternal as to shame the stars.

Like the mathematician. For the novelist to be at all, in any way, like a mathematician is shocking. It's worse than discovering your privates are plastic. Because there's no narration among numbers. It is logically impossible. Time's lacking.

When David Hilbert,[3] the great logician, heard that a student had given up mathematics to write novels, he is supposed to have said: "It was just as well; he did not have enough imagination to become a first-rate mathematician."

The yammer of thought, the constant one-after-another of sounds, the shapes of words, the terrible specter of spelling, are each due to this fact that meanings are heavenly bodies which, to our senses, must somehow announce themselves. A word is a concept made flesh, if you like—the eternal presented as noise. When I spell, then, let's say, "avoirdupois,"[4] I am forming our name for that meaning, but it might, just as well, be written down "dozzo," or still more at length, with the same lack of logic, "typary," "snoddle," or "willmullynull." "Avoirdupois." An unreasonable body. Nonetheless lovely. "Avoirdupois."

There is a fundamental contradiction in our medium.[5] We work with a marble of flaws. My mind is utterly unlike my body,[6] and unless you're an angel, so, I am certain, is yours. Poor Descartes[7] really wrote on the problems of poets: word sense and word sound, math and mechanics, the mind and its body, can they touch? And how, pray God, can they resemble? In the

---

3. Russian-born German mathematician (1862–1943).
4. Weight measure based on sixteen ounces to a pound.
5. See "Gertrude Stein: Her Escape from Protective Language" [Gass's note; this essay appears later in his collection; Stein (1874–1946) was an American poet and novelist active in France].

6. The contrast which is meant here is not that often alleged to exist between thought and feeling, but that between consciousness and things [Gass's note].
7. René Descartes (1596–1650), French philosopher and mathematician best known for the formulation "Cogito ergo sum," Latin for "I think, therefore I am."

act of love, as in all the arts, the soul should be felt by the tongue and the fingers, felt in the skin. So should our sounds come to color up the surface of our stories like a blush. This adventitious music is the only sensory quality our books can have. As Frost[8] observed, even the empty sentence has a sound, or rather—I should say—*is* a series of nervous tensions and resolves. No artist dares neglect his own world's body, for *nothing else*, nothing else about his book is physical.

In the hollow of a jaw, the ear, upon the page, concepts now begin to move: they appear, accelerate, they race, they hesitate a moment, slow, turn, break, join, modify, and it becomes reasonable to speak of the problems of narration for the first time. Truly (that is to say, technically), narration is that part of the art of fiction concerned with the coming on and passing off of words— not the familiar arrangement of words in dry strings like so many shriveled worms, but their formal direction and rapidity. But this is not what's usually meant.

For most people, fiction is history; fiction is history without tables, graphs, dates, imports, edicts, evidence, laws; history without hiatus—intelligible, simple, smooth. Fiction is sociology freed of statistics, politics with no real party in the opposition; it's a world where play money buys you cardboard squares of colored country; a world where everyone is obediently psychological, economic, ethnic, geographical—framed in a keyhole and always nude, each figure fashioned from the latest thing in cello-see-through, so we may observe our hero's guts, too, if we choose: ah, they're blue, and squirming like a tickled river. For truth without effort, thought without rigor, feeling without form, existence without commitment: what will you give? for a wind-up world, a toy life? . . . six bits?[9] for a book with a thicker skin? . . . six bucks? I am a man, myself, intemperately mild, and though it seems to me as much deserved as it's desired, I have no wish to steeple quires of paper passion up so many sad unelevating rears.

Nay, not *seems*, it *is* a stubborn, country-headed thing to say: that there are no events but words in fiction. Words mean things. Thus we use them every day: make love, buy bread, and blow up bridges. But the use of language in fiction only mimics its use in life. A sign like GENTS, for instance, tells me where to pee. It conveys information; it produces feelings of glad relief. I use the sign, but I dare not dawdle under it. It might have read MEN or borne a moustache. This kind of sign passes out of consciousness, is extinguished by its use. In literature, however, the sign remains; it sings; and we return to it again and again.

In contrast, the composer's medium is pure; that is, the tones he uses exist for music, and are made by instruments especially designed. Imagine his feelings, then, if he were forced to employ the meaningful noises of every day: bird calls, sirens, screams, alarm bells, whistles, ticks, and human chatter. He could plead all he liked that his music was pure, but we would know that he'd written down sounds from a play unseen, and we would insist that it told a story. Critics would describe the characters (one wears a goatee) and quarrel over their motives, marriages, or mothers, all their dark genes. Although no one wonders, of a painted peach, whether the tree it grew on was watered properly, we are happily witness, week after week, to further

---

8. Robert Frost (1874–1963), American poet.   9. Slang for seventy-five cents.

examination of Hamlet or Madame Bovary,[1] quite as if they were real. And they are so serious, so learned, so certain—so laughable—these ladies and gentlemen. Ah well, it's merely energy which might otherwise elucidate the Trinity.[2]

So the novelist makes his book from boards which say LADIES and GENTS. Every scrap has been worn, every item handled; most of the pieces are dented or split. The writer may choose to be heroic—poets often are—he may strive to purify his diction and achieve an exclusively literary language. He may pretend that every syllable he speaks hasn't been spit, sometimes, in someone else's mouth. Such poets scrub, they clean, they smooth, they polish, until we can scarcely recognize their words on the page. "A star glide, a single frantic sullenness, a single financial grass greediness," wrote Gertrude Stein. *"Toute Pensée émet un Coup de Dés,"* wrote Mallarmé.[3] Most novelists, however (it is one of the things that make them one), try to turn the tattering to account— incorporate it cleverly—as the painter does when he pastes up a collage of newspaper, tin foil, and postage stamps. He will recognize, for example, that stories are wonderful devices for controlling the speed of the mind, for resting it after hard climbs; they give a reassuring light to a dark place, and help the reader hold, like handsome handles, heavy luggage on long trips.

A dedicated storyteller, though—a true lie-minded man—will serve his history best, and guarantee its popularity, not by imitating nature, since nature's no source of verisimilitude, but by following as closely as he can our simplest, most direct and unaffected forms of daily talk, for we report real things, things which intrigue and worry us, and such resembling gossip in a book allows us to believe in figures and events we cannot see, shall never touch, with an assurance of safety which sets our passions free. He will avoid recording consciousness since consciousness is private—we do not normally "take it down"—and because no one really believes in any other feelings than his own. However, the moment our writer concentrates on sound, the moment he formalizes his sentences, the moment he puts in a figure of speech or turns a phrase, shifts a tense or alters tone, the moment he carries description, or any account, beyond need, he begins to turn his reader's interest away from the world which lies among his words like a beautiful woman among her slaves, and directs him toward the slaves themselves. This illustrates a basic principle: if I describe my peach too perfectly, it's the poem which will make my mouth water . . . while the real peach spoils.

Sculptures take up space and gather dust. Concepts do not. They take up us. They invade us as we read, and they achieve, as our resistance and their forces vary, every conceivable degree of occupation. Imagine a worry or a pain, an obsessive thought, a jealousy or hate so strong it renders you insensible to all else. Then while it lasts, you are that fear, that ache, for consciousness is always smaller than its opportunities, and can contract around a kernel like a shell. A piece of music can drive you out and take your place. The purpose of a literary work is the capture of consciousness, and the consequent creation, in you, of an imagined sensibility, so that while you read you are that patient pool or cataract of concepts which the author has

1. Protagonists, respectively, of Shakespeare's play (1602) and of the novel (1857) by the French writer Gustave Flaubert (1821–1880).
2. Christian conception of a three-person God

(Father, Son, and Holy Spirit).
3. Every thought is a roll of the dice (French). Stéphane Mallarmé (1842–1898), French poet.

constructed; and though at first it might seem as if the richness of life had been replaced by something less so—senseless noises, abstract meanings, mere shadows of worldly employment—yet the new self with which fine fiction and good poetry should provide you is as wide as the mind is, and musicked deep with feeling. While listening to such symbols sounding, the blind perceive; thought seems to grow a body; and the will is at rest amid that moving like a gull asleep on the sea. Perhaps we'll be forgiven, then, if we fret about our words and continue country-headed. It is not a refusal to please. There's no willfulness, disdain, exile . . . no anger. Because a consciousness electrified by beauty—is that not the aim and emblem and the ending of all finely made love?

Are you afraid?

1970

CHARLES OLSON

Charles Olson (1910–1970) first published "Projective Verse" in a pamphlet, *Poetry New York*, in 1950. Two years earlier he had joined the faculty of North Carolina's Black Mountain College, where his colleagues included the choreographer Merce Cunningham (1919–2009), the painter Josef Albers (1888–1976), and the poet Robert Creeley (1926–2005), from whom Olson borrowed the statement "FORM IS NEVER MORE THAN AN EXTENSION OF CONTENT." By advocating a set of formal principles based on the breath as a unit of measure, Olson described a new form of poetic measure unfolding on the "open field" of the page. His essay became a manifesto for poets reacting against the strictures of traditional forms.

From Projective Verse

(projectile   (percussive   (prospective
vs.
The Non-Projective

❊   ❊   ❊

I

First, some simplicities that a man learns, if he works in OPEN, or what can also be called COMPOSITION BY FIELD, as opposed to inherited line, stanza, over-all form, what is the "old" base of the non-projective.

(1) the *kinetics* of the thing. A poem is energy transferred from where the poet got it (he will have some several causations), by way of the poem itself to, all the way over to, the reader. Okay. Then the poem itself must, at all points, be a high energy-construct and, at all points, an energy-discharge. So: how is the poet to accomplish same energy, how is he, what is the process by which a poet gets in, at all points energy at least the equivalent of the energy which propelled him in the first place, yet an

energy which is peculiar to verse alone and which will be, obviously, also different from the energy which the reader, because he is a third term, will take away?

This is the problem which any poet who departs from closed form is specially confronted by. And it involves a whole series of new recognitions. From the moment he ventures into FIELD COMPOSITION—puts himself in the open—he can go by no track other than the one the poem under hand declares, for itself. Thus he has to behave, and be, instant by instant, aware of some several forces just now beginning to be examined. (It is much more, for example, this push, than simply such a one as Pound[1] put, so wisely, to get us started: "the musical phrase," go by it, boys, rather than by, the metronome.)

(2) is the *principle*, the law which presides conspicuously over such composition, and, when obeyed, is the reason why a projective poem can come into being. It is this: FORM IS NEVER MORE THAN AN EXTENSION OF CONTENT. (Or so it got phrased by one, R. Creeley, and it makes absolute sense to me, with this possible corollary, that right form, in any given poem, is the only and exclusively possible extension of content under hand.) There it is, brothers, sitting there, for USE.

Now (3) the *process* of the thing, how the principle can be made so to shape the energies that the form is accomplished. And I think it can be boiled down to one statement (first pounded into my head by Edward Dahlberg):[2] ONE PERCEPTION MUST IMMEDIATELY AND DIRECTLY LEAD TO A FURTHER PERCEPTION. It means exactly what it says, is a matter of, at *all* points (even, I should say, of our management of daily reality as of the daily work) get on with it, keep moving, keep in, speed, the nerves, their speed, the perceptions, theirs, the acts, the split second acts, the whole business, keep it moving as fast as you can, citizen. And if you also set up as a poet, USE USE USE the process at all points, in any given poem always, always one perception must must must MOVE, INSTANTER, ON ANOTHER!

So there we are, fast, there's the dogma. And its excuse, its usableness, in practice. Which gets us, it ought to get us, inside the machinery, now, 1950, of how projective verse is made.

If I hammer, if I recall in, and keep calling in, the breath, the breathing as distinguished from the hearing, it is for cause, it is to insist upon a part that breath plays in verse which has not (due, I think, to the smothering of the power of the line by too set a concept of foot) has not been sufficiently observed or practiced, but which has to be if verse is to advance to its proper force and place in the day, now, and ahead. I take it that PROJECTIVE VERSE teaches, is, this lesson, that that verse will only do in which a poet manages to register both the acquisitions of his ear *and* the pressures of his breath.

1950

---

1. Ezra Pound (1885–1972), American poet and critic, a major figure of the modernist movement in early 20th-century poetry.

2. American novelist and essayist (1900–1977).

FRANK O'HARA

On August 27, 1959, the poet Frank O'Hara (1926–1966) had a lunchtime conversation with the poet and playwright then known as LeRoi Jones, later as Amiri Baraka (1934–2014). (Selections from the work of both these writers appear elsewhere in this anthology.) It was a heady period of multiplying literary "movements," and the two decided, as a joke, to invent their own movement. A week later O'Hara wrote "Personism," which presents "a movement I recently founded and which nobody yet knows about," and sent it as a letter to Donald Allen (1912–2004), who published it in the anthology *The New American Poetry 1945–1960* (1960). Allen's anthology, a kind of midcentury avant-garde cultural manifesto, became one of the most influential collections of poetry and poetics published since World War II. O'Hara's contribution retains the original mocking spirit of his lunchtime conversation, but it also offers a lively description of poetry as an address from one person to another. "In all modesty, I confess it may be the death of literature as we know it," O'Hara jokes, but his effort to loosen poetry from the academic debates about meaning and from an elite idea of "literature," and to restore it to the immediacy of one person speaking to another, was serious and proved influential.

From Personism: A Manifesto

Everything is in the poems, but at the risk of sounding like the poor wealthy man's Allen Ginsberg[1] I will write to you because I just heard that one of my fellow poets thinks that a poem of mine that can't be got at one reading is because I was confused too. Now, come on. I don't believe in god, so I don't have to make elaborately sounded structures. I hate Vachel Lindsay,[2] always have, I don't even like rhythm, assonance, all that stuff. You just go on your nerve. If someone's chasing you down the street with a knife you just run, you don't turn around and shout, "Give it up! I was a track star for Mineola Prep."

That's for the writing poems part. As for their reception, suppose you're in love and someone's mistreating (*mal aimé*)[3] you, you don't say, "Hey, you can't hurt me this way, I *care*!" you just let all the different bodies fall where they may, and they always do may after a few months. But that's not why you fell in love in the first place, just to hang onto life, so you have to take your chances and try to avoid being logical. Pain always produces logic, which is very bad for you.

I'm not saying that I don't have practically the most lofty ideas of anyone writing today, but what difference does that make? they're just ideas. The only good thing about it is that when I get lofty enough I've stopped thinking and that's when refreshment arrives.

1. American poet (1926–1997) and member of the Beat generation.
2. American poet (1879–1931) famous for his emphatic use of sound and rhythm.

3. Poorly loved (French). *La Chanson du mal-aimé* (The Song of the Poorly Loved) is a poem by the French Symbolist poet Guillaume Apollinaire (1880–1918).

But how can you really care if anybody gets it, or gets what it means, or if it improves them. Improves them for what? for death? Why hurry them along? Too many poets act like a middle-aged mother trying to get her kids to eat too much cooked meat, and potatoes with drippings (tears). I don't give a damn whether they eat or not. Forced feeding leads to excessive thinness (effete). Nobody should experience anything they don't need to, if they don't need poetry bully for them, I like the movies too. And after all, only Whitman and Crane and Williams,[4] of the American poets, are better than the movies. As for measure and other technical apparatus, that's just common sense: if you're going to buy a pair of pants you want them to be tight enough so everyone will want to go to bed with you. There's nothing metaphysical about it. Unless, of course, you flatter yourself into thinking that what you're experiencing is "yearning."

Abstraction in poetry, which Allen recently commented on in *It is*, is intriguing.[5] I think it appears mostly in the minute particulars where decision is necessary. Abstraction (in poetry, not in painting) involves personal removal by the poet. For instance, the decision involved in the choice between "the nostalgia of the infinite" and "the nostalgia *for* the infinite" defines an attitude towards degree of abstraction. The nostalgia *of* the infinite representing the greater degree of abstraction, removal, and negative capability (as in Keats and Mallarmé).[6] Personism, a movement which I recently founded and which nobody yet knows about, interests me a great deal, being so totally opposed to this kind of abstract removal that it is verging on a true abstraction for the first time, really, in the history of poetry. Personism is to Wallace Stevens what *la poésie pure* was to Béranger.[7] Personism has nothing to do with philosophy, it's all art. It does not have to do with personality or intimacy, far from it! But to give you a vague idea, one of its minimal aspects is to address itself to one person (other than the poet himself), thus evoking overtones of love without destroying love's life-giving vulgarity, and sustaining the poet's feelings towards the poem while preventing love from distracting him into feeling about the person. That's part of personism. It was founded by me after lunch with LeRoi Jones on August 27, 1959, a day in which I was in love with someone (not Roi, by the way, a blond). I went back to work and wrote a poem for this person. While I was writing it I was realizing that if I wanted to I could use the telephone instead of writing the poem, and so Personism was born. It's a very exciting movement which will undoubtedly have lots of adherents. It puts the poem squarely between the poet and the person, Lucky Pierre style,[8] and the poem is correspondingly gratified. The poem is at last between two persons instead of two pages. In all modesty, I confess that it may be the death of literature as we know it. * * *

September 3, 1959

1960

4. Walt Whitman (1819–1892), Hart Crane (1899–1932), and William Carlos Williams (1883–1963).
5. Donald Allen (1912–2004), a poet and the editor of the anthology in which O'Hara's essay appeared, wrote frequently about abstraction in poetry.
6. John Keats (1795–1821), English Romantic poet. Stéphane Mallarmé (1842–1898), French

Symbolist poet and critic.
7. Wallace Stevens (1879–1955), American poet. Pierre-Jean de Béranger (1780–1857), French poet and songwriter who became determined to sing for the people.
8. "Lucky Pierre": slang phrase for either a man in a sexual threesome of two women and one man or the middle man in a threesome of sexually entwined men.

RICHARD FOREMAN

Born in New York on June 10, 1937, the experimental director and playwright Richard Foreman graduated from Brown University with a B.A. in 1959 and received an M.F.A. in playwriting from the Yale School of Drama in 1962. He founded his Ontological-Hysteric Theater in 1968 and became a leading writer, practitioner, and theorist of avant-garde theater. In his essay "Foundations for a Theater" (1993), Foreman wrote, "I try to make plays as hard to remember as a vivid dream which, when awake, you know you've lived with intensity, yet try as you might you can't remember."

For Foreman, drama is about consciousness, about how we experience the present. Inspired by the early twentieth-century writer Gertrude Stein, he crafted plays that, like hers, lack narrative and plot and do not progress from beginning to middle to end. Rather, they constitute a "continuous present" in which audience members experience their own sensory responses to what appears on the stage. Foreman's plays typically have flat characters who deliver their lines in a slow, clear, unemotional manner. His goal is to startle the spectator into a fresh awareness of his or her own perceiving mind. This "mental awakening" is foundational to Foreman's theater, and is similar to the modern playwright Bertolt Brecht's *verfremden-effekt*— "distancing effect." Rather than losing oneself in the experience of theater, one becomes self-consciously aware of what it is like to experience it.

Foreman's stage is often replete with objects such as skulls, flowers, globes, mirrors, stuffed animals, crutches, and radios. These objects are most often simply there; some seem to have symbolic significance for the play in progress, others are harder to relate to the action. The objects gesture toward the "ontological" aspect of Foreman's theater—the aspect that relates to *being*. Like the bodies of the audience and the actors, they are there to be present, and to be experienced, in the shared space and time of the performance. In the brief selection reprinted here, taken from the first part of a three-part manifesto filled with photographs, line drawings, and fragments of text, Foreman sums up his aim for experimental theater. He envisions a new kind of theater that can run without the "fuel" of an audience's desire, a kind of art that can attain its own unique form of being.

From Ontological-Hysteric Manifesto I

Art is not beauty of description or depth of emotion, it is making a machine, not to do something to audience, but that makes <u>itself</u> run on <u>new</u> fuel. Can this machine run? Most machines (art) run on audience fuel—(Man's piggish desire to be at the center, to be made to feel there is "caringness" built into the world: old art manipulates that, tries to get a response: fuel is DESIRE in that case.

FIND FUEL OTHER THAN DESIRE! Nervous energy? Basic hum of life? vibration?) (Desire kills vibration, gets too crude)

<u>WE MAKE A PERPETUAL MOTION MACHINE</u>[1]. (The closer to that ideal the better. Run on less and less fuel . . . that's the goal of the new art machine.)

1. Machine designed to sustain motion without application of outside force; actual perpetual motion machines have proven impossible to construct.

CHARLES LUDLAM

Charles Ludlam was born April 12, 1943, on Long Island, New York. He studied dramatic literature at Hofstra University, graduating in 1964. Ludlam began to live an openly gay life in college, and his career unfolded in the heart of New York's gay community in the West Village. Ludlam formed his Ridiculous Theatrical Company in Sheridan Square in the West Village in 1967, just a block from the Stonewall Inn—the location of the 1969 "Stonewall riots" that spurred the gay liberation movement. The political fervor of the 1960s and early '70s marks Ludlam's work, though he does not address politics directly in his plays. He preferred to think of his work as "queer theater" rather than an art form representing politicized identities. A prolific writer, Ludlam has been widely published and anthologized. He died of AIDS in 1987, and his obituary was printed on the front page of the *New York Times*, confirming both his influence and his successful integration of the avant-garde into the mainstream.

Ludlam was one of the few in the American avant-garde theater scene interested both in the dramatic "text" and in the traditional aim of moving the audience emotionally. Speaking of the avant-garde, he declared, "I hate minimal art. I hate conceptual art. I am for execution. I am for maximal art. Minimal art is inflationary art: less for your money. . . . Art is for the body. It has a soul but it also has a body." Usually performed in drag, his "highly charged shenanigans" came to be associated closely with the "camp" aesthetic. He is most famous for his *Camille* (1973), in which he starred in the title role, in drag, *Galas* (1983), inspired by Maria Callas, who is also an inspiration for Frank Bidart's poem "Ellen West," included in this volume, and *The Mystery of Irma Vep* (1984), inspired by Victorian melodrama.

Aspiring to the "actor-manager" role usually associated with the nineteenth-century British theater industry, Ludlam wrote, directed, and starred in many of the Ridiculous Theatrical Company's plays. Known for his warmth and larger-than-life personality, Ludlam was beloved among his friends and peers in the avant-garde theater world. He would influence a wide variety of queer performance artists—both male and female—including the playwright Tony Kushner, author and director of *Angels in America* (1993). In 1999, Kushner provided the introduction for a collection of Ludlam's plays.

"Ridiculous Theatre, Scourge of Human Folly," a Ludlam manifesto, is reprinted here in full. Written as a series of axioms in numerical order—suggesting straightforward logic—the manifesto is in fact more farcical than logical. The "instructions for use" highlight the performative nature of the manifesto as a genre: manifestos do not just *say*, they *do*.

Ridiculous Theatre, Scourge of Human Folly

Aim: To get beyond nihilism[1] by revaluing combat.

Axioms to a theatre for ridicule:

---

1. Total rejection of prevailing beliefs, usually out of a sense that the world is meaningless.

1. You are a living mockery of your own ideals. If not, you have set your ideals too low.
2. The things one takes seriously are one's weaknesses.
3. Just as many people who claim a belief in God disprove it with their every act, so too there are those whose every deed, though they say there is no God, is an act of faith.
4. Evolution is a conscious process.
5. Bathos is that which is intended to be sorrowful but because of the extremity of its expression becomes comic. Pathos is that which is meant to be comic but because of the extremity of its expression becomes sorrowful. Some things which seem to be opposites are actually different degrees of the same thing.
6. The comic hero thrives by his vices. The tragic hero is destroyed by his virtue. Moral paradox is the crux of the drama.
7. The theatre is a humble materialist enterprise which seeks to produce riches of the imagination, not the other way around. The theatre is an event and not an object. Theatre workers need not blush and conceal their desperate struggle to pay the landlords their rents. Theatre without the stink of art.

Instructions for use:
This is farce not Sunday school. Illustrate hedonistic[2] calculus. Test out a dangerous idea, a theme that threatens to destroy one's whole value system. Treat the material in a madly farcical manner without losing the seriousness of the theme. Show how paradoxes arrest the mind. Scare yourself a bit along the way.

1975

2. Pleasure-seeking.

A. R. AMMONS

A mmons (1926–2001), represented elsewhere in this anthology by a selection of his poems, delivered "A Poem Is a Walk" as a lecture for teachers at the International Poetry Forum in Pittsburgh, Pennsylvania, in April 1967. It was published in 1968 in Cornell University's literary journal, *Epoch*. By 1964 Ammons had joined the English faculty at Cornell (in Ithaca, New York), where he was a much-loved teacher. His concerns as a poet and as a teacher of poetry are evident in this essay, which provides an account of poetry as an "interior seeking," its shape unfolding through a process of discovery. In the essay Ammons locates the essential rhythms of poetry in the motions of the body as it moves through the world. A peripatetic writer and theorist, Ammons employs this essay's principles in his poetry. "A Poem Is a Walk" also connects Ammons to the American Transcendentalist tradition. It recalls the famous essay "Walking" (1862), by Henry David Thoreau (1817–1862), in which this activity is figured as inward exploration, and the poems of Robert Frost (1874–1963), many of which are structured as a walk. A similar impulse can be found in such American poets as Robert Creeley, Frank O'Hara, and Jorie Graham.

From A Poem Is a Walk

What justification is there for comparing a poem with a walk rather than with something else? I take the walk to be the externalization of an interior seeking so that the analogy is first of all between the external and the internal. Poets not only do a lot of walking but talk about it in their poems: "I wandered lonely as a cloud," "Now I out walking," and "Out walking in the frozen swamp one gray day."[1] There are countless examples, and many of them suggest that both the real and the fictive walk are externalizations of an inward seeking. The walk magnified is the journey, and probably no figure has been used more often than the journey for both the structure and concern of an interior seeking.

How does a poem resemble a walk? First, each makes use of the whole body, involvement is total, both mind and body. You can't take a walk without feet and legs, without a circulatory system, a guidance and coordinating system, without eyes, ears, desire, will, need: the total person. This observation is important not only for what it includes but for what it rules out: as with a walk, a poem is not simply a mental activity: it has body, rhythm, feeling, sound, and mind, conscious and subconscious. The pace at which a poet walks (and thinks), his natural breath-length, the line he pursues, whether forthright and straight or weaving and meditative, his whole "air," whether of aimlessness or purpose—all these things and many more figure into the "physiology" of the poem he writes.

A second resemblance is that every walk is unreproducible, as is every poem. Even if you walk exactly the same route each time—as with a sonnet—the events along the route cannot be imagined to be the same from day to day, as the poet's health, sight, his anticipations, moods, fears, thoughts cannot be the same. There are no two identical sonnets or villanelles. If there were, we would not know how to keep the extra one: it would have no separate existence. If a poem is each time new, then it is necessarily an act of discovery, a chance taken, a chance that may lead to fulfillment or disaster. The poet exposes himself to the risk. All that has been said about poetry, all that he has learned about poetry, is only a partial assurance.

The third resemblance between a poem and a walk is that each turns, one or more times, and eventually returns. It's conceivable that a poem could rake out and go through incident after incident without ever returning, merely ending in the poet's return to dust. But most poems and most walks return. I have already quoted the first line from Frost's "The Wood-Pile." Now, here are the first three lines:

> Out walking in the frozen swamp one gray day,
> I paused and said, 'I will turn back from here.
> No, I will go on farther—and we shall see.'

The poet is moving outward seeking the point from which he will turn back. In "The Wood-Pile" there is no return: return is implied. The poet

---

1. Lines from, respectively, "I Wandered, Lonely as a Cloud" by English poet William Wordsworth, and "Away!" and "The Wood-Pile," both by American poet Robert Frost.

goes farther and farther into the swamp until he finds by accident the point of illumination with which he closes the poem.

But the turns and returns or implied returns give shape to the walk and to the poem. With the first step, the number of shapes the walk might take is infinite, but then the walk begins to "define" itself as it goes along, though freedom remains total with each step: any tempting side road can be turned into on impulse, or any wild patch of woods can be explored. The pattern of the walk is to come true, is to be recognized, discovered. The pattern, when discovered, may be found to apply to the whole walk, or only a segment of the walk may prove to have contour and therefore suggestion and shape. From previous knowledge of the terrain, inner and outer, the poet may have before the walk an inkling of a possible contour. Taking the walk would then be searching out or confirming, giving actuality to, a previous intuition.

The fourth resemblance has to do with the motion common to poems and walks. The motion may be lumbering, clipped, wavering, tripping, mechanical, dance-like, awkward, staggering, slow, etc. But the motion occurs only in the body of the walker or in the body of the words. It can't be extracted and contemplated. It is nonreproducible and nonlogical. It can't be translated into another body. There is only one way to know it and that is to enter into it.

To summarize, a walk involves the whole person; it is not reproducible: its shape occurs, unfolds: it has a motion characteristic of the walker.

*　*　*

There is no ideal walk, then, though I haven't taken the time to prove it out completely, except the useless, meaningless walk. Only uselessness is empty enough for the presence of so many uses, and only through uselessness can the ideal walk come into the sum total of its uses. Only uselessness can allow the walk to be totally itself.

I hope you are, now, if you were not before, ready to agree with me that the greatest wrong that can be done a poem is to substitute a known part for an unknown whole and that the choice to be made is the freedom of nothingness: that our experience of poetry is least injured when we accept it as useless, meaningless, and nonrational.

* * * Poetry is a mode of discourse that differs from logical exposition. It is the mode I spoke of earlier, that can reconcile opposites into a "real" world both concrete and universal. Teach that. Teach the distinction.

Second, I would suggest you teach that poetry leads us to the unstructured sources of our beings, to the unknown, and returns us to our rational, structured selves refreshed. Having once experienced the mystery, plenitude, contradiction, and composure of a work of art, we afterward have a built-in resistance to the slogans and propaganda of oversimplification that have often contributed to the destruction of human life. Poetry is a verbal means to a nonverbal source. It is a motion to no-motion, to the still point of contemplation and deep realization. Its knowledges are all negative and, therefore, more positive than any knowledge. Nothing that can be said about it in words is worth saying.

April 1967   1968

AUDRE LORDE

As a black feminist, lesbian, poet, cancer survivor, and social activist, Audre Lorde (1934–1992) felt compelled to respond to the frequent assertion among activists that writing poetry is a luxury. Her essay "Poetry Is Not a Luxury" originally appeared in *Chrysalis: A Magazine of Female Culture* in 1977 and was reprinted in her well-known collection of essays, *Sister, Outsider* (1989). Lorde argued that, rather than being a luxury, poetry is "a vital necessity" because it creates a language in which to express women's hopes and dreams. The writing process, as she describes it, gives life and voice to what is unnamed and as yet unthought, and thus overcomes the forces in society that silence women's experiences. In this sense poetry articulates the vision necessary for social change to occur. Lorde's life and work reflected her belief that poetry is a form of empowerment and a tool for survival. A selection of her poems can be found elsewhere in this anthology.

From Poetry Is Not a Luxury

For women, then, poetry is not a luxury. It is a vital necessity of our existence. It forms the quality of the light within which we predicate our hopes and dreams toward survival and change, first made into language, then into idea, then into more tangible action. Poetry is the way we help give name to the nameless so it can be thought. The farthest external horizons of our hopes and fears are cobbled by our poems, carved from the rock experiences of our daily lives.

As they become known and accepted to ourselves, our feelings, and the honest exploration of them, become sanctuaries and fortresses and spawning grounds for the most radical and daring of ideas, the house of difference so necessary to change and the conceptualization of any meaningful action. Right now, I could name at least ten ideas I would once have found intolerable or incomprehensible and frightening, except as they came after dreams and poems. This is not idle fantasy, but the true meaning of "It feels right to me." We can train ourselves to respect our feelings and to discipline (transpose) them into a language that catches those feelings so they can be shared. And where that language does not yet exist, it is our poetry which helps to fashion it. Poetry is not only dream or vision, it is the skeleton architecture of our lives.

1977   1978

DENISE LEVERTOV
1923–1997

Denise Levertov once wrote of her predecessor, the poet H. D.: "She showed a way to penetrate mystery; which means, not to flood darkness with light so that darkness is destroyed, but to *enter into* darkness, mystery, so that it is experienced." Along with Robert Duncan, Levertov carried out in her own distinctive way H. D.'s tradition of visionary poetry. More grounded than her predecessor in observing the natural world and in appreciating daily life, Levertov connected the concrete to the invisible, as suggested by the image of *The Jacob's Ladder* (1961), the title of her fifth book. She desired that a poem be "hard as a floor, sound as a bench" but also that it be "mysterious" ("Illustrious Ancestors"), and in her poems ordinary events open into the unknown. The origins of Levertov's magical sense of the world are not difficult to trace. She was born in England and wrote of her parents: "My mother was descended from the Welsh tailor and mystic Angel Jones of Mold, my father from the noted Hasid, Schneour Zaiman [d. 1831], the 'Rav of Northern White Russia.'" In "Illustrious Ancestors" Levertov claimed a connection to her forefathers, both mystical and Hasidic: "some line still taut between me and them." Hasidism, a sect of Judaism that emphasizes the soul's communion with God rather than formal religious observance and encourages what Levertov called "a wonder at creation," was an important influence on her father, Paul Philip Levertoff. He had converted to Christianity as a student and later became an Anglican priest, but he retained his interest in Judaism and told Hasidic legends to Levertov and her older sister, Olga, throughout their childhoods. From her mother, Beatrice Spooner-Jones, Levertov learned to look closely at the world around her, and we might say of her work what she said of her mother: "with how much gazing / her life had paid tribute to the world's body" ("The 90th Year").

In 1947 Levertov married an American, Mitchell Goodman (they later divorced), and moved to the United States. She described this move as crucial to her development as a poet; it "necessitated the finding of new rhythms in which to write, in accordance with new rhythms of life and speech." In this discovery of a new idiom the stylistic influence of William Carlos Williams was especially important to her; without it, she said, "I could not have developed from a British Romantic with an almost Victorian background to an American poet of any vitality." Levertov embraced Williams's interest in an organic poetic form, growing out of the poet's relation to her subject, and like Duncan and Robert Creeley, she actively explored the relations between the line and the unit of breath as they control rhythm, melody, and emphasis. But if Levertov became the poet she was by becoming an American poet, her European heritage also enriched her sense of influence. Although her poem "September 1961" acknowledges her link to "the old great ones" (Ezra Pound, Williams, and H. D.), she was as at home with the German lyric poet Rainer Maria Rilke as with the American Transcendentalist Ralph Waldo Emerson. And in the United States she discovered the work of the Jewish theologian and philosopher Martin Buber, which renewed her interest "in the Hasidic ideas with which I was dimly acquainted as a child." Her eclecticism let her move easily between plain and richly descriptive language, between a vivid perception of the "thing itself" and the often radiant mystery that, for Levertov, arose from such seeing.

From 1956 to 1959 Levertov lived with her husband and son in Mexico. They were joined there by her mother, who, after her daughter's departure, remained in Mexico for the final eighteen years of her life (she died in 1977). Several moving poems in Levertov's collection *Life in the Forest* (1978), among them "The 90th Year" and "Death in Mexico," address her mother's last years. In the late 1960s the political crisis prompted by the Vietnam War turned Levertov's work more directly to public woes, as reflected in her following four books. Not all the poems in these books explicitly concern political issues ("The Sorrow Dance," for example, contains her sequence in memory of her sister, Olga, one of her finest, most powerful poems); nonetheless, many poems originated in a need for public testimony. Her overtly political poems are not often among her best, however; their very explicitness restricted her distinctive strengths as a poet, which included a feeling for the inexplicable, a language lyrical enough to express wish and desire, and a capacity for playfulness. But it is a mistake to separate too rigidly the political concerns in her work from a larger engagement with the world. As she wrote: "If a degree of intimacy is a condition of lyric expression, surely—at times when events make feelings run high—that intimacy between writer and political belief does exist, and is as intense as other emotions."

The power of Levertov's poems depends on her capacity to balance, however precariously, her two-sided vision, to keep alive both terms of what one critic called her "magical realism." At its best her work seems to spring from experience deep within her, stirred into being by a source beyond herself (as "Caedmon" is suddenly "affrighted" by an angel, or the poet at the age of sixteen dreams deeply, "sunk in the well"). Her finest poems render the inexplicable nature of our ordinary lives and their capacity for unexpected beauty. But Levertov's capacity for pleasure in the world never strays too far from the knowledge that the very landscapes that delight us contain places "that can pull you / down" ("Zeroing In"), as our inner landscapes also contain places "'that are bruised forever, that time / never assuages, never.'"

Levertov published several collections of prose, including *The Poet in the World* (1973), *Light Up the Cave* (1981), and *New and Selected Essays* (1992). In 1987 she published her fifteenth book of poems, *Breathing the Water*. This book contains a long sequence, "The Showings: Lady Julian of Norwich, 1342–1416," which continues the link between Levertov's work and a visionary tradition. She published three subsequent collections: *A Door in the Hive* (1989), *Evening Train* (1992), and *Tesserae* (1995). Levertov taught widely and from 1982 until her death was professor of English at Stanford University, where she was an important teacher for a younger generation of writers.

To the Snake

Green Snake, when I hung you round my neck
and stroked your cold, pulsing throat
   as you hissed to me, glinting
arrowy gold scales, and I felt
   the weight of you on my shoulders,   5
and the whispering silver of your dryness
   sounded close at my ears—
Green Snake—I swore to my companions that certainly
   you were harmless! But truly
I had no certainty, and no hope, only desiring   10
   to hold you, for that joy,
       which left
a long wake of pleasure, as the leaves moved

and you faded into the pattern
of grass and shadows, and I returned   15
smiling and haunted, to a dark morning.

                                                                    1960

The Jacob's Ladder[1]

The stairway is not
a thing of gleaming strands
a radiant evanescence
for angels' feet that only glance in their tread, and need not
touch the stone.   5

It is of stone.
A rosy stone that takes
a glowing tone of softness
only because behind it the sky is a doubtful, a doubting
night gray.   10

A stairway of sharp
angles, solidly built.
One sees that the angels must spring
down from one step to the next, giving a little
lift of the wings: 15

and a man climbing
must scrape his knees, and bring
the grip of his hands into play. The cut stone
consoles his groping feet. Wings brush past him.
The poem ascends.   20

                                                                    1961

In Mind

There's in my mind a woman
of innocence, unadorned but

fair-featured, and smelling of
apples or grass. She wears

a utopian smock or shift, her hair   5
is light brown and smooth, and she

---

1. Jacob dreamed of "a ladder set up on the earth, and the top of it reached to heaven: and behold the angels of God ascending and descending on it" (Genesis 28.12).

is kind and very clean without
ostentation—

        but she has
no imagination.   10

             And there's a
turbulent moon-ridden girl

or old woman, or both,
dressed in opals and rags, feathers

and torn taffeta,   15
who knows strange songs—

but she is not kind.

                        1964

What Were They Like?

1) Did the people of Vietnam
   use lanterns of stone?
2) Did they hold ceremonies
   to reverence the opening of buds?
3) Were they inclined to quiet laughter?   5
4) Did they use bone and ivory,
   jade and silver, for ornament?
5) Had they an epic poem?
6) Did they distinguish between speech and singing?

1) Sir, their light hearts turned to stone.   10
   It is not remembered whether in gardens
   stone lanterns illumined pleasant ways.
2) Perhaps they gathered once to delight in blossom,
   but after the children were killed
   there were no more buds.   15
3) Sir, laughter is bitter to the burned mouth.
4) A dream ago, perhaps. Ornament is for joy.
   All the bones were charred.
5) It is not remembered. Remember,
   most were peasants; their life   20
   was in rice and bamboo.
   When peaceful clouds were reflected in the paddies
   and the water buffalo stepped surely along terraces,
   maybe fathers told their sons old tales.
   When bombs smashed those mirrors   25
   there was time only to scream.
6) There is an echo yet
   of their speech which was like a song.

It was reported their singing resembled
the flight of moths in moonlight.   30
Who can say? It is silent now.

1971

Caedmon[1]

All others talked as if
talk were a dance.
Clodhopper I, with clumsy feet
would break the gliding ring.
Early I learned to   5
hunch myself
close by the door:
then when the talk began
I'd wipe my
mouth and wend   10
unnoticed back to the barn
to be with the warm beasts,
dumb among body sounds
of the simple ones.
I'd see by a twist   15
of lit rush[2] the motes
of gold moving
from shadow to shadow
slow in the wake
of deep untroubled sighs.   20
The cows
munched or stirred or were still. I
was at home and lonely,
both in good measure. Until
the sudden angel affrighted me—light effacing   25
my feeble beam,
a forest of torches, feathers of flame, sparks upflying:
but the cows as before
were calm, and nothing was burning,
                nothing but I, as that hand of fire   30
touched my lips and scorched my tongue
and pulled my voice
                        into the ring of the dance.

1987

1. "The story comes, of course, from the Venerable Bede's *History of the English Church and
People*, but I first read it as a child in John Richard Green's *History of the English People*, 1855"
[Levertov's note]. Caedmon (fl. 658–680) was,
according to the story, an illiterate cowherd
employed by a monastery; one night he received
a divine call to sing verses in praise of God. He is
the earliest known Christian poet in English.
2. The piths of rush plants were used for
candlewicks.

JAMES BALDWIN
1924–1987

I n the early 1940s, the African American writer James Baldwin was once refused service at a restaurant in New Jersey, and he reacted with anger, finally throwing a water glass at the waitress. He fled, pursued by police. Reflecting later on the experience in his essay "Notes of a Native Son" (1955), Baldwin wrote that he was struck by two facts, "both equally difficult for the imagination to grasp, and one was that I could have been murdered. But the other was that I had been ready to commit murder." Baldwin's ability to speak honestly about race in America—in widely read essays as well as in fiction—and to analyze the inner dynamics of race in a way that was both gripping and intellectual made him a key figure in the history of civil rights in America from the 1940s right up to his death in 1987. Though he mainly lived abroad in Paris and other European cities from 1949 onward, his voice was heard back home, distinguished by an emphasis on shared humanity and the possibility of love across racial lines.

Baldwin was brought up in a poor and strictly religious household in Harlem with an authoritarian father—later revealed to be his stepfather—his beloved mother, and eight siblings. His reading began at home, where he read and reread the Bible and Harriet Beecher Stowe's *Uncle Tom's Cabin*. He attended public schools in New York City alongside black Harlem neighbors and Jewish, Irish, and Eastern European immigrants from other parts of the city. A theater teacher at his middle school introduced him to the writings of Charles Dickens and took him to see Shakespeare plays in the city. He then attended DeWitt Clinton High School, which reached a peak enrollment of twelve thousand students in the 1930s and was reputed to be the largest high school in the world; the photographer Richard Avedon was a classmate. At DeWitt Clinton he met remarkable teachers—including the poet Countee Cullen—who further opened the worlds of literature and intellectual life to the young James. Baldwin briefly became a child preacher at the age of fourteen. When he abandoned preaching he also left the church, but the church never left him. Its message of love, suffering, and redemption in a violent world remained rooted in his imagination; its lyrical cadences, found in scripture, oratory, and ecstatic music, recur as both the themes and the models for his prose.

Starting in the late 1940s, Baldwin published essays on topics ranging from art and literature to history to black life in Harlem, Atlanta, and Paris. His fame grew when he found a voice in fiction, publishing the critically acclaimed realist novel *Go Tell It on the Mountain* in 1953, a story about the teenage son of a black preacher in Harlem that hewed closely to his own biography. *Go Tell It on the Mountain* was followed by a play, *Amen Corner*, which was staged once in 1955 by the Howard University Players and was not produced again for over a decade. It was published in full in 1968. A second novel, *Giovanni's Room* (1956), departed from the subject of black life in Harlem. Baldwin did not want to be pigeonholed as the new "Negro writer" on the scene. *Giovanni's Room* was a tragic love story about a white American named David and his relationship with Giovanni, the beautiful and doomed lover he meets in Paris. Written by a black writer through the first-person perspective of a white gay man, and openly sympathetic to the plight of its central characters, *Giovanni's Room* was both a professionally risky and a beautifully crafted novel. But Baldwin would soon become too indispensable a participant in the evolving civil rights movement to be dismissed by readers who found gay subject matter offensive. His essays on the experience of being black in the United States and in postwar Europe had already established him as a serious thinker about race. In his notable 1962 essay "Letter from a Region of my Mind," he analyzed religion's relationship to race as well as the fraught psychology of black-white relations in America, using terms that explored the sexualized emotional dependency of white America on black inferiority. The *New Yorker* featured the essay, cementing Baldwin's reputation as the writer who seemed best able to explain black and white America to itself.

Baldwin continued to write fiction and essays throughout his life. In novels and short stories, his preoccupations were remarkably consistent: doomed black and white men, strong but tired black women, jazz or church musicians, preachers and hustlers, brothers and mothers and sons, the experience of racial violence and the lives of expatriates. Having lived a bravely open homosexual life since his teens, Baldwin stood out for his humane representations of masculine gay men and for his candid reflections on love between men of different races.

He ultimately published six novels, two plays, and a collection of short stories. The early novels, including *Another Country* (1962), are regarded as his best. His nonfiction was collected in *Notes of a Native Son* (1955), *The Price of the Ticket* (1985), and various other volumes, including *Collected Essays* (1998) and *The Cross of Redemption* (2010).

The stories reprinted here represent high points in his literary oeuvre. In "Going to Meet the Man" (1965), Baldwin dares to write from the perspectives of a white deputy sheriff and his young son and thus to fully engage the horror of lynching. Baldwin shocks the reader with racist language and sexualized violence while showing how easily a young boy becomes complicit with a racist culture. "Sonny's Blues" is a classic Baldwin story, imagining music as a source of redemption within the black community, despite the realities of poverty, incarceration, and addiction.

Going to Meet the Man

"What's the matter?" she asked.

"I don't know," he said, trying to laugh, "I guess I'm tired."

"You've been working too hard," she said. "I keep telling you."

"Well, goddammit, woman," he said, "it's not my fault!" He tried again; he wretchedly failed again. Then he just lay there, silent, angry, and helpless. Excitement filled him like a toothache, but it refused to enter his flesh. He stroked her breast. This was his wife. He could not ask her to do just a little thing for him, just to help him out, just for a little while, the way he could ask a nigger girl to do it. He lay there, and he sighed. The image of a black girl caused a distant excitement in him, like a far-away light; but, again, the excitement was more like pain; instead of forcing him to act, it made action impossible.

"Go to sleep," she said, gently, "you got a hard day tomorrow."

"Yeah," he said, and rolled over on his side, facing her, one hand still on one breast. "Goddamn the niggers. The black stinking coons. You'd think they'd learn. Wouldn't you think they'd learn? I mean, *wouldn't* you?"

"They going to be out there tomorrow," she said, and took his hand away, "get some sleep."

He lay there, one hand between his legs, staring at the frail sanctuary of his wife. A faint light came from the shutters; the moon was full. Two dogs, far away, were barking at each other, back and forth, insistently, as though they were agreeing to make an appointment. He heard a car coming north on the road and he half sat up, his hand reaching for his holster, which was on a chair near the bed, on top of his pants. The lights hit the shutters and seemed to travel across the room and then went out. The sound of the car slipped away, he heard it hit gravel, then heard it no more. Some liver-lipped students, probably, heading back to that college—but coming from where? His watch said it was two in the morning. They could be coming from anywhere, from out of state most likely, and they would be at the courthouse tomorrow. The niggers were getting ready. Well, they would be ready, too.

He moaned. He wanted to let whatever was in him out; but it wouldn't come out. Goddamn! he said aloud, and turned again, on his side, away from Grace, staring at the shutters. He was a big, healthy man and he had never had any trouble sleeping. And he wasn't old enough yet to have any trouble getting it up—he was only forty-two. And he was a good man, a God-fearing man, he had tried to do his duty all his life, and he had been a deputy sheriff for several years. Nothing had ever bothered him before, certainly not getting it up. Sometimes, sure, like any other man, he knew that he wanted a little more spice than Grace could give him and he would drive over yonder and pick up a black piece or arrest her, it came to the same thing, but he couldn't do that now, no more. There was no telling what might happen once your ass was in the air. And they were low enough to kill a man then, too, every one of them, or the girl herself might do it, right while she was making believe you made her feel so good. The niggers. What had the good Lord Almighty had in mind when he made the niggers? Well. They were pretty good at that, all right. Damn. Damn. Goddamn.

This wasn't helping him to sleep. He turned again, toward Grace again, and moved close to her warm body. He felt something he had never felt before. He felt that he would like to hold her, hold her, hold her, and be buried in her like a child and never have to get up in the morning again and go downtown to face those faces, good Christ, they were ugly! and never have to enter that jailhouse again and smell that smell and hear that singing; never again feel that filthy, kinky, greasy hair under his hand, never again watch those black breasts leap against the leaping cattle prod, never hear those moans again or watch that blood run down or the fat lips split or the sealed eyes struggle open. They were animals, they were no better than animals, what could be done with people like that? Here they had been in a civilized country for years and they still lived like animals. Their houses were dark, with oil cloth or cardboard in the windows, the smell was enough to make you puke your guts out, and there they sat, a whole tribe, pumping out kids, it looked like, every damn five minutes, and laughing and talking and playing music like they didn't have a care in the world, and he reckoned they didn't, neither, and coming to the door, into the sunlight, just standing there, just looking foolish, not thinking of anything but just getting back to what they were doing, saying, Yes suh, Mr. Jesse. I surely will, Mr. Jesse. Fine weather, Mr. Jesse. Why, I thank you, Mr. Jesse. He had worked for a mail-order house for a while and it had been his job to collect the payments for the stuff they bought. They were too dumb to know that they were being cheated blind, but that was no skin off his ass—he was just supposed to do his job. They would be late—they didn't have the sense to put money aside;

but it was easy to scare them, and he never really had any trouble. Hell, they all liked him, the kids used to smile when he came to the door. He gave them candy, sometimes, or chewing gum, and rubbed their rough bullet heads—maybe the candy should have been poisoned. Those kids were grown now. He had had trouble with one of them today.

"There was this nigger today," he said; and stopped; his voice sounded peculiar. He touched Grace. "You awake?" he asked. She mumbled something, impatiently, she was probably telling him to go to sleep. It was all right. He knew that he was not alone.

"What a funny time," he said, "to be thinking about a thing like that—you listening?" She mumbled something again. He rolled over on his back. "This nigger's one of the ringleaders. We had trouble with him before. We must have had him out there at the work farm three or four times. Well, Big Jim C. and some of the boys really had to whip that nigger's ass today." He looked over at Grace; he could not tell whether she was listening or not; and he was afraid to ask again. "They had this line you know, to register"—he laughed, but she did not—"and they wouldn't stay where Big Jim C. wanted them, no, they had to start blocking traffic all around the courthouse so couldn't nothing or nobody get through, and Big Jim C. told them to disperse and they wouldn't move, they just kept up that singing, and Big Jim C. figured that the others would move if this nigger would move, him being the ringleader, but he wouldn't move and he wouldn't let the others move, so they had to beat him and a couple of the others and they threw them in the wagon—but *I* didn't see this nigger till I got to the jail. They were still singing and I was supposed to make them stop. Well, I couldn't make them stop for me but I knew he could make them stop. He was lying on the ground jerking and moaning, they had threw him in a cell by himself, and blood was coming out his ears from where Big Jim C. and his boys had whipped him. Wouldn't you think they'd learn? I put the prod to him and he jerked some more and he kind of screamed—but he didn't have much voice left. 'You make them stop that singing,' I said to him, 'you hear me? You make them stop that singing.' He acted like he didn't hear me and I put it to him again, under his arms, and he just rolled around on the floor and blood started coming from his mouth. He'd pissed his pants already." He paused. His mouth felt dry and his throat was as rough as sandpaper; as he talked, he began to hurt all over with that peculiar excitement which refused to be released. "You all are going to stop your singing, I said to him, and you are going to stop coming down to the courthouse and disrupting traffic and molesting the people and keeping us from our duties and keeping doctors from getting to sick white women and getting all them Northerners in this town to give our town a bad name—!" As he said this, he kept prodding the boy, sweat pouring from beneath the helmet he had not yet taken off. The boy rolled around in his own dirt and water and blood and tried to scream again as the prod hit his testicles, but the scream did not come out, only a kind of rattle and a moan. He stopped. He was not supposed to kill the nigger. The cell was filled with a terrible odor. The boy was still. "You hear me?" he called. "You had enough?" The singing went on. "You had enough?" His foot leapt out, he had not known it was going to, and caught the boy flush on the jaw. *Jesus*, he thought, *this ain't no nigger, this is a goddamn bull*, and he screamed again, "You had enough? You going to make them stop that singing now?"

But the boy was out. And now he was shaking worse than the boy had been shaking. He was glad no one could see him. At the same time, he felt very close to a very peculiar, particular joy; something deep in him and deep in his memory was stirred, but whatever was in his memory eluded him. He took off his helmet. He walked to the cell door.

"White man," said the boy, from the floor, behind him.

He stopped. For some reason, he grabbed his privates.

"You remember Old Julia?"

The boy said, from the floor, with his mouth full of blood, and one eye, barely open, glaring like the eye of a cat in the dark, "My grandmother's name was Mrs. Julia Blossom. *Mrs.* Julia Blossom. You going to call our women by their right names yet.—And those kids ain't going to stop singing. We going to keep on singing until every one of you miserable white mothers go stark raving out of your minds." Then he closed the one eye; he spat blood; his head fell back against the floor.

He looked down at the boy, whom he had been seeing, off and on, for more than a year, and suddenly remembered him: Old Julia had been one of his mail-order customers, a nice old woman. He had not seen her for years, he supposed that she must be dead.

He had walked into the yard, the boy had been sitting in a swing. He had smiled at the boy, and asked, "Old Julia home?"

The boy looked at him for a long time before he answered. "Don't no Old Julia live here."

"This is her house. I know her. She's lived here for years."

The boy shook his head. "You might know a Old Julia someplace else, white man. But don't nobody by that name live here."

He watched the boy; the boy watched him. The boy certainly wasn't more than ten. *White man.* He didn't have time to be fooling around with some crazy kid. He yelled, "Hey! Old Julia!"

But only silence answered him. The expression on the boy's face did not change. The sun beat down on them both, still and silent; he had the feeling that he had been caught up in a nightmare, a nightmare dreamed by a child; perhaps one of the nightmares he himself had dreamed as a child. It had that feeling—everything familiar, without undergoing any other change, had been subtly and hideously displaced: the trees, the sun, the patches of grass in the yard, the leaning porch and the weary porch steps and the card-board in the windows and the black hole of the door which looked like the entrance to a cave, and the eyes of the pickaninny, all, all, were charged with malevolence. *White man.* He looked at the boy. "She's gone out?"

The boy said nothing.

"Well," he said, "tell her I passed by and I'll pass by next week." He started to go; he stopped. "You want some chewing gum?"

The boy got down from the swing and started for the house. He said, "I don't want nothing you got, white man." He walked into the house and closed the door behind him.

Now the boy looked as though he were dead. Jesse wanted to go over to him and pick him up and pistol whip him until the boy's head burst open like a melon. He began to tremble with what he believed was rage, sweat, both cold and hot, raced down his body, the singing filled him as though it were a weird, uncontrollable, monstrous howling rumbling up from the depths of his own belly, he felt an icy fear rise in him and raise him up, and he shouted, he howled, "You lucky we *pump* some white blood into you every once in a while—your women! Here's what I got for all the black bitches in the world—!" Then he was, abruptly, almost too weak to stand; to his bewilderment, his horror, beneath his own fingers, he felt himself violently stiffen—with no warning at all; he dropped his hands and he stared at the boy and he left the cell.

"All that singing they do," he said. "All that singing." He could not remember the first time he had heard it; he had been hearing it all his life. It was the sound with which he was most familiar—though it was also the sound of which he had been least conscious—and it had always contained an obscure comfort. They were singing to God. They were singing for mercy and they hoped to go to heaven, and he had even sometimes felt, when looking into the eyes of some of the old women, a few of the very old men, that they were singing for mercy for his soul, too. Of course he had never thought of their heaven or of what God was, or could be, for them; God was the same for everyone, he supposed, and heaven was where good people went—he supposed. He had never thought much about what it meant to be a good person. He tried to be a good person and treat everybody right: it wasn't his fault if the niggers had taken it into their heads to fight against God and go against the rules laid down in the Bible for everyone to read! Any preacher would tell you that. He was only doing his duty: protecting white people from the niggers and the niggers from themselves. And there were still lots of good niggers around—he had to remember that; they weren't all like that boy this afternoon; and the good niggers must be mighty sad to see what was happening to their people. They would thank him when this was over. In that way they had, the best of them, not quite looking him in the eye, in a low voice, with a little smile: We surely thanks you, Mr. Jesse. From the bottom of our hearts, we thanks you. He smiled. They hadn't all gone crazy. This trouble would pass.—He knew that the young people had changed some of the words to the songs. He had scarcely listened to the words before and he did not listen to them now; but he knew that the words were different; he could hear that much. He did not know if the faces were different, he had never, before this trouble began, watched them as they sang, but he certainly did not like what he saw now. They hated him, and this hatred was blacker than their hearts, blacker than their skins, redder than their blood, and harder, by far, than his club. Each day, each night, he felt worn out, aching, with their smell in his nostrils and filling his lungs, as though he were drowning—drowning in niggers; and it was all to be done again when he awoke. It would never end. It would never end. Perhaps this was what the singing had meant all along. They had not been singing black folks into heaven, they had been singing white folks into hell.

Everyone felt this black suspicion in many ways, but no one knew how to express it. Men much older than he, who had been responsible for law and order much longer than he, were now much quieter than they had been, and the tone of their jokes, in a way that he could not quite put his finger on, had changed. These men were his models, they had been friends to his father, and they had taught him what it meant to be a man. He looked to them for courage now. It wasn't that he didn't know that what he was doing was right—he knew that, nobody had to tell him that; it was only that he missed the ease of former years. But they didn't have much time to hang out with each other these days. They tended to stay close to their families every free minute because nobody knew what might happen next. Explosions rocked the night of their tranquil town. Each time each man wondered silently if perhaps this time the dynamite had not fallen into the wrong hands. They thought that they knew where all the guns were; but they could not possibly know every move that was made in that secret place where the darkies lived. From time to time it was suggested that they form a posse and search the home of every nigger, but they hadn't done it yet. For one thing, this might have brought the bastards from the North down on their backs; for another, although the niggers were scattered throughout the town— down in the hollow near the railroad tracks, way west near the mills, up on the hill, the well-off ones, and some out near the college—nothing seemed to happen in one part of town without the niggers immediately knowing it in the other. This meant that they could not take them by surprise. They rarely mentioned it, but they *knew* that some of the niggers had guns. It stood to reason, as they said, since, after all, some of them had been in the Army. There were niggers in the Army right now and God knows they wouldn't have had any trouble stealing this half-assed government blind—the whole world was doing it, look at the European countries and all those countries in Africa. They made jokes about it—bitter jokes; and they cursed the government in Washington, which had betrayed them; but they had not yet formed a posse. Now, if their town had been laid out like some towns in the North, where all the niggers lived together in one locality, they could have gone down and set fire to the houses and brought about peace that way. If the niggers had all lived in one place, they could have kept the fire in one place. But the way this town was laid out, the fire could hardly be controlled. It would spread all over town—and the niggers would probably be helping it to spread. Still, from time to time, they spoke of doing it, anyway; so that now there was a real fear among them that somebody might go crazy and light the match.

They rarely mentioned anything not directly related to the war that they were fighting, but this had failed to establish between them the unspoken communication of soldiers during a war. Each man, in the thrilling silence which sped outward from their exchanges, their laughter, and their anecdotes, seemed wrestling, in various degrees of darkness, with a secret which he could not articulate to himself, and which, however directly it related to the war, related yet more surely to his privacy and his past. They could no longer be sure, after all, that they had all done the same things. They had never dreamed that their privacy could contain any element of terror, could threaten, that is, to reveal itself, to the scrutiny of a judgment day, while remaining unreadable and inaccessible to themselves; nor had they dreamed that the past, while certainly refusing to be forgotten, could yet so stubbornly refuse to be remembered. They felt themselves mysteriously set at naught, as no longer entering into the real concerns of other people—while here they were, out-numbered, fighting to save the civilized world. They had thought that people would care—people didn't care; not enough, anyway, to help them. It would have been a help, really, or at least a relief, even to have been forced to surrender. Thus they had lost, probably forever, their old and easy connection with each other. They were forced to depend on each other more and, at the same time, to trust each other less. Who could tell when one of them might not betray them all, for money, or for the ease of confession? But no one dared imagine what there might be to confess. They were soldiers fighting a war, but their relationship to each other was that of accomplices in a crime. They all had to keep their mouths shut.

I stepped in the river at Jordan.

Out of the darkness of the room, out of nowhere, the line came flying up at him, with the melody and the beat. He turned wordlessly toward his sleeping wife. *I stepped in the river at Jordan.* Where had he heard that song?

"Grace," he whispered. "You awake?"

She did not answer. If she was awake, she wanted him to sleep. Her breathing was slow and easy, her body slowly rose and fell.

I stepped in the river at Jordan.
The water came to my knees.

He began to sweat. He felt an overwhelming fear, which yet contained a curious and dreadful pleasure.

I stepped in the river at Jordan.
The water came to my waist.

It had been night, as it was now, he was in the car between his mother and his father, sleepy, his head in his mother's lap, sleepy, and yet full of excitement. The singing came from far away, across the dark fields. There were no lights anywhere. They had said good-bye to all the others and turned off on this dark dirt road. They were almost home.

I stepped in the river at Jordan,
The water came over my head,
I looked way over to the other side,
He was making up my dying bed!

"I guess they singing for him," his father said, seeming very weary and subdued now. "Even when they're sad, they sound like they just about to go and tear off a piece." He yawned and leaned across the boy and slapped his wife lightly on the shoulder, allowing his hand to rest there for a moment. "Don't they?"

"Don't talk that way," she said.

"Well, that's what we going to do," he said, "you can make up your mind to that." He started whistling. "You see? When I begin to feel it, I gets kind of musical, too."

Oh, Lord! Come on and ease my troubling mind!

He had a black friend, his age, eight, who lived nearby. His name was Otis. They wrestled together in the dirt. Now the thought of Otis made him sick. He began to shiver. His mother put her arm around him.

"He's tired," she said.

"We'll be home soon," said his father. He began to whistle again.

"We didn't see Otis this morning," Jesse said. He did not know why he said this. His voice, in the darkness of the car, sounded small and accusing.

"You haven't seen Otis for a couple of mornings," his mother said.

That was true. But he was only concerned about *this* morning.

"No," said his father, "I reckon Otis's folks was afraid to let him show himself this morning."

"But Otis didn't do nothing!" Now his voice sounded questioning.

"Otis *can't* do nothing," said his father, "he's too little." The car lights picked up their wooden house, which now solemnly approached them, the lights falling around it like yellow dust. Their dog, chained to a tree, began to bark.

"We just want to make sure Otis *don't* do nothing," said his father, and stopped the car. He looked down at Jesse. "And you tell him what your Daddy said, you hear?"

"Yes sir," he said.

His father switched off the lights. The dog moaned and pranced, but they ignored him and went inside. He could not sleep. He lay awake, hearing the night sounds, the dog yawning and moaning outside, the sawing of the crickets, the cry of the owl, dogs barking far away, then no sounds at all, just the heavy, endless buzzing of the night. The darkness pressed on his eyelids like a scratchy blanket. He turned, he turned again. He wanted to call his mother, but he knew his father would not like this. He was terribly afraid. Then he heard his father's voice in the other room, low, with a joke in it; but this did not help him, it frightened him more, he knew what was going to happen. He put his head under the blanket, then pushed his head out again, for fear, staring at the dark window. He heard his mother's moan, his father's sigh; he gritted his teeth. Then their bed began to rock. His father's breathing seemed to fill the world.

That morning, before the sun had gathered all its strength, men and women, some flushed and some pale with excitement, came with news. Jesse's father seemed to know what the news was before the first jalopy stopped in the yard, and he ran out, crying, "They got him, then? They got him?"

The first jalopy held eight people, three men and two women and three children. The children were sitting on the laps of the grown-ups. Jesse knew two of them, the two boys; they shyly and uncomfortably greeted each other. He did not know the girl.

"Yes, they got him," said one of the women, the older one, who wore a wide hat and a fancy, faded blue dress. "They found him early this morning."

"How far had he got?" Jesse's father asked.

"He hadn't got no further than Harkness," one of the men said. "Look like he got lost up there in all them trees—or maybe he just got so scared he couldn't move." They all laughed.

"Yes, and you know it's near a graveyard, too," said the younger woman, and they laughed again.

"Is that where they got him now?" asked Jesse's father.

By this time there were three cars piled behind the first one, with everyone looking excited and shining, and Jesse noticed that they were carrying food. It was like a Fourth of July picnic.

"Yeah, that's where he is," said one of the men, "declare, Jesse, you going to keep us here all day long, answering your damn fool questions. Come on, we ain't got no time to waste."

"Don't bother putting up no food," cried a woman from one of the other cars, "we got enough. Just come on."

"Why, thank you," said Jesse's father, "we be right along, then."

"I better get a sweater for the boy," said his mother, "in case it turns cold."

Jesse watched his mother's thin legs cross the yard. He knew that she also wanted to comb her hair a little and maybe put on a better dress, the dress she wore to church. His father guessed this, too, for he yelled behind her, "Now don't you go trying to turn yourself into no movie star. You just come on." But he laughed as he said this, and winked at the men; his wife was younger and prettier than most of the other women. He clapped Jesse on the head and started pulling him toward the car. "You all go on," he said, "I'll be right behind you. Jesse, you go tie up that there dog while I get this car started."

The cars sputtered and coughed and shook; the caravan began to move; bright dust filled the air. As soon as he was tied up, the dog began to bark. Jesse's mother came out of the house, carrying a jacket for his father and a sweater for Jesse. She had put a ribbon in her hair and had an old shawl around her shoulders.

"Put these in the car, son," she said, and handed everything to him. She bent down and stroked the dog, looked to see if there was water in his bowl, then went back up the three porch steps and closed the door.

"Come on," said his father, "ain't nothing in there for nobody to steal." He was sitting in the car, which trembled and belched. The last car of the caravan had disappeared but the sound of singing floated behind them.

Jesse got into the car, sitting close to his father, loving the smell of the car, and the trembling, and the bright day, and the sense of going on a great and unexpected journey. His mother got in and closed the door and the car began to move. Not until then did he ask, "Where are we going? Are we going on a picnic?"

He had a feeling that he knew where they were going, but he was not sure.

"That's right," his father said, "we're going on a picnic. You won't ever forget *this* picnic—!"

"Are we," he asked, after a moment, "going to see the bad nigger—the one that knocked down old Miss Standish?"

"Well, I reckon," said his mother, "that we *might* see him."

He started to ask, *Will a lot of niggers be there? Will Otis be there?*—but he did not ask his question, to which, in a strange and uncomfortable way, he already knew the answer. Their friends, in the other cars, stretched up the road as far as he could see; other cars had joined them; there were cars behind them. They were singing. The sun seemed suddenly very hot, and he was at once very happy and a little afraid. He did not quite understand what was happening, and he did not know what to ask—he had no one to ask. He had grown accustomed, for the solution of such mysteries, to go to Otis. He felt that Otis knew everything. But he could not ask Otis about this. Anyway, he had not seen Otis for two days; he had not seen a black face anywhere for more than two days; and he now realized, as they began chugging up the long hill which eventually led to Harkness, that there were no black faces on the road this morning, no black people anywhere. From the houses in which they lived, all along the road, no smoke curled, no life stirred—maybe one or two chickens were to be seen, that was all. There was no one at the windows, no one in the yard, no one sitting on the porches, and the doors were closed. He had come this road many a time and seen women washing in the yard (there were no clothes on the clotheslines), men working in the fields, children playing in the dust; black men passed them on the road other mornings, other days, on foot, or in wagons, sometimes in cars, tipping their hats, smiling, joking, their teeth a solid white against their skin, their eyes as warm as the sun, the blackness of their skin like dull fire against the white or the blue or the grey of their torn clothes. They passed the nigger church—dead-white, desolate, locked up; and the graveyard, where no one knelt or walked, and he saw no flowers. He wanted to ask, *Where are they? Where are they all?* But he did not dare. As the hill grew steeper, the sun grew colder. He looked at his mother and his father. They looked straight ahead, seeming to be listening to the singing which echoed and echoed in this graveyard silence. They were strangers to him now. They were looking at something he could not see. His father's lips had a strange, cruel curve, he wet his lips from time to time, and swallowed. He was terribly aware of his father's tongue, it was as though he had never seen it before. And his father's body suddenly seemed immense, bigger than a mountain. His eyes, which were grey-green, looked yellow in the sunlight; or at least there was a light in them which he had never seen before. His mother patted her hair and adjusted the ribbon, leaning forward to look into the car mirror. "You look all right," said his father, and laughed. "When that nigger looks at you, he's going to swear he threw his life away for nothing. Wouldn't be surprised if he don't come back to haunt you." And he laughed again.

The singing now slowly began to cease; and he realized that they were nearing their destination. They had reached a straight, narrow, pebbly road, with trees on either side. The sunlight filtered down on them from a great height, as though they were underwater; and the branches of the trees scraped against the cars with a tearing sound. To the right of them, and beneath them, invisible now, lay the town; and to the left, miles of trees which led to the high mountain range which his ancestors had crossed in order to settle in this valley. Now, all was silent, except for the bumping of the tires against the rocky road, the sputtering of motors, and the sound of a crying child. And they seemed to move more slowly. They were beginning to climb again. He watched the cars ahead as they toiled patiently upward, disappearing into the sunlight of the clearing. Presently, he felt their vehicle also rise, heard his father's changed breathing, the sunlight hit his face, the trees moved away from them, and they were there. As their car crossed the clearing, he looked around. There seemed to be millions, there were certainly hundreds of people in the clearing, staring toward something he could not see. There was a fire. He could not see the flames, but he smelled the smoke. Then they were on the other side of the clearing, among the trees again. His father drove off the road and parked the car behind a great many other cars. He looked down at Jesse.

"You all right?" he asked.

"Yes sir," he said.

"Well, come on, then," his father said. He reached over and opened the door on his mother's side. His mother stepped out first. They followed her into the clearing. At first he was aware only of confusion, of his mother and father greeting and being greeted, himself being handled, hugged, and patted, and told how much he had grown. The wind blew the smoke from the fire across the clearing into his eyes and nose. He could not see over the backs of the people in front of him. The sounds of laughing and cursing and wrath—and something else—rolled in waves from the front of the mob to the back. Those in front expressed their delight at what they saw, and this delight rolled backward, wave upon wave, across the clearing, more acrid than the smoke. His father reached down suddenly and sat Jesse on his shoulders.

Now he saw the fire—of twigs and boxes, piled high; flames made pale orange and yellow and thin as a veil under the steadier light of the sun; grey-blue smoke rolled upward and poured over their heads. Beyond the shifting curtain of fire and smoke, he made out first only a length of gleaming chain, attached to a great limb of the tree; then he saw that this chain bound two black hands together at the wrist, dirty yellow palm facing dirty yellow palm. The smoke poured up; the hands dropped out of sight; a cry went up from the crowd. Then the hands slowly came into view again, pulled upward by the chain. This time he saw the kinky, sweating, bloody head—he had never before seen a head with so much hair on it, hair so black and so tangled that it seemed like another jungle. The head was hanging. He saw the forehead, flat and high, with a kind of arrow of hair in the center, like he had, like his father had; they called it a widow's peak; and the mangled eyebrows, the wide nose, the closed eyes, and the glinting eyelashes and the hanging lips, all streaming with blood and sweat. His hands were straight above his head. All his weight pulled downward from his hands; and he was a big man, a bigger man than his father, and black as an African jungle cat, and naked. Jesse pulled upward; his father's hands held him firmly by the ankles. He wanted to say something, he did not know what, but nothing he said could have been heard, for now the crowd roared again as a man stepped forward and put more wood on the fire. The flames leapt up. He thought he heard the hanging man scream, but he was not sure. Sweat was pouring from the hair in his armpits, poured down his sides, over his chest, into his navel and his groin. He was lowered again; he was raised again. Now Jesse knew that he heard him scream. The head went back, the mouth wide open, blood bubbling from the mouth; the veins of the neck jumped out; Jesse clung to his father's neck in terror as the cry rolled over the crowd. The cry of all the people rose to answer the dying man's cry. He wanted death to come quickly. They wanted to make death wait: and it was they who held death, now, on a leash which they lengthened little by little. *What did he do?* Jesse wondered. *What did the man do? What did he do?*—but he could not ask his father. He was seated on his father's shoulders, but his father was far away. There were two older men, friends of his father's, raising and lowering the chain; everyone, indiscriminately, seemed to be responsible for the fire. There was no hair left on the nigger's privates, and the eyes, now, were wide open, as white as the eyes of a clown or a doll. The smoke now carried a terrible odor across the clearing, the odor of something burning which was both sweet and rotten.

He turned his head a little and saw the field of faces. He watched his mother's face. Her eyes were very bright, her mouth was open: she was more beautiful than he had ever seen her, and more strange. He began to feel a joy he had never felt before. He watched the hanging, gleaming body, the most beautiful and terrible object he had ever seen till then. One of his father's friends reached up and in his hands he held a knife: and Jesse wished that he had been that man. It was a long, bright knife and the sun seemed to catch it, to play with it, to caress it—it was brighter than the fire. And a wave of laughter swept the crowd. Jesse felt his father's hands on his ankles slip and tighten. The man with the knife walked toward the crowd, smiling slightly; as though this were a signal, silence fell; he heard his mother cough. Then the man with the knife walked up to the hanging body. He turned and smiled again. Now there was a silence all over the field. The hanging head looked up. It seemed fully conscious now, as though the fire had burned out terror and pain. The man with the knife took the nigger's privates in his hand, one hand, still smiling, as though he were weighing them. In the cradle of the one white hand, the nigger's privates seemed as remote as meat being weighed in the scales; but seemed heavier, too, much heavier, and Jesse felt his scrotum tighten; and huge, huge, much bigger than his father's, flaccid, hairless, the largest thing he had ever seen till then, and the blackest. The white hand stretched them, cradled them, caressed them. Then the dying man's eyes looked straight into Jesse's eyes—it could not have been as long as a second, but it seemed longer than a year. Then Jesse screamed, and the crowd screamed as the knife flashed, first up, then down, cutting the dreadful thing away, and the blood came roaring down. Then the crowd rushed forward, tearing at the body with their hands, with knives, with rocks, with stones, howling and cursing. Jesse's head, of its own weight, fell downward toward his father's head. Someone stepped forward and drenched the body with kerosene. Where the man had been, a great sheet of flame appeared. Jesse's father lowered him to the ground.

"Well, I told you," said his father, "you wasn't never going to forget *this* picnic." His father's face was full of sweat, his eyes were very peaceful. At that moment Jesse loved his father more than he had ever loved him. He felt that his father had carried him through a mighty test, had revealed to him a great secret which would be the key to his life forever.

"I reckon," he said. "I reckon."

Jesse's father took him by the hand and, with his mother a little behind them, talking and laughing with the other women, they walked through the crowd, across the clearing. The black body was on the ground, the chain which had held it was being rolled up by one of his father's friends. Whatever the fire had left undone, the hands and the knives and the stones of the people had accomplished. The head was caved in, one eye was torn out, one ear was hanging. But one had to look carefully to realize this, for it was, now, merely, a black charred object on the black, charred ground. He lay spread-eagled with what had been a wound between what had been his legs.

"They going to leave him here, then?" Jesse whispered.

"Yeah," said his father, "they'll come and get him by and by. I reckon we better get over there and get some of that food before it's all gone."

"I reckon," he muttered now to himself, "I reckon." Grace stirred and touched him on the thigh: the moonlight covered her like glory. Something bubbled up in him, his nature again returned to him. He thought of the boy in the cell; he thought of the man in the fire; he thought of the knife and grabbed himself and stroked himself and a terrible sound, something between a high laugh and a howl, came out of him and dragged his sleeping wife up on one elbow. She stared at him in a moonlight which had now grown cold as ice. He thought of the morning and grabbed her, laughing and crying, crying and laughing, and he whispered, as he stroked her, as he took her, "Come on, sugar, I'm going to do you like a nigger, just like a nigger, come on, sugar, and love me just like you'd love a nigger." He thought of the morning as he labored and she moaned, thought of morning as he labored harder than he ever had before, and before his labors had ended, he heard the first cock crow and the dogs begin to bark, and the sound of tires on the gravel road.

1965

Sonny's Blues

I read about it in the paper, in the subway, on my way to work. I read it, and I couldn't believe it, and I read it again. Then perhaps I just stared at it, at the newsprint spelling out his name, spelling out the story. I stared at it in the swinging lights of the subway car, and in the faces and bodies of the people, and in my own face, trapped in the darkness which roared outside.

It was not to be believed and I kept telling myself that, as I walked from the subway station to the high school. And at the same time I couldn't doubt it. I was scared, scared for Sonny. He became real to me again. A great block of ice got settled in my belly and kept melting there slowly all day long, while I taught my classes algebra. It was a special kind of ice. It kept melting, sending trickles of ice water all up and down my veins, but it never got less. Sometimes it hardened and seemed to expand until I felt my guts were going to come spilling out or that I was going to choke or scream. This would always be at a moment when I was remembering some specific thing Sonny had once said or done.

When he was about as old as the boys in my classes his face had been bright and open, there was a lot of copper in it; and he'd had wonderfully direct brown eyes, and great gentleness and privacy. I wondered what he looked like now. He had been picked up, the evening before, in a raid on an apartment downtown, for peddling and using heroin.

I couldn't believe it: but what I mean by that is that I couldn't find any room for it anywhere inside me. I had kept it outside me for a long time. I hadn't wanted to know. I had had suspicions, but I didn't name them, I kept putting them away. I told myself that Sonny was wild, but he wasn't crazy. And he'd always been a good boy, he hadn't ever turned hard or evil or disrespectful, the way kids can, so quick, so quick, especially in Harlem. I didn't want to believe that I'd ever see my brother going down, coming to nothing, all that light in his face gone out, in the condition I'd already seen so many others. Yet it had happened and here I was, talking about algebra to a lot of boys who might, every one of them for all I knew, be popping off needles every time they went to the head.[1] Maybe it did more for them than algebra could.

I was sure that the first time Sonny had ever had horse,[2] he couldn't have been much older than these boys were now. These boys, now, were living as we'd been living then, they were growing up with a rush and their heads bumped abruptly against the low ceiling of their actual possibilities. They were filled with rage. All they really knew were two darknesses, the darkness of their lives, which was now closing in on them, and the darkness of the movies, which had blinded them to that other darkness, and in which they now, vindictively, dreamed, at once more together than they were at any other time, and more alone.

When the last bell rang, the last class ended, I let out my breath. It seemed I'd been holding it for all that time. My clothes were wet—I may have looked as though I'd been sitting in a steam bath, all dressed up, all afternoon. I sat alone in the classroom a long time. I listened to the boys outside, downstairs,

---

1. Lavatory. 2. Slang term for heroin.

shouting and cursing and laughing. Their laughter struck me for perhaps the first time. It was not the joyous laughter which—God knows why—one associates with children. It was mocking and insular, its intent was to denigrate. It was disenchanted, and in this, also, lay the authority of their curses. Perhaps I was listening to them because I was thinking about my brother and in them I heard my brother. And myself.

One boy was whistling a tune, at once very complicated and very simple, it seemed to be pouring out of him as though he were a bird, and it sounded very cool and moving through all that harsh, bright air, only just holding its own through all those other sounds.

I stood up and walked over to the window and looked down into the courtyard. It was the beginning of the spring and the sap was rising in the boys. A teacher passed through them every now and again, quickly, as though he or she couldn't wait to get out of that courtyard, to get those boys out of their sight and off their minds. I started collecting my stuff. I thought I'd better get home and talk to Isabel.

The courtyard was almost deserted by the time I got downstairs. I saw this boy standing in the shadow of a doorway, looking just like Sonny. I almost called his name. Then I saw that it wasn't Sonny, but somebody we used to know, a boy from around our block. He'd been Sonny's friend. He'd never been mine, having been too young for me, and, anyway, I'd never liked him. And now, even though he was a grown-up man, he still hung around that block, still spent hours on the street corners, was always high and raggy. I used to run into him from time to time and he'd often work around to asking me for a quarter or fifty cents. He always had some real good excuse, too, and I always gave it to him, I don't know why.

But now, abruptly, I hated him. I couldn't stand the way he looked at me, partly like a dog, partly like a cunning child. I wanted to ask him what the hell he was doing in the school courtyard.

He sort of shuffled over to me, and he said, "I see you got the papers. So you already know about it."

"You mean about Sonny? Yes, I already know about it. How come they didn't get you?"

He grinned. It made him repulsive and it also brought to mind what he'd looked like as a kid. "I wasn't there. I stay away from them people."

"Good for you." I offered him a cigarette and I watched him through the smoke. "You come all the way down here just to tell me about Sonny?"

"That's right." He was sort of shaking his head and his eyes looked strange, as though they were about to cross. The bright sun deadened his damp dark brown skin and it made his eyes look yellow and showed up the dirt in his kinked hair. He smelled funky. I moved a little away from him and I said, "Well, thanks. But I already know about it and I got to get home."

"I'll walk you a little ways," he said. We started walking. There were a couple of kids still loitering in the courtyard and one of them said goodnight to me and looked strangely at the boy beside me.

"What're you going to do?" he asked me. "I mean, about Sonny?"

"Look. I haven't seen Sonny for over a year, I'm not sure I'm going to do anything. Anyway, what the hell *can* I do?"

"That's right," he said quickly, "ain't nothing you can do. Can't much help old Sonny no more, I guess."

It was what I was thinking and so it seemed to me he had no right to say it.

"I'm surprised at Sonny, though," he went on—he had a funny way of talking, he looked straight ahead as though he were talking to himself—"I thought Sonny was a smart boy, I thought he was too smart to get hung."[3]

"I guess he thought so too," I said sharply, "and that's how he got hung. And how about you? You're pretty goddamn smart, I bet."

Then he looked directly at me, just for a minute. "I ain't smart," he said. "If I was smart, I'd have reached for a pistol a long time ago."

"Look. Don't tell *me* your sad story, if it was up to me, I'd give you one." Then I felt guilty—guilty, probably, for never having supposed that the poor bastard *had* a story of his own, much less a sad one, and I asked, quickly, "What's going to happen to him now?"

He didn't answer this. He was off by himself some place. "Funny thing," he said, and from his tone we might have been discussing the quickest way to get to Brooklyn, "when I saw the papers this morning, the first thing I asked myself was if I had anything to do with it. I felt sort of responsible."

I began to listen more carefully. The subway station was on the corner, just before us, and I stopped. He stopped, too. We were in front of a bar and he ducked slightly, peering in, but whoever he was looking for didn't seem to be there. The juke box was blasting away with something black and bouncy and I half watched the barmaid as she danced her way from the juke box to her place behind the bar. And I watched her face as she laughingly responded to something someone said to her, still keeping time to the music. When she smiled one saw the little girl, one sensed the doomed, still-struggling woman beneath the battered face of the semi-whore.

"I never *give* Sonny nothing," the boy said finally, "but a long time ago I come to school high and Sonny asked me how it felt." He paused, I couldn't bear to watch him, I watched the barmaid, and I listened to the music which seemed to be causing the pavement to shake. "I told him it felt great." The music stopped, the barmaid paused and watched the juke box until the music began again. "It did."

All this was carrying me some place I didn't want to go. I certainly didn't want to know how it felt. It filled everything, the people, the houses, the music, the dark, quicksilver barmaid, with menace; and this menace was their reality.

"What's going to happen to him now?" I asked again.

"They'll send him away some place and they'll try to cure him." He shook his head. "Maybe he'll even think he's kicked the habit. Then they'll let him loose"—he gestured, throwing his cigarette into the gutter. "That's all."

"What do you mean, that's *all*?"

But I knew what he meant.

"I *mean*, that's *all*." He turned his head and looked at me, pulling down the corners of his mouth. "Don't you know what I mean?" he asked, softly.

"How the hell *would* I know what you mean?" I almost whispered it, I don't know why.

"That's right," he said to the air, "how would *he* know what I mean?" He turned toward me again, patient and calm, and yet I somehow felt him

3. Become an addict.

shaking, shaking as though he were going to fall apart. I felt that ice in my guts again, the dread I'd felt all afternoon; and again I watched the barmaid, moving about the bar, washing glasses, and singing. "Listen. They'll let him out and then it'll just start all over again. That's what I mean."

"You mean—they'll let him out. And then he'll just start working his way back in again. You mean he'll never kick the habit. Is that what you mean?"

"That's right," he said, cheerfully. "*You* see what I mean."

"Tell me," I said at last, "why does he want to die? He must want to die, he's killing himself, why does he want to die?"

He looked at me in surprise. He licked his lips. "He don't want to die. He wants to live. Don't nobody want to die, ever."

Then I wanted to ask him—too many things. He could not have answered, or if he had, I could not have borne the answers. I started walking. "Well, I guess it's none of my business."

"It's going to be rough on old Sonny," he said. We reached the subway station. "This is your station?" he asked. I nodded. I took one step down. "Damn!" he said, suddenly. I looked up at him. He grinned again. "Damn it if I didn't leave all my money home. You ain't got a dollar on you, have you? Just for a couple of days, is all."

All at once something inside gave and threatened to come pouring out of me. I didn't hate him anymore. I felt that in another moment I'd start crying like a child.

"Sure," I said. "Don't sweat." I looked in my wallet and didn't have a dollar, I only had a five. "Here," I said. "That hold you?"

He didn't look at it—he didn't want to look at it. A terrible, closed look came over his face, as though he were keeping the number on the bill a secret from him and me. "Thanks," he said, and now he was dying to see me go. "Don't worry about Sonny. Maybe I'll write him or something."

"Sure," I said. "You do that. So long."

"Be seeing you," he said. I went on down the steps.

And I didn't write Sonny or send him anything for a long time. When I finally did, it was just after my little girl died, he wrote me back a letter which made me feel like a bastard.

Here's what he said:

Dear brother,

You don't know how much I needed to hear from you. I wanted to write you many a time but I dug how much I must have hurt you and so I didn't write. But now I feel like a man who's been trying to climb up out of some deep, real deep and funky hole and just saw the sun up there, outside. I got to get outside.

I can't tell you much about how I got here. I mean I don't know how to tell you. I guess I was afraid of something or I was trying to escape from something and you know I have never been very strong in the head (smile). I'm glad Mama and Daddy are dead and can't see what's happened to their son and I swear if I'd known what I was doing I would never have hurt you so, you and a lot of other fine people who were nice to me and who believed in me.

I don't want you to think it had anything to do with me being a musician. It's more than that. Or maybe less than that. I can't get anything straight in my head down here and I try not to think about what's going to happen to me when I get outside again. Sometime I think I'm going to flip and *never* get outside and sometime I think I'll come straight back. I tell you one thing, though, I'd rather blow my brains out than go through this again. But that's what they all say, so they tell me. If I tell you when I'm coming to New York and if you could meet me, I sure would appreciate it. Give my love to Isabel and the kids and I was sure sorry to hear about little Gracie. I wish I could be like Mama and say the Lord's will be done, but I don't know it seems to me that trouble is the one thing that never does get stopped and I don't know what good it does to blame it on the Lord. But maybe it does some good if you believe it.

Your brother,
Sonny

Then I kept in constant touch with him and I sent him whatever I could and I went to meet him when he came back to New York. When I saw him many things I thought I had forgotten came flooding back to me. This was because I had begun, finally, to wonder about Sonny, about the life that Sonny lived inside. This life, whatever it was, had made him older and thinner and it had deepened the distant stillness in which he had always moved. He looked very unlike my baby brother. Yet, when he smiled, when we shook hands, the baby brother I'd never known looked out from the depths of his private life, like an animal waiting to be coaxed into the light.

"How you been keeping?" he asked me.

"All right. And you?"

"Just fine." He was smiling all over his face. "It's good to see you again."

"It's good to see you."

The seven years' difference in our ages lay between us like a chasm: I wondered if these years would ever operate between us as a bridge. I was remembering, and it made it hard to catch my breath, that I had been there when he was born; and I had heard the first words he had ever spoken. When he started to walk, he walked from our mother straight to me. I caught him just before he fell when he took the first steps he ever took in this world.

"How's Isabel?"

"Just fine. She's dying to see you."

"And the boys?"

"They're fine, too. They're anxious to see their uncle."

"Oh, come on. You know they don't remember me."

"Are you kidding? Of course they remember you."

He grinned again. We got into a taxi. We had a lot to say to each other, far too much to know how to begin.

As the taxi began to move, I asked, "You still want to go to India?"

He laughed. "You still remember that. Hell, no. This place is Indian enough for me."

"It used to belong to them,"[4] I said.

---

4. Manhattan Island, in the center of New York City, was purchased by Dutch settlers from the Lenape tribe, circa 1626.

And he laughed again. "They damn sure knew what they were doing when they got rid of it."

Years ago, when he was around fourteen, he'd been all hipped on the idea of going to India. He read books about people sitting on rocks, naked, in all kinds of weather, but mostly bad, naturally, and walking barefoot through hot coals and arriving at wisdom. I used to say that it sounded to me as though they were getting away from wisdom as fast as they could. I think he sort of looked down on me for that.

"Do you mind," he asked, "if we have the driver drive alongside the park?[5] On the west side—I haven't seen the city in so long."

"Of course not," I said. I was afraid that I might sound as though I were humoring him, but I hoped he wouldn't take it that way.

So we drove along, between the green of the park and the stony, lifeless elegance of hotels and apartment buildings, toward the vivid, killing streets of our childhood. These streets hadn't changed, though housing projects jutted up out of them now like rocks in the middle of a boiling sea. Most of the houses in which we had grown up had vanished, as had the stores from which we had stolen, the basements in which we had first tried sex, the rooftops from which we had hurled tin cans and bricks. But houses exactly like the houses of our past yet dominated the landscape, boys exactly like the boys we once had been found themselves smothering in these houses, came down into the streets for light and air and found themselves encircled by disaster. Some escaped the trap, most didn't. Those who got out always left something of themselves behind, as some animals amputate a leg and leave it in the trap. It might be said, perhaps, that I had escaped, after all, I was a school teacher; or that Sonny had, he hadn't lived in Harlem for years. Yet, as the cab moved uptown through streets which seemed, with a rush, to darken with dark people, and as I covertly studied Sonny's face, it came to me that what we both were seeking through our separate cab windows was that part of ourselves which had been left behind. It's always at the hour of trouble and confrontation that the missing member aches.

We hit 110th Street and started rolling up Lenox Avenue. And I'd known this avenue all my life, but it seemed to me again, as it had seemed on the day I'd first heard about Sonny's trouble, filled with a hidden menace which was its very breath of life.

"We almost there," said Sonny.

"Almost." We were both too nervous to say anything more.

We live in a housing project. It hasn't been up long. A few days after it was up it seemed uninhabitably new, now, of course, it's already rundown. It looks like a parody of the good, clean, faceless life—God knows the people who live in it do their best to make it a parody. The beat-looking grass lying around isn't enough to make their lives green, the hedges will never hold out the streets, and they know it. The big windows fool no one, they aren't big enough to make space out of no space. They don't bother with the windows, they watch the TV screen instead. The playground is most popular with the children who don't play at jacks, or skip rope, or roller skate, or swing, and they can be found in it after dark. We moved in partly because it's not too far from where I teach, and partly for the kids; but it's really just like the houses

5. Central Park.

in which Sonny and I grew up. The same things happen, they'll have the same things to remember. The moment Sonny and I started into the house I had the feeling that I was simply bringing him back into the danger he had almost died trying to escape.

Sonny has never been talkative. So I don't know why I was sure he'd be dying to talk to me when supper was over the first night. Everything went fine, the oldest boy remembered him, and the youngest boy liked him, and Sonny had remembered to bring something for each of them; and Isabel, who is really much nicer than I am, more open and giving, had gone to a lot of trouble about dinner and was genuinely glad to see him. And she's always been able to tease Sonny in a way that I haven't. It was nice to see her face so vivid again and to hear her laugh and watch her make Sonny laugh. She wasn't, or, anyway, she didn't seem to be, at all uneasy or embarrassed. She chatted as though there were no subject which had to be avoided and she got Sonny past his first, faint stiffness. And thank God she was there, for I was filled with that icy dread again. Everything I did seemed awkward to me, and everything I said sounded freighted with hidden meaning. I was trying to remember everything I'd heard about dope addiction and I couldn't help watching Sonny for signs. I wasn't doing it out of malice. I was trying to find out something about my brother. I was dying to hear him tell me he was safe.

"Safe!" my father grunted, whenever Mama suggested trying to move to a neighborhood which might be safer for children. "Safe, hell! Ain't no place safe for kids, nor nobody."

He always went on like this, but he wasn't, ever, really as bad as he sounded, not even on weekends, when he got drunk. As a matter of fact, he was always on the lookout for "something a little better," but he died before he found it. He died suddenly, during a drunken weekend in the middle of the war, when Sonny was fifteen. He and Sonny hadn't ever got on too well. And this was partly because Sonny was the apple of his father's eye. It was because he loved Sonny so much and was frightened for him, that he was always fighting with him. It doesn't do any good to fight with Sonny. Sonny just moves back, inside himself, where he can't be reached. But the principal reason that they never hit it off is that they were so much alike. Daddy was big and rough and loud-talking, just the opposite of Sonny, but they both had—that same privacy.

Mama tried to tell me something about this, just after Daddy died. I was home on leave from the army.

This was the last time I ever saw my mother alive. Just the same, this picture gets all mixed up in my mind with pictures I had of her when she was younger. The way I always see her is the way she used to be on a Sunday afternoon, say, when the old folks were talking after the big Sunday dinner. I always see her wearing pale blue. She'd be sitting on the sofa. And my father would be sitting in the easy chair, not far from her. And the living room would be full of church folks and relatives. There they sit, in chairs all around the living room, and the night is creeping up outside, but nobody knows it yet. You can see the darkness growing against the windowpanes and you hear the street noises every now and again, or maybe the jangling beat of a tambourine from one of the churches close by, but it's real quiet in the room. For a moment nobody's talking, but every face looks darkening, like the sky outside. And my mother rocks a little from the waist, and my father's eyes are closed. Everyone is looking at something a child can't see. For a minute they've forgotten the children. Maybe a kid is lying on the rug, half asleep. Maybe somebody's got a kid in his lap and is absent-mindedly stroking the kid's head. Maybe there's a kid, quiet and big-eyed, curled up in a big chair in the corner. The silence, the darkness coming, and the darkness in the faces frightens the child obscurely. He hopes that the hand which strokes his forehead will never stop—will never die. He hopes that there will never come a time when the old folks won't be sitting around the living room, talking about where they've come from, and what they've seen, and what's happened to them and their kinfolk.

But something deep and watchful in the child knows that this is bound to end, is already ending. In a moment someone will get up and turn on the light. Then the old folks will remember the children and they won't talk anymore that day. And when light fills the room, the child is filled with darkness. He knows that every time this happens he's moved just a little closer to that darkness outside. The darkness outside is what the old folks have been talking about. It's what they've come from. It's what they endure. The child knows that they won't talk anymore because if he knows too much about what's happened to *them*, he'll know too much too soon, about what's going to happen to *him*.

The last time I talked to my mother, I remember I was restless. I wanted to get out and see Isabel. We weren't married then and we had a lot to straighten out between us.

There Mama sat, in black, by the window. She was humming an old church song, *Lord, you brought me from a long ways off*. Sonny was out somewhere. Mama kept watching the streets.

"I don't know," she said, "if I'll ever see you again, after you go off from here. But I hope you'll remember the things I tried to teach you."

"Don't talk like that," I said, and smiled. "You'll be here a long time yet."

She smiled, too, but she said nothing. She was quiet for a long time. And I said, "Mama, don't you worry about nothing. I'll be writing all the time, and you be getting the checks. . . ."

"I want to talk to you about your brother," she said, suddenly. "If anything happens to me he ain't going to have nobody to look out for him."

"Mama," I said, "ain't nothing going to happen to you *or* Sonny. Sonny's all right. He's a good boy and he's got good sense."

"It ain't a question of his being a good boy," Mama said, "nor of his having good sense. It ain't only the bad ones, nor yet the dumb ones that gets sucked under." She stopped, looking at me. "Your Daddy once had a brother," she said, and she smiled in a way that made me feel she was in pain. "You didn't never know that, did you?"

"No," I said, "I never knew that," and I watched her face.

"Oh, yes," she said, "your Daddy had a brother." She looked out of the window again. "I know you never saw your Daddy cry. But *I* did—many a time, through all these years."

I asked her, "What happened to his brother? How come nobody's ever talked about him?"

This was the first time I ever saw my mother look old.

"His brother got killed," she said, "when he was just a little younger than you are now. I knew him. He was a fine boy. He was maybe a little full of the devil, but he didn't mean nobody no harm."

Then she stopped and the room was silent, exactly as it had sometimes been on those Sunday afternoons. Mama kept looking out into the streets.

"He used to have a job in the mill," she said, "and, like all young folks, he just liked to perform on Saturday nights. Saturday nights, him and your father would drift around to different places, go to dances and things like that, or just sit around with people they knew, and your father's brother would sing, he had a fine voice, and play along with himself on his guitar. Well, this particular Saturday night, him and your father was coming home from some place, and they were both a little drunk and there was a moon that night, it was bright like day. Your father's brother was feeling kind of good, and he was whistling to himself, and he had his guitar slung over his shoulder. They was coming down a hill and beneath them was a road that turned off from the highway. Well, your father's brother, being always kind of frisky, decided to run down this hill, and he did, with that guitar banging and clanging behind him, and he ran across the road, and he was making water behind a tree. And your father was sort of amused at him and he was still coming down the hill, kind of slow. Then he heard a car motor and that same minute his brother stepped from behind the tree, into the road, in the moonlight. And he started to cross the road. And your father started to run down the hill, he says he don't know why. This car was full of white men. They was all drunk, and when they seen your father's brother they let out a great whoop and holler and they aimed the car straight at him. They was having fun, they just wanted to scare him, the way they do sometimes, you know. But they was drunk. And I guess the boy, being drunk, too, and scared, kind of lost his head. By the time he jumped it was too late. Your father says he heard his brother scream when the car rolled over him, and he heard the wood of that guitar when it give, and he heard them strings go flying, and he heard them white men shouting, and the car kept on a-going and it ain't stopped till this day. And, time your father got down the hill, his brother weren't nothing but blood and pulp."

Tears were gleaming on my mother's face. There wasn't anything I could say.

"He never mentioned it," she said, "because I never let him mention it before you children. Your Daddy was like a crazy man that night and for many a night thereafter. He says he never in his life seen anything as dark as that road after the lights of that car had gone away. Weren't nothing, weren't nobody on that road, just your Daddy and his brother and that busted guitar. Oh, yes. Your Daddy never did really get right again. Till the day he died he weren't sure but that every white man he saw was the man that killed his brother."

She stopped and took out her handkerchief and dried her eyes and looked at me.

"I ain't telling you all this," she said, "to make you scared or bitter or to make you hate nobody. I'm telling you this because you got a brother. And the world ain't changed."

I guess I didn't want to believe this. I guess she saw this in my face. She turned away from me, toward the window again, searching those streets.

"But I praise my Redeemer," she said at last, "that He called your Daddy home before me. I ain't saying it to throw no flowers at myself, but, I declare, it keeps me from feeling too cast down to know I helped your father get safely through this world. Your father always acted like he was the roughest, strongest man on earth. And everybody took him to be like that. But if he hadn't had *me* there—to see his tears!"

She was crying again. Still, I couldn't move. I said, "Lord, Lord, Mama, I didn't know it was like that."

"Oh, honey," she said, "there's a lot that you don't know. But you are going to find it out." She stood up from the window and came over to me. "You got to hold on to your brother," she said, "and don't let him fall, no matter what it looks like is happening to him and no matter how evil you gets with him. You going to be evil with him many a time. But don't you forget what I told you, you hear?"

"I won't forget," I said. "Don't you worry, I won't forget. I won't let nothing happen to Sonny."

My mother smiled as though she were amused at something she saw in my face. Then, "You may not be able to stop nothing from happening. But you got to let him know you's *there*."

Two days later I was married, and then I was gone. And I had a lot of things on my mind and I pretty well forgot my promise to Mama until I got shipped home on a special furlough for her funeral.

And, after the funeral, with just Sonny and me alone in the empty kitchen, I tried to find out something about him.

"What do you want to do?" I asked him.

"I'm going to be a musician," he said.

For he had graduated, in the time I had been away, from dancing to the juke box to finding out who was playing what, and what they were doing with it, and he had bought himself a set of drums.

"You mean, you want to be a drummer?" I somehow had the feeling that being a drummer might be all right for other people but not for my brother Sonny.

"I don't think," he said, looking at me very gravely, "that I'll ever be a good drummer. But I think I can play a piano."

I frowned. I'd never played the role of the older brother quite so seriously before, had scarcely ever, in fact, *asked* Sonny a damn thing. I sensed myself in the presence of something I didn't really know how to handle, didn't understand. So I made my frown a little deeper as I asked: "What kind of musician do you want to be?"

He grinned. "How many kinds do you think there are?"

"Be *serious*," I said.

He laughed, throwing his head back, and then looked at me. "I *am* serious."

"Well, then, for Christ's sake, stop kidding around and answer a serious question. I mean, do you want to be a concert pianist, you want to play classical music and all that, or—or what?" Long before I finished he was laughing again. "For Christ's *sake*, Sonny!"

He sobered, but with difficulty. "I'm sorry. But you sound so—*scared*!" and he was off again.

"Well, you may think it's funny now, baby, but it's not going to be so funny when you have to make your living at it, let me tell you *that*." I was furious because I knew he was laughing at me and I didn't know why.

"No," he said, very sober now, and afraid, perhaps, that he'd hurt me, "I don't want to be a classical pianist. That isn't what interests me. I mean"—he paused, looking hard at me, as though his eyes would help me to understand, and then gestured helplessly, as though perhaps his hand would help—"I mean, I'll have a lot of studying to do, and I'll have to study *everything*, but, I mean, I want to play *with*—jazz musicians." He stopped. "I want to play jazz," he said.

Well, the word had never before sounded as heavy, as real, as it sounded that afternoon in Sonny's mouth. I just looked at him and I was probably frowning a real frown by this time. I simply couldn't see why on earth he'd want to spend his time hanging around nightclubs, clowning around on bandstands, while people pushed each other around a dance floor. It seemed—beneath him, somehow. I had never thought about it before, had never been forced to, but I suppose I had always put jazz musicians in a class with what Daddy called "good-time people."

"Are you *serious*?"

"Hell, *yes*, I'm serious."

He looked more helpless than ever, and annoyed, and deeply hurt.

I suggested, helpfully: "You mean—like Louis Armstrong?"[6]

His face closed as though I'd struck him. "No. I'm not talking about none of that old-time, down-home crap."

"Well, look, Sonny, I'm sorry, don't get mad. I just don't altogether get it, that's all. Name somebody—you know, a jazz musician you admire."

"Bird."

"Who?"

"Bird! Charlie Parker![7] Don't they teach you nothing in the goddamn army?"

I lit a cigarette. I was surprised and then a little amused to discover that I was trembling. "I've been out of touch," I said. "You'll have to be patient with me. Now. Who's this Parker character?"

"He's just one of the greatest jazz musicians alive," said Sonny, sullenly, his hands in his pockets, his back to me. "Maybe *the* greatest," he added, bitterly, "that's probably why *you* never heard of him."

"All right," I said, "I'm ignorant. I'm sorry. I'll go out and buy all the cat's records right away, all right?"

"It don't," said Sonny, with dignity, "make any difference to me. I don't care what you listen to. Don't do me no favors."

I was beginning to realize that I'd never seen him so upset before. With another part of my mind I was thinking that this would probably turn out to be one of those things kids go through and that I shouldn't make it seem important by pushing it too hard. Still, I didn't think it would do any harm to ask: "Doesn't all this take a lot of time? Can you make a living at it?"

He turned back to me and half leaned, half sat, on the kitchen table. "Everything takes time," he said, "and—well, yes, sure, I can make a living

6. American jazz trumpeter (1901–1971).
7. Charles Christopher Parker Jr. (1920–1955), nicknamed "Yardbird" or simply "Bird," American jazz saxophonist credited with inventing the experimental "bebop" style of jazz. He died from the effects of long-term heroin addiction.

at it. But what I don't seem to be able to make you understand is that it's the only thing I want to do."

"Well, Sonny," I said, gently, "you know people can't always do exactly what they *want* to do—"

"*No*, I don't know that," said Sonny, surprising me. "I think people *ought* to do what they want to do, what else are they alive for?"

"You getting to be a big boy," I said desperately, "it's time you started thinking about your future."

"I'm thinking about my future," said Sonny, grimly. "I think about it all the time."

I gave up. I decided, if he didn't change his mind, that we could always talk about it later. "In the meantime," I said, "you got to finish school." We had already decided that he'd have to move in with Isabel and her folks. I knew this wasn't the ideal arrangement because Isabel's folks are inclined to be dicty[8] and they hadn't especially wanted Isabel to marry me. But I didn't know what else to do. "And we have to get you fixed up at Isabel's."

There was a long silence. He moved from the kitchen table to the window. "That's a terrible idea. You know it yourself."

"Do you have a *better* idea?"

He just walked up and down the kitchen for a minute. He was as tall as I was. He had started to shave. I suddenly had the feeling that I didn't know him at all.

He stopped at the kitchen table and picked up my cigarettes. Looking at me with a kind of mocking, amused defiance, he put one between his lips. "You mind?"

"You smoking already?"

He lit the cigarette and nodded, watching me through the smoke. "I just wanted to see if I'd have the courage to smoke in front of you." He grinned and blew a great cloud of smoke to the ceiling. "It was easy." He looked at my face. "Come on, now. I bet you was smoking at my age, tell the truth."

I didn't say anything but the truth was on my face, and he laughed. But now there was something very strained in his laugh. "Sure. And I bet that ain't all you was doing."

He was frightening me a little. "Cut the crap," I said. "We already decided that you was going to go and live at Isabel's. Now what's got into you all of a sudden?"

"*You* decided it," he pointed out. "*I* didn't decide nothing." He stopped in front of me, leaning against the stove, arms loosely folded. "Look, brother. I don't want to stay in Harlem no more, I really don't." He was very earnest. He looked at me, then over toward the kitchen window. There was something in his eyes I'd never seen before, some thoughtfulness, some worry all his own. He rubbed the muscle of one arm. "It's time I was getting out of here."

"Where do you want to *go*, Sonny?"

"I want to join the army. Or the navy, I don't care. If I say I'm old enough, they'll believe me."

Then I got mad. It was because I was so scared. "You must be crazy. You goddamn fool, what the hell do you want to go and join the *army* for?"

8. Slang for "snobbish."

"I just told you. To get out of Harlem."

"Sonny, you haven't even finished *school*. And if you really want to be a musician, how do you expect to study if you're in the *army*?"

He looked at me, trapped, and in anguish. "There's ways. I might be able to work out some kind of deal. Anyway, I'll have the G.I. Bill[9] when I come out."

"*If* you come out." We stared at each other. "Sonny, please. Be reasonable. I know the setup is far from perfect. But we got to do the best we can."

"I ain't learning nothing in school," he said. "Even when I go." He turned away from me and opened the window and threw his cigarette out into the narrow alley. I watched his back. "At least, I ain't learning nothing you'd want me to learn." He slammed the window so hard I thought the glass would fly out, and turned back to me. "And I'm sick of the stink of these garbage cans!"

"Sonny," I said, "I know how you feel. But if you don't finish school now, you're going to be sorry later that you didn't." I grabbed him by the shoulders. "And you only got another year. It ain't so bad. And I'll come back and I swear I'll help you do *whatever* you want to do. Just try to put up with it till I come back. Will you please do that? For me?"

He didn't answer and he wouldn't look at me.

"Sonny. You hear me?"

He pulled away. "I hear you. But you never hear anything *I* say."

I didn't know what to say to that. He looked out of the window and then back at me. "OK," he said, and sighed. "I'll try."

Then I said, trying to cheer him up a little, "They got a piano at Isabel's. You can practice on it."

And as a matter of fact, it did cheer him up for a minute. "That's right," he said to himself. "I forgot that." His face relaxed a little. But the worry, the thoughtfulness, played on it still, the way shadows play on a face which is staring into the fire.

But I thought I'd never hear the end of that piano. At first, Isabel would write me, saying how nice it was that Sonny was so serious about his music and how, as soon as he came in from school, or wherever he had been when he was supposed to be at school, he went straight to that piano and stayed there until suppertime. And, after supper, he went back to that piano and stayed there until everybody went to bed. He was at the piano all day Saturday and all day Sunday. Then he bought a record player and started playing records. He'd play one record over and over again, all day long sometimes, and he'd improvise along with it on the piano. Or he'd play one section of the record, one chord, one change, one progression, then he'd do it on the piano. Then back to the record. Then back to the piano.

Well, I really don't know how they stood it. Isabel finally confessed that it wasn't like living with a person at all, it was like living with sound. And the sound didn't make any sense to her, didn't make any sense to any of them— naturally. They began, in a way, to be afflicted by this presence that was living in their home. It was as though Sonny were some sort of god, or

9. The Servicemen's Readjustment Act (1944), known as the G.I. Bill, provided educational and other benefits to World War II veterans.

monster. He moved in an atmosphere which wasn't like theirs at all. They fed him and he ate, he washed himself, he walked in and out of their door; he certainly wasn't nasty or unpleasant or rude, Sonny isn't any of those things; but it was as though he were all wrapped up in some cloud, some fire, some vision all his own; and there wasn't any way to reach him.

At the same time, he wasn't really a man yet, he was still a child, and they had to watch out for him in all kinds of ways. They certainly couldn't throw him out. Neither did they dare to make a great scene about that piano because even they dimly sensed, as I sensed, from so many thousands of miles away, that Sonny was at that piano playing for his life.

But he hadn't been going to school. One day a letter came from the school board and Isabel's mother got it—there had, apparently, been other letters but Sonny had torn them up. This day, when Sonny came in, Isabel's mother showed him the letter and asked where he'd been spending his time. And she finally got it out of him that he'd been down in Greenwich Village,[1] with musicians and other characters, in a white girl's apartment. And this scared her and she started to scream at him and what came up, once she began—though she denies it to this day—was what sacrifices they were making to give Sonny a decent home and how little he appreciated it.

Sonny didn't play the piano that day. By evening, Isabel's mother had calmed down but then there was the old man to deal with, and Isabel herself. Isabel says she did her best to be calm but she broke down and started crying. She says she just watched Sonny's face. She could tell, by watching him, what was happening with him. And what was happening was that they penetrated his cloud, they had reached him. Even if their fingers had been a thousand times more gentle than human fingers ever are, he could hardly help feeling that they had stripped him naked and were spitting on that nakedness. For he also had to see that his presence, that music, which was life or death to him, had been torture for them and that they had endured it, not at all for his sake, but only for mine. And Sonny couldn't take that. He can take it a little better today than he could then but he's still not very good at it and, frankly, I don't know anybody who is.

The silence of the next few days must have been louder than the sound of all the music ever played since time began. One morning, before she went to work, Isabel was in his room for something and she suddenly realized that all of his records were gone. And she knew for certain that he was gone. And he was. He went as far as the navy would carry him. He finally sent me a postcard from some place in Greece and that was the first I knew that Sonny was still alive. I didn't see him anymore until we were both back in New York and the war had long been over.

He was a man by then, of course, but I wasn't willing to see it. He came by the house from time to time, but we fought almost every time we met. I didn't like the way he carried himself, loose and dreamlike all the time, and I didn't like his friends, and his music seemed to be merely an excuse for the life he led. It sounded just that weird and disordered.

Then we had a fight, a pretty awful fight, and I didn't see him for months. By and by I looked him up, where he was living, in a furnished room in the

---

1. Neighborhood in Lower Manhattan where artists, musicians, writers, and intellectuals gathered in the mid-20th century.

Village, and I tried to make it up. But there were lots of other people in the room and Sonny just lay on his bed, and he wouldn't come downstairs with me, and he treated these other people as though they were his family and I weren't. So I got mad and then he got mad, and then I told him that he might just as well be dead as live the way he was living. Then he stood up and he told me not to worry about him anymore in life, that he *was* dead as far as I was concerned. Then he pushed me to the door and the other people looked on as though nothing were happening, and he slammed the door behind me. I stood in the hallway, staring at the door. I heard somebody laugh in the room and then the tears came to my eyes. I started down the steps, whistling to keep from crying, I kept whistling to myself, *You going to need me, baby, one of these cold, rainy days.*[2]

I read about Sonny's trouble in the spring. Little Grace died in the fall. She was a beautiful little girl. But she only lived a little over two years. She died of polio and she suffered. She had a slight fever for a couple of days, but it didn't seem like anything and we just kept her in bed. And we would certainly have called the doctor, but the fever dropped, she seemed to be all right. So we thought it had just been a cold. Then, one day, she was up, playing, Isabel was in the kitchen fixing lunch for the two boys when they'd come in from school, and she heard Grace fall down in the living room. When you have a lot of children you don't always start running when one of them falls, unless they start screaming or something. And, this time, Grace was quiet. Yet, Isabel says that when she heard that *thump* and then that silence, something happened in her to make her afraid. And she ran to the living room and there was little Grace on the floor, all twisted up, and the reason she hadn't screamed was that she couldn't get her breath. And when she did scream, it was the worst sound, Isabel says, that she'd ever heard in all her life, and she still hears it sometimes in her dreams. Isabel will sometimes wake me up with a low, moaning, strangled sound and I have to be quick to awaken her and hold her to me and where Isabel is weeping against me seems a mortal wound.

I think I may have written Sonny the very day that little Grace was buried. I was sitting in the living room in the dark, by myself, and I suddenly thought of Sonny. My trouble made his real.

One Saturday afternoon, when Sonny had been living with us, or, anyway, been in our house, for nearly two weeks, I found myself wandering aimlessly about the living room, drinking from a can of beer, and trying to work up the courage to search Sonny's room. He was out, he was usually out whenever I was home, and Isabel had taken the children to see their grandparents. Suddenly I was standing still in front of the living room window, watching Seventh Avenue. The idea of searching Sonny's room made me still. I scarcely dared to admit to myself what I'd be searching for. I didn't know what I'd do if I found it. Or if I didn't.

On the sidewalk across from me, near the entrance to a barbecue joint, some people were holding an old-fashioned revival meeting. The barbecue cook, wearing a dirty white apron, his conked[3] hair reddish and metallic in

2. Possibly based on Bertha "Chippie" Hill's 1928 recording of the song "Some Cold Rainy Day."
3. Chemically straightened.

the pale sun, and a cigarette between his lips, stood in the doorway, watching them. Kids and older people paused in their errands and stood there, along with some older men and a couple of very tough-looking women who watched everything that happened on the avenue, as though they owned it, or were maybe owned by it. Well, they were watching this, too. The revival was being carried on by three sisters in black, and a brother. All they had were their voices and their Bibles and a tambourine. The brother was testifying and while he testified two of the sisters stood together, seeming to say, amen, and the third sister walked around with the tambourine outstretched and a couple of people dropped coins into it. Then the brother's testimony ended and the sister who had been taking up the collection dumped the coins into her palm and transferred them to the pocket of her long black robe. Then she raised both hands, striking the tambourine against the air, and then against one hand, and she started to sing. And the two other sisters and the brother joined in.

It was strange, suddenly, to watch, though I had been seeing these street meetings all my life. So, of course, had everybody else down there. Yet, they paused and watched and listened and I stood still at the window. *"Tis the old ship of Zion,"* they sang, and the sister with the tambourine kept a steady, jangling beat, *"it has rescued many a thousand!"*[4] Not a soul under the sound of their voices was hearing this song for the first time, not one of them had been rescued. Nor had they seen much in the way of rescue work being done around them. Neither did they especially believe in the holiness of the three sisters and the brother, they knew too much about them, knew where they lived, and how. The woman with the tambourine, whose voice dominated the air, whose face was bright with joy, was divided by very little from the woman who stood watching her, a cigarette between her heavy, chapped lips, her hair a cuckoo's nest, her face scarred and swollen from many beatings, and her black eyes glittering like coal. Perhaps they both knew this, which was why, when, as rarely, they addressed each other, they addressed each other as Sister. As the singing filled the air the watching, listening faces underwent a change, the eyes focusing on something within; the music seemed to soothe a poison out of them; and time seemed, nearly, to fall away from the sullen, belligerent, battered faces, as though they were fleeing back to their first condition, while dreaming of their last. The barbecue cook half shook his head and smiled, and dropped his cigarette and disappeared into his joint. A man fumbled in his pockets for change and stood holding it in his hand impatiently, as though he had just remembered a pressing appointment further up the avenue. He looked furious. Then I saw Sonny, standing on the edge of the crowd. He was carrying a wide, flat notebook with a green cover, and it made him look, from where I was standing, almost like a schoolboy. The coppery sun brought out the copper in his skin, he was very faintly smiling, standing very still. Then the singing stopped, the tambourine turned into a collection plate again. The furious man dropped in his coins and vanished, so did a couple of the women, and Sonny dropped some change in the plate, looking directly at the woman with a little smile. He started across the avenue, toward the house. He has a slow, loping walk, something like the way

---

4. From the song "The Old Ship of Zion," a 19th-century Christian spiritual.

Harlem hipsters walk, only he's imposed on this his own half-beat. I had never really noticed it before.

I stayed at the window, both relieved and apprehensive. As Sonny disappeared from my sight, they began singing again. And they were still singing when his key turned in the lock.

"Hey," he said.

"Hey, yourself. You want some beer?"

"No. Well, maybe." But he came up to the window and stood beside me, looking out. "What a warm voice," he said.

They were singing *If I could only hear my mother pray again!*[5]

"Yes," I said, "and she can sure beat that tambourine."

"But what a terrible song," he said, and laughed. He dropped his notebook on the sofa and disappeared into the kitchen. "Where's Isabel and the kids?"

"I think they went to see their grandparents. You hungry?"

"No." He came back into the living room with his can of beer. "You want to come some place with me tonight?"

I sensed, I don't know how, that I couldn't possibly say no. "Sure. Where?"

He sat down on the sofa and picked up his notebook and started leafing through it. "I'm going to sit in with some fellows in a joint in the Village."

"You mean, you're going to play, tonight?"

"That's right." He took a swallow of his beer and moved back to the window. He gave me a sidelong look. "If you can stand it."

"I'll try," I said.

He smiled to himself and we both watched as the meeting across the way broke up. The three sisters and the brother, heads bowed, were singing *God be with you till we meet again.*[6] The faces around them were very quiet. Then the song ended. The small crowd dispersed. We watched the three women and the lone man walk slowly up the avenue.

"When she was singing before," said Sonny, abruptly, "her voice reminded me for a minute of what heroin feels like sometimes—when it's in your veins. It makes you feel sort of warm and cool at the same time. And distant. And—and sure." He sipped his beer, very deliberately not looking at me. I watched his face. "It makes you feel—in control. Sometimes you've got to have that feeling."

"Do you?" I sat down slowly in the easy chair.

"Sometimes." He went to the sofa and picked up his notebook again. "Some people do."

"In order," I asked, "to play?" And my voice was very ugly, full of contempt and anger.

"Well"—he looked at me with great troubled eyes, as though, in fact, he hoped his eyes would tell me things he could never otherwise say—"they *think* so. And *if* they think so—!"

"And what do *you* think?" I asked.

He sat on the sofa and put his can of beer on the floor. "I don't know," he said, and I couldn't be sure if he were answering my question or pursuing his

5. Traditional Christian spiritual.
6. Christian spiritual by Jeremiah E. Rankin (1828–1904).

thoughts. His face didn't tell me. "It's not so much to *play*. It's to *stand* it, to be able to make it at all. On any level." He frowned and smiled: "In order to keep from shaking to pieces."

"But these friends of yours," I said, "they seem to shake themselves to pieces pretty goddamn fast."

"Maybe." He played with the notebook. And something told me that I should curb my tongue, that Sonny was doing his best to talk, that I should listen. "But of course you only know the ones that've gone to pieces. Some don't—or at least they haven't *yet* and that's just about all *any* of us can say." He paused. "And then there are some who just live, really, in hell, and they know it and they see what's happening and they go right on. I don't know." He sighed, dropped the notebook, folded his arms. "Some guys, you can tell from the way they play, they on something *all* the time. And you can see that, well, it makes something real for them. But of course," he picked up his beer from the floor and sipped it and put the can down again, "they *want* to, too, you've got to see that. Even some of them that say they don't—*some*, not all."

"And what about you?" I asked—I couldn't help it. "What about you? Do *you* want to?"

He stood up and walked to the window and remained silent for a long time. Then he sighed. "Me," he said. Then: "While I was downstairs before, on my way here, listening to that woman sing, it struck me all of a sudden how much suffering she must have had to go through—to sing like that. It's *repulsive* to think you have to suffer that much."

I said: "But there's no way not to suffer—is there, Sonny?"

"I believe not," he said and smiled, "but that's never stopped anyone from trying." He looked at me. "Has it?" I realized, with this mocking look, that there stood between us, forever, beyond the power of time or forgiveness, the fact that I had held silence—so long!—when he had needed human speech to help him. He turned back to the window. "No, there's no way not to suffer. But you try all kinds of ways to keep from drowning in it, to keep on top of it, and to make it seem—well, like *you*. Like you did something, all right, and now you're suffering for it. You know?" I said nothing. "Well you know," he said, impatiently, "why *do* people suffer? Maybe it's better to do something to give it a reason, *any* reason."

"But we just agreed," I said, "that there's no way not to suffer. Isn't it better, then, just to—take it?"

"But nobody just takes it," Sonny cried, "that's what I'm telling you! *Everybody* tries not to. You're just hung up on the *way* some people try—it's not *your* way!"

The hair on my face began to itch, my face felt wet. "That's not true," I said, "that's not true. I don't give a damn what other people do, I don't even care how they suffer. I just care how *you* suffer." And he looked at me. "Please believe me," I said, "I don't want to see you—die—trying not to suffer."

"I won't," he said, flatly, "die trying not to suffer. At least, not any faster than anybody else."

"But there's no need," I said, trying to laugh, "is there? in killing yourself."

I wanted to say more, but I couldn't. I wanted to talk about willpower and how life could be—well, beautiful. I wanted to say that it was all within; but was it? or, rather, wasn't that exactly the trouble? And I wanted to promise that I would never fail him again. But it would all have sounded—empty words and lies.

So I made the promise to myself and prayed that I would keep it.

"It's terrible sometimes, inside," he said, "that's what's the trouble. You walk these streets, black and funky and cold, and there's not really a living ass to talk to, and there's nothing shaking, and there's no way of getting it out—that storm inside. You can't talk it and you can't make love with it, and when you finally try to get with it and play it, you realize *nobody's* listening. So *you've* got to listen. You got to find a way to listen."

And then he walked away from the window and sat on the sofa again, as though all the wind had suddenly been knocked out of him. "Sometimes you'll do *anything* to play, even cut your mother's throat." He laughed and looked at me. "Or your brother's." Then he sobered. "Or your own." Then: "Don't worry. I'm all right now and I think I'll *be* all right. But I can't forget—where I've been. I don't mean just the physical place I've been, I mean where I've *been*. And *what* I've been."

"What have you been, Sonny?" I asked.

He smiled—but sat sideways on the sofa, his elbow resting on the back, his fingers playing with his mouth and chin, not looking at me. "I've been something I didn't recognize, didn't know I could be. Didn't know anybody could be." He stopped, looking inward, looking helplessly young, looking old. "I'm not talking about it now because I feel *guilty* or anything like that—maybe it would be better if I did, I don't know. Anyway, I can't really talk about it. Not to you, not to anybody," and now he turned and faced me. "Sometimes, you know, and it was actually when I was most *out* of the world, I felt that I was in it, that I was *with* it, really, and I could play or I didn't really have to *play*, it just came out of me, it was there. And I don't know how I played, thinking about it now, but I know I did awful things, those times, sometimes, to people. Or it wasn't that I *did* anything to them—it was that they weren't real." He picked up the beer can; it was empty; he rolled it between his palms: "And other times—well, I needed a fix, I needed to find a place to lean, I needed to clear a space to *listen*—and I couldn't find it, and I—went crazy, I did terrible things to *me*, I was terrible *for* me." He began pressing the beer can between his hands, I watched the metal begin to give. It glittered, as he played with it, like a knife, and I was afraid he would cut himself, but I said nothing. "Oh well. I can never tell you. I was all by myself at the bottom of something, stinking and sweating and crying and shaking, and I smelled it, you know? *my* stink, and I thought I'd die if I couldn't get away from it and yet, all the same, I knew that everything I was doing was just locking me in with it. And I didn't know," he paused, still flattening the beer can, "I didn't know, I still *don't* know, something kept telling me that maybe it was good to smell your own stink, but I didn't think that *that* was what I'd been trying to do—and—who can stand it?" and he abruptly dropped the ruined beer can, looking at me with a small, still smile, and then rose, walking to the window as though it were the lodestone rock.[7] I watched his face, he watched the avenue. "I couldn't tell you when Mama died—but the reason I wanted to leave Harlem so bad was to get away from drugs. And then, when I ran away, that's what I was running from—really. When I came

---

7. Naturally magnetized rock.

back, nothing had changed, *I* hadn't changed, I was just—older." And he stopped, drumming with his fingers on the windowpane. The sun had vanished, soon darkness would fall. I watched his face. "It can come again," he said, almost as though speaking to himself. Then he turned to me. "It can come again," he repeated. "I just want you to know that."

"All right," I said, at last. "So it can come again. All right."

He smiled, but the smile was sorrowful. "I had to try to tell you," he said.

"Yes," I said. "I understand that."

"You're my brother," he said, looking straight at me, and not smiling at all.

"Yes," I repeated, "yes. I understand that."

He turned back to the window, looking out. "All that hatred down there," he said, "all that hatred and misery and love. It's a wonder it doesn't blow the avenue apart."

We went to the only nightclub on a short, dark street, downtown. We squeezed through the narrow, chattering, jam-packed bar to the entrance of the big room, where the bandstand was. And we stood there for a moment, for the lights were very dim in this room and we couldn't see. Then, "Hello, boy," said a voice and an enormous black man, much older than Sonny or myself, erupted out of all that atmospheric lighting and put an arm around Sonny's shoulder. "I been sitting right here," he said, "waiting for you."

He had a big voice, too, and heads in the darkness turned toward us.

Sonny grinned and pulled a little away, and said, "Creole, this is my brother. I told you about him."

Creole shook my hand. "I'm glad to meet you, son," he said, and it was clear that he was glad to meet me *there*, for Sonny's sake. And he smiled, "You got a real musician in *your* family," and he took his arm from Sonny's shoulder and slapped him, lightly, affectionately, with the back of his hand.

"Well. Now I've heard it all," said a voice behind us. This was another musician, and a friend of Sonny's, a coal-black, cheerful-looking man, built close to the ground. He immediately began confiding to me, at the top of his lungs, the most terrible things about Sonny, his teeth gleaming like a lighthouse and his laugh coming up out of him like the beginning of an earthquake. And it turned out that everyone at the bar knew Sonny, or almost everyone; some were musicians, working there, or nearby, or not working, some were simply hangers-on, and some were there to hear Sonny play. I was introduced to all of them and they were all very polite to me. Yet, it was clear that, for them, I was only Sonny's brother. Here, I was in Sonny's world. Or, rather: his kingdom. Here, it was not even a question that his veins bore royal blood.

They were going to play soon and Creole installed me, by myself, at a table in a dark corner. Then I watched them, Creole, and the little black man, and Sonny, and the others, while they horsed around, standing just below the bandstand. The light from the bandstand spilled just a little short of them and, watching them laughing and gesturing and moving about, I had the feeling that they, nevertheless, were being most careful not to step into that circle of light too suddenly: that if they moved into the light too suddenly, without thinking, they would perish in flame. Then, while I watched, one of them, the small, black man, moved into the light and crossed the bandstand and started fooling around with his drums. Then—being funny and being, also, extremely ceremonious—Creole took Sonny by the arm and led him to the piano. A woman's voice called Sonny's name and a few hands started clapping. And Sonny, also being funny and being ceremonious, and so touched, I think, that he could have cried, but neither hiding it nor showing it, riding it like a man, grinned, and put both hands to his heart and bowed from the waist.

Creole then went to the bass fiddle and a lean, very bright-skinned brown man jumped up on the bandstand and picked up his horn. So there they were, and the atmosphere on the bandstand and in the room began to change and tighten. Someone stepped up to the microphone and announced them. Then there were all kinds of murmurs. Some people at the bar shushed others. The waitress ran around, frantically getting in the last orders, guys and chicks got closer to each other, and the lights on the bandstand, on the quartet, turned to a kind of indigo. Then they all looked different there. Creole looked about him for the last time, as though he were making certain that all his chickens were in the coop, and then he—jumped and struck the fiddle. And there they were.

All I know about music is that not many people ever really hear it. And even then, on the rare occasions when something opens within, and the music enters, what we mainly hear, or hear corroborated, are personal, private, vanishing evocations. But the man who creates the music is hearing something else, is dealing with the roar rising from the void and imposing order on it as it hits the air. What is evoked in him, then, is of another order, more terrible because it has no words, and triumphant, too, for that same reason. And his triumph, when he triumphs, is ours. I just watched Sonny's face. His face was troubled, he was working hard, but he wasn't with it. And I had the feeling that, in a way, everyone on the bandstand was waiting for him, both waiting for him and pushing him along. But as I began to watch Creole, I realized that it was Creole who held them all back. He had them on a short rein. Up there, keeping the beat with his whole body, wailing on the fiddle, with his eyes half closed, he was listening to everything, but he was listening to Sonny. He was having a dialogue with Sonny. He wanted Sonny to leave the shoreline and strike out for the deep water. He was Sonny's witness that deep water and drowning were not the same thing— he had been there, and he knew. And he wanted Sonny to know. He was waiting for Sonny to do the things on the keys which would let Creole know that Sonny was in the water.

And, while Creole listened, Sonny moved, deep within, exactly like someone in torment. I had never before thought of how awful the relationship must be between the musician and his instrument. He has to fill it, this instrument, with the breath of life, his own. He has to make it do what he wants it to do. And a piano is just a piano. It's made out of so much wood and wires and little hammers and big ones, and ivory. While there's only so much you can do with it, the only way to find this out is to try; to try and make it do everything.

And Sonny hadn't been near a piano for over a year. And he wasn't on much better terms with his life, not the life that stretched before him now. He and the piano stammered, started one way, got scared, stopped; started another way, panicked, marked time, started again; then seemed to have found a direction, panicked again, got stuck. And the face I saw on Sonny

I'd never seen before. Everything had been burned out of it, and, at the same time, things usually hidden were being burned in, by the fire and fury of the battle which was occurring in him up there.

Yet, watching Creole's face as they neared the end of the first set, I had the feeling that something had happened, something I hadn't heard. Then they finished, there was scattered applause, and then, without an instant's warning, Creole started into something else, it was almost sardonic, it was *Am I Blue*.[8] And, as though he commanded, Sonny began to play. Something began to happen. And Creole let out the reins. The dry, low, black man said something awful on the drums, Creole answered, and the drums talked back. Then the horn insisted, sweet and high, slightly detached perhaps, and Creole listened, commenting now and then, dry, and driving, beautiful and calm and old. Then they all came together again, and Sonny was part of the family again. I could tell this from his face. He seemed to have found, right there beneath his fingers, a damn brand-new piano. It seemed that he couldn't get over it. Then, for awhile, just being happy with Sonny, they seemed to be agreeing with him that brand-new pianos certainly were a gas.

Then Creole stepped forward to remind them that what they were playing was the blues. He hit something in all of them, he hit something in me, myself, and the music tightened and deepened, apprehension began to beat the air. Creole began to tell us what the blues were all about. They were not about anything very new. He and his boys up there were keeping it new, at the risk of ruin, destruction, madness, and death, in order to find new ways to make us listen. For, while the tale of how we suffer, and how we are delighted, and how we may triumph is never new, it always must be heard. There isn't any other tale to tell, it's the only light we've got in all this darkness.

And this tale, according to that face, that body, those strong hands on those strings, has another aspect in every country, and a new depth in every generation. Listen, Creole seemed to be saying, listen. Now these are Sonny's blues. He made the little black man on the drums know it, and the bright, brown man on the horn. Creole wasn't trying any longer to get Sonny in the water. He was wishing him Godspeed. Then he stepped back, very slowly, filling the air with the immense suggestion that Sonny speak for himself.

Then they all gathered around Sonny and Sonny played. Every now and again one of them seemed to say, amen. Sonny's fingers filled the air with life, his life. But that life contained so many others. And Sonny went all the way back, he really began with the spare, flat statement of the opening phrase of the song. Then he began to make it his. It was very beautiful because it wasn't hurried and it was no longer a lament. I seemed to hear with what burning he had made it his, with what burning we had yet to make it ours, how we could cease lamenting. Freedom lurked around us and I understood, at last, that he could help us to be free if we would listen, that he would never be free until we did. Yet, there was no battle in his face now. I heard what he had gone through, and would continue to go through until he came to rest in earth. He had made it his: that long line, of which we knew only Mama and Daddy. And he was giving it back, as everything must be given back, so that, passing through death, it can live forever. I saw my

---

8. Jazz standard by Harry Akst and Grant Clarke (1929).

mother's face again, and felt, for the first time, how the stones of the road she had walked on must have bruised her feet. I saw the moonlit road where my father's brother died. And it brought something else back to me, and carried me past it, I saw my little girl again and felt Isabel's tears again, and I felt my own tears begin to rise. And I was yet aware that this was only a moment, that the world waited outside, as hungry as a tiger, and that trouble stretched above us, longer than the sky.

Then it was over. Creole and Sonny let out their breath, both soaking wet, and grinning. There was a lot of applause and some of it was real. In the dark, the girl came by and I asked her to take drinks to the bandstand. There was a long pause, while they talked up there in the indigo light and after awhile I saw the girl put a Scotch and milk on top of the piano for Sonny. He didn't seem to notice it, but just before they started playing again, he sipped from it and looked toward me, and nodded. Then he put it back on top of the piano. For me, then, as they began to play again, it glowed and shook above my brother's head like the very cup of trembling.[9]

1957

9. See Isaiah 51.22: "Thus saith thy lord the LORD, and thy God that pleadeth the cause of his people, Behold, I have taken out of thine hand the cup of trembling, even the dregs of the cup of my fury; thou shalt no more drink it again."

FLANNERY O'CONNOR
1925–1964

Flannery O'Connor, one of the twentieth century's finest short-story writers, was born in Savannah, Georgia; lived with her mother in Milledgeville, Georgia, for much of her life; and died before her fortieth birthday—a victim of lupus, which had also killed her father. Her life and fiction thus tracked a southern orbit, and she was considered an important figure among the southern writers who have grown popular since the 1930s, including novelist William Faulkner, the poet and novelist Robert Penn Warren (included in this volume), and novelists Katherine Ann Porter, Carson McCullers, Harper Lee, and Caroline Gordon (O'Connor's longtime mentor), to name a few. But O'Connor was also one of the early graduates of the Iowa Writers Workshop, completing her M.F.A. degree there in 1947. What she learned at the Workshop about the craft and discipline of story writing informed her practice for the rest of her life. One textbook she encountered there—Cleanth Brooks and Robert Penn Warren's *Understanding Fiction* (1943)—became, as she said, her "Bible," and, indeed, teachers have often turned to O'Connor's work to illustrate key elements of the short story. Her story "A Good Man Is Hard to Find" (1955) was ultimately included as a model in the 1959 edition of *Understanding Fiction*.

To call a textbook scripture speaks, in O'Connor's case, to the weight of a third influence that shapes her work, alongside southern culture and the literary formalism she learned at Iowa: Roman Catholicism. She sought, as she said, to write "Christian realism," where the ugly, the stubborn, and the sinful take center stage in dramas of violence and redemption, played out on a small scale to universal consequences. Her stories are often dark comedies; O'Connor's understanding of divine mercy included a generous irony that she turned on villains and heroes alike. She turned that irony on herself, too. As a result of her lupus, O'Connor had to use crutches from 1955 onward; she remarked, apropos of a trip to the healing waters at Lourdes, France, "I had the best-looking crutches in Europe." She refused to indulge either in pity or in self-pity in the face of what she saw as pervasive human imperfection in a fallen world.

O'Connor published two novels, *Wise Blood* (1952) and *The Violent Bear It Away* (1960). They are weighty with religious symbolism, dense with cultural observation, and ingeniously contrived in the black-humored manner of Nathanael West, her American predecessor in this mode. But her most memorable characters and plots can be found in the stories, which are extremely funny, sometimes unbearably so. O'Connor often leaves readers wondering just what they are laughing at. Upon consideration, the jokes appear dreadful, as with Manley Pointer's treatment of Joy Hopewell's artificial leg in "Good Country People" or Mr. Shiftlet's of his bride in "The Life You Save May Be Your Own." A typical Flannery O'Connor story consists at its most vital level of people talking, clucking their clichés about life, death, and the universe. These clichés are captured with beautiful accuracy by an artist who had spent her life listening to them, lovingly and maliciously keeping track until she could put them to use. Early in her life she hoped to be a cartoonist, and there is cartoonlike mastery in her vivid renderings of character through speech and gesture. O'Connor's art lies partly in making it impossible for us merely to scorn the banalities of expression and behavior by which these people get through their lives. Critics have called her a maker of grotesques, a label that like other ones— regionalist, southern lady, or Roman Catholic writer—might have annoyed her if it didn't obviously amuse her, too. She once remarked tartly that "anything that comes out of the South is going to be called grotesque by the Northern reader, unless it is grotesque, in which case it is going to be called realistic."

Although O'Connor's stories are filled with religious allusions and parodies, they do not preach. One of her best is titled "Revelation," but O'Connor seldom concludes any story with a simple, unambiguous sense of what has been revealed. "A Good Man Is Hard to Find," reprinted here, has famously flummoxed readers in this regard ever since its publication. The stories included in this selection are from her collection *A Good Man Is Hard to Find* (1955).

The Life You Save May Be Your Own

The old woman and her daughter were sitting on their porch when Mr. Shiftlet came up their road for the first time. The old woman slid to the edge of her chair and leaned forward, shading her eyes from the piercing sunset with her hand. The daughter could not see far in front of her and continued to play with her fingers. Although the old woman lived in this desolate spot with only her daughter and she had never seen Mr. Shiftlet before, she could tell, even from a distance, that he was a tramp and no one to be afraid of. His left coat sleeve was folded up to show there was only half an arm in it and his gaunt figure listed slightly to the side as if the breeze were pushing him. He had on a black town suit and a brown felt hat that was turned up in the front and down in the back and he carried a tin tool box by a handle. He came on, at an amble, up her road, his face turned toward the sun which appeared to be balancing itself on the peak of a small mountain.

The old woman didn't change her position until he was almost into her yard; then she rose with one hand fisted on her hip. The daughter, a large girl in a short blue organdy dress, saw him all at once and jumped up and began to stamp and point and make excited speechless sounds.

Mr. Shiftlet stopped just inside the yard and set his box on the ground and tipped his hat at her as if she were not in the least afflicted; then he turned toward the old woman and swung the hat all the way off. He had long black slick hair that hung flat from a part in the middle to beyond the tips of his ears on either side. His face descended in forehead for more than half its length and ended suddenly with his features just balanced over a jutting steel-trap jaw. He seemed to be a young man but he had a look of composed dissatisfaction as if he understood life thoroughly.

"Good evening," the old woman said. She was about the size of a cedar fence post and she had a man's gray hat pulled down low over her head.

The tramp stood looking at her and didn't answer. He turned his back and faced the sunset. He swung both his whole and his short arm up slowly so that they indicated an expanse of sky and his figure formed a crooked cross. The old woman watched him with her arms folded across her chest as if she were the owner of the sun, and the daughter watched, her head thrust forward and her fat helpless hands hanging at the wrists. She had long pink-gold hair and eyes as blue as a peacock's neck.

He held the pose for almost fifty seconds and then he picked up his box and came on to the porch and dropped down on the bottom step. "Lady," he said in a firm nasal voice, "I'd give a fortune to live where I could see me a sun do that every evening."

"Does it every evening," the old woman said and sat back down. The daughter sat down too and watched him with a cautious sly look as if he were a bird that had come up very close. He leaned to one side, rooting in his pants pocket, and in a second he brought out a package of chewing gum and offered her a piece. She took it and unpeeled it and began to chew without taking her eyes off him. He offered the old woman a piece but she only raised her upper lip to indicate she had no teeth.

Mr. Shiftlet's pale sharp glance had already passed over everything in the yard—the pump near the corner of the house and the big fig tree that three or four chickens were preparing to roost in—and had moved to a shed where he saw the square rusted back of an automobile. "You ladies drive?" he asked.

"That car ain't run in fifteen year," the old woman said. "The day my husband died, it quit running."

"Nothing is like it used to be, lady," he said. "The world is almost rotten."

"That's right," the old woman said. "You from around here?"

"Name Tom T. Shiftlet," he murmured, looking at the tires.

"I'm pleased to meet you," the old woman said. "Name Lucynell Crater and daughter Lucynell Crater. What you doing around here, Mr. Shiftlet?"

He judged the car to be about a 1928 or '29 Ford. "Lady," he said, and turned and gave her his full attention, "lemme tell you something. There's one of these doctors in Atlanta that's taken a knife and cut the human heart—the human heart," he repeated, leaning forward, "out of a man's chest and held it in his hand," and he held his hand out, palm up, as if it were slightly weighted with the human heart, "and studied it like it was a day-old chicken, and lady," he said, allowing a long significant pause in which his head slid forward and his clay-colored eyes brightened, "he don't know no more about it than you or me."

"That's right," the old woman said.

"Why, if he was to take that knife and cut into every corner of it, he still wouldn't know no more than you or me. What you want to bet?"

"Nothing," the old woman said wisely. "Where you come from, Mr. Shiftlet?"

He didn't answer. He reached into his pocket and brought out a sack of tobacco and a package of cigarette papers and rolled himself a cigarette, expertly with one hand, and attached it in a hanging position to his upper lip. Then he took a box of wooden matches from his pocket and struck one on his shoe. He held the burning match as if he were studying the mystery of flame while it traveled dangerously toward his skin. The daughter began to make loud noises and to point to his hand and shake her finger at him, but when the flame was just before touching him, he leaned down with his hand cupped over it as if he were going to set fire to his nose and lit the cigarette.

He flipped away the dead match and blew a stream of gray into the evening. A sly look came over his face. "Lady," he said, "nowadays, people'll do anything anyways. I can tell you my name is Tom T. Shiftlet and I come from Tarwater, Tennessee, but you never have seen me before: how you know I ain't lying? How you know my name ain't Aaron Sparks, lady, and I come from Singleberry, Georgia, or how you know it's not George Speeds and I come from Lucy, Alabama, or how you know I ain't Thompson Bright from Toolafalls, Mississippi?"

"I don't know nothing about you," the old woman muttered, irked.

"Lady," he said, "people don't care how they lie. Maybe the best I can tell you is, I'm a man; but listen lady," he said and paused and made his tone more ominous still, "what is a man?"

The old woman began to gum a seed. "What you carry in that tin box, Mr. Shiftlet?" she asked.

"Tools," he said, put back. "I'm a carpenter."

"Well, if you come out here to work, I'll be able to feed you and give you a place to sleep but I can't pay. I'll tell you that before you begin," she said.

There was no answer at once and no particular expression on his face. He leaned back against the two-by-four that helped support the porch roof. "Lady," he said slowly, "there's some men that some things mean more to them than money." The old woman rocked without comment and the daughter watched the trigger that moved up and down in his neck. He told the old woman then that all most people were interested in was money, but he asked what a man was made for. He asked her if a man was made for money, or what. He asked her what she thought she was made for but she didn't answer, she only sat rocking and wondered if a one-armed man could put a new roof on her garden house. He asked a lot of questions that she didn't answer. He told her that he was twenty-eight years old and had lived a varied life. He had been a gospel singer, a foreman on the railroad, an assistant in an undertaking parlor, and he come over the radio for three months with Uncle Roy and his Red Creek Wranglers. He said he had fought and bled in the Arm Service of his country and visited every foreign land and that everywhere he had seen people that didn't care if they did a thing one way or another. He said he hadn't been raised thataway.

A fat yellow moon appeared in the branches of the fig tree as if it were going to roost there with the chickens. He said that a man had to escape to the country to see the world whole and that he wished he lived in a desolate place like this where he could see the sun go down every evening like God made it to do.

"Are you married or are you single?" the old woman asked.

There was a long silence. "Lady," he asked finally, "where would you find you an innocent woman today? I wouldn't have any of this trash I could just pick up."

The daughter was leaning very far down, hanging her head almost between her knees watching him through a triangular door she had made in her over-turned hair; and she suddenly fell in a heap on the floor and began to whimper. Mr. Shiftlet straightened her out and helped her get back in the chair.

"Is she your baby girl?" he asked.

"My only," the old woman said "and she's the sweetest girl in the world. I would give her up for nothing on earth. She's smart too. She can sweep the floor, cook, wash, feed the chickens, and hoe. I wouldn't give her up for a casket of jewels."

"No," he said kindly, "don't ever let any man take her away from you."

"Any man come after her," the old woman said, "'ll have to stay around the place."

Mr. Shiftlet's eye in the darkness was focused on a part of the automobile bumper that glittered in the distance. "Lady," he said, jerking his short arm up as if he could point with it to her house and yard and pump, "there ain't a broken thing on this plantation that I couldn't fix for you, one-arm jackleg or not. I'm a man," he said with a sullen dignity, "even if I ain't a whole one. I got," he said, tapping his knuckles on the floor to emphasize the immensity of what he was going to say, "a moral intelligence!" and his face pierced out of the darkness into a shaft of doorlight and he stared at her as if he were astonished himself at this impossible truth.

The old woman was not impressed with the phrase. "I told you you could hang around and work for food," she said, "if you don't mind sleeping in that car yonder."

"Why listen, lady," he said with a grin of delight, "the monks of old slept in their coffins!"

"They wasn't as advanced as we are," the old woman said.

The next morning he began on the roof of the garden house while Lucynell, the daughter, sat on a rock and watched him work. He had not been around a week before the change he had made in the place was apparent. He had patched the front and back steps, built a new hog pen, restored a fence, and taught Lucynell, who was completely deaf and had never said a word in her life, to say the word "bird." The big rosy-faced girl followed him everywhere, saying "Burrttddt ddbirrrttdt," and clapping her hands. The old woman watched from a distance, secretly pleased. She was ravenous for a son-in-law.

Mr. Shiftlet slept on the hard narrow back seat of the car with his feet out the side window. He had his razor and a can of water on a crate that served him as a bedside table and he put up a piece of mirror against the back glass and kept his coat neatly on a hanger that he hung over one of the windows.

In the evenings he sat on the steps and talked while the old woman and Lucynell rocked violently in their chairs on either side of him. The old woman's three mountains were black against the dark blue sky and were visited off and on by various planets and by the moon after it had left the chickens. Mr. Shiftlet pointed out that the reason he had improved this plantation was because he had taken a personal interest in it. He said he was even going to make the automobile run.

He had raised the hood and studied the mechanism and he said he could tell that the car had been built in the days when cars were really built. You take now, he said, one man puts in one bolt and another man puts in another bolt and another man puts in another bolt so that it's a man for a bolt. That's why you have to pay so much for a car: you're paying all those men. Now if you didn't have to pay but one man, you could get you a cheaper car and one that had had a personal interest taken in it, and it would be a better car. The old woman agreed with him that this was so.

Mr. Shiftlet said that the trouble with the world was that nobody cared, or stopped and took any trouble. He said he never would have been able to teach Lucynell to say a word if he hadn't cared and stopped long enough.

"Teach her to say something else," the old woman said.

"What you want her to say next?" Mr. Shiftlet asked.

The old woman's smile was broad and toothless and suggestive. "Teach her to say 'sugarpie,'" she said.

Mr. Shiftlet already knew what was on her mind.

The next day he began to tinker with the automobile and that evening he told her that if she would buy a fan belt, he would be able to make the car run.

The old woman said she would give him the money. "You see that girl yonder?" she asked, pointing to Lucynell who was sitting on the floor a foot away, watching him, her eyes blue even in the dark. "If it was ever a man wanted to take her away, I would say, 'No man on earth is going to take that sweet girl of mine away from me!' but if he was to say, 'Lady, I don't want to take her away, I want her right here,' I would say, 'Mister, I don't blame you none. I wouldn't pass up a chance to live in a permanent place and get the sweetest girl in the world myself. You ain't no fool,' I would say."

"How old is she?" Mr. Shiftlet asked casually.

"Fifteen, sixteen," the old woman said. The girl was nearly thirty but because of her innocence it was impossible to guess.

"It would be a good idea to paint it too," Mr. Shiftlet remarked. "You don't want it to rust out."

"We'll see about that later," the old woman said.

The next day he walked into town and returned with the parts he needed and a can of gasoline. Late in the afternoon, terrible noises issued from the shed and the old woman rushed out of the house, thinking Lucynell was somewhere having a fit. Lucynell was sitting on a chicken crate, stamping her feet and screaming, "Burrddttt! bddurrddtttt!" but her fuss was drowned out by the car. With a volley of blasts it emerged from the shed, moving in a fierce and stately way. Mr. Shiftlet was in the driver's seat, sitting very erect. He had an expression of serious modesty on his face as if he had just raised the dead.

That night, rocking on the porch, the old woman began her business, at once. "You want you an innocent woman, don't you," she asked sympathetically. "You don't want none of this trash."

"No'm, I don't," Mr. Shiftlet said.

"One that can't talk," she continued, "can't sass you back or use foul language. That's the kind for you to have. Right there," and she pointed to Lucynell sitting cross-legged in her chair, holding both feet in her hands.

"That's right," he admitted. "She wouldn't give me any trouble."

"Saturday," the old woman said, "you and her and me can drive into town and get married."

Mr. Shiftlet eased his position on the steps.

"I can't get married right now," he said. "Everything you want to do takes money and I ain't got any."

"What you need with money?" she asked.

"It takes money," he said. "Some people'll do anything anyhow these days, but the way I think, I wouldn't marry no woman that I couldn't take on a trip like she was somebody. I mean take her to a hotel and treat her. I wouldn't marry the Duchesser Windsor,"[1] he said firmly, "unless I could take her to a hotel and giver something good to eat."

"I was raised thataway and there ain't a thing I can do about it. My old mother taught me how to do."

"Lucynell don't even know what a hotel is," the old woman muttered. "Listen here, Mr. Shiftlet," she said, sliding forward in her chair, "you'd be getting a permanent house and a deep well and the most innocent girl in the world. You don't need no money. Lemme tell you something: there ain't any place in the world for a poor disabled friendless drifting man."

The ugly words settled in Mr. Shiftlet's head like a group of buzzards in the top of a tree. He didn't answer at once. He rolled himself a cigarette and lit it and then he said in an even voice, "Lady, a man is divided into two parts, body and spirit."

The old woman clamped her gums together.

"A body and a spirit," he repeated. "The body, lady, is like a house: it don't go anywhere; but the spirit, lady, is like a automobile: always on the move, always . . ."

"Listen, Mr. Shiftlet," she said, "my well never goes dry and my house is always warm in the winter and there's no mortgage on a thing about this place. You can go to the courthouse and see for yourself. And yonder under that shed is a fine automobile." She laid the bait carefully. "You can have it painted by Saturday. I'll pay for the paint."

In the darkness, Mr. Shiftlet's smile stretched like a weary snake waking up by a fire. After a second he recalled himself and said, "I'm only saying a man's spirit means more to him than anything else. I would have to take my wife off for the weekend without no regards at all for cost. I got to follow where my spirit says to go."

"I'll give you fifteen dollars for a weekend trip," the old woman said in a crabbed voice. "That's the best I can do."

---

1. I.e., the Duchess of Windsor, Wallis Warfield Simpson (1896–1986), American-born wife of the British king Edward VIII.

"That wouldn't hardly pay for more than the gas and the hotel," he said. "It wouldn't feed her."

"Seventeen-fifty," the old woman said. "That's all I got so it isn't any use you trying to milk me. You can take a lunch."

Mr. Shiftlet was deeply hurt by the word "milk." He didn't doubt that she had more money sewed up in her mattress but he had already told her he was not interested in her money. "I'll make that do," he said and rose and walked off without treating with her further.

On Saturday the three of them drove into town in the car that the paint had barely dried on and Mr. Shiftlet and Lucynell were married in the Ordinary's office[2] while the old woman witnessed. As they came out of the courthouse, Mr. Shiftlet began twisting his neck in his collar. He looked morose and bitter as if he had been insulted while someone held him. "That didn't satisfy me none," he said. "That was just something a woman in an office did, nothing but paper work and blood tests. What do they know about my blood? If they was to take my heart and cut it out," he said, "they wouldn't know a thing about me. It didn't satisfy me at all."

"It satisfied the law," the old woman said sharply.

"The law," Mr. Shiftlet said and spit. "It's the law that don't satisfy me."

He had painted the car dark green with a yellow band around it just under the windows. The three of them climbed in the front seat and the old woman said, "Don't Lucynell look pretty? Looks like a baby doll." Lucynell was dressed up in a white dress that her mother had uprooted from a trunk and there was a Panama hat on her head with a bunch of red wooden cherries on the brim. Every now and then her placid expression was changed by a sly isolated little thought like a shoot of green in the desert. "You got a prize!" the old woman said.

Mr. Shiftlet didn't even look at her.

They drove back to the house to let the old woman off and pick up the lunch. When they were ready to leave, she stood staring in the window of the car, with her fingers clenched around the glass. Tears began to seep sideways out of her eyes and ran along the dirty creases in her face. "I ain't ever been parted with her for two days before," she said.

Mr. Shiftlet started the motor.

"And I wouldn't let no man have her but you because I seen you would do right. Good-bye, Sugarbaby," she said, clutching at the sleeve of the white dress. Lucynell looked straight at her and didn't seem to see her there at all. Mr. Shiftlet eased the car forward so that she had to move her hands.

The early afternoon was clear and open and surrounded by pale blue sky. Although the car would go only thirty miles an hour, Mr. Shiftlet imagined a terrific climb and dip and swerve that went entirely to his head so that he forgot his morning bitterness. He had always wanted an automobile but he had never been able to afford one before. He drove very fast because he wanted to make Mobile by nightfall.

Occasionally he stopped his thoughts long enough to look at Lucynell in the seat beside him. She had eaten the lunch as soon as they were out of the yard and now she was pulling the cherries off the hat one by one and throwing them out the window. He became depressed in spite of the car. He had

2. Chambers in which this justice of the peace performs the marriage ceremony.

driven about a hundred miles when he decided that she must be hungry again and at the next small town they came to, he stopped in front of an aluminum-painted eating place called The Hot Spot and took her in and ordered her a plate of ham and grits. The ride had made her sleepy and as soon as she got up on the stool, she rested her head on the counter and shut her eyes. There was no one in The Hot Spot but Mr. Shiftlet and the boy behind the counter, a pale youth with a greasy rag hung over his shoulder. Before he could dish up the food, she was snoring gently.

"Give it to her when she wakes up," Mr. Shiftlet said. "I'll pay for it now."

The boy bent over her and stared at the long pink-gold hair and the half-shut sleeping eyes. Then he looked up and stared at Mr. Shiftlet. "She looks like an angel of Gawd," he murmured.

"Hitchhiker," Mr. Shiftlet explained. "I can't wait. I got to make Tuscaloosa."

The boy bent over again and very carefully touched his finger to a strand of the golden hair and Mr. Shiftlet left.

He was more depressed than ever as he drove on by himself. The late afternoon had grown hot and sultry and the country had flattened out. Deep in the sky a storm was preparing very slowly and without thunder as if it meant to drain every drop of air from the earth before it broke. There were times when Mr. Shiftlet preferred not to be alone. He felt too that a man with a car had a responsibility to others and he kept his eye out for a hitchhiker. Occasionally he saw a sign that warned: "Drive carefully. The life you save may be your own."

The narrow road dropped off on either side into dry fields and here and there a shack or a filling station stood in a clearing. The sun began to set directly in front of the automobile. It was a reddening ball that through his windshield was slightly flat on the bottom and top. He saw a boy in overalls and a gray hat standing on the edge of the road and he slowed the car down and stopped in front of him. The boy didn't have his hand raised to thumb the ride, he was only standing there, but he had a small cardboard suitcase and his hat was set on his head in a way to indicate that he had left somewhere for good. "Son," Mr. Shiftlet said, "I see you want a ride."

The boy didn't say he did or he didn't but he opened the door of the car and got in, and Mr. Shiftlet started driving again. The child held the suitcase on his lap and folded his arms on top of it. He turned his head and looked out the window away from Mr. Shiftlet. Mr. Shiftlet felt oppressed. "Son," he said after a minute, "I got the best old mother in the world so I reckon you only got the second best."

The boy gave him a quick dark glance and then turned his face back out the window.

"It's nothing so sweet," Mr. Shiftlet continued, "as a boy's mother. She taught him his first prayers at her knee, she give him love when no other would, she told him what was right and what wasn't, and she seen that he done the right thing. Son," he said, "I never rued a day in my life like the one I rued when I left that old mother of mine."

The boy shifted in his seat but he didn't look at Mr. Shiftlet. He unfolded his arms and put one hand on the door handle.

"My mother was a angel of Gawd," Mr. Shiftlet said in a very strained voice. "He took her from heaven and giver to me and I left her." His eyes were instantly clouded over with a mist of tears. The car was barely moving.

The boy turned angrily in the seat. "You go to the devil!" he cried. "My old woman is a flea bag and yours is a stinking pole cat!" and with that he flung the door open and jumped out with his suitcase into the ditch.

Mr. Shiftlet was so shocked that for about a hundred feet he drove along slowly with the door still open. A cloud, the exact color of the boy's hat and shaped like a turnip, had descended over the sun, and another, worse looking, crouched behind the car. Mr. Shiftlet felt that the rottenness of the world was about to engulf him. He raised his arm and let it fall again to his breast. "Oh Lord!" he prayed. "Break forth and wash the slime from this earth!"

The turnip continued slowly to descend. After a few minutes there was a guffawing peal of thunder from behind and fantastic raindrops, like tin-can tops, crashed over the rear of Mr. Shiftlet's car. Very quickly he stepped on the gas and with his stump sticking out the window he raced the galloping shower into Mobile.

1955

Good Country People

Besides the neutral expression that she wore when she was alone, Mrs. Freeman had two others, forward and reverse, that she used for all her human dealings. Her forward expression was steady and driving like the advance of a heavy truck. Her eyes never swerved to left or right but turned as the story turned as if they followed a yellow line down the center of it. She seldom used the other expression because it was not often necessary for her to retract a statement, but when she did, her face came to a complete stop, there was an almost imperceptible movement of her black eyes, during which they seemed to be receding, and then the observer would see that Mrs. Freeman, though she might stand there as real as several grain sacks thrown on top of each other, was no longer there in spirit. As for getting anything across to her when this was the case, Mrs. Hopewell had given it up. She might talk her head off. Mrs. Freeman could never be brought to admit herself wrong on any point. She would stand there and if she could be brought to say anything, it was something like, "Well, I wouldn't of said it was and I wouldn't of said it wasn't," or letting her gaze range over the top kitchen shelf where there was an assortment of dusty bottles, she might remark, "I see you ain't ate many of them figs you put up last summer."

They carried on their important business in the kitchen at breakfast. Every morning Mrs. Hopewell got up at seven o'clock and lit her gas heater and Joy's. Joy was her daughter, a large blonde girl who had an artificial leg. Mrs. Hopewell thought of her as a child though she was thirty-two years old and highly educated. Joy would get up while her mother was eating and lumber into the bathroom and slam the door, and before long, Mrs. Freeman would arrive at the back door. Joy would hear her mother call, "Come on in," and then they would talk for a while in low voices that were indistinguishable in the bathroom. By the time Joy came in, they had usually finished the weather report and were on one or the other of Mrs. Freeman's daughters, Glynese or Carramae. Joy called them Glycerin and Caramel. Glynese, a redhead, was eighteen and had many admirers; Carramae, a blonde, was only fifteen but already married and pregnant. She could not keep anything on her stomach. Every morning Mrs. Freeman told Mrs. Hopewell how many times she had vomited since the last report.

Mrs. Hopewell liked to tell people that Glynese and Carramae were two of the finest girls she knew and that Mrs. Freeman was a *lady* and that she was never ashamed to take her anywhere or introduce her to anybody they might meet. Then she would tell how she had happened to hire the Freemans in the first place and how they were a godsend to her and how she had had them four years. The reason for her keeping them so long was that they were not trash. They were good country people. She had telephoned the man whose name they had given as a reference and he had told her that Mr. Freeman was a good farmer but that his wife was the nosiest woman ever to walk the earth. "She's got to be into everything," the man said. "If she don't get there before the dust settles, you can bet she's dead, that's all. She'll want to know all your business. I can stand him real good," he had said, "but me nor my wife neither could have stood that woman one more minute on this place." That had put Mrs. Hopewell off for a few days.

She had hired them in the end because there were no other applicants but she had made up her mind beforehand exactly how she would handle the woman. Since she was the type who had to be into everything, then, Mrs. Hopewell had decided, she would not only let her be into everything, she would *see to it* that she was into everything—she would give her the responsibility of everything, she would put her in charge. Mrs. Hopewell had no bad qualities of her own but she was able to use other people's in such a constructive way that she never felt the lack. She had hired the Freemans and she had kept them four years.

Nothing is perfect. This was one of Mrs. Hopewell's favorite sayings. Another was: that is life! And still another, the most important, was: well, other people have their opinions too. She would make these statements, usually at the table, in a tone of gentle insistence as if no one held them but her, and the large hulking Joy, whose constant outrage had obliterated every expression from her face, would stare just a little to the side of her, her eyes icy blue, with the look of someone who has achieved blindness by an act of will and means to keep it.

When Mrs. Hopewell said to Mrs. Freeman that life was like that, Mrs. Freeman would say, "I always said so myself." Nothing had been arrived at by anyone that had not first been arrived at by her. She was quicker than Mr. Freeman. When Mrs. Hopewell said to her after they had been on the place a while, "You know, you're the wheel behind the wheel," and winked, Mrs. Freeman had said, "I know it. I've always been quick. It's some that are quicker than others."

"Everybody is different," Mrs. Hopewell said.

"Yes, most people is," Mrs. Freeman said.

"It takes all kinds to make the world."

"I always said it did myself."

The girl was used to this kind of dialogue for breakfast and more of it for dinner; sometimes they had it for supper too. When they had no guest they ate in the kitchen because that was easier. Mrs. Freeman always managed to arrive at some point during the meal and to watch them finish it. She would stand in the doorway if it were summer but in the winter she would stand with one elbow on top of the refrigerator and look down on them, or she would stand by the gas heater, lifting the back of her skirt slightly. Occasionally she would stand against the wall and roll her head from side to side. At no time was she in any hurry to leave. All this was very trying on Mrs. Hopewell but she was a woman of great patience. She realized that nothing is perfect and that in the Freemans she had good country people and that if, in this day and age, you get good country people, you had better hang onto them.

She had had plenty of experience with trash. Before the Freemans she had averaged one tenant family a year. The wives of these farmers were not the kind you would want to be around you for very long. Mrs. Hopewell, who had divorced her husband long ago, needed someone to walk over the fields with her; and when Joy had to be impressed for these services, her remarks were usually so ugly and her face so glum that Mrs. Hopewell would say, "If you can't come pleasantly, I don't want you at all," to which the girl, standing square and rigid-shouldered with her neck thrust slightly forward, would reply, "If you want me, here I am—LIKE I AM."

Mrs. Hopewell excused this attitude because of the leg (which had been shot off in a hunting accident when Joy was ten). It was hard for Mrs. Hopewell to realize that her child was thirty-two now and that for more than twenty years she had had only one leg. She thought of her still as a child because it tore her heart to think instead of the poor stout girl in her thirties who had never danced a step or had any *normal* good times. Her name was really Joy but as soon as she was twenty-one and away from home, she had had it legally changed. Mrs. Hopewell was certain that she had thought and thought until she had hit upon the ugliest name in any language. Then she had gone and had the beautiful name, Joy, changed without telling her mother until after she had done it. Her legal name was Hulga.

When Mrs. Hopewell thought the name, Hulga, she thought of the broad blank hull of a battleship. She would not use it. She continued to call her Joy to which the girl responded but in a purely mechanical way.

Hulga had learned to tolerate Mrs. Freeman who saved her from taking walks with her mother. Even Glynese and Carramae were useful when they occupied attention that might otherwise have been directed at her. At first she had thought she could not stand Mrs. Freeman for she had found that it was not possible to be rude to her. Mrs. Freeman would take on strange resentments and for days together she would be sullen but the source of her displeasure was always obscure; a direct attack, a positive leer, blatant ugliness to her face—these never touched her. And without warning one day, she began calling her Hulga.

She did not call her that in front of Mrs. Hopewell who would have been incensed but when she and the girl happened to be out of the house together, she would say something and add the name Hulga to the end of it, and the big spectacled Joy-Hulga would scowl and redden as if her privacy had been intruded upon. She considered the name her personal affair. She had arrived at it first purely on the basis of its ugly sound and then the full genius of its fitness had struck her. She had a vision of the name working like the ugly sweating Vulcan who stayed in the furnace and to whom, presumably, the goddess had to come when called.[1] She saw it as the name of her highest creative act. One of her major triumphs was that her mother had not been able to turn her dust into Joy, but the greater one was that she had been able to turn it herself into Hulga. However, Mrs. Freeman's relish for using the name only irritated her. It was as if Mrs. Freeman's beady steel-pointed eyes had penetrated far enough behind her face to reach some secret fact. Something about her seemed to fascinate Mrs. Freeman and then one day Hulga realized that it was the artificial leg. Mrs. Freeman had a special fondness for the details of secret infections, hidden deformities, assaults upon children. Of diseases, she preferred the lingering or incurable. Hulga had heard Mrs. Hopewell give her the details of the hunting accident, how the leg had been literally blasted off, how she had never lost consciousness. Mrs. Freeman could listen to it any time as if it had happened an hour ago.

When Hulga stumped into the kitchen in the morning (she could walk without making the awful noise but she made it—Mrs. Hopewell was certain—because it was ugly-sounding), she glanced at them and did not speak. Mrs. Hopewell would be in her red kimono with her hair tied around her head in rags. She would be sitting at the table, finishing her breakfast and Mrs. Freeman would be hanging by her elbow outward from the refrigerator, looking down at the table. Hulga always put her eggs on the stove to boil and then stood over them with her arms folded, and Mrs. Hopewell would look at her—a kind of indirect gaze divided between her and Mrs. Freeman— and would think that if she would only keep herself up a little, she wouldn't be so bad looking. There was nothing wrong with her face that a pleasant expression wouldn't help. Mrs. Hopewell said that people who looked on the bright side of things would be beautiful even if they were not.

Whenever she looked at Joy this way, she could not help but feel that it would have been better if the child had not taken the Ph.D. It had certainly not brought her out any and now that she had it, there was no more excuse for her to go to school again. Mrs. Hopewell thought it was nice for girls to go to school to have a good time but Joy had "gone through." Anyhow, she would not have been strong enough to go again. The doctors had told Mrs. Hopewell that with the best of care, Joy might see forty-five. She had a weak heart. Joy had made it plain that if it had not been for this condition, she would be far from these red hills and good country people. She would be in a university lecturing to people who knew what she was talking about. And Mrs. Hopewell could very well picture her there, looking like a scarecrow and lecturing to more of the same. Here she went about all day in a six-year-old skirt and a yellow sweat shirt with a faded cowboy on a horse embossed on it. She thought this was funny; Mrs. Hopewell thought it was idiotic and showed simply that she was still a child. She was brilliant but she didn't have a grain of sense. It seemed to Mrs. Hopewell that every year she grew less like other people and more like herself—bloated, rude, and squint-eyed. And she said such strange things! To her own mother she had said—without warning, without excuse, standing up in the middle of a meal with her face purple and her mouth half full—"Woman! do you ever look inside? Do you ever look inside and see what you are *not*? God!" she

---

1. Vulcan was the Greek god of fire, whom Venus, goddess of love, "presumably" obeyed as her consort.

had cried sinking down again and staring at her plate, "Malebranche[2] was right: we are not our own light. We are not our own light!" Mrs. Hopewell had no idea to this day what brought that on. She had only made the remark, hoping Joy would take it in, that a smile never hurt anyone.

The girl had taken the Ph.D. in philosophy and this left Mrs. Hopewell at a complete loss. You could say, "My daughter is a nurse," or "My daughter is a school teacher," or even, "My daughter is a chemical engineer." You could not say, "My daughter is a philosopher." That was something that had ended with the Greeks and Romans. All day Joy sat on her neck in a deep chair, reading. Sometimes she went for walks but she didn't like dogs or cats or birds or flowers or nature or nice young men. She looked at nice young men as if she could smell their stupidity.

One day Mrs. Hopewell had picked up one of the books the girl had just put down and opening it at random, she read, "Science, on the other hand, has to assert its soberness and seriousness afresh and declare that it is concerned solely with what-is. Nothing—how can it be for science anything but a horror and a phantasm? If science is right, then one thing stands firm: science wishes to know nothing of nothing. Such is after all the strictly scientific approach to Nothing. We know it by wishing to know nothing of Nothing." These words had been underlined with a blue pencil and they worked on Mrs. Hopewell like some evil incantation in gibberish. She shut the book quickly and went out of the room as if she were having a chill.

This morning when the girl came in, Mrs. Freeman was on Carramae. "She thrown up four times after supper," she said, "and was up twict in the night after three o'clock. Yesterday she didn't do nothing but ramble in the bureau drawer. All she did. Stand up there and see what she could run up on."

"She's got to eat," Mrs. Hopewell muttered, sipping her coffee, while she watched Joy's back at the stove. She was wondering what the child had said to the Bible salesman. She could not imagine what kind of a conversation she could possibly have had with him.

He was a tall gaunt hatless youth who had called yesterday to sell them a Bible. He had appeared at the door, carrying a large black suitcase that weighted him so heavily on one side that he had to brace himself against the door facing. He seemed on the point of collapse but he said in a cheerful voice, "Good morning, Mrs. Cedars!" and set the suitcase down on the mat. He was not a bad-looking young man though he had on a bright blue suit and yellow socks that were not pulled up far enough. He had prominent face bones and a streak of sticky-looking brown hair falling across his forehead.

"I'm Mrs. Hopewell," she said.

"Oh!" he said, pretending to look puzzled but with his eyes sparkling, "I saw it said 'The Cedars' on the mailbox so I thought you was Mrs. Cedars!" and he burst out in a pleasant laugh. He picked up the satchel and under cover of a pant, he fell forward into her hall. It was rather as if the suitcase had moved first, jerking him after it. "Mrs. Hopewell!" he said and grabbed her hand. "I hope you are well!" and he laughed again and then all at once

2. Nicolas Malebranche (1638–1715), French philosopher.

his face sobered completely. He paused and gave her a straight earnest look and said, "Lady, I've come to speak of serious things."

"Well, come in," she muttered, none too pleased because her dinner was almost ready. He came into the parlor and sat down on the edge of a straight chair and put the suitcase between his feet and glanced around the room as if he were sizing her up by it. Her silver gleamed on the two sideboards; she decided he had never been in a room as elegant as this.

"Mrs. Hopewell," he began, using her name in a way that sounded almost intimate, "I know you believe in Chrustian service."

"Well yes," she murmured.

"I know," he said and paused, looking very wise with his head cocked on one side, "that you're a good woman. Friends have told me."

Mrs. Hopewell never liked to be taken for a fool. "What are you selling?" she asked.

"Bibles," the young man said and his eye raced around the room before he added, "I see you have no family Bible in your parlor, I see that is the one lack you got!"

Mrs. Hopewell could not say, "My daughter is an atheist and won't let me keep the Bible in the parlor." She said, stiffening slightly, "I keep my Bible by my bedside." This was not the truth. It was in the attic somewhere.

"Lady," he said, "the word of God ought to be in the parlor."

"Well, I think that's a matter of taste," she began. "I think . . ."

"Lady," he said, "for a Chrustian, the word of God ought to be in every room in the house besides in his heart. I know you're a Chrustian because I can see it in every line of your face."

She stood up and said, "Well, young man, I don't want to buy a Bible and I smell my dinner burning."

He didn't get up. He began to twist his hands and looking down at them, he said softly, "Well lady, I'll tell you the truth—not many people want to buy one nowadays and besides, I know I'm real simple. I don't know how to say a thing but to say it. I'm just a country boy." He glanced up into her unfriendly face. "People like you don't like to fool with country people like me!"

"Why!" she cried, "good country people are the salt of the earth! Besides, we all have different ways of doing, it takes all kinds to make the world go 'round. That's life!"

"You said a mouthful," he said.

"Why, I think there aren't enough good country people in the world!" she said, stirred. "I think that's what's wrong with it!"

His face had brightened. "I didn't inraduce myself," he said. "I'm Manley Pointer from out in the country around Willohobie, not even from a place, just from near a place."

"You wait a minute," she said. "I have to see about my dinner." She went out to the kitchen and found Joy standing near the door where she had been listening.

"Get rid of the salt of the earth," she said, "and let's eat."

Mrs. Hopewell gave her a pained look and turned the heat down under the vegetables. "I can't be rude to anybody," she murmured and went back into the parlor.

He had opened the suitcase and was sitting with a Bible on each knee.

"You might as well put those up," she told him. "I don't want one."

"I appreciate your honesty," he said. "You don't see any more real honest people unless you go way out in the country."

"I know," she said, "real genuine folks!" Through the crack in the door she heard a groan.

"I guess a lot of boys come telling you they're working their way through college," he said, "but I'm not going to tell you that. Somehow," he said, "I don't want to go to college. I want to devote my life to Chrustian service. See," he said, lowering his voice, "I got this heart condition. I may not live long. When you know it's something wrong with you and you may not live long, well then, lady . . ." He paused, with his mouth open, and stared at her.

He and Joy had the same condition! She knew that her eyes were filling with tears but she collected herself quickly and murmured, "Won't you stay for dinner? We'd love to have you!" and was sorry the instant she heard herself say it.

"Yes mam," he said in an abashed voice, "I would sher love to do that!"

Joy had given him one look on being introduced to him and then throughout the meal had not glanced at him again. He had addressed several remarks to her, which she had pretended not to hear. Mrs. Hopewell could not understand deliberate rudeness, although she lived with it, and she felt she had always to overflow with hospitality to make up for Joy's lack of courtesy. She urged him to talk about himself and he did. He said he was the seventh child of twelve and that his father had been crushed under a tree when he himself was eight years old. He had been crushed very badly, in fact, almost cut in two and was practically not recognizable. His mother had got along the best she could by hard working and she had always seen that her children went to Sunday School and that they read the Bible every evening. He was now nineteen years old and he had been selling Bibles for four months. In that time he had sold seventy-seven Bibles and had the promise of two more sales. He wanted to become a missionary because he thought that was the way you could do most for people. "He who losest his life shall find it," he said simply and he was so sincere, so genuine and earnest that Mrs. Hopewell would not for the world have smiled. He prevented his peas from sliding onto the table by blocking them with a piece of bread which he later cleaned his plate with. She could see Joy observing sidewise how he handled his knife and fork and she saw too that every few minutes, the boy would dart a keen appraising glance at the girl as if he were trying to attract her attention.

After dinner Joy cleared the dishes off the table and disappeared and Mrs. Hopewell was left to talk with him. He told her again about his childhood and his father's accident and about various things that had happened to him. Every five minutes or so she would stifle a yawn. He sat for two hours until finally she told him she must go because she had an appointment in town. He packed his Bibles and thanked her and prepared to leave, but in the doorway he stopped and wrung her hand and said that not on any of his trips had he met a lady as nice as her and he asked if he could come again. She had said she would always be happy to see him.

Joy had been standing in the road, apparently looking at something in the distance, when he came down the steps toward her, bent to the side with his heavy valise. He stopped where she was standing and confronted her directly. Mrs. Hopewell could not hear what he said but she trembled to think what

Joy would say to him. She could see that after a minute Joy said something and that then the boy began to speak again, making an excited gesture with his free hand. After a minute Joy said something else at which the boy began to speak once more. Then to her amazement, Mrs. Hopewell saw the two of them walk off together, toward the gate. Joy had walked all the way to the gate with him and Mrs. Hopewell could not imagine what they had said to each other, and she had not yet dared to ask.

Mrs. Freeman was insisting upon her attention. She had moved from the refrigerator to the heater so that Mrs. Hopewell had to turn and face her in order to seem to be listening. "Glynese gone out with Harvey Hill again last night," she said. "She had this sty."

"Hill," Mrs. Hopewell said absently, "is that the one who works in the garage?"

"Nome, he's the one that goes to chiropracter school," Mrs. Freeman said. "She had this sty. Been had it two days. So she says when he brought her in the other night he says, 'Lemme get rid of that sty for you,' and she says, 'How?' and he says, 'You just lay yourself down acrost the seat of that car and I'll show you.' So she done it and he popped her neck. Kept on a-popping it several times until she made him quit. This morning," Mrs. Freeman said, "she ain't got no sty. She ain't got no traces of a sty."

"I never heard of that before," Mrs. Hopewell said.

"He ast her to marry him before the Ordinary,"[3] Mrs. Freeman went on, "and she told him she wasn't going to be married in no *office*."

"Well, Glynese is a fine girl," Mrs. Hopewell said. "Glynese and Carramae are both fine girls."

"Carramae said when her and Lyman was married Lyman said it sure felt sacred to him. She said he said he wouldn't take five hundred dollars for being married by a preacher."

"How much would he take?" the girl asked from the stove.

"He said he wouldn't take five hundred dollars," Mrs. Freeman repeated.

"Well we all have work to do," Mrs. Hopewell said.

"Lyman said it just felt more sacred to him," Mrs. Freeman said. "The doctor wants Carramae to eat prunes. Says instead of medicine. Says them cramps is coming from pressure. You know where I think it is?"

"She'll be better in a few weeks," Mrs. Hopewell said.

"In the tube," Mrs. Freeman said. "Else she wouldn't be as sick as she is."

Hulga had cracked her two eggs into a saucer and was bringing them to the table along with a cup of coffee that she had filled too full. She sat down carefully and began to eat, meaning to keep Mrs. Freeman there by questions if for any reason she showed an inclination to leave. She could perceive her mother's eye on her. The first round-about question would be about the Bible salesman and she did not wish to bring it on. "How did he pop her neck?" she asked.

Mrs. Freeman went into a description of how he had popped her neck. She said he owned a '55 Mercury but that Glynese said she would rather marry a man with only a '36 Plymouth who would be married by a preacher. The girl asked what if he had a '32 Plymouth and Mrs. Freeman said what Glynese had said was a '36 Plymouth.

---

3. Justice of the peace who performs the marriage ceremony in chambers rather than in public.

Mrs. Hopewell said there were not many girls with Glynese's common sense. She said what she admired in those girls was their common sense. She said that reminded her that they had had a nice visitor yesterday, a young man selling Bibles. "Lord," she said, "he bored me to death but he was so sincere and genuine I couldn't be rude to him. He was just good country people, you know," she said, "—just the salt of the earth."

"I seen him walk up," Mrs. Freeman said, "and then later—I seen him walk off," and Hulga could feel the slight shift in her voice, the slight insinuation, that he had not walked off alone, had he? Her face remained expressionless but the color rose into her neck and she seemed to swallow it down with the next spoonful of egg. Mrs. Freeman was looking at her as if they had a secret together.

"Well, it takes all kinds of people to make the world go 'round," Mrs. Hopewell said. "It's very good we aren't all alike."

"Some people are more alike than others," Mrs. Freeman said.

Hulga got up and stumped, with about twice the noise that was necessary, into her room and locked the door. She was to meet the Bible salesman at ten o'clock at the gate. She had thought about it half the night. She had started thinking of it as a great joke and then she had begun to see profound implications in it. She had lain in bed imagining dialogues for them that were insane on the surface but that reached below to depths that no Bible salesman would be aware of. Their conversation yesterday had been of this kind.

He had stopped in front of her and had simply stood there. His face was bony and sweaty and bright, with a little pointed nose in the center of it, and his look was different from what it had been at the dinner table. He was gazing at her with open curiosity, with fascination, like a child watching a new fantastic animal at the zoo, and he was breathing as if he had run a great distance to reach her. His gaze seemed somehow familiar but she could not think where she had been regarded with it before. For almost a minute he didn't say anything. Then on what seemed an insuck of breath, he whispered, "You ever ate a chicken that was two days old?"

The girl looked at him stonily. He might have just put this question up for consideration at the meeting of a philosophical association. "Yes," she presently replied as if she had considered it from all angles.

"It must have been mighty small!" he said triumphantly and shook all over with little nervous giggles, getting very red in the face, and subsiding finally into his gaze of complete admiration, while the girl's expression remained exactly the same.

"How old are you?" he asked softly.

She waited some time before she answered. Then in a flat voice she said, "Seventeen."

His smiles came in succession like waves breaking on the surface of a little lake. "I see you got a wooden leg," he said. "I think you're brave. I think you're real sweet."

The girl stood blank and solid and silent.

"Walk to the gate with me," he said. "You're a brave sweet little thing and I liked you the minute I seen you walk in the door."

Hulga began to move forward.

"What's your name?" he asked, smiling down on the top of her head.

"Hulga," she said.

"Hulga," he murmured, "Hulga. Hulga. I never heard of anybody name Hulga before. You're shy, aren't you, Hulga?" he asked.

She nodded, watching his large red hand on the handle of the giant valise.

"I like girls that wear glasses," he said. "I think a lot. I'm not like these people that a serious thought don't ever enter their heads. It's because I may die."

"I may die too," she said suddenly and looked up at him. His eyes were very small and brown, glittering feverishly.

"Listen," he said, "don't you think some people was meant to meet on account of what all they got in common and all? Like they both think serious thoughts and all?" He shifted the valise to his other hand so that the hand nearest her was free. He caught hold of her elbow and shook it a little. "I don't work on Saturday," he said. "I like to walk in the woods and see what Mother Nature is wearing. O'er the hills and far away. Pic-nics and things. Couldn't we go on a pic-nic tomorrow? Say yes, Hulga," he said and gave her a dying look as if he felt his insides about to drop out of him. He had even seemed to sway slightly toward her.

During the night she had imagined that she seduced him. She imagined that the two of them walked on the place until they came to the storage barn beyond the two back fields and there, she imagined, that things came to such a pass that she very easily seduced him and that then, of course, she had to reckon with his remorse. True genius can get an idea across even to an inferior mind. She imagined that she took his remorse in hand and changed it into a deeper understanding of life. She took all his shame away and turned it into something useful.

She set off for the gate at exactly ten o'clock, escaping without drawing Mrs. Hopewell's attention. She didn't take anything to eat, forgetting that food is usually taken on a picnic. She wore a pair of slacks and a dirty white shirt, and as an afterthought, she had put some Vapex on the collar of it since she did not own any perfume. When she reached the gate no one was there.

She looked up and down the empty highway and had the furious feeling that she had been tricked, that he had only meant to make her walk to the gate after the idea of him. Then suddenly he stood up, very tall, from behind a bush on the opposite embankment. Smiling, he lifted his hat which was new and wide-brimmed. He had not worn it yesterday and she wondered if he had bought it for the occasion. It was toast-colored with a red and white band around it and was slightly too large for him. He stepped from behind the bush still carrying the black valise. He had on the same suit and the same yellow socks sucked down in his shoes from walking. He crossed the highway and said, "I knew you'd come!"

The girl wondered acidly how he had known this. She pointed to the valise and asked, "Why did you bring your Bibles?"

He took her elbow, smiling down on her as if he could not stop. "You can never tell when you'll need the word of God, Hulga," he said. She had a moment in which she doubted that this was actually happening and then they began to climb the embankment. They went down into the pasture toward the woods. The boy walked lightly by her side, bouncing on his toes. The valise did not seem to be heavy today; he even swung it. They crossed half the pasture without saying anything and then, putting his hand easily on the small of her back, he asked softly, "Where does your wooden leg join on?"

She turned an ugly red and glared at him and for an instant the boy looked abashed. "I didn't mean you no harm," he said. "I only meant you're so brave and all. I guess God takes care of you."

"No," she said, looking forward and walking fast, "I don't even believe in God."

At this he stopped and whistled. "No!" he exclaimed as if he were too astonished to say anything else.

She walked on and in a second he was bouncing at her side, fanning with his hat. "That's very unusual for a girl," he remarked, watching her out of the corner of his eye. When they reached the edge of the wood, he put his hand on her back again and drew her against him without a word and kissed her heavily.

The kiss, which had more pressure than feeling behind it, produced that extra surge of adrenalin in the girl that enables one to carry a packed trunk out of a burning house, but in her, the power went at once to the brain. Even before he released her, her mind, clear and detached and ironic anyway, was regarding him from a great distance, with amusement but with pity. She had never been kissed before and she was pleased to discover that it was an unexceptional experience and all a matter of the mind's control. Some people might enjoy drain water if they were told it was vodka. When the boy, looking expectant but uncertain, pushed her gently away, she turned and walked on, saying nothing as if such business, for her, were common enough.

He came along panting at her side, trying to help her when he saw a root that she might trip over. He caught and held back the long swaying blades of thorn vine until she had passed beyond them. She led the way and he came breathing heavily behind her. Then they came out on a sunlit hillside, sloping softly into another one a little smaller. Beyond, they could see the rusted top of the old barn where the extra hay was stored.

The hill was sprinkled with small pink weeds. "Then you ain't saved?" he asked suddenly, stopping.

The girl smiled. It was the first time she had smiled at him at all. "In my economy," she said, "I'm saved and you are damned but I told you I didn't believe in God."

Nothing seemed to destroy the boy's look of admiration. He gazed at her now as if the fantastic animal at the zoo had put its paw through the bars and given him a loving poke. She thought he looked as if he wanted to kiss her again and she walked on before he had the chance.

"Ain't there somewheres we can sit down sometime?" he murmured, his voice softening toward the end of the sentence.

"In that barn," she said.

They made for it rapidly as if it might slide away like a train. It was a large two-story barn, cool and dark inside. The boy pointed up the ladder that led into the loft and said, "It's too bad we can't go up there."

"Why can't we?" she asked.

"Yer leg," he said reverently.

The girl gave him a contemptuous look and putting both hands on the ladder, she climbed it while he stood below, apparently awestruck. She pulled herself expertly through the opening and then looked down at him and said, "Well, come on if you're coming," and he began to climb the ladder, awkwardly bringing the suitcase with him.

"We won't need the Bible," she observed.

"You never can tell," he said, panting. After he had got into the loft, he was a few seconds catching his breath. She had sat down in a pile of straw. A wide sheath of sunlight, filled with dust particles, slanted over her. She lay back against a bale, her face turned away, looking out the front opening of the barn where hay was thrown from a wagon into the loft. The two pink-speckled hillsides lay back against a dark ridge of woods. The sky was cloudless and cold blue. The boy dropped down by her side and put one arm under her and the other over her and began methodically kissing her face, making little noises like a fish. He did not remove his hat but it was pushed far enough back not to interfere. When her glasses got in his way, he took them off of her and slipped them into his pocket.

The girl at first did not return any of the kisses but presently she began to and after she had put several on his cheek, she reached his lips and remained there, kissing him again and again as if she were trying to draw all the breath out of him. His breath was clear and sweet like a child's and the kisses were sticky like a child's. He mumbled about loving her and about knowing when he first seen her that he loved her, but the mumbling was like the sleepy fretting of a child being put to sleep by his mother. Her mind, throughout this, never stopped or lost itself for a second to her feelings. "You ain't said you loved me none," he whispered finally, pulling back from her. "You got to say that."

She looked away from him off into the hollow sky and then down at a black ridge and then down farther into what appeared to be two green swelling lakes. She didn't realize he had taken her glasses but this landscape could not seem exceptional to her for she seldom paid any close attention to her surroundings.

"You got to say it," he repeated. "You got to say you love me."

She was always careful how she committed herself. "In a sense," she began, "if you use the word loosely, you might say that. But it's not a word I use. I don't have illusions. I'm one of those people who see *through* to nothing."

The boy was frowning. "You got to say it. I said it and you got to say it," he said.

The girl looked at him almost tenderly. "You poor baby," she murmured. "It's just as well you don't understand," and she pulled him by the neck, facedown against her. "We are all damned," she said, "but some of us have taken off our blindfolds and see that there's nothing to see. It's a kind of salvation."

The boy's astonished eyes looked blankly through the ends of her hair. "Okay," he almost whined, "but do you love me or don'tcher?"

"Yes," she said and added, "in a sense. But I must tell you something. There mustn't be anything dishonest between us." She lifted his head and looked him in the eye. "I am thirty years old," she said. "I have a number of degrees."

The boy's look was irritated but dogged. "I don't care," he said. "I don't care a thing about what all you done. I just want to know if you love me or don'tcher?" and he caught her to him and wildly planted her face with kisses until she said, "Yes, yes."

"Okay then," he said, letting her go. "Prove it."

She smiled, looking dreamily out on the shifty landscape. She had seduced him without even making up her mind to try. "How?" she asked, feeling that he should be delayed a little.

He leaned over and put his lips to her ear. "Show me where your wooden leg joins on," he whispered.

The girl uttered a sharp little cry and her face instantly drained of color. The obscenity of the suggestion was not what shocked her. As a child she had sometimes been subject to feelings of shame but education had removed the last traces of that as a good surgeon scrapes for cancer; she would no more have felt it over what he was asking than she would have believed in his Bible. But she was as sensitive about the artificial leg as a peacock about his tail. No one ever touched it but her. She took care of it as someone else would his soul, in private and almost with her own eyes turned away. "No," she said.

"I known it," he muttered, sitting up. "You're just playing me for a sucker."

"Oh no no!" she cried. "It joins on at the knee. Only at the knee. Why do you want to see it?"

The boy gave her a long penetrating look. "Because," he said, "it's what makes you different. You ain't like anybody else."

She sat staring at him. There was nothing about her face or her round freezing-blue eyes to indicate that this had moved her; but she felt as if her heart had stopped and left her mind to pump her blood. She decided that for the first time in her life she was face to face with real innocence. This boy, with an instinct that came from beyond wisdom, had touched the truth about her. When after a minute, she said in a hoarse high voice, "All right," it was like surrendering to him completely. It was like losing her own life and finding it again, miraculously, in his.

Very gently he began to roll the slack leg up. The artificial limb, in a white sock and brown flat shoe, was bound in a heavy material like canvas and ended in an ugly jointure where it was attached to the stump. The boy's face and his voice were entirely reverent as he uncovered it and said, "Now show me how to take it off and on."

She took it off for him and put it back on again and then he took it off himself, handling it as tenderly as if it were a real one. "See!" he said with a delighted child's face. "Now I can do it myself!"

"Put it back on," she said. She was thinking that she would run away with him and that every night he would take the leg off and every morning put it back on again. "Put it back on," she said.

"Not yet," he murmured, setting it on its foot out of her reach. "Leave it off for a while. You got me instead."

She gave a cry of alarm but he pushed her down and began to kiss her again. Without the leg she felt entirely dependent on him. Her brain seemed to have stopped thinking altogether and to be about some other function that it was not very good at. Different expressions raced back and forth over her face. Every now and then the boy, his eyes like two steel spikes, would glance behind him where the leg stood. Finally she pushed him off and said, "Put it back on me now."

"Wait," he said. He leaned the other way and pulled the valise toward him and opened it. It had a pale blue spotted lining and there were only two Bibles in it. He took one of these out and opened the cover of it. It was hollow and contained a pocket flask of whiskey, a pack of cards, and a small blue box with printing on it. He laid these out in front of her one at a time in an evenly-spaced row, like one presenting offerings at the shrine of a goddess. He put the blue box in her hand. THIS PRODUCT TO BE USED ONLY FOR THE PREVENTION OF DISEASE, she read, and dropped it. The boy was unscrewing the top of the flask. He stopped and pointed, with a smile, to the deck of cards. It was not an ordinary deck but one with an obscene picture on the back of each card. "Take a swig," he said, offering her the bottle first. He held it in front of her, but like one mesmerized, she did not move.

Her voice when she spoke had an almost pleading sound. "Aren't you," she murmured, "aren't you just good country people?"

The boy cocked his head. He looked as if he were just beginning to understand that she might be trying to insult him. "Yeah," he said, curling his lip slightly, "but it ain't held me back none. I'm as good as you any day in the week."

"Give me my leg," she said.

He pushed it farther away with his foot. "Come on now, let's begin to have us a good time," he said coaxingly. "We ain't got to know one another good yet."

"Give me my leg!" she screamed and tried to lunge for it but he pushed her down easily.

"What's the matter with you all of a sudden?" he asked, frowning as he screwed the top on the flask and put it quickly back inside the Bible. "You just a while ago said you didn't believe in nothing. I thought you was some girl!"

Her face was almost purple. "You're a Christian!" she hissed. "You're a fine Christian! You're just like them all—say one thing and do another. You're a perfect Christian, you're . . ."

The boy's mouth was set angrily. "I hope you don't think," he said in a lofty indignant tone, "that I believe in that crap! I may sell Bibles but I know which end is up and I wasn't born yesterday and I know where I'm going!"

"Give me my leg!" she screeched. He jumped up so quickly that she barely saw him sweep the cards and the blue box into the Bible and throw the Bible into the valise. She saw him grab the leg and then she saw it for an instant slanted forlornly across the inside of the suitcase with a Bible at either side of its opposite ends. He slammed the lid shut and snatched up the valise and swung it down the hole and then stepped through himself.

When all of him had passed but his head, he turned and regarded her with a look that no longer had any admiration in it. "I've gotten a lot of interesting things," he said. "One time I got a woman's glass eye this way. And you needn't to think you'll catch me because Pointer ain't really my name. I use a different name at every house I call at and don't stay nowhere long. And I'll tell you another thing, Hulga," he said, using the name as if he didn't think much of it, "you ain't so smart. I been believing in nothing every since I was born!" and then the toast-colored hat disappeared down the hole and the girl was left, sitting on the straw in the dusty sunlight. When she turned her churning face toward the opening, she saw his blue figure struggling successfully over the green speckled lake.

Mrs. Hopewell and Mrs. Freeman, who were in the back pasture, digging up onions, saw him emerge a little later from the woods and head across the meadow toward the highway. "Why, that looks like that nice dull young man that tried to sell me a Bible yesterday," Mrs. Hopewell said, squinting. "He must have been selling them to the Negroes back in there. He was so simple," she said, "but I guess the world would be better off if we were all that simple."

Mrs. Freeman's gaze drove forward and just touched him before he disappeared under the hill. Then she returned her attention to the evil-smelling onion shoot she was lifting from the ground. "Some can't be that simple," she said. "I know I never could."

1955

A Good Man Is Hard to Find

The grandmother didn't want to go to Florida. She wanted to visit some of her connections in east Tennessee and she was seizing at every chance to change Bailey's mind. Bailey was the son she lived with, her only boy. He was sitting on the edge of his chair at the table, bent over the orange sports section of the *Journal*. "Now look here, Bailey," she said, "see here, read this," and she stood with one hand on her thin hip and the other rattling the newspaper at his bald head. "Here this fellow that calls himself The Misfit is aloose from the Federal Pen[1] and headed toward Florida and you read here what it says he did to these people. Just you read it. I wouldn't take my children in any direction with a criminal like that aloose in it. I couldn't answer to my conscience if I did."

Bailey didn't look up from his reading so she wheeled around then and faced the children's mother, a young woman in slacks, whose face was as broad and innocent as a cabbage and was tied around with a green head-kerchief that had two points on the top like a rabbit's ears. She was sitting on the sofa, feeding the baby his apricots out of a jar. "The children have been to Florida before," the old lady said. "You all ought to take them somewhere else for a change so they would see different parts of the world and be broad. They never have been to east Tennessee."

The children's mother didn't seem to hear her but the eight-year-old boy, John Wesley, a stocky child with glasses, said, "If you don't want to go to Florida, why dontcha stay at home?" He and the little girl, June Star, were reading the funny papers[2] on the floor.

"She wouldn't stay at home to be queen for a day,"[3] June Star said without raising her yellow head.

"Yes and what would you do if this fellow, The Misfit, caught you?" the grandmother asked.

"I'd smack his face," John Wesley said.

"She wouldn't stay at home for a million bucks," June Star said. "Afraid she'd miss something. She has to go everywhere we go."

---

1. Federal Penitentiary.
2. Comics.
3. Reference to a long-running radio and then television program, *Queen for a Day,* in which women competed to tell the most heartbreaking stories of personal hardship in order to be crowned "Queen for a Day" and win valuable prizes.

"All right, Miss," the grandmother said. "Just remember that the next time you want me to curl your hair."

June Star said her hair was naturally curly.

The next morning the grandmother was the first one in the car, ready to go. She had her big black valise that looked like the head of a hippopotamus in one corner, and underneath it she was hiding a basket with Pitty Sing, the cat, in it. She didn't intend for the cat to be left alone in the house for three days because he would miss her too much and she was afraid he might brush against one of the gas burners and accidentally asphyxiate himself. Her son, Bailey, didn't like to arrive at a motel with a cat.

She sat in the middle of the back seat with John Wesley and June Star on either side of her. Bailey and the children's mother and the baby sat in front and they left Atlanta at eight forty-five with the mileage on the car at 55890. The grandmother wrote this down because she thought it would be interesting to say how many miles they had been when they got back. It took them twenty minutes to reach the outskirts of the city.

The old lady settled herself comfortably, removing her white cotton gloves and putting them up with her purse on the shelf in front of the back window. The children's mother still had on slacks and still had her head tied up in a green kerchief, but the grandmother had on a navy blue straw sailor hat with a bunch of white violets on the brim and a navy blue dress with a small white dot in the print. Her collars and cuffs were white organdy trimmed with lace and at her neckline she had pinned a purple spray of cloth violets containing a sachet. In case of an accident, anyone seeing her dead on the highway would know at once that she was a lady.

She said she thought it was going to be a good day for driving, neither too hot nor too cold, and she cautioned Bailey that the speed limit was fifty-five miles an hour and that the patrolmen hid themselves behind billboards and small clumps of trees and sped out after you before you had a chance to slow down. She pointed out interesting details of the scenery: Stone Mountain; the blue granite that in some places came up to both sides of the highway; the brilliant red clay banks slightly streaked with purple; and the various crops that made rows of green lace-work on the ground. The trees were full of silver-white sunlight and the meanest of them sparkled. The children were reading comic magazines and their mother had gone back to sleep.

"Let's go through Georgia fast so we won't have to look at it much," John Wesley said.

"If I were a little boy," said the grandmother, "I wouldn't talk about my native state that way. Tennessee has the mountains and Georgia has the hills."

"Tennessee is just a hillbilly dumping ground," John Wesley said, "and Georgia is a lousy state too."

"You said it," June Star said.

"In my time," said the grandmother, folding her thin veined fingers, "children were more respectful of their native states and their parents and everything else. People did right then. Oh look at the cute little pickaninny[4]!" she said and pointed to a Negro child standing in the door of a shack.

4. Derogatory term for an African American child.

"Wouldn't that make a picture, now?" she asked and they all turned and looked at the little Negro out of the back window. He waved.

"He didn't have any britches on," June Star said.

"He probably didn't have any," the grandmother explained. "Little niggers in the country don't have things like we do. If I could paint, I'd paint that picture," she said.

The children exchanged comic books.

The grandmother offered to hold the baby and the children's mother passed him over the front seat to her. She set him on her knee and bounced him and told him about the things they were passing. She rolled her eyes and screwed up her mouth and stuck her leathery thin face into his smooth bland one. Occasionally he gave her a faraway smile. They passed a large cotton field with five or six graves fenced in the middle of it, like a small island. "Look at the graveyard!" the grandmother said, pointing it out. "That was the old family burying ground. That belonged to the plantation."

"Where's the plantation?" John Wesley asked.

"Gone with the Wind,"[5] said the grandmother. "Ha. Ha."

When the children finished all the comic books they had brought, they opened the lunch and ate it. The grandmother ate a peanut butter sandwich and an olive and would not let the children throw the box and the paper napkins out the window. When there was nothing else to do they played a game by choosing a cloud and making the other two guess what shape it suggested. John Wesley took one the shape of a cow and June Star guessed a cow and John Wesley said, no, an automobile, and June Star said he didn't play fair, and they began to slap each other over the grandmother.

The grandmother said she would tell them a story if they would keep quiet. When she told a story, she rolled her eyes and waved her head and was very dramatic. She said once when she was a maiden lady she had been courted by a Mr. Edgar Atkins Teagarden from Jasper, Georgia. She said he was a very good-looking man and a gentleman and that he brought her a watermelon every Saturday afternoon with his initials cut in it, E. A. T. Well, one Saturday, she said, Mr. Teagarden brought the watermelon and there was nobody at home and he left it on the front porch and returned in his buggy to Jasper, but she never got the watermelon, she said, because a nigger boy ate it when he saw the initials, E. A. T.! This story tickled John Wesley's funny bone and he giggled and giggled but June Star didn't think it was any good. She said she wouldn't marry a man that just brought her a watermelon on Saturday. The grandmother said she would have done well to marry Mr. Teagarden because he was a gentleman and had bought Coca-Cola stock when it first came out and that he had died only a few years ago, a very wealthy man.

They stopped at The Tower for barbecued sandwiches. The Tower was a part stucco and part wood filling station and dance hall set in a clearing outside of Timothy. A fat man named Red Sammy Butts ran it and there were signs stuck here and there on the building and for miles up and down the highway saying, TRY RED SAMMY'S FAMOUS BARBECUE. NONE

5. Margaret Mitchell's 1936 southern romance novel, *Gone with the Wind*, won the Pulitzer Prize and was made into a popular 1939 film starring Clark Gable and Vivien Leigh.

LIKE FAMOUS RED SAMMY'S! RED SAM! THE FAT BOY WITH THE HAPPY LAUGH! A VETERAN! RED SAMMY'S YOUR MAN!

Red Sammy was lying on the bare ground outside The Tower with his head under a truck while a gray monkey about a foot high, chained to a small chinaberry tree, chattered nearby. The monkey sprang back into the tree and got on the highest limb as soon as he saw the children jump out of the car and run toward him.

Inside, The Tower was a long dark room with a counter at one end and tables at the other and dancing space in the middle. They all sat down at a board table next to the nickelodeon[6] and Red Sam's wife, a tall burnt-brown woman with hair and eyes lighter than her skin, came and took their order. The children's mother put a dime in the machine and played "The Tennessee Waltz," and the grandmother said that tune always made her want to dance. She asked Bailey if he would like to dance but he only glared at her. He didn't have a naturally sunny disposition like she did and trips made him nervous. The grandmother's brown eyes were very bright. She swayed her head from side to side and pretended she was dancing in her chair. June Star said play something she could tap to so the children's mother put in another dime and played a fast number and June Star stepped out onto the dance floor and did her tap routine.

"Ain't she cute?" Red Sam's wife said, leaning over the counter. "Would you like to come be my little girl?"

"No I certainly wouldn't," June Star said. "I wouldn't live in a broken-down place like this for a million bucks!" and she ran back to the table.

"Ain't she cute?" the woman repeated, stretching her mouth politely.

"Aren't you ashamed?" hissed the grandmother.

Red Sam came in and told his wife to quit lounging on the counter and hurry up with these people's order. His khaki trousers reached just to his hip bones and his stomach hung over them like a sack of meal swaying under his shirt. He came over and sat down at a table nearby and let out a combination sigh and yodel. "You can't win," he said. "You can't win," and he wiped his sweating red face off with a gray handkerchief. "These days you don't know who to trust," he said. "Ain't that the truth?"

"People are certainly not nice like they used to be," said the grandmother.

"Two fellers come in here last week," Red Sammy said, "driving a Chrysler. It was a old beat-up car but it was a good one and these boys looked all right to me. Said they worked at the mill and you know I let them fellers charge[7] the gas they bought? Now why did I do that?"

"Because you're a good man!" the grandmother said at once.

"Yes'm, I suppose so," Red Sam said as if he were struck with this answer.

His wife brought the orders, carrying the five plates all at once without a tray, two in each hand and one balanced on her arm. "It isn't a soul in this green world of God's that you can trust," she said. "And I don't count nobody out of that, not nobody," she repeated, looking at Red Sammy.

"Did you read about that criminal, The Misfit, that's escaped?" asked the grandmother.

6. Jukebox.
7. To buy with a promise to pay the shopkeeper later.

"I wouldn't be a bit surprised if he didn't attack this place right here," said the woman. "If he hears about it being here, I wouldn't be none surprised to see him. If he hears it's two cent in the cash register, I wouldn't be a tall surprised if he . . ."

"That'll do," Red Sam said. "Go bring these people their Co'-Colas," and the woman went off to get the rest of the order.

"A good man is hard to find," Red Sammy said. "Everything is getting terrible. I remember the day you could go off and leave your screen door unlatched. Not no more."

He and the grandmother discussed better times. The old lady said that in her opinion Europe was entirely to blame for the way things were now. She said the way Europe acted you would think we were made of money and Red Sam said it was no use talking about it, she was exactly right.[8] The children ran outside into the white sunlight and looked at the monkey in the lacy chinaberry tree. He was busy catching fleas on himself and biting each one carefully between his teeth as if it were a delicacy.

They drove off again into the hot afternoon. The grandmother took cat naps and woke up every few minutes with her own snoring. Outside of Toombsboro she woke up and recalled an old plantation that she had visited in this neighborhood once when she was a young lady. She said the house had six white columns across the front and that there was an avenue of oaks leading up to it and two little wooden trellis arbors on either side in front where you sat down with your suitor after a stroll in the garden. She recalled exactly which road to turn off to get to it. She knew that Bailey would not be willing to lose any time looking at an old house, but the more she talked about it, the more she wanted to see it once again and find out if the little twin arbors were still standing. "There was a secret panel in this house," she said craftily, not telling the truth but wishing that she were, "and the story went that all the family silver was hidden in it when Sherman[9] came through but it was never found . . ."

"Hey!" John Wesley said. "Let's go see it! We'll find it! We'll poke all the woodwork and find it! Who lives there? Where do you turn off at? Hey Pop, can't we turn off there?"

"We never have seen a house with a secret panel!" June Star shrieked. "Let's go to the house with the secret panel! Hey Pop, can't we go see the house with the secret panel!"

"It's not far from here, I know," the grandmother said. "It wouldn't take over twenty minutes."

Bailey was looking straight ahead. His jaw was as rigid as a horseshoe. "No," he said.

The children began to yell and scream that they wanted to see the house with the secret panel. John Wesley kicked the back of the front seat and June Star hung over her mother's shoulder and whined desperately into her ear that they never had any fun even on their vacation, that they could never do what THEY wanted to do. The baby began to scream and John

8. Referring to money supplied by the United States for the reconstruction of Europe after World War II.
9. William Tecumseh Sherman (1820–1891), commander of the Union army that devastated much of Georgia during the American Civil War (1861–65).

Wesley kicked the back of the seat so hard that his father could feel the blows in his kidney.

"All right!" he shouted and drew the car to a stop at the side of the road. "Will you all shut up? Will you all just shut up for one second? If you don't shut up, we won't go anywhere."

"It would be very educational for them," the grandmother murmured.

"All right," Bailey said, "but get this: this is the only time we're going to stop for anything like this. This is the one and only time."

"The dirt road that you have to turn down is about a mile back," the grandmother directed. "I marked it when we passed."

"A dirt road," Bailey groaned.

After they had turned around and were headed toward the dirt road, the grandmother recalled other points about the house, the beautiful glass over the front doorway and the candle-lamp in the hall. John Wesley said that the secret panel was probably in the fireplace.

"You can't go inside this house," Bailey said. "You don't know who lives there."

"While you all talk to the people in front, I'll run around behind and get in a window," John Wesley suggested.

"We'll all stay in the car," his mother said.

They turned onto the dirt road and the car raced roughly along in a swirl of pink dust. The grandmother recalled the times when there were no paved roads and thirty miles was a day's journey. The dirt road was hilly and there were sudden washes in it and sharp curves on dangerous embankments. All at once they would be on a hill, looking down over the blue tops of trees for miles around, then the next minute, they would be in a red depression with the dust-coated trees looking down on them.

"This place had better turn up in a minute," Bailey said, "or I'm going to turn around."

The road looked as if no one had traveled on it in months.

"It's not much farther," the grandmother said and just as she said it, a horrible thought came to her. The thought was so embarrassing that she turned red in the face and her eyes dilated and her feet jumped up, upsetting her valise in the corner. The instant the valise moved, the newspaper top she had over the basket under it rose with a snarl and Pitty Sing, the cat, sprang onto Bailey's shoulder.

The children were thrown to the floor and their mother, clutching the baby, was thrown out the door onto the ground; the old lady was thrown into the front seat. The car turned over once and landed right-side-up in a gulch off the side of the road. Bailey remained in the driver's seat with the cat—gray-striped with a broad white face and an orange nose—clinging to his neck like a caterpillar.

As soon as the children saw they could move their arms and legs, they scrambled out of the car, shouting, "We've had an ACCIDENT!" The grandmother was curled up under the dashboard, hoping she was injured so that Bailey's wrath would not come down on her all at once. The horrible thought she had had before the accident was that the house she had remembered so vividly was not in Georgia but in Tennessee.

Bailey removed the cat from his neck with both hands and flung it out the window against the side of a pine tree. Then he got out of the car and started looking for the children's mother. She was sitting against the side of the red gutted ditch, holding the screaming baby, but she only had a cut down her face and a broken shoulder. "We've had an ACCIDENT!" the children screamed in a frenzy of delight.

"But nobody's killed," June Star said with disappointment as the grandmother limped out of the car, her hat still pinned to her head but the broken front brim standing up at a jaunty angle and the violet spray hanging off the side. They all sat down in the ditch, except the children, to recover from the shock. They were all shaking.

"Maybe a car will come along," said the children's mother hoarsely.

"I believe I have injured an organ," said the grandmother, pressing her side, but no one answered her. Bailey's teeth were clattering. He had on a yellow sport shirt with bright blue parrots designed in it and his face was as yellow as the shirt. The grandmother decided that she would not mention that the house was in Tennessee.

The road was about ten feet above and they could see only the tops of the trees on the other side of it. Behind the ditch they were sitting in there were more woods, tall and dark and deep. In a few minutes they saw a car, some distance away on top of a hill, coming slowly as if the occupants were watching them. The grandmother stood up and waved both arms dramatically to attract their attention. The car continued to come on slowly, disappeared around a bend and appeared again, moving even slower, on top of the hill they had gone over. It was a big black battered hearse-like automobile. There were three men in it.

It came to a stop just over them and for some minutes, the driver looked down with a steady expressionless gaze to where they were sitting, and didn't speak. Then he turned his head and muttered something to the other two and they got out. One was a fat boy in black trousers and a red sweat shirt with a silver stallion embossed on the front of it. He moved around on the right side of them and stood staring, his mouth partly open in a kind of loose grin. The other had on khaki pants and a blue striped coat and a gray hat pulled down very low, hiding most of his face. He came around slowly on the left side. Neither spoke.

The driver got out of the car and stood by the side of it, looking down at them. He was an older man than the other two. His hair was just beginning to gray and he wore silver-rimmed spectacles that gave him a scholarly look. He had a long creased face and didn't have on any shirt or undershirt. He had on blue jeans that were too tight for him and was holding a black hat and a gun. The two boys also had guns.

"We've had an ACCIDENT!" the children screamed.

The grandmother had the peculiar feeling that the bespectacled man was someone she knew. His face was as familiar to her as if she had known him all her life but she could not recall who he was. He moved away from the car and began to come down the embankment, placing his feet carefully so that he wouldn't slip. He had on tan and white shoes and no socks, and his ankles were red and thin. "Good afternoon," he said. "I see you all had you a little spill."

"We turned over twice!" said the grandmother.

"Oncet," he corrected. "We seen it happen. Try their car and see will it run, Hiram," he said quietly to the boy with the gray hat.

"What you got that gun for?" John Wesley asked. "Whatcha gonna do with that gun?"

"Lady," the man said to the children's mother, "would you mind calling them children to sit down by you? Children make me nervous. I want all you all to sit down right together there where you're at."

"What are you telling US what to do for?" June Star asked.

Behind them the line of woods gaped like a dark open mouth. "Come here," said their mother.

"Look here now," Bailey began suddenly, "we're in a predicament! We're in . . ."

The grandmother shrieked. She scrambled to her feet and stood staring. "You're The Misfit!" she said. "I recognized you at once!"

"Yes'm," the man said, smiling slightly as if he were pleased in spite of himself to be known, "but it would have been better for all of you, lady, if you hadn't of reckernized me."

Bailey turned his head sharply and said something to his mother that shocked even the children. The old lady began to cry and The Misfit reddened.

"Lady," he said, "don't you get upset. Sometimes a man says things he don't mean. I don't reckon he meant to talk to you thataway."

"You wouldn't shoot a lady, would you?" the grandmother said and removed a clean handkerchief from her cuff and began to slap at her eyes with it.

The Misfit pointed the toe of his shoe into the ground and made a little hole and then covered it up again. "I would hate to have to," he said.

"Listen," the grandmother almost screamed, "I know you're a good man. You don't look a bit like you have common blood. I know you must come from nice people!"

"Yes mam," he said, "finest people in the world." When he smiled he showed a row of strong white teeth. "God never made a finer woman than my mother and my daddy's heart was pure gold," he said. The boy with the red sweat shirt had come around behind them and was standing with his gun at his hip. The Misfit squatted down on the ground. "Watch them children, Bobby Lee," he said. "You know they make me nervous." He looked at the six of them huddled together in front of him and he seemed to be embarrassed as if he couldn't think of anything to say. "Ain't a cloud in the sky," he remarked, looking up at it. "Don't see no sun but don't see no cloud neither."

"Yes, it's a beautiful day," said the grandmother. "Listen," she said, "you shouldn't call yourself The Misfit because I know you're a good man at heart. I can just look at you and tell."

"Hush!" Bailey yelled. "Hush! Everybody shut up and let me handle this!" He was squatting in the position of a runner about to sprint forward but he didn't move.

"I pre-chate that, lady," The Misfit said and drew a little circle in the ground with the butt of his gun.

"It'll take a half a hour to fix this here car," Hiram called, looking over the raised hood of it.

"Well, first you and Bobby Lee get him and that little boy to step over yonder with you," The Misfit said, pointing to Bailey and John Wesley. "The boys want to ast you something," he said to Bailey. "Would you mind stepping back in them woods there with them?"

"Listen," Bailey began, "we're in a terrible predicament! Nobody realizes what this is," and his voice cracked. His eyes were as blue and intense as the parrots in his shirt and he remained perfectly still.

The grandmother reached up to adjust her hat brim as if she were going to the woods with him but it came off in her hand. She stood staring at it and after a second she let it fall on the ground. Hiram pulled Bailey up by the arm as if he were assisting an old man. John Wesley caught hold of his father's hand and Bobby Lee followed. They went off toward the woods and just as they reached the dark edge, Bailey turned and supporting himself against a gray naked pine trunk, he shouted, "I'll be back in a minute, Mamma, wait on me!"

"Come back this instant!" his mother shrilled but they all disappeared into the woods.

"Bailey Boy!" the grandmother called in a tragic voice but she found she was looking at The Misfit squatting on the ground in front of her. "I just know you're a good man," she said desperately. "You're not a bit common!"

"Nome, I ain't a good man," The Misfit said after a second as if he had considered her statement carefully, "but I ain't the worst in the world nei-ther. My daddy said I was a different breed of dog from my brothers and sisters. 'You know,' Daddy said, 'it's some that can live their whole life out without asking about it and it's others has to know why it is, and this boy is one of the latters. He's going to be into everything!'" He put on his black hat and looked up suddenly and then away deep into the woods as if he were embarrassed again. "I'm sorry I don't have on a shirt before you ladies," he said, hunching his shoulders slightly. "We buried our clothes that we had on when we escaped and we're just making do until we can get better. We borrowed these from some folks we met," he explained.

"That's perfectly all right," the grandmother said. "Maybe Bailey has an extra shirt in his suitcase."

"I'll look and see terrectly," The Misfit said.

"Where are they taking him?" the children's mother screamed.

"Daddy was a card[1] himself," The Misfit said. "You couldn't put anything over on him. He never got in trouble with the Authorities though. Just had the knack of handling them."

"You could be honest too if you'd only try," said the grandmother. "Think how wonderful it would be to settle down and live a comfortable life and not have to think about somebody chasing you all the time."

The Misfit kept scratching in the ground with the butt of his gun as if he were thinking about it. "Yes'm, somebody is always after you," he murmured.

The grandmother noticed how thin his shoulder blades were just behind his hat because she was standing up looking down on him. "Do you ever pray?" she asked.

He shook his head. All she saw was the black hat wiggle between his shoulder blades. "Nome," he said.

There was a pistol shot from the woods, followed closely by another. Then silence. The old lady's head jerked around. She could hear the wind move through the tree tops like a long satisfied insuck of breath. "Bailey Boy!" she called.

1. A clever man.

"I was a gospel singer for a while," The Misfit said. "I been most everything. Been in the arm service, both land and sea, at home and abroad, been twict married, been an undertaker, been with the railroads, plowed Mother Earth, been in a tornado, seen a man burnt alive oncet," and looked up at the children's mother and the little girl who were sitting close together, their faces white and their eyes glassy; "I even seen a woman flogged," he said.

"Pray, pray," the grandmother began, "pray, pray . . ."

"I never was a bad boy that I remember of," The Misfit said in an almost dreamy voice, "but somewheres along the line I done something wrong and got sent to the penitentiary. I was buried alive," and he looked up and held her attention to him by a steady stare.

"That's when you should have started to pray," she said. "What did you do to get sent to the penitentiary that first time?"

"Turn to the right, it was a wall," The Misfit said, looking up again at the cloudless sky. "Turn to the left, it was a wall. Look up it was a ceiling, look down it was a floor. I forget what I done, lady. I set there and set there, trying to remember what it was I done and I ain't recalled it to this day. Oncet in a while, I would think it was coming to me, but it never come."

"Maybe they put you in by mistake," the old lady said vaguely.

"Nome," he said. "It wasn't no mistake. They had the papers on me."

"You must have stolen something," she said.

The Misfit sneered slightly. "Nobody had nothing I wanted," he said. "It was a head-doctor[2] at the penitentiary said what I had done was kill my daddy but I known that for a lie. My daddy died in nineteen ought nineteen of the epidemic flu and I never had a thing to do with it. He was buried in the Mount Hopewell Baptist churchyard and you can go there and see for yourself."

"If you would pray," the old lady said, "Jesus would help you."

"That's right," The Misfit said.

"Well then, why don't you pray?" she asked trembling with delight suddenly.

"I don't want no hep," he said. "I'm doing all right by myself."

Bobby Lee and Hiram came ambling back from the woods. Bobby Lee was dragging a yellow shirt with bright blue parrots in it.

"Thow me that shirt, Bobby Lee," The Misfit said. The shirt came flying at him and landed on his shoulder and he put it on. The grandmother couldn't name what the shirt reminded her of. "No, lady," The Misfit said while he was buttoning it up, "I found out the crime don't matter. You can do one thing or you can do another, kill a man or take a tire off his car, because sooner or later you're going to forget what it was you done and just be punished for it."

The children's mother had begun to make heaving noises as if she couldn't get her breath. "Lady," he asked, "would you and that little girl like to step off yonder with Bobby Lee and Hiram and join your husband?"

"Yes, thank you," the mother said faintly. Her left arm dangled helplessly and she was holding the baby, who had gone to sleep, in the other. "Hep that lady up, Hiram," The Misfit said as she struggled to climb out of the ditch, "and Bobby Lee, you hold onto that little girl's hand."

---

2. A psychiatrist.

"I don't want to hold hands with him," June Star said. "He reminds me of a pig."

The fat boy blushed and laughed and caught her by the arm and pulled her off into the woods after Hiram and her mother.

Alone with The Misfit, the grandmother found that she had lost her voice. There was not a cloud in the sky nor any sun. There was nothing around her but woods. She wanted to tell him that he must pray. She opened and closed her mouth several times before anything came out. Finally she found herself saying, "Jesus, Jesus," meaning, Jesus will help you, but the way she was saying it, it sounded as if she might be cursing.

"Yes'm," The Misfit said as if he agreed. "Jesus thown everything off balance. It was the same case with Him as with me except He hadn't committed any crime and they could prove I had committed one because they had the papers on me. Of course," he said, "they never shown me my papers. That's why I sign myself now. I said long ago, you get you a signature and sign everything you do and keep a copy of it. Then you'll know what you done and you can hold up the crime to the punishment and see do they match and in the end you'll have something to prove you ain't been treated right. I call myself The Misfit," he said, "because I can't make what all I done wrong fit what all I gone through in punishment."

There was a piercing scream from the woods, followed closely by a pistol report. "Does it seem right to you, lady, that one is punished a heap and another ain't punished at all?"

"Jesus!" the old lady cried. "You've got good blood! I know you wouldn't shoot a lady! I know you come from nice people! Pray! Jesus, you ought not to shoot a lady. I'll give you all the money I've got!"

"Lady," The Misfit said, looking beyond her far into the woods, "there never was a body that give the undertaker a tip."

There were two more pistol reports and the grandmother raised her head like a parched old turkey hen crying for water and called, "Bailey Boy, Bailey Boy!" as if her heart would break.

"Jesus was the only One that ever raised the dead."[3] The Misfit continued, "and He shouldn't have done it. He thrown everything off balance. If He did what He said, then it's nothing for you to do but throw away everything and follow Him, and if He didn't, then it's nothing for you to do but enjoy the few minutes you got left the best way you can—by killing somebody or burning down his house or doing some other meanness to him. No pleasure but meanness," he said and his voice had become almost a snarl.

"Maybe He didn't raise the dead," the old lady mumbled, not knowing what she was saying and feeling so dizzy that she sank down in the ditch with her legs twisted under her.

"I wasn't there so I can't say He didn't," The Misfit said. "I wisht I had of been there," he said, hitting the ground with his fist. "It ain't right I wasn't there because if I had of been there I would of known. Listen lady," he said in a high voice, "if I had of been there I would of known and I wouldn't be like I am now." His voice seemed about to crack and the grandmother's

---

3. Chapter 11 of the Gospel of John tells of Jesus bringing a man named Lazarus back to life four days after Lazarus had died.

head cleared for an instant. She saw the man's face twisted close to her own as if he were going to cry and she murmured, "Why you're one of my babies. You're one of my own children!" She reached out and touched him on the shoulder. The Misfit sprang back as if a snake had bitten him and shot her three times through the chest. Then he put his gun down on the ground and took off his glasses and began to clean them.

Hiram and Bobby Lee returned from the woods and stood over the ditch, looking down at the grandmother who half sat and half lay in a puddle of blood with her legs crossed under her like a child's and her face smiling up at the cloudless sky.

Without his glasses, The Misfit's eyes were red-rimmed and pale and defenseless-looking. "Take her off and throw her where you thrown the others," he said, picking up the cat that was rubbing itself against his leg.

"She was a talker, wasn't she?" Bobby Lee said, sliding down the ditch with a yodel.

"She would of been a good woman," The Misfit said, "if it had been somebody there to shoot her every minute of her life."

"Some fun!" Bobby Lee said.

"Shut up, Bobby Lee," The Misfit said. "It's no real pleasure in life."

1953

A. R. AMMONS
1926–2001

Archie Randolph Ammons wrote that he "was born big and jaundiced (and ugly) on February 18, 1926, in a farmhouse 4 miles southwest of Whiteville, North Carolina, and 2 miles northwest of New Hope Elementary School and New Hope Baptist Church." It was characteristic of Ammons to be laconic, self-deprecating, unfailingly local, and unfailingly exact. He belonged to the homemade strain of American writers rather than the Europeanized or cosmopolitan breed. His poems are filled with the landscapes in which he lived: North Carolina, the southern coast of New Jersey, and the surroundings of Ithaca, New York, where he was a member of the English department of Cornell University.

Ammons's career did not start out with a traditional literary education. At Wake Forest College in North Carolina he studied mostly science, especially biology and chemistry, and that scientific training strongly colored his poems. In 1951–52, after working briefly as a high school principal in North Carolina, he studied English literature for three semesters at the University of California at Berkeley. When he returned from Berkeley he spent twelve years as an executive for a biological-glass manufacturer in New Jersey.

In 1955, his thirtieth year, Ammons published his first book of poems, *Ommateum*. The title refers to the compound structure of an insect's eye and foreshadows a twofold impulse in Ammons's work. On the one hand he is involved in the minute observation of natural phenomena; on the other hand he is frustrated by the physical limitations analogous to those of the insects' vision. We see the world as insects do, in small portions and in impulses that take in but do not totally resolve the many images we receive. "Overall is beyond me," Ammons says in "Corsons Inlet," in which the shifting details of shoreline and dunes represent a severe challenge to the poet-observer. There are no straight lines. The contours differ every day, every hour, and they teach the poet the endless adjustments he must make to nature's fluidity.

"A poem is a walk," Ammons said (his essay of that title is excerpted in the "Post-modern Manifestos" cluster of this anthology). His work is characterized by the motion he found everywhere in nature, a motion answered by his mental activity. Both nearsighted and farsighted, he looks closely at vegetation, small animals, the minute shifts of wind and weather and light, yet over and over again seems drawn to the American Transcendentalist Ralph Waldo Emerson's visionary aspirations for poetry. "Poetry," Emerson remarked, "was all written before time was, and whenever we are so finely organized that we can penetrate into that region where the air is music, we hear those primal warnings and attempt to write them down." Much of Ammons's poetry tests this promise to see if it yields a glimpse of supernatural order.

The self in Ammons's poems is a far more modest presence than in the work of many other American writers. Sometimes he is a "surrendered self among unwelcoming forms" (as he writes in the conclusion of "Gravelly Run"); in many other poems he is at home in a universe, both human and natural, whose variety delights him. He is that rare thing, a contemporary poet of praise, one who says "I can find nothing lowly / in the universe" ("Still") and convinces us he speaks the truth.

Ammons began his career writing short lyrics, almost journal entries in an unending career of observation. But the laconic notations—of a landslide, a shift in the shoreline from one day to the next—often bore abstract titles ("Clarity," "Saliences") as if to suggest the connections he felt between concrete experience and speculative thought. Ammons often experimented with poetic form in his effort to make his verse responsive to the engaging but evasive particularity of natural process. This formal inventiveness is part of his work's appeal. "Stop on any word and language gives way: / the blades of reason, unlightened by motion, sink in," he remarks in his "Essay on Poetics." To create *Tape for the Turn of the Year* (1965) he typed a book-length day-to-day verse diary on a roll of adding-machine tape. The poem ended when the tape did. This was his first and most flamboyant attempt to turn his verse into something beyond mere gatherings. He then discovered that the long poem was the form best adapted to his continuing dialogue between the specific and the general. The appearance in 1993 of *Garbage*, a National Book Award winner, confirmed Ammons's gift for creating a book-length, immensely readable, moving, and funny poem, structured around a recurring set of images and ideas but full of digressions.

Ammons tended to use the colon—what one critic calls "the most democratic punctuation," suggesting as it does equivalence on both sides. Used in place of the period, it keeps a line from coming to a halt or stopping the flow in which the mind feverishly suggests analogies among its minutely perceived experiences. Many notable examples of Ammons's extended forms are gathered in *The Selected Longer Poems* (1980), although that book does not include his remarkable *Sphere: The Form of a Motion* (1974). A book-length poem with no full stops, 155 sections of four tercets each, it aspires to be what Ammons's predecessor Wallace Stevens called "the poem of the act of the mind." The only unity in *Sphere* is the mind's power to make analogies between the world's constant "diversifications." Ammons was committed to the provisional, the self-revising, and this commitment kept his poetry fresh over a long career. Writing of his sense of the world in "The Dwelling," from *Sumerian Vistas* (1987), Ammons says, "here the plainest / majesty gave us what it could." The same might be said of his wonderfully generous and witty poems, which constitute a distinctive and invaluable legacy for American poetry.

So I Said I Am Ezra

So I said I am Ezra
and the wind whipped my throat
gaming for the sounds of my voice
   I listened to the wind
go over my head and up into the night   5
Turning to the sea I said
         I am Ezra
but there were no echoes from the waves
The words were swallowed up
   in the voice of the surf   10
or leaping over the swells
lost themselves oceanward
   Over the bleached and broken fields
I moved my feet and turning from the wind
   that ripped sheets of sand   15
   from the beach and threw them
   like seamists across the dunes
swayed as if the wind were taking me away
and said
         I am Ezra   20
As a word too much repeated
falls out of being
so I Ezra went out into the night
like a drift of sand
and splashed among the windy oats   25
that clutch the dunes
of unremembered seas

                                                       1955

Corsons Inlet

I went for a walk over the dunes again this morning
to the sea,
then turned right along
   the surf
                 rounded a naked headland   5
                 and returned

  along the inlet shore:

it was muggy sunny, the wind from the sea steady and high,
crisp in the running sand,
   some breakthroughs of sun   10
  but after a bit

continuous overcast:

the walk liberating, I was released from forms,
from the perpendiculars,
    straight lines, blocks, boxes, binds   15
of thought
into the hues, shadings, rises, flowing bends and blends
      of sight:

           I allow myself eddies of meaning:
yield to a direction of significance   20
running
like a stream through the geography of my work:
   you can find
in my sayings
        swerves of action   25
        like the inlet's cutting edge:
     there are dunes of motion,
organizations of grass, white sandy paths of remembrance
in the overall wandering of mirroring mind:

but Overall is beyond me: is the sum of these events   30
I cannot draw, the ledger I cannot keep, the accounting
beyond the account:

in nature there are few sharp lines: there are areas of
primrose
    more or less dispersed;   35
disorderly orders of bayberry; between the rows
of dunes,
irregular swamps of reeds,
though not reeds alone, but grass, bayberry, yarrow, all . . .
predominantly reeds: 40

I have reached no conclusions, have erected no boundaries,
shutting out and shutting in, separating inside
      from outside: I have
      drawn no lines:
      as   45

manifold events of sand
change the dune's shape that will not be the same shape
tomorrow,

so I am willing to go along, to accept
the becoming   50
thought, to stake off no beginnings or ends, establish
      no walls:

by transitions the land falls from grassy dunes to creek
to undercreek: but there are no lines, though
    change in that transition is clear   55

as any sharpness: but "sharpness" spread out,
allowed to occur over a wider range
than mental lines can keep:

the moon was full last night: today, low tide was low:
black shoals of mussels exposed to the risk   60
of air
and, earlier, of sun,
waved in and out with the waterline, waterline inexact,
caught always in the event of change:
     a young mottled gull stood free on the shoals   65
     and ate
to vomiting: another gull, squawking possession, cracked a crab,
picked out the entrails, swallowed the soft-shelled legs, a ruddy
turnstone[1] running in to snatch leftover bits:

risk is full: every living thing in   70
siege: the demand is life, to keep life: the small
white blacklegged egret, how beautiful, quietly stalks and spears
     the shallows, darts to shore
        to stab—what? I couldn't
     see against the black mudflats—a frightened   75
     fiddler crab?

     the news to my left over the dunes and
reeds and bayberry clumps was
     fall: thousands of tree swallows
     gathering for flight: 80
     an order held
     in constant change: a congregation
rich with entropy: nevertheless, separable, noticeable
     as one event,
        not chaos: preparations for   85
flight from winter,
cheet, cheet, cheet, cheet, wings rifling the green clumps,
beaks
at the bayberries
     a perception full of wind, flight, curve,   90
     sound:
     the possibility of rule as the sum of rulelessness:
the "field" of action
with moving, incalculable center:

in the smaller view, order tight with shape: 95
blue tiny flowers on a leafless weed: carapace of crab:
snail shell:
     pulsations of order
     in the bellies of minnows: orders swallowed,
broken down, transferred through membranes   100
to strengthen larger orders: but in the large view, no

---

1. A ploverlike migratory bird.

lines or changeless shapes: the working in and out, together
       and against, of millions of events: this,
              so that I make
              no form of   105
              formlessness:

orders as summaries, as outcomes of actions override
or in some way result, not predictably (seeing me gain
the top of a dune,
the swallows   110
could take flight—some other fields of bayberry
          could enter fall
          berryless) and there is serenity:

          no arranged terror: no forcing of image, plan,
or thought: 115
no propaganda, no humbling of reality to precept:

terror pervades but is not arranged, all possibilities
of escape open: no route shut, except in
   the sudden loss of all routes:

          I see narrow orders, limited tightness, but will   120
not run to that easy victory:
          still around the looser, wider forces work:
          I will try
   to fasten into order enlarging grasps of disorder, widening
scope, but enjoying the freedom that   125
Scope eludes my grasp, that there is no finality of vision,
that I have perceived nothing completely,
          that tomorrow a new walk is a new walk.

                                      1965

Easter Morning

I have a life that did not become,
that turned aside and stopped,
astonished:
I hold it in me like a pregnancy or
as on my lap a child   5
not to grow or grow old but dwell on

it is to his grave I most
frequently return and return
to ask what is wrong, what was
wrong, to see it all by   10
the light of a different necessity
but the grave will not heal
and the child,

stirring, must share my grave
with me, an old man having   15
gotten by on what was left

when I go back to my home country in these
fresh far-away days, it's convenient to visit
everybody, aunts and uncles, those who used to say,
look how he's shooting up, and the   20
trinket aunts who always had a little
something in their pocketbooks, cinnamon bark
or a penny or nickel, and uncles who
were the rumored fathers of cousins
who whispered of them as of great, if   25
troubled, presences, and school
teachers, just about everybody older
(and some younger) collected in one place
waiting, particularly, but not for
me, mother and father there, too, and others   30
close, close as burrowing
under skin, all in the graveyard
assembled, done for, the world they
used to wield, have trouble and joy
in, gone   35

the child in me that could not become
was not ready for others to go,
to go on into change, blessings and
horrors, but stands there by the road
where the mishap occurred, crying out for   40
help, come and fix this or we
can't get by, but the great ones who
were to return, they could not or did
not hear and went on in a flurry and
now, I say in the graveyard, here   45
lies the flurry, now it can't come
back with help or helpful asides, now
we all buy the bitter
incompletions, pick up the knots of
horror, silently raving, and go on   50
crashing into empty ends not
completions, not rondures the fullness
has come into and spent itself from
I stand on the stump
of a child, whether myself   55
or my little brother who died, and
yell as far as I can, I cannot leave this place, for
for me it is the dearest and the worst,
it is life nearest to life which is
life lost: it is my place where   60
I must stand and fail,
calling attention with tears
to the branches not lofting

boughs into space, to the barren
air that holds the world that was my world 65

though the incompletions
(& completions) burn out
standing in the flash high-burn
momentary structure of ash, still it
is a picture-book, letter-perfect 70
Easter morning: I have been for a
walk: the wind is tranquil: the brook
works without flashing in an abundant
tranquility: the birds are lively with
voice: I saw something I had 75
never seen before: two great birds,
maybe eagles, blackwinged, whitenecked
and -headed, came from the south oaring
the great wings steadily; they went
directly over me, high up, and kept on 80
due north: but then one bird,
the one behind, veered a little to the
left and the other bird kept on seeming
not to notice for a minute: the first
began to circle as if looking for 85
something, coasting, resting its wings
on the down side of some of the circles:
the other bird came back and they both
circled, looking perhaps for a draft;
they turned a few more times, possibly 90
rising—at least, clearly resting—
then flew on falling into distance till
they broke across the local bush and
trees: it was a sight of bountiful
majesty and integrity: the having 95
patterns and routes, breaking
from them to explore other patterns or
better way to routes, and then the
return: a dance sacred as the sap in
the trees, permanent in its descriptions 100
as the ripples round the brook's
ripplestone: fresh as this particular
flood of burn breaking across us now
from the sun.

1981

Singling & Doubling Together

My nature singing in me is your nature singing:
you have means to veer down, filter through,
and, coming in,

harden into vines that break back with leaves,
so that when the wind stirs   5
I know you are there and I hear you in leafspeech,

though of course back into your heightenings I
can never follow: you are there beyond
tracings flesh can take,
and farther away surrounding and informing the systems,   10
you are as if nothing, and
where you are least knowable I celebrate you most

or here most when near dusk the pheasant squawks and
lofts at a sharp angle to the roost cedar,
I catch in the angle of that ascent,   15
in the justness of that event your pheasant nature,
and when dusk settles, the bushes creak and
snap in their natures with your creaking

and snapping nature: I catch the impact and turn
it back: cut the grass and pick up branches   20
under the elm, rise to the several tendernesses
and griefs, and you will fail me only as from the still
of your great high otherness you fail all things,
somewhere to lift things up, if not those things again:

even you risked all the way into the taking on of shape   25
and time fail and fail with me, as me,
and going hence with me know the going hence
and in the cries of that pain it is you crying and
you know of it and it is my pain, my tears, my loss—
what but grace   30

have I to bear in every motion,
embracing or turning away, staggering or standing still,
while your settled kingdom sways in the distillations of light
and plunders down into the darkness with me
and comes nowhere up again but changed into your   35
singing nature when I need sing my nature nevermore.

                                                                          1983

From Garbage

2

garbage has to be the poem of our time because
garbage is spiritual, believable enough

to get our attention, getting in the way, piling
up, stinking, turning brooks brownish and

creamy white: what else deflects us from the   5
errors of our illusionary ways, not a temptation

to trashlessness, that is too far off, and,
anyway, unimaginable, unrealistic: I'm a

hole puncher or hole plugger: stick a finger
in the dame (*dam*, damn, dike), hold back the issue   10

of creativity's floor, the forthcoming, futuristic,
the origins feeding trash: down by I-95 in

Florida where flatland's ocean- and gulf-flat,
mounds of disposal rise (for if you dug

something up to make room for something to put   15
in, what about the something dug up, as with graves:)

the garbage trucks crawl as if in obeisance,
as if up ziggurats[1] toward the high places gulls

and garbage keep alive, offerings to the gods
of garbage, or retribution, of realistic   20

expectation, the deities of unpleasant
necessities: refined, young earthworms,

drowned up in macadam pools by spring rains, moisten
out white in a day or so and, round spots,

look like sputum or creamy-rich, broken-up cold   25
clams: if this is not the best poem of the

century, can it be about the worst poem of the
century: it comes, at least, toward the end,

so a long tracing of bad stuff can swell
under its measure: but there on the heights   30

a small smoke wafts the sacrificial bounty
day and night to layer the sky brown, shut us

in as into a lidded kettle, the everlasting
flame these acres-deep of tendance keep: a

free offering of a crippled plastic chair: 35
a played-out sports outfit: a hill-myna

---

1. The temple towers of the Babylonians, which consisted of a lofty pyramidal structure, built in successive stages, with outside staircases and a religious shrine on top.

print stained with jelly: how to write this
poem, should it be short, a small popping of

duplexes, or long, hunting wide, coming home
late, losing the trail and recovering it: 40

should it act itself out, illustrations,
examples, colors, clothes or intensify

reductively into statement, bones any corpus
would do to surround, or should it be nothing

at all unless it finds itself: the poem,   45
which is about the pre-socratic idea of the

dispositional axis from stone to wind, wind
to stone (with my elaborations, if any)

is complete before it begins, so I needn't
myself hurry into brevity, though a weary reader   50

might briefly be done: the axis will be clear
enough daubed here and there with a little ink

or fined out into every shade and form of its
revelation: this is a scientific poem,

asserting that nature models values, that we   55
have invented little (copied), reflections of

possibilities already here, this where we came
to and how we came: a priestly director behind the

black-chuffing dozer leans the gleanings and
reads the birds, millions of loners circling   60

a common height, alighting to the meaty streaks
and puffy muffins (puffins?): there is a mound,

too, in the poet's mind dead language is hauled
off to and burned down on, the energy held and

shaped into new turns and clusters, the mind   65
strengthened by what it strengthens: for

where but in the very asshole of comedown is
redemption: as where but brought low, where

but in the grief of failure, loss, error do we
discern the savage afflictions that turn us around: 70

where but in the arrangements love crawls us
through, not a thing left in our self-display

unhumiliated, do we find the sweet seed of
new routes; but we are natural: nature, not

we, gave rise to us; we are not, though, though   75
natural, divorced from higher, finer configurations:

tissues and holograms of energy circulate in
us and seek and find representations of themselves

outside us, so that we can participate in
celebrations high and know reaches of feeling   80

and sight and thought that penetrate (really
penetrate) far, far beyond these our wet cells,

right on up past our stories, the planets, moons,
and other bodies locally to the other end of

the pole where matter's forms diffuse and   85
energy loses all means to express itself except

as spirit, there, oh, yes, in the abiding where
mind but nothing else abides, the eternal,

until it turns into another pear or sunfish,
that momentary glint in the fisheye having   90

been there so long, coming and going, it's
eternity's glint: it all wraps back round,

into and out of form, palpable and impalpable,
and in one phase, the one of grief and love,

we know the other, where everlastingness comes to   95
sway, okay and smooth: the heaven we mostly

want, though, is this jet-hoveled hell back,
heaven's daunting asshole: one must write and

rewrite till one writes it right: if I'm in
touch, she said, then I've got an edge: what   100

the hell kind of talk is that: I can't believe
I'm merely an old person: whose mother is dead,

whose father is gone and many of whose
friends and associates have wended away to the

ground, which is only heavy wind, or to ashes,   105
a lighter breeze: but it was all quite frankly

to be expected and not looked forward to: even
old trees, I remember some of them, where they

used to stand: pictures taken by some of them:
and old dogs, specially one imperial black one,   110

quad dogs with their hier*archies* (another *archie*)[2]
one succeeding another, the barking and romping

sliding away like slides from a projector: what
were they then that are what they are now:

1993

2. The A. R. in Ammons's name stands for Archie Randolph.

JAMES MERRILL
1926–1995

When James Merrill's *First Poems* was published in 1950, he was immediately recognized as one of the most gifted and polished poets of his generation. But not until *Water Street* (1962), his third volume of poems, did Merrill begin to enlist his brilliant technique and sophisticated tone in developing a poetic autobiography. The book takes its title from the street where he lived in the seaside village of Stonington, Connecticut. The opening poem, "An Urban Convalescence," explores his decision to leave New York, which he sees as a distracting city that destroys its past. He portrays his move as a rededication to his past and an attempt through poetry "to make some kind of house / Out of the life lived, out of the love spent."

The metaphor of "home" is an emotional center to which Merrill's writing often returns, as in "The Broken Home," which recalls elements of Merrill's experience as the son of parents who divorced when he was young. He had been born to the second marriage of Charles E. Merrill, financier and founder of the best-known brokerage firm in America. "The Broken Home" shows how memory and writing have the power to reshape boyhood pain and conflict so as to achieve "the unstiflement of the entire story." Such an attitude distinguishes Merrill from his contemporaries (Robert Lowell, Anne Sexton, Sylvia Plath) whose autobiographical impulse expresses itself primarily in the present tense and the use of poems as an urgent journal true to the moment.

As an undergraduate at Amherst College, Merrill had written an honors thesis on the French novelist Marcel Proust (1871–1922). His poetry was clearly affected by Proust's notion that the literary exercise of memory slowly discloses the patterns of childhood experience that we are destined to relive. Proust showed in his *In Search of Lost Time* (1913–27) how such power over chaotic past material is often triggered involuntarily by an object or an episode in the present whose associations reach back into formative childhood encounters. The questions he asked were asked by Sigmund Freud (1856–1939), the founder of psychoanalysis, as well: What animates certain scenes—and not others—for us? To answer such questions Merrill presents some of his poems from the viewpoint of an observant child. In other poems the poet is explicitly present, at his desk, trying to incorporate into his adult understanding of the contours of his life the pain and freshness of childhood memories. The poems are narrative (one of his early books was called *Short Stories*) as often as lyric, in the hope that dramatic *action* will reveal the meanings with which certain objects have become charged. As Merrill sees it, "You hardly ever need to *state* your feelings. The point is to feel and keep the eyes open. Then what you feel is expressed, is mimed back at you by the scene. A room, a landscape. I'd go a step further. We don't *know* what we feel until we see it distanced by this kind of translation."

Merrill traveled extensively and presented landscapes from his travels as ways of exploring alternative or buried states of his own mind, the "translations" of which he speaks. Poems such as "Days of 1964" and "After the Fire" reflect his experiences in Greece, where he spent a portion of each year. They respectively anticipate and comment on *The Fire Screen* (1969), a sequence describing the rising and falling curve of a love affair partly in terms of an initiation into Greece with its power to strip away urban sophistication. The books that followed served as initiations into other psychic territories. Problems of family relationships and the erotic entanglements of homosexual love previously seen on an intimate scale were in *Braving the Elements* (1972) acted out against a wider backdrop: the long landscapes, primitive geological perspectives, and erosions of the American Far West. Here human experience, examined in his earlier work in close-up, is seen as part of a longer process of evolution comprehensible in terms of enduring nonhuman patterns.

In *Divine Comedies* (which received the Pulitzer Prize in 1977) Merrill began his most ambitious work: two-thirds of it is devoted to "The Book of Ephraim," a long narrative. It not only recapitulates his career but also attempts to locate individual psychic energies as part of a larger series of nourishing influences: friends living and dead, literary predecessors, scientific theories of the growth of the universe and the mind, the life of other periods and even other universes— all conducted through a set of encounters with the "other world" in séances at the Ouija board. It is a witty and original and assured attempt to take the intimate material of the short lyric that characterized his earlier work and cast it onto an epic scale. The second and third volumes of the trilogy, *Mirabell: Books of Number* and *Scripts for the Pageant*, appeared in 1978 and 1980, respectively; the entire work was collected in 1982 under the title *The Changing Light at Sandover*. By the time of his death, Merrill had established himself as an American formal master, one whose grace and wit made his remarkable variations on traditional forms seem as easy as casual speech. This mastery is evident in his sequence "Family Week at Oracle Ranch" (from his last book, *A Scattering of Salts*, 1995), where Merrill's formal daring is matched by an equally remarkable emotional daring. An edition of his *Collected Prose* (2004) further confirmed his stature in American letters.

An Urban Convalescence

Out for a walk, after a week in bed,
I find them tearing up part of my block
And, chilled through, dazed and lonely, join the dozen
In meek attitudes, watching a huge crane
Fumble luxuriously in the filth of years.   5
Her jaws dribble rubble. An old man
Laughs and curses in her brain,
Bringing to mind the close of *The White Goddess*.[1]

As usual in New York, everything is torn down
Before you have had time to care for it.   10
Head bowed, at the shrine of noise, let me try to recall
What building stood here. Was there a building at all?
I have lived on this same street for a decade.

Wait. Yes. Vaguely a presence rises
Some five floors high, of shabby stone   15
—Or am I confusing it with another one
In another part of town, or of the world?—
And over its lintel into focus vaguely
Misted with blood (my eyes are shut)
A single garland sways, stone fruit, stone leaves,   20
Which years of grit had etched until it thrust
Roots down, even into the poor soil of my seeing.
When did the garland become part of me?
I ask myself, amused almost,
Then shiver once from head to toe,   25
Transfixed by a particular cheap engraving of garlands
Bought for a few francs long ago,
All calligraphic tendril and cross-hatched rondure,
Ten years ago, and crumpled up to stanch
Boughs dripping, whose white gestures filled a cab,   30
And thought of neither then nor since.
Also, to clasp them, the small, red-nailed hand
Of no one I can place. Wait. No. Her name, her features
Lie toppled underneath that year's fashions.
The words she must have spoken, setting her face   35
To fluttering like a veil, I cannot hear now,
Let alone understand.

So that I am already on the stair,
As it were, of where I lived,
When the whole structure shudders at my tread   40
And soundlessly collapses, filling
The air with motes of stone.

1. The book (1948) in which the English poet Robert Graves sets forth the theory that authentic poetry is inspired by a primitive goddess who is both creative and destructive. The crane is her sacred bird, which through a pun Merrill here associates with the mechanical crane. Its operator seems like a crazed parody poet, committed only to demolition.

Onto the still erect building next door
Are pressed levels and hues—
Pocked rose, streaked greens, brown whites.   45
Who drained the pousse-café?[2]
Wires and pipes, snapped off at the roots, quiver.

Well, that is what life does. I stare
A moment longer, so. And presently
The massive volume of the world   50
Closes again.

Upon that book I swear
To abide by what it teaches:
Gospels of ugliness and waste,
Of towering voids, of soiled gusts,   55
Of a shrieking to be faced
Full into, eyes astream with cold—

With cold?
All right then. With self-knowledge.

Indoors at last, the pages of *Time* are apt   60
To open, and the illustrated mayor of New York,
Given a glimpse of how and where I work,
To note yet one more house that can be scrapped.

Unwillingly I picture
My walls weathering in the general view.   65
It is not even as though the new
Buildings did very much for architecture.

Suppose they did. The sickness of our time requires
That these as well be blasted in their prime.
You would think the simple fact of having lasted   70
Threatened our cities like mysterious fires.

There are certain phrases which to use in a poem
Is like rubbing silver with quicksilver. Bright
But facile, the glamour deadens overnight.
For instance, how "the sickness of our time"   75

Enhances, then debases, what I feel.
At my desk I swallow in a glass of water
No longer cordial, scarcely wet, a pill
They had told me not to take until much later.

With the result that back into my imagination   80
The city glides, like cities seen from the air,
Mere smoke and sparkle to the passenger
Having in mind another destination

2. An after-dinner drink made up of layers of different-colored cordials.

Which now is not that honey-slow descent
Of the Champs-Elysées,[3] her hand in his,   85
But the dull need to make some kind of house
Out of the life lived, out of the love spent.

1962

The Broken Home

Crossing the street,
I saw the parents and the child
At their window, gleaming like fruit
With evening's mild gold leaf.

In a room on the floor below,   5
Sunless, cooler—a brimming
Saucer of wax, marbly and dim—
I have lit what's left of my life.

I have thrown out yesterday's milk
And opened a book of maxims.   10
The flame quickens. The word stirs.

Tell me, tongue of fire,
That you and I are as real
At least as the people upstairs.
•
My father, who had flown in World War I,   15
Might have continued to invest his life
In cloud banks well above Wall Street and wife.
But the race was run below, and the point was to win.

Too late now, I make out in his blue gaze
(Through the smoked glass of being thirty-six)   20
The soul eclipsed by twin black pupils, sex
And business; time was money in those days.

Each thirteenth year he married. When he died
There were already several chilled wives
In sable orbit—rings, cars, permanent waves.   25
We'd felt him warming up for a green bride.

He could afford it. He was "in his prime"
At three score ten. But money was not time.
•
When my parents were younger this was a popular act:
A veiled woman would leap from an electric, wine-dark car   30

3. A stylish boulevard in Paris.

To the steps of no matter what—the Senate or the Ritz Bar—
And bodily, at newsreel speed, attack

No matter whom—Al Smith or José Maria Sert
Or Clemenceau[1]—veins standing out on her throat
As she yelled *War mongerer! Pig! Give us the vote!*,   35
And would have to be hauled away in her hobble skirt.

What had the man done? Oh, made history.
Her business (he had implied) was giving birth,
Tending the house, mending the socks.

Always that same old story—   40
Father Time and Mother Earth,[2]
A marriage on the rocks.
                              •
One afternoon, red, satyr-thighed
Michael, the Irish setter, head
Passionately lowered, led   45
The child I was to a shut door. Inside,

Blinds beat sun from the bed.
The green-gold room throbbed like a bruise.
Under a sheet, clad in taboos
Lay whom we sought, her hair undone, outspread,   50

And of a blackness found, if ever now, in old
Engravings where the acid bit.
I must have needed to touch it
Or the whiteness—was she dead?
Her eyes flew open, startled strange and cold.   55
The dog slumped to the floor. She reached for me. I fled.
                              •
Tonight they have stepped out onto the gravel.
The party is over. It's the fall
Of 1931. They love each other still.

She: Charlie, I can't stand the pace.   60
He: Come on, honey—why, you'll bury us all!

A lead soldier guards my windowsill:
Khaki rifle, uniform, and face.
Something in me grows heavy, silvery, pliable.

How intensely people used to feel!   65
Like metal poured at the close of a proletarian novel,[3]

1. Georges Clemenceau (1841–1929), premier of
France during World War I, visited the United
States in 1922. Alfred E. Smith (1873–1944), a
governor of New York and in 1928 the Democratic party's nominee for the presidency. Sert
(1876–1945), a Spanish painter who in 1930
decorated the lobby of the Waldorf-Astoria
Hotel in New York.
2. A reference to Cronus (Greek for "Time"),
ruler of the ancient Titans, and to his wife, Rhea,
an earth deity known as Mother of the Gods.
Because Cronus ate their children as soon as they
were born, Rhea plotted his overthrow.
3. Socialist novel that romanticized laborers.

Refined and glowing from the crucible,
I see those two hearts, I'm afraid,
Still. Cool here in the graveyard of good and evil,
They are even so to be honored and obeyed.   70

                              •

. . . Obeyed, at least, inversely. Thus
I rarely buy a newspaper, or vote.
To do so, I have learned, is to invite
The tread of a stone guest[4] within my house.

Shooting this rusted bolt, though, against him,   75
I trust I am no less time's child than some
Who on the heath impersonate Poor Tom[5]
Or on the barricades risk life and limb.

Nor do I try to keep a garden, only
An avocado in a glass of water—   80
Roots pallid, gemmed with air. And later,

When the small gilt leaves have grown
Fleshy and green, I let them die, yes, yes,
And start another. I am earth's no less.

                              •

A child, a red dog roam the corridors,   85
Still, of the broken home. No sound. The brilliant
Rag runners halt before wide-open doors.
My old room! Its wallpaper—cream, medallioned
With pink and brown—brings back the first nightmares,
Long summer colds, and Emma, sepia-faced,   90
Perspiring over broth carried upstairs
Aswim with golden fats I could not taste.

The real house became a boarding-school.
Under the ballroom ceiling's allegory
Someone at last may actually be allowed   95
To learn something; or, from my window, cool
With the unstiflement of the entire story,
Watch a red setter stretch and sink in cloud.

                                              1966

Dead Center

Upon reflection, as I dip my pen
Tonight, forth ripple messages in code.
In Now's black waters burn the stars of Then.

---

4. The *commendatore* in Mozart's *Don Giovanni*
(1787) returns as a statue to get his revenge.
5. In Shakespeare's *King Lear*, Edgar, disowned
by his father, wanders the heath disguised as a
madman.

Seen from the embankment, marble men
Sleep upside down, bat-wise, the sleep bestowed   5
Upon reflection. As I dip my pen

Thinking how others, deeper into Zen,
Blew on immediacy until it glowed,
In Now's black waters burn the stars of Then.

Or else I'm back at Grandmother's. I'm ten,   10
Dust hides my parents' roadster from the road
Which dips—*into* reflection, with my pen.

Breath after breath, harsh O's of oxygen—
Never deciphered, what do they forebode?
In Now's black waters burn the stars. Ah then   15

Leap, Memory, supreme equestrienne,
Through hoops of fire, circuits you overload!
Beyond reflection, as I dip my pen
In Now's black waters, burn the stars of Then.

1984

Family Week at Oracle Ranch

1 The Brochure

The world outstrips us. In my day,
Had such a place existed,
It would have been advertised with photographs
Of doctors—silver hair, pince-nez—

Above detailed credentials,   5
Not this wide-angle moonscape, lawns and pool,
Patients sharing pain like fudge from home—
As if these were the essentials,

As if a month at what it invites us to think
Is little more than a fat farm for Anorexics,   10
Substance Abusers, Love & Relationship Addicts
Could help *you*, light of my life, when even your shrink . . .

The message, then? That costly folderol,
Underwear made to order in Vienna,
Who needs it! Let the soul hang out   15
At Benetton[1]—stone-washed, one size fits all.

1. A chain of clothing stores.

2 Instead of Complexes

Simplicities. Just seven words—AFRAID,
HURT, LONELY, etc.—to say it with.
Shades of the first watercolor box
(I "felt blue," I "saw red").   20

Also some tips on brushwork. Not to say
"Your silence hurt me,"
Rather, "When you said nothing I felt hurt."
No blame, that way.

Dysfunctionals like us fail to distinguish   25
Between the two modes at first.
While the connoisseur of feeling throws up his hands:
Used to depicting personal anguish

With a full palette—hues, oils, glazes, thinner—
He stares into these withered wells and feels,   30
Well . . . SAD and ANGRY? Future lavender!
An infant Monet[2] blinks beneath his skin.

3 The Counsellors

They're in recovery, too, and tell us from what,
And that's as far as it goes.
Like the sun-priests' in *The Magic Flute*[3]   35
Their ritualized responses serve the plot.

Ken, for example, blond brows knitted: "When
James told the group he worried about dying
Without his lover beside him, I felt SAD."
Thank you for sharing, Ken,   40

I keep from saying; it would come out snide.
Better to view them as deadpan panels
Storing up sunlight for the woebegone,
Prompting from us lines electrified

By buried switches flipped (after how long!) . . .   45
But speak in private meanwhile? We may not
Until a voice within the temple lifts
Bans yet unfathomed into song.

2. Claude Monet (1840–1926), French impressionist painter.
3. One of the most famous of Wolfgang Amadeus Mozart's works, *The Magic Flute* is a *singspiel*—i.e., a combination of songs and dialogue.

4 Gestalt[4]

Little Aileen is a gray plush bear
With button eyes and nose.   50
Perky in flowered smock and clean white collar,
She occupies the chair

Across from the middleaged Big Aileen, face hid
In hands and hands on knees.
Her sobs break. In great waves it's coming back.   55
The uncle. What he did.

Little Aileen is her Inner Child
Who didn't . . . who didn't deserve. . . .
The horror kissed asleep, round Big Aileen
Fairytale thorns grow wild.   60

SADNESS and GUILT entitle us to watch
The survivor compose herself,
Smoothing the flowered stuff, which has ridden up,
Over an innocent gray crotch.

5 Effects of Early "Religious Abuse"

The great recurrent "sinner" found   65
In Dostoevsky[5]—twisted mouth,
Stormlit eyes—before whose irresistible
Unworthiness the pure in heart bow down . . .

Cockcrow. Back across the frozen Neva
To samovar and warm, untubercular bed,   70
Far from the dens of vodka, mucus and semen,
They dream. I woke, the fever

Dripping insight, a spring thaw.
You and the others, wrestling with your demons,
Christs of self-hatred, Livingstones[6] of pain,   75
Had drawn the lightning. In a flash I saw

My future: medic at some Armageddon
Neither side wins. I burned with SHAME for the years
You'd spent among sufferings uncharted—
Not even my barren love to rest your head on.   80

---

4. A configuration or pattern having specific properties that cannot be derived from the sum of its component parts (German); in psychology, the name for a theory that physiological or psychological phenomena do not occur through the summation of individual elements but through gestalts functioning separately or interrelatedly.

5. Fyodor Dostoyevsky (1821–1881), Russian novelist whose work probes the religious questions of sin and redemption.
6. Those resembling David Livingstone (1813–1873), a Scottish missionary and explorer in Africa who sought the source of the Nile River.

6 *The Panic*

Except that Oracle has maps
Of all those badlands. Just now, when you lashed out,
"There's a lot of disease in this room!"
And we felt our faith in one another lapse,

Ken had us break the circle and repair   85
To "a safe place in the room." Faster than fish
We scattered—Randy ducking as from a sniper,
Aileen, wedged in a corner, cradling her bear.

You and I stood flanking the blackboard,
Words as usual between us,   90
But backs to the same wall, for solidarity.
This magical sureness of movement no doubt scored

Points for all concerned, yet the only
Child each had become trembled for you
Thundering forth into the corridors,   95
Decibels measuring how HURT, how LONELY—

7 *Tunnel Vision*

New Age music. "Close your eyes now. You
Are standing," says the lecturer on Grief,
"At a tunnel's mouth. There's light at the end.
The walls, as you walk through   100

Are hung with images: who you loved that year,
An island holiday, a highschool friend.
Younger and younger, step by step—
And suddenly you're here,

At home. Go in. It's your whole life ago."   105
A pink eye-level sun flows through the hall.
"Smell the smells. It's supper time.
Go to the table." Years have begun to flow

Unhindered down my face. Why?
Because nobody's there. The grown-ups? Shadows.   110
The meal? A mirror. Reflect upon it. Before
Reentering the tunnel say goodbye,

8 *Time Recaptured*[7]

Goodbye to childhood, that unhappy haven.
It's over, weep your fill. Let go

---

7. The title evokes Marcel Proust's novel *Remembrance of Things Past*; the title of the final volume is
sometimes translated as *The Past Recaptured*, sometimes as *Time Regained*.

Of the dead dog, the lost toy. Practise grieving 115
At funerals—anybody's. Let go even

Of those first ninety seconds missed,
Fifty-three years ago, of a third-rate opera
Never revived since then. The GUILT you felt,
Adding it all the same to your master list! 120

Which is why, this last morning, when I switch
The FM on, halfway to Oracle,
And hear the announcer say
(Invisibly reweaving the dropped stitch),

"We bring you now the Overture 125
To Ambroise Thomas's seldom-heard *Mignon*,"[8]
Joy (word rusty with disuse)
Flashes up, deserved and pure.

9 Leading the Blind

Is this you—smiling helplessly? Pinned to your chest,
A sign: *Confront Me If I Take Control*. 130
Plus you must wear (till sundown) a black eyeshade.
All day you've been the littlest, the clumsiest.

We're seated face to face. Take off your mask,
Ken says. Now look into each other deeply. Speak,
As far as you can trust, the words of healing. 135
Your pardon for my own blindness I ask;

You mine, for all you hid from me. Two old
Crackpot hearts once more aswim with color,
Our Higher Power has but to dip his brush—
Lo and behold! 140

The group approves. The ban lifts. Let me guide you,
Helpless but voluble, into a dripping music.
The rainbow brightens with each step. Go on,
Take a peek. This once, no one will chide you.

10 The Desert Museum

—Or, as the fat, nearsighted kid ahead 145
Construes his ticket, "Wow, Dessert Museum!"
I leave tomorrow, so you get a pass.
Safer, both feel, instead

Of checking into the No-Tell Motel,
To check it out—our brave new dried-out world. 150

---

8. An opera by French operatic composer Ambroise Thomas (1811–1896).

Exhibits: crystals that for eons glinted
Before the wits did; fossil shells

From when this overlook lay safely drowned;
Whole spiny families repelled by sex,
Whom dying men have drunk from (Randy, frightened,   155
Hugging Little Randy, a red hound). . . .

At length behind a wall of glass, in shade,
The mountain lioness too indolent
To train them upon us unlids her gems
Set in the saddest face Love ever made.   160

11 The Twofold Message

(a) You are a brave and special person, (b)
There are far too many people in the world
For this to still matter for very long.
But (Ken goes on) since you obviously

Made the effort to attend Family Week,   165
We hope that we have shown you just how much
You have in common with everybody else.
Not to be "terminally unique"

Will be the consolation you take home.
Remember, Oracle is only the first step   170
In your recovery. The rest is up to you
And the twelve-step program you become

Involved in. An amazing forty per cent
Of our graduates are still clean after two years.
The rest? Well. . . . Given our society,   175
Sobriety is hard to implement.

12 And If

And if it were all like the moon?
Full this evening, bewitchingly
Glowing in a dark not yet complete
Above the world, explicit rune   180

Of change. Change is the "feeling" that dilutes
Those seven others to uncertain washes
Of soot and silver, inks unknown in my kit.
Change sends out shoots

Of FEAR and LONELINESS; of GUILT, as well,   185
Towards the old, abandoned patterns;
Of joy eventually, and self-forgiveness—
Colors few of us brought to Oracle . . .

And if the old patterns recur?
Ask how the co-dependent moon, another night,
Feels when the light drains wholly from her face.
Ask what that cold comfort means to her.

ALLEN GINSBERG
1926–1997

" Hold back the edges of your gowns, Ladies, we are going through hell." William Carlos Williams's introduction to Allen Ginsberg's *Howl* (1956) was probably the most auspicious public welcome from one poet to another since, one hundred years before, the American Transcendentalist Ralph Waldo Emerson had hailed the unknown Walt Whitman in a letter that Whitman used as a preface to the second edition of *Leaves of Grass. Howl* combined apocalyptic criticism of the dull, prosperous Eisenhower years with exuberant celebration of an emerging counterculture. It was the best-known and most widely circulated book of poems of its time, and with its appearance Ginsberg became part of the history of publicity as well as the history of poetry. *Howl* and Jack Kerouac's novel *On the Road* (1957) were the pocket Bibles of the generation whose name Kerouac had coined—"Beat," with its punning overtones of "beaten down" and "beatified."

Ginsberg was the son of Louis Ginsberg, a poet and schoolteacher in New Jersey, and of Naomi Ginsberg, a Russian émigré, whose madness and eventual death her son memorialized in "Kaddish" (1959). His official education took place at Columbia University, but for him as for Kerouac the presence of William Burroughs in New York was equally influential. Burroughs (1914–1997), later the author of *Naked Lunch* (1959), one of the most inventive experiments in American prose, was at that time a drug addict about to embark on an expatriate life in Mexico and Tangier. He helped Ginsberg discover modern writers: Kafka, Yeats, Céline, Rimbaud. Ginsberg responded to Burroughs's liberated kind of life, to his comic-apocalyptic view of American society, and to his bold literary use of autobiography, as when writing about his own experience with addicts and addiction in *Junkie*, whose chapters Ginsberg was reading in manuscript form in 1950.

Ginsberg's New York career has passed into mythology for a generation of poets and readers. In 1945, his sophomore year, he was expelled from Columbia: he had sketched some obscene drawings and phrases in the dust of his dormitory window to draw the attention of a neglectful cleaning woman to the grimy state of his room. Then, living periodically with Burroughs and Kerouac, he shipped out for short trips as a messman on merchant tankers and worked in addition as a welder, a night porter, and a dishwasher.

One summer, in a Harlem apartment, Ginsberg underwent what he always represented as the central conversion experience of his life. He had an "auditory vision" of the English poet William Blake reciting his poems: first "Ah! Sunflower," and then a few minutes later the same oracular voice intoning "The Sick Rose." It was "like hearing the doom of the whole universe, and at the same time the inevitable auty of that doom." Ginsberg was convinced that the presence of "this big god over all . . . and that the whole purpose of being born was to wake up to Him."

Ginsberg eventually finished Columbia in 1948 with high grades but under a legal cloud. Herbert Huncke, a colorful but irresponsible addict friend, had been using Ginsberg's apartment as a storage depot for the goods he stole to support his drug habit. To avoid prosecution as an accomplice, Ginsberg had to plead insanity and spent eight months in the Columbia Psychiatric Institute.

After more odd jobs and considerable success as a market researcher in San Francisco, Ginsberg left the straight, nine-to-five world for good. He was drawn to San Francisco, he said, by its "long honorable . . . tradition of Bohemian—Buddhist—Wobbly [the I.W.W., an early radical labor movement]—mystical—anarchist social involvement." In the years after 1954 he met San Francisco poets such as Robert Duncan, Kenneth Rexroth, Gary Snyder (who was studying Chinese and Japanese at Berkeley), and Lawrence Ferlinghetti, whose City Lights Bookshop became the publisher of *Howl*. The night Ginsberg read the new poem aloud at the Six Gallery has been called "the birth trauma of the Beat Generation."

The spontaneity of surface in *Howl* conceals but grows out of Ginsberg's care and self-consciousness about rhythm and meter. Under the influence of William Carlos Williams, who had befriended him in Paterson after he left the mental hospital, Ginsberg had started carrying around a notebook to record the rhythms of voices around him. Kerouac's *On the Road* gave him further examples of "frank talk" and, in addition, of an "oceanic" prose "sometimes as sublime as epic line." Under Kerouac's influence Ginsberg began the long tumbling lines that were to become his trademark. He carefully explained that all of *Howl and Other Poems* was an experiment in what could be done with the long line, the longer unit of breath that seemed natural for him. "My feeling is for a big long clanky statement," one that accommodates "not the way you would *say* it, a thought, but the way you would think it—i.e., we think rapidly,

Ginsberg reading *Howl* in New York City in 1966, nine years after the court ruling finding it of redeeming social value and declaring it not obscene.

in visual images as well as words, and if each successive thought were transcribed in its confusion . . . you get a slightly different prosody than if you were talking slowly."

Ginsberg learned the long line as well from biblical rhetoric, from the eighteenth-century English poet Christopher Smart, and above all, from Whitman and Blake. His first book pays tribute to both of these latter poets. "A Supermarket in California," with its movement from exclamations to sad questioning, is Ginsberg's melancholy reminder of what has become, after a century, of Whitman's vision of American plenty. In "Sunflower Sutra" he celebrates the battered nobility beneath our industrial "skin of grime." Ginsberg at his best gives a sense of doom and beauty, whether in the denunciatory impatient prophecies of *Howl* or in the catalog of suffering in "Kaddish." His disconnected phrases can accumulate as narrative shrieks or, at other moments, can build as a litany of praise.

By the end of the 1960s Ginsberg was widely known and widely traveled. He had conducted publicly his own pursuit of inner peace during a long stay with Buddhist instructors in India and at home served as a kind of guru for many young people disoriented by the Vietnam War. Ginsberg read his poetry and held "office hours" in universities all over America, a presence at everything from "be-ins"—mass outdoor festivals of chanting, costumes, and music—to antiwar protests. He was a gentle and persuasive presence at hearings for many kinds of reform: revision of severe drug laws and laws against homosexuality. Ginsberg had lived for years with the poet Peter Orlovsky and wrote frankly about their relationship. His poems record his drug experiences as well, and "The Change," written in Japan in 1963, marks his decision to keep away from what he considered the nonhuman domination of drugs and to lay new stress on "living in and inhabiting the human form."

In *The Fall of America* (1972) Ginsberg created an "epic" that included history and registered the ups and downs of his travels across the United States. These "transit" poems sometimes seem like tape-recorded random lists of sights, sounds, and names, but at their best they give a sense of how far America has fallen, by measuring the provisional and changing world of nuclear America against the traces of nature still visible in our landscape and place-names. With Ginsberg's death, contemporary American poetry lost one of its most definitive and revolutionary figures. Happily, the poems endure.

Howl

for Carl Solomon[1]

I

I saw the best minds of my generation destroyed by madness, starving
    hysterical naked,
dragging themselves through the negro streets at dawn looking for an angry
    fix,
angelheaded hipsters burning for the ancient heavenly connection[2] to the
    starry dynamo in the machinery of night,

1. Ginsberg met Solomon (1928–1993) while both were patients at the Columbia Psychiatric Institute in 1949 and called him "an intuitive Bronx Dadaist and prose-poet." Many details in *Howl* come from the "apocryphal history" that Solomon told Ginsberg in 1949. In "More Mis-haps" (1968) Solomon admits that these adventures were "compounded partly of truth, but for the most [of] raving self-justification, crypto-bohemian boasting . . . effeminate prancing and esoteric aphorisms."

2. In one sense, a person who can supply drugs.

who poverty and tatters and hollow-eyed and high sat up smoking in the
    supernatural darkness of cold-water flats floating across the tops of
    cities contemplating jazz,
who bared their brains to Heaven under the El and saw Mohammedan[3]
    angels staggering on tenement roofs illuminated,   5
who passed through universities with radiant cool eyes hallucinating
    Arkansas and Blake-light[4] tragedy among the scholars of war,
who were expelled from the academies for crazy & publishing obscene odes
    on the windows of the skull,
who cowered in unshaven rooms in underwear, burning their money in
    wastebaskets and listening to the Terror through the wall,
who got busted in their pubic beards returning through Laredo with a belt
    of marijuana for New York,
who ate fire in paint hotels or drank turpentine in Paradise Alley,[5] death, or
    purgatoried their torsos night after night   10
with dreams, with drugs, with waking nightmares, alcohol and cock and
    endless balls,
incomparable blind streets of shuddering cloud and lightning in the mind
    leaping toward poles of Canada & Paterson,[6] illuminating all the
    motionless world of Time between,
Peyote solidities of halls, backyard green tree cemetery dawns, wine
    drunkenness over the rooftops, storefront boroughs of teahead joyride
    neon blinking traffic light, sun and moon and tree vibrations in the
    roaring winter dusks of Brooklyn, ashcan rantings and kind king light
    of mind,
who chained themselves to subways for the endless ride from Battery to
    holy Bronx[7] on benzedrine until the noise of wheels and children
    brought them down shuddering mouth-wracked and battered bleak of
    brain all drained of brilliance in the drear light of Zoo,
who sank all night in submarine light of Bickford's floated out and sat
    through the stale beer afternoon in desolate Fugazzi's,[8] listening to the
    crack of doom on the hydrogen jukebox,   15
who talked continuously seventy hours from park to pad to bar to Bellevue[9]
    to museum to the Brooklyn Bridge,
a lost battalion of platonic conversationalists jumping down the stoops off
    fire escapes off windowsills off Empire State out of the moon,
yacketayakking screaming vomiting whispering facts and memories and
    anecdotes and eyeball kicks and shocks of hospitals and jails and wars,
whole intellects disgorged in total recall for seven days and nights with
    brilliant eyes, meat for the Synagogue cast on the pavement,

3. An English term for a Muslim, commonly used in Western literature until the mid-twentieth century; now considered offensive by many Muslims because it implies that they worship the prophet Mohammed (or Muhammad) in the same way that Christians worship Christ. "The El": the elevated railway in New York City; also a Hebrew word for God.
4. Refers to Ginsberg's apocalyptic vision of the English poet William Blake (1757–1827).
5. A tenement courtyard in New York's East Village; setting of Kerouac's *The Subterraneans* (1958).
6. Ginsberg's hometown; also the town celebrated by William Carlos Williams in his long poem *Paterson* (1946–58).
7. Opposite ends of a New York subway line running from the Battery (the southern tip of Manhattan) to the Bronx Zoo as its northern terminus.
8. New York bar that was a hipster hangout in the 1950s and 1960s. "Bickford's": a line of restaurants and cafeterias in the New York area from the 1920s to the 1960s.
9. New York public hospital to which psychiatric patients may be committed.

who vanished into nowhere Zen New Jersey leaving a trail of ambiguous
    picture postcards of Atlantic City Hall,   20

suffering Eastern sweats and Tangerian bone-grindings and migraines of
    China[1] under junk-withdrawal in Newark's bleak furnished room,

who wandered around and around at midnight in the railroad yard
    wondering where to go, and went, leaving no broken hearts,

who lit cigarettes in boxcars boxcars boxcars racketing through snow
    toward lonesome farms in grandfather night,

who studied Plotinus Poe St. John of the Cross[2] telepathy and bop kaballah[3]
    because the cosmos instinctively vibrated at their feet in Kansas,

who loned it through the streets of Idaho seeking visionary indian angels
    who were visionary indian angels,   25

who thought they were only mad when Baltimore gleamed in supernatural
    ecstasy,

who jumped in limousines with the Chinaman of Oklahoma on the impulse
    of winter midnight streetlight smalltown rain,

who lounged hungry and lonesome through Houston seeking jazz or sex or
    soup, and followed the brilliant Spaniard to converse about America
    and Eternity, a hopeless task, and so took ship to Africa,

who disappeared into the volcanoes of Mexico leaving behind nothing but
    the shadow of dungarees and the lava and ash of poetry scattered in
    fireplace Chicago,

who reappeared on the West Coast investigating the FBI in beards and
    shorts with big pacifist eyes sexy in their dark skin passing out
    incomprehensible leaflets,   30

who burned cigarette holes in their arms protesting the narcotic tobacco
    haze of Capitalism,

who distributed Supercommunist pamphlets in Union Square weeping and
    undressing while the sirens of Los Alamos[4] wailed them down, and
    wailed down Wall,[5] and the Staten Island ferry also wailed,

who broke down crying in white gymnasiums naked and trembling before
    the machinery of other skeletons,

who bit detectives in the neck and shrieked with delight in policecars for
    committing no crime but their own wild cooking pederasty and
    intoxication,

who howled on their knees in the subway and were dragged off the roof
    waving genitals and manuscripts,   35

who let themselves be fucked in the ass by saintly motorcyclists, and
    screamed with joy,

who blew and were blown by those human seraphim, the sailors, caresses
    of Atlantic and Caribbean love,

who balled in the morning in the evenings in rosegardens and the grass of
    public parks and cemeteries scattering their semen freely to whomever
    come who may,

---

1. African and Asian sources of drugs.
2. Spanish visionary and poet (1542–1591), author of *The Dark Night of the Soul*. Plotinus (205–270), visionary Roman philosopher. Edgar Allan Poe (1809–1849), American poet and author of supernatural tales.
3. A mystical tradition of interpreting Hebrew scripture. "Bop": jazz style of the 1940s.
4. New Mexico center for the development of the atomic bomb. In New York in the 1930s Union Square was a gathering place for radical speakers.
5. Wall Street; but also alludes to the Wailing Wall, a place of public lamentation and prayer in Jerusalem.

who hiccupped endlessly trying to giggle but wound up with a sob behind a
   partition in a Turkish Bath when the blonde & naked angel came to
   pierce them with a sword,[6]

who lost their loveboys to the three old shrews of fate[7] the one eyed shrew
   of the heterosexual dollar the one eyed shrew that winks out of the
   womb and the one eyed shrew that does nothing but sit on her ass and
   snip the intellectual golden threads of the craftsman's loom,   40

who copulated ecstatic and insatiate with a bottle of beer a sweetheart a
   package of cigarettes a candle and fell off the bed, and continued
   along the floor and down the hall and ended fainting on the wall with
   a vision of ultimate cunt and come eluding the last gyzym of
   consciousness,

who sweetened the snatches of a million girls trembling in the sunset, and
   were red eyed in the morning but prepared to sweeten the snatch of
   the sunrise, flashing buttocks under barns and naked in the lake,

who went out whoring through Colorado in myriad stolen nightcars, N.C.,[8]
   secret hero of these poems, cocksman and Adonis of Denver—joy to
   the memory of his innumerable lays of girls in empty lots & diner
   backyards, moviehouses' rickety rows, on mountaintops in caves or
   with gaunt waitresses in familiar roadside lonely petticoat upliftings &
   especially secret gas-station solipsisms of johns, & hometown alleys
   too,

who faded out in vast sordid movies, were shifted in dreams, woke on a
   sudden Manhattan, and picked themselves up out of basements
   hungover with heartless Tokay[9] and horrors of Third Avenue iron
   dreams & stumbled to unemployment offices,

who walked all night with their shoes full of blood on the snowbank docks
   waiting for a door in the East River to open to a room full of steamheat
   and opium,   45

who created great suicidal dramas on the apartment cliff-banks of the
   Hudson under the wartime blue floodlight of the moon & their heads
   shall be crowned with laurel in oblivion,

who ate the lamb stew of the imagination or digested the crab at the muddy
   bottom of the rivers of Bowery,[1]

who wept at the romance of the streets with their pushcarts full of onions
   and bad music,

who sat in boxes breathing in the darkness under the bridge, and rose up to
   build harpsichords in their lofts,

who coughed on the sixth floor of Harlem crowned with flame under the
   tubercular sky surrounded by orange crates of theology,   50

who scribbled all night rocking and rolling over lofty incantations which
   in the yellow morning were stanzas of gibberish,

who cooked rotten animals lung heart feet tail borsht & tortillas dreaming
   of the pure vegetable kingdom,

who plunged themselves under meat trucks looking for an egg,

6. An allusion to *The Ecstasy of St. Teresa*, a
sculpture by Lorenzo Bernini (1598–1680) based
on St. Teresa of Ávila's (1515–1582) distinctly
erotic description of a religious vision.
7. In Greek mythology, goddesses who determine
a mortal's life by spinning out a length of thread
and cutting it at the time of death.

8. Neal Cassady, hip companion of Jack Kerouac and the original Dean Moriarty, one of the
leading figures in *On the Road*.
9. A naturally sweet wine made in Hungary.
1. Southern extension of Third Avenue in New
York City; traditional haunt of derelicts and
alcoholics.

who threw their watches off the roof to cast their ballot for Eternity outside
of Time, & alarm clocks fell on their heads every day for the next
decade,

who cut their wrists three times successively unsuccessfully, gave up and
were forced to open antique stores where they thought they were
growing old and cried,   55

who were burned alive in their innocent flannel suits on Madison Avenue[2]
amid blasts of leaden verse & the tanked-up clatter of the iron
regiments of fashion & the nitroglycerine shrieks of the fairies of
advertising & the mustard gas of sinister intelligent editors, or were
run down by the drunken taxicabs of Absolute Reality,

who jumped off the Brooklyn Bridge this actually happened and walked
away unknown and forgotten into the ghostly daze of Chinatown soup
alleyways & firetrucks, not even one free beer,

who sang out of their windows in despair, fell out of the subway window,
jumped in the filthy Passaic,[3] leaped on negroes, cried all over the
street, danced on broken wineglasses barefoot smashed phonograph
records of nostalgic European 1930's German jazz finished the
whiskey and threw up groaning into the bloody toilet, moans in their
ears and the blast of colossal steamwhistles,

who barreled down the highways of the past journeying to each other's
hotrod-Golgotha[4] jail-solitude watch or Birmingham jazz incarnation,

who drove crosscountry seventytwo hours to find out if I had a vision or you
had a vision or he had a vision to find out Eternity,   60

who journeyed to Denver, who died in Denver, who came back to Denver &
waited in vain, who watched over Denver & brooded & loned in
Denver and finally went away to find out the Time, & now Denver is
lonesome for her heroes,

who fell on their knees in hopeless cathedrals praying for each other's
salvation and light and breasts, until the soul illuminated its hair for a
second,

who crashed through their minds in jail waiting for impossible criminals
with golden heads and the charm of reality in their hearts who sang
sweet blues to Alcatraz,

who retired to Mexico to cultivate a habit, or Rocky Mount to tender
Buddha or Tangiers to boys or Southern Pacific to the black
locomotive or Harvard to Narcissus to Woodlawn[5] to the daisychain or
grave,

who demanded sanity trials accusing the radio of hypnotism & were left
with their insanity & their hands & a hung jury,   65

who threw potato salad at CCNY lecturers on Dadaism[6] and subsequently
presented themselves on the granite steps of the madhouse with
shaven heads and harlequin speech of suicide, demanding
instantaneous lobotomy,

---

2. Center of New York advertising agencies.
3. River flowing past Paterson, New Jersey.
4. The place just outside the walls of Jerusalem
where Jesus was believed to have been crucified;
also known as Calvary.
5. A cemetery in the Bronx. The Southern
Pacific is a railroad company. The references in

this line are to the lives of Kerouac, Cassady, and
William Burroughs (an author and fellow Beat).
6. Artistic cult of absurdity (c. 1916–20).
"CCNY": City College of New York. This and the
following incidents probably derived from the
"apocryphal history of my adventures" related by
Solomon to Ginsberg.

and who were given instead the concrete void of insulin metrasol electricity hydrotherapy psychotherapy occupational therapy pingpong & amnesia,

who in humorless protest overturned only one symbolic pingpong table, resting briefly in catatonia,

returning years later truly bald except for a wig of blood, and tears and fingers, to the visible madman doom of the wards of the madtowns of the East,

Pilgrim State's Rockland's and Greystone's[7] foetid halls, bickering with the echoes of the soul, rocking and rolling in the midnight solitude-bench dolmen-realms of love, dream of life a nightmare, bodies turned to stone as heavy as the moon,   70

with mother finally*******, and the last fantastic book flung out of the tenement window, and the last door closed at 4 AM and the last telephone slammed at the wall in reply and the last furnished room emptied down to the last piece of mental furniture, a yellow paper rose twisted on a wire hanger in the closet, and even that imaginary, nothing but a hopeful little bit of hallucination—

ah, Carl,[8] while you are not safe I am not safe, and now you're really in the total animal soup of time—

and who therefore ran through the icy streets obsessed with a sudden flash of the alchemy of the use of the ellipse the catalog the meter & the vibrating plane,

who dreamt and made incarnate gaps in Time & Space through images juxtaposed, and trapped the archangel of the soul between 2 visual images and joined the elemental verbs and set the noun and dash of consciousness together jumping with sensation of Pater Omnipotens Aeterna Deus[9]

to recreate the syntax and measure of poor human prose and stand before you speechless and intelligent and shaking with shame, rejected yet confessing out the soul to conform to the rhythm of thought in his naked and endless head,   75

the madman bum and angel beat in Time, unknown, yet putting down here what might be left to say in time come after death,

and rose reincarnate in the ghostly clothes of jazz in the goldhorn shadow of the band and blew the suffering of America's naked mind for love into an eli eli lamma lamma sabacthani[1] saxophone cry that shivered the cities down to the last radio

with the absolute heart of the poem of life butchered out of their own bodies good to eat a thousand years.

II

What sphinx of cement and aluminum bashed open their skulls and ate up their brains and imagination?

7. Three psychiatric hospitals near New York. Solomon was institutionalized at Pilgrim State and Rockland; Ginsberg's mother, Naomi, was permanently institutionalized at Greystone after years of suffering hallucinations and paranoid attacks. She died there in 1956, the year after *Howl* was written.
8. Solomon.
9. All-Powerful Father, Eternal God (Latin). An allusion to a phrase used by the French painter Paul Cézanne (1839–1906), in a 1904 letter describing the effects of nature. In an interview, Ginsberg compared his own method of sharply juxtaposed images with Cézanne's foreshortening of perspective in landscape painting.
1. Christ's last words on the Cross: My God, my God, why have you forsaken me? (Aramaic).

Moloch![2] Solitude! Filth! Ugliness! Ashcans and unobtainable dollars!
Children screaming under the stairways! Boys sobbing in armies! Old
men weeping in the parks!   80
Moloch! Moloch! Nightmare of Moloch! Moloch the loveless! Mental
Moloch! Moloch the heavy judger of men!
Moloch the incomprehensible prison! Moloch the crossbone soulless
jailhouse and Congress of sorrows! Moloch whose buildings are
judgment! Moloch the vast stone of war! Moloch the stunned
governments!
Moloch whose mind is pure machinery! Moloch whose blood is running
money! Moloch whose fingers are ten armies! Moloch whose breast is
a cannibal dynamo! Moloch whose ear is a smoking tomb!
Moloch whose eyes are a thousand blind windows! Moloch whose
skyscrapers stand in the long streets like endless Jehovahs! Moloch
whose factories dream and croak in the fog! Moloch whose
smokestacks and antennae crown the cities!
Moloch whose love is endless oil and stone! Moloch whose soul is
electricity and banks! Moloch whose poverty is the specter of genius!
Moloch whose fate is a cloud of sexless hydrogen! Moloch whose
name is the Mind!   85
Moloch in whom I sit lonely! Moloch in whom I dream Angels! Crazy in
Moloch! Cocksucker in Moloch! Lacklove and manless in Moloch!
Moloch who entered my soul early! Moloch in whom I am a consciousness
without a body! Moloch who frightened me out of my natural ecstasy!
Moloch whom I abandon! Wake up in Moloch! Light streaming out of
the sky!
Moloch! Moloch! Robot apartments! invisible suburbs! skeleton treasuries!
blind capitals! demonic industries! spectral nations! invincible
madhouses! granite cocks! monstrous bombs!
They broke their backs lifting Moloch to Heaven! Pavements, trees, radios,
tons! lifting the city to Heaven which exists and is everywhere about
us!
Visions! omens! hallucinations! miracles! ecstasies! gone down the Ameri-
can river!   90
Dreams! adorations! illuminations! religions! the whole boatload of
sensitive bullshit!
Breakthroughs! over the river! flips and crucifixions! gone down the flood!
Highs! Epiphanies! Despairs! Ten years' animal screams and suicides!
Minds! New loves! Mad generation! down on the rocks of Time!
Real holy laughter in the river! They saw it all! the wild eyes! the holy yells!
They bade farewell! They jumped off the roof! to solitude! waving!
carrying flowers! Down to the river! into the street!

III

Carl Solomon! I'm with you in Rockland
    where you're madder than I am   95
I'm with you in Rockland
    where you must feel very strange

2. Ginsberg's own annotation in the facsimile edition of the poem reads: "'Moloch': or Molech, the
Canaanite fire god, whose worship was marked by
parents' burning their children as proprietary sacrifice. 'And thou shalt not let any of thy seed pass
through the fire to Molech' [Leviticus 18:21]."

I'm with you in Rockland
    where you imitate the shade of my mother
I'm with you in Rockland
    where you've murdered your twelve secretaries
I'm with you in Rockland
    where you laugh at this invisible humor
I'm with you in Rockland
    where we are great writers on the same dreadful typewriter
I'm with you in Rockland
    where your condition has become serious and is reported on the radio
I'm with you in Rockland
    where the faculties of the skull no longer admit the worms of the
    senses
I'm with you in Rockland
    where you drink the tea of the breasts of the spinsters of Utica[3]
I'm with you in Rockland
    where you pun on the bodies of your nurses the harpies of the Bronx
I'm with you in Rockland
    where you scream in a straightjacket that you're losing the game of
    the actual pingpong of the abyss
I'm with you in Rockland
    where you bang on the catatonic piano the soul is innocent and
    immortal it should never die ungodly in an armed madhouse
I'm with you in Rockland
    where fifty more shocks will never return your soul to its body again
    from its pilgrimage to a cross in the void
I'm with you in Rockland
    where you accuse your doctors of insanity and plot the Hebrew
    socialist revolution against the fascist national Golgotha
I'm with you in Rockland
    where you will split the heavens of Long Island and resurrect your
    living human Jesus from the superhuman tomb
I'm with you in Rockland
    where there are twenty five thousand mad comrades all together
    singing the final stanzas of the Internationale[4]
I'm with you in Rockland
    where we hug and kiss the United States under our bedsheets the
    United States that coughs all night and won't let us sleep
I'm with you in Rockland
    where we wake up electrified out of the coma by our own souls'
    airplanes roaring over the roof they've come to drop angelic bombs
    the hospital illuminates itself imaginary walls collapse O skinny
    legions run outside O starry-spangled shock of mercy the eternal
    war is here O victory forget your underwear we're free
I'm with you in Rockland
    in my dreams you walk dripping from a sea-journey on the highway
    across America in tears to the door of my cottage in the Western night

San Francisco, 1955–56   1956

3. Town in central New York.
4. Former socialist and Communist song; the official Soviet anthem until 1944.

Footnote to Howl

Holy ! Holy ! Holy ! Holy ! Holy ! Holy ! Holy ! Holy ! Holy ! Holy ! Holy !
   Holy ! Holy ! Holy ! Holy !
The world is holy ! The soul is holy ! The skin is holy ! The nose is holy !
   The tongue and cock and hand and asshole holy !
Everything is holy ! everybody's holy ! everywhere is holy ! everyday is in
   eternity ! Everyman's an angel !
The bum's as holy as the seraphim ! the madman is holy as you my soul are
   holy !
The typewriter is holy the poem is holy the voice is holy the hearers are
   holy the ecstasy is holy !   5
Holy Peter holy Allen holy Solomon holy Lucien holy Kerouac holy Huncke
   holy Burroughs holy Cassady[1] holy the unknown buggered and
   suffering beggars holy the hideous human angels !
Holy my mother in the insane asylum ! Holy the cocks of the grandfathers
   of Kansas !
Holy the groaning saxophone ! Holy the bop apocalypse ! Holy the
   jazzbands marijuana hipsters peace & junk & drums !
Holy the solitudes of skyscrapers and pavements ! Holy the cafeterias filled
   with the millions ! Holy the mysterious rivers of tears under the
   streets !
Holy the lone juggernaut ! Holy the vast lamb of the middle-class ! Holy the
   crazy shepherds of rebellion ! Who digs Los Angeles IS Los Angeles !   10
Holy New York Holy San Francisco Holy Peoria & Seattle Holy Paris Holy
   Tangiers Holy Moscow Holy Istanbul !
Holy time in eternity holy eternity in time holy the clocks in space holy the
   fourth dimension holy the fifth International holy the Angel in
   Moloch !

1955–56   1956, 1959

A Supermarket in California

What thoughts I have of you tonight, Walt Whitman,[1] for I walked down
the sidestreets under the trees with a headache self-conscious looking at
the full moon.
   In my hungry fatigue, and shopping for images, I went into the neon
fruit supermarket, dreaming of your enumerations!

1. All the figures mentioned here are Americans who shared or inspired a literary bohemia of the time. "Peter": Peter Orlovsky (1933–2010), Beat poet and Ginsberg's partner for four decades. "Allen": Ginsberg. "Solomon": Carl Solomon (1928–1993), whom Ginsberg met at the psychiatric hospital where Ginsberg's mother was being treated and to whom Ginsberg dedicated "Howl." "Lucien": Lucien Carr (1923–2005), one of the Beats and Ginsberg's roommate at Columbia University in the 1940s. "Kerouac": Jack Kerouac (1922–1969), novelist and founding figure of the Beat generation. "Huncke": Herbert Huncke (1915–1996), writer who influenced Ginsberg and who introduced Ginsberg and Kerouac to the term "beat." "Burroughs": William Burroughs (1914–1997), writer, spoken-word performer, and social critic most famous for the novel Naked Lunch (1959). "Cassady": Neal Cassady (1926–1968), an icon of the Beat generation and the inspiration for the character Dean Moriarty in Kerouac's best-known work, On the Road (1957).
1. American poet (1819–1892), author of Leaves of Grass, against whose homosexuality and vision of American plenty Ginsberg measures himself.

What peaches and what penumbras![2] Whole families shopping at night! Aisles full of husbands! Wives in the avocados, babies in the tomatoes!— and you, Garcia Lorca,[3] what were you doing down by the watermelons?

I saw you, Walt Whitman, childless, lonely old grubber, poking among the meats in the refrigerator and eyeing the grocery boys.

I heard you asking questions of each: Who killed the pork chops? What price bananas? Are you my Angel?   5

I wandered in and out of the brilliant stacks of cans following you, and followed in my imagination by the store detective.

We strode down the open corridors together in our solitary fancy tasting artichokes, possessing every frozen delicacy, and never passing the cashier.

Where are we going, Walt Whitman? The doors close in an hour. Which way does your beard point tonight?

(I touch your book and dream of our odyssey in the supermarket and feel absurd.)

Will we walk all night through solitary streets? The trees add shade to shade, lights out in the houses, we'll both be lonely.   10

Will we stroll dreaming of the lost America of love past blue automobiles in driveways, home to our silent cottage?

Ah, dear father, graybeard, lonely old courage-teacher, what America did you have when Charon quit poling his ferry and you got out on a smoking bank and stood watching the boat disappear on the black waters of Lethe?[4]

Berkeley, 1955   1956

*[handwritten annotation: (1st) * locomotive here means industrial revolution of 19th c & the way that revolution ended up paving a path of devastation]*

Sunflower Sutra[1]

[handwritten marginal annotation: natural imagery to depict industrial blight — not really tree's roots but machinery / rusted iron I reader b/c 3 disappointed as nothing is as beautiful as it should be]

I walked on the banks of the tincan banana dock and sat down under the
  huge shade of a Southern Pacific locomotive to look at the sunset over
  the box house hills and cry.
Jack Kerouac[2] sat beside me on a busted rusty iron pole, companion, we
  thought the same thoughts of the soul, bleak and blue and sad-eyed,
  surrounded by the gnarled steel roots of trees of machinery.
The oily water on the river mirrored the red sky, sun sank on top of final
  Frisco[3] peaks, no fish in that stream, no hermit in those mounts, just
  ourselves rheumy-eyed and hung-over like old bums on the riverbank,
  tired and wily.
Look at the Sunflower, he said, there was a dead gray *[handwritten: holy]* shadow against the
  sky, big as a man, sitting dry on top of a pile of ancient sawdust—

2. Partial shadows.
3. Federico García Lorca (1898–1936), Spanish poet and dramatist and author of "A Poet in New York," whose work is characterized by surrealist and homoerotic inspiration.
4. Forgetfulness. In Greek mythology, one of the rivers of Hades, the Underworld. Charon was the boatman who ferried the dead to Hades.

1. Sanskrit for "thread"; the word refers to Brahmin or Buddhist religious texts of ritual instruction.
2. Fellow Beat (1922–1969), author of *On the Road* (1957).
3. San Francisco.

[handwritten: sees both beauty & horror]

—I rushed up enchanted—it was my first sunflower, memories of
     Blake[4]—my visions—Harlem

and Hells of the Eastern rivers, bridges clanking Joes Greasy Sandwiches,
     dead baby carriages, black treadless tires forgotten and unretreaded,
     the poem of the riverbank, condoms & pots, steel knives, nothing
     stainless, only the dank muck and the razor sharp artifacts passing into
     the past—

and the gray Sunflower poised against the sunset, crackly bleak and dusty
     with the smut and smog and smoke of olden locomotives in its eye—

corolla[5] of bleary spikes pushed down and broken like a battered crown,
     seeds fallen out of its face, soon-to-be-toothless mouth of sunny air,
     sunrays obliterated on its hairy head like a dried wire spiderweb,

leaves stuck out like arms out of the stem, gestures from the sawdust root,
     broke pieces of plaster fallen out of the black twigs, a dead fly in its
     ear,

Unholy battered old thing you were, my sunflower O my soul, I loved you
     then!

The grime was no man's grime but death and human locomotives,

all that dress of dust, that veil of darkened railroad skin, that smog of
     cheek, that eyelid of black mis'ry, that sooty hand or phallus or
     protuberance of artificial worse-than-dirt—industrial—modern—all
     that civilization spotting your crazy golden crown—

and those blear thoughts of death and dusty loveless eyes and ends and
     withered roots below, in the home-pile of sand and sawdust, rubber
     dollar bills, skin of machinery, the guts and innards of the weeping
     coughing car, the empty lonely tincans with their rusty tongues alack,
     what more could I name, the smoked ashes of some cock cigar, the
     cunts of wheelbarrows and the milky breasts of cars, wornout asses out
     of chairs & sphincters of dynamos—all these

entangled in your mummied roots—and you there standing before me in
     the sunset, all your glory in your form!

A perfect beauty of a sunflower! a perfect excellent lovely sunflower
     existence! a sweet natural eye to the new hip moon, woke up alive
     and excited grasping in the sunset shadow sunrise golden monthly
     breeze!

How many flies buzzed round you innocent of your grime, while you
     cursed the heavens of the railroad and your flower soul?

Poor dead flower? when did you forget you were a flower? when did you
     look at your skin and decide you were an impotent dirty old
     locomotive? the ghost of a locomotive? the specter and shade of a once
     powerful mad American locomotive?

You were never no locomotive, Sunflower, you were a sunflower!

And you Locomotive, you are a locomotive, forget me not!

So I grabbed up the skeleton thick sunflower and stuck it at my side like a
     scepter,

and deliver my sermon to my soul, and Jack's soul too, and anyone who'll
     listen,

[handwritten margin notes, line numbers 5, 10, 15, 20]

[handwritten right margin: Sunflower meant to be object of beauty but taken over by grime & pollution of environment — but sees it persevering as spite of in hardships]

[handwritten: (2nd) locomotive changed meaning to Beat poets / characteristics taken always in motion, powerful & dominant]

[handwritten: The holy bums of the Beat must do the same]

*[handwritten: * Sunflower represents America, a land once filled w/ promise]*

[handwritten bottom: That's not who America is really & shouldn't give up / of progress & advancement—locomotive was the symbol of that progress. yet both locomotive & sunflower have lost their luster & have in a way died]

4. In Harlem in 1948 Ginsberg had a hallucinatory revelation in which he heard the English
poet William Blake (1757–1827) reciting Blake's
poems "Ah! Sunflower" and "The Sick Rose."
5. Petals forming the inner envelope of a flower.

[handwritten bottom: New vision of America that remembers it Progressive roots]

Sermon:

—We're not our skin of grime, we're not our dread bleak dusty imageless
locomotive, we're all golden sunflowers inside, blessed by our own
seed & hairy naked accomplishment-bodies growing into mad black
formal sunflowers in the sunset, spied on by our eyes under the
shadow of the mad locomotive riverbank sunset Frisco hilly tincan
evening sitdown vision.

Berkeley, 1955 *Humanity & America are not* 1956
*composed of the grime of industry, greed
of corporation & violence of war — Vision of
America as a new kind of locomotive and a
vision of desolate landscape as a picture of
beauty*

To Aunt Rose

Aunt Rose—now—might I see you
with your thin face and buck tooth smile and pain
            of rheumatism—and a long black heavy shoe
                  for your bony left leg
      limping down the long hall in Newark on the running carpet   5
            past the black grand piano
                  in the day room
                        where the parties were
      and I sang Spanish loyalist[1] songs
            in a high squeaky voice   10
                  (hysterical) the committee listening
      while you limped around the room
            collected the money—
      Aunt Honey, Uncle Sam, a stranger with a cloth arm
            in his pocket   15
                  and huge young bald head
                        of Abraham Lincoln Brigade[2]

—your long sad face
      your tears of sexual frustration
            (what smothered sobs and bony hips   20
                  under the pillows of Osborne Terrace)
—the time I stood on the toilet seat naked
      and you powdered my thighs with Calomine
            against the poison ivy—my tender
                  and shamed first black curled hairs   25
      what were you thinking in secret heart then
            knowing me a man already—
      and I an ignorant girl of family silence on the thin pedestal
            of my legs in the bathroom—Museum of Newark.

                        Aunt Rose   30
      Hitler is dead, Hitler is in Eternity; Hitler is with
            Tamburlane and Emily Brontë[3]

---

1. During the Spanish Civil War (1936–39) many left-wing Americans—among them Ginsberg's relatives in Newark—sympathized with the Spanish loyalists who were resisting Francisco Franco's (1892–1975) efforts to become Fascist dictator of Spain.

2. American volunteers who fought against the Fascists in the Spanish Civil War.
3. English poet and novelist (1818–1848), author of *Wuthering Heights*. Tamburlane was a Mideastern "scourge" and conqueror (hero of Christopher Marlowe's *Tamburlane*, 1588).

Though I see you walking still, a ghost on Osborne Terrace
 down the long dark hall to the front door
  limping a little with a pinched smile   35
   in what must have been a silken
    flower dress
welcoming my father, the Poet, on his visit to Newark
 —see you arriving in the living room
  dancing on your crippled leg   40
  and clapping hands his book
   had been accepted by Liveright[4]

Hitler is dead and Liveright's gone out of business
The Attic of the Past and *Everlasting Minute* are out of print
  Uncle Harry sold his last silk stocking 45
  Claire quit interpretive dancing school
   Buba sits a wrinkled monument in Old
    Ladies Home blinking at hew babies

last time I saw you was the hospital
  pale skull protruding under ashen skin 50
   blue veined unconscious girl
    in an oxygen tent
  the war in Spain has ended long ago
   Aunt Rose

Paris, 1958   1961

4. Leading American publisher of the 1920s and 1930s (Liveright is now an imprint of W. W. Norton); published *The Everlasting Minute* (1937), poems by Allen Ginsberg's father, Louis, whose first book was *The Attic of the Past* (1920).

FRANK O'HARA
1926–1966

After Frank O'Hara's death, the critic Donald Allen gathered O'Hara's *Collected Poems* and was surprised to discover that there were more than five hundred, many not published before. Some had to be retrieved from letters or from scraps of paper in boxes and trunks. O'Hara's poems were often spontaneous acts, revised minimally or not at all, then scattered generously, half forgotten. His work was published not by large commercial presses but by small presses and by art galleries such as Tibor de Nagy. These influential but fugitive paperbacks—*A City Winter* (1952), *Meditations in an Emergency* (1956), *Lunch Poems* (1964), and *Second Avenue* (1960)—included love poems, "letter" poems, "postcards," and odes, each bearing the mark of its occasion: a birthday, a thank-you, memories of a lunch hour, or simply "Having a Coke with You." They are filled, like diaries, with the names of Manhattan streets, writers, artists, restaurants, cafés, and films. O'Hara practiced what he once called, in mockery of pompous poetic manifestos, "personism." The term came to him one day at the office when he was writing a poem for someone he loved. "While I was writing it I was realizing that if I wanted to I could use the telephone instead of writing the poem, and so Personism was born. . . . It puts the poem squarely between the poet and the person, Lucky Pierre style, and the poem is correspondingly grati- fied. The poem is at last between two persons instead of two pages." (O'Hara's essay "Personism" is excerpted in the "Postmodern Manifestos" cluster of this anthology.)

O'Hara moved to New York City in 1951. He was born in Baltimore and grew up in Worcester, Massachusetts. He had served in the navy for two years (and been sta- tioned in the South Pacific and Japan), then studied at Harvard, where he majored in music and English. In New York he became involved in the art world, working at dif- ferent times as an editor and critic for *Art News* and a curator for the Museum of Modern Art. But he was not simply making a living; he was also making a life. In these years abstract expressionism—nonrepresentational painting—flourished, and New York replaced Paris as the art capital of the world. O'Hara met and wrote about painters such as Willem de Kooning, Franz Kline, and Jackson Pollock, then produc- ing their most brilliant work. After 1955, as a special assistant in the International Program of the Museum of Modern Art, O'Hara helped organize important traveling exhibitions that introduced the new American painting to the art world abroad.

As friends, many of these painters (and sculptors) were the occasions for and recipients of O'Hara's poems. Even more important, their way of working served as a model for his own style of writing. As the poet John Ashbery puts it, "The poem [is] the chronicle of the creative act that produces it." At the simplest level this means including the random jumps, distractions, and loose associations involved in writing about a particular moment, and sometimes recording the pauses in the writing of the poem ("And now that I have finished dinner I can continue"). In O'Hara's work the casual is often, unexpectedly, the launching point for the visionary. The offhand chronicle of a lunch-hour walk can suddenly crystallize around a thunderclap mem- ory of three friends, artists who died young: "First / Bunny died, then John Latouche, / then Jackson Pollock. But is the / earth as full as life was full, of them?"

O'Hara was indisputably, for his generation, *the* poet of New York; the city was for him what pastoral or rural worlds were for other writers, a source of refreshment and fantasy. But behind the exultation of O'Hara's cityscapes, a reader can often sense the melancholy that is made explicit in poems such as "A Step Away from Them." Part of the city's allure was that it answered O'Hara's driving need to reach out for friends, events, animation. His eagerness is balanced on "the wilderness wish / of wanting to be everything to everybody everywhere." O'Hara's poetry also displays an understanding of the intersections between the fast-paced energy of urban life and the world of machines.

O'Hara's example of a resonant casualness encouraged other poets—Ashbery, Ken- neth Koch, and James Schuyler. Loosely known as the "New York school" of poets, they occasionally collaborated on poems, plays, and happenings. O'Hara's bravado was a rallying point for these writers outside the more traditional and historically con- scious modernism of Ezra Pound and T. S. Eliot. His poems were like "inspired ram- bling," open to all levels and areas of experience, expressed in a colloquial tone that could easily shade into surrealistic dream. "I'm too blue, / An elephant takes up his trumpet, / money flutters from the windows of cries." More recently the influence of O'Hara's casual and often comic voice makes itself felt in the work of Billy Collins.

A few days after his fortieth birthday, in 1966, O'Hara was struck down at night by a beach buggy on Fire Island, New York, and died a few hours later. Despite his pre- mature death he enabled a nourishing interaction of painting, writing, dance, and theater.

To the Harbormaster

I wanted to be sure to reach you;
though my ship was on the way it got caught
in some moorings. I am always tying up
and then deciding to depart. In storms and
at sunset, with the metallic coils of the tide   5
around my fathomless arms, I am unable
to understand the forms of my vanity
or I am hard alee with my Polish rudder[1]
in my hand and the sun sinking. To
you I offer my hull and the tattered cordage   10
of my will. The terrible channels where
the wind drives me against the brown lips
of the reeds are not all behind me. Yet
I trust the sanity of my vessel; and
if it sinks, it may well be in answer   15
to the reasoning of the eternal voices,
the waves which have kept me from reaching you.

1954?   1957

Why I Am Not a Painter

I am not a painter, I am a poet.
Why? I think I would rather be
a painter, but I am not. Well,

for instance, Mike Goldberg
is starting a painting. I drop in.   5
"Sit down and have a drink" he
says. I drink; we drink. I look
up. "You have SARDINES in it."
"Yes, it needed something there."
"Oh." I go and the days go by   10
and I drop in again. The painting
is going on, and I go, and the days
go by. I drop in. The painting is
finished. "Where's SARDINES?"
All that's left is just   15
letters, "It was too much," Mike says.

But me? One day I am thinking of
a color: orange. I write a line

1. Probably a submerged comic reference to *The Polish Rider*, by the Dutch painter Rembrandt Harmensz van Rijn (1606–1669). O'Hara said this poem was about his friend the painter Larry Rivers (1923–2002), who expressed a continuing fascination with Rembrandt's painting of a knight on horseback. "Hard alee": a movement toward the lee, or sheltered side, of a sailboat, i.e., away from the wind.

about orange. Pretty soon it is a
whole page of words, not lines.
Then another page. There should be   20
so much more, not of orange, of
words, of how terrible orange is
and life. Days go by. It is even in
prose, I am a real poet. My poem   25
is finished and I haven't mentioned
orange yet. It's twelve poems, I call
it ORANGES. And one day in a gallery
I see Mike's painting, called SARDINES.

                                                    1957

A Step Away from Them

It's my lunch hour, so I go
for a walk among the hum-colored
cabs. First, down the sidewalk
where laborers feed their dirty
glistening torsos sandwiches   5
and Coca-Cola, with yellow helmets
on. They protect them from falling
bricks, I guess. Then onto the
avenue where skirts are flipping
above heels and blow up over   10
grates. The sun is hot, but the
cabs stir up the air. I look
at bargains in wristwatches. There
are cats playing in sawdust.
                        On   15
to Times Square, where the sign
blows smoke over my head,[1] and higher
the waterfall pours lightly. A
Negro stands in a doorway with a
toothpick, languorously agitating.   20
A blonde chorus girl clicks: he
smiles and rubs his chin. Everything
suddenly honks: it is 12:40 of
a Thursday.
                Neon in daylight is a   25
great pleasure, as Edwin Denby[2] would
write, as are light bulbs in daylight.
I stop for a cheeseburger at JULIET's
CORNER. Giulietta Masina, wife of
Federico Fellini, è bell' attrice.[3]   30

---

1. Famous steam-puffing billboard, advertising cigarettes.
2. Fellow poet (1903–1983) and influential ballet critic.

3. Is [a] beautiful actress (Italian). Masina (1921–1994), Italian film actress, starred in many films by her husband, the Italian filmmaker Fellini (1920–1993), including *Juliet of the Spirits* (1965).

And chocolate malted. A lady in
foxes on such a day puts her poodle
in a cab.
      There are several Puerto
Ricans on the avenue today, which   35
makes it beautiful and warm. First
Bunny died, then John Latouche,
then Jackson Pollock.[4] But is the
earth as full as life was full, of them?
And one has eaten and one walks,   40
past the magazines with nudes
and the posters for bullfight and
the Manhattan Storage Warehouse,
which they'll soon tear down. I
used to think they had the Armory   45
Show[5] there.
      A glass of papaya juice
and back to work. My heart is in my
pocket, it is Poems by Pierre Reverdy.[6]

1956   1964

The Day Lady[1] Died

It is 12:20 in New York a Friday
three days after Bastille day,[2] yes
it is 1959 and I go get a shoeshine
because I will get off the 4:19 in Easthampton[3]
at 7:15 and then go straight to dinner   5
and I don't know the people who will feed me

I walk up the muggy street beginning to sun
and have a hamburger and a malted and buy
an ugly new world writing to see what the poets
in Ghana are doing these days   10
                          I go on to the bank
and Miss Stillwagon (first name Linda I once heard)
doesn't even look up my balance for once in her life
and in the GOLDEN GRIFFIN I get a little Verlaine
for Patsy[4] with drawings by Bonnard although I do   15

4. Abstract expressionist painter (1912–1956), considered the originator of "action" painting. "Bunny": V. R. Lang (1924–1956), poet and director of The Poet's Theater in Cambridge, Massachusetts, where she produced several of O'Hara's plays. Latouche (1917–1956), lyricist for several New York musicals, such as *The Golden Apple*. All three were gifted friends of the poet who met tragic deaths.
5. Site in 1913 of the influential and controversial first American showing of European postimpressionist painters.

6. French poet (1899–1960) whose work strongly influenced O'Hara's writing.
1. Billie Holiday (1915–1959), also known as Lady Day, classic blues and jazz singer.
2. July 14, the French national holiday.
3. Town in eastern Long Island, a summer resort then popular among New York artists.
4. Patsy Southgate, an artist and friend of the poet. "Golden Griffin": a bookstore that was located close to the Museum of Modern Art. "Verlaine": Paul Verlaine (1844–1896), French poet.

think of Hesiod, trans. Richmond Lattimore or
Brendan Behan's new play or *Le Balcon* or *Les Nègres*
of Genet,[5] but I don't, I stick with Verlaine
after practically going to sleep with quandariness

and for Mike I just stroll into the PARK LANE   20
Liquor Store and ask for a bottle of Strega and
then I go back where I came from to 6th Avenue
and the tobacconist in the Ziegfeld Theatre and
casually ask for a carton of Gauloises and a carton
of Picayunes, and a NEW YORK POST with her face on it   25
and I am sweating a lot by now and thinking of
leaning on the john door in the 5 SPOT
while she whispered a song along the keyboard
to Mal Waldron[6] and everyone and I stopped breathing

1959   1960

A True Account of Talking to the Sun at Fire Island

The Sun woke me this morning loud
and clear, saying "Hey! I've been
trying to wake you up for fifteen
minutes. Don't be so rude, you are
only the second poet I've ever chosen   5
to speak to personally
                        so why
aren't you more attentive? If I could
burn you through the window I would
to wake you up. I can't hang around   10
here all day."
                "Sorry, Sun, I stayed
up late last night talking to Hal."

"When I woke up Mayakovsky[1] he was
a lot more prompt" the Sun said   15
petulantly. "Most people are up
already waiting to see if I'm going
to put in an appearance."
                        I tried
to apologize "I missed you yesterday."   20
"That's better" he said. "I didn't
know you'd come out." "You may be
wondering why I've come so close?"

5. Plays (*The Balcony* and *The Blacks*, both
1955) by the French writer Jean Genet (1910–
1986?), whose subjects were often the homosexual world and the lives of the dispossessed.
"Bonnard": Pierre Bonnard (1867–1947), French
painter and printmaker. "Hesiod": early Greek
poet (c. 700 B.C.E.) and author of *Works and*

Days, translated by the American poet Richmond Lattimore (1906–1984). Brendan Behan
(1923–1964), Irish writer and dramatist.
6. Billie Holiday's accompanist (1926–2002).
1. Vladimir Mayakovsky (1893–1930), Russian
poet and representative of early-20th-century
Futurism.

"Yes" I said beginning to feel hot
wondering if maybe he wasn't burning me   25
anyway.
                "Frankly I wanted to tell you
I like your poetry. I see a lot
on my rounds and you're okay. You may
not be the greatest thing on earth, but   30
you're different. Now, I've heard some
say you're crazy, they being excessively
calm themselves to my mind, and other
crazy poets think that you're a boring
reactionary. Not me.   35
                Just keep on
like I do and pay no attention. You'll
find that people always will complain
about the atmosphere, either too hot
or too cold too bright or too dark, days   40
too short or too long.
                If you don't appear
at all one day they think you're lazy
or dead. Just keep right on, I like it.

And don't worry about your lineage   45
poetic or natural. The Sun shines on
the jungle, you know, on the tundra
the sea, the ghetto. Wherever you were
I knew it and saw you moving. I was waiting
for you to get to work.   50

                And now that you
are making your own days, so to speak,
even if no one reads you but me
you won't be depressed. Not
everyone can look up, even at me. It   55
hurts their eyes."
                "Oh Sun, I'm so grateful to you!"

"Thanks and remember I'm watching. It's
easier for me to speak to you out
here. I don't have to slide down   60
between buildings to get your ear.
I know you love Manhattan, but
you ought to look up more often.
                And
always embrace things, people earth   65
sky stars, as I do, freely and with
the appropriate sense of space. That
is your inclination, known in the heavens
and you should follow it to hell, if
necessary, which I doubt.   70
                Maybe we'll
speak again in Africa, of which I too

506 | GALWAY KINNELL

am specially fond. Go back to sleep now
Frank, and I may leave a tiny poem
in that brain of yours as my farewell."   75

"Sun, don't go!" I was awake
at last. "No, go I must, they're calling
me."
    "Who are they?"
                      Rising he said "Some   80
day you'll know. They're calling to you
too." Darkly he rose, and then I slept.

                                           1971

GALWAY KINNELL
1927–2014

I n a 1971 interview, Galway Kinnell praised Walt Whitman's *Song of Myself*: "The final action of the poem where Whitman dissolves into the air and into the ground, is for me one of the great moments of self-transcendence in poetry. In one way or another, consciously or not, all poems try to pass beyond the self." This capacity for self-transcendence is dramatized in Kinnell's work, where he enters the lives of animals ("The Porcupine," "The Bear") and experiences himself as part of the natural world, like the flower he speaks for in "Flower Herding on Mount Monadnock." "Part of poetry's usefulness in the world," he said, "is that it pays some of our huge unpaid tribute to the things and creatures that share the earth with us." His work moves between a vivid sense of the world's physical actuality and an equally vivid sense of its dissolution, for mortality is Kinnell's great theme. It appears in his work both as extinction and as "the flowing away into the universe which we desire." This theme is worked out at length in his sequence *The Book of Nightmares* (1978).

Kinnell grew up in Providence, Rhode Island, and attended Princeton University, where he and a classmate, W. S. Merwin, sometimes read each other their poems. He wrote continuously, combining his life of poetry with political commitments. In the course of his life, Kinnell was the director of an adult-education program in Chicago, a journalist in Iran, and a field-worker for the Congress of Racial Equality in Louisiana. Later he taught at a large number of colleges and universities.

Kinnell's experiences working for voter registration in the South in the 1960s made their way into his long poem "The Last River" (*Body Rags*, 1969). Over the years Kinnell frequently wrote poems that united his personal life with the events of the nation. His work includes powerful war poems such as "Vapor Trail Reflected in the Frog Pond" and "The Dead Shall Be Raised Incorruptible," and in "The Past" (1985) he meditates on, and imagines his way into, the consequences of the dropping of the atomic bombs on Hiroshima and Nagasaki. Elsewhere he suggested that poetry is an alternative to a technological world in which domination of nature represses the knowledge of death. In 1994 his collection *Imperfect Thirst* extended his meditation on mortality into the arena of family history and personal memory. In a moving poem, "Neverland," on his sister's confrontation with death's agony and mystery, the last words she speaks are, "Now is when the point of the story changes."

Kinnell's earliest work, as seen in *What a Kingdom It Was* (1960) and *First Poems 1946–1954* (1970), is formally intricate. The course of his career was a movement to a looser line, a more uncluttered diction. His sense of form arises from what he called the "inner shape" of the poem: "saying in its own music what matters most." Over the years he came to write poems that maintain musicality and a richness of language while never departing too far from the speaking voice. Kinnell's attraction to the nonhuman world, which may remind us of Theodore Roethke and Gary Snyder, gives his work a vivid sense of life's diversity. But he sometimes elevated the instinctual at the expense of a shaping, conscious awareness and wrote as if the very need for poetic form were, in and of itself, repressive. The finest of Kinnell's poems combine self-transcendence with self-awareness in rhythms that convey a powerful physical energy and an empathetic imagination. His description of Whitman can serve as a description of Kinnell's best work: "All his feelings for existence, for himself, for his own place, come out in what he says about them. . . . He rescues these things from death and lets them live in his poems and, in turn, they save him from incoherence and silence."

The Porcupine

1

Fatted
on herbs, swollen on crabapples,
puffed up on bast and phloem,[1] ballooned
on willow flowers, poplar catkins, first
leafs of aspen and larch,   5
the porcupine
drags and bounces his last meal through ice,
mud, roses and goldenrod, into the stubbly high fields.

2

In character
he resembles us in seven ways: 10
he puts his mark on outhouses,
he alchemizes by moonlight,
he shits on the run,
he uses his tail for climbing,
he chuckles softly to himself when scared,   15
he's overcrowded if there's more than one of him per five acres,
his eyes have their own inner redness.

3

Digger of
goings across floors, of hesitations
at thresholds, of   20
handprints of dread
at doorpost or window jamb, he would

---

1. I.e., on plant tissues.

gouge the world
empty of us, hack and crater
it
until it is nothing, if that
could rinse it of all our sweat and pathos.

25

Adorer of ax
handles aflow with grain, of arms
of Morris chairs,[2] of hand
crafted objects
steeped in the juice of fingertips,
of surfaces wetted down
with fist grease and elbow oil,
of clothespins that have
grabbed our body-rags by underarm and crotch . . .

30

35

Unimpressed—bored—
by the whirl of the stars, by *these*
he's astonished, ultra-
Rilkean[3] angel!

40

for whom the true
portion of the sweetness of earth
is one of those bottom-heavy, glittering, saccadic
bits
of salt water that splash down
the haunted ravines of a human face.

45

4

A farmer shot a porcupine three times
as it dozed on a tree limb. On
the way down it tore open its belly
on a broken
branch, hooked its gut,
and went on falling. On the ground
it sprang to its feet, and
paying out gut heaved
and spartled[4] through a hundred feet of goldenrod
before
the abrupt emptiness.

50

55

5

The Avesta[5]
puts porcupine killers

2. Easy chairs.
3. The German poet Rainer Maria Rilke (1875–1926) wrote in a letter that "the 'angel' of [Rilke's Duino] Elegies has nothing to do with the angel of the Christian heaven. . . . The angel of the Elegies is that being which stands for the idea of recogniz-ing a higher order of reality in invisibility."
4. Variant of "sprottle," to sprawl or struggle helplessly.
5. Book of the sacred writings of Zoroastrianism, a Persian religion.

into hell for nine generations, sentencing them   60
to gnaw out
each other's hearts for the
salts of desire.

I roll
this way and that in the great bed, under   65
the quilt
that mimics this country of broken farms and woods,
the fatty sheath of the man
melting off,
the self-stabbing coil   70
of bristles reversing, blossoming outward—
a red-eyed, hard-toothed, arrow-stuck urchin
tossing up mattress feathers,
pricking the
woman beside me until she cries.   75

6

In my time I have
crouched, quills erected,
Saint
Sebastian[6] of the
scared heart, and been   80
beat dead with a locust club
on the bare snout.
And fallen from high places
I have fled, have
jogged   85
over fields of goldenrod,
terrified, seeking home,
and among flowers
I have come to myself empty, the rope
strung out behind me   90
in the fall sun
suddenly glorified with all my blood.

7

And tonight I think I prowl broken
skulled or vacant as a
sucked egg in the wintry meadow, softly chuckling, blank   95
template of myself, dragging
a starved belly through the lichflowered acres,
where
burdock looses the ark of its seed
and thistle holds up its lost blooms   100

6. Early Christian saint and martyr (d. 288); he was shot full of arrows by an execution squad and miraculously survived, only to be beaten to death later.

and rosebushes in the wind scrape their dead limbs
for the forced-fire
of roses.

1969

Blackberry Eating

I love to go out in late September
among the fat, overripe, icy, black blackberries
to eat blackberries for breakfast,
the stalks very prickly, a penalty
they earn for knowing the black art   5
of blackberry-making; and as I stand among them
lifting the stalks to my mouth, the ripest berries
fall almost unbidden to my tongue,
as words sometimes do, certain peculiar words
like *strengths* or *squinched*,   10
many-lettered, one-syllabled lumps,
which I squeeze, squinch open, and splurge well
in the silent, startled, icy, black language
of blackberry-eating in late September.

1980

After Making Love We Hear Footsteps

For I can snore like a bullhorn
or play loud music
or sit up talking with any reasonably sober Irishman
and Fergus will only sink deeper
into his dreamless sleep, which goes by all in one flash,   5
but let there be that heavy breathing
or a stifled come-cry anywhere in the house
and he will wrench himself awake
and make for it on the run—as now, we lie together,
after making love, quiet, touching along the length of our bodies,   10
familiar touch of the long-married,
and he appears—in his baseball pajamas, it happens,
the neck opening so small he has to screw them on—
and flops down between us and hugs us and snuggles himself to sleep,
his face gleaming with satisfaction at being this very child.   15

In the half darkness we look at each other
and smile
and touch arms across this little, startlingly muscled body—
this one whom habit of memory propels to the ground of his making,

sleeper only the mortal sounds can sing awake,   20
this blessing love gives again into our arms.

1980

Cemetery Angels

On these cold days
they stand over
our dead, who will
erupt into flower as soon
as memory and human shape   5
rot out of them, each bent
forward and with wings
partly opened as though
warming itself at a fire.

1985

JOHN ASHBERY
b. 1927

John Ashbery has described his writing this way: "I think that any one of my poems might be considered to be a snapshot of whatever is going on in my mind at the time—first of all the desire to write a poem, after that wondering if I've left the oven on or thinking about where I must be in the next hour." Ashbery has developed a style hospitable to quicksilver changes in tone and attention. His work often moves freely between different modes of discourse, between a language of popular culture and commonplace experience and a heightened rhetoric often associated with poetic vision. Ashbery's poems show an awareness of the various linguistic codes (including clichés and conventional public speech) by which we live and through which we define ourselves. This awareness includes an interest in what he has called "prose voices," and he has often written in a way that challenges the supposed boundaries between poetry and prose.

Ashbery's poetry was not always so open to contradictory notions and impulses. His early books rejected the mere surfaces of realism and the momentary in order to get at "remoter areas of consciousness." The protagonist of "Illustration" (from his first book, *Some Trees*) is a cheerful nun about to leave behind the irrelevancies of the world by leaping from a skyscraper. Her act implies "Much that is beautiful must be discarded / So that we may resemble a taller / impression of ourselves." To reach the "remoter areas of consciousness," Ashbery tried various technical experiments. He used highly patterned forms such as the sestina in "Some Trees" and "The Tennis Court Oath" (1962) not with any show of mechanical brilliance but to explore: "I once told somebody that writing a sestina was rather like riding downhill on a bicycle and having the pedals push your feet. I wanted my feet to be pushed into places they wouldn't normally have taken."

Ashbery was born in Rochester, New York. He attended Deerfield Academy and Harvard, from which he graduated in 1949. He received an M.A. in English from Columbia in 1951. After a preliminary stay in France as a Fulbright scholar, he returned in 1958 for eight years and was art critic for the European edition of the *New York Herald Tribune* and reported the European shows and exhibitions for *Art News* and *Arts International*. He returned to New York in 1965 to be executive editor of *Art News*, a position he held until 1972. He has taught creative writing at Brooklyn College, Bard College, Wesleyan University, and other institutions over his long career.

Ashbery's interest in art played a formative role in his poetry. He is often associated with Frank O'Hara, James Schuyler, and Kenneth Koch as part of the "New York school" of poets. The name refers to their common interest in the New York school of abstract painters of the 1940s and 1950s, some of whose techniques they wished to adapt to poetry. These painters avoided realism in order to stress the work of art as a representation of the creative act that produced it—as in the action paintings of Jackson Pollock. Ashbery's long poem *Self-Portrait in a Convex Mirror* gives as much attention to the rapidly changing feelings of the poet in the act of writing his poem as it does to the Renaissance painting that inspired him. The poem moves back and forth between the distracted energies that feed a work of art and the completed composition, which the artist feels as both a triumph and a falsification of complex feelings. Ashbery shares with O'Hara a sense of the colloquial brilliance of daily life in New York and sets this in tension with the concentration and stasis of art.

Ashbery has published prolifically since his first collection, *Self-Portrait in a Convex Mirror*, appeared in 1975. His important book-length poem, *Flow Chart*, appeared in 1991. His entertaining and provocative *Other Traditions* (2000) is a collection of his Norton Lectures on poetry at Harvard. Ashbery's work, especially his earlier, more highly experimental poems, has become particularly influential for a younger generation identified as "Language" poets, such as Charles Bernstein, Lyn Hejinian, Michael Palmer, and Susan Howe. They have been attracted to the linguistic playfulness of Ashbery's poetry and to its resistance to being read as a single, personal voice. Exposing and sometimes breaking through the world's dominant uses of language, Ashbery's poems open new possibilities of meaning: "We are all talkers / It is true, but underneath the talk lies / The moving and not wanting to be moved, the loose / Meaning, untidy and simple like the threshing floor" ("Soonest Mended").

Illustration

I

A novice[1] was sitting on a cornice
High over the city. Angels

Combined their prayers with those
Of the police, begging her to come off it.

One lady promised to be her friend.   5
"I do not want a friend," she said.

---

1. Student in the first stage of instruction to be a nun.

ILLUSTRATION | 513

A mother offered her some nylons
Stripped from her very legs. Others brought

Little offerings of fruit and candy,
The blind man all his flowers. If any   10

Could be called successful, these were,
For that the scene should be a ceremony

Was what she wanted. "I desire
Monuments," she said. "I want to move

Figuratively, as waves caress   15
The thoughtless shore. You people I know

Will offer me every good thing
I do not want. But please remember

I died accepting them." With that, the wind
Unpinned her bulky robes, and naked   20

As a roc's[2] egg, she drifted softly downward
Out of the angels' tenderness and the minds of men.

II

Much that is beautiful must be discarded
So that we may resemble a taller

Impression of ourselves. Moths climb in the flame,   25
Alas, that wish only to be the flame:

They do not lessen our stature.
We twinkle under the weight

Of indiscretions. But how could we tell
That of the truth we know, she was   30

The somber vestment? For that night, rockets sighed
Elegantly over the city, and there was feasting:

There is so much in that moment!
So many attitudes toward that flame,

We might have soared from earth, watching her glide   35
Aloft, in her peplum[3] of bright leaves.

But she, of course, was only an effigy
Of indifference, a miracle

---

2. Legendary bird of prey.
3. In ancient Greece, a drapery about the upper part of the body.

Not meant for us, as the leaves are not
Winter's because it is the end.   40

1956

Soonest Mended

Barely tolerated, living on the margin
In our technological society, we were always having to be rescued
On the brink of destruction, like heroines in *Orlando Furioso*[1]
Before it was time to start all over again.
There would be thunder in the bushes, a rustling of coils,   5
And Angelica, in the Ingres painting,[2] was considering
The colorful but small monster near her toe, as though wondering
        whether forgetting
The whole thing might not, in the end, be the only solution.
And then there always came a time when
Happy Hooligan[3] in his rusted green automobile   10
Came plowing down the course, just to make sure everything was O.K.,
Only by that time we were in another chapter and confused
About how to receive this latest piece of information.
Was it information? Weren't we rather acting this out
For someone else's benefit, thoughts in a mind   15
With room enough and to spare for our little problems (so they began
        to seem),
Our daily quandary about food and the rent and bills to be paid?
To reduce all this to a small variant,
To step free at last, minuscule on the gigantic plateau—
This was our ambition: to be small and clear and free.   20
Alas, the summer's energy wanes quickly.
A moment and it is gone. And no longer
May we make the necessary arrangements, simple as they are.
Our star was brighter perhaps when it had water in it.
Now there is no question even of that, but only   25
Of holding on to the hard earth so as not to get thrown off,
With an occasional dream, a vision: a robin flies across
The upper corner of the window, you brush your hair away
And cannot quite see, or a wound will flash
Against the sweet faces of the others, something like: 30
This is what you wanted to hear, so why
Did you think of listening to something else? We are all talkers
It is true, but underneath the talk lies
The moving and not wanting to be moved, the loose
Meaning, untidy and simple like a threshing floor.[4]   35

---

1. Fantastical epic poem by Ludovico Ariosto
(1474–1533), whose romantic heroine Angelica
is constantly being rescued from imminent per-
ils such as monsters and storms at sea.
2. *Roger Delivering Angelica* (1819), a painting
based on a scene from Ariosto, by French artist
Jean-Auguste-Dominique Ingres (1780–1867).
3. The good-natured, simple title character of a
popular comic strip of the 1920s and 1930s.
4. Used at harvest time to separate the wheat
from the chaff, which is to be discarded.

These then were some hazards of the course,
Yet though we knew the course *was* hazards and nothing else
It was still a shock when, almost a quarter of a century later,
The clarity of the rules dawned on you for the first time.
They were the players, and we who had struggled at the game   40
Were merely spectators, though subject to its vicissitudes
And moving with it out of the tearful stadium, borne on shoulders,
        at last.
Night after night this message returns, repeated
In the flickering bulbs of the sky, raised past us, taken away from us,
Yet ours over and over until the end that is past truth,   45
The being of our sentences, in the climate that fostered them,
Not ours to own, like a book, but to be with, and sometimes
To be without, alone and desperate.
But the fantasy makes it ours, a kind of fence-sitting
Raised to the level of an esthetic ideal. These were moments, years,   50
Solid with reality, faces, namable events, kisses, heroic acts,
But like the friendly beginning of a geometrical progression
Not too reassuring, as though meaning could be cast aside some day
When it had been outgrown. Better, you said, to stay cowering
Like this in the early lessons, since the promise of learning   55
Is a delusion, and I agreed, adding that
Tomorrow would alter the sense of what had already been learned,
That the learning process is extended in this way, so that from this
        standpoint
None of us ever graduates from college,
For time is an emulsion,[5] and probably thinking not to grow up   60
Is the brightest kind of maturity for us, right now at any rate.
And you see, both of us were right, though nothing
Has somehow come to nothing; the avatars[6]
Of our conforming to the rules and living
Around the home have made—well, in a sense, "good citizens" of us,   65
Brushing the teeth and all that, and learning to accept
The charity of the hard moments as they are doled out,
For this is action, this not being sure, this careless
Preparing, sowing the seeds crooked in the furrow,
Making ready to forget, and always coming back   70
To the mooring of starting out, that day so long ago.

                                                1970

Self-Portrait in a Convex Mirror[1]

As Parmigianino did it, the right hand
Bigger than the head, thrust at the viewer
And swerving easily away, as though to protect

---

5. A chemical solution in which the particles of
one liquid are suspended in another.
6. Incarnations.
1. This self-portrait, by the Italian Mannerist

Parmigianino (Girolamo Francesco Mazzola,
1503–1540) on a convex piece of poplar wood,
hangs in the Kunsthistorisches Museum in
Vienna.

What it advertises. A few leaded panes, old beams,
Fur, pleated muslin, a coral ring run together   5
In a movement supporting the face, which swims
Toward and away like the hand
Except that it is in repose. It is what is
Sequestered. Vasari[2] says, "Francesco one day set himself
To take his own portrait, looking at himself for that purpose   10
In a convex mirror, such as is used by barbers . . .
He accordingly caused a ball of wood to be made
By a turner, and having divided it in half and
Brought it to the size of the mirror, he set himself
With great art to copy all that he saw in the glass,"   15
Chiefly his reflection, of which the portrait
Is the reflection once removed.
The glass chose to reflect only what he saw
Which was enough for his purpose: his image
Glazed, embalmed, projected at a 180-degree angle.   20
The time of day or the density of the light
Adhering to the face keeps it
Lively and intact in a recurring wave
Of arrival. The soul establishes itself.
But how far can it swim out through the eyes   25
And still return safely to its nest? The surface
Of the mirror being convex, the distance increases
Significantly; that is, enough to make the point
That the soul is a captive, treated humanely, kept
In suspension, unable to advance much farther   30
Than your look as it intercepts the picture.
Pope Clement and his court were "stupefied"
By it,[3] according to Vasari, and promised a commission
That never materialized. The soul has to stay where it is,
Even though restless, hearing raindrops at the pane,   35
The sighing of autumn leaves thrashed by the wind,
Longing to be free, outside, but it must stay
Posing in this place. It must move
As little as possible. This is what the portrait says.
But there is in that gaze a combination   40
Of tenderness, amusement and regret, so powerful
In its restraint that one cannot look for long.
The secret is too plain. The pity of it smarts,
Makes hot tears spurt: that the soul is not a soul,
Has no secret, is small, and it fits   45
Its hollow perfectly: its room, our moment of attention.
That is the tune but there are no words.
The words are only speculation
(From the Latin speculum, mirror):
They seek and cannot find the meaning of the music.   50

2. Giorgio Vasari (1511–1574), Italian architect, painter, and art historian whose *Lives of the Most Eminent Italian Painters, Sculptors, and Architects* is the principal source of information about those artists.

3. When Parmigianino moved from his native Parma to Rome in 1524, he presented the self-portrait to Pope Clement VII as a credential for papal patronage.

We see only postures of the dream,
Riders of the motion that swings the face
Into view under evening skies, with no
False disarray as proof of authenticity.
But it is life englobed.   55
One would like to stick one's hand
Out of the globe, but its dimension,
What carries it, will not allow it.
No doubt it is this, not the reflex
To hide something, which makes the hand loom large   60
As it retreats slightly. There is no way
To build it flat like a section of wall:
It must join the segment of a circle,
Roving back to the body of which it seems
So unlikely a part, to fence in and shore up the face   65
On which the effort of this condition reads
Like a pinpoint of a smile, a spark
Or star one is not sure of having seen
As darkness resumes. A perverse light whose
Imperative of subtlety dooms in advance its   70
Conceit to light up: unimportant but meant.
Francesco, your hand is big enough
To wreck the sphere, and too big,
One would think, to weave delicate meshes
That only argue its further detention.   75
(Big, but not coarse, merely on another scale,
Like a dozing whale on the sea bottom
In relation to the tiny, self-important ship
On the surface.) But your eyes proclaim
That everything is surface. The surface is what's there   80
And nothing can exist except what's there.
There are no recesses in the room, only alcoves,
And the window doesn't matter much, or that
Sliver of window or mirror on the right, even
As a gauge of the weather, which in French is   85
Le temps, the word for time, and which
Follows a course wherein changes are merely
Features of the whole. The whole is stable within
Instability, a globe like ours, resting
On a pedestal of vacuum, a ping-pong ball   90
Secure on its jet of water.
And just as there are no words for the surface, that is,
No words to say what it really is, that it is not
Superficial but a visible core, then there is
No way out of the problem of pathos vs. experience.   95
You will stay on, restive, serene in
Your gesture which is neither embrace nor warning
But which holds something of both in pure
Affirmation that doesn't affirm anything.

The balloon pops, the attention   100
Turns dully away. Clouds

In the puddle stir up into sawtoothed fragments.
I think of the friends
Who came to see me, of what yesterday
Was like. A peculiar slant   105
Of memory that intrudes on the dreaming model
In the silence of the studio as he considers
Lifting the pencil to the self-portrait.
How many people came and stayed a certain time,
Uttered light or dark speech that became part of you   110
Like light behind windblown fog and sand,
Filtered and influenced by it, until no part
Remains that is surely you. Those voices in the dusk
Have told you all and still the tale goes on
In the form of memories deposited in irregular   115
Clumps of crystals. Whose curved hand controls,
Francesco, the turning seasons and the thoughts
That peel off and fly away at breathless speeds
Like the last stubborn leaves ripped
From wet branches? I see in this only the chaos   120
Of your round mirror which organizes everything
Around the polestar[4] of your eyes which are empty,
Know nothing, dream but reveal nothing.
I feel the carousel starting slowly
And going faster and faster: desk, papers, books,   125
Photographs of friends, the window and the trees
Merging in one neutral band that surrounds
Me on all sides, everywhere I look.
And I cannot explain the action of leveling,
Why it should all boil down to one   130
Uniform substance, a magma[5] of interiors.
My guide in these matters is your self,
Firm, oblique, accepting everything with the same
Wraith of a smile, and as time speeds up so that it is soon
Much later, I can know only the straight way out,   135
The distance between us. Long ago
The strewn evidence meant something,
The small accidents and pleasures
Of the day as it moved gracelessly on,
A housewife doing chores. Impossible now   140
To restore those properties in the silver blur that is
The record of what you accomplished by sitting down
"With great art to copy all that you saw in the glass"
So as to perfect and rule out the extraneous
Forever. In the circle of your intentions certain spars[6] 145
Remain that perpetuate the enchantment of self with self:
Eyebeams, muslin, coral. It doesn't matter
Because these are things as they are today
Before one's shadow ever grew
Out of the field into thoughts of tomorrow.   150

---

4. The North Star; the center of attraction.
5. Soft mixture of organic or mineral materials.

6. Pieces of lustrous mineral; also, round timbers
used to support rigging and sails on a ship or boat.

Tomorrow is easy, but today is uncharted,
Desolate, reluctant as any landscape
To yield what are laws of perspective
After all only to the painter's deep
Mistrust, a weak instrument though   155
Necessary. Of course some things
Are possible, it knows, but it doesn't know
Which ones. Some day we will try
To do as many things as are possible
And perhaps we shall succeed at a handful   160
Of them, but this will not have anything
To do with what is promised today, our
Landscape sweeping out from us to disappear
On the horizon. Today enough of a cover burnishes
To keep the supposition of promises together   165
In one piece of surface, letting one ramble
Back home from them so that these
Even stronger possibilities can remain
Whole without being tested. Actually
The skin of the bubble-chamber's as tough as   170
Reptile eggs; everything gets "programmed" there
In due course: more keeps getting included
Without adding to the sum, and just as one
Gets accustomed to a noise that
Kept one awake but now no longer does,   175
So the room contains this flow like an hourglass
Without varying in climate or quality
(Except perhaps to brighten bleakly and almost
Invisibly, in a focus sharpening toward death—more
Of this later). What should be the vacuum of a dream   180
Becomes continually replete as the source of dreams
Is being tapped so that this one dream
May wax, flourish like a cabbage rose,
Defying sumptuary laws,[7] leaving us
To awake and try to begin living in what   185
Has now become a slum. Sydney Freedberg in his
Parmigianino says of it: "Realism in this portrait
No longer produces an objective truth, but a *bizarria*[8] . . .
However its distortion does not create
A feeling of disharmony. . . . The forms retain   190
A strong measure of ideal beauty," because
Fed by our dreams, so inconsequential until one day
We notice the hole they left. Now their importance
If not their meaning is plain. They were to nourish
A dream which includes them all, as they are   195
Finally reversed in the accumulating mirror.
They seemed strange because we couldn't actually see them.
And we realize this only at a point where they lapse
Like a wave breaking on a rock, giving up

---

7. Laws regulating private behavior, in this case
mode of dress.

8. Distortion. Sydney J. Freedberg, *Parmigianino:
His Works in Painting* (1950).

Its shape in a gesture which expresses that shape.   200
The forms retain a strong measure of ideal beauty
As they forage in secret on our idea of distortion.
Why be unhappy with this arrangement, since
Dreams prolong us as they are absorbed?
Something like living occurs, a movement   205
Out of the dream into its codification.

As I start to forget it
It presents its stereotype again
But it is an unfamiliar stereotype, the face
Riding at anchor, issued from hazards, soon   210
To accost others, "rather angel than man" (Vasari).
Perhaps an angel looks like everything
We have forgotten, I mean forgotten
Things that don't seem familiar when
We meet them again, lost beyond telling,   215
Which were ours once. This would be the point
Of invading the privacy of this man who
"Dabbled in alchemy, but whose wish
Here was not to examine the subtleties of art
In a detached, scientific spirit: he wished through them   220
To impart the sense of novelty and amazement to the spectator"
(Freedberg). Later portraits such as the Uffizi
"Gentleman," the Borghese "Young Prelate" and
The Naples "Antea" issue from Mannerist
Tensions,[9] but here, as Freedberg points out,   225
The surprise, the tension are in the concept
Rather than its realization.
The consonance of the High Renaissance[1]
Is present, though distorted by the mirror.
What is novel is the extreme care in rendering   230
The velleities[2] of the rounded reflecting surface
(It is the first mirror portrait),
So that you could be fooled for a moment
Before you realize the reflection
Isn't yours. You feel then like one of those   235
Hoffmann[3] characters who have been deprived
Of a reflection, except that the whole of me
Is seen to be supplanted by the strict
Otherness of the painter in his
Other room. We have surprised him   240
At work, but no, he has surprised us
As he works. The picture is almost finished,
The surprise almost over, as when one looks out,
Startled by a snowfall which even now is

9. Mannerism was a style of painting in 16th-century Italy in which proportions or the laws of perspective were distorted to produce effects of tension or disturbance. "Uffizi" and "Borghese": galleries in Florence and Rome, respectively.
1. In Italian painting and architecture, the period in the late 15th and early 16th centuries in which the harmonious proportions ("consonance") of classical art were emulated and honored.
2. Subtle tendencies.
3. E. T. A. Hoffman (1776–1822), German author known for his tales of the supernatural.

Ending in specks and sparkles of snow. 245
It happened while you were inside, asleep,
And there is no reason why you should have
Been awake for it, except that the day
Is ending and it will be hard for you
To get to sleep tonight, at least until late. 250

The shadow of the city injects its own
Urgency: Rome where Francesco
Was at work during the Sack:[4] his inventions
Amazed the soldiers who burst in on him;
They decided to spare his life, but he left soon after; 255
Vienna where the painting is today, where
I saw it with Pierre in the summer of 1959; New York
Where I am now, which is a logarithm[5]
Of other cities. Our landscape
Is alive with filiations, shuttlings; 260
Business is carried on by look, gesture,
Hearsay. It is another life to the city,
The backing of the looking glass of the
Unidentified but precisely sketched studio. It wants
To siphon off the life of the studio, deflate 265
Its mapped space to enactments, island it.
That operation has been temporarily stalled
But something new is on the way, a new preciosity
In the wind. Can you stand it,
Francesco? Are you strong enough for it? 270
This wind brings what it knows not, is
Self-propelled, blind, has no notion
Of itself. It is inertia that once
Acknowledged saps all activity, secret or public:
Whispers of the word that can't be understood 275
But can be felt, a chill, a blight
Moving outward along the capes and peninsulas
Of your nervures and so to the archipelagoes
And to the bathed, aired secrecy of the open sea.
This is its negative side. Its positive side is 280
Making you notice life and the stresses
That only seemed to go away, but now,
As this new mode questions, are seen to be
Hastening out of style. If they are to become classics
They must decide which side they are on. 285
Their reticence has undermined
The urban scenery, made its ambiguities
Look willful and tired, the games of an old man.
What we need now is this unlikely
Challenger pounding on the gates of an amazed 290

4. In 1527 troops of the Hapsburg emperor Charles V sacked Rome in an assertion of power against Pope Clement VII.
5. Mathematical term referring to the power to which a fixed number (the base) must be raised to obtain a given number or variable. In Ashbery's work this is less a mathematical concept than an image of the way an apparently fixed concept can multiply or divide into other forms.

Castle. Your argument, Francesco,
Had begun to grow stale as no answer
Or answers were forthcoming. If it dissolves now
Into dust, that only means its time had come
Some time ago, but look now, and listen: 295
It may be that another life is stocked there
In recesses no one knew of; that it,
Not we, are the change; that we are in fact it
If we could get back to it, relive some of the way
It looked, turn our faces to the globe as it sets   300
And still be coming out all right:
Nerves normal, breath normal. Since it is a metaphor
Made to include us, we are a part of it and
Can live in it as in fact we have done,
Only leaving our minds bare for questioning   305
We now see will not take place at random
But in an orderly way that means to menace
Nobody—the normal way things are done,
Like the concentric growing up of days
Around a life: correctly, if you think about it.   310

A breeze like the turning of a page
Brings back your face: the moment
Takes such a big bite out of the haze
Of pleasant intuition it comes after.
The locking into place is "death itself,"   315
As Berg said of a phrase in Mahler's Ninth,[6]
Or, to quote Imogen in *Cymbeline*, "There cannot
Be a pinch in death more sharp than this,"[7] for,
Though only exercise or tactic, it carries
The momentum of a conviction that had been building.   320
Mere forgetfulness cannot remove it
Nor wishing bring it back, as long as it remains
The white precipitate[8] of its dream
In the climate of sighs flung across our world,
A cloth over a birdcage. But it is certain that   325
What is beautiful seems so only in relation to a specific
Life, experienced or not, channeled into some form
Steeped in the nostalgia of a collective past.
The light sinks today with an enthusiasm
I have known elsewhere, and known why   330
It seemed meaningful, that others felt this way
Years ago. I go on consulting
This mirror that is no longer mine
For as much brisk vacancy as is to be
My portion this time. And the vase is always full   335
Because there is only just so much room
And it accommodates everything. The sample

---

6. Alban Berg (1885–1935), Viennese composer
of twelve-tone music, speaking of the Ninth
Symphony of his predecessor, the Austrian composer Gustav Mahler (1860–1911).

7. Shakespeare, *Cymbeline* 1.1.131–32.
8. In chemistry, a solid deposit separated from a
solution.

One sees is not to be taken as
Merely that, but as everything as it
May be imagined outside time—not as a gesture   340
But as all, in the refined, assimilable state.
But what is this universe the porch of
As it veers in and out, back and forth,
Refusing to surround, us and still the only
Thing we can see? Love once   345
Tipped the scales but now is shadowed, invisible,
Though mysteriously present, around somewhere.
But we know it cannot be sandwiched
Between two adjacent moments, that its windings
Lead nowhere except to further tributaries   350
And that these empty themselves into a vague
Sense of something that can never be known
Even though it seems likely that each of us
Knows what it is and is capable of
Communicating it to the other. But the look   355
Some wear as a sign makes one want to
Push forward ignoring the apparent
Naïveté of the attempt, not caring
That no one is listening, since the light
Has been lit once and for all in their eyes   360
And is present, unimpaired, a permanent anomaly,
Awake and silent. On the surface of it
There seems no special reason why that light
Should be focused by love, or why
The city falling with its beautiful suburbs   365
Into space always less clear, less defined,
Should read as the support of its progress,
The easel upon which the drama unfolded
To its own satisfaction and to the end
Of our dreaming, as we had never imagined   370
It would end, in worn daylight with the painted
Promise showing through as a gage, a bond.
This nondescript, never-to-be defined daytime is
The secret of where it takes place
And we can no longer return to the various   375
Conflicting statements gathered, lapses of memory
Of the principal witnesses. All we know
Is that we are a little early, that
Today has that special, lapidary[9]
Todayness that the sunlight reproduces   380
Faithfully in casting twig-shadows on blithe
Sidewalks. No previous day would have been like this.
I used to think they were all alike,
That the present always looked the same to everybody
But this confusion drains away as one   385
Is always cresting into one's present.
Yet the "poetic," straw-colored space

9. Gemlike, precisely cut.

Of the long corridor that leads back to the painting,
Its darkening opposite—is this
Some figment of "art," not to be imagined
As real, let alone special? Hasn't it too its lair   390
In the present we are always escaping from
And falling back into, as the waterwheel of days
Pursues its uneventful, even serene course?
I think it is trying to say it is today   395
And we must get out of it even as the public
Is pushing through the museum now so as to
Be out by closing time. You can't live there.
The gray glaze of the past attacks all know-how:
Secrets of wash and finish that took a lifetime   400
To learn and are reduced to the status of
Black-and-white illustrations in a book where colorplates
Are rare. That is, all time
Reduces to no special time. No one
Alludes to the change; to do so might   405
Involve calling attention to oneself
Which would augment the dread of not getting out
Before having seen the whole collection
(Except for the sculptures in the basement:
They are where they belong).   410
Our time gets to be veiled, compromised
By the portrait's will to endure. It hints at
Our own, which we were hoping to keep hidden.
We don't need paintings or
Doggerel written by mature poets when   415
The explosion is so precise, so fine.
Is there any point even in acknowledging
The existence of all that? Does it
Exist? Certainly the leisure to
Indulge stately pastimes doesn't,   420
Any more. Today has no margins, the event arrives
Flush with its edges, is of the same substance,
Indistinguishable. "Play" is something else;
It exists, in a society specifically
Organized as a demonstration of itself.   425
There is no other way, and those assholes
Who would confuse everything with their mirror games
Which seem to multiply stakes and possibilities, or
At least confuse issues by means of an investing
Aura that would corrode the architecture   430
Of the whole in a haze of suppressed mockery,
Are beside the point. They are out of the game,
Which doesn't exist until they are out of it.
It seems like a very hostile universe
But as the principle of each individual thing is   435
Hostile to, exists at the expense of all the others
As philosophers have often pointed out, at least
This thing, the mute, undivided present,
Has the justification of logic, which

In this instance isn't a bad thing   440
Or wouldn't be, if the way of telling
Didn't somehow intrude, twisting the end result
Into a caricature of itself. This always
Happens, as in the game where
A whispered phrase passed around the room   445
Ends up as something completely different.
It is the principle that makes works of art so unlike
What the artist intended. Often he finds
He has omitted the thing he started out to say
In the first place. Seduced by flowers,   450
Explicit pleasures, he blames himself (though
Secretly satisfied with the result), imagining
He had a say in the matter and exercised
An option of which he was hardly conscious,
Unaware that necessity circumvents such resolutions   455
So as to create something new
For itself, that there is no other way,
That the history of creation proceeds according to
Stringent laws, and that things
Do get done in this way, but never the things   460
We set out to accomplish and wanted so desperately
To see come into being. Parmigianino
Must have realized this as he worked at his
Life-obstructing task. One is forced to read
The perfectly plausible accomplishment of a purpose   465
Into the smooth, perhaps even bland (but so
Enigmatic) finish. Is there anything
To be serious about beyond this otherness
That gets included in the most ordinary
Forms of daily activity, changing everything   470
Slightly and profoundly, and tearing the matter
Of creation, any creation, not just artistic creation
Out of our hands, to install it on some monstrous, near
Peak, too close to ignore, too far
For one to intervene? This otherness, this   475
"Not-being-us" is all there is to look at
In the mirror, though no one can say
How it came to be this way. A ship
Flying unknown colors has entered the harbor.
You are allowing extraneous matters   480
To break up your day, cloud the focus
Of the crystal ball. Its scene drifts away
Like vapor scattered on the wind. The fertile
Thought-associations that until now came
So easily, appear no more, or rarely. Their   485
Colorings are less intense, washed out
By autumn rains and winds, spoiled, muddied,
Given back to you because they are worthless.
Yet we are such creatures of habit that their
Implications are still around *en permanence*, confusing   490
Issues. To be serious only about sex

Is perhaps one way, but the sands are hissing
As they approach the beginning of the big slide
Into what happened. This past
Is now here: the painter's   495
Reflected face, in which we linger, receiving
Dreams and inspirations on an unassigned
Frequency, but the hues have turned metallic,
The curves and edges are not so rich. Each person
Has one big theory to explain the universe   500
But it doesn't tell the whole story
And in the end it is what is outside him
That matters, to him and especially to us
Who have been given no help whatever
In decoding our own man-size quotient and must rely   505
On second-hand knowledge. Yet I know
That no one else's taste is going to be
Any help, and might as well be ignored.
Once it seemed so perfect—gloss on the fine
Freckled skin, lips moistened as though about to part   510
Releasing speech, and the familiar look
Of clothes and furniture that one forgets.
This could have been our paradise: exotic
Refuge within an exhausted world, but that wasn't
In the cards, because it couldn't have been   515
The point. Aping naturalness may be the first step
Toward achieving an inner calm
But it is the first step only, and often
Remains a frozen gesture of welcome etched
On the air materializing behind it,   520
A convention. And we have really
No time for these, except to use them
For kindling. The sooner they are burnt up
The better for the roles we have to play.
Therefore I beseech you, withdraw that hand,   525
Offer it no longer as shield or greeting,
The shield of a greeting, Francesco:
There is room for one bullet in the chamber:
Our looking through the wrong end
Of the telescope as you fall back at a speed   530
Faster than that of light to flatten ultimately
Among the features of the room, an invitation
Never mailed, the "it was all a dream"
Syndrome, though the "all" tells tersely
Enough how it wasn't. Its existence   535
Was real, though troubled, and the ache
Of this waking dream can never drown out
The diagram still sketched on the wind,
Chosen, meant for me and materialized
In the disguising radiance of my room.   540
We have seen the city; it is the gibbous[1]

---

1. Irregularly rounded or convex (for example, the form of the moon between half moon and full moon).

Mirrored eye of an insect. All things happen
On its balcony and are resumed within,
But the action is the cold, syrupy flow
Of a pageant. One feels too confined,   545
Sifting the April sunlight for clues,
In the mere stillness of the ease of its
Parameter.[2] The hand holds no chalk
And each part of the whole falls off
And cannot know it knew, except   550
Here and there, in cold pockets
Of remembrance, whispers out of time.

       1975

Myrtle

How funny your name would be
if you could follow it back to where
the first person thought of saying it,
naming himself that, or maybe
some other persons thought of it   5
and named that person. It would
be like following a river to its source,
which would be impossible. Rivers have no source.
They just automatically appear at a place
where they get wider, and soon a real   10
river comes along, with fish and debris,
regal as you please, and someone
has already given it a name: St. Benno[1]
(saints are popular for this purpose) or, or
some other name, the name of his   15
long-lost girlfriend, who comes
at long last to impersonate that river,
on a stage, her voice clanking
like its bed, her clothing of sand
and pasted paper, a piece of real technology,   20
while all along she is thinking, I can
do what I want to do. But I want to stay here.

       1996

2. A constant whose values characterize the variables in a system.
1. St. Benno of Meissen (1010–1106), patron of angling.

W. S. MERWIN
b. 1927

" I started writing hymns for my father almost as soon as I could write at all, illus-trating them," W. S. Merwin has said. "I recall some rather stern little pieces addressed . . . to backsliders, but I can remember too wondering whether there might not be some liberating mode." William Stanley Merwin's father was a Presby-terian minister in Union, New Jersey, and Scranton, Pennsylvania, where Merwin grew up. Apart from hymn writing Merwin had almost no acquaintance with poetry until, on a scholarship, he entered Princeton University. There he read verse steadily and began to write with the encouragement of the poet John Berryman and the critic R. P. Blackmur, as well as his classmate, Galway Kinnell. Then Merwin's extensive study of foreign languages and literatures enabled him to find work as a tutor abroad. He remained, like Ezra Pound, apart from American literary institu-tions and became a translator of European literature, especially medieval romance and modern Symbolist poetry.

Merwin's continuing activity as a translator has been a resource and stimulus for his own poetry. In translating two great medieval epics, the French *Song of Roland* (1963) and the Spanish *The Poem of the Cid* (1959), his object was to bring into English a diction "rough, spare, sinewy, rapid" that would transmit the directness and energy of the world of chivalric imagination. His first book, *A Masque for Janus* (1952), includes ballads, songs, and carols—often based on medieval verse forms— the slightly antique diction of which gives an air of simple mystery to poems about love, inner heroism, and death.

In later books Merwin drew his subjects from a more clearly contemporary con-text. Many of the poems in *The Drunk in the Furnace* (1960) and *The Moving Target* (1963) are about members of his family and memories of his boyhood in Scranton. A further change came with *The Lice* (1967), a volume whose brief, prophetic poems reflect Merwin's despair at that time: he believed "the future was so bleak that there was no point in writing anything at all"; what happened was that "the poems kind of pushed their way upon me when I wasn't thinking about writing." This despair and an accompanying anger are palpable in a poem like "For a Coming Extinction." In many of these poems and those of volumes immediately following, Merwin tries to reach below the surface of urban American experience but without the benefit of narrative or preestablished metrical forms. He speaks through humble figures, as in "Peasant: His Prayer to the Powers of This World." Or he uses the most commonplace occurrences as a point of departure for meditation: "Evening, or Daybreak." His poems quickly become parables, spoken in a voice concerned less with descriptive detail than with archetypal elements: the ways in which each eve-ning prefigures death, each dawn the passing of time.

Of these short poems Merwin says: "What is needed for any particular nebulous unwritten hope that may become a poem is not a manipulable, more or less predict-able recurring pattern, but an unduplicatable resonance, something that would be like an echo except that it is repeating no sound." Hence his unpunctuated lines of varying lengths, which seem a series of related oracular phrases, each correspond-ing to a breath. The poems frequently use the metaphor of a threshold or door, locating the reader at a moment between life and death or between life and a visionary afterlife. The poet is stationed at that imagined spot between the past and the present or between the present and the future. In 1973 he prepared *Asian Figures*, a series of adaptations of Asian proverbs, that reflect his continuing interest in compact meditative forms such as rituals and prayers.

Merwin has always been concerned with absence, with what is silent, vanished, invisible, yet real. In many of the poems gathered in his *Selected Poems* (1988) and *The Rain in the Trees* (1988), this concern focuses on forms of life endangered by ecological destruction. Merwin resides primarily in Hawaii, and his book-length narrative poem *The Folding Cliffs* (1998) explores Hawaiian history while gathering together, in his description, "almost all of my interests—interests in nonliterate peoples, in their and our relation to the earth, to the primal sources of things, our relation to the natural world, . . . the destruction of the earth for abstract and greedy reasons." Merwin's singular power in both shorter and longer poems is beautifully evident in his collection *The River Sound* (1999). His *Migration: New and Selected Poems* (2005), which gathers work from the 1960s through 2005, received the National Book Award for poetry. *The Shadow of Sirius* (2008) won the Pulitzer Prize, and a two-volume edition of his *Collected Poems* was published by The Library of America in 2013. In 2010 Merwin was appointed the seventeenth Poet Laureate Consultant in Poetry to the Library of Congress.

The Drunk in the Furnace

For a good decade
The furnace stood in the naked gully, fireless
And vacant as any hat. Then when it was
No more to them than a hulking black fossil
To erode unnoticed with the rest of the junk-hill   5
By the poisonous creek, and rapidly to be added
    To their ignorance.

They were afterwards astonished
To confirm, one morning, a twist of smoke like a pale
Resurrection, staggering out of its chewed hole,   10
And to remark then other tokens that someone,
Cosily bolted behind the eye-holed iron
Door of the drafty burner, had there established
    His bad castle.

Where he gets his spirits   15
It's a mystery. But the stuff keeps him musical:
Hammer-and-anvilling with poker and bottle
To his jugged bellowings, till the last groaning clang
As he collapses onto the rioting
Springs of a litter of car-seats ranged on the grates,   20
    To sleep like an iron pig.

In their tar-paper church
On a text about stoke-holes that are sated never
Their Reverend lingers. They nod and hate trespassers.
When the furnace wakes, though, all afternoon   25

Their witless offspring flock like piped rats[1] to its siren
Crescendo, and agape on the crumbling ridge
        Stand in a row and learn.

                                                    1960

For the Anniversary of My Death

Every year without knowing it I have passed the day
When the last fires will wave to me
And the silence will set out
Tireless traveller
Like the beam of a lightless star   5

Then I will no longer
Find myself in life as in a strange garment
Surprised at the earth
And the love of one woman
And then shamelessness of men   10
As today writing after three days of rain
Hearing the wren sing and the falling cease
And bowing not knowing to what

                                                    1967

For a Coming Extinction

Gray whale
Now that we are sending you to The End
That great god
Tell him
That we who follow you invented forgiveness   5
And forgive nothing

I write as though you could understand
And I could say it
One must always pretend something
Among the dying   10
When you have left the seas nodding on their stalks
Empty of you

Tell him that we were made
On another day[1]

1. Allusion to the Pied Piper of Hamelin, whose piping lured the rats from the town; when he was not paid, he lured away the children as well.
1. In Genesis 1, God creates humans on the sixth day and gives them dominion over all other creatures in the world. The animals had been created on the fifth and sixth days.

The bewilderment will diminish like an echo   15
Winding along your inner mountains
Unheard by us
And find its way out
Leaving behind it the future
Dead   20
And ours

When you will not see again
The whale calves trying the light
Consider what you will find in the black garden
And its court   25
The sea cows the Great Auks the gorillas[2]
The irreplaceable hosts ranged countless
And fore-ordaining as stars
Our sacrifices
Join your word to theirs   30
Tell him
That it is we who are important

                                                            1967

Losing a Language

A breath leaves the sentences and does not come back
yet the old still remember something that they could say

but they know now that such things are no longer believed
and the young have fewer words

many of the things the words were about   5
no longer exist

the noun for standing in mist by a haunted tree
the verb for I

the children will not repeat
the phrases their parents speak   10

somebody has persuaded them
that it is better to say everything differently

so that they can be admired somewhere
farther and farther away

where nothing that is here is known   15
we have little to say to each other

---

2. Animals extinct or endangered. Sea cows are large walruslike animals. The great auks were large flightless sea birds.

we are wrong and dark
in the eyes of the new owners

the radio is incomprehensible
the day is glass   20

when there is a voice at the door it is foreign
everywhere instead of a name there is a lie

nobody has seen it happening
nobody remembers

this is what the words were made   25
to prophesy

here are the extinct feathers
here is the rain we saw

1988

Lament for the Makers[1]

I that all through my early days
I remember well was always
    the youngest of the company
    save for one sister after me

from the time when I was able   5
to walk under the dinner table
    and be punished for that promptly
    because its leaves could fall on me

father and mother overhead
who they talked with and what they said   10
    were mostly clouds that knew already
    directions far too old for me

at school I skipped a grade so that
whatever I did after that
    each year everyone would be   15
    older and hold it up to me

at college many of my friends
were returning veterans

---

1. The title and stanza form of this poem are taken from the Scots poet William Dunbar (c. 1460–c. 1520), whose "Lament for the Makers" mourns the passing of fellow poets and confesses the poet's fear of mortality. Merwin's poem like- wise commemorates the passing of fellow poets, a number of whom are represented in this anthology and can be found by consulting the index. Only the names of those poets not repre- sented in this volume are annotated here.

equipped with an authority
I admired and they treated me   20

as the kid some years below them
so I married half to show them
    and listened with new vanity
    when I heard it said to me

how young I was and what a shock   25
I was the youngest on the block
    I thought I had it coming to me
    and I believe it mattered to me

and seemed my own and there to stay
for a while then came the day   30
    I was in another country
    other older friends around me

my youth by then taken for granted
and found that it had been supplanted
    the notes in some anthology   35
    listed persons born after me

how long had that been going on
how could I be not quite so young
    and not notice and nobody
    even bother to inform me   40

though my fond hopes were taking longer
than I had hoped when I was younger
    a phrase that came more frequently
    to suggest itself to me

but the secret was still there   45
safe in the unprotected air
    that breath that in its own words only
    sang when I was a child to me

and caught me helpless to convey it
with nothing but the words to say it   50
    though it was those words completely
    and they rang it was clear to me

with a changeless overtone
I have listened for since then
    hearing that note endlessly   55
    vary every time beyond me

trying to find where it comes from
and to what words it may come
    and forever after be
    present for the thought kept at me   60

that my mother and every day
of our lives would slip away
    like the summer and suddenly
    all would have been taken from me

but that presence I had known   65
sometimes in words would not be gone
    and if it spoke even once for me
    it would stay there and be me

however few might choose those words
for listening to afterwards   70
    there I would be awake to see
    a world that looked unchanged to me

I suppose that was what I thought
young as I was then and that note
    sang from the words of somebody   75
    in my twenties I looked around me

to all the poets who were then
living and whose lines had been
    sustenance and company
    and a light for years to me   80

I found the portraits of their faces
first in the rows of oval spaces
    in Oscar Williams' Treasury[2]
    so they were settled long before me

and they would always be the same   85
in that distance of their fame
    affixed in immortality
    during their lifetimes while around me

all was woods seen from a train
no sooner glimpsed than gone again   90
    but those immortals constantly
    in some measure reassured me

then first there was Dylan Thomas
from the White Horse[3] taken from us
    to the brick wall I woke to see   95
    for years across the street from me

then word of the death of Stevens
brought a new knowledge of silence

---

2. Oscar Williams's *A Little Treasury of Modern Poetry* (1950), an anthology containing some of the major English and American modernists, featured on its cover oval portraits of the poets represented.

3. Thomas (1914–1953), a Welsh poet, collapsed at the White Horse Tavern in Greenwich Village, and subsequently died, after drinking heavily while in New York City to take part in a reading of his play, *Under Milk Wood* (1954).

the nothing but there finally
the sparrow saying *Be thou me*   100

how long his long auroras had
played on the darkness overhead
 since I looked up from my Shelley
 and Arrowsmith[4] first showed him to me

and not long from his death until   105
Edwin Muir[5] had fallen still
 that fine bell of the latter day
 not well heard yet it seems to me

Sylvia Plath then took her own
direction into the unknown   110
 from her last stars and poetry
 in the house a few blocks from me

Williams[6] a little afterwards
was carried off by the black rapids
 that flowed through Paterson as he   115
 said and their rushing sound is in me

that was the time that gathered Frost[7]
into the dark where he was lost
 to us but from too far to see
 his voice keeps coming back to me   120

at the number he had uttered
to the driver a last word
 then that watchful and most lonely
 wanderer whose words went with me

everywhere Elizabeth   125
Bishop lay alone in death
 they were leaving the party early
 our elders it came home to me

but the needle moved among us
taking always by surprise   130
 flicking by too fast to see
 to touch a friend born after me

4. William Arrowsmith (1924–1992), scholar and translator, was a classmate and friend of Merwin's when they were undergraduates at Princeton University. "Be Thou Me" appears in canto VI of "It Must Change," from Wallace Stevens's long poem *Notes Toward a Supreme Fiction*: "Bethou me, said sparrow, to the crackled blade, / And you, and you, bethou me as you blow, / When in my coppice you behold me be." Stevens (1879–1955) is echoing canto V of Percy Bysshe Shelley (1792–1822), "Ode to the West Wind":

"Be thou, Spirit Fierce, / My spirit. Be thou me, impetuous one!" Another of Stevens's long poems is titled "The Auroras of Autumn."
5. Scottish poet (1887–1963).
6. William Carlos Williams (1883–1963), American modernist poet whose work includes the long autobiographical poem *Paterson*.
7. Robert Frost (1874–1963), American poet whose works include "Stopping by Woods on a Snowy Evening."

and James Wright by his darkened river
heard the night heron pass over
    took his candle down the frosty 135
    road and disappeared before me

Howard Moss[8] had felt the gnawing
at his name and found that nothing
    made it better he was funny
    even so about it to me 140

Graves[9] in his nineties lost the score
forgot that he had died before
    found his way back innocently
    who once had been a guide to me

Nemerov[1] sadder than his verse 145
said a new year could not be worse
    then the black flukes of agony
    went down leaving the words with me

Stafford[2] watched his hand catch the light
seeing that it was time to write 150
    a memento of their story
    signed and is a plain before me

then the sudden news that Ted
Roethke had been found floating dead
    in someone's pool at night but he 155
    still rises from his lines for me

and on the rimless wheel in turn
Eliot[3] spun and Jarrell was borne
    off by a car who had loved to see
    the racetrack then there came to me 160

one day the knocking at the garden
door and the news that Berryman
    from the bridge had leapt who twenty
    years before had quoted to me

the passage where *a jest* wrote Crane 165
falls from the speechless caravan[4]
    with a wave to bones and Henry[5]
    and to all that he had told me

---

8. American poet (1922–1987).
9. Robert Graves (1895–1985), poet and translator whose work includes *The White Goddess* (1944). As a young man Merwin worked for a short time as a tutor for Graves's children.
1. Howard Nemerov (1920–1991), American poet.
2. William Stafford (1914–1993), American poet.

3. T. S. Eliot (1888–1965), Anglo-American modernist poet.
4. Hart Crane (1899–1952), American poet, author of the poetic sequence *The Bridge* (1930), from which the lines in italics are taken.
5. Characters in John Berryman's *Dream Songs*, selections from which appear in this volume.

I dreamed that Auden[6] sat up in bed
but I could not catch what he said   170
   by the time he was already
   dead someone next morning told me

and Marianne Moore entered the ark
Pound[7] would say no more from the dark
   who once had helped to set me free   175
   I thought of the prose around me

and David Jones[8] would rest until
the turn of time under the hill
   but from the sleep of Arthur[9] he
   wakes an echo that follows me   180

Lowell thought the shadow skyline
coming toward him was Manhattan
   but it blacked out in the taxi
   once he read his *Notebook* to me

now Jimmy Merrill's voice is heard   185
like an aria afterward
   and we know he will never be
   old after all who spoke to me

on the cold street that last evening
of his heart that leapt at finding   190
   some yet unknown poetry
   then waved through the window to me

in that city we were born in
one by one they have all gone
   out of the time and language we   195
   had in common which have brought me

to this season after them
the best words did not keep them from
   leaving themselves finally
   as this day is going from me   200

and the clear note they were hearing
never promised anything
   but the true sound of brevity
   that will go on after me

1996

---

6. W. H. Auden (1907–1973), Anglo-American poet.
7. Marianne Moore (1887–1972) and Ezra Pound (1885–1972), American modernist poets.
8. Anglo-Welsh artist and poet (1895–1974).
9. The legendary King Arthur, who ruled over the Knights of the Round Table, figures in several of David Jones's poems and essays.

Ceremony after an Amputation

Spirits of the place who were here before I saw it
    to whom I have made such offerings as I have known how to make
    wanting from the first to approach you with recognition
    bringing for your swept ridge trees lining the wind with seedlings
    that have grown now to become these long wings in chorus   5
    where the birds assemble and settle their flying lives
    you have taught me without meaning and have lifted me up
    without talk or promise and again and again reappeared to me
    unmistakable and changing and unpronounceable as a face

dust of the time a day in late spring after the silk of rain   10
    had fallen softly through the night and after the green morning
    the afternoon floating brushed with gold and then the sounds
    of machines erupting across the valley and elbowing up the slopes
    pushing themselves forward to occupy you to be more of you
    who remain the untouched silence through which they are passing   15
    I try to hear you remembering that we are not separate
    to find you who cannot be lost or elsewhere or incomplete

nature of the solitary machine coming into the story
    from the minds that conceived you and the hands that first
        conjured up
    the phantom of you in fine lines on the drawing board   20
    you for whom function is all the good that exists
    you to whom I have come with nothing but purpose
    a purpose of my own as though it was something we shared
    you that were pried from the earth without anyone
    consulting you and were carried off burned beaten metamorphosed 25
    according to plans and lives to which you owed nothing

let us be at peace with each other let peace be what is between us
    and you now single vanished part of my left hand bit of bone
        finger-end index
    who began with me in the dark that was already my mother
    you who touched whatever I could touch of the beginning   30
    and were how I touched and who remembered the sense of it
    when I thought I had forgotten it you in whom it waited
    under your only map of one untrodden mountain
    you who did as well as we could through all the hours at the piano
    and who helped undo the bras and found our way to the treasure   35

and who held the fruit and the pages and knew how to button
    my right cuff and to wash my left ear and had taken in
    heart beats of birds and beloved faces and hair by day and by night
    fur of dogs ears of horses tongues and the latches of doors
    so that I still feel them clearly long after they are gone   40
    and lake water beside the boat one evening of an ancient summer
    and the vibration of a string over which a bow was moving
    as though the sound of the note were still playing
    and the hand of my wife found in the shallows of waking

you who in a flicker of my inattention   45
      signalled to me once only my error telling me
      of the sudden blow from the side so that I looked down
      to see not you any longer but instead a mouth
      full of blood calling after you who had already gone gone
      gone ahead into what I cannot know or reach or touch   50
      leaving in your place only the cloud of pain rising
      into the day filling the light possessing every sound
      becoming the single color and taste and direction

yet as the pain recedes and the moment of it
      you remain with me even in the missing of you   55
      small boat moving before me on the current under the daylight
      whatever you had touched and had known and took with you
      is with me now as you are when you are already there
      unseen part of me reminding me warning me
      pointing to what I cannot see never letting me forget   60
      you are my own speaking only to me going with me
      all the rest of the way telling me what is still here

                                                                          2000

JAMES WRIGHT
1927–1980

"My name is James A. Wright, and I was born / Twenty-five miles from this infected grave, / In Martins Ferry, Ohio, where one slave / To Hazel-Atlas Glass became my father"; so James Wright introduced himself in an early poem, "At the Executed Murderer's Grave." The angry assertiveness in these lines suggests his embattled relations with an America he loves and hates. This America is symbolized for him by the landscape of Ohio, in particular by Martins Ferry, just across the Ohio River from Wheeling, West Virginia, the home of Wheeling Steel and of the glass factory where his father worked for fifty years. In Wright's work this landscape is harsh evidence of the way the social world has contaminated a natural world infinitely more beautiful and self-restoring. The same social world that destroys the landscape also turns its back on those whose lives meet failure or defeat, and Wright's deep knowledge of defeat and his anger at this exclusion lead him to the murderer's grave. It is not simply that Wright sympathizes with social outcasts, but rather, as Robert Hass acutely pointed out, "the suffering of other people, particularly the lost and the derelict, is actually a part of his own emotional life. It is what he writes from, not what he writes about." As a poet who writes out of loss, Wright is elegiac, memorializing a vanished beauty and lost hopes. So deep is his sense of loss that he will sometimes identify with anyone and anything that is scarred or wounded ("I am not a happy man by talent," he once said. "Sometimes I have been very happy, but characteristically I'm a miserable son of a bitch"). Any serious reading of his work has to contend with sorting out those poems in which this identification is unthinking and sentimental, poems where Wright suggests that all forms of suffering and defeat are equal and alike. What remains in some of his best work is a curiously tough-minded tenderness at work in his exploration of despair. He admires, for example, the sumac flourishing in the Ohio landscape, its bark so tough it "will turn aside hatchets and knife blades" ("The Sumac in Ohio").

When Wright finished high school, he joined the army. In 1948 he left the military to attend Kenyon College in Ohio on the G.I. Bill. ("I applied to several schools in Ohio," he once said, "and they all said no except Kenyon College. So I went there.") He was lucky in his teachers; at Kenyon he studied with John Crowe Ransom and, after a Fulbright scholarship to the University of Vienna, he went to the University of Washington, where he studied with the poet Theodore Roethke and also became a close friend of Richard Hugo's. At Washington he wrote a Ph.D. dissertation on Charles Dickens and received the degree in 1959. Thereafter he became a teacher, first at the University of Minnesota, Minneapolis (1957–64), and later at Hunter College, New York (1966–80).

From both Ransom and Roethke, Wright learned poetic form. From Ransom in particular he took what he called "the Horatian ideal" of the carefully made, unified poem. Wright would later say that were he to choose a master, he would choose the Latin poet Horace, "who was able to write humorously and kindly in flawless verse." The Horatian impulse in Wright—restrained, formal, sometimes satirical— helps hold in check a deep-seated romanticism that idealizes nature and the unconscious. His first two books, *The Green Wall* (1957), chosen to appear in the Yale Younger Poets series, and *Saint Judas* (1959), are formal and literary in style although much of their subject matter (the murderer, the lunatic, a deaf child) might be called Romantic. Wright seems in these books closest to Thomas Hardy, Robert Frost, and Edwin Arlington Robinson. But in the 1960s, like a great many other American poets, he moved away from traditional forms, explored more open and improvisatory poetic structures, and began to depend heavily on what his fellow poet Robert Bly called "the deep image." Wright had been translating the work of Spanish poets often associated with surrealism—Pablo Neruda, César Vallejo, and Juan Ramón Jiménez—as well as the German Georg Trakl (whom he translated in collaboration with Bly), and he took from them, in part, a reliance on the power of a poetic image to evoke association deep within the unconscious. He followed his volume *The Branch Will Not Break* (1963) with two books, *Shall We Gather at the River* (1968) and *Two Citizens* (1974), in which he began to overwork certain images ("stone," "dark"), as if repetition were a substitute for clarity. Some of the poems in these books succeed in carrying us into areas of experience that resist the discursive, but the effect of a number of poems is to exclude conscious intelligence, to celebrate "whatever is not mind," as Robert Hass has pointed out. It is as if Wright responded to the scarred landscape outside (and inside) him by fleeing to an inwardness so deep it could not partake of thought or expression.

But Wright's love of clarity and form and his ability to see through pretensions (including his own) resurface in *Moments of the Italian Summer* (1976), *To a Blossoming Pear Tree* (1977), and his posthumous last collection, *This Journey* (1982). Restored to a unity of thinking and feeling, many of the poems in these books convey the flawed beauty of the world with a loving and witty tenderness. He often writes with particular feeling about creatures—finches, lizards, hermit crabs— whose liveliness and fragility touch him (in this and other regards his work has been important to the poet Mary Oliver). In "A Finch Sitting Out a Windstorm," his final portrait of the finch suggests admiration of its stubborness in the face of loss: "But his face is as battered / As Carmen Basilio's. / He never listens / To me."

Though the poems of his final book do not abandon the anger he feels thinking of the ruined landscapes of Ohio, the European setting of many of the poems extends his sense of ruin into a knowledge of how time chips away at all human creation,

with or without the help of men and women. Although he had claimed to be consti-
tutionally unhappy, the poems of *This Journey* suggest that before his death from
cancer a deep happiness took him by surprise. We turn to Wright's work for its fierce
understanding of defeat, for its blend of American speech rhythms with the formal
music of poetry, and for the loveliness he finds in the imperfect and neglected.
Accustomed to expect the worst, he had an enduring capacity to be astonished by
this loveliness, as in this childhood memory of a trip to the icehouse with his father:
"We stood and breathed the rising steam of that amazing winter, and carried away
in our wagon the immense fifty-pound diamond, while the old man chipped us each
a jagged little chunk and then walked behind us, his hands so calm they were trembling for us, trembling with exquisite care" ("The Ice House").

Autumn Begins in Martins Ferry, Ohio

In the Shreve High football stadium,
I think of Polacks nursing long beers in Tiltonsville,
And gray faces of Negroes in the blast furnace at Benwood,[1]
And the ruptured night watchman of Wheeling Steel,
Dreaming of heroes.   5

All the proud fathers are ashamed to go home.
Their women cluck like starved pullets,
Dying for love.

Therefore,
Their sons grow suicidally beautiful   10
At the beginning of October,
And gallop terribly against each other's bodies.

                                                              1963

To the Evening Star: Central Minnesota

Under the water tower at the edge of town
A huge Airedale ponders a long ripple
In the grass fields beyond.
Miles off, a whole grove silently
Flies up into the darkness.   5
One light comes on in the sky,
One lamp on the prairie.

Beautiful daylight of the body, your hands carry seashells.
West of this wide plain,
Animals wilder than ours   10
Come down from the green mountains in the darkness.

---

1. A town south of Martins Ferry, where the Wheeling Steel Works are located. Tiltonsville is a town in
easternmost Ohio, north of Martins Ferry.

Now they can see you, they know
The open meadows are safe.

1963

A Blessing

Just off the highway to Rochester, Minnesota,
Twilight bounds softly forth on the grass.
And the eyes of those two Indian ponies
Darken with kindness.
They have come gladly out of the willows   5
To welcome my friend and me.
We step over the barbed wire into the pasture
Where they have been grazing all day, alone.
They ripple tensely, they can hardly contain their happiness
That we have come.   10
They bow shyly as wet swans. They love each other.
There is no loneliness like theirs.
At home once more,
They begin munching the young tufts of spring in the darkness.
I would like to hold the slenderer one in my arms,   15
For she has walked over to me
And nuzzled my left hand.
She is black and white,
Her mane falls wild on her forehead,
And the light breeze moves me to caress her long ear   20
That is delicate as the skin over a girl's wrist.
Suddenly I realize
That if I stepped out of my body I would break
Into blossom.

1963

A Centenary Ode: Inscribed to Little Crow,
Leader of the Sioux Rebellion in Minnesota, 1862[1]

I had nothing to do with it. I was not here.
I was not born.
In 1862, when your hotheads
Raised hell from here to South Dakota,
My own fathers scattered into West Virginia   5
And southern Ohio.
My family fought the Confederacy

1. Under Little Crow a group of Sioux attacked and killed more than eight hundred settlers and soldiers in Minnesota. They were eventually routed by federal troops. About a month later Little Crow, while foraging for food, was shot by white farmers.

And fought the Union.[2]
None of them got killed.
But for all that, it was not my fathers   10
Who murdered you.
Not much.

I don't know
Where the fathers of Minneapolis finalized
Your flayed carcass.   15
Little Crow, true father
Of my dark America.
When I close my eyes I lose you among
Old loneliness.
My family were a lot of singing drunks and good carpenters.   20
We had brothers who loved one another no matter what they did.
And they did plenty.

I think they would have run like hell from your Sioux.
And when you caught them you all would have run like hell
From the Confederacy and from the Union   25
Into the hills and hunted for a few things,
Some bull-cat under the stones, a gar[3] maybe,
If you were hungry, and if you were happy,
Sunfish and corn.

If only I knew where to mourn you,   30
I would surely mourn.

But I don't know.

I did not come here only to grieve
For my people's defeat.
The troops of the Union, who won,   35
Still outnumber us.
Old Paddy Beck, my great-uncle, is dead
At the old soldiers' home near Tiffen, Ohio.
He got away with every last stitch
Of his uniform, save only   40
The dress trousers.

Oh all around us,
The hobo jungles of America grow wild again.
The pick handles bloom like your skinned spine.
I don't even know where   45
My own grave is.

1971

---

2. During the Civil War members of Wright's family fought on both sides of the conflict.

3. Long pikelike freshwater fish. "Bull-cat": catfish.

With the Shell of a Hermit Crab

Lugete, O Veneres Cupidinesque[1]
—Catullus

This lovely little life whose toes
Touched the white sand from side to side,
How delicately no one knows,
Crept from his loneliness, and died.

From deep waters long miles away   5
He wandered, looking for his name,
And all he found was you and me,
A quick life and a candle flame.

Today, you happen to be gone.
I sit here in the raging hell,   10
The city of the dead, alone,
Holding a little empty shell.

I peer into his tiny face.
It looms too huge for me to bear.
Two blocks away the sea gives place   15
To river. Both are everywhere.

I reach out and flick out the light.
Darkly I touch his fragile scars,
So far away, so delicate,
Stars in a wilderness of stars.   20

1977

1. Mourn, O Venuses and Cupids (Latin). The opening line of the ancient Roman poet Catullus's "Poem 3," a mock-elegy on the death of his mistress's bird.

PHILIP LEVINE
1928–2015

In one of his poems Philip Levine imagines a former life "as a small, quick fox" who stands "in the pathway shouting and refusing / to budge, feeling the dignity / of the small creature menaced / by the many and larger" ("The Fox"). This self-portrait has Levine's characteristic humor, but it aptly renders his deep, even stubborn, sympathy with ordinary men and women and his equally stubborn antipathy toward those who look down on ordinary life. Levine shared the faith of his favorite poet, Walt Whitman, in an inclusive, democratic poetry, and, with Whitman, he could boast that he was "one of the roughs."

Levine was born to a Jewish family in Detroit, Michigan, and began factory work at fourteen, during the war years. He continued to work while he attended Wayne (now Wayne State) University in Detroit and had what he called "a succession of stupid jobs"—working in a bottling corporation, for Cadillac, for Chevrolet Gear and Axle, and for Wyandotte Chemical Company. At one point in his life he also trained as a boxer. In 1957 he received an MFA from the University of Iowa, where the poets John Berryman and Robert Lowell were his teachers. In 1958 he moved to California and taught for many years at California State University at Fresno, where his students included Sherley Ann Williams, David St. John, Luis Omar Salinas, and Gary Soto. In the mid-1960s he went to Spain for the first time and felt "when I looked at the Spanish landscape I was looking at a part of myself. . . . In a year I began to become Catalan in a small way." He would later edit and translate the work of two Spanish poets, Gloria Fuentes and Jaime Sabines. For many years he taught at New York University.

His fellow poet Galway Kinnell once suggested that Levine "used to hold something back as if for fear poetry would betray him into tenderness. In his recent poems, it has done exactly that." Although an anger at society energizes many Levine poems—including the title poem of his book *They Feed They Lion* (1972), a response to the 1967 riots in his native Detroit—his twenty-some volumes of poetry demonstrate a wide range of feeling. At heart he is a narrative poet, even in his brief lyrics, like Thomas Hardy or Robert Penn Warren—both of whom he admired. His stories most often tell of loss and remembrance, and Levine's elegiac strain is one source of his tenderness. Feeling himself in a world where "No One Remembers" (the title of one of his poems), where life is characterized by impermanence, his poems re-create the people, landscapes, and events that make up—as the title of his 1976 collection puts it—*The Names of the Lost*. His books, *What Work Is* (1991), *The Simple Truth* (1994), *The Mercy* (1999), *Breath* (2004), and *News of the World* (2007), show Levine using the full range of his gifts—his narrative skill, his affection and respect for the ordinary person, his acute sense of place—with increasing ambition and rhythmic power.

With its rapid motion between the colloquial and the lyrical, Levine's best work has a distinctively gritty radiance. A strong, physical sense grounds his powerful nostalgia, giving us a world we can see and touch. Levine called himself a Romantic, and one of the dangers in his work is its tendency to inflate experience. Saving him from such inflation, though, is a lively, subversive, comic sense often directed at himself. His memorable poems are energetic; they vary the stresses of syntax against the short, trimeter line in which he often composes and accumulate power as they move along. But Levine's lines can sometimes seem arbitrary, as if what we really had was prose broken into pieces. In the work of the poets he most admired, Levine often argued, the failures do not matter—all that matters are the genuine poems. His own best poems rise out of a world we inhabit in common, where the experiences of ordinary life and work are transfused with energy and feeling. On Levine's appointment as Poet Laureate for 2011–12, he was called a laureate "of the industrial heartland."

Animals Are Passing from Our Lives

It's wonderful how I jog
on four honed-down ivory toes
my massive buttocks slipping
like oiled parts with each light step.

I'm to market. I can smell   5
the sour, grooved block, I can smell
the blade that opens the hole
and the pudgy white fingers

that shake out the intestines
like a hankie. In my dreams   10
the snouts drool on the marble,
suffering children, suffering flies,

suffering the consumers
who won't meet their steady eyes
for fear they could see. The boy   15
who drives me along believes

that any moment I'll fall
on my side and drum my toes
like a typewriter or squeal
and shit like a new housewife   20

discovering television,
or that I'll turn like a beast
cleverly to hook his teeth
with my teeth. No. Not this pig.

                                                          1968

Detroit Grease Shop Poem

Four bright steel crosses,
universal joints,[1] plucked
out of the burlap sack—
"the heart of the drive train,"
the book says. Stars   5
on Lemon's wooden palm,
stars that must be capped,
rolled, and anointed,
that have their orders
and their commands as he   10
has his.
                    Under the blue
hesitant light another day
at Automotive
in the city of dreams.
We're all here to count   15
and be counted, Lemon,
Rosie, Eugene, Luis,
and me, too young to know

---

1. Shaft couplings designed to transmit rotation from one shaft to another.

this is for keeps, pinning   20
on my apron, rolling up
my sleeves.
         The roof leaks
from yesterday's rain,
the waters gather above us   25
waiting for one mistake.
When a drop falls on Lemon's
corded arm, he looks at it
as though it were something
rare or mysterious   30
like a drop of water or
a single lucid meteor
fallen slowly from
nowhere and burning on
his skin like a tear.   35

1972

Starlight

My father stands in the warm evening
on the porch of my first house.
I am four years old and growing tired.
I see his head among the stars,
the glow of his cigarette, redder   5
than the summer moon riding
low over the old neighborhood: We
are alone, and he asks me if I am happy.
"Are you happy?" I cannot answer.
I do not really understand the word,   10
and the voice, my father's voice, is not
his voice, but somehow thick and choked,
a voice I have not heard before, but
heard often since. He bends and passes
a thumb beneath each of my eyes.   15
The cigarette is gone, but I can smell
the tiredness that hangs on his breath.
He has found nothing, and he smiles
and holds my head with both his hands.
Then he lifts me to his shoulder,   20
and now I too am there among the stars,
as tall as he. Are you happy? I say.
He nods in answer, Yes! oh yes! oh yes!
And in that new voice he says nothing,
holding my head tight against his head,   25
his eyes closed up against the starlight,
as though those tiny blinking eyes
of light might find a tall, gaunt child

holding his child against the promises
of autumn, until the boy slept   30
never to waken in that world again.

                                                                    1979

The Simple Truth

I bought a dollar and a half's worth of small red potatoes,
took them home, boiled them in their jackets
and ate them for dinner with a little butter and salt.
Then I walked through the dried fields
on the edge of town. In middle June the light   5
hung on in the dark furrows at my feet,
and in the mountain oaks overhead the birds
were gathering for the night, the jays and mockers
squawking back and forth, the finches still darting
into the dusty light. The woman who sold me   10
the potatoes was from Poland; she was someone
out of my childhood in a pink spangled sweater and sunglasses
praising the perfection of all her fruits and vegetables
at the road-side stand and urging me to taste
even the pale, raw sweet corn trucked all the way,   15
she swore, from New Jersey. "Eat, eat," she said,
"Even if you don't I'll say you did."
                                        Some things
you know all your life. They are so simple and true
they must be said without elegance, meter and rhyme,   20
they must be laid on the table beside the salt shaker,
the glass of water, the absence of light gathering
in the shadows of picture frames, they must be
naked and alone, they must stand for themselves.
My friend Henri and I arrived at this together in 1965   25
before I went away, before he began to kill himself,
and the two of us to betray our love. Can you taste
what I'm saying? It is onions or potatoes, a pinch
of simple salt, the wealth of melting butter, it is obvious,
it stays in the back of your throat like a truth   30
you never uttered because the time was always wrong,
it stays there for the rest of your life, unspoken,
made of that dirt we call earth, the metal we call salt,
in a form we have no words for, and you live on it.

                                                                    1996

ANNE SEXTON
1928–1974

Anne Sexton's first book of poems, *To Bedlam and Part Way Back* (1960), was published at a time when the label "confessional" came to be attached to poems more frankly autobiographical than had been usual in American verse. For Sexton the term is particularly apt. Although she had abandoned the Roman Catholicism into which she was born, her poems enact something analogous to preparing for and receiving religious absolution.

Sexton's confessions were to be made in terms more startling than the traditional Catholic images of her childhood. The purpose of her poems was not to analyze or explain behavior but to make it palpable in all its ferocity of feeling. Poetry "should be a shock to the senses. It should also hurt." This is apparent in both her themes and the ways in which she exhibits her subjects. Sexton writes about sex, illegitimacy, guilt, madness, and suicide. *To Bedlam* portrays her breakdown, her time in a mental hospital, her efforts at reconciliation with her daughter and husband when she returns. Her second book, *All My Pretty Ones* (1962), takes its title from Shakespeare's *Macbeth* and refers to the deaths of both her parents within three months of one another. Later books—*Live or Die* (1966), *The Death Notebooks* (1974), and *The Awful Rowing toward God* (1975; posthumous)—act out a debate about suicide and prefigure Sexton's taking of her own life. And yet, as the poet's tender address to her daughter in "Little Girl, My String Bean, My Lovely Woman" suggests, Sexton's work ranges beyond an obsession with death.

Sexton spoke of images as "the heart of poetry. Images come from the unconscious. Imagination and the unconscious are one and the same." Powerful images substantiate the strangeness of feelings and through them the poet attempts to redefine experiences so as to gain understanding, absolution, or revenge. Sexton's poems, poised between, as her titles suggest, life and death or "bedlam and part way back," are efforts at establishing a middle ground of self-assertion, substituting surreal images for the reductive versions of life visible to the exterior eye.

Sexton was born in 1928 in Newton, Massachusetts, and attended Garland Junior College. She came to poetry fairly late—when she was twenty-eight, after seeing the critic I. A. Richards lecturing about the sonnet on television. In the late 1950s she attended poetry workshops in the Boston area, including Robert Lowell's poetry seminars at Boston University. One of her fellow students was Sylvia Plath, whose suicide she commemorated in a poem, "Sylvia's Death." Sexton claimed that she was less influenced by Lowell's *Life Studies* than by W. D. Snodgrass's autobiographical *Heart's Needle* (1959), but certainly Lowell's support and the association with Plath left their mark on her and made it possible for her to publish. Although her career was relatively brief, she received several major literary prizes, including the Pulitzer Prize for *Live or Die* and an American Academy of Arts and Letters traveling fellowship. Her suicide came after a series of mental breakdowns.

The Truth the Dead Know

For My Mother, Born March 1902, Died March 1959
and My Father, Born February 1900, Died June 1959

Gone, I say and walk from church,
refusing the stiff procession to the grave,
letting the dead ride alone in the hearse.
It is June. I am tired of being brave.

We drive to the Cape. I cultivate   5
myself where the sun gutters from the sky,
where the sea swings in like an iron gate
and we touch. In another country people die.

My darling, the wind falls in like stones
from the whitehearted water and when we touch   10
we enter touch entirely. No one's alone.
Men kill for this, or for as much.

And what of the dead? They lie without shoes
in their stone boats. They are more like stone
than the sea would be if it stopped. They refuse   15
to be blessed, throat, eye and knucklebone.

                                                    1962

The Starry Night

That does not keep me from having a terrible
need of—shall I say the word—religion.
Then I go out at night to paint the stars.
—Vincent Van Gogh[1]
in a letter to his brother

The town does not exist
except where one black-haired tree slips
up like a drowned woman into the hot sky.
The town is silent. The night boils with eleven stars.
Oh starry starry night! This is how   5
I want to die.

It moves. They are all alive.
Even the moon bulges in its orange irons
to push children, like a god, from its eye.
The old unseen serpent swallows up the stars.   10
Oh starry starry night! This is how
I want to die:

---

1. Dutch painter (1853–1890) who in his thirties committed suicide. This letter to his brother—his only
confidant—was written in September 1888. At the time he was painting *Starry Night on the Rhône*.

into that rushing beast of the night,
sucked up by that great dragon, to split
from my life with no flag,   15
no belly,
no cry.

1962

Sylvia's Death

for Sylvia Plath[1]

Oh Sylvia, Sylvia,
with a dead box of stones and spoons,

with two children, two meteors
wandering loose in the tiny playroom,

with your mouth into the sheet,   5
into the roofbeam, into the dumb prayer,

(Sylvia, Sylvia,
where did you go
after you wrote me
from Devonshire   10
about raising potatoes
and keeping bees?)

what did you stand by,
just how did you lie down into?

Thief!—   15
how did you crawl into,

crawl down alone
into the death I wanted so badly and for so long,

the death we said we both outgrew,
the one we wore on our skinny breasts,   20

the one we talked of so often each time
we downed three extra dry martinis in Boston,

the death that talked of analysts and cures,
the death that talked like brides with plots,

---

1. American poet (1932–1963) and friend of Sexton's who committed suicide. Plath was living in
England with her children, having separated from her husband, the poet Ted Hughes.

the death we drank to,   25
the motives and then the quiet deed?

(In Boston
the dying
ride in cabs,
yes death again,   30
that ride home
with *our* boy.)

O Sylvia, I remember the sleepy drummer
who beat on our eyes with an old story,

how we wanted to let him come   35
like a sadist or a New York fairy

to do his job,
a necessity, a window in a wall or a crib,

and since that time he waited
under our heart, our cupboard,   40

and I see now that we store him up
year after year, old suicides

and I know at the news of your death,
a terrible taste for it, like salt.

(And me,   45
me too.
And now, Sylvia,
you again
with death again,
that ride home   50
with *our* boy.)

And I say only
with my arms stretched out into that stone place,

what is your death
but an old belonging,   55

a mole that fell out
of one of your poems?

(O friend,
while the moon's bad,
and the king's gone,   60
and the queen's at her wit's end
the bar fly ought to sing!)

O tiny mother,
you too!
O funny duchess!   65
O blonde thing!

February 17, 1963   1966

Little Girl, My String Bean, My Lovely Woman

My daughter, at eleven
(almost twelve), is like a garden.

Oh darling! Born in that sweet birthday suit
and having owned it and known it for so long,
now you must watch high noon enter—   5
noon, that ghost hour.
Oh, funny little girl—this one under a blueberry sky,
this one! How can I say that I've known
just what you know and just where you are?

It's not a strange place, this odd home   10
where your face sits in my hand
so full of distance,
so full of its immediate fever.
The summer has seized you,
as when, last month in Amalfi,[1] I saw   15
lemons as large as your desk-side globe—
that miniature map of the world—
and I could mention, too,
the market stalls of mushrooms
and garlic buds all engorged.   20
Or I think even of the orchard next door,
where the berries are done
and the apples are beginning to swell.
And once, with our first backyard,
I remember I planted an acre of yellow beans   25
we couldn't eat.

Oh, little girl,
my stringbean,
how do you grow?
You grow this way.   30
You are too many to eat.

I hear
as in a dream
the conversation of the old wives

---

1. A seaport town in Campania, Italy.

speaking of *womanhood*.   35
I remember that I heard nothing myself.
I was alone.
I waited like a target.

Let high noon enter—
the hour of the ghosts.   40
Once the Romans believed
that noon was the ghost hour,
and I can believe it, too,
under that startling sun,
and someday they will come to you,   45
someday, men bare to the waist, young Romans
at noon where they belong,
with ladders and hammers
while no one sleeps.

But before they enter   50
I will have said,
Your bones are lovely,
and before their strange hands
there was always this hand that formed.

Oh, darling, let your body in,   55
let it tie you in,
in comfort.
What I want to say, Linda,
is that women are born twice.

If I could have watched you grow   60
as a magical mother might,
if I could have seen through my magical transparent belly,
there would have been such ripening within:
your embryo,
the seed taking on its own,   65
life clapping the bedpost,
bones from the pond,
thumbs and two mysterious eyes,
the awfully human head,
the heart jumping like a puppy,   70
the important lungs,
the becoming—
while it becomes!
as it does now,
a world of its own,   75
a delicate place.

I say hello
to such shakes and knockings and high jinks,
such music, such sprouts,
such dancing-mad-bears of music,   80
such necessary sugar,
such goings-on!

Oh, little girl,
my stringbean,
how do you grow? 85
You grow this way.
You are too many to eat.

What I want to say, Linda,
is that there is nothing in your body that lies.
All that is new is telling the truth. 90
I'm here, that somebody else,
an old tree in the background.

Darling,
stand still at your door,
sure of yourself, a white stone, a good stone— 95
as exceptional as laughter
you will strike fire,
that new thing!

July 14, 1964   1966

From The Death of the Fathers[1]

2. *How We Danced*

The night of my cousin's wedding
I wore blue. 25
I was nineteen
and we danced, Father, we orbited.
We moved like angels washing themselves.
We moved like two birds on fire.
Then we moved like the sea in a jar, 30
slower and slower.
The orchestra played
"Oh how we danced on the night we were wed."
And you waltzed me like a lazy Susan
and we were dear, 35
very dear.
Now that you are laid out,
useless as a blind dog,
now that you no longer lurk,
the song rings in my head. 40
Pure oxygen was the champagne we drank
and clicked our glasses, one to one.
The champagne breathed like a skin diver
and the glasses were crystal and the bride
and groom gripped each other in sleep 45
like nineteen-thirty marathon dancers.

---

1. Printed here are parts 2 and 3 of a six-part sequence.

Mother was a belle and danced with twenty men.
You danced with me never saying a word.
Instead the serpent spoke as you held me close.
The serpent, that mocker, woke up and pressed against me   50
like a great god and we bent together
like two lonely swans.

3. The Boat

Father
(he calls himself
"old sea dog"),   55
in his yachting cap
at the wheel of the Chris-Craft,
a mahogany speedboat
named Go Too III,
speeds out past Cuckold's Light[2]   60
over the dark brainy blue.
I in the very back
with an orange life jacket on.
I in the dare seat.
Mother up front.   65
Her kerchief flapping.
The waves deep as whales.
(Whales in fact have been sighted.
A school two miles out of Boothbay Harbor.)[3]
It is bumpy and we are going too fast.   70
The waves are boulders that we ride upon.
I am seen and we are riding
to Pemaquid[4] or Spain.
Now the waves are higher;
they are round buildings.   75
We start to go through them
and the boat shudders.
Father is going faster.
I am wet.
I am tumbling on my seat   80
like a loose kumquat.
Suddenly
a wave that we go under.
Under. Under. Under.
We are daring the sea.   85
We have parted it.
We are scissors.
Here in the green room
the dead are very close.
Here in the pitiless green   90
where there are no keepsakes
or cathedrals an angel spoke:

2. A Maine lighthouse.   4. A coastal village in Maine.
3. A coastal town in Maine.

You have no business.
No business here.
Give me a sign,   95
cried Father,
and the sky breaks over us.
There is air to have.
There are gulls kissing the boat.
There is the sun as big as a nose.   100
And here are the three of us
dividing our deaths,
bailing the boat
and closing out
the cold wing that has clasped us   105
this bright August day.

1972

PHILIP K. DICK
1928–1982

66 I am a fictionalizing philosopher, not a novelist," proclaimed Philip K. (Kindred) Dick, the author of forty-four novels and over a hundred short stories, most of them works of science fiction. He once remarked that his fiction took up two large questions: "What is Human?" and "What is Real?" Dick led a tumultuous life that added to the urgency with which he explored such questions. He struggled for decades with paranoia, mental illness, and drug addiction, and spent the last eight years of his life trying to interpret a mystical experience that occurred on February 3, 1974—"2-3-74" in the shorthand of his most ardent fans. His 1978 novel, *VALIS*, and his extensive journals deal with the revelations of that day. These experiences were informed by his interest in alternative religions and mystical traditions, particularly Gnosticism, and by his reading in the works of Plato and the influential early-twentieth-century psychologist Carl Jung (who coined the concept of the "archetype"—still in use today—a term based on the idea of a collective human unconscious). Dick wrote for those who, like himself, could not or would not, as he put it, "blunt their own intimations about the irrational, mysterious nature of reality."

Dick was born in Chicago in 1928, and as a small child moved with his divorced mother to Berkeley, California, where he lived for much of his life. Dick's twin sister, Jane, died of malnourishment eight weeks after birth, a fact that haunted Dick until his own death in 1982. He briefly attended the University of California at Berkeley (he didn't like his ROTC training, though he enjoyed reading the philosopher David Hume), but never completed college. He was married five times and fathered three children.

Science fiction in lowbrow pulp magazines and (as with Patricia Highsmith) comics attracted the young Philip, and when he was fourteen he tried his hand at writing a science fiction novel. His passion for science fiction met the forces of history in the 1950s and '60s, when the birth of the atomic age in America, the intensifying Cold War, and the advent of space exploration made futuristic scenarios and apocalyptic violence seem ever closer to the real world. The genre's popularity began to take off in these decades. Dick's success in this niche—in the course of his career he won several Nebula and Hugo awards, the highest honors for science fiction writing—was matched by his growing fame among a wide range of readers. In the early 1970s he was interviewed by *Rolling Stone*, featured in the *New Yorker*, and visited for a night by an admirer named Art Spiegelman (later the author of the graphic narrative *Maus*, excerpted in this volume). His work became important to scholars of postmodernism as well as to a broad swath of the general public, who saw film adaptations of his work in *Blade Runner* (1982), *Total Recall* (1990), *Minority Report* (2002), and *The Adjustment Bureau* (2011), among numerous other films based on his writings.

Dick's stories can read like logic problems. He once pointed out that "Precious Artifact," included here, demonstrated a particular story form that he explained this way: "What appears to be the case is Y but we find out the opposite is true (null-Y). But then that turns out not to be true, so are we back to Y? . . . Either I've invented a whole new logic or, ahem, I'm not playing with a full deck." Whatever his logic, Dick was adept at exploring fundamental longings, and that skill allowed his stories to transcend their heady structures. In them we find characters—and whole cultures—longing for the solace of animals, sex, companionship, social status, the beauty of the natural world, and some semblance of truth.

Precious Artifact

Below the 'copter of Milt Biskle lay newly fertile lands. He had done well with his area of Mars, verdant from his reconstruction of the ancient water-network. Spring, two springs each year, had been brought to this autumn world of sand and hopping toads, a land once made of dried soil cracking with the dust of former times, of a dreary and unwatered waste. Victim of the recent Prox-Terra conflict.

Quite soon the first Terran emigrants would appear, stake their claims, and take over. He could retire. Perhaps he could return to Terra or bring his own family here, receive priority of land-acquisition—as a reconstruct engineer he deserved it. Area Yellow had progressed far faster than the other engineers' sections. And now his reward came.

Reaching forward, Milt Biskle touched the button of his long-range transmitter. "This is Reconstruct Engineer Yellow," he said. "I'd like a psychiatrist. Anyone will do, so long as he's immediately available."

When Milt Biskle entered the office Dr. DeWinter rose and held out his hand. "I've heard," Dr. DeWinter said, "that you, of all the forty-odd reconstruct engineers, have been the most creative. It's no wonder you're tired. Even God had to rest after six days of such work, and you've been at it for years. As I was waiting for you to reach me I received a news memo from Terra that will interest you." He picked the memo up from his desk. "The initial transport of settlers is about to arrive here on Mars . . . and they'll go directly into your area. Congratulations, Mr. Biskle."

Rousing himself Milt Biskle said, "What if I returned to Earth?"

"But if you mean to stake a claim for your family, here—"

Milt Biskle said, "I want you to do something for me. I feel too tired, too—" He gestured. "Or depressed, maybe. Anyhow I'd like you to make arrangements for my gear, including my wug-plant, to be put aboard a transport returning to Terra."

"Six years of work," Dr. DeWinter said. "And now you're abandoning your recompense. Recently I visited Earth and it's just as you remember—"

"How do you know how I remember it?"

"Rather," DeWinter corrected himself smoothly, "I should say it's just as it was. Overcrowded, tiny conapts with seven families to a single cramped kitchen. Autobahns[1] so crowded you can't make a move until eleven in the morning."

"For me," Milt Biskle said, "the overcrowding will be a relief after six years of robot autonomic[2] equipment." He had made up his mind. In spite of what he had accomplished here, or perhaps because of it, he intended to go home. Despite the psychiatrist's arguments.

Dr. DeWinter purred, "What if your wife and children, Milt, are among the passengers of this first transport?" Once more he lifted a document from his neatly arranged desk. He studied the paper, then said, "Biskle, Fay, Mrs. Laura C. June C. Woman and two girl children. Your family?"

"Yes," Milt Biskle admitted woodenly; he stared straight ahead.

"So you see you can't head back to Earth. Put on your hair and prepare to meet them at Field Three. And exchange your teeth. You've got the stainless steel ones in, at the moment."

Chagrined, Biskle nodded. Like all Terrans he had lost his hair and teeth from the fallout during the war. For everyday service in his lonely job of re-reconstructing Yellow Area of Mars he made no use of the expensive wig which he had brought from Terra, and as to the teeth he personally found the steel ones far more comfortable than the natural-color plastic set. It indicated how far he had drifted from social interaction. He felt vaguely guilty; Dr. DeWinter was right.

But he had felt guilty ever since the defeat of the Proxmen. The war had embittered him; it didn't seem fair that one of the two competing cultures would have to suffer, since the needs of both were legitimate.

Mars itself had been the locus of contention. Both cultures needed it as a colony on which to deposit surplus populations. Thank God Terra had managed to gain tactical mastery during the last year of the war . . . hence it was Terrans such as himself, and not Proxmen, patching up Mars.

"By the way," Dr. DeWinter said. "I happen to know of your intentions regarding your fellow reconstruct engineers."

Milt Biskle glanced up swiftly.

"As a matter of fact," Dr. DeWinter said, "we know they're at this moment gathering in Red Area to hear your account." Opening his desk drawer he got out a yo-yo, stood up, and began to operate it expertly doing *walking the dog*.[3] "Your panic-stricken speech to the effect that something is wrong, although you can't seem to say just what it might be."

1. Highways (German).
2. Autonomous.

3. A yo-yo trick, as is *around the world* (next page).

Watching the yo-yo Biskle said, "That's a toy popular in the Prox system. At least so I read in a homeopape article, once."

"Hmm. I understood it originated in the Philippines." Engrossed, Dr. DeWinter now did *around the world*. He did it well. "I'm taking the liberty of sending a disposition to the reconstruct engineers' gathering, testifying to your mental condition. It will be read aloud—sorry to say."

"I still intend to address the gathering," Biskle said.

"Well, then there's a compromise that occurs to me. Greet your little family when it arrives here on Mars and then we'll arrange a trip to Terra for you. At our expense. And in exchange you'll agree not to address the gathering of reconstruct engineers or burden them in any way with your nebulous forebodings." DeWinter eyed him keenly. "After all, this is a critical moment. The first emigrants are arriving. We don't want trouble; we don't want to make anyone uneasy."

"Would you do me a favor?" Biskle asked. "Show me that you've got a wig on. And that your teeth are false. Just so I can be sure that you're a Terran."

Dr. DeWinter tilted his wig and plucked out his set of false teeth.

"I'll take the offer," Milt Biskle said. "If you'll agree to make certain that my wife obtains the parcel of land I set aside for her."

Nodding, DeWinter tossed him a small white envelope. "Here's your ticket. Round-trip, of course, since you'll be coming back."

I hope so, Biskle thought as he picked up the ticket. But it depends on what I see on Terra. Or rather on what they *let* me see.

He had a feeling they'd let him see very little. In fact as little as Proxmanly possible.

When his ship reached Terra a smartly uniformed guide waited for him. "Mr. Biskle?" Trim and attractive and exceedingly young, she stepped forward alertly. "I'm Mary Ableseth, your Tourplan companion. I'll show you around the planet during your brief stay here." She smiled brightly and very professionally. He was taken aback. "I'll be with you constantly, night and day."

"Night, too?" he managed to say.

"Yes, Mr. Biskle. That's my job. We expect you to be disoriented due to your years of labor on Mars . . . labor we of Terra applaud and honor, as is right." She fell in beside him, steering him toward a parked 'copter. "Where would you like to go first? New York City? Broadway? To the night clubs and theaters and restaurants . . ."

"No, to Central Park. To sit on a bench."

"But there is no more Central Park, Mr. Biskle. It was turned into a parking lot for government employees while you were on Mars."

"I see," Milt Biskle said. "Well, then Portsmouth Square in San Francisco will do." He opened the door of the 'copter.

"That, too, has become a parking lot," Miss Ableseth said, with a sad shake of her long, luminous red hair. "We're so darn overpopulated. Try again, Mr. Biskle; there are a few parks left, one in Kansas, I believe, and *two* in Utah in the south part near St. George."

"This is bad news," Milt said. "May I stop at that amphetamine dispenser and put in my dime? I need a stimulant to cheer me up."

"Certainly," Miss Ableseth said, nodding graciously.

Milt Biskle walked to the spaceport's nearby stimulant dispenser, reached into his pocket, found a dime, and dropped the dime in the slot.

The dime fell completely through the dispenser and bounced onto the pavement.

"Odd," Biskle said, puzzled.

"I think I can explain that," Miss Ableseth said. "That dime of yours is a Martian dime, made for a lighter gravity."

"Hmm," Milt Biskle said, as he retrieved the dime. As Miss Ableseth had predicted, he felt disoriented. He stood by as she put in a dime of her own and obtained the small tube of amphetamine stimulants for him. Certainly her explanation seemed adequate. But—

"It is now eight P.M. local time," Miss Ableseth said. "And I haven't had dinner, although of course you have, aboard your ship. Why not take me to dinner? We can talk over a bottle of Pinot Noir[4] and you can tell me these vague forebodings which have brought you to Terra, that something dire is wrong and that all your marvelous reconstruct work is pointless. I'd adore to hear about it." She guided him back to the 'copter and the two of them entered, squeezing into the back seat together. Milt Biskle found her to be warm and yielding, decidedly Terran; he became embarrassed and felt his heart pounding in effort-syndrome. It had been some time since he had been this close to a woman.

"Listen," he said, as the automatic circuit of the 'copter caused it to rise from the spaceport parking lot, "I'm married. I've got two children and I came here on business. I'm on Terra to prove that the Proxmen really won and that we few remaining Terrans are slaves of the Prox authorities, laboring for—" He gave up; it was hopeless. Miss Ableseth remained pressed against him.

"You really think," Miss Ableseth said presently, as the 'copter passed above New York City, "that I'm a Prox agent?"

"N-no," Milt Biskle said. "I guess not." It did not seem likely, under the circumstances.

"While you're on Terra," Miss Ableseth said, "why stay in an overcrowded, noisy hotel? Why not stay with me at my conapt in New Jersey? There's plenty of room and you're more than welcome."

"Okay," Biskle agreed, feeling the futility of arguing.

"Good." Miss Ableseth gave an instruction to the 'copter; it turned north. "We'll have dinner there. It'll save money, and at all the decent restaurants there's a two-hour line this time of night, so it's almost impossible to get a table. You've probably forgotten. How wonderful it'll be when half our population can emigrate!"

"Yes," Biskle said tightly. "And they'll like Mars; we've done a good job." He felt a measure of enthusiasm returning to him, a sense of pride in the reconstruct work he and his compatriots had done. "Wait until you see it, Miss Ableseth."

"Call me Mary," Miss Ableseth said, as she arranged her heavy scarlet wig; it had become dislodged during the last few moments in the cramped quarters of the 'copter.

4. A type of red wine.

"Okay," Biskle said, and, except for a nagging awareness of disloyalty to Fay, he felt a sense of well-being.

"Things happen fast on Terra," Mary Ableseth said. "Due to the terrible pressure of overpopulation." She pressed her teeth in place; they, too, had become dislodged.

"So I see," Milt Biskle agreed, and straightened his own wig and teeth, too. *Could I have been mistaken?* he asked himself. After all he could see the lights of New York below; Terra was decidedly not a depopulated ruin and its civilization was intact.

Or was this all an illusion, imposed on his percept-system by Prox psychiatric techniques unfamiliar to him? It was a fact that his dime had fallen completely through the amphetamine dispenser. Didn't that indicate something was subtly, terribly wrong?

Perhaps the dispenser hadn't really been there.

The next day he and Mary Ableseth visited one of the few remaining parks. In the southern part of Utah, near the mountains, the park, although small, was bright green and attractive. Milt Biskle lolled on the grass watching a squirrel progressing toward a tree in wicket-like[5] leaps, its tail flowing behind it in a gray stream.

"No squirrels on Mars," Milt Biskle said sleepily.

Wearing a slight sunsuit, Mary Ableseth stretched out on her back, eyes shut. "It's nice here, Milt. I imagine Mars is like this." Beyond the park heavy traffic moved along the freeway; the noise reminded Milt of the surf of the Pacific Ocean. It lulled him. All seemed well, and he tossed a peanut to the squirrel. The squirrel veered, wicket-hopped toward the peanut, its intelligent face twitching in response.

As it sat upright, holding the nut, Milt Biskle tossed a second nut off to the right. The squirrel heard it land among the maple leaves; its ears pricked up, and this reminded Milt of a game he once had played with a cat, an old sleepy tom which had belonged to him and his brother in the days before Terra had been so overpopulated, when pets were still legal. He had waited until Pumpkin—the tomcat—was almost asleep and then he had tossed a small object into the corner of the room. Pumpkin woke up. His eyes had flown open and his ears had pricked, turned, and he had sat for fifteen minutes listening and watching, brooding as to what had made the noise. It was a harmless way of teasing the old cat, and Milt felt sad, thinking how many years Pumpkin had been dead now, his last legal pet. On Mars, though, pets would be legal again. That cheered him.

In fact on Mars, during his years of reconstruct work, he had possessed a pet. A Martian plant. He had brought it with him to Terra and it now stood on the living-room coffee table in Mary Ableseth's conapt, its limbs draped rather unhappily. It had not prospered in the unfamiliar Terran climate.

"Strange," Milt murmured, "that my wug-plant isn't thriving. I'd have thought in such a moist atmosphere . . ."

"It's the gravity," Mary said, eyes still shut, her bosom rising and falling regularly. She was almost asleep. "Too much for it."

---

5. In the shape of a curved hoop used in the lawn game of croquet.

Milt regarded the supine form of the woman, remembering Pumpkin under similar circumstances. The hypnogogic moment, between waking and sleeping, when consciousness and unconsciousness became blended . . . reaching, he picked up a pebble.

He tossed the pebble into the leaves near Mary's head.

At once she sat up, eyes open startled, her sunsuit falling from her.

Both her ears pricked up.

"But we Terrans," Milt said, "have lost control of the musculature of our ears, Mary. On even a reflex basis."

"What?" she murmured, blinking in confusion as she retied her sunsuit.

"Our ability to prick up our ears has atrophied," Milt explained. "Unlike the dog and cat. Although to examine us morphologically you wouldn't know because the muscles are still there. So you made an error."

"I don't know what you're talking about," Mary said, with a trace of sullenness. She turned her attention entirely to arranging the bra of her sunsuit, ignoring him.

"Let's go back to the conapt," Milt said, rising to his feet. He no longer felt like lolling in the park, because he could no longer believe in the park. Unreal squirrel, unreal grass . . . was it actually? Would they ever show him the substance beneath the illusion? He doubted it.

The squirrel followed them a short way as they walked to their parked 'copter, then turned its attention to a family of Terrans which included two small boys; the children threw nuts to the squirrel and it scampered in vigorous activity.

"Convincing," Milt said. And it really was.

Mary said, "Too bad you couldn't have seen Dr. DeWinter more, Milt. He could have helped you." Her voice was oddly hard.

"I have no doubt of that," Milt Biskle agreed as they re-entered the parked 'copter.

When they arrived back at Mary's conapt he found his Martian wugplant dead. It had evidently perished of dehydration.

"Don't try to explain this," he said to Mary as the two of them stood gazing down at the parched, dead stalks of the once active plant. "You know what it shows. Terra is supposedly more humid than Mars, even reconstructed Mars at its best. Yet this plant has completely dried out. There's no moisture left on Terra because I suppose the Prox blasts emptied the seas. Right?"

Mary said nothing.

"What I don't understand," Milt said, "is why it's worth it to you people to keep the illusion going. *I've finished my job.*"

After a pause Mary said, "Maybe there're more planets requiring reconstruct work, Milt."

"Your population is that great?"

"I was thinking of Terra. Here," Mary said. "Reconstruct work on it will take generations; all the talent and ability you reconstruct engineers possess will be required." She added, "I'm just following your hypothetical logic, of course."

"So Terra's our next job. That's why you let me come here. In fact I'm going to *stay* here." He realized that, thoroughly and utterly, in a flash of insight. "I won't be going back to Mars and I won't see Fay again. You're replacing her." It all made sense.

"Well," Mary said, with a faint wry smile, "let's say I'm attempting to." She stroked his arm. Barefoot, still in her sunsuit, she moved slowly closer and closer to him.

Frightened, he backed away from her. Picking up the dead wug-plant, he numbly carried it to the apt's disposal chute and dropped the brittle, dry remains in. They vanished at once.

"And now," Mary said busily, "we're going to visit the Museum of Modern Art in New York and then, if we have time, the Smithsonian in Washington, D.C. They've asked me to keep you busy so you don't start brooding."

"But I am brooding," Milt said as he watched her change from her sunsuit to a gray wool knit dress. Nothing can stop that, he said to himself. And you know it now. And as each reconstruct engineer finishes his area it's going to happen again. I'm just the first.

At least I'm not alone, he realized. And felt somewhat better.

"How do I look?" Mary asked as she put on lipstick before the bedroom mirror.

"Fine," he said listlessly, and wondered if Mary would meet each reconstruct engineer in turn, become the mistress of each. Not only is she not what she seems, he thought, but I don't even get to keep her.

It seemed a gratuitous loss, easily avoided.

He was, he realized, beginning to like her. *Mary was alive*, that much was real. Terran or not. At least they had not lost the war to shadows; they had lost to authentic living organisms. He felt somewhat cheered.

"Ready for the Museum of Modern Art?" Mary said briskly, with a smile.

Later, at the Smithsonian, after he had viewed the Spirit of St. Louis and the Wright brothers'[6] incredibly ancient plane—it appeared to be at least a million years old—he caught sight of an exhibit which he had been anticipating.

Saying nothing to Mary—she was absorbed in studying a case of semiprecious stones in their natural uncut state—he slipped off and, a moment later, stood before a glass-walled section entitled

PROX MILITARY OF 2014

Three Prox soldiers stood frozen, their dark muzzles stained and grimy, sidearms ready, in a makeshift shelter composed of the remains of one of their transports. A bloody Prox flag hung drably. This was a defeated enclave of the enemy; these three creatures were about to surrender or be killed.

A group of Terran visitors stood before the exhibit, gawking. Milt Biskle said to the man nearest him, "Convincing, isn't it?"

"Sure is," the man, middle-aged, with glasses and gray hair, agreed. "Were you in the war?" he asked Milt, glancing at him.

"I'm in reconstruct," Milt said. "Yellow Engineer."

---

6. Orville (1871–1948) and Wilbur (1867–1912) Wright, brothers and inventors of the first airplane, flown in 1903. "Spirit of St. Louis": plane in which airman Charles Lindbergh (1902–1974) made the first transatlantic flight in 1927.

"Oh." The man nodded, impressed. "Boy, these Proxmen look scary. You'd almost expect them to step out of that exhibit and fight us to the death." He grinned. "They put up a good fight before they gave in, those Proxmen; you have to give 'em credit for that."

Beside him the man's gray, taut wife said, "Those guns of theirs make me shiver. It's too realistic." Disapproving, she walked on.

"You're right," Milt Biskle said. "They do look frighteningly real, because of course they are." There was no point in creating an illusion of this sort because the genuine thing lay immediately at hand, readily available. Milt swung himself under the guardrail, reached the transparent glass of the exhibit, raised his foot, and smashed the glass; it burst and rained down with a furious racket of shivering fragments.

As Mary came running, Milt snatched a rifle from one of the frozen Proxmen in the exhibit and turned it toward her.

She halted, breathing rapidly, eyeing him but saying nothing.

"I am willing to work for you," Milt said to her, holding the rifle expertly. "After all, if my own race no longer exists I can hardly reconstruct a colony world for them; even I can see that. But I want to know the truth. Show it to me and I'll go on with my job."

Mary said, "No, Milt, if you knew the truth you wouldn't go on. You'd turn that gun on yourself." She sounded calm, even compassionate, but her eyes were bright and enlarged, wary.

"Then I'll kill you," he said. And, after that, himself.

"Wait." She pondered. "Milt—this is difficult. You know absolutely nothing and yet look how miserable you are. How do you expect to feel when you can see your planet as it is? It's almost too much for me and I'm—" She hesitated.

"Say it."

"I'm just a—" she choked out the word—"a visitor."

"But I am right," he said. "Say it. Admit it."

"You're right, Milt," she sighed.

Two uniformed museum guards appeared, holding pistols. "You okay, Miss Ableseth?"

"For the present," Mary said. She did not take her eyes off Milt and the rifle which he held. "Just wait," she instructed the guards.

"Yes ma'am." The guards waited. No one moved.

Milt said, "Did any Terran women survive?"

After a pause, Mary said, "No, Milt. But we Proxmen are within the same genus, as you well know. We can interbreed. Doesn't that make you feel better?"

"Sure," he said. "A lot better." And he did feel like turning the rifle on himself now, without waiting. It was all he could do to resist the impulse. So he had been right; that thing had not been Fay, there at Field Three on Mars. "Listen," he said to Mary Ableseth, "I want to go back to Mars again. I came here to learn something. I learned it, now I want to go back. Maybe I'll talk to Dr. DeWinter again, maybe he can help me. Any objection to that?"

"No." She seemed to understand how he felt. "After all, you did all your work there. You have a right to return. But eventually you have to begin here on Terra. We can wait a year or so, perhaps even two. But eventually Mars will be filled up and we'll need the room. And it's going to be so much harder

566 | PHILIP K. DICK

here . . . as you'll discover." She tried to smile but failed; he saw the effort. "I'm sorry, Milt."

"So am I," Milt Biskle said. "Hell, I was sorry when that wug-plant died. I knew the truth then. It wasn't just a guess."

"You'll be interested to know that your fellow reconstruct engineer Red, Cleveland Andre, addressed the meeting in your place. And passed your intimations on to them all, along with his own. They voted to send an official delegate here to Terra to investigate; he's on his way now."

"I'm interested," Milt said. "But it doesn't really matter. It hardly changes things." He put down the rifle. "Can I go back to Mars now?" He felt tired. "Tell Dr. DeWinter I'm coming." Tell him, he thought, to have every psychiatric technique in his repertory ready for me, because it will take a lot. "What about Earth's animals?" he asked. "Did any forms at all survive? How about the dog and the cat?"

Mary glanced at the museum guards; a flicker of communication passed silently between them and then Mary said, "Maybe it's all right after all."

"What's all right?" Milt Biskle said.

"For you to see. Just for a moment. You seem to be standing up to it better than we had expected. In our opinion you *are* entitled to that." She added, "Yes, Milt, the dog and cat survived; they live here among the ruins. Come along and look."

He followed after her, thinking to himself, Wasn't she right the first time? Do I really want to look? Can I stand up to what exists in actuality—what they've felt the need of keeping from me up until now?

At the exit ramp of the museum Mary halted and said, "Go on outside, Milt. I'll stay here. I'll be waiting for you when you come back in."

Haltingly, he descended the ramp.

And saw.

It was, of course, as she had said, ruins. The city had been decapitated, leveled three feet above ground level; the buildings had become hollow squares, without contents, like some infinite arrangements of useless, ancient courtyards. He could not believe that what he saw was *new*, it seemed to him as if these abandoned remnants had always been there, exactly as they were now. And—how long would they remain this way?

To the right an elaborate but small-scale mechanical system had plopped itself down on a debris-filled street. As he watched, it extended a host of pseudopodia which burrowed inquisitively into the nearby foundations. The foundations, steel and cement, were abruptly pulverized; the bare ground, exposed, lay naked and dark brown, seared over from the atomic heat generated by the repair autonomic rig—a construct, Milt Biskle thought, not much different from those I employ on Mars. At least to some meager extent the rig had the task of clearing away the old. He knew from his own reconstruct work on Mars that it would be followed, probably within minutes, by an equally elaborate mechanism which would lay the groundwork for the new structures to come.

And, standing off to one side in the otherwise deserted street, watching this limited clearing-work in progress, two gray, thin figures could be made out. Two hawk-nosed Proxmen with their pale, natural hair arranged in high coils, their earlobes elongated with heavy weights.

The victors, he thought to himself. Experiencing the satisfaction of this spectacle, witnessing the last artifacts of the defeated race being obliterated. Someday a purely Prox city will rise up here: Prox architecture, streets of the odd, wide Prox pattern, the uniform box-like buildings with their many subsurface levels. And citizens such as these will be treading the ramps, accepting the high-speed runnels[7] in their daily routines. And what, he thought, about the Terran dogs and cats which now inhabit these ruins, as Mary said? Will even they disappear? Probably not entirely. There will be room for them, perhaps in museums and zoos, as oddities to be gaped at. Survivals of an ecology which no longer obtained. Or even mattered.

And yet—Mary was right. The Proxmen were within the same genus. Even if they did not interbreed with the remaining Terrans, the species as he had known it would go on. And they would interbreed, he thought. His own relationship with Mary was a harbinger. As individuals they were not so far apart. The results might even be good.

The results, he thought as he turned away and started back into the museum, may be a race not quite Prox and not quite Terran; something that is genuinely new may come from the melding. At least we can hope so.

Terra would be rebuilt. He had seen slight but real work in progress with his own eyes. Perhaps the Proxmen lacked the skill that he and his fellow reconstruct engineers possessed . . . but now that Mars was virtually done they could begin here. It was not absolutely hopeless. Not *quite*.

Walking up to Mary he said hoarsely, "Do me a favor. Get me a cat I can take back to Mars with me. I've always liked cats. Especially the orange ones with stripes."

One of the museum guards, after a glance at his companion, said, "We can arrange that, Mr. Biskle. We can get a—cub, is that the word?"

"Kitten, I think," Mary corrected.

On the trip back to Mars, Milt Biskle sat with the box containing the orange kitten on his lap, working out his plans. In fifteen minutes the ship would land on Mars and Dr. DeWinter—or the thing that posed as Dr. DeWinter anyhow—would be waiting to meet him. And it would be too late. From where he sat he could see the emergency escape hatch with its red warning light. His plans had become focused around the hatch. It was not ideal but it would serve.

In the box the orange kitten reached up a paw and batted at Milt's hand. He felt the sharp, tiny claws rake across his hand and he absently disengaged his flesh, retreating from the probing reach of the animal. You wouldn't have liked Mars anyhow, he thought, and rose to his feet.

Carrying the box, he strode swiftly toward the emergency hatch. Before the stewardess could reach him he had thrown open the hatch. He stepped forward and the hatch locked behind him. For an instant he was within the cramped unit, and then he began to twist open the heavy outer door.

"Mr. Biskle!" the stewardess's voice came, muffled by the door behind him. He heard her fumbling to reach him, opening the door and groping to catch hold of him.

As he twisted open the outer door the kitten within the box under his arm snarled.

You, too? Milt Biskle thought, and paused.

---

7. Grooves or narrow channels.

Death, the emptiness and utter lack of warmth of 'tween space, seeped around him, filtering past the partly opened outer door. He smelled it and something within him, as in the kitten, retreated by instinct. He paused, holding the box, not trying to push the outer door any farther open, and in that moment the stewardess grabbed him.

"Mr. Biskle," she said with a half-sob, "are you out of your mind? Good God, what are you doing?" She managed to tug the outer door shut, screw the emergency section back into shut position.

"You know exactly what I'm doing," Milt Biskle said as he allowed her to propel him back into the ship and to his seat. And don't think you stopped me, he said to himself. Because it wasn't you. I could have gone ahead and done it. But I decided not to.

He wondered why.

Later, at Field Three on Mars, Dr. DeWinter met him as he had expected.

The two of them walked to the parked 'copter and DeWinter in a worried tone of voice said, "I've just been informed that during the trip—"

"That's right. I attempted suicide. But I changed my mind. Maybe you know why. You're the psychologist, the authority as to what goes on inside us." He entered the 'copter, being careful not to bang the box containing the Terran kitten.

"You're going to go ahead and stake your landparcel with Fay?" Dr. DeWinter asked presently as the 'copter flew above green, wet fields of high-protein wheat. "Even though—you know?"

"Yes." He nodded. After all, there was nothing else for him, as far as he could make out.

"You Terrans." DeWinter shook his head. "Admirable." Now he noticed the box on Milt Biskle's lap. "What's that you have there? A creature from Terra?" He eyed it suspiciously; obviously to him it was a manifestation of an alien form of life. "A rather peculiar-looking organism."

"It's going to keep me company," Milt Biskle said. "While I go on with my work, either building up my private parcel or—" Or helping you Proxmen with Terra, he thought.

"Is that what was called a 'rattlesnake'? I detect the sound of its rattles." Dr. DeWinter edged away.

"It's purring." Milt Biskle stroked the kitten as the autonomic circuit of the 'copter guided it across the dully red Martian sky. Contact with the one familiar life-form, he realized, will keep me sane. It will make it possible for me to go on. He felt grateful. My race may have been defeated and destroyed, but not all Terran creatures have perished. When we reconstruct Terra maybe we can induce the authorities to allow us to set up game preserves. We'll make that part of our task, he told himself, and again he patted the kitten. At least we can hope for that much.

Next to him, Dr. DeWinter was also deep in thought. He appreciated the intricate workmanship, by engineers stationed on the third planet,[8] which had gone into the simulacrum resting in the box on Milt Biskle's lap. The technical achievement was impressive, even to him, and he saw clearly—as

8. Earth, or Terra.

Milt Biskle of course did not. This artifact, accepted by the Terran as an authentic organism from his familiar past, would provide a pivot by which the man would hang onto his psychic balance.

But what about the other reconstruct engineers? What would carry each of them through and past the moment of discovery as each completed his work and had to—whether he liked it or not—awake?

It would vary from Terran to Terran. A dog for one, a more elaborate simulacrum, possibly that of a nubile human female, for another. In any case, each would be provided with an "exception" to the true state. One essential surviving entity, selected out of what had in fact totally vanished. Research into the past of each engineer would provide the clue, as it had in Biskle's instance; the cat-simulacrum had been finished weeks before his abrupt, panic-stricken trip home to Terra. For instance, in Andre's case a parrot-simulacrum was already under construction. It would be done by the time he made *his* trip home.

"I call him Thunder," Milt Biskle explained.

"Good name," Dr. DeWinter—as he titled himself these days—said. And thought, A shame we could not have shown him the real situation of Terra. Actually it's quite interesting that he accepted what he saw, because on some level he must realize that nothing survives a war of the kind we conducted. Obviously he desperately wanted to believe that a remnant, even though no more than rubble, endures. But it's typical of the Terran mind to fasten onto phantoms. That might help explain their defeat in the conflict; they were simply not realists.

"This cat," Milt Biskle said, "is going to be a mighty hunter of Martian sneak-mice."

"Right," Dr. DeWinter agreed, and thought, *As long as its batteries don't run down.* He, too, patted the kitten.

A switch closed and the kitten purred louder.

1964

ADRIENNE RICH
1929–2012

A childhood of reading and hearing poems taught Adrienne Rich to love the sound of words; her adult life taught her that poetry must "consciously situate itself amid political conditions." Over the years she conducted a passionate struggle to honor these parts of herself, in her best poems brilliantly mixing what she called "the poetry of the actual world with the poetry of sound." Extending a dialogue—between art and politics—that she first discovered in W. B. Yeats, whose poems she read as an undergraduate at Radcliffe, her work addresses with particular power the experiences of women, experiences often omitted from history and misrepresented in literature. Our culture, she believes, is "split at the root" (to adapt the title of one of her essays); art is separated from politics, and the poet's identity as a woman is separated from her art. Rich's work seeks a language that will expose and integrate these divisions in the self and in the world. To do this she wrote "directly and overtly as a woman, out of a woman's body and experience," for "to take women's existence seriously as theme and source for art, was something I had been hungering to do, needing to do, all my writing life."

Rich's first book was published in the Yale Younger Poets series, a prize particularly important for poets of her generation (others in the series have included James Wright, John Ashbery, and W. S. Merwin). W. H. Auden, the judge for the series in the 1950s, said of Rich's volume *A Change of World* (1951) that her poems "were neatly and modestly dressed . . . respect their elders, but are not cowed by them and do not tell fibs." Rich, looking back at that period from the vantage point of 1972, renders a more complicated sense of things. In an influential essay, "When We Dead Awaken," she recalls this period as one in which the chief models for poetry were men; from those models she first learned her craft. Even in reading the poetry of older women writers she found herself "looking . . . for the same things I found in the poetry of men . . . , to be equal was still confused with sounding the same." Twenty years and five volumes after *A Change of World* she published *The Will to Change*, taking its title from the opening line of Charles Olson's *The Kingfishers*: "What does not change / is the will to change." The shift of emphasis in Rich's titles signals an important turn in her work—from acceptance of change as a way of the world to an active sense of change as willed or desired.

In 1953 Rich married and in her twenties gave birth to three children within four years—"a radicalizing experience," she said. It was during this time that Rich experienced most severely that gap between what she calls the "energy of creation" and the "energy of relation. . . . In those early years I always felt the conflict as a failure of love in myself." In her later work Rich came to identify the source of that conflict not as individual but as social, and in 1976 she published a book of prose, *Of Woman Born: Motherhood as Experience and Institution*, in which she contrasts the actual experience of bearing and raising children with the myths fostered by our medical, social, and political institutions.

With her third and fourth books, *Snapshots of a Daughter-in-Law* (1963) and *Necessities of Life* (1966), Rich began explicitly to treat problems that engaged her throughout her writing life. The title poem of *Snapshots* exposes the gap between literary versions of women's experience and the day-to-day truths of their lives.

Rich's poems aim at self-definition, at establishing boundaries of the self, but they also fight off the notion that insights remain solitary and unshared. Many of her poems proceed by means of intimate argument, sometimes with externalized parts of herself, as if to dramatize the way identity forms from the self's movement beyond fixed boundaries. In some of her most powerful later poems she pushes her imagination to recognize the multiple aspects of the self ("My selves," she calls them in her poem "Integrity"); in "Transcendental Etude," she writes: *"I am the lover and the loved, / home and wanderer, she who splits / firewood and she who knocks, a stranger / in the storm."* In other important later poems she carried out a dialogue with lives similar to and different from her own, as in the generous and powerful title poem of her collection *An Atlas of the Difficult World* (1991). As she writes in the essay "Blood, Bread, and Poetry," in her development as a poet she came to feel "more and more urgently the dynamic between poetry as language and poetry as a kind of action, probing, burning, stripping, placing itself in dialogue with others."

After Rich and her husband moved to New York City in 1966 they became increasingly involved in radical politics, especially in the opposition to the Vietnam War. These concerns are reflected in the poems of *Leaflets* (1969) and *The Will to Change* (1971). Along with new subject matter came equally important changes in style.

Rich's poems throughout the 1960s moved away from formal verse patterns to more jagged utterance. Devices such as sentence fragments, lines of varying length, and irregular spacing to mark off phrases emphasized a voice of greater urgency. With "Snapshots of a Daughter-in-Law" Rich began dating her poems, as if to mark each one as provisional, true to the moment but an instrument of passage, like an entry in a journal in which feelings are subject to continual revision.

In the 1970s Rich dedicated herself increasingly to feminism. Her work as a poet, a prose writer, and a public speaker took on a new unity and intensity. The continuing task was to see herself—as she put it in 1984—as neither "unique nor universal, but a person in history, a woman and not a man, a white and also Jewish inheritor of a particular Western consciousness, from the making of which most women have been excluded." She says in "Planetarium": "I am an instrument in the shape / of a woman trying to translate pulsations / into images for the relief of the body / and the reconstruction of the mind."

Rich's collections of prose—*Of Woman Born*; *On Lies, Secrets, and Silences: Selected Prose 1966–1978*; *Blood, Bread, and Poetry: Selected Prose 1979–1985*; *What Is Found There: Notebooks on Poetry and Politics* (1993); and *Arts of the Possible* (2001)—provide an important context for her poems. In these works she addresses issues of women's education and their literary traditions, Jewish identity, the relations between poetry and politics, and what she has called "the erasure of lesbian existence." As a young woman Rich had been stirred by James Baldwin's comment that "any real change implies the breakup of the world as one has always known it, the loss of all that gave one an identity, the end of safety." In many ways her essays, like her poems, track the forces that resist such change and the human conditions that require it. Her essay "Compulsory Heterosexuality and Lesbian Existence" is an important example of such an examination.

Although Rich's individual poems do not consistently succeed in expressing a political vision without sacrificing "intensity of language," her work is best read as a continuous process. The books have an air of ongoing, pained investigation, almost scientific in intention but with an ardor suggested by their titles: *The Dream of a Common Language* (1977), *A Wild Patience Has Taken Me This Far* (1981), *The Fact of a Doorframe* (1984), and *Your Native Land, Your Life* (1986). Rich's later books, *Time's Power* (1989), *An Atlas of the Difficult World* (1991), *Dark Fields of the Republic: Poems 1991–1995* (1995), *Midnight Salvage: Poems 1995–1998* (1999), *Fox* (2001), and *The School Among the Ruins* (2004), demonstrate an ongoing power of language and deepening poetic vision. *Telephone Ringing in the Labyrinth* (2007) collects poems from 2004–06. Late in her life, Rich published *A Human Eye: Essays on Art in Society, 1997–2008*, *Tonight No Poetry Will Serve: Poems 2007–2010*, and *Later Poems: Selected and New, 1971–2012*. Reading through her poems we may sometimes wish for more relaxation and playfulness, for a liberating comic sense of self almost never present in her work. What we find, however, is invaluable—a poet whose imagination confronts and resists the harsh necessities of our times and keeps alive a vision of what is possible: "a whole new poetry beginning here" ("Transcendental Etude").

Snapshots of a Daughter-in-Law

1

You, once a belle in Shreveport,
with henna-colored hair, skin like a peachbud,
still have your dresses copied from that time,
and play a Chopin prelude

called by Cortot: *"Delicious recollections*   5
float like perfume through the memory."[1]

Your mind now, moldering like wedding-cake,
heavy with useless experience, rich
with suspicion, rumor, fantasy,
crumbling to pieces under the knife-edge   10
of mere fact. In the prime of your life.

Nervy, glowering, your daughter
wipes the teaspoons, grows another way.

2

Banging the coffee-pot into the sink
she hears the angels chiding, and looks out   15
past the raked gardens to the sloppy sky.
Only a week since They said: *Have no patience.*

The next time it was: *Be insatiable.*
Then: *Save yourself; others you cannot save.*
Sometimes she's let the tapstream scald her arm,   20
a match burn to her thumbnail,

or held her hand above the kettle's snout
right in the woolly steam. They are probably angels,
since nothing hurts her anymore, except
each morning's grit blowing into her eyes.   25

3

A thinking woman sleeps with monsters.[2]
The beak that grips her, she becomes. And Nature,
that sprung-lidded, still commodious
steamer-trunk of *tempora* and *mores*[3]
gets stuffed with it all: the mildewed orange-flowers,   30
the female pills, the terrible breasts
of Boadicea[4] beneath flat foxes' heads and orchids.

Two handsome women, gripped in argument,
each proud, acute, subtle, I hear scream
across the cut glass and majolica   35

---

1. A remark made by Alfred Cortot (1877–1962), a well-known French pianist, in his *Chopin: 24 Preludes* (1930); he is referring specifically to Chopin's Prelude No. 7, Andantino, A Major.
2. A reference to W. B. Yeats's "Leda and the Swan," a poem about the rape of a maiden by Zeus in the form of a giant bird. The poem ends: "Did she put on his knowledge with his power / Before the indifferent beak could let her drop?"

3. Times and customs (Latin), an allusion to the Roman orator Cicero's famous phrase "O Tempora! O Mores!" ("Alas for the degeneracy of our times and the low standard of our morals!").
4. British queen in the time of the Emperor Nero; she led her people in a large, ultimately unsuccessful revolt against Roman rule. "Female pills": remedies for menstrual pain.

like Furies[5] cornered from their prey:
The argument *ad feminam*,[6] all the old knives
that have rusted in my back, I drive in yours,
ma semblable, ma soeur![7]

4

Knowing themselves too well in one another: 40
their gifts no pure fruition, but a thorn,
the prick filed sharp against a hint of scorn . . .
Reading while waiting
for the iron to heat,
writing, *My Life had stood—a Loaded Gun*[8]— 45
in that Amherst pantry while the jellies boil and scum,
or, more often,
iron-eyed and beaked and purposed as a bird,
dusting everything on the whatnot every day of life.

5

Dulce ridens, dulce loquens,[9] 50
she shaves her legs until they gleam
like petrified mammoth-tusk.

6

When to her lute Corinna sings[1]
neither words nor music are her own;
only the long hair dipping 55
over her cheek, only the song
of silk against her knees
and these
adjusted in reflections of an eye.

Poised, trembling and unsatisfied, before 60
an unlocked door, that cage of cages,
tell us, you bird, you tragical machine—
is this *fertilisante douleur*?[2] Pinned down
by love, for you the only natural action,
are you edged more keen 65

---

5. Greek goddesses of vengeance. "Majolica": a kind of earthenware with a richly colored glaze.
6. Feminine version of the Latin phrase *ad hominem* (literally, "to the man"), referring to an argument directed not to reason but to personal prejudices and emotions.
7. The last line of Charles Baudelaire's French poem "Au Lecteur" addresses *"Hypocrite lecteur!—mon semblable—mon frère!"* (Hypocrite reader, like me, my brother!); Rich here instead addresses *"ma soeur"* (my sister). See also T. S. Eliot, "The Waste Land," line 76.

8. *"Emily Dickinson, Complete Poems*, ed. T. H. Johnson, 1960, p. 369" [Rich's note]; this is the poem numbered 754 in the Johnson edition. Amherst, Massachusetts, is the town where Dickinson lived her entire life (1830–1886).
9. Sweetly laughing, sweetly speaking (Latin, from Horace, *Odes*, 22.23–24).
1. First line of a lyric poem by Thomas Campion (1567–1620) about the extent to which a courtier is moved by Corinna's beautiful music.
2. Fertilizing (or life-giving) sorrow (French).

to prise the secrets of the vault? has Nature shown
her household books to you, daughter-in-law,
that her sons never saw?

7

"To have in this uncertain world some stay
which cannot be undermined, is   70
of the utmost consequence."[3]
             Thus wrote
a woman, partly brave and partly good,
who fought with what she partly understood.
Few men about her would or could do more,   75
hence she was labeled harpy, shrew and whore.

8

"You all die at fifteen," said Diderot,[4]
and turn part legend, part convention.
Still, eyes inaccurately dream
behind closed windows blankening with steam.   80
Deliciously, all that we might have been,
all that we were—fire, tears,
wit, taste, martyred ambition—
stirs like the memory of refused adultery
the drained and flagging bosom of our middle years.   85

9

Not that it is done well, but
that it is done at all?[5] Yes, think
of the odds! or shrug them off forever.
This luxury of the precocious child,
Time's precious chronic invalid,—   90
would we, darlings, resign it if we could?
Our blight has been our sinecure:
mere talent was enough for us—
glitter in fragments and rough drafts.

Sigh no more, ladies.   95
            Time is male
and in his cups drinks to the fair.
Bemused by gallantry, we hear
our mediocrities over-praised,
indolence read as abnegation,   100

3. "From Mary Wollstonecraft, *Thoughts on the Education of Daughters*, London, 1787" [Rich's note]. Wollstonecraft (1759–1797), one of the first feminist thinkers, is best-known for her "Vindication of the Rights of Woman."
4. Denis Diderot (1713–1784), French philosopher, encyclopedist, playwright, and critic. " 'You all die at fifteen': 'Vous mourez toutes à quinze ans,' from the *Lettres à Sophie Volland*, quoted by Simone de Beauvoir in *Le Deuxième Sexe*, Vol. II, pp. 123–24" [Rich's note].
5. An allusion to Samuel Johnson's remark to James Boswell: "Sir, a woman's preaching is like a dog's walking on his hinder legs. It is not done well; but you are surprised to find it done at all" (July 31, 1763).

slattern thought styled intuition,
every lapse forgiven, our crime
only to cast too bold a shadow
or smash the mold straight off.

For that, solitary confinement,   105
tear gas, attrition shelling.
Few applicants for that honor.

                              10

                    Well,
she's long about her coming, who must be
more merciless to herself than history.   110
Her mind full to the wind, I see her plunge
breasted and glancing through the currents,
taking the light upon her
at least as beautiful as any boy
or helicopter,[6]   115
                    poised, still coming,
her fine blades making the air wince

but her cargo
no promise then:
delivered   120
palpable
ours.

1958–60   1963

              "I Am in Danger—Sir—"[1]

"Half-cracked" to Higginson,[2] living,
afterward famous in garbled versions,
your hoard of dazzling scraps a battlefield,
now your old snood

mothballed at Harvard   5
and you in your variorum monument[3]

6. "She comes down from the remoteness of ages, from Thebes, from Crete, from Chichén-Itzá; and she is also the totem set deep in the African jungle; she is a helicopter and she is a bird; and there is this, the greatest wonder of all: under her tinted hair the forest murmur becomes a thought, and words issue from her breasts" (Simone de Beauvoir, *The Second Sex*, trans. H. M. Parshley [New York, 1953], 729). (A translation of the passage from *Le Deuxième Sexe*, Vol. II, 574, cited in French by Rich.)
1. A sentence in a letter from Emily Dickinson to Thomas Wentworth Higginson (1823–1911), a critic and editor with whom she opened correspondence in 1862 and to whom she sent some of her poems. She writes: "You think my gait 'spasmodic'—I am in danger—Sir—You think me 'uncontrolled'—I have no Tribunal."
2. In a letter Higginson described Dickinson as "my partially cracked Poetess at Amherst."
3. *The Poems of Emily Dickinson*, ed. Thomas H. Johnson, 3 vols. (Cambridge, Mass., 1955) is a "variorum" in that it contains all the variant readings in her manuscripts. "Mothballed at Harvard": the Houghton Rare Books Library at Harvard University has a collection of Emily Dickinson manuscripts and memorabilia.

equivocal to the end—
who are you?

Gardening the day-lily,
wiping the wine-glass stems,   10
your thought pulsed on behind
a forehead battered paper-thin,

you, woman, masculine
in single-mindedness,
for whom the word was more   15
than a symptom—

a condition of being.
Till the air buzzing with spoiled language
sang in your ears
of Perjury   20

and in your half-cracked way you chose
silence for entertainment,
chose to have it out at last
on your own premises.

1964   1966

A Valediction Forbidding Mourning[1]

My swirling wants. Your frozen lips.
The grammar turned and attacked me.
Themes, written under duress.
Emptiness of the notations.

They gave me a drug that slowed the healing of wounds.   5

I want you to see this before I leave:
the experience of repetition as death
the failure of criticism to locate the pain
the poster in the bus that said:
my bleeding is under control.   10

A red plant in a cemetery of plastic wreaths.

A last attempt: the language is a dialect called metaphor.
These images go unglossed: hair, glacier, flashlight.
When I think of a landscape I am thinking of a time.
When I talk of taking a trip I mean forever.   15

---

1. Title of a famous poem by John Donne (1572–1631) in which the English poet forbids his wife to lament his departure for a trip to the Continent.

I could say: those mountains have a meaning
but further than that I could not say.

To do something very common, in my own way.

1970   1971

Diving into the Wreck

First having read the book of myths,
and loaded the camera,
and checked the edge of the knife-blade,
I put on
the body-armor of black rubber   5
the absurd flippers
the grave and awkward mask.
I am having to do this
not like Cousteau[1] with his
assiduous team   10
aboard the sun-flooded schooner
but here alone.

There is a ladder.
The ladder is always there
hanging innocently   15
close to the side of the schooner.
We know what it is for,
we who have used it.
Otherwise
it's a piece of maritime floss   20
some sundry equipment.

I go down.
Rung after rung and still
the oxygen immerses me
the blue light   25
the clear atoms
of our human air.
I go down.
My flippers cripple me,
I crawl like an insect down the ladder   30
and there is no one
to tell me when the ocean
will begin.

First the air is blue and then
it is bluer and then green and then   35
black I am blacking out and yet

1. Jacques-Yves Cousteau (1910–1997), French underwater explorer and author.

my mask is powerful
it pumps my blood with power
the sea is another story
the sea is not a question of power   40
I have to learn alone
to turn my body without force
in the deep element.

And now: it is easy to forget
what I came for   45
among so many who have always
lived here
swaying their crenellated fans
between the reefs
and besides   50
you breathe differently down here.

I came to explore the wreck.
The words are purposes.
The words are maps.
I came to see the damage that was done   55
and the treasures that prevail.
I stroke the beam of my lamp
slowly along the flank
of something more permanent
than fish or weed   60

the thing I came for:
the wreck and not the story of the wreck
the thing itself and not the myth
the drowned face[2] always staring
toward the sun   65
the evidence of damage
worn by salt and sway into this threadbare beauty
the ribs of the disaster
curving their assertion
among the tentative haunters.   70

This is the place.
And I am here, the mermaid whose dark hair
streams black, the merman in his armored body
We circle silently
about the wreck   75
we dive into the hold.
I am she: I am he

whose drowned face sleeps with open eyes
whose breasts still bear the stress
whose silver, copper, vermeil cargo lies   80

2. Referring to the ornamental female figurehead that formed the prow of many old sailing ships.

obscurely inside barrels
half-wedged and left to rot
we are the half-destroyed instruments
that once held to a course
the water-eaten log   85
the fouled compass

We are, I am, you are
by cowardice or courage
the one who find our way
back to this scene   90
carrying a knife, a camera
a book of myths
in which
our names do not appear.

1972   1973

Power

Living   in the earth-deposits   of our history

Today a backhoe divulged   out of a crumbling flank of earth
one bottle   amber   perfect   a hundred-year-old
cure for fever   or melancholy   a tonic
for living on this earth   in the winters of this climate   5

Today I was reading about Marie Curie:[1]
she must have known she suffered   from radiation sickness
her body bombarded for years   by the element
she had purified
It seems she denied to the end   10
the source of the cataracts on her eyes
the cracked and suppurating[2] skin   of her finger-ends
till she could no longer hold   a test-tube or a pencil

She died   a famous woman   denying
her wounds   15
denying
her wounds   came   from the same source as her power

1974   1978

---

1. Physical chemist (1867–1934) who with her husband investigated radioactivity and on her own discovered polonium and radium; she received the Nobel Prize in 1911.
2. Discharging pus.

Transcendental Etude[1]

for Michelle Cliff

This August evening I've been driving
over backroads fringed with queen anne's lace
my car startling young deer in meadows—one
gave a hoarse intake of her breath and all
four fawns sprang after her   5
into the dark maples.
Three months from today they'll be fair game
for the hit-and-run hunters, glorying
in a weekend's destructive power,
triggers fingered by drunken gunmen, sometimes   10
so inept as to leave the shattered animal
stunned in her blood. But this evening deep in summer
the deer are still alive and free,
nibbling apples from early-laden boughs
so weighted, so englobed   15
with already yellowing fruit
they seem eternal, Hesperidean[2]
in the clear-tuned, cricket-throbbing air.

Later I stood in the dooryard,
my nerves singing the immense   20
fragility of all this sweetness,
this green world already sentimentalized, photographed,
advertised to death. Yet, it persists
stubbornly beyond the fake Vermont
of antique barnboards glazed into discothèques,   25
artificial snow, the sick Vermont of children
conceived in apathy, grown to winters
of rotgut violence,
poverty gnashing its teeth like a blind cat at their lives.
Still, it persists. Turning off onto a dirt road   30
from the raw cuts bulldozed through a quiet village
for the tourist run to Canada,
I've sat on a stone fence above a great, soft, sloping field
of musing heifers, a farmstead
slanting its planes calmly in the calm light,   35
a dead elm raising bleached arms
above a green so dense with life,
minute, momentary life—slugs, moles, pheasants, gnats,
spiders, moths, hummingbirds, groundhogs, butterflies—
a lifetime is too narrow   40
to understand it all, beginning with the huge
rockshelves that underlie all that life.

---

1. "Etude": a piece of music played for the practice of a point of technique or a composition built on technique but played for its artistic value.

2. I.e., like the golden apples of the tree guarded by the Hesperides, daughters of Atlas, in Greek mythology.

No one ever told us we had to study our lives,
make of our lives a study, as if learning natural history
or music, that we should begin   45
with the simple exercises first
and slowly go on trying
the hard ones, practicing till strength
and accuracy became one with the daring
to leap into transcendence, take the chance   50
of breaking down in the wild arpeggio
or faulting the full sentence of the fugue.[3]
—And in fact we can't live like that: we take on
everything at once before we've even begun
to read or mark time, we're forced to begin   55
in the midst of the hardest movement,
the one already sounding as we are born.
At most we're allowed a few months
of simply listening to the simple line
of a woman's voice singing a child   60
against her heart. Everything else is too soon,
too sudden, the wrenching-apart, that woman's heartbeat
heard ever after from a distance,
the loss of that ground-note echoing
whenever we are happy, or in despair.   65

Everything else seems beyond us,
we aren't ready for it, nothing that was said
is true for us, caught naked in the argument,
the counterpoint, trying to sightread
what our fingers can't keep up with, learn by heart   70
what we can't even read. And yet
it *is* this we were born to. We aren't virtuosi
or child prodigies, there are no prodigies
in this realm, only a half-blind, stubborn
cleaving to the timbre, the tones of what we are   75
—even when all the texts describe it differently.

And we're not performers, like Liszt,[4] competing
against the world for speed and brilliance
(the 79-year-old pianist said, when I asked her
What makes a virtuoso?—Competitiveness.)   80
The longer I live the more I mistrust
theatricality, the false glamour cast
by performance, the more I know its poverty beside
the truths we are salvaging from
the splitting-open of our lives.   85
The woman who sits watching, listening,
eyes moving in the darkness

---

3. Musical piece characterized by the interweaving of several voices. "Arpeggio": production of a chord's tones in succession.

4. Franz Liszt (1811–1886), Hungarian composer
and pianist noted for his virtuoso performances.

in rehearsing in her body, hearing-out in her blood
a score touched off in her perhaps
by some words, a few chords, from the stage: 90
a tale only she can tell.

But there come times—perhaps this is one of them—
when we have to take ourselves more seriously or die;
when we have to pull back from the incantations,
rhythms we've moved to thoughtlessly,   95
and disenthrall ourselves, bestow
ourselves to silence, or a severer listening, cleansed
of oratory, formulas, choruses, laments, static
crowding the wires. We cut the wires,
find ourselves in free-fall, as if   100
our true home were the undimensional
solitudes, the rift
in the Great Nebula.[5]
No one who survives to speak
new language, has avoided this: 105
the cutting-away of an old force that held her
rooted to an old ground
the pitch of utter loneliness
where she herself and all creation
seem equally dispersed, weightless, her being a cry   110
to which no echo comes or can ever come.

But in fact we were always like this,
rootless, dismembered: knowing it makes the difference.
Birth stripped our birthright from us,
tore us from a woman, from women, from ourselves   115
so early on
and the whole chorus throbbing at our ears
like midges, told us nothing, nothing
of origins, nothing we needed
to know, nothing that could re-member us.   120

Only: that it is unnatural,
the homesickness for a woman, for ourselves,
for that acute joy at the shadow her head and arms
cast on a wall, her heavy or slender
thighs on which we lay, flesh against flesh,   125
eyes steady on the face of love; smell of her milk, her sweat,
terror of her disappearance, all fused in this hunger
for the element they have called most dangerous, to be
lifted breathtaken on her breast, to rock within her
—even if beaten back, stranded against, to apprehend   130
in a sudden brine-clear thought

5. A nebula is an immense body of rarefied gas or dust in interstellar space. Rich may be referring to the Great Nebula in the Orion constellation or to a body of dark nebulae, usually called the "Great Rift," which in photographs appears to divide the Milky Way.

trembling like the tiny, orbed, endangered
egg-sac of a new world:
This is what she was to me, and this
is how I can love myself—   135
as only a woman can love me.

Homesick for myself, for her—as, after the heatwave
breaks, the clear tones of the world
manifest: cloud, bough, wall, insect, the very soul of light:
homesick as the fluted vault of desire   140
articulates itself: *I am the lover and the loved,*
home and wanderer, she who splits
firewood and she who knocks, a stranger
in the storm, two women, eye to eye
measuring each other's spirit, each other's   145
limitless desire,
                    a whole new poetry beginning here.

Vision begins to happen in such a life
as if a woman quietly walked away
from the argument and jargon in a room   150
and sitting down in the kitchen, began turning in her lap
bits of yarn, calico and velvet scraps,
laying them out absently on the scrubbed boards
in the lamplight, with small rainbow-colored shells
sent in cotton-wool from somewhere far away,   155
and skeins of milkweed from the nearest meadow—
original domestic silk, the finest findings—
and the darkblue petal of the petunia,
and the dry darkbrown lace of seaweed;
not forgotten either, the shed silver   160
whisker of the cat,
the spiral of paper-wasp-nest curling
beside the finch's yellow feather.
Such a composition has nothing to do with eternity,
the striving for greatness, brilliance—   165
only with the musing of a mind
one with her body, experienced fingers quietly pushing
dark against bright, silk against roughness,
pulling the tenets of a life together
with no mere will to mastery,   170
only care for the many-lived, unending
forms in which she finds herself,
becoming now the sherd of broken glass
slicing light in a corner, dangerous
to flesh, now the plentiful, soft leaf   175
that wrapped round the throbbing finger, soothes the wound;
and now the stone foundation, rockshelf further
forming underneath everything that grows.

1977   1978

Shattered Head

A life hauls itself uphill
    through hoar-mist steaming
the sun's tongue licking
    leaf upon leaf into stricken liquid
When? When? cry the soothseekers   5
    but time is a bloodshot eye
seeing its last of beauty its own
    foreclosure
                a bloodshot mind
finding itself unspeakable   10
    What is the last thought?
Now I will let you know?
    or, *Now I know?*
(porridge of skull-splinters, brain tissue
    mouth and throat membrane, cranial fluid)   15

Shattered head on the breast
    of a wooded hill
laid down there endlessly so
    tendrils soaked into matted compost
become a root   20
    torqued over the faint springhead
groin whence illegible
    matter leaches: worm-borings, spurts of silt
volumes of sporic changes
    hair long blown into far follicles   25
blasted into a chosen place

Revenge on the head (genitals, breast, untouched)
    revenge on the mouth
packed with its inarticulate confessions
    revenge on the eyes   30
green-gray and restless
    revenge on the big and searching lips
                the tender tongue
revenge on the sensual, on the nose the
    carrier of history   35
revenge on the life devoured
in another incineration

You can walk by such a place, the earth is made of them
where the stretched tissue of a field or woods is humid
        with belovéd matter   40
the soothseekers have withdrawn
you feel no ghost, only a sporic chorus
when that place utters its worn sigh
    let us have peace

And the shattered head answers back   45
   I believed I was loved, I believed I loved,
     who did this to us?

1996–97   1999

Five O'Clock, January 2003

Tonight as cargoes of my young
fellow countrymen and women are being hauled
into positions aimed at death, positions
they who did not will it suddenly
have to assume   5
I am thinking of Ed Azevedo
half-awake in recovery
if he has his arm whole
and how much pain he must bear
under the drugs   10
On cliffs above a beach
luxuriant in low tide after storms
littered with driftwood hurled and piled and
humanly arranged in fantastic
installations and beyond   15
silk-blue and onion-silver-skinned
Jeffers' "most glorious creature on earth"[1]
we passed, greeting, I saw his arm
bandaged to the elbow
asked and he told me: It was just   20
a small cut, nothing, on the hand he'd
washed in peroxide thinking
that was it until the pain began
traveling up his arm
and then the antibiotics the splint the   25
numbing drugs the sick sensation
and this evening at five o'clock the emergency
surgery and last summer
the train from Czechoslovakia to Spain
with his girl, cheap wine, bread and cheese   30
room with a balcony, ocean like this
nobody asking for pay in advance
kindness of foreigners
in that country, sick sensation now
needing to sit in his brother's truck again   35
even the accident on the motorcycle

1. See Robinson Jeffers, "Ninth Anniversary," in *The Wild God of the World: An Anthology of Robinson Jeffers*, ed. Albert Gelpi (Stanford, Calif.: Stanford University Press, 2003), p. 52: "there the most glorious / Creature on earth shines in the nights or glitters in the suns, / Or feels of its stone in the blind fog" [Rich's note].

was nothing like this
I'll be thinking of you at five
this evening I said
afterward you'll feel better, your body   40
will be clean of this poison
I didn't say Your war is here
but could you have believed
that from a small thing infection
would crawl through the blood   45
and the enormous ruffled shine
of an ocean wouldn't tell you.

2003   2004

Wait

In paradise every
the desert wind is rising
third thought
in hell there are no thoughts
is of earth   5
sand screams against your government
issued tent   hell's noise
in your nostrils   crawl
into your ear-shell
wrap ourself in no-thought   10
wait   no place for the little lyric
wedding-ring glint the reason why
on earth
they never told you

2003   2004

URSULA K. LE GUIN
b. 1929

Gender, social behavior, and art combine in Ursula K. Le Guin's fiction to create model worlds, all with their own systems of organized belief. In doing so this author inquires more broadly and with more depth than is usual in science fiction. Traditionally, science fiction writers have been at their best when dealing with dystopian worlds, projecting alternative visions in which their satiric powers criticize contemporary tendencies gone bad in a nightmare future; utopias within this subgenre are more often declarative statements of what would be good—and therefore less interesting and less engaging as art. Le Guin distinguishes herself by demonstrating a sincere interest in exploring the legitimacy of other styles of existence—not just what they are but how they work. Her utopian creations are tested against all we know not just about physical and mechanical science but about anthropology in general and gender relationships in particular.

Drawing on what she first learned from Alfred L. and Theodora K. Kroeber, her anthropologist father and folklorist/writer mother, Le Guin has produced science fiction that shifts readers' interests from the pageantry of outer-space discovery and battle to the more subtle dimensions of human identity and communication. Foremost is the power of art. In "A Wizard of Earthsea" (1968) the power of naming something brings it into being; a similar creative effect is apparent in "She Unnames Them" (printed here), in which Eve revises Adam's masculine, typifying style by introducing an ethic representative of woman's feelings. Her novel *The Left Hand of Darkness* (1969) shows a human ethnologist investigating a world in which gender does not shape reality at all. In this society of hermaphrodites who experience sexual distinctions only for a short time during reproduction, such limitations as binary thinking disappear. Yet this is no simple utopia, for the author believes that any reality is a cultural rather than strictly scientific description—and that one description is superior to another only in its functional persuasiveness. Hence even her creatures in *The Left Hand of Darkness* need to overcome the restrictions of their society and develop secure identities capable of sharing love. This same appraisal informs her story "Schrödinger's Cat" (printed here), in which the famous Austrian physicist's great *Gedankenexperiment* (literally "thought experiment," as opposed to a demonstration with physical matter) is examined in terms of its cultural implications, not its scientific truth. A similarly complex understanding of socioeconomics informs the action of "The Dispossessed" (1974), in which a scientist compares visits to an outworn anarchistic utopia with a younger world whose capitalistic versus communistic rivalries are much like our own. Here, as is usual in her work, Le Guin dresses her thought with rich nuances of character and motivated behavior; the intelligence behind her work is always accessible in human terms—sometimes uncomfortably revealing terms, as is apparent in the manner of her narrators in "She Unnames Them" and "Schrödinger's Cat."

Born in Berkeley, California, where her father taught at the University of California, Le Guin was raised in this academic environment before attending Radcliffe College (for an undergraduate degree in French) and Columbia University (for a master's degree in romance languages). Her longtime residence has been in Oregon, and the ecology of the Pacific Northwest figures as an element in her fiction as well as in the amazing amount and variety of her other work. In addition to many novels (often written in trilogies), she has written poetry, essays, children's books, and ecological statements and has collaborated on photographic and cinematic projects. As a science fictionist she is one of the most highly honored writers in her field, a consistent winner of the subgenre's highest awards, including the Hugo and the Nebula several times.

Both of the following texts are from *The Compass Rose* (1982).

Schrödinger's Cat[1]

As things appear to be coming to some sort of climax, I have withdrawn to this place. It is cooler here, and nothing moves fast.

On the way here I met a married couple who were coming apart. She had pretty well gone to pieces, but he seemed, at first glance, quite hearty. While he was telling me that he had no hormones of any kind, she pulled herself together and, by supporting her head in the crook of her right knee and hopping on the toes of the right foot, approached us shouting, "Well what's *wrong* with a person trying to express themselves?" The left leg, the arms, and the trunk, which had remained lying in the heap, twitched and jerked in sympathy. "Great legs," the husband pointed out, looking at the slim ankle. "My wife has great legs."

A cat has arrived, interrupting my narrative. It is a striped yellow tom with white chest and paws. He has long whiskers and yellow eyes. I never noticed before that cats had whiskers above their eyes; is that normal? There is no way to tell. As he has gone to sleep on my knee, I shall proceed.

Where?

Nowhere, evidently. Yet the impulse to narrate remains. Many things are not worth doing, but almost anything is worth telling. In any case, I have a severe congenital case of *Ethica laboris puritanica*,[2] or Adam's Disease. It is incurable except by total decapitation. I even like to dream when asleep, and to try and recall my dreams: it assures me that I haven't wasted seven or eight hours just lying there. Now here I am, lying, here. Hard at it.

Well, the couple I was telling you about finally broke up. The pieces of him trotted around bouncing and cheeping, like little chicks, but she was finally reduced to nothing but a mass of nerves: rather like fine chicken wire, in fact, but hopelessly tangled.

So I came on, placing one foot carefully in front of the other, and grieving. This grief is with me still. I fear it is part of me, like foot or loin or eye, or may even be myself: for I seem to have no other self, nothing further, nothing that lies outside the borders of grief.

Yet I don't know what I grieve for: my wife? my husband? my children, or myself? I can't remember. Most dreams are forgotten, try as one will to remember. Yet later music strikes the note, and the harmonic rings along the mandolin strings of the mind, and we find tears in our eyes. Some note keeps playing that makes me want to cry; but what for? I am not certain.

---

1. The Austrian physicist Erwin Schrödinger (1887–1961) proposed the following thought experiment in 1935: if a cat is sealed in a box such that it will die in the event of a random and unpredictable atomic-level event, then, according to quantum theory, the cat is simultane- ously alive and dead until the box is opened for inspection.

2. Puritan work ethic (Latin); a trait the narra- tor sees as a necessary consequence of the bibli- cal expulsion from the Garden of Eden ("Adam's Disease").

The yellow cat, who may have belonged to the couple that broke up, is dreaming. His paws twitch now and then, and once he makes a small, suppressed remark with his mouth shut. I wonder what a cat dreams of, and to whom he was speaking just then. Cats seldom waste words. They are quiet beasts. They keep their counsel, they reflect. They reflect all day, and at night their eyes reflect. Overbred Siamese cats may be as noisy as little dogs, and then people say, "They're talking," but the noise is farther from speech than is the deep silence of the hound or the tabby. All this cat can say is meow, but maybe in his silences he will suggest to me what it is that I have lost, what I am grieving for. I have a feeling that he knows. That's why he came here. Cats look out for Number One.

It was getting awfully hot. I mean, you could touch less and less. The stove burners, for instance. Now I know that stove burners always used to get hot; that was their final cause, they existed in order to get hot. But they began to get hot without having been turned on. Electric units or gas rings, there they'd be when you came into the kitchen for breakfast, all four of them glaring away, the air above them shaking like clear jelly with the heat waves. It did no good to turn them off, because they weren't on in the first place. Besides, the knobs and dials were also hot, uncomfortable to the touch.

Some people tried hard to cool them off. The favorite technique was to turn them on. It worked sometimes, but you could not count on it. Others investigated the phenomenon, tried to get at the root of it, the cause. They were probably the most frightened ones, but man is most human at his most frightened. In the face of the hot stove burners they acted with exemplary coolness. They studied, they observed. They were like the fellow in Michelangelo's *Last Judgment*,[3] has clapped his hands over his face in horror as the devils drag him down to Hell—but only over one eye. The other eye is busy looking. It's all he can do, but he does it. He observes. Indeed, one wonders if Hell would exist, if he did not look at it. However, neither he, nor the people I am talking about, had enough time left to do much about it. And then finally of course there were the people who did not try to do or think anything about it at all.

When the water came out of the cold-water taps hot one morning, however, even people who had blamed it all on the Democrats began to feel a more profound unease. Before long, forks and pencils and wrenches were too hot to handle without gloves; and cars were really terrible. It was like opening the door of an oven going full blast, to open the door of your car. And by then, other people almost scorched your fingers off. A kiss was like a branding iron. Your child's hair flowed along your hand like fire.

Here, as I said, it is cooler; and, as a matter of fact, this animal is cool. A real cool cat. No wonder it's pleasant to pet his fur. Also he moves slowly, at least for the most part, which is all the slowness one can reasonably expect of a cat. He hasn't that frenetic quality most creatures acquired—all they did was ZAP and gone. They lacked presence. I suppose birds always tended to be that way, but even the hummingbird used to halt for a second in the very center of his metabolic frenzy, and hang, still as a hub, present, above the fuchsias—then gone again, but you knew something was there besides

3. Monumental fresco in the Vatican's Sistine Chapel by the Italian Renaissance painter Michelangelo Buonarotti (1475–1564).

the blurring brightness. But it got so that even robins and pigeons, the heavy impudent birds, were a blur; and as for swallows, they cracked the sound barrier. You knew of swallows only by the small, curved sonic booms that looped about the eaves of old houses in the evening.

Worms shot like subway trains through the dirt of gardens, among the writhing roots of roses.

You could scarcely lay a hand on children, by then: too fast to catch, too hot to hold. They grew up before your eyes.

But then, maybe that's always been true.

I was interrupted by the cat, who woke and said meow once, then jumped down from my lap and leaned against my legs diligently. This is a cat who knows how to get fed. He also knows how to jump. There was a lazy fluidity to his leap, as if gravity affected him less than it does other creatures. As a matter of fact there were some localised cases, just before I left, of the failure of gravity; but this quality in the cat's leap was something quite else. I am not yet in such a state of confusion that I can be alarmed by grace. Indeed, I found it reassuring. While I was opening a can of sardines, a person arrived.

Hearing the knock, I thought it might be the mailman. I miss mail very much, so I hurried to the door and said, "Is it the mail?"

A voice replied, "Yah!" I opened the door. He came in, almost pushing me aside in his haste. He dumped down an enormous knapsack he had been carrying, straightened up, massaged his shoulders, and said, "Wow!"

"How did you get here?"

He stared at me and repeated, "How?"

At this my thoughts concerning human and animal speech recurred to me, and I decided that this was probably not a man, but a small dog. (Large dogs seldom go yah, wow, how, unless it is appropriate to do so.)

"Come on, fella," I coaxed him. "Come, come on, that's a boy, good doggie!" I opened a can of pork and beans for him at once, for he looked half starved. He ate voraciously, gulping and lapping. When it was gone he said "Wow!" several times. I was just about to scratch him behind the ears when he stiffened, his hackles bristling, and growled deep in his throat. He had noticed the cat.

The cat had noticed him some time before, without interest, and was now sitting on a copy of *The Well-Tempered Clavier*[4] washing sardine oil off its whiskers.

"Wow!" the dog, whom I had thought of calling Rover, barked. "Wow! Do you know what that is? *That's Schrödinger's cat!*"

"No it's not, not any more; it's my cat," I said, unreasonably offended.

"Oh, well, Schrödinger's dead, of course, but it's his cat. I've seen hundreds of pictures of it. Erwin Schrödinger, the great physicist, you know. Oh, wow! To think of finding it here!"

The cat looked coldly at him for a moment, and began to wash its left shoulder with negligent energy. An almost religious expression had come into Rover's face. "It was meant," he said in a low, impressive tone. "Yah. It was *meant*. It can't be a mere coincidence. It's too improbable. Me, with the box; you, with the cat; to meet—here—now." He looked up at me, his eyes

---

4. Keyboard music by the German Baroque-era composer Johann Sebastian Bach (1685–1750).

shining with happy fervor. "Isn't it wonderful?" he said. "I'll get the box set up right away." And he started to tear open his huge knapsack.

While the cat washed its front paws, Rover unpacked. While the cat washed its tail and belly, regions hard to reach gracefully, Rover put together what he had unpacked, a complex task. When he and the cat finished their operations simultaneously and looked at me, I was impressed. They had come out even, to the very second. Indeed it seemed that something more than chance was involved. I hoped it was not myself.

"What's that?" I asked, pointing to a protuberance on the outside of the box. I did not ask what the box was as it was quite clearly a box.

"The gun," Rover said with excited pride.

"The gun?"

"To shoot the cat."

"To shoot the cat?"

"Or to *not shoot* the cat. Depending on the photon."

"The photon?"

"Yah! It's Schrödinger's great Gedankenexperiment.[5] You see, there's a little emitter here. At Zero Time, five seconds after the lid of the box is closed, it will emit one photon. The photon will strike a half-silvered mirror. The quantum mechanical probability of the photon passing through the mirror is exactly one half, isn't it? So! If the photon passes through, the trigger will be activated and the gun will fire. If the photon is deflected, the trigger will not be activated and the gun will not fire. Now, you put the cat in. The cat is in the box. You close the lid. You go away! You stay away! What happens?" Rover's eyes were bright.

"The cat gets hungry?"

"The cat gets shot—or not shot," he said, seizing my arm, though not, fortunately, in his teeth. "But the gun is silent, perfectly silent. The box is soundproof. There is no way to know whether or not the cat has been shot, until you lift the lid of the box. There is *no* way! Do you see how central this is to the whole of quantum theory? Before Zero Time the whole system, on the quantum level or on our level, is nice and simple. But after Zero Time the whole system can be represented only by a linear combination of two waves. We cannot predict the behavior of the photon, and thus, once it has behaved, we cannot predict the state of the system it has determined. We cannot predict it! God plays dice with the world![6] So it is beautifully demonstrated that if you desire certainty, any certainty, you must create it yourself!"

"How?"

"By lifting the lid of the box, of course," Rover said, looking at me with sudden disappointment, perhaps a touch of suspicion, like a Baptist who finds he has been talking church matters not to another Baptist as he thought, but a Methodist, or even, God forbid, an Episcopalian. "To find out whether the cat is dead or not."

"Do you mean," I said carefully, "that until you lift the lid of the box, the cat has neither been shot nor not been shot?"

"Yah!" Rover said, radiant with relief, welcoming me back to the fold. "Or maybe, you know, both."

5. Thought experiment (German, literal trans.); the intellectual demonstration of a theory, often making use of analogy.

6. The German-born American physicist Albert Einstein (1879–1955) stated that God *did not* play dice with the universe.

"But why does opening the box and looking reduce the system back to one probability, either live cat or dead cat? Why don't we get included in the system when we lift the lid of the box?"

There was a pause. "How?" Rover barked, distrustfully.

"Well, we would involve ourselves in the system, you see, the superposition of two waves. There's no reason why it should only exist *inside* an open box, is there? So when we came to look, there we would be, you and I, both looking at a live cat, and both looking at a dead cat. You see?"

A dark cloud lowered on Rover's eyes and brow. He barked twice in a subdued, harsh voice, and walked away. With his back turned to me he said in a firm, sad tone, "You must not complicate the issue. It is complicated enough."

"Are you sure?"

He nodded. Turning, he spoke pleadingly. "Listen. It's all we have—the box. Truly it is. The box. And the cat. And they're here. The box, the cat, at last. Put the cat in the box. Will you? Will you let me put the cat in the box?"

"No," I said, shocked.

"Please. Please. Just for a minute. Just for half a minute! Please let me put the cat in the box!"

"Why?"

"I can't stand this terrible uncertainty," he said, and burst into tears.

I stood some while indecisive. Though I felt sorry for the poor son of a bitch, I was about to tell him, gently, No; when a curious thing happened. The cat walked over to the box, sniffed around it, lifted his tail and sprayed a corner to mark his territory, and then lightly, with that marvellous fluid ease, leapt into it. His yellow tail just flicked the edge of the lid as he jumped, and it closed, falling into place with a soft, decisive click.

"The cat is in the box," I said.

"The cat is in the box," Rover repeated in a whisper, falling to his knees. "Oh, wow. Oh, wow. Oh, wow."

There was silence then: deep silence. We both gazed, I afoot, Rover kneeling, at the box. No sound. Nothing happened. Nothing would happen. Nothing would ever happen, until we lifted the lid of the box.

"Like Pandora,"[7] I said in a weak whisper. I could not quite recall Pandora's legend. She had let all the plagues and evils out of the box, of course, but there had been something else, too. After all the devils were let loose, something quite different, quite unexpected, had been left. What had it been? Hope? A dead cat? I could not remember.

Impatience welled up in me. I turned on Rover, glaring. He returned the look with expressive brown eyes. You can't tell me dogs haven't got souls.

"Just exactly what are you trying to prove?" I demanded.

"That the cat will be dead, or not dead," he murmured submissively. "Certainty. All I want is certainty. To know for *sure* that God *does* play dice with the world."

I looked at him for a while with fascinated incredulity. "Whether he does, or doesn't," I said, "do you think he's going to leave you a note about it in the box?" I went to the box, and with a rather dramatic gesture, flung the lid back. Rover staggered up from his knees, gasping, to look. The cat was, of course, not there.

---

7. In Greek mythology the first mortal woman, who out of curiosity opened a box and released human ills into the world; another version has her losing all human blessings except hope.

Rover neither barked, nor fainted, nor cursed, nor wept. He really took it very well.

"Where is the cat?" he asked at last.

"Where is the box?"

"Here."

"Where's here?"

"Here is now."

"We used to think so," I said, "but really we should use larger boxes."

He gazed about him in mute bewilderment, and did not flinch even when the roof of the house was lifted off just like the lid of a box, letting in the unconscionable, inordinate light of the stars. He had just time to breathe, "Oh, wow!"

I have identified the note that keeps sounding. I checked it on the mandolin before the glue melted. It is the note A, the one that drove the composer Schumann mad.[8] It is a beautiful, clear tone, much clearer now that the stars are visible. I shall miss the cat. I wonder if he found what it was we lost?

1982

She Unnames Them

Most of them accepted namelessness with the perfect indifference with which they had so long accepted and ignored their names. Whales and dolphins, seals and sea otters consented with particular grace and alacrity, sliding into anonymity as into their element. A faction of yaks, however, protested. They said that "yak" sounded right, and that almost everyone who knew they existed called them that. Unlike the ubiquitous creatures such as rats or fleas who had been called by hundreds or thousands of different names since Babel,[1] the yaks could truly say, they said, that they had *a name*. They discussed the matter all summer. The councils of the elderly females finally agreed that though the name might be useful to others, it was so redundant from the yak point of view that they never spoke it themselves, and hence might as well dispense with it. After they presented the argument in this light to their bulls, a full consensus was delayed only by the onset of severe early blizzards. Soon after the beginning of the thaw their agreement was reached and the designation "yak" was returned to the donor.

Among the domestic animals, few horses had cared what anybody called them since the failure of Dean Swift's[2] attempt to name them from their own vocabulary. Cattle, sheep, swine, asses, mules, and goats, along with chickens, geese, and turkeys, all agreed enthusiastically to give their names back to the people to whom—as they put it—they belonged.

A couple of problems did come up with pets. The cats of course steadfastly denied ever having had any name other than those self-given, unspoken,

---

8. The German Romantic composer and pianist Robert Schumann (1810–1856) died from mental stress that included tinnitus, a persistent ringing in the ears.

1. Biblical city where God determined people wouldn't speak just one language.

2. Anglo-Irish satirist Jonathan Swift (1667–1745), who in book IV of *Gulliver's Travels* (1726) depicts horses who are smarter and more humane than people as a way to mock human pretensions of higher intelligence.

effanineffably personal names which, as the poet named Eliot[3] said, they spend long hours daily contemplating—though none of the contemplators has ever admitted that what they contemplate is in fact their name, and some onlookers have wondered if the object of that meditative gaze might not in fact be the Perfect, or Platonic,[4] Mouse. In any case it is a moot point now. It was with the dogs, and with some parrots, lovebirds, ravens, and mynahs that the trouble arose. These verbally talented individuals insisted that their names were important to them, and flatly refused to part with them. But as soon as they understood that the issue was precisely one of individual choice, and that anybody who wanted to be called Rover, or Froufrou, or Polly, or even Birdie in the personal sense, was perfectly free to do so, not one of them had the least objection to parting with the lower case (or, as regards German creatures, uppercase) generic appellations poodle, parrot, dog, or bird, and all the Linnaean[5] qualifiers that had trailed along behind them for two hundred years like tin cans tied to a tail.

The insects parted with their names in vast clouds and swarms of ephemeral syllables buzzing and stinging and humming and flitting and crawling and tunneling away.

As for the fish of the sea, their names dispersed from them in silence throughout the oceans like faint, dark blurs of cuttlefish ink, and drifted off on the currents without a trace.

None were left now to unname, and yet how close I felt to them when I saw one of them swim or fly or trot or crawl across my way or over my skin, or stalk me in the night, or go along beside me for a while in the day. They seemed far closer than when their names had stood between myself and them like a clear barrier: so close that my fear of them and their fear of me became one same fear. And the attraction that many of us felt, the desire to smell one another's smells, feel or rub or caress one another's scales or skin or feathers or fur, taste one another's blood or flesh, keep one another warm,—that attraction was now all one with the fear, and the hunter could not be told from the hunted, nor the eater from the food.

This was more or less the effect I had been after. It was somewhat more powerful than I had anticipated, but I could not now, in all conscience, make an exception for myself. I resolutely put anxiety away, went to Adam, and said, "You and your father lent me this—gave it to me, actually. It's been really useful, but it doesn't exactly seem to fit very well lately. But thanks very much! It's really been very useful."

It is hard to give back a gift without sounding peevish or ungrateful, and I did not want to leave him with that impression of me. He was not paying much attention, as it happened, and said only, "Put it down over there, OK?" and went on with what he was doing.

One of my reasons for doing what I did was that talk was getting us nowhere; but all the same I felt a little let down. I had been prepared to defend my decision. And I thought that perhaps when he did notice he might

3. T. S. Eliot (1888–1965), American-born British poet and author of *Old Possum's Practical Book of Cats* (1939).
4. The Greek philosopher Plato (427–347 B.C.E.) posited that perfect archetypal forms underlie the many imperfect manifestations of things in the real world.
5. Swedish botanist Carolus Linnaeus (1707–1778) classified plants and animals by using a double Latin name designating genus and species. "Uppercase": in German, all nouns are capitalized.

be upset and want to talk. I put some things away and fiddled around a little, but he continued to do what he was doing and to take no notice of anything else. At last I said, "Well, goodbye, dear. I hope the garden key turns up."

He was fitting parts together, and said without looking around, "OK, fine, dear. When's dinner?"

"I'm not sure," I said. "I'm going now. With the—" I hesitated, and finally said, "With them, you know," and went on. In fact I had only just then realized how hard it would have been to explain myself. I could not chatter away as I used to do, taking it all for granted. My words now must be as slow, as new, as single, as tentative as the steps I took going down the path away from the house, between the dark-branched, tall dancers motionless against the winter shining.

1982

GARY SNYDER
b. 1930

"I try to hold both history and wildness in my mind, that my poems may approach the true measure of things and stand against the unbalance and ignorance of our time," Gary Snyder has said. Throughout his life Snyder has sought alternatives to this imbalance. His quest has led him to the natural world, to the study of mythology and the discipline of Eastern religions, and to living oral traditions including those of Native American societies. Snyder understands the work of poetry as recovery and healing. Like the shaman-poet of primitive cultures whose power to "heal disease and resist death" is "acquired from dreams" (as he writes in the essay "Poetry and the Primitive"), he seeks to restore contact with a vital universe in which all things are interdependent. The journey of Snyder's life and work has taken him back to what he calls "the most archaic values on earth." His poems are acts of cultural criticism, challenges to the dominant values of the contemporary world.

The American West Coast is Snyder's native landscape; its forests and mountains have always attracted him, and they inspire many of his poems. He was born in San Francisco, grew up in Washington State, and later moved with his family to Portland, Oregon. In 1947 he entered Reed College, where he studied anthropology and developed a special interest in Native American cultures (Northwest Coast Indian myths and tales inform his second book, *Myths and Texts*, 1960). After doing graduate work in linguistics at Indiana University, he returned to the West, where he became associated with Kenneth Rexroth and Philip Whalen as well as Jack Kerouac and Allen Ginsberg, all of whom participated in what came to be called the San Francisco Renaissance. In this period Snyder also studied classical Chinese at the University of California at Berkeley and translated some of the Cold Mountain poems of the Zen poet Han-shan. In the mid-1950s Snyder went to Japan, where he resided, except intermittently, until 1968; in Japan he took formal instruction in Buddhism under Zen masters. The various traditions Snyder has studied come together in his varied vision-quest poems.

Snyder's poems, like his life, combine reading and formal study with physical activity; he has worked as a timber scaler, a forest-fire lookout (one of his lookouts inspired "August on Sourdough"), a logger, and a crewman on a tanker in the South Pacific. "My poems follow the rhythms of the physical work I'm doing and the life I'm leading at any given time," he has remarked. The title of his first book, *Riprap* (1959), is a forester's term for, he explains, "a cobble of stone laid on steep slick rock to make a trail for horses in the mountains." Snyder's poems often follow a trail of ascent or descent, as in "Straight-Creek–Great Burn" from his Pulitzer Prize–winning volume *Turtle Island* (1975). Hiking with friends, he experiences the world as dynamic and flowing (running water and "changing clouds"), but the journey brings the walkers to a still point; they lie "resting on dry fern and / watching." From such a stillness the central image of a Snyder poem often rises, like the birds that "arch and loop," then "settle down." The achievement of stillness in a universe of change is, for Snyder, pivotal. The mind empties itself, the individual ego is erased, and the local place reveals the universal.

If Snyder's poems contain a Zenlike stillness, they also exhibit an appealing energy, one source of which is his love of wildness. Like the Henry David Thoreau of *Walden*, explicitly evoked in sections of *Myths and Texts*, Snyder finds a tonic wildness in the natural world, but unlike Thoreau he is an unabashed celebrant of erotic experience (his earlier poems show that he also knows its destructive possibilities). He renders one of the various faces of Eros in "Beneath My Hand and Eye the Distant Hills. Your Body" (from *The Back Country*, 1968).

Some of Snyder's numerous essays on politics and ecology are included in his influential *Earth House Hold* (1969), *The Practice of the Wild* (1990), and *A Place in Space: Ethics, Aesthetics, and Watersheds* (1995). His collections *Axe Handles* (1983), *Left Out in the Rain* (1986), and *No Nature: New and Selected Poems* (1992) confirm that his poems are bound up in the same concerns. *Danger on Peaks* (2004) continues Snyder's explorations of landscape and ecology and also registers the upheavals of change in the earth and in the body, including the world-changing events of September 11, 2001, memorialized in "Falling from a Height, Holding Hands." Although his didactic impulse sometimes leads him to oversimplification, Snyder's political vision remains one strength of his poetry. The potential in this vision for self-importance and over-seriousness is tempered by his sense of humor and the conviction, palpable in his best poems, that his experiences are common and shared. Snyder's poems suggest diverse contexts: his belief in the writer as cultural critic links him to Thoreau and Robert Duncan, his rhythms and strong images recall Ezra Pound, his meticulous attention to the natural world reminds us of Robert Frost and A. R. Ammons. Eclectic yet respectful of ancient traditions, Snyder is an American original who sees his own work as part of a "continual creation," one manifestation of the energy that sustains all life.

Milton[1] by Firelight

Piute Creek,[2] August 1955

"O hell, what do mine eyes
       with grief behold?"[3]
Working with an old
Singlejack miner, who can sense

---

1. John Milton (1608–1674), major English poet and author of *Paradise Lost*, which retells the biblical story of humanity's Fall from Grace.
2. Part of Yosemite National Park, where Snyder served as a fire lookout. The Sierra Nevada mountain range includes Yosemite in its span.
3. Satan's words when he first sees Adam and Eve in the Garden of Eden (*Paradise Lost* 4.358).

The vein and cleavage   5
In the very guts of rock, can
Blast granite, build
Switchbacks⁴ that last for years
Under the beat of snow, thaw, mule-hooves.
What use, Milton, a silly story   10
Of our lost general⁵ parents,
                    eaters of fruit?

The Indian, the chainsaw boy,
And a string of six mules
Came riding down to camp   15
Hungry for tomatoes and green apples.
Sleeping in saddle blankets
Under a bright night-sky
Han River slantwise by morning.
Jays squall   20
Coffee boils

In ten thousand years the Sierras
Will be dry and dead, home of the scorpion.
Ice-scratched slabs and bent trees.
No paradise, no fall,   25
Only the weathering land
The wheeling sky,
Man, with his Satan
Scouring the chaos of the mind.
Oh Hell!   30

Fire down
Too dark to read, miles from a road
The bell-mare clangs in the meadow
That packed dirt for a fill-in
Scrambling through loose rocks   35
On an old trail
All of a summer's day.⁶

                                                    1959

Riprap¹

Lay down these words
Before your mind like rocks.
                    placed solid, by hands
In choice of place, set
Before the body of the mind   5

---

4. Roads ascending a steep incline in a zigzag
pattern.
5. I.e., shared by all of humankind.
6. Alludes to an epic simile describing Satan's fall:
"From morn / to noon he fell, from noon to dewy

eve, / A summer's day" (*Paradise Lost* 1.742–44).
1. A cobble of stone laid on steep slick rock to
make a trail for horses in the mountains [Sny-
der's note].

in space and time:
Solidity of bark, leaf, or wall
           riprap of things:
Cobble of milky way,
           straying planets,   10
These poems, people,
           lost ponies with
Dragging saddles—
           and rocky sure-foot trails.
The worlds like an endless   15
           four-dimensional
Game of Go.[2]
           ants and pebbles
In the thin loam, each rock a word
           a creek-washed stone   20
Granite: ingrained
           with torment of fire and weight
Crystal and sediment linked hot
           all change, in thoughts,
As well as things.   25

           1959

August on Sourdough,[1] A Visit from Dick Brewer

You hitched a thousand miles
           north from San Francisco
Hiked up the mountainside   a mile in the air
The little cabin—one room—
           walled in glass   5
Meadows and snowfields,   hundreds of peaks.
We lay in our sleeping bags
           talking half the night;
Wind in the guy-cables   this summer mountain rain.
Next morning I went with you   10
           as far as the cliffs,
Loaned you my poncho—   the rain across the shale—
You down the snowfield
           flapping in the wind
Waving a last goodbye   half hidden in the clouds   15
To go on hitching
           clear to New York;
Me back to my mountain   and far, far, west.

           1968

2. An ancient Japanese game played with black and white stones, placed one after the other on a checkered board.

1. Mountain in Washington State, where Snyder worked as a fire-watcher during summer 1953.

Beneath My Hand and Eye the Distant Hills. Your Body

What my hand follows on your body
Is the line. A stream of love
   of heat, of light,   what my
   eye   lascivious
         licks   5
   over, watching
   far snow-dappled Uintah mountains[1]
Is that stream.
Of power.   what my
   hand curves over, following the line.   10
   "hip" and "groin"

Where "I"
   follow by hand and eye
   the swimming limit of your body.
As when vision idly dallies on the hills   15
Loving what it feeds on.
   soft cinder cones and craters;
   —Drum Hadley in the Pinacate[2]
     took ten minutes more to look again—
A leap of power unfurling: 20
     left,   right—right—
My heart beat faster looking
   at the snowy Uintah mountains.

As my hand feeds on you
   runs down your side and curls beneath your hip.   25
oil pool; stratum; water—

What "is" within   not known
   but feel it
   sinking with a breath
   pusht ruthless, surely, down.   30

     Beneath this long caress of hand and eye
       "we" learn the flower burning,
         outward, from "below".

                            1968

---

1. In northeastern Utah.   2. California town.

Ripples on the Surface

"Ripples on the surface of the water
were silver salmon passing under—different
from the sorts of ripples caused by breezes"

A scudding plume on the wave—
a humpback whale is   5
breaking out in air up
gulping herring
  —Nature not a book, but a *performance*, a
high old culture

Ever-fresh events   10
scraped out, rubbed out, and used, used, again—
the braided channels of the rivers
hidden under fields of grass—

  The vast wild.
    the house, alone.   15
  the little house in the wild,
    the wild in the house.

  both forgotten.

    No nature.

  Both together, one big empty house   20

           1993

Falling from a Height, Holding Hands

  What was *that*?
  storms of flying glass
  & billowing flames

  a clear day to the far sky—

  better than burning,   5
  hold hands.

  We will be
  two peregrines diving

  all the way down

           2004

DONALD BARTHELME
1931–1989

B orn in Philadelphia, where his parents were attending college, Donald Barthelme was raised in Houston, Texas, where his father became a prominent architect. The author's collegiate experience as a reporter for and editor of the student
newspaper at the University of Houston influenced his career and his literary style.
After army service he returned to Houston and worked on the city newspaper, wrote
publicity for the university, edited the school's quarterly magazine of the arts, *Forum,*
and directed the Contemporary Arts Museum. During these years Barthelme became
fascinated with the mechanical workings of language, from the appearance of type
on the page to verbal equivalents for nonverbal popular artifacts. When in 1962
he moved to New York to edit *Location*, a short-lived journal of literature and art,
and started writing short stories and parodies for the *New Yorker*, Barthelme
began to have a unique impact on literature through his recognition that language,
rather than what language represents, could be the subject of fiction.

Lives, his narratives show, are influenced by the quality of language within which
they are conducted. In today's world a material culture and a communications
medium given to advertising and promotion feed each other in a frenzy of consumption; everything is ingested, nothing is digested, with the result that meaning
becomes a casualty of process. Danger exists in letting fine-sounding words and
phrases pass without questioning the motives that inform them—something that
Barthelme's engineers get away with in "Report" (collected in *Unspeakable Practices,
Unnatural Acts*, 1968) when they propose to work on "realtime online computer-
controlled wish evaporation" (a task they believe necessary in "meeting the rising
expectations of the world's peoples, which are as you know rising entirely too fast").
Witty and satirical, Barthelme could be especially adept at making sophisticated
philosophical points within mundane situations. "Me and Miss Mandible," from his
first collection, *Come Back, Dr. Caligari* (1964), argues a postmodern understanding of semiotics from a sixth-grade classroom to which an adult has been mysteriously returned to suffer, with all his experience, in the company of twelve-year-olds.
What he learns, and wishes he could teach the others now struggling through
behavior molded by television and movies, is that "signs are signs, and that some of
them are lies."

Barthelme's four novels move in the same direction as his ten volumes of short
stories. *Snow White* (1967), like his early fiction, uses a preposterous situation—
the fairy tale character living with seven small men in a contemporary Greenwich
Village apartment—to show how modern life lacks heroism and romance. *The Dead
Father* (1975) is more weighted with psychological issues, principally the power of
fatherhood and how that power is absurdly clung to. Here the author began relying
less on satirical references to current life and more on narrative statement. In the
middle to late 1970s Barthelme's fiction also became more comfortable in describing
life as lived without the superimposition of defamiliarizing actions; *Paradise* (1986)
reads almost conventionally. Yet as had happened so productively in such early work
as "The Balloon" (printed here), Barthelme wondered at existence. At his death he
had completed a fanciful romance, *The King* (published posthumously in 1990); in it
he recasts the situation of Britain in the early years of World War II, applying literally the Arthurian terms to which commentators of the time liked to allude.

The following text is from *Unspeakable Practices, Unnatural Acts* (1968).

The Balloon

The balloon, beginning at a point on Fourteenth Street, the exact location of which I cannot reveal, expanded northward all one night, while people were sleeping, until it reached the Park. There, I stopped it; at dawn the northernmost edges lay over the Plaza,[1] the free-hanging motion was frivolous and gentle. But experiencing a faint irritation at stopping, even to protect the trees, and seeing no reason the balloon should not be allowed to expand upward, over the parts of the city it was already covering, into the "air space" to be found there, I asked the engineers to see to it. This expansion took place throughout the morning, soft imperceptible sighing of gas through the valves. The balloon then covered forty-five blocks north-south and an irregular area east-west, as many as six crosstown blocks on either side of the Avenue[2] in some places. That was the situation, then.

But it is wrong to speak of "situations," implying sets of circumstances leading to some resolution, some escape of tension; there were no situations, simply the balloon hanging there—muted heavy grays and browns for the most part, contrasting with walnut and soft yellows. A deliberate lack of finish, enhanced by skillful installation, gave the surface a rough, forgotten quality; sliding weights on the inside, carefully adjusted, anchored the great, vari-shaped mass at a number of points. Now we have had a flood of original ideas in all media, works of singular beauty as well as significant milestones in the history of inflation, but at that moment there was only *this balloon*, concrete particular, hanging there.

There were reactions. Some people found the balloon "interesting." As a response this seemed inadequate to the immensity of the balloon, the suddenness of its appearance over the city; on the other hand, in the absence of hysteria or other societally induced anxiety, it must be judged a calm "mature" one. There was a certain amount of initial argumentation about the "meaning" of the balloon; this subsided, because we have learned not to insist on meanings, and they are rarely even looked for now, except in cases involving the simplest, safest phenomena. It was agreed that since the meaning of the balloon could never be known absolutely, extended discussion was pointless, or at least less purposeful than the activities of those who, for example, hung green and blue paper lanterns from the warm gray underside, in certain streets, or seized the occasion to write messages on the surface, announcing their availability for the performance of unnatural acts, or the availability of acquaintances.

Daring children jumped, especially at those points where the balloon hovered close to a building, so that the gap between balloon and building was a matter of a few inches, or points where the balloon actually made contact, exerting an ever-so-slight pressure against the side of a building, so that balloon and building seemed a unity. The upper surface was so structured that a "landscape" was presented, small valleys as well as slight knolls, or mounds; once atop the balloon, a stroll was possible, or even a trip, from one place to another. There was pleasure in being able to run down an incline, then up

---

1. Grand Army Plaza, site of the Plaza Hotel (also called the Plaza), at the southeastern corner of Central Park in New York City, approxi- mately 2.5 miles north of Fourteenth Street, the northern boundary of Greenwich Village.
2. Fifth Avenue.

the opposing slope, both gently graded, or in making a leap from one side to the other. Bouncing was possible, because of the pneumaticity of the surface, and even falling, if that was your wish. That all these varied motions, as well as others, were within one's possibilities, in experiencing the "up" side of the balloon, was extremely exciting for children, accustomed to the city's flat, hard skin. But the purpose of the balloon was not to amuse children.

Too, the number of people, children and adults, who took advantage of the opportunities described was not so large as it might have been: a certain timidity, lack of trust in the balloon, was seen. There was, furthermore, some hostility. Because we had hidden the pumps, which fed helium to the interior, and because the surface was so vast that the authorities could not determine the point of entry—that is, the point at which the gas was injected—a degree of frustration was evidenced by those city officers into whose province such manifestations normally fell. The apparent purposelessness of the balloon was vexing (as was the fact that it was "there" at all). Had we painted, in great letters, "LABORATORY TESTS PROVE" OR "18% MORE EFFECTIVE" on the sides of the balloon, this difficulty would have been circumvented. But I could not bear to do so. On the whole, these officers were remarkably tolerant, considering the dimensions of the anomaly, this tolerance being the result of, first, secret tests conducted by night that convinced them that little or nothing could be done in the way of removing or destroying the balloon, and, secondly, a public warmth that arose (not uncolored by touches of the aforementioned hostility) toward the balloon, from ordinary citizens.

As a single balloon must stand for a lifetime of thinking about balloons, so each citizen expressed, in the attitude he chose, a complex of attitudes. One man might consider that the balloon had to do with the notion *sullied*, as in the sentence *The big balloon sullied the otherwise clear and radiant Manhattan sky.* That is, the balloon was, in this man's view, an imposture, something inferior to the sky that had formerly been there, something interposed between the people and their "sky." But in fact it was January, the sky was dark and ugly; it was not a sky you could look up into, lying on your back in the street, with pleasure, unless pleasure, for you, proceeded from having been threatened, from having been misused. And the underside of the balloon was a pleasure to look up into, we had seen to that, muted grays and browns for the most part, contrasted with walnut and soft, forgotten yellows. And so, while this man was thinking *sullied*, still there was an admixture of pleasurable cognition in his thinking, struggling with the original perception.

Another man, on the other hand, might view the balloon as if it were part of a system of unanticipated rewards, as when one's employer walks in and says, "Here, Henry, take this package of money I have wrapped for you, because we have been doing so well in the business here, and I admire the way you bruise the tulips, without which bruising your department would not be a success, or at least not the success that it is." For this man the balloon might be a brilliantly heroic "muscle and pluck" experience, even if an experience poorly understood.

Another man might say, "Without the example of ———, it is doubtful that ——— would exist today in its present form," and find many to agree with him, or to argue with him. Ideas of "bloat" and "float" were introduced, as well as concepts of dream and responsibility. Others engaged in remarkably detailed fantasies having to do with a wish either to lose themselves in the balloon, or to engorge it. The private character of these wishes, of their origins, deeply buried and unknown, was such that they were not much spoken of; yet there is evidence that they were widespread. It was also argued that what was important was what you felt when you stood under the balloon; some people claimed that they felt sheltered, warmed, as never before, while enemies of the balloon felt, or reported feeling, constrained, a "heavy" feeling.

Critical opinion was divided:

"monstrous pourings"

"harp"

XXXXXXX "certain contrasts with darker portions"

"inner joy"

"large, square corners"

"conservative eclecticism that has so far governed modern balloon design"

::::::: "abnormal vigor"

"warm, soft, lazy passages"

"Has unity been sacrificed for a sprawling quality?"

"*Quelle catastrophe!*"

"munching"

People began, in a curious way, to locate themselves in relation to aspects of the balloon: "I'll be at that place where it dips down into Forty-seventh Street almost to the sidewalk, near the Alamo Chile House," or, "Why don't we go stand on top, and take the air, and maybe walk about a bit, where it forms a tight, curving line with the façade of the Gallery of Modern Art—" Marginal intersections offered entrances within a given time duration, as well as "warm, soft, lazy passages" in which . . . But it is wrong to speak of "marginal intersections," each intersection was crucial, none could be ignored (as if, walking there, you might not find someone capable of turning your attention, in a flash, from old exercises to new exercises, risks and escalations). Each intersection was crucial, meeting of balloon and building, meeting of balloon and man, meeting of balloon and balloon.

It was suggested that what was admired about the balloon was finally this: that it was not limited, or defined. Sometimes a bulge, blister, or subsection would carry all the way east to the river on its own initiative, in the manner of an army's movements on a map, as seen in a headquarters remote from the fighting. Then that part would be, as it were, thrown back again, or would withdraw into new dispositions; the next morning, that part would have made another sortie, or disappeared altogether. This ability of the balloon to shift its shape, to change, was very pleasing, especially to people whose lives were rather rigidly patterned, persons to whom change, although desired, was not available. The balloon, for the twenty-two days of its existence, offered the possibility, in its randomness, of mislocation of the self, in contradistinction to the grid of precise, rectangular pathways under our feet. The amount of specialized training currently needed, and the conse-

1945 to the Present

Autumn Rhythm (Number 30), Jackson Pollock, 1950

With Abstract Expressionism, the style of post–World War II American painting that had international impact, the canvas became less a surface upon which to represent than an arena in which to act. Jackson Pollock (1912–1956) was the most noteworthy of the so-called action painters. One of his favorite methods, working above a canvas stretched on the ground, dancing over and around it, dripping and swirling paint, was dramatic enough to be captured in photographs and film documentaries.

James Baldwin, September 13, 1955, Carl Van Vechten

This portrait is one of a series that Van Vechten took of Baldwin using different backdrops, drapes, and lighting. The photographer captured many of the era's writers and artists in rich color images, working in the medium from 1939 until his death in 1964. This image juxtaposes Baldwin's thoughtful expression—he gazes to his left at something outside the frame—with the images of stylized white women on the poster behind him, whose gazes are similarly distant. All three faces are contemplative, even while they become subjects for the viewer's own contemplation. Baldwin commented throughout his life on what he called his "ugliness" and doodled fashionable white women's faces like those behind him on the backs of his earliest manuscripts. Even while he unpacked the racist norms of beauty in his writing, he thus remained in some ways fascinated by those norms. Van Vechten, revealing Baldwin's classically symmetrical features and rich skin tones in contrast—and parallel—to the faces behind him, offered a different view—a view of Baldwin's beauty.

Blam, Roy Lichtenstein, 1962

Roy Lichtenstein (1923–1997) helped to launch the Pop Art movement. Lichtenstein used bold outlines, vivid colors, and the technique of Benday dots, popular in commercial printing, to simulate with painting the process of mechanical reproduction. This aesthetic clearly defied the expressionist practices of abstract painters like Jackson Pollock. The cartoon style of *Blam* (in fact, Lichtenstein took this image from a comic book) and its onomatopoetic lettering are typical of Lichtenstein's work. The literally explosive image—a fighter plane being blown apart in the air—also suggests the way in which Pop Art sought to explode boundaries between an original and a copy, a unique image and one that is reproduced, and between high and low culture more generally. Fiction writers like Donald Barthelme, poets like John Ashbery, and comic book artists like Art Spiegelman are all indebted in different ways to Pop Art.

Estate, Robert Rauschenberg,
1963

Few artworks reflect the social
and aesthetic nature of their
times as boldly as the combines
and assemblages of Robert
Rauschenberg (b. 1925).
Self-consciousness about his
medium combines with
sociopolitical awareness in
works that address both
concerns and make them the
viewers' own.

    Estate employs brushwork,
silk-screening, photography, and
photocopying to interrogate its
audience as well as itself. Most
important, every image in this
collage remains recognizable,
even as the expressive manner of
combination (including several
brushstrokes and color actions
worthy of Abstract Expressionism) emphasizes the artist's
creative act.

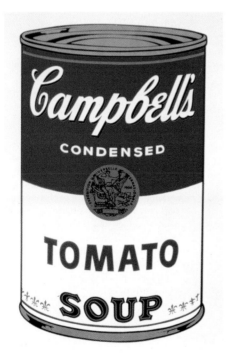

Campbell's Soup 1 (Tomato),
Andy Warhol, 1968

For the Pop artist Andy Warhol (1928–1987),
an object as banal as a Campbell's soup can
could evoke the spirit of the American 1960s.
While both representational and abstract
painting had conventionally been dedicated to
matters of great importance, whether in the
subject portrayed or in the activity of putting
paint to canvas, Warhol's soup can undercut
the premises of both styles while commenting
on the materialism underlying the business of
producing and selling art. Creativity was now a
matter of selection, in this case of lavishing the
artist's considerable talent and technique on
(and commanding a high price for) such an
everyday object. From this decade onward,
literary artists would find success by doing
much the same thing.

Earthrise and Lunar Horizon from Apollo 8, 1968

The photo of "Earthrise" over the lunar horizon was taken by the Apollo 8 crew, astronauts Frank Borman (b. 1928), James Lovell (b. 1928), and William Anders (b. 1933), who were the first humans to leave Earth's orbit, entering into lunar orbit on Christmas Eve, 1968. The photograph showed the Earth for the first time as it appears from deep space. The philosopher Hannah Arendt, in her book *The Human Condition* (1958), anticipated the signifi- cance of this image when she wrote that a shift from seeing men and women as earthbound crea- tures to seeing them as dwellers of the universe would be a radical change in understanding the human condition, as revolutionary as the invention of the telescope.

The American Indian
Fritz Scholder, 1970

The American Indian by Fritz Scholder (1937–2005), a Luiseño Indian, belongs to a series of paintings that blew open the doors of "acceptable" Indian imagery and undermined clichés and stereotypes of the stoic "noble savage." Rather than traditional Indian regalia, the figure wears a judicial robe fashioned from the American flag, as if to suggest that only being wrapped in the symbol of the colonists will certify him as "American." But the whitened face and skeletal rendering of the figure's mouth suggest what colonization cost him. The single feather in his hair, the necklace, and the tomahawk may suggest how the expectations of tourists also shape his depiction.

Untitled, Cindy Sherman, 1981

This photograph by the artist Cindy Sherman (b. 1954) is number 96 of her "Centerfold" series (1981). Like Sherman's earlier, black-and-white "Film Stills," this series consists of "self-portraits" in which the artist explores representations of women by dressing in a variety of costumes and adopting a variety of poses. Sherman's role as both photographer and subject reverses the traditional power of the male gaze, and here she examines and subverts the objectified images of women displayed in magazine centerfolds. Rather than signaling availability, this cropped, color-saturated photograph is enigmatic. Sherman's girlish clothing, evoking the 1950s, conceals more than it reveals, and she holds in her hand a largely unreadable scrap torn from a newspaper. Her gaze, vacant and interior, is also unreadable. Her distinctly unrevealing sweater and the flush on her face become part of the color pattern—oranges and browns forming a series of grids and checks—rather than erotic signs.

Vietnam Veterans Memorial, Maya Lin, 1982

Located on the mall in Washington, D.C., the Vietnam Veterans Memorial is a 246-foot-long, v-shaped sunken wall of black granite. It is engraved with more than fifty-eight thousand names of those who died in the Vietnam conflict. The names are listed in chronological order, and to locate a particular name a visitor walks along the wall searching for it. The polished surface of the granite reflects the sky, the surrounding landscape, and the visitor. Considerable controversy attended the design, by the Chinese American architect Maya Lin (b. 1959), some objecting to its abstraction in place of the realistic statuary of most war memorials, and some finding it too somber. Lin has said she wanted a structure that would carve out a space for the public display of grief and loss, and the memorial has a powerful elegiac quality. Dedicated on Veterans Day, 1982, it has become the most widely visited monument in Washington.

Sonny's Quilt, Faith Ringgold, 1986

In *Sonny's Quilt*, an acrylic painting on canvas with a pieced fabric border, Faith Ringgold (b. 1930) unites two African American art forms: jazz and the quilt. This quilt depicts the jazz saxophonist Theodore Walter "Sonny" Rollins poised high on an imagined intersection of the Williamsburg Bridge, which runs across the quilt, and the Brooklyn Bridge, which recedes into the visual field of the quilt below him. Ringgold's depiction of the two bridges evokes the iconic status of the Brooklyn Bridge in American painting, photography, and literature, while honoring the fact that Rollins chose the Williamsburg Bridge as his favored place to practice.

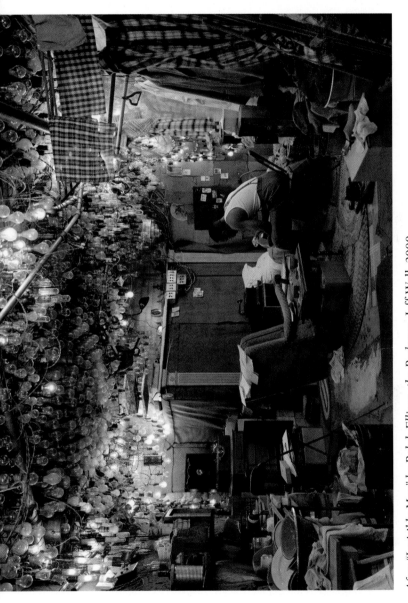

After "Invisible Man" by Ralph Ellison, the Prologue, Jeff Wall, 2000

Ralph Ellison's masterwork, the novel *Invisible Man*, has inspired several prominent photographers to enter its imaginative world. In the introduction to this volume, readers will find an image from Gordon Parks's photo essay on the novel, which appeared in *Life* magazine in 1952, a series that included an image based, like the one above, on the novel's famous scene of the unnamed protagonist in his basement apartment, flooded with the light of over a thousand bulbs. While Parks's photograph is abstract in composition, Jeff Wall creates an elaborately staged but naturalistic space for his version of the scene, directing attention away from the symbolic significance of the bulbs—the sense that no amount of light can make the protagonist socially visible as a human being. Instead, his back is turned to the viewer, and he is dwarfed by the textured clutter of his space.

World Trade Center Burning, Peter Morgan, September 11, 2001

"A screaming comes across the sky." This opening sentence of Thomas Pynchon's 1973 novel *Gravity's Rainbow* had for decades impressed readers with the terrors of modern warfare, in which military technologies at the far edge of human inventiveness were turned against people at home. That Pynchon's scene was London, under attack from German V-2 rockets near the end of World War II, may have allayed readers' most personal fears. Yet on September 11, 2001, another such screaming awoke not just the United States but the whole world to the reality that wholesale destruction was an ever-present possibility. After half a century of Cold War rhetoric that had made such catastrophes unthinkable, the unthinkable happened. Two jet airliners were crashed into the twin towers of New York's World Trade Center in an event witnessed within minutes by television viewers all over the Earth. By the time the buildings collapsed, the whole world was watching. What in normal terms might be a line in a novel or a scene in a movie was now most horribly real.

Screenshot from *The Silent History*, by Eli Horowitz, Kevin Moffett, and Matthew Derby, with app design by Russell Quinn, 2012

The Silent History, the first novel built fully into a mobile app, was released in daily installments to subscribers in 2012 and was thereafter sold as a complete novel through the Apple App Store. A paper version was published in 2014. In the original app format, parts of the novel called "Field Reports" are available only in specific geographic locations tracked by a mobile device's GPS. Horowitz's vision was to create a novel you could "explore" in a physical sense, blending the imaginative world of the story with the reader's presence in real-world locations. *The Silent History* demonstrates how formal innovations in contemporary literature arise as traditional story-telling genres, such as the novel, migrate into ever-changing electronic media.

quent desirability of long-term commitments, has been occasioned by the steadily growing importance of complex machinery, in virtually all kinds of operations; as this tendency increases, more and more people will turn, in bewildered inadequacy, to solutions for which the balloon may stand as a prototype, or "rough draft."

I met you under the balloon, on the occasion of your return from Norway; you asked if it was mine; I said it was. The balloon, I said, is a spontaneous autobiographical disclosure, having to do with the unease I felt at your absence, and with sexual deprivation, but now that your visit to Bergen has been terminated, it is no longer necessary or appropriate. Removal of the balloon was easy; trailer trucks carried away the depleted fabric, which is now stored in West Virginia, awaiting some other time of unhappiness, sometime, perhaps, when we are angry with one another.

1968

TONI MORRISON
b. 1931

The 1993 Nobel Laureate in literature, Toni Morrison is a novelist of great importance in her own right and has been the central figure in putting fiction by and about African American women at the forefront of the late-twentieth-century literary canon. Whereas the legacy of slavery had obscured a usable tradition, and critical stereotypes at times restricted such writers' range, Morrison's fiction serves as a model for reconstructing a culturally empowering past. She joins the great American tradition of self-invention: her example and her editorial work have figured importantly in the careers of other writers, such as Toni Cade Bambara (included in this volume) and Gayl Jones.

Morrison was born in Lorain, Ohio, where much of her fiction is set (a departure from earlier African American narratives typically located in the rural South or urban North). Having earned a B.A. from Howard University with a major in English and a minor in classics, and an M.A. from Cornell University (with a thesis on suicide in the novels of Virginia Woolf and William Faulkner), Morrison began a teaching career in 1955 that reached from Texas Southern University back to Howard, where her students included the future activist Stokeley Carmichael and the future critic Houston A. Baker Jr. At this time she married Harold Morrison, a Jamaican architect, with whom she had two children before ending their marriage in 1964. Already writing, she took a job with the publishing firm Random House and eventually settled in New York City, where she worked until 1983. During these same years she held visiting teaching appointments at institutions including Yale University and Bard College.

As a first novel, *The Bluest Eye* (1970) is uncommonly mature for its confident use of various narrative voices. Throughout her career Morrison has been dedicated to constructing a practical cultural identity of a race and a gender whose self-images have been obscured or denied by dominating forces, and in *The Bluest Eye* she already shows that narrative strategy is an important element in such construction. A girl's need to be loved generates the novel's action, action that involves displaced and alienated affections (and eventually incestuous rape); the family's inability to produce a style of existence in which love can be born and thrive leads to just such a devastating fate for Morrison's protagonist. Love is also denied in *Sula* (1974), in which relationships extend in two directions: between contemporaries (Sula and her friend Nel) and with previous generations.

With *Song of Solomon* (1977) Morrison seeks a more positive redemption of her characters. Turning away from his parents' loveless marriage, Milkman Dead makes a physical and mental journey to his ancestral roots. Here he discovers a more useful legacy in communal tales about Grandmother and Great-Grandfather, each long dead but infusing the local culture with emotionally sustaining lore. Milkman uses this lore to learn how the spiritual guidance offered by his aunt Pilate eclipses the material concerns of his parents' world.

Allegory becomes an important strategy in *Tar Baby* (1981), drawing on the strong folk culture of Haiti, where two contrasting persons form a troubled relationship based on their distinct searches for and rejections of a heritage. Yet it is in a rebuilding of history, rather than allegory or myth, that Morrison achieved her great strength as a novelist in *Beloved* (1987), the winner of her first major award, the Pulitzer Prize. Set in the middle 1870s, when race relations in America were at their most crucial juncture (slavery having ended and the course of the South's Reconstruction not yet fully determined), this novel shows a mother (Sethe) being haunted and eventually destroyed by the ghost of a daughter (Beloved) whom she had killed eighteen years earlier rather than allow to be taken by a vicious slavemaster. This novel is central to Morrison's canon because it involves so many important themes and techniques, from love and guilt to history's role in clarifying the past's influence on the present, all told in an experimental style of magical realism that draws upon techniques from both oral storytelling and modernist fiction.

Paradise (1988) takes a nineteenth-century utopia and reexamines its ideals in the face of 1970s realities—a reminder of how neither past nor present can be insulated from the other. *Jazz* (1992) finds Morrison modeling her narrative voice on the progression of a jazz solo to demonstrate how improvisation with detail can change the nature of what is expressed. Present and past weave together in her characters' lives as the narrative seeks to understand the jealousies of love and the sometimes macabre manifestations of hatred. *Love* (2003), with its murder, arson, pedophilia, and several rapes punctuating a narrative in which arguments over a legacy dislodge awkward elements of the past, is a reminder of how disturbing Morrison's fiction can be. *A Mercy* (2008) explores the contradictions between American and pastoral ideals, and the realities of Native American extermination and African American slavery. Her most recent novel is *God Help the Child* (2015).

Presently serving as the prestigious Goheen Professor of the Humanities at Princeton University, Morrison has moved easily into the role of spokesperson for literary issues. Together with her Nobel lecture, her essays collected as *Playing in the Dark: Whiteness and the Literary Imagination* (1992) challenge stereotypes in white critical thinking about black literature. Her short story "Recitatif," written for *Confirmation*, the 1983 anthology edited by Amiri and Amina Baraka, directly addresses the issues of individual and family, past and present, and race and its effacements that motivate the larger sense of her work. A "recitatif" is a vocal performance in which a narrative is not stated but sung. In her work Morrison's voice sings proudly of a past that in the artistic nature of its reconstruction puts all Americans in touch with a more positively usable heritage.

The following text is from *Confirmation*.

Recitatif

My mother danced all night and Roberta's was sick. That's why we were taken to St. Bonny's. People want to put their arms around you when you tell them you were in a shelter, but it really wasn't bad. No big long room with one hundred beds like Bellevue.[1] There were four to a room, and when Roberta and me came, there was a shortage of state kids, so we were the only ones assigned to 406 and could go from bed to bed if we wanted to. And we wanted to, too. We changed beds every night and for the whole four months we were there we never picked one out as our own permanent bed.

It didn't start out that way. The minute I walked in and the Big Bozo introduced us, I got sick to my stomach. It was one thing to be taken out of your own bed early in the morning—it was something else to be stuck in a strange place with a girl from a whole other race. And Mary, that's my mother, she was right. Every now and then she would stop dancing long enough to tell me something important and one of the things she said was that they never washed their hair and they smelled funny. Roberta sure did. Smell funny, I mean. So when the Big Bozo (nobody ever called her Mrs. Itkin, just like nobody ever said St. Bonaventure)—when she said, "Twyla, this is Roberta. Roberta, this is Twyla. Make each other welcome." I said, "My mother won't like you putting me in here."

"Good," said Bozo. "Maybe then she'll come and take you home."

How's that for mean? If Roberta had laughed I would have killed her, but she didn't. She just walked over to the window and stood with her back to us.

"Turn around," said the Bozo. "Don't be rude. Now Twyla. Roberta. When you hear a loud buzzer, that's the call for dinner. Come down to the first floor. Any fights and no movie." And then, just to make sure we knew what we would be missing, *"The Wizard of Oz."*[2]

Roberta must have thought I meant that my mother would be mad about my being put in the shelter. Not about rooming with her, because as soon as Bozo left she came over to me and said, "Is your mother sick too?"

"No," I said. "She just likes to dance all night."

"Oh," she nodded her head and I liked the way she understood things so fast. So for the moment it didn't matter that we looked like salt and pepper standing there and that's what the other kids called us sometimes. We were eight years old and got F's all the time. Me because I couldn't remember what I read or what the teacher said. And Roberta because she couldn't read at all and didn't even listen to the teacher. She wasn't good at anything except jacks, at which she was a killer: pow scoop pow scoop pow scoop.

We didn't like each other all that much at first, but nobody else wanted to play with us because we weren't real orphans with beautiful dead parents in the sky. We were dumped. Even the New York City Puerto Ricans and the upstate Indians ignored us. All kinds of kids were in there, black ones, white ones, even two Koreans. The food was good, though. At least I thought so. Roberta hated it and left whole pieces of things on her plate: Spam, Salisbury steak—even jello with fruit cocktail in it, and she didn't care if I ate what

---

1. Bellevue Hospital in New York City is known for its psychiatric ward. St. Bonaventure's offers the services of a youth shelter and school.

2. The 1939 film based on the 1900 children's book by the American writer L. Frank Baum (1856–1919).

she wouldn't. Mary's idea of supper was popcorn and a can of Yoo-Hoo.[3] Hot mashed potatoes and two weenies was like Thanksgiving for me.

It really wasn't bad, St. Bonny's. The big girls on the second floor pushed us around now and then. But that was all. They wore lipstick and eyebrow pencil and wobbled their knees while they watched TV. Fifteen, sixteen, even, some of them were. They were put-out girls, scared runaways most of them. Poor little girls who fought their uncles off but looked tough to us, and mean. God did they look mean. The staff tried to keep them separate from the younger children, but sometimes they caught us watching them in the orchard where they played radios and danced with each other. They'd light out after us and pull our hair or twist our arms. We were scared of them, Roberta and me, but neither of us wanted the other one to know it. So we got a good list of dirty names we could shout back when we ran from them through the orchard. I used to dream a lot and almost always the orchard was there. Two acres, four maybe, of these little apple trees. Hundreds of them. Empty and crooked like beggar women when I first came to St. Bonny's but fat with flowers when I left. I don't know why I dreamt about that orchard so much. Nothing really happened there. Nothing all that important, I mean. Just the big girls dancing and playing the radio. Roberta and me watching. Maggie fell down there once. The kitchen woman with legs like parentheses. And the big girls laughed at her. We should have helped her up, I know, but we were scared of those girls with lipstick and eyebrow pencil. Maggie couldn't talk. The kids said she had her tongue cut out, but I think she was just born that way: mute. She was old and sandy-colored and she worked in the kitchen. I don't know if she was nice or not. I just remember her legs like parentheses and how she rocked when she walked. She worked from early in the morning till two o'clock, and if she was late, if she had too much cleaning and didn't get out till two-fifteen or so, she'd cut through the orchard so she wouldn't miss her bus and have to wait another hour. She wore this really stupid little hat—a kid's hat with ear flaps—and she wasn't much taller than we were. A really awful little hat. Even for a mute, it was dumb—dressing like a kid and never saying anything at all.

"But what about if somebody tries to kill her?" I used to wonder about that. "Or what if she wants to cry? Can she cry?"

"Sure," Roberta said. "But just tears. No sounds come out."

"She can't scream?"

"Nope. Nothing."

"Can she hear?"

"I guess."

"Let's call her," I said. And we did.

"Dummy! Dummy!" She never turned her head.

"Bow legs! Bow legs!" Nothing. She just rocked on, the chin straps of her baby-boy hat swaying from side to side. I think we were wrong. I think she could hear and didn't let on. And it shames me even now to think there was somebody in there after all who heard us call her those names and couldn't tell on us.

We got along all right, Roberta and me. Changed beds every night, got F's in civics and communication skills and gym. The Bozo was disappointed in us, she said. Out of 130 of us state cases, 90 were under twelve. Almost

---

3. A chocolate soft drink.

all were real orphans with beautiful dead parents in the sky. We were the only ones dumped and the only ones with F's in three classes including gym. So we got along—what with her leaving whole pieces of things on her plate and being nice about not asking questions.

I think it was the day before Maggie fell down that we found out our mothers were coming to visit us on the same Sunday. We had been at the shelter twenty-eight days (Roberta twenty-eight and a half) and this was their first visit with us. Our mothers would come at ten o'clock in time for chapel, then lunch with us in the teachers' lounge. I thought if my dancing mother met her sick mother it might be good for her. And Roberta thought her sick mother would get a big bang out of a dancing one. We got excited about it and curled each other's hair. After breakfast we sat on the bed watching the road from the window. Roberta's socks were still wet. She washed them the night before and put them on the radiator to dry. They hadn't, but she put them on anyway because their tops were so pretty—scalloped in pink. Each of us had a purple construction-paper basket that we had made in craft class. Mine had a yellow crayon rabbit on it. Roberta's had eggs with wiggly lines of color. Inside were cellophane grass and just the jelly beans because I'd eaten the two marshmallow eggs they gave us. The Big Bozo came herself to get us. Smiling she told us we looked very nice and to come downstairs. We were so surprised by the smile we'd never seen before, neither of us moved.

"Don't you want to see your mommies?"

I stood up first and spilled the jelly beans all over the floor. Bozo's smile disappeared while we scrambled to get the candy up off the floor and put it back in the grass.

She escorted us downstairs to the first floor, where the other girls were lining up to file into the chapel. A bunch of grown-ups stood to one side. Viewers mostly. The old biddies who wanted servants and the fags who wanted company looking for children they might want to adopt. Once in a while a grandmother. Almost never anybody young or anybody whose face wouldn't scare you in the night. Because if any of the real orphans had young relatives they wouldn't be real orphans. I saw Mary right away. She had on those green slacks I hated and hated even more now because didn't she know we were going to chapel? And that fur jacket with the pocket linings so ripped she had to pull to get her hands out of them. But her face was pretty—like always, and she smiled and waved like she was the little girl looking for her mother—not me.

I walked slowly, trying not to drop the jelly beans and hoping the paper handle would hold. I had to use my last Chiclet because by the time I finished cutting everything out, all the Elmer's was gone. I am left-handed and the scissors never worked for me. It didn't matter, though; I might just as well have chewed the gum. Mary dropped to her knees and grabbed me, mashing the basket, the jelly beans, and the grass into her ratty fur jacket.

"Twyla, baby. Twyla, baby!"

I could have killed her. Already I heard the big girls in the orchard the next time saying, "Twyyyyyla, baby!" But I couldn't stay mad at Mary while she was smiling and hugging me and smelling of Lady Esther dusting powder. I wanted to stay buried in her fur all day.

To tell the truth I forgot about Roberta. Mary and I got in line for the traipse into chapel and I was feeling proud because she looked so beautiful even in those ugly green slacks that made her behind stick out. A pretty mother on earth is better than a beautiful dead one in the sky even if she did leave you all alone to go dancing.

I felt a tap on my shoulder, turned, and saw Roberta smiling. I smiled back, but not too much lest somebody think this visit was the biggest thing that ever happened in my life. Then Roberta said, "Mother, I want you to meet my roommate, Twyla. And that's Twyla's mother."

I looked up it seemed for miles. She was big. Bigger than any man and on her chest was the biggest cross I'd ever seen. I swear it was six inches long each way. And in the crook of her arm was the biggest Bible ever made.

Mary, simple-minded as ever, grinned and tried to yank her hand out of the pocket with the raggedy lining—to shake hands, I guess. Roberta's mother looked down at me and then looked down at Mary too. She didn't say anything, just grabbed Roberta with her Bible-free hand and stepped out of line, walking quickly to the rear of it. Mary was still grinning because she's not too swift when it comes to what's really going on. Then this light bulb goes off in her head and she says "That bitch!" really loud and us almost in the chapel now. Organ music whining; the Bonny Angels singing sweetly. Everybody in the world turned around to look. And Mary would have kept it up—kept calling names if I hadn't squeezed her hand as hard as I could. That helped a little, but she still twitched and crossed and uncrossed her legs all through service. Even groaned a couple of times. Why did I think she would come there and act right? Slacks. No hat like the grandmothers and viewers, and groaning all the while. When we stood for hymns she kept her mouth shut. Wouldn't even look at the words on the page. She actually reached in her purse for a mirror to check her lipstick. All I could think of was that she really needed to be killed. The sermon lasted a year, and I knew the real orphans were looking smug again.

We were supposed to have lunch in the teachers' lounge, but Mary didn't bring anything, so we picked fur and cellophane grass off the mashed jelly beans and ate them. I could have killed her. I sneaked a look at Roberta. Her mother had brought chicken legs and ham sandwiches and oranges and a whole box of chocolate-covered grahams. Roberta drank milk from a thermos while her mother read the Bible to her.

Things are not right. The wrong food is always with the wrong people. Maybe that's why I got into waitress work later—to match up the right people with the right food. Roberta just let those chicken legs sit there, but she did bring a stack of grahams up to me later when the visit was over. I think she was sorry that her mother would not shake my mother's hand. And I liked that and I liked the fact that she didn't say a word about Mary groaning all the way through the service and not bringing any lunch.

Roberta left in May when the apple trees were heavy and white. On her last day we went to the orchard to watch the big girls smoke and dance by the radio. It didn't matter that they said, "Twyyyyyla, baby." We sat on the ground and breathed. Lady Esther. Apple blossoms. I still go soft when I smell one or the other. Roberta was going home. The big cross and the big Bible was coming to get her and she seemed sort of glad and sort of not. I thought I would die in that room of four beds without her and I knew Bozo had plans to move some other dumped kid in there with me. Roberta promised to write every day, which was really sweet of her because she couldn't read a lick so how could she write anybody. I would have drawn pictures and sent them to her but she never gave me her address. Little by little she faded. Her wet socks with the pink scalloped tops and her big serious-looking eyes—that's all I could catch when I tried to bring her to mind.

I was working behind the counter at the Howard Johnson's on the Thruway just before the Kingston exit. Not a bad job. Kind of a long ride from Newburgh,[4] but okay once I got there. Mine was the second night shift—eleven to seven. Very light until a Greyhound checked in for breakfast around six-thirty. At that hour the sun was all the way clear of the hills behind the restaurant. The place looked better at night—more like shelter—but I loved it when the sun broke in, even if it did show all the cracks in the vinyl and the speckled floor looked dirty no matter what the mop boy did.

It was August and a bus crowd was just unloading. They would stand around a long while: going to the john, and looking at gifts and junk-for-sale machines, reluctant to sit down so soon. Even to eat. I was trying to fill the coffee pots and get them all situated on the electric burners when I saw her. She was sitting in a booth smoking a cigarette with two guys smothered in head and facial hair. Her own hair was so big and wild I could hardly see her face. But the eyes. I would know them anywhere. She had on a powder-blue halter and shorts outfit and earrings the size of bracelets. Talk about lipstick and eyebrow pencil. She made the big girls look like nuns. I couldn't get off the counter until seven o'clock, but I kept watching the booth in case they got up to leave before that. My replacement was on time for a change, so I counted and stacked my receipts as fast as I could and signed off. I walked over to the booth, smiling and wondering if she would remember me. Or even if she wanted to remember me. Maybe she didn't want to be reminded of St. Bonny's or to have anybody know she was ever there. I know I never talked about it to anybody.

I put my hands in my apron pockets and leaned against the back of the booth facing them.

"Roberta? Roberta Fisk?"

She looked up. "Yeah?"

"Twyla."

She squinted for a second and then said, "Wow."

"Remember me?"

"Sure. Hey. Wow."

"It's been a while," I said, and gave a smile to the two hairy guys.

"Yeah. Wow. You work here?"

"Yeah," I said. "I live in Newburgh."

"Newburgh? No kidding?" She laughed then a private laugh that included the guys but only the guys, and they laughed with her. What could I do but laugh too and wonder why I was standing there with my knees showing out from under that uniform. Without looking I could see the blue and white triangle on my head, my hair shapeless in a net, my ankles thick in white oxfords. Nothing could have been less sheer than my stockings. There was this silence that came down right after I laughed. A silence it was her turn to fill up. With introductions, maybe, to her boyfriends or an invitation to sit down and have a Coke. Instead she lit a cigarette off the one she'd just

4. A city beside the Hudson River, located eighty miles north of New York City.

finished and said, "We're on our way to the Coast. He's got an appointment with Hendrix."[5] She gestured casually toward the boy next to her.

"Hendrix? Fantastic," I said. "Really fantastic. What's she doing now?"

Roberta coughed on her cigarette and the two guys rolled their eyes up at the ceiling.

"Hendrix. Jimi Hendrix, asshole. He's only the biggest—Oh, wow. Forget it."

I was dismissed without anyone saying goodbye, so I thought I would do it for her.

"How's your mother?" I asked. Her grin cracked her whole face. She swallowed. "Fine," she said. "How's yours?"

"Pretty as a picture," I said and turned away. The backs of my knees were damp. Howard Johnson's really was a dump in the sunlight.

James is as comfortable as a house slipper. He liked my cooking and I liked his big loud family. They have lived in Newburgh all of their lives and talk about it the way people do who have always known a home. His grandmother is a porch swing older than his father and when they talk about streets and avenues and buildings they call them names they no longer have. They still call the A & P[6] Rico's because it stands on property once a mom and pop store owned by Mr. Rico. And they call the new community college Town Hall because it once was. My mother-in-law puts up jelly and cucumbers and buys butter wrapped in cloth from a dairy. James and his father talk about fishing and baseball and I can see them all together on the Hudson in a raggedy skiff. Half the population of Newburgh is on welfare now, but to my husband's family it was still some upstate paradise of a time long past. A time of ice houses and vegetable wagons, coal furnaces and children weeding gardens. When our son was born my mother-in-law gave me the crib blanket that had been hers.

But the town they remembered had changed. Something quick was in the air. Magnificent old houses, so ruined they had become shelter for squatters and rent risks, were bought and renovated. Smart IBM people[7] moved out of their suburbs back into the city and put shutters up and herb gardens in their backyards. A brochure came in the mail announcing the opening of a Food Emporium. Gourmet food it said—and listed items the rich IBM crowd would want. It was located in a new mall at the edge of town and I drove out to shop there one day—just to see. It was late in June. After the tulips were gone and the Queen Elizabeth roses were open everywhere. I trailed my cart along the aisle tossing in smoked oysters and Robert's sauce and things I knew would sit in my cupboard for years. Only when I found some Klondike ice cream bars did I feel less guilty about spending James's fireman's salary so foolishly. My father-in-law ate them with the same gusto little Joseph did.

Waiting in the check-out line I heard a voice say, "Twyla!"

The classical music piped over the aisles had affected me and the woman leaning toward me was dressed to kill. Diamonds on her hand, a smart white summer dress. "I'm Mrs. Benson," I said.

---

5. Jimi Hendrix (1942–1970), African American musician and rock star.
6. Supermarket, part of a national chain once called the Great Atlantic and Pacific Tea Company.
7. High-salaried employees of the International Business Machine Corporation, headquartered in the suburbs north of New York City.

"Ho. Ho. The Big Bozo," she sang.

For a split second I didn't know what she was talking about. She had a bunch of asparagus and two cartons of fancy water.

"Roberta!"

"Right."

"For heaven's sake. Roberta."

"You look great," she said.

"So do you. Where are you? Here? In Newburgh?"

"Yes. Over in Annandale."

I was opening my mouth to say more when the cashier called my attention to her empty counter.

"Meet you outside." Roberta pointed her finger and went into the express line.

I placed the groceries and kept myself from glancing around to check Roberta's progress. I remembered Howard Johnson's and looking for a chance to speak only to be greeted with a stingy "wow." But she was waiting for me and her huge hair was sleek now, smooth around a small, nicely shaped head. Shoes, dress, everything lovely and summery and rich. I was dying to know what happened to her, how she got from Jimi Hendrix to Annandale, a neighborhood full of doctors and IBM executives. Easy, I thought. Everything is so easy for them. They think they own the world.

"How long," I asked her. "How long have you been here?"

"A year. I got married to a man who lives here. And you, you're married too, right? Benson, you said."

"Yeah. James Benson."

"And is he nice?"

"Oh, is he nice?"

"Well, is he?" Roberta's eyes were steady as though she really meant the question and wanted an answer.

"He's wonderful, Roberta. Wonderful."

"So you're happy."

"Very."

"That's good," she said and nodded her head. "I always hoped you'd be happy. Any kids? I know you have kids."

"One. A boy. How about you?"

"Four."

"Four?"

She laughed. "Step kids. He's a widower."

"Oh."

"Got a minute? Let's have a coffee."

I thought about the Klondikes melting and the inconvenience of going all the way to my car and putting the bags in the trunk. Served me right for buying all that stuff I didn't need. Roberta was ahead of me.

"Put them in my car. It's right here."

And then I saw the dark blue limousine.

"You married a Chinaman?"

"No," she laughed. "He's the driver."

"Oh, my. If the Big Bozo could see you now."

We both giggled. Really giggled. Suddenly, in just a pulse beat, twenty years disappeared and all of it came rushing back. The big girls (whom we called gar girls—Roberta's misheard word for the evil stone faces described in a civics class) there dancing in the orchard, the ploppy mashed potatoes, the double weenies, the Spam with pineapple. We went into the coffee shop holding on to one another and I tried to think why we were glad to see each other this time and not before. Once, twelve years ago, we passed like strangers. A black girl and a white girl meeting in a Howard Johnson's on the road and having nothing to say. One in a blue and white triangle waitress hat—the other on her way to see Hendrix. Now we were behaving like sisters separated for much too long. Those four short months were nothing in time. Maybe it was the thing itself. Just being there, together. Two little girls who knew what nobody else in the world knew—how not to ask questions. How to believe what had to be believed. There was politeness in that reluctance and generosity as well. Is your mother sick too? No, she dances all night. Oh—and an understanding nod.

We sat in a booth by the window and fell into recollection like veterans.

"Did you ever learn to read?"

"Watch." She picked up the menu. "Special of the day. Cream of corn soup. Entrées. Two dots and a wriggly line. Quiche. Chef salad, scallops . . ."

I was laughing and applauding when the waitress came up.

"Remember the Easter baskets?"

"And how we tried to *introduce* them?"

"Your mother with that cross like two telephone poles."

"And yours with those tight slacks."

We laughed so loudly heads turned and made the laughter harder to suppress.

"What happened to the Jimi Hendrix date?"

Roberta made a blow-out sound with her lips.

"When he died I thought about you."

"Oh, you heard about him finally?"

"Finally. Come on, I was a small-town country waitress."

"And I was a small-town country dropout. God, were we wild. I still don't know how I got out of there alive."

"But you did."

"I did. I really did. Now I'm Mrs. Kenneth Norton."

"Sounds like a mouthful."

"It is."

"Servants and all?"

Roberta held up two fingers.

"Ow! What does he do?"

"Computers and stuff. What do I know?"

"I don't remember a hell of a lot from those days, but Lord, St. Bonny's is as clear as daylight. Remember Maggie? The day she fell down and those gar girls laughed at her?"

Roberta looked up from her salad and stared at me. "Maggie didn't fall," she said.

"Yes, she did. You remember."

"No, Twyla. They knocked her down. Those girls pushed her down and tore her clothes. In the orchard."

"I don't—that's not what happened."

"Sure it is. In the orchard. Remember how scared we were?"

"Wait a minute. I don't remember any of that."

"And Bozo was fired."

"You're crazy. She was there when I left. You left before me."

"I went back. You weren't there when they fired Bozo."

"What?"

"Twice. Once for a year when I was about ten, another for two months when I was fourteen. That's when I ran away."

"You ran away from St. Bonny's?"

"I had to. What do you want? Me dancing in that orchard?"

"Are you sure about Maggie?"

"Of course I'm sure. You've blocked it, Twyla. It happened. Those girls had behavior problems, you know."

"Didn't they, though. But why can't I remember the Maggie thing?"

"Believe me. It happened. And we were there."

"Who did you room with when you went back?" I asked her as if I would know her. The Maggie thing was troubling me.

"Creeps. They tickled themselves in the night."

My ears were itching and I wanted to go home suddenly. This was all very well but she couldn't just comb her hair, wash her face and pretend everything was hunky-dory. After the Howard Johnson's snub. And no apology. Nothing.

"Were you on dope or what that time at Howard Johnson's?" I tried to make my voice sound friendlier than I felt.

"Maybe, a little. I never did drugs much. Why?"

"I don't know; you acted sort of like you didn't want to know me then."

"Oh, Twyla, you know how it was in those days: black—white. You know how everything was."

But I didn't know. I thought it was just the opposite. Busloads of blacks and whites came into Howard Johnson's together. They roamed together then: students, musicians, lovers, protesters. You got to see everything at Howard Johnson's and blacks were very friendly with whites in those days. But sitting there with nothing on my plate but two hard tomato wedges wondering about the melting Klondikes it seemed childish remembering the slight. We went to her car, and with the help of the driver, got my stuff into my station wagon.

"We'll keep in touch this time," she said.

"Sure," I said. "Sure. Give me a call."

"I will," she said, and then just as I was sliding behind the wheel, she leaned into the window. "By the way. Your mother. Did she ever stop dancing?"

I shook my head. "No. Never."

Roberta nodded.

"And yours? Did she ever get well?"

She smiled a tiny sad smile. "No. She never did. Look, call me, okay?"

"Okay," I said, but I knew I wouldn't. Roberta had messed up my past somehow with that business about Maggie. I wouldn't forget a thing like that. Would I?

Strife came to us that fall. At least that's what the paper called it. Strife. Racial strife. The word made me think of a bird—a big shrieking bird out of 1,000,000,000 B.C. Flapping its wings and cawing. Its eye with no lid always bearing down on you. All day it screeched and at night it slept on the rooftops. It woke you in the morning and from the *Today* show to the eleven o'clock news it kept you an awful company. I couldn't figure it out from one day to the next. I knew I was supposed to feel something strong, but I didn't know what, and James wasn't any help. Joseph was on the list of kids to be transferred from the junior high school to another one at some far-out-of-the-way place and I thought it was a good thing until I heard it was a bad thing. I mean I didn't know. All the schools seemed dumps to me, and the fact that one was nicer looking didn't hold much weight. But the papers were full of it and then the kids began to get jumpy. In August, mind you. Schools weren't even open yet. I thought Joseph might be frightened to go over there, but he didn't seem scared so I forgot about it, until I found myself driving along Hudson Street out there by the school they were trying to integrate and saw a line of women marching. And who do you suppose was in line, big as life, holding a sign in front of her bigger than her mother's cross? MOTHERS HAVE RIGHTS TOO! it said.

I drove on, and then changed my mind. I circled the block, slowed down, and honked my horn.

Roberta looked over and when she saw me she waved. I didn't wave back, but I didn't move either. She handed her sign to another woman and came over to where I was parked.

"Hi."

"What are you doing?"

"Picketing. What's it look like?"

"What for?"

"What do you mean 'What for?' They want to take my kids and send them out of the neighborhood. They don't want to go."

"So what if they go to another school? My boy's being bussed too, and I don't mind. Why should you?"

"It's not about us, Twyla. Me and you. It's about our kids."

"What's more *us* than that?"

"Well, it is a free country."

"Not yet, but it will be."

"What the hell does that mean? I'm not doing anything to you."

"You really think that?"

"I know it."

"I wonder what made me think you were different."

"I wonder what made me think you were different."

"Look at them," I said. "Just look. Who do they think they are? Swarming all over the place like they own it. And now they think they can decide where my child goes to school. Look at them, Roberta. They're Bozos."

Roberta turned around and looked at the women. Almost all of them were standing still now, waiting. Some were even edging toward us. Roberta looked at me out of some refrigerator behind her eyes. "No, they're not. They're just mothers."

"And what am I? Swiss cheese?"

"I used to curl your hair."

"I hated your hands in my hair."

The women were moving. Our faces looked mean to them of course and they looked as though they could not wait to throw themselves in front of a police car, or better yet, into my car and drag me away by my ankles. Now they surrounded my car and gently, gently began to rock it. I swayed back and forth like a sideways yo-yo. Automatically I reached for Roberta, like the old days in the orchard when they saw us watching them and we had to get out of there, and if one of us fell the other pulled her up and if one of us was caught the other stayed to kick and scratch, and neither would leave the other behind. My arm shot out of the car window but no receiving hand was there. Roberta was looking at me sway from side to side in the car and her face was still. My purse slid from the car seat down under the dashboard. The four policemen who had been drinking Tab[8] in their car finally got the message and strolled over, forcing their way through the women. Quietly, firmly they spoke. "Okay, ladies. Back in line or off the streets."

Some of them went away willingly; others had to be urged away from the car doors and the hood. Roberta didn't move. She was looking steadily at me. I was fumbling to turn on the ignition, which wouldn't catch because the gearshift was still in drive. The seats of the car were a mess because the swaying had thrown my grocery coupons all over it and my purse was sprawled on the floor.

"Maybe I am different now, Twyla. But you're not. You're the same little state kid who kicked a poor old black lady when she was down on the ground. You kicked a black lady and you have the nerve to call me a bigot."

The coupons were everywhere and the guts of my purse were bunched under the dashboard. What was she saying? Black? Maggie wasn't black.

"She wasn't black," I said.

"Like hell she wasn't, and you kicked her. We both did. You kicked a black lady who couldn't even scream."

"Liar!"

"You're the liar! Why don't you just go on home and leave us alone, huh?"

She turned away and I skidded away from the curb.

The next morning I went into the garage and cut the side out of the carton our portable TV had come in. It wasn't nearly big enough, but after a while I had a decent sign: red spray-painted letters on a white background—AND SO DO CHILDREN * * * *. I meant just to go down to the school and tack it up somewhere so those cows on the picket line across the street could see it, but when I got there, some ten or so others had already assembled—protesting the cows across the street. Police permits and everything. I got in line and we strutted in time on our side while Roberta's group strutted on theirs. That first day we were all dignified, pretending the other side didn't exist. The second day there was name calling and finger gestures. But that was about all. People changed signs from time to time, but Roberta never did and neither did I. Actually my sign didn't make sense without Roberta's. "And so do children what?" one of the women on my side asked me. Have rights, I said, as though it was obvious.

Roberta didn't acknowledge my presence in any way and I got to thinking maybe she didn't know I was there. I began to pace myself in the line, jostling people one minute and lagging behind the next, so Roberta and I could reach the end of our respective lines at the same time and there would be a moment in our turn when we would face each other. Still, I couldn't tell whether she saw me and knew my sign was for her. The next day I went early

8. A diet soda.

before we were scheduled to assemble. I waited until she got there before I exposed my new creation. As soon as she hoisted her MOTHERS HAVE RIGHTS TOO I began to wave my new one, which said, HOW WOULD YOU KNOW? I know she saw that one, but I had gotten addicted now. My signs got crazier each day, and the women on my side decided that I was a kook. They couldn't make heads or tails out of my brilliant screaming posters.

I brought a painted sign in queenly red with huge black letters that said, IS YOUR MOTHER WELL? Roberta took her lunch break and didn't come back for the rest of the day or any day after. Two days later I stopped going too and couldn't have been missed because nobody understood my signs anyway.

It was a nasty six weeks. Classes were suspended and Joseph didn't go to anybody's school until October. The children—everybody's children—soon got bored with that extended vacation they thought was going to be so great. They looked at TV until their eyes flattened. I spent a couple of mornings tutoring my son, as the other mothers said we should. Twice I opened a text from last year that he had never turned in. Twice he yawned in my face. Other mothers organized living room sessions so the kids would keep up. None of the kids could concentrate so they drifted back to *The Price Is Right* and *The Brady Bunch*.[9] When the school finally opened there were fights once or twice and some sirens roared through the streets every once in a while. There were a lot of photographers from Albany. And just when ABC was about to send up a news crew, the kids settled down like nothing in the world had happened. Joseph hung my HOW WOULD YOU KNOW? sign in his bedroom. I don't know what became of AND SO DO CHILDREN * * * *. I think my father-in-law cleaned some fish on it. He was always puttering around in our garage. Each of his five children lived in Newburgh and he acted as though he had five extra homes.

I couldn't help looking for Roberta when Joseph graduated from high school, but I didn't see her. It didn't trouble me much what she had said to me in the car. I mean the kicking part. I know I didn't do that, I couldn't do that. But I was puzzled by her telling me Maggie was black. When I thought about it I actually couldn't be certain. She wasn't pitch-black, I knew, or I would have remembered that. What I remember was the kiddie hat, and the semicircle legs. I tried to reassure myself about the race thing for a long time until it dawned on me that the truth was already there, and Roberta knew it. I didn't kick her; I didn't join in with the gar girls and kick that lady, but I sure did want to. We watched and never tried to help her and never called for help. Maggie was my dancing mother. Deaf, I thought, and dumb. Nobody inside. Nobody who would hear you if you cried in the night. Nobody who could tell you anything important that you could use. Rocking, dancing, swaying as she walked. And when the gar girls pushed her down, and started roughhousing, I knew she wouldn't scream, couldn't—just like me—and I was glad about that.

We decided not to have a tree, because Christmas would be at my mother-in-law's house, so why have a tree at both places? Joseph was at SUNY New Paltz[1] and we had to economize, we said. But at the last minute, I changed

---

9. Popular television programs of the 1970s; respectively, a game show and a situation comedy.

1. A campus in the State University of New York system, located 70 miles north of New York City.

my mind. Nothing could be that bad. So I rushed around town looking for a tree, something small but wide. By the time I found a place, it was snowing and very late. I dawdled like it was the most important purchase in the world and the tree man was fed up with me. Finally I chose one and had it tied onto the trunk of the car. I drove away slowly because the sand trucks were not out yet and the streets could be murder at the beginning of a snowfall. Downtown the streets were wide and rather empty except for a cluster of people coming out of the Newburgh Hotel. The one hotel in town that wasn't built out of cardboard and Plexiglas. A party, probably. The men huddled in the snow were dressed in tails and the women had on furs. Shiny things glittered from underneath their coats. It made me tired to look at them. Tired, tired, tired. On the next corner was a small diner with loops and loops of paper bells in the window. I stopped the car and went in. Just for a cup of coffee and twenty minutes of peace before I went home and tried to finish everything before Christmas Eve.

"Twyla?"

There she was. In a silvery evening gown and dark fur coat. A man and another woman were with her, the man fumbling for change to put in the cigarette machine. The woman was humming and tapping on the counter with her fingernails. They all looked a little bit drunk.

"Well. It's you."

"How are you?"

I shrugged. "Pretty good. Frazzled. Christmas and all."

"Regular?" called the woman from the counter.

"Fine," Roberta called back and then, "Wait for me in the car."

She slipped into the booth beside me. "I have to tell you something, Twyla. I made up my mind if I ever saw you again, I'd tell you."

"I'd just as soon not hear anything, Roberta. It doesn't matter now, anyway."

"No," she said. "Not about that."

"Don't be long," said the woman. She carried two regulars to go and the man peeled his cigarette pack as they left.

"It's about St. Bonny's and Maggie."

"Oh, please."

"Listen to me. I really did think she was black. I didn't make that up. I really thought so. But now I can't be sure. I just remember her as old, so old. And because she couldn't talk—well, you know, I thought she was crazy. She'd been brought up in an institution like my mother was and like I thought I would be too. And you were right. We didn't kick her. It was the gar girls. Only them. But, well, I wanted to. I really wanted them to hurt her. I said we did it, too. You and me, but that's not true. And I don't want you to carry that around. It was just that I wanted to do it so bad that day— wanting to is doing it."

Her eyes were watery from the drinks she'd had, I guess. I know it's that way with me. One glass of wine and I start bawling over the littlest thing.

"We were kids, Roberta."

"Yeah. Yeah. I know, just kids."

"Eight."

"Eight."

"And lonely."

"Scared, too."

She wiped her cheeks with the heel of her hand and smiled. "Well, that's all I wanted to say."

I nodded and couldn't think of any way to fill the silence that went from the diner past the paper bells on out into the snow. It was heavy now. I thought I'd better wait for the sand trucks before starting home.

"Thanks, Roberta."

"Sure."

"Did I tell you? My mother, she never did stop dancing."

"Yes. You told me. And mine, she never got well." Roberta lifted her hands from the tabletop and covered her face with her palms. When she took them away she really was crying. "Oh shit, Twyla. Shit, shit, shit. What the hell happened to Maggie?"

1983

SYLVIA PLATH
1932–1963

I n an introduction to Sylvia Plath's *Ariel* (1965), published two years after her suicide in London, Robert Lowell wrote: "In these poems . . . Sylvia Plath becomes
herself, becomes something imaginary, newly, wildly, and subtly created— . . . one
of those super-real, hypnotic great classical heroines." Lowell had first met Plath in
1958, during her regular visits to his poetry seminar at Boston University, where he
remembered her "air of maddening docility." Later, writing his introduction, he recognized her astonishing creation of a poetic self. The poems of *Ariel* were written at
white heat, two or three a day, in the last months of Plath's life, but there is nothing
hurried in their language or structure. When they are taken together with the poems
posthumously published in *Crossing the Water* (1971) and *Winter Trees* (1972), a
coherent persona emerges: larger than life, operatic in feeling. Although this focus on
the self often excludes attention to the larger world, it generates the dynamic energy of
her work. Plath appropriates a centrally American tradition, the heroic ego confronting the sublime, but she brilliantly revises this tradition by turning what the American Transcendentalist Ralph Waldo Emerson called the "great and crescive self" into
a heroine instead of a hero. Seizing a mythic power, the Plath of the poems trans-
mutes the domestic and the ordinary into the hallucinatory, the utterly strange. Her
revision of the romantic ego dramatizes its tendency toward disproportion and excess,
and she is fully capable of both using and mocking this heightened sense of self, as
she does in her poem "Lady Lazarus."

Plath's well-known autobiographical novel, *The Bell Jar* (1963), has nothing of the
brilliance of her poems, but it effectively dramatizes the stereotyping of women's
roles in the 1950s and the turmoil of a young woman only partly aware that her gifts
and ambitions greatly exceed the options available to her. In the novel Plath uses her
experience as a guest editor of a young-women's magazine (in real life, *Mademoiselle*)
and then, in an abrupt shift, presents her heroine's attempted suicide and hospitalization. Plath herself had suffered a serious breakdown and attempted suicide

between her junior and senior years in college. The popularity of *The Bell Jar* may be one reason why attention to Plath's life has sometimes obscured the accomplishments of her art. While her poems often begin in autobiography, their success depends on Plath's imaginative transformations of experience into myth, as in a number of her poems (such as "Daddy") where the figure of her Prussian father is transformed into an emblem for masculine authority. Otto Plath was an entomologist and the author of a treatise on bumblebees. His death in 1940 from gangrene (the consequence of a diabetic condition he refused to treat), when Plath was eight, was the crucial event of her childhood. After his death her mother, Aurelia, while struggling to support two small children, encouraged her daughter's literary ambitions.

In many ways Plath embodied the bright, young, middle-class woman of the 1950s. She went to Smith College on a scholarship and graduated summa cum laude. On a Fulbright grant she studied in England at Cambridge University, where she met and married the poet Ted Hughes. On the face of it her marriage must have seemed the perfect fate for such a young woman; it combined romance, two poets beginning careers together (Plath's first book, *The Colossus*, appeared in 1960, three years after Hughes's first collection, *The Hawk in the Rain*), and two children (Frieda, born in 1960, and Nicholas, born in 1962), with a country house in Devon, England. In her poems, however, we find the strains of such a life; the work is galvanized by suffering, by a terrible constriction against which she unlooses "The lioness, / The shriek in the bath, / The cloak of holes" ("Purdah"). In articulating a dark vision of domestic life, Plath adopted the license of Robert Lowell and Anne Sexton, a fellow student in Lowell's poetry seminar, to write about "private and taboo subjects."

While still living in Devon, Plath wrote most of the poems that were to make up *Ariel* (by Christmas 1962, she had gathered them in a black binder and arranged them in a careful sequence). The marriage broke up in the summer of 1962, and at the beginning of the new year Plath found herself with two small children, living in a London flat during one of the coldest winters in recent British history. There she began new poems, writing furiously until February 1963, when she took her own life. The *Ariel* collection published by Hughes in 1965 does not follow Plath's intended sequence; it omits what Hughes called "some of the more personally aggressive poems from 1962" and includes the dozen or so poems Plath wrote in the months before her death and that she had envisioned as the beginnings of a third book. Nonetheless, the powerful, angry poems of *Ariel*, mining a limited range of deep feeling, are Plath's best-known work. Fueled by an anger toward her husband and her father, she speaks in these poems as one whose feelings are more than her own; it is as if she were the character in George Eliot's *Daniel Deronda* (1876) who appears suddenly before the novel's heroine and says, "I am a woman's life." Other poems, however, demonstrate her ability to render a wider variety of emotion; they include poems about her children (such as "Morning Song," "Child," and "Parliament Hill Fields") and a number of arresting poems about the natural world. In the vastness of natural processes the Romantic ego finds something as large as itself, and Plath's response to nature is intense, often uncanny. Her poems offer an eccentric vision where (as in "Blackberrying") the appearance of the natural world is never separable from the consciousness of the one who sees it.

For all her courting of excess Plath is a remarkably controlled writer; her lucid stanzas, her clear diction, and her dazzling alterations of sound all display that control. The imaginative intensity of her poems is her own triumphant creation out of the difficult circumstances of her life. She once remarked, "I cannot sympathize with those cries from the heart that are informed by nothing except a needle or a knife. . . . I believe that one should be able to control and manipulate experiences, even the most terrifying . . . with an informed and intelligent mind." The influence of her style, and of the persona she created, continues to be felt in the work of a wide variety of contemporary poets.

Morning Song

Love set you going like a fat gold watch.
The midwife slapped your footsoles, and your bald cry
Took its place among the elements.

Our voices echo, magnifying your arrival. New statue.
In a drafty museum, your nakedness   5
Shadows our safety. We stand round blankly as walls.

I'm no more your mother
Than the cloud that distills a mirror to reflect its own slow
Effacement at the wind's hand.

All night your moth-breath   10
Flickers among the flat pink roses. I wake to listen:
A far sea moves in my ear.

One cry, and I stumble from bed, cow-heavy and floral
In my Victorian nightgown.
Your mouth opens clean as a cat's. The window square   15

Whitens and swallows its dull stars. And now you try
Your handful of notes;
The clear vowels rise like balloons.

1961   1966

Lady Lazarus[1]

I have done it again.
One year in every ten
I manage it—

A sort of walking miracle, my skin
Bright as a Nazi lampshade,[2]   5
My right foot

A paperweight,
My face a featureless, fine
Jew linen.

Peel off the napkin   10
O my enemy.
Do I terrify?——

1. Lazarus was raised from the dead by Jesus   2. In the Nazi death camps, the victims' skins
(John 11.1–45).   were sometimes used to make lampshades.

The nose, the eye pits, the full set of teeth?
The sour breath
Will vanish in a day.   15

Soon, soon the flesh
The grave cave ate will be
At home on me

And I a smiling woman.
I am only thirty.   20
And like the cat I have nine times to die.

This is Number Three.
What a trash
To annihilate each decade.

What a million filaments.   25
The peanut-crunching crowd
Shoves in to see

Them unwrap me hand and foot——
The big strip tease.
Gentlemen, ladies   30

These are my hands
My knees.
I may be skin and bone,

Nevertheless, I am the same, identical woman.
The first time it happened I was ten.   35
It was an accident.

The second time I meant
To last it out and not come back at all.
I rocked shut

As a seashell.   40
They had to call and call
And pick the worms off me like sticky pearls.

Dying
Is an art, like everything else.
I do it exceptionally well.   45

I do it so it feels like hell.
I do it so it feels real.
I guess you could say I've a call.

It's easy enough to do it in a cell.
It's easy enough to do it and stay put.   50
It's the theatrical

Comeback in broad day
To the same place, the same face, the same brute
Amused shout:

'A miracle!'   55
That knocks me out.
There is a charge

For the eyeing of my scars, there is a charge
For the hearing of my heart——
It really goes.   60

And there is a charge, a very large charge
For a word or a touch
Or a bit of blood

Or a piece of my hair or my clothes.
So, so, Herr[3] Doktor.   65
So, Herr Enemy.

I am your opus,
I am your valuable,
The pure gold baby

That melts to a shriek.   70
I turn and burn.
Do not think I underestimate your great concern.

Ash, ash——
You poke and stir.
Flesh, bone, there is nothing there——   75

A cake of soap,
A wedding ring,
A gold filling.[4]

Herr God, Herr Lucifer
Beware   80
Beware.

Out of the ash[5]
I rise with my red hair
And I eat men like air.

1962   1966

---

3. Mr. (German).
4. The Nazis used human remains in the making of soap and scavenged corpses for jewelry and gold teeth.

5. An allusion to the phoenix, a mythical bird that dies by fire and is reborn out of its own ashes.

Ariel[1]

Stasis in darkness.
Then the substanceless blue
Pour of tor[2] and distances.

God's lioness,
How one we grow,   5
Pivot of heels and knees!—The furrow

Splits and passes, sister to
The brown arc
Of the neck I cannot catch,

Nigger-eye   10
Berries cast dark
Hooks——

Black sweet blood mouthfuls,
Shadows.
Something else   15

Hauls me through air——
Thighs, hair;
Flakes from my heels.

White
Godiva,[3] I unpeel——   20
Dead hands, dead stringencies.

And now I
Foam to wheat, a glitter of seas.
The child's cry

Melts in the wall.   25
And I
Am the arrow,

The dew that flies
Suicidal, at one with the drive
Into the red   30

Eye, the cauldron of morning.

1962   1966

---

1. The spirit of fire and air in Shakespeare's
Tempest. Ariel was also the name of the horse
Plath rode weekly in 1961–62, when she lived in
Devon, England.
2. A rocky peak.

3. According to legend, in 1040 Lady Godiva
rode naked on horseback through the streets of
Coventry to win a remission of feudal obligations
and taxes.

Daddy

You do not do, you do not do
Any more, black shoe
In which I have lived like a foot
For thirty years, poor and white,
Barely daring to breathe or Achoo.   5

Daddy, I have had to kill you.
You died before I had time——
Marble-heavy, a bag full of God,
Ghastly statue with one grey toe[1]
Big as a Frisco seal   10

And a head in the freakish Atlantic
Where it pours bean green over blue
In the waters of beautiful Nauset.[2]
I used to pray to recover you.
Ach, du.[3]   15

In the German tongue, in the Polish town[4]
Scraped flat by the roller
Of wars, wars, wars.
But the name of the town is common.
My Polack friend   20

Says there are a dozen or two.
So I never could tell where you
Put your foot, your root,
I never could talk to you.
The tongue stuck in my jaw.   25

It stuck in a barb wire snare.
Ich,[5] ich, ich, ich,
I could hardly speak.
I thought every German was you.
And the language obscene   30

An engine, an engine
Chuffing me off like a Jew.
A Jew to Dachau, Auschwitz, Belsen.[6]
I began to talk like a Jew.
I think I may well be a Jew.   35

---

1. Plath's father's toe turned black from gangrene, a complication of diabetes.
2. Massachusetts beach.
3. Ah, you (German): the first of a series of references to her father's German origins.

4. The poet's father, of German descent, was born in Grabow, Poland.
5. I (German).
6. German concentration camps, where millions of Jews were murdered during World War II.

The snows of the Tyrol,[7] the clear beer of Vienna
Are not very pure or true.
With my gypsy ancestress and my weird luck
And my Taroc[8] pack and my Taroc pack
I may be a bit of a Jew.   40

I have always been scared of *you*,
With your Luftwaffe,[9] your gobbledygoo.
And your neat mustache
And your Aryan eye, bright blue.
Panzer[1]-man, panzer-man, O You——   45

Not God but a swastika
So black no sky could squeak through.
Every woman adores a Fascist,
The boot in the face, the brute
Brute heart of a brute like you.   50

You stand at the blackboard, daddy,
In the picture I have of you,
A cleft in your chin instead of your foot
But no less a devil for that, no not
And less the black man who   55

Bit my pretty red heart in two.
I was ten when they buried you.
At twenty I tried to die
And get back, back, back to you.
I thought even the bones would do.   60

But they pulled me out of the sack,
And they stuck me together with glue.[2]
And then I knew what to do.
I made a model of you,
A man in black with a Meinkampf[3] look   65

And a love of the rack and the screw.
And I said I do, I do.
So daddy, I'm finally through.
The black telephone's off at the root,
The voices just can't worm through.   70

If I've killed one man, I've killed two——
The vampire who said he was you
And drank my blood for a year,

7. Austrian Alpine region.
8. Variation of Tarot, ancient fortune-telling cards. Gypsies, like Jews, were objects of Nazi genocidal ambition; many died in the concentration camps.
9. The German air force.
1. Armor (German); refers to the German army's tank corps in World War II. Hitler preached the superiority of the Aryans—people of German stock with blond hair and blue eyes.
2. An allusion to Plath's first suicide attempt.
3. A reference to Hitler's political autobiography, *Mein Kampf* (*My Struggle*), written and published before his rise to power, in which the future dictator outlined his plans for world conquest.

Seven years, if you want to know.
Daddy, you can lie back now.   75

There's a stake in your fat black heart
And the villagers never liked you.
They are dancing and stamping on you.
They always *knew* it was you.
Daddy, daddy, you bastard, I'm through.   80

1962   1966

Words

Axes
After whose stroke the wood rings,
And the echoes!
Echoes traveling
Off from the centre like horses.   5

The sap
Wells like tears, like the
Water striving
To re-establish its mirror
Over the rock   10

That drops and turns,
A white skull,
Eaten by weedy greens.
Years later I
Encounter them on the road——   15

Words dry and riderless,
The indefatigable hoof-taps.
While
From the bottom of the pool, fixed stars
Govern a life.   20

1963   1966

Blackberrying

Nobody in the lane, and nothing, nothing but blackberries,
Blackberries on either side, though on the right mainly,
A blackberry alley, going down in hooks, and a sea
Somewhere at the end of it, heaving. Blackberries
Big as the ball of my thumb, and dumb as eyes   5
Ebon in the hedges, fat
With blue-red juices. These they squander on my fingers.

I had not asked for such a blood sisterhood; they must love me.
They accommodate themselves to my milkbottle, flattening their sides.

Overhead go the choughs[1] in black, cacophonous flocks—   10
Bits of burnt paper wheeling in a blown sky.
Theirs is the only voice, protesting, protesting.
I do not think the sea will appear at all.
The high, green meadows are glowing, as if lit from within.
I come to one bush of berries so ripe it is a bush of flies,   15
Hanging their bluegreen bellies and their wing panes in a Chinese screen.
The honey-feast of the berries has stunned them; they believe in heaven.
One more hook, and the berries and bushes end.

The only thing to come now is the sea.
From between two hills a sudden wind funnels at me,   20
Slapping its phantom laundry in my face.
These hills are too green and sweet to have tasted salt.
I follow the sheep path between them. A last hook brings me
To the hills' northern face, and the face is orange rock
That looks out on nothing, nothing but a great space   25
Of white and pewter lights, and a din like silversmiths
Beating and beating at an intractable metal.

1961   1971

Purdah[1]

Jade—
Stone of the side,
The agonized

Side of green Adam, I
Smile, cross-legged,   5
Enigmatical,

Shifting my clarities.
So valuable!
How the sun polishes this shoulder!

And should   10
The moon, my
Indefatigable cousin

Rise, with her cancerous pallors,
Dragging trees—
Little bushy polyps,[2]   15

---

1. Small, chattering birds of the crow family.
1. Among Muslims and some Hindu sects, seclusion of women from public observation.
2. Animals that have many feet or tentacles, like octopuses, cuttlefish, and smaller coelenterates; also a general term for tumors that have tentacle-like protrusions.

Little nets,
My visibilities hide.
I gleam like a mirror.

At this facet the bridegroom arrives
Lord of the mirrors!   20
It is himself he guides

In among these silk
Screens, these rustling appurtenances.
I breathe, and the mouth

Veil stirs its curtain   25
My eye
Veil is

A concatenation of rainbows.
I am his.
Even in his   30

Absence, I
Revolve in my
Sheath of impossibles,

Priceless and quiet
Among these parakeets, macaws!³   35
O chatterers

Attendants of the eyelash!
I shall unloose
One feather, like the peacock.

Attendants of the lip!   40
I shall unloose
One note

Shattering
The chandelier
Of air that all day flies   45

Its crystals
A million ignorants.
Attendants!

Attendants!
And at his next step   50
I shall unloose

3. Two kinds of parrots.

I shall unloose—
From the small jeweled
Doll he guards like a heart—

The lioness,   55
The shriek in the bath,
The cloak of holes.

1962   1972

The Applicant

First, are you our sort of a person?
Do you wear
A glass eye, false teeth or a crutch,
A brace or a hook,
Rubber breasts or a rubber crotch,   5

Stitches to show something's missing? No, no? Then
How can we give you a thing?
Stop crying.
Open your hand.
Empty? Empty. Here is a hand   10

To fill it and willing
To bring teacups and roll away headaches
And do whatever you tell it.
Will you marry it?
It is guaranteed   15

To thumb shut your eyes at the end
And dissolve of sorrow.
We make new stock from the salt.
I notice you are stark naked.
How about this suit——   20

Black and stiff, but not a bad fit.
Will you marry it?
It is waterproof, shatterproof, proof
Against fire and bombs through the roof.
Believe me, they'll bury you in it.   25

Now your head, excuse me, is empty.
I have the ticket for that.
Come here, sweetie, out of the closet.
Well, what do you think of *that*?
Naked as paper to start   30

But in twenty-five years she'll be silver,
In fifty, gold.

A living doll, everywhere you look.
It can sew, it can cook,
It can talk, talk, talk.   35

It works, there is nothing wrong with it.
You have a hole, it's a poultice.
You have an eye, it's an image.
My boy, it's your last resort.
Will you marry it, marry it, marry it.   40

1962   1965

Child

Your clear eye is the one absolutely beautiful thing.
I want to fill it with color and ducks,
The zoo of the new

Whose names you meditate—
April snowdrop, Indian pipe,   5
Little

Stalk without wrinkle,
Pool in which images
Should be grand and classical

Not this troublous   10
Wringing of hands, this dark
Ceiling without a star.

1963   1972

JOHN UPDIKE
1932–2009

" To transcribe middleness with all its grits, bumps and anonymities, in its
fullness of satisfaction and mystery: is it possible . . . or worth doing?" John
Updike's novels and stories give a positive answer to the question he asks in his early
memoir, *The Dogwood Tree: A Boyhood*; for he is arguably the most significant tran-
scriber, or creator rather, of "middleness" in American writing since William Dean
Howells (about whom he has written appreciatively) a century earlier. Falling in love
in high school, meeting a college roommate, going to the eye doctor or dentist, eating
supper on Sunday night, visiting your mother with your wife and son—these activities

are made to yield up their possibilities to a writer as responsively curious in imagination and delicately precise in his literary expression as Updike showed himself to be.

Born in Shillington, Pennsylvania, John Updike was an only child. He was gifted at drawing and caricature, and after graduating summa cum laude from Harvard in 1954, he spent a year studying art in England, then returned to America and went to work for the *New Yorker*, where his first stories appeared and to which he contributed regularly for five decades. When later in the 1950s he left the magazine, he also left New York City and with his wife and children settled in Ipswich, Massachusetts. There he pursued "his solitary trade as methodically as the dentist practiced his," resisting the temptations of university teaching as successfully as he did the blandishments of media talk shows. His ample output was achieved through dedicated, steady work; his books are the fruit of patience, leisure, and craft.

Since 1959, when his first novel, *The Poorhouse Fair*, appeared, Updike published not only many novels and stories but also eight books of poetry, a play, and a vast store of book reviews and other prose writings. He is most admired by some readers as the author of the "Olinger" stories (included in *The Early Stories: 1953–1975*, 2003) about life in an imaginary Pennsylvania town that takes on its colors from the real Shillington of his youth. The heroes of these stories are adolescents straining to break out of their fast-perishing environments, as they grow up and as their small town turns into something else. Updike treats them with a blend of affection and ironic humor that is wonderfully assured in its touch, although his sense of place, of growing up during the Depression and the years of World War II, is always vividly present. Like Howells (whose fine memoir of his youthful days in Ohio, *A Boy's Town*, is an ancestor of Updike's *The Dogwood Tree*), he shows how one's spirit takes on its coloration from the material circumstances—houses, clothes, landscape, food, parents—one is bounded by.

This sense of place, which is also a sense of life, is found in the stories and in the novels, too, although Updike found it harder to invent convincing forms in which to tell longer tales. His most ambitious novel is probably *The Centaur* (1964), memorable for its portrayal of three days of confusion and error in the life of an American high school teacher seen through his son's eyes, but the book is also burdened with an elaborate set of mythical trappings that seem less than inevitable. *Couples* (1968), a novel that gained him a good deal of notoriety as a chronicler of sexual relationships, both marital and adulterous, is jammed with much interesting early-1960s lore about suburban life but seems uncertain whether it is an exercise in realism or a creative fantasy, as does *Marry Me* (1976).

In the four "Rabbit" novels, Updike found his most congenial and engaging subject for longer fiction. In each book he rendered the sense of an era—the 1950s in *Rabbit, Run*; the late 1960s in *Rabbit Redux*; the great gasoline crisis of 1979 in *Rabbit Is Rich*; the end of the Reagan era (and the end of Rabbit) in *Rabbit at Rest* (1990)—through the eyes of a hero who both is and is not like his creator. Harry "Rabbit" Angstrom, ex–high school basketball star, perpetually prey to nostalgia and in love with his own past, lives in a present he can't abide. *Rabbit, Run* shows him trying to escape from his town, his job, his wife, and his child by a series of disastrously sentimental and humanly irresponsible actions; yet Updike makes us feel Rabbit's yearnings even as we judge the painful consequences of yielding to them. Ten years later the fading basketball star has become a fortyish, dispirited printer with a wayward wife and a country that is both landing on the moon and falling to pieces. *Rabbit Redux* is masterly in presenting a small town rotting away from its past certainties; it also attempts to deal with the Vietnam War and the black revolution. *Rabbit Is Rich* is a gentler, sadder chronicling of the hero's settling into grandfatherhood as he draws ever closer to death; while *Rabbit at Rest*, the longest and richest of the four novels, brings him to a moving conclusion. Rabbit's coda is presented in the reflections of his son and illegitimate daughter in "Rabbit Remembered," collected in *Licks of Love* (2000). In *Roger's Version* (1986) and *S* (1988), Updike adopted—or permitted his protagonists to adopt—a more broadly, sometimes a harsher, satiric view of contemporary religion, computer technology, feminism, and other forms of "liberation." Still, for all his virtuosity as a novelist, his best work may be found in the stories and in his short novel *Of the Farm* (1965). In "Separating" (printed here) the boy from "The Happiest I've Been" (*The Same Door,* 1959) has grown up, married, and fathered children and is now about to leave them as he moves into divorce. It is a beautiful example of Updike's careful, poised sense of how things work, a sense that can also be observed in the poem "Dog's Death" and in his memoir *Self-Consciousness* (1989).

Near the end of "The Dogwood Tree," he summarized his boyish dream of becoming an artist:

> He saw art—between drawing and writing he ignorantly made no distinction—as a method of riding a thin pencil out of Shillington, out of time altogether, into an infinity of unseen and even unborn hearts. He pictured this infinity as radiant. How innocent!

Most writers would name that innocence only to deplore it. Updike maintained instead that, as with the Christian faith he professed, succeeding years gave him no better assumptions with which to replace it. In any case, his fine sense of fact protected him from fashionable extravagances in black humor and experimental narratives, while enabling him to be both a satirist and a celebrator of our social and domestic conditions. In the last decade of his life a fabulative, almost magical atmosphere appeared in some works, as with his 2000 novel, *Gertrude and Claudius.* Yet even here John Updike showed himself to be our era's most sensitive craftsman of personal and societal manners, as he did in the generational family saga based on spiritual perceptions, *In the Beauty of the Lilies* (1996), in *Villages* (2004), a bildungsroman about a protagonist's marriages, careers, and communities, and in the sociopolitical challenge of *Terrorist* (2006).

The following text is from the *New Yorker* (June 23, 1975).

Separating

The day was fair. Brilliant. All that June the weather had mocked the Maples' internal misery with solid sunlight—golden shafts and cascades of green in which their conversations had wormed unseeing, their sad murmuring selves the only stain in Nature. Usually by this time of the year they had acquired tans; but when they met their elder daughter's plane on her return from a year in England they were almost as pale as she, though Judith was too dazzled by the sunny opulent jumble of her native land to notice. They did not spoil her homecoming by telling her immediately. Wait a few days, let her recover from jet lag, had been one of their formulations, in that string of gray dialogues—over coffee, over cocktails, over Cointreau—that had shaped the strategy of their dissolution, while the earth performed its annual stunt of renewal unnoticed beyond their closed windows. Richard had thought to leave at Easter; Joan had insisted they wait until the four children were at last assembled, with all exams passed and ceremonies attended, and the bauble of summer to console them. So he had drudged away, in love, in dread, repairing screens, getting the mowers sharpened, rolling and patching their new tennis court.

The court, clay, had come through its first winter pitted and windswept bare of redcoat. Years ago the Maples had observed how often, among their friends, divorce followed a dramatic home improvement, as if the marriage were making one last twitchy effort to live; their own worst crisis had come amid the plaster dust and exposed plumbing of a kitchen renovation. Yet, a summer ago, as canary-yellow bulldozers gaily churned a grassy, daisy-dotted knoll into a muddy plateau, and a crew of pigtailed young men raked and tamped clay into a plane, this transformation did not strike them as ominous, but festive in its impudence; their marriage could rend the earth for fun. The next spring, waking each day at dawn to a sliding sensation as if the bed were being tipped, Richard found the barren tennis court, its net and tapes still rolled in the barn, an environment congruous with his mood of purposeful desolation, and the crumbling of handfuls of clay into cracks and holes (dogs had frolicked on the court in a thaw; rivulets had evolved trenches) an activity suitably elemental and interminable. In his sealed heart he hoped the day would never come.

Now it was here. A Friday. Judith was reacclimated; all four children were assembled, before jobs and camps and visits again scattered them. Joan thought they should be told one by one. Richard was for making an announcement at the table. She said, "I think just making an announcement is a cop-out. They'll start quarrelling and playing to each other instead of focussing. They're each individuals, you know, not just some corporate obstacle to your freedom."

"O.K., O.K. I agree." Joan's plan was exact. That evening, they were giving Judith a belated welcome-home dinner, of lobster and champagne. Then, the party over, they, the two of them, who nineteen years before would push her in a baby carriage along Tenth Street to Washington Square,[1] were to walk her out of the house, to the bridge across the salt creek, and tell her, swearing her to secrecy. Then Richard Jr., who was going directly from work to a rock concert in Boston, would be told, either late when he returned on the train or early Saturday morning before he went off to his job; he was seventeen and employed as one of a golf-course maintenance crew. Then the two younger children, John and Margaret, could, as the morning wore on, be informed.

"Mopped up, as it were," Richard said.

"Do you have any better plan? That leaves you the rest of Saturday to answer any questions, pack, and make your wonderful departure."

"No," he said, meaning he had no better plan, and agreed to hers, though it had an edge of false order, a plea for control in the semblance of its achievement, like Joan's long chore lists and financial accountings and, in the days when he first knew her, her too copious lecture notes. Her plan turned one hurdle for him into four—four knife-sharp walls, each with a sheer blind drop on the other side.

All spring he had been morbidly conscious of insides and outsides, of barriers and partitions. He and Joan stood as a thin barrier between the children and the truth. Each moment was a partition, with the past on one side and the future on the other, a future containing this unthinkable *now*. Beyond four knifelike walls a new life for him waited vaguely. His skull cupped a secret, a white face, a face both frightened and soothing, both strange and known, that he wanted to shield from tears, which he felt all about him,

---

1. In Greenwich Village, an area in lower Manhattan, New York City.

solid as the sunlight. So haunted, he had become obsessed with battening down the house against his absence, replacing screens and sash cords, hinges and latches—a Houdini[2] making things snug before his escape.

The lock. He had still to replace a lock on one of the doors of the screened porch. The task, like most such, proved more difficult than he had imagined. The old lock, aluminum frozen by corrosion, had been deliberately rendered obsolete by manufacturers. Three hardware stores had nothing that even approximately matched the mortised hole its removal (surprisingly easy) left. Another hole had to be gouged, with bits too small and saws too big, and the old hole fitted with a block of wood—the chisels dull, the saw rusty, his fingers thick with lack of sleep. The sun poured down, beyond the porch, on a world of neglect. The bushes already needed pruning, the windward side of the house was shedding flakes of paint, rain would get in when he was gone, insects, rot, death. His family, all those he would lose, filtered through the edges of his awareness as he struggled with screw holes, splinters, opaque instructions, minutiae of metal.

Judith sat on the porch, a princess returned from exile. She regaled them with stories of fuel shortages, of bomb scares in the Underground, of Pakistani workmen loudly lusting after her as she walked past on her way to dance school. Joan came and went, in and out of the house, calmer than she should have been, praising his struggles with the lock as if this were one more and not the last of their chain of shared chores. The younger of his sons, John, now at fifteen suddenly, unwittingly handsome, for a few minutes held the rickety screen door while his father clumsily hammered and chiselled, each blow a kind of sob in Richard's ears. His younger daughter, having been at a slumber party, slept on the porch hammock through all the noise—heavy and pink, trusting and forsaken. Time, like the sunlight, continued relentlessly; the sunlight slowly slanted. Today was one of the longest days. The lock clicked, worked. He was through. He had a drink; he drank it on the porch, listening to his daughter. "It was so sweet," she was saying, "during the worst of it, how all the butcher's and bakery shops kept open by candlelight. They're all so plucky and cute. From the papers, things sounded so much worse here—people shooting people in gas lines, and everybody freezing."

Richard asked her, "Do you still want to live in England forever?" *Forever*: the concept, now a reality upon him, pressed and scratched at the back of his throat.

"No," Judith confessed, turning her oval face to him, its eyes still childishly far apart, but the lips set as over something succulent and satisfactory. "I was anxious to come home. I'm an American." She was a woman. They had raised her; he and Joan had endured together to raise her, alone of the four. The others had still some raising left in them. Yet it was the thought of telling Judith—the image of her, their first baby, walking between them arm in arm to the bridge—that broke him. The partition between himself and the tears broke. Richard sat down to the celebratory meal with the back

---

2. Harry Houdini (1874–1926), American magician and escape artist.

of his throat aching; the champagne, the lobster seemed phases of sunshine; he saw them and tasted them through tears. He blinked, swallowed, croakily joked about hay fever. The tears would not stop leaking through; they came not through a hole that could be plugged but through a permeable spot in a membrane, steadily, purely, endlessly, fruitfully. They became, his tears, a shield for himself against these others—their faces, the fact of their assembly, a last time as innocents, at a table where he sat the last time as head. Tears dropped from his nose as he broke the lobster's back; salt flavored his champagne as he sipped it; the raw clench at the back of his throat was delicious. He could not help himself.

His children tried to ignore his tears. Judith on his right, lit a cigarette, gazed upward in the direction of her too energetic, too sophisticated exhalation; on her other side, John earnestly bent his face to the extraction of the last morsels—legs, tail segments—from the scarlet corpse. Joan, at the opposite end of the table, glanced at him surprised, her reproach displaced by a quick grimace, of forgiveness, or of salute to his superior gift of strategy. Between them, Margaret, no longer called Bean, thirteen and large for her age, gazed from the other side of his pane of tears as if into a shopwindow at something she coveted—at her father, a crystalline heap of splinters and memories. It was not she, however, but John who, in the kitchen, as they cleared the plates and carapaces away, asked Joan the question: *"Why is Daddy crying?"*

Richard heard the question but not the murmured answer. Then he heard Bean cry, "Oh, no-oh!"—the faintly dramatized exclamation of one who had long expected it.

John returned to the table carrying a bowl of salad. He nodded tersely at his father and his lips shaped the conspiratorial words "She told."

"Told what?" Richard asked aloud, insanely.

The boy sat down as if to rebuke his father's distraction with the example of his own good manners and said quietly, "The separation."

Joan and Margaret returned; the child, in Richard's twisted vision, seemed diminished in size, and relieved, relieved to have had the boogeyman at last proved real. He called out to her—the distances at the table had grown immense—"You knew, you always knew," but the clenching at the back of his throat prevented him from making sense of it. From afar he heard Joan talking, levelly, sensibly, reciting what they had prepared: it was a separation for the summer, an experiment. She and Daddy both agreed it would be good for them; they needed space and time to think; they liked each other but did not make each other happy enough, somehow.

Judith, imitating her mother's factual tone, but in her youth off-key, too cool, said, "I think it's silly. You should either live together or get divorced."

Richard's crying, like a wave that has crested and crashed, had become tumultuous; but it was overtopped by another tumult, for John, who had been so reserved, now grew larger and larger at the table. Perhaps his younger sister's being credited with knowing set him off. "Why didn't you *tell* us?" he asked, in a large round voice quite unlike his own. "You should have *told* us you weren't getting along."

Richard was startled into attempting to force words through his tears. "We *do* get along, that's the trouble, so it doesn't show even to us—"

"That we do not love each other" was the rest of the sentence; he couldn't finish it.

Joan finished for him, in her style. "And we've always, *especially*, loved our children."

John was not mollified. "What do you care about *us*?" he boomed. "We're just little things you *had*." His sisters' laughing forced a laugh from him, which he turned hard and parodistic: "Ha ha *ha*." Richard and Joan realized simultaneously that the child was drunk, on Judith's homecoming champagne. Feeling bound to keep the center of the stage, John took a cigarette from Judith's pack, poked it into his mouth, let it hang from his lower lip, and squinted like a gangster.

"You're not little things we had," Richard called to him. "You're the whole point. But you're grown. Or almost."

The boy was lighting matches. Instead of holding them to his cigarette (for they had never seen him smoke; being "good" had been his way of setting himself apart), he held them to his mother's face, closer and closer, for her to blow out. Then he lit the whole folder—a hiss and then a torch, held against his mother's face. Prismed by tears, the flame filled Richard's vision; he didn't know how it was extinguished. He heard Margaret say, "Oh stop showing off," and saw John, in response, break the cigarette in two and put the halves entirely into his mouth and chew, sticking out his tongue to display the shreds to his sister.

Joan talked to him, reasoning—a fountain of reason, unintelligible. "Talked about it for years . . . our children must help us . . . Daddy and I both want . . ." As the boy listened, he carefully wadded a paper napkin into the leaves of his salad, fashioned a ball of paper and lettuce, and popped it into his mouth, looking around the table for the expected laughter. None came. Judith said, "Be mature," and dismissed a plume of smoke.

Richard got up from this stifling table and led the boy outside. Though the house was in twilight, the outdoors still brimmed with light, the long waste light of high summer. Both laughing, he supervised John's spitting out the lettuce and paper and tobacco into the pachysandra.[3] He took him by the hand—a square gritty hand, but for its softness a man's. Yet, it held on. They ran together up into the field, past the tennis court. The raw banking left by the bulldozers was dotted with daisies. Past the court and a flat stretch where they used to play family baseball stood a soft green rise glorious in the sun, each weed and species of grass distinct as illumination on parchment. "I'm sorry, so sorry," Richard cried. "You were the only one who ever tried to help me with all the goddam jobs around this place."

Sobbing, safe within his tears and the champagne, John explained, "It's not just the separation, it's the whole crummy year, I *hate* that school, you can't make any friends, the history teacher's a scud."[4]

They sat on the crest of the rise, shaking and warm from their tears but easier in their voices, and Richard tried to focus on the child's sad year—the weekdays long with homework, the weekends spent in his room with model airplanes, while his parents murmured down below, nursing their

---

3. Green, leafy plant, frequently used as ground cover.
4. Dull, disagreeable, objectionable person.

separation. How selfish, how blind, Richard thought; his eyes felt scoured. He told his son, "We'll think about getting you transferred. Life's too short to be miserable."

They had said what they could, but did not want the moment to heal, and talked on, about the school, about the tennis court, whether it would ever again be as good as it had been that first summer. They walked to inspect it and pressed a few more tapes more firmly down. A little stiltedly, perhaps trying to make too much of the moment, to prolong it, Richard led the boy to the spot in the field where the view was best, of the metallic blue river, the emerald marsh, the scattered islands velvet with shadow in the low light, the white bits of beach far away. "See," he said. "It goes on being beautiful. It'll be here tomorrow."

"I know," John answered, impatiently. The moment had closed.

Back in the house, the others had opened some white wine, the champagne being drunk, and still sat at the table, the three females, gossiping. Where Joan sat had become the head. She turned, showing him a tearless face, and asked, "All right?"

"We're fine," he said, resenting it, though relieved, that the party went on without him.

In bed she explained, "I couldn't cry I guess because I cried so much all spring. It really wasn't fair. It's your idea, and you made it look as though I was kicking you out."

"I'm sorry," he said. "I couldn't stop. I wanted to but couldn't."

"You *didn't* want to. You loved it. You were having your way, making a general announcement."

"I love having it over," he admitted. "God, those kids were great. So brave and funny." John, returned to the house, had settled to a model airplane in his room, and kept shouting down to them, "I'm O.K. No sweat." "And the way," Richard went on, cozy in his relief, "they never questioned the reasons we gave. No thought of a third person. Not even Judith."

"That *was* touching," Joan said.

He gave her a hug. "You were great too. Thank you." Guiltily, he realized he did not feel separated.

"You still have Dickie to do," she told him. These words set before him a black mountain in the darkness; its cold breath, its near weight affected his chest. Of the four children Dickie was most nearly his conscience. Joan did not need to add, "That's one piece of your dirty work I won't do for you."

"I know. I'll do it. You go to sleep."

Within minutes, her breathing slowed, became oblivious and deep. It was quarter to midnight. Dickie's train from the concert would come in at one-fourteen. Richard set the alarm for one. He had slept atrociously for weeks. But whenever he closed his lids some glimpse of the last hours scorched them—Judith exhaling toward the ceiling in a kind of aversion, Bean's mute staring, the sunstruck growth of the field where he and John had rested. The mountain before him moved closer, moved within him; he was huge, momentous. The ache at the back of his throat felt stale. His wife slept as if slain beside him. When, exasperated by his hot lids, his crowded heart, he rose from bed and dressed, she awoke enough to turn over. He told her then, "If I could undo it all, I would."

"Where would you begin?" she asked. There was no place. Giving him courage, she was always giving him courage. He put on shoes without socks in the dark. The children were breathing in their rooms, the downstairs was hollow. In their confusion they had left lights burning. He turned off all but one, the kitchen overhead. The car started. He had hoped it wouldn't. He met only moonlight on the road; it seemed a diaphanous companion, flickering in the leaves along the roadside, haunting his rearview mirror like a pursuer, melting under his headlights. The center of town, not quite deserted, was eerie at this hour. A young cop in uniform kept company with a gang of T-shirted kids on the steps of the bank. Across from the railroad station, several bars kept open. Customers, mostly young, passed in and out of the warm night, savoring summer's novelty. Voices shouted from cars as they passed; an immense conversation seemed in progress. Richard parked and in his weariness put his head on the passenger seat, out of the commotion and wheeling lights. It was as when, in the movies, an assassin grimly carries his mission through the jostle of a carnival—except the movies cannot show the precipitous, palpable slope you cling to within. You cannot climb back down; you can only fall. The synthetic fabric of the car seat, warmed by his cheek, confided to him an ancient, distant scent of vanilla.

A train whistle caused him to lift his head. It was on time; he had hoped it would be late. The slender drawgates descended. The bell of approach tingled happily. The great metal body, horizontally fluted, rocked to a stop, and sleepy teen-agers disembarked, his son among them. Dickie did not show surprise that his father was meeting him at this terrible hour. He sauntered to the car with two friends, both taller than he. He said "Hi" to his father and took the passenger's seat with an exhausted promptness that expressed gratitude. The friends got into the back, and Richard was grateful; a few more minutes' postponement would be won by driving them home.

He asked, "How was the concert?"

"Groovy," one boy said from the back seat.

"It bit," the other said.

"It was O.K.," Dickie said, moderate by nature, so reasonable that in his childhood the unreason of the world had given him headaches, stomach aches, nausea. When the second friend had been dropped off at his dark house, the boy blurted, "Dad, my eyes are killing me with hay fever! I'm out there cutting that mothering grass all day!"

"Do we still have those drops?"

"They didn't do any good last summer."

"They might this." Richard swung a U-turn on the empty street. The drive home took a few minutes. The mountain was here, in his throat. "Richard," he said, and felt the boy, slumped and rubbing his eyes, go tense at his tone, "I didn't come to meet you just to make your life easier. I came because your mother and I have some news for you, and you're a hard man to get ahold of these days. It's sad news."

"That's O.K." The reassurance came out soft, but quick, as if released from the tip of a spring.

Richard had feared that his tears would return and choke him, but the boy's manliness set an example, and his voice issued forth steady and dry. "It's sad news, but it needn't be tragic news, at least for you. It should have no practical effect on your life, though it's bound to have an emotional effect. You'll work at your job, and go back to school in September. Your mother and I are really proud of what you're making of your life; we don't want that to change at all."

"Yeah," the boy said lightly, on the intake of his breath, holding himself up. They turned the corner; the church they went to loomed like a gutted fort. The home of the woman Richard hoped to marry stood across the green. Her bedroom light burned.

"Your mother and I," he said, "have decided to separate. For the summer. Nothing legal, no divorce yet. We want to see how it feels. For some years now, we haven't been doing enough for each other, making each other as happy as we should be. Have you sensed that?"

"No," the boy said. It was an honest, unemotional answer: true or false in a quiz.

Glad for the factual basis, Richard pursued, even garrulously, the details. His apartment across town, his utter accessibility, the split vacation arrangements, the advantages to the children, the added mobility and variety of the summer. Dickie listened, absorbing. "Do the others know?"

Richard described how they had been told.

"How did they take it?"

"The girls pretty calmly. John flipped out; he shouted and ate a cigarette and made a salad out of his napkin and told us how much he hated school."

His brother chuckled. "He did?"

"Yeah. The school issue was more upsetting for him than Mom and me. He seemed to feel better for having exploded."

"He did?" The repetition was the first sign that he was stunned.

"Yes. Dickie, I want to tell you something. This last hour, waiting for your train to get in, has been about the worst of my life. I hate this. *Hate* it. My father would have died before doing it to me." He felt immensely lighter, saying this. He had dumped the mountain on the boy. They were home. Moving swiftly as a shadow, Dickie was out of the car, through the bright kitchen. Richard called after him, "Want a glass of milk or anything?"

"No thanks."

"Want us to call the course tomorrow and say you're too sick to work?"

"No, that's all right." The answer was faint, delivered at the door to his room; Richard listened for the slam of a tantrum. The door closed normally. The sound was sickening.

Joan had sunk into that first deep trough of sleep and was slow to awake. Richard had to repeat, "I told him."

"What did he say?"

"Nothing much. Could you go say good night to him? Please."

She left their room, without putting on a bathrobe. He sluggishly changed back into his pajamas and walked down the hall. Dickie was already in bed, Joan was sitting beside him, and the boy's bedside clock radio was murmuring music. When she stood, an inexplicable light—the moon?—outlined her body through the nightie. Richard sat on the warm place she had indented on the child's narrow mattress. He asked him, "Do you want the radio on like that?"

"It always is."

"Doesn't it keep you awake? It would me."

"No."

"Are you sleepy?"

"Yeah."

"Good. Sure you want to get up and go to work? You've had a big night."

"I want to."

Away at school this winter he had learned for the first time that you can go short of sleep and live. As an infant he had slept with an immobile, sweating intensity that had alarmed his babysitters. As the children aged, he became the first to go to bed, earlier for a time than his younger brother and sister. Even now, he would go slack in the middle of a television show, his sprawled legs hairy and brown. "O.K. Good boy. Dickie, listen. I love you so much, I never knew how much until now. No matter how this works out, I'll always be with you. Really."

Richard bent to kiss an averted face but his son, sinewy, turned and with wet cheeks embraced him and gave him a kiss, on the lips, passionate as a woman's. In his father's ear he moaned one word, the crucial, intelligent word: "Why?"

Why. It was a whistle of wind in a crack, a knife thrust, a window thrown open on emptiness. The white face was gone, the darkness was featureless. Richard had forgotten why.

1975

PHILIP ROTH
b. 1933

From the moment Philip Roth's collection of stories *Goodbye, Columbus* won the Houghton Mifflin Literary Fellowship for 1959, his career has received the ambiguous reward of much anxious concern from critics, centered on whether he would develop the promise displayed in this first book. Ten years later, with *Portnoy's Complaint*, Roth became overnight the famous author of a "dirty" bestseller, yet his success only made his critics more uneasy. Was this gifted portrayer of Jewish middle-class life really more interested in scoring points off caricatures than in creating and exploring characters? Did his very facility with words inhibit the exercise of deeper sympathies and more humanly generous purposes?

Roth grew up in Newark, New Jersey, attended the branch of Rutgers University there, graduated from Bucknell University, took an M.A. in English literature at the University of Chicago, then served in the army. Over the years he has taught at a number of universities while receiving many awards and fellowships. Like John Barth, another "university" writer, Roth is an ironic humorist, although the impulse behind his early stories is darker and less playful. *Goodbye, Columbus* is about Jews on the verge of being or already having been assimilated into the larger American culture, and the stories confidently take the measure of their embattled heroes, as in "The Conversion of the Jews" or "Epstein" or the long title story. "Defender of the Faith" (printed here), arguably the best piece in the collection, is distinguished for the way Roth explores rather than exploits the conflict between personal feelings and religious loyalties as they are felt by Nathan Marx, a U.S. Army sergeant in a Missouri training company near the end of World War II. Throughout *Goodbye, Columbus* the narrator's voice is centrally important: in some stories it is indistinguishable from that of a campus wiseguy; in others it reaches out to a calmer and graver sense of disparities between promises and performance.

Roth's first two novels, *Letting Go* (1962) and *When She Was Good* (1967), markedly extended the territory charted in *Goodbye, Columbus* and showed him eager and equipped to write about people other than Jews. *Letting Go* is conventional in technique and in its subjects—love, marriage, university life—but Roth's easy mastery of the look and feel of places and things is everywhere evident. F. Scott Fitzgerald is the American writer whose presence in these early novels is most strongly felt; in particular, the section from *Letting Go* told in the first person by a graduate student in English betrays its indebtedness to Fitzgerald's Nick Carraway, the narrator of *The Great Gatsby*. This Fitzgeraldian atmosphere, with its nostalgic evocation of adolescence and early romantic visions, is even more evident in *When She Was Good*, which is strong in its rendering of middle-American living rooms and kitchens, the flushed atmosphere of late-night 1950s sex in parked cars, or the lyrics of popular songs—bits of remembered trivia that Roth, like his predecessor, has a genius for bringing to life.

The less-than-overwhelming reception of his second novel probably helped Roth move away from relatively sober realism; certainly *Portnoy's Complaint* (1969) is a louder and more virtuoso performance than the earlier books. Alexander Portnoy's recollections of early childhood miseries are really a pretext for Roth to perform a succession of clever numbers in the inventive mode of a stand-up comic. Memories of growing up in New Jersey, listening to radio programs, playing softball, ogling girls at the ice-skating rink, or (most sensationally) masturbating in outlandish ways add up to an entertaining narrative that is sometimes crude but more often delicate and precise.

After *Portnoy* Roth moved toward fantasy and further showmanly operations: *Our Gang* (1970) attempted to do for Richard Nixon and his associates what actual events were to do one better; *The Breast* (1971) is a rather unamusing fable about a man's metamorphosis into that object; *The Great American Novel* (1973) threatened to sink under its weight of baseball lore dressed up in tall tales and sick jokes. But in *My Life as a Man* (1974) and *The Professor of Desire* (1977) he returned to matters that have traditionally preoccupied the social novelist and that inform his own best work: marriage, divorce, the family, Jewishness, and psychoanalysis—the pressures of civilization and the resultant individual discontents.

His finest work is to be found in the Zuckerman novels, beginning with *Zuckerman Bound* (1985) and its successor, *The Counterlife* (1987). In these novels Roth created a hero-as-novelist whose experience parallels in important ways that of his creator. A scandalous novel, *Carnovsky*, recalls *Portnoy's Complaint*; a critic named Milton Appel is a stand-in for the real critic Irving Howe, who once subjected Roth's work to hostile criticism. Yet for all the dangers of self-pity or self-absorption such autobiographical reference involves, the novels add up to something much deeper, more comic and touching, than self-advertisement and complaint. Scenes like the death of Zuckerman's father in a Florida hospital and the subsequent return of the son to the vanished Newark where he grew up are moving expressions of the generous purposes and human sympathies we find in Roth's work at its best. And those purposes and sympathies are also evident in his autobiographical writing: in *The Facts* (1988) and especially in *Patrimony* (1991), a poignant memoir of his father.

In the 1990s and into the twenty-first century, Roth has developed his art of impersonation into audacious and sometimes excessive forms. *Operation Shylock* (1993) poses a presumably real Philip Roth who encounters an impostor; *Sabbath's Theater* (1995) recasts his typical protagonist as a puppeteer who manipulates women in much the same way; *American Pastoral* (1997) brings back Nathan

Zuckerman for a high school reunion and the investigation of a "more ordinary" classmate's life. Zuckerman remains on hand for *I Married a Communist* (1998) and *The Human Stain* (2000), while David Kepesh (who had turned into a female breast in the author's much earlier fantasy) reappears as a professor who seduces his students in *The Dying Animal* (2001). Further seduction takes place in *Everyman* (2006), although the author's most disturbing projections are reserved for *The Plot against America* (2004), in which a fictive Charles A. Lindbergh becomes president and initiates repression of American Jews. *Exit Ghost* (2007) has Nathan Zuckerman return to New York City and reencounter characters from previous novels. *Indignation* (2008) sets a young man's maturation against the looming threat of military service in the Korean War. *The Humbling* (2009) projects Roth's late-life anxieties as a writer onto the career of an actor in decline. *Nemesis* (2010), his twenty-fourth and, he says, final novel, expands the author's concerns with human morality (and the role of a God who allows such suffering) to encompass a polio epidemic in the Newark of his childhood. Throughout his work, Roth's emphasis remains on invention, reminding readers that the writerly self is a virtually inexhaustible resource for the imagination. Nevertheless, in 2012 Roth announced his retirement from writing, saying he had "done my best with what I had."

The following text is from *Goodbye, Columbus* (1959).

Defender of the Faith

In May of 1945, only a few weeks after the fighting had ended in Europe, I was rotated back to the States, where I spent the remainder of the war with a training company at Camp Crowder, Missouri. We had been racing across Germany so swiftly during the late winter and spring that when I boarded the plane that drizzly morning in Berlin, I couldn't believe our destination lay to the west. My mind might inform me otherwise, but there was an inertia of the spirit that told me we were flying to a new front where we would disembark and continue our push eastward—eastward until we'd circled the globe, marching through villages along whose twisting, cobbled streets crowds of the enemy would watch us take possession of what up till then they'd considered their own. I had changed enough in two years not to mind the trembling of the old people, the crying of the very young, the uncertain fear in the eyes of the once-arrogant. After two years I had been fortunate enough to develop an infantryman's heart which, like his feet, at first aches and swells, but finally grows horny enough for him to travel the weirdest paths without feeling a thing.

Captain Paul Barrett was to be my C.O. at Camp Crowder. The day I reported for duty he came out of his office to shake my hand. He was short, gruff, and fiery, and indoors or out he wore his polished helmet liner[1] down on his little eyes. In Europe he had received a battlefield commission and a serious chest wound, and had been returned to the States only a few months before. He spoke easily to me, but was, I thought, unnecessarily abusive towards the troops. At the evening formation, he introduced me.

"Gentlemen," he called. "Sergeant Thurston, as you know, is no longer with this Company. Your new First Sergeant is Sergeant Nathan Marx here. He is a veteran of the European theater and consequently will take no shit."

---

1. Plastic liner worn under a helmet to prevent chafing and bruising.

I sat up late in the orderly room that evening, trying halfheartedly to solve the riddle of duty rosters, personnel forms, and morning reports. The CQ[2] slept with his mouth open on a mattress on the floor. A trainee stood reading the next day's duty roster, which was posted on the bulletin board directly inside the screen door. It was a warm evening and I could hear the men's radios playing dance music over in the barracks.

The trainee, who I knew had been staring at me whenever I looked groggily into the forms, finally took a step in my direction.

"Hey, Sarge—we having a G.I. party tomorrow night?" A G.I. party is a barracks-cleaning.

"You usually have them on Friday nights?"

"Yes," and then he added mysteriously, "that's the whole thing."

"Then you'll have a G.I. party."

He turned away and I heard him mumbling. His shoulders were moving and I wondered if he was crying.

"What's your name, soldier?" I asked.

He turned, not crying at all. Instead his green-speckled eyes, long and narrow, flashed like fish in the sun. He walked over to me and sat on the edge of my desk.

He reached out a hand. "Sheldon," he said.

"Stand on your own two feet, Sheldon."

Climbing off the desk, he said, "Sheldon Grossbart." He smiled wider at the intimacy into which he'd led me.

"You against cleaning the barracks Friday night, Grossbart? Maybe we shouldn't have G.I. parties—maybe we should get a maid." My tone startled me: I felt like a Charlie McCarthy, with every top sergeant I had ever known as my Edgar Bergen.[3]

"No, Sergeant." He grew serious, but with a seriousness that seemed only to be the stifling of a smile. "It's just G.I. parties on Friday night, of all nights . . ."

He slipped up to the corner of the desk again—not quite sitting, but not quite standing either. He looked at me with those speckled eyes flashing and then made a gesture with his hand. It was very slight, no more than a rotation back and forth of the wrist, and yet it managed to exclude from our affairs everything else in the orderly room, to make the two of us the center of the world. It seemed, in fact, to exclude everything about the two of us except our hearts. "Sergeant Thurston was one thing," he whispered, an eye flashing to the sleeping CQ, "but we thought with you here, things might be a little different."

"We?"

"The Jewish personnel."

"Why?" I said, harshly.

He hesitated a moment, and then, uncontrollably, his hand went up to his mouth. "I mean . . ." he said.

"What's on your mind?" Whether I was still angry at the "Sheldon" business or something else, I hadn't a chance to tell—but clearly I was angry.

2. Noncommissioned officer in charge of quarters at night or on weekends.

3. A ventriloquist who, with Charlie McCarthy, his dummy, was a popular radio comedian.

". . . we thought you . . . Marx, you know, like Karl Marx. The Marx brothers. Those guys are all . . . M-A-R-X, isn't that how you spell it, Sergeant?"

"M-A-R-X."

"Fishbein said—" He stopped. "What I mean to say, Sergeant—" His face and neck were red, and his mouth moved but no words came out. In a moment, he raised himself to attention, gazing down at me. It was as though he had suddenly decided he could expect no more sympathy from me than from Thurston, the reason being that I was of Thurston's faith and not his. The young man had managed to confuse himself as to what my faith really was, but I felt no desire to straighten him out. Very simply, I didn't like him.

When I did nothing but return his gaze, he spoke, in an altered tone. "You see, Sergeant," he explained to me, "Friday nights, Jews are supposed to go to services."

"Did Sergeant Thurston tell you you couldn't go to them when there was a G.I. party?"

"No."

"Did he say you had to stay and scrub the floors?"

"No, Sergeant."

"Did the Captain say you had to stay and scrub the floors?"

"That isn't it, Sergeant. It's the other guys in the barracks." He leaned toward me. "They think we're goofing off. But we're not. That's when Jews go to services, Friday night. We have to."

"Then go."

"But the other guys make accusations. They have no right."

"That's not the Army's problem, Grossbart. It's a personal problem you'll have to work out yourself."

"But it's un*fair*."

I got up to leave. "There's nothing I can do about it," I said.

Grossbart stiffened in front of me. "But this is a matter of *religion*, sir."

"Sergeant."

"I mean 'Sergeant,'" he said, almost snarling.

"Look, go see the chaplain. The I.G.[4] You want to see Captain Barrett, I'll arrange an appointment."

"No, no. I don't want to make trouble, Sergeant. That's the first thing they throw up to you. I just want my rights!"

"Damn it, Grossbart, stop whining. You have your rights. You can stay and scrub floors or you can go to *shul*[5]—"

The smile swam in again. Spittle gleamed at the corners of his mouth. "You mean church, Sergeant."

"I mean *shul*, Grossbart!" I walked past him and outside. Near me I heard the scrunching of a guard's boots on gravel. In the lighted windows of the barracks the young men in T-shirts and fatigue pants were sitting on their bunks, polishing their rifles. Suddenly there was a light rustling behind me. I turned and saw Grossbart's dark frame fleeing back to the barracks, racing to tell his Jewish friends that they were right—that like Karl and Harpo, I was one of them.

---

4. Inspector general, who, apart from the chaplain, provided the only route by which complaints could be registered.

5. Synagogue (Yiddish).

The next morning, while chatting with the Captain, I recounted the incident of the previous evening, as if to unburden myself of it. Somehow in the telling it seemed to the Captain that I was not so much explaining Grossbart's position as defending it.

"Marx, I'd fight side by side with a nigger if the fellow proved to me he was a man. I pride myself," the Captain said looking out the window, "that I've got an open mind. Consequently, Sergeant, nobody gets special treatment here, for the good *or* the bad. All a man's got to do is prove himself. A man fires well on the range, I give him a weekend pass. He scores high in PT, he gets a weekend pass. He *earns* it." He turned from the window and pointed a finger at me. "You're a Jewish fellow, am I right, Marx?"

"Yes, sir."

"And I admire you. I admire you because of the ribbons on your chest, not because you had a hem stitched on your dick before you were old enough to even know you had one. I judge a man by what he shows me on the field of battle, Sergeant. It's what he's got *here*," he said, and then, though I expected he would point to his heart, he jerked a thumb towards the buttons straining to hold his blouse across his belly. "Guts," he said.

"Okay, sir, I only wanted to pass on to you how the men felt."

"Mr. Marx, you're going to be old before your time if you worry about how the men feel. Leave that stuff to the Chaplain—pussy, the clap, church picnics with the little girls from Joplin, that's all his business, not yours. Let's us train these fellas to shoot straight. If the Jewish personnel feels the other men are accusing them of goldbricking . . . well, I just don't know. Seems awful funny how suddenly the Lord is calling so loud in Private Grossman's ear he's just got to run to church."

"Synagogue," I said.

"Synagogue is right, Sergeant. I'll write that down for handy reference. Thank you for stopping by."

That evening, a few minutes before the company gathered outside the orderly room for the chow formation, I called the CQ, Corporal Robert LaHill, in to see me. LaHill was a dark burly fellow whose hair curled out of his clothes wherever it could. He carried a glaze in his eyes that made one think of caves and dinosaurs. "LaHill," I said, "when you take the formation, remind the men that they're free to attend church services *whenever* they are held, provided they report to the orderly room before they leave the area."

LaHill didn't flicker; he scratched his wrist, but gave no indication that he'd heard or understood.

"LaHill," I said, "*church*. You remember? Church, priest, Mass, confession . . ."

He curled one lip into a ghastly smile; I took it for a signal that for a second he had flickered back up into the human race.

"Jewish personnel who want to attend services this evening are to fall out in front of the orderly room at 1900." And then I added, "By order of Captain Barrett."

A little while later, as a twilight softer than any I had seen that year dropped over Camp Crowder, I heard LaHill's thick, inflectionless voice outside my window: "Give me your ears, troopers. Toppie says for me to tell you that at 1900 hours all Jewish personnel is to fall out in front here if they wants to attend the Jewish Mass."

At seven o'clock, I looked out of the orderly-room window and saw three soldiers in starched khakis standing alone on the dusty quadrangle. They looked at their watches, and fidgeted while they whispered back and forth. It was getting darker, and alone on the deserted field they looked tiny. When I walked to the door I heard the noises of the G.I. party coming from the surrounding barracks—bunks being pushed to the wall, faucets pounding water into buckets, brooms whisking at the wooden floors. In the windows big puffs of cloth moved round and round, cleaning the dirt away for Saturday's inspection. I walked outside and the moment my foot hit the ground I thought I heard Grossbart, who was now in the center, call to the other two, "Ten-*hut!*" Or maybe when they all three jumped to attention, I imagined I heard the command.

At my approach, Grossbart stepped forward. "Thank you, sir," he said.

"Sergeant, Grossbart," I reminded him. "You call officers 'Sir.' I'm not an officer. You've been in the Army three weeks—you know that."

He turned his palms out at his sides to indicate that, in truth, he and I lived beyond convention. "Thank you, anyway," he said.

"Yes," the tall boy behind him said. "Thanks a lot."

And the third whispered, "Thank you," but his mouth barely fluttered so that he did not alter by more than a lip's movement, the posture of attention.

"For what?" I said.

Grossbart snorted, happily. "For the announcement before. The Corporal's announcement. It helped. It made it . . ."

"Fancier." It was the tall boy finishing Grossbart's sentence.

Grossbart smiled. "He means formal, sir. Public," he said to me. "Now it won't seem as though we're just taking off, goldbricking, because the work has begun."

"It was by order of Captain Barrett," I said.

"Ahh, but you pull a little weight . . ." Grossbart said. "So we thank you." Then he turned to his companions. "Sergeant Marx, I want you to meet Larry Fishbein."

The tall boy stepped forward and extended his hand. I shook it. "You from New York?" he asked.

"Yes."

"Me too." He had a cadaverous face that collapsed inward from his cheekbone to his jaw, and when he smiled—as he did at the news of our communal attachment—revealed a mouthful of bad teeth. He blinked his eyes a good deal, as though he were fighting back tears. "What borough?" he asked.

I turned to Grossbart. "It's five after seven. What time are services?"

"*Shul,*" he smiled, "is in ten minutes. I want you to meet Mickey Halpern. This is Nathan Marx, our Sergeant."

The third boy hopped forward. "Private Michael Halpern." He saluted.

"Salute officers, Halpern." The boy dropped his hand, and in his nervousness checked to see if his shirt pockets were buttoned on the way down.

"Shall I march them over, sir?" Grossbart asked, "or are you coming along?"

From behind Grossbart, Fishbein piped up. "Afterwards they're having refreshments. A Ladies' Auxiliary from St. Louis, the rabbi told us last week."

"The chaplain," whispered Halpern.

"You're welcome to come along," Grossbart said.

To avoid his plea, I looked away, and saw, in the windows of the barracks, a cloud of faces staring out at the four of us.

"Look, hurry out of here, Grossbart."

"Okay, then," he said. He turned to the others. "Double time, *march!*" and they started off, but ten feet away Grossbart spun about, and running backwards he called to me, "Good *shabus,*[6] sir." And then the three were swallowed into the Missouri dusk.

Even after they'd disappeared over the parade grounds, whose green was now a deep twilight blue, I could hear Grossbart singing the double-time cadence, and as it grew dimmer and dimmer it suddenly touched some deep memory—as did the slant of light—and I was remembering the shrill sounds of a Bronx playground, where years ago, beside the Grand Concourse,[7] I had played on long spring evenings such as this. Those thin fading sounds . . . It was a pleasant memory for a young man so far from peace and home, and it brought so very many recollections with it that I began to grow exceedingly tender about myself. In fact, I indulged myself to a reverie so strong that I felt within as though a hand had opened and was reaching down inside. It had to reach so very far to touch me. It had to reach past those days in the forests of Belgium and the dying I'd refused to weep over; past the nights in those German farmhouses whose books we'd burned to warm us, and which I couldn't bother to mourn; past those endless stretches when I'd shut off all softness I might feel for my fellows, and managed even to deny myself the posture of a conqueror—the swagger that I, as a Jew, might well have worn as my boots whacked against the rubble of Münster, Braunschweig, and finally Berlin.

But now one night noise, one rumor of home and time past, and memory plunged down through all I had anesthetized and came to what I suddenly remembered to be myself. So it was not altogether curious that in search of more of me I found myself following Grossbart's tracks to Chapel No. 3 where the Jewish services were being held.

I took a seat in the last row, which was empty. Two rows in front sat Grossbart, Fishbein, and Halpern, each holding a little white dixie cup. Fishbein was pouring the contents of his cup into Grossbart's, and Grossbart looked mirthful as the liquid drew a purple arc between his hand and Fishbein's. In the glary yellow light, I saw the chaplain on the pulpit chanting the first line of the responsive reading. Grossbart's prayerbook remained closed on his lap; he swished the cup around. Only Halpern responded in prayer. The fingers of his right hand were spread wide across the cover of the book, and his cap was pulled down low onto his brow so that it was round like a *yarmulke*[8] rather than long and pointed. From time to time, Grossbart wet his lips at the cup's edge; Fishbein, his long yellow face, a dying light bulb, looked from here to there, leaning forward at the neck to catch sight of the faces down the row, in front—then behind. He saw me

6. Sabbath (Yiddish).
7. Avenue in the Bronx, New York.

8. Skullcap (Yiddish).

and his eyelids beat a tattoo. His elbow slid into Grossbart's side, his neck inclined towards his friend, and then, when the congregation responded, Grossbart's voice was among them. Fishbein looked into his book now too; his lips, however, didn't move.

Finally it was time to drink the wine. The chaplain smiled down at them as Grossbart swigged in one long gulp, Halpern sipped, meditating, and Fishbein faked devotion with an empty cup.

At last the chaplain spoke: "As I look down amongst the congregation—" he grinned at the word, "this night, I see many new faces, and I want to welcome you to Friday night services here at Camp Crowder. I am Major Leo Ben Ezra, your chaplain . . ." Though an American, the chaplain spoke English very deliberately, syllabically almost, as though to communicate, above all, to the lip-readers in the audience. "I have only a few words to say before we adjourn to the refreshment room where the kind ladies of the Temple Sinai, St. Louis, Missouri, have a nice setting for you."

Applause and whistling broke out. After a momentary grin, the chaplain raised his palms to the congregation, his eyes flicking upward a moment, as if to remind the troops where they were and Who Else might be in attendance. In the sudden silence that followed, I thought I heard Grossbart's cackle—"Let the goyim[9] clean the floors!" Were those the words? I wasn't sure, but Fishbein, grinning, nudged Halpern. Halpern looked dumbly at him, then went back to his prayerbook, which had been occupying him all through the rabbi's talk. One hand tugged at the black kinky hair that stuck out under his cap. His lips moved.

The rabbi continued. "It is about the food that I want to speak to you for a moment. I know, I know, I know," he intoned, wearily, "how in the mouths of most of you the *trafe*[1] food tastes like ashes. I know how you gag, some of you, and how your parents suffer to think of their children eating foods unclean and offensive to the palate. What can I tell you? I can only say close your eyes and swallow as best you can. Eat what you must to live and throw away the rest. I wish I could help more. For those of you who find this impossible, may I ask that you try and try, but then come to see me in private where, if your revulsion is such, we will have to seek aid from those higher up."

A round of chatter rose and subsided; then everyone sang "Ain Keloha-noh," after all those years I discovered I still knew the words.

Suddenly, the service over, Grossbart was upon me. "Higher up? He means the General?"

"Hey, Shelly," Fishbein interrupted, "he means God." He smacked his face and looked at Halpern. "How high can you go!"

"Shhh!" Grossbart said. "What do you think, Sergeant?"

"I don't know. You better ask the chaplain."

"I'm going to. I'm making an appointment to see him in private. So is Mickey."

Halpern shook his head. "No, no, Sheldon . . ."

"You have rights, Mickey. They can't push us around."

"It's okay. It bothers my mother, not me . . ."

---

9. Gentiles (Yiddish).　　　　1. Unkosher—unfit to eat (Yiddish).

Grossbart looked at me. "Yesterday he threw up. From the hash. It was all ham and God knows what else."

"I have a cold—that was why," Halpern said. He pushed his *yamalkah* back into a cap.

"What about you, Fishbein?" I asked. "You kosher too?"

He flushed, which made the yellow more gray than pink. "A little. But I'll let it ride. I have a very strong stomach. And I don't eat a lot anyway . . ." I continued to look at him, and he held up his wrist to re-enforce what he'd just said. His watch was tightened to the last hole and he pointed that out to me. "So I don't mind."

"But services are important to you?" I asked him.

He looked at Grossbart. "Sure, sir."

"Sergeant."

"Not so much at home," said Grossbart, coming between us, "but away from home it gives one a sense of his Jewishness."

"We have to stick together," Fishbein said.

I started to walk towards the door; Halpern stepped back to make way for me.

"That's what happened in Germany," Grossbart was saying, loud enough for me to hear. "They didn't stick together. They let themselves get pushed around."

I turned. "Look, Grossbart, this is the Army, not summer camp."

He smiled. "So?" Halpern tried to sneak off, but Grossbart held his arm. "So?" he said again.

"Grossbart," I asked, "how old are you?"

"Nineteen."

"And you?" I said to Fishbein.

"The same. The same month even."

"And what about him?" I pointed to Halpern, who'd finally made it safely to the door.

"Eighteen," Grossbart whispered. "But he's like he can't tie his shoes or brush his teeth himself. I feel sorry for him."

"I feel sorry for all of us, Grossbart, but just act like a man. Just don't overdo it."

"Overdo what, sir?"

"The sir business. Don't overdo that," I said, and I left him standing there. I passed by Halpern but he did not look up. Then I was outside, black surrounded me—but behind I heard Grossbart call, "Hey, Mickey, *liebschen*,[2] come on back. Refreshments!"

Liebschen! My grandmother's word for me!

One morning, a week later, while I was working at my desk, Captain Barrett shouted for me to come into his office. When I entered, he had his helmet liner squashed down so that I couldn't even see his eyes. He was on the phone, and when he spoke to me, he cupped one hand over the mouthpiece.

"Who the fuck is Grossbart?"

"Third platoon, Captain," I said. "A trainee."

2. Darling (German).

"What's all this stink about food? His mother called a goddam congress-man about the food . . ." He uncovered the mouthpiece and slid his helmet up so I could see the curl of his bottom eyelash. "Yes, sir," he said into the phone. "Yes, sir. I'm still here, sir. I'm asking Marx here right now . . ."

He covered the mouthpiece again and looked back to me. "Lightfoot Har-ry's on the phone," he said, between his teeth. "This congressman calls General Lyman who calls Colonel Sousa who calls the Major who calls me. They're just dying to stick this thing on me. What's a matter," he shook the phone at me, "I don't feed the troops? What the hell is this?"

"Sir, Grossbart is strange . . ." Barrett greeted that with a mockingly indulgent smile. I altered my approach. "Captain, he's a very orthodox Jew and so he's only allowed to eat certain foods."

"He throws up, the congressman said. Every time he eats something his mother says he throws up!"

"He's accustomed to observing the dietary laws, Captain."

"So why's his old lady have to call the White House!"

"Jewish parents, sir, they're apt to be more protective than you expect. I mean Jews have a very close family life. A boy goes away from home, some-times the mother is liable to get very upset. Probably the boy *mentioned* something in a letter and his mother misinterpreted."

"I'd like to punch him one right in the mouth. There's a goddam war on and he wants a silver platter!"

"I don't think the boy's to blame, sir. I'm sure we can straighten it out by just asking him. Jewish parents worry—"

"*All* parents worry, for Christ sake. But they don't get on their high horse and start pulling strings—"

I interrupted, my voice higher, tighter than before. "The home life, Cap-tain, is so very important . . . but you're right, it may sometimes get out of hand. It's a very wonderful thing, Captain, but because it's so close, this kind of thing—"

He didn't listen any longer to my attempt to present both myself and Lightfoot Harry with an explanation for the letter. He turned back to the phone. "Sir?" he said. "Sir, Marx here tells me Jews have a tendency to be pushy. He says he thinks he can settle it right here in the Company . . . Yes, sir . . . I *will* call back, sir, soon as I can . . ." He hung up. "Where are the men, Sergeant?"

"On the range."

With a whack on the top, he crushed his helmet over his eyes, and charged out of his chair. "We're going for a ride."

The Captain drove and I sat beside him. It was a hot spring day and under my newly starched fatigues it felt as though my armpits were melting down onto my sides and chest. The roads were dry and by the time we reached the firing range, my teeth felt gritty with dust though my mouth had been shut the whole trip. The Captain slammed the brakes on and told me to get the hell out and find Grossbart.

I found him on his belly, firing wildly at the 500 feet target. Waiting their turns behind him were Halpern and Fishbein. Fishbein, wearing a pair of rimless G.I. glasses I hadn't seen on him before, gave the appearance of an old peddler who would gladly have sold you the rifle and cartridges that were slung all over him. I stood back by the ammo boxes, waiting for Grossbart to finish spraying the distant targets. Fishbein straggled back to stand near me.

"Hello, Sergeant Marx."

"How are you?" I mumbled.

"Fine, thank you. Sheldon's really a good shot."

"I didn't notice."

"I'm not so good, but I think I'm getting the hang of it now . . . Sergeant, I don't mean to, you know, ask what I shouldn't . . ." The boy stopped. He was trying to speak intimately but the noise of the shooting necessitated that he shout at me.

"What is it?" I asked. Down the range I saw Captain Barrett standing up in the jeep, scanning the line for me and Grossbart.

"My parents keep asking and asking where we're going. Everybody says the Pacific. I don't care, but my parents . . . If I could relieve their minds I think I could concentrate more on my shooting."

"I don't know where, Fishbein. Try to concentrate anyway."

"Sheldon says you might be able to find out—"

"I don't know a thing, Fishbein. You just take it easy, and don't let Sheldon—"

"*I'm* taking it easy, Sergeant. It's at home—"

Grossbart had just finished on the line and was dusting his fatigues with one hand. I left Fishbein's sentence in the middle.

"Grossbart, the Captain wants to see you."

He came toward us. His eyes blazed and twinkled. "Hi!"

"Don't point that goddam rifle!"

"I wouldn't shoot you, Sarge." He gave me a smile wide as a pumpkin as he turned the barrel aside.

"Damn you, Grossbart—this is no joke! Follow me."

I walked ahead of him and had the awful suspicion that behind me Grossbart was *marching*, his rifle on his shoulder, as though he were a one-man detachment.

At the jeep he gave the Captain a rifle salute. "Private Sheldon Grossbart, sir."

"At ease, Grossman." The Captain slid over to the empty front seat, and crooking a finger, invited Grossbart closer.

"Bart, sir. Sheldon Gross*bart*. It's a common error." Grossbart nodded to me—*I understand*, he indicated. I looked away, just as the mess truck pulled up to the range, disgorging a half dozen K.P.'s with rolled-up sleeves. The mess sergeant screamed at them while they set up the chow line equipment.

"Grossbart, your mama wrote some congressman that we don't feed you right. Do you know that?" the Captain said.

"It was my father, sir. He wrote to Representative Franconi that my religion forbids me to eat certain foods."

"What religion is that, Grossbart?"

"Jewish."

"Jewish, *sir*," I said to Grossbart.

"Excuse me, sir. 'Jewish, sir.'"

"What have you been living on?" the Captain asked. "You've been in the Army a month already. You don't look to me like you're falling to pieces."

"I eat because I have to, sir. But Sergeant Marx will testify to the fact that I don't eat one mouthful more than I need to in order to survive."

"Marx," Barrett asked, "is that so?"

"I've never seen Grossbart eat, sir," I said.

"But you heard the rabbi," Grossbart said. "He told us what to do, and I listened."

The Captain looked at me. "Well, Marx?"

"I still don't know what he eats and doesn't eat, sir."

Grossbart raised his rifle, as though to offer it to me. "But, Sergeant—"

"Look, Grossbart, just answer the Captain's questions!" I said sharply.

Barrett smiled at me and I resented it. "All right, Grossbart," he said, "What is it you want? The little piece of paper? You want out?"

"No, sir. Only to be allowed to live as a Jew. And for the others, too."

"What others?"

"Fishbein, sir, and Halpern."

"They don't like the way we serve either?"

"Halpern throws up, sir. I've seen it."

"I thought *you* threw up."

"Just once, sir. I didn't know the sausage was sausage."

"We'll give menus, Grossbart. We'll show training films about the food, so you can identify when we're trying to poison you."

Grossbart did not answer. Out before me, the men had been organized into two long chow lines. At the tail end of one I spotted Fishbein—or rather, his glasses spotted me. They winked sunlight back at me like a friend. Halpern stood next to him, patting inside his collar with a khaki handkerchief. They moved with the line as it began to edge up towards the food. The mess sergeant was still screaming at the K.P.'s, who stood ready to ladle out the food, bewildered. For a moment I was actually terrorized by the thought that somehow the mess sergeant was going to get involved in Grossbart's problem.

"Come over here, Marx," the Captain said to me. "Marx, you're a Jewish fella, am I right?"

I played straight man. "Yes, sir."

"How long you been in the Army? Tell this boy."

"Three years and two months."

"A year in combat, Grossbart. Twelve goddam months in combat all through Europe. I admire this man," the Captain said, snapping a wrist against my chest. But do you hear him peeping about the food? Do you? I want an answer, Grossbart. Yes or no."

"No, sir."

"And why not? He's a Jewish fella."

"Some things are more important to some Jews than other things to other Jews."

Barrett blew up. "Look, Grossbart, Marx here is a good man, a goddam *hero*. When you were sitting on your sweet ass in high school, Sergeant Marx was killing Germans. Who does more for the Jews, you by throwing up over a lousy piece of sausage, a piece of firstcut meat—or Marx by killing those Nazi bastards? If I was a Jew, Grossbart, I'd kiss this man's feet. He's a goddam hero, you know that? And *he* eats what we give him. Why do you have to cause trouble is what I want to know! What is it you're buckin' for, a discharge?"

"No, sir."

"I'm talking to a *wall*! Sergeant, get him out of my way." Barrett pounced over to the driver's seat. "I'm going to see the chaplain!" The engine roared, the jeep spun around, and then, raising a whirl of dust, the Captain was headed back to camp.

For a moment, Grossbart and I stood side by side, watching the jeep. Then he looked at me and said, "I don't want to start trouble. That's the first thing they toss up to us."

When he spoke I saw that his teeth were white and straight, and the sight of them suddenly made me understand that Grossbart actually did have parents: that once upon a time someone had taken little Sheldon to the dentist. He was someone's son. Despite all the talk about his parents, it was hard to believe in Grossbart as a child, an heir—as related by blood to anyone, mother, father, or, above all, to me. This realization led me to another.

"What does your father do, Grossbart?" I asked, as we started to walk back towards the chow line.

"He's a tailor."

"An American?"

"Now, yes. A son in the Army," he said, jokingly.

"And your mother?" I asked.

He winked. "A *ballabusta*[3]—she practically sleeps with a dustcloth in her hand."

"She's also an immigrant?"

"All she talks is Yiddish, still."

"And your father too?"

"A little English. 'Clean,' 'Press,' 'Take the pants in . . .' That's the extent of it. But they're good to me . . ."

"Then, Grossbart—" I reached out and stopped him. He turned towards me and when our eyes met his seemed to jump back, shiver in their sockets. He looked afraid. "Grossbart, then you were the one who wrote that letter, weren't you?"

It took only a second or two for his eyes to flash happy again. "Yes." He walked on, and I kept pace. "It's what my father *would* have written if he had known how. It was his name, though. *He* signed it. He even mailed it. I sent it home. For the New York postmark."

I was astonished, and he saw it. With complete seriousness, he thrust his right arm in front of me. "Blood is blood, Sergeant," he said, pinching the blue vein in his wrist.

"What the hell *are* you trying to do, Grossbart? I've seen you eat. Do you know that? I told the Captain I don't know what you eat, but I've seen you eat like a hound at chow."

"We work hard, Sergeant. We're in training. For a furnace to work, you've got to feed it coal."

"If you wrote the letter, Grossbart, then why did you say you threw up all the time?"

"I was really talking about Mickey there. But he would never write, Sergeant, though I pleaded with him. He'll waste away to nothing if I don't

---

3. Good housekeeper (Yiddish).

help. Sergeant, I used my name, my father's name, but it's Mickey and Fishbein too I'm watching out for."

"You're a regular Messiah,[4] aren't you?"

We were at the chow line now.

"That's a good one, Sergeant." He smiled. "But who knows? Who can tell? Maybe you're the Messiah . . . a little bit. What Mickey says is the Messiah is a collective idea. He went to Yeshivah,[5] Mickey, for a while. He says *together* we're the Messiah. Me a little bit, you a little bit . . . You should hear that kid talk, Sergeant, when he gets going."

"Me a little bit, you a little bit. You'd like to believe that, wouldn't you, Grossbart? That makes everything so clean for you."

"It doesn't seem too bad a thing to believe, Sergeant. It only means we should all give a little, is all . . ."

I walked off to eat my rations with the other noncoms.[6]

Two days later a letter addressed to Captain Barrett passed over my desk. It had come through the chain of command—from the office of Congressman Franconi, where it had been received, to General Lyman, to Colonel Sousa, to Major Lamont, to Captain Barrett. I read it over twice while the Captain was at the officers' mess. It was dated May 14th, the day Barrett had spoken with Grossbart on the rifle range.

Dear Congressman:

First let me thank you for your interest in behalf of my son, Private Sheldon Grossbart. Fortunately, I was able to speak with Sheldon on the phone the other night, and I think I've been able to solve our problem. He is, as I mentioned in my last letter, a very religious boy, and it was only with the greatest difficulty that I could persuade him that the religious thing to do—what God Himself would want Sheldon to do—would be to suffer the pangs of religious remorse for the good of his country and all mankind. It took some doing, Congressman, but finally he saw the light. In fact, what he said (and I wrote down the words on a scratch pad so as never to forget), what he said was, "I guess you're right, Dad. So many millions of my fellow Jews gave up their lives to the enemy, the least I can do is live for a while minus a bit of my heritage so as to help end this struggle and regain for all the children of God dignity and humanity." That, Congressman, would make any father proud.

By the way, Sheldon wanted me to know—and to pass on to you—the name of a soldier who helped him reach this decision: SERGEANT NATHAN MARX. Sergeant Marx is a combat veteran who is Sheldon's First Sergeant. This man has helped Sheldon over some of the first hurdles he's had to face in the Army, and is in part responsible for Sheldon's changing his mind about the dietary laws. I know Sheldon would appreciate any recognition Marx could receive.

Thank you and good luck. I look forward to seeing your name on the next election ballot.

Respectfully,
Samuel E. Grossbart

---

4. The deliverer who will rule over the people of Israel at the end of time.

5. Jewish institution of learning.

6. Noncommissioned officers.

Attached to the Grossbart communiqué was a communiqué addressed to General Marshall Lyman, the post commander, and signed by Representative Charles E. Franconi of the House of Representatives. The communiqué informed General Lyman that Sergeant Nathan Marx was a credit to the U.S. Army and the Jewish people.

What was Grossbart's motive in recanting? Did he feel he'd gone too far? Was the letter a strategic retreat—a crafty attempt to strengthen what he considered our alliance? Or had he actually changed his mind, via an imaginary dialogue between Grossbart *père* and *fils*?[7] I was puzzled, but only for a few days—that is, only until I realized that whatever his reasons, he had actually decided to disappear from my life: he was going to allow himself to become just another trainee. I saw him at inspection but he never winked; at chow formations but he never flashed me a sign; on Sundays, with the other trainees, he would sit around watching the noncoms' softball team, for whom I pitched, but not once did he speak an unnecessary or unusual word to me. Fishbein and Halpern retreated from sight too, at Grossbart's command I was sure. Apparently he'd seen that wisdom lay in turning back before he plunged us over into the ugliness of privilege undeserved. Our separation allowed me to forgive him our past encounters, and, finally, to admire him for his good sense.

Meanwhile, free of Grossbart, I grew used to my job and my administrative tasks. I stepped on a scale one day and discovered I had truly become a noncombatant: I had gained seven pounds. I found patience to get past the first three pages of a book. I thought about the future more and more, and wrote letters to girls I'd known before the war—I even got a few answers. I sent away to Columbia for a Law School catalogue. I continued to follow the war in the Pacific, but it was not my war and I read of bombings and battles like a civilian. I thought I could see the end in sight and sometimes at night I dreamed that I was walking on the streets of Manhattan—Broadway, Third Avenue, and 116th Street, where I had lived those three years I'd attended Columbia College. I curled myself around these dreams and I began to be happy.

And then one Saturday when everyone was away and I was alone in the orderly room reading a month-old copy of the *Sporting News*, Grossbart reappeared.

"You a baseball fan, Sergeant?"

I looked up. "How are you?"

"Fine," Grossbart said. "They're making a soldier out of me."

"How are Fishbein and Halpern?"

"Coming along," he said. "We've got no training this afternoon. They're at the movies."

"How come you're not with them?"

"I wanted to come over and say hello."

He smiled—a shy, regular-guy smile, as though he and I well knew that our friendship drew its sustenance from unexpected visits, remembered birthdays, and borrowed lawnmowers. At first it offended me, and then the feeling was swallowed by the general uneasiness I felt at the thought that

7. Father and son (French).

everyone on the post was locked away in a dark movie theater and I was here alone with Grossbart. I folded my paper.

"Sergeant," he said, "I'd like to ask a favor. It is a favor and I'm making no bones about it."

He stopped, allowing me to refuse him a hearing—which, of course, forced me into a courtesy I did not intend. "Go ahead."

"Well, actually it's two favors."

I said nothing.

"The first one's about these rumors. Everybody says we're going to the Pacific."

"As I told your friend Fishbein, I don't know. You'll just have to wait to find out. Like everybody else."

"You think there's a chance of any of us going East?"

"Germany," I said, "maybe."

"I meant New York."

"I don't think so, Grossbart. Offhand."

"Thanks for the information, Sergeant," he said.

"It's not information, Grossbart. Just what I surmise."

"It certainly would be good to be near home. My parents . . . you know." He took a step towards the door and then turned back. "Oh the other thing. May I ask the other?"

"What is it?"

"The other thing is—I've got relatives in St. Louis and they say they'll give me a whole Passover dinner if I can get down there. God, Sergeant, that'd mean an awful lot to me."

I stood up. "No passes during basic, Grossbart."

"But we're off from now till Monday morning, Sergeant. I could leave the post and no one would even know."

"I'd know. You'd know."

"But that's all. Just the two of us. Last night I called my aunt and you should have heard her. 'Come, come,' she said. 'I got gefilte fish, *chrain*,[8] the works!' Just a day, Sergeant, I'd take the blame if anything happened."

"The captain isn't here to sign a pass."

"You could sign."

"Look, Grossbart—"

"Sergeant, for two months practically I've been eating *trafe* till I want to die."

"I thought you'd made up your mind to live with it. To be minus a little bit of heritage."

He pointed a finger at me. "You!" he said. "That wasn't for you to read!"

"I read it. So what."

"That letter was addressed to a congressman."

"Grossbart, don't feed me any crap. You *wanted* me to read it."

"Why are you persecuting me, Sergeant?"

"Are you kidding!"

"I've run into this before," he said, "but never from my own!"

"Get out of here, Grossbart! Get the hell out of my sight!"

---

8. Horseradish, traditionally eaten as part of the Passover meal.

He did not move. "Ashamed, that's what you are. So you take it out on the rest of us. They say Hitler himself was half a Jew. Seeing this, I wouldn't doubt it!"

"What are you trying to do with me, Grossbart? What are you after? You want me to give you special privileges, to change the food, to find out about your orders, to give you weekend passes."

"You even talk like a goy!" Grossbart shook his fist. "Is this a weekend pass I'm asking for? Is a Seder[9] sacred or not?"

Seder! It suddenly occurred to me that Passover had been celebrated weeks before. I confronted Grossbart with the fact.

"That's right," he said. "Who says no? A month ago, and *I* was in the field eating hash! And now all I ask is a simple favor—a Jewish boy I thought would understand. My aunt's willing to go out of her way—to make a Seder a month later—" He turned to go, mumbling.

"Come back here!" I called. He stopped and looked at me. "Grossbart, why can't you be like the rest? Why do you have to stick out like a sore thumb? Why do you beg for special treatment?"

"Because I'm a Jew, Sergeant. I *am* different. Better, maybe not. But different."

"This is a war, Grossbart. For the time being *be* the same."

"I refuse."

"What?"

"I refuse. I can't stop being me, that's all there is to it." Tears came to his eyes. "It's a hard thing to be a Jew. But now I see what Mickey says—it's a harder thing to stay one." He raised a hand sadly toward me. "Look at you."

"Stop crying!"

"Stop this, stop that, stop the other thing! You stop, Sergeant. Stop closing your heart to your own!" And wiping his face with his sleeve, he ran out the door. "The least we can do for one another . . . the least . . ."

An hour later I saw Grossbart headed across the field. He wore a pair of starched khakis and carried only a little leather ditty bag. I went to the door and from the outside felt the heat of the day. It was quiet—not a soul in sight except over by the mess hall four K.P.'s sitting round a pan, sloped forward from the waists, gabbing and peeling potatoes in the sun.

"Grossbart!" I called.

He looked toward me and continued walking.

"Grossbart, get over here!"

He turned and stepped into his long shadow. Finally he stood before me.

"Where are you going?" I said.

"St. Louis. I don't care."

"You'll get caught without a pass."

"So I'll get caught without a pass."

"You'll go to the stockade."

"I'm in the stockade." He made an about-face and headed off.

I let him go only a step: "Come back here," I said, and he followed me into the office, where I typed out a pass and signed the Captain's name and my own initials after it.

9. Ceremonial dinner on the first evening of Passover.

He took the pass from me and then, a moment later, he reached out and grabbed my hand. "Sergeant, you don't know how much this means to me."

"Okay. Don't get in any trouble."

"I wish I could show you how much this means to me."

"Don't do me any favors. Don't write any more congressmen for citations."

Amazingly, he smiled. "You're right. I won't. But let me do something."

"Bring me a piece of that gefilte fish. Just get out of here."

"I will! With a slice of carrot and a little horseradish. I won't forget."

"All right. Just show your pass at the gate. And don't tell *anybody*."

"I won't. It's a month late, but a good Yom Tov[1] to you."

"Good Yom Tov, Grossbart," I said.

"You're a good Jew, Sergeant. You like to think you have a hard heart, but underneath you're a fine decent man. I mean that."

Those last three words touched me more than any words from Grossbart's mouth had the right to. "All right, Grossbart. Now call me 'sir' and get the hell out of here."

He ran out the door and was gone. I felt very pleased with myself—it was a great relief to stop fighting Grossbart. And it had cost me nothing. Barrett would never find out, and if he did, I could manage to invent some excuse. For a while I sat at my desk, comfortable in my decision. Then the screen door flew back and Grossbart burst in again. "Sergeant!" he said. Behind him I saw Fishbein and Halpern, both in starched khakis, both carrying ditty bags exactly like Grossbart's.

"Sergeant, I caught Mickey and Larry coming out of the movies. I almost missed them."

"Grossbart, did I say tell no one?"

"But my aunt said I could bring friends. That I should, in fact."

"I'm the Sergeant, Grossbart—not your aunt!"

Grossbart looked at me in disbelief; he pulled Halpern up by his sleeve. "Mickey, tell the Sergeant what this would mean to you."

"Grossbart, for God's sake, spare us—"

"Tell him what you told me, Mickey. How much it would mean."

Halpern looked at me and, shrugging his shoulders, made his admission. "A lot."

Fishbein stepped forward without prompting. "This would mean a great deal to me and my parents, Sergeant Marx."

"No!" I shouted.

Grossbart was shaking his head. "Sergeant, I could see you denying me, but how you can deny Mickey, a Yeshivah boy, that's beyond me."

"I'm not denying Mickey anything. You just pushed a little too hard, Grossbart. *You* denied him."

"I'll give him my pass, then," Grossbart said. "I'll give him my aunt's address and a little note. At least let him go."

In a second he had crammed the pass into Halpern's pants'pocket. Halpern looked at me, Fishbein too. Grossbart was at the door, pushing it open. "Mickey, bring me a piece of gefilte fish at least." And then he was outside again.

1. Holiday (Yiddish).

The three of us looked at one another and then I said, "Halpern, hand that pass over."

He took it from his pocket and gave it to me. Fishbein had now moved to the doorway, where he lingered. He stood there with his mouth slightly open and then pointed to himself. "And me?" he asked.

His utter ridiculousness exhausted me. I slumped down in my seat and I felt pulses knocking at the back of my eyes. "Fishbein," I said, "you understand I'm not trying to deny you anything, don't you? If it was my Army I'd serve gefilte fish in the mess hall. I'd sell kugel[2] in the PX, honest to God."

Halpern smiled.

"You understand, don't you, Halpern?"

"Yes, Sergeant."

"And you, Fishbein? I don't want enemies. I'm just like you—I want to serve my time and go home. I miss the same things you miss."

"Then, Sergeant," Fishbein interrupted, "Why don't you come too?"

"Where?"

"To St. Louis. To Shelley's aunt. We'll have a regular Seder. Play hide-the-matzah." He gave a broad, black-toothed smile.

I saw Grossbart in the doorway again, on the other side of the screen.

"Pssst!" He waved a piece of paper. "Mickey, here's the address. Tell her I couldn't get away."

Halpern did not move. He looked at me and I saw the shrug moving up his arms into his shoulders again. I took the cover off my typewriter and made out passes for him and Fishbein. "Go," I said, "the three of you."

I thought Halpern was going to kiss my hand.

That afternoon, in a bar in Joplin, I drank beer and listened with half an ear to the Cardinal game. I tried to look squarely at what I'd become involved in, and began to wonder if perhaps the struggle with Grossbart wasn't as much my fault as his. What was I that I had to *muster* generous feelings? Who was I to have been feeling so grudging, so tight-hearted? After all, I wasn't being asked to move the world. Had I a right, then, or a reason, to clamp down on Grossbart, when that meant clamping down on Halpern, too? And Fishbein, that ugly agreeable soul, wouldn't he suffer in the bargain also? Out of the many recollections that had tumbled over me these past few days, I heard from some childhood moment my grandmother's voice: "What are you making a *tsimas*?"[3] It was what she would ask my mother when, say, I had cut myself with a knife and her daughter was busy bawling me out. I would need a hug and a kiss and my mother would moralize! But my grandmother knew—mercy overrides justice. I should have known it, too. Who was Nathan Marx to be such a pennypincher with kindness? Surely, I thought, the Messiah himself—if he should ever come—won't niggle over nickels and dimes. God willing, he'll hug and kiss.

The next day, while we were playing softball over on the Parade Grounds, I decided to ask Bob Wright, who was noncom in charge over at Classification and Assignment, where he thought our trainees would be sent when their cycle ended in two weeks. I asked casually, between innings, and he

---

2. Baked pudding of noodles or potatoes.
3. Fuss (Yiddish, literal trans.); here a side dish made of mixed cooked vegetables and fruit.

said, "They're pushing them all into the Pacific. Shulman cut the orders on your boys the other day."

The news shocked me, as though I were father to Halpern, Fishbein, and Grossbart.

That night I was just sliding into sleep when someone tapped on the door. "What is it?"

"Sheldon."

He opened the door and came in. For a moment I felt his presence without being able to see him. "How was it?" I asked, as though to the darkness.

He popped into sight before me. "Great, Sergeant." I felt my springs sag; Grossbart was sitting on the edge of the bed. I sat up.

"How about you?" he asked. "Have a nice weekend?"

"Yes."

He took a deep paternal breath. "The others went to sleep . . ." We sat silently for a while, as a homey feeling invaded my ugly little cubicle: the door was locked, the cat out, the children safely in bed.

"Sergeant, can I tell you something? Personal?"

I did not answer and he seemed to know why. "Not about me. About Mickey. Sergeant, I never felt for anybody like I feel for him. Last night I heard Mickey in the bed next to me. He was crying so, it could have broken your heart. Real sobs."

"I'm sorry to hear that."

"I had to talk to him to stop him. He held my hand, Sergeant—he wouldn't let it go. He was almost hysterical. He kept saying if he only knew where we were going. Even if he knew it *was* the Pacific, that would be better than nothing. Just to know."

Long ago, someone had taught Grossbart the sad law that only lies can get the truth. Not that I couldn't believe in Halpern's crying—his eyes *always* seemed red-rimmed. But, fact or not, it became a lie when Grossbart uttered it. He was entirely strategic. But then—it came with the force of indictment—so was I! There are strategies of aggression, but there are strategies of retreat, as well. And so, recognizing that I myself, had not been without craft and guile, I told him what I knew. "It is the Pacific."

He let out a small gasp, which was not a lie. "I'll tell him. I wish it was otherwise."

"So do I."

He jumped on my words. "You mean you think you could do something? A change maybe?"

"No, I couldn't do a thing."

"Don't you know anybody over at C & A?"

"Grossbart, there's nothing I can do. If your orders are for the Pacific then it's the Pacific."

"But Mickey."

"Mickey, you, me—everybody, Grossbart. There's nothing to be done. Maybe the war'll end before you go. Pray for a miracle."

"But—"

"Good night, Grossbart." I settled back, and was relieved to feel the springs upbend again as Grossbart rose to leave. I could see him clearly now; his jaw had dropped and he looked like a dazed prizefighter. I noticed for the first time a little paper bag in his hand.

"Grossbart"—I smiled—"my gift?"

"Oh, yes, Sergeant. Here, from all of us." He handed me the bag. "It's egg roll."

"Egg roll?" I accepted the bag and felt a damp grease spot on the bottom. I opened it, sure that Grossbart was joking.

"We thought you'd probably like it. You know, Chinese egg roll. We thought you'd probably have a taste for—"

"Your aunt served egg roll?"

"She wasn't home."

"Grossbart, she invited you. You told me she invited you and your friends."

"I know. I just reread the letter. *Next* week."

I got out of bed and walked to the window. It was black as far off as I could see. "Grossbart," I said. But I was not calling him.

"What?"

"What are you, Grossbart? Honest to God, what are you?"

I think it was the first time I'd asked him a question for which he didn't have an immediate answer.

"How can you do this to people?" I asked.

"Sergeant, the day away did us all a world of good. Fishbein, you should see him, he *loves* Chinese food."

"But the Seder," I said.

"We took second best, Sergeant."

Rage came charging at me. I didn't sidestep—I grabbed it, pulled it in, hugged it to my chest.

"Grossbart, you're a liar! You're a schemer and a crook! You've got no respect for anything! Nothing at all! Not for me, for the truth, not even for poor Halpern! You use us all—"

"Sergeant, Sergeant, I feel for Mickey, honest to God, I do. I *love* Mickey. I try—"

"You try! You feel!" I lurched towards him and grabbed his shirt front. I shook him furiously. "Grossbart, get out. Get out and stay the hell away from me! Because if I see you, I'll make your life miserable. *You understand that?*"

"Yes."

I let him free, and when he walked from the room I wanted to spit on the floor where he had stood. I couldn't stop the fury from rising in my heart. It engulfed me, owned me, till it seemed I could only rid myself of it with tears or an act of violence. I snatched from the bed the bag Grossbart had given me and with all my strength threw it out the window. And the next morning, as the men policed the area around the barracks, I heard a great cry go up from one of the trainees who'd been anticipating only his morning handful of cigarette butts and candy wrappers. "Egg roll!" he shouted. "Holy Christ, Chinese goddam egg roll!"

A week later, when I read the orders that had come down from C & A, I couldn't believe my eyes. Every single trainee was to be shipped to Camp Stoneham, California, and from there to the Pacific. Every trainee but one: Private Sheldon Grossbart was to be sent to Fort Monmouth, New Jersey. I read the mimeographed sheet several times. Dee, Farrell, Fishbein, Fuselli, Fylypowycz, Glinicki, Gromke, Gucwa, Halpern, Hardy, Helebrandt . . . right down to Anton Zygadlo, all were to be headed West before the month was out. All except Grossbart. He had pulled a string and I wasn't it.

I lifted the phone and called C & A.

The voice on the other end said smartly, "Corporal Shulman, sir."

"Let me speak to Sergeant Wright."

"Who is this calling, sir?"

"Sergeant Marx."

And to my surprise, the voice said, *"Oh."* Then: "Just a minute, Sergeant."

Shulman's *oh* stayed with me while I waited for Wright to come to the phone. Why *oh?* Who was Shulman? And then, so simply, I knew I'd discovered the string Grossbart had pulled. In fact, I could hear Grossbart the day he'd discovered Shulman, in the PX, or the bowling alley, or maybe even at services. "Glad to meet you. Where you from? Bronx? Me too. Do you know so-and-so? And so-and-so? Me too! You work at C & A? Really? Hey, how's chances of getting East? Could you do something? Change something? Swindle, cheat, lie? We gotta help each other, you know . . . if the Jews in Germany . . ."

At the other end Bob Wright answered. "How are you, Nate? How's the pitching arm?"

"Good. Bob, I wonder if you could do me a favor." I heard clearly my own words and they so reminded me of Grossbart that I dropped more easily than I could have imagined into what I had planned. "This may sound crazy, Bob, but I got a kid here on orders to Monmouth who wants them changed. He had a brother killed in Europe and he's hot to go to the Pacific. Says he'd feel like a coward if he wound up stateside. I don't know, Bob, can anything be done? Put somebody else in the Monmouth slot?"

"Who?" he asked cagily.

"Anybody. First guy on the alphabet. I don't care. The kid just asked if something could be done."

"What's his name?"

"Grossbart, Sheldon."

Wright didn't answer.

"Yeah," I said, "he's a Jewish kid, so he thought I could help him out. You know."

"I guess I can do something," he finally said. "The Major hasn't been around here for weeks—TDY[4] to the golf course. I'll try, Nate that's all I can say."

"I'd appreciate it, Bob. See you Sunday," and I hung up, perspiring.

And the following day the corrected orders appeared: Fishbein, Fuselli, Fylypowycz, Glinicki, Grossbart, Gucwa, Halpern, Hardy . . . Lucky Private Harley Alton was to go to Fort Monmouth, New Jersey, where for some reason or other, they wanted an enlisted man with infantry training.

After chow that night I stopped back at the orderly room to straighten out the guard duty roster. Grossbart was waiting for me. He spoke first.

"You son of a bitch!"

---

4. Temporary Duty, an army orders term used ironically here.

I sat down at my desk and while he glared down at me I began to make the necessary alterations in the duty roster.

"What do you have against me?" he cried. "Against my family? Would it kill you for me to be near my father, God knows how many months he has left to him."

"Why?"

"His heart," Grossbart said. "He hasn't had enough troubles in a lifetime, you've got to add to them. I curse the day I ever met you, Marx! Shulman told me what happened over there. There's no limit to your anti-Semitism, is there! The damage you've done here isn't enough. You have to make a special phone call! You really want me dead!"

I made the last few notations in the duty roster and got up to leave. "Good night, Grossbart."

"You owe me an explanation!" He stood in my path.

"Sheldon, you're the one who owes explanations."

He scowled. "To *you*?"

"To me, I think so, yes. Mostly to Fishbein and Halpern."

"That's right, twist things around. I owe nobody nothing, I've done all I could do for them. Now I think I've got the right to watch out for myself."

"For each other we have to learn to watch out, Sheldon. You told me yourself."

"You call this watching out for me, what you did?"

"No. For all of us."

I pushed him aside and started for the door. I heard his furious breathing behind me, and it sounded like steam rushing from the engine of his terrible strength.

"You'll be all right," I said from the door. And, I thought, so would Fishbein and Halpern be all right, even in the Pacific, if only Grossbart could continue to see in the obsequiousness of the one, the soft spirituality of the other, some profit for himself.

I stood outside the orderly room, and I heard Grossbart weeping behind me. Over in the barracks, in the lighted windows, I could see the boys in their T-shirts sitting on their bunks talking about their orders, as they'd been doing for the past two days. With a kind of quiet nervousness, they polished shoes, shined belt buckles, squared away underwear, trying as best they could to accept their fate. Behind me, Grossbart swallowed hard, accepting his. And then, resisting with all my will an impulse to turn and seek pardon for my vindictiveness, I accepted my own.

1959

AMIRI BARAKA (LEROI JONES)
1934–2014

When in 1967 LeRoi Jones assumed the Bantuized Muslim name Amiri Baraka (meaning Prince, a Blessed One), he was undergoing one of several changes in his progression as a maker of literature. Born Everett Leroy Jones, he was the child of middle-class African American parents in Newark, New Jersey, where his scholastic abilities took him to the best schools available; as Baraka recalls in his autobiography, his classmates were more often white suburbanites than inner-city children of his own race. He restyled his name as "LeRoi" during his undergraduate years at Howard University (a traditionally African American institution), to which he had transferred from the mostly white campus of Rutgers University (where he had won a scholarship). After leaving Howard in 1954 and serving in the U.S. Air Force, from which he was discharged for unapproved political activities, Jones moved to New York City's Greenwich Village and became prominent on the avant-garde poetry scene. His friends were white innovators—Gilbert Sorrentino, Diane DiPrima, and Frank O'Hara among them—with whom he worked on the magazine *Kulchur* in addition to editing and publishing his own journal, *Yugen*. Married to Hettie Cohen, he began an interracial family and wrote record reviews for mainstream jazz magazines.

Jones was well established in the more intellectually elite quarters of New York's world of poetry, art, and music. Yet as racial tensions mounted, with the assassination of Medgar Evers, fatal church bombings in Alabama, and the murder of civil rights workers James Chaney, Andrew Goodman, and Michael Schwerner in Mississippi, Jones's life underwent major changes as well. In 1965, following the assassination of Malcolm X, he left his wife and children and moved to Harlem, where as a newly declared black cultural nationalist he founded the Black Arts Repertory Theater, dedicated to taking socially militant drama directly to the people it represented.

Poetry as a vehicle of popular encouragement remained central to Baraka's belief. He may well have agreed with the judge who once convicted him of incitement to riot that his poems could motivate people to act (whether such influence or intent had been proven in legal form is another matter, and his incitement conviction was later overturned on appeal). As opposed to his very first work, which conveyed a personal anguish for which the poet projected no political solution ("I am inside someone / who hates me, I look / out from his eyes") and whose collective title conveys little hope other than in the act of expression (*Preface to a Twenty Volume Suicide Note*, 1961), his later work is replete with exhortations, capitalized imperatives for action, and chantlike repetitions designed to arouse a fury for action and then direct it toward the achievement of specific social goals. Much like his drama, this poetry is overtly presentational, declaring what the reader needs to think about and then providing the stimulus to act. Yet all the while the personal nature of Baraka stands behind it, making clear that a deep and complex imagination has been brought to bear on the issues. The range and intensity of Baraka's poetry is evident in his 1995 collection, *Transbluesency: The Selected Poems of Amiri Baraka/LeRoi Jones (1961–1995)*. His 2004 collection, *Somebody Blew Up America & Other Poems*, contains Baraka's controversial poem of the same name, written after 9/11, during a period in which he was New Jersey's poet laureate. After the poem's publication, public outcry became so great that the governor of New Jersey took action to abolish the position.

Although Baraka sued, the United States Court of Appeals eventually ruled that state officials were immune from such lawsuits. Baraka never feared controversy; he remained an influence for many younger writers both as a major poet and as a cultural and political leader.

Beginning in the 1980s Baraka taught in the African Studies Department at the State University of New York, Stony Brook. In addition to poetry and drama, he continued to write essays on social subjects and on jazz.

An Agony. As Now.

I am inside someone
who hates me. I look
out from his eyes. Smell
what fouled tunes come in
to his breath. Love his   5
wretched women.

Slits in the metal, for sun. Where
my eyes sit turning, at the cool air
the glance of light, or hard flesh
rubbed against me, a woman, a man,   10
without shadow, or voice, or meaning.

This is the enclosure (flesh,
where innocence is a weapon. An
abstraction. Touch. (Not mine,
Or yours, if you are the soul I had   15
and abandoned when I was blind and had
my enemies carry me as a dead man
(if he is beautiful, or pitied.

It can be pain. (As now, as all his
flesh hurts me.) It can be that. Or   20
pain. As when she ran from me into
that forest.
          Or pain, the mind
silver spiraled whirled against the
sun, higher than even old men thought   25
God would be. Or pain. And the other. The
yes. (Inside his books, his fingers. They
are withered yellow flowers and were never
beautiful.) The yes. You will, lost soul, say
'beauty.' Beauty, practiced, as the tree. The   30
slow river. A white sun in its wet sentences.

Or, the cold men in their gale. Ecstasy. Flesh
or soul. The yes. (Their robes blown. Their bowls
empty. They chant at my heels, not at yours.) Flesh
or soul, as corrupt. Where the answer moves too quickly.   35
Where the God is a self, after all.)

Cold air blown through narrow blind eyes. Flesh,
white hot metal. Glows as the day with its sun.
It is a human love, I live inside. A bony skeleton
you recognize as words or simple feeling.   40

But it has no feeling. As the metal, is hot, it is not,
given to love.

It burns the thing
inside it. And that thing
screams.   45

1964

A Poem for Willie Best[1]

I

The face sings, alone
at the top
          of the body. All
flesh, all song, aligned. For hell
is silent, at those cracked lips   5
flakes of skin and mind
twist and whistle softly
as they fall.
          It was your own death
you saw. Your own face, stiff   10
and raw. This
without sound, or
movement. Sweet afton,[2] the
dead beggar bleeds
yet. His blood, for a time   15
alive, and huddled in a door
way, struggling to sing. Rain
washes it into cracks. Pits
whose bottoms are famous. Whose sides
are innocent broadcasts   20
of another life.

II

At this point, neither
front nor back. A point, the
dimensionless line. The top
of a head, seen from Christ's   25
heaven, stripped of history
or desire.

1. Willie Best was a negro character actor whose
Hollywood name was Sleep'n'eat [Baraka's note].
2. "Flow Gently Sweet Afton," a poem by the
Scottish poet Robert Burns (1759–1796), refers
to the river Afton in Ayrshire, Scotland.

      Fixed, perpendicular
to shadow. (Even speech, vertical,
leaves no trace. Born in to death   30
held fast to it, where
the lover spreads his arms, the line
he makes to threaten Gods with history.
The fingers stretch to emptiness. At
each point, after flesh, even light   35
is speculation. But an end, his end,
failing a beginning.

2

A cross. The gesture, symbol, line
arms held stiff, nailed stiff, with
no sign, of what gave them strength.   40
The point, become a line, a cross, or
the man, and his material, driven in
the ground. If the head rolls back
and the mouth opens, screamed into
existence, there will be perhaps   45
only the slightest hint of movement
a smear; no help will come. No one
will turn to that station again.

III

At a cross roads, sits the
player. No drum, no umbrella, even   50
though it's raining. Again, and we
are somehow less miserable because
here is a hero, used to being wet.
One road is where you are standing now
(reading this, the other, crosses then   55
rushes into a wood.
                  5 lbs neckbones.
                  5 lbs hog innards.
                  10 bottles cheap wine.
                                (the contents   60
of a paper bag, also shoes, with holes
for the big toe, and several rusted
knives. This is a literature, of
symbols. And it is his gift, as the
bag is.   65
          (The contents
again, holy saviours,
                  300 men on horseback
                  75 bibles
                  the quietness   70
of a field. A rich
man, though wet through
by the rain.

I said,
         47 howitzers[3]
         7 polished horse jaws
         a few trees being waved
softly back under
the black night
                  All this should be
invested.

IV

         Where
         ever,
                  he has gone. Who ever
         mourns
         or sits silent
         to remember

         There is nothing of pity
         here. Nothing
         of sympathy.

V

This is the dance of the raised
leg. Of the hand on the knee
quickly.
         As a dance it punishes
speech. 'The house burned. The
old man killed.'
                  As a dance it
is obscure.

VI

This is the song
of the highest C.
                  The falsetto. An elegance
that punishes silence. This is the song
of the toes pointed inward, the arms swung, the
hips, moved, for fucking, slow, from side
to side. He is quoted
saying, "My father was
never a jockey,
                  but
   he did teach me
            how to ride."

---

3. Short, relatively light cannons for the high-angle firing of shells at a low velocity.

VII

The balance.
        (Rushed in, swarmed of dark, cloaks,
and only red lights pushed a message
to the street. Rub.
        This is the lady,   115
I saw you with.
This is your mother.
This is the lady I wanted
some how to sleep with.
        As a dance, or   120
our elegant song. Sun red and grown
from trees, fences, mud roads in dried out
river beds. This is for me, with no God
but what is given. Give me
        Something more   125
than what is here. I must tell you
my body hurts.

The balance.
        Can you hear? Here
I am again. Your boy, dynamite. Can   130
you hear? My soul is moved. The soul
you gave me. I say, my soul, and it
is moved. That soul
you gave me.
        Yes, I'm sure   135
this is the lady. You
slept with her. Witness, your boy,
here, dynamite. Hear?
        I mean
can you?   140
The balance.
        He was tired of losing. (And
his walking buddies tired
of walking.
        Bent slightly,   145
at the waist. Left hand low, to flick
quick showy jabs ala Sugar.[4] The right
cocked, to complete,
        any combination.
        He was   150
tired of losing, but he was fighting
a big dumb "farmer."
        Such a blue bright
afternoon, and only a few hundred yards
from the beach. He said, I'm tired   155
of losing.
        "I *got* ta cut'cha."

---

4. Sugar Ray Robinson (1921–1989), American boxer.

VIII

A renegade
behind the mask. And even
the mask, a renegade   160
disguise. Black skin
and hanging lip.

         Lazy
         Frightened
         Thieving   165
         Very potent sexually
         Scars
         Generally inferior
                    (but natural
rhythms.   170

His head is
at the window. The only
part
    that sings.
(The word he used   175
          (we are passing St. Mark's place[5]
         and those crazy jews who fuck)
                         to provoke
in neon, still useful
in the rain,   180
         to provoke
some meaning, where before
there was only hell. I said
silence, at his huddled blood.
                 It is an obscene invention.   185
                 A white sticky discharge.
                 "Jism," in white chalk
                 on the back of Angel's garage.
                 Red jackets with the head of
                 Hobbes[6] staring into space. "Jasm"   190
                 the name the leader took, had it
                 stenciled on his chest.
                       And he sits
wet at the crossroads, remembering distinctly
each weightless face that eases by. (Sun at   195
the back door, and that hideous mindless grin.
                    (Hear?

                               1964

---

5. Street in New York City's East Village.
6. Thomas Hobbes (1588–1679), English philosopher who believed a "social contract" was necessary between rulers and the ruled. Here he
represents the Western, white, materialist
tradition.

Will They Cry When You're Gone, You Bet

You leave dead friends in
a desert. But they've deserted
you, and them-
selves, and are leaving
themselves,   5
in the foot paths
of madmen and saints
enough sense to get away
from the dryness and uselessness
of such relaxation, dying in the dry   10
light, sand packed in their mouths
eyes burning, white women serenade them
in mystic deviousness, which is another
way of saying they're seeing things, which
are not really there, except for them,   15
never to find an oasis, even bitter water
which we get used to, is better than
white drifting fairies, muses, singing
to us, in calm tones, about how it is better to die
etcetera, than go off from them, how it is better to   20
lie in the cruel sun with your eyes turning to dunes
than leave them alone in that white heat.

1969

N. SCOTT MOMADAY
b. 1934

" I n a certain sense," writes N. Scott Momaday in the nonfiction collection *The Man Made of Words* (1997), "we are all made of words; . . . our most essential being consists in language. It is the element in which we think and dream and act, in which we live our daily lives." Since the publication of his Pulitzer Prize–winning novel *House Made of Dawn* (1968), Momaday's writing has crossed boundaries of language, form, and genre, thereby creating for Momaday, through will and imagination, an American Indian identity in words.

Navarre Scott Momaday was born at the Kiowa and Comanche Indian Hospital in Lawton, Oklahoma, the only child of Al Momaday, a Kiowa, and Natachee Scott, who was part Cherokee. He spent most of his early years in New Mexico and Arizona, moving in 1946 to Jemez Pueblo in New Mexico's Rio Grande Valley. There his parents, both artists and teachers, took jobs at a small day school. Growing up on reservations, including those of the Navajo and the Apache, Momaday experienced the rhythms of traditional tribal life, but saw, too, the changes wrought by

674 | N. SCOTT MOMADAY

postwar material culture, and their human costs—the alcoholism, unemployment, and personal disintegration that mark the life of Abel, the returning veteran in *House Made of Dawn*. Early on, Momaday's mother instilled in him the value of a bicultural education that would open the future without closing off his native heritage. Momaday attended reservation, public, and mission schools, then graduated from military high school in Virginia and the University of New Mexico. He received his Ph.D. in 1963 from Stanford University, where his mentor in American and English literature was the poet and critic Yvor Winters. Since then his teaching career has taken him to Santa Barbara, Berkeley, the University of Moscow, Stanford, and the University of Arizona.

What some scholars call the "Native American Renaissance" is usually said to have begun with the publication of *House Made of Dawn* in 1968 and its being awarded the Pulitzer Prize the following year. And, indeed, from 1968 to the present Native American writers have published a substantial body of fine poetry, fiction, and autobiography, gaining considerable notice in the United States and abroad. Over the decades since the publication of *House Made of Dawn*, Momaday himself has published a second novel, *The Ancient Child* (1989), as well as several volumes of poems, short stories, memoirs, and critical works. His deliberate engagement with a variety of forms—oral and written poetry, prose fiction and nonfiction, autobiography, legend, history, photography, painting (all "forms of discovery," in Winters's words)—has helped him lay claim to his Kiowa past.

Momaday's idea of the past as a journey is consciously expressed in *The Journey of Tai-me*, which offers his translations of the Kiowa myths he learned as a child from his grandmother, Aho. This work relates the story of the Sun Dance—a ceremony for spiritual guidance and power performed by many Plains Indian groups—to his revelatory memory of journeying to Oklahoma to see the sacred Tai-me bundle: "I became more keenly aware of myself as someone who had walked through time and in whose blood there is something inestimably old and undying. It was as if I had remembered something that happened two hundred years ago. I meant then to seek after the source of my memory and myself." In *The Way to Rainy Mountain* (1969) Momaday undertakes this search, collecting, with his father as translator, Kiowa tales and myths and clustering them with brief, loose historical commentaries and personal family stories. What seem to be fragments come together in a complex structure—twenty-four "quintessential novels," divided into three sections, framed by poems and prose pieces—that follow the Kiowa from emergence through maturity to decline as a Plains Indian culture. Central to *Rainy Mountain* and to all of Momaday's writing is the land—the focal point of memory, the defining place for Kiowa culture. The same rootedness that defines Momaday's ancestors gives his work its conjuring power, a power that comes from distilling in words and pictures, as Momaday writes, "the glare of noon and all the colors of the dawn and dusk."

From The Way to Rainy Mountain

Headwaters

Noon in the intermountain plain:
There is scant telling of the marsh—
A log, hollow and weather-stained,
An insect at the mouth, and moss—
Yet waters rise against the roots,   5
Stand brimming to the stalks. What moves?

What moves on this archaic force
Was wild and welling at the source.

Introduction

A single knoll rises out of the plain in Oklahoma, north and west of the Wichita Range. For my people, the Kiowas,[1] it is an old landmark, and they gave it the name Rainy Mountain. The hardest weather in the world is there. Winter brings blizzards, hot tornadic winds arise in the spring, and in summer the prairie is an anvil's edge. The grass turns brittle and brown, and it cracks beneath your feet. There are green belts along the rivers and creeks, linear groves of hickory and pecan, willow and witch hazel. At a distance in July or August the steaming foliage seems almost to writhe in fire. Great green and yellow grasshoppers are everywhere in the tall grass, popping up like corn to sting the flesh, and tortoises crawl about on the red earth, going nowhere in the plenty of time. Loneliness is an aspect of the land. All things in the plain are isolate; there is no confusion of objects in the eye, but *one* hill or *one* tree or *one* man. To look upon that landscape in the early morning, with the sun at your back, is to lose the sense of proportion. Your imagination comes to life, and this, you think, is where Creation was begun.

I returned to Rainy Mountain in July. My grandmother had died in the spring, and I wanted to be at her grave. She had lived to be very old and at last infirm. Her only living daughter was with her when she died, and I was told that in death her face was that of a child.

I like to think of her as a child. When she was born, the Kiowas were living the last great moment of their history. For more than a hundred years they had controlled the open range from the Smoky Hill River to the Red, from the headwaters of the Canadian to the fork of the Arkansas and Cimarron. In alliance with the Comanches, they had ruled the whole of the southern Plains. War was their sacred business, and they were among the finest horsemen the world has ever known. But warfare for the Kiowas was preeminently a matter of disposition rather than of survival, and they never understood the grim, unrelenting advance of the U.S. Cavalry. When at last, divided and ill-provisioned, they were driven onto the Staked Plains in the cold rains of autumn, they fell into panic. In Palo Duro Canyon[2] they abandoned their crucial stores to pillage and had nothing then but their lives. In order to save themselves, they surrendered to the soldiers at Fort Sill[3] and were imprisoned in the old stone corral that now stands as a military museum. My grandmother was spared the humiliation of those high gray walls by eight or ten years, but she must have known from birth the affliction of defeat, the dark brooding of old warriors.

Her name was Aho, and she belonged to the last culture to evolve in North America. Her forebears came down from the high country in western Montana nearly three centuries ago. They were a mountain people, a mysterious tribe of hunters whose language has never been positively classified

---

1. The Kiowa were a nomadic hunting and gathering people of the Southern Plains.
2. On the Staked Plains, or the Texas Panhandle, that part of the state jutting north between New Mexico and Oklahoma.
3. U.S. Cavalry fort in Oklahoma and site of the Kiowa-Comanche Agency.

in any major group. In the late seventeenth century they began a long migration to the south and east. It was a journey toward the dawn, and it led to a golden age. Along the way the Kiowas were befriended by the Crows, who gave them the culture and religion of the Plains. They acquired horses, and their ancient nomadic spirit was suddenly free of the ground. They acquired Tai-me,[4] the sacred Sun Dance doll, from that moment the object and symbol of their worship, and so shared in the divinity of the sun. Not least, they acquired the sense of destiny, therefore courage and pride. When they entered upon the southern Plains they had been transformed. No longer were they slaves to the simple necessity of survival; they were a lordly and dangerous society of fighters and thieves, hunters and priests of the sun. According to their origin myth, they entered the world through a hollow log. From one point of view, their migration was the fruit of an old prophecy, for indeed they emerged from a sunless world.

Although my grandmother lived out her long life in the shadow of Rainy Mountain, the immense landscape of the continental interior lay like memory in her blood. She could tell of the Crows, whom she had never seen, and of the Black Hills, where she had never been. I wanted to see in reality what she had seen more perfectly in the mind's eye, and traveled fifteen hundred miles to begin my pilgrimage.

Yellowstone, it seemed to me, was the top of the world, a region of deep lakes and dark timber, canyons and waterfalls. But, beautiful as it is, one might have the sense of confinement there. The skyline in all directions is close at hand, the high wall of the woods and deep cleavages of shade. There is a perfect freedom in the mountains, but it belongs to the eagle and the elk, the badger and the bear. The Kiowas reckoned their stature by the distance they could see, and they were bent and blind in the wilderness.

Descending eastward, the highland meadows are a stairway to the plain. In July the inland slope of the Rockies is luxuriant with flax and buckwheat, stonecrop and larkspur. The earth unfolds and the limit of the land recedes. Clusters of trees, and animals grazing far in the distance, cause the vision to reach away and wonder to build upon the mind. The sun follows a longer course in the day, and the sky is immense beyond all comparison. The great billowing clouds that sail upon it are shadows that move upon the grain like water, dividing light. Farther down, in the land of the Crows and Blackfeet, the plain is yellow. Sweet clover takes hold of the hills and bends upon itself to cover and seal the soil. There the Kiowas paused on their way; they had come to the place where they must change their lives. The sun is at home on the plains. Precisely there does it have the certain character of a god. When the Kiowas came to the land of the Crows, they could see the dark lees of the hills at dawn across the Bighorn River, the profusion of light on the grain shelves, the oldest deity ranging after the solstices. Not yet would they veer southward to the caldron of the land that lay below; they must wean their blood from the northern winter and hold the mountains a while longer in their view. They bore Tai-me in procession to the east.

A dark mist lay over the Black Hills, and the land was like iron. At the top of a ridge I caught sight of Devil's Tower upthrust against the gray sky as if

4. The sacred being who aids the Kiowa in times of trouble; this being is embodied in the holy doll central to Kiowa ritual.

in the birth of time the core of the earth had broken through its crust and the motion of the world was begun. There are things in nature that engender an awful quiet in the heart of man; Devil's Tower is one of them. Two centuries ago, because they could not do otherwise, the Kiowas made a legend at the base of the rock. My grandmother said:

> Eight children were there at play, seven sisters and their brother. Suddenly the boy was struck dumb; he trembled and began to run upon his hands and feet. His fingers became claws, and his body was covered with fur. Directly there was a bear where the boy had been. The sisters were terrified; they ran, and the bear after them. They came to the stump of a great tree, and the tree spoke to them. It bade them climb upon it, and as they did so it began to rise into the air. The bear came to kill them, but they were just beyond its reach. It reared against the tree and scored the bark all around with its claws. The seven sisters were borne into the sky, and they became the stars of the Big Dipper.

From that moment, and so long as the legend lives, the Kiowas have kinsmen in the night sky. Whatever they were in the mountains, they could be no more. However tenuous their well-being, however much they had suffered and would suffer again, they had found a way out of the wilderness.

My grandmother had a reverence for the sun, a holy regard that now is all but gone out of mankind. There was a wariness in her, and an ancient awe. She was a Christian in her later years, but she had come a long way about, and she never forgot her birthright. As a child she had been to the Sun Dances; she had taken part in those annual rites, and by them she had learned the restoration of her people in the presence of Tai-me. She was about seven when the last Kiowa Sun Dance was held in 1887 on the Washita River above Rainy Mountain Creek. The buffalo were gone. In order to consummate the ancient sacrifice—to impale the head of a buffalo bull upon the medicine tree—a delegation of old men journeyed into Texas, there to beg and barter for an animal from the Goodnight herd. She was ten when the Kiowas came together for the last time as a living Sun Dance culture. They could find no buffalo; they had to hang an old hide from the sacred tree. Before the dance could begin, a company of soldiers rode out from Fort Sill under orders to disperse the tribe. Forbidden without cause the essential act of their faith,[5] having seen the wild herds slaughtered and left to rot upon the ground, the Kiowas backed away forever from the medicine tree. That was July 20, 1890, at the great bend of the Washita. My grandmother was there. Without bitterness, and for as long as she lived, she bore a vision of deicide.

Now that I can have her only in memory, I see my grandmother in the several postures that were peculiar to her: standing at the wood stove on a winter morning and turning meat in a great iron skillet; sitting at the south window, bent above her beadwork, and afterwards, when her vision failed, looking down for a long time into the fold of her hands; going out upon a cane, very slowly as she did when the weight of age came upon her; praying. I remember her most often at prayer. She made long, rambling prayers out of suffering and hope, having seen many things. I was never sure that I had the right to hear, so exclusive were they of all mere custom and company.

---

5. From the 1880s on, the U.S. government sought to ban all "heathenish" practices among Native American peoples in a continuing effort to Christianize and "civilize" them.

The last time I saw her she prayed standing by the side of her bed at night, naked to the waist, the light of a kerosene lamp moving upon her dark skin. Her long, black hair, always drawn and braided in the day, lay upon her shoulders and against her breasts like a shawl. I do not speak Kiowa, and I never understood her prayers, but there was something inherently sad in the sound, some merest hesitation upon the syllables of sorrow. She began in a high and descending pitch, exhausting her breath to silence; then again and again—and always the same intensity of effort, of something that is, and is not, like urgency in the human voice. Transported so in the dancing light among the shadows of her room, she seemed beyond the reach of time. But that was illusion; I think I knew then that I should not see her again.

Houses are like sentinels in the plain, old keepers of the weather watch. There, in a very little while, wood takes on the appearance of great age. All colors wear soon away in the wind and rain, and then the wood is burned gray and the grain appears and the nails turn red with rust. The window-panes are black and opaque; you imagine there is nothing within, and indeed there are many ghosts, bones given up to the land. They stand here and there against the sky, and you approach them for a longer time than you expect. They belong in the distance; it is their domain.

Once there was a lot of sound in my grandmother's house, a lot of coming and going, feasting and talk. The summers there were full of excitement and reunion. The Kiowas are a summer people; they abide the cold and keep to themselves, but when the season turns and the land becomes warm and vital they cannot hold still; an old love of going returns upon them. The aged visitors who came to my grandmother's house when I was a child were made of lean and leather, and they bore themselves upright. They wore great black hats and bright ample shirts that shook in the wind. They rubbed fat upon their hair and wound their braids with strips of colored cloth. Some of them painted their faces and carried the scars of old and cherished enmities. They were an old council of warlords, come to remind and be reminded of who they were. Their wives and daughters served them well. The women might indulge themselves; gossip was at once the mark and compensation of their servitude. They made loud and elaborate talk among themselves, full of jest and gesture, fright and false alarm. They went abroad in fringed and flowered shawls, bright beadwork and German silver. They were at home in the kitchen, and they prepared meals that were banquets.

There were frequent prayer meetings, and great nocturnal feasts. When I was a child I played with my cousins outside, where the lamplight fell upon the ground and the singing of the old people rose up around us and carried away into the darkness. There were a lot of good things to eat, a lot of laughter and surprise. And afterwards, when the quiet returned, I lay down with my grandmother and could hear the frogs away by the river and feel the motion of the air.

Now there is a funeral silence in the rooms, the endless wake of some final word. The walls have closed in upon my grandmother's house. When I returned to it in mourning, I saw for the first time in my life how small it was. It was late at night, and there was a white moon, nearly full. I sat for a long time on the stone steps by the kitchen door. From there I could see out across the land; I could see the long row of trees by the creek, the low light upon the rolling plains, and the stars of the Big Dipper. Once I looked at the moon and caught sight of a strange thing. A cricket had perched upon the handrail, only a few inches away from me. My line of vision was such that the creature filled the moon like a fossil. It had gone there, I thought, to live and die, for there, of all places, was its small definition made whole and eternal. A warm wind rose up and purled like the longing within me.

The next morning I awoke at dawn and went out on the dirt road to Rainy Mountain. It was already hot, and the grasshoppers began to fill the air. Still, it was early in the morning, and the birds sang out of the shadows. The long yellow grass on the mountain shone in the bright light, and a scissortail hied above the land. There, where it ought to be, at the end of a long and legendary way, was my grandmother's grave. Here and there on the dark stones were ancestral names. Looking back once, I saw the mountain and came away.

IV

They lived at first in the mountains. They did not yet know of Tai-me, but this is what they knew: There was a man and his wife. They had a beautiful child, a little girl whom they would not allow to go out of their sight. But one day a friend of the family came and asked if she might take the child outside to play. The mother guessed that would be all right, but she told the friend to leave the child in its cradle and to place the cradle in a tree. While the child was in the tree, a redbird came among the branches. It was not like any bird that you have seen; it was very beautiful, and it did not fly away. It kept still upon a limb, close to the child. After a while the child got out of its cradle and began to climb after the redbird. And at the same time the tree began to grow taller, and the child was borne up into the sky. She was then a woman, and she found herself in a strange place. Instead of a redbird, there was a young man standing before her. The man spoke to her and said: "I have been watching you for a long time, and I knew that I would find a way to bring you here. I have brought you here to be my wife." The woman looked all around; she saw that he was the only living man there. She saw that he was the sun.

There the land itself ascends into the sky. These mountains lie at the top of the continent, and they cast a long rain shadow on the sea of grasses to the east. They arise out of the last North American wilderness, and they have wilderness names: Wasatch, Bitterroot, Bighorn, Wind River.

I have walked in a mountain meadow bright with Indian paintbrush, lupine, and wild buckwheat, and I have seen high in the branches of a lodgepole pine the male pine grosbeak, round and rose-colored, its dark, striped wings nearly invisible in the soft, mottled light. And the uppermost branches of the tree seemed very slowly to ride across the blue sky.

XIII

If an arrow is well made, it will have tooth marks upon it. That is how you know. The Kiowas made fine arrows and straightened them in their teeth. Then they drew them to the bow to see if they were straight. Once there was a man and his wife. They were alone at night in their tipi. By the light of the fire the man was making arrows. After a while he caught sight of something. There was a small opening in the tipi where two hides were sewn together. Someone was there on the outside, looking in. The man went on with his work, but he said to his wife: "Someone is standing outside. Do not be afraid. Let us talk easily, as of ordinary things." He took up an arrow and straightened it in his teeth; then, as it was right for him to do, he drew it to the bow and took aim, first in this direction and then in that. And all the while he was talking, as if to his wife. But this is how he spoke: "I know that you are there on the outside, for I can feel your eyes upon me. If you are a Kiowa, you will understand what I am saying, and you will speak your name." But there was no answer, and the man went on in the same way, pointing the arrow all around. At last his aim fell upon the place where his enemy stood, and he let go of the string. The arrow went straight to the enemy's heart.

The old men were the best arrow-makers, for they could bring time and patience to their craft. The young men—the fighters and hunters—were willing to pay a high price for arrows that were well made.

When my father was a boy, an old man used to come to Mammedaty's[6] house and pay his respects. He was a lean old man in braids and was impressive in his age and bearing. His name was Cheney, and he was an arrowmaker. Every morning, my father tells me, Cheney would paint his wrinkled face, go out, and pray aloud to the rising sun. In my mind I can see that man as if he were there now. I like to watch him as he makes his prayer. I know where he stands and where his voice goes on the rolling grasses and where the sun comes up on the land. There, at dawn, you can feel the silence. It is cold and clear and deep like water. It takes hold of you and will not let you go.

XVII

Bad women are thrown away. Once there was a handsome young man. He was wild and reckless, and the chief talked to the wind about him. After that, the man went hunting. A great whirlwind passed by, and he was blind. The Kiowas have no need

In the Kiowa calendars[7] there is graphic proof that the lives of women were hard, whether they were "bad women" or not. Only the captives, who were slaves, held lower status. During the Sun Dance of 1843, a man stabbed his wife in

6. Momaday's paternal grandfather.
7. The Kiowa recorded their history in pictures that functioned as calendars.

of a blind man; they left him alone with his wife and child. The winter was coming on and food was scarce. In four days the man's wife grew tired of caring for him. A herd of buffalo came near, and the man knew the sound. He asked his wife to hand him a bow and an arrow. "You must tell me," he said, "when the buffalo are directly in front of me." And in that way he killed a bull, but his wife said that he had missed. He asked for another arrow and killed another bull, but again his wife said that he had missed. Now the man was a hunter, and he knew the sound an arrow makes when it strikes home, but he said nothing. Then his wife helped herself to the meat and ran away with her child. The man was blind; he ate grass and kept himself alive. In seven days a band of Kiowas found him and took him to their camp. There in the firelight a woman was telling a story. She told of how her husband had been killed by enemy warriors. The blind man listened, and he knew her voice. That was a bad woman. At sunrise they threw her away.

the breast because she accepted Chief Dohasan's invitation to ride with him in the ceremonial procession. And in the winter of 1851–52, Big Bow stole the wife of a man who was away on a raiding expedition. He brought her to his father's camp and made her wait outside in the bitter cold while he went in to collect his things. But his father knew what was going on, and he held Big Bow and would not let him go. The woman was made to wait in the snow until her feet were frozen.

Mammedaty's grandmother, Kau-au-ointy,[8] was a Mexican captive, taken from her homeland when she was a child of eight or ten years. I never knew her, but I have been to her grave at Rainy Mountain.

KAU-AU-OINTY

BORN 1834

DIED 1929

AT REST

She raised a lot of eyebrows, they say, for she would not play the part of a Kiowa woman. From slavery she rose up to become a figure in the tribe. She owned a great herd of cattle, and she could ride as well as any man. She had blue eyes.

XXIV

East of my grandmother's house, south of the pecan grove, there is buried a woman in a beautiful dress. Mammedaty used to know where she is buried, but now no one knows. If you stand on the front porch of the house and look eastward towards Carnegie, you know that the woman is buried somewhere within the range of your vision. But her grave is unmarked. She was buried in a cabinet, and she wore a beautiful dress.

Aho's high moccasins are made of softest, cream-colored skins. On each instep there is a bright disc of beadwork—an eight-pointed star, red and pale blue on a white field—and there are bands of beadwork at the soles and ankles. The flaps of the leggings are wide and richly ornamented with blue and red and green and white and lavender beads.

East of my grandmother's house the sun rises out of the plain. Once in his

8. Momaday's great-great-grandmother.

How beautiful it was! It was one of those fine buckskin dresses, and it was decorated with elk's teeth and beadwork. That dress is still there, under the ground.

life a man ought to concentrate his mind upon the remembered earth, I believe. He ought to give himself up to a particular landscape in his experience, to look at it from as many angles as he can, to wonder about it, to dwell upon it. He ought to imagine that he touches it with his hands at every season and listens to the sounds that are made upon it. He ought to imagine the creatures there and all the faintest motions of the wind. He ought to recollect the glare of noon and all the colors of the dawn and dusk.

Epilogue

During the first hours after midnight on the morning of November 13, 1833, it seemed that the world was coming to an end. Suddenly the stillness of the night was broken; there were brilliant flashes of light in the sky, light of such intensity that people were awakened by it. With the speed and density of a driving rain, stars were falling in the universe. Some were brighter than Venus; one was said to be as large as the moon.

That most brilliant shower of Leonid meteors[9] has a special place in the memory of the Kiowa people. It is among the earliest entries in the Kiowa calendars, and it marks the beginning as it were of the historical period in the tribal mind. In the preceding year Tai-me had been stolen by a band of Osages, and although it was later returned, the loss was an almost unimaginable tragedy; and in 1837 the Kiowas made the first of their treaties[1] with the United States. The falling stars seemed to image the sudden and violent disintegration of an old order.

But indeed the golden age of the Kiowas had been short-lived, ninety or a hundred years, say, from about 1740. The culture would persist for a while in decline, until about 1875, but then it would be gone, and there would be very little material evidence that it had ever been. Yet it is within the reach of memory still, though tenuously now, and moreover it is even defined in a remarkably rich and living verbal tradition which demands to be preserved for its own sake. The living memory and the verbal tradition which transcends it were brought together for me once and for all in the person of Ko-sahn.

A hundred-year-old woman came to my grandmother's house one afternoon in July. Aho was dead; Mammedaty had died before I was born. There were very few Kiowas left who could remember the Sun Dances; Ko-sahn was one of them; she was a grown woman when my grandparents came into the world. Her body was twisted and her face deeply lined with age. Her thin white hair was held in place by a cap of black netting, though she wore braids as well, and she had but one eye. She was dressed in the manner of a Kiowa matron, a dark, full-cut dress that reached nearly to the ankles, full, flowing sleeves, and

9. Annual meteor shower that appears to emanate from the constellation Leo; the Leonid shower of 1833 was spectactar to observers in North America east of the Rocky Mountains.
1. This treaty provided for settlers' passage through Kiowa and Comanche lands.

a wide, apron-like sash. She sat on a bench in the arbor so concentrated in her great age that she seemed extraordinarily small. She was quiet for a time—she might almost have been asleep—and then she began to speak and to sing. She spoke of many things, and once she spoke of the Sun Dance:

> My sisters and I were very young; that was a long time ago. Early one morning they came to wake us up. They had brought a great buffalo in from the plain. Everyone went out to see and to pray. We heard a great many voices. One man said that the lodge was almost ready. We were told to go there, and someone gave me a piece of cloth. It was very beautiful. Then I asked what I ought to do with it, and they said that I must tie it to the Tai-me tree. There were other pieces of cloth on the tree, and so I put mine there as well.
>
> When the lodge frame was finished, a woman—sometimes a man—began to sing. It was like this:
>
> > *Everything is ready.*
> > *Now the four societies must go out.*
> > *They must go out and get the leaves,*
> > > *the branches for the lodge.*
>
> And when the branches were tied in place, again there was singing:
>
> > *Let the boys go out.*
> > *Come on, boys, now we must get the earth.*
>
> The boys began to shout. Now they were not just ordinary boys, not all of them; they were those for whom prayers had been made, and they were dressed in different ways. There was an old, old woman. She had something on her back. The boys went out to see. The old woman had a bag full of earth on her back. It was a certain kind of sandy earth. That is what they must have in the lodge. The dancers must dance upon the sandy earth. The old woman held a digging tool in her hand. She turned towards the south and pointed with her lips. It was like a kiss, and she began to sing:
>
> > *We have brought the earth.*
> > *Now it is time to play;*
> > *As old as I am, I still have the feeling of play.*
>
> That was the beginning of the Sun Dance. The dancers treated themselves with buffalo medicine, and slowly they began to take their steps. . . . And all the people were around, and they wore splendid things—beautiful buckskin and beads. The chiefs wore necklaces, and their pendants shone like the sun. There were many people, and oh, it was beautiful! That was the beginning of the Sun Dance. It was all for Tai-me, you know, and it was a long time ago.

It was—all of this and more—a quest, a going forth upon the way to Rainy Mountain. Probably Ko-sahn too is dead now. At times, in the quiet of evening, I think she must have wondered, dreaming, who she was. Was she become in her sleep that old purveyor of the sacred earth, perhaps, that ancient one who, old as she was, still had the feeling of play? And in her mind, at times, did she see the falling stars?

Rainy Mountain Cemetery

Most is your name the name of this dark stone.
Deranged in death, the mind to be inheres
Forever in the nominal unknown,
The wake of nothing audible he hears
Who listens here and now to hear your name.   5

The early sun, red as a hunter's moon,
Runs in the plain. The mountain burns and shines;
And silence is the long approach of noon
Upon the shadow that your name defines—
And death this cold, black density of stone.   10

1969

AUDRE LORDE
1934-1992

Audre Lorde's poetry wages what she called "a war against the tyrannies of silence"; it articulates what has been passed over out of fear or discomfort, what has been kept hidden and secret. Reading her we feel the violence inherent in breaking a silence, perhaps most often as she probes the experience of anger—the anger of black toward white or white toward black, a woman's anger at men and other women, and men's anger toward women. "My Black woman's anger," she wrote in her collection of essays, *Sister Outsider*, "is a molten pond at the core of me, my most fiercely guarded secret." Having admitted this secret into her poems, Lorde transforms our expectations of what is a fit subject for the lyric. Her work is often deliberately disturbing, the powerful voice of the poem cutting through denial, politeness, and fear. In developing this voice Lorde drew on African resources, especially the matriarchal mythology and history of West Africa. Her seventh book, *The Black Unicorn* (1978), reflects the time she spent in Africa studying, in particular, Yoruba mythology and reclaiming her connection to the rich African cultures. The African presence is evident in one of her last books, *Our Dead Behind Us* (1986), as well. Lorde's work suggests that she always connected poetry to the speaking voice, but her study of African materials deepened her connection to oral traditions (like the chant or the call) and taught her the power of voice to cut across time and place. From African writers, she said, she learned that "we live in accordance with, in a kind of correspondence with, the rest of the world as a whole." A powerful voice informed by personal and cultural history creates the possibility, for Lorde, of bridging the differences her work does not seek to erase. "It is not difference that immobilizes us," she wrote, "but silence."

Her work celebrates difference and confounds it. In Adrienne Rich's words, Lorde wrote "as a Black woman, a mother, a daughter, a Lesbian, a feminist, a visionary." Her poem "Coal" affirms an *I* that is "the total black, being spoken / from the earth's inside." This total blackness was, for her, also associated with Eros and with creativity; she celebrated this source as what she called "woman's place of power within each of us," which is "neither white nor surface; it is dark, it is ancient; and it is deep." Her best work calls on the deepest places of her own life—on the pain she experienced, on her rage (her second book, in 1972, was titled *Cables to Rage*), on her longing and desire. One of the silences her poems broke concerns love between women, and she wrote a number of poems that are erotic, precise, and true to both the power and delicacy of feeling. Unafraid of anger, she was also capable of tenderness; this is perhaps most clear not only in her love poems but in poems that address a younger generation.

Lorde was born in New York City and lived in New York almost all her life. Her parents were West Indian, and her mother was light skinned. "I grew up in a genuine confusion / between grass and weeds and flowers / and what colored meant," Lorde wrote in her poem "Outside." Part of that confusion was the conflict represented by her father's blackness and her mother's desire for whiteness (in "Black Mother Woman" Lorde speaks of the mother as "split with deceitful longings"). Lorde's understanding of identity forged out of conflict began for her, then, in her own family history with its legacy of "conflicting rebellions" ("Black Mother Woman"). In 1961 she received a B.A. from Hunter College and later a Master's of Library Science from Columbia University. The following year she married and the marriage produced a daughter and a son (she divorced in 1970). In 1968 she became poet-in-residence for a year at Tougaloo College in Mississippi, her first experience in the American South. Thereafter she knew her work to be that of a writer and teacher; she taught at John Jay College of Criminal Justice in New York City and, from 1981, was professor of English at Hunter College. In the last years of her life Lorde traveled extensively, not only to Africa but to Australia (where she met with aborigine women) and Germany. During her last years she lived much of the time in St. Croix.

"I have come to believe over and over again," Lorde said, "that what is most important to me must be spoken, made verbal and shared, even at the risk of having it bruised or misunderstood." (Her essay "Poetry Is Not a Luxury" [1977] makes the case for poetry's essential speaking of what is otherwise unnamed and unthought. A selection from this essay appears in the "Postmodern Manifestos" cluster of this anthology.) The drive toward expression made Lorde a prolific writer and led her to compose several prose works in which she shared experiences often restricted to privacy: *The Cancer Journals* (1980), an account of her struggle with breast cancer, and *Zami: A New Spelling of My Name* (1982), a "biomythography" of her growing up and her emergent lesbian identity. The urgency Lorde felt to make experience "verbal and shared," however, sometimes overrode a distinction crucial to her work: that between poetry and rhetoric. She preserved this distinction in her best work by listening and responding to other voices in herself and in the world around her. With their combination of pain, anger, and tenderness, her finest poems are poetry as illumination, poetry in which, as she said, "we give name to those ideas which are—until the poem—nameless, formless, about to be birthed, but already felt."

Coal

I
is the total black, being spoken
from the earth's inside.
There are many kinds of open
how a diamond comes into a knot of flame   5
how sound comes into a word, coloured
by who pays what for speaking.

Some words are open like a diamond
on glass windows

singing out within the passing crash of sun   10
Then there are words like stapled wagers
in a perforated book,—buy and sign and tear apart—
and come whatever wills all chances
the stub remains
an ill-pulled tooth with a ragged edge.   15
Some words live in my throat
breeding like adders. Others know sun
seeking like gypsies over my tongue
to explode through my lips
like young sparrows bursting from shell.   20
Some words
bedevil me.

Love is a word, another kind of open.
As the diamond comes into a knot of flame
I am Black because I come from the earth's inside   25
now take my word for jewel in the open light.

                                                                           1968

The Woman Thing

The hunters are back from beating the winter's face
in search of a challenge or task
in search of food
making fresh tracks for their children's hunger
they do not watch the sun   5
they cannot wear its heat for a sign
of triumph or freedom;
The hunters are treading heavily homeward
through snow that is marked
with their own bloody footprints.   10
emptyhanded, the hunters return
snow-maddened, sustained by their rages.

In the night after food they may seek
young girls for their amusement. But now
the hunters are coming   15
and the unbaked girls flee from their angers.
All this day I have craved
food for my child's hunger
Emptyhanded the hunters come shouting
injustices drip from their mouths   20
like stale snow melted in sunlight.

Meanwhile
the woman thing my mother taught me
bakes off its covering of snow
like a rising blackening sun.   25

                                                                           1968

Black Mother Woman

I cannot recall you gentle
yet through your heavy love
I have become
an image of your once delicate flesh
split with deceitful longings.   5

When strangers come and compliment me
your aged spirit takes a bow
jingling with pride
but once you hid that secret
in the center of furies   10
hanging me
with deep breasts and wiry hair
with your own split flesh
and long suffering eyes
buried in myths of little worth.   15

But I have peeled away your anger
down to the core of love
and look mother
I Am
a dark temple where your true spirit rises   20
beautiful
and tough as chestnut
stanchion[1] against your nightmare of weakness
and if my eyes conceal
a squadron of conflicting rebellions   25
I learned from you
to define myself
through your denials.

                                                                1971

1. Upright bar or post (for supporting, e.g., a railing).

MARY OLIVER
b. 1935

"[O]f course / loss is the great lesson," Mary Oliver writes in her poem "Poppies." "But also I say this: that light / is an invitation to happiness / and that happiness, when it's done right / is a kind of holiness." What we experience first and most intensely in Mary Oliver's poetry is the earthly delight that constitutes her vision of happiness and holiness. That delight is founded in the world of the alligator, the deer, the bear, the black oak, the trumpet vine, the wild mushroom. This variegated natural world is precisely recorded in Oliver's poetry, from her first book, *No Voyage and Other Poems* (1963), to her collection of prose, poems, and prose poems, *Winter Hours* (2000). But a river of loss runs underground in her poems, whose deeper currents are sometimes an unspoken source propelling the poet out into the natural world; that world restores her to herself; its vitality and beauty open her heart. Yet in Oliver's best work the natural world does more than restore or console; it also teaches the "great lesson" of loving and letting go.

Oliver was born in Maple Heights, Ohio, and attended Vassar College. She lives in Provincetown, Massachusetts, and Bennington, Vermont; not surprisingly, the New England landscape is as central to her work as it is to Robert Frost's. But perhaps the poet she most closely resembles is James Wright (also born in Ohio), to whose memory her Pulitzer Prize–winning *American Primitive* (1983) is dedicated; she shares Wright's capacity for wonder, as well as his movement away from a social world into a natural one. Digging for mussels or spotting bear in the Truro Woods (in poems from *Twelve Moons*, 1979), watching humpback whales or blue herons on the ponds (in *American Primitive*), observing the hummingbird (in *New and Selected Poems*, 1992), Oliver endows her regional landscape with the spaciousness and depth the American Transcendentalist Henry David Thoreau gave to Walden Pond. Indeed, the very title of *American Primitive* suggests her self-conscious participation in an American impulse toward something primary and primal in the self and in the world.

One of the pleasures of reading Oliver's work is the education it provides about plants and animals in its detailed and knowledgeable observation—as when, for example, in "Skunk Cabbage" (*American Primitive*) she sees the "turnip-hearted skunk cabbage / slinging its bunched leaves up / through the chilly mud." The power and precision of her descriptions make it seem that, in lines from her "Alligator Poem" (*New and Selected Poems*), we "saw the world as if for a second time, / the way it really is." But Oliver's poems are as much about transformation as about observation, for in her work—as in "Alligator Poem"—the secret life of the world seems to open itself, for a moment, to human apprehension, transforming the world and the self. For Oliver the natural world casts a spell of amazement over poet and reader (this amazement— the stance of wonder at what is—is frequently registered by Oliver's use of the interrogative). Those moments when she is "washed and washed / in the river / of earthly delight" ("Poppies") restore the poet to her faith in the world that made her. These rapturous antidotes heal night's pain, mitigate loneliness, turn the heaviness of "the great bones of my life" ("Spring Azures") into wings. They are also the antidote to psychic pain, and to a social world with which Mary Oliver's poems want little to do. That world occasionally intrudes into Oliver's poems in the form of disturbing figures, like the woman in the airport restroom in "Singapore," the disfigured boy in "Acid," or, more ominously and persistently, the father who "knocks / wildly at the door" in "A Visitor." These figures unsettle the poet's solitude and threaten a vision of happiness and holiness sometimes too easily affirmed in her work. Though such human and social intrusions are intermittent in Oliver's poems, they seem to gesture toward injuries this poet keeps hidden.

There is such naturalness to Oliver's poems that we may fail to notice their craft. Oliver's language stays close to the spoken American idiom but infuses it with music, and creates, through verbal design, images of startling vividness (in "Alligator Poem" the birds "shook open the snowy pleats of their wings, and drifted away"). In a poetry so attentive to detail, where line breaks focus our attention on particulars—"the line is the device upon which the poem spins itself into being," she has said—there is also extraordinary power. Oliver builds her stanzas so they interlock, one into another, and the reader is pulled through a series of perceptions into the poet's insight. In certain poems the movement of her lines across the page rhythmically enacts the reaching forward and pulling back of the poet's walks into the landscape. Of course, making the design of a poem seem as natural as the hummingbird pausing at the trumpet vine is one sign of how gifted a poet Oliver is.

Her *New and Selected Poems* won the National Book Award in 1992 and includes work from six previous books. She has published prolifically throughout her career, with over a dozen books since 1992, including several essay collections and handbooks on writing.

The Black Snake

When the black snake
flashed onto the morning road,
and the truck could not swerve—
death, that is how it happens.

Now he lies looped and useless   5
as an old bicycle tire.
I stop the car
and carry him into the bushes.

He is as cool and gleaming
as a braided whip, he is as beautiful and quiet   10
as a dead brother.
I leave him under the leaves

and drive on, thinking
about *death*: its suddenness,
its terrible weight,   15
its certain coming. Yet under

reason burns a brighter fire, which the bones
have always preferred.
It is the story of endless good fortune.
It says to oblivion: not me!   20

It is the light at the center of every cell.
It is what sent the snake coiling and flowing forward
happily all spring through the green leaves before
he came to the road.

                                                   1979

In Blackwater Woods

Look, the trees
are turning
their own bodies
into pillars

of light,
are giving off the rich   5
fragrance of cinnamon
and fulfillment,

the long tapers
of cattails   10
are bursting and floating away over
the blue shoulders

of the ponds,
and every pond,
no matter what its   15
name is, is

nameless now.
Every year
everything
I have ever learned   20

in my lifetime
leads back to this: the fires
and the black river of loss
whose other side

is salvation,   25
whose meaning
none of us will ever know.
To live in this world

you must be able
to do three things: 30
to love what is mortal;
to hold it

against your bones knowing
your own life depends on it;
and, when the time comes to let it go,   35
to let it go.

                                                                    1983

Wild Geese

You do not have to be good.
You do not have to walk on your knees
for a hundred miles through the desert, repenting.
You only have to let the soft animal of your body
        love what it loves.   5
Tell me about despair, yours, and I will tell you mine.

Meanwhile the world goes on.
Meanwhile the sun and the dear pebbles of the rain
are moving across the landscapes,
over the prairies and the deep trees,   10
the mountains and the rivers.
Meanwhile the wild geese, high in the clean blue air,
are heading home again.
Whoever you are, no matter how lonely,
the world offers itself to your imagination,   15
calls to you like the wild geese, harsh and exciting—
over and over announcing your place
in the family of things.

                                                            1986

Poppies

The poppies send up their
orange flares; swaying
in the wind, their congregations
are a levitation

of bright dust, of thin   5
and lacy leaves.
There isn't a place
in this world that doesn't

sooner or later drown
in the indigos of darkness,   10
but now, for a while,
the roughage

shines like a miracle
as it floats above everything
with its yellow hair.   15
Of course nothing stops the cold,

black, curved blade
from hooking forward—
of course
loss is the great lesson.   20

But also I say this: that light
is an invitation
to happiness,
and that happiness,

when it's done right,   25
is a kind of holiness,
palpable and redemptive.
Inside the bright fields,

touched by their rough and spongy gold,
I am washed and washed   30
in the river
of earthly delight—

and what are you going to do—
what can you do
about it—   35
deep, blue night?

1991–92   1992

Hummingbird Pauses at the Trumpet Vine

Who doesn't love
roses, and who
doesn't love the lilies
of the black ponds

floating like flocks   5
of tiny swans,
and of course the flaming
trumpet vine

where the hummingbird comes
like a small green angel, to soak   10
his dark tongue
in happiness—

and who doesn't want
to live with the brisk
motor of his heart   15
singing

like a Schubert,[1]
and his eyes
working and working like those days of rapture,
by van Gogh,[2] in Arles?   20

Look! for most of the world
is waiting
or remembering—
most of the world is time

when we're not here,   25
not born yet, or died—
a slow fire
under the earth with all

1. Franz Schubert (1797–1828), Austrian composer and proponent of musical Romanticism.
2. Vincent Van Gogh (1853–1890), Dutch Postimpressionist painter who produced much of his
best-known work in Arles in the south of France.

our dumb wild blind cousins
who also   30
can't even remember anymore
their own happiness—

Look! and then we will be
like the pale cool
stones, that last almost   35
forever.

1991–92   1992

Alligator Poem

I knelt down
at the edge of the water,
and if the white birds standing
in the tops of the trees whistled any warning
I didn't understand,   5
I drank up to the very moment it came
crashing toward me,
its tail flailing
like a bundle of swords,
slashing the grass,   10
and the inside of its cradle-shaped mouth
gaping,
and rimmed with teeth—
and that's how I almost died
of foolishness   15
in beautiful Florida.
But I didn't.
I leaped aside, and fell,
and it streamed past me, crushing everything in its path
as it swept down to the water   20
and threw itself in,
and, in the end,
this isn't a poem about foolishness
but about how I rose from the ground
and saw the world as if for the second time,   25
the way it really is.
The water, that circle of shattered glass,
healed itself with a slow whisper
and lay back
with the back-lit light of polished steel,   30
and the birds, in the endless waterfalls of the trees,
shook open the snowy pleats of their wings, and drifted away,
while, for a keepsake, and to steady myself,
I reached out,
I picked the wild flowers from the grass around me—   35
blue stars

and blood-red trumpets
on long green stems—
for hours in my trembling hands they glittered
like fire.   40

1992

LUCILLE CLIFTON
1936–2010

Lucille Clifton seemed able to lift the poem off the page and return it to the air we breathe. Like the work of Langston Hughes or William Carlos Williams, her poems allow us to hear the language of our daily lives as poetry and to experience the poetry in our ordinary lives. Although a closer look reveals the subtle craft of her poems (for example, the slant rhymes and the carefully paced repetitions), they appear deceptively simple. Their frankness and directness close the distance between poet and reader, especially when these poems are read aloud. Clifton emphasized the informality in her work through the lowercase letters she preferred and through her frequent omission of titles. The language of her poems reflects her identity; "I am a black woman poet," she said, "and I sound like one." Grounded in realistic details, her poems do not shy away from what is harsh and painful, including incest, suicide, mental illness, and the effects of poverty and racism. But while Clifton's anger fueled many poems, her imagination found beauty and humor in unexpected places; indeed, she seemed able to make poetry out of anything. In this she resembles the African American quilters who rework the materials of ordinary experience into distinctive and compelling designs. Indeed, she titled one of her books *Quilting* (1991) and borrowed its section headings from the names of traditional quilt patterns.

Born in Depew, New York, to a father who worked in the steel mills and a mother who was a launderer and a homemaker (and who wrote poems but burned them), Clifton was the first person in her family to attend college. "I had a very regular life, the life of a poor black person," Clifton once said; but her background and her gifts sometimes made her feel that "there is no planet stranger / than the one I'm from" ("note, passed to superman"). At sixteen she began her studies at Howard University in Washington, D.C., and she later attended Fredonia State Teachers College in New York State. She went on to work as a claims clerk in the New York State Division of Employment (1958–60) and as a literature assistant at the Office of Education in Washington (1960–71). Clifton never formally studied creative writing, but she wrote poems and thought of herself as a poet from a young age. However, her work did not receive public recognition until she was in her thirties. In 1969 she sent a poem to the poet Robert Hayden at the National Endowment for the Arts. Hayden had left the NEA, but his successor, Carolyn Kizer, read the work and submitted it to the YW-YMHA Poetry Center Discovery Award competition in New York City. Clifton won the competition and at the award ceremony, after she read her poems, an editor from Random House in the audience offered to publish her first book, *Good Times* (1969). *Good Times* appeared when she was thirty-three, a wife and mother with six children under the age of eleven. During these years her method of composition followed those writers, many of them women, who compose lines of poetry in the mind until there is time to write them down.

Clifton came from a line of African American storytellers extending from her great-grandmother, Caroline Donald, who was born in Dahomey, Africa, sold into slavery, and taken to America. Clifton's memoir, *Generations* (1976), chronicles the history of her family, including the genealogy and the tradition of strong women passed down to Clifton through her father's stories. In much of her work, Clifton consciously sought to recover an African American past that has too often been omitted from standard histories and to retell history from previously unacknowledged points of view.

In a poem beginning "the light that came to Lucille Clifton," a voice from "the non-dead past" speaks this message to her: "You might as well open the door, my child / for truth is furiously knocking." Throughout her long and productive career as a poet, and as a writer of memoirs and children's books, she transmitted the voices of a living past. Like Toni Morrison's fiction, Clifton's poems are full of ghosts: her mother and father, her unborn children, her ancestors, and sometimes mythical and biblical figures. These presences in her work bear witness to a legacy of pain, wisdom, and survival. As a writer brave enough to open the door to the truths of her life and her world, Clifton possessed a "gift of understanding" that put her in touch with the suffering of the "holy lost" ("Wild Blessing"), but the spiritual dimension of her work also reveals the possibility of joy and transformation, evident in "blessing the boats."

Clifton's books include *Good News about the Earth* (1972) and *Two-Headed Woman* (1980), which received the University of Massachusetts Juniper Prize. Both of these volumes were nominated for the Pulitzer Prize. Subsequent collections include *Next* (1987), *The Book of Light* (1993), *Blessing the Boats: New and Selected Poems 1988–2000* (2000), *Mercy* (2004), and *Voices* (2008). Clifton's work for children includes *The Black BCs* (1970), *The Times They Used to Be* (1974), and an award-winning series of books featuring events in the life of Everett Anderson, a young black boy. In 1999 she was elected a chancellor of the Academy of American Poets. She served as poet laureate for the State of Maryland and as distinguished professor of humanities at St. Mary's College in Maryland.

[handwritten annotation: ➔ condemns neglect of elderly]

miss rosie

[handwritten annotation: → homeless, not "all there"]

when i watch you
wrapped up like garbage
sitting, surrounded by the smell
of too old potato peels
or
when i watch you
in your old man's shoes
with the little toe cut out
sitting, waiting for your mind
like next week's grocery   10
i say
when i watch you
you wet brown bag of a woman
who used to be the best looking gal in georgia
used to be called the Georgia Rose
i stand up

[handwritten annotation: Pay respect & homage to a lady who's a representative of every old person who once mattered & was so respected & cared for in their best years]

[handwritten annotation: respect she once had & still has despite her deteriorating conditions]

through your destruction
i stand up

[handwritten: Statement shows respect & gives value to Miss Rosie as a human being]

1969   1987

[handwritten: MON]

the lost baby poem

[handwritten: Abortion?]

the time i dropped your almost body down
down to meet the waters under the city
and run one with the sewage to the sea
what did i know about waters rushing back
what did i know about drowning
or being drowned   5

[handwritten: drowning in regret/guilt?]

you would have been born into winter
in the year of the disconnected gas
and no car we would have made the thin
walk over genesee hill[1] into the canada wind   10
to watch you slip like ice into strangers' hands
you would have fallen naked as snow into winter
if you were here i could tell you these
and some other things

[handwritten: reasoning behind the abortion? So poor that she couldn't take care of a baby]

if i am ever less than a mountain   15
for your definite brothers and sisters
let the rivers pour over my head
let the sea take me for a spiller
of seas let black men call me stranger
always for your never named sake   20

[handwritten: Learned from her mistakes maybe? A promise to her unborn child that she will do her best for the children she has now or else she should be punished in some way.]

[handwritten: coming up for air/that pause to emphasize]

1972

[handwritten: mantra- or manifesto- entire of life]

homage to my hips

[handwritten: Owning who you are not willing to be trapped in a petty understanding of who/what she is. Not contained by stereotypes]

these hips are big hips
they need space to
move around in.
they don't fit into little
petty places, these hips.
are free hips.   5
they don't like to be held back.
these hips have never been enslaved,
they go where they want to go
they do what they want to do.   10
these hips are mighty hips.
these hips are magic hips.
i have known them
to put a spell on a man and
spin him like a top!   15

*[handwritten: hips stands for the woman (synecdoche) * part stands for a whole]*

[handwritten: Not interested in how her hips look but rather how they act — she's a woman of action]

[handwritten: unapologetic]

*[handwritten: *has power of * celebration of body]*

1980

---

1. Genesee County is in western New York State.

wild blessings

licked in the palm of my hand
by an uninvited woman, so i have held
in that hand the hand of a man who
emptied into his daughter, the hand
of a girl who threw herself
from a tenement window, the trembling
junkie hand of a priest, of a boy who
shattered across viet nam
someone resembling his mother,
and more, and more.
do not ask me to thank the tongue
that circled my fingers
or pride myself on the attentions
of the holy lost.
i am grateful for many blessings
but the gift of understanding,
the wild one, maybe not.

1991

wishes for sons

i wish them cramps.
i wish them a strange town
and the last tampon.
i wish them no 7–11.

i wish them one week early
and wearing a white skirt.
i wish them one week late.

later i wish them hot flashes
and clots like you
wouldn't believe. let the
flashes come when they
meet someone special.
let the clots come
when they want to.

let them think they have accepted   15
arrogance in the universe,
then bring them to gynecologists
not unlike themselves.

1991

Handwritten annotations:

solidarity? everyone has a darkness inside them

shepherd wed to sheep?

a poem about understanding — although she is grateful for many of her blessings, she doesn't really feel grateful for her deep understanding of the terrible things about others (child abusers & junkies, soldiers who killed innocents just like their mom, suicides)

primitive ability to see/understand — there's no changing it

mom

adolescence associated w/ ignorance

guys don't have to think about these things the same way women do

directed to the sons of men wishing them all the pain & embarrassment of the female gender to gain empathy & understanding (maybe for the women in their lives)

first and only you. men.

the frustration of having to deal w/ that ignorance

directed towards arrogant, ignorant men who think being a woman isn't hard & they know a woman's body better than she does & then to interact w/ someone who is exactly the kind of arrogance he exhibited

blessing the boats

(*at St. Mary's*)[1]

may the tide
that is entering even now
the lip of our understanding
carry you out
beyond the face of fear   5
may you kiss
the wind then turn from it
certain that it will
love your back   may you
open your eyes to water   10
water waving forever
and may you in your innocence
sail through this to that

1991

the mississippi river empties into the gulf

and the gulf enters the sea and so forth,
none of them emptying anything,
all of them carrying yesterday
forever on their white tipped backs,
all of them dragging forward tomorrow.   5
it is the great circulation
of the earth's body, like the blood
of the gods, this river in which the past
is always flowing, every water
is the same water coming round.   10
everyday someone is standing on the edge
of this river, staring into time,
whispering mistakenly:
only here, only now.

1996

moonchild[1]

whatever slid into my mother's room that
late June night, tapping her great belly,

---

1. A county in southern Maryland that is a tide-water peninsula bordered by the Chesapeake Bay and three rivers: the Patuxent, the Potomac, and the Wicomico. It is also the location of St. Mary's College, where Clifton taught.

1. *Moonchild* (1917), a novel by the English occultist Aleister Crowley (1875–1947), involves a magical war between practitioners of white magic and practitioners of black magic over an unborn child.

summoned me out roundheaded and unsmiling.
is this the moon, my father used to grin,
cradling me?   it was the moon   5
but nobody knew it then.

the moon understands dark places.
the moon has secrets of her own.
she holds what light she can.

we girls were <u>ten years old</u> and giggling
in our hand-me-downs, we wanted breasts,
pretended that we had them, tissued
our undershirts, jay Johnson is teaching
me to french kiss, ella bragged, who
is teaching you? how do you say; my father?   15

the moon is queen of everything.
she rules the oceans, rivers, rain.
when I am asked whose tears these are
I always blame the moon.

2000

Handwritten annotations:

juxtaposition of light & childhood
light is what which is what also it should be but had to what she go through in her childhood
molesting his daughter — this darkness juxtaposed the light

Is she the moon? is this her way of seperating herself from what happened & giving herself some power

blame her mother for not protecting her from her father?

[oh antic god]

oh antic God
return to me
my mother in her thirties[1]
leaned across the front porch
the huge pillow of her breasts   5
pressing against the rail
summoning me in for bed.

I am almost the dead woman's age times two.

I can barely recall her song
the scent of her hands   10
though her wild hair scratches my dreams
at night.   return to me, oh Lord of then
and now, my mother's calling,
her young voice humming my name.

2004

---

1. Thelma Moore Sayles, Clifton's mother, died at age forty-four.

DON DeLILLO
b. 1936

D on DeLillo's best-known novels evoke twentieth- and twenty-first-century American culture and global history on its grandest scale. Encompassing big-league sports, atomic bombs, space exploration, the 9/11 attacks, international business, environmental disasters, huge art installations, and glittering supermarkets, his sixteen novels have captured the preoccupations of his times. Not historical novels in the traditional sense, DeLillo's works allow readers to hear how people of all ages speak, think, and experience the world as massive forces bear down upon them. He observes modern experience with an eye that is both critical and loving. Touched always with humor that makes the reader see cultural absurdities in a new light, his attention to the human dimensions of mass culture has made his work popular since his breakthrough novel, *White Noise*, was published in 1985.

"The future belongs to crowds." The narrator of *Mao II* makes this prophecy on the heels of a prologue describing the mass wedding of 13,000 followers of the Reverend Sun Myung Moon in Yankee Stadium. This kind of spectacle appears frequently in DeLillo's work. His millennial novel, *Underworld* (1998), begins with one of his best-known crowd scenes, set at the Polo Grounds baseball stadium in New York: it is 1951, the famous playoff game between two New York City teams, the Giants and the Dodgers. In the stands we find power brokers and celebrities and thousands of ordinary New Yorkers. In *Libra* (1988), DeLillo conjures up the mass of humanity lining the presidential motorcade route in Dallas, Texas, on November 22, 1963, a scene the reader experiences through the eyes of President Kennedy's assassin, Lee Harvey Oswald.

DeLillo's crowds reflect the vibrant city where the author has lived throughout his life. "New York made me," he once declared. "There's a sensibility, a sense of humor, an approach, a sort of dark approach to things that's part New York, and maybe part growing up Catholic, and that . . . shapes my work far more than anything I read." Born in New York City in 1936 and raised in a tight-knit Southern Italian neighborhood in the Bronx, DeLillo attended Catholic schools, graduating from Fordham University in the late fifties. In Catholic ritual, and in the modern art and jazz he discovered in the city in the sixties, he found his most enduring preoccupations as a writer of fiction.

For all their fascination with crowds, DeLillo's novels are grounded in the lives of their characters. In any DeLillo crowd scene, the reader will find individuals the novel will follow closely. *Underworld*, DeLillo's most massive novel, follows Cotter, a black child from the projects, as he jumps the stiles to see the Giants-Dodgers playoff game. The boy later escapes from the stands with the game-winning homerun ball off Bobby Thompson's bat, and the ball becomes a precious object that carries characters' stories and American history along with it to the start of the new century five decades later. Through such characters, DeLillo ushers readers into the place where recorded history gives way to the novelist's imagination. Shuttling between mass culture and the private lives contained in crowds, DeLillo's fiction diagrams the machinery of transcendence: how does an immigrant or outcast become an American? How does a soldier decide to assassinate a president? How does a believer connect to the cosmos? How does a wildly diverse city become a human community? And how do the decisions of individuals add up to History?

DeLillo is renowned for understanding how media of all kinds penetrate deep into modern life. That wisdom has resonated steadily with readers as the Internet age dawned and flourished over the course of his writing career. His characters strive for authentic human connection within the flow of advertising, television, film, radio, gossip, misinformation, and mass hysteria that swirls around their living rooms, bedrooms, cars, and kitchen tables. Children have a special role in countering these forces. In *The Names* (1982), a child writes mystical stories filled with misspellings. His estranged parents and their friends make the plot run—the novel follows a cult that is methodically committing murders in small villages along the Mediterranean coast of Greece—but the novel's transcendent passages come from the boy's pen. Through him DeLillo presents an innocent, authentic, and nonviolent mysticism that counters the cult's murderous rituals. A toddler in *White Noise* gradually gives up words in favor of more-visceral forms of human communication—he cries steadily for twenty-four hours and then stops. These strange speakers, or nonspeakers, draw others beyond ordinary language to a deeper experience of the human condition.

The form and style of DeLillo's novels reflect his shifts in scale from the crowd to the individual, from panoramic scenes to family bedrooms. His epic novels are built from multiple individual stories that braid together into a broad view of an era, a nation, or even the whole globe. Within each story DeLillo's fine-tuned ear for dialogue allows the reader to hear the very words through which his characters put their lives together. As the digital age took hold in the early twenty-first century, even his early novels seemed both prophetic and redemptive to contemporary readers looking to find coherent stories that could hold their own within the torrent of words and pictures flowing over us every day.

When *White Noise* was published, DeLillo was considered a practitioner of the "paranoid school" of American fiction: part of a group of writers, including Thomas Pynchon, John Barth, William Gaddis, and Richard Powers, whose novels represented massive institutions or conspiracies in which characters could not hope to shape their own lives. The novel's funny, satirical picture of fragmented American family life in a leafy suburb seemed to capture what was "postmodern" in middle-class life—the way television seemed to generate reality, the encompassing aura of consumer culture, the morphing domestic scene shaped by divorce, remarriage, international careers, and blended families. DeLillo's dark humor cast a critical light on middle-class achievements—the main character of *White Noise* is a failing professor of "Hitler Studies" who, try as he might, cannot learn German. But for all the novel's satire and fragmentation, classic moments of transcendence and community emerge from *White Noise*. Such elements return in all of DeLillo's major novels and set him apart from his paranoid peers, putting him ultimately closer to a school of religiously inflected American novelists that would include secular Jewish writers, American Catholic novelists, and those Protestant writers who reserve a place for mysticism and grace.

DeLillo has garnered several major prizes in his long career, starting with the National Book Award for *White Noise*, later followed by the Jerusalem Prize and the William Dean Howells Medal for *Underworld*. In 2013 he was awarded the first Library of Congress Prize for American Fiction, which honors "strong, unique, enduring voices that—throughout long, consistently accomplished careers—have told us something about the American experience." Receiving news of the award, DeLillo said that his "first thoughts were of my mother and father, who came to this country the hard way, as young people confronting a new language and culture." The prize, he said, "is the culmination of their efforts and a tribute to their memory."

In the selection from *White Noise* that follows, the main character, Professor Jack Gladney, and his family have been evacuated from their home, joining the mass of humanity converging upon a school gym to shelter from an environmental disaster that the media have dubbed the "Airborne Toxic Event." Arriving at the gym in the family car, Gladney, his wife, Babette, and their four children are suddenly thrown out of their suburban security. Each must find a place in the unfolding American spectacle.

From White Noise

Part II: Airborne Toxic Event

Small crowds collected around certain men. Here were the sources of information and rumor. One person worked in a chemical plant, another had overheard a remark, a third was related to a clerk in a state agency. True, false, and other kinds of news radiated through the dormitory from these dense clusters.

It was said that we would be allowed to go home first thing in the morning; that the government was engaged in a cover-up; that a helicopter had entered the toxic cloud and never reappeared; that the dogs had arrived from New Mexico, parachuting into a meadow in a daring night drop; that the town of Farmington would be uninhabitable for forty years.

Remarks existed in a state of permanent flotation. No one thing was either more or less plausible than any other thing. As people jolted out of reality, we were released from the need to distinguish.

Some families chose to sleep in their cars, others were forced to do so because there was no room for them in the seven or eight buildings on the grounds. We were in a large barracks, one of three such buildings at the camp, and with the generator now working we were fairly comfortable. The Red Cross had provided cots, portable heaters, sandwiches and coffee. There were kerosene lamps to supplement the existing overhead lights. Many people had radios, extra food to share with others, blankets, beach chairs, extra clothing. The place was crowded, still quite cold, but the sight of nurses and volunteer workers made us feel the children were safe, and the presence of other stranded souls, young women with infants, old and infirm people, gave us a certain staunchness and will, a selfless bent that was pronounced enough to function as a common identity. This large gray area, dank and bare and lost to history just a couple of hours ago, was an oddly agreeable place right now, filled with an eagerness of community and voice.

Seekers of news moved from one cluster of people to another, tending to linger at the larger groups. In this way I moved slowly through the barracks. There were nine evacuation centers, I learned, including this one and the Kung Fu Palace. Iron City had not been emptied out; nor had most of the other towns in the area. It was said that the governor was on his way from the capitol in an executive helicopter. It would probably set down in a bean field outside a deserted town, allowing the governor to emerge, square-jawed and confident, in a bush jacket, within camera range, for ten or fifteen seconds, as a demonstration of his imperishability.

What a surprise it was to ease my way between people at the outer edges of one of the largest clusters and discover that my own son was at the center of things, speaking in his new-found voice, his tone of enthusiasm for runaway calamity. He was talking about the airborne toxic event in a technical way, although his voice all but sang with prophetic disclosure. He pronounced the name itself, Nyodene Derivative,[1] with an unseemly relish, taking morbid delight in the very sound. People listened attentively to this adolescent boy in a field jacket and cap, with binoculars strapped around his neck and an Instamatic[2] fastened to his belt. No doubt his listeners were influenced by his age. He would be truthful and earnest, serving no special interest; he would have an awareness of the environment; his knowledge of chemistry would be fresh and up-to-date.

I heard him say, "The stuff they sprayed on the big spill at the train yard was probably soda ash. But it was a case of too little too late. My guess is they'll get some crop dusters up in the air at daybreak and bombard the toxic cloud with lots more soda ash, which could break it up and scatter it into a million harmless puffs. Soda ash is the common name for sodium carbonate, which is used in the manufacture of glass, ceramics, detergents, and soaps. It's also what they use to make bicarbonate of soda, something a lot of you have probably guzzled after a night on the town."

People moved in closer, impressed by the boy's knowledgeability and wit. It was remarkable to hear him speak so easily to a crowd of strangers. Was he finding himself, learning how to determine his worth from the reactions of others? Was it possible that out of the turmoil and surge of this dreadful event he would learn to make his way in the world?

"What you're probably all wondering is what exactly is this Nyodene D. we keep hearing about? A good question. We studied it in school, we saw movies of rats having convulsions and so on. So, okay, it's basically simple. Nyodene D. is a whole bunch of things thrown together that are byproducts of the manufacture of insecticide. The original stuff kills roaches, the byproducts kill everything left over. A little joke our teacher made."

He snapped his fingers, let his left leg swing a bit.

"In powder form it's colorless, odorless, and very dangerous, except no one seems to know exactly what it causes in humans or in the offspring of humans. They tested for years and either they don't know for sure or they know and aren't saying. Some things are too awful to publicize."

He arched his brows and began to twitch comically, his tongue lolling in a corner of his mouth. I was astonished to hear people laugh.

"Once it seeps into the soil, it has a life span of forty years. This is longer than a lot of people. After five years you'll notice various kinds of fungi appearing between your regular windows and storm windows as well as in your clothes and food. After ten years your screens will turn rusty and begin to pit and rot. Siding will warp. There will be glass breakage and trauma to pets. After twenty years you'll probably have to seal yourself in the attic and just wait and see. I guess there's a lesson in all this. Get to know your chemicals."

I didn't want him to see me there. It would make him self-conscious, remind him of his former life as a gloomy and fugitive boy. Let him bloom, if that's what he was doing, in the name of mischance, dread, and random disaster. So I slipped away, passing a man who wore snow boots wrapped in

1. Fictional toxic substance; elsewhere in the novel it is referred to as "Nyodene D." and is said to be "packed with chlorides, benzines, phenols, hydrocarbons."
2. Inexpensive and popular point-and-shoot camera made by Kodak between 1963 and 1988.

plastic, and headed for the far end of the barracks, where we'd earlier made camp.

We were next to a black family of Jehovah's Witnesses.[3] A man and woman with a boy about twelve. Father and son were handing out tracts to people nearby and seemed to have no trouble finding willing recipients and listeners.

The woman said to Babette, "Isn't this something?"

"Nothing surprises me anymore," Babette said.

"Isn't that the truth."

"What would surprise me would be if there were no surprises."

"That sounds about right."

"Or if there were little bitty surprises. That would be a surprise. Instead of things like this."

"God Jehovah's got a bigger surprise in store than this," the woman said.

"God Jehovah?"

"That's the one."

Steffie and Wilder were asleep in one of the cots. Denise sat at the other end engrossed in the *Physicians' Desk Reference*. Several air mattresses were stacked against the wall. There was a long line at the emergency telephone, people calling relatives or trying to reach the switchboard at one or another radio call-in show. The radios here were tuned mainly to just such shows. Babette sat in a camp chair, going through a canvas bag full of snack thins and other provisions. I noticed jars and cartons that had been sitting in the refrigerator or cabinet for months.

"I thought this would be a good time to cut down on fatty things," she said.

"Why now especially?"

"This is a time for discipline, mental toughness. We're practically at the edge."

"I think it's interesting that you regard a possible disaster for yourself, your family, and thousands of other people as an opportunity to cut down on fatty foods."

"You take discipline where you can find it," she said. "If I don't eat my yogurt now, I may as well stop buying the stuff forever. Except I think I'll skip the wheat germ."

The brand name was foreign-looking. I picked up the jar of wheat germ and examined the label closely.

"It's German," I told her. "Eat it."

There were people in pajamas and slippers. A man with a rifle slung over his shoulder. Kids crawling into sleeping bags. Babette gestured, wanting me to lean closer.

"Let's keep the radio turned off," she whispered. "So the girls can't hear. They haven't gotten beyond *déjà vu*. I want to keep it that way."

"What if the symptoms are real?"

"How could they be real?"

"Why couldn't they be real?"

---

3. Christian denomination founded in America by Charles Taze Russell in the 1870s. Practitioners are known for their door-to-door evangelism and belief that the end of the world is near.

"They get them only when they're broadcast," she whispered.

"Did Steffie hear about *déjà vu* on the radio?"

"She must have."

"How do you know? Were you with her when it was broadcast?"

"I'm not sure."

"Think hard."

"I can't remember."

"Do you remember telling her what *déjà vu* means?"

She spooned some yogurt out of the carton, seemed to pause, deep in thought.

"This happened before," she said finally.

"What happened before?"

"Eating yogurt, sitting here, talking about *déjà vu*."

"I don't want to hear this."

"The yogurt was on my spoon. I saw it in a flash. The whole experience. Natural, whole-milk, low-fat."

The yogurt was still on the spoon. I watched her put the spoon to her mouth, thoughtfully, trying to measure the action against the illusion of a matching original. From my squatting position I motioned her to lean closer.

"Heinrich seems to be coming out of his shell," I whispered.

"Where is he? I haven't seen him."

"See that knot of people? He's right in the middle. He's telling them what he knows about the toxic event."

"What does he know?"

"Quite a lot, it turns out."

"Why didn't he tell us?" she whispered.

"He's probably tired of us. He doesn't think it's worth his while to be funny and charming in front of his family. That's the way sons are. We represent the wrong kind of challenge."

"Funny and charming?"

"I guess he had it in him all the while. It was a question of finding the right time to exercise his gifts."

She moved closer, our heads almost touching.

"Don't you think you ought to go over there?" she said. "Let him see you in the crowd. Show him that his father is present at his big moment."

"He'll only get upset if he sees me in the crowd."

"Why?"

"I'm his father."

"So if you go over there, you'll ruin things by embarrassing him and cramping his style because of the father-son thing. And if you don't go over, he'll never know you saw him in his big moment and he'll think he has to behave in your presence the way he's always behaved, sort of peevishly and defensive, instead of in this new, delightful, and expansive manner."

"It's a double bind."

"What if I went over?" she whispered.

"He'll think I sent you."

"Would that be so awful?"

"He thinks I use you to get him to do what I want."

"There may be some truth in that, Jack. But then what are stepparents for if they can't be used in little skirmishes between blood relatives?"

I moved still closer, lowered my voice even more.

"Just a Life Saver,"[4] I said.

"What?"

"Just some saliva that you didn't know what to do with."

"It was a Life Saver," she whispered, making an O with her thumb and index finger.

"Give me one."

"It was the last one."

"What flavor—*quick*."

"Cherry."

I puckered my lips and made little sucking sounds. The black man with the tracts came over and squatted next to me. We engaged in an earnest and prolonged handshake. He studied me openly, giving the impression that he had traveled this rugged distance, uprooting his family, not to escape the chemical event but to find the one person who would understand what he had to say.

"It's happening everywhere, isn't it?"

"More or less," I said.

"And what's the government doing about it?"

"Nothing."

"You said it, I didn't. There's only one word in the language to describe what's being done and you found it exactly. I'm not surprised at all. But when you think about it, what *can* they do? Because what is coming is definitely coming. No government in the world is big enough to stop it. Does a man like yourself know the size of India's standing army?"

"One million."

"I didn't say it, you did. One million soldiers and they can't stop it. Do you know who's got the biggest standing army in the world?"

"It's either China or Russia, although the Vietnamese ought to be mentioned."

"Tell me this," he said. "Can the Vietnamese stop it?"

"No."

"It's here, isn't it? People feel it. We know in our bones. God's kingdom is coming."

He was a rangy man with sparse hair and a gap between his two front teeth. He squatted easily, seemed loose-jointed and comfortable. I realized he was wearing a suit and tie with running shoes.

"Are these great days?" he said.

I studied his face, trying to find a clue to the right answer.

"Do you feel it coming? Is it on the way? Do you *want* it to come?"

He bounced on his toes as he spoke.

"Wars, famines, earthquakes, volcanic eruptions. It's all beginning to jell. In your own words, is there anything that can stop it from coming once it picks up momentum?"

"No."

"You said it, I didn't. Floods, tornados, epidemics of strange new diseases. Is it a sign? Is it the truth? Are you ready?"

---

4. Jack had caught Babette taking an experimental pill meant to cure the fear of death; she claimed she was swallowing a Life Saver candy or saliva. Jack also wants a supply of these pills.

"Do people really feel it in their bones?" I said.

"Good news travels fast."

"Do people talk about it? On your door-to-door visits, do you get the impression they want it?"

"It's not do they want it. It's where do I go to sign up. It's get me out of here right now. People ask, 'Is there seasonal change in God's kingdom?' They ask, 'Are there bridge tolls and returnable bottles?' In other words I'm saying they're getting right down to it."

"You feel it's a ground swell."

"A sudden gathering. Exactly put. I took one look and I knew. This is a man who understands."

"Earthquakes are not up, statistically."

He gave me a condescending smile. I felt it was richly deserved, although I wasn't sure why. Maybe it was prissy to be quoting statistics in the face of powerful beliefs, fears, desires.

"How do you plan to spend your resurrection?" he said, as though asking about a long weekend coming up.

"We all get one?"

"You're either among the wicked or among the saved. The wicked get to rot as they walk down the street. They get to feel their own eyes slide out of their sockets. You'll know them by their stickiness and lost parts. People tracking slime of their own making. All the flashiness of Armageddon is in the rotting. The saved know each other by their neatness and reserve. He doesn't have showy ways is how you know a saved person."

He was a serious man, he was matter-of-fact and practical, down to his running shoes. I wondered about his eerie self-assurance, his freedom from doubt. Is this the point of Armageddon? No ambiguity, no more doubt. He was ready to run into the next world. He was forcing the next world to seep into my consciousness, stupendous events that seemed matter-of-fact to him, self-evident, reasonable, imminent, true. I did not feel Armageddon in my bones but I worried about all those people who did, who were ready for it, wishing hard, making phone calls and bank withdrawals. If enough people want it to happen, will it happen? How many people are enough people? Why are we talking to each other from this aboriginal crouch?

He handed me a pamphlet called "Twenty Common Mistakes About the End of the World." I struggled out of the squatting posture, feeling dizziness and back-pain. At the front of the hall a woman was saying something about exposure to toxic agents. Her small voice was almost lost in the shuffling roar of the barracks, the kind of low-level rumble that humans routinely make in large enclosed places. Denise had put down her reference work and was giving me a hard-eyed look. It was the look she usually saved for her father and his latest loss of foothold.

"What's wrong?" I said to her.

"Didn't you hear what the voice said?"

"Exposure."

"That's right," she said sharply.

"What's that got to do with us?"

"Not us," she said. "You."

"Why me?"

"Aren't you the one who got out of the car to fill the gas tank?"

"Where was the airborne event when I did that?"

"Just ahead of us. Don't you remember? You got back in the car and we went a little ways and then there it was in all those lights."

"You're saying when I got out of the car, the cloud may have been close enough to rain all over me."

"It's not your fault," she said impatiently, "but you were practically right in it for about two and a half minutes."

I made my way up front. Two lines were forming. A to M and N to Z. At the end of each line was a folding table with a microcomputer on it. Technicians milled about, men and women with lapel badges and color-coded armbands. I stood behind the life-jacket-wearing family. They looked bright, happy, and well-drilled. The thick orange vests did not seem especially out of place even though we were on more or less dry land, well above sea level, many miles from the nearest ominous body of water. Stark upheavals bring out every sort of quaint aberration by the very suddenness of their coming. Dashes of color and idiosyncrasy marked the scene from beginning to end.

The lines were not long. When I reached the A-to-M desk, the man seated there typed out data on his keyboard. My name, age, medical history, so on. He was a gaunt young man who seemed suspicious of conversation that strayed outside certain unspecified guidelines. Over the left sleeve on his khaki jacket he wore a green armband bearing the word SIMUVAC.

I related the circumstances of my presumed exposure.

"How long were you out there?"

"Two and a half minutes," I said. "Is that considered long or short?"

"Anything that puts you in contact with actual emissions means we have a situation."

"Why didn't the drifting cloud disperse in all that wind and rain?"

"This is not your everyday cirrus. This is a high-definition event. It is packed with dense concentrations of byproduct. You could almost toss a hook in there and tow it out to sea, which I'm exaggerating to make a point."

"What about people in the car? I had to open the door to get out and get back in."

"There are known degrees of exposure. I'd say their situation is they're minimal risks. It's the two and a half minutes standing right in it that makes me wince. Actual skin and orifice contact. This is Nyodene D. A whole new generation of toxic waste. What we call state of the art. One part per million million can send a rat into a permanent state."

He regarded me with the grimly superior air of a combat veteran. Obviously he didn't think much of people whose complacent and overprotected lives did not allow for encounters with brain-dead rats. I wanted this man on my side. He had access to data. I was prepared to be servile and fawning if it would keep him from dropping casually shattering remarks about my degree of exposure and chances for survival.

"That's quite an armband you've got there. What does SIMUVAC mean? Sounds important."

"Short for simulated evacuation. A new state program they're still battling over funds for."

"But this evacuation isn't simulated. It's real."

"We know that. But we thought we could use it as a model."

"A form of practice? Are you saying you saw a chance to use the real event in order to rehearse the simulation?"

"We took it right into the streets."

"How is it going?" I said.

"The insertion curve isn't as smooth as we would like. There's a probability excess. Plus which we don't have our victims laid out where we'd want them if this was an actual simulation. In other words we're forced to take our victims as we find them. We didn't get a jump on computer traffic. Suddenly it just spilled out, three-dimensionally, all over the landscape. You have to make allowances for the fact that everything we see tonight is real. There's a lot of polishing we still have to do. But that's what this exercise is all about."

"What about the computers? Is that real data you're running through the system or is it just practice stuff?"

"You watch," he said.

He spent a fair amount of time tapping on the keys and then studying coded responses on the data screen—a considerably longer time, it seemed to me, than he'd devoted to the people who'd preceded me in line. In fact I began to feel that others were watching me. I stood with my arms folded, trying to create a picture of an impassive man, someone in line at a hardware store waiting for the girl at the register to ring up his heavy-duty rope. It seemed the only way to neutralize events, to counteract the passage of computerized dots that registered my life and death. Look at no one, reveal nothing, remain still. The genius of the primitive mind is that it can render human helplessness in noble and beautiful ways.

"You're generating big numbers," he said, peering at the screen.

"I was out there only two and a half minutes. That's how many seconds?"

"It's not just you were out there so many seconds. It's your whole data profile. I tapped into your history. I'm getting bracketed numbers with pulsing stars."

"What does that mean?"

"You'd rather not know."

He made a silencing gesture as if something of particular morbid interest was appearing on the screen. I wondered what he meant when he said he'd tapped into my history. Where was it located exactly? Some state or federal agency, some insurance company or credit firm or medical clearinghouse? What history was he referring to? I'd told him some basic things. Height, weight, childhood diseases. What else did he know? Did he know about my wives, my involvement with Hitler, my dreams and fears?[5]

He had a skinny neck and jug-handle ears to go with his starved skull— the innocent prewar look of a rural murderer.

"Am I going to die?"

"Not as such," he said.

"What do you mean?"

"Not in so many words."

"How many words does it take?"

"It's not a question of words. It's a question of years. We'll know more in fifteen years. In the meantime we definitely have a situation."

5. Jack has been married five times to four different women; his academic field is called Hitler Studies.

"What will we know in fifteen years?"

"If you're still alive at the time, we'll know that much more than we do now. Nyodene D. has a life span of thirty years. You'll have made it halfway through."

"I thought it was forty years."

"Forty years in the soil. Thirty years in the human body."

"So, to outlive this substance, I will have to make it into my eighties. Then I can begin to relax."

"Knowing what we know at this time."

"But the general consensus seems to be that we don't know enough at this time to be sure of anything."

"Let me answer like so. If I was a rat I wouldn't want to be anywhere within a two hundred mile radius of the airborne event."

"What if you were a human?"

He looked at me carefully. I stood with my arms folded, staring over his head toward the front door of the barracks. To look at him would be to declare my vulnerability.

"I wouldn't worry about what I can't see or feel," he said. "I'd go ahead and live my life. Get married, settle down, have kids. There's no reason you can't do these things, knowing what we know."

"But you said we have a situation."

"I didn't say it. The computer did. The whole system says it. It's what we call a massive data-base tally. Gladney, J. A. K. I punch in the name, the substance, the exposure time and then I tap into your computer history. Your genetics, your personals, your medicals, your psychologicals, your police-and-hospitals. It comes back pulsing stars. This doesn't mean anything is going to happen to you as such, at least not today or tomorrow. It just means you are the sum total of your data. No man escapes that."

"And this massive so-called tally is not a simulation despite that armband you're wearing. It is real."

"It is real," he said.

I stood absolutely still. If they thought I was already dead, they might be inclined to leave me alone. I think I felt as I would if a doctor had held an X-ray to the light showing a star-shaped hole at the center of one of my vital organs. Death has entered. It is inside you. You are said to be dying and yet are separate from the dying, can ponder it at your leisure, literally see on the X-ray photograph or computer screen the horrible alien logic of it all. It is when death is rendered graphically, is televised so to speak, that you sense an eerie separation between your condition and yourself. A network of symbols has been introduced, an entire awesome technology wrested from the gods. It makes you feel like a stranger in your own dying.

I wanted my academic gown[6] and dark glasses.

When I got back to the other end of the barracks, the three younger children were asleep, Heinrich was making notations on a road map and Babette was seated some distance away with Old Man Treadwell and a number of other blind people. She was reading to them from a small and brightly colored stack of supermarket tabloids.

---

6. The ceremonial robe whose color and style indicates the level, subject, and often the place, of the wearer's education; the robes are worn by scholars during commencement and other ritual occasions.

I needed a distraction. I found a camp chair and set it near the wall behind Babette. There were four blind people, a nurse and three sighted people arranged in a semicircle facing the reader. Others occasionally paused to listen to an item or two, then moved on. Babette employed her storytelling voice, the same sincere and lilting tone she used when she read fairy tales to Wilder or erotic passages to her husband in their brass bed high above the headlong traffic hum.

She reported a front-page story. "Life After Death Guaranteed with Bonus Coupons." Then turned to the designated page.

"Scientists at Princeton's famed Institute for Advanced Studies have stunned the world by presenting absolute and undeniable proof of life after death. A researcher at the world-renowned Institute has used hypnosis to induce hundreds of people to recall their previous-life experiences as pyramid-builders, exchange students, and extraterrestrials."

Babette changed her voice to do dialogue.

"'In the last year alone,' declares reincarnation hypnotist Ling Ti Wan, 'I have helped hundreds to regress to previous lives under hypnosis. One of my most amazing subjects was a woman who was able to recall her life as a hunter-gatherer in the Mesolithic era ten thousand years ago. It was remarkable to hear this tiny senior citizen in polyester slacks describe her life as a hulking male chieftain whose band inhabited a peat bog and hunted wild boar with primitive bow and arrow. She was able to identify features of that era which only a trained archaeologist could know about. She even spoke several phrases in the language of that day, a tongue remarkably similar to modern-day German.'"

Babette's voice resumed its tone of straight narration.

"Dr. Shiv Chatterjee, fitness guru and high-energy physicist, recently stunned a live TV audience by relating the well-documented case of two women, unknown to each other, who came to him for regression in the same week, only to discover that they had been twin sisters in the lost city of Atlantis fifty thousand years ago. Both women describe the city, before its mysterious and catastrophic plunge into the sea, as a clean and well-run municipality where you could walk safely almost any time of day or night. Today they are food stylists for NASA.[7]

"Even more startling is the case of five-year-old Patti Weaver who has made convincing claims to Dr. Chatterjee that in her previous-life experience she was the secret KGB[8] assassin responsible for the unsolved murders of famed personalities Howard Hughes, Marilyn Monroe, and Elvis Presley. Known in international espionage circles as 'the Viper' for the deadly and untraceable venom he injected into the balls of the feet of his celebrity victims, the assassin died in a fiery Moscow helicopter crash just hours before little Patti Weaver was born in Popular Mechanics, Iowa. She not only has the same bodily markings as the Viper but seems to have a remarkable knack for picking up Russian words and phrases.

"'I regressed this subject at least a dozen times,' says Dr. Chatterjee. 'I used the toughest professional techniques to get her to contradict herself.

7. National Aeronautics and Space Administration, the government agency responsible for space exploration.
8. Komitet Gosudarstvennoy Bezopasnosti (KGB)

or "Committee for State Security," the Soviet Union's secretive national spy and security agency, in operation from the 1950s through the 1980s.

But her story is remarkably consistent. It is a tale of the good that can come from evil.' Says little Patti, 'At the moment of my death as the Viper, I saw a glowing circle of light. It seemed to welcome me, to beckon. It was a warm spiritual experience. I just walked right toward it. I was not sad at all.'"

Babette did the voices of Dr. Chatterjee and Patti Weaver. Her Chatterjee was a warm and mellow Indian-accented English, with clipped phrasing. She did Patti as a child-hero in a contemporary movie, the only person on screen who is unawed by mysterious throbbing phenomena.

"In a further startling development it was revealed by little Patti that the three supercelebrities were murdered for the same astonishing reason. Each of them at the time of his or her death was in secret possession of the Holy Shroud of Turin,[9] famed for its sacred curative powers. Entertainers Elvis and Marilyn were drink-and-drug nightmare victims and secretly hoped to restore spiritual and bodily calm to their lives by actually drying themselves with the Holy Shroud after pore-cleansing sessions in the sauna. Multifaceted billionaire Howard Hughes suffered from stop-action blink syndrome, a bizarre condition which prevented his eyes from reopening for hours after a simple blink, and he obviously hoped to utilize the amazing power of the Shroud until the Viper intervened with a swift injection of phantom venom. Patti Weaver has further revealed under hypnosis that the KGB has long sought possession of the Shroud of Turin on behalf of the rapidly aging and pain-racked members of the Politburo, the famed executive committee of the Communist Party. Possession of the Shroud is said to be the real motive behind the attempted assassination of Pope John Paul II at the Vatican—an attempt that failed only because the Viper had already died in a horror helicopter crash and been reborn as a freckle-faced girl in Iowa.

"The no-risk bonus coupon below gives you guaranteed access to dozens of documented cases of life after death, everlasting life, previous-life experiences, posthumous life in outer space, transmigration of souls, and personalized resurrection through stream-of-consciousness computer techniques."

I studied the faces in the semicircle. No one seemed amazed by this account. Old Man Treadwell lit a cigarette, impatient with his own trembling hand, forced to shake out the flame before it burned him. There was no interest shown in discussion, The story occupied some recess of passive belief. There it was, familiar and comforting in its own strange way, a set of statements no less real than our daily quota of observable household fact. Even Babette in her tone of voice betrayed no sign of skepticism or condescension. Surely I was in no position to feel superior to these elderly listeners, blind or sighted. Little Patti's walk toward the warm welcoming glow found me in a weakened and receptive state. I wanted to believe at least this part of the tale.

Babette read an ad. The Stanford Linear Accelerator 3-Day Particle-Smashing Diet.

She picked up another tabloid. The cover story concerned the country's leading psychics and their predictions for the coming year. She read the items slowly.

9. A linen cloth, bearing the likeness of the front and back of a man's face and body marked with the wounds of crucifixion, that is believed by some to be the cloth that wrapped the body of Jesus following his death on the cross.

"Squadrons of UFOs will invade Disney World and Cape Canaveral.[1] In a startling twist, the attack will be revealed as a demonstration of the folly of war, leading to a nuclear test-ban treaty between the U.S. and Russia.

"The ghost of Elvis Presley will be seen taking lonely walks at dawn around Graceland, his musical mansion.

"A Japanese consortium will buy Air Force One[2] and turn it into a luxury flying condominium with midair refueling privileges and air-to-surface missile capability.

"Bigfoot will appear dramatically at a campsite in the rugged and scenic Pacific Northwest. The hairy, upright man-beast, who stands eight feet tall and may be evolution's missing link, will gently welcome tourists to gather around him, revealing himself to be an apostle of peace.

"UFOs will raise the lost city of Atlantis from its watery grave in the Caribbean by telekinetic means and the help of powerful cables with properties not known in earthlike materials. The result will be a 'city of peace' where money and passports are totally unknown.

"The spirit of Lyndon B. Johnson[3] will contact CBS executives to arrange an interview on live TV in order to defend itself against charges made in recent books.

"Beatle assassin Mark David Chapman[4] will legally change his name to John Lennon and begin a new career as a rock lyricist from his prison cell on murderer's row.

"Members of an air-crash cult will hijack a jumbo jet and crash it into the White House in an act of blind devotion to their mysterious and reclusive leader, known only as Uncle Bob. The President and First Lady will miraculously survive with minor cuts, according to close friends of the couple.

"Dead multibillionaire Howard Hughes will mysteriously appear in the sky over Las Vegas.

"Wonder drugs mass-produced aboard UFO pharmaceutical labs in the weightless environment of space will lead to cures for anxiety, obesity, and mood swings.

"From beyond the grave, dead living legend John Wayne will communicate telepathically with President Reagan[5] to help frame U.S. foreign policy. Mellowed by death, the strapping actor will advocate a hopeful policy of peace and love.

"Sixties superkiller Charles Manson will break out of prison and terrorize the California countryside for weeks before negotiating a surrender on live TV in the offices of International Creative Management.[6]

"Earth's only satellite, the moon, will explode on a humid night in July, playing havoc with tides and raining dirt and debris over much of our

1. Cape Canaveral, Florida; location of the John F. Kennedy Space Center.
2. The plane that carries the president of the United States.
3. Lyndon B. Johnson (1908–1973), 36th president of the United States (1963–69).
4. Mark David Chapman shot and killed the musician John Lennon, founding member of the Beatles, outside Lennon's apartment in New York City on December 8, 1980.
5. Ronald Reagan (1911–2004), 40th president of the United States (1981–89). He had been a well-

known film and television actor from the 1930s to the late '60s. John Wayne (1907–1979), American movie actor famed for his roles in Westerns.
6. A talent agency with offices in Los Angeles, New York, Washington, D.C., and London. "Manson": Charles Manson (b. 1934), leader of the Manson Family, a cult he founded in California in the late 1960s. Manson was convicted in 1971 of conspiracy to murder seven people; these and other murders were carried out on his orders by members of his cult.

planet. But UFO cleanup crews will help avert a worldwide disaster, signalling an era of peace and harmony."

I watched the audience. Folded arms, heads slightly tilted. The predictions did not seem reckless to them. They were content to exchange brief and unrelated remarks, as during a break for a commercial on TV. The tabloid future, with its mechanism of a hopeful twist to apocalyptic events, was perhaps not so very remote from our own immediate experience. Look at us, I thought. Forced out of our homes, sent streaming into the bitter night, pursued by a toxic cloud, crammed together in makeshift quarters, ambiguously death-sentenced. We'd become part of the public stuff of media disaster. The small audience of the old and blind recognized the predictions of the psychics as events so near to happening that they had to be shaped in advance to our needs and wishes. Out of some persistent sense of large-scale ruin, we kept inventing hope.

Babette read an ad for diet sunglasses. The old people listened with interest. I went back to our area. I wanted to be near the children, watch them sleep. Watching children sleep makes me feel devout, part of a spiritual system. It is the closest I can come to God. If there is a secular equivalent of standing in a great spired cathedral with marble pillars and streams of mystical light slanting through two-tier Gothic windows, it would be watching children in their little bedrooms fast asleep. Girls especially.

Most of the lights were out now. The barracks roar had subsided. People were settling in. Heinrich was still awake, sitting on the floor, fully dressed, his back to the wall, reading a Red Cross resuscitation manual. He was not, in any case, a child whose lustrous slumber brought me peace. A restless, teeth-grinding, and erratic sleeper, the boy sometimes fell from his bed, to be found in a fetal bundle by early light, shivering on the hardwood floor.

"They seem to have things under control," I said.

"Who?"

"Whoever's in charge out there."

"Who's in charge?"

"Never mind."

"It's like we've been flung back in time," he said. "Here we are in the Stone Age, knowing all these great things after centuries of progress but what can we do to make life easier for the Stone Agers? Can we make a refrigerator? Can we even explain how it works? What is electricity? What is light? We experience these things every day of our lives but what good does it do if we find ourselves hurled back in time and we can't even tell people the basic principles much less actually make something that would improve conditions. Name one thing you could make. Could you make a simple wooden match that you could strike on a rock to make a flame? We think we're so great and modern. Moon landings, artificial hearts. But what if you were hurled into a time warp and came face to face with the ancient Greeks. The Greeks invented trigonometry. They did autopsies and dissections. What could you tell an ancient Greek that he couldn't say, 'Big deal.' Could you tell him about the atom? Atom is a Greek word. The Greeks knew that the major events in the universe can't be seen by the eye of man. It's waves, it's rays, it's particles."

"We're doing all right."

"We're sitting in this huge moldy room. It's like we're flung back."

"We have heat, we have light."

"These are Stone Age things. They had heat and light. They had fire. They rubbed flints together and made sparks. Could you rub flints together? Would you know a flint if you saw one? If a Stoner Ager asked you what a nucleotide is, could you tell him? How do we make carbon paper?[7] What is glass? If you came awake tomorrow in the Middle Ages and there was an epidemic raging, what could you do to stop it, knowing what you know about the progress of medicines and diseases? Here it is practically the twenty-first century and you've read hundreds of books and magazines and seen a hundred TV shows about science and medicine. Could you tell those people one little crucial thing that might save a million and a half lives?"

"'Boil your water,' I'd tell them."

"Sure. What about 'Wash behind your ears.' That's about as good."

"I still think we're doing fairly well. There was no warning. We have food, we have radios."

"What is a radio? What is the principle of a radio? Go ahead, explain. You're sitting in the middle of this circle of people. They use pebble tools. They eat grubs. Explain a radio."

"There's no mystery. Powerful transmitters send signals. They travel through the air, to be picked up by receivers."

"They travel through the air. What, like birds? Why not tell them magic? They travel through the air in magic waves. What is a nucleotide? You don't know, do you? Yet these are the building blocks of life. What good is knowledge if it just floats in the air? It goes from computer to computer. It changes and grows every second of every day. But nobody actually knows anything."

"You know something. You know about Nyodene D. I saw you with those people."

"That was a one-time freak," he told me.

He went back to his reading. I decided to get some air. Outside there were several groups of people standing around fires in fifty-five-gallon drums. A man sold soft drinks and sandwiches from an open-sided vehicle. Parked nearby were school buses, motorcycles, smallish vans called ambulettes. I walked around a while. There were people asleep in cars, others pitching tents. Beams of light swung slowly through the woods, searching out sounds, calm voices calling. I walked past a carload of prostitutes from Iron City. The interior light was on, the faces occupied the windows. They resembled the checkout women at the supermarket, blondish, double-chinned, resigned. A man leaned against the front door on the driver's side, speaking through a small opening in the window, his breath showing white. A radio said: "Hog futures[8] have declined in sympathy, adding bearishness to that market."

I realized the man talking to the prostitutes was Murray Jay Siskind. I walked over there, waited for him to finish his sentence before addressing him. He took off his right glove to shake my hand. The car window went up.

"I thought you were in New York for the term break."

---

7. A special kind of paper coated on one side with solid ink, used for making copies of documents produced on a typewriter.

8. Financial contract in which the price of a certain good (hogs) is agreed upon today, with the sale taking place in the future at the agreed-upon price. Profits depend upon what happens to the good's value between contract and sale.

"I came back early to look at car-crash movies. Alfonse arranged a week of screenings to help me prepare for my seminar. I was on the airport bus heading in from Iron City when sirens started blowing. The driver didn't have much choice but to follow the traffic out here."

"Where are you spending the night?"

"The whole bus was assigned to one of the outbuildings. I heard a rumor about painted women and came out to investigate. One of them is dressed in leopard loungewear under her coat. She showed me. Another one says she has a snap-off crotch. What do you think she means by that? I'm a little worried, though, about all these outbreaks of life-style diseases. I carry a reinforced ribbed condom at all times. One size fits all. But I have a feeling it's not much protection against the intelligence and adaptability of the modern virus."

"The women don't seem busy," I said.

"I don't think this is the kind of disaster that leads to sexual abandon. One or two fellows might come skulking out eventually but there won't be an orgiastic horde, not tonight anyway."

"I guess people need time to go through certain stages."

"It's obvious," he said.

I told him I'd spent two and a half minutes exposed to the toxic cloud. Then I summarized the interview I'd had with the SIMUVAC man.

"That little breath of Nyodene has planted a death in my body. It is now official, according to the computer. I've got death inside me. It's just a question of whether or not I can outlive it. It has a life span of its own. Thirty years. Even if it doesn't kill me in a direct way, it will probably outlive me in my own body. I could die in a plane crash and the Nyodene D. would be thriving as my remains were laid to rest."

"This is the nature of modern death," Murray said. "It has a life independent of us. It is growing in prestige and dimension. It has a sweep it never had before. We study it objectively. We can predict its appearance, trace its path in the body. We can take cross-section pictures of it, tape its tremors and waves. We've never been so close to it, so familiar with its habits and attitudes. We know it intimately. But it continues to grow, to acquire breadth and scope, new outlets, new passages and means. The more we learn, the more it grows. Is this some law of physics? Every advance in knowledge and technique is matched by a new kind of death, a new strain. Death adapts, like a viral agent. Is it a law of nature? Or some private superstition of mine? I sense that the dead are closer to us than ever. I sense that we inhabit the same air as the dead. Remember Lao Tse.[9] There is no difference between the quick and the dead. They are one channel of vitality.' He said this six hundred years before Christ. It is true once again, perhaps more true than ever."

He placed his hands on my shoulders and looked sadly into my face. He told me in the simplest words how sorry he was about what had happened. He talked to me about the likelihood of a computer error. Computers make mistakes, he said. Carpet static can cause a mistake. Some lint or hair in the circuits. He didn't believe this and neither did I. But he spoke convincingly, his eyes filled with spontaneous emotion, a broad and profound feeling.

9. Chinese Taoist poet and philosopher (571–531 B.C.E.).

I felt oddly rewarded. His compassion was equal to the occasion, an impressive pity and grief. The bad news was almost worth it.

"Ever since I was in my twenties, I've had the fear, the dread. Now it's been realized. I feel enmeshed, I feel deeply involved. It's no wonder they call this thing the airborne toxic event. It's an event all right. It marks the end of uneventful things. This is just the beginning. Wait and see."

A talk-show host said: "You are on the air." The fires burned in the oil drums. The sandwich vendor closed down his van.

"Any episodes of *déjà vu* in your group?"

"Wife and daughter," I said.

"There's a theory about *déjà vu*."

"I don't want to hear it."

"Why do we think these things happened before? Simple. They did happen before, in our minds, as visions of the future. Because these are precognitions, we can't fit the material into our system of consciousness as it is now structured. This is basically supernatural stuff. We're seeing into the future but haven't learned how to process the experience. So it stays hidden until the precognition comes true, until we come face to face with the event. Now we are free to remember it, to experience it as familiar material."

"Why are so many people having these episodes now?"

"Because death is in the air," he said gently. "It is liberating suppressed material. It is getting us closer to things we haven't learned about ourselves. Most of us have probably seen our own death but haven't known how to make the material surface. Maybe when we die, the first thing we'll say is, 'I know this feeling. I was here before.'"

He put his hands back on my shoulders, studied me with renewed and touching sadness. We heard the prostitutes call out to someone.

"I'd like to lose interest in myself," I told Murray. "Is there any chance of that happening?"

"None. Better men have tried."

"I guess you're right."

"It's obvious."

"I wish there was something I could do. I wish I could out-think the problem."

"Work harder on your Hitler," he said.

I looked at him. How much did he know?

The car window opened a crack. One of the women said to Murray, "All right, I'll do it for twenty-five."

"Have you checked with your representative?" he said.

She rolled down the window to peer at him. She had the opaque look of a hair-curlered woman on the evening news whose house had been buried in mud.

"You know who I mean," Murray said. "The fellow who sees to your emotional needs in return for one hundred percent of your earnings. The fellow you depend on to beat you up when you're bad."

"Bobby? He's in Iron City, keeping out of the cloud. He doesn't like to expose himself unless it's absolutely necessary."

The women laughed, six heads bobbing. It was insider's laughter, a little overdone, meant to identify them as people bound together in ways not easily appreciated by the rest of us.

A second window opened half an inch, a bright mouth appeared. "The type pimp Bobby is, he likes to use his mind."

A second round of laughter. We weren't sure whether it was at Bobby's expense, or ours, or theirs. The windows went up.

"It's none of my business," I said, "but what is it she's willing to do with you for twenty-five dollars?"

"The Heimlich maneuver."[1]

I studied the part of his face that lay between the touring cap and beard. He seemed deep in thought, gazing at the car. The windows were fogged, the women's heads capped in cigarette smoke.

"Of course we'd have to find a vertical space," he said absently.

"You don't really expect her to lodge a chunk of food in her windpipe."

He looked at me, half startled. "What? No, no, that won't be necessary. As long as she makes gagging and choking sounds. As long as she sighs deeply when I jolt the pelvis. As long as she collapses helplessly backward into my life-saving embrace."

He took off his glove to shake my hand. Then he went over to the car to work out details with the woman in question. I watched him knock on the rear door. After a moment it opened and he squeezed into the back seat. I walked over to one of the oil drums. Three men and a woman stood around the fire, passing rumors back and forth.

Three of the live deer at the Kung Fu Palace were dead. The governor was dead, his pilot and co-pilot seriously injured after a crash landing in a shopping mall. Two of the men at the switching yard were dead, tiny acid burns visible in their Mylex suits. Packs of German shepherds, the Nyodene-sniffing dogs, had shed their parachutes and were being set loose in the affected communities. There was a rash of UFO sightings in the area. There was widespread looting by men in plastic sheets. Two looters were dead. Six National Guardsmen were dead, killed in a firefight that broke out after a racial incident. There were reports of miscarriages, babies born prematurely. There were sightings of additional billowing clouds.

The people who relayed these pieces of unverified information did so with a certain respectful dread, bouncing on their toes in the cold, arms crossed on their chests. They were fearful that the stories might be true but at the same time impressed by the dramatic character of things. The toxic event had released a spirit of imagination. People spun tales, others listened spellbound. There was a growing respect for the vivid rumor, the most chilling tale. We were no closer to believing or disbelieving a given story than we had been earlier. But there was a greater appreciation now. We began to marvel at our own ability to manufacture awe.

German shepherds. That was the reassuring news I took inside with me. The sturdy body, dense and darkish coat, fierce head, long lapping tongue. I pictured them prowling the empty streets, heavy-gaited, alert. Able to hear sounds we couldn't hear, able to sense changes in the flow of information. I saw them in our house, snouting into closets, tall ears pointed, a smell about them of heat and fur and stored power.

In the barracks almost everyone was sleeping. I made my way along a dim wall. The massed bodies lay in heavy rest, seeming to emit a single nasal

---

1. First-aid technique for dislodging an obstruction from the windpipe of someone who is choking.

sigh. Figures stirred; a wide-eyed Asian child watched me step among a dozen clustered sleeping bags. Colored lights skipped past my right ear. I heard a toilet flush.

Babette was curled on an air mattress, covered in her coat. My son slept sitting in a chair like some boozed commuter, head rolling on his chest. I carried a camp chair over to the cot where the younger children were. Then I sat there, leaning forward, to watch them sleep.

A random tumble of heads and dangled limbs. In those soft warm faces was a quality of trust so absolute and pure that I did not want to think it might be misplaced. There must be something, somewhere, large and grand and redoubtable enough to justify this shining reliance and implicit belief. A feeling of desperate piety swept over me. It was cosmic in nature, full of yearnings and reachings. It spoke of vast distances, awesome but subtle forces. These sleeping children were like figures in an ad for the Rosicrucians,[2] drawing a powerful beam of light from somewhere off the page. Steffie turned slightly, then muttered something in her sleep. It seemed important that I know what it was. In my current state, bearing the death impression of the Nyodene cloud, I was ready to search anywhere for signs and hints, intimations of odd comfort. I pulled my chair up closer. Her face in pouchy sleep might have been a structure designed solely to protect the eyes, those great, large and apprehensive things, prone to color phases and a darting alertness, to a perception of distress in others. I sat there watching her. Moments later she spoke again. Distinct syllables this time, not some dreamy murmur—but a language not quite of this world. I struggled to understand. I was convinced she was saying something, fitting together units of stable meaning. I watched her face, waited. Ten minutes passed. She uttered two clearly audible words, familiar and elusive at the same time, words that seemed to have a ritual meaning, part of a verbal spell or ecstatic chant.

Toyota Celica.

A long moment passed before I realized this was the name of an automobile. The truth only amazed me more. The utterance was beautiful and mysterious, gold-shot with looming wonder. It was like the name of an ancient power in the sky, tablet-carved in cuneiform.[3] It made me feel that something hovered. But how could this be? A simple brand name, an ordinary car. How could these near-nonsense words, murmured in a child's restless sleep, make me sense a meaning, a presence? She was only repeating some TV voice. Toyota Corolla, Toyota Celica, Toyota Cressida. Supranational names, computer-generated, more or less universally pronounceable. Part of every child's brain noise, the substatic regions too deep to probe. Whatever its source, the utterance struck me with the impact of a moment of splendid transcendence.

I depend on my children for that.

I sat a while longer, watching Denise, watching Wilder, feeling selfless and spiritually large. There was an empty air mattress on the floor but I wanted to

2. Originally a secretive anti-Catholic philosophical society, founded in Germany in the 17th century. Modern branches of the Rosicrucians, both Christian and Masonic, continue to propound secret knowledge and to recruit followers.

3. System of writing used in ancient Mesopotamia, with characters pressed into clay tablets.

share Babette's and eased myself next to her body, a dreaming mound. Her hands, feet, and face were drawn under the sheltering coat; only a burst of hair remained. I fell at once into marine oblivion, a deep-dwelling crablike consciousness, silent and dreamless.

1985

RUDOLFO ANAYA
b. 1937

L *lano* is a Spanish adjective meaning "plain, simple, even, smooth, level"; as a noun, its feminine form (*llana*) indicates a "mason's trowel," while the masculine, *llano*, signifies an area of plain, flat ground. On the eastern *llanos* of New Mexico, in the village of Pastura, Rudolfo Anaya was born. This high, arid, windy landscape figures in much of Anaya's fiction, suggesting the way that nature's trowel works incessantly to level out human effort. As a Hispanic American, the author can trace his ancestry back through four centuries of activity in this region. As critic Margarite Fernández Olmos notes, Anaya's parents' backgrounds combined both sides of the region's rural life: his mother's family were farmers growing crops and raising pigs, sheep, and cows in the Puerto de Luna valley, while his father was a free-ranging vaquero, a cowboy whose family tradition was to work with cattle herds in the open rather than settling the land. After Anaya's father was killed in an accident, his mother married another vaquero, who helped raise his stepson with an understanding of both farming and ranching lifestyles. When still a small child, Anaya moved with his family to the town of Santa Rosa, New Mexico—"the social hub of the surrounding rural communities," as Olmos describes it, where on busy Highway 66 Anaya could witness the transcontinental link between East Coast and West Coast cultures. Yet the nearby Pecos River and its opportunities for hunting and fishing let the author grow up in close proximity to nature, an experience he would appreciate for its spiritual dimensions. By age fifteen he and his family joined the urban migration that had begun in the years following World War II and moved to a barrio (Hispanic neighborhood) in Albuquerque. Here he learned the ways of big cities, another influence on his subsequent fiction. But an accident more typical of rural life directed his interests to literature: while diving into an irrigation ditch that he and his friends were using as a swimming hole, Anaya fractured two vertebrae in his neck and spent much of his seventeenth year recovering in a world of books and meditation. After a false start in business school he became an English major at the University of New Mexico, where he began writing fiction (for himself) and went on to earn M.A. degrees in English and in counseling, and then found work as a high school teacher and guidance counselor.

Bless Me, Ultima (1972) was Anaya's first novel, published to acclaim within the just-emerging network of the Chicano arts movement that would eventually include recognition of such writers as Rolando Hinojosa, Estella Portillo, Bernice Zamora, and Ricardo Sánchez. As a result of the book's success Anaya was appointed to a professorship at the University of New Mexico, where he taught until achieving emeritus status in 1993. In the novel, Ultima is a practitioner of folk-healing arts developed by women; she serves as mentor to the boy Antonio, who in the coming-of-age tradition of the *bildungsroman* (think *David Copperfield*, *A Portrait of the Artist as a Young Man*, *The Magic Mountain*) must make the choices that will define his adult life. In Antonio's case these conflicts reflect the alternatives of Anaya's boyhood: farming one's land or wandering as a vaquero, taking one's cultural lead from the Hispanic or the Anglo, and sorting out the gender biases in competing systems of religious belief. *Heart of Aztlán* (1976) and *Tortuga* (1979) complete what critics describe as a trilogy of Chicano novels, as the narrative action shifts from the countryside to the city and then to the experiences of a teenager recovering from a paralyzing accident. In all three works the author blends the modern with the ancient, the formalities of culture with folklorish roots, and the plainly discursive with the richly allegorical, producing narratives that proceed on many different levels all at one time.

"Dos," the second chapter of *Bless Me, Ultima*, displays Anaya's characteristic literary techniques, including the mix of Hispanic and Anglo references that helps create the Chicano experience—a condition of living in the borderland area that until 1848 was part of Mexico and that today retains many aspects of Mexican culture, including both Hispanic and Indian elements. In recent years his writing has expanded from autobiography to a more general social vision of Chicano life. *Alburquque* (1992)—the title reflects the original spelling of the city's name—follows the quest of a young boxer who must look beyond his adoptive family to find his roots. With *Zia Summer* (1995) Anaya writes a full-fledged detective novel, introducing a private eye named Sonny Baca, who seeks the murderer of a prominent politician's wife by sorting through the type of social and ethnic issues the author had treated previously in a more personal manner.

Other Sonny Baca novels have followed, all of them reminders of how far "Alburquque," the largest city in New Mexico, has come from its days as a frontier outpost (while retaining its mix of Spanish, Native American, and mestizo cultures).

The following text is from *Bless Me, Ultima* (1972).

From Bless Me, Ultima

Dos[1]

Ultima slipped easily into the routine of our daily life. The first day she put on her apron and helped my mother with breakfast, later she swept the house and then helped my mother wash our clothes in the old washing machine they pulled outside where it was cooler under the shade of the young elm trees. It was as if she had always been here. My mother was very happy because now she had someone to talk to and she didn't have to wait until Sunday when her women friends from the town came up the dusty path to sit in the sala[2] and visit.

Deborah and Theresa were happy because Ultima did many of the household chores they normally did, and they had more time to spend in the attic and cut out an interminable train of paper dolls which they dressed, gave names to, and most miraculously, made talk.

My father was also pleased. Now he had one more person to tell his dream to. My father's dream was to gather his sons around him and move westward to the land of the setting sun, to the vineyards of California. But the war had taken his three sons and it had made him bitter. He often got

---

1. Two (Spanish). 2. Living room (Spanish).

drunk on Saturday afternoons and then he would rave against old age, he would rage against the town on the opposite side of the river which drained a man of his freedom, and he would cry because the war had ruined his dream. It was very sad to see my father cry, but I understood it, because sometimes a man has to cry. Even if he is a man.

And I was happy with Ultima. We walked together in the llano[3] and along the river banks to gather herbs and roots for her medicines. She taught me the names of plants and flowers, of trees and bushes, of birds and animals; but most important, I learned from her that there was a beauty in the time of day and in the time of night, and that there was peace in the river and in the hills. She taught me to listen to the mystery of the groaning earth and to feel complete in the fulfillment of its time. My soul grew under her careful guidance.

I had been afraid of the awful *presence* of the river, which was the soul of the river, but through her I learned that my spirit shared in the spirit of all things. But the innocence which our isolation sheltered could not last forever, and the affairs of the town began to reach across our bridge and enter my life. Ultima's owl gave the warning that the time of peace on our hill was drawing to an end.

It was Saturday night. My mother had laid out our clean clothes for Sunday mass, and we had gone to bed early because we always went to early mass. The house was quiet, and I was in the mist of some dream when I heard the owl cry its warning. I was up instantly, looking through the small window at the dark figure that ran madly towards the house. He hurled himself at the door and began pounding.

"¡Márez!" he shouted, "¡Márez! ¡Ándale, hombre!"[4]

I was frightened, but I recognized the voice. It was Jasón's father.

"¡Un momento!" I heard my father call. He fumbled with the farol.[5]

"¡Ándale, hombre, ándale!" Chávez cried pitifully, "mataron a mi hermano—"[6]

"Ya vengo—"[7] My father opened the door and the frightened man burst in. In the kitchen I heard my mother moan, "Ave María Purísima, mis hijos—"[8] She had not heard Chávez' last words, and so she assumed the aviso[9] was one that brought bad news about her sons.

"Chávez, ¿qué pasa?"[1] My father held the trembling man.

"¡Mi hermano, mi hermano!" Chávez sobbed, "He has killed my brother!"

"¿Pero qué dices, hombre?"[2] my father exclaimed. He pulled Chávez into the hall and held up the farol. The light cast by the farol revealed the wild, frightened eyes of Chávez.

"¡Gabriel!" my mother cried and came forward, but my father pushed her back. He did not want her to see the monstrous mask of fear on the man's face.

"It is not our sons, it is something in town—get him some water."

"Lo mató, lo mató—"[3] Chávez repeated.

---

3. Plain (Spanish).
4. Come on, man (Spanish).
5. Lantern (Spanish). "Un momento": Just a minute (Spanish).
6. They killed my brother (Spanish).
7. I'm coming now (Spanish).
8. Hail Virgin Mary, my sons (Spanish).
9. Warning (Spanish).
1. Chávez, what's happening? (Spanish).
2. But what are you saying, man? (Spanish).
3. He killed him, he killed him (Spanish).

"Get hold of yourself, hombre, tell me what has happened!" My father shook Chávez and the man's sobbing subsided. He took the glass of water and drank, then he could talk.

"Reynaldo has just brought the news, my brother is dead," he sighed and slumped against the wall. Chávez' brother was the sheriff of the town. The man would have fallen if my father had not held him up.

"¡Madre de Dios![4] Who? How?"

"¡Lupito!" Chávez cried out. His face corded with thick veins. For the first time his left arm came up and I saw the rifle he held.

"Jesús, María y José,"[5] my mother prayed.

My father groaned and slumped against the wall. "Ay que Lupito," he shook his head, "the war[6] made him crazy—"

Chávez regained part of his composure. "Get your rifle, we must go to the bridge—"

"The bridge?"

"Reynaldo said to meet him there—The crazy bastard has taken to the river—"

My father nodded silently. He went to the bedroom and returned with his coat. While he loaded his rifle in the kitchen Chávez related what he knew.

"My brother had just finished his rounds," he gasped, "he was at the bus depot cafe, having coffee, sitting without a care in the world—and the bastard came up to where he sat and without warning shot him in the head—" His body shook as he retold the story.

"Perhaps it is better if you wait here, hombre," my father said with consolation.

"No!" Chávez shouted. "I must go. He was my brother!"

My father nodded. I saw him stand beside Chávez and put his arm around his shoulders. Now he too was armed. I had only seen him shoot the rifle when we slaughtered pigs in the fall. Now they were going armed for a man.

"Gabriel, be careful," my mother called as my father and Chávez slipped out into the dark.

"Sí,"[7] I heard him answer, then the screen door banged. "Keep the doors locked—" My mother went to the door and shut the latch. We never locked our doors, but tonight there was something strange and fearful in the air.

Perhaps this is what drew me out into the night to follow my father and Chávez down to the bridge, or perhaps it was some concern I had for my father. I do not know. I waited until my mother was in the sala then dressed and slipped downstairs. I glanced down the hall and saw candlelight flickering from the sala. That room was never entered unless there were Sunday visitors, or unless my mother took us in to pray novenas and rosaries for my brothers at war. I knew she was kneeling at her altar now, praying. I knew she would pray until my father returned.

I slipped out the kitchen door and into the night. It was cool. I sniffed the air, there was a tinge of autumn in it. I ran up the goat path until I caught sight of two dark shadows ahead of me. Chávez and my father.

---

4. Mother of God (Spanish).
5. Jesus, Mary, and Joseph (Spanish).
6. World War II. "Ay que Lupito": Oh, that Lupito

(Spanish).
7. Yes (Spanish).

We passed Fío's dark house and then the tall juniper tree that stood where the hill sloped down to the bridge. Even from this distance I could hear the commotion on the bridge. As we neared the bridge I was afraid of being discovered as I had no reason for being there. My father would be very angry. To escape detection I cut to the right and was swallowed up by the dark brush of the river. I pushed through the dense bosque[8] until I came to the bank of the river. From where I stood I could look up into the flooding beams of light that were pointed down by the excited men. I could hear them giving frenzied, shouted instructions. I looked to my left where the bridge started and saw my father and Chávez running towards the excitement at the center of the bridge.

My eyes were now accustomed to the dark, but it was a glint of light that made me turn and look at a clump of bullrushes in the sweeping water of the river just a few yards away. What I saw made my blood run cold. Crouched in the reeds and half submerged in the muddy waters lay the figure of Lupito, the man who had killed the sheriff. The glint of light was from the pistol he held in his hand.

It was frightening enough to come upon him so suddenly, but as I dropped to my knees in fright I must have uttered a cry because he turned and looked directly at me. At that same moment a beam of light found him and illuminated a face twisted with madness. I do not know if he saw me, or if the light cut off his vision, but I saw his bitter, contorted grin. As long as I live I will never forget those wild eyes, like the eyes of a trapped, savage animal.

At the same time someone shouted from the bridge, "There!" Then all the lights found the crouched figure. He jumped and I saw him as clear as if it were daylight.

"Ayeeeeee!" He screamed a blood curdling cry that echoed down the river. The men on the bridge didn't know what to do. They stood transfixed, looking down at the mad man waving the pistol in the air. "Ayeeeeeeee!" He cried again. It was a cry of rage and pain, and it made my soul sick. The cry of a tormented man had come to the peaceful green mystery of my river, and the great *presence* of the river watched from the shadows and deep recesses, as I watched from where I crouched at the bank.

"Japanese sol'jer, Japanese sol'jer!" he cried, "I am wounded. Come help me—" he called to the men on the bridge. The rising mist of the river swirled in the beams of spotlights. It was like a horrible nightmare.

Suddenly he leaped up and ran splashing through the water towards me. The lights followed him. He grew bigger, I heard his panting, the water his feet kicked up splashed on my face, and I thought he would run over me. Then as quickly as he had sprinted in my direction he turned and disappeared again into the dark clumps of reeds in the river. The lights moved in all directions, but they couldn't find him. Some of the lights swept over me and I trembled with fear that I would be found out, or worse, that I would be mistaken for Lupito and shot.

"The crazy bastard got away!" someone shouted on the bridge.

"Ayeeeeee!" the scream sounded again. It was a cry that I did not understand, and I am sure the men on the bridge did not either. The man they

8. Wood, forest (Spanish).

hunted had slipped away from human understanding; he had become a wild animal, and they were afraid.

"Damn!" I heard them cursing themselves. Then a car with a siren and flashing red light came on the bridge. It was Vigil, the state policeman who patrolled our town.

"Chávez is dead!" I heard him shout. "He never had a chance. His brains blown out—" There was silence.

"We have to kill him!" Jasón's father shouted. His voice was full of anger, rage and desperation.

"I have to deputize you—" Vigil started to say.

"The hell with deputizing!" Chávez shouted. "He killed my brother! ¡Está loco!"[9] The men agreed with their silence.

"Have you spotted him?" Vigil asked.

"Just now we saw him, but we lost him—"

"He's down there," someone added.

"He is an animal! He has to be shot!" Chávez cried out.

"¡Sí!" the men agreed.

"Now wait a moment—" It was my father who spoke. I do not know what he said because of the shouting. In the meantime I searched the dark of the river for Lupito. I finally saw him. He was about forty feet away, crouched in the reeds as before. The muddy waters of the river lapped and gurgled savagely around him. Before the night had been only cool, now it turned cold and I shivered. I was torn between a fear that made my body tremble, and a desire to help the poor man. But I could not move, I could only watch like a chained spectator.

"Márez is right!" I heard a booming voice on the bridge. In the lights I could make out the figure of Narciso. There was only one man that big and with that voice in town. I knew that Narciso was one of the old people from Las Pasturas, and that he was a good friend to my father. I knew they often drank together on Saturdays, and once or twice he had been to our house.

"¡Por Dios, hombres!"[1] he shouted, "let us act like men! That is not an animal down there, that is a man. Lupito. You all know Lupito. You know that the war made him sick—" But the men would not listen to Narciso. I guess it was because he was the town drunk, and they said he never did anything useful.

"Go back to your drinking and leave this job to men," one of them jeered at him.

"He killed the sheriff in cold blood," another added. I knew that the sheriff had been greatly admired.

"I am not drinking," Narciso persisted, "it is you men who are drunk for blood. You have lost your reason—"

"Reason!" Chávez countered. "What reason did he have for killing my brother. You know," he addressed the men, "my brother did no one harm. Tonight a mad animal crawled behind him and took his life. You call that reason! That animal has to be destroyed!"

"¡Sí! ¡Sí!" the men shouted in unison.

"At least let us try to talk to him," Narciso begged. I knew that it was hard for a man of the llano to beg.

9. He's crazy (Spanish).　　　　1. By God, men (Spanish).

"Yes," Vigil added, "perhaps he will give himself up—"

"Do you think he'll listen to talk!" Chávez jumped forward. "He's down there, and he still has the pistol that killed my brother! Go down and talk to him!" I could see Chávez shouting in Vigil's face, and Vigil said nothing. Chávez laughed. "This is the only talk he will understand—" he turned and fired over the railing of the bridge. His shots roared then whined away down the river. I could hear the bullets make splashing noises in the water.

"Wait!" Narciso shouted. He took Chávez' rifle and with one hand held it up. Chávez struggled against him but Narciso was too big and strong. "I will talk to him," Narciso said. He pushed Chávez back. "I understand your sorrow Chávez," he said, "but one killing is enough for tonight—" The men must have been impressed by his sincerity because they stood back and waited.

Narciso leaned over the concrete railing and shouted down into the darkness. "Hey Lupito! It is me, Narciso. It is me, hombre, your compadre. Listen my friend, a very bad business has happened tonight, but if we act like men we can settle it—Let me come down and talk to you, Lupito. Let me help you—"

I looked at Lupito. He had been watching the action on the bridge, but now as Narciso talked to him I saw his head slump on his chest. He seemed to be thinking. I prayed that he would listen to Narciso and that the angry and frustrated men on the bridge would not commit mortal sin. The night was very quiet. The men on the bridge awaited an answer. Only the lapping water of the river made a sound.

"¡Amigo!"[2] Narciso shouted, "You know I am your friend, I want to help you, hombre—" He laughed softly. "Hey, Lupito, you remember just a few years ago, before you went to the war, you remember the first time you came into the Eight Ball to gamble a little. Remember how I taught you how Juan Botas marked the aces with a little tobacco juice, and he thought you were green, but you beat him!" He laughed again. "Those were good times, Lupito, before the war came. Now we have this bad business to settle. But we are friends who will help you—"

I saw Lupito's tense body shake. A low, sad mournful cry tore itself from his throat and mixed into the lapping sound of the waters of the river. His head shook slowly, and I guess he must have been thinking and fighting between surrendering or remaining free, and hunted. Then like a coiled spring he jumped up, his pistol aimed straight up. There was a flash of fire and the loud report of the pistol. But he had not fired at Narciso or at any of the men on the bridge! The spotlights found him.

"There's your answer!" Chávez shouted.

"He's firing! He's firing!" Another voice shouted. "He's crazy!"

Lupito's pistol sounded again. Still he was not aiming at the men on the bridge. He was shooting to draw their fire!

"Shoot! Shoot!" someone on the bridge called.

"No, no," I whispered through clenched lips. But it was too late for anything. The frightened men responded by aiming their rifles over the side of the bridge. One single shot sounded then a barrage followed it like the roar of a canon, like the rumble of thunder in a summer thunderstorm.

2. Friend (Spanish).

Many shots found their mark. I saw Lupito lifted off his feet and hurled backward by the bullets. But he got up and ran limping and crying towards the bank where I lay.

"Bless me—" I thought he cried, and the second volley of shots from the bridge sounded, but this time they sounded like a great whirling of wings, like pigeons swirling to roost on the church top. He fell forward then clawed and crawled out of the holy water of the river onto the bank in front of me. I wanted to reach out and help him, but I was frozen by my fear. He looked up at me and his face was bathed in water and flowing, hot blood, but it was also dark and peaceful as it slumped into the sand of the riverbank. He made a strange gurgling sound in his throat, then he was still. Up on the bridge a great shout went up. The men were already running to the end of the bridge to come down and claim the man whose dead hands dug into the soft, wet sand in front of me.

I turned and ran. The dark shadows of the river enveloped me as I raced for the safety of home. Branches whipped at my face and cut it, and vines and tree trunks caught at my feet and tripped me. In my headlong rush I disturbed sleeping birds and their shrill cries and slapping wings hit at my face. The horror of darkness had never been so complete as it was for me that night.

I had started praying to myself from the moment I heard the first shot and I never stopped praying until I reached home. Over and over through my mind ran the words of the Act of Contrition. I had not yet been to catechism nor had I made my first holy communion, but my mother had taught me the Act of Contrition. It was to be said after one made his confession to the priest, and as the last prayer before death.

Did God listen? Would he hear? Had he seen my father on the bridge? And where was Lupito's soul winging to, or was it washing down the river to the fertile valley of my uncles' farms?

A priest could have saved Lupito. Oh why did my mother dream for me to be a priest! How would I ever wash away the stain of blood from the sweet waters of my river! I think at that time I began to cry because as I left the river brush and headed up the hills I heard my sobs for the first time.

It was also then that I heard the owl. Between my gasps for air and my sobs I stopped and listened for its song. My heart was pounding and my lungs hurt, but a calmness had come over the moonlit night when I heard the hooting of Ultima's owl. I stood still for a long time. I realized that the owl had been with me throughout the night. It had watched over all that had happened on the bridge. Suddenly the terrible, dark fear that had possessed me was gone.

I looked at the house that my father and my brothers had built on the juniper-patched hill; it was quiet and peaceful in the blue night. The sky sparkled with a million stars and the Virgin's horned moon, the moon of my mother's people, the moon of the Lunas.[3] My mother would be praying for the soul of Lupito.

Again the owl sang, Ultima's spirit bathed me with its strong resolution. I turned and looked across the river. Some lights shone in the town. In the

3. "Lunas": moons. "Virgin": Virgin Mary.

moonlight I could make out the tower of the church, the school house top, and way beyond the glistening of the town's water tank. I heard the soft wail of a siren and I knew the men would be pulling Lupito from the river.

The river's brown waters would be stained with blood, forever and ever and ever . . .

In the autumn I would have to go to the school in the town, and in a few years I would go to catechism lessons in the church. I shivered. My body began to hurt from the beating it had taken from the brush of the river. But what hurt more was that I had witnessed for the first time the death of a man.

My father did not like the town or its way. When we had first moved from Las Pasturas we had lived in a rented house in the town. But every evening after work he had looked across the river to these barren, empty hills, and finally he had bought a couple of acres and began building our house. Everyone told him he was crazy, that the rocky, wild hill could sustain no life, and my mother was more than upset. She wanted to buy along the river where the land was fertile and there was water for the plants and trees. But my father won the fight to be close to his llano, because truthfully our hill was the beginning of the llano, from here it stretched away as far as the eye could see, to Las Pasturas and beyond.

The men of the town had murdered Lupito. But he had murdered the sheriff. They said the war had made him crazy. The prayers for Lupito mixed into prayers for my brothers. So many different thoughts raced through my mind that I felt dizzy, and very weary and sick. I ran the last of the way and slipped quietly into the house. I groped for the stair railing in the dark and felt a warm hand take mine. Startled, I looked up into Ultima's brown, wrinkled face.

"You knew!" I whispered. I understood that she did not want my mother to hear.

"Sí," she replied.

"And the owl—" I gasped. My mind searched for answers, but my body was so tired that my knees buckled and I fell forward. As small and thin as Ultima was she had the strength to lift me in her arms and carry me into her room. She placed me on her bed and then by the light of a small, flickering candle she mixed one of her herbs in a tin cup, held it over the flame to warm, then gave it to me to drink.

"They killed Lupito," I said as I gulped the medicine.

"I know," she nodded. She prepared a new potion and with this she washed the cuts on my face and feet.

"Will he go to hell?" I asked.

"That is not for us to say, Antonio. The war-sickness was not taken out of him, he did not know what he was doing—"

"And the men on the bridge, my father!"

"Men will do what they must do," she answered. She sat on the bed by my side. Her voice was soothing, and the drink she had given me made me sleepy. The wild, frightening excitement in my body began to die.

"The ways of men are strange, and hard to learn," I heard her say.

"Will I learn them?" I asked. I felt the weight on my eyelids.

"You will learn much, you will see much," I heard her far-away voice. I felt a blanket cover me. I felt safe in the warm sweetness of the room. Outside the owl sang its dark questioning to the night, and I slept.

But even into my deep sleep my dreams came. In my dream I saw my three brothers. I saw them as I remembered them before they went away to war, which seemed so very long ago. They stood by the house that we rented in town and they looked across the river at the hills of the llano.

Father says that the town steals our freedom; he says that we must build a castle across the river, on the lonely hill of the mockingbirds. I think it was León who spoke first, he was the eldest, and his voice always had a sad note to it. But in the dark mist of the dream I could not be sure.

His heart has been heavy since we came to the town, the second figure spoke, his forefathers were men of the sea, the Márez people, they were conquistadores, men whose freedom was unbounded.

It was Andrew who said that! It was Andrew! I was sure because his voice was husky like his thick and sturdy body.

Father says the freedom of the wild horse is in the Márez blood, and his gaze is always westward. His fathers before him were vaqueros,[4] *and so he expects us to be men of the llano. I was sure the third voice belonged to Eugene.*

I longed to touch them. I was hungry for their company. Instead I spoke.

We must all gather around our father, I heard myself say. His dream is to ride westward in search of new adventure. He builds highways that stretch into the sun, and we must travel that road with him.

My brothers frowned. You are a Luna, they chanted in unison, you are to be a farmer-priest for mother!

The doves came to drink in the still pooh of the river and their cry was mournful in the darkness of my dream.

My brothers laughed. You are but a baby, Tony, you are our mother's dream. Stay and sleep to the doves cou-rou while we cross the mighty River of the Carp to build our father's castle in the hills.

I must go! I cried to the three dark figures. I must lift the muddy waters of the river in blessing to our new home!

Along the river the tormented cry of a lonely goddess filled the valley. The winding wail made the blood of men run cold.

It is la llorona,[5] *my brothers cried in fear, the old witch who cries along the river banks and seeks the blood of boys and men to drink!*

La llorona seeks the soul of Antonioooooooooo . . .

It is the soul of Lupito, they cried in fear, doomed to wander the river at night because the waters washed his soul away!

Lupito seeks his blessingggggggggg . . .

It is neither! I shouted. I swung the dark robe of the priest over my shoulders then lifted my hands in the air. The mist swirled around me and sparks flew when I spoke. It is the presence of the river!

Save us, my brothers cried and cowered at my words.

I spoke to the presence of the river and it allowed my brothers to cross with their carpenter tools to build our castle on the hill.

Behind us I heard my mother moan and cry because with each turning of the sun her son was growing old . . .

1972

---

4. Cowboys (Spanish).
5. A ghost (Spanish); in Chicana/o and Mexican lore, a spurned mistress who drowned her children and was fated to eternally seek their recovery.

THOMAS PYNCHON
b. 1937

Thomas Pynchon has remained the most private of contemporary American writers, without so much as a photograph of him in circulation. A few facts are known: born on Long Island, graduated from Cornell University—where he was a student in Vladimir Nabokov's European literature course—in the late 1950s, served a term in the navy, and now lives—it is said—in southern (or is it northern?) California. He appeared twice as a character with a paper bag over his head on the cartoon comedy show *The Simpsons*, in 2004, voicing himself. Beyond that, silence, which has been broken only by eight strange and distinctive novels, plus a few short stories.

"Entropy," one of Pynchon's first publications (1960), is printed here as an introduction to his work. Its thematics of an elusive order within radical disorder anticipates his first novel, *V.* (1963), particularly in its reference to modern physics. That complex novel cannot be understood by reference to convenient fictional signposts. Although it showed an indebtedness to Faulkner and Joyce (an indebtedness shared by most serious American novelists), Pynchon's style was already wholly his own. In writing that was by turns labyrinthine, eloquent, and colloquial, he showed a particular fondness for imitating and parodying various styles. But instead of disparaging or minimizing their subjects, these imitations and parodies radiated a generous exuberance that extended to the many characters who inhabit *V.* and whose individual paranoias—Pynchon's word to characterize attempts to make connections between events—propel them into unbelievably complicated and absurd plots. The interest of *V.* was largely in the inventiveness with which Pynchon developed those plots, which might involve anything from diplomatic spy stories in nineteenth-century Africa to the bombing of Malta during World War II to the surgical reconstruction of a young woman's nose to a hunt for alligators in New York City sewers.

The comic talent shown in various New York episodes from *V.* was also evident in *The Crying of Lot 49* (1966). This short, perfectly controlled novel teases us and itself with questions about the meaning of our American heritage, as embodied in the form of the mysterious legacy left to its heroine, Oedipa Maas. (The jokey yet portentous name exemplifies Pynchon's way of playing at "significance.") What is the connection between this legacy and the mysterious alternative to the U.S. Postal System on which Oedipa believes she has stumbled? Is there a secret network of alienated citizens carrying on their lives outside the ordinary systems and institutions of American life? Or is it all Oedipa's delusion, her private paranoia? These questions are considered through a style that continually surprises and unsettles us, though it is less discontinuous than *V.*'s. In Pynchon's world everything serious has its silly aspects (inspired by the Marx Brothers and countless other comic acts), while bits of trivia and foolery are suddenly elevated, through the style, into objects of sublime contemplation—as at the novel's end, when Oedipa thinks of "squatters" who "slept in junkyards in the stripped shells of wrecked Plymouths, or even, daring, spent the night up some pole in a lineman's tent like caterpillars, swung among a web of telephone wires, living in the very copper rigging and secular miracle of communication, untroubled by the dumb voltages flickering their miles, the night long, in the thousands of unheard messages." Often Pynchon's sentences enact the daring freedom he admires, in contrast to the institutions of a technological society.

Pynchon's longest and most daring and exhaustive effort came with the publication, in 1973, of *Gravity's Rainbow*. This encyclopedic fantasy operates through brilliant improvisations, tall tales, obscene parables, and burlesque stage routines, all of which work together into a story of supersonic capabilities and annihilative retributions. A huge cast of characters, each with a crazy name and a plot to unravel, is located all over the map, but mainly in World War II London and in postwar Germany. As the four main and the countless subsidiary plots take shape, characters—and the reader—attempt to "read" the messages flickering, the dumb intent to communicate, in the most casual as well as the most portentous sign. Pynchon's knowingness and fascination with popular culture are overwhelmingly evident in *Gravity's Rainbow*, as is his preoccupation with the lore of theoretical science, of obscure historical tales, and of contemporary comic books. No one denies the formidably encyclopedic nature of this astonishing effort; the question is, as Warner Berthoff has asked, whether that effort may not also be "encyclopedically monotonous and static." More readers begin *Gravity's Rainbow* than finish it.

After 1973, except for the publication in 1984 of some of his early stories (in *Slow Learner*), all was silent on the Pynchon front until *Vineland* appeared in 1990, followed by *Mason & Dixon* in 1997 and *Against the Day* in 2006. *Vineland* is wonderful on the California terrain and has much freewheeling and funny inventiveness; at other times Pynchon seems to be flogging his material and repeating himself. *Mason & Dixon*, about the plotters of the line that would differentiate the American North and South, is written in the manner of his more ambitious works, a massive "mega-novel" that by its very excesses of character, plot, and references to history (arcane and otherwise) seeks to overwhelm the reader with its display of authority. *Against the Day* (2006) and *Inherent Vice* (2009) have more conventional subjects—family-revenge drama and crime solving, respectively—yet the author still dotes on fantastic inventions and overwritten prose. *Bleeding Edge* (2013) was a National Book Award finalist; it is a detective story set in New York City in the early days of the Internet and during the months prior to the attacks of September 11. Although there is still no consensus on his stature as an enduring American writer, there is general recognition of the quirky, uncanny exactitude of his imagination, evident across his oeuvre. Pynchon's theatrical spellbindings as a man of metaphor, and his feats of association (in Robert Frost's phrase), are employed on subjects—like the rocket in *Gravity's Rainbow*—that were thought to be beyond words. For daring, wit, and exuberance, no contemporary writer excels him.

The following text is from *Slow Learner* (1984).

Entropy

> Boris has just given me a summary of his views. He is a weather prophet. The weather will continue bad, he says. There will be more calamities, more death, more despair. Not the slightest indication of a change anywhere. . . . We must get into step, a lockstep toward the prison of death. There is no escape. The weather will not change.
>
> —*Tropic of Cancer*[1]

Downstairs, Meatball Mulligan's lease-breaking party was moving into its 40th hour. On the kitchen floor, amid a litter of empty champagne fifths, were Sandor Rojas and three friends, playing spit in the ocean and staying

1. Novel (1934) by the American writer Henry Miller (1891–1980).

awake on Heidseck[2] and benzedrine pills. In the living room Duke, Vincent, Krinkles and Paco sat crouched over a 15-inch speaker which had been bolted into the top of a wastepaper basket, listening to 27 watts' worth of *The Heroes' Gate at Kiev.*[3] They all wore hornrimmed sunglasses and rapt expressions, and smoked funny-looking cigarettes which contained not, as you might expect, tobacco, but an adulterated form of *cannabis sativa.*[4] This group was the Duke di Angelis quartet. They recorded for a local label called Tambú and had to their credit one 10' LP entitled *Songs of Outer Space.* From time to time one of them would flick the ashes from his cigarette into the speaker cone to watch them dance around. Meatball himself was sleeping over by the window, holding an empty magnum to his chest as if it were a teddy bear. Several government girls, who worked for people like the State Department and NSA, had passed out on couches, chairs and in one case the bathroom sink.

This was in early February of '57 and back then there were a lot of American expatriates around Washington, D.C., who would talk, every time they met you, about how someday they were going to go over to Europe for real but right now it seemed they were working for the government. Everyone saw a fine irony in this. They would stage, for instance, polyglot parties where the newcomer was sort of ignored if he couldn't carry on simultaneous conversations in three or four languages. They would haunt Armenian delicatessens for weeks at a stretch and invite you over for bulghour and lamb in tiny kitchens whose walls were covered with bullfight posters. They would have affairs with sultry girls from Andalucía or the Midi[5] who studied economics at Georgetown. Their Dôme was a collegiate Rathskeller out on Wisconsin Avenue called the Old Heidelberg and they had to settle for cherry blossoms instead of lime trees when spring came, but in its lethargic way their life provided, as they said, kicks.

At the moment, Meatball's party seemed to be gathering its second wind. Outside there was rain. Rain splatted against the tar paper on the roof and was fractured into a fine spray off the noses, eyebrows and lips of wooden gargoyles under the eaves, and ran like drool down the windowpanes. The day before, it had snowed and the day before that there had been winds of gale force and before that the sun had made the city glitter bright as April, though the calendar read early February. It is a curious season in Washington, this false spring. Somewhere in it are Lincoln's Birthday and the Chinese New Year, and a forlornness in the streets because cherry blossoms are weeks away still and, as Sarah Vaughan has put it, spring will be a little late this year. Generally crowds like the one which would gather in the Old Heidelberg on weekday afternoons to drink Würtzburger and to sing Lili Marlene (not to mention The Sweetheart of Sigma Chi) are inevitably and incorrigibly Romantic. And as every good Romantic knows, the soul (*spiritus, ruach, pneuma*)[6] is nothing, substantially, but air; it is only natural that warpings in the atmosphere should be recapitulated in those who breathe it. So that over and above the public components—holidays, tour-

---

2. A very dry champagne. "Spit in the ocean": a form of poker.
3. Music by the Russian composer Modest Mussorgsky (1839–1881) from his *Pictures at an Exhibition.*

4. Marijuana.
5. Regions of Spain and France, respectively.
6. "Soul" (and also "breath") in, respectively, Latin, Hebrew, and Greek.

The Gerry Mulligan Quartet premiered in Los Angeles in 1952 with Mulligan on baritone saxophone, Chet Baker on trumpet, Bob Whitlock on bass, and Chico Hamilton on drums. There was no pianist, an innovation for small ensemble jazz, leaving harmonic silences for the other instruments to fill.

ist attractions—there are private meanderings, linked to the climate as if this spell were a *stretto* passage in the year's fugue: haphazard weather, aimless loves, unpredicted commitments: months one can easily spend *in* fugue, because oddly enough, later on, winds, rains, passions of February and March are never remembered in that city, it is as if they had never been.

The last bass notes of *The Heroes' Gate* boomed up through the floor and woke Callisto from an uneasy sleep. The first thing he became aware of was a small bird he had been holding gently between his hands, against his body. He turned his head sidewise on the pillow to smile down at it, at its blue hunched-down head and sick, lidded eyes, wondering how many more nights he would have to give it warmth before it was well again. He had been holding the bird like that for three days: it was the only way he knew to restore its health. Next to him the girl stirred and whimpered, her arm thrown across her face. Mingled with the sounds of the rain came the first tentative, querulous morning voices of the other birds, hidden in philodendrons and small fan palms: patches of scarlet, yellow and blue laced through this Rousseau-like[7] fantasy, this hothouse jungle it had taken him seven years to weave together. Hermetically sealed, it was a tiny enclave of regularity in the city's chaos, alien to the vagaries of the weather, of national politics, of any civil disorder. Through trial-and-error Callisto had perfected its ecological balance, with the help of the girl its artistic harmony, so that the swayings of its plant life, the stirrings of its birds and human inhabitants

7. Henri Rousseau (1844–1910), French primitive painter of exotic landscapes.

were all as integral as the rhythms of a perfectly-executed mobile. He and the girl could no longer, of course, be omitted from that sanctuary; they had become necessary to its unity. What they needed from outside was delivered. They did not go out.

"Is he all right," she whispered. She lay like a tawny question mark facing him, her eyes suddenly huge and dark and blinking slowly. Callisto ran a finger beneath the feathers at the base of the bird's neck; caressed it gently. "He's going to be well, I think. See: he hears his friends beginning to wake up." The girl had heard the rain and the birds even before she was fully awake. Her name was Aubade: she was part French and part Annamese, and she lived on her own curious and lonely planet, where the clouds and the odor of poincianas, the bitterness of wine and the accidental fingers at the small of her back or feathery against her breasts came to her reduced inevitably to the terms of sound: of music which emerged at intervals from a howling darkness of discordancy. "Aubade," he said, "go see." Obedient, she arose; padded to the window, pulled aside the drapes and after a moment said: "It is 37. Still 37." Callisto frowned. "Since Tuesday, then," he said. "No change." Henry Adams,[8] three generations before his own, had stared aghast at Power; Callisto found himself now in much the same state over Thermodynamics, the inner life of that power, realizing like his predecessor that the Virgin and the dynamo stand as much for love as for power; that the two are indeed identical; and that love therefore not only makes the world go round but also makes the boccie ball spin, the nebula precess. It was this latter or sidereal element which disturbed him. The cosmologists had predicted an eventual heat-death for the universe (something like Limbo: form and motion abolished, heat-energy identical at every point in it); the meteorologists, day-to-day, staved it off by contradicting with a reassuring array of varied temperatures.

But for three days now, despite the changeful weather, the mercury had stayed at 37 degrees Fahrenheit. Leery at omens of apocalypse, Callisto shifted beneath the covers. His fingers pressed the bird more firmly, as if needing some pulsing or suffering assurance of an early break in the temperature.

It was that last cymbal crash that did it. Meatball was hurled wincing into consciousness as the synchronized wagging of heads over the wastebasket stopped. The final hiss remained for an instant in the room, then melted into the whisper of rain outside. "Aarrgghh," announced Meatball in the silence, looking at the empty magnum. Krinkles, in slow motion, turned, smiled and held out a cigarette. "Tea time, man," he said. "No, no," said Meatball. "How many times I got to tell you guys. Not at my place. You ought to know, Washington is lousy with Feds." Krinkles looked wistful. "Jeez, Meatball," he said, "you don't want to do nothing no more." "Hair of dog," said Meatball. "Only hope. Any juice left?" He began to crawl toward the kitchen. "No champagne, I don't think," Duke said. "Case of tequila behind the icebox." They put on an Earl Bostic[9] side. Meatball paused at the kitchen door, glowering at Sandor Rojas. "Lemons," he said after some thought. He crawled to the refrigerator and got out three lemons and some cubes, found

8. American historian and man of letters (1838–1918) whose writings explore the nature of power, cultural figurations of which ranged from the Virgin Mary to the modern dynamo engine.
9. American jazz musician (1913–1965) who also recorded rhythm-and-blues material.

the tequila and set about restoring order to his nervous system. He drew blood once cutting the lemons and had to use two hands squeezing them and his foot to crack the ice tray but after about ten minutes he found himself, through some miracle, beaming down into a monster tequila sour. "That looks yummy," Sandor Rojas said. "How about you make me one." Meatball blinked at him. *"Kitchi lofass a shegithe,"*[1] he replied automatically, and wandered away into the bathroom. "I say," he called out a moment later to no one in particular. "I say, there seems to be a girl or something sleeping in the sink." He took her by the shoulders and shook. "Wha," she said. "You don't look too comfortable," Meatball said. "Well," she agreed. She stumbled to the shower, turned on the cold water and sat down crosslegged in the spray. "That's better," she smiled.

"Meatball," Sandor Rojas yelled from the kitchen. "Somebody is trying to come in the window. A burglar, I think. A second-story man." "What are you worrying about," Meatball said. "We're on the third floor." He loped back into the kitchen. A shaggy woebegone figure stood out on the fire escape, raking his fingernails down the windowpane. Meatball opened the window. "Saul," he said.

"Sort of wet out," Saul said. He climbed in, dripping. "You heard, I guess."

"Miriam left you," Meatball said, "or something, is all I heard."

There was a sudden flurry of knocking at the front door. "Do come in," Sandor Rojas called. The door opened and there were three coeds from George Washington, all of whom were majoring in philosophy. They were each holding a gallon of Chianti. Sandor leaped up and dashed into the living room. "We heard there was a party," one blonde said. "Young blood," Sandor shouted. He was an ex-Hungarian freedom fighter who had easily the worst chronic case of what certain critics of the middle class have called Don Giovannism in the District of Columbia. *Purchè porti la gonnella, voi sapete quel che fa.*[2] Like Pavlov's dog: a contralto voice or a whiff of Arpège and Sandor would begin to salivate. Meatball regarded the trio blearily as they filed into the kitchen; he shrugged. "Put the wine in the icebox," he said, "and good morning."

Aubade's neck made a golden bow as she bent over the sheets of foolscap, scribbling away in the green murk of the room. "As a young man at Princeton," Callisto was dictating, nestling the bird against the gray hairs of his chest, "Callisto had learned a mnemonic device for remembering the Laws of Thermodynamics: you can't win, things are going to get worse before they get better, who says they're going to get better. At the age of 54, confronted with Gibbs'[3] notion of the universe, he suddenly realized that undergraduate cant had been oracle, after all. That spindly maze of equations became, for him, a vision of ultimate, cosmic heat-death. He had known all along, of course, that nothing but a theoretical engine or system ever runs at 100% efficiency; and about the theorem of Clausius, which states that the entropy of an isolated system always continually increases. It was not,

1. Little horse prick in your asshole (Hungarian).
2. As long as she wears a skirt, you know what he does (Italian); from Lorenzo da Ponte's libretto to Mozart's opera *Don Giovanni* (1787).

3. Josiah Willard Gibbs (1839–1903), American physicist and chemist, a founder of statistical mechanics.

however, until Gibbs and Boltzmann[4] brought to this principle the methods of statistical mechanics that the horrible significance of it all dawned on him: only then did he realize that the isolated system—galaxy, engine, human being, culture, whatever—must evolve spontaneously toward the Condition of the More Probable. He was forced, therefore, in the sad dying fall of middle age, to a radical reëvaluation of everything he had learned up to then; all the cities and seasons and casual passions of his days had now to be looked at in a new and elusive light. He did not know if he was equal to the task. He was aware of the dangers of the reductive fallacy and, he hoped, strong enough not to drift into the graceful decadence of an enervated fatalism. His had always been a vigorous, Italian sort of pessimism: like Machiavelli, he allowed the forces of *virtù* and *fortuna*[5] to be about 50/50; but the equations now introduced a random factor which pushed the odds to some unutterable and indeterminate ratio which he found himself afraid to calculate." Around him loomed vague hothouse shapes; the pitifully small heart fluttered against his own. Counterpointed against his words the girl heard the chatter of birds and fitful car honkings scattered along the wet morning and Earl Bostic's alto rising in occasional wild peaks through the floor. The architectonic purity of her world was constantly threatened by such hints of anarchy: gaps and excrescences and skew lines, and a shifting or tilting of planes to which she had continually to readjust lest the whole structure shiver into a disarray of discrete and meaningless signals. Callisto had described the process once as a kind of "feedback": she crawled into dreams each night with a sense of exhaustion, and a desperate resolve never to relax that vigilance. Even in the brief periods when Callisto made love to her, soaring above the bowing of taut nerves in haphazard double-stops would be the one singing string of her determination.

"Nevertheless," continued Callisto, "he found in entropy or the measure of disorganization for a closed system an adequate metaphor to apply to certain phenomena in his own world. He saw, for example, the younger generation responding to Madison Avenue with the same spleen his own had once reserved for Wall Street: and in American 'consumerism' discovered a similar tendency from the least to the most probable, from differentiation to sameness, from ordered individuality to a kind of chaos. He found himself, in short, restating Gibbs' prediction in social terms, and envisioned a heat-death for his culture in which ideas, like heat-energy, would no longer be transferred, since each point in it would ultimately have the same quantity of energy; and intellectual motion would, accordingly, cease." He glanced up suddenly. "Check it now," he said. Again she rose and peered out at the thermometer. "37," she said. "The rain has stopped." He bent his head quickly and held his lips against a quivering wing. "Then it will change soon," he said, trying to keep his voice firm.

Sitting on the stove Saul was like any big rag doll that a kid has been taking out some incomprehensible rage on. "What happened," Meatball said. "If you feel like talking, I mean."

"Of course I feel like talking," Saul said. "One thing I did, I slugged her."

4. Ludwig Boltzmann (1844–1906), Austrian physicist who studied how atoms determine visual properties of matter. Rudolf Clausius (1822–1888), German physicist, developer of the science of thermodynamics.
5. Niccolò Machiavelli (1469–1527), Florentine statesman and writer on government, contrasted virtuous behavior (*virtù*) with good luck (*fortuna*).

"Discipline must be maintained."

"Ha, ha. I wish you'd been there. Oh Meatball, it was a lovely fight. She ended up throwing a *Handbook of Chemistry and Physics* at me, only it missed and went through the window, and when the glass broke I reckon something in her broke too. She stormed out of the house crying, out in the rain. No raincoat or anything."

"She'll be back."

"No."

"Well!" Soon Meatball said: "It was something earthshattering, no doubt. Like who is better, Sal Mineo or Ricky Nelson."[6]

"What it was about," Saul said, "was communication theory. Which of course makes it very hilarious."

"I don't know anything about communication theory."

"Neither does my wife. Come right down to it, who does? That's the joke." When Meatball saw the kind of smile Saul had on his face he said: "Maybe you would like tequila or something."

"No. I mean, I'm sorry. It's a field you can go off the deep end in, is all. You get where you're watching all the time for security cops: behind bushes, around corners. MUFFET is top secret."

"Wha."

"Multi-unit factorial field electronic tabulator."

"You were fighting about that."

"Miriam has been reading science fiction again. That and *Scientific American.* It seems she is, as we say, bugged at this idea of computers acting like people. I made the mistake of saying you can just as well turn that around, and talk about human behavior like a program fed into an IBM machine."

"Why not," Meatball said.

"Indeed, why not. In fact it is sort of crucial to communication, not to mention information theory. Only when I said that she hit the roof. Up went the balloon. And I can't figure out *why*. If anybody should know why, I should. I refuse to believe the government is wasting taxpayers' money on me, when it has so many bigger and better things to waste it on."

Meatball made a moue. "Maybe she thought you were acting like a cold, dehumanized amoral scientist type."

"My god," Saul flung up an arm. "Dehumanized. How much more human can I get? I worry, Meatball, I do. There are Europeans wandering around North Africa these days with their tongues torn out of their heads because those tongues have spoken the wrong words. Only the Europeans thought they were the right words."

"Language barrier," Meatball suggested.

Saul jumped down off the stove. "That," he said, angry, "is a good candidate for sick joke of the year. No, ace, it is *not* a barrier. If it is anything it's a kind of leakage. Tell a girl: 'I love you.' No trouble with two-thirds of that, it's a closed circuit. Just you and she. But that nasty four-letter word in the middle, *that's* the one you have to look out for. Ambiguity. Redundance. Irrelevance, even. Leakage. All this is noise. Noise screws up your signal, makes for disorganization in the circuit."

---

6. Contemporary figures from film and television who were icons of bad and good teenage behavior, respectively.

Meatball shuffled around. "Well, now, Saul," he muttered, "you're sort of, I don't know, expecting a lot from people. I mean, you know. What it is is, most of the things we say, I guess, are mostly noise."

"Ha! Half of what you just said, for example."

"Well, you do it too."

"I know." Saul smiled grimly. "It's a bitch, ain't it."

"I bet that's what keeps divorce lawyers in business. Whoops."

"Oh I'm not sensitive. Besides," frowning, "you're right. You find I think that most 'successful' marriages—Miriam and me, up to last night—are sort of founded on compromises. You never run at top efficiency, usually all you have is a minimum basis for a workable thing. I believe the phrase is Togetherness."

"Aarrgghh."

"Exactly. You find that one a bit noisy, don't you. But the noise content is different for each of us because you're a bachelor and I'm not. Or wasn't. The hell with it."

"Well sure," Meatball said, trying to be helpful, "you were using different words. By 'human being' you meant something that you can look at like it was a computer. It helps you think better on the job or something. But Miriam meant something entirely—"

"The hell with it."

Meatball fell silent. "I'll take that drink," Saul said after a while.

The card game had been abandoned and Sandor's friends were slowly getting wasted on tequila. On the living room couch, one of the coeds and Krinkles were engaged in amorous conversation. "No," Krinkles was saying, "no, I can't put Dave *down*. In fact I give Dave a lot of credit, man. Especially considering his accident and all." The girl's smile faded. "How terrible," she said. "What accident?" "Hadn't you heard?" Krinkles said. "When Dave was in the army, just a private E-2, they sent him down to Oak Ridge on special duty. Something to do with the Manhattan Project.[7] He was handling hot stuff one day and got an overdose of radiation. So now he's got to wear lead gloves all the time." She shook her head sympathetically. "What an awful break for a piano player."

Meatball had abandoned Saul to a bottle of tequila and was about to go to sleep in a closet when the front door flew open and the place was invaded by five enlisted personnel of the U.S. Navy, all in varying stages of abomination. "This is the place," shouted a fat, pimply seaman apprentice who had lost his white hat. "This here is the hoorhouse that chief was telling us about." A stringy-looking 3rd class boatswain's mate pushed him aside and cased the living room. "You're right, Slab," he said. "But it don't look like much, even for Stateside. I seen better tail in Naples, Italy." "How much, hey," boomed a large seaman with adenoids, who was holding a Mason jar full of white lightning. "Oh, my god," said Meatball.

Outside the temperature remained constant at 37 degrees Fahrenheit. In the hothouse Aubade stood absently caressing the branches of a young mimosa, hearing a motif of sap-rising, the rough and unresolved anticipatory theme of those fragile pink blossoms which, it is said, insure fertility.

---

7. The research program that developed the atomic bomb for use at the end of World War II.

That music rose in a tangled tracery: arabesques of order competing fugally with the improvised discords of the party downstairs, which peaked sometimes in cusps and ogees of noise. That precious signal-to-noise ratio, whose delicate balance required every calorie of her strength, seesawed inside the small tenuous skull as she watched Callisto, sheltering the bird. Callisto was trying to confront any idea of the heat-death now, as he nuzzled the feathery lump in his hands. He sought correspondences. Sade, of course. And Temple Drake, gaunt and hopeless in her little park in Paris, at the end of *Sanctuary*.[8] Final equilibrium. *Nightwood*.[9] And the tango. Any tango, but more than any perhaps the sad sick dance in Stravinsky's *L'Histoire du Soldat*.[1] He thought back: what had tango music been for them after the war, what meanings had he missed in all the stately coupled automatons in the *cafés'-dansants*,[2] or in the metronomes which had ticked behind the eyes of his own partners? Not even the clean constant winds of Switzerland could cure the *grippe espagnole*.[3] Stravinsky had had it, they all had had it. And how many musicians were left after Passchendaele, after the Marne?[4] It came down in this case to seven: violin, double-bass. Clarinet, bassoon. Cornet, trombone. Tympani. Almost as if any tiny troupe of saltimbanques had set about conveying the same information as a full pit-orchestra. There was hardly a full complement left in Europe. Yet with violin and tympani Stravinsky had managed to communicate in that tango the same exhaustion, the same airlessness one saw in the slicked-down youths who were trying to imitate Vernon Castle, and in their mistresses, who simply did not care. *Ma maîtresse*.[5] Celeste. Returning to Nice after the second war he had found that café replaced by a perfume shop which catered to American tourists. And no secret vestige of her in the cobblestones or in the old pension next door; no perfume to match her breath heavy with the sweet Spanish wine she always drank. And so instead he had purchased a Henry Miller novel and left for Paris,[6] and read the book on the train so that when he arrived he had been given at least a little forewarning. And saw that Celeste and the others and even Temple Drake were not all that had changed. "Aubade," he said, "my head aches." The sound of his voice generated in the girl an answering scrap of melody. Her movement toward the kitchen, the towel, the cold water, and his eyes following her formed a weird and intricate canon; as she placed the compress on his forehead his sigh of gratitude seemed to signal a new subject, another series of modulations.

"No," Meatball was still saying, "no, I'm afraid not. This is not a house of ill repute. I'm sorry, really I am." Slab was adamant. "But the chief said," he kept repeating. The seaman offered to swap the moonshine for a good piece. Meatball looked around frantically, as if seeking assistance. In the middle of the room, the Duke di Angelis quartet were engaged in a historic

8. Sexually notorious novel published in 1931 by the American writer William Faulkner (1897–1962).
9. Novel published in 1936 by the American expatriate writer Djuna Barnes (1892–1982).
1. "The Story of the soldier" (French), a 1918 work by the Russian composer Igor Stravinsky (1882–1971).

2. Café dancers (French).
3. Spanish flu (French).
4. Battle sites in World War I noted for their extremely high casualties.
5. My mistress (French).
6. Miller was famous for his overtly sexual novels written in Paris during the 1930s.

moment. Vincent was seated and the others standing: they were going through the motions of a group having a session, only without instruments. "I say," Meatball said. Duke moved his head a few times, smiled faintly, lit a cigarette, and eventually caught sight of Meatball. "Quiet, man," he whispered. Vincent began to fling his arms around, his fists clenched; then, abruptly, was still, then repeated the performance. This went on for a few minutes while Meatball sipped his drink moodily. The navy had withdrawn to the kitchen. Finally at some invisible signal the group stopped tapping their feet and Duke grinned and said, "At least we ended together."

Meatball glared at him. "I say," he said. "I have this new conception, man," Duke said. "You remember your namesake. You remember Gerry."

"No," said Meatball. "I'll remember April, if that's any help."

"As a matter of fact," Duke said, "it was Love for Sale. Which shows how much you know. The point is, it was Mulligan, Chet Baker[7] and that crew, way back then, out yonder. You dig?"

"Baritone sax," Meatball said. "Something about a baritone sax."

"But no piano, man. No guitar. Or accordion. You know what that means."

"Not exactly," Meatball said.

"Well first let me just say, that I am no Mingus, no John Lewis.[8] Theory was never my strong point. I mean things like reading were always difficult for me and all—"

"I know," Meatball said drily. "You got your card taken away because you changed key on Happy Birthday at a Kiwanis Club picnic."

"Rotarian. But it occurred to me, in one of these flashes of insight, that if that first quartet of Mulligan's had no piano, it could only mean one thing."

"No chords," said Paco, the baby-faced bass.

"What he is trying to say," Duke said, "is no root chords. Nothing to listen to while you blow a horizontal line. What one does in such a case is, one *thinks* the roots."

A horrified awareness was dawning on Meatball. "And the next logical extension," he said.

"Is to think everything," Duke announced with simple dignity. "Roots, line, everything."

Meatball looked at Duke, awed. "But," he said.

"Well," Duke said modestly, "there are a few bugs to work out."

"But," Meatball said.

"Just listen," Duke said. "You'll catch on." And off they went again into orbit, presumably somewhere around the asteroid belt. After a while Krinkles made an embouchure and started moving his fingers and Duke clapped his hand to his forehead. "Oaf!" he roared. "The new head we're using, you remember, I wrote last night?" "Sure," Krinkles said, "the new head. I come in on the bridge. All your heads I come in then." "Right," Duke said. "So why—" "Wha," said Krinkles, "16 bars, I wait, I come in—" "16?" Duke said. "No. No, Krinkles. Eight you waited. You want me to sing it? A ciga-

---

7. In 1952 the American jazz musicians Gerry Mulligan (1927–1996) and Chet Baker (1929–1988) became famous for their revolutionary pianoless quartet.

8. Charles Mingus (1922–1979) and John Lewis (1920–2001), American jazz musicians noted for their compositions.

rette that bears a lipstick's traces, an airline ticket to romantic places." Krinkles scratched his head. "These Foolish Things, you mean." "Yes," Duke said, "yes, Krinkles. Bravo." "Not I'll Remember April," Krinkles said. "*Minghe morte*,"[9] said Duke. "I *figured* we were playing it a little slow," Krinkles said. Meatball chuckled. "Back to the old drawing board," he said. "No, man," Duke said, "back to the airless void." And they took off again, only it seemed Paco was playing in G sharp while time rest were in E flat, so they had to start all over.

In the kitchen two of the girls from George Washington and the sailors were singing Let's All Go Down and Piss on the Forrestal.[1] There was a two-handed, bilingual *morra*[2] game on over by the icebox. Saul had filled several paper bags with water and was sitting on the fire escape, dropping them on passersby in the street. A fat government girl in a Bennington sweatshirt, recently engaged to an ensign attached to the Forrestal, came charging into the kitchen, head lowered, and butted Slab in the stomach. Figuring this was as good an excuse for a fight as any, Slab's buddies piled in. The *morra* players were nose-to-nose, screaming *trois, sette* at the tops of their lungs. From the shower the girl Meatball had taken out of the sink announced that she was drowning. She had apparently sat on the drain and the water was now up to her neck. The noise in Meatball's apartment had reached a sustained, ungodly crescendo.

Meatball stood and watched, scratching his stomach lazily. The way he figured, there were only about two ways he could cope: (a) lock himself in the closet and maybe eventually they would all go away, or (b) try to calm everybody down, one by one. (a) was certainly the more attractive alternative. But then he started thinking about that closet. It was dark and stuffy and he would be alone. He did not feature being alone. And then this crew off the good ship Lollipop[3] or whatever it was might take it upon themselves to kick down the closet door, for a lark. And if that happened he would be, at the very least, embarrassed. The other way was more a pain in the neck, but probably better in the long run.

So he decided to try and keep his lease-breaking party from deteriorating into total chaos: he gave wine to the sailors and separated the *morra* players; he introduced the fat government girl to Sandor Rojas, who would keep her out of trouble; he helped the girl in the shower to dry off and get into bed; he had another talk with Saul; he called a repairman for the refrigerator, which someone had discovered was on the blink. This is what he did until nightfall, when most of the revellers had passed out and the party trembled on the threshold of its third day.

Upstairs Callisto, helpless in the past, did not feel the faint rhythm inside the bird begin to slacken and fail. Aubade was by the window, wandering the ashes of her own lovely world; the temperature held steady, the sky had become a uniform darkening gray. Then something from downstairs—a girl's scream, an overturned chair, a glass dropped on the floor, he would never know what exactly—pierced that private time-warp and he became

---

9. Dead prick (Italian).
1. Aircraft carrier in the U.S. Navy.
2. Finger game originally played by Italians. The commands are numbers; below, three (*trois*,

French) and seven (*sette*, Italian).
3. The subject of film and song popularized in the 1930s by the American child actress Shirley Temple (1928–2014).

aware of the faltering, the constriction of muscles, the tiny tossings of the bird's head; and his own pulse began to pound more fiercely, as if trying to compensate. "Aubade," he called weakly, "he's dying." The girl, flowing and rapt, crossed the hothouse to gaze down at Callisto's hands. The two remained like that, poised, for one minute, and two, while the heartbeat ticked a graceful diminuendo down at last into stillness. Callisto raised his head slowly. "I held him," he protested, impotent with the wonder of it, "to give him the warmth of my body. Almost as if I were communicating life to him, or a sense of life. What has happened? Has the transfer of heat ceased to work? Is there no more . . ." He did not finish.

"I was just at the window," she said. He sank back, terrified. She stood a moment more, irresolute; she had sensed his obsession long ago, realized somehow that that constant 37 was now decisive. Suddenly then, as if seeing the single and unavoidable conclusion to all this she moved swiftly to the window before Callisto could speak; tore away the drapes and smashed out the glass with two exquisite hands which came away bleeding and glistening with splinters; and turned to face the man on the bed and wait with him until the moment of equilibrium was reached, when 37 degrees Fahrenheit should prevail both outside and inside, and forever, and the hovering, curious dominant of their separate lives should resolve into a tonic of darkness and the final absence of all motion.

1984

RAYMOND CARVER
1938–1988

Minimal fiction; designer fiction; even "dirty fiction," a phrase the British magazine *Granta* used to characterize the new style of American writing that was supposedly polluting the realistic short story with unconventional, irrealistic techniques—these terms were tossed around by critics of an abruptly new style of work that at times seemed to dominate the 1980s. Popularized by Bobbie Ann Mason, Ann Beattie, Frederick Barthelme, and Barry Hannah as well, its chief practitioner was a master of fine arts graduate from the University of Iowa's Writers Workshop, Raymond Carver, whose collections *Will You Please Be Quiet, Please?* (1976), *What We Talk About When We Talk About Love* (1981), and *Cathedral* (1983) set the most imitated style of their generation. Moved to put some order to these many definitions, writer John Barth—whose nonrealistic, innovative work had helped characterize the writing of the decades before—coined the term Post-Alcoholic Blue-Collar Minimalist Hyperrealism to describe the school Carver may have inadvertently founded. A recovering alcoholic, Carver had worked as a janitor, sawmill hand, delivery person, and sales representative, suggesting the profile Barth had in mind. But more pertinent to the style of his fiction was his training at Iowa and teaching in creative writing programs at universities around the country.

By the time of his death, his became the most accepted style in such academic programs and in the literary magazines they generated.

This style's success is important. With conventions of literary realism having been challenged and theorists questioning all such previously stable assumptions, readers of Barth, Donald Barthelme, Kurt Vonnegut, and other such experimenters may have felt that simple realism was no longer an up-to-date way in which to write. Raymond Carver proved that it was, and that previous challenges to realistic tradition had only made it all the more effective, especially when those challenges are incorporated in the new style. Carver's patient narration does not strive for a reader's suspension of disbelief. Rather, as in the introduction of the bizarre situation experienced in "Cathedral" (printed here), its plain, even flat statement presents matter unadorned by devices meant to persuade or convince. So a blind man wants to learn what the architecture of a cathedral suggests? Here it is, Carver's story says: what you see is what there is; take it or leave it; if you are blind, he will help you feel your way through, but never as a direction to meaning, only to an apprehension of the facts. Carver's characters are usually working-class people somewhat down on their luck. Often, alcohol figures in their lives, less as a stimulant than as a further depressant. Totally unexceptional, their failures, like their hopes, are small, even puny. But from such stripped-down essentials the author is able to write in a plain, simple manner, sticking to the absolute minimum so that no one can accuse him of trying to create illusions.

Much was made of Raymond Carver's alcoholism and recovery. He made no apologies for his hard, sometimes abusive life, the rigors of which contributed to ill health and an early death. His stories and poems have the same quiet toughness to them, not flamboyant in confrontation with life's meanness but dedicated to holding on against time's slowly destructive friction with a grittiness all their own.

The following text is from *Cathedral* (1983).

Cathedral

This blind man, an old friend of my wife's, he was on his way to spend the night. His wife had died. So he was visiting the dead wife's relatives in Connecticut. He called my wife from his in-laws'. Arrangements were made. He would come by train, a five-hour trip, and my wife would meet him at the station. She hadn't seen him since she worked for him one summer in Seattle ten years ago. But she and the blind man had kept in touch. They made tapes and mailed them back and forth. I wasn't enthusiastic about his visit. He was no one I knew. And his being blind bothered me. My idea of blindness came from the movies. In the movies, the blind moved slowly and never laughed. Sometimes they were led by seeing-eye dogs. A blind man in my house was not something I looked forward to.

That summer in Seattle she had needed a job. She didn't have any money. The man she was going to marry at the end of the summer was in officers' training school. He didn't have any money, either. But she was in love with the guy, and he was in love with her, etc. She'd seen something in the paper: HELP WANTED—*Reading to Blind Man*, and a telephone number. She phoned and went over, was hired on the spot. She'd worked with this blind man all summer. She read stuff to him, case studies, reports, that sort of thing. She helped him organize his little office in the county social-service department. They'd become good friends, my wife and the blind man. How do I know these things? She told me. And she told me something else. On her last day in the office, the blind man asked if he could touch her face. She agreed to this. She told me he touched his fingers to every part of her face, her nose—even her neck! She never forgot it. She even tried to write a poem about it. She was always trying to write a poem. She wrote a poem or two every year, usually after something really important had happened to her.

When we first started going out together, she showed me the poem. In the poem, she recalled his fingers and the way they had moved around over her face. In the poem, she talked about what she had felt at the time, about what went through her mind when the blind man touched her nose and lips. I can remember I didn't think much of the poem. Of course, I didn't tell her that. Maybe I just don't understand poetry. I admit it's not the first thing I reach for when I pick up something to read.

Anyway, this man who'd first enjoyed her favors, the officer-to-be, he'd been her childhood sweetheart. So okay. I'm saying that at the end of the summer she let the blind man run his hands over her face, said goodbye to him, married her childhood etc., who was now a commissioned officer, and she moved away from Seattle. But they'd kept in touch, she and the blind man. She made the first contact after a year or so. She called him up one night from an Air Force base in Alabama. She wanted to talk. They talked. He asked her to send him a tape and tell him about her life. She did this. She sent the tape. On the tape, she told the blind man about her husband and about their life together in the military. She told the blind man she loved her husband but she didn't like it where they lived and she didn't like it that he was a part of the military-industrial thing. She told the blind man she'd written a poem and he was in it. She told him that she was writing a poem about what it was like to be an Air Force officer's wife. The poem wasn't finished yet. She was still writing it. The blind man made a tape. He sent her the tape. She made a tape. This went on for years. My wife's officer was posted to one base and then another. She sent tapes from Moody AFB,[1] McGuire, McConnell, and finally Travis, near Sacramento, where one night she got to feeling lonely and cut off from people she kept losing in that moving-around life. She got to feeling she couldn't go it another step. She went in and swallowed all the pills and capsules in the medicine chest and washed them down with a bottle of gin. Then she got into a hot bath and passed out.

But instead of dying, she got sick. She threw up. Her officer—why should he have a name? he was the childhood sweetheart, and what more does he want?—came home from somewhere, found her, and called the ambulance. In time, she put it all on a tape and sent the tape to the blind man. Over the years, she put all kinds of stuff on tapes and sent the tapes off lickety-split. Next to writing a poem every year, I think it was her chief means of recreation. On one tape, she told the blind man she'd decided to live away from her officer for a time. On another tape, she told him about her divorce. She and I began going out, and of course she told her blind man about it. She told him everything, or so it seemed to me. Once she asked me if I'd like to

---

1. Air force base. Names of other air force bases follow.

hear the latest tape from the blind man. This was a year ago. I was on the tape, she said. So I said okay, I'd listen to it. I got us drinks and we settled down in the living room. We made ready to listen. First she inserted the tape into the player and adjusted a couple of dials. Then she pushed a lever. The tape squeaked and someone began to talk in this loud voice. She lowered the volume. After a few minutes of harmless chitchat, I heard my own name in the mouth of this stranger, this blind man I didn't even know! And then this: "From all you've said about him, I can only conclude—" But we were interrupted, a knock at the door, something, and we didn't ever get back to the tape. Maybe it was just as well. I'd heard all I wanted to.

Now this same blind man was coming to sleep in my house.

"Maybe I could take him bowling," I said to my wife. She was at the draining board doing scalloped potatoes. She put down the knife she was using and turned around.

"If you love me," she said, "you can do this for me. If you don't love me, okay. But if you had a friend, any friend, and the friend came to visit, I'd make him feel comfortable." She wiped her hands with the dish towel.

"I don't have any blind friends," I said.

"You don't have *any* friends," she said. "Period. Besides," she said, "goddam it, his wife's just died! Don't you understand that? The man's lost his wife!"

I didn't answer. She'd told me a little about the blind man's wife. Her name was Beulah. Beulah! That's a name for a colored woman.

"Was his wife a Negro?" I asked.

"Are you crazy?" my wife said. "Have you just flipped or something?" She picked up a potato. I saw it hit the floor, then roll under the stove. "What's wrong with you?" she said. "Are you drunk?"

"I'm just asking," I said.

Right then my wife filled me in with more detail than I cared to know. I made a drink and sat at the kitchen table to listen. Pieces of the story began to fall into place.

Beulah had gone to work for the blind man the summer after my wife had stopped working for him. Pretty soon Beulah and the blind man had themselves a church wedding. It was a little wedding—who'd want to go to such a wedding in the first place?—just the two of them, plus the minister and the minister's wife. But it was a church wedding just the same. It was what Beulah had wanted, he'd said. But even then Beulah must have been carrying the cancer in her glands. After they had been inseparable for eight years—my wife's word, *inseparable*—Beulah's health went into a rapid decline. She died in a Seattle hospital room, the blind man sitting beside the bed and holding on to her hand. They'd married, lived and worked together, slept together—had sex, sure—and then the blind man had to bury her. All this without his having ever seen what the goddamned woman looked like. It was beyond my understanding. Hearing this, I felt sorry for the blind man for a little bit. And then I found myself thinking what a pitiful life this woman must have led. Imagine a woman who could never see herself as she was seen in the eyes of her loved one. A woman who could go on day after day and never receive the smallest compliment from her beloved. A woman whose husband could never read the expression on her face, be it misery or something better. Someone who could wear makeup or not—what difference to him? She could, if she wanted, wear green eye-shadow around one eye, a straight pin in her nostril, yellow slacks and purple shoes, no matter. And then to slip off into death, the blind man's hand on her hand, his blind eyes streaming tears—I'm imagining now—her last thought maybe this: that he never even knew what she looked like, and she on an express to the grave. Robert was left with a small insurance policy and half of a twenty-peso Mexican coin. The other half of the coin went into the box with her. Pathetic.

So when the time rolled around, my wife went to the depot to pick him up. With nothing to do but wait—sure, I blamed him for that—I was having a drink and watching the TV when I heard the car pull into the drive. I got up from the sofa with my drink and went to the window to have a look.

I saw my wife laughing as she parked the car. I saw her get out of the car and shut the door. She was still wearing a smile. Just amazing. She went around to the other side of the car to where the blind man was already starting to get out. This blind man, feature this, he was wearing a full beard! A beard on a blind man! Too much, I say. The blind man reached into the back seat and dragged out a suitcase. My wife took his arm, shut the car door, and, talking all the way, moved him down the drive and then up the steps to the front porch. I turned off the TV. I finished my drink, rinsed the glass, dried my hands. Then I went to the door.

My wife said, "I want you to meet Robert. Robert, this is my husband. I've told you all about him." She was beaming. She had this blind man by his coat sleeve.

The blind man let go of his suitcase and up came his hand.

I took it. He squeezed hard, held my hand, and then he let it go.

"I feel like we've already met," he boomed.

"Likewise," I said. I didn't know what else to say. Then I said, "Welcome. I've heard a lot about you." We began to move then, a little group, from the porch into the living room, my wife guiding him by the arm. The blind man was carrying his suitcase in his other hand. My wife said things like, "To your left here, Robert. That's right. Now watch it, there's a chair. That's it. Sit down right here. This is the sofa. We just bought this sofa two weeks ago."

I started to say something about the old sofa. I'd liked that old sofa. But I didn't say anything. Then I wanted to say something else, small-talk, about the scenic ride along the Hudson. How going *to* New York, you should sit on the right-hand side of the train, and coming *from* New York, the left-hand side.

"Did you have a good train ride?" I said. "Which side of the train did you sit on, by the way?"

"What a question, which side!" my wife said. "What's it matter which side?" she said.

"I just asked," I said.

"Right side," the blind man said. "I hadn't been on a train in nearly forty years. Not since I was a kid. With my folks. That's been a long time. I'd nearly forgotten the sensation. I have winter in my beard now," he said. "So I've been told, anyway. Do I look distinguished, my dear?" the blind man said to my wife.

"You look distinguished, Robert," she said. "Robert," she said. "Robert, it's just so good to see you."

My wife finally took her eyes off the blind man and looked at me. I had the feeling she didn't like what she saw. I shrugged.

I've never met, or personally known, anyone who was blind. This blind man was late forties, a heavy-set, balding man with stooped shoulders, as if he carried a great weight there. He wore brown slacks, brown shoes, a light-brown shirt, a tie, a sports coat. Spiffy. He also had this full beard. But he didn't use a cane and he didn't wear dark glasses. I'd always thought dark glasses were a must for the blind. Fact was, I wished he had a pair. At first glance, his eyes looked like anyone else's eyes. But if you looked close, there was something different about them. Too much white in the iris, for one thing, and the pupils seemed to move around in the sockets without his knowing it or being able to stop it. Creepy. As I stared at his face, I saw the left pupil turn in toward his nose while the other made an effort to keep in one place. But it was only an effort, for that eye was on the roam without his knowing it or wanting it to be.

I said, "Let me get you a drink. What's your pleasure? We have a little of everything. It's one of our pastimes."

"Bub, I'm a Scotch man myself," he said fast enough in this big voice.

"Right," I said. Bub! "Sure you are. I knew it."

He let his fingers touch his suitcase, which was sitting alongside the sofa. He was taking his bearings. I didn't blame him for that.

"I'll move that up to your room," my wife said.

"No, that's fine," the blind man said loudly. "It can go up when I go up."

"A little water with the Scotch?" I said.

"Very little," he said.

"I knew it," I said.

He said, "Just a tad. The Irish actor, Barry Fitzgerald?[2] I'm like that fellow. When I drink water, Fitzgerald said, I drink water. When I drink whiskey, I drink whiskey." My wife laughed. The blind man brought his hand up under his beard. He lifted his beard slowly and let it drop.

I did the drinks, three big glasses of Scotch with a splash of water in each. Then we made ourselves comfortable and talked about Robert's travels. First the long flight from the West Coast to Connecticut, we covered that. Then from Connecticut up here by train. We had another drink concerning that leg of the trip.

I remembered having read somewhere that the blind didn't smoke because, as speculation had it, they couldn't see the smoke they exhaled. I thought I knew that much and that much only about blind people. But this blind man smoked his cigarette down to the nubbin and then lit another one. This blind man filled his ashtray and my wife emptied it.

When we sat down at the table for dinner, we had another drink. My wife heaped Robert's plate with cube steak, scalloped potatoes, green beans. I buttered him up two slices of bread. I said, "Here's bread and butter for you." I swallowed some of my drink. "Now let us pray," I said, and the blind man lowered his head. My wife looked at me, her mouth agape. "Pray the phone won't ring and the food doesn't get cold," I said.

---

2. Noted for his stock characterizations of Irish figures (often priests) in American films of the 1940s and 1950s.

We dug in. We ate everything there was to eat on the table. We ate like there was no tomorrow. We didn't talk. We ate. We scarfed. We grazed that table. We were into serious eating. The blind man had right away located his foods, he knew just where everything was on his plate. I watched with admiration as he used his knife and fork on the meat. He'd cut two pieces of meat, fork the meat into his mouth, and then go all out for the scalloped potatoes, the beans next, and then he'd tear off a hunk of buttered bread and eat that. He'd follow this up with a big drink of milk. It didn't seem to bother him to use his fingers once in a while, either.

We finished everything, including half a strawberry pie. For a few moments, we sat as if stunned. Sweat beaded on our faces. Finally, we got up from the table and left the dirty plates. We didn't look back. We took ourselves into the living room and sank into our places again. Robert and my wife sat on the sofa. I took the big chair. We had us two or three more drinks while they talked about the major things that had come to pass for them in the past ten years. For the most part, I just listened. Now and then I joined in. I didn't want him to think I'd left the room, and I didn't want her to think I was feeling left out. They talked of things that had happened to them—to them!—these past ten years. I waited in vain to hear my name on my wife's sweet lips: "And then my dear husband came into my life"— something like that. But I heard nothing of the sort. More talk of Robert. Robert had done a little of everything, it seemed, a regular blind jack-of-all-trades. But most recently he and his wife had had an Amway[3] distributor-ship, from which, I gathered, they'd earned their living, such as it was. The blind man was also a ham radio operator. He talked in his loud voice about conversations he'd had with fellow operators in Guam, in the Philippines, in Alaska, and even in Tahiti. He said he'd have a lot of friends there if he ever wanted to go visit those places. From time to time, he'd turn his blind face toward me, put his hand under his beard, ask me something. How long had I been in my present position? (Three years.) Did I like my work? (I didn't.) Was I going to stay with it? (What were the options?) Finally, when I thought he was beginning to run down, I got up and turned on the TV.

My wife looked at me with irritation. She was heading toward a boil. Then she looked at the blind man and said, "Robert, do you have a TV?"

The blind man said, "My dear, I have two TVs. I have a color set and a black-and-white thing, an old relic. It's funny, but if I turn the TV on, and I'm always turning it on, I turn on the color set. It's funny, don't you think?"

I didn't know what to say to that. I had absolutely nothing to say to that. No opinion. So I watched the news program and tried to listen to what the announcer was saying.

"This is a color TV," the blind man said. "Don't ask me how, but I can tell."

"We traded up a while ago," I said.

The blind man had another taste of his drink. He lifted his beard, sniffed it, and let it fall. He leaned forward on the sofa. He positioned his ashtray on the coffee table, then put the lighter to his cigarette. He leaned back on the sofa and crossed his legs at the ankles.

---

3. A retail sales business operated by selling directly to consumers in their homes.

My wife covered her mouth, and then she yawned. She stretched. She said, "I think I'll go upstairs and put on my robe. I think I'll change into something else. Robert, you make yourself comfortable," she said.

"I'm comfortable," the blind man said.

"I want you to feel comfortable in this house," she said.

"I am comfortable," the blind man said.

After she'd left the room, he and I listened to the weather report and then to the sports roundup. By that time, she'd been gone so long I didn't know if she was going to come back. I thought she might have gone to bed. I wished she'd come back downstairs. I didn't want to be left alone with a blind man. I asked him if he wanted another drink, and he said sure. Then I asked if he wanted to smoke some dope with me. I said I'd just rolled a number. I hadn't, but I planned to do so in about two shakes.

"I'll try some with you," he said.

"Damn right," I said. "That's the stuff."

I got our drinks and sat down on the sofa with him. Then I rolled us two fat numbers. I lit one and passed it. I brought it to his fingers. He took it and inhaled.

"Hold it as long as you can," I said. I could tell he didn't know the first thing.

My wife came back downstairs wearing her pink robe and her pink slippers.

"What do I smell?" she said.

"We thought we'd have us some cannabis," I said.

My wife gave me a savage look. Then she looked at the blind man and said, "Robert, I didn't know you smoked."

He said, "I do now, my dear. There's a first time for everything. But I don't feel anything yet."

"This stuff is pretty mellow," I said. "This stuff is mild. It's dope you can reason with," I said. "It doesn't mess you up."

"Not much it doesn't, bub," he said, and laughed.

My wife sat on the sofa between the blind man and me. I passed her the number. She took it and toked and then passed it back to me. "Which way is this going?" she said. Then she said, "I shouldn't be smoking this. I can hardly keep my eyes open as it is. That dinner did me in. I shouldn't have eaten so much."

"It was the strawberry pie," the blind man said. "That's what did it," he said, and he laughed his big laugh. Then he shook his head.

"There's more strawberry pie," I said.

"Do you want some more, Robert?" my wife said.

"Maybe in a little while," he said.

We gave our attention to the TV. My wife yawned again. She said, "Your bed is made up when you feel like going to bed, Robert. I know you must have had a long day. When you're ready to go to bed, say so." She pulled his arm. "Robert?"

He came to and said, "I've had a real nice time. This beats tapes, doesn't it?"

I said, "Coming at you," and I put the number between his fingers. He inhaled, held the smoke, and then let it go. It was like he'd been doing it since he was nine years old.

"Thanks, bub," he said. "But I think this is all for me. I think I'm beginning to feel it," he said. He held the burning roach out for my wife.

"Same here," she said. "Ditto. Me, too." She took the roach and passed it to me. "I may just sit here for a while between you two guys with my eyes closed. But don't let me bother you, okay? Either one of you. If it bothers you, say so. Otherwise, I may just sit here with my eyes closed until you're ready to go to bed," she said. "Your bed's made up, Robert, when you're ready. It's right next to our room at the top of the stairs. We'll show you up when you're ready. You wake me up now, you guys, if I fall asleep." She said that and then she closed her eyes and went to sleep.

The news program ended. I got up and changed the channel. I sat back down on the sofa. I wished my wife hadn't pooped out. Her head lay across the back of the sofa, her mouth open. She'd turned so that her robe had slipped away from her legs, exposing a juicy thigh. I reached to draw her robe back over her, and it was then that I glanced at the blind man. What the hell! I flipped the robe open again.

"You say when you want some strawberry pie," I said.

"I will," he said.

I said, "Are you tired? Do you want me to take you up to your bed? Are you ready to hit the hay?"

"Not yet," he said. "No, I'll stay up with you, bub. If that's all right. I'll stay up until you're ready to turn in. We haven't had a chance to talk. Know what I mean? I feel like me and her monopolized the evening." He lifted his beard and he let it fall. He picked up his cigarettes and his lighter.

"That's all right," I said. Then I said, "I'm glad for the company."

And I guess I was. Every night I smoked dope and stayed up as long as I could before I fell asleep. My wife and I hardly ever went to bed at the same time. When I did go to sleep, I had these dreams. Sometimes I'd wake up from one of them, my heart going crazy.

Something about the church and the Middle Ages was on the TV. Not your run-of-the-mill TV fare. I wanted to watch something else. I turned to the other channels. But there was nothing on them, either. So I turned back to the first channel and apologized.

"Bub, it's all right," the blind man said. "It's fine with me. Whatever you want to watch is okay. I'm always learning something. Learning never ends. It won't hurt me to learn something tonight. I got ears," he said.

We didn't say anything for a time. He was leaning forward with his head turned at me, his right ear aimed in the direction of the set. Very disconcerting. Now and then his eyelids drooped and then they snapped open again. Now and then he put his fingers into his beard and tugged, like he was thinking about something he was hearing on the television.

On the screen, a group of men wearing cowls was being set upon and tormented by men dressed in skeleton costumes and men dressed as devils. The men dressed as devils wore devil masks, horns, and long tails. This pageant was part of a procession. The Englishman who was narrating the thing said it took place in Spain once a year. I tried to explain to the blind man what was happening.

"Skeletons," he said. "I know about skeletons," he said, and he nodded.

The TV showed this one cathedral. Then there was a long, slow look at another one. Finally, the picture switched to the famous one in Paris, with its flying buttresses and its spires reaching up to the clouds. The camera pulled away to show the whole of the cathedral rising above the skyline.

There were times when the Englishman who was telling the thing would shut up, would simply let the camera move around over the cathedrals. Or else the camera would tour the countryside, men in fields walking behind oxen. I waited as long as I could. Then I felt I had to say something. I said, "They're showing the outside of this cathedral now. Gargoyles. Little statues carved to look like monsters. Now I guess they're in Italy. Yeah, they're in Italy. There's paintings on the walls of this one church."

"Are those fresco paintings, bub?" he asked, and he sipped from his drink.

I reached for my glass. But it was empty. I tried to remember what I could remember. "You're asking me are those frescoes?" I said. "That's a good question. I don't know."

The camera moved to a cathedral outside Lisbon. The differences in the Portuguese cathedral compared with the French and Italian were not that great. But they were there. Mostly the interior stuff. Then something occurred to me, and I said, "Something has occurred to me. Do you have any idea what a cathedral is? What they look like, that is? Do you follow me? If somebody says cathedral to you, do you have any notion what they're talking about? Do you know the difference between that and a Baptist church, say?"

He let the smoke dribble from his mouth. "I know they took hundreds of workers fifty or a hundred years to build," he said. "I just heard the man say that, of course. I know generations of the same families worked on a cathedral. I heard him say that, too. The men who began their life's work on them, they never lived to see the completion of their work. In that wise, bub, they're no different from the rest of us, right?" He laughed. Then his eyelids drooped again. His head nodded. He seemed to be snoozing. Maybe he was imagining himself in Portugal. The TV was showing another cathedral now. This one was in Germany. The Englishman's voice droned on. "Cathedrals," the blind man said. He sat up and rolled his head back and forth. "If you want the truth, bub, that's about all I know. What I just said. What I heard him say. But maybe you could describe one to me? I wish you'd do it. I'd like that. If you want to know, I really don't have a good idea."

I stared hard at the shot of the cathedral on the TV. How could I even begin to describe it? But say my life depended on it. Say my life was being threatened by an insane guy who said I had to do it or else.

I stared some more at the cathedral before the picture flipped off into the countryside. There was no use. I turned to the blind man and said, "To begin with, they're very tall." I was looking around the room for clues. "They reach way up. Up and up. Toward the sky. They're so big, some of them, they have to have these supports. To help hold them up, so to speak. These supports are called buttresses. They remind me of viaducts, for some reason. But maybe you don't know viaducts, either? Sometimes the cathedrals have devils and such carved into the front. Sometimes lords and ladies. Don't ask me why this is," I said.

He was nodding. The whole upper part of his body seemed to be moving back and forth.

"I'm not doing so good, am I?" I said.

He stopped nodding and leaned forward on the edge of the sofa. As he listened to me, he was running his fingers through his beard. I wasn't getting through to him, I could see that. But he waited for me to go on just the same. He nodded, like he was trying to encourage me. I tried to think what else to say. "They're really big," I said. "They're massive. They're built of stone. Marble, too, sometimes. In those olden days, when they built cathedrals, men wanted to be close to God. In those olden days, God was an important part of everyone's life. You could tell this from their cathedral-building. I'm sorry," I said, "but it looks like that's the best I can do for you. I'm just no good at it."

"That's all right, bub," the blind man said. "Hey, listen. I hope you don't mind my asking you. Can I ask you something? Let me ask you a simple question, yes or no. I'm just curious and there's no offense. You're my host. But let me ask if you are in any way religious? You don't mind my asking?"

I shook my head. He couldn't see that, though. A wink is the same as a nod to a blind man. "I guess I don't believe in it. In anything. Sometimes it's hard. You know what I'm saying?"

"Sure, I do," he said.

"Right," I said.

The Englishman was still holding forth. My wife sighed in her sleep. She drew a long breath and went on with her sleeping.

"You'll have to forgive me," I said. "But I can't tell you what a cathedral looks like. It just isn't in me to do it. I can't do any more than I've done."

The blind man sat very still, his head down, as he listened to me.

I said, "The truth is, cathedrals don't mean anything special to me. Nothing. Cathedrals. They're something to look at on late-night TV. That's all they are."

It was then that the blind man cleared his throat. He brought something up. He took a handkerchief from his back pocket. Then he said, "I get it, bub. It's okay. It happens. Don't worry about it," he said. "Hey, listen to me. Will you do me a favor? I got an idea. Why don't you find us some heavy paper? And a pen. We'll do something. We'll draw one together. Get us a pen and some heavy paper. Go on, bub, get the stuff," he said.

So I went upstairs. My legs felt like they didn't have any strength in them. They felt like they did after I'd done some running. In my wife's room, I looked around. I found some ballpoints in a little basket on her table. And then I tried to think where to look for the kind of paper he was talking about.

Downstairs, in the kitchen, I found a shopping bag with onion skins in the bottom of the bag. I emptied the bag and shook it. I brought it into the living room and sat down with it near his legs. I moved some things, smoothed the wrinkles from the bag, spread it out on the coffee table.

The blind man got down from the sofa and sat next to me on the carpet.

He ran his fingers over the paper. He went up and down the sides of the paper. The edges, even the edges. He fingered the corners.

"All right," he said. "All right, let's do her."

He found my hand, the hand with the pen. He closed his hand over my hand. "Go ahead, bub, draw," he said. "Draw. You'll see. I'll follow along with you. It'll be okay. Just begin now like I'm telling you. You'll see. Draw," the blind man said.

So I began. First I drew a box that looked like a house. It could have been the house I lived in. Then I put a roof on it. At either end of the roof, I drew spires. Crazy.

"Swell," he said. "Terrific. You're doing fine," he said. "Never thought anything like this could happen in your lifetime, did you, bub? Well, it's a strange life, we all know that. Go on now. Keep it up."

I put in windows with arches. I drew flying buttresses. I hung great doors. I couldn't stop. The TV station went off the air. I put down the pen and closed and opened my fingers. The blind man felt around over the paper. He moved the tips of his fingers over the paper, all over what I had drawn, and he nodded.

"Doing fine," the blind man said.

I took up the pen again, and he found my hand. I kept at it. I'm no artist. But I kept drawing just the same.

My wife opened up her eyes and gazed at us. She sat up on the sofa, her robe hanging open. She said, "What are you doing? Tell me, I want to know."

I didn't answer her.

The blind man said, "We're drawing a cathedral. Me and him are working on it. Press hard," he said to me. "That's right. That's good," he said. "Sure. You got it, bub. I can tell. You didn't think you could. But you can, can't you? You're cooking with gas now. You know what I'm saying? We're going to really have us something here in a minute. How's the old arm?" he said. "Put some people in there now. What's a cathedral without people?"

My wife said, "What's going on? Robert, what are you doing? What's going on?"

"It's all right," he said to her. "Close your eyes now," the blind man said to me.

I did it. I closed them just like he said.

"Are they closed?" he said. "Don't fudge."

"They're closed," I said.

"Keep them that way," he said. He said, "Don't stop now. Draw."

So we kept on with it. His fingers rode my fingers as my hand went over the paper. It was like nothing else in my life up to now.

Then he said, "I think that's it. I think you got it," he said. "Take a look. What do you think?"

But I had my eyes closed. I thought I'd keep them that way for a little longer. I thought it was something I ought to do.

"Well?" he said. "Are you looking?"

My eyes were still closed. I was in my house. I knew that. But I didn't feel like I was inside anything.

"It's really something," I said.

1983

ISHMAEL REED
b. 1938

shmael Reed's love-hate affair with American popular culture has led him to both literary successes and entanglements with sociocultural obstacles. On the positive side his appreciation of America's cultural riches, including such American-born art forms as jazz, rhythm and blues, detective novels, comic books, and the rich blend of all the world's cultures and their unique vernaculars, has enabled him to champion a truly native literature apart from the standards imposed (in a colonial manner) from European culture. Perhaps partly in recognition of this versatility, Reed was awarded a MacArthur Foundation "genius" fellowship. Negatively, his unbounded sense of satire has managed to offend almost every interest group in the profession of literature, from feminists to creative-writing-program teachers of poetry. In the chapter from his novel *The Last Days of Louisiana Red* (1974) printed here, Reed humorously critiques a presumed ally, someone who teaches African American literature. The text being taught, Richard Wright's *Native Son* (1940), is one of the most important novels in American literature. Yet Reed objects to the stereotyping that this very success makes possible. So too for his character Minnie the Moocher from this same novel. The satire is especially cutting in naming the novel's chief feminist after a figure in bandleader Cab Calloway's song from the 1940s, an era of popular culture heavy with now-abhorrent sexual caricatures; it is effective, however, because of the way Reed shows how people like Minnie cooperate with their own oppression by maintaining forces of exclusion. It is to Reed's credit that he uses history and folklore to subvert such exclusionary processes, just as his novel employs figures from classic radio comedy such as Amos and Andy and their friend Kingfish to undermine ideas that, when stated by others, pass for the logic of a black bourgeoisie.

Reed draws a good picture of himself in the biographical note to his second novel, *Yellow Back Radio Broke-Down* (1969):

> Ishmael Reed was born in Chattanooga, Tennessee, on February 22, 1938. Chattanooga built a monument to every Confederate soldier killed in the Civil War, so Ishmael Reed spent his early years bumping into stone. He grew up in Buffalo, New York, where "polack" is scribbled on the bust of Chopin in Humboldt Park.
>
> Ishmael Reed attended the University of Buffalo and left after receiving rude phone calls from an anti-Gnostic bursar. At 20 he was stranded in North Platte, Nebraska. Buffalo Bill once had a drink there. He has taught American fiction at the University of California at Berkeley, and the University of Washington at Seattle.
>
> He startled the scientific community by making his home in New York City. Ishmael Reed has been buffaloed by many aspects of American society, which makes him uniquely qualified to write about the West.

Yellow Back Radio Broke-Down is indeed about the West, but a West in which a band of cowboy rustlers is confronted by the pope in a helicopter. Similar absurdities and anachronisms distinguish Reed's other novels, including the Egyptology and Haitian Voodoo of *Mumbo Jumbo* (1972), in which West Indian religion is employed for its imaginative resources, and the Civil War slave narrative of *Flight to*

Canada (1976). Subsequent novels lampoon contemporary politics, including political correctness; notable among these are *Reckless Eyeballing* (1986), *Japanese by Spring* (1993), and *Juice!* (2011).

Most of Ishmael Reed's literary methods are evident in *The Last Days of Louisiana Red*. Hoodoo is present in the folklore practices of Papa LaBas and his Solid Gumbo Works, an enterprise that, much like this native religion, draws on the spiritual nature of life, especially in contrast to the materialism of its rivals, Louisiana Red and the Moochers. It is set in a Berkeley, California, rife with early 1970s turbulence, including a university curriculum destabilized by an intellectual who, in the chapter printed here, dreams he has become the character Mary Dalton in Richard Wright's *Native Son*, a novel in which a rich, young white woman is inadvertently killed by her family's physically intimidating black chauffeur, Bigger Thomas. Sexual, racial, intellectual, and religious issues are thrown together in a mixed bag of popular references, all of which Reed shakes up and displays in fresh new postures. Like all good satirists, he exposes his subjects' weaknesses by emphasizing problems in their own terms.

Reed's poetry is an even more direct introduction to his general literary activity, for here is seen the blending of popular forms from many different cultures that to him constitutes truly American expression. His "Neo-HooDoo Manifesto," presented as a poem, is in fact a program for what Reed would write himself and help others publish (via his *Yardbird Reader* series of books and anthologies produced with the Before Columbus Foundation). His message is that a rich culture, an original culture, exists within the very forms that older European standards disallow as lowbrow. He catalogs a wide range of popular entertainment figures and devises a poetic language that employs the power of expression so evident in the rhythms of such music. His editing and anthologizing and small-press productions have called on the resources not just of African Americans but of Chinese Americans, Japanese Americans, white Americans of various ethnic backgrounds, and Native Americans, a blending of influences into non-Eurocentric aesthetic forms that is unique to America.

From The Last Days of Louisiana Red

Chapter 36

[MARY DALTON'S DREAM]

He was a blonde. He lay in the bed, tossing and turning. His room. What was that odor? The pungent odor of middle-class perfume making the air misty. He didn't feel right. His hair. What on earth was the matter with his hair? It was long and was covering the pillow. The pillows? They had a flower print and were pink. Pink? He rose in his bed and his breasts jiggled. BREASTS? THE BREASTS?? He looked back into the mirror next to the bed and his mouth made a black hollow hole of horror. "O MY GOD. MY GOD." He was a woman. You know what he said next, don't you, reader? He's from New York and so . . . you guessed it! "Kafka.[1] Pure Kafka," he said. A feeling crept over him. Tingly. What could he do? He felt like screaming, but he couldn't scream. Was that someone coming down the hall? He ran and jumped back into the bed, pulled the covers up to his neck

---

1. Franz Kafka (1883–1924), Austrian-Czech author of *The Metamorphosis*, in which the protagonist awakes to find himself turned into a giant insect.

and pretended to be asleep. Someone *was* coming down the hall. They stood for a moment outside in the hall. And then the knob slowly turned. Someone was now in the room; a dark foreboding shadow crept to the foot of the bed. A giant colored man—an Olmec-headed[2] giant wearing a chauffeur's cap. Max started to really scream this time.

"Please, Ms. Dalton,[3] you will wake the whole house," the figure says. *Look at that white bitch laying there. Sloppy drunk. Probably wants some peter too. That's all they think about anyway. I'll fuck her into a cunt energy crisis she mess with me. That's probably what she wont. Been hittin on me all night. Probably pretending to be drunk. Wonts to see how far I go. I know Jan ain't gettin any. One simple dude. Tried to give me that old PROGRESSIVE LABOR[4] line. Who don't know that? Who don't know that old simple ass mutherfuckin bullshit? Them mens was working at the Ford plant. Had some good jobs too. Then here come this Progressive Labor bullshit and them niggers lost they job after it was over. Ha! When is this bitch going to go to sleep? I wont to take that dark blue Buick with steel spoke wheels over to the South Side. Man, will them mo'fugs be mad when they see. Think I'm a pimp. Then I'll go up to the counter and roll out my 75 dollars. Man, they think I'm one of them pimps. Then I go get me some rangs. Lots of them. Have them all shining on my fingers. Shining. Justa shining. Gee. Bet I could have me plenty ol stankin bitches. Commisstee. That shit ain't nothing but some bunk. Roosia. Shhhhhhit. Started to bust that mo'fug Jan right in the mouf. Must be a sissy. . . . The door opens and in comes a woman tapping a cane. Ahhhh-shitt. Here come that other old crazy white woman down the hall. Look like Ms. Mary trying to say something. I better do something quick.*

Max finally realized the situation. He made a futile effort to move his lips. "Bigggg. Bigggggg." Meanwhile the cane tapping comes closer to the door. Bigger picks up the pillow and starts towards Mary Dalton when—

Max wakes up from the nightmare.

There was some bamming at the door real rough. Bam! Bam! Bam! Bam! Bam, Bam! Max leaped out of his dream and rushed to the door. Who could this be bamming at his door this time of night? The woman, trembling, rushed into the room.

"What do you want? I told you to never come here."

She wriggled out of her raincoat, then nervously wrung out a match after lighting a cigarette. She plopped down in a chair and drew her breath. It was Lisa, stripped of her Nanny's rags, sharp, voluptuous.

"It's LaBas. He called. He wants to talk about Ed's killing. Suppose he starts to ask me a lot of questions? You know I can't stand up under a lot of questions."

"You fool. You come here for that? I told you never to contact me here on this assignment."

"Look, you've only been here for a few years. I've been here more than ten, ever since his wife Ruby left. I've worked on that household and put my conjure all over the place. Then they sent you in to begin this organization

---

2. Large-headed statues were a cultural characteristic of the Olmec, pre-Aztec Indian peoples of what is now Tabasco and Veracruz in Mexico.
3. The character murdered by Bigger Thomas in

Native Son (1940), a novel by the American writer Richard Wright (1908–1960).
4. A Marxist magazine and political party active in the United States beginning in the 1930s.

to add to Ed's problems. Just as I had worked hard to prepare Minnie to do that. We've done enough damage to that family. When will it end?"

"It will end when Solid Gumbo Works has folded."

"I can't wait any longer. Since Wolf was killed, she's brought those Moochers into the household. I have to shuffle about like Hattie McDaniel[5] to take care of their needs. They write slogans all over the walls and sleep on stained mattresses. They leave rings in the bathtub. They've been up all night with the mimeograph machine, trying to free Kingfish and Andy."[6]

"Yes, I know," Max said. "I wrote the copy."

"I have to fix breakfast and clean up their mess. You know how Moochers are, never clean up after themselves, always expect someone else to do their cleaning for them. I told you not to draw the girl into that organization. I was doing O.K. All I needed was some more time."

"You were taking too long. Besides, the Moochers provided us with the numbers to wear down Solid Gumbo Works."

"Well, I still maintain that if it had been left to me, I would have put her on Ed. I never did go along with his killing."

"It was necessary. You know that. If we hadn't butchered him that night, he would have discovered the cure for heroin addiction. That was the industrial secret you passed on to me; the papers of his you Xeroxed. We had to do it. If he had found a legitimate cure, our quack operation would have shut down: the southern mailhouse empire we built would shut down. Heroin, jukeboxes, our black record company in the east, The House of Cocaine. Everybody would have been asking for Ed's Gumbo. Wasn't it enough that he found a cure for cancer?"

"You thought you'd gotten rid of that threat when you killed that Chinese acupuncturist, but Ed found different means."

"You always respected him a bit, didn't you?"

"He was a man. Ed was a hard-working man. Sometimes I wanted to tell him who I was, where I was from, and what was wrong with me. That I had been sent into his house to train his child to drive him crazy."

"You can't quit. I received orders from Louisiana Red that we have one more job. You think you have problems. Do you think I like posing as a visiting lecturer at the University of California at Berkeley? The way the women in the English Department office whisper about my lack of potency and sometimes refuse to file for my office post box.

"Do you think that I enjoy it when they refuse to mimeograph copies of lecture notes for my students? Why, this campus reminds me of the set of *I Was a Teenage Werewolf*.[7] If Louisiana Red hadn't promised me this one-million-dollar retirement money, I never would have taken care of this assignment. I was doing all right with my New York industrial spy firm. But you, you have to stay until it's over. They have you where they want you."

---

5. An actress known for portraying African American maids in American films of the 1930s and 1940s, including *Gone with the Wind* (1939), for which she won the Academy Award for Best Supporting Actress.

6. African American characters in the *Amos 'n' Andy* radio and television comedy show of the 1930s, '40s, and '50s.
7. Popular American film of the 1950s.

"I'm leaving."

Max pulls out a sheet of paper from a desk drawer. "You know that Louisiana Red doesn't play. They will get to you through your police record. You are a fugitive from justice, you know, you bag woman. (Reads) 'Real name: The Hammerhead Shark.' The title you picked up in that caper when you hit a man on the head with a hammer, put a hex on a congressman, double-crossed Jack Johnson, stabbed Martin Luther King, brought charges against Father Divine, brought down Sam Cooke in a blaze of gunfire and bad-mouthed Joe Louis.[8] They know your penchant for Coon-Can and about your scar too. Not only are the law enforcement bureaus after you, but you know the consequences of crossing the Louisiana Red Corporation."

"I'm not frightened any more. I've sent a message to the Red Rooster and told him that I want out, Max."

"I've thought about leaving myself."

"You have? Why, Max, we can leave together, go to Reno; why, I can get a job as a waitress, you can deal blackjack."

"But they'll follow us."

"Not if we move fast enough."

"Maybe we ought to. You know how I missed you during those long days. When you couldn't be with me in my arms. How we had to limit ourselves to meeting every other Thursday, your day off. There must be thousands of us all over the country, meeting like this out of public view."

"Yes, my dearest, the American underground of Desire, the name of the first American slaver; we know each other on the street and recognize each other's signals. How we pay subscriptions to our propaganda organs which convince the public that it's only the Jim Brown and Racquel Welch[9] bedroom scene that's the problem. We rule America, all of it, my Nanny and me. The 'Every Other Thursday Society.' Yes, I want to leave, Lisa. My cover is getting to me."

"I don't understand."

"That book I'm doing—the one on Richard Wright's book." He rushes to the bar, makes a drink and gulps it down. Then he slams the empty glass on the bar. "It's getting to me. I'm having these dreams. Just before you knocked on the door, I had one. I was the murder victim and this big brute was coming towards me with a pillow."

"That dream will come true if you won't move over to the wall."

The startled couple turned around to see the gunman standing in the doorway.

"Son of a bitch. So you were going to take it on the lam and leave me stranded now that the assignment has heated up."

"T, take it easy, have a drink."

"No thanks, I'm not thirsty. Here I have been playing the fool for these past years, helping you set up Ed Yellings, and now you are going to drop me. Years of swallowing my pride and acting like a kookie rookie when all

8. Popular figures from African American culture. Johnson (1878–1946), first black heavyweight champion of the world. King (1929–1968), civil rights leader. Father Divine, born George Baker (1877–1965), American religious leader.

Cooke (1935–1964), popular singer. Louis (1914–1981), world heavyweight boxing champion.
9. Then current film stars, respectively African American and white.

along you two were carrying on. I'm finished with this assignment. I feel sick about what has happened to Minnie. She wants more power now than Marie Laveau,[1] and you two did it to her. I'm going to call the Director of Louisiana Red Corporation, the Red Rooster, and tell him everything I know about you two. You see, it's all over. That's what I came up here to tell you about."

"What's all over?" Lisa says. "You don't make sense."

"About an hour ago Minnie busted George Kingfish Stevens and Andy Brown out of jail and then commandeered an airplane after miraculously evading San Francisco security, which was as tight as a drum. You don't have anything else to use against Solid Gumbo Works because Minnie has been shot."

"Shot," both Lisa and Max exclaim.

"Yes, she was shot by a passenger. The poor child was rushed to a New York hospital. It sickens me, my part in this whole thing."

He walks over to the telephone and dials.

"Hello, operator, give me Louisiana Red Corporation in New Orleans, person to person to the Red Rooster, the number is area code 504—" but before he could say anything Max lunged for him and with incredible strength wrestled him to the floor. The gun went off, killing T Feeler.

"Max, let's get out of here. We really must go now."

Max slowly looked up from where he knelt over the corpse. "Who you callin Max, bitch? I'll whip you into bad health."

"Max, what's the matter with you? Why are you talking that way?"

"I'm gone fix you good. Killing you won't count. Not even the best critics will notice it. I'm going to kill you." He walks towards her. She screams.

"Max! Stop!"

"Max? Who Max? I'm Bigger," Max growls.

1974

Neo-HooDoo Manifesto[1]

Neo-HooDoo is a "Lost American Church" updated. Neo-HooDoo is the music of James Brown[2] without the lyrics and ads for Black Capitalism. Neo-HooDoo is the 8 basic dances of 19-century New Orleans' *Place Congo*—the Calinda the Bamboula the Chacta the Babouille the Conjaille the Juba the Congo and the VooDoo—modernized into the Philly Dog, the Hully Gully, the Funky Chicken, the Popcorn, the Boogaloo and the dance of great American choreographer Buddy Bradley.

Neo-HooDoos would rather "shake that thing" than be stiff and erect. (There were more people performing a Neo-HooDoo sacred dance, the Boogaloo, at Woodstock than chanting Hare Krishna . . . Hare Hare!) All

---

1. Quasi-legendary hoodoo priestess in old New Orleans.
1. From *Conjure: Selected Poems, 1963–1970*

(1972).
2. African American rhythm-and-blues singer and bandleader (1933–2006).

so-called "Store Front Churches" and "Rock Festivals"[3] receive their matrix in the HooDoo rites of Marie Laveau[4] conducted at New Orleans' Lake Pontchartrain, and Bayou St. John in the 1880's. The power of HooDoo challenged the stability of civil authority in New Orleans and was driven underground where to this day it flourishes in the Black ghettos throughout the country. Thats why in Ralph Ellison's[5] modern novel *Invisible Man* New Orleans is described as "The Home of Mystery." "Everybody from New Orleans got that thing," Louis Armstrong[6] said once.

HooDoo is the strange and beautiful "fits" the Black slave Tituba gave the children of Salem.[7] (Notice the arm waving ecstatic females seemingly possessed at the "Pentecostal," "Baptist," and "Rock Festivals," [all fronts for Neo-HooDoo]). The reason that HooDoo isn't given the credit it deserves in influencing American Culture is because the students of that culture both "overground" and "underground" are uptight closet Jeho-vah revisionists. They would assert the American and East Indian and Chinese thing before they would the Black thing. Their spiritual leaders Ezra Pound and T. S. Eliot[8] hated Africa and "Darkies." In Theodore Roszak's book *The Making of a Counter Culture*[9]—there is barely any mention of the Black influence on this culture even though its members dress like Blacks talk like Blacks walk like Blacks, gesture like Blacks wear Afros and indulge in Black music and dance (Neo-HooDoo).

Neo-HooDoo is sexual, sensual and digs the old "heathen" good good loving. An early American HooDoo song says:

> Now lady I ain't no mill man
> Just the mill man's son
> But I can do your grinding
> till the mill man comes

Which doesn't mean that women are treated as "sexual toys" in Neo-HooDoo or as one slick Jeho-vah Revisionist recently said, "victims of a raging hormone imbalance." Neo-HooDoo claims many women philosophers and theoreticians which is more than ugh religions Christianity and its offspring Islam can claim. When our theoretician Zora Neale Hurston[1] asked a *Mambo* (a female priestess in the Haitian VooDoo) a definition of VooDoo the Mambo lifted her skirts and exhibited her Erzulie Seal, her Isis seal. Neo-HooDoo identifies with Julia Jackson[2] who stripped HooDoo of its oppressive Catholic layer—Julia Jackson said when asked the origin of the amulets and talismans in her studio, "I make all my own stuff. It saves money and it's as good. People who has to buy their stuff ain't using their heads."

3. Massively attended concerts, often outdoors, popular in the 1960s and 1970s; Woodstock was the major one. "Store Front Churches": small churches with improvised sites in neighborhood shops.
4. See n. 1, p. 759.
5. African American writer (1914–1994).
6. American jazz musician and vocalist (1900–1971).
7. A town in Massachusetts that was the site of witchcraft hysteria in 1692.
8. Pound (1885–1972) and Eliot (1888–1965) were modernist American and Anglo-American poets, respectively.
9. A 1969 study of contemporary young people's revolt against establishment codes and traditions.
1. American fiction writer, poet, and folklorist (1891–1960).
2. Prominent hoodoo practitioner in New Orleans in the 1940s.

Neo-HooDoo is not a church for egotripping—it takes its "organization" from Haitian VooDoo of which Milo Rigaud wrote:

Unlike other established religions, there is no hierarchy of bishops, archbishops, cardinals, or a pope in VooDoo. Each oum'phor is a law unto itself, following the traditions of VooDoo but modifying and changing the ceremonies and rituals in various ways. Secrets of VooDoo.

Neo-HooDoo believes that every man is an artist and every artist a priest. You can bring your own creative ideas to Neo-HooDoo. Charlie "Yardbird (Thoth)" Parker[3] is an example of the Neo-HooDoo artist as an innovator and improvisor.

In Neo-HooDoo, Christ the landlord deity ("render unto Caesar") is on probation. This includes "The Black Christ" and "The Hippie Christ." Neo-HooDoo tells Christ to get lost. (Judas Iscariot holds an honorary degree from Neo-HooDoo.)

Whereas at the center of Christianity lies the graveyard the organ-drone and the cross, the center of Neo-HooDoo is the drum the anhk and the Dance. So Fine, Barefootin, Heard it Through the Grapevine,[4] are all Neo-HooDoos.

Neo-HooDoo has "seen a lot of things in this old world."

Neo-HooDoo borrows from Ancient Egyptians (ritual accessories of Ancient Egypt are still sold in the House of Candles and Talismans on Stanton Street in New York, the Botanical Gardens in East Harlem, and Min and Mom on Haight Street in San Francisco, examples of underground centers found in ghettos throughout America).

Neo-HooDoo borrows from Haiti Africa and South America. Neo-HooDoo comes in all styles and moods. Louis Jordon Nellie Lutcher John Lee Hooker Ma Rainey Dinah Washington the Temptations Ike and Tina Turner Aretha Franklin Muddy Waters Otis Redding Sly and the Family Stone B. B. King Junior Wells Bessie Smith Jelly Roll Morton Ray Charles Jimi Hendrix Buddy Miles the 5th Dimension the Chambers Brothers Etta James and acolytes Creedence Clearwater Revival the Flaming Embers Procol Harum are all Neo-HooDoos. Neo-HooDoo never turns down pork. In fact Neo-HooDoo is the Bar-B-Cue of Amerika. The Neo-HooDoo cuisine is Geechee Gree Gree Verta Mae's *Vibration Cooking*.[5] (Ortiz Walton's Neo-HooDoo Jass Band performs at the Native Son Restaurant in Berkeley, California. Joe Overstreet's[6] Neo-HooDoo exhibit will happen at the Berkeley Gallery Sept. 1, 1970 in Berkeley.)

---

3. American jazz musician (1920–1955), pioneer of the bebop style of modern jazz.
4. Popular rock 'n' roll and rhythm-and-blues songs that inspired new dances.
5. This paragraph lists a mélange of contemporary popular musicians and musical groups from a wide range of musical styles, including the blues, jazz, rock 'n' roll, and Motown.
6. American painter (b. 1934)

Neo-HooDoo ain't Negritude.[7] Neo-HooDoo never been to France. Neo-HooDoo is "your Mama" as Larry Neal[8] said. Neo-HooDoos Little Richard and Chuck Berry nearly succeeded in converting the Beatles.[9] When the Beatles said they were more popular than Christ they seemed astonished at the resulting outcry. This is because although they could feebly through amplification and technological sham "mimic" (as if Little Richard and Chuck Berry were Loa [Spirits] practicing ventriloquism on their "Horses") the Beatles failed to realize that they were conjuring the music and ritual (although imitation) of a Forgotten Faith, a traditional enemy of Christianity which Christianity the Cop Religion has had to drive underground each time they meet. Neo-HooDoo now demands a rematch, the referees were bribed and the adversary had resin on his gloves.

The Vatican Forbids Jazz Masses in Italy
Rome, Aug. 6 (UPI)—The Vatican today barred jazz and popular music from masses in Italian churches and forbade young Roman Catholics to change prayers or readings used on Sundays and holy days.

It said such changes in worship were "eccentric and arbitrary."

A Vatican document distributed to all Italian bishops did not refer to similar experimental masses elsewhere in the world, although Pope Paul VI and other high-ranking churchmen are known to dislike the growing tendency to deviate from the accepted form of the mass.

Some Italian churches have permitted jazz masses played by combos while youthful worshipers sang such songs as "We Shall Overcome."

Church leaders two years ago rebuked priests who permitted such experiments. The New York Times, August 7, 1970.

Africa is the home of the Ioa (Spirits) of Neo-HooDoo although we are building our own American "pantheon." Thousands of "Spirits" (Ka) who would laugh at Jeho-vah's fury concerning "false idols" (translated everybody else's religion) or "fetishes." Moses, Jeho-vah's messenger and zombie swiped the secrets of VooDoo from old Jethro but nevertheless ended up with a curse. (Warning, many White "Black delineators" who practiced HooDoo VooDoo for gain and did not "feed" the Black Spirits of HooDoo ended up tragically. Bix Beiderbecke and Irene Castle (who exploited Black Dance in the 1920s and relished in dressing up as a Nun) are examples of this tragic tendency.

Moses had a near heart attack when he saw his sons dancing nude before the Black Bull God Apis. They were dancing to a "heathen sound" that Moses had "heard before in Egypt" (probably a mixture of Sun Ra and Jimmy Reed[1] played in the nightclub district of ancient Egypt's "The Domain of Osiris"—named after the god who enjoyed the fancy footwork of the pigmies).

---

7. A 20th-century literary school of poetry written in French by African authors.
8. Music critic, theoretician of African American literature, and anthologist (1937–1981).
9. British rock group of the 1960s. Little Richard (b. 1932) and Chuck Berry (b. 1926), African American rock 'n' rollers who had a formative influence on the Beatles.
1. Blues musician (1925–1976) from the 1950s. Sun Ra (1914–1993), avant-garde jazz musician of the 1950s.

The continuing war between Moses and his "Sons" was recently acted out in Chicago in the guise of an American "trial."

I have called Jeho-vah (most likely Set the Egyptian Sat-on [a pun on the fiend's penalty] Satan) somewhere "a party-pooper and hater of dance." Neo-HooDoos are detectives of the metaphysical about to make a pinch. We have issued warrants for a god arrest. If Jeho-vah reveals his real name he will be released on his own recognizance de-horned and put out to pasture.

A dangerous paranoid pain-in-the-neck a CopGod from the git-go, Jeho-vah was the successful law and order candidate in the mythological relay of the 4th century A.D. Jeho-vah is the God of punishment. The H-Bomb is a typical Jeho-vah "miracle." Jeho-vah is why we are in Vietnam.[2] He told Moses to go out and "subdue" the world.

There has never been in history another such culture as the Western civilization—a culture which has practiced the belief that the physical and social environment of man is subject to rational manipulation and that history is subject to the will and action of man; whereas central to the traditional cultures of the rivals of Western civilization, those of Africa and Asia, is a belief that it is environment that dominates man. The Politics of Hysteria, *Edmund Stillman and William Pfaff.*

"Political leaders" are merely altar boys from Jeho-vah. While the targets of some "revolutionaries" are laundramats and candy stores, Neo-HooDoo targets are TV the museums the symphony halls and churches art music and literature departments in Christianizing (education I think they call it!) universities which propogate the Art of Jeho-vah—much Byzantine Middle Ages Renaissance painting of Jeho-vah's "500 years of civilization" as Nixon[3] put it are Jeho-vah propaganda. Many White revolutionaries can only get together with 3rd world people on the most mundane 'political' level because they are of Jeho-vah's party and don't know it. How much Black music do so-called revolutionary underground radio stations play. On the other hand how much Bach?[4]

Neo-HooDoos are Black Red (Black Hawk an American Indian was an early philosopher of the HooDoo Church) and occasionally White (Mademoiselle Charlotte is a Haitian Loa [Spirit]).

Neo-HooDoo is a litany seeking its text
Neo-HooDoo is a Dance and Music closing in on its words
Neo-HooDoo is a Church finding its lyrics
Cecil Brown Al Young Calvin Hernton

---

2. The war in Vietnam was being waged at the time this essay was written. In 1965 then president Lyndon Johnson delivered a famous speech, "Why We Are in Vietnam."
3. Richard Nixon (1913–1994) was president of the United States at the time this essay was written.
4. Johann Sebastian Bach (1685–1750), German organist and composer.

David Henderson Steven Cannon Quincy Troupe
Ted Joans Victor Cruz N. H. Pritchard Ishmael Reed
Lennox Raphael Sarah Fabio Ron Welburn[5] are Neo-
HooDoo's "Manhattan Project"[6] of writing . . .

A Neo-HooDoo celebration will involve the dance music
and poetry of Neo-HooDoo and whatever ideas the
participating artists might add. A Neo-HooDoo seal
is the Face of an Old American Train.
Neo-HooDoo signs are everywhere!
Neo-HooDoo is the Now Locomotive swinging
up the Tracks of the American Soul.

Almost 100 years ago HooDoo was forced to say
Goodbye to America. Now HooDoo is
back as Neo-HooDoo
You can't keep a good church down!

1972

---

5. These lines list contemporary multicultural writers.
6. The research program that developed the atomic bomb for use at the end of World War II.

CHARLES SIMIC
b. 1938

Charles Simic came to the United States from Belgrade, Yugoslavia, at the age of sixteen. When in 2007 he was named as poet laureate of the United States for the coming year, he responded that he was "especially touched and honored to be selected because I am an immigrant boy who didn't speak English until I was fifteen." His earliest childhood memories are of bombs dropping, people disappearing, and buildings in ruins. "My own home movie begins with the German bombing of Belgrade on April 6, 1941," he has said, "when a bomb hit the building across the street. I flew out of my bed all the way across the room. I was three years old and more astonished than I actually was frightened by the flames that rose everywhere." The unpredictability of Simic's poetry, with its feeling for the bizarre and irrational quality of ordinary things, may have originated in his childhood. During the German occupation of Yugoslavia a civil war broke out among the partisans; before long the communist Marshal Tito emerged as the Yugoslav leader. In 1944 the American and British forces bombed German-occupied Belgrade, where the Simics continued to live. After the war Tito established a repressive communist regime: "People were being arrested left and right. Everybody was afraid. In school there was indoctrination," Simic writes in his memoir *A Fly in the Soup* (2000). During those years Simic, his mother, and his brother spent time in refugee camps and prisons; they were finally able to leave Yugoslavia for Paris in 1953. A year later they immigrated to the United States, where his father was already living. "After what we had been through," he writes, "the wildest lies seemed plausible and the poems that I was going to write had to take that into account."

Simic's poetry is often full of mysterious fragments, as if some unspecified force has detonated both the larger, cohesive structure of the world and the narrative of the poem. At the same time Simic's stanzas function as regulating and balancing structures in tension with what is incomprehensible and often absurd. This tension, along with Simic's deadpan tone, renders the comic and the frightening qualities of a world where truth and justice are "The Famous No-Shows" and existence is a cosmic joke. It is not surprising that Simic admires the early film comedian Buster Keaton (1895–1966) for his "serenity in the face of chaos." The joke in Simic's poems is also a form of black humor, born of a historical dread that Simic attributes to life in the twentieth century. Menace permeates the ordinary and domestic moments in Simic's poems. In "A Book Full of Pictures" a child is reading, a father studying, a mother knitting, but the quiet of the poem is disturbing. A "black rain-coat / in the upstairs bedroom" sways from the ceiling. The declarative statements of the poem, like the click of the knitting needles, seem designed to fend off violence within and without the scene.

Simic's years in a Yugoslavia that monitored dissent through a secret police taught him the brutal consequences of a politically repressive conformity, and he has always been attracted to irreverence and unpredictability. As a young man he lived in New York and was drawn to surrealist poetry and to the wild flights of twentieth-century Latin American verse. Impatient with what he saw as the academic conservatism of poetry in the 1950s and early 1960s, he wrote verse that celebrated surreal and associative leaps (exemplified by the "controlled anarchy" of the jazz saxophonist Sonny Rollins, who is depicted in Faith Ringgold's painting *Sonny's Quilt*, reproduced in the color insert in this anthology) and untamable erotic impulses. His work since that period continues to celebrate irreverence and humor. Along with such outward wildness, Simic's poetry is full of secrets, and the presence of something hidden frequently disturbs or haunts a Simic poem. Often the poems read like enigmatic disclosures in the form of riddles or jokes. He loves metaphysical speculation and can suggest philosophical questions through the most particular and even ordinary things, such as a fork or a glove; he has said that he practices "a kind of bedroom and kitchen metaphysics."

Among Simic's many books are *Selected Poems 1963–1983* (1985, revised and expanded 1990), *The Book of Gods and Devils* (1990), *Hotel Insomnia* (1992), *Walking the Black Cat* (1996), *Jackstraws* (1999), *Night Picnic* (2001), *The Voice at 3:00 A.M.: Selected Late and New Poems* (2003), *My Noiseless Entourage* (2005), *That Little Something* (2008), and *The Monster Loves the Labyrinth* (2008). *Master of Disguises* (2010) shows Simic at the height of his powers. His *New and Selected Poems, 1962–2012* appeared in 2013 and he has continued to publish since. In addition he has edited and translated the work of Eastern European poets such as Vasko Popa and Tomaz Salamun. His collections of essays and memoirs include *The Uncertain Certainty* (1985), *Wonderful Words Silent Truth* (1990), and *A Fly in the Soup* (2000). Simic has described his work as a kind of "nonsense made up of fiction, autobiography, the essay, poetry, and, of course, the joke." With their mixture of the comic and the terrible and with their surreal storytelling power, Simic's poems haunt the mind long after one has read them.

Fork

This strange thing must have crept
Right out of hell.
It resembles a bird's foot
Worn around the cannibal's neck.

As you hold it in your hand,   5
As you stab with it into a piece of meat,
It is possible to imagine the rest of the bird:
Its head which like your fist
Is large, bald, beakless and blind.

                                                    1971

Prodigy

I grew up bent over
a chessboard.

I loved the word *endgame*.[1]

All my cousins looked worried.

It was a small house   5
near a Roman graveyard.
Planes and tanks
shook its windowpanes.

A retired professor of astronomy
taught me how to play.   10

That must have been in 1944.

In the set we were using,
the paint had almost chipped off
the black pieces.

The white King was missing   15
and had to be substituted for.

I'm told but do not believe
that that summer I witnessed
men hung from telephone poles.

I remember my mother   20
blindfolding me a lot.
She had a way of tucking my head
suddenly under her overcoat.

In chess, too, the professor told me,
the masters play blindfolded,   25
the great ones on several boards
at the same time.

                                                    1980

1. Late stage of a chess game after the major reduction of forces.

A Book Full of Pictures

Father studied theology through the mail
And this was exam time.
Mother knitted. I sat quietly with a book
Full of pictures. Night fell.
My hands grew cold touching the faces   5
Of dead kings and queens.

There was a black raincoat
   in the upstairs bedroom
Swaying from the ceiling,
But what was it doing there?   10
Mother's long needles made quick crosses.
They were black
Like the inside of my head just then.

The pages I turned sounded like wings.
"The soul is a bird," he once said.   15
In my book full of pictures
A battle raged: lances and swords
Made a kind of wintry forest
With my heart spiked and bleeding in its branches.

1992

Arriving Celebrities

Tragedy and Comedy
Stepping out of a limousine
In ritzy furs;
Diminutive skirts,
Blowing kisses   5
Left and right.

Bedlam of adoring fans,
Pushing and squeezing,
Hollering for a glimpse,
When—all of a sudden!   10
A hush.
An all-inclusive clam-up.

Is someone, I inquired
Of my neighbors,
Already lying knifed   15
On the dance floor
Mouthing the name
We are all straining to overhear?

The towering bodyguards
With shaved heads   20
And mirror-tinted shades,
Don't hear me right,
Or will not deign
To grant my presence.

1999

MICHAEL S. HARPER
1938–2016

"I've been listening to music all my life," Michael S. Harper once said, and his first book of poems, *Dear John, Dear Coltrane* (1970), took its title from his poem to the great American jazz saxophonist. Recalling Coltrane's life in his prose piece "Don't They Speak Jazz," Harper told this story: "Trane was searching for a particular tone on his horn; he had what we thought was a perfect embouchure, but his teeth hurt constantly, so he searched for the soft reed which would ease the pain. After searching for a year, each session killing his chops, he gave it up completely; there was no easy way to get that sound: play through the pain to *a love supreme*." Playing through the pain is a part of what Harper brought to his poetry. Like the great blues singers and jazz musicians, his work celebrates life as song, especially as tragic song, full of losses and griefs, but song nevertheless. Sometimes the pain Harper sings through is personal, like the death of one of his sons in "Deathwatch" (he and his wife lost two of their infant sons shortly after birth); sometimes the pain belongs to family history (as in "Grandfather"). Sometimes it is the pain of history more generally, its violence and oppression.

History was Harper's second love as a poet, following right behind music. His poem to Coltrane, while dependent on the techniques of jazz and the blues, reflects Harper's concern with an imaginative recovery of history, especially black history, in an America where (as he once put it) the "amnesia level" is high. "I think the important thing about Americans is that they're not very good historians," Harper has said. "And Americans are really bad historians when it comes to moral ideas because they can't keep them in their heads very long." For Harper, to be a poet was to be a good historian; history identifies and inscribes moral issues that continue to engage us in the present. In college, Harper recalled, he read William Carlos Williams's *In the American Grain* (1925), in which Williams announces that "History for us begins with murder and enslavement, not with discovery." Like Williams, Harper wanted to bring his personal imagination in contact with an American history (black and white) essentially tragic, tragic because, he said, "so many possibilities exist and there's been so much waste." This tragic sense informs Harper's work perhaps most clearly in his volume *Nightmare Begins Responsibility* (1975)—the title is a variation on one of the Irish poet William Butler Yeats's epigraphs—where a personal sense of loss is never separable from the sufferings of black history or of human history more generally. *Honorable Amendments* appeared in 1995, and *Songlines in Michaeltree: New and Collected Poems* was published in 2000.

Born in Brooklyn, New York, Harper remembered a childhood in which "my parents weren't rich, but they had a good record collection." He grew up hearing the blues and jazz, but also reading the work of Langston Hughes and, later, James Baldwin and Ralph Ellison, and his poetic technique owed something to his literary as well as to his musical sensibility. An additional resource was a family tradition of oral storytelling ("My people were good storytellers," he has said), out of which some of his poems have grown. In fact, the jazz techniques of variation on a theme, of improvisation around an existing form, recall traditions of oral storytelling and both the jazz and oral traditions that influenced the formal experiments of an Ellison or a Baldwin. After high school Harper earned a B.A. and an M.A. at what is now California State University, Los Angeles, then went to the University of Iowa for an MFA. His travels abroad, first to Mexico and Europe and later (1977) to South Africa, intensified his historical sense both of his own family roots and of their connection with racial history. From 1970 until his death in 2016, Harper taught at Brown University, where he was a professor of English and director of the writing program.

"Most great art is finally testamental," Harper wrote; "its technical brilliance never shadows the content of the song." Harper wrote poems to remember and to witness, but at times the urgency of the content overpowered his form and his language could not sustain the urgency the poem asserted. This may be the cost for a poet whose engagement with moral issues, whose deep historical sense, and whose rhythmic inventiveness enabled him to create powerful and moving poems. His finest work possesses what he admired in Coltrane: "the energy and passion with which he approached his instrument and music," resembling the energy it takes "to break oppressive conditions, oppressive musical structures, and oppressive societal structures." Harper's inclusive sense of history let him write (in "Blue Ruth: America") that "history is your own heartbeat," but also let him hear his own heart beat in time with those who lived in other times, other places. Responsible to memory, Harper also shared the affirmative impulse found in the blues: "The blues say 'Yes' to life no matter what it is. That doesn't mean you're going to survive it. But it means you're going to say yes to it."

Dear John, Dear Coltrane[1]

a love supreme, a love supreme
a love supreme, a love supreme

Sex fingers toes
in the marketplace
near your father's church
in Hamlet, North Carolina[2]—
witness to this love   5
in this calm fallow
of these minds,
there is no substitute for pain:
genitals gone or going,
seed burned out,   10
you tuck the roots in the earth,
turn back, and move

---

1. John Coltrane (1926–1967), avant-garde jazz musician. The epigraph is a phrase chanted at the beginning of his four-part composition *A* *Love Supreme*.

2. Coltrane's birthplace.

by river through the swamps,
singing: *a love supreme, a love supreme*;
what does it all mean? 15
Loss, so great each black
woman expects your failure
in mute change, the seed gone.
You plod up into the electric city—
your song now crystal and 20
the blues. You pick up the horn
with some will and blow
into the freezing night:
a love supreme, a love supreme—

Dawn comes and you cook 25
up the thick sin 'tween
impotence and death, fuel
the tenor sax cannibal
heart, genitals and sweat
that makes you clean— 30
a love supreme, a love supreme—

Why you so black?
cause I am
why you so funky?
cause I am 35
why you so black?
cause I am
why you so sweet?
cause I am
why you so black? 40
cause I am
a love supreme, a love supreme:

So sick
you couldn't play *Naima*,[3]
so flat we ached 45
for song you'd concealed
with your own blood,
your diseased liver gave
out its purity,
the inflated heart 50
pumps out, the tenor[4] kiss,
tenor love:
a love supreme, a love supreme—
a love supreme, a love supreme—

1970

---

3. One of Coltrane's most famous songs named for his wife.

4. Perhaps an allusion to the tenor saxophone, Coltrane's instrument.

American History

for John Callahan

Those four black girls blown up
in that Alabama church[1]
remind me of five hundred
middle passage blacks,[2]
in a net, under water   5
in Charleston harbor
so redcoats[3] wouldn't find them.
Can't find what you can't see
can you?

1970

Martin's Blues[1]

He came apart in the open,
the slow motion cameras
falling quickly
neither alive nor kicking;
stone blind dead   5
on the balcony
that old melody
etched his black lips
in a pruned echo:
We shall overcome   10
some day—[2]
Yes we did!
Yes we did!

1971

"*Bird Lives*": Charles Parker[1] in St. Louis

Last on legs, last on sax,
last in Indian wars, last on *smack*,
Bird is specious, *Bird* is alive,

---

1. On September 15, 1963, the Sixteenth Street Baptist Church in Birmingham, Alabama, was bombed by white racists as a reprisal against civil rights demonstrations.
2. Captured and en route from Africa (along the "Middle Passage," the usual route for slave ships) to be sold as slaves.
3. I.e., British soldiers.

1. Martin Luther King Jr. (1929–1968), American civil rights leader, was assassinated on a motel balcony in Memphis, Tennessee.
2. Line from "we shall overcome," a hymn that became an anthem of the Civil Rights Movement.
1. American jazz musician (1920–1955), known as "Bird"; he was a heroin (smack) addict.

horn, unplayable, before, after,
right now: it's heroin time: 5
smack, in the melody a trip;
smack, in the Mississippi;
smack, in the drug merchant trap;
smack, in St. Louis, Missouri.

We knew you were through—   10
trying to get out of town,
unpaid bills, connections
unmet, unwanted, unasked,
Bird's in the last arc
of his own light: *blow Bird!*   15
And you did—
screaming, screaming, baby,
for life, after it, around it,
screaming for life, *blow Bird!*

What is the meaning of music?   20
What is the meaning of war?
What is the meaning of oppression?
Blow Bird! Ripped up and down
into the interior of life, the pain,
Bird, the embraceable you,[2]   25
how many brothers gone,
smacked out: blues and racism,
the hardest, longest penis
in the Mississippi urinal:
Blow Bird!   30

Taught more musicians, then forgot,
space loose, fouling the melodies,
the marching songs, the fine white
geese from the plantations,
syrup in this pork barrel,   35
Kansas City, the even teeth
of the mafia, the big band:
Blow Bird! Inside out Charlie's
guts, *Blow Bird!* get yourself killed.

In the first wave, the musicians,   40
out there, alone, in the first wave;
everywhere you went, Massey Hall,
Sweden, New Rochelle, *Birdland*,
nameless bird, Blue Note, Carnegie,[3]
tuxedo junction, out of nowhere,   45

2. Title of a 1928 song by George and Ira Gersh- land, the landmark New York City jazz club
win; Parker recorded a memorable version in 1947. named after him; the Blue Note, another New
3. Among the places where Parker performed York City jazz club; and Carnegie Hall, the
were Massey Concert Hall in Toronto, Canada; famous New York City concert hall.
Malmo, Sweden; New Rochelle, New York; Bird-

confirmation, confirmation, confirmation:
Bird Lives! Bird Lives! and you do:
Dead—

1972

Nightmare Begins Responsibility[1]

I place these numbed wrists to the pane
watching white uniforms whisk over
him in the tube-kept
prison
fear what they will do in experiment   5
watch my gloved stickshifting gasolined hands
breathe *boxcar-information-please* infirmary tubes
distrusting white-pink mending paperthin
silkened end hairs, distrusting tubes
shrunk in his *trunk-skincapped*   10
shaven head, in thighs
distrusting-white-hands-picking-baboon-light
on this son who will not make his second night
of this wardstrewn intensive airpocket
where his father's asthmatic   15
hymns of *night-train,* train done gone
his mother can only know that he has flown
up into essential calm unseen corridor
going boxscarred home, *mamaborn, sweetsonchild*
gonedowntown into *researchtestingwarehousebatteryacid*   20
mama-son-done-gone / me telling her 'nother
train tonight, no music, no breathstroked
heartbeat in my infinite distrust of them:

and of my distrusting self
white-doctor-who-breathed-for-him-all-night   25
say it for two sons gone,
say nightmare, say it loud
panebreaking heartmadness:
nightmare begins responsibility.

1975

---

1. Cf. the title of a book by American poet Delmore Schwartz, *In Dreams Begin Responsibilities* (1938); Schwartz took the title from a line in the Irish poet William Butler Yeats's "Responsibilities" (1913).

TONI CADE BAMBARA
1939–1995

" Her writing is woven, aware of its music, its overlapping waves of scenic action, so clearly on its way," Toni Morrison wrote about editing the work of her friend Toni Cade Bambara, "like a magnet collecting details in its wake, each of which is essential to the final effect." In her preface to the posthumous collection of fiction, essays, and conversations *Deep Sightings and Rescue Missions* (1996), Morrison describes Bambara as an "ever vocal woman," and the remarkable presence of a living voice distinguishes the stories collected in *Gorilla, My Love* (1972) and *The Sea Birds Are Still Alive* (1977), as well as Bambara's novels, *The Salt Eaters* (1981) and the posthumously published *Those Bones Are Not My Child* (1999).

Born and raised in New York City, Bambara was as much a social activist as a writer. She worked in organizations dedicated to the most practical day-to-day benefits for minority city dwellers and also traveled to Cuba and Vietnam to lobby for reformed national politics. She spent the last fifteen years of her professional life working on television documentaries, including *The Bombing of Orange Avenue* (about the Philadelphia police department's deadly assault on the MOVE organization). Yet she will be remembered for her short stories, particularly the first-person narratives of her women storytellers about their experiences in the black community. Her protagonists are activists in their societies, societies that in their flux demand creative readjustment at every stage. Such is the dynamic of "Medley" (printed here), in which a culture's music indexes the pace and rhythms of its social existence. As in this story, Bambara's plots are always moving, existing in a state of being "on their way" toward an imperatively stated conclusion, as Toni Morrison has said of this writer's prose style.

As her novel *The Salt Eaters* shows, Bambara was sensitive to the role storytelling plays in healthy communities. Here, when an activist is frustrated over divisiveness in the people she wishes to help, a traditional healer comes to the rescue with her tales of folk values. Life is change, Bambara understood; the fluid nature of language teaches that no stable, secure place exists beyond the voice's constant ability to reinvent itself. Hence Bambara meant to be of service in editing *Tales and Stories of Black Folks* (1971), an anthology that provides ample evidence for how African Americans not only created folk legends but adapted European and African materials to their own uniquely American ends. In this writer's fiction readers can see the same process taking place, a joyful embrace of voice as the most personal statement possible in a world dependent on self-invention for survival.

The following text is from *The Sea Birds Are Still Alive* (1977).

Medley

I could tell the minute I got in the door and dropped my bag, I wasn't staying. Dishes piled sky-high in the sink looking like some circus act. Glasses all ghosty on the counter. Busted tea bags, curling canteloupe rinds, white cartons from the Chinamen, green sacks from the deli, and that damn dog creeping up on me for me to wrassle his head or kick him in the ribs one.

No, I definitely wasn't staying. Couldn't even figure why I'd come. But picked my way to the hallway anyway till the laundry-stuffed pillowcases stopped me. Larry's bass blocking the view to the bedroom.

"That you, Sweet Pea?"

"No, man, ain't me at all," I say, working my way back to the suitcase and shoving that damn dog out the way. "See ya round," I holler, the door slamming behind me, cutting off the words abrupt.

Quite naturally sitting cross-legged at the club, I embroider a little on the homecoming tale, what with an audience of two crazy women and a fresh bottle of Jack Daniels.[1] Got so I could actually see shonuff toadstools growing in the sink. Canteloupe seeds sprouting in the muck. A goddamn compost heap breeding near the stove, garbage gardens on the grill.

"Sweet Pea, you oughta hush, cause you can't possibly keep on lying so," Pot Limit's screaming, tears popping from her eyes. "Lawd hold my legs, cause this liar bout to kill me off."

"Never mind about Larry's housekeeping, girl," Sylvia's soothing me, sloshing perfectly good bourbon all over the table. "You can come and stay with me till your house comes through. It'll be like old times at Aunt Merriam's."

I ease back into the booth to wait for the next set. The drummer's fooling with the equipment, tapping the mikes, hoping he's watched, so I watch him. But feeling worried in my mind about Larry, cause I've been through days like that myself. Cold cream caked on my face from the day before, hair matted, bathrobe funky, not a clean pair of drawers to my name. Even the emergency ones, the draggy cotton numbers stuffed way in the back of the drawer under the scented paper gone. And no clean silverware in the box and the last of the paper cups gone too. Icebox empty cept for a rock of cheese and the lone water jug that ain't even half full that's how anyhow the thing's gone on. And not a clue as to the next step. But then Pot Limit'll come bamming on the door to say So-and-so's in town and can she have the card table for a game. Or Sylvia'll send a funny card inviting herself to dinner and even giving me the menu. Then I zoom through that house like a manic work brigade till me and the place ready for white-glove inspection. But what if some somebody or other don't intervene for Larry, I'm thinking.

The drummer's messin round on the cymbals, head cocked to the side, rings sparkling. The other dudes are stepping out from behind the curtain. The piano man playing with the wah-wah doing splashy, breathy science fiction stuff. Sylvia checking me out to make sure I ain't too blue. Blue got hold to me, but I lean foward out of the shadows and babble something about how off the bourbon tastes these days. Hate worryin Sylvia, who is the kind of friend who bleeds at the eyes with your pain. I drain my glass and hum along with the opening riff of the guitar and I keep my eyes strictly off the bass player, whoever he is.

Larry Landers looked more like a bass player than ole Mingus[2] himself. Got these long arms that drape down over the bass like they were grown

---

1. Jack Daniel's brand of Tennessee bourbon whisky.

2. Charles Mingus (1922–1979), African American jazz bassist, band leader, and composer.

special for that purpose. Fine, strong hands with long fingers and muscular knuckles, the dimples deep black at the joints. His calluses so other-colored and hard, looked like Larry had swiped his grandmother's tarnished thimbles to play with. He'd move in on that bass like he was going to hump it or something, slide up behind it as he lifted it from the rug, all slinky. He'd become one with the wood. Head dipped down sideways bobbing out the rhythm, feet tapping, legs jiggling, he'd look good. Thing about it, though, ole Larry couldn't play for shit. Couldn't never find the right placement for the notes. Never plucking with enough strength, despite the perfectly capable hands. Either you didn't hear him at all or what you heard was off. The man couldn't play for nuthin is what I'm saying. But Larry Landers was baad in the shower, though.

He'd soap me up and down with them great, fine hands, doing a deep bass walking in the back of his mouth. And I'd just have to sing, though I can't sing to save my life. But we'd have one hellafyin musical time in the shower, lemme tell you. "Green Dolphin Street"[3] never sounded like nuthin till Larry bopped out them changes and actually made me sound good. On "My Funny Valentine"[4] he'd do a whizzing sounding bow thing that made his throat vibrate real sexy and I'd cutesy up the introduction, which is, come to think of it, my favorite part. But the main number when the hot water started running out was "I Feel Like Making Love." That was usually the wind up of our repertoire cause you can imagine what that song can do to you in the shower and all.

Got so we spent a helluva lotta time in the shower. Just as well, cause didn't nobody call Larry for gigs. He a nice man, considerate, generous, baad in the shower, and good taste in music. But he just wasn't nobody's bass player. Knew all the stances, though, the postures, the facial expressions, had the choreography down. And right in the middle of supper he'd get some Ron Carter[5] thing going in his head and hop up from the table to go get the bass. Haul that sucker right in the kitchen and do a number in dumb show, all the playing in his throat, the acting with his hands. But that ain't nuthin. I mean that can't get it. I can impersonate Betty Carter[6] if it comes to that. The arms crooked just so, the fingers popping, the body working, the cap and all, the teeth, authentic. But I got sense enough to know I ain't nobody's singer. Actually, I am a mother, though I'm only just now getting it together. And too, I'm an A-1 manicurist.

Me and my cousin Sinbad come North working our show in cathouses at first. Set up a salon right smack in the middle of Miz Maybry's Saturday traffic. But that wasn't no kind of life to be bringing my daughter into. So I parked her at a boarding school till I could make some other kind of life. Wasn't no kind of life for Sinbad either, so we quit.

Our first shop was a three-chair affair on Austin. Had a student barber who could do anything—blow-outs, do's, corn rows, weird cuts, afros, press and curl, whatever you wanted. Plus he din't gab you to death. And he always brought his sides and didn't blast em neither. He went on to New York and

---

3. That is, "On Green Dolphin Street," a 1947 song that has become a modern jazz classic.
4. Popular 1937 song by Richard Rodgers and

Lorenz Hart that has become a jazz standard.
5. Contemporary jazz bassist (b. 1937).
6. Contemporary jazz singer (1929–1998).

opened his own shop. Was a bootblack too then, an old dude named James Noughton, had a crooked back and worked at the post office at night, and knew everything about everything, read all the time.

"Whatcha want to know about Marcus Garvey,[7] Sweet Pea?"

If it wasn't Garvey, it was the rackets or the trucking industry or the flora and fauna of Greenland or the planets or how the special effects in the disaster movies were done. One Saturday I asked him to tell me about the war, cause my nephew'd been drafted and it all seemed so wrong to me, our men over there in Nam fighting folks who fighting for the same things we are, to get that blood-sucker off our backs.

Well, what I say that for. Old dude gave us a deep knee bend, straight up eight-credit dissertation on World Wars I and II—the archduke getting offed, Africa cut up like so much cake, Churchill and his cigars, Gabriel Heatter on the radio, Hitler at the Olympics igging Owens, Red Cross doing Bloods dirty refusing donuts and bandages, A. Philip Randolph scaring the white folks to death, Mary McLeod Bethune[8] at the White House, Liberty Bond drives, the Russian front, frostbite of the feet, the Jew stiffs, the gypsies no one mourned . . . the whole johnson. Talked straight through the day, Miz Mary's fish dinner growing cold on the radiator, his one and only customer walking off with one dull shoe. Fell out exhausted, his shoe rag limp in his lap, one arm draped over the left foot platform, the other clutching his heart. Took Sinbad and our cousin Pepper to get the old man home. I stayed with him all night with the ice pack and a fifth of Old Crow.[9] He liked to die.

After while trade picked up and with a better class of folk too. Then me and Sinbad moved to North and Gaylord and called the shop Chez Sinbad. No more winos stumbling in or deadbeats wasting my time talking raunchy shit. The paperboy, the numbers man, the dudes with classier hot stuff coming in on Tuesday mornings only. We did up the place nice. Light globes from a New Orleans whorehouse, Sinbad likes to lie. Brown-and-black-and-silver-striped wallpaper. Lots of mirrors and hanging plants. Them old barber chairs spruced up and called antiques and damn if someone didn't buy one off us for eight hundred, cracked me up.

I cut my schedule down to ten hours in the shop so I could do private sessions with the gamblers and other business men and women who don't like sitting around the shop even though it's comfy, specially my part. Got me a cigar showcase with a marble top for serving coffee in clear glass mugs with heatproof handles too. My ten hours in the shop are spent leisurely. And my twenty hours out are making me a mint. Takes dust to be a mother, don't you know.

It was a perfect schedule once Larry Landers came into my life. He parttimed at a record shop and bartended at Topp's on the days and nights I worked at the shops. That gave us most of Monday and Wednesdays to listen to sides and hit the clubs. Gave me Fridays all to myself to study in the

---

7. American black nationalist leader (1887–1940).
8. American educator and founder of the National Council of Negro Women (1875–1955). Chancellor Adolf Hitler (1889–1945), representing Germany as host of the 1936 Olympic Games, refused to honor the African American track and field star Jessie Owens (1913–1980), who had won four gold medals. Randolph (1889–1979), American labor leader and organizer of the Brotherhood of Sleeping Car Porters.
9. A common brand of whiskey.

library and wade through them college bulletins and get to the museum and generally chart out a routine for when Debbie and me are a team. Sundays I always drive to Delaware to see her, and Larry detours to D.C. to see his sons. My bankbook started telling me I was soon going to be a full-time mama again and a college girl to boot, if I can ever talk myself into doing a school thing again, old as I am.

Life with Larry was cool. Not just cause he wouldn't hear about me going halves on the bills. But cause he was an easy man to be easy with. He liked talking softly and listening to music. And he liked having folks over for dinner and cards. Larry a real nice man and I liked him a lot. And I liked his friend Hector, who lived in the back of the apartment. Ole moon-face Hector went to school with Larry years ago and is some kind of kin. And they once failed in the funeral business together and I guess those stories of them times kinda keep them friends.

The time they had to put Larry's brother away is their best story, Hector's story really, since Larry got to play a little grief music round the edges. They decided to pass up a church service, since Bam was such a treacherous desperado wouldn't nobody want to preach over his body and wouldn't nobody want to come to hear no lies about the dearly departed untimely ripped or cut down or whatever. So Hector and Larry set up some kind of pop stand awning right at the gravesite, expecting close blood only. But seems the whole town turned out to make sure ole evil, hell-raising Bam was truly dead. Dudes straight from the barber chair, the striped ponchos blowing like wings, fuzz and foam on they face and all, lumbering up the hill to the hole taking bets and talking shit, relating how Ole Crazy Bam had shot up the town, shot up the jail, shot up the hospital pursuing some bootlegger who'd come up one keg short of the order. Women from all around come to demand the lid be lifted so they could check for themselves and be sure that Bam was stone cold. No matter how I tried I couldn't think of nobody bad enough to think on when they told the story of the man I'd never met.

Larry and Hector so bent over laughing bout the funeral, I couldn't hardly put the events in proper sequence. But I could surely picture some neighbor lady calling on Larry and Bam's mama reporting how the whole town had turned out for the burying. And the mama snatching up the first black thing she could find to wrap around herself and make an appearance. No use passing up a scene like that. And Larry prancing round the kitchen being his mama. And I'm too stunned to laugh, not at somebody's mama, and somebody's brother dead. But him and Hector laughing to beat the band and I can't help myself.

Thing about it, though, the funeral business stories are Hector's stories and he's not what you'd call a good storyteller. He never gives you the names, so you got all these he's and she's floating around. And he don't believe in giving details, so you got to scramble to paint your own pictures. Toward the end of that particular tale of Bam, all I could picture was the townspeople driving a stake through the dead man's heart, then hurling that coffin into the hole right quick. There was also something in that story about the civil rights workers wanting to make a case cause a white cop had cut Bam down. But looked like Hector didn't have a hold to that part of the story, so I just don't know.

Stories are not Hector's long suit. But he is an absolute artist on windows. Ole Moon-Face can wash some windows and make you cry about it too. Makes these smooth little turns out there on that little bitty sill just like he wasn't four stories up without a belt. I'd park myself at the breakfast counter and thread the new curtains on the rods while Hector mixed up the vinegar solution real chef-like. Wring out the rags just so, scrunch up the newspapers into soft wads that make you think of cat's paws. Hector was a cat himself out there on the sill, making these marvelous circles in the glass, rubbing the hardhead spots with a strip of steel wool he had pinned to his overalls.

Hector offered to do my car once. But I put a stop to that after that first time. My windshield so clear and sparkling felt like I was in an accident and heading over the hood, no glass there. But it was a pleasure to have coffee and watch Hector. After while, though, Larry started hinting that the apartment wasn't big enough for four. I agreed, thinking he meant Earl had to go. Come to find Larry meant Hector, which was a real drag. I love to be around people who do whatever it is they do with style and care.

Larry's dog's named Earl P. Jessup Bowers, if you can get ready for that. And I should mention straightaway that I do not like dogs one bit, which is why I was glad when Larry said somebody had to go. Cats are bad enough. Horses are a total drag. By the age of nine I was fed up with all that noble horse this and noble horse that. They got good PR,[1] horses. But I really can't use em. Was a fire once when I was little and some dumb horse almost burnt my daddy up messin around, twisting, snorting, broncing, rearing up, doing everything but comin on out the barn like even the chickens had sense enough to do. I told my daddy to let that horse's ass burn. Horses be as dumb as cows. Cows just don't have good press agents at all.

I used to like cows when I was real little and needed to hug me something bigger than a goldfish. But don't let it rain, the dumbbells'll fall right in a ditch and you break a plow and shout yourself hoarse trying to get them fools to come up out the ditch. Chipmunks I don't mind when I'm at the breakfast counter with my tea and they're on their side of the glass doing Disney things in the yard. Blue jays are law-and-order birds, thoroughly despicable. And there's one prize fool in my Aunt Merriam's yard I will one day surely kill. He tries to "whip whip whippoorwill" like the Indians do in the Fort This or That movies when they're signaling to each other closing in on George Montgomery but don't never get around to wiping that sucker out. But dogs are one of my favorite hatreds. All the time woofing, bolting down their food, slopping water on the newly waxed linoleum, messin with you when you trying to read, chewin on the slippers.

Earl P. Jessup Bowers was an especial drag. But I could put up with Earl when Hector was around. Once Hector was gone and them windows got cloudy and gritty, I was through. Kicked that dog every chance I got. And after thinking what it meant, how the deal went down, place too small for four and it was Hector not Earl—I started moving up my calendar so I could get out of there. I ain't the kind of lady to press no ultimatum on no man. Like "Choose, me or the dog." That's unattractive. Kicking Hector out was too. An insult to me, once I got to thinking on it. Especially since I had carefully explained from jump street to Larry that I got one item on my

---

1. Public relations; here suggesting a good image, good reputation.

agenda, making a home for me and my kid. So if anybody should've been given walking papers, should've been me.

Anyway. One day Moody comes waltzing into Chez Sinbad's and tips his hat. He glances at his nails and glances at me. And I figure here is my house in a green corduroy suit. Pot Limit had just read my cards and the jack of diamonds kept coming up on my resource side. Sylvia and me put our heads together and figure it got to be some gambler or hustler who wants his nails done. What other jacks do I know to make my fortune? I'm so positive about Moody, I whip out a postcard from the drawer where I keep the emeries and write my daughter to start packing.

"How much you make a day, Miss Lady?"

"Thursdays are always good for fifty," I lie.

He hands me fifty and glances over at Sinbad, who nods that it's cool. "I'd like my nails done at four-thirty. My place."

"Got a customer at that time, Mr. Moody, and I like to stay reliable. How bout five-twenty?"

He smiles a slow smile and glances at Sinbad, who nods again, everything's cool. "Fine," he says. "And do you think you can manage a shave without cutting a person's throat?"

"Mr. Moody, I don't know you well enough to have just cause. And none of your friends have gotten to me yet with that particular proposition. Can't say what I'm prepared to do in the future, but for now I can surely shave you real careful-like."

Moody smiles again, then turns to Sinbad, who says it's cool and he'll give me the address. This look-nod dialogue burns my ass. That's like when you take a dude to lunch and pay the check and the waiter's standing there with *your* money in his paws asking *the dude* was everything all right and later for *you*. Shit. But I take down Moody's address and let the rest roll off me like so much steaming lava. I start packing up my little alligator case—buffer, batteries, clippers, emeries, massager, sifter, arrowroot and cornstarch, clear sealer, magnifying glass, and my own mixture of green and purple pigments.

"Five-twenty ain't five-twenty-one, is it, Miss Lady?"

"Not in my book," I say, swinging my appointment book around so he can see how full it is and how neatly the times are printed in. Course I always fill in phony names case some creep starts pressing me for a session.

For six Thursdays running and two Monday nights, I'm at Moody's bending over them nails with a miner's light strapped to my forehead, the magnifying glass in its stand, nicking just enough of the nails at the sides, tinting just enough with the color so he can mark them cards as he shuffles. Takes an hour to do it proper. Then I sift my talc concoction and brush his hands till they're smooth. Them cards move around so fast in his hands, he can actually tell me he's about to deal from the bottom in the next three moves and I miss it and I'm not new to this. I been a gambler's manicurist for more years than I care to mention. Ten times he'll cut and each time the same fifteen cards in the top cut and each time in exactly the same order. Incredible.

Now, I've known hands. My first husband, for instance. To see them hands work their show in the grandstands, at a circus, in a parade, the parimutuels—

artistry in action. We met on the train. As a matter of fact, he was trying to burgle my bag. Some story to tell the grandchildren, hunh? I had to get him straight about robbing from folks. I don't play that. Ya gonna steal, hell, steal back some of them millions we got in escrow is my opinion. We spent three good years on the circuit. Then credit cards moved in. Then choke-and-grab muggers killed the whole tradition. He was reduced to a mere shell of his former self, as they say, and took to putting them hands on me. I try not to think on when things went sour. Try not to think about them big slapping hands, only of them working hands. Moody's working hands were something like that, but even better. So I'm impressed and he's impressed. And he pays me fifty and tips me fifty and shuts up when I shave him and keeps his hands off my lovely person.

I'm so excited counting up my bread, moving up the calendar, making impulsive calls to Delaware and the two of us squealing over the wire like a coupla fools, that what Larry got to say about all these goings-on just rolls off my back like so much molten lead.

"Well, who be up there while he got his head in your lap and you squeezing his goddamn blackheads?"

"I don't squeeze his goddamn blackheads, Larry, on account of he don't have no goddamn blackheads. I give him a shave, a steam, and an egg-white face mask. And when I'm through, his face is as smooth as his hands."

"I'll bet," Larry says. That makes me mad cause I expect some kind of respect for my work, which is better than just good.

"And he doesn't have his head in my lap. He's got a whole barbershop set up on his solarium."

"His what?" Larry squinting at me, raising the wooden spoon he stirring the spaghetti with, and I raise the knife I'm chopping the onions with. Thing about it, though, he don't laugh. It's funny as hell to me, but Larry got no sense of humor sometimes, which is too bad cause he's a lotta fun when he's laughing and joking.

"It's not a bedroom. He's got this screened-in sun porch where he raises African violets and—"

"Please, Sweet Pea. Why don't you quit? You think I'm dumb?"

"I'm serious. I'm serious and I'm mad cause I ain't got no reason to lie to you whatever was going on, Larry." He turns back to the pot and I continue working on the sauce and I'm pissed off cause this is silly. "He sits in the barber chair and I shave him and give him a manicure."

"What else you be giving him? A man don't be paying a good-looking woman to come to his house and all and don't—"

"Larry, if you had the dough and felt like it, wouldn't you pay Pot Limit to come read your cards? And couldn't you keep your hands to yourself and she a good-looking woman? And couldn't you see yourself paying Sylvia to come and cook for you and no funny stuff, and she's one of the best-looking women in town?"

Larry cooled out fast. My next shot was to bring up the fact that he was insulting my work. Do I go around saying the women who pass up Bill the bartender and come to him are after his joint? No, cause I respect the fact that Larry Landers mixes the best piña coladas this side of Barbados. And he's flashy with the blender and the glasses and the whole show. He's good and I respect that. But he cooled out so fast I didn't have to bring it up. I don't believe in overkill, besides I like to keep some things in reserve. He cooled out so fast I realized he wasn't really jealous. He was just going through one of them obligatory male numbers, all symbolic, no depth.

Like the time this dude came into the shop to talk some trash and Sinbad got his ass on his shoulders, talking about the dude showed no respect for him cause for all he knew I could be Sinbad's woman. And me arguing that since that ain't the case, what's the deal? I mean why get hot over what if if what if ain't. Men are crazy. Now there is Sinbad, my blood cousin who grew up right in the same house like a brother damn near, putting me through simple-ass changes like that. Who's got time for grand opera and comic strips, I'm trying to make a life for me and my kid. But men are like that. Gorillas, if you know what I mean.

Like at Topp's sometimes. I'll drop in to have a drink with Larry when he's on the bar and then I leave. And maybe some dude'll take it in his head to walk me to the car. That's cool. I lay it out right quick that me and Larry are a we and then we take it from there, just two people gassing in the summer breeze and that's just fine. But don't let some other dude holler over something like "Hey, man, can you handle all that? Why don't you step aside, junior, and let a man . . ." and blah-de-da-de-dah. They can be the best of friends or total strangers just kidding around, but right away they two gorillas pounding on their chest, pounding on their chest and talking over my head, yelling over the tops of cars just like I'm not a person with some say-so in the matter. It's a man-to-man ritual that ain't got nothing to do with me. So I just get in my car and take off and leave them to get it on if they've a mind to. They got it.

But if one of the gorillas is a relative, or a friend of mine, or a nice kinda man I got in mind for one of my friends, I will stick around long enough to shout em down and point out that they are some ugly gorillas and are showing no respect for me and therefore owe me an apology. But if they don't fit into one of them categories, I figure it ain't my place to try to develop them so they can make the leap from gorilla to human. If their own mamas and daddies didn't care whether they turned out to be amoebas or catfish or whatever, it ain't my weight. I got my own weight. I'm a mother. So they got it.

Like I use to tell my daughter's daddy, the key to getting along and living with other folks is to keep clear whose weight is whose. His drinking, for instance, was not my weight. And him waking me up in the night for them long, rambling, ninety-proof monologues bout how the whole world's made up of victims, rescuers, and executioners and I'm the dirty bitch cause I ain't rescuing him fast enough to suit him. Then got so I was the executioner, to hear him tell it. I don't say nuthin cause my philosophy of life and death is this—I'll go when the wagon comes, but I ain't going out behind somebody else's shit. I arranged my priorities long ago when I jumped into my woman stride. Some things I'll go off on. Some things I'll hold my silence and wait it out. Some things I just bump off, cause the best solution to some problems is to just abandon them.

But I struggled with Mac, Debbie's daddy. Talked to his family, his church, AA, hid the bottles, threatened the liquor man, left a good job to play nurse, mistress, kitten, buddy. But then he stopped calling me Dahlin and started calling me Mama. I don't play that. I'm my daughter's mama. So

I split. Did my best to sweeten them last few months, but I'd been leaving for a long time.

The silliest thing about all of Larry's grumblings back then was Moody had no eyes for me and vice versa. I just like the money. And I like watching him mess around with the cards. He's exquisite, dazzling, stunning shuffling, cutting, marking, dealing from the bottom, the middle, the near top. I ain't never seen nothing like it, and I seen a whole lot. The thing that made me mad, though, and made me know Larry Landers wasn't ready to deal with no woman full grown was the way he kept bringing it up, always talking about what he figured was on Moody's mind, like what's on my mind don't count. So I finally did have to use up my reserves and point out to Larry that he was insulting my work and that I would never dream of accusing him of not being a good bartender, of just being another pretty face, like they say.

"You can't tell me he don't have eyes," he kept saying.

"What about my eyes? Don't my eyes count?" I gave it up after a coupla tries. All I know is, Moody wasn't even thinking about me. I was impressed with his work and needed the trade and vice versa.

One time, for instance, I was doing his hands on the solarium and thought I saw a glint of metal up under his jacket. I rearranged myself in the chair so I could work my elbow in there to see if he was carrying heat. I thought I was being cool about it.

"How bout keeping your tits on your side of the table, Miss Lady."

I would rather he think anything but that. I would rather he think I was clumsy in my work even. "Wasn't about tits, Moody. I was just trying to see if you had a holster on and was too lazy to ask."

"Would have expected you too. You a straight-up, direct kind of person." He opened his jacket away with the heel of his hand, being careful with his nails. I liked that.

"It's not about you," he said quietly, jerking his chin in the direction of the revolver. "Had to transport some money today and forgot to take it off. Sorry."

I gave myself two demerits. One for the tits, the other for setting up a situation where he wound up telling me something about his comings and goings. I'm too old to be making mistakes like that. So I apologized. Then gave myself two stars. He had a good opinion of me and my work. I did an extra-fine job on his hands that day.

Then the house happened. I had been reading the rental ads and For Sale columns for months and looking at some awful, tacky places. Then one Monday me and Sylvia lucked up on this cute little white-brick job up on a hill away from the street. Lots of light and enough room and not too much yard to kill me off. I paid my money down and rushed them papers through. Got back to Larry's place all excited and found him with his mouth all poked out.

Half grumbling, half proposing, he hinted around that we all should live at his place like a family. Only he didn't quite lay it out plain in case of rejection. And I'll tell you something, I wouldn't want to be no man. Must be hard on the heart always having to get out there, setting yourself up to be possibly shot down, approaching the lady, calling, the invitation, the rap. I don't think I could handle it myself unless everybody was just straight up at all times from day one till the end. I didn't answer Larry's nonproposed proposal cause it didn't come clear to me till after dinner. So I just let my silence carry

whatever meaning it will. Ain't nuthin too much changed from the first day
he came to get me from my Aunt Merriam's place. My agenda is still to make
a home for my girl. Marriage just ain't one of the things on my mind no more,
not after two. Got no regrets or bad feelings about them husbands neither.
Like the poem says, when you're handed a lemon, make lemonade, honey,
make lemonade. That's Gwen Brooks'[2] motto, that's mine too. You get a
lemon, well, just make lemonade.

"Going on the road next week," Moody announces one day through the steam
towel. "Like you to travel with me, keep my hands in shape. Keep the women
off my neck. Check the dudes at my back. Ain't asking you to carry heat or
money or put yourself in no danger. But I could use your help." He pauses and
I ease my buns into the chair, staring at the steam curling from the towel.

"Wicked schedule though—Mobile, Birmingham, Sarasota Springs,
Jacksonville, then Puerto Rico and back. Can pay you two thousand and
expenses. You're good, Miss Lady. You're good and you got good sense. And
while I don't believe in nothing but my skill and chance, I gotta say you've
brought me luck. You a lucky lady, Miss Lady."

He raises his hands and cracks his knuckles and it's like the talking towel
has eyes as well cause damn if he ain't checking his cuticles.

"I'll call you later, Moody," I manage to say, mind reeling. With two thousand I can get my stuff out of storage, and buy Debbie a real nice bedroom
set, pay tuition at the college too and start my three-credit-at-a-time grind.

Course I never dreamed the week would be so unnerving, exhausting, constantly on my feet, serving drinks, woofing sisters, trying to distract dudes,
keeping track of fifty-leven umpteen goings on. Did have to carry the heat on
three occasions and had to do a helluva lotta driving. Plus was most of the
time holed up in the hotel room close to the phone. I had pictured myself
lazying on the beach in Florida dreaming up cruises around the world with
two matching steamer trunks with the drawers and hangers and stuff. I'd
pictured traipsing through the casinos in Puerto Rico ordering chicken salad
and coffee liqueur and tipping the croupiers with blue chips. Shit no. Was
work. And I sure as hell learned how Moody got his name. Got so we didn't
even speak, but I kept those hands in shape and his face smooth and placid.
And whether he won, lost, broke even, or got wiped out, I don't even know.
He gave me my money and took off for New Orleans. That trip liked to
kill me.

"You never did say nothing interesting about Moody," Pot Limit says
insinuatingly, swinging her legs in from the aisle cause ain't nobody there
to snatch so she might as well sit comfortable.

"Yeah, she thought she'd put us off the trail with a rip-roaring tale about
Larry's housekeeping."

They slapping five and hunching each other and making a whole lotta
noise, spilling Jack Daniels on my turquoise T-straps from Puerto Rico.

"Come on, fess up, Sweet Pea," they crooning. "Did you give him some?"

"Ahhh, yawl bitches are tiresome, you know that?"

"Naaw, naaw," say Sylvia, grabbing my arm. "You can tell us. We wantta
know all about the trip, specially the nights." She winks at Pot Limit.

2. Gwendolyn Brooks (1917–2000), American poet, novelist, and autobiographer.

"Tell us about this Moody man and his wonderful hands one more time, cept we want to hear how the hands feel on the flesh, honey." Pot Limit doing a bump and grind in the chair that almost makes me join in the fun, except I'm worried in my mind about Larry Landers.

Just then the piano player comes by and leans over Sylvia, blowing in her ear. And me and Pot Limit mimic the confectionary goings-on. And just as well, cause there's nothin to tell about Moody. It wasn't a movie after all. And in real life the good-looking gambler's got cards on his mind. Just like I got my child on my mind. Onliest thing to say about the trip is I'm five pounds lighter, not a shade darker, but two thousand closer toward my goal.

"Ease up," Sylvia says, interrupting the piano player to fuss over me. Then the drummer comes by and eases in on Pot Limit. And I ease back into the shadows of the booth to think Larry over.

I'm staring at the entrance half expecting Larry to come into Topps, but it's not his night. Then too, the thing is ended if I'd only know it. Larry the kind of man you're either living with him or you're out. I for one would've liked us to continue, me and Debbie in our place, him and Earl at his. But he got so grumpy the time I said that, I sure wasn't gonna bring it up again. Got grumpy in the shower too, got so he didn't want to wash my back.

But that last night fore I left for Birmingham, we had us one crazy musical time in the shower. I kept trying to lure him into "Maiden Voyage," which I really can't do without back-up, cause I can't sing all them changes. After while he come out from behind his sulk and did a Jon Lucien[3] combination on vocal and bass, alternating the sections, eight bars of singing words, eight bars of singing bass. It was baad. Then he insisted on doing "I Love You More Today Than Yesterday." And we like to break our arches, stomping out the beat against the shower mat.

The bathroom was all steamy and we had the curtains open so we could see the plants and watch the candles burning. I had bought us a big fat cake of sandalwood soap and it was matching them candles scent for scent. Must've been two o'clock in the morning and looked like the hot water would last forever and ever and ever. Larry finally let go of the love songs, which were making me feel kinda funny cause I thought it was understood that I was splitting, just like he'd always made it clear either I was there or nowhere.

Then we hit on a tune I don't even know the name of cept I like to scat and do my thing Larry calls Swahili wailing. He laid down the most intricate weaving, walking, bopping, strutting bottom to my singing I ever heard. It inspired me. Took that melody and went right on out that shower, them candles bout used up, the fatty soap long since abandoned in the dish, our bodies barely visible in the steamed-up mirrors walling his bathroom. Took that melody right on out the room and out of doors and somewhere out this world. Larry changing instruments fast as I'm changing moods, colors. Took an alto solo and gave me a rest, worked an intro up on the piano playing the chords across my back, drove me all up into the high register while he weaved in and out around my head on a flute sounding like them chilly pipes of the Andes.[4] And I was Yma Sumac[5] for one minute there, up there breathing some rare

3. Caribbean-born American jazz vocalist and musician (1942–2007).
4. Mountain range in South America. "Chilly pipes": i.e., panpipes, common in Chilean folk music.
5. Peruvian singer (1922–2008) popular with American audiences in the 1950s.

air and losing my mind, I was so high on just sheer music. Music and water, the healthiest things in the world. And that hot water pounding like it was part of the group with a union card and all. And I could tell that if that bass could've fit in the tub, Larry would've dragged that bad boy in there and played the hell out of them soggy strings once and for all.

I dipped way down and reached way back for snatches of Jelly Roll Morton's "Deep Creek Blues"[6] and Larry so painful, so stinging on the bass, could make you cry. Then I'm racing fast through Bessie and all the other Smith singers, Mildred Bailey, Billie and imitators, Betty Roche, Nat King Cole vintage 46, a little Joe Carroll, King Pleasure, some Babs.[7] Found myself pulling lines out of songs I don't even like, but ransacked songs just for the meaningful lines or two cause I realized we were doing more than just making music together, and it had to be said just how things stood.

Then I was off again and lost Larry somewhere down there doing scales, sound like. And he went back to that first supporting line that had drove me up into the Andes. And he stayed there waiting for me to return and do some more Swahili wailing. But I was elsewhere and liked it out there and ignored the fact that he was aiming for a wind-up of "I Love You More Today Than Yesterday." I sang myself out till all I could ever have left in life was "Brown Baby" to sing to my little girl. Larry stayed on the ground with the same supporting line, and the hot water started getting funny and I knew my time was up. So I came crashing down, jarring the song out of shape, diving back into the melody line and somehow, not even knowing what song each other was doing, we finished up together just as the water turned cold.

1977

6. Dixieland jazz classic of the 1920s.

7. Blues and jazz musicians of the 1920s, 1930s, and 1940s.

FRANK BIDART
b. 1939

Frank Bidart's poems make disembodied human voices into fully-fleshed characters. Influenced by the dramatic monologues of the early-twentieth-century poet Robert Frost, Bidart tells of hearing a character's voice in his head as he writes, a voice that becomes more and more real on the typed page until, he says, "something very odd happens: the 'being' of the poem suddenly becomes the poem on paper, and no longer the 'voice' in my head. The poem on paper suddenly seems a truer embodiment of the poem's voice. . . . I've learned to trust this when it happens— at that point, the entire process is finished." Bidart's finished poems are distinctive on the page: white space, indentations, line breaks, parentheses, block capitals, and dramatic punctuation sculpt the tone and cadence of the voice, rendering it dynamic to both eye and ear.

Often working in longer verse forms inspired by Walt Whitman's capacious poetry from the nineteenth century, Bidart invites all manner of people and cultural artifacts into his poems. Mythology, translations of poets such as Ovid, Catullus, and Dante, bits of pop culture, and pornography all find a place; he once made a poem out of quotations from the actor Heath Ledger. The best-known poem from his first collection, *Golden State* (1973), is "Herbert White," whose narrator is a necrophiliac and murderer of young girls. (In 2010 the poem was adapted into a short film by actor and director James Franco, who is friendly with Bidart.) To date, he is the author of nine books of poetry, and since 1972 has taught in the English department at Wellesley College in Massachusetts. He is the editor of Robert Lowell's selected poems. Though his own poetry was seen as unconventional when he began, his work's significance has been widely recognized over time. *Desire* (1997) was nominated for the Pulitzer Prize, the National Book Award, and the National Book Critics Circle Award; it received the 1998 Rebekah Johnson Bobbitt Prize from the Library of Congress. He was awarded the Bollingen Prize in 2007. *Metaphysical Dog* (2013) won the National Books Critics Circle Award and was a finalist for the National Book Award.

Bidart was raised in a Roman Catholic family in Bakersfield, California. In the words of the poet and critic Dan Chaisson, his "father was a potato farmer who dreamed of being a cowboy. His mother considered herself a great, undiscovered beauty." He attended graduate school in English at Harvard, where he became acquainted with Robert Lowell and Elizabeth Bishop (both poets are in this volume). While Lowell and many other poets turned to autobiographical, "confessional" writing, Bidart's poems stood out. They sounded like confessional poems, but the confessors were characters that embodied, as Bidart says, the "anti-self"— "someone who is all the things that one is not." In poetry, he has said, one might confront "one's shadow." He has been known as a gay poet since the publication of his second book, *The Book of the Body* (1977), and while his work is included in anthologies of gay writers, he has said that he does not write for a particular audience in this regard. "The mystery of art, if you get it right," he says, is that "the specific is felt as universal."

Bidart's poetry examines the tensions between body and mind, desire and disgust, guilt and aspiration. The poem included here, "Ellen West," takes up these themes through the voice of an anorexic woman. It is one of Bidart's best-known works, important enough to his own vision that he later wrote a poem about its composition called "Writing 'Ellen West.'" The character speaking is based on a real woman of the same name, born in 1888, whose case Bidart studied in an undergraduate psychology class. Bidart himself had been "heavier before I began graduate school, and I had always hated it." Fifteen years later, he returned to West, exploring the idea that the body is somehow at odds with the mind. Between body and mind, the poem seems to ask, where do we locate the voice that speaks and sings?

Ellen West

I love sweets,—
        heaven
would be dying on a bed of vanilla ice cream . . .

But my true self
is thin, all profile

and effortless gestures, the sort of blond

elegant girl whose
                    body is the image of her soul.

—My doctors tell me I must give up
this ideal;
          but I
WILL NOT . . . cannot.

Only to my husband I'm not simply a "case."

But he is a fool. He married
meat, and thought it was a wife.

                  • • •

Why am I a girl?

I ask my doctors, and they tell me they
don't know, that it is just "given."

But it has such
implications—;
               and sometimes,
I even feel like a girl.

                  • • •

Now, at the beginning of Ellen's thirty-second year, her physical condition has deteriorated still further. Her use of laxatives increases beyond measure. Every evening she takes sixty to seventy tablets of a laxative, with the result that she suffers tortured vomiting at night and violent diarrhea by day, often accompanied by a weakness of the heart. She has thinned down to a skeleton, and weighs only 92 pounds.

                  • • •

About five years ago, I was in a restaurant,
eating alone
          with a book. I was
not married, and often did that . . .

—I'd turn down
dinner invitations, so I could eat alone;

I'd allow myself two pieces of bread, with
butter, at the beginning, and three scoops of
vanilla ice cream, at the end,—

                         sitting there alone
with a book, both in the book
and out of it, waited on, idly
watching people,—

                    when an attractive young man
and woman, both elegantly dressed,
sat next to me.
                    She was beautiful—;   45

with sharp, clear features, a good
bone structure—;
                    if she took her make-up off
in front of you, rubbing cold cream
again and again across her skin, she still would be   50
beautiful—
              more beautiful.

And he,—
              I couldn't remember when I had seen a man
so attractive. I didn't know why. He was almost   55

a male version
              of her,—

I had the sudden, mad notion that I
wanted to be his lover . . .

—Were they married?   60
                    were *they* lovers?

They didn't wear wedding rings.

Their behavior was circumspect. They discussed
politics. They didn't touch . . .

—How could I discover?   65
                    Then, when the first course
arrived, I noticed the way

each held his fork out for the other

to taste what he had ordered . . .

                              They did this   70
again and again, with pleased looks, indulgent
smiles, for each course,
                    more than once for *each* dish—;
much too much for just friends . . .

—Their behavior somehow sickened me;   75

the way each *gladly*
put the *food* the other had offered *into his mouth*—;

I knew what they were. I knew they slept together.

An immense depression came over me . . .

—I knew I could never   80
with such ease allow another to put food into my mouth:

happily *myself* put food into another's mouth—;

I knew that to become a wife I would have to give up my ideal.

● ● ●

Even as a child,
I saw that the "natural" process of aging   85

is for one's middle to thicken—
one's skin to blotch;

as happened to my mother.
And her mother.
                    I loathed "Nature."   90

At twelve, pancakes
became the most terrible thought there is . . .

I shall *defeat* "Nature."

In the hospital, when they
weigh me, I wear weights secretly sewn into my belt.   95

● ● ●

January 16. The patient is allowed to eat in her room, but comes readily
with her husband to afternoon coffee. Previously she had stoutly
resisted this on the ground that she did not really eat but devoured like
a wild animal. This she demonstrated with utmost realism . . . . Her
physical examination showed nothing striking. Salivary glands are   100
markedly enlarged on both sides.
     January 21. Has been reading *Faust*[1] again. In her diary, writes that
art is the "mutual permeation" of the "world of the body" and the
"world of the spirit." Says that her own poems are "hospital poems . . .
weak—without skill or perseverance; only managing to beat their   105
wings softly."
     February 8. Agitation, quickly subsided again. Has attached herself
to an elegant, very thin female patient. Homo-erotic component strik-
ingly evident.
     February 15. Vexation, and torment. Says that her mind forces her   110
always to think of eating. Feels herself degraded by this. Has entirely,
for the first time in years, stopped writing poetry.

● ● ●

1. *Faust* (1808), a play by the German writer Johann Wolfgang von Goethe (1749–1832), tells the story
of a man who sells his soul to the devil in return for knowledge.

Callas[2] is my favorite singer, but I've only
seen her once—;

I've never forgotten that night . . .   115

—It was in *Tosca*,[3] she had long before
lost weight, her voice
had been, for years,
                        deteriorating, half itself . . .

When her career began, of course, she was fat,   120

enormous—; in the early photographs,
sometimes I almost don't recognize her . . .

The voice too then was enormous—

healthy; robust; subtle; but capable of
crude effects, even vulgar,   125
                        almost out of
high spirits, too much health . . .

But soon she felt that she must lose weight,—
that all she was trying to express

was obliterated by her body,   130
buried in flesh—;
                        abruptly, within
four months, she lost at least sixty pounds . . .

—The gossip in Milan was that Callas
had swallowed a tapeworm.   135

But of course she hadn't.
                        The *tapeworm*

was her *soul* . . .

—How her soul, uncompromising,
insatiable,   140
                        must have loved eating the flesh from her bones,

revealing this extraordinarily
mercurial; fragile; masterly creature . . .

—But irresistibly, nothing
stopped there; the huge voice   145

---

2. Maria Callas (1923–1977), renowned American opera singer of Greek descent.

3. Opera (1899) by Italian composer Giacomo
Puccini (1858–1924).

also began to change: at first, it simply diminished
in volume, in size,
                    then the top notes became
shrill, unreliable—at last,
usually not there at all . . .   150

—No one knows *why*. Perhaps her mind,
ravenous, still insatiable, sensed

that to struggle with the *shreds* of a voice

must make her artistry subtler, more refined,
more capable of expressing humiliation,   155
rage, betrayal . . .

—Perhaps the opposite. Perhaps her spirit
loathed the unending struggle

to *embody* itself, to *manifest* itself, on a stage whose

mechanics, and suffocating customs,   160
seemed expressly designed to annihilate spirit . . .

—I know that in *Tosca*, in the second act,
when, humiliated, hounded by Scarpia,[4]
she sang *Vissi d'arte*
                    —"I lived for art"—   165

and in torment, bewilderment, at the end she asks,
with a voice reaching
                    harrowingly for the notes,

"Art has *repaid* me LIKE THIS?"
                              I felt I was watching   170

autobiography—
               an art; skill;
virtuosity

miles distant from the usual soprano's
athleticism,—   175
               the usual musician's dream
of virtuosity *without* content . . .

—I wonder what she feels, now,
listening to her recordings.

For they have already, within a few years,   180
begun to date . . .

---

4. In *Tosca*, the Roman Chief of Police, Scarpia, offers to spare the life of the singer Tosca's lover—
whose execution Scarpia has ordered—if she will sleep with him.

Whatever they express
they express through the style of a decade
and a half—;
    a style *she* helped create . . .   185

—She must know that now
she probably would *not* do a trill in
exactly that way,—
      that the whole sound, atmosphere,
dramaturgy of her recordings   190

have just slightly become those of the past . . .

—Is it bitter? Does her soul
tell her

that she was an *idiot* ever to think
anything   195
    material wholly could satisfy? . . .

—Perhaps it says: *The only way*
to escape
the History of Styles

is not to have a body.   200

       ● ● ●

When I open my eyes in the morning, my great
mystery
    stands before me . . .

—I *know* that I am intelligent; therefore

the inability not to fear food   205
day-and-night; this unending hunger
ten minutes after I have eaten . . .
       a childish
dread of eating; hunger which can have no cause,—

half my mind says that all this   210
is demeaning . . .

      Bread
for days on end
drives all real thought from my brain . . .

—Then I think, No. The ideal of being thin   215

conceals the ideal
not to have a body—;
     which is NOT trivial . . .

This wish seems now as much a "given" of my existence

as the intolerable   220
fact that I am dark-complexioned; big-boned;
and once weighed
one hundred and sixty-five pounds . . .

—But then I think, *No*. That's too simple,—

without a body, who can   225
know himself at all?
                              Only by
acting; choosing; rejecting; have I
made myself—
                              discovered who and what *Ellen* can be . . .   230

—But then again I think, *NO*. This *I* is anterior

to name; gender; action;
fashion;
        MATTER ITSELF,—

. . . trying to stop my hunger with FOOD   235
is like trying to appease thirst
                              with ink.

                              • • •

March 30. Result of the consultation: Both gentlemen agree completely with my prognosis and doubt any therapeutic usefulness of
commitment[5] even more emphatically than I. All three of us are   240
agreed that it is not a case of obsessional neurosis and not one of
manic-depressive psychosis, and that no definitely reliable therapy is
possible. We therefore resolved to give in to the patient's demand for
discharge.

                              • • •

The train-ride yesterday   245
was far *worse* than I expected . . .

                              In our compartment
were ordinary people: a student;
a woman; her child;—

they had ordinary bodies, pleasant faces;   250
                              but I thought
I was surrounded by creatures

with the pathetic, desperate

---

5. That is, voluntary or involuntary confinement in an inpatient mental health facility.

desire to be *not* what they were:—

the student was short,   255
and carried his body as if forcing
it to be taller—;

the woman showed her gums when she smiled,
and often held her
hand up to hide them—;   260

the child
seemed to cry simply because it was
small; a dwarf, and helpless . . .

—I was hungry. I had insisted that my husband
not bring food . . .   265

After about thirty minutes, the woman
peeled an orange

to quiet the child. She put a section
into its mouth—;
                    immediately it spit it out.   270

The piece fell to the floor.

—She pushed it with her foot through the dirt
toward me
several inches.

My husband saw me staring   275
down at the piece . . .

—I didn't move; how I wanted
to reach out,
             and as if invisible

shove it in my mouth—;   280

my body
became rigid. As I stared at him,
I could see him staring

at me,—
          then he looked at the student—; at the woman—; then   285
back to me . . .

I didn't move.

—At last, he bent down, and
casually
          threw it out the window.   290

He looked away.

—I got up to leave the compartment, then
saw his face,—

his eyes
were red;   295
       and I saw

—*I'm sure I saw*—

disappointment.

• • •

On the third day of being home she is as if transformed. At breakfast
she eats butter and sugar, at noon she eats so much that—for the first   300
time in thirteen years!—she is satisfied by her food and gets really
full. At afternoon coffee she eats chocolate creams and Easter eggs.
She takes a walk with her husband, reads poems, listens to recordings, is in a positively festive mood, and all heaviness seems to have
fallen away from her. She writes letters, the last one a letter to the   305
fellow patient here to whom she had become so attached. In the evening she takes a lethal dose of poison, and on the following morning
she is dead. "She looked as she had never looked in life—calm and
happy and peaceful."

• • •

Dearest.—I remember how   310
at eighteen,
       on hikes with friends, when
they rested, sitting down to joke or talk,

I circled
around them, afraid to hike ahead alone,   315

yet afraid to rest
when I was not yet truly thin.

You and, yes, my husband,—
you and he

have by degrees drawn me within the circle;   320
forced me to sit down at last on the ground.

I am grateful.

But something in me *refuses* it.

—How eager I have been
to compromise, to kill this *refuser*,   325

but each compromise, each attempt
to poison an ideal
which often seemed to *me* sterile and unreal,

heightens my hunger.

I am crippled. I disappoint you.   330

Will you greet with anger, or
happiness,

the news which might well reach you
before this letter?

                    Your *Ellen*.   335

                           1977

MAXINE HONG KINGSTON
b. 1940

Maxine Hong Kingston was born in Stockton, California, to Chinese immigrant parents. Before they emigrated from China, Kingston's father had been a schoolteacher and a poet; her mother had been a rural doctor in a profession consisting almost entirely of men. In America they took on quite different identities: her father, at times unemployed, worked in a gambling house and a laundry; her mother raised six children, of whom Kingston was the eldest.

Kingston graduated from the University of California at Berkeley, studying there in the turbulent middle sixties. Her debut as a writer was auspicious: in 1976, an unknown, she published her first and most widely read book, *The Woman Warrior*, and was catapulted to literary fame. Subtitled "Memoirs of a Girlhood among Ghosts," it combines autobiographical fact with legends, especially Asian ones, to make a distinct imaginative creation. Reviews of the book, almost universally laudatory, emphasized its poetic and lyric beauty. *The Woman Warrior* is about the cultural conflicts Chinese Americans must confront. Still, what remains in the mind is its quality of vivid particularity, as for example at the beginning of "Shaman," the book's third section:

> Once in a long while, four times so far for me, my mother brings out the metal tube that holds her medical diploma. On the tube are gold circles crossed with seven red lines each—"joy" ideographs in abstract. There are also little flowers that look like gears for a gold machine. . . . When I open it the smell of China flies out, a thousand-year-old bat flying heavy-handed out of the Chinese caverns where bats are as white as dust, a smell that comes from long ago, far back in my brain.

Although *The Woman Warrior* received the National Book Critics' Circle award for general nonfiction, there is nothing "general" in the richness of its language.

The importance of storytelling to Kingston's enterprise in *The Woman Warrior* and its successor, *China Men* (1980), cannot be overemphasized. In an interview with Bill Moyers on public television, Kingston said that her attempt was to push the account toward "form" by giving it a "redemptive" meaning, making it a "beautiful" story rather than a sordid one. As is typically the case with her practice as a writer, her effort is to mediate between present and past: "I think that my stories have a constant breaking in and out of the present and past. So the reader might be walking along very well in the present, but the past breaks through and changes and enlightens the present and vice versa."

Kingston had originally conceived of *The Woman Warrior* and *China Men* as one long book, but decided to preserve an overall division by gender: *Warrior* is about her female antecedents; while *China Men*, which won the 1980 National Book Award for nonfiction, deals with her relation to her father and complements that relation by providing epic-like biographies of earlier male forebears, especially those Chinese who came to America and worked on building the railroads. In a final section she writes about her brother who served in the U.S. Navy during the Vietnam War. As she discusses in the interview with Moyers, her father annotated both of these memoir-meditations, carrying further the conversation between the generations.

Tripmaster Monkey (1989), presented more deliberately as a novel, is an exercise as excessive as the young fifth-generation American hero, Wittman Ah Sing, who is portrayed there. Subtitled "His Fake Book," the novel is an extended, picaresque account of Wittman's adventures as an aspiring playwright who imagines himself to be an incarnation of the legendary Monkey King—a trickster hero said to have brought the Buddha's teaching to China. Combining magic, realism, and black humor, *Tripmaster Monkey* is about a young man's search for a community in America. Although Kingston's myth-laden narratives have been called "exotic," she dislikes the word, since she has dedicated her art to exploring what it means to be a human being in American society. In fact, she thinks of her books as more American than Chinese, sees the American poet William Carlos Williams's *In the American Grain* as a true prose predecessor, and probably would be happy to think of the hero of *Tripmaster Monkey* as a later, different version of Huck Finn (in Mark Twain's novel) or Augie March (in Saul Bellow's). As the critic Jennie Wang explains in even larger dimensions, Kingston's Wittman Ah Sing, "the maker/magician . . . conceived in the mind's fancy of a metafictionist," joins in his multiculturalism American and postmodern ambitions.

In 2011 Kingston celebrated her sixty-fifth birthday by publishing a memoir, *I Love a Broad Margin to My Life*. Written in verse form, this work engages issues of aging as the writer recalls incidents in her marriage, her career, and her involvement with social causes. She considers imaginative elements as well, including the ultimate fate of her Woman Warrior and the experiences of her protagonist in *Tripmaster Monkey* in a projected visit to China.

The following text is from *The Woman Warrior* (1976).

From The Woman Warrior

No Name Woman

"You must not tell anyone," my mother said, "what I am about to tell you. In China your father had a sister who killed herself. She jumped into the family well. We say that your father has all brothers because it is as if she had never been born.

"In 1924 just a few days after our village celebrated seventeen hurry-up weddings—to make sure that every young man who went 'out on the road' would responsibly come home—your father and his brothers and your grandfather and his brothers and your aunt's new husband sailed for America, the Gold Mountain. It was your grandfather's last trip. Those lucky enough to get contracts waved good-bye from the decks. They fed and guarded the stowaways and helped them off in Cuba, New York, Bali, Hawaii. 'We'll meet in California next year,' they said. All of them sent money home.

"I remember looking at your aunt one day when she and I were dressing; I had not noticed before that she had such a protruding melon of a stomach. But I did not think, 'She's pregnant,' until she began to look like other pregnant women, her shirt pulling and the white tops of her black pants showing. She could not have been pregnant, you see, because her husband had been gone for years. No one said anything. We did not discuss it. In early summer she was ready to have the child, long after the time when it could have been possible.

"The village had also been counting. On the night the baby was to be born the villagers raided our house. Some were crying. Like a great saw, teeth strung with lights, files of people walked zigzag across our land, tearing the rice. Their lanterns doubled in the disturbed black water, which drained away through the broken bunds.[1] As the villagers closed in, we could see that some of them, probably men and women we knew well, wore white masks. The people with long hair hung it over their faces. Women with short hair made it stand up on end. Some had tied white bands around their foreheads, arms, and legs.

"At first they threw mud and rocks at the house. Then they threw eggs and began slaughtering our stock. We could hear the animals scream their deaths—the roosters, the pigs, a last great roar from the ox. Familiar wild heads flared in our night windows; the villagers encircled us. Some of the faces stopped to peer at us, their eyes rushing like searchlights. The hands flattened against the panes, framed heads, and left red prints.

"The villagers broke in the front and the back doors at the same time, even though we had not locked the doors against them. Their knives dripped with the blood of our animals. They smeared blood on the doors and walls. One woman swung a chicken, whose throat she had slit, splattering blood in red arcs about her. We stood together in the middle of our house, in the family hall with the pictures and tables of the ancestors around us, and looked straight ahead.

"At that time the house had only two wings. When the men came back, we would build two more to enclose our courtyard and a third one to begin a second courtyard. The villagers pushed through both wings, even your grandparents' rooms, to find your aunt's, which was also mine until the men returned. From this room a new wing for one of the younger families would grow. They ripped up her clothes and shoes and broke her combs, grinding them underfoot. They tore her work from the loom. They scattered the cooking fire and rolled the new weaving in it. We could hear them in the kitchen breaking our bowls and banging the pots. They overturned the great waist-high earthenware jugs; duck eggs, pickled fruits, vegetables burst out and mixed in acrid torrents. The old woman from the next field swept a broom

---

1. Embankments built to enclose rice paddies and control the flow of irrigation water.

through the air and loosed the spirits-of-the-broom over our heads. 'Pig,' 'Ghost.' 'Pig,' they sobbed and scolded while they ruined our house.

"When they left, they took sugar and oranges to bless themselves. They cut pieces from the dead animals. Some of them took bowls that were not broken and clothes that were not torn. Afterward we swept up the rice and sewed it back up into sacks. But the smells from the spilled preserves lasted. Your aunt gave birth in the pigsty that night. The next morning when I went for the water, I found her and the baby plugging up the family well.

"Don't let your father know that I told you. He denies her. Now that you have started to menstruate, what happened to her could happen to you. Don't humiliate us. You wouldn't like to be forgotten as if you had never been born. The villagers are watchful."

Whenever she had to warn us about life, my mother told stories that ran like this one, a story to grow up on. She tested our strength to establish realities. Those in the emigrant generations who could not reassert brute survival died young and far from home. Those of us in the first American generations have had to figure out how the invisible world the emigrants built around our childhoods fits in solid America.

The immigrants confused the gods by diverting their curses, misleading them with crooked streets and false names. They must try to confuse their offspring as well, who, I suppose, threaten them in similar ways—always trying to get things straight, always trying to name the unspeakable. The Chinese I know hide their names; sojourners take new names when their lives change and guard their real names with silence.

Chinese-Americans, when you try to understand what things in you are Chinese, how do you separate what is peculiar to childhood, to poverty, insanities, one family, your mother who marked your growing with stories, from what is Chinese? What is Chinese tradition and what is the movies?

If I want to learn what clothes my aunt wore, whether flashy or ordinary, I would have to begin. "Remember Father's drowned-in-the-well sister?" I cannot ask that. My mother has told me once and for all the useful parts. She will add nothing unless powered by Necessity, a riverbank that guides her life. She plants vegetable gardens rather than lawns, she carries the odd-shaped tomatoes home from the fields and eats food left for the gods.

Whenever we did frivolous things, we used up energy, we flew high kites. We children came up off the ground over the melting cones our parents brought home from work and the American movie on New Year's Day—*Oh, You Beautiful Doll* with Betty Grable one year, and *She Wore a Yellow Ribbon* with John Wayne another year. After the one carnival ride each, we paid in guilt; our tired father counted his change on the dark walk home.

Adultery is extravagance. Could people who hatch their own chicks and eat the embryos and the heads for delicacies and boil the feet in vinegar for party food, leaving only the gravel, eating even the gizzard lining—could such people engender a prodigal aunt? To be a woman, to have a daughter in starvation time was a waste enough. My aunt could not have been the lone romantic who gave up everything for sex. Women in the old China did not choose. Some man had commanded her to lie with him and be his secret evil. I wonder whether he masked himself when he joined the raid on her family.

Perhaps she had encountered him in the fields or on the mountain where the daughters-in-law collected fuel. Or perhaps he first noticed her in the marketplace. He was not a stranger because the village housed no strangers. She had to have dealings with him other than sex. Perhaps he worked an adjoining field, or he sold her the cloth for the dress she sewed and wore. His demand must have surprised, then terrified her. She obeyed him; she always did as she was told.

When the family found a young man in the next village to be her husband, she had stood tractably beside the best rooster, his proxy,[2] and promised before they met that she would be his forever. She was lucky that he was her age and she would be the first wife, an advantage secure now. The night she first saw him, he had sex with her. Then he left for America. She had almost forgotten what he looked like. When she tried to envision him, she only saw the black and white face in the group photograph the men had had taken before leaving.

The other man was not, after all, much different from her husband. They both gave orders: she followed. "If you tell your family, I'll beat you. I'll kill you. Be here again next week." No one talked sex, ever. And she might have separated the rapes from the rest of living if only she did not have to buy her oil from him or gather wood in the same forest. I want her fear to have lasted just as long as rape lasted so that the fear could have been contained. No drawnout fear. But women at sex hazarded birth and hence lifetimes. The fear did not stop but permeated everywhere. She told the man, "I think I'm pregnant." He organized the raid against her.

On nights when my mother and father talked about their life back home, sometimes they mentioned an "outcast table" whose business they still seemed to be settling, their voices tight. In a commensal tradition,[3] where food is precious, the powerful older people made wrongdoers eat alone. Instead of letting them start separate new lives like the Japanese, who could become samurais and geishas,[4] the Chinese family, faces averted but eyes glowering sideways, hung on to the offenders and fed them leftovers. My aunt must have lived in the same house as my parents and eaten at an outcast table. My mother spoke about the raid as if she had seen it, when she and my aunt, a daughter-in-law to a different household, should not have been living together at all. Daughters-in-law lived with their husbands' parents, not their own; a synonym for marriage in Chinese is "taking a daughter-in-law." Her husband's parents could have sold her, mortgaged her, stoned her. But they had sent her back to her own mother and father, a mysterious act hinting at disgraces not told me. Perhaps they had thrown her out to deflect the avengers.

She was the only daughter; her four brothers went with her father, husband, and uncles "out on the road" and for some years became western men. When the goods were divided among the family, three of the brothers took land, and the youngest, my father, chose an education. After my grandparents gave their daughter away to her husband's family, they had dispensed all the adventure and all the property. They expected her alone to keep the traditional ways, which her brothers, now among the barbarians,

2. Someone or something that has the power to substitute or act for another.
3. A tradition in which people eat together at the same table.
4. In Japanese society, women trained to entertain men. "Samurai": the Japanese warrior elite.

could fumble without detection. The heavy, deep-rooted women were to maintain the past against the flood, safe for returning. But the rare urge west had fixed upon our family, and so my aunt crossed boundaries not delineated in space.

The work of preservation demands that the feelings playing about in one's guts not be turned into action. Just watch their passing like cherry blossoms. But perhaps my aunt, my forerunner, caught in a slow life, let dreams grow and fade and after some months or years went toward what persisted. Fear at the enormities of the forbidden kept her desires delicate, wire and bone. She looked at a man because she liked the way the hair was tucked behind his ears, or she liked the question-mark line of a long torso curving at the shoulder and straight at the hip. For warm eyes or a soft voice or a slow walk— that's all—a few hairs, a line, a brightness, a sound, a pace, she gave up family. She offered us up for a charm that vanished with tiredness, a pigtail that didn't toss when the wind died. Why, the wrong lighting could erase the dearest thing about him.

It could very well have been, however, that my aunt did not take subtle enjoyment of her friend, but, a wild woman, kept rollicking company. Imagining her free with sex doesn't fit, though. I don't know any women like that, or men either. Unless I see her life branching into mine, she gives me no ancestral help.

To sustain her being in love, she often worked at herself in the mirror, guessing at the colors and shapes that would interest him, changing them frequently in order to hit on the right combination. She wanted him to look back.

On a farm near the sea, a woman who tended her appearance reaped a reputation for eccentricity. All the married women blunt-cut their hair in flaps about their ears or pulled it back in tight buns. No nonsense. Neither style blew easily into heart-catching tangles. And at their weddings they displayed themselves in their long hair for the last time. "It brushed the backs of my knees," my mother tells me. "It was braided, and even so, it brushed the backs of my knees."

At the mirror my aunt combed individuality into her bob. A bun could have been contrived to escape into black streamers blowing in the wind or in quiet wisps about her face, but only the older women in our picture album wear buns. She brushed her hair back from her forehead, tucking the flaps behind her ears. She looped a piece of thread, knotted into a circle between her index fingers and thumbs, and ran the double strand across her forehead. When she closed her fingers as if she were making a pair of shadow geese bite, the string twisted together catching the little hairs. Then she pulled the thread away from her skin, ripping the hair out neatly, her eyes watering from the needles of pain. Opening her fingers, she cleaned the thread, then rolled it along her hairline and the tops of her eyebrows. My mother did the same to me and my sisters and herself. I used to believe that the expression "caught by the short hairs" meant a captive held with a depilatory string. It especially hurt at the temples, but my mother said we were lucky we didn't have to have our feet bound when we were seven. Sisters used to sit on their beds and cry together, she said, as their mothers or their slave removed the bandages for a few minutes each night and let the blood gush back into their veins. I hope that the man my aunt loved appreciated a smooth brow, that he wasn't just a tits-and-ass man.

Once my aunt found a freckle on her chin, at a spot that the almanac said predestined her for unhappiness. She dug it out with a hot needle and washed the wound with peroxide.

More attention to her looks than these pullings of hairs and pickings at spots would have caused gossip among the villagers. They owned work clothes and good clothes, and they wore good clothes for feasting the new seasons. But since a woman combing her hair hexes beginnings, my aunt rarely found an occasion to look her best. Women looked like great sea snails—the corded wood, babies, and laundry they carried were the whorls on their backs. The Chinese did not admire a bent back; goddesses and warriors stood straight. Still there must have been a marvelous freeing of beauty when a worker laid down her burden and stretched and arched.

Such commonplace loveliness, however, was not enough for my aunt. She dreamed of a lover for the fifteen days of New Year's, the time for families to exchange visits, money, and food. She plied her secret comb. And sure enough she cursed the year, the family, the village, and herself.

Even as her hair lured her imminent lover, many other men looked at her. Uncles, cousins, nephews, brothers would have looked, too, had they been home between journeys. Perhaps they had already been restraining their curiosity, and they left, fearful that their glances, like a field of nesting birds, might be startled and caught. Poverty hurt, and that was their first reason for leaving. But another, final reason for leaving the crowded house was the never-said.

She may have been unusually beloved, the precious only daughter, spoiled and mirror gazing because of the affection the family lavished on her. When her husband left, they welcomed the chance to take her back from the in-laws; she could live like the little daughter for just a while longer. There are stories that my grandfather was different from other people, "crazy ever since the little Jap bayoneted him in the head." He used to put his naked penis on the dinner table, laughing. And one day he brought home a baby girl, wrapped up inside his brown western-style greatcoat.[5] He had traded one of his sons, probably my father, the youngest, for her. My grandmother made him trade back. When he finally got a daughter of his own, he doted on her. They must have all loved her, except perhaps my father, the only brother who never went back to China, having once been traded for a girl.

Brothers and sisters, newly men and women, had to efface their sexual color and present plain miens. Disturbing hair and eyes, a smile like no other, threatened the ideal of five generations living under one roof. To focus blurs, people shouted face to face and yelled from room to room. The immigrants I know have loud voices, unmodulated to American tones even after years away from the village where they called their friendships out across the fields. I have not been able to stop my mother's screams in public libraries or over telephones. Walking erect (knees straight, toes pointed forward, not pigeon-toed, which is Chinese-feminine) and speaking in an inaudible voice, I have tried to turn myself American-feminine. Chinese

5. A heavy overcoat.

communication was loud, public. Only sick people had to whisper. But at the dinner table, where the family members came nearest one another, no one could talk, not the outcasts nor any eaters. Every word that falls from the mouth is a coin lost. Silently they gave and accepted food with both hands. A preoccupied child who took his bowl with one hand got a sideways glare. A complete moment of total attention is due everyone alike. Children and lovers have no singularity here, but my aunt used a secret voice, a separate attentiveness.

She kept the man's name to herself throughout her labor and dying; she did not accuse him that he be punished with her. To save her inseminator's name she gave silent birth.

He may have been somebody in her own household, but intercourse with a man outside the family would have been no less abhorrent. All the village were kinsmen, and the titles shouted in loud country voices never let kinship be forgotten. Any man within visiting distance would have been neutralized as a lover—"brother," "younger brother," "older brother"—one hundred and fifteen relationship titles. Parents researched birth charts probably not so much to assure good fortune as to circumvent incest in a population that has but one hundred surnames. Everybody has eight million relatives. How useless then sexual mannerisms, how dangerous.

As if it came from an atavism[6] deeper than fear, I used to add "brother" silently to boys' names. It hexed the boys, who would or would not ask me to dance, and made them less scary and as familiar and deserving of benevolence as girls.

But, of course, I hexed myself also—no dates. I should have stood up, both arms waving, and shouted out across libraries, "Hey, you! Love me back." I had no idea, though, how to make attraction selective, how to control its direction and magnitude. If I made myself American-pretty so that the five or six Chinese boys in the class fell in love with me, everyone else—the Caucasian, Negro, and Japanese boys—would too. Sisterliness, dignified and honorable, made much more sense.

Attraction eludes control so stubbornly that whole societies designed to organize relationships among people cannot keep order, not even when they bind people to one another from childhood and raise them together. Among the very poor and the wealthy, brothers married their adopted sisters, like doves. Our family allowed some romance, paying adult brides' prices and providing dowries so that their sons and daughters could marry strangers. Marriage promises to turn strangers into friendly relatives—a nation of siblings.

In the village structure, spirits shimmered among the live creatures, balanced and held in equilibrium by time and land. But one human being flaring up into violence could open up a black hole; a maelstrom[7] that pulled in the sky. The frightened villagers, who depended on one another to maintain the real, went to my aunt to show her a personal, physical representation of the break she had made in the "roundness." Misallying couples snapped off the future, which was to be embodied in true offspring. The villagers punished her for acting as if she could have a private life, secret and apart from them.

---

6. A trait with origins further back than the preceding generation; a throwback.

7. A powerful, violent whirlpool.

If my aunt had betrayed the family at a time of large grain yields and peace, when many boys were born, and wings were being built on many houses, perhaps she might have escaped such severe punishment. But the men— hungry, greedy, tired of planting in dry soil—had been forced to leave the village in order to send food-money home. There were ghost plagues, bandit plagues, wars with the Japanese, floods. My Chinese brother and sister had died of an unknown sickness. Adultery, perhaps only a mistake during good times, became a crime when the village needed food.

The round moon cakes and round doorways, the round tables of graduated size that fit one roundness inside another, round windows and rice bowls—these talismans had lost their power to warn this family of the law: a family must be whole, faithfully keeping the descent line by having sons to feed the old and the dead, who in turn look after the family. The villagers came to show my aunt and her lover in hiding a broken house. The villagers were speeding up the circling of events because she was too shortsighted to see that her infidelity had already harmed the village, that waves of consequences would return unpredictably, sometimes in disguise, as now, to hurt her. This roundness had to be made coin-sized so that she would see its circumference: punish her at the birth of her baby. Awaken her to the inexorable. People who refused fatalism because they could invent small resources insisted on culpability. Deny accidents and wrest fault from the stars.

After the villagers left, their lanterns now scattering in various directions toward home, the family broke their silence and cursed her. "Aiaa, we're going to die. Death is coming. Death is coming. Look what you've done. You've killed us. Ghost! Dead ghost! Ghost! You've never been born." She ran out into the fields, far enough from the house so that she could no longer hear their voices, and pressed herself against the earth, her own land no more. When she felt the birth coming, she thought that she had been hurt. Her body seized together. "They've hurt me too much," she thought. "This is gall, and it will kill me." With forehead and knees against the earth, her body convulsed and then relaxed. She turned on her back, lay on the ground. The black well of sky and stars went out and out and out forever; her body and her complexity seemed to disappear. She was one of the stars, a bright dot in blackness, without home, without a companion, in eternal cold and silence. An agoraphobia[8] rose in her, speeding higher and higher, bigger and bigger; she would not be able to contain it; there would be no end to fear.

Flayed, unprotected against space, she felt pain return, focusing her body. This pain chilled her—a cold, steady kind of surface pain. Inside, spasmodically, the other pain, the pain of the child, heated her. For hours she lay on the ground, alternately body and space. Sometimes a vision of normal comfort obliterated reality: she saw the family in the evening gambling at the dinner table, the young people massaging their elder's backs. She saw them congratulating one another, high joy on the mornings the rice shoots came up. When these pictures burst, the stars drew yet further apart. Black space opened.

She got to her feet to fight better and remembered that old-fashioned women gave birth in their pigsties to fool the jealous, pain-dealing gods, who

8. An abnormal fear of open space.

do not snatch piglets. Before the next spasms could stop her, she ran to the pigsty, each step a rushing out into emptiness. She climbed over the fence and knelt in the dirt. It was good to have a fence enclosing her, a tribal person alone.

Laboring, this woman who had carried her child as a foreign growth that sickened her every day, expelled it at last. She reached down to touch the hot, wet, moving mass, surely smaller than anything human, and could feel that it was human after all—fingers, toes, nails, nose. She pulled it up on to her belly, and it lay curled there, but in the air, feet precisely tucked one under the other. She opened her loose shirt and buttoned the child inside. After resting, it squirmed and thrashed and she pushed it up to her breast. It turned its head this way and that until it found her nipple. There, it made little snuffling noises. She clenched her teeth at its preciousness, lovely as a young calf, a piglet, a little dog.

She may have gone to the pigsty as a last act of responsibility: she would protect this child as she had protected its father. It would look after her soul, leaving supplies on her grave. But how would this tiny child without family find her grave when there would be no marker for her anywhere, neither in the earth nor the family hall? No one would give her a family hall name. She had taken the child with her into the wastes. At its birth the two of them had felt the same raw pain of separation, a wound that only the family pressing tight could close. A child with no descent line would not soften her life but only trail after her, ghostlike, begging her to give it purpose. At dawn the villagers on their way to the fields would stand around the fence and look.

Full of milk, the little ghost slept. When it awoke, she hardened her breasts against the milk that crying loosens. Toward morning she picked up the baby and walked to the well.

Carrying the baby to the well shows loving. Otherwise abandon it. Turn its face into the mud. Mothers who love their children take them along. It was probably a girl; there is some hope of forgiveness for boys.

"Don't tell anyone you had an aunt. Your father does not want to hear her name. She has never been born." I have believed that sex was unspeakable and words so strong and fathers so frail that "aunt" would do my father mysterious harm. I have thought that my family, having settled among immigrants who had also been their neighbors in the ancestral land, needed to clean their name, and a wrong word would incite the kinspeople even here. But there is more to this silence: they want me to participate in her punishment. And I have.

In the twenty years since I heard this story I have not asked for details nor said my aunt's name; I do not know it. People who can comfort the dead can also chase after them to hurt them further—a reverse ancestor worship. The real punishment was not the raid swiftly inflicted by the villagers, but the family's deliberately forgetting her. Her betrayal so maddened them, they saw to it that she would suffer forever, even after death. Always hungry, always needing, she would have to beg food from other ghosts, snatch and steal it from those whose living descendants give them gifts. She would have to fight the ghosts massed at crossroads for the buns a few thoughtful citizens leave to decoy her away from village and home so that the ancestral spirits could feast unharassed. At peace, they could act like gods, not ghosts, their descent lines providing them with paper suits and dresses, spirit money, paper houses, paper automobiles, chicken, meat, and rice[9] into eternity—essences delivered up in smoke and flames, steam and incense rising from each rice bowl. In an attempt to make the Chinese care for people outside the family, Chairman Mao[1] encourages us now to give our paper replicas to the spirits of outstanding soldiers and workers, no matter whose ancestors they may be. My aunt remains forever hungry. Goods are not distributed evenly among the dead.

My aunt haunts me—her ghost drawn to me because now, after fifty years of neglect, I alone devote pages of paper to her, though not origamied into houses and clothes. I do not think she always means me well. I am telling on her, and she was a spite suicide, drowning herself in the drinking water. The Chinese are always very frightened of the drowned one, whose weeping ghost, wet hair hanging and skin bloated, waits silently by the water to pull down a substitute.

1976

9. Traditionally, offerings left at the graves of ancestors.
1. Mao Zedong (1893–1976), head of the Chinese Communist Party and leader of China from 1949 to 1976.

ROBERT PINSKY
b. 1940

A poet, critic, and translator, Robert Pinsky is a remarkable and influential figure in contemporary poetry. His appointment in 1997 for a two-year term as the ninth poet laureate of the United States (among his predecessors in this position were Rita Dove, Robert Penn Warren, and Richard Wilbur, also represented in this anthology) confirmed the range and ambition of his work. In his first collection of poetry, *Sadness and Happiness* (1975), Pinsky staked out a territory neglected by most image-dominated American poetry in the 1970s: the discursiveness that poetry shares with prose and speech, including declaration, statement, and abstract definition. A year later, his influential book of criticism, *The Situation of Poetry* (1976), argued for a poetry with the prose virtues of "Clarity, Flexibility, Efficiency, and Cohesiveness." In Pinsky's hands this "drab, unglamorous group" of virtues produced the winning and pleasurable poems of his first book and two following collections: *An Explanation of America* (1980) and *History of My Heart* (1984). Like William Carlos Williams and Elizabeth Bishop before him, Pinsky endows his poems with the casualness of prose inflections; the result is a wonderfully sociable body of poetry, with a relaxed and familiar sense of middle-class life. Here are poems of tennis and psychiatrists, baseball and daughters in school, high school dances, movies, "the small-town main street" ("History of My Heart").

But Pinsky's emphasis on the explanatory and the domestic can obscure his ambition and his formal virtuosity. The long title poem of *An Explanation of America* bespeaks his desire to bring together domestic life (the poem is addressed to his daughter) and the nation, to unite private feeling with "general Happiness and Safety." The poems of *History of My Heart* call on the personal memories at work in his first book but also introduce another sort of music, more mysterious and—what other word?—poetic. The publication of *The Want Bone* in 1990 and a book of new and collected poems, *The Figured Wheel*, in 1996, further demonstrated that the language of Pinsky's best poems is ordinary and yet also transcendent. If one of his strengths is the way he makes poetry a conversation about ideas, increasingly he also summons the power of poetry to sing what is "impossible to say." Pinsky's formal virtuosity lies in his ability to marry variations on traditional poetic rhythms (like the pentameter line at work in "The Want Bone," "At Pleasure Bay," and "Shirt") with American speech rhythms. This ability to shape a poetic line close to ordinary rhythms of speech and prose, and thus to render and deepen the everyday, connects him to Frank Bidart and James McMichael, two contemporary poets he admires. Pinsky is also an American master of the half or slant rhyme (like "twice" and "police" in "At Pleasure Bay" and the alliterative echo, like "bell" and "blue" in "The Want Bone," which gives his work a sense of both formal music and relaxation; there is the repeated echo of sound within and between stanzas, without the closure of full rhyme. The sensuousness of poetry, Pinsky remarks in his collection of essays *Poetry and the World* (1988), gives "elegance and significance to the sounds that breath makes vibrating in the mouth and throat." In "The Want Bone" (the dried jawbone of a shark, which he saw on a friend's mantle) he renders the sound vibrating in "this scalded toothless harp" as song: "my food my parent my child I want you my own / My flower my fin my life my lightness my O." Reading these lines we might easily forget that this poet has argued for poetry's discursive qualities. At the same time Pinsky's work continues to include what is sometimes excluded from American poetry, such as explanation or back-slapping ethnic jokes (in "Impossible to Tell" from *The Figured Wheel*).

Pinsky grew up in what he has called a "nominally orthodox" Jewish family in Long Branch, New Jersey. He later attended Rutgers and then Stanford University (where he studied with Yvor Winters). Though he lived in California for several years and now teaches in the graduate writing program at Boston University, Long Branch is Pinsky's middle America, despite its location at the ocean's edge ("bounded on three sides by similar places / and on one side by vast, uncouth houses / A glum boardwalk and, / as we say, the beach"). In Long Branch are his childhood memories and streets, as well as his sense of ethnic experience. With its fading boardwalk and movie houses, it also exemplifies an American popular culture for which Pinsky has unabashed appreciation. "At Pleasure Bay" (from *The Want Bone*), included here, beautifully commingles childhood memory and a sense of place with a feeling for the larger historical forces shaping the lives of local inhabitants. Though it is unlike Pinsky to move too far afield from everyday life, "At Pleasure Bay" and poems like it reveal the ways that Pinsky's vision extends beyond the personal and local into a deeper past and (in the poem's closing vision) future. The same process of enlarging a sense of community and connection while not straying too far from daily experience unfolds in "Shirt," which works its own variations on the pentameter line and is beautifully shaped by Pinsky's trademark half rhymes, here working within a single line as well as between lines.

The pleasures of Pinsky's poetry are also literary; he is unabashed in his references to literary antecedents but in no sense narrowly academic. Instead his work acknowledges and celebrates the way literature shapes his (and our) sense of life and experience, as well as his (and our) use of language. Pinsky's poetry is so distinctively American in its diction and subjects that his important work as a translator can come as a surprise. Among the poets he has translated are Czeslaw Milosz (the two worked together on the translations) and Paul Célan. In 1994 Pinsky published *The Inferno of Dante*, recipient of the Academy of American Poets translation award, in which his formal gifts allowed him to re-create an American version of Dante's interlocked rhyme scheme, the terza rima. In a review of this translation in the *New York Times*, Edward Hirsch described the effect of Pinsky's stanzas as "moving through a series of interpenetrating rooms . . . or going down a set of winding stairs." While his sense of literary tradition is deep and wide-ranging, Pinsky is also engaged with new possibilities for literature created by computer technology. In 1985, in collaboration with computer programmers, he created an interactive text adventure game, *Mind-wheel*, and he has served as the poetry editor of the weekly online magazine *Slate*. Computer software and poetry, Pinsky has said, "share a great human myth or trope, an image that could be called the secret passage: the discovery of large manifold channels through a small, ordinary-looking or all but invisible aperture. . . . This passage to vast complexities is what writing through the machine might become."

The Figured Wheel

The figured wheel rolls through shopping malls and prisons,
Over farms, small and immense, and the rotten little downtowns.
Covered with symbols, it mills everything alive and grinds
The remains of the dead in the cemeteries, in unmarked graves and oceans.

Sluiced by salt water and fresh, by pure and contaminated rivers, 5
By snow and sand, it separates and recombines all droplets and grains,
Even the infinite sub-atomic particles crushed under the illustrated,
Varying treads of its wide circumferential track.

Spraying flecks of tar and molten rock it rumbles
Through the Antarctic station of American sailors and technicians, 10
And shakes the floors and windows of whorehouses for diggers and
  smelters
From Bethany, Pennsylvania to a practically nameless, semi-penal New
  Town

In the mineral-rich tundra of the Soviet northernmost settlements.
Artists illuminate it with pictures and incised mottoes
Taken from the Ten Thousand Stories and the Register of True Dramas. 15
They hang it with colored ribbons and with bells of many pitches.

With paints and chisels and moving lights they record
On its rotating surface the elegant and terrifying doings
Of the inhabitants of the Hundred Pantheons of major Gods
Disposed in iconographic stations at hub, spoke and concentric bands, 20

And also the grotesque demi-Gods, Hopi gargoyles and Ibo dryads.[1]
They cover it with wind-chimes and electronic instruments
That vibrate as it rolls to make an all-but-unthinkable music,
So that the wheel hums and rings as it turns through the births of stars

---

1. Woodland spirits. "Ibo": a West African tribe, many of whose members were sent as slaves to America.

And through the dead-world of bomb, fireblast and fallout   25
Where only a few doomed races of insects fumble in the smoking grasses.
It is Jesus oblivious to hurt turning to give words to the unrighteous,
And is also Gogol's[2] feeding pig that without knowing it eats a baby chick

And goes on feeding. It is the empty armor of My Cid,[3] clattering
Into the arrows of the credulous unbelievers, a metal suit   30
Like the lost astronaut revolving with his useless umbilicus
Through the cold streams, neither energy nor matter, that agitate

The cold, cyclical dark, turning and returning.
Even in the scorched and frozen world of the dead after the holocaust
The wheel as it turns goes on accreting ornaments.   35
Scientists and artists festoon it from the grave with brilliant

Toys and messages, jokes and zodiacs, tragedies conceived
From among the dreams of the unemployed and the pampered,
The listless and the tortured. It is hung with devices
By dead masters who have survived by reducing themselves magically   40

To tiny organisms, to wisps of matter, crumbs of soil,
Bits of dry skin, microscopic flakes, which is why they are called "great,"
In their humility that goes on celebrating the turning
Of the wheel as it rolls unrelentingly over

A cow plodding through car-traffic on a street in *Iasi*,[4]   45
And over the haunts of Robert Pinsky's mother and father
And wife and children and his sweet self
Which he hereby unwillingly and inexpertly gives up, because it is

There, figured and pre-figured in the nothing-transfiguring wheel.

                                                                        1984

The Street

Streaked and fretted with effort, the thick
Vine of the world, red nervelets
Coiled at its tips.

All roads lead from it. All night
Wainwrights and upholsterers work finishing   5
The wheeled coffin

Of the dead favorite of the Emperor,
The child's corpse propped seated
On brocade, with yellow

---

2. Nikolai Gogol (1809–1852), Russian novelist, short-story writer, and playwright.
3. The Castillian epic *Poem of the Cid* (c. 1140)
celebrates the legendary Spanish hero, the Cid.
4. City in Moldavia, Romania.

Oiled curls, kohl on the stiff lids.   10
Slaves throw petals on the roadway
For the cortege, white

Languid flowers shooting from dark
Blisters on the vine, ramifying
Into streets. On mine,   15

Rockwell Avenue, it was embarrassing:
Trouble—fights, the police, sickness—
Seemed never to come

For anyone when they were fully dressed.
It was always underwear or dirty pyjamas,   20
Unseemly stretches

Of skin showing through a torn housecoat.
Once a stranger drove off in a car
With somebody's wife,

And he ran after them in his undershirt   25
And threw his shoe at the car. It bounced
Into the street

Harmlessly, and we carried it back to him;
But the man had too much dignity
To put it back on,   30

So he held it and stood crying in the street:
"He's breaking up my home," he said,
"The son of a bitch

Bastard is breaking up my home." The street
Rose undulant in pavement-breaking coils   35
And the man rode it,

Still holding his shoe and stiffly upright
Like a trick rider in the circus parade
That came down the street

Each August. As the powerful dragonlike   40
Hump swelled he rose cursing and ready
To throw his shoe—woven

Angular as a twig into the fabulous
Rug or brocade with crowns and camels,
Leopards and rosettes,   45

All riding the vegetable wave of the street
From the John Flock Mortuary Home
Down to the river.

It was a small place, and off the center,
But so much a place to itself, I felt   50
Like a young prince

Or aspirant squire. I knew that *Ivanhoe*[1]
Was about race. The Saxons were Jews,
Or even Coloreds,

With their low-ceilinged, unbelievably   55
Sour-smelling houses down by the docks.
Everything was written

Or woven, ivory and pink and emerald—
Nothing was too ugly or petty or terrible
To be weighed in the immense   60

Silver scales of the dead: the looming
Balances set right onto the live, dangerous
Gray bark of the street.

                                                        1984

The Want Bone

The tongue of the waves tolled in the earth's bell.
Blue rippled and soaked in the fire of blue.
The dried mouthbones of a shark in the hot swale
Gaped on nothing but sand on either side.

The bone tasted of nothing and smelled of nothing,   5
A scalded toothless harp, uncrushed, unstrung.
The joined arcs made the shape of birth and craving
And the welded-open shape kept mouthing O.

Ossified cords held the corners together
In groined spirals pleated like a summer dress.   10
But where was the limber grin, the gash of pleasure?
Infinitesimal mouths bore it away,

The beach scrubbed and etched and pickled it clean.
But O I love you it sings, my little my country
My food my parent my child I want you my own   15
My flower my fin my life my lightness my O.

                                                        1990

1. The title and hero of Sir Walter Scott's romance novel (1819), set in 12th-century England, in which the hero wins the Saxon princess Rowena and champions a Jewish woman, Rebecca.

Shirt

The back, the yoke, the yardage. Lapped seams,[1]
The nearly invisible stitches along the collar
Turned in a sweatshop by Koreans or Malaysians

Gossiping over tea and noodles on their break
Or talking money or politics while one fitted   5
This armpiece with its overseam to the band

Of cuff I button at my wrist. The presser, the cutter,
The wringer, the mangle. The needle, the union,
The treadle, the bobbin. The code. The infamous blaze

At the Triangle Factory[2] in nineteen-eleven   10
One hundred and forty-six died in the flames
On the ninth floor, no hydrants, no fire escapes—

The witness in a building across the street
Who watched how a young man helped a girl to step
up to the windowsill, then held her out   15

Away from the masonry wall and let her drop.
And then another. As if he were helping them up
To enter a streetcar, and not eternity.

A third before he dropped her put her arms
Around his neck and kissed him. Then he held   20
Her into space, and dropped her. Almost at once

He stepped to the sill himself, his jacket flared
And fluttered up from his shirt as he came down,
Air filling up the legs of his gray trousers—

Like Hart Crane's Bedlamite,[3] "shrill shirt ballooning."   25
Wonderful how the pattern matches perfectly
Across the placket and over the twin bar-tacked

Corners of both pockets, like a strict rhyme
Or a major chord. Prints, plaids, checks,
Houndstooth, Tattersall, Madras. The clan tartans   30

---

1. Overlapping seams used to join fabric in interfacings to make them less bulky.
2. In 1911 the Triangle shirtwaist factory in New York City was the scene of a notorious fire in which 146 women who worked in the factory jumped to their deaths to escape the flames. This event marked the beginning of rigorous efforts to enforce workplace safety.
3. A reference to lines from the opening section ("To Brooklyn Bridge") of the American poet Hart Crane's sequence *The Bridge* (1930): "Out of some subway scuttle, cell or loft / A bedlamite speeds to thy parapets." A bedlamite is an inmate of a hospital for the mentally ill.

Invented by mill-owners inspired by the hoax of Ossian,[4]
To control their savage Scottish workers, tamed
By a fabricated heraldry: MacGregor,

Bailey, MacMartin. The kilt, devised for workers
To wear among the dusty clattering looms.   35
Weavers, carders, spinners. The loader,

The docker, the navvy.[5] The planter, the picker, the sorter
Sweating at her machine in a litter of cotton
As slaves in calico headrags sweated in fields:

George Herbert,[6] your descendant is a Black   40
Lady in South Carolina, her name is Irma
And she inspected my shirt. Its color and fit

And feel and its clean smell have satisfied
Both her and me. We have culled its cost and quality
Down to the buttons of simulated bone,   45

The buttonholes, the sizing, the facing, the characters
Printed in black on neckband and tail. The shape,
The label, the labor, the color, the shade. The shirt.

1990

At Pleasure Bay

In the willows along the river at Pleasure Bay
A catbird singing, never the same phrase twice.
Here under the pines a little off the road
In 1927 the Chief of Police
And Mrs. W. killed themselves together,   5
Sitting in a roadster. Ancient unshaken pilings
And underwater chunks of still-mortared brick
In shapes like bits of puzzle strew the bottom
Where the landing was for Price's Hotel and Theater.
And here's where boats blew two blasts for the keeper   10
To shunt the iron swing-bridge. He leaned on the gears
Like a skipper in the hut that housed the works
And the bridge moaned and turned on its middle pier
To let them through. In the middle of the summer
Two or three cars might wait for the iron trusswork   15
Winching aside, with maybe a child to notice
A name on the stern in black-and-gold on white,

---

4. In 1760 James Macpherson published *Poems of Ossian*, which falsely claimed to be a translation of a text by the 3rd-century Irish hero of that name.

5. An unskilled laborer, especially one engaged in excavating or construction.
6. English poet (1593–1633).

Sandpiper, Patsy Ann, Do Not Disturb,
The Idler. If a boat was running whiskey,
The bridge clanged shut behind it as it passed   20
And opened up again for the Coast Guard cutter
Slowly as a sundial, and always jammed halfway.
The roadbed whole, but opened like a switch,
The river pulling and coursing between the piers.
Never the same phrase twice, the catbird filling   25
The humid August evening near the inlet
With borrowed music that he melds and changes.
Dragonflies and sandflies, frogs in the rushes, two bodies
Not moving in the open car among the pines,
A sliver of story. The tenor at Price's Hotel,   30
In clown costume, unfurls the sorrow gathered
In ruffles at his throat and cuffs, high quavers
That hold like splashes of light on the dark water,
The aria's closing phrases, changed and fading.
And after a gap of quiet, cheers and applause   35
Audible in the houses across the river,
Some in the audience weeping as if they had melted
Inside the music. Never the same. In Berlin
The daughter of an English lord, in love
With Adolf Hitler, whom she has met. She is taking   40
Possession of the apartment of a couple,
Elderly well-off Jews. They survive the war
To settle here in the Bay, the old lady
Teaches piano, but the whole world swivels
And gapes at their feet as the girl and a high-up Nazi   45
Examine the furniture, the glass, the pictures,
The elegant story that was theirs and now
Is a part of hers. A few months later the English
Enter the war and she shoots herself in a park,
An addled, upper-class girl, her life that passes   50
Into the lives of others or into a place.
The taking of lives—the Chief and Mrs. W.
Took theirs to stay together, as local ghosts.
Last flurries of kisses, the revolver's barrel,
Shivers of a story that a child might hear   55
And half remember, voices in the rushes,
A singing in the willows. From across the river,
Faint quavers of music, the same phrase twice and again,
Ranging and building. Over the high new bridge
The flashing of traffic homeward from the racetrack,   60
With one boat chugging under the arches, outward
Unnoticed through Pleasure Bay to the open sea.
Here's where the people stood to watch the theater
Burn on the water. All that night the fireboats
Kept playing their spouts of water into the blaze.   65
In the morning, smoking pilasters and beams.
Black smell of char for weeks, the ruin already
Soaking back into the river. After you die
You hover near the ceiling above your body

And watch the mourners awhile. A few days more 70
You float above the heads of the ones you knew
And watch them through a twilight. As it grows darker
You wander off and find your way to the river
And wade across. On the other side, night air,
Willows, the smell of the river, and a mass 75
Of sleeping bodies all along the bank,
A kind of singing from among the rushes
Calling you further forward in the dark.
You lie down and embrace one body, the limbs
Heavy with sleep reach eagerly up around you 80
And you make love until your soul brims up
And burns free out of you and shifts and spills
Down over into that other body, and you
Forget the life you had and begin again
On the same crossing—maybe as a child who passes 85
Through the same place. But never the same way twice.
Here in the daylight, the catbird in the willows,
The new café, with a terrace and a landing,
Frogs in the cattails where the swing-bridge was—
Here's where you might have slipped across the water 90
When you were only a presence, at Pleasure Bay.

1990

SIMON J. ORTIZ
b. 1941

In his poem "A Designated National Park," Simon J. Ortiz tells of visiting Monte-zuma Castle in Verde Valley, Arizona, where he experiences as present in himself the life of the people there: "Hear / in my cave, sacred song. / Morning feeling, sacred song. / We shall plant today." His connection to that landscape, however, is complicated by the fact that it is now a "DESIGNATED FEDERAL RECREATION FEE AREA": "This morning / I have to buy a permit to get back home." Ortiz's treat-ment of Verde Valley is characteristic of the way he inhabits a conflicted landscape. He was born and raised in the Acoma Pueblo Community in Albuquerque, New Mexico. One meaning of the name *Acoma* is "the place that always was," and in this sense it transcends the poet's place of origin and represents for him the Native American way of life. Ortiz continually returns to this abiding sense of origin after traveling great distances from it. Often his poems enact a journey, and as Joseph Bruhac reminds us, in American Indian cultures the theme of traveling implicitly recalls the "tragic epic movements of Native American nations." Many of Ortiz's poems dramatize his disorientation as he moves within an America where Indian names are reduced to billboard signs, where rivers burn from industrial wastes and construction fills up the spaces of the earth. His sense of contemporary life, espe-cially its absurdities, is acute.

But the America he travels conceals within it an older landscape animated by spirit, where the earth is alive with "wind visions" and "The Mountains dream / about pine brothers and friends" ("Vision Shadows"); to travel it is to seek "the center of the center" ("Between Albuquerque and Santa Fe"), the place where the spirits enter the world. Asked in an interview, "Why do you write?" Ortiz once responded, "Because Indians always tell a story. . . . The only way to continue is to tell a story and there is no other way. Your children will not survive unless you tell something about them—how they were born, how they came to this certain place, how they continued." Tellingly, Ortiz chose to reprint these comments at the beginning of his collection A Good Journey (1977). The stories his poems narrate are evidence that the Native American way of life is continuous, despite all the forces that attempt to eradicate it. But his work also tells of the painful costs that come with survival.

After receiving his early education at a Bureau of Indian Affairs school on the Acoma Reservation, Ortiz later attended the University of New Mexico and the University of Iowa. He has since taught at San Diego State University and the University of New Mexico. "I never decided to become a poet," Ortiz has said, suggesting that his relatives transmitted to him the power of words. "An old-man relative with a humpback used to come to our home when I was a child, and he would carry me on his back. He told me stories. . . . That contact must have contributed the language of myself." His father, a stonemason, carpenter, and woodcarver, would talk and sing as he worked. In "A Story of How a Wall Stands," he remembers his father saying "Underneath / what looks like loose stone, / there is stone woven together." This sense of underlying connection is true of Ortiz's poetry as well, often at its finest when revealing how a moment or event fits into the ongoing cycles celebrated by ritual. His best poems are sometimes surprising in the way the apparently loose details suddenly blaze into an arrangement. Characteristically, this happens through powerful repetitions culminating in the last movements of a poem, a technique that depends on rereading. Ortiz's collection Going for Rain appeared in 1976; its poems sometimes show a writer whose strong feelings have not yet found a distinctive language or rhythm. His next book, The Good Journey, is more assured and its range significantly broader. His work also includes From Sand Creek, which won the 1982 Pushcart Prize, as well as A Poem Is a Journey (1981) and an edition that collects earlier volumes together with new work, Woven Stone (1992). After and Before the Lightning was published in 1994; his short stories were collected in Men on the Moon (1999). Ortiz's mission—continuance and preservation—sometimes allows a didactic impulse to shape his work too rigidly. But his finest poems have a richness of experience and a vital, imaginative sense of the earth that refuses any single conceptual or moral frame.

A recurring image in several Ortiz poems is the "Wisconsin horse" he once saw standing "within a fence // silent in the hot afternoon" while one mile away new construction was going on: "I tell the horse, / 'That's America building something'" ("The Wisconsin Horse"). The spirit of the horse, restrained by the chainlink fence and threatened by the approaching construction, suggests Ortiz's sense of constriction in the VA hospitals (his experience in one of these prompted his sequence Poems from the Veterans Hospital), as well as in small-town bars, in the Salvation Army store, or in the boundaries of the designated National Parks. Something threatens to break loose in these poems; feelings precariously held in check shake the formal structures. Other poems, like "Earth and Rain, the Plants & Sun," have the freedom and buoyancy of the hawk's flight; the words move in a space that seems immense. Instead of explosive anger or despair, the tone of the poem is close to song or prayer. What is so moving in Ortiz's work is that these voices are both his; together they suggest the fracture of identity and the possibility of reintegration.

Passing through Little Rock

The old Indian ghosts—
                                        "Quapaw"
"Waccamaw"[1]—
                            are just billboard words
in this crummy town.   5

"You know, I'm worrying a lot lately,"
he says in the old hotel bar.

"You're getting older and scared ain't you?"

I just want to cross the next hill,
through that clump of trees   10
and come out the other side

and see a clean river,
the whole earth new
and hear the noise it makes
at birth.   15

                                                            1976

Earth and Rain, the Plants & Sun

        Once near San Ysidro
        on the way to Colorado,
        I stopped and looked.
        The sound of a meadowlark
        through smell of fresh cut alfalfa.   5

        Raho would say,
        "Look, Dad." A hawk

        sweeping
                    its wings

        clear through   10
                    the blue
        of whole and pure
                    the wind
                            the sky.

        It is writhing   15
        overhead.
        Hear. The Bringer.
                The Thunderer.

1. Names of Native American tribes formerly living in Arkansas.

Sunlight falls
through cloud curtains,   20
a straight bright shaft.

It falls,
      it falls,
   down
      to earth,   25
a green plant.

Today, the Katzina[1] come.
The dancing prayers.

Many times, the Katzina.
The dancing prayers.   30
It shall not end,
son, it will not end,
this love.

Again and again,
the earth is new again.   35
They come, listen, listen.
Hold on to your mother's hand.
They come

O great joy, they come.
The plants with bells.   40
The stones with voices.
Listen, son, hold my hand.

                                                    1977

Vision Shadows

Wind visions are honest.
Eagles clearly soar
to the craggy peaks
of the mind.
The mind is full   5
of sunprayer
and childlaughter.

The Mountains dream
about pine brothers and friends,
the mystic realm of boulders   10

---

1. Or Kachina; spirits of the invisible life forces of the Pueblo Indians of North America. The Kachinas are impersonated by elaborately costumed masked men and boys of the tribes who visit Pueblo villages the first half of the year. Although not worshiped as gods, Kachinas are greatly revered; one of their main purposes is to bring rain for the spring crops.

which shelter
rabbits, squirrels, wrens.
They believe in the power.
They also believe
in quick eagle death.   15

The eagle loops
into the wind power.
He can see a million miles
and more because of it.

All believe things   20
of origin and solitude.

          But what has happened
(I hear strange news from Wyoming
of thallium sulphate. Ranchers
bearing arms in helicopters.[1])   25
to these visions?
I hear foreign tremors.
Breath comes thin and shredded.
I hear the scabs of strange deaths
falling off.   30

Snake hurries through the grass.
Coyote is befuddled by his own tricks.
And Bear whimpers pain into the wind.

Poisonous fumes cross our sacred paths.
The wind is still.   35
O Blue Sky, O Mountain, O Spirit, O
what has stopped?

Eagles tumble dumbly into shadows
that swallow them with dull thuds.
The sage can't breathe.   40
Jackrabbit is lonely and alone
with eagle gone.

It is painful, aiiee, without visions
to soothe dry whimpers
or repair the flight of eagle, our own brother.   45

                                                      1977

---

1. In 1971 the owner of Wyoming's largest sheep ranch was found to have hired a helicopter in order to shoot bald eagles, which he claimed were preying on his lambs. He was later found to be responsible for the deaths of more than 700 eagles by aerial shooting and by poisoning with thallium sulphate, a chemical used as rat poison.

From Poems from the Veterans Hospital

Travelling

A man has been in the VAH Library all day long,
looking at the maps, the atlas, and the globe,
finding places.
              Acapulco, the Bay of Bengal,
Antarctica, Madagascar, Rome, Luxembourg,   5
places.

He writes their names on a letter pad, hurries
to another source, asks the librarian for a book
but it is out and he looks hurt and then he rushes
back to the globe, turns it a few times and finds   10
Yokohama and then the Aleutian Islands.

Later on, he studies Cape Cod for a moment,
a faraway glee on his face, in his eyes.
He is Gauguin, he is Coyote,[1] he is who he is,
travelling the known and unknown places,   15
travelling, travelling.

                                    1977

From From Sand Creek

At the Salvation Army
a clerk
caught me
wandering
among old spoons   5
        and knives,
             sweaters and shoes.

I couldn't have stolen anything;
my life was stolen already.

In protest though,   10
I should have stolen.
My life. My life.

She caught me;
Carson[1] caught Indians,

---

1. The trickster figure in southwestern and other Native American tales. The French painter Paul Gauguin (1848–1903) left his home in France for Tahiti and the Marquesas Islands.
1. Christopher ("Kit") Carson (1809–1868), trapper, scout, Indian agent, and soldier, was hired by the government to help control the Navajo. Beginning in 1863 he waged a brutal economic war against the tribe, marching through the heart of their territory to destroy their crops, orchards, and livestock. In 1864 most Navajo surrendered to Carson, who forced nearly 8,000 Navajo men, women, and children to take what came to be called the "Long Walk" of 300 miles from Arizona to Fort Sumner, New Mexico, where they remained in disease-ridden confinement until 1868.

secured them with his lies.   15
Bound them with his belief.

After winter,
our own lives fled.

I reassured her
what she believed.   20
Bought a sweater.

And fled.

I should have stolen.
My life. My life.

1981

BILLY COLLINS
b. 1941

The voice in a Billy Collins poem is so intimate and immediate that we feel we are in the same room with the poet. Collins imagines poet and reader sitting together at a breakfast table: "I will lean forward, / elbows on the table, / with something to tell you / and you will look up, as always, / your spoon dripping with milk, ready to listen" ("A Portrait of the Reader with a Bowl of Cereal"). The colloquial voice in his poems charms us with its air of spontaneous expression, its modesty, its humor. If some of his poems coast on charm alone, Collins's best work takes us on a surprising ride: its strange and unexpected associations deepen the familiar into the mysterious or make the mysterious familiar.

Describing the structures of his poetry, Collins says, "We are attempting, all the time, to create a logical, rational path through the day. To the left and right there are an amazing set of distractions that we can't afford to follow. But the poet is willing to stop anywhere." His poems often proceed as accounts of a day and its distractions, as in "Tuesday, June 4, 1991." At the same time the formal shapeliness of Collins's work endows ordinary activity with a strange and pleasing formality and turns it, line by measured line and stanza by stanza, into a ritual including both the pleasures and the pathos of life. These poems present a humorous self-awareness about the speaker's dramatizing and obsessive love of distraction—anything, no matter how insignificant, can carry off his attention—and one thing that is so welcome about Collins's poems is that they are funny. Only on later readings do we realize that they are also sad. When he looks over the edges of domestic life there is blankness; unlike the work of a Jorie Graham or a Charles Wright, a Collins poem evokes no metaphysical structures that might sustain this fragile world. Yet (in the Irish poet William Butler Yeats's phrase) Collins loves "what vanishes"—the day in June, the good meal, even one's memories. This knowledge of how things large and small disappear is a great equalizer. The humor in Collins's poetry puts this equalizing principle to work; he deflates the grandiose and subjects large statements of truth to the test of the particular. Collins's titles, imaginative and playful, suggest the way he alights on small, usually trivial instances in which life's strangeness and mystery flash out: "Weighing the Dog," "I Chop Some Parsley While Listening to Art Blakey's Version of 'Three Blind Mice.'" Other titles signal the way he grounds the improbable within the everyday: "Taking Off Emily Dickinson's Clothes," "Shoveling Snow with Buddha."

Collins's collections of poems include *Questions about Angels* (1977), *The Art of Drowning* (1995), *Picnic, Lightning* (1998), *Sailing Alone Around the World: New and Selected Poems* (2001), *Nine Horses* (2003), *The Trouble with Poetry and Other Poems* (2005), *Ballistics* (2008), *Horoscopes for the Dead* (2011), and *Aimless Love: New and Selected Poems* (2013). He served as poet laureate of the United States from 2001 to 2003. Born in New York City (in a hospital where, as he likes to note, William Carlos Williams worked as a pediatric resident), Collins teaches at Lehman College of the City University. Walking the city streets animates him and inflects some of his poems in a way that recalls the work of Frank O'Hara, with whom Collins shares an idiomatic American voice, colloquial and understated, shaped by jazz and the blues. Collins's work often plays with the melody of a pentameter line as a jazz musician plays on and off the melody of a song; the pentameter is an undertone from which a more idiosyncratic rhythm moves around and away. While the rhythms of Collins's poetry often enforce a slowing-down, a tender lingering over everyday life, their breezy tone and quick humor seem to suggest that nothing too serious is going on. It is as if Collins were fending off the large, prophetic claims made by visionary poets (early in his career he earned a Ph.D. at the University of California at Riverside, specializing in the Romantic period), even as some of his poems are riffs on the Romantic tradition. Such Collins poems as "Keats's Handwriting" and "Lines Composed Over Three Thousand Miles from Tintern Abbey" deflate the romantic sublime and substitute for it a vision self-deprecating and humorous. Thus when we hear nightingales in a Collins poem, they're a group singing on the gospel radio station ("Sunday Morning with the Sensational Nightingales").

Collins's modest claims for poetry and the fact that his work is so appealing and accessible can lead us to underestimate the necessity and reward of rereading him. The best of his poems open up a moment like a series of nested boxes; if we read too quickly, we miss the pleasure and surprise of intricate connections and deepening discoveries. A Collins poem has a spontaneity that yields immediate pleasure, but only when we listen again more attentively do we recognize the art that makes itself look easy.

Forgetfulness

The name of the author is the first to go
followed obediently by the title, the plot,
the heartbreaking conclusion, the entire novel
which suddenly becomes one you have never read, never even heard of,

as if, one by one, the memories you used to harbor   5
decided to retire to the southern hemisphere of the brain,
to a little fishing village where there are no phones.

Long ago you kissed the names of the nine Muses goodbye,
and watched the quadratic equation pack its bag,
and even now as you memorize the order of the planets,   10

something else is slipping away, a state flower perhaps,
the address of an uncle, the capital of Paraguay.

Whatever it is you are struggling to remember
it is not poised on the tip of your tongue,
not even lurking in some obscure corner of your spleen.   15

It has floated away down a dark mythological river
whose name begins with an *L* as far as you can recall,[1]
well on your own way to oblivion where you will join those
who have even forgotten how to swim and how to ride a bicycle.

No wonder you rise in the middle of the night   20
to look up the date of a famous battle in a book on war.
No wonder the moon in the window seems to have drifted
out of a love poem that you used to know by heart.

                                                                      1991

Osso Buco[1]

I love the sound of the bone against the plate
and the fortress-like look of it
lying before me in a moat of risotto,[2]
the meat soft as the leg of an angel
who has lived a purely airborne existence.   5
And best of all, the secret marrow,
the invaded privacy of the animal
prized out with a knife and swallowed down
with cold, exhilarating wine.

I am swaying now in the hour after dinner,   10
a citizen tilted back on his chair,
a creature with a full stomach—
something you don't hear much about in poetry,
that sanctuary of hunger and deprivation.
You know: the driving rain, the boots by the door,   15
small birds searching for berries in winter.

But tonight, the lion of contentment
has placed a warm, heavy paw on my chest,
and I can only close my eyes and listen
to the drums of woe throbbing in the distance   20
and the sound of my wife's laughter
on the telephone in the next room,
the woman who cooked the savory osso buco,
who pointed to show the butcher the ones she wanted.

1. In Greek mythology, Lethe is the river of forgetfulness in Hades.

1. An Italian dish made with veal shanks.
2. An Italian rice dish.

She who talks to her faraway friend   25
while I linger here at the table
with a hot, companionable cup of tea,
feeling like one of the friendly natives,
a reliable guide, maybe even the chief's favorite son.

Somewhere, a man is crawling up a rocky hillside   30
on bleeding knees and palms, an Irish penitent
carrying the stone of the world in his stomach;
and elsewhere people of all nations stare
at one another across a long, empty table.

But here, the candles give off their warm glow,   35
the same light that Shakespeare and Izaac Walton[3] wrote by,
the light that lit and shadowed the faces of history.
Only now it plays on the blue plates,
the crumpled napkins, the crossed knife and fork.

In a while, one of us will go up to bed   40
and the other one will follow.
Then we will slip below the surface of the night
into miles of water, drifting down and down
to the dark, soundless bottom
until the weight of dreams pulls us lower still,   45
below the shale and layered rock,
beneath the strata of hunger and pleasure,
into the broken bones of the earth itself,
into the marrow of the only place we know.

                                                                    1995

Tuesday, June 4, 1991

By the time I get myself out of bed, my wife has left
the house to take her botany final and the painter
has arrived in his van and is already painting
the columns of the front porch white and the decking gray.

It is early June, a breezy and sun-riddled Tuesday   5
that would quickly be forgotten were it not for my
writing these few things down as I sit here empty-headed
at the typewriter with a cup of coffee, light and sweet.

I feel like the secretary to the morning whose only
responsibility is to take down its bright, airy dictation   10
until it's time to go to lunch with the other girls,
all of us ordering the cottage cheese with half a pear.

---

3. English writer (1593–1683), author of *The Compleat Angler*, a treatise on fishing and a picture of peace and simple virtues; it is among the most republished books in English literature.

This is what stenographers do in courtrooms, too,
alert at their miniature machines taking down every word.
When there is a silence they sit still as I do, waiting   15
and listening, fingers resting lightly on the keys.

This is also what Samuel Pepys[1] did, jotting down in
private ciphers minor events that would have otherwise
slipped into the dark amnesiac waters of the Thames.
His vigilance finally paid off when London caught fire   20

as mine does when the painter comes in for coffee
and says how much he likes this slow vocal rendition
of "You Don't Know What Love Is"[2] and I figure I will
make him a tape when he goes back to his brushes and pails.

Under the music I can hear the rush of cars and trucks   25
on the highway and every so often the new kitten, Felix,
hops into my lap and watches my fingers drumming out
a running record of this particular June Tuesday

as it unrolls before my eyes, a long intricate carpet
that I am walking on slowly with my head bowed   30
knowing that it is leading me to the quiet shrine
of the afternoon and the melancholy candles of evening.

If I look up, I see out the window the white stars
of clematis climbing a ladder of strings, a woodpile,
a stack of faded bricks, a small green garden of herbs,   35
things you would expect to find outside a window,

all written down now and placed in the setting
of a stanza as unalterably as they are seated
in their chairs in the ontological[3] rooms of the world.
Yes, this is the kind of job I could succeed in,   40

an unpaid but contented amanuensis[4] whose hands
are two birds fluttering on the lettered keys,
whose eyes see sunlight splashing through the leaves,
and the bright pink asterisks of honeysuckle

and the piano at the other end of this room with   45
its small vase of faded flowers and its empty bench.
So convinced am I that I have found my vocation,
tomorrow I will begin my chronicling earlier, at dawn,

a time when hangmen and farmers are up and doing,
when men holding pistols stand in a field back to back.   50

1. English writer (1633–1703), known primarily
for his diaries.
2. A song from the jazz repertoire, written by
Gene de Paul in 1941.

3. Having to do with the branch of metaphysics
that deals with the nature of being.
4. One employed to write from dictation or to
copy manuscripts.

It is the time the ancients imagined in robes, as Eos
or Aurora,[5] who would leave her sleeping husband in bed,

not to take her botany final, but to pull the sun,
her brother, over the horizon's brilliant rim,
her four-horse chariot aimed at the zenith of the sky,   55
But tomorrow, dawn will come the way I picture her,

barefoot and disheveled, standing outside my window
in one of the fragile cotton dresses of the poor.
She will look in at me with her thin arms extended,
offering a handful of birdsong and a small cup of light.   60

1995

I Chop Some Parsley While Listening to Art Blakey's[1] Version of "Three Blind Mice"

And I start wondering how they came to be blind.
If it was congenital, they could be brothers and sisters,
and I think of the poor mother
brooding over her sightless young triplets.

Or was it a common accident, all three caught   5
in a searing explosion, a fireworks perhaps?
If not,
if each came to his or her blindness separately,

how did they ever manage to find one another?
Would it not be difficult for a blind mouse   10
to locate even one fellow mouse with vision
let alone two other blind ones?

And how, in their tiny darkness,
could they possibly have run after a farmer's wife
or anyone else's wife for that matter?   15
Not to mention why.

Just so she could cut off their tails
with a carving knife, is the cynic's answer,
but the thought of them without eyes
and now without tails to trail through the moist grass   20

or slip around the corner of a baseboard
has the cynic who always lounges within me
up off his couch and at the window
trying to hide the rising softness that he feels.

5. The Greek and Roman goddesses of dawn.   1. Jazz drummer and bandleader (1919–1990).

Art Blakey on the drums.

By now I am on to dicing an onion   25
which might account for the wet stinging
in my own eyes, though Freddie Hubbard's
mournful trumpet on "Blue Moon,"

which happens to be the next cut,[2]
cannot be said to be making matters any better.   30

1998

The Night House

Every day the body works in the fields of the world
mending a stone wall
or swinging a sickle through the tall grass—
the grass of civics, the grass of money—
and every night the body curls around itself   5
and listens for the soft bells of sleep.

But the heart is restless and rises
from the body in the middle of the night,

---

2. The next song (or "cut" on a vinyl record) on *Three Blind Mice, Vol. 1*, a 1962 live recording by Art
Blakey's Jazz Messengers, which included Freddie Hubbard (1938–2008).

leaves the trapezoidal bedroom
with its thick, pictureless walls 10
to sit by herself at the kitchen table
and heat some milk in a pan.

And the mind gets up too, puts on a robe
and goes downstairs, lights a cigarette,
and opens a book on engineering. 15
Even the conscience awakens
and roams from room to room in the dark,
darting away from every mirror like a strange fish.

And the soul is up on the roof
in her nightdress, straddling the ridge, 20
singing a song about the wildness of the sea
until the first rip of pink appears in the sky.
Then, they all will return to the sleeping body
the way a flock of birds settles back into a tree,

resuming their daily colloquy, 25
talking to each other or themselves
even through the heat of the long afternoons.
Which is why the body—that house of voices—
sometimes puts down its metal tongs, its needle, or its pen
to stare into the distance, 30

to listen to all its names being called
before bending again to its labor.

1998

Litany

You are the bread and the knife,
The crystal goblet and the wine.

Jacques Crickillon

You are the bread and the knife,
the crystal goblet and the wine.
You are the dew on the morning grass,
and the burning wheel of the sun.
You are the white apron of the baker 5
and the marsh birds suddenly in flight.

However, you are not the wind in the orchard,
the plums on the counter,
or the house of cards.
And you are certainly not the pine-scented air. 10
There is no way you are the pine-scented air.

It is possible that you are the fish under the bridge,
maybe even the pigeon on the general's head,

but you are not even close
to being the field of cornflowers at dusk.   15

And a quick look in the mirror will show
that you are neither the boots in the corner
nor the boat asleep in its boathouse.

It might interest you to know,
speaking of the plentiful imagery of the world,   20
that I am the sound of rain on the roof.

I also happen to be the shooting star,
the evening paper blowing down an alley,
and the basket of chestnuts on the kitchen table.

I am also the moon in the trees   25
and the blind woman's teacup.
But don't worry, I am not the bread and the knife.
You are still the bread and the knife.
You will always be the bread and the knife,
not to mention the crystal goblet and—somehow—the wine.   30

2002

Sonnet

All we need is fourteen lines,[1] well, thirteen now,
and after this one just a dozen
to launch a little ship on love's storm-tossed seas,
then only ten more left like rows of beans.
How easily it goes unless you get Elizabethan[2]   5
and insist the iambic[3] bongos must be played
and rhymes positioned at the ends of lines,
one for every station of the cross.
But hang on here while we make the turn[4]
into the final six where all will be resolved,   10
where longing and heartache will find an end,
where Laura will tell Petrarch[5] to put down his pen,
take off those crazy medieval tights,
blow out the lights, and come at last to bed.

2001

1. The line count typical of a sonnet.
2. A sonnet composed of three quatrains and a terminal couplet, in iambic pentameter, with the rhyme pattern *abab cdcd efef gg* (also called Shakespearean).
3. A metrical foot consisting of one unstressed syllable followed by one stressed syllable.
4. In an Elizabethan sonnet, the turn is typically the ninth line, often marked by a change in tone or mood.
5. The sight of a woman named "Laura" spurred Francesco Petrarch (1304–1374), an Italian scholar, poet, and Renaissance humanist, to write a collection mostly of sonnets entitled *Il Canzoniere*.

GLORIA ANZALDÚA
1942–2004

The term "Chicano" was originally pejorative, used on both sides of the border to identify Mexican Americans of the lowest social class. Just as the once demeaning label "black" was appropriated and revalued by African Americans during the civil rights, black power, and black arts movements of the 1960s, so "Chicano" was embraced by Hispanic activists as a badge of pride, especially among university students and farm workers. By 1987, when the first edition of Gloria Anzaldúa's *Borderlands / La Frontera: The New Mestiza* appeared, two more politically sensitive terms had been added to the sociocultural lexicon: "Chicana," specifically identifying Mexican American women, particularly in light of their announced aims and the general interests of the Chicano movement, and "mestiza," describing Chicana women who are especially concerned with a heritage that is both Chicana and Native American. Together with Cherríe Moraga, her coeditor on *This Bridge Called My Back: Writings by Radical Women of Color* (1981), Anzaldúa emerged as a pioneer in both the writing and the study of Chicana literature.

The daughter of ranchers in Jesus Maria of the Valley, Texas, Anzaldúa labored as a migrant fieldworker before earning a B.A. from Pan American University (1969) and an M.A. from the University of Texas at Austin (1973); she did further graduate study at the University of California at Santa Cruz. She taught creative writing, Chicano studies, and feminist studies at major universities from Texas to California. She published the novel *La Prieta* (Spanish for "the dark one," 1997), other anthologies, and a series of children's books, the most notable of which—*Prietita and the Ghost Woman / Prietita y La Llorona* (1996)—introduces young readers to an important figure in Chicana culture.

La Llorona is one of the three principal representations of women in Mexican culture: *La Virgen de Guadalupe*, a vision of the Virgin Mary who appeared to an Indian, Juan Diego, in 1531 on a hillside outside Mexico City that was sacred to the worship of Tonantzín, the Indian "Mother of Heaven"; *La Chingada*, incorrectly translated as "The Raped One" but whom Anzaldúa insists be accurately identified as "The Fucked One," the deposed Aztec princess (also known as La Malinche, Doña Marina, and Malintzín Tenepal) who served the Spanish military leader Hernan Cortés as translator and lover during his consolidation of colonial power between 1519 and 1522; and *La Llorona*, "The Woman Who Cries," a spurned mistress of Mexican legend who drowned her children and was fated to eternally seek their recovery. Each of these representations metaphorically controls a certain distinct realm of possibility for Chicanas. At the core of Anzaldúa's work is the belief that because metaphors structure the way we think, the metaphorical influences of these types of women must be reshaped so that Chicanas can escape the binary constraint of being judged as either a virgin or a whore (and nothing else). *Borderlands/La Frontera* is Anzaldúa's most comprehensive effort toward that restructuring.

Although written mainly in English, the personal essays and narrative poem printed here reflect another key part of Anzaldúa's art: not only did she wish to write in Spanish from time to time but she did not always translate that Spanish into English. When she did not provide such a translation in a piece primarily in English, she wanted to speak directly to those who either could not or chose not to communicate in English. This practice, much like her blending of fiction, poetry, social commentary, and personal memoir, helps create the narrative richness that characterizes her work.

The following texts are from the second edition of *Borderlands/La Frontera* (1999).

La conciencia de la mestiza / Towards a New Consciousness

Por la mujer de mi raza
hablará el espíritu.[1]

José Vasconcelos, Mexican philosopher, envisaged *una raza mestiza, una mezcla de razas afines, una raza de color—la primera raza síntesis del globo.* He called it a cosmic race, *la raza cósmica,* a fifth race embracing the four major races of the world.[2] Opposite to the theory of the pure Aryan,[3] and to the policy of racial purity that white America practices, his theory is one of inclusivity. At the confluence of two or more genetic streams, with chromosomes constantly "crossing over," this mixture of races, rather than resulting in an inferior being, provides hybrid progeny, a mutable, more malleable species with a rich gene pool. From this racial, ideological, cultural and biological cross-pollinization, an "alien" consciousness is presently in the making—a new *mestiza* consciousness, *una conciencia de mujer.* It is a consciousness of the Borderlands.

Una lucha de fronteras / A Struggle of Borders

Because I, a *mestiza,*
continually walk out of one culture
and into another,
because I am in all cultures at the same time,
alma entre dos mundos, tres, cuatro,
me zumba la cabeza con lo contradictorio.
Estoy norteada por todas las voces que me hablan
simultáneamente.

The ambivalence from the clash of voices results in mental and emotional states of perplexity. Internal strife results in insecurity and indecisiveness. The *mestiza*'s dual or multiple personality is plagued by psychic restlessness.

In a constant state of mental nepantilism, an Aztec[4] word meaning torn between ways, *la mestiza* is a product of the transfer of the cultural and spiritual values of one group to another. Being tricultural, monolingual, bilingual, or multilingual, speaking a patois, and in a state of perpetual transition, the *mestiza* faces the dilemma of the mixed breed: which collectivity does the daughter of a darkskinned mother listen to?

El choque de un alma atrapado entire el mundo del espíritu y el mundo de la técnica a veces la deja entullada. Cradled in one culture, sandwiched between

---

1. "This is my own 'take off' on Jose Vasconcelos' idea. José Vasconcelos, *La Raza Cósmica: Misión de la Raza Ibero-Americana* (México: Aguilar S.A. de Ediciones, 1961)" [Anzaldúa's note]. José Vasconcelos (1882–1959) was a Mexican philosopher.

2. Vasconcelos [Anzaldúa's note].
3. Nazi misnomer for Caucasians of non-Jewish descent.
4. A precolonial people of Mexico with a highly developed civilization.

two cultures, straddling all three cultures and their value systems, *la mestiza* undergoes a struggle of flesh, a struggle of borders, an inner war. Like all people, we perceive the version of reality that our culture communicates. Like others having or living in more than one culture, we get multiple, often opposing messages. The coming together of two self-consistent but habitually incompatible frames of reference[5] causes *un choque*, a cultural collision.

Within us and within *la cultura chicana*, commonly held beliefs of the white culture attack commonly held beliefs of the Mexican culture, and both attack commonly held beliefs of the indigenous culture. Subconsciously, we see an attack on ourselves and our beliefs as a threat and we attempt to block with a counterstance.

But it is not enough to stand on the opposite river bank, shouting questions, challenging patriarchal, white conventions. A counterstance locks one into a duel of oppressor and oppressed; locked in mortal combat, like the cop and the criminal, both are reduced to a common denominator of violence. The counterstance refutes the dominant culture's views and beliefs, and, for this, it is proudly defiant. All reaction is limited by, and dependent on, what it is reacting against. Because the counterstance stems from a problem with authority—outer as well as inner—it's a step towards liberation from cultural domination. But it is not a way of life. At some point, on our way to a new consciousness, we will have to leave the opposite bank, the split between the two mortal combatants somehow healed so that we are on both shores at once and, at once, see through serpent and eagle[6] eyes. Or perhaps we will decide to disengage from the dominant culture, write it off altogether as a lost cause, and cross the border into a wholly new and separate territory. Or we might go another route. The possibilities are numerous once we decide to act and not react.

A Tolerance for Ambiguity

These numerous possibilities leave *la mestiza* floundering in uncharted seas. In perceiving conflicting information and points of view, she is subjected to a swamping of her psychological borders. She has discovered that she can't hold concepts or ideas in rigid boundaries. The borders and walls that are supposed to keep the undesirable ideas out are entrenched habits and patterns of behavior; these habits and patterns are the enemy within. Rigidity means death. Only by remaining flexible is she able to stretch the psyche horizontally and vertically. *La mestiza* constantly has to shift out of habitual formations; from convergent thinking, analytical reasoning that tends to use rationality to move toward a single goal (a Western mode), to divergent thinking,[7] characterized by movement away from set patterns and goals and toward a more whole perspective, one that includes rather than excludes.

The new *mestiza* copes by developing a tolerance for contradictions, a tolerance for ambiguity. She learns to be an Indian in Mexican culture, to be Mexican from an Anglo point of view. She learns to juggle cultures. She has

5. Arthur Koestler [(1905–1983), Hungarian-born writer active in Germany and Britain] termed this term "bisociation." Albert Rothenberg, *The Creative Process in Art, Science, and Other Fields* (Chicago, IL: University of Chicago Press, 1979), 12 [Anzaldúa's note].

6. Female and male, respectively; a binarism in traditional Mexican culture.
7. In part, I derive my definitions for "convergent" and "divergent" thinking from Rothenberg, 12–13 [Anzaldúa's note].

a plural personality, she operates in a pluralistic mode—nothing is thrust out, the good the bad and the ugly, nothing rejected, nothing abandoned. Not only does she sustain contradictions, she turns the ambivalence into something else.

She can be jarred out of ambivalence by an intense, and often painful, emotional event which inverts or resolves the ambivalence. I'm not sure exactly how. The work takes place underground—subconsciously. It is work that the soul performs. That focal point or fulcrum, that juncture where the *mestiza* stands, is where phenomena tend to collide. It is where the possibility of uniting all that is separate occurs. This assembly is not one where severed or separated pieces merely come together. Nor is it a balancing of opposing powers. In attempting to work out a synthesis, the self has added a third element which is greater than the sum of its severed parts. That third element is a new consciousness—a *mestiza* consciousness—and though it is a source of intense pain, its energy comes from continual creative motion that keeps breaking down the unitary aspect of each new paradigm.

En unas pocas centurias, the future will belong to the *mestiza*. Because the future depends on the breaking down of paradigms, it depends on the straddling of two or more cultures. By creating a new mythos—that is, a change in the way we perceive reality, the way we see ourselves, and the ways we behave—*la mestiza* creates a new consciousness.

The work of *mestiza* consciousness is to break down the subject-object duality that keeps her a prisoner and to show in the flesh and through the images in her work how duality is transcended. The answer to the problem between the white race and the colored, between males and females, lies in healing the split that originates in the very foundation of our lives, our culture, our languages, our thoughts. A massive uprooting of dualistic thinking in the individual and collective consciousness is the beginning of a long struggle, but one that could, in our best hopes, bring us to the end of rape, of violence, of war.

La encrucijada / The Crossroads

A chicken is being sacrificed
    at a crossroads, a simple mound of earth
a mud shrine for *Eshu*,
    Yoruba[8] god of indeterminacy,
who blesses her choice of path.
    She begins her journey.

Su cuerpo es una bocacalle. La mestiza has gone from being the sacrificial goat to becoming the officiating priestess at the crossroads.

As a *mestiza* I have no country, my homeland cast me out; yet all countries are mine because I am every woman's sister or potential lover. (As a lesbian I have no race, my own people disclaim me; but I am all races because there is the queer of me in all races.) I am cultureless because, as a feminist, I challenge the collective cultural/religious male-derived beliefs of Indo-

---

8. Large ethnic group of southwest Nigeria and southeast Benin, in Africa.

Hispanics and Anglos; yet I am cultured because I am participating in the creation of yet another culture, a new story to explain the world and our participation in it, a new value system with images and symbols that connect us to each other and to the planet. *Soy un amasamiento*, I am an act of kneading, of uniting and joining that not only has produced both a creature of darkness and a creature of light, but also a creature that questions the definitions of light and dark and gives them new meanings.

We are the people who leap in the dark, we are the people on the knees of the gods. In our very flesh, (r)evolution works out the clash of cultures. It makes us crazy constantly, but if the center holds, we've made some kind of evolutionary step forward. *Nuestra alma el trabajo*, the opus, the great alchemical work; spiritual *mestizaje*, a "morphogenesis,"[9] an inevitable unfolding. We have become the quickening serpent movement.

Indigenous like corn, like corn, the *mestiza* is a product of crossbreeding, designed for preservation under a variety of conditions. Like an ear of corn—a female seed-bearing organ—the *mestiza* is tenacious, tightly wrapped in the husks of her culture. Like kernels she clings to the cob; with thick stalks and strong brace roots, she holds tight to the earth—she will survive the crossroads.

Lavando y remojando el maíz en agua de cal, despojando el pellejo. Moliendo, mixteando, amasando, haciendo tortillas de masa.[1] She steeps the corn in lime, it swells, softens. With stone roller on *metate*, she grinds the corn, then grinds again. She kneads and moulds the dough, pats the round balls into *tortillas*.

> We are the porous rock in the stone *metate*
> squatting on the ground.
> We are the rolling pin, *el maíz y agua*,
> la masa harina. Somos el amasijo.
> Somos lo molido en el metate.
> We are the *comal* sizzling hot,
> the hot *tortilla*, the hungry mouth.
> We are the coarse rock.
> We are the grinding motion,
> the mixed potion, *somos el molcajete*.
> We are the pestle, the *comino, ajo, pimienta*,
> We are the *chile colorado*,
> the green shoot that cracks the rock.
> We will abide.

---

9. "To borrow from chemist Ilya Prigogine's theory of 'dissipative structures.' Prigogine discovered that substances interact not in predictable ways as it was taught in science, but in different and fluctuating ways to produce new and more complex structures, a kind of birth he called 'morphogenesis,' which created unpredictable innovations. Harold Gilliam, 'Searching for a New World View,' *This World* (January, 1981), 23" [Anzaldúa's note]. Ilya Prigogine (1917–2003), Russian-born Belgian physical chemist active in the United States.
1. *Tortillas de masa harina*: corn tortillas are of two types, the smooth uniform ones made in a tortilla press and usually bought at a tortilla factory or supermarket, and *gorditas*, made by mixing *masa* with lard or shortening or butter (my mother sometimes puts in bits of bacon or chicharones [Anzaldúa's note].

El camino de la mestiza / The Mestiza Way

Caught between the sudden contraction, the breath sucked in and the endless space, the brown woman stands still, looks at the sky. She decides to go down, digging her way along the roots of trees. Sifting through the bones, she shakes them to see if there is any marrow in them. Then, touching the dirt to her forehead, to her tongue, she takes a few bones, leaves the rest in their burial place.

She goes through her backpack, keeps her journal and address book, throws away the muni-bart metromaps. The coins are heavy and they go next, then the greenbacks flutter through the air. She keeps her knife, can opener and eyebrow pencil. She puts bones, pieces of bark, *hierbas*, eagle feather, snakeskin, tape recorder, the rattle and drum in her pack and she sets out to become the complete *tolteca*.[2]

Her first step is to take inventory. *Despojando, desgranando, quitando paja.* Just what did she inherit from her ancestors? This weight on her back—which is the baggage from the Indian mother, which the baggage from the Spanish father, which the baggage from the Anglo?

Pero es difícil differentiating between *lo heredado, lo adquirido, lo impuesto.* She puts history through a sieve, winnows out the lies, looks at the forces that we as a race, as women, have been a part of. *Luego bota lo que no vale, los desmientos, los desencuentros, el embrutecimiento. Aguarda el juicio, hondo y enraízado, de la gente antigua.* This step is a conscious rupture with all oppressive traditions of all cultures and religions. She communicates that rupture, documents the struggle. She reinterprets history and, using new symbols, she shapes new myths. She adopts new perspectives toward the darkskinned, women and queers. She strengthens her tolerance (and intolerance) for ambiguity. She is willing to share, to make herself vulnerable to foreign ways of seeing and thinking. She surrenders all notions of safety of the familiar. Deconstruct, construct. She becomes a *nahual*, able to transform herself into a tree, a coyote, into another person. She learns to transform the small "I" into the total Self. *Se hace moldeadora de su alma. Según la concepción que tiene de sí misma, así será.*

Que no se nos olviden los hombres

> *"Tú no sirves pa'nada—*
> you're good for nothing.
> *Eres pura vieja."*

"You're nothing but a woman" means you are defective. Its opposite is to be *un macho*. The modern meaning of the word "machismo," as well as the concept, is actually an Anglo invention. For men like my father, being "macho" meant being strong enough to protect and support my mother and us, yet being able to show love. Today's macho has doubts about his ability to feed and protect his family. His "machismo" is an adaptation to oppression and poverty and low self-esteem. It is the result of hierarchical male dominance.

---

2. Female member of the ancient Toltec group of Nahuatl Indians who lived in Mexico before the Aztecs. "Muni-bart metromaps": maps of the public-transit systems of the Bay Area in California.

The Anglo, feeling inadequate and inferior and powerless, displaces or transfers these feelings to the Chicano by shaming him. In the Gringo world, the Chicano suffers from excessive humility and self-effacement, shame of self and self-deprecation. Around Latinos he suffers from a sense of language inadequacy and its accompanying discomfort; with Native Americans he suffers from a racial amnesia which ignores our common blood, and from guilt because the Spanish part of him took their land and oppressed them. He has an excessive compensatory hubris when around Mexicans from the other side. It overlays a deep sense of racial shame.

The loss of a sense of dignity and respect in the macho breeds a false machismo which leads him to put down women and even to brutalize them. Coexisting with his sexist behavior is a love for the mother which takes precedence over that of all others. Devoted son, macho pig. To wash down the shame of his acts, of his very being, and to handle the brute in the mirror, he takes to the bottle, the snort, the needle, and the fist.

Though we "understand" the root causes of male hatred and fear, and the subsequent wounding of women, we do not excuse, we do not condone, and we will no longer put up with it. From the men of our race, we demand the admission/acknowledgment/disclosure/testimony that they wound us, violate us, are afraid of us and of our power. We need them to say they will begin to eliminate their hurtful put-down ways. But more than the words, we demand acts. We say to them: We will develop equal power with you and those who have shamed us.

It is imperative that *mestizas* support each other in changing the sexist elements in the Mexican-Indian culture. As long as woman is put down, the Indian and the Black in all of us is put down. The struggle of the *mestiza* is above all a feminist one. As long as *los hombres* think they have to *chingar mujeres* and each other to be men, as long as men are taught that they are superior and therefore culturally favored over *la mujer*, as long as to be a *vieja* is a thing of derision, there can be no real healing of our psyches. We're halfway there—we have such love of the Mother, the good mother. The first step is to unlearn the *puta/virgen* dichotomy and to see *Coatlalopeuh-Coatlicue* in the Mother, *Guadalupe.*[3]

Tenderness, a sign of vulnerability, is so feared that it is showered on women with verbal abuse and blows. Men, even more than women, are fettered to gender roles. Women at least have had the guts to break out of bondage. Only gay men have had the courage to expose themselves to the woman inside them and to challenge the current masculinity. I've encountered a few scattered and isolated gentle straight men, the beginnings of a new breed, but they are confused, and entangled with sexist behaviors that they have not been able to eradicate. We need a new masculinity and the new man needs a movement.

Lumping the males who deviate from the general norm with man, the oppressor, is a gross injustice. *Asombra pensar que nos hemos quedado en ese pozo oscuro donde el mundo encierra a las lesbianas. Asombra pensar que hemos,*

3. The Virgin of Guadalupe, patron saint of Mexico. In matriarchal Olmec culture Coatl was a figuration of the sacred womb from which all things were born and to which they returned. Coatlicue is the Meso-American serpent that is half male, half female.

como femenistas y lesbianas, cerrado nuestros corazónes a los hombres, a nuestros hermanos los jotos, desheredados y marginales como nosotros. Being the supreme crossers of cultures, homosexuals have strong bonds with the queer white, Black, Asian, Native American, Latino, and with the queer in Italy, Australia and the rest of the planet. We come from all colors, all classes, all races, all time periods. Our role is to link people with each other—the Blacks with Jews with Indians with Asians with whites with extraterrestrials. It is to transfer ideas and information from one culture to another. Colored homosexuals have more knowledge of other cultures; have always been at the forefront (although sometimes in the closet) of all liberation struggles in this country; have suffered more injustices and have survived them despite all odds. Chicanos need to acknowledge the political and artistic contributions of their queer. People, listen to what your *jotería* is saying.

The *mestizo* and the queer exist at this time and point on the evolutionary continuum for a purpose. We are a blending that proves that all blood is intricately woven together, and that we are spawned out of similar souls.

Somos una gente

Hay tantísimas fronteras
que dividen a la gente,
pero por cada frontera
existe también un puente.
—Gina Valdés[4]

Divided Loyalties. Many women and men of color do not want to have any dealings with white people. It takes too much time and energy to explain to the downwardly mobile, white middle-class women that it's okay for us to want to own "possessions," never having had any nice furniture on our dirt floors or "luxuries" like washing machines. Many feel that whites should help their own people rid themselves of race hatred and fear first. I, for one, choose to use some of my energy to serve as mediator. I think we need to allow whites to be our allies. Through our literature, art, *corridos*, and folktales we must share our history with them so when they set up committees to help Big Mountain *Navajos* or the Chicano farmworkers or *los Nicaragüenses*[5] they won't turn people away because of their racial fears and ignorances. They will come to see that they are not helping us but following our lead.

Individually, but also as a racial entity, we need to voice our needs. We need to say to white society: We need you to accept the fact that Chicanos are different, to acknowledge your rejection and negation of us. We need you to own the fact that you looked upon us as less than human, that you stole our lands, our personhood, our self-respect. We need you to make public restitution: to say that, to compensate for your own sense of defectiveness, you strive for power over us, you erase our history and our experience

4. Gina Valdés, *Puentes y Fronteras: Coplas Chicanas* (Los Angeles, CA: Castle Lithograph, 1982), 2 [Anzaldúa's note].
5. Nicaraguans; here a reference to the Sandinista government, which was opposed covertly by the United States in the 1980s. "Big Mountain Navajos": Dineh people of Big Mountain, Arizona, forcibly removed in a land dispute with energy companies in 1997. "Farmworkers": members of the United Farm Workers, a union founded in 1962.

because it makes you feel guilty—you'd rather forget your brutish acts. To say you've split yourself from minority groups, that you disown us, that your dual consciousness splits off parts of yourself, transferring the "negative" parts onto us. (Where there is persecution of minorities, there is shadow projection. Where there is violence and war, there is repression of shadow.) To say that you are afraid of us, that to put distance between us, you wear the mask of contempt. Admit that Mexico is your double, that she exists in the shadow of this country, that we are irrevocably tied to her. Gringo, accept the doppelganger[6] in your psyche. By taking back your collective shadow the intracultural split will heal. And finally, tell us what you need from us.

By Your True Faces We Will Know You

I am visible—see this Indian face—yet I am invisible. I both blind them with my beak nose and am their blind spot. But I exist, we exist. They'd like to think I have melted in the pot. But I haven't, we haven't.

The dominant white culture is killing us slowly with its ignorance. By taking away our self-determination, it has made us weak and empty. As a people we have resisted and we have taken expedient positions, but we have never been allowed to develop unencumbered—we have never been allowed to be fully ourselves. The whites in power want us people of color to barricade ourselves behind our separate tribal walls so they can pick us off one at a time with their hidden weapons; so they can whitewash and distort history. Ignorance splits people, creates prejudices. A misinformed people is a subjugated people.

Before the Chicano and the undocumented worker and the Mexican from the other side can come together, before the Chicano can have unity with Native Americans and other groups, we need to know the history of their struggle and they need to know ours. Our mothers, our sisters and brothers, the guys who hang out on street corners, the children in the playgrounds, each of us must know our Indian lineage, our afro-*mestizaje*, our history of resistance.

To the immigrant *mexicano* and the recent arrivals we must teach our history. The 80 million *mexicanos* and the Latinos from Central and South America must know of our struggles. Each one of us must know basic facts about Nicaragua, Chile and the rest of Latin America. The Latinoist movement (Chicanos, Puerto Ricans, Cubans and other Spanish-speaking people working together to combat racial discrimination in the marketplace) is good but it is not enough. Other than a common culture we will have nothing to hold us together. We need to meet on a broader communal ground.

The struggle is inner: Chicano, *indio*, American Indian, *mojado*, *mexicano*, immigrant Latino, Anglo in power, working class Anglo, Black, Asian—our psyches resemble the bordertowns and are populated by the same people. The struggle has always been inner, and is played out in the outer terrains. Awareness of our situation must come before inner changes, which in turn

6. Literally, "double-goer" (German); an alter ego or the ghost of a living person.

come before changes in society. Nothing happens in the "real" world unless it first happens in the images in our heads.

El día de la Chicana

I will not be shamed again
Nor will I shame myself.

I am possessed by a vision: that we Chicanas and Chicanos have taken back or uncovered our true faces, our dignity and self-respect. It's a validation vision.

Seeing the Chicana anew in light of her history, I seek an exoneration, a seeing through the fictions of white supremacy, a seeing of ourselves in our true guises and not as the false racial personality that has been given to us and that we have given to ourselves. I seek our woman's face, our true features, the positive and the negative seen clearly, free of the tainted biases of male dominance. I seek new images of identity, new beliefs about ourselves, our humanity and worth no longer in question.

Estamos viviendo en la noche de la Raza, un tiempo cuando el trabajo se hace a lo quieto, en lo oscuro. El día cuando aceptamos tal y como somos y para donde vamos y porque—ese día será el día de la Raza. Yo tengo el conpromiso de expresar mi visión, mi sensibilidad, mi percepción de la revalidación de la gente mexicana, su mérito, estimación, honra, aprecio, y validez.

On December 2nd when my sun goes into my first house, I celebrate *el día de la Chicana y el Chicano:* On that day I clean my altars, light my *Coatlalopeuh* candle, burn sage and copal,[7] take *el baño para espantar basura;* sweep my house. On that day I bare my soul, make myself vulnerable to friends and family by expressing my feelings. On that day I affirm who we are.

On that day I look inside our conflicts and our basic introverted racial temperament. I identify our needs, voice them. I acknowledge that the self and the race have been wounded. I recognize the need to take care of our personhood, of our racial self. On that day I gather the splintered and disowned parts of *la gente mexicana* and hold them in my arms. *Todas las partes de nosotros valen.*

On that day I say, "Yes, all you people wound us when you reject us. Rejection strips us of self-worth; our vulnerability exposes us to shame. It is our innate identity you find wanting. We are ashamed that we need your good opinion, that we need your acceptance. We can no longer camouflage our needs, can no longer let defenses and fences sprout around us. We can no longer withdraw. To rage and look upon you with contempt is to rage and be contemptuous of ourselves. We can no longer blame you, nor disown the white parts, the male parts, the pathological parts, the queer parts, the vulnerable parts. Here we are weaponless with open arms, with only our magic. Let's try it our way, the *mestiza* way, the Chicana way, the woman way."

---

7. Amber fossilized resin from tropical trees.

On that day, I search for our essential dignity as a people, a people with a sense of purpose—to belong and contribute to something greater than our *pueblo*. On that day I seek to recover and reshape my spiritual identity. *¡Anímate! Raza, a celebrar el día de la Chicana.*

El retorno

All movements are accomplished in six stages,
and the seventh brings return.
   —I Ching[8]

Tanto tiempo sin verte casa mía,
mi cuna, mi bondo nido de la huerta.
   —"Soledad"[9]

I stand at the river, watch the curving, twisting serpent, a serpent nailed to the fence where the mouth of the Rio Grande empties into the Gulf.

I have come back. *Tanto dolor me costó el alejamiento.* I shade my eyes and look up. The bone beak of a hawk slowly circling over me, checking me out as potential carrion. In its wake a little bird flickering its wings, swimming sporadically like a fish. In the distance the expressway and the slough of traffic like an irritated sow. The sudden pull in my gut, *la tierra, los aguaceros.* My land, *el viento soplando la arena, el lagartijo debajo de un nopalito. Me acuerdo como era antes. Una región desértica de vasta llanuras, costeras de baja altura, de escasa lluvia, de chaparrales formados por mesquites y huizaches.* If I look real hard I can almost see the Spanish fathers who were called "the cavalry of Christ" enter this valley riding their *burros*, see the clash of cultures commence.

Tierra natal. This is home, the small towns in the Valley, *los pueblitos* with chicken pens and goats picketed to mesquite shrubs. *En las colonias* on the other side of the tracks, junk cars line the front yards of hot pink and lavender-trimmed houses—Chicano architecture we call it, self-consciously. I have missed the TV shows where hosts speak in half and half, and where awards are given in the category of Tex-Mex music. I have missed the Mexican cemeteries blooming with artificial flowers, the fields of aloe vera and red pepper, rows of sugar cane, of corn hanging on the stalks, the cloud of *polvareda* in the dirt roads behind a speeding pickup truck, *el sabor de tamales de rez y venado* I have missed *la yegua colorada* gnawing the wooden gate of her stall, the smell of horse flesh from Carito's corrals. *Hecho menos las noches calientes sin aire, noches de linternas y lechuzas* making holes in the night.

I still feel the old despair when I look at the unpainted, dilapidated, scrap lumber houses consisting mostly of corrugated aluminum. Some of the poorest people in the U.S. live in the Lower Rio Grande Valley, and arid and semiarid land of irrigated farming, intense sunlight and heat, citrus groves next to chaparral and cactus. I walk through the elementary school

---

8. "Richard Wilhelm, *The I Ching or Book of Changes,* trans. Cary F. Baynes (Princeton: Princeton University Press, 1950), 98" [Anzaldúa's note]. A central text of Confucianism dating from the first millennium B.C.E.

9. *Soledad* is sung by the group Haciendo Punto en Otro Son [Anzaldúa's note].

I attended so long ago, that remained segregated until recently. I remember how the white teachers used to punish us for being Mexican.

How I love this tragic valley of South Texas, as Ricardo Sánchez calls it; this borderland between the Nueces and the Rio Grande.[1] This land has survived possession and ill-use by five countries: Spain, Mexico, the Republic of Texas, the U.S., the Confederacy,[2] and the U.S. again. It has survived Anglo-Mexican blood feuds, lynchings, burnings, rapes, pillage.

Today I see the Valley still struggling to survive. Whether it does or not, it will never be as I remember it. The borderlands depression that was set off by the 1982 peso devaluation in Mexico resulted in the closure of hundreds of Valley businesses. Many people lost their homes, cars, land. Prior to 1982, U.S. store owners thrived on retail sales to Mexicans who came across the border for groceries and clothes and appliances. While goods on the U.S. side have become 10, 100, 1000 times more expensive for Mexican buyers, goods on the Mexican side have become 10, 100, 1000 times cheaper for Americans. Because the Valley is heavily dependent on agriculture and Mexican retail trade, it has the highest unemployment rates along the entire border region; it is the Valley that has been hardest hit.[3]

"It's been a bad year for corn," my brother, Nune, says. As he talks, I remember my father scanning the sky for a rain that would end the drought, looking up into the sky, day after day, while the corn withered on its stalk. My father has been dead for 29 years, having worked himself to death. The life span of a Mexican farm laborer is 56—he lived to be 38. It shocks me that I am older than he. I, too, search the sky for rain. Like the ancients, I worship the rain god and the maize goddess, but unlike my father I have recovered their names. Now for rain (irrigation) one offers not a sacrifice of blood, but of money.

"Farming is in a bad way," my brother says. "Two to three thousand small and big farmers went bankrupt in this country last year. Six years ago the price of corn was $8.00 per hundred pounds," he goes on. "This year it is $3.90 per hundred pounds." And, I think to myself, after taking inflation into account, not planting anything puts you ahead.

I walk out to the back yard, stare at *los rosales de mamá*. She wants me to help her prune the rose bushes, dig out the carpet grass that is choking them. *Mamagrande Ramona también tenía rosales*. Here every Mexican grows flowers. If they don't have a piece of dirt, they use car tires, jars, cans, shoe boxes. Roses are the Mexican's favorite flower. I think, how symbolic—thorns and all.

Yes, the Chicano and Chicana have always taken care of growing things and the land. Again I see the four of us kids getting off the school bus, changing into our work clothes, walking into the field with Papi and Mami, all six

1. Rivers in southern Texas. Sánchez (1941–1995), Chicano poet, educator, and activist.
2. I.e., the Confederate States of America, made up of eleven southern states (including Texas) that seceded from the Union at the start of the U.S. Civil War (1861–65). After it won independence from Mexico (1836) and before it was admitted as a state to the United States (1845), Texas was a republic.
3. Out of the twenty-two border counties in the four border states, Hidalgo County (named for Father Hidalgo who was shot in 1810 after instigating Mexico's revolt against Spanish rule under the banner of *la Virgen de Guadalupe*) is the most poverty-stricken county in the nation as well as the largest home base (along with Imperial in California) for migrant farmworkers. It was here I was born and raised. I am amazed that both it and I have survived [Anzaldúa's note].

of us bending to the ground. Below our feet, under the earth lie the watermelon seeds. We cover them with paper plates, putting *terremotes* on top of the plates to keep them from being blown away by the wind. The paper plates keep the freeze away. Next day or the next, we remove the plates, bare the tiny green shoots to the elements. They survive and grow, give fruit hundreds of times the size of the seed. We water them and hoe them. We harvest them. The vines dry, rot, are plowed under. Growth, death, decay, birth. The soil prepared again and again, impregnated, worked on. A constant changing of forms, *renacimientos de la tierra madre*.

> This land was Mexican once
> was Indian always
> and is.
> And will be again.

1987

How to Tame a Wild Tongue

"We're going to have to control your tongue," the dentist says, pulling out all the metal from my mouth. Silver bits plop and tinkle into the basin. My mouth is a motherlode.

The dentist is cleaning out my roots. I get a whiff of the stench when I gasp. "I can't cap that tooth yet, you're still draining," he says.

"We're going to have to do something about your tongue," I hear the anger rising in his voice. My tongue keeps pushing out the wads of cotton, pushing back the drills, the long thin needles. "I've never seen anything as strong or as stubborn," he says. And I think, how do you tame a wild tongue, train it to be quiet, how do you bridle and saddle it? How do you make it lie down?

> "Who is to say that robbing a people of
> its language is less violent than war?"
> —Ray Gwyn Smith[1]

I remember being caught speaking Spanish at recess—that was good for three licks on the knuckles with a sharp ruler. I remember being sent to the corner of the classroom for "talking back" to the Anglo teacher when all I was trying to do was tell her how to pronounce my name. "If you want to be American, speak 'American.' If you don't like it, go back to Mexico where you belong."

"I want you to speak English. *Pa'hallar buen trabajo tienes que saber hablar el inglés bien. Qué vale toda tu educación si todavía hablas inglés con un* 'accent,'" my mother would say, mortified that I spoke English like a Mexican. At Pan American University, I, and all Chicano students were required to take two speech classes. Their purpose: to get rid of our accents.

1. Ray Gwyn Smith [(b. 1944), Welsh painter and art educator active in the United States], *Moorland Is Cold Country*, unpublished book [Anzaldúa's note].

Attacks on one's form of expression with the intent to censor are a viola-tion of the First Amendment. *El Anglo con cara de inocente nos arrancó la lengua.* Wild tongues can't be tamed, they can only be cut out.

Overcoming the Tradition of Silence

Ahogadas, escupimos el oscuro.
Peleando con nuestra propia sombra
el silencio nos sepulta.

En boca cerrada no entran moscas. "Flies don't enter a closed mouth" is a say-ing I kept hearing when I was a child. *Ser habladora* was to be a gossip and a liar, to talk too much. *Muchachitas bien criadas*, well-bred girls don't answer back. *Es una falta de respeto* to talk back to one's mother or father. I remem-ber one of the sins I'd recite to the priest in the confession box the few times I went to confession: talking back to my mother, *hablar pa' 'trás, repelar. Hoci-cona, repelona, chismosa*, having a big mouth, questioning, carrying tales are all signs of being *mal criada*. In my culture they are all words that are deroga-tory if applied to women—I've never heard them applied to men.

The first time I heard two women, a Puerto Rican and a Cuban, say the word *"nosotras,"* I was shocked. I had not known the word existed. Chicanas use *nosotros* whether we're male or female. We are robbed of our female being by the masculine plural. Language is a male discourse.

> And our tongues have become
> dry   the wilderness has
> dried out our tongues   and
> we have forgotten speech.
> —Irena Klepfisz[2]

Even our own people, other Spanish speakers *nos quieren poner candados en la boca.* They would hold us back with their bag of *reglas de academia.*

Oyé como ladra: el lenguaje de la frontera

> *Quien tiene boca se equivoca.*
> —Mexican saying

"*Pocho*,[3] cultural traitor, you're speaking the oppressor's language by speaking English, you're ruining the Spanish language," I have been accused by vari-ous Latinos and Latinas. Chicano Spanish is considered by the purist and by most Latinos deficient, a mutilation of Spanish.

But Chicano Spanish is a border tongue which developed naturally. Change, *evolución, enriquecimiento de palabras nuevas por invención o adopción* have created variants of Chicano Spanish, *un nuevo lenguaje. Un lenguaje que cor-responde a un modo de vivir.* Chicano Spanish is not incorrect, it is a living language.

---

2. Irena Klepfisz [(b. 1941), North American critic], "*Di rayze aheym / The Journey Home*," in *The Tribe of Dina: A Jewish Women's Anthology*, Melanie Kaye/Kantrowitz and Irena Klepfisz, eds. (Montpelier, VT: Sinister Wisdom Books, 1986), 49 [Anzaldúa's note].

3. An anglicized Mexican or American of Mexi-can origin who speaks Spanish with an accent characteristic of North Americans and who dis-torts and reconstructs the language according to the influence of English. Anzaldúa offers a defi-nition later in this selection.

For a people who are neither Spanish nor live in a country in which Spanish is the first language; for a people who live in a country in which English is the reigning tongue but who are not Anglo; for a people who cannot entirely identify with either standard (formal, Castillian) Spanish nor standard English, what recourse is left to them but to create their own language? A language which they can connect their identity to, one capable of communicating the realities and values true to themselves—a language with terms that are neither *español ni inglés*, but both. We speak a patois, a forked tongue, a variation of two languages.

Chicano Spanish sprang out of the Chicanos' need to identify ourselves as a distinct people. We needed a language with which we could communicate with ourselves, a secret language. For some of us, language is a homeland closer than the Southwest—for many Chicanos today live in the Midwest and the East. And because we are a complex, heterogeneous people, we speak many languages. Some of the languages we speak are:

1. Standard English
2. Working class and slang English
3. Standard Spanish
4. Standard Mexican Spanish
5. North Mexican Spanish dialect
6. Chicano Spanish (Texas, New Mexico, Arizona and California have regional variations)
7. Tex-Mex
8. *Pachuco* (called *caló*)

My "home" tongues are the languages I speak with my sister and brothers, with my friends. They are the last five listed, with 6 and 7 being closest to my heart. From school, the media and job situations, I've picked up standard and working class English. From Mamagrande Locha and from reading Spanish and Mexican literature, I've picked up Standard Spanish and Standard Mexican Spanish. From *los recién llegados*, Mexican immigrants, and *braceros*, I learned the North Mexican dialect. With Mexicans I'll try to speak either Standard Mexican Spanish or the North Mexican dialect. From my parents and Chicanos living in the Valley,[4] I picked up Chicano Texas Spanish, and I speak it with my mom; younger brother (who married a Mexican and who rarely mixes Spanish with English), aunts and older relatives.

With Chicanas from *Nuevo México* or *Arizona* I will speak Chicano Spanish a little, but often they don't understand what I'm saying. With most California Chicanas I speak entirely in English (unless I forget). When I first moved to San Francisco, I'd rattle off something in Spanish, unintentionally embarrassing them. Often it is only with another Chicana *tejana* that I can talk freely.

Words distorted by English are known as anglicisms or *pochismos*. The *pocho* is an anglicized Mexican or American of Mexican origin who speaks Spanish with an accent characteristic of North Americans and who distorts and reconstructs the language according to the influence of English.[5] Tex-

4. I.e., of the Rio Grande in southern Texas, bordering Mexico.
5. R. C. Ortega, *Dialectología Del Barrio*, trans. Hortencia S. Alwan (Los Angeles, CA: R. C. Ortega Publisher & Bookseller, 1977), 132 [Anzaldúa's note].

Mex, or Spanglish, comes most naturally to me. I may switch back and forth from English to Spanish in the same sentence or in the same word. With my sister and my brother Nune and with Chicano *tejano* contemporaries I speak in Tex-Mex.

From kids and people my own age I picked up *Pachuco*. *Pachuco* (the language of the zoot suiters) is a language of rebellion, both against Standard Spanish and Standard English. It is a secret language. Adults of the culture and outsiders cannot understand it. It is made up of slang words from both English and Spanish. *Ruca* means girl or woman, *vato* means guy or dude, *chale* means no, *simón* means yes, *churo* is sure, talk is *periquiar*, *pigionear* means petting, *que gacho* means how nerdy, *ponte águila* means watch out, death is called *la pelona*. Through lack of practice and not having others who can speak it, I've lost most of the *Pachuco* tongue.

Chicano Spanish

Chicanos, after 250 years of Spanish/Anglo colonization have developed significant differences in the Spanish we speak. We collapse two adjacent vowels into a single syllable and sometimes shift the stress in certain words such as *maíz / maiz, cohete / cuete*. We leave out certain consonants when they appear between vowels: *lado/lao, mojado/mojao*. Chicanos from South Texas pronounced *f* as *j* as in *jue* (*fue*). Chicanos use "archaisms," words that are no longer in the Spanish language, words that have been evolved out. We say *semos, truje, haiga, ansina*, and *naiden*. We retain the "archaic" *j*, as in *jalar*, that derives from an earlier *h*, (the French *halar* or the Germanic *halon* which was lost to standard Spanish in the 16th century), but which is still found in several regional dialects such as the one spoken in South Texas. (Due to geography, Chicanos from the Valley of South Texas were cut off linguistically from other Spanish speakers. We tend to use words that the Spaniards brought over from Medieval Spain. The majority of the Spanish colonizers in Mexico and the Southwest came from Extremadura—Hernán Cortés was one of them—and Andalucía.[6] Andalucians pronounce *ll* like a *y*, and their *d*'s tend to be absorbed by adjacent vowels: *tirado* becomes *tirao*. They brought *el lenguaje popular, dialectos y regionalismos*.)[7]

Chicanos and other Spanish speakers also shift *ll* to *y* and *z* to *s*.[8] We leave out initial syllables, saying *tar* for *estar, toy* for *estoy*; *hora* for *ahora* (*cubanos* and *puertorriqueños* also leave out initial letters of some words.) We also leave out the final syllable such as *pa* for *para*. The intervocalic *y*, the *ll* as in *tortilla, ella, botella*, gets replaced by *tortia* or *tortiya, ea, botea*. We add an additional syllable at the beginning of certain words: *atocar* for *tocar, agastar* for *gastar*. Sometimes we'll say *lavaste las vacijas*, other times *lavates* (substituting the *ates* verb endings for the *aste*).

We use anglicisms, words borrowed from English: *bola* from ball, *carpeta* from carpet, *máchina de lavar* (instead of *lavadora*) from washing machine. Tex-Mex argot, created by adding a Spanish sound at the beginning or end

---

6. Region in southern Spain. Extremadura is a city in central Spain. Cortés (1485–1547), Spanish soldier and explorer who conquered the Aztecs and claimed Mexico for Spain.
7. Eduardo Hernández-Chávez, Andrew D. Cohen, and Anthony F. Beltramo, *El Lenguaje de*

los Chicanos: Regional and Social Characteristics of Language Used by Mexican Americans (Arlington, VA: Center for Applied Linguistics, 1975), 39 [Anzaldúa's note].
8. Hernández-Chávez, xvii [Anzaldúa's note].

of an English word such as *cookiar* for cook, *watchar* for watch, *parkiar* for park, and *rapiar* for rape, is the result of the pressures on Spanish speakers to adapt to English.

We don't use the word *vosotros/as* or its accompanying verb form. We don't say *claro* (to mean yes), *imagínate*, or *me emociona*, unless we picked up Spanish from Latinas, out of a book, or in a classroom. Other Spanish-speaking groups are going through the same, or similar, development in their Spanish.

Linguistic Terrorism

> *Deslenguadas. Somos los del español deficiente.* We are your linguistic nightmare, your linguistic aberration, your linguistic *mestizaje*, the subject of your *burla*. Because we speak with tongues of fire we are culturally crucified. Racially, culturally and linguistically *somos huérfanos*—we speak an orphan tongue.

Chicanas who grew up speaking Chicano Spanish have internalized the belief that we speak poor Spanish. It is illegitimate, a bastard language. And because we internalize how our language has been used against us by the dominant culture, we use our language differences against each other.

Chicana feminists often skirt around each other with suspicion and hesitation. For the longest time I couldn't figure it out. Then it dawned on me. To be close to another Chicana is like looking into the mirror. We are afraid of what we'll see there. *Pena.* Shame. Low estimation of self. In childhood we are told that our language is wrong. Repeated attacks on our native tongue diminish our sense of self. The attacks continue throughout our lives.

Chicanas feel uncomfortable talking in Spanish to Latinas, afraid of their censure. Their language was not outlawed in their countries. They had a whole lifetime of being immersed in their native tongue; generations, centuries in which Spanish was a first language, taught in school, heard on radio and TV, and read in the newspaper.

If a person, Chicana or Latina, has a low estimation of my native tongue, she also has a low estimation of me. Often with *mexicanas y latinas* we'll speak English as a neutral language. Even among Chicanas we tend to speak English at parties or conferences. Yet, at the same time, we're afraid the other will think we're *agringadas* because we don't speak Chicano Spanish. We oppress each other trying to out-Chicano each other, vying to be the "real" Chicanas, to speak like Chicanos. There is no one Chicano language just as there is no one Chicano experience. A monolingual Chicana whose first language is English or Spanish is just as much a Chicana as one who speaks several variants of Spanish. A Chicana from Michigan or Chicago or Detroit is just as much a Chicana as one from the Southwest. Chicano Spanish is as diverse linguistically as it is regionally.

By the end of this century, Spanish speakers will comprise the biggest minority group in the U.S., a country where students in high schools and colleges are encouraged to take French classes because French is considered more "cultured." But for a language to remain alive it must be used.[9]

---

9. Irena Klepfisz, "Secular Jewish Identity: Yidishkayt in America," in *The Tribe of Dina*, Kaye/Kantrowitz, eds., 43 [Anzaldúa's note].

By the end of this century English, and not Spanish, will be the mother tongue of most Chicanos and Latinos.

So, if you want to really hurt me, talk badly about my language. Ethnic identity is twin skin to linguistic identity—I am my language. Until I can take pride in my language, I cannot take pride in myself. Until I can accept as legitimate Chicano Texas Spanish, Tex-Mex and all the other languages I speak, I cannot accept the legitimacy of myself. Until I am free to write bilingually and to switch codes without having always to translate, while I still have to speak English or Spanish when I would rather speak Spanglish, and as long as I have to accommodate the English speakers rather than having them accommodate me, my tongue will be illegitimate.

I will no longer be made to feel ashamed of existing. I will have my voice: Indian, Spanish, white. I will have my serpent's tongue—my woman's voice, my sexual voice, my poet's voice. I will overcome the tradition of silence.

> My fingers
> move sly against your palm
> Like women everywhere, we speak in code. . . .
>
> —Melanie Kaye/Kantrowitz[1]

"Vistas," corridos, y comida: My Native Tongue

In the 1960s, I read my first Chicano novel. It was *City of Night* by John Rechy[2] a gay Texan, son of a Scottish father and a Mexican mother. For days I walked around in stunned amazement that a Chicano could write and could get published. When I read *I Am Joaquín*[3] I was surprised to see a bilingual book by a Chicano in print. When I saw poetry written in Tex-Mex for the first time, a feeling of pure joy flashed through me. I felt like we really existed as a people. In 1971, when I started teaching High School English to Chicano students, I tried to supplement the required texts with works by Chicanos, only to be reprimanded and forbidden to do so by the principal. He claimed that I was supposed to teach "American" and English literature. At the risk of being fired, I swore my students to secrecy and slipped in Chicano short stories, poems, a play. In graduate school, while working toward a Ph.D., I had to "argue" with one advisor after the other, semester after semester, before I was allowed to make Chicano literature an area of focus.

Even before I read books by Chicanos or Mexicans, it was the Mexican movies I saw at the drive-in—the Thursday night special of $1.00 a carload—that gave me a sense of belonging. *"Vámonos a las vistas,"* my mother would call out and we'd all—grandmother, brothers, sister and cousins—squeeze into the car. We'd wolf down cheese and bologna white bread sandwiches while watching Pedro Infante in melodramatic tear-jerkers like *Nosotros los pobres*,[4]

---

1. Melanie Kaye/Kantrowitz, "Sign," in *We Speak in Code: Poems and Other Writings* (Pittsburgh, PA: Motheroot Publications, Inc., 1980), 85 [Anzaldúa's note].
2. American novelist (b. 1931). The book was published in 1963.

3. Rodolfo Gonzales [(1928–2005), Chicano novelist], *I Am Joaquín Yo Soy Joaquín* (New York, NY: Bantam Books, 1972). It was first published in 1967 [Anzaldúa's note].
4. A 1947 film. Infante (1917–1957), Mexican film actor and singer.

the first "real" Mexican movie (that was not an imitation of European movies). I remember seeing *Cuando los hijos se van*[5] and surmising that all Mexican movies played up the love a mother has for her children and what ungrateful sons and daughters suffer when they are not devoted to their mothers. I remember the singing-type "westerns" of Jorge Negrete and Miguel Aceves Mejía.[6] When watching Mexican movies, I felt a sense of homecoming as well as alienation. People who were to amount to something didn't go to Mexican movies, or *bailes* or tune their radios to *bolero, rancherita,* and *corrido* music.

The whole time I was growing up, there was *norteño* music sometimes called North Mexican border music, or Tex-Mex music, or Chicano music, or *cantina* (bar) music. I grew up listening to *conjuntos,* three- or four-piece bands made up of folk musicians playing guitar, *bajo sexto,*[7] drums and button accordion, which Chicanos had borrowed from the German immigrants who had come to Central Texas and Mexico to farm and build breweries. In the Rio Grande Valley, Steve Jordan and Little Joe Hernández were popular, and Flaco Jiménez[8] was the accordion king. The rhythms of Tex-Mex music are those of the polka, also adapted from the Germans, who in turn had borrowed the polka from the Czechs and Bohemians.

I remember the hot, sultry evenings when *corridos*—songs of love and death on the Texas-Mexican borderlands—reverberated out of cheap amplifiers from the local *cantinas* and wafted in through my bedroom window.

Corridos first became widely used along the South Texas / Mexican border during the early conflict between Chicanos and Anglos. The *corridos* are usually about Mexican heroes who do valiant deeds against the Anglo oppressors. Pancho Villa's song, *"La cucaracha,"* is the most famous one. *Corridos* of John F. Kennedy[9] and his death are still very popular in the Valley. Older Chicanos remember Lydia Mendoza,[1] one of the great border *corrido* singers who was called *la Gloria de Tejas.* Her *"El tango negre,"* sung during the Great Depression, made her a singer of the people. The everpresent *corridos* narrated one hundred years of border history, bringing news of events as well as entertaining. These folk musicians and folk songs are our chief cultural mythmakers, and they made our hard lives seem bearable.

I grew up feeling ambivalent about our music. Country-western and rock-and-roll had more status. In the 50s and 60s, for the slightly educated and *agringado* Chicanos, there existed a sense of shame at being caught listening to our music. Yet I couldn't stop my feet from thumping to the music, could not stop humming the words, nor hide from myself the exhilaration I felt when I heard it.

There are more subtle ways that we internalize identification, especially in the forms of images and emotions. For me food and certain smells are tied

5. A 1941 film.
6. Mexican singer and film actor (1916–2006). Negrete (1911–1953), Mexican singing actor.
7. Twelve-string guitar tuned one octave lower than normal.
8. Mexican American musicians. Esteban Jordán (1939–2010). José María De Leon Hérnandez (b.

1940), Leonardo "Flaco" Jiménez (b. 1939).
9. Thirty-fifth U.S. president (1917–1963), assassinated in Dallas, Texas. Villa (ca. 1877–1923), born Doroteo Arango, Mexican revolutionary leader.
1. Mexican American singer, songwriter, and musician (1916–2007).

to my identity, to my homeland. Woodsmoke curling up to an immense blue sky; woodsmoke perfuming my grandmother's clothes, her skin. The stench of cow manure and the yellow patches on the ground; the crack of a .22 rifle and the reek of cordite. Homemade white cheese sizzling in a pan, melting inside a folded *tortilla*. My sister Hilda's hot, spicy *menudo*[2] *chile colorado* making it deep red, pieces of *panza* and hominy floating on top. My brother Carito barbecuing *fajitas* in the backyard. Even now and 3,000 miles away, I can see my mother spicing the ground beef, pork and venison with *chile*. My mouth salivates at the thought of the hot steaming *tamales* I would be eating if I were home.

> *Si le preguntas a mi mamá, "¿Qué eres?"*

> "Identity is the essential core of who
> we are as individuals, the conscious
> experience of the self inside."
> —Kaufman[3]

Nosotros los Chicanos straddle the borderlands. On one side of us, we are constantly exposed to the Spanish of the Mexicans, on the other side we hear the Anglos' incessant clamoring so that we forget our language. Among ourselves we don't say *nosotros los americanos, o nosotros los españoles, o nosotros los hispanos.* We say *nosotros los mexicanos* (by *mexicanos* we do not mean citizens of Mexico; we do not mean a national identity, but a racial one). We distinguish between *mexicanos del otro lado* and *mexicanos de este lado.* Deep in our hearts we believe that being Mexican has nothing to do with which country one lives in. Being Mexican is a state of soul—not one of mind, not one of citizenship. Neither eagle nor serpent,[4] but both. And like the ocean, neither animal respects borders.

> *Dime con quien andas y te diré quien eres.*
> (Tell me who your friends are and I'll tell you who
> you are.)
> —Mexican saying

Si le preguntas a mi mamá, "¿Qué eres?" te dirá, "Soy mexicana." My brothers and sister say the same. I sometimes will answer *"soy mexicana"* and at others will say *"soy Chicana" o "soy tejana."* But I identified as *"Raza"* before I ever identified as *"mexicana"* or "Chicana."

As a culture, we call ourselves Spanish when referring to ourselves as a linguistic group and when copping out. It is then that we forget our predominant Indian genes. We are 70 to 80 percent Indian.[5] We call ourselves Hispanic[6] or Spanish-American or Latin American or Latin when linking ourselves to other Spanish-speaking peoples of the Western hemisphere

---

2. Mexican soup made of simmered tripe, onion, garlic, chili, and hominy.
3. Gershen Kaufman [(b. 1943), American psychologist], *Shame: The Power of Caring* (Cambridge: Schenkman Books, Inc. 1980), 68. This book was instrumental in my understanding of shame [from Anzaldúa's note].
4. Respectively, male and female cultural figurations.
5. John R. Chávez [(b. 1949), American scholar

and educator], *The Lost Land: The Chicano Images of the Southwest* (Albuquerque, NM: University of New Mexico Press, 1984), 88–90 [from Anzaldúa's note].
6. "Hispanic" is derived from Hispanis (*España*, a name given to the Iberian Peninsula in ancient times when it was a part of the Roman Empire) and is a term designated by the U.S. government to make it easier to handle us on paper [Anzaldúa's note].

and when copping out. We call ourselves Mexican-American[7] to signify we are neither Mexican nor American, but more the noun "American" than the adjective "Mexican" (and when copping out).

Chicanos and other people of color suffer economically for not acculturating. This voluntary (yet forced) alienation makes for psychological conflict, a kind of dual identity—we don't identify with the Anglo-American cultural values and we don't totally identify with the Mexican cultural values. We are a synergy of two cultures with various degrees of Mexicanness or Angloness. I have so internalized the borderland conflict that sometimes I feel like one cancels out the other and we are zero, nothing, no one. *A veces no soy nada ni nadie. Pero hasta cuando no lo soy, lo soy.*

When not copping out, when we know we are more than nothing, we call ourselves Mexican, referring to race and ancestry; *mestizo* when affirming both our Indian and Spanish (but we hardly ever own our Black ancestry); Chicano when referring to a politically aware people born and/or raised in the U.S.; *Raza* when referring to Chicanos; *tejanos* when we are Chicanos from Texas.

Chicanos did not know we were a people until 1965 when Cesar Chavez[8] and the farmworkers united and *I Am Joaquín* was published and *la Raza Unida* party[9] was formed in Texas. With that recognition, we became a distinct people. Something momentous happened to the Chicano soul—we became aware of our reality and acquired a name and a language (Chicano Spanish) that reflected that reality. Now that we had a name, some of the fragmented pieces began to fall together—who we were, what we were, how we had evolved. We began to get glimpses of what we might eventually become.

Yet the struggle of identities continues, the struggle of borders is our reality still. One day the inner struggle will cease and a true integration take place. In the meantime, *tenemos que hacerla lucha. ¿Quién está protegiendo los ranchos de mi gente? ¿Quién está tratando de cerrar la fisura entre la india y el bianco en nuestra sangre? El Chicano, sí, el Chicano que anda como un ladrón en su propia casa.*[1]

Los Chicanos, how patient we seem, how very patient. There is the quiet of the Indian about us. We know how to survive. When other races have given up their tongue, we've kept ours. We know what it is to live under the hammer blow of the dominant *norteamericano* culture. But more than we count the blows, we count the days the weeks the years the centuries the eons until the white laws and commerce and customs will rot in the deserts they've created, lie bleached. *Humildes* yet proud, *quietos* yet wild, *nosotros los mexicanos* Chicanos will walk by the crumbling ashes as we go about our business. Stubborn, persevering, impenetrable as stone, yet possessing a malleability that renders us unbreakable, we, the *mestizas* and *mestizos*, will remain.

1987

---

7. The Treaty of Guadalupe Hidalgo created the Mexican-American in 1848 [Anzaldúa's note].
8. Chicano union organizer (1927–1993).
9. Known in America as the United Farm Workers; founded in 1962.
1. Anglos, in order to alleviate their guilt for dispossessing the Chicano, stressed the Spanish part of us and perpetrated the myth of the Spanish Southwest. We have accepted the fiction that we are Hispanic, that is Spanish, in order to accommodate ourselves to the dominant culture and its abhorrence of Indians. Chávez, 88–91 [Anzaldúa's note].

El sonavabitche

(for Aishe Berger)

Car flowing down a lava of highway
just happened to glance out the window
in time to see brown faces bent backs
like prehistoric boulders in a field
so common a sight no one   5
notices
blood rushes to my face
twelve years I'd sat on the memory
the anger scorching me
my throat so tight I can   10
barely get the words out.

I got to the farm
in time to hear the shots
ricochet off barn,
spit into the sand,   15
in time to see tall men in uniforms
thumping fists on doors
metallic voices yelling Halt!
their hawk eyes constantly shifting.

When I hear the words, *"Corran muchachos"*[1]   20
I run back to the car, ducking,
see the glistening faces, arms outflung,
of the *mexicanos* running headlong
through the fields
kicking up clouds of dirt   25

see them reach the tree line
foliage opening, swishing closed behind them.
I hear the tussling of bodies, grunts, panting
squeak of leather squawk of walkie-talkies
sun reflecting off gunbarrels   30
the world a blinding light
a great buzzing in my ears
my knees like aspens in the wind.
I see that wide cavernous look of the hunted
the look of hares   35
thick limp blue-black hair
The bare heads humbly bent
of those who do not speak
the ember in their eyes extinguished.

I lean on the shanty wall of that migrant camp   40
north of Muncie, Indiana.
Wets, a voice says.

---

1. Run boys [Anzaldúa's note].

I turn to see a Chicano pushing
the head of his *muchachita*[2]
back into the *naguas*[3] of the mother   45
a tin plate face down on the floor
tortillas scattered around them.
His other hand signals me over.
He too is from *el valle de Tejas*[4]
I had been his kid's teacher.   50
I'd come to get the grower
to fill up the sewage ditch near the huts
saying it wouldn't do for the children
to play in it.
    Smoke from a cooking fire and   55
    shirtless *niños* gather around us.

    Mojados[5] he says again,
leaning on his chipped Chevy station wagon
Been here two weeks
about a dozen of them.   60
The *sonavabitche* works them
from sunup to dark—15 hours sometimes.
Como mulas los trabaja[6]
no saben como hacer la perra.[7]
Last Sunday they asked for a day off   65
wanted to pray and rest,
write letters to their *familias*.
¿Y sabes lo que hizo el sonavabitche?[8]
He turns away and spits.
Says he has to hold back half their wages   70
that they'd eaten the other half:
sack of beans, sack of rice, sack of flour.
Frijoleros sí lo son[9] but no way
could they have eaten that many *frijoles*.
I nod.   75

Como le dije, son doce[1]—started out 13
five days packed in the back of a pickup
boarded up tight
fast cross-country run no stops
except to change drivers, to gas up   80
no food they pissed into their shoes—
those that had *guaraches*[2]
slept slumped against each other
sabe Dios[3] where they shit.
One smothered to death on the way here   85

---

2. Little girl [Anzaldúa's note].
3. Skirt [Anzaldúa's note].
4. Rio Grande Valley in Texas [Anzaldúa's note].
5. Wetbacks, undocumented workers, illegal immigrants from Mexico and parts south [Anzaldúa's note].
6. He works them like mules [Anzaldúa's note].
7. They don't know how to make the work easier for themselves [Anzaldúa's note].
8. And you know what the son of a bitch did? [Anzaldúa's note].
9. Bean eaters they are [Anzaldúa's note].
1. Like I told you, they're 12 [Anzaldúa's note].
2. Sandals [Anzaldúa's note].
3. God knows [Anzaldúa's note].

Miss, you should've seen them when they
stumbled out.
First thing the *sonavabitche* did was clamp
a handkerchief over his nose
then ordered them stripped   90
hosed them down himself
in front of everybody.
They hobbled about
learning to walk all over again.
Flacos con caras de viejos[4]   95
aunque la mita'eran jóvenes.[5]

Como le estaba diciendo[6]
today was payday.
You saw them, *la migra*[7] came busting in
waving their *pinche pistolas.*[8]   100
Said someone made a call,
what you call it? Anonymous.
Guess who? That *sonavabitche*, who else?
Done this three times since we've been coming here
Sepa Dios how many times in between.   105
Wets, free labor, *esclavos.*[9]
Pobres jijos de la Chingada.[1]
This the last time we work for him
no matter how *fregados*[2] we are
he said, shaking his head,   110
spitting at the ground.
Vámonos, mujer, empaca el mugrero.[3]

He hands me a cup of coffee,
half of it sugar, half of it milk
my throat so dry I even down the dregs.   115
It has to be done.
Steeling myself
I take that walk to the big house.

Finally the big man lets me in.
How about a drink? I shake my head.   120
He looks me over, opens his eyes wide
and smiles, says how sorry he is immigration[4]
is getting so tough
a poor Mexican can't make a living
and they sure do need the work.   125
My throat so thick the words stick.

4. Skinny with old faces [Anzaldúa's note].
5. Though half were youths [Anzaldúa's note].
6. As I was telling you [Anzaldúa's note].
7. Slang for immigration officials [Anzaldúa's note].
8. Guns [Anzaldúa's note].
9. Slaves [Anzaldúa's note].
1. "Poor sons of the fucked one" [Anzaldúa's note]. *La Chingada* is the preferred Chicana term for *La Malinche* or *Malintzin*, the deposed Aztec princess who served Hernan Cortés as translator and became his lover during the Spanish Conquest of Mexico (1519–22).
2. Poor, beaten, downtrodden, in need [Anzaldúa's note].
3. Let's go, woman, pack our junk [Anzaldúa's note].
4. The U.S. Immigration and Naturalization Service.

He studies me, then says,
Well, what can I do you for?
I want two weeks wages
including two Saturdays and Sundays,   130
minimum wage, 15 hours a day.
I'm more startled than he.
Whoa there, sinorita,
wets work for whatever you give them
the season hasn't been good.   135
Besides most are halfway to Mexico by now.
Two weeks wages, I say,
the words swelling in my throat.

    Miss uh what did you say your name was?
    I fumble for my card.   140
    You can't do this,
    I haven't broken no law,
    his lidded eyes darken, I step back.
    I'm leaving in two minutes and I want cash
    the whole amount right here in my purse   145
    when I walk out.
    No hoarseness, no trembling.
    It startled both of us.

You want me telling every single one
of your neighbors what you've been doing   150
all these years? The mayor, too?
Maybe make a call to Washington?
Slitted eyes studied the card again.
They had no cards, no papers.
I'd seen it over and over.   155
Work them, then turn them in before paying them.

    Well, now, he was saying,
    I know we can work something out,
    a sweet young thang like yourself.
    Cash, I said. I didn't know anyone in D.C.   160
    now I didn't have to.
    You want to keep it for yourself?
    That it? His eyes were pin pricks.
    Sweat money, Mister, blood money,
    not my sweat, but same blood.   165
    Yeah, but who's to say you won't abscond with it?
    If I ever hear that you got illegals on your land
    even a single one, I'm going to come here
    in broad daylight and have you
    hung by your balls.   170
    He walks slowly to his desk.
    Knees shaking, I count every bill
    taking my time.

1987

SHARON OLDS
b. 1942

L ike Whitman, Sharon Olds celebrates the body and writes about it without shame. And like Whitman, her candor arouses a mixed response among contemporary readers. Some find Olds's poems, with their close observations about sexuality, family life, and family pathology, disturbingly graphic, while many others find them moving and brave. Nonetheless, her second book, *The Dead and the Living* (1984), won the National Book Award and has gone on to become one of the best-selling volumes in contemporary poetry. The fact that Olds is a woman who writes about desire and sexual pleasure, or who describes her father's genitals ("My Father Speaks to Me from the Dead"), may intensify reader response. We are far more accustomed to male writers exploring the sexual and bodily terrain. In her poems Olds lays out the domestic territory of erotic life, which extends to motherhood, daughterhood, and the body's life of sensation. She is unabashed about the ways in which pleasure can be entangled with pain, especially in her numerous poems about parents and parental cruelty. In "I Go Back to May 1937" the speaker warns younger versions of her parents, about to get married, "you are going to do things / you cannot imagine you would ever do, / you are going to do bad things to children."

Olds's examination of intimate subjects has a distinctive quality of fascination and even tenderness. As she writes in "Little Things": "I am doing something I learned early to do, I am / paying attention to the small beauties, / whatever I have—as if it were our duty / to find things to love, to bind ourselves to this world." These lines articulate a central strategy in Olds's work: paying attention to what otherwise might be overlooked, finding beauty in surprising places. They also provide an example of how carefully her poems are shaped. Working from the base of an iambic pentameter line, Olds fashions a freer, more conversational style and binds the lines together with a series of subtle rhymes, or half rhymes, several of them internal to the line ("do/beauties/duty"; "find/bind"). Olds has a particular gift for metaphor that transfigures the ordinary without forsaking its ordinariness. Metaphor renders the "small beauties" she discovers even in embarrassing or painful experience: applying spermicide to a slippery diaphragm ("I'd decorate it / like a cake" in "Adolescence") or imagining the parents as paper dolls from which she "strikes sparks" ("I go Back to May 1937"), or seeing the navel as "thistle / seed fossil" ("My Father Speaks to Me from the Dead"). Because so many of Olds's poems focus on intimate experience, it is perhaps too easy to assume that the work is simply autobiographical or confessional (a description Olds herself rejects; she calls the work "apparently very personal"). The candor in these poems is an imaginative creation; it is not make-believe but, in the critic Elaine Scarry's phrase, "made-real."

Sharon Olds grew up in Berkeley, California, and attended Stanford University, then earned her Ph.D. at Columbia. She published her first book of poems, *Satan Says* (1980), when she was thirty-seven years old. Since then she has published numerous additional volumes besides *The Dead and the Living*, among them *The Gold Cell* (1987), *The Father* (1992), *Blood, Tin, Straw* (1999), and *Strike Sparks: Selected Poems* 1980–2002 (2002). In 1984 she started a poetry workshop at Goldwater Hospital for the severely disabled on Roosevelt Island, and since 1992 has taught in the Graduate Creative Writing Program at NYU.

Sex Without Love

How do they do it, the ones who make love
without love? Formal as dancers,
gliding over each other like ice-skaters
over the ice, fingers hooked
inside each other's bodies, faces   5
red as steak, wine, wet as the
children at birth whose mothers are going to
give them away. How do they come to the
come to the   come to the   God   come to the
still waters, and not love   10
the one who came there with them, heat
rising slowly as steam off their joined
skin? I guess they are the true religious,
the purists, the pros, the ones who will not
accept a false Messiah, love the   15
priest instead of the God. They do not
mistake the partner for their own pleasure,
they are like great runners: they know they are alone
with the road surface, the cold, the wind,
the fit of their shoes, their overall cardio-   20
vascular health—just factors, like the other
in the bed, and not their truth, which is
the single body alone in the universe
against its own best time.

                                                          1984

I Go Back to May 1937

I see them standing at the formal gates of their colleges,
I see my father strolling out
under the ochre sandstone arch, the
red tiles glinting like bent
plates of blood behind his head, I   5
see my mother with a few light books at her hip
standing at the pillar made of tiny bricks,
the wrought-iron gate still open behind her, its
sword-tips aglow in the May air,
they are about to graduate, they are about to get married,   10
they are kids, they are dumb, all they know is they are
innocent, they would never hurt anybody.
I want to go up to them and say Stop,
don't do it—she's the wrong woman,
he's the wrong man, you are going to do things   15
you cannot imagine you would ever do,
you are going to do bad things to children,
you are going to suffer in ways you have not heard of,
you are going to want to die. I want to go

up to them there in the late May sunlight and say it,   20
her hungry pretty face turning to me,
her pitiful beautiful untouched body,
his arrogant handsome face turning to me,
his pitiful beautiful untouched body,
but I don't do it I want to live. I   25
take them up like the male and female
paper dolls and bang them together
at the hips, like chips of flint, as if to
strike sparks from them, I say
Do what you are going to do, and I will tell about it.   30

1987

Little Things

After she's gone to camp, in the early
evening I clear our girl's breakfast dishes
from the rosewood table, and find a dinky
crystallized pool of maple syrup, the
grains standing there, round, in the night, I   5
rub it with my fingertip
as if I could read it, this raised dot of
amber sugar, and this time,
when I think of my father, I wonder why
I think of my father, of the Vulcan[1] blood-red   10
glass in his hand, or his black hair gleaming like a
broken-open coal. I think I learned
to love the little things about him
because of all the big things
I could not love, no one could, it would be wrong to.   15
So when I fix on this image of resin,
or sweep together with the heel of my hand a
pile of my son's sunburn peels like
insect wings, where I peeled his back the night before camp,
I am doing something I learned early to do, I am   20
paying attention to small beauties,
whatever I have—as if it were our duty
to find things to love, to bind ourselves to this world.

1987

My Father Speaks to Me from the Dead

I seem to have woken up in a pot-shed,
on clay, on shards, the glitter paths
of slugs kiss-crossing my body. I don't know
where to start, with this grime on me.

---

1. The ancient Roman mythological god of fire and metal working.

I take the spider glue-net, plug
of the dead, out of my mouth, let's see
if where I have been I can do this.
I love your feet. I love your knees,
I love your our my legs, they are so
long because they are yours and mine
both. I love your—what can I call it,
between your legs, we never named it, the
glint and purity of its curls. I love
your rear end, I changed you once,
washed the detritus off your tiny
bottom, with my finger rubbed
the oil on you; when I touched your little
anus I crossed wires with God for a moment.
I never hated your shit—that was
your mother. I love your navel, thistle
seed fossil, even though
it's her print on you. Of course I love
your breasts—did you see me looking up
from within your daughter's face, as she nursed?
I love your bony shoulders and you know I
love your hair, thick and live
as earth. And I never hated your face,
I hated its eruptions. You know what I love?
I love your brain, its halves and silvery
folds, like a woman's labia.
I love in you
even what comes
from deep in your mother—your heart, that hard worker,
and your womb, it is a heaven to me,
I lie on its gentle hills and gaze up
at its rosy vault.
I have been in a body without breath,
I have been in the morgue, in fire, in the slagged
chimney, in the air over the earth,
and buried in the earth, and pulled down
into the ocean—where I have been
I understand this life, I am matter,
your father, I made you, when I say now that I love you
I mean look down at your hand, move it,
that action is matter's love, for human
love go elsewhere.

1992

Adolescence

When I think of my adolescence, I think
of the bathroom of that seedy hotel
in San Francisco, where my boyfriend would take me.
I had never seen a bathroom like that—

no curtains, no towels, no mirror, just 5
a sink green with grime and a toilet
yellow and rust-colored—like something in a science experiment,
growing the plague in bowls.
Sex was still a crime, then,
I'd sign out of my college dorm 10
to a false destination, sign into
the flophouse under a false name,
go down the hall to the one bathroom
and lock myself in. And I could not learn to get that
diaphragm in, I'd decorate it 15
like a cake, with glistening spermicide,
and lean over, and it would leap from my fingers
and sail, into a corner, to land
in a concave depression like a rat's nest,
I'd bend and pluck it out and wash it 20
and wash it down to that fragile dome,
I'd frost it again till it was shimmering
and bend it into its tensile arc and it would
fly through the air, rim humming
like Saturn's ring,[1] I would bow down and crawl to retrieve it. 25
When I think of being eighteen,
that's what I see, that brimmed disc
floating through the air and descending, I see myself
kneeling and reaching, reaching for my own life.

1996

The Talkers

All week, we talked. We talked
in the morning on the porch, when I combed my hair
and flung the comb-hair out into the air,
it floated down the slope, toward the valley.
We talked while walking to the car, talked 5
over its mild, belled roof,
while opening the doors, then ducked down
and there we were, bent toward the interior, talking.
Meeting, in the middle of the day,
the first thing when we saw each other 10
we opened our mouths. All day,
we sang to each other the level music
of spoken language. Even while we ate
we did not pause, I'd speak to him through
the broken body of the butter cookie, 15
gently spraying him with crumbs. We talked
and walked, we leaned against the opposite sides of the
car and talked in the parking lot

---

1. Also the name of a contraceptive vaginal ring.

until everyone else had driven off, we clung to its
dark cold raft and started a new subject.   20
We did not talk about his wife, much,
or my husband, but to everything else
we turned the workings of our lips and tongues
—up to our necks in the hot tub, or
walking up the steep road,   25
stepping into the hot dust as if
down into the ions of a wing, and on the
sand, next to each other, as we turned
the turns that upon each other would be the
turnings of joy—even under   30
water there trailed from our mouths the delicate
chains of our sentences. But mostly at night, and
far into the night, we talked until we
dropped, as if, stopping for an instant, we might
move right toward each other. Today,   35
he said he felt he could talk to me forever,
it must be the way the angels live,
sitting across from each other, deep
in the bliss of their shared spirit. My God,
they are not going to touch each other.   40

1999

SAM SHEPARD
b. 1943

Assessing Sam Shepard's importance, the critic Richard Gilman finds the key in his fascination with rootlessness. In this quality are his works' greatest difficulties and their deepest appeal, a dramaturgy famous for what Gilman describes as "the frantic efforts of so many of his characters to make themselves felt, often by violence (or cartoon violence—blows without injuries, bullets without death: dream or make-believe, something filmed), of the great strand in his work of the ego run wild, of the craving for altered states of being and the power to transcend physical or moral limitations." Whether monologues or dialogues, his actors' lines are more than contributions to plot and action—they are "outcries of characters craving to be known."

Because of his success as an actor in a score of major motion pictures, including *The Right Stuff* (1983), *Steel Magnolias* (1989), and *Black Hawk Down* (2002), Shepard is one of America's most recognizable contemporary dramatists. His image is a strongly self-created one, as he transformed himself from Samuel Shepard Rogers III (called "Steve" at home, the son of career-military parents who later became ranchers in rural California) into Sam Shepard, underground rock musician and experimental Off-Broadway playwright. Doing this meant abandoning studies he had begun at an agricultural college and giving up work as a horseman and ranch hand. Arriving in New York City as a nineteen-year-old, he found work as a waiter at The Village Gate, Greenwich

Village's top jazz club at the time, where he met musicians, actors and actresses, and most helpfully Ralph Cook, founder and director of Theater Genesis (whose company included actress O-Lan Johnson, later to be Shepard's wife). His one-act plays were first presented by the Theater Genesis ensemble at St. Mark's-in-the-Bowery in 1964, beginning a prolific Off-Broadway career that would win him eleven Obie awards. By 1979 he had won a Pulitzer Prize as well (for his three-act play *Buried Child*). Also a short-story writer and essayist, Shepard was invited by the German filmmaker Wim Wenders to adapt some of this nontheatrical material for the motion picture *Paris, Texas*, which won the Palm d'Or award when it premiered at the Cannes Film Festival in 1984. By then his marriage with O-Lan Johnson had ended; a long-term relationship with the film actress Jessica Lange followed. *Far North* (1988) displays Shepard's skills as a cinematic director, and his playwriting career has continued with such works as *Eyes for Consuela* (1998), *The Late Henry Moss* (2002), and *The God of Hell* (2004).

True West (1980) finds Shephard expanding his dramaturgy from the one-act vignette to a more conventional running time, channeling his earlier penchant for symbolic abstraction into the suggestions (if not always the practicalities) of realism. As in many of his plays the American West, past and present, shares attention with family concerns, as an undercurrent of violence sets the deliberately uneasy tone. In a style that draws from the works of Samuel Beckett and Edward Albee, *True West* is starkly minimal, putting just four characters in a single set, here a familiar kitchen-dinette scene. The play's general aura is what Shepard scholars have called "frontier gothic," in which themes from the American West of pioneer days (independence, isolation, a climate of physical violence) appear in contemporary life, especially within familial and social relationships.

The text is from *Seven Plays* (1981).

True West

Characters

AUSTIN: *early thirties, light blue sports shirt, light tan cardigan sweater, clean blue jeans, white tennis shoes*

LEE: *his older brother, early forties, filthy white t-shirt, tattered brown overcoat covered with dust, dark blue baggy suit pants from the Salvation Army, pink suede belt, pointed black forties dress shoes scuffed up, holes in the soles, no socks, no hat, long pronounced sideburns, "Gene Vincent" hairdo,*[1] *two days' growth of beard, bad teeth*

SAUL KIMMER: *late forties, Hollywood producer, pink and white flower print sports shirt, white sports coat with matching polyester slacks, black and white loafers*

MOM: *early sixties, mother of the brothers, small woman, conservative white skirt and matching jacket, red shoulder bag, two pieces of matching red luggage*

True West was first performed at the Magic Theatre in San Francisco on July 10, 1980. The director was Robert Woodruff, and the cast was as follows:

AUSTIN	Peter Coyote
LEE	Jim Haynie
SAUL KIMMER	Tom Dahlgren
MOM	Carol McElheney

---

1. Pompadour style favored by some American rock 'n' roll musicians of the late 1950s.

SCENE: *All nine scenes take place on the same set; a kitchen and adjoining alcove of an older home in a Southern California suburb, about 40 miles east of Los Angeles. The kitchen takes up most of the playing area to stage left. The kitchen consists of a sink, upstage center, surrounded by counter space, a wall telephone, cupboards, and a small window just above it bordered by neat yellow curtains. Stage left of sink is a stove. Stage right, a refrigerator. The alcove adjoins the kitchen to stage right. There is no wall division or door to the alcove. It is open and easily accessible from the kitchen and defined only by the objects in it: a small round glass breakfast table mounted on white iron legs, two matching white iron chairs set across from each other. The two exterior walls of the alcove which prescribe a corner in the upstage right are composed of many small windows, beginning from a solid wall about three feet high and extending to the ceiling. The windows look out to bushes and citrus trees. The alcove is filled with all sorts of house plants in various pots, mostly Boston ferns hanging in planters at different levels. The floor of the alcove is composed of green synthetic grass.*

All entrances and exits are made stage left from the kitchen. There is no door. The actors simply go off and come onto the playing area.

NOTE ON SET AND COSTUME: *The set should be constructed realistically with no attempt to distort its dimensions, shapes, objects, or colors. No objects should be introduced which might draw special attention to themselves other than the props demanded by the script. If a stylistic "concept" is grafted onto the set design it will only serve to confuse the evolution of the characters' situation, which is the most important focus of the play.*

Likewise, the costumes should be exactly representative of who the characters are and not added onto for the sake of making a point to the audience.

NOTE ON SOUND: *The Coyote of Southern California has a distinct yapping, dog-like bark, similar to a Hyena. This yapping grows more intense and maniacal as the pack grows in numbers, which is usually the case when they lure and kill pets from suburban yards. The sense of growing frenzy in the pack should be felt in the background, particularly in Scenes 7 and 8. In any case, these Coyotes never make the long, mournful, solitary howl of the Hollywood stereotype.*

The sound of Crickets can speak for itself.

These sounds should also be treated realistically even though they sometimes grow in volume and numbers.

Act One

SCENE 1

Night. Sound of crickets in dark. Candlelight appears in alcove, illuminating AUSTIN, *seated at glass table hunched over a writing notebook, pen in hand, cigarette burning in ashtray, cup of coffee, typewriter on table, stacks of paper, candle burning on table.*

Soft moonlight fills kitchen illuminating LEE, *beer in hand, six-pack on counter behind him. He's leaning against the sink, mildly drunk; takes a slug of beer.*

LEE   So, Mom took off for Alaska, huh?
AUSTIN   Yeah.
LEE   Sorta' left you in charge.
AUSTIN   Well, she knew I was coming down here so she offered me the place.

LEE You keepin' the plants watered?

AUSTIN Yeah.

LEE Keepin' the sink clean? She don't like even a single tea leaf in the sink ya' know.

AUSTIN [*trying to concentrate on writing*] Yeah, I know.
[*Pause.*]

LEE She gonna' be up there a long time?

AUSTIN I don't know.

LEE Kinda' nice for you, huh? Whole place to yourself.

AUSTIN Yeah, it's great.

LEE Ya' got crickets anyway. Tons a' crickets out there. [*looks around kitchen*] Ya' got groceries? Coffee?

AUSTIN [*looking up from writing*] What?

LEE You got coffee?

AUSTIN Yeah.

LEE At's good, [*short pause*] Real coffee? From the bean?

AUSTIN Yeah. You want some?

LEE Naw. I brought some uh—[*motions to beer*]

AUSTIN Help yourself to whatever's—[*motions to refrigerator*]

LEE I will. Don't worry about me. I'm not the one to worry about. I mean I can uh—[*pause*] You always work by candlelight?

AUSTIN No—uh—Not always.

LEE Just sometimes?

AUSTIN [*puts pen down, rubs his eyes*] Yeah. Sometimes it's soothing.

LEE Isn't that what the old guys did?

AUSTIN What old guys?

LEE The Forefathers.[2] You know.

AUSTIN Forefathers?

LEE Isn't that what they did? Candlelight burning into the night? Cabins in the wilderness.

AUSTIN [*rubs hand through his hair*] I suppose.

LEE I'm not botherin' you am I? I mean I don't wanna break into yer uh—concentration or nothin'.

AUSTIN No, it's all right.

LEE That's good. I mean I realize that yer line a' work demands a lota' concentration.

AUSTIN It's okay.

LEE You probably think that I'm not fully able to comprehend somethin' like that, huh?

AUSTIN Like what?

LEE That stuff yer doin'. That art. You know. Whatever you call it.

AUSTIN It's just a little research.

LEE You may not know it but I did a little art myself once.

AUSTIN You did?

LEE Yeah! I did some a' that. I fooled around with it. No future in it.

AUSTIN What'd you do?

LEE Never mind what I did! Just never mind about that. [*pause*] It was ahead of its time.

---

2. Common term for the founders of the United States.

[*Pause.*]

AUSTIN So, you went out to see the old man, huh?

LEE Yeah, I seen him.

AUSTIN How's he doing?

LEE Same. He's doin' just about the same.

AUSTIN I was down there too, you know.

LEE What d'ya' want, an award? You want some kinda' medal? You were down there. He told me all about you.

AUSTIN What'd he say?

LEE He told me. Don't worry.

[*Pause.*]

AUSTIN Well—

LEE You don't have to say nothin'.

AUSTIN I wasn't.

LEE Yeah, you were gonna' make somethin' up. Somethin' brilliant.

[*Pause.*]

AUSTIN You going to be down here very long, Lee?

LEE Might be. Depends on a few things.

AUSTIN You got some friends down here?

LEE [*laughs*] I know a few people. Yeah.

AUSTIN Well, you can stay here as long as I'm here.

LEE I don't need your permission do I?

AUSTIN No.

LEE I mean she's my mother too, right?

AUSTIN Right.

LEE She might've just as easily asked me to take care of her place as you.

AUSTIN That's right.

LEE I mean I know how to water plants.

[*Long pause.*]

AUSTIN So you don't know how long you'll be staying then?

LEE Depends mostly on houses, ya' know.

AUSTIN Houses?

LEE Yeah. Houses. Electric devices. Stuff like that. I gotta' make a little tour first.

[*Short pause.*]

AUSTIN Lee, why don't you just try another neighborhood, all right?

LEE [*laughs.*] What'sa' matter with this neighborhood? This is a great neighborhood. Lush. Good class a' people. Not many dogs.

AUSTIN Well, our uh—Our mother just happens to live here. That's all.

LEE Nobody's gonna' know. All they know is somethin's missing. That's all. She'll never even hear about it. Nobody's gonna' know.

AUSTIN You're going to get picked up if you start walking around here at night.

LEE Me? I'm gonna' git picked up? What about you? You stick out like a sore thumb. Look at you. You think yer regular lookin'?

AUSTIN I've got too much to deal with here to be worrying about—

LEE Yer not gonna' have to worry about me! I've been doin' all right without you. I haven't been anywhere near you for five years! Now isn't that true?

AUSTIN Yeah.

LEE   So you don't have to worry about me. I'm a free agent.

AUSTIN   All right.

LEE   Now all I wanna' do is borrow yer car.

AUSTIN   No!

LEE   Just fer a day. One day.

AUSTIN   No!

LEE   I won't take it outside a twenty mile radius. I promise ya'. You can check the speedometer.

AUSTIN   You're not borrowing my car! That's all there is to it.
   [*Pause.*]

LEE   Then I'll just take the damn thing.

AUSTIN   Lee, look—I don't want any trouble, all right?

LEE   That's a dumb line. That is a dumb fuckin' line. You git paid fer dreamin' up a line like that?

AUSTIN   Look, I can give you some money if you need money.
   [LEE *suddenly lunges at* AUSTIN, *grabs him violently by the shirt and shakes him with tremendous power.*]

LEE   Don't you say that to me! Don't you ever say that to me! [*just as suddenly he turns him loose, pushes him away and backs off*] You may be able to git away with that with the Old Man. Git him tanked up for a week! Buy him off with yer Hollywood blood money, but not me! I can git my own money my own way. Big money!

AUSTIN   I was just making an offer.

LEE   Yeah, well keep it to yourself!
   [*Long pause.*]
Those are the most monotonous fuckin' crickets I ever heard in my life.

AUSTIN   I kinda' like the sound.

LEE   Yeah. Supposed to be able to tell the temperature by the number a' pulses. You believe that?

AUSTIN   The temperature?

LEE   Yeah. The air. How hot it is.

AUSTIN   How do you do that?

LEE   I don't know. Some woman told me that. She was a Botanist. So I believed her.

AUSTIN   Where'd you meet her?

LEE   What?

AUSTIN   The woman Botanist?

LEE   I met her on the desert. I been spendin' a lota' time on the desert.

AUSTIN   What were you doing out there?

LEE   [*pause, stares in space*]   I forgit. Had me a Pit Bull there for a while but I lost him.

AUSTIN   Pit Bull?

LEE   Fightin' dog. Damn I made some good money off that little dog. Real good money.
   [*Pause.*]

AUSTIN   You could come up north with me, you know.

LEE   What's up there?

AUSTIN   My family.

LEE   Oh, that's right, you got the wife and kiddies now don't ya'. The house, the car, the whole slam. That's right.

AUSTIN You could spend a couple days. See how you like it. I've got an extra room.

LEE Too cold up there.
     [*Pause.*]

AUSTIN You want to sleep for a while?

LEE [*pause, stares at* AUSTIN]   I don't sleep.
     [*Lights to black.*]

SCENE 2

Morning. AUSTIN *is watering plants with a vaporizer,* LEE *sits at glass table in alcove drinking beer.*

LEE I never realized the old lady was so security-minded.

AUSTIN How do you mean?

LEE Made a little tour this morning. She's got locks on everything. Locks and double-locks and chain locks and—What's she got that's so valuable?

AUSTIN Antiques I guess. I don't know.

LEE Antiques? Brought everything with her from the old place, huh. Just the same crap we always had around. Plates and spoons.

AUSTIN I guess they have personal value to her.

LEE Personal value. Yeah. Just a lota' junk. Most of it's phony anyway. Idaho decals. Now who in the hell wants to eat offa' plate with the State of Idaho starin' ya' in the face. Every time ya' take a bite ya' get to see a little bit more.

AUSTIN Well it must mean something to her or she wouldn't save it.

LEE Yeah, well personally I don't wann' be invaded by Idaho when I'm eatin'. When I'm eatin' I'm home. Ya' know what I'm sayin'? I'm not driftin', I'm home. I don't need my thoughts swept off to Idaho. I don't need that!
     [*Pause.*]

AUSTIN Did you go out last night?

LEE Why?

AUSTIN I thought I heard you go out.

LEE Yeah, I went out. What about it?

AUSTIN Just wondered.

LEE Damn coyotes kept me awake.

AUSTIN Oh yeah, I heard them. They must've killed somebody's dog or something.

LEE Yappin' their fool heads off. They don't yap like that on the desert. They howl. These are city coyotes here.

AUSTIN Well, you don't sleep anyway do you?
     [*Pause,* LEE *stares at him.*]

LEE You're pretty smart aren't ya?

AUSTIN How do you mean?

LEE I mean you never had any more on the ball than I did. But here you are gettin' invited into prominent people's houses. Sittin' around talkin' like you know somethin'.

AUSTIN They're not so prominent.

LEE They're a helluva' lot more prominent than the houses I get invited into.

AUSTIN   Well you invite yourself.

LEE   That's right. I do. In fact I probably got a wider range a' choices than you do, come to think of it.

AUSTIN   I wouldn't doubt it.

LEE   In fact I been inside some pretty classy places in my time. And I never even went to an Ivy League school either.

AUSTIN   You want some breakfast or something?

LEE   Breakfast?

AUSTIN   Yeah. Don't you eat breakfast?

LEE   Look, don't worry about me pal. I can take care a' myself. You just go ahead as though I wasn't even here, all right?
　　　[AUSTIN *goes into kitchen, makes coffee.*]

AUSTIN   Where'd you walk to last night?
　　　[*Pause.*]

LEE   I went up in the foothills there. Up in the San Gabriels.[3] Heat was drivin' me crazy.

AUSTIN   Well, wasn't it hot out on the desert?

LEE   Different kinda' heat. Out there it's clean. Cools off at night. There's a nice little breeze.

AUSTIN   Where were you, the Mojave?

LEE   Yeah. The Mojave. That's right.

AUSTIN   I haven't been out there in years.

LEE   Out past Needles there.

AUSTIN   Oh yeah.

LEE   Up here it's different. This country's real different.

AUSTIN   Well, it's been built up.

LEE   Built up? Wiped out is more like it. I don't even hardly recognize it.

AUSTIN   Yeah. Foothills are the same though, aren't they?

LEE   Pretty much. It's funny goin' up in there. The smells and everything. Used to catch snakes up there, remember?

AUSTIN   You caught snakes.

LEE   Yeah. And you'd pretend you were Geronimo or some damn thing. You used to go right out to lunch.

AUSTIN   I enjoyed my imagination.

LEE   That what you call it? Looks like yer still enjoyin' it.

AUSTIN   So you just wandered around up there, huh?

LEE   Yeah. With a purpose.

AUSTIN   See any houses?
　　　[*Pause.*]

LEE   Couple. Couple a' real nice ones. One of 'em didn't even have a dog. Walked right up and stuck my head in the window. Not a peep. Just a sweet kinda' surburban silence.

AUSTIN   What kind of a place was it?

LEE   Like a paradise. Kinda' place that sorta' kills ya' inside. Warm yellow lights. Mexican tile all around. Copper pots hangin' over the stove. Ya' know like they got in the magazines. Blonde people movin' in and outa'

3. Mountains between Los Angeles and the Mojave Desert in Southern California; the Mojave Desert stretches from this mountain barrier east of Los Angeles to Arizona and Nevada; Needles, mentioned below, is a city in California on the Colorado River in the Mojave Valley, which straddles the California-Arizona border.

the rooms, talkin' to each other. [*pause*] Kinda' place you wish you sorta' grew up in, ya' know.

AUSTIN   That's the kind of place you wish you'd grown up in?

LEE   Yeah, why not?

AUSTIN   I thought you hated that kind of stuff.

LEE   Yeah, well you never knew too much about me did ya'?
       [*Pause.*]

AUSTIN   Why'd you go out to the desert in the first place?

LEE   I was on my way to see the old man.

AUSTIN   You mean you just passed through there?

LEE   Yeah. That's right. Three months of passin' through.

AUSTIN   Three months?

LEE   Somethin' like that. Maybe more. Why?

AUSTIN   You lived on the Mojave for three months?

LEE   Yeah. What'sa' matter with that?

AUSTIN   By yourself?

LEE   Mostly. Had a couple a' visitors. Had that dog for a while.

AUSTIN   Didn't you miss people?

LEE [*laughs*]   People?

AUSTIN   Yeah. I mean I go crazy if I have to spend three nights in a motel by myself.

LEE   Yer not in a motel now.

AUSTIN   No, I know. But sometimes I have to stay in motels.

LEE   Well, they got people in motels don't they?

AUSTIN   Strangers.

LEE   Yer friendly aren't ya'? Aren't you the friendly type?
       [*Pause.*]

AUSTIN   I'm going to have somebody coming by here later, Lee.

LEE   Ah! Lady friend?

AUSTIN   No, a producer.

LEE   Aha! What's he produce?

AUSTIN   Film. Movies. You know.

LEE   Oh, movies. Motion Pictures! A Big Wig huh?

AUSTIN   Yeah.

LEE   What's he comin' by here for?

AUSTIN   We have to talk about a project.

LEE   Whadya' mean, "a project"? What's "a project"?

AUSTIN   A script.

LEE   Oh. That's what yer doin' with all these papers?

AUSTIN   Yeah.

LEE   Well, what's the project about?

AUSTIN   We're uh—it's a period piece.

LEE   What's "a period piece"?

AUSTIN   Look, it doesn't matter. The main thing is we need to discuss this alone. I mean—

LEE   Oh, I get it. You want me outa' the picture.

AUSTIN   Not exactly. I just need to be alone with him for a couple of hours. So we can talk.

LEE   Yer afraid I'll embarrass ya' huh?

AUSTIN   I'm not afraid you'll embarrass me!

LEE Well, I tell ya' what—Why don't you just gimme the keys to yer car and I'll be back here around six o'clock or so. That give ya' enough time?

AUSTIN I'm not loaning you my car, Lee.

LEE You want me to just git lost huh? Take a hike? Is that it? Pound the pavement for a few hours while you bullshit yer way into a million bucks.

AUSTIN Look, it's going to be hard enough for me to face this character on my own without—

LEE You don't know this guy?

AUSTIN No I don't know—He's a producer. I mean I've been meeting with him for months but you never get to know a producer.

LEE Yer tryin' to hustle him? Is that it?

AUSTIN I'm not trying to hustle him! I'm trying to work out a deal! It's not easy.

LEE What kinda' deal?

AUSTIN Convince him it's a worthwhile story.

LEE He's not convinced? How come he's comin' over here if he's not convinced? I'll convince him for ya'.

AUSTIN You don't understand the way things work down here.

LEE How do things work down here?

[*Pause.*]

AUSTIN Look, if I loan you my car will you have it back here by six?

LEE On the button. With a full tank a' gas.

AUSTIN [*digging in his pocket for keys*] Forget about the gas.

LEE Hey, these days gas is gold, old buddy.

[AUSTIN *hands the keys to* LEE.]

You remember that car I used to loan you?

AUSTIN Yeah.

LEE Forty Ford. Flathead.[4]

AUSTIN Yeah.

LEE Sucker hauled ass didn't it?

AUSTIN Lee, it's not that I don't want to loan you my car—

LEE You are loanin' me yer car.

[LEE *gives* AUSTIN *a pat on the shoulder, pause.*]

AUSTIN I know. I just wish—

LEE What? You wish what?

AUSTIN I don't know. I wish I wasn't—I wish I didn't have to be doing business down here. I'd like to just spend some time with you.

LEE I thought it was "Art" you were doin'.

[LEE *moves across kitchen toward exit, tosses keys in his hand.*]

AUSTIN Try to get it back here by six, okay?

LEE No sweat. Hey, ya' know, if that uh—story of yours doesn't go over with the guy—tell him I got a couple a' "projects" he might be interested in. Real commercial. Full a' suspense. True-to-life stuff.

[LEE *exits,* AUSTIN *stares after* LEE *then turns, goes to papers at table, leafs through pages, lights fade to black.*]

---

4. Type of internal combustion engine, here used in a 1940 Ford automobile, at this time popular as a hotrod.

SCENE 3

Afternoon. Alcove, SAUL KIMMER *and* AUSTIN *seated across from each other at table.*

SAUL   Well, to tell you the truth Austin, I have never felt so confident about a project in quite a long time.

AUSTIN   Well, that's good to hear, Saul.

SAUL   I am absolutely convinced we can get this thing off the ground. I mean we'll have to make a sale to television and that means getting a major star. Somebody bankable. But I think we can do it. I really do.

AUSTIN   Don't you think we need a first draft before we approach a star?

SAUL   No, no, not at all. I don't think it's necessary. Maybe a brief synopsis. I don't want you to touch the typewriter until we have some seed money.

AUSTIN   That's fine with me.

SAUL   I mean it's a great story. Just the story alone. You've really managed to capture something this time.

AUSTIN   I'm glad you like it, Saul.
   [LEE *enters abruptly into kitchen carrying a stolen television set, short pause.*]

LEE   Aw shit, I'm sorry about that. I am really sorry Austin.

AUSTIN [*standing*]   That's all right.

LEE [*moving toward them*]   I mean I thought it was way past six already. You said to have it back here by six.

AUSTIN   We were just finishing up. [*to Saul*]. This is my, uh—brother, Lee.

SAUL [*standing*]   Oh, I'm very happy to meet you.
   [LEE *sets T.V. on sink counter, shakes hands with* SAUL.]

LEE   I can't tell ya' how happy I am to meet you sir.

SAUL   Saul Kimmer.

LEE   Mr. Kipper.

SAUL   Kimmer.

AUSTIN   Lee's been living out on the desert and he just uh—

SAUL   Oh, that's terrific! [*to* LEE] Palm Springs?[5]

LEE   Yeah. Yeah, right. Right around in that area. Near uh—Bob Hope[6] Drive there.

SAUL   Oh I love it out there. I just love it. The air is wonderful.

LEE   Yeah. Sure is. Healthy.

SAUL   And the golf. I don't know if you play golf, but the golf is just about the best.

LEE   I play a lota' golf.

SAUL   Is that right?

LEE   Yeah. In fact I was hoping I'd run into somebody out here who played a little golf. I've been lookin' for a partner.

SAUL   Well, I uh—

AUSTIN   Lee's just down for a visit while our mother's in Alaska.

5. City in south-central California where streets are named for stars in the Hollywood entertainment industry.
6. American film comedian (1903–2003).

SAUL   Oh, your mother's in Alaska?

AUSTIN   Yes. She went up there on a little vacation. This is her place.

SAUL   I see. Well isn't that something. Alaska.

LEE   What kinda' handicap do ya' have, Mr. Kimmer?

SAUL   Oh I'm just a Sunday duffer really. You know.

LEE   That's good 'cause I haven't swung a club in months.

SAUL   Well we ought to get together sometime and have a little game. Austin, do you play?

[SAUL *mimes a Johnny Carson golf swing for* AUSTIN.]

AUSTIN   No. I don't uh—I've watched it on TV.

LEE   [*to* SAUL]   How 'bout tomorrow morning? Bright and early. We could get out there and put in eighteen holes before breakfast.

SAUL   Well, I've got uh—I have several appointments—

LEE   No, I mean real early. Crack a' dawn. While the dew's still thick on the fairway.

SAUL   Sounds really great.

LEE   Austin could be our caddie.

SAUL   Now that's an idea. [*laughs*]

AUSTIN   I don't know the first thing about golf.

LEE   There's nothin' to it. Isn't that right, Saul? He'd pick it up in fifteen minutes.

SAUL   Sure. Doesn't take long. 'Course you have to play for years to find your true form. [*chuckles*]

LEE   [*to* AUSTIN]   We'll give ya' a quick run-down on the club faces. The irons, the woods. Show ya' a couple pointers on the basic swing. Might even let ya' hit the ball a couple times. Whadya' think, Saul?

SAUL   Why not. I think it'd be great. I haven't had any exercise in weeks.

LEE   'At's the spirit! We'll have a little orange juice right afterwards.
    [*Pause.*]

SAUL   Orange juice?

LEE   Yeah! Vitamin C! Nothin' like a shot a' orange juice after a round a' golf. Hot shower. Snappin' towels at each others' privates. Real sense a' fraternity.

SAUL   [*smiles at* AUSTIN]   Well, you make it sound very inviting, I must say. It really does sound great.

LEE   Then it's a date.

SAUL   Well, I'll call the country club and see if I can arrange something.

LEE   Great! Boy, I sure am sorry that I busted in on ya' all in the middle of yer meeting.

SAUL   Oh that's quite all right. We were just about finished anyway.

LEE   I can wait out in the other room if you want.

SAUL   No really—

LEE   Just got Austin's color TV back from the shop. I can watch a little amateur boxing now.
    [LEE *and* AUSTIN *exchange looks.*]

SAUL   Oh—Yes.

LEE   You don't fool around in Television, do you Saul?

SAUL   Uh—I have in the past. Produced some TV Specials. Network stuff. But it's mainly features now.

LEE   That's where the big money is, huh?

SAUL   Yes. That's right.

AUSTIN   Why don't I call you tomorrow, Saul and we'll get together. We can have lunch or something.

SAUL   That'd be terrific.

LEE   Right after the golf.
        [*Pause.*]

SAUL   What?

LEE   You can have lunch right after the golf.

SAUL   Oh, right.

LEE   Austin was tellin' me that yer interested in stories.

SAUL   Well, we develop certain projects that we feel have commercial potential.

LEE   What kinda' stuff do ya' go in for?

SAUL   Oh, the usual. You know. Good love interest. Lots of action. [*chuckles at* AUSTIN]

LEE   Westerns?

SAUL   Sometimes.

AUSTIN   I'll give you a ring, Saul.
        [AUSTIN *tries to move* SAUL *across the kitchen but* LEE *blocks their way.*]

LEE   I got a Western that'd knock yer lights out.

SAUL   Oh really?

LEE   Yeah. Contemporary Western. Based on a true story. 'Course I'm not a writer like my brother here. I'm not a man of the pen.

SAUL   Well—

LEE   I mean I can tell ya' a story off the tongue but I can't put it down on paper. That don't make any difference though does it?

SAUL   No, not really.

LEE   I mean plenty a' guys have stories don't they? True-life stories. Musta' been a lota' movies made from real life.

SAUL   Yes. I suppose so.

LEE   I haven't seen a good Western since "Lonely Are the Brave."[7] You remember that movie?

SAUL   No, I'm afraid I—

LEE   Kirk Douglas. Helluva' movie. You remember that movie, Austin?

AUSTIN   Yes.

LEE   [*to* SAUL]   The man dies for the love of a horse.

SAUL   Is that right.

LEE   Yeah. Ya' hear the horse screamin' at the end of it. Rain's comin' down. Horse is screamin'. Then there's a shot. BLAM! Just a single shot like that. Then nothin' but the sound of rain. And Kirk Douglas is ridin' in the ambulance. Ridin' away from the scene of the accident. And when he hears that shot he knows that his horse has died. He knows. And you see his eyes. And his eyes die. Right inside his face. And then his eyes close. And you know that he's died too. You know that Kirk Douglas has died from the death of his horse.

SAUL   [*eyes* AUSTIN *nervously*]   Well, it sounds like a great movie. I'm sorry I missed it.

---

7. Film (1962) directed by David Miller, starring the American film actor Kirk Douglas (b. 1916).

LEE   Yeah, you shouldn't a' missed that one.

SAUL   I'll have to try to catch it some time. Arrange a screening or something. Well, Austin, I'll have to hit the freeway before rush hour.

AUSTIN [*ushers him toward exit*]   It's good seeing you, Saul.
      [AUSTIN *and* SAUL *shake hands.*]

LEE   So ya' think there's room for a real Western these days? A true-to-life Western?

SAUL   Well, I don't see why not. Why don't you uh—tell the story to Austin and have him write a little outline.

LEE   You'd take a look at it then?

SAUL   Yes. Sure. I'll give it a read-through. Always eager for new material.
      [*smiles at* AUSTIN]

LEE   That's great! You'd really read it then huh?

SAUL   It would just be my opinion of course.

LEE   That's all I want. Just an opinion. I happen to think it has a lota' possibilities.

SAUL   Well, it was great meeting you and I'll—
      [SAUL *and* LEE *shake.*]

LEE   I'll call you tomorrow about the golf.

SAUL   Oh. Yes, right.

LEE   Austin's got your number, right?

SAUL   Yes.

LEE   So long Saul. [*gives* SAUL *a pat on the back*]
      [SAUL *exits,* AUSTIN *turns to* LEE, *looks at T.V. then back to* LEE.]

AUSTIN   Give me the keys.
      [AUSTIN *extends his hand toward* LEE, LEE *doesn't move, just stares at* AUSTIN, *smiles, lights to black.*]

SCENE 4

Night. Coyotes in distance, fade, sound of typewriter in dark, crickets, candle-light in alcove, dim light in kitchen, lights reveal AUSTIN *at glass table typing,* LEE *sits across from him, foot on table, drinking beer and whiskey, the T.V. is still on sink counter,* AUSTIN *types for a while, then stops.*

LEE   All right, now read it back to me.

AUSTIN   I'm not reading it back to you, Lee. You can read it when we're finished. I can't spend all night on this.

LEE   You got better things to do?

AUSTIN   Let's just go ahead. Now what happens when he leaves Texas?

LEE   Is he ready to leave Texas yet? I didn't know we were that far along. He's not ready to leave Texas.

AUSTIN   He's right at the border.

LEE [*sitting up*]   No, see this is one a' the crucial parts. Right here. [*taps paper with beer can*] We can't rush through this. He's not right at the border. He's a good fifty miles from the border. A lot can happen in fifty miles.

AUSTIN   It's only an outline. We're not writing an entire script now.

LEE   Well ya' can't leave things out even if it is an outline. It's one a' the most important parts. Ya' can't go leavin' it out.

AUSTIN   Okay, okay. Let's just—get it done.

LEE   All right. Now. He's in the truck and he's got his horse trailer and his horse.

AUSTIN   We've already established that.

LEE   And he sees this other guy comin' up behind him in another truck. And that truck is pullin' a gooseneck.

AUSTIN   What's a gooseneck?

LEE   Cattle trailer. You know the kind with a gooseneck, goes right down in the bed a' the pick-up.

AUSTIN   Oh. All right. [*types*]

LEE   It's important.

AUSTIN   Okay. I got it.

LEE   All these details are important.
     [AUSTIN *types as they talk.*]

AUSTIN   I've got it.

LEE   And this other guy's got his horse all saddled up in the back a' the gooseneck.

AUSTIN   Right.

LEE   So both these guys have got their horses right along with 'em, see.

AUSTIN   I understand.

LEE   Then this first guy suddenly realizes two things.

AUSTIN   The guy in front?

LEE   Right. The guy in front realizes two things almost at the same time. Simultaneous.

AUSTIN   What were the two things?

LEE   Number one, he realizes that the guy behind him is the husband of the woman he's been—
     [LEE *makes gesture of screwing by pumping his arm.*]

AUSTIN   [*sees* LEE's *gesture*]   Oh. Yeah.

LEE   And number two, he realizes he's in the middle of Tornado Country.

AUSTIN   What's "Tornado Country"?

LEE   Panhandle.[8]

AUSTIN   Panhandle?

LEE   Sweetwater.[9] Around in that area. Nothin'. Nowhere. And number three—

AUSTIN   I thought there was only two.

LEE   There's three. There's a third unforeseen realization.

AUSTIN   And what's that?

LEE   That he's runnin' outa' gas.

AUSTIN   [*stops typing*]   Come on, Lee.
     [AUSTIN *gets up, moves to kitchen, gets a glass of water.*]

LEE   Whadya' mean, "come on"? That's what it is. Write it down! He's runnin' outa' gas.

AUSTIN   It's too—

LEE   What? It's too what? It's too real! That's what ya' mean isn't it? It's too much like real life!

---

8. Northern extension of Texas or western extension of Oklahoma.

9. City at the southern extreme of the Texas Panhandle.

AUSTIN   It's not like real life! It's not enough like real life. Things don't happen like that.

LEE   What! Men don't fuck other men's women?

AUSTIN   Yes. But they don't end up chasing each other across the Panhandle. Through "Tornado Country."

LEE   They do in this movie!

AUSTIN   And they don't have horses conveniently along with them when they run out of gas! And they don't run out of gas either!

LEE   These guys run outa' gas! This is my story and one a' these guys runs outa' gas!

AUSTIN   It's just a dumb excuse to get them into a chase scene. It's contrived.

LEE   It is a chase scene! It's already a chase scene. They been chasin' each other fer days.

AUSTIN   So now they're supposed to abandon their trucks, climb on their horses and chase each other into the mountains?

LEE   [*standing suddenly*]   There aren't any mountains in the Panhandle! It's flat!

> [LEE *turns violently toward windows in alcove and throws beer can at them.*]

LEE   Goddamn these crickets! [*yells at crickets*] Shut up out there! [*pause, turns back toward table*] This place is like a fuckin' rest home here. How're you supposed to think!

AUSTIN   You wanna' take a break?

LEE   No, I don't wanna' take a break! I wanna' get this done! This is my last chance to get this done.

AUSTIN   [*moves back into alcove*]   All right. Take it easy.

LEE   I'm gonna' be leavin' this area. I don't have time to mess around here.

AUSTIN   Where are you going?

LEE   Never mind where I'm goin'! That's got nothin' to do with you. I just gotta' get this done. I'm not like you. Hangin' around bein' a parasite offa' other fools. I gotta' do this thing and get out.

> [*Pause.*]

AUSTIN   A parasite? Me?

LEE   Yeah, you!

AUSTIN   After you break into people's houses and take their televisions?

LEE   They don't need their televisions! I'm doin' them a service.

AUSTIN   Give me back my keys, Lee.

LEE   Not until you write this thing! You're gonna' write this outline thing for me or that car's gonna' wind up in Arizona with a different paint job.

AUSTIN   You think you can force me to write this? I was doing you a favor.

LEE   Git off yer high horse will ya'! Favor! Big favor. Handin' down favors from the mountain top.

AUSTIN   Let's just write it, okay? Let's sit down and not get upset and see if we can just get through this.

> [AUSTIN *sits at typewriter.*]
> [*Long pause.*]

LEE   Yer not gonna' even show it to him, are ya'?

AUSTIN   What?

LEE   This outline. You got no intention of showin' it to him. Yer just doin' this 'cause yer afraid a' me.

AUSTIN   You can show it to him yourself.

LEE   I will, boy! I'm gonna' read it to him on the golf course.

AUSTIN   And I'm not afraid of you either.

LEE   Then how come yer doin' it?

AUSTIN   [*pause*]   So I can get my keys back.
   [*Pause as* LEE *takes keys out of his pocket slowly and throws them on table, long pause,* AUSTIN *stares at keys.*]

LEE   There. Now you got yer keys back.
   [AUSTIN *looks up at* LEE *but doesn't take keys.*]

LEE   Go ahead. There's yer keys.
   [AUSTIN *slowly takes keys off table and puts them back in his own pocket.*]
   Now what're you gonna' do? Kick me out?

AUSTIN   I'm not going to kick you out, Lee.

LEE   You couldn't kick me out, boy.

AUSTIN   I know.

LEE   So you can't even consider that one. [*pause*] You could call the police. That'd be the obvious thing.

AUSTIN   You're my brother.

LEE   That don't mean a thing. You go down to the L.A. Police Department there and ask them what kinda' people kill each other the most. What do you think they'd say?

AUSTIN   Who said anything about killing?

LEE   Family people. Brothers. Brothers-in-law. Cousins. Real American-type people. They kill each other in the heat mostly. In the Smog-Alerts. In the Brush Fire Season. Right about this time a' year.

AUSTIN   This isn't the same.

LEE   Oh no? What makes it different?

AUSTIN   We're not insane. We're not driven to acts of violence like that. Not over a dumb movie script. Now sit down.
   [*Long pause,* LEE *considers which way to go with it.*]

LEE   Maybe not. [*he sits back down at table across from* AUSTIN] Maybe you're right. Maybe we're too intelligent, huh? [*pause*] We got our heads on our shoulders. One of us has even got a Ivy League diploma. Now that means somethin' don't it? Doesn't that mean somethin'?

AUSTIN   Look, I'll write this thing for you, Lee. I don't mind writing it. I just don't want to get all worked up about it. It's not worth it. Now, come on. Let's just get through it, okay?

LEE   Nah. I think there's easier money. Lotsa' places I could pick up thousands. Maybe millions. I don't need this shit. I could go up to Sacramento Valley and steal me a diesel. Ten thousand a week dismantling one a' those suckers. Ten thousand a week!
   [LEE *opens another beer, puts his foot back up on table.*]

AUSTIN   No, really, look, I'll write it out for you. I think it's a great idea.

LEE   Nah, you got yer own work to do. I don't wanna' interfere with yer life.

AUSTIN   I mean it'd be really fantastic if you could sell this. Turn it into a movie. I mean it.

[*Pause.*]

LEE   Ya' think so huh?

AUSTIN   Absolutely. You could really turn your life around, you know. Change things.

LEE   I could get me a house maybe.

AUSTIN   Sure you could get a house. You could get a whole ranch if you wanted to.

LEE   [*laughs*] A ranch? I could get a ranch?

AUSTIN   'Course you could. You know what a screenplay sells for these days?

LEE   No. What's it sell for?

AUSTIN   A lot. A whole lot of money.

LEE   Thousands?

AUSTIN   Yeah. Thousands.

LEE   Millions?

AUSTIN   Well—

LEE   We could get the old man outa' hock then.

AUSTIN   Maybe.

LEE   Maybe? Whadya' mean, maybe?

AUSTIN   I mean it might take more than money.

LEE   You were just tellin' me it'd change my whole life around. Why wouldn't it change his?

AUSTIN   He's different.

LEE   Oh, he's of a different ilk huh?

AUSTIN   He's not gonna' change. Let's leave the old man out of it.

LEE   That's right. He's not gonna' change but I will. I'll just turn myself right inside out. I could be just like you then, huh? Sittin' around dreamin' stuff up. Gettin' paid to dream. Ridin' back and forth on the freeway just dreamin' my fool head off.

AUSTIN   It's not all that easy.

LEE   It's not, huh?

AUSTIN   No. There's a lot of work involved.

LEE   What's the toughest part? Deciding whether to jog or play tennis?
      [*Long pause.*]

AUSTIN   Well, look. You can stay here—do whatever you want to. Borrow the car. Come in and out. Doesn't matter to me. It's not my house. I'll help you write this thing or—not. Just let me know what you want. You tell me.

LEE   Oh. So now suddenly you're at my service. Is that it?

AUSTIN   What do you want to do Lee?
      [*Long pause,* LEE *stares at him then turns and dreams at windows.*]

LEE   I tell ya' what I'd do if I still had that dog. Ya' wanna' know what I'd do?

AUSTIN   What?

LEE   Head out to Ventura. Cook up a little match. God that little dog could bear down. Lota' money in dog fightin'. Big money.
      [*Pause.*]

AUSTIN   Why don't we try to see this through, Lee. Just for the hell of it. Maybe you've really got something here. What do you think?
      [*Pause,* LEE *considers.*]

LEE Maybe so. No harm in tryin' I guess. You think it's such a hot idea. Besides, I always wondered what'd be like to be you.

AUSTIN You did?

LEE Yeah, sure. I used to picture you walkin' around some campus with yer arms fulla' books. Blondes chasin' after ya'.

AUSTIN Blondes? That's funny.

LEE What's funny about it?

AUSTIN Because I always used to picture you somewhere.

LEE Where'd you picture me?

AUSTIN Oh, I don't know. Different places. Adventures. You were always on some adventure.

LEE Yeah.

AUSTIN And I used to say to myself, "Lee's got the right idea. He's out there in the world and here I am. What am I doing?"

LEE Well you were settin' yourself up for somethin'.

AUSTIN I guess.

LEE We better get started on this thing then.

AUSTIN Okay.

    [AUSTIN *sits up at typewriter, puts new paper in.*]

LEE Oh. Can I get the keys back before I forget?

    [AUSTIN *hesitates.*]

You said I could borrow the car if I wanted, right? Isn't that what you said?

AUSTIN Yeah. Right.

    [AUSTIN *takes keys out of his pocket, sets them on table,* LEE *takes keys slowly, plays with them in his hand.*]

LEE I could get a ranch, huh?

AUSTIN Yeah. We have to write it first though.

LEE Okay. Let's write it.

    [*Lights start dimming slowly to end of scene as* AUSTIN *types,* LEE *speaks.*]
So they take off after each other straight into an endless black prairie. The sun is just comin' down and they can feel the night on their backs. What they don't know is that each one of 'em is afraid, see. Each one separately thinks that he's the only one that's afraid. And they keep ridin' like that straight into the night. Not knowing. And the one who's chasin' doesn't know where the other one is taking him. And the one who's being chased doesn't know where he's going.

    [*Lights to black, typing stops in the dark, crickets fade.*]

Act Two

SCENE 5

Morning. LEE *at the table in alcove with a set of golf clubs in a fancy leather bag,* AUSTIN *at sink washing a few dishes.*

AUSTIN He really liked it, huh?

LEE He wouldn't a' gave me these clubs if he didn't like it.

AUSTIN He gave you the clubs?

LEE Yeah. I told ya' he gave me the clubs. The bag too.

AUSTIN   I thought he just loaned them to you.

LEE   He said it was part a' the advance. A little gift like. Gesture of his good faith.

AUSTIN   He's giving you an advance?

LEE   Now what's so amazing about that? I told ya' it was a good story. You even said it was a good story.

AUSTIN   Well that is really incredible Lee. You know how many guys spend their whole lives down here trying to break into this business? Just trying to get in the door?

LEE   [pulling clubs out of bag, testing them]   I got no idea. How many?
          [Pause.]

AUSTIN   How much of an advance is he giving you?

LEE   Plenty. We were talkin' big money out there. Ninth hole is where I sealed the deal.

AUSTIN   He made a firm commitment?

LEE   Absolutely.

AUSTIN   Well, I know Saul and he doesn't fool around when he says he likes something.

LEE   I thought you said you didn't know him.

AUSTIN   Well, I'm familiar with his tastes.

LEE   I let him get two up on me goin' into the back nine. He was sure he had me cold. You shoulda' seen his face when I pulled out the old pitching wedge and plopped it pin-high, two feet from the cup. He 'bout shit his pants. "Where'd a guy like you ever learn how to play golf like that?" he says.
          [LEE laughs, AUSTIN stares at him.]

AUSTIN   'Course there's no contract yet. Nothing's final until it's on paper.

LEE   It's final, all right. There's no way he's gonna' back out of it now. We gambled for it.

AUSTIN   Saul, gambled?

LEE   Yeah, sure. I mean he liked the outline already so he wasn't risking that much. I just guaranteed it with my short game.
          [Pause.]

AUSTIN   Well, we should celebrate or something. I think Mom left a bottle of champagne in the refrigerator. We should have a little toast.
          [AUSTIN gets glasses from cupboard, goes to refrigerator, pulls out bottle of champagne.]

LEE   You shouldn't oughta' take her champagne, Austin. She's gonna' miss that.

AUSTIN   Oh, she's not going to mind. She'd be glad we put it to good use. I'll get her another bottle. Besides, it's perfect for the occasion.
          [Pause.]

LEE   Yer gonna' get a nice fee fer writin' the script a' course. Straight fee.
          [AUSTIN stops, stares at LEE, puts glasses and bottle on table, pause.]

AUSTIN   I'm writing the script?

LEE   That's what he said. Said we couldn't hire a better screenwriter in the whole town.

AUSTIN   But I'm already working on a script. I've got my own project. I don't have time to write two scripts.

LEE   No, he said he was gonna' drop that other one.

[*Pause.*]

AUSTIN   What? You mean mine? He's going to drop mine and do yours instead?

LEE [*Smiles*]   Now look, Austin, it's jest beginner's luck ya' know. I mean I sank a fifty foot putt for this deal. No hard feelings.
[AUSTIN *goes to phone on wall, grabs it, starts dialing.*] He's not gonna' be in, Austin. Told me he wouldn't be in 'till late this afternoon.

AUSTIN   [*stays on phone, dialing, listens*] I can't believe this. I just can't believe it. Are you sure he said that? Why would he drop mine?

LEE   That's what he told me.

AUSTIN   He can't do that without telling me first. Without talking to me at least. He wouldn't just make a decision like that without talking to me!

LEE   Well I was kinda' surprised myself. But he was real enthusiastic about my story.
[AUSTIN *hangs up phone violently, paces.*]

AUSTIN   What'd he say! Tell me everything he said!

LEE   I been tellin' ya'! He said he liked the story a whole lot. It was the first authentic Western to come along in a decade.

AUSTIN   He liked that story! Your story?

LEE   Yeah! What's so surprisin' about that?

AUSTIN   It's stupid! It's the dumbest story I ever heard in my life.

LEE   Hey, hold on! That's my story yer talkin' about!

AUSTIN   It's a bullshit story! It's idiotic. Two lamebrains chasing each other across Texas! Are you kidding? Who do you think's going to go see a film like that?

LEE   It's not a film! It's a movie. There's a big difference. That's somethin' Saul told me.

AUSTIN   Oh he did, huh?

LEE   Yeah, he said, "In this business we make movies, American movies. Leave the films to the French."

AUSTIN   So you got real intimate with old Saul huh? He started pouring forth his vast knowledge of Cinema.

LEE   I think he liked me a lot, to tell ya' the truth. I think he felt I was somebody he could confide in.

AUSTIN   What'd you do, beat him up or something?

LEE [stands fast]   Hey, I've about had it with the insults buddy! You think yer the only one in the brain department here? Yer the only one that can sit around and cook things up? There's other people got ideas too, ya' know!

AUSTIN   You must've done something. Threatened him or something. Now what'd you do Lee?

LEE   I convinced him!
[LEE *makes sudden menacing lunge toward* AUSTIN, *wielding golf club above his head, stops himself, frozen moment, long pause,* LEE *lowers club.*]

AUSTIN   Oh, Jesus. You didn't hurt him did you?
[*Long silence,* LEE *sits back down at table.*]
Lee! Did you hurt him?

LEE   I didn't do nothin' to him! He liked my story. Pure and simple. He said it was the best story he's come across in a long, long time.

AUSTIN That's what he told me about my story! That's the same thing he said to me.

LEE Well, he musta' been lyin'. He musta' been lyin' to one of us anyway.

AUSTIN You can't come into this town and start pushing people around. They're gonna' put you away!

LEE I never pushed anybody around! I beat him fair and square. [*pause*] They can't touch me anyway. They can't put a finger on me. I'm gone. I can come in through the window and go out through the door. They never knew what hit 'em. You, yer stuck. Yer the one that's stuck. Not me. So don't be warnin' me what to do in this town.

[*Pause,* AUSTIN *crosses to table, sits at typewriter, rests.*]

AUSTIN Lee, come on, level with me will you? It doesn't make any sense that suddenly he'd throw my idea out the window. I've been talking to him for months. I've got too much at stake. Everything's riding on this project.

LEE What's yer idea?

AUSTIN It's just a simple love story.

LEE What kinda' love story?

AUSTIN [*stands, crosses into kitchen*] I'm not telling you!

LEE Ha! 'Fraid I'll steal it huh? Competition's gettin' kinda' close to home isn't it?

AUSTIN Where did Saul say he was going?

LEE He was gonna' take my story to a couple studios.

AUSTIN That's *my* outline you know! I wrote that outline! You've got no right to be peddling it around.

LEE You weren't ready to take credit for it last night.

AUSTIN Give me my keys!

LEE What?

AUSTIN The keys! I want my keys back!

LEE Where you goin'?

AUSTIN Just give me my keys! I gotta' take a drive. I gotta' get out of here for a while.

LEE Where you gonna' go, Austin?

AUSTIN [*pause*] I might just drive out to the desert for a while. I gotta' think.

LEE You can think here just as good. This is the perfect setup for thinkin'. We got some writin' to do here, boy. Now let's just have us a little toast. Relax. We're partners now.

[LEE *pops the cork of the champagne bottle, pours two drinks as the lights fade to black.*]

SCENE 6

Afternoon. LEE *and* SAUL *in kitchen,* AUSTIN *in alcove.*

LEE Now you tell him. You tell him, Mr. Kipper.

SAUL Kimmer.

LEE Kimmer. You tell him what you told me. He don't believe me.

AUSTIN I don't want to hear it.

SAUL It's really not a big issue, Austin. I was simply amazed by your brother's story and—

AUSTIN Amazed? You lost a bet! You gambled with my material!

SAUL That's really beside the point, Austin. I'm ready to go all the way with your brother's story. I think it has a great deal of merit.

AUSTIN I don't want to hear about it, okay? Go tell it to the executives! Tell it to somebody who's going to turn it into a package deal or something. A T.V. series. Don't tell it to me.

SAUL But I want to continue with your project too, Austin. It's not as though we can't do both. We're big enough for that aren't we?

AUSTIN "We"? *I* can't do both! I don't know about "we."

LEE [*to* SAUL] See, what'd I tell ya'. He's totally unsympathetic.

SAUL Austin, there's no point in our going to another screenwriter for this. It just doesn't make sense. You're brothers. You know each other. There's a familiarity with the material that just wouldn't be possible otherwise.

AUSTIN There's no familiarity with the material! None! I don't know what "Tornado Country" is. I don't know what a "gooseneck" is. And I don't want to know! [*pointing to* LEE] He's a hustler! He's a bigger hustler than you are! If you can't see that, then—

LEE [*to* AUSTIN] Hey, now hold on. I didn't have to bring this bone back to you, boy. I persuaded Saul here that you were the right man for the job. You don't have to go throwin' up favors in my face.

AUSTIN Favors! I'm the one who wrote the fuckin' outline! You can't even spell.

SAUL [*to* AUSTIN] Your brother told me about the situation with your father. [*Pause.*]

AUSTIN What? [*looks at* LEE]

SAUL That's right. Now we have a clear-cut deal here, Austin. We have big studio money standing behind this thing. Just on the basis of your outline.

AUSTIN [*to* SAUL] What'd he tell you about my father?

SAUL Well—that he's destitute. He needs money.

LEE That's right. He does.

[AUSTIN *shakes his head, stares at them both.*]

AUSTIN [*to* LEE] And this little assignment is supposed to go toward the old man? A charity project? Is that what this is? Did you cook this up on the ninth green too?

SAUL It's a big slice, Austin.

AUSTIN [*to* LEE] I gave him money! I already gave him money. You know that. He drank it all up!

LEE This is a different deal here.

SAUL We can set up a trust for your father. A large sum of money. It can be doled out to him in parcels so he can't misuse it.

AUSTIN Yeah, and who's doing the doling?

SAUL Your brother volunteered.

[AUSTIN *laughs.*]

LEE That's right. I'll make sure he uses it for groceries.

AUSTIN [*to* SAUL] I'm not doing this script! I'm not writing this crap for you or anybody else. You can't blackmail me into it. You can't threaten me into it. There's no way I'm doing it. So just give it up. Both of you.

[*Long pause.*]

SAUL Well, that's it then. I mean this is an easy three hundred grand. Just for a first draft. It's incredible, Austin. We've got three different studios all trying to cut each other's throats to get this material. In one morning. That's how hot it is.

AUSTIN Yeah, well you can afford to give me a percentage on the outline then. And you better get the genius here an agent before he gets burned.

LEE Saul's gonna' be my agent. Isn't that right, Saul?

SAUL That's right, [to AUSTIN] Your brother has really got something, Austin. I've been around too long not to recognize it. Raw talent.

AUSTIN He's got a lota' balls is what he's got. He's taking you right down the river.

SAUL Three hundred thousand, Austin. Just for a first draft. Now you've never been offered that kind of money before.

AUSTIN I'm not writing it.
[Pause.]

SAUL I see. Well—

LEE We'll just go to another writer then. Right, Saul? Just hire us somebody with some enthusiasm. Somebody who can recognize the value of a good story.

SAUL I'm sorry about this, Austin.

AUSTIN Yeah.

SAUL I mean I was hoping we could continue both things but now I don't see how it's possible.

AUSTIN So you're dropping my idea altogether. Is that it? Just trade horses in midstream? After all these months of meetings.

SAUL I wish there was another way.

AUSTIN I've got everything riding on this, Saul. You know that. It's my only shot. If this falls through—

SAUL I have to go with what my instincts tell me—

AUSTIN Your instincts!

SAUL My gut reaction.

AUSTIN You lost! That's your gut reaction. You lost a gamble. Now you're trying to tell me you like his story? How could you possibly fall for that story? It's as phony as Hoppalong Cassidy.[1] What do you see in it? I'm curious.

SAUL It has the ring of truth, Austin.

AUSTIN [Laughs] Truth?

LEE It is true.

SAUL Something about the real West.

AUSTIN Why? Because it's got horses? Because it's got grown men acting like little boys?

SAUL Something about the land. Your brother is speaking from experience.

AUSTIN So am I!

SAUL But nobody's interested in love these days, Austin. Let's face it.

LEE That's right.

---

1. Popular television Western in the early 1950s, based on the central character from motion pictures, mostly serials, produced between 1935 and 1948.

AUSTIN [*to* SAUL]   He's been camped out on the desert for three months. Talking to cactus. What's he know about what people wanna' see on the screen! I drive on the freeway every day. I swallow the smog. I watch the news in color. I shop in the Safeway.[2] I'm the one who's in touch! Not him!

SAUL   I have to go now, Austin.

[SAUL *starts to leave.*]

AUSTIN   There's no such thing as the West anymore! It's a dead issue! It's dried up, Saul, and so are you.

[SAUL *stops and turns to* AUSTIN.]

SAUL   Maybe you're right. But I have to take the gamble, don't I?

AUSTIN   You're a fool to do this, Saul.

SAUL   I've always gone on my hunches. Always. And I've never been wrong. [*to* LEE] I'll talk to you tomorrow, Lee.

LEE   All right, Mr. Kimmer.

SAUL   Maybe we could have some lunch.

LEE   Fine with me. [*smiles at* AUSTIN]

SAUL   I'll give you a ring.

[SAUL *exits, lights to black as brothers look at each other from a distance.*]

SCENE 7

Night. Coyotes, crickets, sound of typewriter in dark, candlelight up on LEE *at typewriter struggling to type with one finger system,* AUSTIN *sits sprawled out on kitchen floor with whiskey bottle, drunk.*

AUSTIN [*singing, from floor*]
"Red sails in the sunset
Way out on the blue
Please carry my loved one
Home safely to me

Red sails in the sunset—"[3]

LEE [*slams fist on table*]   Hey! Knock it off will ya'! I'm tryin' to concentrate here.

AUSTIN [*laughs*]   You're tryin' to concentrate?

LEE   Yeah. That's right.

AUSTIN   Now you're tryin' to concentrate.

LEE   Between you, the coyotes and the crickets a thought don't have much of a chance.

AUSTIN   "Between me, the coyotes and the crickets." What a great title.

LEE   I don't need a title! I need a thought.

AUSTIN [*laughs*]   A thought! Here's a thought for ya'—

LEE   I'm not askin' fer yer thoughts! I got my own. I can do this thing on my own.

AUSTIN   You're going to write an entire script on your own?

LEE   That's right.

[*Pause.*]

AUSTIN   Here's a thought. Saul Kimmer—

2. Major grocery store chain, mainly in California and throughout the West and Midwest.
3. From "Red Sails in the Sunset," American song

by Hugh Williams and Jimmy Kennedy published in 1935 and popularly revived in 1951 by Nat King Cole.

LEE Shut up will ya'!

AUSTIN He thinks we're the same person.

LEE Don't get cute.

AUSTIN He does! He's lost his mind. Poor old Saul. [*giggles*] Thinks we're one and the same.

LEE Why don't you ease up on that champagne.

AUSTIN [*holding up bottle*] This isn't champagne anymore. We went through the champagne a long time ago. This is serious stuff. The days of champagne are long gone.

LEE Well, go outside and drink it.

AUSTIN I'm enjoying your company, Lee. For the first time since your arrival I am finally enjoying your company. And now you want me to go outside and drink alone?

LEE That's right.

[LEE *reads through paper in typewriter, makes an erasure.*]

AUSTIN You think you'll make more progress if you're alone? You might drive yourself crazy.

LEE I could have this thing done in a night if I had a little silence.

AUSTIN Well you'd still have the crickets to contend with. The coyotes. The sounds of the Police Helicopters prowling above the neighborhood. Slashing their searchlights down through the streets. Hunting for the likes of you.

LEE I'm a screenwriter now! I'm legitimate.

AUSTIN [*laughing*] A screenwriter!

LEE That's right. I'm on salary. That's more'n I can say for you. I got an advance coming.

AUSTIN This is true. This is very true. An advance. [*pause*] Well, maybe I oughta' go out and try my hand at your trade. Since you're doing so good at mine.

LEE Ha!

[LEE *attempts to type some more but gets the ribbon tangled up, starts trying to re-thread it as they continue talking.*]

AUSTIN Well why not? You don't think I've got what it takes to sneak into people's houses and steal their T.V.s?

LEE You couldn't steal a toaster without losin' yer lunch.

[AUSTIN *stands with a struggle, supports himself by the sink.*]

AUSTIN You don't think I could sneak into somebody's house and steal a toaster?

LEE Go take a shower or somethin' will ya!

[LEE *gets more tangled up with the typewriter ribbon, pulling it out of the machine as though it was fishing line.*]

AUSTIN You really don't think I could steal a crumby toaster? How much you wanna' bet I can't steal a toaster! How much? Go ahead! You're a gambler aren't you? Tell me how much yer willing to put on the line. Some part of your big advance? Oh, you haven't got that yet have you. I forgot.

LEE All right. I'll bet you your car that you can't steal a toaster without gettin' busted.

AUSTIN You already got my car!

LEE Okay, your house then.

AUSTIN What're you gonna' give me! I'm not talkin' about my house and my car, I'm talkin' about what are you gonna' give me. You don't have nothin' to give me.

LEE I'll give you—shared screen credit. How 'bout that? I'll have it put in the contract that this was written by the both of us.

AUSTIN I don't want my name on that piece of shit! I want something of value. You got anything of value? You got any tidbits from the desert? Any Rattlesnake bones? I'm not a greedy man. Any little personal treasure will suffice.

LEE I'm gonna' just kick yer ass out in a minute.

AUSTIN Oh, so now you're gonna' kick me out! Now I'm the intruder. I'm the one who's invading your precious privacy.

LEE I'm trying to do some screenwriting here!!
    [LEE *stands, picks up typewriter, slams it down hard on table, pause, silence except for crickets.*]

AUSTIN Well, you got everything you need. You got plenty a' coffee? Groceries. You got a car. A contract. [*pause*] Might need a new typewriter ribbon but other than that you're pretty well fixed. I'll just leave ya' alone for a while.
    [AUSTIN *tries to steady himself to leave,* LEE *makes a move toward him.*]

LEE Where you goin'?

AUSTIN Don't worry about me. I'm not the one to worry about.
    [AUSTIN *weaves toward exit, stops.*]

LEE What're you gonna' do? Just go wander out into the night?

AUSTIN I'm gonna' make a little tour.

LEE Why don't ya' just go to bed for Christ's sake. Yer makin' me sick.

AUSTIN I can take care a' myself. Don't worry about me.
    [AUSTIN *weaves badly in another attempt to exit, he crashes to the floor,* LEE *goes to him but remains standing.*]

LEE You want me to call your wife for ya' or something?

AUSTIN [*from floor*] My wife?

LEE Yeah. I mean maybe she can help ya' out. Talk to ya' or somethin'.

AUSTIN [*struggles to stand again*] She's five hundred miles away. North. North of here. Up in the North country where things are calm. I don't need any help. I'm gonna' go outside and I'm gonna' steal a toaster. I'm gonna' steal some other stuff too. I might even commit bigger crimes. Bigger than you ever dreamed of. Crimes beyond the imagination!
    [AUSTIN *manages to get himself vertical, tries to head for exit again.*]

LEE Just hang on a minute, Austin.

AUSTIN Why? What for? You don't need my help, right? You got a handle on the project. Besides, I'm lookin' forward to the smell of the night. The bushes. Orange blossoms. Dust in the driveways. Rain bird sprinklers. Lights in people's houses. You're right about the lights, Lee. Everybody else is livin' the life. Indoors. Safe. This is a Paradise down here. You know that? We're livin' in a Paradise. We've forgotten about that.

LEE You sound just like the old man now.

AUSTIN Yeah, well we all sound alike when we're sloshed. We just sorta' echo each other.

LEE Maybe if we could work on this together we could bring him back out here. Get him settled down some place.

[AUSTIN *turns violently toward* LEE, *takes a swing at him, misses and crashes to the floor again,* LEE *stays standing.*]

AUSTIN   I don't want him out here! I've had it with him! I went all the way out there! I went out of my way. I gave him money and all he did was play Al Jolson[4] records and spit at me! I gave him money!
      [*Pause.*]

LEE   Just help me a little with the characters, all right? You know how to do it, Austin.

AUSTIN [*on floor, laughs*]   The characters!

LEE   Yeah. You know. The way they talk and stuff. I can hear it in my head but I can't get it down on paper.

AUSTIN   What characters?

LEE   The guys. The guys in the story.

AUSTIN   Those aren't characters.

LEE   Whatever you call 'em then. I need to write somethin' out.

AUSTIN   Those are illusions of characters.

LEE   I don't give a damn what ya' call 'em! You know what I'm talkin' about!

AUSTIN   Those are fantasies of a long lost boyhood.

LEE   I gotta' write somethin' out on paper!!
      [*Pause.*]

AUSTIN   What for? Saul's gonna' get you a fancy screenwriter isn't he?

LEE   I wanna' do it myself!

AUSTIN   Then do it! Yer on your own now, old buddy. You bulldogged yer way into contention. Now you gotta' carry it through.

LEE   I will but I need some advice. Just a couple a' things. Come on, Austin. Just help me get 'em talkin' right. It won't take much.

AUSTIN   Oh, now you're having a little doubt huh? What happened? The pressure's on, boy. This is it. You gotta' come up with it now. You don't come up with a winner on your first time out they just cut your head off. They don't give you a second chance ya' know.

LEE   I got a good story! I know it's a good story. I just need a little help is all.

AUSTIN   Not from me. Not from yer little old brother. I'm retired.

LEE   You could save this thing for me, Austin. I'd give ya' half the money. I would. I only need half anyway. With this kinda' money I could be a long time down the road. I'd never bother ya' again. I promise. You'd never even see me again.

AUSTIN [*still on floor*]   You'd disappear?

LEE   I would for sure.

AUSTIN   Where would you disappear to?

LEE   That don't matter. I got plenty a' places.

AUSTIN   Nobody can disappear. The old man tried that. Look where it got him. He lost his teeth.

LEE   He never had any money.

AUSTIN   I don't mean that. I mean his teeth! His real teeth. First he lost his real teeth, then he lost his false teeth. You never knew that did ya'? He never confided in you.

LEE   Nah, I never knew that.

---

4. American popular singer (1886–1950), depicted in blackface makeup on his record covers and in films; a purveyor of songs in the minstrel manner.

AUSTIN   You wanna' drink?
> [AUSTIN *offers bottle to* LEE, LEE *takes it, sits down on kitchen floor with* AUSTIN, *they share the bottle.*]

Yeah, he lost his real teeth one at a time. Woke up every morning with another tooth lying on the mattress. Finally, he decides he's gotta' get 'em all pulled out but he doesn't have any money. Middle of Arizona with no money and no insurance and every morning another tooth is lying on the mattress. [*takes a drink*] So what does he do?

LEE   I dunno'. I never knew about that.

AUSTIN   He begs the government. G.I. Bill[5] or some damn thing. Some pension plan he remembers in the back of his head. And they send him out the money.

LEE   They did?
> [*They keep trading the bottle between them, taking drinks.*]

AUSTIN   Yeah. They send him the money but it's not enough money. Costs a lot to have all yer teeth yanked. They charge by the individual tooth, ya' know. I mean one tooth isn't equal to another tooth. Some are more expensive. Like the big ones in the back—

LEE   So what happened?

AUSTIN   So he locates a Mexican dentist in Juarez[6] who'll do the whole thing for a song. And he takes off hitchhiking to the border.

LEE   Hitchhiking?

AUSTIN   Yeah. So how long you think it takes him to get to the border? A man his age.

LEE   I dunno.

AUSTIN   Eight days it takes him. Eight days in the rain and the sun and every day he's droppin' teeth on the blacktop and nobody'll pick him up 'cause his mouth's full a' blood.
> [*Pause, they drink.*]

So finally he stumbles into the dentist. Dentist takes all his money and all his teeth. And there he is, in Mexico, with his gums sewed up and his pockets empty.
> [*Long silence,* AUSTIN *drinks.*]

LEE   That's it?

AUSTIN   Then I go out to see him, see. I go out there and I take him out for a nice Chinese dinner. But he doesn't eat. All he wants to do is drink Martinis outa' plastic cups. And he takes his teeth out and lays 'em on the table 'cause he can't stand the feel of 'em. And we ask the waitress for one a' those doggie bags to take the Chop Suey home in. So he drops his teeth in the doggie bag along with the Chop Suey. And then we go out to hit all the bars up and down the highway. Says he wants to introduce me to all his buddies. And in one a' those bars, in one a' those bars up and down the highway, he left that doggie bag with his teeth laying in the Chop Suey.

LEE   You never found it?

AUSTIN   We went back but we never did find it. [*pause*] Now that's a true story. True to life.
> [*They drink as lights fade to black.*]

---

5. Post–World War II legislation according housing and educational benefits to military veterans.

6. Mexican city immediately across the Rio Grande from El Paso, Texas.

SCENE 8

*Very early morning, between night and day. No crickets, coyotes yapping fever-
ishly in distance before light comes up, a small fire blazes up in the dark from
alcove area, sound of* LEE *smashing typewriter with a golf club, lights coming
up,* LEE *seen smashing typewriter methodically then dropping pages of his script
into a burning bowl set on the floor of alcove, flames leap up,* AUSTIN *has a whole
bunch of stolen toasters lined up on the sink counter along with* LEE's *stolen T.V.,
the toasters are of a wide variety of models, mostly chrome,* AUSTIN *goes up and
down the line of toasters, breathing on them and polishing them with a dish
towel, both men are drunk, empty whiskey bottles and beer cans litter floor of
kitchen, they share a half empty bottle on one of the chairs in the alcove,* LEE
*keeps periodically taking deliberate ax-chops at the typewriter using a nine-iron
as* AUSTIN *speaks, all of their mother's house plants are dead and drooping.*

AUSTIN [*polishing toasters*]   There's gonna' be a general lack of toast in the
neighborhood this morning. Many, many unhappy, bewildered breakfast faces. I guess it's best not to even think of the victims. Not to even
entertain it. Is that the right psychology?

LEE [*pause*]   What?

AUSTIN   Is that the correct criminal psychology? Not to think of the victims?

LEE   What victims?
[LEE *takes another swipe at typewriter with nine-iron, adds pages to the
fire.*]

AUSTIN   The victims of crime. Of breaking and entering. I mean is it a
prerequisite for a criminal not to have a conscience?

LEE   Ask a criminal.
[*Pause,* LEE *stares at* AUSTIN.]
What're you gonna' do with all those toasters? That's the dumbest thing
I ever saw in my life.

AUSTIN   I've got hundreds of dollars worth of household appliances here.
You may not realize that.

LEE   Yeah, and how many hundreds of dollars did you walk right past?

AUSTIN   It was toasters you challenged me to. Only toasters. I ignored
every other temptation.

LEE   I never challenged you! That's no challenge. Anybody can steal a
toaster.
[LEE *smashes typewriter again.*]

AUSTIN   You don't have to take it out on my typewriter ya' know. It's not
the machine's fault that you can't write. It's a sin to do that to a good
machine.

LEE   A sin?

AUSTIN   When you consider all the writers who never even had a
machine. Who would have given an eyeball for a good typewriter. Any
typewriter.
[LEE *smashes typewriter again.*]

AUSTIN [*polishing toaster*]   All the ones who wrote on matchbook covers.
Paper bags. Toilet paper. Who had their writing destroyed by their jailers.
Who persisted beyond all odds. Those writers would find it hard to
understand your actions.

[LEE *comes down on typewriter with one final crushing blow of the nine-iron then collapses in one of the chairs, takes a drink from bottle, pause.*]

AUSTIN [*after pause*]   Not to mention demolishing a perfectly good golf club. What about all the struggling golfers? What about Lee Trevino?[7] What do you think he would've said when he was batting balls around with broomsticks at the age of nine. Impoverished.

[*Pause.*]

LEE   What time is it anyway?

AUSTIN   No idea. Time stands still when you're havin' fun.

LEE   Is it too late to call a woman? You know any women?

AUSTIN   I'm a married man.

LEE   I mean a local woman.

[AUSTIN *looks out at light through window above sink.*]

AUSTIN   It's either too late or too early. You're the nature enthusiast. Can't you tell the time by the light in the sky? Orient yourself around the North Star or something?

LEE   I can't tell anything.

AUSTIN   Maybe you need a little breakfast. Some toast! How 'bout some toast?

[AUSTIN *goes to cupboard, pulls out loaf of bread and starts dropping slices into every toaster, LEE stays sitting, drinks, watches AUSTIN.*]

LEE   I don't need toast. I need a woman.

AUSTIN   A woman isn't the answer. Never was.

LEE   I'm not talkin' about permanent. I'm talkin' about temporary.

AUSTIN [*putting toast in toasters*]   We'll just test the merits of these little demons. See which brands have a tendency to burn. See which one can produce a perfectly golden piece of fluffy toast.

LEE   How much gas you got in yer car?

AUSTIN   I haven't driven my car for days now. So I haven't had an opportunity to look at the gas gauge.

LEE   Take a guess. You think there's enough to get me to Bakersfield?[8]

AUSTIN   Bakersfield? What's in Bakersfield?

LEE   Just never mind what's in Bakersfield! You think there's enough goddamn gas in the car!

AUSTIN   Sure.

LEE   Sure. You could care less, right. Let me run outa' gas on the Grapevine.[9] You could give a shit.

AUSTIN   I'd say there was enough gas to get you just about anywhere, Lee. With your determination and guts.

LEE   What the hell time is it anyway?

[LEE *pulls out his wallet, starts going through dozens of small pieces of paper with phone numbers written on them, drops some on the floor, drops others in the fire.*]

AUSTIN   Very early. This is the time of morning when the coyotes kill people's cocker spaniels. Did you hear them? That's what they were doing out there. Luring innocent pets away from their homes.

---

7. American golf champion (b. 1939).
8. City in Kern County, California, about 115 miles north-northwest of Los Angeles.

9. Steep, winding section of the Ridge Route, the highway linking Los Angeles and Bakersfield.

LEE [*searching through his papers*]   What's the area code for Bakersfield? You know?

AUSTIN   You could always call the operator.

LEE   I can't stand that voice they give ya'.

AUSTIN   What voice?

LEE   That voice that warns you that if you'd only tried harder to find the number in the phone book you wouldn't have to be calling the operator to begin with.

> [LEE *gets up, holding a slip of paper from his wallet, stumbles toward phone on wall, yanks receiver, starts dialing.*]

AUSTIN   Well I don't understand why you'd want to talk to anybody else anyway. I mean you can talk to me. I'm your brother.

LEE [*dialing*]   I wanna' talk to a woman. I haven't heard a woman's voice in a long time.

AUSTIN   Not since the Botanist?

LEE   What?

AUSTIN   Nothing. [*starts singing as he tends toast*]
"Red sails in the sunset
Way out on the blue
Please carry my loved one
Home safely to me"

LEE   Hey, knock it off will ya'! This is long distance here.

AUSTIN   Bakersfield?

LEE   Yeah, Bakersfield. It's Kern County.

AUSTIN   Well, what County are *we* in?

LEE   You better get yourself a 7-Up, boy.

AUSTIN   One County's as good as another.

> [AUSTIN *hums "Red Sails" softly as* LEE *talks on phone.*]

LEE [*to phone*]   Yeah, operator look—first off I wanna' know the area code for Bakersfield. Right. Bakersfield! Okay. Good. Now I wanna' know if you can help me track somebody down. [*pause*] No, no I mean a phone number. Just a phone number. Okay. [*holds a piece of paper up and reads it*] Okay, the name is Melly Ferguson. Melly. [*pause*] I dunno'. Melly. Maybe. Yeah. Maybe Melanie. Yeah. Melanie Ferguson. Okay. [*pause*] What? I can't hear ya' so good. Sounds like yer under the ocean. [*pause*] You got ten Melanie Fergusons? How could that be? Ten Melanie Fergusons in Bakersfield? Well gimme all of 'em then. [*pause*] What d'ya' mean? Gimmie all ten Melanie Fergusons! That's right. Just a second. [*to* AUSTIN] Gimme a pen.

AUSTIN   I don't have a pen.

LEE   Gimme a pencil then!

AUSTIN   I don't have a pencil.

LEE [*to phone*]   Just a second, operator. [*to* AUSTIN] Yer a writer and ya' don't have a pen or a pencil!

AUSTIN   I'm not a writer. You're a writer.

LEE   I'm on the phone here! Get me a pen or a pencil.

AUSTIN   I gotta' watch the toast.

LEE [*to phone*]   Hang on a second, operator.

> [LEE *lets the phone drop then starts pulling all the drawers in the kitchen out on the floor and dumping the contents, searching for a pencil,* AUSTIN *watches him casually.*]

LEE [*crashing through drawers, throwing contents around kitchen*] This is the last time I try to live with people, boy! I can't believe it. Here I am! Here I am again in a desperate situation! This would never happen out on the desert. I would never be in this kinda' situation out on the desert. Isn't there a pen or a pencil in this house! Who lives in this house anyway!

AUSTIN Our mother.

LEE How come she don't have a pen or a pencil! She's a social person isn't she? Doesn't she have to make shopping lists? She's gotta' have a pencil. [*finds a pencil*] Aaha! [*he rushes back to phone, picks up receiver*] All right operator. Operator? Hey! Operator! Goddamnit!
[LEE *rips the phone off the wall and throws it down, goes back to chair and falls into it, drinks, long pause.*]

AUSTIN She hung up?

LEE Yeah, she hung up. I knew she was gonna' hang up. I could hear it in her voice.
[LEE *starts going through his slips of paper again.*]

AUSTIN Well, you're probably better off staying here with me anyway. I'll take care of you.

LEE I don't need takin' care of! Not by you anyway.

AUSTIN Toast is almost ready.
[AUSTIN *starts buttering all the toast as it pops up.*]

LEE I don't want any toast!
[*Long pause.*]

AUSTIN You gotta' eat something. Can't just drink. How long have we been drinking, anyway?

LEE [*looking through slips of paper*] Maybe it was Fresno.[1] What's the area code for Fresno? How could I have lost that number! She was beautiful.
[*Pause.*]

AUSTIN Why don't you just forget about that, Lee. Forget about the woman.

LEE She had green eyes. You know what green eyes do to me?

AUSTIN I know but you're not gonna' get it on with her now anyway. It's dawn already. She's in Bakersfield for Christ's sake.
[*Long pause, LEE considers the situation.*]

LEE Yeah, [*looks at windows*] It's dawn?

AUSTIN Let's just have some toast and—

LEE What is this bullshit with the toast anyway! You make it sound like salvation or something. I don't want any goddamn toast! How many times I gotta' tell ya'! [LEE *gets up, crosses upstage to windows in alcove, looks out,* AUSTIN *butters toast*]

AUSTIN Well it is like salvation sort of. I mean the smell. I love the smell of toast. And the sun's coming up. It makes me feel like anything's possible. Ya' know?

LEE [*back to* AUSTIN, *facing windows upstage*] So go to church why don't ya'.

AUSTIN Like a beginning. I love beginnings.

LEE Oh yeah. I've always been kinda' partial to endings myself.

AUSTIN What if I come with you, Lee?

LEE [*pause as* LEE *turns toward* AUSTIN] What?

AUSTIN What if I come with you out to the desert?

LEE Are you kiddin'?

---

1. City in central California.

AUSTIN   No. I'd just like to see what it's like.

LEE   You wouldn't last a day out there pal.

AUSTIN   That's what you said about the toasters. You said I couldn't steal a toaster either.

LEE   A toaster's got nothin' to do with the desert.

AUSTIN   I could make it, Lee. I'm not that helpless. I can cook.

LEE   Cook?

AUSTIN   I can.

LEE   So what! You can cook. Toast.

AUSTIN   I can make fires. I know how to get fresh water from condensation.

[AUSTIN *stacks buttered toast up in a tall stack on plate.*]
[LEE *slams table.*]

LEE   It's not somethin' you learn out of a Boy Scout handbook!

AUSTIN   Well how do you learn it then! How're you supposed to learn it!
[*Pause.*]

LEE   Ya' just learn it, that's all. Ya' learn it 'cause ya' have to learn it. You don't *have* to learn it.

AUSTIN   You could teach me.

LEE   [*stands*]   What're you, crazy or somethin'? You went to college. Here, you are down here, rollin' in bucks. Floatin' up and down in elevators. And you wanna' learn how to live on the desert!

AUSTIN   I do, Lee. I really do. There's nothin' down here for me. There never was. When we were kids here it was different. There was a life here then. But now—I keep comin' down here thinkin' it's the fifties or somethin'. I keep finding myself getting off the freeway at familiar landmarks that turn out to be unfamiliar. On the way to appointments. Wandering down streets I thought I recognized that turn out to be replicas of streets I remember. Streets I misremember. Streets I can't tell if I lived on or saw in a postcard. Fields that don't even exist anymore.

LEE   There's no point cryin' about that now.

AUSTIN   There's nothin' real down here, Lee! Least of all me!

LEE   Well I can't save you from that!

AUSTIN   You can let me come with you.

LEE   No dice, pal.

AUSTIN   You could let me come with you, Lee!

LEE   Hey, do you actually think I chose to live out in the middle a' nowhere? Do ya'? Ya' think it's some kinda' philosophical decision I took or somethin'? I'm livin' out there 'cause I can't make it here! And yer bitchin' to me about all yer success!

AUSTIN   I'd cash it all in in a second. That's the truth.

LEE   [*Pause, shakes his head*]   I can't believe this.

AUSTIN   Let me go with you.

LEE   Stop sayin' that will ya'! Yer worse than a dog.

[AUSTIN *offers out the plate of neatly stacked toast to* LEE.]

AUSTIN   You want some toast?

[LEE *suddenly explodes and knocks the plate out of* AUSTIN'S *hand, toast goes flying, long frozen moment where it appears* LEE *might go all the way this time when* AUSTIN *breaks it by slowly lowering himself to his knees and begins gathering the scattered toast from the floor and stacking it back on the plate,* LEE *begins to circle* AUSTIN *in a slow, predatory way, crushing pieces of toast in his wake, no words for a while,* AUSTIN *keeps gathering toast, even the crushed pieces.*]

LEE   Tell ya' what I'll do, little brother. I might just consider makin' you a deal. Little trade, [AUSTIN *continues gathering toast as* LEE *circles him through this*] You write me up this screenplay thing just like I tell ya'. I mean you can use all yer usual tricks and stuff. Yer fancy language. Yer artistic hocus pocus. But ya' gotta' write everything like I say. Every move. Every time they run outa' gas, they run outa' gas. Every time they wanna' jump on a horse, they do just that. If they wanna' stay in Texas, by God they'll stay in Texas! [*Keeps circling*] And you finish the whole thing up for me. Top to bottom. And you put my name on it. And I own all the rights. And every dime goes in my pocket. You do that and I'll sure enough take ya' with me to the desert, [LEE *stops, pause, looks down at* AUSTIN] How's that sound?

[*Pause as* AUSTIN *stands slowly holding plate of demolished toast, their faces are very close, pause.*]

AUSTIN   It's a deal.

[LEE *stares straight into* AUSTIN's *eyes, then he slowly takes a piece of toast off the plate, raises it to his mouth and takes a huge crushing bite never taking his eyes off* AUSTIN's, *as* LEE *crunches into the toast the lights black out.*]

SCENE 9

Midday. No sound, blazing heat, the stage is ravaged; bottles, toasters, smashed typewriter, ripped out telephone, etc. All the debris from previous scene is now starkly visible in intense yellow light, the effect should be like a desert junkyard at high noon, the coolness of the preceding scenes is totally obliterated. AUSTIN *is seated at table in alcove, shirt open, pouring with sweat, hunched over a writing notebook, scribbling notes desperately with a ballpoint pen.* LEE *with no shirt, beer in hand, sweat pouring down his chest, is walking a slow circle around the table, picking his way through the objects, sometimes kicking them aside.*

LEE [*as he walks*]   All right, read it back to me. Read it back to me!

AUSTIN [*scribbling at top speed*]   Just a second.

LEE   Come on, come on! Just read what ya' got.

AUSTIN   I can't keep up! It's not the same as if I had a typewriter.

LEE   Just read what we got so far. Forget about the rest.

AUSTIN   All right. Let's see—okay—[*wipes sweat from his face, reads as* LEE *circles*] Luke says uh—

LEE   Luke?

AUSTIN   Yeah.

LEE   His name's Luke? All right, all right—we can change the names later. What's he say? Come on, come on.

AUSTIN   He says uh—[*reading*] "I told ya' you were a fool to follow me in here. I know this prairie like the back a' my hand."

LEE   No, no, no! That's not what I said. I never said that.

AUSTIN   That's what I wrote.

LEE   It's not what I said. I never said "like the back a' my hand." That's stupid. That's one a' those—whadya' call it? Whadya' call that?

AUSTIN What?

LEE Whadya' call it when somethin's been said a thousand times before. Whadya' call that?

AUSTIN Um—a cliché?

LEE Yeah. That's right. Cliché. That's what that is. A cliché. "The back a' my hand." That's stupid.

AUSTIN That's what you said.

LEE I never said that! And even if I did, that's where yer supposed to come in. That's where yer supposed to change it to somethin' better.

AUSTIN Well how am I supposed to do that and write down what you say at the same time?

LEE Ya' just do, that's all! You hear a stupid line you change it. That's yer job.

AUSTIN All right, [makes more notes]

LEE What're you changin' it to?

AUSTIN I'm not changing it. I'm just trying to catch up.

LEE Well change it! We gotta' change that, we can't leave that in there like that. ". . . the back a' my hand." That's dumb.

AUSTIN [stops writing, sits back] All right.

LEE [pacing] So what'll we change it to?

AUSTIN Um—How 'bout—"I'm on intimate terms with this prairie."

LEE [to himself considering line as he walks] "I'm on intimate terms with this prairie." Intimate terms, intimate terms. Intimate—that means like uh—sexual right?

AUSTIN Well—yeah—or—

LEE He's on sexual terms with the prairie? How dya' figure that?

AUSTIN Well it doesn't necessarily have to mean sexual.

LEE What's it mean then?

AUSTIN It means uh—close—personal—

LEE All right. How's it sound? Put it into the uh—the line there. Read it back. Let's see how it sounds. [to himself]. "Intimate terms."

AUSTIN [scribbles in notebook] Okay. It'd go something like this: [reads] "I told ya' you were a fool to follow me in here. I'm on intimate terms with this prairie."

LEE That's good. I like that. That's real good.

AUSTIN You do?

LEE Yeah. Don't you?

AUSTIN Sure.

LEE Sounds original now. "Intimate terms." That's good. Okay. Now we're cookin! That has a real ring to it.

> [AUSTIN makes more notes, LEE walks around, pours beer on his arms and rubs it over his chest feeling good about the new progress, as he does this MOM enters unobtrusively down left with her luggage, she stops and stares at the scene still holding luggage as the two men continue, unaware of her presence, AUSTIN absorbed in his writing, LEE cooling himself off with beer.]

LEE [continues] "He's on intimate terms with this prairie." Sounds real mysterious and kinda' threatening at the same time.

AUSTIN [writing rapidly] Good.

LEE Now—[LEE *turns and suddenly sees* MOM, *he stares at her for a while,
she stares back,* AUSTIN *keeps writing feverishly, not noticing,* LEE *walks
slowly over to* MOM *and takes a closer look, long pause.*]

LEE Mom?
[AUSTIN *looks up suddenly from his writing, sees* MOM, *stands quickly,
long pause,* MOM *surveys the damage.*]

AUSTIN Mom. What're you doing back?

MOM I'm back.

LEE Here, lemme take those for ya.
[LEE *sets beer on counter then takes both her bags but doesn't know
where to set them down in the sea of junk so he just keeps holding them.*]

AUSTIN I wasn't expecting you back so soon. I thought uh—How was
Alaska?

MOM Fine.

LEE See any igloos?

MOM No. Just glaciers.

AUSTIN Cold huh?

MOM What?

AUSTIN It must've been cold up there?

MOM Not really.

LEE Musta' been colder than this here. I mean we're havin' a real scorcher
here.

MOM Oh? [*she looks at damage*]

LEE Yeah. Must be in the hundreds.

AUSTIN You wanna' take your coat off, Mom?

MOM No. [*pause, she surveys space*] What happened in here?

AUSTIN Oh um—Me and Lee were just sort of celebrating and uh—

MOM Celebrating?

AUSTIN Yeah. Uh—Lee sold a screenplay. A story, I mean.

MOM Lee did?

AUSTIN Yeah.

MOM Not you?

AUSTIN No. Him.

MOM [*to* LEE] You sold a screenplay?

LEE Yeah. That's right. We're just sorta' finishing it up right now. That's
what we're doing here.

AUSTIN Me and Lee are going out to the desert to live.

MOM You and Lee?

AUSTIN Yeah. I'm taking off with Lee.

MOM [*she looks back and forth at each of them, pause*] You gonna go live
with your father?

AUSTIN No. We're going to a different desert Mom.

MOM I see. Well, you'll probably wind up on the same desert sooner or
later. What're all these toasters doing here?

AUSTIN Well—we had kind of a contest.

MOM Contest?

LEE Yeah.

AUSTIN Lee won.

MOM Did you win a lot of money, Lee?

LEE   Well not yet. It's comin' in any day now.

MOM   [*to* LEE]   What happened to your shirt?

LEE   Oh. I was sweatin' like a pig and I took it off.
      [AUSTIN *grabs* LEE's *shirt off the table and tosses it to him,* LEE *sets down suitcases and puts his shirt on.*]

MOM   Well it's one hell of a mess in here isn't it?

AUSTIN   Yeah, I'll clean it up for you, Mom. I just didn't know you were coming back so soon.

MOM   I didn't either.

AUSTIN   What happened?

MOM   Nothing. I just started missing all my plants.
      [*She notices dead plants.*]

AUSTIN   Oh.

MOM   Oh, they're all dead aren't they, [*she crosses toward them, examines them closely*] You didn't get a chance to water I guess.

AUSTIN   I was doing it and then Lee came and—

LEE   Yeah I just distracted him a whole lot here, Mom. It's not his fault.
      [*Pause, as* MOM *stares at plants.*]

MOM   Oh well, one less thing to take care of I guess, [*turns toward brothers*] Oh, that reminds me—You boys will probably never guess who's in town. Try and guess.
      [*Long pause, brothers stare at her.*]

AUSTIN   Whadya' mean, Mom?

MOM   Take a guess. Somebody very important has come to town. I read it, coming down on the Greyhound.

LEE   Somebody very important?

MOM   See if you can guess. You'll never guess.

AUSTIN   Mom—we're trying to uh—[*points to writing pad*]

MOM   Picasso.[1] [*pause*] Picasso's in town. Isn't that incredible? Right now.
      [*Pause.*]

AUSTIN   Picasso's dead, Mom.

MOM   No, he's not dead. He's visiting the museum. I read it on the bus. We have to go down there and see him.

AUSTIN   Mom—

MOM   This is the chance of a lifetime. Can you imagine? We could all go down and meet him. All three of us.

LEE   Uh—I don't think I'm really up fer meetin' anybody right now. I'm uh—What's his name?

MOM   Picasso! Picasso! You've never heard of Picasso? Austin, you've heard of Picasso.

AUSTIN   Mom, we're not going to have time.

MOM   It won't take long. We'll just hop in the car and go down there. An opportunity like this doesn't come along every day.

AUSTIN   We're gonna' be leavin' here, Mom!
      [*Pause.*]

MOM   Oh.

LEE   Yeah.
      [*Pause.*]

1. Pablo Picasso (1881–1973), Spanish-born modernist painter.

MOM   You're both leaving?

LEE [*looks at* AUSTIN]   Well we were thinkin' about that before but now I—

AUSTIN   No, we are! We're both leaving. We've got it all planned.

MOM [*to* AUSTIN]   Well you can't leave. You have a family.

AUSTIN   I'm leaving. I'm getting out of here.

LEE [*to* MOM]   I don't really think Austin's cut out for the desert do you?

MOM   No. He's not.

AUSTIN   I'm going with you, Lee!

MOM   He's too thin.

LEE   Yeah, he'd just burn up out there.

AUSTIN [*to* LEE]   We just gotta' finish this screenplay and then we're gonna' take off. That's the plan. That's what you said. Come on, let's get back to work, Lee.

LEE   I can't work under these conditions here. It's too hot.

AUSTIN   Then we'll do it on the desert.

LEE   Don't be tellin' me what we're gonna' do!

MOM   Don't shout in the house.

LEE   We're just gonna' have to postpone the whole deal.

AUSTIN   I can't postpone it! It's gone past postponing! I'm doing everything you said. I'm writing down exactly what you tell me.

LEE   Yeah, but you were right all along see. It is a dumb story. "Two lame-brains chasin' each other across Texas." That's what you said, right?

AUSTIN   I never said that.

     [LEE *sneers in* AUSTIN's *face then turns to* MOM.]

LEE   I'm gonna' just borrow some a' your antiques, Mom. You don't mind do ya'? Just a few plates and things. Silverware.

     [LEE *starts going through all the cupboards in kitchen pulling out plates and stacking them on counter as* MOM *and* AUSTIN *watch*.]

MOM   You don't have any utensils on the desert?

LEE   Nah, I'm fresh out.

AUSTIN [*to* LEE]   What're you doing?

MOM   Well some of those are very old. Bone China.

LEE   I'm tired of eatin' outa' my bare hands, ya' know. It's not civilized.

AUSTIN [*to* LEE]   What're you doing? We made a deal!

MOM   Couldn't you borrow the plastic ones instead? I have plenty of plastic ones.

LEE [*as he stacks plates*]   It's not the same. Plastic's not the same at all. What I need is somethin' authentic. Somethin' to keep me in touch. It's easy to get outa' touch out there. Don't worry I'll get 'em back to ya'.

     [AUSTIN *rushes up to* LEE, *grabs him by shoulders*.]

AUSTIN   You can't just drop the whole thing, Lee!

     [LEE *turns, pushes* AUSTIN *in the chest knocking him backwards into the alcove*, MOM *watches numbly*, LEE *returns to collecting the plates, silverware, etc*.]

MOM   You boys shouldn't fight in the house. Go outside and fight.

LEE   I'm not fightin'. I'm leavin'.

MOM   There's been enough damage done already.

LEE [*his back to* AUSTIN *and* MOM, *stacking dishes on counter*]   I'm clearin' outa' here once and for all. All this town does is drive a man insane. Look what it's done to Austin there. I'm not lettin' that happen to me.

Sell myself down the river. No sir. I'd rather be a hundred miles from nowhere than let that happen to me.

[*During this* AUSTIN *has picked up the ripped-out phone from the floor and wrapped the cord tightly around both his hands, he lunges at* LEE *whose back is still to him, wraps the cord around* LEE'S *neck, plants a foot in* LEE'S *back and pulls back on the cord, tightening it,* LEE *chokes desperately, can't speak and can't reach* AUSTIN *with his arms,* AUSTIN *keeps applying pressure on* LEE'S *back with his foot, bending him into the sink,* MOM *watches.*]

AUSTIN [*tightening cord*]   You're not goin' anywhere! You're not takin' anything with you. You're not takin' my car! You're not takin' the dishes! You're not takin' anything! You're stayin' right here!

MOM   You'll have to stop fighting in the house. There's plenty of room outside to fight. You've got the whole outdoors to fight in.

[LEE *tries to tear himself away, he crashes across the stage like an enraged bull dragging* AUSTIN *with him, he snorts and bellows but* AUSTIN *hangs on and manages to keep clear of* LEE'S *attempts to grab him, they crash into the table, to the floor,* LEE *is face down thrashing wildly and choking,* AUSTIN *pulls cord tighter, stands with one foot planted on* LEE'S *back and the cord stretched taut.*]

AUSTIN [*holding cord*]   Gimme back my keys, Lee! Take the keys out! Take 'em out!

[LEE *desperately tries to dig in his pockets, searching for the car keys,* MOM *moves closer.*]

MOM [*calmly to* AUSTIN.]   You're not killing him are you?

AUSTIN   I don't know. I don't know if I'm killing him. I'm stopping him. That's all. I'm just stopping him.

[LEE *thrashes but* AUSTIN *is relentless.*]

MOM   You oughta' let him breathe a little bit.

AUSTIN   Throw the keys out, Lee!

[LEE *finally gets keys out and throws them on floor but out of* AUSTIN'S *reach,* AUSTIN *keeps pressure on cord, pulling* LEE'S *neck back,* LEE *gets one hand to the cord but can't relieve the pressure.*]

Reach me those keys would ya', Mom.

MOM [*not moving*]   Why are you doing this to him?

AUSTIN   Reach me the keys!

MOM   Not until you stop choking him.

AUSTIN   I can't stop choking him! He'll kill me if I stop choking him!

MOM   He won't kill you. He's your brother.

AUSTIN   Just get me the keys would ya'!

[*Pause* MOM *picks keys up off floor, hands them to* AUSTIN.]

AUSTIN [*to* MOM]   Thanks.

MOM   Will you let him go now?

AUSTIN   I don't know. He's not gonna' let me get outa' here.

MOM   Well you can't kill him.

AUSTIN   I can kill him! I can easily kill him. Right now. Right here. All I gotta' do is just tighten up. See? [*he tightens cord,* LEE *thrashes wildly,* AUSTIN *releases pressure a little, maintaining control*] Ya' see that?

MOM   That's a savage thing to do.

AUSTIN   Yeah well don't tell me I can't kill him because I can. I can just twist. I can just keep twisting. [AUSTIN *twists the cord tighter,* LEE *weakens, his breathing changes to a short rasp*]

MOM   Austin!

[AUSTIN *relieves pressure,* LEE *breathes easier but* AUSTIN *keeps him under control.*]

AUSTIN [*eyes on* LEE, *holding cord*]   I'm goin' to the desert. There's nothing stopping me. I'm going by myself to the desert.

[MOM *moving toward her luggage.*]

MOM   Well, I'm going to go check into a motel. I can't stand this anymore.

AUSTIN   Don't go yet!

[MOM *pauses.*]

MOM   I can't stay here. This is worse than being homeless.

AUSTIN   I'll get everything fixed up for you, Mom. I promise. Just stay for a while.

MOM [*picking up luggage*]   You're going to the desert.

AUSTIN   Just wait!

[LEE *thrashes,* AUSTIN *subdues him,* MOM *watches holding luggage, pause.*]

MOM   It was the worst feeling being up there. In Alaska. Staring out a window. I never felt so desperate before. That's why when I saw that article on Picasso I thought—

AUSTIN   Stay here, Mom. This is where you live.

[*She looks around the stage.*]

MOM   I don't recognize it at all.

[*She exits with luggage,* AUSTIN *makes a move toward her but* LEE *starts to struggle and* AUSTIN *subdues him again with cord, pause.*]

AUSTIN [*holding cord*]   Lee? I'll make ya' a deal. You let me get outa' here. Just let me get to my car. All right, Lee? Gimme a little headstart and I'll turn you loose. Just gimme a little headstart. All right?

[LEE *makes no response,* AUSTIN *slowly releases tension cord, still nothing from* LEE.]

AUSTIN   Lee?

[LEE *is motionless,* AUSTIN *very slowly begins to stand, still keeping a tenuous hold on the cord and his eyes riveted to* LEE *for any sign of movement,* AUSTIN *slowly drops the cord and stands, he stares down at* LEE *who appears to be dead.*]

AUSTIN [*whispers*]   Lee?

[*Pause,* AUSTIN *considers, looks toward exit, back to* LEE, *then makes a small movement as if to leave. Instantly* LEE *is on his feet and moves toward exit, blocking* AUSTIN's *escape. They square off to each other, keeping a distance between them. Pause, a single coyote heard in distance, lights fade softly into moonlight, the figures of the brothers now appear to be caught in a vast desert-like landscape, they are very still but watchful for the next move, lights go slowly to black as the after-image of the brothers pulses in the dark, coyote fades.*]

1980

LOUISE GLÜCK
b. 1943

"I was born to a vocation: / to bear witness / to the great mysteries," Louise Glück writes in "Parados." Apparently, she took the vocation of poet seriously from a young age. As a child, asked by a friend's mother to recite a poem she had written for an assignment, Glück readily complied: "My special triumph with this poem," she recounts in her essay "The Education of the Poet," "had involved a metrical inversion in the last line (not that I called it that), an omission of the final rhyme: to my ear it was exhilarating, a kind of explosion of form." The friend's mother congratulated her: "'a very good poem,' she said, 'right until the last line,'" which she then proceeded to rearrange aloud into the order I had explicitly intended to violate. 'You see,' she told me, 'all that was missing was that last rhyme.' I was furious" (*Proofs and Theories*, 1994). In part this portrait of a superior, knowing child anticipates the oracular, prophetic tone we sometimes hear in Glück's work. As with the declaration "I was born to a vocation," the poet seems elevated from the ordinary world and set apart by her knowledge. At the same time Glück's childhood memory suggests what she has elsewhere called "the mandarin in my nature which would have to be checked," which is to say, her exceptional intelligence had to be schooled in common experience; she had to learn to identify with rather than to separate herself from others. The lesson of such schooling, enacted in some of Glück's best poems, such as the sequence "October," is this: what makes the poet exceptional is her ability to render the representative experience she also recognizes as her own.

Glück's work illuminates with particular power the mysteries of those utterly common experiences, pain and loss. The title of Glück's first collection of poetry, *Firstborn* (1968), refers to two firstborn children: a sister who died as an infant before Glück was born, and the poet herself, the older of two surviving sisters. "I have always been, in one way or another, obsessed with sisters, the dead and the living both," she writes in "Death and Absences." Glück saw herself as the dead sister's substitute; at the same time, she says, "I took on the guilty responsibility of the survivor." Although in her early volumes—*Firstborn*, *The House on Marshland* (1975), *Descending Figure* (1980), and *The Triumph of Achilles* (1985)—the traces of autobiography are distanced and mythic, much of Glück's work revisits the lost sister and explores the poet's feelings of grief and insufficiency. Few contemporary poets have registered so powerfully the self's compulsive efforts, inevitably failing, to become invulnerable to loss and absence, though her mythic transformations of biography can be compared to the work of Sylvia Plath and the early Stanley Kunitz, and her articulation of pain has an affinity with the poems of Frank Bidart.

Nevertheless, Glück has always refused any easy equation of art with personal experience (one of her essays is titled "Against Sincerity"), and it is therefore striking that in an essay on her education as a poet she gives a remarkably acute account of her struggle with anorexia, which came to a crisis when she was sixteen. This struggle, she writes, was shaped by a terror of "incompleteness and ravenous need" and by the concomitant desire to appear "completely free of all forms of dependency, to appear complete, self-contained." She was saved from dying, she believes, by psychoanalysis ("analysis taught me to think") and by her experience at the School of General Studies at Columbia, which she entered at eighteen. Her teachers, Leonie Adams and Stanley Kunitz, provided her work with "the steady application of scrutiny." Glück's poetry demonstrates that she took the lesson of this scrutiny and trained it on herself and her world. The intensity of perception in her poems—whether of an infant son, a father's gesture of good-bye, or her own childhood portrait—can be startling.

Her poetry is often impatient with the transitory and hungry for the unchanging—the "blue and permanent" water of "The Drowned Children," the eternal world that stands in implicit contrast to earthly loss and change (the blighted tomato plants in "Vespers"). In this regard she shares the "religious mind" she describes in her essay on T. S. Eliot, the mind that craves "what is final, immutable" and "cannot sustain itself on matter and process." But the impulse of "repulsion" toward the physical world F. R. Leavis once noted in Eliot is countered in Glück by an engagement with complex family relations and with the beauty of the natural world. Her collection *The Wild Iris* (1992), a series of flower poems spoken to and by a divinity, expresses the longing for what is eternal and an arresting sense of the earth's transient loveliness. In *The Meadowlands* (1996) the warring parties in an unraveling marriage (they are modeled on characters in the *Odyssey*) are depicted in wickedly comic tones.

Glück has sought to vary her stylistic habits and preoccupations from one book to another ("Each book I've written has culminated in a conscious diagnostic act, a swearing off"). Clearly the child exulting in a metrical inversion anticipates Glück's lifelong attention to and experiment with form. While her work provides some haunting and resonant images, the resources of syntax generate much of her poems' power. Glück's sentences are muscles of perception, capable of complex extension and retraction, at times unwinding in a stanza to bring together opposing forces or experiences (like authority and woundedness, or the timeless and the transient). Her work moves, in varying degrees from poem to poem, between syntactical control and giving way (what she has called "abandon"). Sometimes her complex sentences spill forward from one clause into another, but line breaks or the beginning of a new sentence midline interrupt this motion, giving her work the consistent sense of something incomplete, clipped off, unsaid (she shares this quality with her predecessors George Oppen and Emily Dickinson). At other times, as in parts of her sequence "October," Glück's equation of the sentence with the line ("It does me no good; violence has changed me") has an authoritative tone and declarative control simultaneously undermined by the way one sentence is laid against another without transition or copula. Characteristically for this poet, the pressure of what is unsaid fills the spaces between sentences, between lines, and between stanzas. The distinctive voice we hear in Glück—part oracle, part acute observer, part hapless participant in the rush of feeling and experience—often arises from the way her poems (like certain of Dickinson's) move between statement and mystery, between words and silences. Her response to the events of September 11, 2001, in "October," displays all of these qualities.

Glück teaches at Boston University and at Yale University. She received the 1993 Pulitzer Prize for *The Wild Iris* and the PEN Award for her indispensible collection of essays on poetic vocation, *Proofs and Theories* (1994). More recent volumes include *Vita Nova* (1999), *The Seven Ages* (2001), *Averno* (2006), *A Village Life* (2009) and *Faithful and Virtuous Night* (2014). Her *Poems, 1962–2012* appeared in 2013. Glück received the Bollingen Prize for poetry in 2001.

The Drowned Children

You see, they have no judgment.
So it is natural that they should drown,
first the ice taking them in
and then, all winter, their wool scarves
floating behind them as they sink   5
until at last they are quiet.
And the pond lifts them in its manifold dark arms.

But death must come to them differently,
so close to the beginning.
As though they had always been   10
blind and weightless. Therefore
the rest is dreamed, the lamp,
the good white cloth that covered the table,
their bodies.

And yet they hear the names they used   15
like lures slipping over the pond:
What are you waiting for
come home, come home, lost
in the waters, blue and permanent.

1980

From Descending Figure[1]

2 *The Sick Child*

—Rijksmuseum[2]

A small child
is ill, has wakened.
It is winter, past midnight   20
in Antwerp.[3] Above a wooden chest,
the stars shine.
And the child
relaxes in her mother's arms.
The mother does not sleep;   25
she stares
fixedly into the bright museum.
By spring the child will die.
Then it is wrong, wrong
to hold her—   30
Let her be alone,
without memory, as the others wake
terrified, scraping the dark
paint from their faces.

3 *For My Sister*

Far away my sister is moving in her crib.   35
The dead ones are like that,
always the last to quiet.

Because, however long they lie in the earth,
they will not learn to speak

---

1. Printed here are parts 2 and 3 of the three-part sequence.
2. The national museum of the Netherlands, in Amsterdam.
3. A city in Belgium.

but remain uncertainly pressing against the wooden bars,   40
so small the leaves hold them down.

Now, if she had a voice,
the cries of hunger would be beginning.
I should go to her;
perhaps if I sang very softly,   45
her skin so white,
her head covered with black feathers. . . .

1980

Appearances

When we were children, my parents had our portraits painted,
then hung them side by side, over the mantel,
where we couldn't fight.
I'm the dark one, the older one. My sister's blond,
the one who looks angry because she can't talk.   5

It never bothered me, not talking.
That hasn't changed much. My sister's still blond, not different
from the portrait. Except we're adults now, we've been analyzed:
we understand our expressions.

My mother tried to love us equally,   10
dressed us in the same dresses; she wanted us
perceived as sisters.
That's what she wanted from the portraits:
you need to see them hanging together, facing one another—
separated, they don't make the same statement.   15
You wouldn't know what the eyes were fixed on;
they'd seem to be staring into space.

This was the summer we went to Paris, the summer I was seven.
Every morning, we went to the convent.
Every afternoon, we sat still, having the portraits painted,   20
wearing green cotton dresses, the square neck marked with a ruffle.
Monsieur Davanzo added the flesh tones: my sister's ruddy; mine, faintly
    bluish.
To amuse us, Madame Davanzo hung cherries over our ears.

It was something I was good at: sitting still, not moving.
I did it to be good, to please my mother, to distract her from the child that
    died.   25
I wanted to be child enough. I'm still the same,
like a toy that can stop and go, but not change direction.

Anyone can love a dead child, love an absence.
My mother's strong; she doesn't do what's easy.

She's like her mother: she believes in family, in order.   30
She doesn't change her house, just freshens the paint occasionally.
Sometimes something breaks, gets thrown away, but that's all.
She likes to sit there, on the blue couch, looking up at her daughters,
at the two who lived. She can't remember how it really was,
how anytime she ministered to one child, loved that child,   35
she damaged the other. You could say
she's like an artist with a dream, a vision.
Without that, she'd have been torn apart.
We were like the portraits, always together: you had to shut out one child
      to see the other.   40
That's why only the painter noticed: a face already so controlled, so
      withdrawn,
and too obedient, the clear eyes saying
If you want me to be a nun, I'll be a nun.

                                                                                          1990

Vespers[1]

In your extended absence, you permit me
use of earth, anticipating
some return on investment. I must report
failure in my assignment, principally
regarding the tomato plants.   5
I think I should not be encouraged to grow
tomatoes. Or, if I am, you should withhold
the heavy rains, the cold nights that come
so often here, while other regions get
twelve weeks of summer. All this   10
belongs to you: on the other hand,
I planted the seeds, I watched the first shoots
like wings tearing the soil, and it was my heart
broken by the blight, the black spot so quickly
multiplying in the rows. I doubt   15
you have a heart, in our understanding of
that term. You who do not discriminate
between the dead and the living, who are, in consequence,
immune to foreshadowing, you may not know
how much terror we bear, the spotted leaf,   20
the red leaves of the maple falling
even in August, in early darkness: I am responsible
for these vines.

                                                                                          1992

---

1. Evening prayers. Also, the sixth and next to last of the canonical hours, whose office of prayer services is said before nightfall in, e.g., a Roman Catholic monastery.

October

1

Is it winter again, is it cold again,
didn't Frank just slip on the ice,
didn't he heal, weren't the spring seeds planted

didn't the night end,
didn't the melting ice
flood the narrow gutters

wasn't my body
rescued, wasn't it safe

didn't the scar form, invisible
above the injury

terror and cold,
didn't they just end, wasn't the back garden
harrowed and planted—

I remember how the earth felt, red and dense,
in stiff rows, weren't the seeds planted,
didn't vines climb the south wall

I can't hear your voice
for the wind's cries, whistling over the bare ground

I no longer care
what sound it makes

when was I silenced, when did it first seem
pointless to describe that sound

what it sounds like can't change what it is—

didn't the night end, wasn't the earth
safe when it was planted

didn't we plant the seeds,
weren't we necessary to the earth,

the vines, were they harvested?

2

Summer after summer has ended,
balm after violence:
it does me no good
to be good to me now;
violence has changed me.

Daybreak. The low hills shine
ochre and fire, even the fields shine.
I know what I see; sun that could be   35
the August sun, returning
everything that was taken away—

You hear this voice? This is my mind's voice;
you can't touch my body now.   40
It has changed once, it has hardened,
don't ask it to respond again.

A day like a day in summer.
Exceptionally still. The long shadows of the maples
nearly mauve on the gravel paths.   45
And in the evening, warmth. Night like a night in summer.

It does me no good; violence has changed me.
My body has grown cold like the stripped fields;
now there is only my mind, cautious and wary,
with the sense it is being tested.   50

Once more, the sun rises as it rose in summer;
bounty, balm after violence.
Balm after the leaves have changed, after the fields
have been harvested and turned.

Tell me this is the future,   55
I won't believe you.
Tell me I'm living,
I won't believe you.

                            3

Snow had fallen. I remember
music from an open window.   60

Come to me, said the world.
This is not to say
it spoke in exact sentences
but that I perceived beauty in this manner.

Sunrise. A film of moisture   65
on each living thing. Pools of cold light
formed in the gutters.

I stood
at the doorway,
ridiculous as it now seems.   70

What others found in art,
I found in nature. What others found

in human love, I found in nature.
Very simple. But there was no voice there.

Winter was over. In the thawed dirt, 75
bits of green were showing.

Come to me, said the world. I was standing
in my wool coat at a kind of bright portal—
I can finally say
long age; it gives me considerable pleasure. Beauty 80
the healer, the teacher—

death cannot harm me
more than you have harmed me,
my beloved life.

4

The light has changed; 85
middle C[1] is tuned darker now.
And the songs of morning sound over-rehearsed.

This is the light of autumn, not the light of spring.
The light of autumn: *you will not be spared.*

The songs have changed; the unspeakable 90
has entered them.

This is the light of autumn, not the light that says
I am reborn.

Not the spring dawn: *I strained, I suffered, I was delivered.*
This is the present, an allegory of waste. 95

So much has changed. And still, you are fortunate:
the ideal burns in you like a fever.
Or not like a fever, like a second heart.

The songs have changed, but really they are still quite beautiful.
They have been concentrated in a smaller space, the space of the mind. 100
They are dark, now, with desolation and anguish.

And yet the notes recur. They hover oddly
in anticipation of silence.
The ear gets used to them.
The eye gets used to them. 105
The eye gets used to disappearances.

---

1. A tone represented by the note "C," located on the grand staff between the bass and treble clefs, the
middle of the piano keyboard; the piano key used as a reference for all other notes.

You will not be spared, nor will what you love be spared.

A wind has come and gone, taking apart the mind;
it has left in its wake a strange lucidity.

How privileged you are, to be still passionately   110
clinging to what you love;
the forfeit of hope has not destroyed you.

Maestoso, doloroso:[2]

This is the light of autumn; it has turned on us.
Surely it is a privilege to approach the end   115
still believing in something.

                                    5

It is true there is not enough beauty in the world.
It is also true that I am not competent to restore it.
Neither is there candor, and here I may be of some use.

I am   120
at work, though I am silent.

The bland

misery of the world
bounds us on either side, an alley

lined with trees, we are   125

companions here, not speaking,
each with his own thoughts;

behind the trees, iron
gates of private houses,
the shuttered rooms   130

somehow deserted, abandoned,

as though it were the artist's
duty to create
hope, but out of what? what?

the word itself   135
false, a device to refute
perception—At the intersection,

2. Italian musical terms, directing the play of the music to have grand, dignified, majestic phrasing,
and to carry a sorrowful, melancholy, plaintive tone.

ornamental lights of the season.

I was young here. Riding
the subway with my small book   140
as though to defend myself against

this same world:

you are not alone,
the poem said,
in the dark tunnel.   145

6

The brightness of the day becomes
the brightness of the night;
the fire becomes the mirror.

My friend the earth is bitter; I think
sunlight has failed her.   150
Bitter or weary, it is hard to say.

Between herself and the sun,
something has ended.
She wants, now, to be left alone;
I think we must give up   155
turning to her for affirmation.

Above the fields,
above the roofs of the village houses,
the brilliance that made all life possible
becomes the cold stars.   160

Lie still and watch:
they give nothing but ask nothing.

From within the earth's
bitter disgrace, coldness and barrenness

my friend the moon rises: 165
she is beautiful tonight, but when is she not beautiful?

2006

ALICE WALKER
b. 1944

Of the two daughters at odds over family heirlooms in the story "Everyday Use" (included here), Alice Walker resembles each one. Like the burned Maggie, she spent a childhood even more limited than her family's rural poverty dictated, for as a little girl she was shot in the eye with a BB gun; the disfigurement plagued her until it was corrected during her college years. Like Dee, she was able to attend college— first Spelman College and then Sarah Lawrence College on a scholarship—and acquire urban sophistication from the North. Many of Walker's characters become adept in the new cultural language of the Black Arts and black power movements to which the author contributed as a young writer—and all of them are subjected to the same dismay Dee's mother feels at having to rule against this daughter's wishes. Like the mother, therefore, Walker is given to seeing both sides of a situation; and when it comes to choosing between her characters' opposing positions, she tends to be critical of her own personality first and extremely sparing in her judgment of others.

From her native Eatonton, Georgia, Walker gained an understanding of the rural South. In her essay "Beyond the Peacock," Walker evaluates both the older white writer Flannery O'Connor, who lived in nearby Milledgeville, and the perspectives from which readers see the region and its heritage. Visitors to O'Connor's home, for example, often romanticize the house's handmade bricks; Walker points out that the slaves who made those bricks surely suffered in the process. As the educated child of sharecroppers, Walker can critically reexamine the myths in and around O'Connor's life while doing justice to the complexity of O'Connor's work.

After college Walker returned to the South, first to work in the civil rights movement against segregation and then to teach at Jackson State College in Mississippi. Her first novel, *The Third Life of Grange Copeland* (1970), follows its protagonist through three generations of domestic experience. In *Meridian* (1976), Walker presents fragmentary recollections of the 1960s among characters trying to make sense of their recent past. This novel reflects many of the topics treated in the author's short-story collection, *In Love & Trouble* (1973), in which a range of African American women almost always have unhappy relationships with men. Walker's third novel, *The Color Purple* (1982), makes her strongest narrative statement, formulated from what she calls a "womanist" (as opposed to strictly feminist) perspective. This approach draws on the black folk expression "womanish," which in a mother-to-daughter context signifies a call to adult, mature, responsible (and courageous) behavior. Such behavior benefits women and men and is necessary, Walker argues, for the survival of all African Americans by keeping creativity alive. The plot and the style of *The Color Purple* show how this happens, as the young black woman Celie draws on her sister's letters (written from Africa) for her own letters to God. Though Celie's life by any other terms could be considered disastrous (including rape, incest, and the killing of her babies by her father, and both physical and psychological abuse by her husband), her actions and her ability to express herself give her status as an individual. To everyone who will listen, Celie says: "I am here."

Walker has continued to publish novels, short stories, poetry, and essays. In *The Same River Twice* (1996) she writes about how the filming of *The Color Purple* challenged and changed her life. As a sociocultural critic she has examined the atrocity of female genital mutilation in parts of Africa, also incorporating her conclusions in her novel *Possessing the Secret of Joy* (1992), and as a literary critic she has spoken for a richer and more complete understanding of Zora Neale Hurston, whose employment of folk materials in narrative anticipates Walker's. Throughout her career she has spoken about the need for strength from African American women, and her writing seeks workable models for such strength.

The following text is from *In Love & Trouble* (1973).

Everyday Use

For Your Grandmama

I will wait for her in the yard that Maggie and I made so clean and wavy yesterday afternoon. A yard like this is more comfortable than most people know. It is not just a yard. It is like an extended living room. When the hard clay is swept clean as a floor and the fine sand around the edges lined with tiny, irregular grooves, anyone can come and sit and look up into the elm tree and wait for the breezes that never come inside the house.

Maggie will be nervous until after her sister goes: she will stand hopelessly in corners, homely and ashamed of the burn scars down her arms and legs, eyeing her sister with a mixture of envy and awe. She thinks her sister has held life always in the palm of one hand, that "no" is a word the world never learned to say to her.

You've no doubt seen those TV shows where the child who has "made it" is confronted, as a surprise, by her own mother and father, tottering in weakly from backstage. (A pleasant surprise, of course: What would they do if parent and child came on the show only to curse out and insult each other?) On TV mother and child embrace and smile into each other's faces. Sometimes the mother and father weep, the child wraps them in her arms and leans across the table to tell how she would not have made it without their help. I have seen these programs.

Sometimes I dream a dream in which Dee and I are suddenly brought together on a TV program of this sort. Out of a dark and soft-seated limousine I am ushered into a bright room filled with many people. There I meet a smiling, gray, sporty man like Johnny Carson who shakes my hand and tells me what a fine girl I have. Then we are on the stage and Dee is embracing me with tears in her eyes. She pins on my dress a large orchid, even though she has told me once that she thinks orchids are tacky flowers.

In real life I am a large, big-boned woman with rough, man-working hands. In the winter I wear flannel nightgowns to bed and overalls during the day. I can kill and clean a hog as mercilessly as a man. My fat keeps me hot in zero weather. I can work outside all day, breaking ice to get water for washing; I can eat pork liver cooked over the open fire minutes after it comes steaming from the hog. One winter I knocked a bull calf straight in the brain between the eyes with a sledge hammer and had the meat hung up to chill before nightfall. But of course all this does not show on television. I am the way my daughter would want me to be: a hundred pounds lighter, my skin like an uncooked barley pancake. My hair glistens in the hot bright lights. Johnny Carson has much to do to keep up with my quick and witty tongue.

But that is a mistake. I know even before I wake up. Who ever knew a Johnson with a quick tongue? Who can even imagine me looking a strange white man in the eye? It seems to me I have talked to them always with one foot raised in flight, with my head turned in whichever way is farthest from them. Dee, though. She would always look anyone in the eye. Hesitation was no part of her nature.

"How do I look, Mama?" Maggie says, showing just enough of her thin body enveloped in pink skirt and red blouse for me to know she's there, almost hidden by the door.

"Come out into the yard," I say.

Have you ever seen a lame animal, perhaps a dog run over by some careless person rich enough to own a car, sidle up to someone who is ignorant enough to be kind to them? That is the way my Maggie walks. She has been like this, chin on chest, eyes on ground, feet in shuffle, ever since the fire that burned the other house to the ground.

Dee is lighter than Maggie, with nicer hair and a fuller figure. She's a woman now, though sometimes I forget. How long ago was it that the other house burned? Ten, twelve years? Sometimes I can still hear the flames and feel Maggie's arms sticking to me, her hair smoking and her dress falling off her in little black papery flakes. Her eyes seemed stretched open, blazed open by the flames reflected in them. And Dee. I see her standing off under the sweet gum tree she used to dig gum out of; a look of concentration on her face as she watched the last dingy gray board of the house fall in toward the red-hot brick chimney. Why don't you do a dance around the ashes? I'd wanted to ask her. She had hated the house that much.

I used to think she hated Maggie, too. But that was before we raised the money, the church and me, to send her to Augusta to school. She used to read to us without pity; forcing words, lies, other folks' habits, whole lives upon us two, sitting trapped and ignorant underneath her voice. She washed us in a river of make-believe, burned us with a lot of knowledge we didn't necessarily need to know. Pressed us to her with the serious way she read, to shove us away at just the moment, like dimwits, we seemed about to understand.

Dee wanted nice things. A yellow organdy dress to wear to her graduation from high school; black pumps to match a green suit she'd made from an old suit somebody gave me. She was determined to stare down any disaster in her efforts. Her eyelids would not flicker for minutes at a time. Often I fought off the temptation to shake her. At sixteen she had a style of her own: and knew what style was.

I never had an education myself. After second grade the school was closed down. Don't ask me why: in 1927 colored asked fewer questions than they do now. Sometimes Maggie reads to me. She stumbles along good-naturedly but can't see well. She knows she is not bright. Like good looks and money, quickness passed her by. She will marry John Thomas (who has mossy teeth in an earnest face) and then I'll be free to sit here and I guess just sing church songs to myself. Although I never was a good singer. Never could carry a tune. I was always better at a man's job. I used to love to milk till I was hooked in the side in '49. Cows are soothing and slow and don't bother you, unless you try to milk them the wrong way.

I have deliberately turned my back on the house. It is three rooms, just like the one that burned, except the roof is tin; they don't make shingle roofs any more. There are no real windows, just some holes cut in the sides, like the portholes in a ship, but not round and not square, with rawhide holding the shutters up on the outside. This house is in a pasture, too, like the other one. No doubt when Dee sees it she will want to tear it down. She wrote me once that no matter where we "choose" to live, she will manage to come see us. But she will never bring her friends. Maggie and I thought about this and Maggie asked me, "Mama, when did Dee ever *have* any friends?"

She had a few. Furtive boys in pink shirts hanging about on washday after school. Nervous girls who never laughed. Impressed with her they worshiped the well-turned phrase, the cute shape, the scalding humor that erupted like bubbles in lye. She read to them.

When she was courting Jimmy T she didn't have much time to pay to us, but turned all her faultfinding power on him. He *flew* to marry a cheap city girl from a family of ignorant flashy people. She hardly had time to recompose herself.

When she comes I will meet—but there they are!

Maggie attempts to make a dash for the house, in her shuffling way, but I stay her with my hand. "Come back here," I say. And she stops and tries to dig a well in the sand with her toe.

It is hard to see them clearly through the strong sun. But even the first glimpse of leg out of the car tells me it is Dee. Her feet were always neat-looking, as if God himself had shaped them with a certain style. From the other side of the car comes a short, stocky man. Hair is all over his head a foot long and hanging from his chin like a kinky mule tail. I hear Maggie suck in her breath. "Uhnnnh," is what it sounds like. Like when you see the wriggling end of a snake just in front of your foot on the road. "Uhnnnh."

Dee next. A dress down to the ground, in this hot weather. A dress so loud it hurts my eyes. There are yellows and oranges enough to throw back the light of the sun. I feel my whole face warming from the heat waves it throws out. Earrings gold, too, and hanging down to her shoulders. Bracelets dangling and making noises when she moves her arm up to shake the folds of the dress out of her armpits. The dress is loose and flows, and as she walks closer, I like it. I hear Maggie go "Uhnnnh" again. It is her sister's hair. It stands straight up like the wool on a sheep. It is black as night and around the edges are two long pigtails that rope about like small lizards disappearing behind her ears.

"Wa-su-zo-Tean-o!" she says, coming on in that gliding way the dress makes her move. The short stocky fellow with the hair to his navel is all grinning and he follows up with "Asalamalakim, my mother and sister!" He moves to hug Maggie but she falls back, right up against the back of my chair. I feel her trembling there and when I look up I see the perspiration falling off her chin.

"Don't get up," says Dee. Since I am stout it takes something of a push. You can see me trying to move a second or two before I make it. She turns, showing white heels through her sandals, and goes back to the car. Out she peeks next with a Polaroid. She stoops down quickly and lines up picture after picture of me sitting there in front of the house with Maggie cowering behind me. She never takes a shot without making sure the house is included. When a cow comes nibbling around the edge of the yard she snaps it and me and Maggie *and* the house. Then she puts the Polaroid in the back seat of the car, and comes up and kisses me on the forehead.

Meanwhile Asalamalakim is going through motions with Maggie's hand. Maggie's hand is as limp as a fish, and probably as cold, despite the sweat, and she keeps trying to pull it back. It looks like Asalamalakim wants to shake hands but wants to do it fancy. Or maybe he don't know how people shake hands. Anyhow, he soon gives up on Maggie.

"Well," I say. "Dee."

"No, Mama," she says. "Not 'Dee,' Wangero Leewanika Kemanjo!"

"What happened to 'Dee'?" I wanted to know.

"She's dead," Wangero said. "I couldn't bear it any longer, being named after the people who oppress me."

"You know as well as me you was named after your aunt Dicie," I said. Dicie is my sister. She named Dee. We called her "Big Dee" after Dee was born.

"But who was *she* named after?" asked Wangero.

"I guess after Grandma Dee," I said.

"And who was she named after?" asked Wangero.

"Her mother," I said, and saw Wangero was getting tired. "That's about as far back as I can trace it," I said. Though, in fact, I probably could have carried it back beyond the Civil War through the branches.

"Well," said Asalamalakim, "there you are."

"Uhnnnh," I heard Maggie say.

"There I was not," I said, "before 'Dicie' cropped up in our family, so why should I try to trace it that far back?"

He just stood there grinning, looking down on me like somebody inspecting a Model A car.[1] Every once in a while he and Wangero sent eye signals over my head.

"How do you pronounce this name?" I asked.

"You don't have to call me by it if you don't want to," said Wangero.

"Why shouldn't I?" I asked. "If that's what you want us to call you, we'll call you."

"I know it might sound awkward at first," said Wangero.

"I'll get used to it," I said. "Ream it out again."

Well, soon we got the name out of the way. Asalamalakim had a name twice as long and three times as hard. After I tripped over it two or three times he told me to just call him Hakim-a-barber. I wanted to ask him was he a barber, but I didn't really think he was, so I didn't ask.

"You must belong to those beef-cattle peoples down the road," I said. They said "Asalamalakim" when they met you, too, but they didn't shake hands. Always too busy: feeding the cattle, fixing the fences, putting up salt-lick shelters, throwing down hay. When the white folks poisoned some of the herd the men stayed up all night with rifles in their hands. I walked a mile and a half just to see the sight.

Hakim-a-barber said, "I accept some of their doctrines, but farming and raising cattle is not my style." (They didn't tell me, and I didn't ask, whether Wangero (Dee) had really gone and married him.)

---

1. Popular model of Ford automobile introduced in 1928.

We sat down to eat and right away he said he didn't eat collards and pork was unclean. Wangero, though, went on through the chitlins and corn bread, the greens and everything else. She talked a blue streak over the sweet potatoes. Everything delighted her. Even the fact that we still used the benches her daddy made for the table when we couldn't afford to buy chairs.

"Oh, Mama!" she cried. Then turned to Hakim-a-barber. "I never knew how lovely these benches are. You can feel the rump prints," she said, running her hands underneath her and along the bench. Then she gave a sigh and her hand closed over Grandma Dee's butter dish. "That's it!" she said. "I knew there was something I wanted to ask you if I could have." She jumped up from the table and went over in the corner where the churn stood, the milk in it clabber by now. She looked at the churn and looked at it.

"This churn top is what I need," she said. "Didn't Uncle Buddy whittle it out of a tree you all used to have?"

"Yes," I said.

"Uh huh," she said happily. "And I want the dasher, too."

"Uncle Buddy whittle that, too?" asked the barber.

Dee (Wangero) looked up at me.

"Aunt Dee's first husband whittled the dash," said Maggie so low you almost couldn't hear her. "His name was Henry, but they called him Stash."

"Maggie's brain is like an elephant's," Wangero said, laughing. "I can use the churn top as a centerpiece for the alcove table," she said, sliding a plate over the churn, "and I'll think of something artistic to do with the dasher."

When she finished wrapping the dasher the handle stuck out. I took it for a moment in my hands. You didn't even have to look close to see where hands pushing the dasher up and down to make butter had left a kind of sink in the wood. In fact, there were a lot of small sinks; you could see where thumbs and fingers had sunk into the wood. It was beautiful light yellow wood, from a tree that grew in the yard where Big Dee and Stash had lived.

After dinner Dee (Wangero) went to the trunk at the foot of my bed and started rifling through it. Maggie hung back in the kitchen over the dishpan. Out came Wangero with two quilts. They had been pieced by Grandma Dee and then Big Dee and me had hung them on the quilt frames on the front porch and quilted them. One was in the Lone Star pattern. The other was Walk Around the Mountain. In both of them were scraps of dresses Grandma Dee had worn fifty and more years ago. Bits and pieces of Grandpa Jarrell's Paisley shirts. And one teeny faded blue piece, about the size of a penny matchbox, that was from Great Grandpa Ezra's uniform that he wore in the Civil War.

"Mama," Wangero said sweet as a bird. "Can I have these old quilts?"

I heard something fall in the kitchen, and a minute later the kitchen door slammed.

"Why don't you take one or two of the others?" I asked. "These old things was just done by me and Big Dee from some tops your grandma pieced before she died."

"No," said Wangero. "I don't want those. They are stitched around the borders by machine."

"That'll make them last better," I said.

"That's not the point," said Wangero. "These are all pieces of dresses Grandma used to wear. She did all this stitching by hand. Imagine!" She held the quilts securely in her arms, stroking them.

"Some of the pieces, like those lavender ones, come from old clothes her mother handed down to her," I said, moving up to touch the quilts. Dee (Wangero) moved back just enough so that I couldn't reach the quilts. They already belonged to her.

"Imagine!" she breathed again, clutching them closely to her bosom.

"The truth is," I said, "I promised to give them quilts to Maggie, for when she marries John Thomas."

She gasped like a bee had stung her.

"Maggie can't appreciate these quilts!" she said. "She'd probably be backward enough to put them to everyday use."

"I reckon she would," I said. "God knows I been saving 'em for long enough with nobody using 'em. I hope she will!" I didn't want to bring up how I had offered Dee (Wangero) a quilt when she went away to college. Then she had told me they were old-fashioned, out of style.

"But they're *priceless!*" she was saying now, furiously; for she has a temper. "Maggie would put them on the bed and in five years they'd be in rags. Less than that!"

"She can always make some more," I said. "Maggie knows how to quilt."

Dee (Wangero) looked at me with hatred. "You just will not understand. The point is these quilts, *these* quilts!"

"Well," I said, stumped. "What would *you* do with them?"

"Hang them," she said. As if that was the only thing you *could* do with quilts.

Maggie by now was standing in the door. I could almost hear the sound her feet made as they scraped over each other.

"She can have them, Mama," she said, like somebody used to never winning anything, or having anything reserved for her. "I can 'member Grandma Dee without the quilts."

I looked at her hard. She had filled her bottom lip with checkerberry snuff and it gave her face a kind of dopey, hangdog look. It was Grandma Dee and Big Dee who taught her how to quilt herself. She stood there with her scarred hands hidden in the folds of her skirt. She looked at her sister with something like fear but she wasn't mad at her. This was Maggie's portion. This was the way she knew God to work.

When I looked at her like that something hit me in the top of my head and ran down to the soles of my feet. Just like when I'm in church and the spirit of God touches me and I get happy and shout. I did something I never had done before: hugged Maggie to me, then dragged her on into the room, snatched the quilts out of Miss Wangero's hands and dumped them into Maggie's lap. Maggie just sat there on my bed with her mouth open.

"Take one or two of the others," I said to Dee.

But she turned without a word and went out to Hakim-a-barber.

"You just don't understand," she said, as Maggie and I came out to the car.

"What don't I understand?" I wanted to know.

"Your heritage," she said. And then she turned to Maggie, kissed her, and said, "You ought to try to make something of yourself, too, Maggie. It's really a new day for us. But from the way you and Mama still live you'd never know it."

She put on some sunglasses that hid everything above the tip of her nose and her chin.

Maggie smiled; maybe at the sunglasses. But a real smile, not scared. After we watched the car dust settle I asked Maggie to bring me a dip of snuff. And then the two of us sat there just enjoying, until it was time to go in the house and go to bed.

1973

AUGUST WILSON
1945–2005

In a preface to a collection of three August Wilson plays, their creator noted that "writing a play is for me like walking down the landscape of the self, unattended, unadorned, exploring what D. H. Lawrence called 'the dark forest of the soul.'" The evident sincerity, even solemnity, of this pronouncement indicates the heroic intensity with which Wilson conceived his artistic mission. That mission was nothing less than to provide a collective history of African American experience in the twentieth century. By centering his plays in different decades, Wilson hoped to use them as chronicles on an epic scale of the conflicts, joys, and sufferings of black people— "Put them all together and you have a history," he said about his plays. His first successful one, *Ma Rainey's Black Bottom* (1984), is set in 1920s Chicago and deals with black jazz musicians, their relations with one another and between themselves and their white employers. *Fences* (1985), its successor, is set in Pittsburgh in 1957, where the tensions of a black family play themselves out in various disruptions on a smaller but no less intense scale than would be ushered in, the following decade, by what Wilson calls (referring to the civil rights activism of those years) "the hot winds of change." Subsequent plays explored other decades, but most of them are situated in Wilson's native Pittsburgh in a black section called the Hill.

Wilson dropped out of school in ninth grade and, therefore, conducted his own education, reading widely—especially African American writers—and being particularly touched by Ralph Ellison and Langston Hughes. He founded a community theater called Black Horizon on the Hill and later began to write plays for another black theater in St. Paul, Minnesota. It was *Ma Rainey* that drew the attention of the director of Yale's Repertory Theater, Lloyd Richards, who produced it at Yale, then took it to Broadway. Richards henceforth became the director of Wilson's plays, first through staged readings at the Playwright's Conference, then through performances in New Haven and on Broadway. Wilson has written that one night in 1965 (he was twenty years old) he put on a Bessie Smith record and discovered the blues: at that moment, "the universe stuttered and everything fell to a new place." Like Bessie Smith, Ma Rainey was a legendary African American singer, often regarded as the mother of the blues, and Wilson's play, set in a recording studio where the white producers and the black musicians are waiting for Ma to show up, explores tensions of race and sexuality. Like all his plays, it unfolds leisurely through characters who do little more than talk to each other. But out of this talk is eventually generated a moment of violent action, in the case of *Ma Rainey* the fatal stabbing of one of the musicians by his enraged cohort.

In response to the criticism that his plays are "talky," Wilson pointed out that an oral culture is central to the people he writes about, thus "the talk is the whole point." Most certainly, the talk is liveliest in Wilson's work when it is laced with humor and with the animus one character displays toward another. At times, in dramatizing a number of competing voices raised in harmony or disharmony, Wilson achieved something like an operatic feel to the conversation as the voices—imbued with the rhythms and language of black culture and black music—play against each other in satisfying orchestration (George Bernard Shaw was a master of such operatic effects).

Speaking of *Ma Rainey* and *Fences*, Wilson said that he was concerned in them with the idea of missed possibilities: "Music and sports were the traditional inroads for blacks," and for the protagonist in each play, "even those inroads fail." The hero of *Fences*, perhaps Wilson's most engaging though least experimental play, is Troy Maxson whose color denied him a career in Major League Baseball (in Troy's prime as a player, baseball was still segregated). His stubborn dramatization of himself as a man who missed out on greatness puts him in conflict with both his wife and his son Cory, since Troy tries to repress Cory's potential career as a football star, believing that things haven't improved for black athletes. At certain moments in the play Troy rises to expressive arias in praise of himself as a heroic loser:

> Woman . . . I do the best I can do. I come in here every Friday. I carry a sack of potatoes and a bucket of lard. You all line up at the door with your hands out. I give you the lint from my pockets. I give you my sweat and blood. I ain't got no tears. I don't spend them. We go upstairs in that room at night . . . and I fall down on you and try to blast a hole into forever. I get up Monday morning . . . find my lunch on the table. I go out. Make my way. Find my strength to carry me through the next Friday.

One understands why *Fences* has been compared with Arthur Miller's *Death of a Salesman*. Both plays risk sentimentality in their underlining of the hero's plangent complaints, but at their best those complaints have idiomatic force and resonate with a true voice of feeling.

Wilson went on to write probably his most ambitious and difficult play, *Joe Turner's Come and Gone*, in which the occupants of a Pittsburgh boardinghouse in 1911 rehearse their individual histories, mainly stories of migrating from the South to the North. The most eloquently dark of these stories is that of Herald Loomis, who spent seven years in bondage to the bounty hunter Joe Turner. *Joe Turner* is usually called Wilson's most "poetic" drama, and the critic Frank Rich accurately pointed out that it was a "mixture of the well-made naturalistic boardinghouse drama and the mystical, non-Western theater of ritual and metaphor." The play is about secrets, about the tension between what can be expressed in words and what lies beyond them, inexpressible. In any case, the persistent presence of the vernacular, of folktales and dream visions, takes *Joe Turner* into a different realm from the naturalism of *Fences*. In Wilson's later plays he continued to experiment with this realm and to challenge his audience and his critics.

Fences[1]

CHARACTERS

TROY MAXSON

JIM BONO, TROY's *friend*

ROSE, TROY's *wife*

LYONS, TROY's *oldest son by previous marriage*

GABRIEL, TROY's *brother*

CORY, TROY *and* ROSE's *son*

RAYNELL, TROY's *daughter*

Setting

The setting is the yard which fronts the only entrance to the MAXSON *household, an ancient two-story brick house set back off a small alley in a big-city neighborhood. The entrance to the house is gained by two or three steps leading to a wooden porch badly in need of paint.*

A relatively recent addition to the house and running its full width, the porch lacks congruence. It is a sturdy porch with a flat roof. One or two chairs of dubious value sit at one end where the kitchen window opens onto the porch. An old-fashioned icebox stands silent guard at the opposite end.

The yard is a small dirt yard, partially fenced, except for the last scene, with a wooden sawhorse, a pile of lumber, and other fence-building equipment set off to the side. Opposite is a tree from which hangs a ball made of rags. A baseball bat leans against the tree. Two oil drums serve as garbage receptacles and sit near the house at right to complete the setting.

The Play

Near the turn of the century, the destitute of Europe sprang on the city with tenacious claws and an honest and solid dream. The city devoured them. They swelled its belly until it burst into a thousand furnaces and sewing machines, a thousand butcher shops and bakers' ovens, a thousand churches and hospitals and funeral parlors and money-lenders. The city grew. It nourished itself and offered each man a partnership limited only by his talent, his guile, and his willingness and capacity for hard work. For the immigrants of Europe, a dream dared and won true.

The descendants of African slaves were offered no such welcome or participation. They came from places called the Carolinas and the Virginias, Georgia, Alabama, Mississippi, and Tennessee. They came strong, eager, searching. The city rejected them and they fled and settled along the riverbanks and under bridges in shallow, ramshackle houses made of sticks and tar-paper. They collected rags and wood. They sold the use of their muscles and their bodies. They cleaned houses and washed clothes, they shined shoes, and in quiet desperation and vengeful pride, they stole, and lived in pursuit of their own dream. That they could breathe free, finally, and stand to meet life with the force of dignity and whatever eloquence the heart could call upon.

By 1957, the hard-won victories of the European immigrants had solidified the industrial might of America. War had been confronted and won with new energies that used loyalty and patriotism as its fuel. Life was rich, full, and flourishing. The Milwaukee Braves won the World Series, and the hot winds of

1. The text is from the 4th printing of the NAL edition of the play (1994).

change that would make the sixties a turbulent, racing, dangerous, and pro-
vocative decade had not yet begun to blow full.

Act 1

SCENE 1

It is 1957. TROY *and* BONO *enter the yard, engaged in conversation.* TROY *is fifty-three years old, a large man with thick, heavy hands; it is this largeness that he strives to fill out and make an accommodation with. Together with his blackness, his largeness informs his sensibilities and the choices he has made in his life.*

Of the two men, BONO *is obviously the follower. His commitment to their friendship of thirty-odd years is rooted in his admiration of* TROY's *honesty, capacity for hard work, and his strength, which* BONO *seeks to emulate.*

It is Friday night, payday, and the one night of the week the two men engage in a ritual of talk and drink. TROY *is usually the most talkative and at times he can be crude and almost vulgar, though he is capable of rising to profound heights of expression. The men carry lunch buckets and wear or carry burlap aprons and are dressed in clothes suitable to their jobs as garbage collectors.*

BONO   Troy, you ought to stop that lying!

TROY   I ain't lying! The nigger had a watermelon this big. [*He indicates with his hands.*] Talking about . . . "What watermelon, Mr. Rand?" I liked to fell out! "What watermelon, Mr. Rand?" . . . And it sitting there big as life.

BONO   What did Mr. Rand say?

TROY   Ain't said nothing. Figure if the nigger too dumb to know he carrying a watermelon, he wasn't gonna get much sense out of him. Trying to hide that great big old watermelon under his coat. Afraid to let the white man see him carry it home.

BONO   I'm like you . . . I ain't got no time for them kind of people.

TROY   Now what he look like getting mad cause he see the man from the union talking to Mr. Rand?

BONO   He come to me talking about . . . "Maxson gonna get us fired." I told him to get away from me with that. He walked away from me calling you a troublemaker. What Mr. Rand say?

TROY   Ain't said nothing. He told me to go down the Commissioner's office next Friday. They called me down there to see them.

BONO   Well, as long as you got your complaint filed, they can't fire you. That's what one of them white fellows tell me.

TROY   I ain't worried about them firing me. They gonna fire me cause I asked a question? That's all I did. I went to Mr. Rand and asked him, "Why? Why you got the white mens driving and the colored lifting?" Told him, "what's the matter, don't I count? You think only white fellows got sense enough to drive a truck. That ain't no paper job! Hell, anybody can drive a truck. How come you got all whites driving and the colored lifting?" He told me "take it to the union." Well, hell, that's what I done! Now they wanna come up with this pack of lies.

BONO   I told Brownie if the man come and ask him any questions . . . just tell the truth! It ain't nothing but something they done trumped up on you cause you filed a complaint on them.

TROY   Brownie don't understand nothing. All I want them to do is change the job description. Give everybody a chance to drive the truck. Brownie can't see that. He ain't got that much sense.

BONO   How you figure he be making out with that gal be up at Taylors' all the time . . . that Alberta gal?

TROY   Same as you and me. Getting just as much as we is. Which is to say nothing.

BONO   It is, huh? I figure you doing a little better than me . . . and I ain't saying what I'm doing.

TROY   Aw, nigger, look here . . . I know you. If you had got anywhere near that gal, twenty minutes later you be looking to tell somebody. And the first one you gonna tell . . . that you gonna want to brag to . . . is gonna be me.

BONO   I ain't saying that. I see where you be eyeing her.

TROY   I eye all the women. I don't miss nothing. Don't never let nobody tell you Troy Maxson don't eye the women.

BONO   You been doing more than eyeing her. You done bought her a drink or two.

TROY   Hell yeah, I bought her a drink! What that mean? I bought you one, too. What that mean cause I buy her a drink? I'm just being polite.

BONO   It's alright to buy her one drink. That's what you call being polite. But when you wanna be buying two or three . . . that's what you call eyeing her.

TROY   Look here, as long as you known me . . . you ever known me to chase after women?

BONO   Hell yeah! Long as I done known you. You forgetting I knew you when.

TROY   Naw, I'm talking about since I been married to Rose?

BONO   Oh, not since you been married to Rose. Now, that's the truth, there. I can say that.

TROY   Alright then! Case closed.

BONO   I see you be walking up around Alberta's house. You supposed to be at Taylors' and you be walking around there.

TROY   What you watching where I'm walking for? I ain't watching after you.

BONO   I seen you walking around there more than once.

TROY   Hell, you liable to see me walking anywhere! That don't mean nothing cause you see me walking around there.

BONO   Where she come from anyway? She just kinda showed up one day.

TROY   Tallahassee. You can look at her and tell she one of them Florida gals. They got some big healthy women down there. Grow them right up out the ground. Got a little bit of Indian in her. Most of them niggers down in Florida got some Indian in them.

BONO   I don't know about that Indian part. But she damn sure big and healthy. Woman wear some big stockings. Got them great big old legs and hips as wide as the Mississippi River.

TROY   Legs don't mean nothing. You don't do nothing but push them out of the way. But them hips cushion the ride!

BONO   Troy, you ain't got no sense.

TROY   It's the truth! Like you riding on Goodyears!

[ROSE *enters from the house. She is ten years younger than* TROY, *her devotion to him stems from her recognition of the possibilities of her life without him: a succession of abusive men and their babies, a life of partying and running the streets, the Church, or aloneness with its attendant pain and frustration. She recognizes* TROY's *spirit as a fine and illuminating one and she either ignores or forgives his faults, only some of which she recognizes. Though she doesn't drink, her presence is an integral part of the Friday night rituals. She alternates between the porch and the kitchen, where supper preparations are under way.*]

ROSE   What you all out here getting into?

TROY   What you worried about what we getting into for? This is men talk, woman.

ROSE   What I care what you all talking about? Bono, you gonna stay for supper?

BONO   No, I thank you, Rose. But Lucille say she cooking up a pot of pigfeet.

TROY   Pigfeet! Hell, I'm going home with you! Might even stay the night if you got some pigfeet. You got something in there to top them pigfeet, Rose?

ROSE   I'm cooking up some chicken. I got some chicken and collard greens.

TROY   Well, go on back in the house and let me and Bono finish what we was talking about. This is men talk. I got some talk for you later. You know what kind of talk I mean. You go on and powder it up.

ROSE   Troy Maxson, don't you start that now!

TROY   [*puts his arm around her*]   Aw, woman . . . come here. Look here, Bono . . . when I met this woman . . . I got out that place, say, "Hitch up my pony, saddle up my mare . . . there's a woman out there for me somewhere. I looked here. Looked there. Saw Rose and latched on to her." I latched on to her and told her—I'm gonna tell you the truth—I told her, "Baby, I don't wanna marry, I just wanna be your man." Rose told me . . . tell him what you told me, Rose.

ROSE   I told him if he wasn't the marrying kind, then move out the way so the marrying kind could find me.

TROY   That's what she told me. "Nigger, you in my way. You blocking the view! Move out the way so I can find me a husband." I thought it over two or three days. Come back—

ROSE   Ain't no two or three days nothing. You was back the same night.

TROY   Come back, told her . . . "Okay, baby . . . but I'm gonna buy me a banty rooster and put him out there in the backyard . . . and when he see a stranger come, he'll flap his wings and crow . . ." Look here, Bono, I could watch the front door by myself . . . it was that back door I was worried about.

ROSE   Troy, you ought not talk like that. Troy ain't doing nothing but telling a lie.

TROY   Only thing is . . . when we first got married . . . forget the rooster . . . we ain't had no yard!

BONO   I hear you tell it. Me and Lucille was staying down there on Logan Street. Had two rooms with the outhouse in the back. I ain't mind the outhouse none. But when that goddamn wind blow through there in the winter . . . that's what I'm talking about! To this day I wonder why in the hell I ever stayed down there for six long years. But see, I didn't know I could do no better. I thought only white folks had inside toilets and things.

ROSE There's a lot of people don't know they can do no better than they doing now. That's just something you got to learn. A lot of folks still shop at Bella's.

TROY Ain't nothing wrong with shopping at Bella's. She got fresh food.

ROSE I ain't said nothing about if she got fresh food. I'm talking about what she charge. She charge ten cents more than the A&P.

TROY The A&P ain't never done nothing for me. I spends my money where I'm treated right. I go down to Bella, say, "I need a loaf of bread, I'll pay you on Friday." She give it to me. What sense that make when I got money to go and spend it somewhere else and ignore the person who done right by me? That ain't in the Bible.

ROSE We ain't talking about what's in the Bible. What sense it make to shop there when she overcharge?

TROY You shop where you want to. I'll do my shopping where the people been good to me.

ROSE Well, I don't think it's right for her to overcharge. That's all I was saying.

BONO Look here . . . I got to get on. Lucille going be raising all kind of hell.

TROY Where you going, nigger? We ain't finished this pint. Come here, finish this pint.

BONO Well, hell, I am . . . if you ever turn the bottle loose.

TROY [hands him the bottle] The only thing I say about the A&P is I'm glad Cory got that job down there. Help him take care of his school clothes and things. Gabe done moved out and things getting tight around here. He got that job. . . . He can start to look out for himself.

ROSE Cory done went and got recruited by a college football team.

TROY I told that boy about that football stuff. The white man ain't gonna let him get nowhere with that football. I told him when he first come to me with it. Now you come telling me he done went and got more tied up in it. He ought to go and get recruited in how to fix cars or something where he can make a living.

ROSE He ain't talking about making no living playing football. It's just something the boys in school do. They gonna send a recruiter by to talk to you. He'll tell you he ain't talking about making no living playing football. It's a honor to be recruited.

TROY It ain't gonna get him nowhere. Bono'll tell you that.

BONO If he be like you in the sports . . . he's gonna be alright. Ain't but two men ever played baseball as good as you. That's Babe Ruth and Josh Gibson. Them's the only two men ever hit more home runs than you.

TROY What it ever get me? Ain't got a pot to piss in or a window to throw it out of.

ROSE Times have changed since you was playing baseball, Troy. That was before the war. Times have changed a lot since then.

TROY How in hell they done changed?

ROSE They got lots of colored boys playing ball now. Baseball and football.

BONO You right about that, Rose. Times have changed, Troy. You just come along too early.

TROY There ought not never have been no time called too early! Now you take that fellow . . . what's that fellow they had playing right field for the Yankees back then? You know who I'm talking about, Bono. Used to play right field for the Yankees?

ROSE Selkirk?

TROY Selkirk! That's it! Man batting .269, understand? .269. What kind of sense that make? I was hitting .432 with thirty-seven home runs! Man batting .269 and playing right field for the Yankees! I saw Josh Gibson's daughter yesterday. She walking around with raggedy shoes on her feet. Now I bet you Selkirk's daughter ain't walking around with raggedy shoes on her feet. I bet you that!

ROSE They got a lot of colored baseball players now. Jackie Robinson was the first. Folks had to wait for Jackie Robinson.

TROY I done seen a hundred niggers play baseball better than Jackie Robinson. Hell, I know some teams Jackie Robinson couldn't even make! What you talking about Jackie Robinson. Jackie Robinson wasn't nobody. I'm talking about if you could play ball then they ought to have let you play. Don't care what color you were. Come telling me I come along too early. If you could play . . . then they ought to have let you play. [TROY takes a long drink from the bottle.]

ROSE You gonna drink yourself to death. You don't need to be drinking like that.

TROY Death ain't nothing. I done seen him. Done wrassled with him. You can't tell me nothing about death. Death ain't nothing but a fastball on the outside corner. And you know what I'll do to that! Lookee here, Bono . . . am I lying? You get one of them fastballs, about waist high, over the outside corner of the plate where you can get the meat of the bat on it . . . and good god! You can kiss it goodbye. Now, am I lying?

BONO Naw, you telling the truth there. I seen you do it.

TROY If I'm lying . . . that 450 feet worth of lying! [Pause.] That's all death is to me. A fastball on the outside corner.

ROSE I don't know why you want to get on talking about death.

TROY Ain't nothing wrong with talking about death. That's part of life. Everybody gonna die. You gonna die, I'm gonna die. Bono's gonna die. Hell, we all gonna die.

ROSE But you ain't got to talk about it. I don't like to talk about it.

TROY You the one brought it up. Me and Bono was talking about baseball . . . you tell me I'm gonna drink myself to death. Ain't that right, Bono? You know I don't drink this but one night out of the week. That's Friday night. I'm gonna drink just enough to where I can handle it. Then I cuts it loose. I leave it alone. So don't you worry about me drinking myself to death. 'Cause I ain't worried about Death. I done seen him. I done wrestled with him. Look here, Bono . . . I looked up one day and Death was marching straight at me. Like Soldiers on Parade! The Army of Death marching straight at me. The middle of July, 1941. It got real cold just like it be winter. It seem like Death himself reached out and touched me on the shoulder. He touch me just like I touch you. I got cold as ice and Death standing there grinning at me.

ROSE   Troy, why don't you hush that talk.

TROY   I say . . . "What you want, Mr. Death? You be wanting me? You done brought your army to be getting me?" I looked him dead in the eye. I wasn't fearing nothing. I was ready to tangle. Just like I'm ready to tangle now. The Bible say be ever vigilant. That's why I don't get but so drunk. I got to keep watch.

ROSE   Troy was right down there in Mercy Hospital. You remember he had pneumonia? Laying there with a fever talking plumb out of his head.

TROY   Death standing there staring at me . . . carrying that sickle in his hand. Finally he say, "You want bound over for another year?" See, just like that . . . "You want bound over for another year?" I told him, "Bound over hell! Let's settle this now!" It seem like he kinda fell back when I said that, and all the cold went out of me. I reached down and grabbed that sickle and threw it just as far as I could throw it . . . and me and him commenced to wrestling. We wrestled for three days and three nights. I can't say where I found the strength from. Every time it seemed like he was gonna get the best of me, I'd reach way down deep inside myself and find the strength to do him one better.

ROSE   Every time Troy tell that story he find different ways to tell it. Different things to make up about it.

TROY   I ain't making up nothing. I'm telling you the facts of what happened. I wrestled with Death for three days and three nights and I'm standing here to tell you about it. [Pause.] Alright. At the end of the third night we done weakened each other to where we can't hardly move. Death stood up, throwed on his robe . . . had him a white robe with a hood on it. He throwed on that robe and went off to look for his sickle. Say, "I'll be back." Just like that. "I'll be back." I told him, say, "Yeah, but . . . you gonna have to find me!" I wasn't no fool. I wasn't going looking for him. Death ain't nothing to play with. And I know he's gonna get me. I know I got to join his army . . . his camp followers. But as long as I keep my strength and see him coming . . . as long as I keep up my vigilance . . . he's gonna have to fight to get me. I ain't going easy.

BONO   Well, look here, since you got to keep up your vigilance . . . let me have the bottle.

TROY   Aw hell, I shouldn't have told you that part. I should have left out that part.

ROSE   Troy be talking that stuff and half the time don't even know what he be talking about.

TROY   Bono know me better than that.

BONO   That's right. I know you. I know you got some Uncle Remus[2] in your blood. You got more stories than the devil got sinners.

TROY   Aw hell, I done seen him too! Done talked with the devil.

ROSE   Troy, don't nobody wanna be hearing all that stuff.

[LYONS *enters the yard from the street. Thirty-four years old,* TROY's *son by a previous marriage, he sports a neatly trimmed goatee, sport coat, white shirt, tieless and buttoned at the collar. Though he fancies himself*

2. Old slave and folk philosopher whose proverbs and stories were recorded by Joel Chandler Harris (1848–1908).

a musician, he is more caught up in the rituals and "idea" of being a musician than in the actual practice of the music. He has come to borrow money from TROY, *and while he knows he will be successful, he is uncertain as to what extent his lifestyle will be held up to scrutiny and ridicule.*]

LYONS   Hey, Pop.

TROY   What you come "Hey, Popping" me for?

LYONS   How you doing, Rose? [*He kisses her.*] Mr. Bono, how you doing?

BONO   Hey, Lyons . . . how you been?

TROY   He must have been doing alright. I ain't seen him around here last week.

ROSE   Troy, leave your boy alone. He come by to see you and you wanna start all that nonsense.

TROY   I ain't bothering Lyons. [*Offers him the bottle.*] Here . . . get you a drink. We got an understanding. I know why he come by to see me and he know I know.

LYONS   Come on, Pop . . . I just stopped by to say hi . . . see how you was doing.

TROY   You ain't stopped by yesterday.

ROSE   You gonna stay for supper, Lyons? I got some chicken cooking in the oven.

LYONS   No, Rose . . . thanks. I was just in the neighborhood and thought I'd stop by for a minute.

TROY   You was in the neighborhood alright, nigger. You telling the truth there. You was in the neighborhood cause it's my payday.

LYONS   Well, hell, since you mentioned it . . . let me have ten dollars.

TROY   I'll be damned! I'll die and go to hell and play blackjack with the devil before I give you ten dollars.

BONO   That's what I wanna know about . . . that devil you done seen.

LYONS   What . . . Pop done seen the devil? You too much, Pops.

TROY   Yeah, I done seen him. Talked to him too!

ROSE   You ain't seen no devil. I done told you that man ain't had nothing to do with the devil. Anything you can't understand, you want to call it the devil.

TROY   Look here, Bono . . . I went down to see Hertzberger about some furniture. Got three rooms for two-ninety-eight. That what it say on the radio. "Three rooms . . . two-ninety-eight." Even made up a little song about it. Go down there . . . man tell me I can't get no credit. I'm working every day and can't get no credit. What to do? I got an empty house with some raggedy furniture in it. Cory ain't got no bed. He's sleeping on a pile of rags on the floor. Working every day and can't get no credit. Come back here—Rose'll tell you—madder than hell. Sit down . . . try to figure what I'm gonna do. Come a knock on the door. Ain't been living here but three days. Who know I'm here? Open the door . . . devil standing there bigger than life. White fellow . . . got on good clothes and everything. Standing there with a clipboard in his hand. I ain't had to say nothing. First words come out of his mouth was . . . "I understand you need some furniture and can't get no credit." I liked to fell over. He say "I'll give you all the credit you want, but you got to pay the interest on it." I told him, "Give me three rooms worth and charge whatever you want." Next day a truck pulled up here and two men unloaded them three rooms. Man what drove the truck give me a book. Say send ten dollars, first of every month to the address in the book and everything will be alright. Say if I miss a payment the devil was coming back and it'll be hell to pay. That was fifteen years ago. To this day . . . the first of the month I send my ten dollars, Rose'll tell you.

ROSE   Troy lying.

TROY   I ain't never seen that man since. Now you tell me who else that could have been but the devil? I ain't sold my soul or nothing like that, you understand. Naw, I wouldn't have truck with the devil about nothing like that. I got my furniture and pays my ten dollars the first of the month just like clockwork.

BONO   How long you say you been paying this ten dollars a month?

TROY   Fifteen years!

BONO   Hell, ain't you finished paying for it yet? How much the man done charged you.

TROY   Aw hell, I done paid for it. I done paid for it ten times over! The fact is I'm scared to stop paying it.

ROSE   Troy lying. We got that furniture from Mr. Glickman. He ain't paying no ten dollars a month to nobody.

TROY   Aw hell, woman. Bono know I ain't that big a fool.

LYONS   I was just getting ready to say . . . I know where there's a bridge for sale.

TROY   Look here, I'll tell you this . . . it don't matter to me if he was the devil. It don't matter if the devil give credit. Somebody has got to give it.

ROSE   It ought to matter. You going around talking about having truck with the devil . . . God's the one you gonna have to answer to. He's the one gonna be at the Judgment.

LYONS   Yeah, well, look here, Pop . . . let me have that ten dollars. I'll give it back to you. Bonnie got a job working at the hospital.

TROY   What I tell you, Bono? The only time I see this nigger is when he wants something. That's the only time I see him.

LYONS   Come on, Pop, Mr. Bono don't want to hear all that. Let me have the ten dollars. I told you Bonnie working.

TROY   What that mean to me? "Bonnie working." I don't care if she working. Go ask her for the ten dollars if she working. Talking about "Bonnie working." Why ain't you working?

LYONS   Aw, Pop, you know I can't find no decent job. Where am I gonna get a job at? You know I can't get no job.

TROY   I told you I know some people down there. I can get you on the rubbish if you want to work. I told you that the last time you came by here asking me for something.

LYONS   Naw, Pop . . . thanks. That ain't for me. I don't wanna be carrying nobody's rubbish. I don't wanna be punching nobody's time clock.

TROY   What's the matter, you too good to carry people's rubbish? Where you think that ten dollars you talking about come from? I'm just supposed to haul people's rubbish and give my money to you cause you too lazy to work. You too lazy to work and wanna know why you ain't got what I got.

ROSE   What hospital Bonnie working at? Mercy?

LYONS   She's down at Passavant working in the laundry.

TROY   I ain't got nothing as it is. I give you that ten dollars and I got to eat beans the rest of the week. Naw . . . you ain't getting no ten dollars here.

LYONS   You ain't got to be eating no beans. I don't know why you wanna say that.

TROY   I ain't got no extra money. Gabe done moved over to Miss Pearl's paying her the rent and things done got tight around here. I can't afford to be giving you every payday.

LYONS   I ain't asked you to give me nothing. I asked you to loan me ten dollars. I know you got ten dollars.

TROY   Yeah, I got it. You know why I got it? Cause I don't throw my money away out there in the streets. You living the fast life . . . wanna be a musician . . . running around in them clubs and things . . . then, you learn to take care of yourself. You ain't gonna find me going and asking nobody for nothing. I done spent too many years without.

LYONS   You and me is two different people, Pop.

TROY   I done learned my mistake and learned to do what's right by it. You still trying to get something for nothing. Life don't owe you nothing. You owe it to yourself. Ask Bono. He'll tell you I'm right.

LYONS   You got your way of dealing with the world . . . I got mine. The only thing that matters to me is the music.

TROY   Yeah, I can see that! It don't matter how you gonna eat . . . where your next dollar is coming from. You telling the truth there.

LYONS   I know I got to eat. But I got to live too. I need something that gonna help me to get out of the bed in the morning. Make me feel like I belong in the world. I don't bother nobody. I just stay with my music cause that's the only way I can find to live in the world. Otherwise there ain't no telling what I might do. Now I don't come criticizing you and how you live. I just come by to ask you for ten dollars. I don't wanna hear all that about how I live.

TROY   Boy, your mama did a hell of a job raising you.

LYONS   You can't change me, Pop. I'm thirty-four years old. If you wanted to change me, you should have been there when I was growing up. I come by to see you . . . ask for ten dollars and you want to talk about how I was raised. You don't know nothing about how I was raised.

ROSE   Let the boy have ten dollars, Troy.

TROY   [to LYONS]   What the hell you looking at me for? I ain't got no ten dollars. You know what I do with my money. [to ROSE.] Give him ten dollars if you want him to have it.

ROSE   I will. Just as soon as you turn it loose.

TROY   [handing ROSE the money]   There it is. Seventy-six dollars and forty-two cents. You see this, Bono? Now, I ain't gonna get but six of that back.

ROSE   You ought to stop telling that lie. Here, Lyons. [She hands him the money.]

LYONS   Thanks, Rose. Look . . . I got to run . . . I'll see you later.

TROY   Wait a minute. You gonna say, "thanks, Rose" and ain't gonna look to see where she got that ten dollars from? See how they do me, Bono?

LYONS   I know she got it from you, Pop. Thanks. I'll give it back to you.

TROY   There he go telling another lie. Time I see that ten dollars . . . he'll be owing me thirty more.

LYONS   See you, Mr. Bono.

BONO   Take care, Lyons!

LYONS   Thanks, Pop. I'll see you again. [LYONS *exits the yard.*]

TROY   I don't know why he don't go and get him a decent job and take care of that woman he got.

BONO   He'll be alright, Troy. The boy is still young.

TROY   The *boy* is thirty-four years old.

ROSE   Let's not get off into all that.

BONO   Look here . . . I got to be going. I got to be getting on. Lucille gonna be waiting.

TROY   [*puts his arm around* ROSE]   See this woman, Bono? I love this woman. I love this woman so much it hurts. I love her so much . . . I done run out of ways of loving her. So I got to go back to basics. Don't you come by my house Monday morning talking about time to go to work . . .'cause I'm still gonna be stroking!

ROSE   Troy! Stop it now!

BONO   I ain't paying him no mind, Rose. That ain't nothing but gin-talk. Go on, Troy. I'll see you Monday.

TROY   Don't you come by my house, nigger! I done told you what I'm gonna be doing.
[*The lights go down to black.*]

SCENE 2

The lights come up on ROSE *hanging up clothes. She hums and sings softly to herself. It is the following morning.*

[ROSE *sings*]
Jesus, be a fence all around me every day
Jesus, I want you to protect me as I travel on my way.
Jesus, be a fence all around me every day.
[TROY *enters from the house.*]
[ROSE (*continued*)]
Jesus, I want you to protect me
As I travel on my way.
[*To* TROY]
'Morning. You ready for breakfast? I can fix it soon as I finish hanging up these clothes?

TROY   I got the coffee on. That'll be alright. I'll just drink some of that this morning.

ROSE   That 651 hit yesterday. That's the second time this month. Miss Pearl hit for a dollar . . . seem like those that need the least always get lucky. Poor folks can't get nothing.

TROY   Them numbers don't know nobody. I don't know why you fool with them. You and Lyons both.

ROSE   It's something to do.

TROY   You ain't doing nothing but throwing your money away.

ROSE   Troy, you know I don't play foolishly. I just play a nickel here and a nickel there.

TROY   That's two nickels you done thrown away.

ROSE   Now I hit sometimes . . . that makes up for it. It always comes in handy when I do hit. I don't hear you complaining then.

TROY   I ain't complaining now. I just say it's foolish. Trying to guess out of six hundred ways which way the number gonna come. If I had all the money niggers, these Negroes, throw away on numbers for one week— just one week—I'd be a rich man.

ROSE   Well, you wishing and calling it foolish ain't gonna stop folks from playing numbers. That's one thing for sure. Besides . . . some good things come from playing numbers. Look where Pope done bought him that restaurant off of numbers.

TROY   I can't stand niggers like that. Man ain't had two dimes to rub together. He walking around with his shoes all run over bumming money for cigarettes. Alright. Got lucky there and hit the numbers . . .

ROSE   Troy, I know all about it.

TROY   Had good sense, I'll say that for him. He ain't throwed his money away. I seen niggers hit the numbers and go through two thousand dollars in four days. Man brought him that restaurant down there . . . fixed it up real nice . . . and then didn't want nobody to come in it! A Negro go in there and can't get no kind of service. I seen a white fellow come in there and order a bowl of stew. Pope picked all the meat out the pot for him. Man ain't had nothing but a bowl of meat! Negro come behind him and ain't got nothing but the potatoes and carrots. Talking about what numbers do for people, you picked a wrong example. Ain't done nothing but make a worser fool out of him than he was before.

ROSE   Troy, you ought to stop worrying about what happened at work yesterday.

TROY   I ain't worried. Just told me to be down there at the Commissioner's office on Friday. Everybody think they gonna fire me. I ain't worried about them firing me. You ain't got to worry about that [*Pause.*] Where's Cory? Cory in the house? [*Calls*] Cory?

ROSE   He gone out.

TROY   Out, huh? He gone out 'cause he know I want him to help me with this fence. I know how he is. That boy scared of work.

[GABRIEL *enters. He comes halfway down the alley and, hearing* TROY's *voice, stops.*]

TROY [*continues*]   He ain't done a lick of work in his life.

ROSE   He had to go to football practice. Coach wanted them to get in a little extra practice before the season start.

TROY   I got his practice . . . running out of here before he get his chores done.

ROSE   Troy, what is wrong with you this morning? Don't nothing set right with you. Go on back in there and go to bed . . . get up on the other side.

TROY   Why something got to be wrong with me? I ain't said nothing wrong with me.

ROSE   You got something to say about everything. First it's the numbers . . . then it's the way the man runs his restaurant . . . then you done got on Cory. What's it gonna be next? Take a look up there and see if the weather suits you . . . or is it gonna be how you gonna put up the fence with the clothes hanging in the yard.

TROY   You hit the nail on the head then.

ROSE   I know you like I know the back of my hand. Go on in there and get you some coffee . . . see if that straighten you up. 'Cause you ain't right this morning.

[TROY *starts into the house and sees* GABRIEL. GABRIEL *starts singing.* TROY's *brother, he is seven years younger than* TROY. *Injured in World War II, he has a metal plate in his head. He carries an old trumpet tied around his waist and believes with every fiber of his being that he is the Archangel Gabriel. He carries a chipped basket with an assortment of discarded fruits and vegetables he has picked up in the strip district and which he attempts to sell.*]

[GABRIEL *singing.*]
Yes ma'am, I got plums
You ask me how I sell them
Oh ten cents apiece
Three for a quarter
Come and buy now
'Cause I'm here today
And tomorrow I'll be gone

[GABRIEL *enters.*]

GABRIEL   Hey, Rose!

ROSE   How you doing, Gabe?

GABRIEL   There's Troy . . . Hey, Troy!

TROY   Hey, Gabe. [*Exit into kitchen.*]

ROSE [*to* GABRIEL]   What you got there?

GABRIEL   You know what I got, Rose. I got fruits and vegetables.

ROSE [*looking in basket*]   Where's all these plums you talking about?

GABRIEL   I ain't got no plums today, Rose. I was just singing that. Have some tomorrow. Put me in a big order for plums. Have enough plums tomorrow for St. Peter and everybody. [TROY *re-enters from kitchen, crosses to steps. To* ROSE.] Troy's mad at me.

TROY   I ain't mad at you. What I got to be mad at you about? You ain't done nothing to me.

GABRIEL   I just moved over to Miss Pearl's to keep out from in your way. I ain't mean no harm by it.

TROY   Who said anything about that? I ain't said anything about that.

GABRIEL   You ain't mad at me, is you?

TROY   Naw . . . I ain't mad at you, Gabe. If I was mad at you I'd tell you about it.

GABRIEL   Got me two rooms. In the basement. Got my own door too. Wanna see my key? [*He holds up a key.*] That's my own key! Ain't nobody else got a key like that. That's my key! My two rooms!

TROY   Well, that's good, Gabe. You got your own key . . . that's good.

ROSE   You hungry, Gabe? I was just fixing to cook Troy his breakfast.

GABRIEL   I'll take some biscuits. You got some biscuits? Did you know when I was in heaven . . . every morning me and St. Peter would sit down by the gate and eat some big fat biscuits? Oh, yeah! We had us a good time. We'd sit there and eat us them biscuits and then St. Peter would go off to sleep and tell me to wake him up when it's time to open the gates for the judgment.

ROSE   Well, come on . . . I'll make up a batch of biscuits. [ROSE *exits into the house.*]

GABRIEL   Troy . . . St. Peter got your name in the book. I seen it. It say . . . Troy Maxson. I say . . . I know him! He got the same name like what I got. That's my brother!

TROY   How many times you gonna tell me that, Gabe?

GABRIEL   Ain't got my name in the book. Don't have to have my name. I done died and went to heaven. He got your name though. One morning St. Peter was looking at his book . . . marking it up for the judgment . . . and he let me see your name. Got it in there under M. Got Rose's name . . . I ain't seen it like I seen yours . . . but I know it's in there. He got a great big book. Got everybody's name what was ever been born. That's what he told me. But I seen your name. Seen it with my own eyes.

TROY   Go on in the house there. Rose going to fix you something to eat.

GABRIEL   Oh, I ain't hungry. I done had breakfast with Aunt Jemimah. She come by and cooked me up a whole mess of flapjacks. Remember how we used to eat them flapjacks?

TROY   Go on in the house and get you something to eat now.

GABRIEL   I got to go sell my plums. I done sold some tomatoes. Got me two quarters. Wanna see? [*He shows* TROY *his quarters.*] I'm gonna save them and buy me a new horn so St. Peter can hear me when it's time to open the gates. [GABRIEL *stops suddenly. Listens.*] Hear that? That's the hell-hounds. I got to chase them out of here. Go on get out of here! Get out!

[GABRIEL *exits singing.*]

Better get ready for the judgment
Better get ready for the judgment
My lord is coming down

[ROSE *enters from the house.*]

TROY   He gone off somewhere.

GABRIEL [*offstage*]

Better get ready for the judgment
Better get ready for the judgment morning
Better get ready for the judgment
My God is coming down.

ROSE   He ain't eating right. Miss Pearl say she can't get him to eat nothing.

TROY   What you want me to do about it, Rose? I done did everything I can for the man. I can't make him get well. Man got half his head blown away . . . what you expect?

ROSE   Seem like something ought to be done to help him.

TROY   Man don't bother nobody. He just mixed up from that metal plate he got in his head. Ain't no sense for him to go back into the hospital.

ROSE   Least he be eating right. They can help him take care of himself.

TROY   Don't nobody wanna be locked up, Rose. What you wanna lock him up for? Man go over there and fight the war . . . messin' around with them Japs, get half his head blown off . . . and they give him a lousy three thousand dollars. And I had to swoop down on that.

ROSE   Is you fixing to go into that again?

TROY   That's the only way I got a roof over my head . . . cause of that metal plate.

ROSE   Ain't no sense you blaming yourself for nothing. Gabe wasn't in no condition to manage that money. You done what was right by him. Can't nobody say you ain't done what was right by him. Look how long you took care of him . . . till he wanted to have his own place and moved over there with Miss Pearl.

TROY   That ain't what I'm saying, woman! I'm just stating the facts. If my brother didn't have that metal plate in his head . . . I wouldn't have a pot to piss in or a window to throw it out of. And I'm fifty-three years old. Now see if you can understand that! [TROY *gets up from the porch and starts to exit the yard.*]

ROSE   Where you going off to? You been running out of here every Saturday for weeks. I thought you was gonna work on this fence?

TROY   I'm gonna walk down to Taylors'. Listen to the ball game. I'll be back in a bit. I'll work on it when I get back.
      [*He exits the yard. The lights go to black.*]

SCENE 3

The lights come up on the yard. It is four hours later. ROSE *is taking down the clothes from the line.* CORY *enters carrying his football equipment.*

ROSE   Your daddy liked to had a fit with you running out of here this morning without doing your chores.

CORY   I told you I had to go to practice.

ROSE   He say you were supposed to help him with this fence.

CORY   He been saying that the last four or five Saturdays, and then he don't never do nothing, but go down to Taylors'. Did you tell him about the recruiter?

ROSE   Yeah, I told him.

CORY   What he say?

ROSE   He ain't said nothing too much. You get in there and get started on your chores before he gets back. Go on and scrub down them steps before he gets back here hollering and carrying on.

CORY   I'm hungry. What you got to eat, Mama?

ROSE   Go on and get started on your chores. I got some meat loaf in there. Go on and make you a sandwich . . . and don't leave no mess in there. [CORY *exits into the house.* ROSE *continues to take down the clothes.* TROY *enters the yard and sneaks up and grabs her from behind.*] Troy! Go on, now. You liked to scared me to death. What was the score of the game? Lucille had me on the phone and I couldn't keep up with it.

TROY   What I care about the game? Come here, woman. [*He tries to kiss her.*]

ROSE   I thought you went down Taylors' to listen to the game. Go on, Troy! You supposed to be putting up this fence.

TROY   [*attempting to kiss her again*]   I'll put it up when I finish with what is at hand.

ROSE   Go on, Troy. I ain't studying you.

TROY   [*chasing after her*]   I'm studying you . . . fixing to do my homework!

ROSE   Troy, you better leave me alone.

TROY   Where's Cory? That boy brought his butt home yet?

ROSE   He's in the house doing his chores.

TROY [*calling*]   Cory! Get your butt out here, boy! [ROSE *exits into the house with the laundry.* TROY *goes over to the pile of wood, picks up a board, and starts sawing.* CORY *enters from the house.*] You just now coming in here from leaving this morning?

CORY   Yeah, I had to go to football practice.

TROY   Yeah, what?

CORY   Yessir.

TROY   I ain't but two seconds off you noway. The garbage sitting in there overflowing . . . you ain't done none of your chores . . . and you come in here talking about, "Yeah."

CORY   I was just getting ready to do my chores now, Pop . . .

TROY   Your first chore is to help me with this fence on Saturday. Everything else come after that. Now get that saw and cut them boards.

> [CORY *takes the saw and begins cutting the boards.* TROY *continues working. There is a long pause.*]

CORY   Hey, Pop . . . why don't you buy a TV?

TROY   What I want with a TV? What I want one of them for?

CORY   Everybody got one. Earl, Ba Bra . . . Jesse!

TROY   I ain't asked you who had one. I say what I want with one?

CORY   So you can watch it. They got lots of things on TV. Baseball games and everything. We could watch the World Series.

TROY   Yeah . . . and how much this TV cost?

CORY   I don't know. They got them on sale for around two hundred dollars.

TROY   Two hundred dollars, huh?

CORY   That ain't that much, Pop.

TROY   Naw, it's just two hundred dollars. See that roof you got over your head at night? Let me tell you something about that roof. It's been over ten years since that roof was last tarred. See now . . . the snow come this winter and sit up there on that roof like it is . . . and it's gonna seep inside. It's just gonna be a little bit . . . ain't gonna hardly notice it. Then the next thing you know, it's gonna be leaking all over the house. Then the wood rot from all that water and you gonna need a whole new roof. Now, how much you think it cost to get that roof tarred?

CORY   I don't know.

TROY   Two hundred and sixty-four dollars . . . cash money. While you thinking about a TV, I got to be thinking about the roof . . . and whatever else go wrong around here. Now if you had two hundred dollars, what would you do . . . fix the roof or buy a TV?

CORY   I'd buy a TV. Then when the roof started to leak . . . when it needed fixing . . . I'd fix it.

TROY   Where you gonna get the money from? You done spent it for a TV. You gonna sit up and watch the water run all over your brand new TV.

CORY   Aw, Pop. You got money. I know you do.

TROY   Where I got it at, huh?

CORY   You got it in the bank.

TROY   You wanna see my bankbook? You wanna see that seventy-three dollars and twenty-two cents I got sitting up in there.

CORY   You ain't got to pay for it all at one time. You can put a down payment on it and carry it on home with you.

TROY   Not me. I ain't gonna owe nobody nothing if I can help it. Miss a payment and they come and snatch it right out your house. Then what you got? Now, soon as I get two hundred dollars clear, then I'll buy a TV. Right now, as soon as I get two hundred and sixty-four dollars, I'm gonna have this roof tarred.

CORY   Aw . . . Pop!

TROY   You go on and get you two hundred dollars and buy one if ya want it. I got better things to do with my money.

CORY   I can't get no two hundred dollars. I ain't never seen two hundred dollars.

TROY   I'll tell you what . . . you get you a hundred dollars and I'll put the other hundred with it.

CORY   Alright, I'm gonna show you.

TROY   You gonna show me how you can cut them boards right now.
          [CORY *begins to cut the boards. There is a long pause.*]

CORY   The Pirates won today. That makes five in a row.

TROY   I ain't thinking about the Pirates. Got an all-white team. Got that boy . . . that Puerto Rican boy . . . Clemente. Don't even half-play him. That boy could be something if they give him a chance. Play him one day and sit him on the bench the next.

CORY   He gets a lot of chances to play.

TROY   I'm talking about playing regular. Playing every day so you can get your timing. That's what I'm talking about.

CORY   They got some white guys on the team that don't play every day. You can't play everybody at the same time.

TROY   If they got a white fellow sitting on the bench . . . you can bet your last dollar he can't play! The colored guy got to be twice as good before he get on the team. That's why I don't want you to get all tied up in them sports. Man on the team and what it get him? They got colored on the team and don't use them. Same as not having them. All them teams the same.

CORY   The Braves got Hank Aaron and Wes Covington. Hank Aaron hit two home runs today. That makes forty-three.

TROY   Hank Aaron ain't nobody. That's what you supposed to do. That's how you supposed to play the game. Ain't nothing to it. It's just a matter of timing . . . getting the right follow-through. Hell, I can hit forty-three home runs right now!

CORY   Not off no major-league pitching, you couldn't.

TROY   We had better pitching in the Negro leagues. I hit seven home runs off of Satchel Paige. You can't get no better than that!

CORY   Sandy Koufax. He's leading the league in strikeouts.

TROY   I ain't thinking of no Sandy Koufax.

CORY   You got Warren Spahn and Lew Burdette. I bet you couldn't hit no home runs off of Warren Spahn.

TROY   I'm through with it now. You go on and cut them boards. [*Pause.*] Your mama tells me you got recruited by a college football team? Is that right?

CORY   Yeah. Coach Zellman say the recruiter gonna be coming by to talk to you. Get you to sign the permission papers.

TROY   I thought you supposed to be working down there at the A&P. Ain't you suppose to be working down there after school?

CORY   Mr. Stawicki say he gonna hold my job for me until after the football season. Say starting next week I can work weekends.

TROY   I thought we had an understanding about this football stuff? You suppose to keep up with your chores and hold that job down at the A&P. Ain't been around here all day on a Saturday. Ain't none of your chores done . . . and now you telling me you done quit your job.

CORY   I'm gonna be working weekends.

TROY   You damn right you are! And ain't no need for nobody coming around here to talk to me about signing nothing.

CORY   Hey, Pop . . . you can't do that. He's coming all the way from North Carolina.

TROY   I don't care where he coming from. The white man ain't gonna let you get nowhere with that football noway. You go on and get your book-learning so you can work yourself up in that A&P or learn how to fix cars or build houses or something, get you a trade. That way you can have something can't nobody take away from you. You go on and learn how to put your hands to some good use. Besides hauling people's garbage.

CORY   I get good grades, Pop. That's why the recruiter wants to talk with you. You got to keep up your grades to get recruited. This way I'll be going to college. I'll get a chance . . .

TROY   First, you gonna get your butt down there to the A&P and get your job back.

CORY   Mr. Stawicki done already hired somebody else 'cause I told him I was playing football.

TROY   You a bigger fool than I thought . . . to let somebody take away your job so you can play some football. Where you gonna get your money to take out your girlfriend and whatnot? What kind of foolishness is that to let somebody take away your job?

CORY   I'm still gonna be working weekends.

TROY   Naw . . . naw. You getting your butt out of here and finding you another job.

CORY   Come on, Pop! I got to practice. I can't work after school and play football too. The team needs me. That's what Coach Zellman say . . .

TROY   I don't care what nobody else say. I'm the boss . . . you understand? I'm the boss around here. I do the only saying what counts.

CORY   Come on, Pop!

TROY   I asked you . . . Did you understand?

CORY   Yeah . . .

TROY   What!

CORY   Yessir.

TROY   You go down there to that A&P and see if you can get your job back. If you can't do both . . . then you quit the football team. You've got to take the crookeds with the straights.

CORY   Yessir. [*Pause.*] Can I ask you a question?

TROY   What the hell you wanna ask me? Mr. Stawicki the one you got the questions for.

CORY   How come you ain't never liked me?

TROY   Liked you? Who the hell say I got to like you? What law is there say I got to like you? Wanna stand up in my face and ask a damn fool-ass question like that. Talking about liking somebody. Come here, boy, when

I talk to you. [CORY *comes over to where* TROY *is working. He stands slouched over and* TROY *shoves him on his shoulder.*] Straighten up, goddammit! I asked you a question . . . what law is there say I got to like you?

CORY None.

TROY Well, alright then! Don't you eat every day? [*Pause.*] Answer me when I talk to you! Don't you eat every day?

CORY Yeah.

TROY Nigger, as long as you in my house, you put that sir on the end of it when you talk to me!

CORY Yes . . . sir.

TROY You eat every day.

CORY Yessir!

TROY Got a roof over your head.

CORY Yessir!

TROY Got clothes on your back.

CORY Yessir.

TROY Why you think that is?

CORY 'Cause of you.

TROY Aw, hell I know it's 'cause of me . . . but why do you think that is?

CORY [*hesitant*] 'Cause you like me.

TROY Like you? I go out of here every morning . . . bust my butt . . . putting up with them crackers every day . . . 'cause I like you? You about the biggest fool I ever saw. [*Pause.*] It's my job. It's my responsibility! You understand that? A man got to take care of his family. You live in my house . . . sleep you behind on my bedclothes . . . fill you belly up with my food . . . cause you my son. You my flesh and blood. Not 'cause I like you! 'Cause it's my duty to take care of you. I owe a responsibility to you! Let's get this straight right here . . . before it go along any further . . . I ain't got to like you. Mr. Rand don't give me my money come payday 'cause he likes me. He gives me 'cause he owe me. I done give you everything I had to give you. I gave you your life! Me and your mama worked that out between us. And liking your black ass wasn't part of the bargain. Don't you try and go through life worrying about if somebody like you or not. You best be making sure they doing right by you. You understand what I'm saying, boy?

CORY Yessir.

TROY Then get the hell out of my face, and get on down to that A&P.

[ROSE *has been standing behind the screen door for much of the scene. She enters as* CORY *exits.*]

ROSE Why don't you let the boy go ahead and play football, Troy? Ain't no harm in that. He's just trying to be like you with the sports.

TROY I don't want him to be like me! I want him to move as far away from my life as he can get. You the only decent thing that ever happened to me. I wish him that. But I don't wish him a thing else from my life. I decided seventeen years ago that boy wasn't getting involved in no sports. Not after what they did to me in the sports.

ROSE Troy, why don't you admit you was too old to play in the major leagues? For once . . . why don't you admit that?

TROY What do you mean too old? Don't come telling me I was too old. I just wasn't the right color. Hell, I'm fifty-three years old and I can do better than Selkirk's .269 right now!

ROSE How's was you gonna play ball when you were over forty? Sometimes I can't get no sense out of you.

TROY I got good sense, woman. I got sense enough not to let my boy get hurt over playing no sports. You been mothering that boy too much. Worried about if people like him.

ROSE Everything that boy do . . . he do for you. He wants you to say "Good job, son." That's all.

TROY Rose, I ain't got time for that. He's alive. He's healthy. He's got to make his own way. I made mine. Ain't nobody gonna hold his hand when he get out there in that world.

ROSE Times have changed from when you was young, Troy. People change. The world's changing around you and you can't even see it.

TROY [slow, methodical] Woman . . . I do the best I can do. I come in here every Friday. I carry a sack of potatoes and a bucket of lard. You all line up at the door with your hands out. I give you the lint from my pockets. I give you my sweat and my blood. I ain't got no tears. I done spent them. We go upstairs in that room at night . . . and I fall down on you and try to blast a hole into forever. I get up Monday morning . . . find my lunch on the table. I go out. Make my way. Find my strength to carry me through to the next Friday. [Pause.] That's all I got, Rose. That's all I got to give. I can't give nothing else.

[TROY exits into the house. The lights go down to black.]

SCENE 4

It is Friday. Two weeks later. CORY starts out of the house with his football equipment. The phone rings.

CORY [calling] I got it! [He answers the phone and stands in the screen door talking.] Hello? Hey, Jesse. Naw . . . I was just getting ready to leave now.

ROSE [calling] Cory!

CORY I told you, man, them spikes is all tore up. You can use them if you want, but they ain't no good. Earl got some spikes.

ROSE [calling] Cory!

CORY [calling to ROSE] Mam? I'm talking to Jesse. [Into phone.] When she say that? [Pause.] Aw, you lying, man. I'm gonna tell her you said that.

ROSE [calling] Cory, don't you go nowhere!

CORY I got to go to the game, Ma! [Into the phone.] Yeah, hey, look, I'll talk to you later. Yeah, I'll meet you over Earl's house. Later. Bye, Ma!

[CORY exits the house and starts out the yard.]

ROSE Cory, where you going off to? You got that stuff all pulled out and thrown all over your room.

CORY [in the yard] I was looking for my spikes. Jesse wanted to borrow my spikes.

ROSE Get up there and get that cleaned up before your daddy gets back in here.

CORY I got to go to the game! I'll clean it up when I get back. [CORY exits.]

ROSE That's all he need to do is see that room all messed up.

[ROSE exits into the house. TROY and BONO enter the yard. TROY is dressed in clothes other than his work clothes.]

BONO He told him the same thing he told you. Take it to the union.

TROY   Brownie ain't got that much sense. Man wasn't thinking about nothing. He wait until I confront them on it . . . then he wanna come crying seniority. [*Calls.*] Hey, Rose!

BONO   I wish I could have seen Mr. Rand's face when he told you.

TROY   He couldn't get it out of his mouth! Liked to bit his tongue! When they called me down there to the Commissioner's office . . . he thought they was gonna fire me. Like everybody else.

BONO   I didn't think they was gonna fire you. I thought they was gonna put you on the warning paper.

TROY   Hey, Rose! [*To* BONO.] Yeah, Mr. Rand like to bit his tongue. [TROY *breaks the seal on the bottle, takes a drink, and hands it to* BONO.]

BONO   I see you ran right down to Taylors' and told that Alberta gal.

TROY [*calling*]   Hey Rose! [*To* BONO] I told everybody. Hey Rose! I went down there to cash my check.

ROSE [*entering from the house*]   Hush all that hollering, man! I know you out here. What they say down there at the Commissioner's office?

TROY   You supposed to come when I call you, woman. Bono'll tell you that. [*To* BONO.] Don't Lucille come when you call her?

ROSE   Man, hush your mouth. I ain't no dog . . . talk about "come when you call me."

TROY [*puts his arm around* ROSE]   You hear this, Bono? I had me an old dog used to get uppity like that. You say, "C'mere, Blue!" . . . and he just lay there and look at you. End up getting a stick and chasing him away trying to make him come.

ROSE   I ain't studying you and your dog. I remember you used to sing that old song.

TROY [*He sings.*]   Hear it ring! Hear it ring! I had a dog his name was Blue.

ROSE   Don't nobody wanna hear you sing that old song.

TROY [*sings*]   You know Blue was mighty true.

ROSE   Used to have Cory running around here singing that song.

BONO   Hell, I remember that song myself.

TROY [*sings*]

>   You know Blue was a good old dog.
>   Blue treed a possum in a hollow log.

That was my daddy's song. My daddy made up that song.

ROSE   I don't care who made it up. Don't nobody wanna hear you sing it.

TROY [*makes a song like calling a dog*]   Come here, woman.

ROSE   You come in here carrying on, I reckon they ain't fired you. What they say down there at the Commissioner's office?

TROY   Look here, Rose . . . Mr. Rand called me into his office today when I got back from talking to them people down there . . . it come from up top . . . he called me in and told me they was making me a driver.

ROSE   Troy, you kidding!

TROY   No I ain't. Ask Bono.

ROSE   Well, that's great, Troy. Now you don't have to hassle them people no more.

[LYONS *enters from the street.*]

TROY   Aw hell, I wasn't looking to see you today. I thought you was in jail. Got it all over the front page of the *Courier* about them raiding Sefus' place . . . where you be hanging out with all them thugs.

LYONS   Hey, Pop . . . that ain't got nothing to do with me. I don't go down there gambling. I go down there to sit in with the band. I ain't got nothing to do with the gambling part. They got some good music down there.

TROY   They got some rogues . . . is what they got.

LYONS   How you been, Mr. Bono? Hi, Rose.

BONO   I see where you playing down at the Crawford Grill tonight.

ROSE   How come you ain't brought Bonnie like I told you. You should have brought Bonnie with you, she ain't been over in a month of Sundays.

LYONS   I was just in the neighborhood . . . thought I'd stop by.

TROY   Here he come . . .

BONO   Your daddy got a promotion on the rubbish. He's gonna be the first colored driver. Ain't got to do nothing but sit up there and read the paper like them white fellows.

LYONS   Hey, Pop . . . if you knew how to read you'd be alright.

BONO   Naw . . . naw . . . you mean if the nigger knew how to *drive* he'd be all right Been fighting with them people about driving and ain't even got a license. Mr. Rand know you ain't got no driver's license?

TROY   Driving ain't nothing. All you do is point the truck where you want it to go. Driving ain't nothing.

BONO   Do Mr. Rand know you ain't got no driver's license? That's what I'm talking about. I ain't asked if driving was easy. I asked if Mr. Rand know you ain't got no driver's license.

TROY   He ain't got to know. The man ain't got to know my business. Time he find out, I have two or three driver's licenses.

LYONS   [*going into his pocket*] Say, look here, Pop . . .

TROY   I knew it was coming. Didn't I tell you, Bono? I know what kind of "Look here, Pop" that was. The nigger fixing to ask me for some money. It's Friday night. It's my payday. All them rogues down there on the avenue . . . the ones that ain't in jail . . . and Lyons is hopping in his shoes to get down there with them.

LYONS   See, Pop . . . if you give somebody else a chance to talk sometime, you'd see that I was fixing to pay you back your ten dollars like I told you. Here . . . I told you I'd pay you when Bonnie got paid.

TROY   Naw . . . you go ahead and keep that ten dollars. Put it in the bank. The next time you feel like you wanna come by here and ask me for something . . . you go on down there and get that.

LYONS   Here's your ten dollars, Pop. I told you I don't want you to give me nothing. I just wanted to borrow ten dollars.

TROY   Naw . . . go on and keep that for the next time you want to ask me.

LYONS   Come on, Pop . . . here go your ten dollars.

ROSE   Why don't you go on and let the boy pay you back, Troy?

LYONS   Here you go, Rose. If you don't take it I'm gonna have to hear about it for the next six months. [*He hands her the money.*]

ROSE   You can hand yours over here too, Troy.

TROY   You see this, Bono. You see how they do me.

BONO   Yeah, Lucille do me the same way.

[GABRIEL *is heard singing offstage. He enters.*]

GABRIEL   Better get ready for the Judgment! Better get ready for . . . Hey! . . . Hey! . . . There's Troy's boy!

LYONS   How you doing, Uncle Gabe?

GABRIEL   Lyons . . . the King of the Jungle! Rose . . . hey, Rose. Got a flower for you. [*He takes a rose from his pocket.*] Picked it myself. That's the same rose like you is!

ROSE   That's right nice of you, Gabe.

LYONS   What you been doing, Uncle Gabe?

GABRIEL   Oh, I been chasing hellhounds and waiting on the time to tell St. Peter to open the gates.

LYONS   You been chasing hellhounds, huh? Well . . . you doing the right thing, Uncle Gabe. Somebody got to chase them.

GABRIEL   Oh, yeah . . . I know it. The devil's strong, The devil ain't no pushover. Hellhounds snipping at everybody's heels. But I got my trumpet waiting on the judgment time.

LYONS   Waiting on the Battle of Armageddon, huh?

GABRIEL   Ain't gonna be too much of a battle when God get to waving that Judgment sword. But the peoples gonna have a hell of a time trying to get into heaven if them gates ain't open.

LYONS   [*putting his arm around* GABRIEL]   You hear this, Pop. Uncle Gabe, you alright!

GABRIEL   [*laughing with* LYONS]   Lyons! King of the Jungle.

ROSE   You gonna stay for supper, Gabe. Want me to fix you a plate?

GABRIEL   I'll take a sandwich, Rose. Don't want no plate. Just wanna eat with my hands. I'll take a sandwich.

ROSE   How about you, Lyons? You staying? Got some short ribs cooking.

LYONS   Naw, I won't eat nothing till after we finished playing. [*Pause.*] You ought to come down and listen to me play, Pop.

TROY   I don't like that Chinese music. All that noise.

ROSE   Go on in the house and wash up, Gabe . . . I'll fix you a sandwich.

GABRIEL   [*to* LYONS, *as he exits*]   Troy's mad at me.

LYONS   What you mad at Uncle Gabe for, Pop.

ROSE   He thinks Troy's mad at him 'cause he moved over to Miss Pearl's.

TROY   I ain't mad at the man. He can live where he want to live at.

LYONS   What he move over there for? Miss Pearl don't like nobody.

ROSE   She don't mind him none. She treats him real nice. She just don't allow all that singing.

TROY   She don't mind that rent he be paying . . . that's what she don't mind.

ROSE   Troy, I ain't going through that with you no more. He's over there cause he want to have his own place. He can come and go as he please.

TROY   Hell, he could come and go as he please here. I wasn't stopping him. I ain't put no rules on him.

ROSE   It ain't the same thing, Troy. And you know it. [GABRIEL *comes to the door.*] Now, that's the last I wanna hear about that. I don't wanna hear nothing else about Gabe and Miss Pearl. And next week . . .

GABRIEL   I'm ready for my sandwich, Rose.

ROSE   And next week . . . when that recruiter come from that school . . . I want you to sign that paper and go on and let Cory play football. Then that'll be the last I have to hear about that.

TROY   [*to* ROSE *as she exits into the house*]   I ain't thinking about Cory nothing.

LYONS   What . . . Cory got recruited? What school he going to?

TROY   That boy walking around here smelling his piss . . . thinking he's grown. Thinking he's gonna do what he want, irrespective of what I say. Look here, Bono . . . I left the Commissioner's office and went down to the A&P . . . that boy ain't working down there. He lying to me. Telling me he got his job back . . . telling me he working weekends . . . telling me he working after school . . . Mr. Stawicki tell me he ain't working down there at all!

LYONS   Cory just growing up. He's just busting at the seams trying to fill out your shoes.

TROY   I don't care what he's doing. When he get to the point where he wanna disobey me . . . then it's time for him to move on. Bono'll tell you that. I bet he ain't never disobeyed his daddy without paying the consequences.

BONO   I ain't never had a chance. My daddy came on through . . . but I ain't never knew him to see him . . . or what he had on his mind or where he went. Just moving on through. Searching out the New Land. That's what the old folks used to call it. See a fellow moving around from place to place . . . woman to woman . . . called it searching out the New Land. I can't say if he ever found it. I come along, didn't want no kids. Didn't know if I was gonna be in one place long enough to fix on them right as their daddy. I figured I was going searching too. As it turned out I been hooked up with Lucille near about as long as your daddy been with Rose. Going on sixteen years.

TROY   Sometimes I wish I hadn't known my daddy. My daddy ain't cared nothing about no kids. A kid to him wasn't nothing. All he wanted was for you to learn how to walk so he could start you to working. When it come time for eating . . . he ate first. If there was anything left over, that's what you got. Man would sit down and eat two chickens and give you the wing.

LYONS   You ought to stop that, Pop. Everybody feed their kids. No matter how hard times is . . . everybody care about their kids. Make sure they have something to eat.

TROY   The only thing my daddy cared about was getting them bales of cotton in to Mr. Lubin. That's the only thing that mattered to him. Sometimes I used to wonder why he was living. Wonder why the devil hadn't come and got him. "Get them bales of cotton in to Mr. Lubin" and find out he owe him money . . .

LYONS   He should have just went on and left when he saw he couldn't get nowhere. That's what I would have done.

TROY   How he gonna leave with eleven kids? And where he gonna go? He ain't knew how to do nothing but farm. No, he was trapped and I think he knew it. But I'll say this for him . . . he felt a responsibility toward us. Maybe he ain't treated us the way I felt he should have . . . but without that responsibility he could have walked off and left us . . . made his own way.

BONO   A lot of them did. Back in those days what you talking about . . . they walk out their front door and just take on down one road or another and keep on walking.

LYONS   There you go! That's what I'm talking about.

BONO   Just keep on walking till you come to something else. Ain't you never heard of nobody having the walking blues? Well, that's what you call it when you just take off like that.

TROY   My daddy ain't had them walking blues! What you talking about? He stayed right there with his family. But he was just as evil as he could be. My mama couldn't stand him. Couldn't stand that evilness. She run off when I was about eight. She sneaked off one night after he had gone to sleep. Told me she was coming back for me. I ain't never seen her no more. All his women run off and left him. He wasn't good for nobody. When my turn come to head out, I was fourteen and got to sniffing around Joe Canewell's daughter. Had us an old mule we called Greyboy. My daddy sent me out to do some plowing and I tied up Greyboy and went to fooling around with Joe Canewell's daughter. We done found us a nice little spot, got real cozy with each other. She about thirteen and we done figured we was grown anyway . . . so we down there enjoying ourselves . . . ain't thinking about nothing. We didn't know Greyboy had got loose and wandered back to the house and my daddy was looking for me. We down there by the creek enjoying ourselves when my daddy come up on us. Surprised us. He had them leather straps off the mule and commenced to whupping me like there was no tomorrow. I jumped up, mad and embarrassed. I was scared of my daddy. When he commenced to whupping on me . . . quite naturally I run to get out of the way. [*Pause.*] Now I thought he was mad cause I ain't done my work. But I see where he was chasing me off so he could have the gal for himself. When I see what the matter of it was, I lost all fear of my daddy. Right there is where I become a man . . . at fourteen years of age. [*Pause.*] Now it was my turn to run him off. I picked up them same reins that he had used on me. I picked up them reins and commenced to whupping on him. The gal jumped up and run off . . . and when my daddy turned to face me, I could see why the devil had never come to get him . . . cause he was the devil himself. I don't know what happened. When I woke up, I was laying right there by the creek, and Blue . . . this old dog we had . . . was licking my face. I thought I was blind. I couldn't see nothing. Both my eyes were swollen shut. I layed there and cried. I didn't know what I was gonna do. The only thing I knew was the time had come for me to leave my daddy's house. And right there the world suddenly got big. And it was a long time before I could cut it down to where I could handle it. Part of that cutting down was when I got to the place where I could feel him kicking in my blood and knew that the only thing that separated us was the matter of a few years.

[GABRIEL *enters from the house with a sandwich.*]

LYONS   What you got there, Uncle Gabe?

GABRIEL   Got me a ham sandwich. Rose gave me a ham sandwich.

TROY   I don't know what happened to him. I done lost touch with everybody except Gabriel. But I hope he's dead. I hope he found some peace.

LYONS   That's a heavy story, Pop. I didn't know you left home when you was fourteen.

TROY   And didn't know nothing. The only part of the world I knew was the forty-two acres of Mr. Lubin's land. That's all I knew about life.

LYONS Fourteen's kinda young to be out on your own. [*Phone rings.*] I don't even think I was ready to be out on my own at fourteen. I don't know what I would have done.

TROY I got up from the creek and walked on down to Mobile. I was through with farming. Figured I could do better in the city. So I walked the two hundred miles to Mobile.

LYONS Wait a minute . . . you ain't walked no two hundred miles, Pop. Ain't nobody gonna walk no two hundred miles. You talking about some walking there.

BONO That's the only way you got anywhere back in them days.

LYONS Shhh. Damn if I wouldn't have hitched a ride with somebody!

TROY Who you gonna hitch it with? They ain't had no cars and things like they got now. We talking about 1918.

ROSE [*entering*] What you all out here getting into?

TROY [*to* ROSE] I'm telling Lyons how good he got it. He don't know nothing about this I'm talking.

ROSE Lyons, that was Bonnie on the phone. She say you supposed to pick her up.

LYONS Yeah, okay, Rose.

TROY I walked on down to Mobile and hitched up with some of them fellows that was heading this way. Got up here and found out . . . not only couldn't you get a job . . . you couldn't find no place to live. I thought I was in freedom. Shhh. Colored folks living down there on the riverbanks in whatever kind of shelter they could find for themselves. Right down there under the Brady Street Bridge. Living in shacks made of sticks and tarpaper. Messed around there and went from bad to worse. Started stealing. First it was food. Then I figured, hell, if I steal money I can buy me some food. Buy me some shoes too! One thing led to another. Met your mama. I was young and anxious to be a man. Met your mama and had you. What I do that for? Now I got to worry about feeding you and her. Got to steal three times as much. Went out one day looking for somebody to rob . . . that's what I was, a robber. I'll tell you the truth. I'm ashamed of it today. But it's the truth. Went to rob this fellow . . . pulled out my knife . . . and he pulled out a gun. Shot me in the chest. It felt just like somebody had taken a hot branding iron and laid it on me. When he shot me I jumped at him with my knife. They tell me I killed him and they put me in the penitentiary and locked me up for fifteen years. That's where I met Bono. That's where I learned how to play baseball. Got out that place and your mama had taken you and went on to make life without me. Fifteen years was a long time for her to wait. But that fifteen years cured me of that robbing stuff. Rose'll tell you. She asked me when I met her if I had gotten all that foolishness out of my system. And I told her, "Baby, it's you and baseball all what count with me." You hear me, Bono? I meant it too. She say, "Which one comes first?" I told her, "Baby, there ain't no doubt it's baseball . . . but you stick and get old with me and we'll both outlive this baseball." Am I right, Rose? And it's true.

ROSE Man, hush your mouth. You ain't said no such thing. Talking about, "Baby, you know you'll always be number one with me." That's what you was talking.

TROY   You hear that, Bono? That's why I love her.

BONO   Rose'll keep you straight. You get off the track, she'll straighten you up.

ROSE   Lyons, you better get on up and get Bonnie. She waiting on you.

LYONS [*gets up to go*]   Hey, Pop, why don't you come down to the Grill and hear me play?

TROY   I ain't going down there. I'm too old to be sitting around in them clubs.

BONO   You got to be good to play down at the Grill.

LYONS   Come on, Pop . . .

TROY   I got to get up in the morning.

LYONS   You ain't got to stay long.

TROY   Naw, I'm gonna get my supper and go on to bed.

LYONS   Well, I got to go. I'll see you again.

TROY   Don't you come around my house on my payday!

ROSE   Pick up the phone and let somebody know you coming. And bring Bonnie with you. You know I'm always glad to see her.

LYONS   Yeah, I'll do that, Rose. You take care now. See you, Pop. See you, Mr. Bono. See you, Uncle Gabe.

GABRIEL   Lyons! King of the Jungle!
          [LYONS *exits.*]

TROY   Is supper ready, woman? Me and you got some business to take care of. I'm gonna tear it up too!

ROSE   Troy, I done told you now!

TROY [*puts his arm around* BONO]   Aw hell, woman . . . this is Bono. Bono like family. I done known this nigger since . . . how long I done know you?

BONO   It's been a long time.

TROY   I done known this nigger since Skippy was a pup. Me and him done been through some times.

BONO   You sure right about that.

TROY   Hell, I done know him longer than I known you. And we still standing shoulder to shoulder. Hey, look here, Bono . . . a man can't ask for no more than that. [*Drinks to him.*] I love you, nigger.

BONO   Hell, I love you too . . . but I got to get home see my woman. You got yours in hand. I got to go get mine.
          [BONO *starts to exit as* CORY *enters the yard, dressed in his football uniform. He gives* TROY *a hard, uncompromising look.*]

CORY   What you do that for, Pop? [*He throws his helmet down in the direction of* TROY.]

ROSE   What's the matter? Cory . . . what's the matter?

CORY   Papa done went up to the school and told Coach Zellman I can't play football no more. Wouldn't even let me play the game. Told him to tell the recruiter not to come.

ROSE   Troy . . .

TROY   What you Troying me for. Yeah, I did it. And the boy know why I did it.

CORY   Why you wanna do that to me? That was the one chance I had.

ROSE   Ain't nothing wrong with Cory playing football, Troy.

TROY   The boy lied to me. I told the nigger if he wanna play football . . . to keep up his chores and hold down that job at the A&P. That was the conditions. Stopped down there to see Mr. Stawicki . . .

CORY   I can't work after school during the football season, Pop! I tried to tell you that Mr. Stawicki's holding my job for me. You don't never want to listen to nobody. And then you wanna go and do this to me!

TROY   I ain't done nothing to you. You done it to yourself.

CORY   Just cause you didn't have a chance! You just scared I'm gonna be better than you, that's all.

TROY   Come here.

ROSE   Troy . . .

[CORY *reluctantly crosses over to* TROY.]

TROY   Alright! See. You done made a mistake.

CORY   I didn't even do nothing!

TROY   I'm gonna tell you what your mistake was. See . . . you swung at the ball and didn't hit it. That's strike one. See, you in the batter's box now. You swung and you missed. That's strike one. Don't you strike out!

[*Lights fade to black.*]

Act 2

SCENE 1

The following morning. CORY *is at the tree hitting the ball with the bat. He tries to mimic* TROY, *but his swing is awkward, less sure.* ROSE *enters from the house.*

ROSE   Cory, I want you to help me with this cupboard.

CORY   I ain't quitting the team. I don't care what Poppa say.

ROSE   I'll talk to him when he gets back. He had to go see about your Uncle Gabe. The police done arrested him. Say he was disturbing the peace. He'll be back directly. Come on in here and help me clean out the top of this cupboard. [CORY *exits into the house.* ROSE *sees* TROY *and* BONO *coming down the alley.*] Troy . . . what they say down there?

TROY   Ain't said nothing. I give them fifty dollars and they let him go. I'll talk to you about it. Where's Cory?

ROSE   He's in there helping me clean out these cupboards.

TROY   Tell him to get his butt out here.

[TROY *and* BONO *go over to the pile of wood.* BONO *picks up the saw and begins sawing.*]

TROY [*to* BONO]   All they want is the money. That makes six or seven times I done went down there and got him. See me coming they stick out their *hands.*

BONO   Yeah, I know what you mean. That's all they care about . . . that money. They don't care about what's right. [*Pause.*] Nigger, why you got to go and get some hard wood? You ain't doing nothing but building a little old fence. Get you some soft pine wood. That's all you need.

TROY   I know what I'm doing. This is outside wood. You put pine wood inside the house. Pine wood is inside wood. This here is outside wood. Now you tell me where the fence is gonna be?

BONO   You don't need this wood. You can put it up with pine wood and it'll stand as long as you gonna be here looking at it.

TROY   How you know how long I'm gonna be here, nigger? Hell, I might just live forever. Live longer than old man Horsely.

BONO   That's what Magee used to say.

TROY   Magee's a damn fool. Now you tell me who you ever heard of gonna pull their own teeth with a pair of rusty pliers?

BONO   The old folks . . . my granddaddy used to pull his teeth with pliers. They ain't had no dentists for the colored folks back then.

TROY   Get clean pliers! You understand? Clean pliers! Sterilize them! Besides we ain't living back then. All Magee had to do was walk over to Doc Goldblums.

BONO   I see where you and that Tallahassee gal . . . that Alberta . . . I see where you all done got tight.

TROY   What you mean "got tight"?

BONO   I see where you be laughing and joking with her all the time.

TROY   I laughs and jokes with all of them, Bono. You know me.

BONO   That ain't the kind of laughing and joking I'm talking about.
[CORY *enters from the house.*]

CORY   How you doing, Mr. Bono?

TROY   Cory? Get that saw from Bono and cut some wood. He talking about the wood's too hard to cut. Stand back there, Jim, and let that young boy show you how it's done.

BONO   He's sure welcome to it. [CORY *takes the saw and begins to cut the wood.*] Whew-e-e Look at that. Big old strong boy. Look like Joe Louis.[3] Hell, must be getting old the way I'm watching that boy whip through that wood.

CORY   I don't see why Mama want a fence around the yard noways.

TROY   Damn if I know either. What the hell she keeping out with it? She ain't got nothing nobody want.

BONO   Some people build fences to keep people out . . . and other people build fences to keep people in. Rose wants to hold on to you all. She loves you.

TROY   Hell, nigger, I don't need nobody to tell me my wife loves me, Cory . . . go on in the house and see if you can find that other saw.

CORY   Where's it at?

TROY   I said find it! Look for it till you find it! [CORY *exits into the house.*] What's that supposed to mean? Wanna keep us in?

BONO   Troy . . . I done known you seem like damn near my whole life. You and Rose both. I done know both of you all for a long time. I remember when you met Rose. When you was hitting them baseball out the park. A lot of them old gals was after you then. You had the pick of the litter. When you picked Rose, I was happy for you. That was the first time I knew you had any sense. I said . . . My man Troy knows what he's doing . . . I'm gonna follow this nigger . . . he might take me somewhere. I been following you too. I done learned a whole heap of things about life watching you. I done learned how to tell where the shit lies. How to tell it from the alfalfa. You done learned me a lot of things. You showed me how to not make the same mistakes . . . to take life as it comes along and keep putting one foot in front of the other. [*Pause.*] Rose a good woman, Troy.

---

3. Boxer (1914–1981), heavyweight champion from 1937 to 1949.

TROY   Hell, nigger, I know she a good woman. I been married to her for eighteen years. What you got on your mind, Bono?

BONO   I just say she a good woman. Just like I say anything. I ain't got to have nothing on my mind.

TROY   You just gonna say she a good woman and leave it hanging out there like that? Why you telling me she a good woman?

BONO   She loves you, Troy. Rose loves you.

TROY   You saying I don't measure up. That's what you trying to say. I don't measure up 'cause I'm seeing this other gal. I know what you trying to say.

BONO   I know what Rose means to you, Troy. I'm just trying to say I don't want to see you mess up.

TROY   Yeah, I appreciate that, Bono. If you was messing around on Lucille I'd be telling you the same thing.

BONO   Well, that's all I got to say. I just say that because I love you both.

TROY   Hell, you know me . . . I wasn't out there looking for nothing. You can't find a better woman than Rose. I know that. But seems like this woman just stuck onto me where I can't shake her loose. I done wrestled with it, tried to throw her off me . . . but she just stuck on tighter. Now she's stuck on for good.

BONO   You's in control . . . that's what you tell me all the time. You responsible for what you do.

TROY   I ain't ducking the responsibility of it. As long as it sets right in my heart . . . then I'm okay. Cause that's all I listen to. It'll tell me right from wrong every time. And I ain't talking about doing Rose no bad turn. I love Rose. She done carried me a long ways and I love and respect her for that.

BONO   I know you do. That's why I don't want to see you hurt her. But what you gonna do when she find out? What you got then? If you try and juggle both of them . . . sooner or later you gonna drop one of them. That's common sense.

TROY   Yeah, I hear what you saying, Bono. I been trying to figure a way to work it out.

BONO   Work it out right, Troy. I don't want to be getting all up between you and Rose's business . . . but work it so it come out right.

TROY   Aw hell, I get all up between you and Lucille's business. When you gonna get that woman that refrigerator she been wanting? Don't tell me you ain't got no money now. I know who your banker is. Mellon don't need that money bad as Lucille want that refrigerator. I'll tell you that.

BONO   Tell you what I'll do . . . when you finish building this fence for Rose . . . I'll buy Lucille that refrigerator.

TROY   You done stuck your foot in your mouth now! [TROY *grabs up a board and begins to saw.* BONO *starts to walk out the yard.*] Hey, nigger . . . where you going?

BONO   I'm going home. I know you don't expect me to help you now. I'm protecting my money. I wanna see you put that fence up by yourself. That's what I want to see. You'll be here another six months without me.

TROY   Nigger, you ain't right.

BONO   When it comes to my money . . . I'm right as fireworks on the Fourth of July.

TROY   Alright, we gonna see now. You better get out your bankbook.

[BONO *exits, and* TROY *continues to work.* ROSE *enters from the house.*]

ROSE What they say down there? What's happening with Gabe?

TROY I went down there and got him out. Cost me fifty dollars. Say he was disturbing the peace. Judge set up a hearing for him in three weeks. Say to show cause why he shouldn't be re-committed.

ROSE What was he doing that cause them to arrest him?

TROY Some kids was teasing him and he run them off home. Say he was howling and carrying on. Some folks seen him and called the police. That's all it was.

ROSE Well, what's you say? What'd you tell the judge?

TROY Told him I'd look after him. It didn't make no sense to recommit the man. He stuck out his big greasy palm and told me to give him fifty dollars and take him on home.

ROSE Where's he at now? Where'd he go off to?

TROY He's gone on about his business. He don't need nobody to hold his hand.

ROSE Well, I don't know. Seem like that would be the best place for him if they did put him into the hospital. I know what you're gonna say. But that's what I think would be best.

TROY The man done had his life ruined fighting for what? And they wanna take and lock him up. Let him be free. He don't bother nobody.

ROSE Well, everybody got their own way of looking at it I guess. Come on and get your lunch. I got a bowl of lima beans and some cornbread in the oven. Come on get something to eat. Ain't no sense you fretting over Gabe. [ROSE *turns to go into the house.*]

TROY Rose . . . got something to tell you.

ROSE Well, come on . . . wait till I get this food on the table.

TROY Rose! [*She stops and turns around.*] I don't know how to say this. [*Pause.*] I can't explain it none. It just sort of grows on you till it gets out of hand. It starts out like a little bush . . . and the next thing you know it's a whole forest.

ROSE Troy . . . what are you talking about?

TROY I'm talking, woman, let me talk. I'm trying to find a way to tell you . . . I'm gonna be a daddy. I'm gonna be somebody's daddy.

ROSE Troy . . . you're not telling me this? You're gonna be . . . what?

TROY Rose . . . now . . . see . . .

ROSE You telling me you gonna be somebody's daddy? You telling your *wife* this?

[GABRIEL *enters from the street. He carries a rose in his hand.*]

GABRIEL Hey, Troy! Hey, Rose!

ROSE I have to wait eighteen years to hear something like this.

GABRIEL Hey, Rose . . . I got a flower for you. [*He hands it to her.*] That's a rose. Same rose like you is.

ROSE Thanks, Gabe.

GABRIEL Troy, you ain't mad at me is you? Them bad mens come and put me away. You ain't mad at me is you?

TROY Naw, Gabe, I ain't mad at you.

ROSE Eighteen years and you wanna come with this.

GABRIEL [*takes a quarter out of his pocket*] See what I got? Got a brand new quarter.

TROY Rose . . . it's just . . .

ROSE Ain't nothing you can say, Troy. Ain't no way of explaining that.

GABRIEL Fellow that give me this quarter had a whole mess of them. I'm gonna keep this quarter till it stop shining.

ROSE Gabe, go on in the house there. I got some watermelon in the frigidaire. Go on and get you a piece.

GABRIEL Say, Rose . . . you know I was chasing hellhounds and them bad mens come and get me and take me away. Troy helped me. He come down there and told them they better let me go before he beat them up. Yeah, he did!

ROSE You go on and get you a piece of watermelon, Gabe. Them bad mens is gone now.

GABRIEL Okay, Rose . . . gonna get me some watermelon. The kind with the stripes on it. [GABRIEL *exits into the house.*]

ROSE Why, Troy? Why? After all these years to come dragging this in to me now. It don't make no sense at your age. I could have expected this ten or fifteen years ago, but not now.

TROY Age ain't got nothing to do with it, Rose.

ROSE I done tried to be everything a wife should be. Everything a wife could be. Been married eighteen years and I got to live to see the day you tell me you been seeing another woman and done fathered a child by her. And you know I ain't never wanted no half nothing in my family. My whole family is half. Everybody got different fathers and mothers . . . my two sisters and my brother. Can't hardly tell who's who. Can't never sit down and talk about Papa and Mama. It's your papa and your mama and my papa and my mama . . .

TROY Rose . . . stop it now.

ROSE I ain't never wanted that for none of my children. And now you wanna drag your behind in here and tell me something like this.

TROY You ought to know. It's time for you to know.

ROSE Well, I don't want to know, goddamn it!

TROY I can't just make it go away. It's done now. I can't wish the circumstance of the thing away.

ROSE And you don't want to either. Maybe you want to wish me and my boy away. Maybe that's what you want? Well, you can't wish us away. I've got eighteen years of my life invested in you. You ought to have stayed upstairs in my bed where you belong.

TROY Rose . . . now listen to me . . . we can get a handle on this thing. We can talk this out . . . come to an understanding.

ROSE All of a sudden it's "we." Where was "we" at when you was down there rolling around with some godforsaken woman? "We" should have come to an understanding before you started making a damn fool of yourself. You're a day late and a dollar short when it comes to an understanding with me.

TROY It's just . . . She gives me a different idea . . . a different understanding about myself. I can step out of this house and get away from the pressures and problems . . . be a different man. I ain't got to wonder how I'm gonna pay the bills or get the roof fixed. I can just be a part of myself that I ain't never been.

ROSE What I want to know . . . is do you plan to continue seeing her? That's all you can say to me.

TROY I can sit up in her house and laugh. Do you understand what I'm saying. I can laugh out loud . . . and it feels good. It reaches all the way down to the bottom of my shoes. [*Pause.*] Rose, I can't give that up.

ROSE Maybe you ought to go on and stay down there with her . . . if she a better woman than me.

TROY It ain't about nobody being a better woman or nothing. Rose, you ain't the blame. A man couldn't ask for no woman to be a better wife than you've been. I'm responsible for it. I done locked myself into a pattern trying to take care of you all that I forgot about myself.

ROSE What the hell was I there for? That was my job, not somebody else's.

TROY Rose, I done tried all my life to live decent . . . to live a clean . . . hard . . . useful life. I tried to be a good husband to you. In every way I knew how. Maybe I come into the world backwards, I don't know. But . . . you born with two strikes on you before you come to the plate. You got to guard it closely . . . always looking for the curve-ball on the inside corner. You can't afford to let none get past you. You can't afford a call strike. If you going down . . . you going down swinging. Everything lined up against you. What you gonna do. I fooled them, Rose. I bunted. When I found you and Cory and a halfway decent job . . . I was safe. Couldn't nothing touch me. I wasn't gonna strike out no more. I wasn't going back to the penitentiary. I wasn't gonna lay in the streets with a bottle of wine. I was safe. I had me a family. A job. I wasn't gonna get that last strike. I was on first looking for one of them boys to knock me in. To get me home.

ROSE You should have stayed in my bed, Troy.

TROY Then, when I saw that gal . . . she firmed up my backbone. And I got to thinking that if I tried . . . I just might be able to steal second. Do you understand after eighteen years I wanted to steal second.

ROSE You should have held me tight. You should have grabbed me and held on.

TROY I stood on first base for eighteen years and I thought . . . well, goddamn it . . . go on for it!

ROSE We're not talking about baseball! We're talking about you going off to lay in bed with another woman . . . and then bring it home to me. That's what we're talking about. We ain't talking about no baseball.

TROY Rose, you're not listening to me. I'm trying the best I can to explain it to you. It's not easy for me to admit that I been standing in the same place for eighteen years.

ROSE I been standing with you! I been right here with you, Troy. I got a life too. I gave eighteen years of my life to stand in the same spot with you. Don't you think I ever wanted other things? Don't you think I had dreams and hopes? What about my life? What about me? Don't you think it ever crossed my mind to want to know other men? That I wanted to lay up somewhere and forget about my responsibilities? That I wanted someone to make me laugh so I could feel good? You not the only one who's got wants and needs. But I held on to you, Troy. I took all my feelings, my wants and needs, my dreams . . . and I buried them inside you. I planted a seed and watched and prayed over it. I planted myself inside you and waited to bloom. And it didn't take me no eighteen years to find out the soil was hard and rocky and it wasn't never gonna bloom. But I held on to you, Troy. I held you tighter. You was my husband. I owed you everything I had. Every part of me I could find to give you. And upstairs in that room . . . with the darkness falling in on me . . . I gave everything I had to try and erase the doubt that you wasn't the finest man in the world. And wherever you was going . . . I wanted to be there with you. 'Cause you was my husband. 'Cause that's the only way I was gonna survive as your wife. You always talking about what you give . . . and what you don't have to give. But you take too. You take . . . and don't even know nobody's giving!

[ROSE *turns to exit into the house;* TROY *grabs her arm.*]

TROY   You say I take and don't give!

ROSE   Troy! You're hurting me!

TROY   You say I take and don't give!

ROSE   Troy . . . you're hurting my arm! Let go!

TROY   I done give you everything I got. Don't you tell that lie on me.

ROSE   Troy!

TROY   Don't you tell that lie on me!

[CORY *enters from the house.*]

CORY   Mama!

ROSE   Troy, you're hurting me.

TROY   Don't you tell me about no taking and giving.

[CORY *comes up behind* TROY *and grabs him.* TROY, *surprised, is thrown off balance just as* CORY *throws a glancing blow that catches him on the chest and knocks him down.* TROY *is stunned, as is* CORY.]

ROSE   Troy. Troy. No! [TROY *gets to his feet and starts at* CORY.] Troy no. Please! Troy!

[ROSE *pulls on* TROY *to hold him back.* TROY *stops himself.*]

TROY [*to* CORY]   Alright. That's strike two. You stay away from around me, boy. Don't you strike out. You living with a full count.[4] Don't you strike out.

[TROY *exits out the yard as the lights go down.*]

SCENE 2

It is six months later, early afternoon. TROY *enters from the house and starts to exit the yard.* ROSE *enters from the house.*

ROSE   Troy, I want to talk to you.

TROY   All of a sudden, after all this time, you want to talk to me, huh? You ain't wanted to talk to me for months. You ain't wanted to talk to me last night. You ain't wanted no part of me then. What you wanna talk to me about now?

ROSE   Tomorrow's Friday.

TROY   I know what day tomorrow is. You think I don't know tomorrow's Friday? My whole life I ain't done nothing but look to see Friday coming and you got to tell me it's Friday.

ROSE   I want to know if you're coming home.

TROY   I always come home, Rose. You know that. There ain't never been a night I ain't come home.

---

4. In baseball, a count of three balls and two strikes; one more ball will result in a walk; one more strike will put the batter out.

ROSE That ain't what I mean . . . and you know it. I want to know if you're coming straight home after work.

TROY I figure I'd cash my check . . . hang out at Taylors' with the boys . . . maybe play a game of checkers . . .

ROSE Troy, I can't live like this. I won't live like this. You livin' on borrowed time with me. It's been going on six months now you ain't been coming home.

TROY I be here every night. Every night of the year. That's 365 days.

ROSE I want you to come home tomorrow after work.

TROY Rose . . . I don't mess up my pay. You know that now. I take my pay and I give it to you. I don't have no money but what you give me back. I just want to have a little time to myself . . . a little time to enjoy life.

ROSE What about me? When's my time to enjoy life?

TROY I don't know what to tell you, Rose. I'm doing the best I can.

ROSE You ain't been home from work but time enough to change your clothes and run out . . . and you wanna call that the best you can do?

TROY I'm going over to the hospital to see Alberta. She went into the hospital this afternoon. Look like she might have the baby early. I won't be gone long.

ROSE Well, you ought to know. They went over to Miss Pearl's and got Gabe today. She said you told them to go ahead and lock him up.

TROY I ain't said no such thing. Whoever told you that telling a lie. Pearl ain't doing nothing but telling a big fat lie.

ROSE She ain't had to tell me. I read it on the papers.

TROY I ain't told them nothing of the kind.

ROSE I saw it right there on the papers.

TROY What it say, huh?

ROSE It said you told them to take him.

TROY Then they screwed that up, just the way they screw up everything. I ain't worried about what they got on the paper.

ROSE Say the government send part of his check to the hospital and the other part to you.

TROY I ain't got nothing to do with that if that's the way it works. I ain't made up the rules about how it work.

ROSE You did Gabe just like you did Cory. You wouldn't sign the paper for Cory . . . but you signed for Gabe. You signed that paper.

[*The telephone is heard ringing inside the house.*]

TROY I told you I ain't signed nothing, woman! The only thing I signed was the release form. Hell, I can't read, I don't know what they had on the paper! I ain't signed nothing about sending Gabe away.

ROSE I said send him to the hospital . . . you said let him be free . . . now you done went down there and signed him to the hospital for half his money. You went back on yourself, Troy. You gonna have to answer for that.

TROY See now . . . you been over there talking to Miss Pearl. She done got mad cause she ain't getting Gabe's rent money. That's all it is. She's liable to say anything.

ROSE Troy, I seen where you signed the paper.

TROY You ain't seen nothing I signed. What she doing got papers on my brother anyway? Miss Pearl telling a big fat lie. And I'm gonna tell her about it too! You ain't seen nothing I signed. Say . . . you ain't seen nothing I signed.

[ROSE *exits into the house to answer the telephone. Presently she returns.*]

ROSE Troy . . . that was the hospital. Alberta had the baby.

TROY What she have? What is it?

ROSE It's a girl.

TROY I better get on down to the hospital to see her.

ROSE Troy . . .

TROY Rose . . . I got to go see her now. That's only right . . . what's the matter . . . the baby's alright, ain't it?

ROSE Alberta died having the baby.

TROY Died . . . you say she's dead? Alberta's dead?

ROSE They said they done all they could. They couldn't do nothing for her.

TROY The baby? How's the baby?

ROSE They say it's healthy. I wonder who's gonna bury her.

TROY She had family, Rose. She wasn't living in the world by herself.

ROSE I know she wasn't living in the world by herself.

TROY Next thing you gonna want to know if she had any insurance.

ROSE Troy, you ain't got to talk like that.

TROY That's the first thing that jumped out your mouth. "Who's gonna bury her?" Like I'm fixing to take on that task for myself.

ROSE I am your wife. Don't push me away.

TROY I ain't pushing nobody away. Just give me some space. That's all. Just give me some room to breathe.

[ROSE *exits into the house.* TROY *walks about the yard.*]

TROY [*with a quiet rage that threatens to consume him*] Alright . . . Mr. Death. See now . . . I'm gonna tell you what I'm gonna do. I'm gonna take and build me a fence around this yard. See? I'm gonna build me a fence around what belongs to me. And then I want you to stay on the other side. See? You stay over there until you're ready for me. Then you come on. Bring your army. Bring your sickle. Bring your wrestling clothes. I ain't gonna fall down on my vigilance this time. You ain't gonna sneak up on me no more. When you ready for me . . . when the top of your list say Troy Maxson . . . that's when you come around here. You come up and knock on the front door. Ain't nobody else got nothing to do with this. This is between you and me. Man to man. You stay on the other side of that fence until you ready for me. Then you come up and knock on the front door. Anytime you want. I'll be ready for you.

[*The lights go down to black.*]

SCENE 3

The lights come up on the porch. It is late evening three days later. ROSE *sits listening to the ball game waiting for* TROY. *The final out of the game is made and* ROSE *switches off the radio.* TROY *enters the yard carrying an infant wrapped in blankets. He stands back from the house and calls.*

[ROSE *enters and stands on the porch. There is a long, awkward silence, the weight of which grows heavier with each passing second.*]

TROY Rose . . . I'm standing here with my daughter in my arms. She ain't but a wee bittie little old thing. She don't know nothing about grownups' business. She innocent . . . and she ain't got no mama.

ROSE What you telling me for, Troy? [*She turns and exits into the house.*]

TROY Well . . . I guess we'll just sit out here on the porch. [*He sits down on the porch. There is an awkward indelicateness about the way he handles the baby. His largeness engulfs and seems to swallow it. He speaks loud enough for* ROSE *to hear.*] A man's got to do what's right for him. I ain't sorry for nothing I done. It felt right in my heart. [*To the baby.*] What you smiling at? Your daddy's a big man. Got these great big old hands. But sometimes he's scared. And right now your daddy's scared cause we sitting out here and ain't got no home. Oh, I been homeless before. I ain't had no little baby with me. But I been homeless. You just be out on the road by your lonesome and you see one of them trains coming and you just kinda go like this . . .

[*He sings as a lullaby.*]

Please, Mr. Engineer let a man ride the line
Please, Mr. Engineer let a man ride the line
I ain't got no ticket please let me ride the blinds

[ROSE *enters from the house.* TROY *hearing her steps behind him, stands and faces her.*]

She's my daughter, Rose. My own flesh and blood. I can't deny her no more than I can deny them boys. [*Pause.*] You and them boys is my family. You and them and this child is all I got in the world. So I guess what I'm saying is . . . I'd appreciate it if you'd help me take care of her.

ROSE Okay, Troy . . . you're right. I'll take care of your baby for you . . . cause . . . like you say . . . she's innocent . . . and you can't visit the sins of the father upon the child. A motherless child has got a hard time. [*She takes the baby from him.*] From right now . . . this child got a mother. But you a womanless man.

[ROSE *turns and exits into the house with the baby. Lights go down to black.*]

SCENE 4

It is two months later. LYONS *enters from the street. He knocks on the door and calls.*

LYONS Hey, Rose! [*Pause.*] Rose!

ROSE [*from inside the house*] Stop that yelling. You gonna wake up Raynell. I just got her to sleep.

LYONS I just stopped by to pay Papa this twenty dollars I owe him. Where's Papa at?

ROSE He should be here in a minute. I'm getting ready to go down to the church. Sit down and wait on him.

LYONS I got to go pick up Bonnie over her mother's house.

ROSE Well, sit it down there on the table. He'll get it.

LYONS [*enters the house and sets the money on the table*] Tell Papa I said thanks. I'll see you again.

ROSE Alright, Lyons. We'll see you.

[LYONS *starts to exit as* CORY *enters.*]

CORY   Hey, Lyons.

LYONS   What's happening, Cory. Say man, I'm sorry I missed your graduation. You know I had a gig and couldn't get away. Otherwise, I would have been there. So what you doing?

CORY   I'm trying to find a job.

LYONS   Yeah, I know how that go, man. It's rough out here. Jobs are scarce.

CORY   Yeah, I know.

LYONS   Look here, I got to run. Talk to Papa . . . he know some people. He'll be able to help get you a job. Talk to him . . . see what he say.

CORY   Yeah . . . alright, Lyons.

LYONS   You take care. I'll talk to you soon. We'll find some time to talk.
        [LYONS *exits the yard.* CORY *wanders over to the tree, picks up the bat and assumes a batting stance. He studies an imaginary pitcher and swings. Dissatisfied with the result, he tries again.* TROY *enters. They eye each other for a beat.* CORY *puts the bat down and exits the yard.* TROY *starts into the house as* ROSE *exits with* RAYNELL. *She is carrying a cake.*]

TROY   I'm coming in and everybody's going out.

ROSE   I'm taking this cake down to the church for the bakesale. Lyons was by to see you. He stopped by to pay you your twenty dollars. It's laying in there on the table.

TROY [*going into his pocket*]   Well . . . here go this money.

ROSE   Put it in there on the table, Troy. I'll get it.

TROY   What time you coming back?

ROSE   Ain't no use in you studying me. It don't matter what time I come back.

TROY   I just asked you a question, woman. What's the matter . . . can't I ask you a question?

ROSE   Troy, I don't want to go into it. Your dinner's in there on the stove. All you got to do is heat it up. And don't you be eating the rest of them cakes in there. I'm coming back for them. We having a bakesale at the church tomorrow.
        [ROSE *exits the yard.* TROY *sits down on the steps, takes a pint bottle from his pocket, opens it, and drinks. He begins to sing.*]
        [TROY]
                Hear it ring! Hear it ring!
                Had an old dog his name was Blue
                You know Blue was mighty true
                You know Blue as a good old dog
                Blue trees a possum in a hollow log
                You know from that he was a good old dog
        [BONO *enters the yard.*]

BONO   Hey, Troy.

TROY   Hey, what's happening, Bono?

BONO   I just thought I'd stop by to see you.

TROY   What you stop by and see me for? You ain't stopped by in a month of Sundays. Hell, I must owe you money or something.

BONO   Since you got your promotion I can't keep up with you. Used to see you everyday. Now I don't even know what route you working.

TROY   They keep switching me around. Got me out in Greentree now . . . hauling white folks' garbage.

BONO   Greentree, huh? You lucky, at least you ain't got to be lifting them barrels. Damn if they ain't getting heavier. I'm gonna put in my two years and call it quits.

TROY   I'm thinking about retiring myself. How's Lucille?

BONO   You got it easy. You can *drive* for another five years.

TROY   It ain't the same, Bono. It ain't like working the back of the truck. Ain't got nobody to talk to . . . feel like you working by yourself. Naw, I'm thinking about retiring. How's Lucille?

BONO   She alright. Her arthritis get to acting up on her sometime. Saw Rose on my way in. She going down to the church, huh?

TROY   Yeah, she took up going down there. All them preachers looking for somebody to fatten their pockets. [*Pause.*] Got some gin here.

BONO   Naw, thanks. I just stopped by to say hello.

TROY   Hell, nigger . . . you can take a drink. I ain't never known you to say no to a drink. You ain't got to work tomorrow.

BONO   I just stopped by. I'm fixing to go over to Skinner's. We got us a domino game going over his house every Friday.

TROY   Nigger, you can't play no dominoes. I used to whup you four games out of five.

BONO   Well, that learned me. I'm getting better.

TROY   Yeah? Well, that's alright.

BONO   Look here . . . I got to be getting on. Stop by sometime, huh?

TROY   Yeah, I'll do that, Bono. Lucille told Rose you bought her a new refrigerator.

BONO   Yeah, Rose told Lucille you had finally built your fence . . . so I figured we'd call it even.

TROY   I knew you would.

BONO   Yeah . . . okay. I'll be talking to you.

TROY   Yeah, take care, Bono. Good to see you. I'm gonna stop over.

BONO   Yeah. Okay, Troy.

   [BONO *exits.* TROY *drinks from the bottle.*]

TROY

> Old Blue died and I dig his grave
> Let him down with a golden chain
> Every night when I hear old Blue bark
> I know Blue treed a possum in Noah's Ark.
> Hear it ring! Hear it ring!

   [CORY *enters the yard. They eye each other for a beat.* TROY *is sitting in the middle of the steps.* CORY *walks over.*]

CORY   I got to get by.

TROY   Say what? What's you say?

CORY   You in my way. I got to get by.

TROY   You got to get by where? This is my house. Bought and paid for. In full. Took me fifteen years. And if you wanna go in my house and I'm sitting on the steps . . . you say excuse me. Like your mama taught you.

CORY   Come on, Pop . . . I got to get by.

   [CORY *starts to maneuver his way past* TROY. TROY *grabs his leg and shoves him back.*]

TROY   You just gonna walk over top of me?

CORY I live here too!

TROY [*advancing toward him*] You just gonna walk over top of me in my own house?

CORY I ain't scared of you.

TROY I ain't asked if you was scared of me. I asked you if you was fixing to walk over top of me in my own house? That's the question. You ain't gonna say excuse me? You just gonna walk over top of me?

CORY If you wanna put it like that.

TROY How else am I gonna put it?

CORY I was walking by you to go into the house 'cause you sitting on the steps drunk, singing to yourself. You can put it like that.

TROY Without saying excuse me?? [CORY *doesn't respond.*] I asked you a question. Without saying excuse me??

CORY I ain't got to say excuse me to you. You don't count around here no more.

TROY Oh, I see . . . I don't count around here no more. You ain't got to say excuse me to your daddy. All of a sudden you done got so grown that your daddy don't count around here no more . . . Around here in his own house and yard that he done paid for with the sweat of his brow. You done got so grown to where you gonna take over. You gonna take over my house. Is that right? You gonna wear my pants. You gonna go in there and stretch out on my bed. You ain't got to say excuse me cause I don't count around here no more. Is that right?

CORY That's right. You always talking this dumb stuff. Now, why don't you just get out my way.

TROY I guess you got someplace to sleep and something to put in your belly. You got that, huh? You got that? That's what you need. You got that, huh?

CORY You don't know what I got. You ain't got to worry about what I got.

TROY You right! You one hundred percent right! I done spent the last seventeen years worrying about what you got. Now it's your turn, see? I'll tell you what you do. You grown . . . we done established that. You a man. Now, let's see you act like one. Turn your behind around and walk out this yard. And when you get out there in the alley . . . you can forget about this house. See? 'Cause this is my house. You go on and be a man and get your own house. You can forget about this. 'Cause this is mine. You go on and get yours 'cause I'm through with doing for you.

CORY You talking about what you did for me . . . what'd you ever give me?

TROY Them feet and bones! That pumping heart nigger! I give you more than anybody else is ever gonna give you.

CORY You ain't never gave me nothing! You ain't never done nothing but hold me back. Afraid I was gonna be better than you. All you ever did was try and make me scared of you. I used to tremble every time you called my name. Every time I heard your footsteps in the house. Wondering all the time . . . what's Papa gonna say if I do this? . . . What's he gonna say if I do that? . . . what's Papa gonna say if I turn on the radio? And Mama, too . . . she tries . . . but she's scared of you.

TROY You leave your mama out of this. She ain't got nothing to do with this.

CORY I don't know how she stand you . . . after what you did to her.

TROY   I told you to leave your mama out of this! [*He advances toward* CORY.]

CORY   What you gonna do . . . give me a whupping? You can't whup me no more. You're too old. You just an old man.

TROY [*shoves him on his shoulder*]   Nigger! That's what you are. You just another nigger on the street to me!

CORY   You crazy! You know that?

TROY   Go on now! You got the devil in you. Get on away from me!

CORY   You just a crazy old man . . . talking about I got the devil in me.

TROY   Yeah, I'm crazy! If you don't get on the other side of that yard . . . I'm gonna show you how crazy I am! Go on . . . get the hell out of my yard.

CORY   It ain't your yard. You took Uncle Gabe's money he got from the army to buy this house and then you put him out.

TROY [TROY *advances on* CORY.]   Get your black ass out of my yard!
[TROY's *advance backs* CORY *up against the tree.* CORY *grabs up the bat.*]

CORY   I ain't going nowhere! Come on . . . put me out! I ain't scared of you.

TROY   That's my bat!

CORY   Come on!

TROY   Put my bat down!

CORY   Come on, put me out. [CORY *swings at* TROY, *who backs across the yard.*] What's the matter? You so bad . . . put me out!
[TROY *advances toward* CORY.]

CORY [*backing up*]   Come on! Come on!

TROY   You're gonna have to use it! You wanna draw that bat back on me . . . you're gonna have to use it.

CORY   Come on! . . . Come on!
[CORY *swings the bat at* TROY *a second time. He misses.* TROY *continues to advance toward him.*]

TROY   You're gonna have to kill me! You wanna draw that bat back on me. You're gonna have to kill me.
[CORY, *backed up against the tree, can go no farther.* TROY *taunts him. He sticks out his head and offers him a target.*]

Come on! Come on!
[CORY *is unable to swing the bat.* TROY *grabs it.*]

TROY   Then I'll show you.
[CORY *and* TROY *struggle over the bat. The struggle is fierce and fully engaged.* TROY *ultimately is the stronger, and takes the bat from* CORY *and stands over him ready to swing. He stops himself.*]

Go on and get away from around my house.
[CORY, *stung by his defeat, picks himself up, walks slowly out of the yard and up the alley.*]

CORY   Tell Mama I'll be back for my things.

TROY   They'll be on the other side of that fence.
[CORY *exits.*]

TROY   I can't taste nothing. Helluljah! I can't taste nothing no more. [TROY *assumes a batting posture and begins to taunt Death, the fastball in the outside corner.*] Come on! It's between you and me now! Come on! Anytime you want! Come on! I be ready for you . . . but I ain't gonna be easy.
[*The lights go down on the scene.*]

SCENE 5

The time is 1965. The lights come up in the yard. It is the morning of TROY's *funeral. A funeral plaque with a light hangs beside the door. There is a small garden plot off to the side. There is noise and activity in the house as* ROSE, LYONS *and* BONO *have gathered. The door opens and* RAYNELL, *seven years old, enters dressed in a flannel nightgown. She crosses to the garden and pokes around with a stick.* ROSE *calls from the house.*

ROSE   Raynell!

RAYNELL   Mam?

ROSE   What you doing out there?

RAYNELL   Nothing.

　　　　[ROSE *comes to the door.*]

ROSE   Girl, get in here and get dressed. What you doing?

RAYNELL   Seeing if my garden growed.

ROSE   I told you it ain't gonna grow overnight. You got to wait.

RAYNELL   It don't look like it never gonna grow. Dag!

ROSE   I told you a watched pot never boils. Get in here and get dressed.

RAYNELL   This ain't even no pot, Mama.

ROSE   You just have to give it a chance. It'll grow. Now you come on and do what I told you. We got to be getting ready. This ain't no morning to be playing around. You hear me?

RAYNELL   Yes, mam.

　　　　[ROSE *exits into the house.* RAYNELL *continues to poke at her garden with a stick.* CORY *enters. He is dressed in a Marine corporal's uniform, and carries a duffel bag. His posture is that of a military man, and his speech has a clipped sternness.*]

CORY [*to* RAYNELL]   Hi. [*Pause.*] I bet your name is Raynell.

RAYNELL   Uh huh.

CORY   Is your mama home?

　　　　[RAYNELL *runs up on the porch and calls through the screendoor.*]

RAYNELL   Mama . . . there's some man out here. Mama?

　　　　[ROSE *comes to the door.*]

ROSE   Cory? Lord have mercy! Look here, you all! [ROSE *and* CORY *embrace in a tearful reunion as* BONO *and* LYONS *enter from the house dressed in funeral clothes.*]

BONO   Aw, looka here . . .

ROSE   Done got all grown up!

CORY   Don't cry, Mama. What you crying about?

ROSE   I'm just so glad you made it.

CORY   Hey Lyons. How you doing, Mr. Bono.

　　　　[LYON *goes to embrace* CORY.]

LYONS   Look at you, man. Look at you. Don't he look good, Rose. Got them Corporal stripes.

ROSE   What took you so long?

CORY   You know how the Marines are, Mama. They got to get all their paperwork straight before they let you do anything.

ROSE   Well, I'm sure glad you made it. They let Lyons come. Your Uncle Gabe's still in the hospital. They don't know if they gonna let him out or not. I just talked to them a little while ago.

LYONS   A Corporal in the United States Marines.

BONO   Your daddy knew you had it in you. He used to tell me all the time.

LYONS   Don't he look good, Mr. Bono?

BONO   Yeah, he remind me of Troy when I first met him. [*Pause.*] Say, Rose, Lucille's down at the church with the choir. I'm gonna go down and get the pallbearers lined up. I'll be back to get you all.

ROSE   Thanks, Jim.

CORY   See you, Mr. Bono.

LYONS [*With his arm around* RAYNELL]   Cory . . . look at Raynell. Ain't she precious? She gonna break a whole lot of hearts.

ROSE   Raynell, come and say hello to your brother. This is your brother, Cory. You remember Cory.

RAYNELL   No, Mam.

CORY   She don't remember me, Mama.

ROSE   Well, we talk about you. She heard us talk about you. [*To* RAYNELL.] This is your brother, Cory. Come on and say hello.

RAYNELL   Hi.

CORY   Hi. So you're Raynell. Mama told me a lot about you.

ROSE   You all come on into the house and let me fix you some breakfast. Keep up your strength.

CORY   I ain't hungry, Mama.

LYONS   You can fix me something, Rose. I'll be in there in a minute.

ROSE   Cory, you sure you don't want nothing. I know they ain't feeding you right.

CORY   No, Mama . . . thanks. I don't feel like eating. I'll get something later.

ROSE   Raynell . . . get on upstairs and get that dress on like I told you.
    [ROSE *and* RAYNELL *exit into the house.*]

LYONS   So . . . I hear you thinking about getting married.

CORY   Yeah, I done found the right one, Lyons. It's about time.

LYONS   Me and Bonnie been split up about four years now. About the time Papa retired. I guess she just got tired of all them changes I was putting her through. [*Pause.*] I always knew you was gonna make something out yourself. Your head was always in the right direction. So . . . you gonna stay in . . . make it a career . . . put in your twenty years?

CORY   I don't know. I got six already, I think that's enough.

LYONS   Stick with Uncle Sam and retire early. Ain't nothing out here. I guess Rose told you what happened with me. They got me down the workhouse. I thought I was being slick cashing other people's checks.

CORY   How much time you doing?

LYONS   They give me three years. I got that beat now. I ain't got but nine more months. It ain't so bad. You learn to deal with it like anything else. You got to take the crookeds with the straights. That's what Papa used to say. He used to say that when he struck out. I seen him strike out three times in a row . . . and the next time up he hit the ball over the grandstand. Right out there in Homestead Field. He wasn't satisfied hitting in the seats . . . he want to hit it over everything! After the game he had two hundred people standing around waiting to shake his hand. You got to take the crookeds with the straights. Yeah, Papa was something else.

CORY   You still playing?

LYONS   Cory . . . you know I'm gonna do that. There's some fellows down there we got us a band . . . we gonna try and stay together when we get out . . . but yeah, I'm still playing. It still helps me to get out of bed in the morning. As long as it do that I'm gonna be right there playing and trying to make some sense out of it.

ROSE [calling]   Lyons, I got these eggs in the pan.

LYONS   Let me go on and get these eggs, man. Get ready to go bury Papa. [Pause.] How you doing? You doing alright?

> [CORY nods. LYONS touches him on the shoulder and they share a moment of silent grief. LYONS exits into the house. CORY wanders about the yard. RAYNELL enters.]

RAYNELL   Hi.

CORY   Hi.

RAYNELL   Did you used to sleep in my room?

CORY   Yeah . . . that used to be my room.

RAYNELL   That's what Papa call it. "Cory's room." It got your football in the closet.

> [ROSE comes to the door.]

ROSE   Raynell, get in there and get them good shoes on.

RAYNELL   Mama, can't I wear these. Them other one hurt my feet.

ROSE   Well, they just gonna have to hurt your feet for a while. You ain't said they hurt your feet when you went down to the store and got them.

RAYNELL   They didn't hurt then. My feet done got bigger.

ROSE   Don't you give me no backtalk now. You get in there and get them shoes on. [RAYNELL exits into the house.] Ain't too much changed. He still got that piece of rag tied to that tree. He was out here swinging that bat. I was just ready to go back in the house. He swung that bat and then he just fell over. Seem like he swung it and stood there with this grin on his face . . . and then he just fell over. They carried him on down to the hospital, but I knew there wasn't no need . . . why don't you come on in the house?

CORY   Mama . . . I got something to tell you. I don't know how to tell you this . . . but I've got to tell you . . . I'm not going to Papa's funeral.

ROSE   Boy, hush your mouth. That's your daddy you talking about. I don't want hear that kind of talk this morning. I done raised you to come to this? You standing there all healthy and grown talking about you ain't going to your daddy's funeral?

CORY   Mama . . . listen . . .

ROSE   I don't want to hear it, Cory. You just get that thought out of your head.

CORY   I can't drag Papa with me everywhere I go. I've got to say no to him. One time in my life I've got to say no.

ROSE   Don't nobody have to listen to nothing like that. I know you and your daddy ain't seen eye to eye, but I ain't got to listen to that kind of talk this morning. Whatever was between you and your daddy . . . the time has come to put it aside. Just take it and set it over there on the shelf and forget about it. Disrespecting your daddy ain't gonna make you a man, Cory. You got to find a way to come to that on your own. Not going to your daddy's funeral ain't gonna make you a man.

CORY   The whole time I was growing up . . . living in his house . . . Papa was like a shadow that followed you everywhere. It weighed on you and sunk into your flesh. It would wrap around you and lay there until you couldn't tell which one was you anymore. That shadow digging in your flesh. Trying to crawl in. Trying to live through you. Everywhere I looked, Troy Maxson was staring back at me . . . hiding under the bed . . . in the closet. I'm just saying I've got to find a way to get rid of that shadow, Mama.

ROSE   You just like him. You got him in you good.

CORY   Don't tell me that, Mama.

ROSE   You Troy Maxson all over again.

CORY   I don't want to be Troy Maxson. I want to be me.

ROSE   You can't be nobody but who you are, Cory. That shadow wasn't nothing but you growing into yourself. You either got to grow into it or cut it down to fit you. But that's all you got to make life with. That's all you got to measure yourself against that world out there. Your daddy wanted you to be everything he wasn't . . . and at the same time he tried to make you into everything he was. I don't know if he was right or wrong . . . but I do know he meant to do more good than he meant to do harm. He wasn't always right. Sometimes when he touched he bruised. And sometimes when he took me in his arms he cut. When I first met your daddy I thought . . . Here is a man I can lay down with and make a baby. That's the first thing I thought when I seen him. I was thirty years old and had done seen my share of men. But when he walked up to me and said, "I can dance a waltz that'll make you dizzy," I thought, Rose Lee, here is a man that you can open yourself up to and be filled to bursting. Here is a man that can fill all them empty spaces you been tipping around the edges of. One of them empty spaces was being somebody's mother. I married your daddy and settled down to cooking his supper and keeping clean sheets on the bed. When your daddy walked through the house he was so big he filled it up. That was my first mistake. Not to make him leave some room for me. For my part in the matter. But at that time I wanted that. I wanted a house that I could sing in. And that's what your daddy gave me. I didn't know to keep up his strength I had to give up little pieces of mine. I did that. I took on his life as mine and mixed up the pieces so that you couldn't hardly tell which was which anymore. It was my choice. It was my life and I didn't have to live it like that. But that's what life offered me in the way of being a woman, and I took it. I grabbed hold of it with both hands. By the time Raynell came into the house, me and your daddy had done lost touch with one another. I didn't want to make my blessing off of nobody's misfortune . . . but I took on to Raynell like she was all them babies I had wanted and never had. [*The phone rings.*] Like I'd been blessed to relive a part of my life. And if the Lord see fit to keep up my strength . . . I'm gonna do her just like your daddy did you . . . I'm gonna give her the best of what's in me.

RAYNELL [*entering, still with her old shoes*]   Mama . . . Reverend Tollivier on the phone.

   [ROSE *exits into the house.*]

RAYNELL   Hi.

CORY   Hi.

RAYNELL   You in the Army or the Marines?
CORY   Marines.
RAYNELL   Papa said it was the Army. Did you know Blue?
CORY   Blue? Who's Blue?
RAYNELL   Papa's dog what he sing about all the time.

[CORY *singing.*]
Hear it ring! hear it ring!
I had a dog his name was Blue
You know Blue was mighty true
You know Blue was a good old dog
Blue treed a possum in a hollow log
You know from that he was a good old dog.
Hear it ring! Hear it ring!

[RAYNELL *joins in singing.*]

[CORY *and* RAYNELL]
Blue treed a possum out on a limb
Blue looked at me and I looked at him
Grabbed that possum and put him in a sack
Blue stayed there till I came back
Old Blue's feets was big and round
Never allowed a possum to touch the ground.

Old Blue died and I dug his grave
I dug his grave with a silver spade
Let him down with a golden chain
And every night I call his name
Go on Blue, you good dog you
Go on Blue, you good dog you
[RAYNELL]
Blue laid down and died like a man
Blue laid down and died . . .
[BOTH]
Blue laid down and died like a man
Now he's treeing possums in the Promised Land
I'm gonna tell you this to let you know
Blue's gone where the good dogs go
When I hear old Blue bark
When I heard old Blue bark
Blue treed a possum in Noah's Ark
Blue treed a possum in Noah's Ark.

[ROSE *comes to the screen door.*]
ROSE   Cory, we gonna be ready to go in a minute.
CORY [*to* RAYNELL]   You go on in the house and change them shoes like
    Mama told you so we can go to papa's funeral.
RAYNELL   Okay, I'll be right back.

[RAYNELL *exits into the house.* CORY *gets up and crosses over to the tree.*
ROSE *stands in the screen door watching him.* GABRIEL *enters from the
alley.*]

GABRIEL [*calling*]   Hey, Rose!
ROSE   Gabe?
GABRIEL   I'm here, Rose. Hey Rose, I'm here!

[ROSE *enters from the house.*]

ROSE   Lord . . . Look here, Lyons!

LYONS   See, I told you, Rose . . . I told you they'd let him come.

CORY   How you doing, Uncle Gabe?

LYONS   How you doing, Uncle Gabe?

GABRIEL   Hey, Rose. It's time. It's time to tell St. Peter to open the gates. Troy, you ready? You ready, Troy. I'm gonna tell St. Peter to open the gates. You get ready now.

> [GABRIEL, *with great fanfare, braces himself to blow. The trumpet is without a mouthpiece. He puts the end of it into his mouth and blows with great force, like a man who has been waiting some twenty-odd years for this single moment. No sound comes out of the trumpet. He braces himself and blows again with the same result. A third time he blows. There is a weight of impossible description that falls away and leaves him bare and exposed to a frightful realization. It is a trauma that a sane and normal mind would be unable to withstand. He begins to dance. A slow, strange dance, eerie and life-giving. A dance of atavistic signature and ritual.* LYONS *attempts to embrace him.* GABRIEL *pushes* LYONS *away. He begins to howl in what is an attempt at song, or perhaps a song turning back into itself in an attempt at speech. He finishes his dance and the gates of heaven stand open as wide as God's closet.*]

That's the way that go!

[*BLACKOUT.*]

ANNIE DILLARD
b. 1945

Annie Dillard was born in Pittsburgh, Pennsylvania; was educated at Hollins College, Virginia; and has taught creative writing at Western Washington University and Wesleyan University. She has lived in the Blue Ridge Mountains of the Appalachian chain and among the Cascades of the Pacific Northwest; it is the solitude and close attention to nature and one's own thoughts prompted by rural life in these regions that motivate her writing, which among her generation is stylistically unique. She is deeply meditative, even spiritual, yet she can express herself in a swinging rhythm that sweeps up poetic insight and religious references with the same joyful ease of describing nature at play. *Pilgrim at Tinker Creek* (1974) follows the progress of the seasons as the author lives a quiet, closely observant life in the seclusion of Virginia's Roanoke Valley. Nature is studied, but so are books of a widely ranging theological, philosophical, and scientific nature. The author's subject is nothing less than cosmic, a search for understanding how beauty and violence form necessary parts of the world as we know it. Nature, like human life, is generously productive and violently destructive, equally inclusive and isolative. These tensions reinforce the thoughts Dillard examines: her own, and also those of writers who have formed our intellectual heritage. In this way her work resembles that of the American Transcendentalist Henry David Thoreau in *Walden*, particularly in its appreciation of nature's cyclic patterns. More like Thoreau's friend

Ralph Waldo Emerson, however, Dillard directs her thoughts to metaphysical ends, joining a tradition reaching back to Puritan poetry and sermons. "Seeing," excerpted here, helps establish a rhythm important to all of *Pilgrim at Tinker Creek*, that of paging through nature as though it is a book while reading commentaries by critics as though they are signs of nature. As the critic Wendy Lesser noted about the author's essay "For the Time Being" (1999), Dillard excels with "the conjunction of seemingly disparate facts that eventually add up to a complex whole."

Elsewhere in Dillard's canon are lighter subjects, such as the status of the contemporary novel (*Living by Fiction*, 1982) and accounts of picturesque travel (*Teaching a Stone to Talk*, 1982). The author has written about meeting Chinese writers, reminisced about her childhood, and studied her writing processes. In 1992 she published *The Living*, a historical novel set in the Pacific Northwest that is as much about the landscape as about its inhabitants. A second novel, *The Maytrees* (2007), is very much a product of a writerly mind, in which the progress of a long marriage allows ample time for meditation. As the critic Ihab Hassan has said of Dillard's *Holy the Firm* (1977): "Her language is as textured as her perception, an Orphic poetry with terrors small and near at hand; her path is that of the solitary wanderer, in the wilderness of the Cascades or Blue Ridge Mountains, living in a rough cabin to 'study hard things.'"

The following text is from *Pilgrim at Tinker Creek* (1974).

From Pilgrim at Tinker Creek

Seeing

When I was six or seven years old, growing up in Pittsburgh, I used to take a precious penny of my own and hide it for someone else to find. It was a curious compulsion; sadly, I've never been seized by it since. For some reason I always "hid" the penny along the same stretch of sidewalk up the street. I would cradle it at the roots of a sycamore, say, or in a hole left by a chipped-off piece of sidewalk. Then I would take a piece of chalk, and, starting at either end of the block, draw huge arrows leading up to the penny from both directions. After I learned to write I labeled the arrows: SURPRISE AHEAD or MONEY THIS WAY. I was greatly excited, during all this arrow-drawing, at the thought of the first lucky passer-by who would receive in this way, regardless of merit, a free gift from the universe. But I never lurked about. I would go straight home and not give the matter another thought, until, some months later, I would be gripped again by the impulse to hide another penny.

It is still the first week in January, and I've got great plans. I've been thinking about seeing. There are lots of things to see, unwrapped gifts and free surprises. The world is fairly studded and strewn with pennies cast broadside from a generous hand. But—and this is the point—who gets excited by a mere penny? If you follow one arrow, if you crouch motionless on a bank to watch a tremulous ripple thrill on the water and are rewarded by the sight of a muskrat kit paddling from its den, will you count that sight a chip of copper only, and go your rueful way? It is dire poverty indeed when a man is so malnourished and fatigued that he won't stoop to pick up a penny. But if you cultivate a healthy poverty and simplicity, so that finding a penny will literally make your day, then, since the world is in fact planted in pennies, you have with your poverty bought a lifetime of days. It is that simple. What you see is what you get.

I used to be able to see flying insects in the air. I'd look ahead and see, not the row of hemlocks across the road, but the air in front of it. My eyes would focus along that column of air, picking out flying insects. But I lost interest, I guess, for I dropped the habit. Now I can see birds. Probably some people can look at the grass at their feet and discover all the crawling creatures. I would like to know grasses and sedges—and care. Then my least journey into the world would be a field trip, a series of happy recognitions. Thoreau,[1] in an expansive mood, exulted, "What a rich book might be made about buds, including, perhaps, sprouts!" It would be nice to think so. I cherish mental images I have of three perfectly happy people. One collects stones. Another—an Englishman, say—watches clouds. The third lives on a coast and collects drops of seawater which he examines microscopically and mounts. But I don't see what the specialist sees, and so I cut myself off, not only from the total picture, but from the various forms of happiness.

Unfortunately, nature is very much a now-you-see-it, now-you-don't affair. A fish flashes, then dissolves in the water before my eyes like so much salt. Deer apparently ascend bodily into heaven; the brightest oriole fades into leaves. These disappearances stun me into stillness and concentration; they say of nature that it conceals with a grand nonchalance, and they say of vision that it is a deliberate gift, the revelation of a dancer who for my eyes only flings away her seven veils. For nature does reveal as well as conceal: now-you-don't-see-it, now-you-do. For a week last September migrating red-winged blackbirds were feeding heavily down by the creek at the back of the house. One day I went out to investigate the racket; I walked up to a tree, an Osage orange,[2] and a hundred birds flew away. They simply materialized out of the tree. I saw a tree, then a whisk of color, then a tree again. I walked closer and another hundred blackbirds took flight. Not a branch, not a twig budged: the birds were apparently weightless as well as invisible. Or, it was as if the leaves of the Osage orange had been freed from a spell in the form of red-winged blackbirds; they flew from the tree, caught my eye in the sky, and vanished. When I looked again at the tree the leaves had reassembled as if nothing had happened. Finally I walked directly to the trunk of the tree and a final hundred, the real diehards, appeared, spread, and vanished. How could so many hide in the tree without my seeing them? The Osage orange, unruffled, looked just as it had looked from the house, when three hundred red-winged blackbirds cried from its crown. I looked downstream where they flew, and they were gone. Searching, I couldn't spot one. I wandered downstream to force them to play their hand, but they'd crossed the creek and scattered. One show to a customer. These appearances catch at my throat; they are the free gifts, the bright coppers at the roots of trees.

It's all a matter of keeping my eyes open. Nature is like one of those line drawings of a tree that are puzzles for children: Can you find hidden in the

---

1. Henry David Thoreau (1817–1862), American writer and naturalist associated with the Transcendentalist movement.

2. Hardwood tree of the mulberry family, sometimes called the mock orange.

leaves a duck, a house, a boy, a bucket, a zebra, and a boot? Specialists can find the most incredibly well-hidden things. A book I read when I was young recommended an easy way to find caterpillars to rear: you simply find some fresh caterpillar droppings, look up, and there's your caterpillar. More recently an author advised me to set my mind at ease about those piles of cut stems on the ground in grassy fields. Field mice make them; they cut the grass down by degrees to reach the seeds at the head. It seems that when the grass is tightly packed, as in a field of ripe grain, the blade won't topple at a single cut through the stem; instead, the cut stem simply drops vertically, held in the crush of grain. The mouse severs the bottom again and again, the stem keeps dropping an inch at a time, and finally the head is low enough for the mouse to reach the seeds. Meanwhile, the mouse is positively littering the field with its little piles of cut stems into which, presumably, the author of the book is constantly stumbling.

If I can't see these minutiae, I still try to keep my eyes open. I'm always on the lookout for antlion traps in sandy soil, monarch pupae near milkweed, skipper larvae in locust leaves. These things are utterly common, and I've not seen one. I bang on hollow trees near water, but so far no flying squirrels have appeared. In flat country I watch every sunset in hopes of seeing the green ray. The green ray is a seldom-seen streak of light that rises from the sun like a spurting fountain at the moment of sunset; it throbs into the sky for two seconds and disappears. One more reason to keep my eyes open. A photography professor at the University of Florida just happened to see a bird die in mid-flight; it jerked, died, dropped, and smashed on the ground. I squint at the wind because I read Stewart Edward White.[3] "I have always maintained that if you looked closely enough you could *see* the wind—the dim, hardly-made-out, fine débris fleeing high in the air." White was an excellent observer, and devoted an entire chapter of *The Mountains*[4] to the subject of seeing deer: "As soon as you can forget the naturally obvious and construct an artificial obvious, then you too will see deer."

But the artificial obvious is hard to see. My eyes account for less than one percent of the weight of my head; I'm bony and dense; I see what I expect. I once spent a full three minutes looking at a bullfrog that was so unexpectedly large I couldn't see it even though a dozen enthusiastic campers were shouting directions. Finally I asked, "What color am I looking for?" and a fellow said, "Green." When at last I picked out the frog, I saw what painters are up against: the thing wasn't green at all, but the color of wet hickory bark.

The lover can see, and the knowledgeable. I visited an aunt and uncle at a quarter-horse ranch in Cody, Wyoming.[5] I couldn't do much of anything useful, but I could, I thought, draw. So, as we all sat around the kitchen table after supper, I produced a sheet of paper and drew a horse. "That's one lame horse," my aunt volunteered. The rest of the family joined in: "Only place to saddle that one is his neck"; "Looks like we better shoot the poor thing, on account of those terrible growths." Meekly, I slid the pencil and paper down the table. Everyone in that family, including my three young cousins, could draw a horse. Beautifully. When the paper came back

3. American spiritualist writer (1873–1946).
4. Published in 1904.
5. City in the northwestern section of the state.

"Quarter horse": type of small horse bred for strength, speed, and endurance.

it looked as though five shining, real quarter horses had been corraled by mistake with a papier-mâché moose; the real horses seemed to gaze at the monster with a steady, puzzled air. I stay away from horses now, but I can do a creditable goldfish. The point is that I just don't know what the lover knows; I just can't see the artificial obvious that those in the know construct. The herpetologist asks the native, "Are there snakes in that ravine?" "Nosir." And the herpetologist comes home with, yessir, three bags full. Are there butterflies on that mountain? Are the bluets in bloom, are there arrowheads here, or fossil shells in the shale?

Peeping through my keyhole I see within the range of only about thirty percent of the light that comes from the sun; the rest is infrared and some little ultraviolet, perfectly apparent to many animals, but invisible to me. A nightmare network of ganglia, charged and firing without my knowledge, cuts and splices what I do see, editing it for my brain. Donald E. Carr[6] points out that the sense impressions of one-celled animals are *not* edited for the brain: "This is philosophically interesting in a rather mournful way, since it means that only the simplest animals perceive the universe as it is."

A fog that won't burn away drifts and flows across my field of vision. When you see fog move against a backdrop of deep pines, you don't see the fog itself, but streaks of clearness floating across the air in dark shreds. So I see only tatters of clearness through a pervading obscurity. I can't distinguish the fog from the overcast sky; I can't be sure if the light is direct or reflected. Everywhere darkness and the presence of the unseen appalls. We estimate now that only one atom dances alone in every cubic meter of intergalactic space. I blink and squint. What planet or power yanks Halley's Comet[7] out of orbit? We haven't seen that force yet; it's a question of distance, density, and the pallor of reflected light. We rock, cradled in the swaddling band of darkness. Even the simple darkness of night whispers suggestions to the mind. Last summer, in August, I stayed at the creek too late.

Where Tinker Creek flows under the sycamore log bridge to the tear-shaped island, it is slow and shallow, fringed thinly in cattail marsh. At this spot an astonishing bloom of life supports vast breeding populations of insects, fish, reptiles, birds, and mammals. On windless summer evenings I stalk along the creek bank or straddle the sycamore log in absolute stillness, watching for muskrats. The night I stayed too late I was hunched on the log staring spellbound at spreading, reflected stains of lilac on the water. A cloud in the sky suddenly lighted as if turned on by a switch; its reflection just as suddenly materialized on the water upstream, flat and floating, so that I couldn't see the creek bottom, or life in the water under the cloud. Downstream, away from the cloud on the water, water turtles smooth as beans were gliding down with the current in a series of easy, weightless push-offs, as men bound on the moon. I didn't know whether to trace the progress of one turtle I was sure of, risking sticking my face in one of the bridge's spider webs made invisible by the gathering dark, or take a chance on seeing the carp, or scan the mudbank in hope of seeing a muskrat, or

6. American environmentalist and writer (1903–1986).
7. Observed by the English astronomer Edmond Halley (1656–1742), who predicted that its orbit would return the comet to earthly view every seventy-six years.

follow the last of the swallows who caught at my heart and trailed it after them like streamers as they appeared from directly below, under the log, flying upstream with their tails forked, so fast.

But shadows spread, and deepened, and stayed. After thousands of years we're still strangers to darkness, fearful aliens in an enemy camp with our arms crossed over our chests. I stirred. A land turtle on the bank, startled, hissed the air from its lungs and withdrew into its shell. An uneasy pink here, an unfathomable blue there, gave great suggestion of lurking beings. Things were going on. I couldn't see whether that sere rustle I heard was a distant rattlesnake, slit-eyed, or a nearby sparrow kicking in the dry flood debris slung at the foot of a willow. Tremendous action roiled the water everywhere I looked, big action, inexplicable. A tremor welled up beside a gaping muskrat burrow in the bank and I caught my breath, but no muskrat appeared. The ripples continued to fan upstream with a steady, powerful thrust. Night was knitting over my face an eyeless mask, and I still sat transfixed. A distant airplane, a delta wing out of nightmare, made a gliding shadow on the creek's bottom that looked like a stingray cruising upstream. At once a black fin slit the pink cloud on the water, shearing it in two. The two halves merged together and seemed to dissolve before my eyes. Darkness pooled in the cleft of the creek and rose, as water collects in a well. Untamed, dreaming lights flickered over the sky. I saw hints of hulking underwater shadows, two pale splashes out of the water, and round ripples rolling close together from a blackened center.

At last I stared upstream where only the deepest violet remained of the cloud, a cloud so high its underbelly still glowed feeble color reflected from a hidden sky lighted in turn by a sun halfway to China. And out of that violet, a sudden enormous black body arced over the water. I saw only a cylindrical sleekness. Head and tail, if there was a head and tail, were both submerged in cloud. I saw only one ebony fling, a headlong dive to darkness; then the waters closed, and the lights went out.

I walked home in a shivering daze, up hill and down. Later I lay open-mouthed in bed, my arms flung wide at my sides to steady the whirling darkness. At this latitude I'm spinning 836 miles an hour round the earth's axis; I often fancy I feel my sweeping fall as a breakneck arc like the dive of dolphins, and the hollow rushing of wind raises hair on my neck and the side of my face. In orbit around the sun I'm moving 64,800 miles an hour. The solar system as a whole, like a merry-go-round unhinged, spins, bobs, and blinks at the speed of 43,200 miles an hour along a course set east of Hercules.[8] Someone has piped, and we are dancing a tarantella until the sweat pours. I open my eyes and I see dark, muscled forms curl out of water, with flapping gills and flattened eyes. I close my eyes and I see stars, deep stars giving way to deeper stars, deeper stars bowing to deepest stars at the crown of an infinite cone.

"Still," wrote van Gogh[9] in a letter, "a great deal of light falls on everything." If we are blinded by darkness, we are also blinded by light. When too much light falls on everything, a special terror results. Peter Freuchen[1]

---

8. A large northern constellation, named after the Greek and Roman god.
9. Vincent van Gogh (1853–1890), Dutch Post-

impressionist painter.
1. Danish writer, explorer, and authority on Greenland (1886–1957).

describes the notorious kayak sickness to which Greenland Eskimos are prone. "The Greenland fjords are peculiar for the spells of completely quiet weather, when there is not enough wind to blow out a match and the water is like a sheet of glass. The kayak hunter must sit in his boat without stirring a finger so as not to scare the shy seals away. . . . The sun, low in the sky, sends a glare into his eyes, and the landscape around moves into the realm of the unreal. The reflex from the mirrorlike water hypnotizes him, he seems to be unable to move, and all of a sudden it is as if he were floating in a bottomless void, sinking, sinking, and sinking. . . . Horror-stricken, he tries to stir, to cry out, but he cannot, he is completely paralyzed, he just falls and falls." Some hunters are especially cursed with this panic, and bring ruin and sometimes starvation to their families.

Sometimes here in Virginia at sunset low clouds on the southern or northern horizon are completely invisible in the lighted sky. I only know one is there because I can see its reflection in still water. The first time I discovered this mystery I looked from cloud to no-cloud in bewilderment, checking my bearings over and over, thinking maybe the ark of the covenant[2] was just passing by south of Dead Man Mountain. Only much later did I read the explanation: polarized light from the sky is very much weakened by reflection, but the light in clouds isn't polarized. So invisible clouds pass among visible clouds, till all slide over the mountains; so a greater light extinguishes a lesser as though it didn't exist.

In the great meteor shower of August, the Perseid, I wail all day for the shooting stars I miss. They're out there showering down, committing hara-kiri in a flame of fatal attraction, and hissing perhaps at last into the ocean. But at dawn what looks like a blue dome clamps down over me like a lid on a pot. The stars and planets could smash and I'd never know. Only a piece of ashen moon occasionally climbs up or down the inside of the dome, and our local star without surcease explodes on our heads. We have really only that one light, one source for all power, and yet we must turn away from it by universal decree. Nobody here on the planet seems aware of this strange, powerful taboo, that we all walk about carefully averting our faces, this way and that, lest our eyes be blasted forever.

Darkness appalls and light dazzles; the scrap of visible light that doesn't hurt my eyes hurts my brain. What I see sets me swaying. Size and distance and the sudden swelling of meanings confuse me, bowl me over. I straddle the sycamore log bridge over Tinker Creek in the summer. I look at the lighted creek bottom: snail tracks tunnel the mud in quavering curves. A crayfish jerks, but by the time I absorb what has happened, he's gone in a billowing smokescreen of silt. I look at the water: minnows and shiners. If I'm thinking minnows, a carp will fill my brain till I scream. I look at the water's surface: skaters, bubbles, and leaves sliding down. Suddenly, my own face, reflected, startles me witless. Those snails have been tracking my face! Finally, with a shuddering wrench of the will, I see clouds, cirrus clouds. I'm dizzy, I fall in. This looking business is risky.

Once I stood on a humped rock on nearby Purgatory Mountain, watching through binoculars the great autumn hawk migration below, until I

2. In ancient Israel a chest containing two stone tablets of the Ten Commandments, seen as a symbol of God's presence.

discovered that I was in danger of joining the hawks on a vertical migration of my own. I was used to binoculars, but not, apparently, to balancing on humped rocks while looking through them. I staggered. Everything advanced and receded by turns; the world was full of unexplained fore-shortenings and depths. A distant huge tan object, a hawk the size of an elephant, turned out to be the browned bough of a nearby loblolly pine. I followed a sharp-shinned hawk against a featureless sky, rotating my head unawares as it flew, and when I lowered the glass a glimpse of my own looming shoulder sent me staggering. What prevents the men on Palomar[3] from falling, voiceless and blinded, from their tiny, vaulted chairs?

I reel in confusion; I don't understand what I see. With the naked eye I can see two million light-years to the Andromeda galaxy. Often I slop some creek water in a jar and when I get home I dump it in a white china bowl. After the silt settles I return and see tracings of minute snails on the bottom, a planarian or two winding round the rim of water, roundworms shim-mying frantically, and finally, when my eyes have adjusted to these dimensions, amoebae. At first the amoebae look like muscae volitantes, those curled mov-ing spots you seem to see in your eyes when you stare at a distant wall. Then I see the amoebae as drops of water congealed, bluish, translucent, like chips of sky in the bowl. At length I choose one individual and give myself over to its idea of an evening. I see it dribble a grainy foot before it on its wet, unfath-omable way. Do its unedited sense impressions include the fierce focus of my eyes? Shall I take it outside and show it Andromeda, and blow its little endo-plasm? I stir the water with a finger, in case it's running out of oxygen. Maybe I should get a tropical aquarium with motorized bubblers and lights, and keep this one for a pet. Yes, it would tell its fissioned descendants, the uni-verse is two feet by five, and if you listen closely you can hear the buzzing music of the spheres.

Oh, it's mysterious lamplit evenings, here in the galaxy, one after the other. It's one of those nights when I wander from window to window, look-ing for a sign. But I can't see. Terror and a beauty insoluble are a ribband of blue woven into the fringes of garments of things both great and small. No culture explains, no bivouac offers real haven or rest. But it could be that we are not seeing something. Galileo[4] thought comets were an optical illu-sion. This is fertile ground: since we are certain that they're not, we can look at what our scientists have been saying with fresh hope. What if there are *really* gleaming, castellated cities hung upside-down over the desert sand? What limpid lakes and cool date palms have our caravans always passed untried? Until, one by one, by the blindest of leaps, we light on the road to these places, we must stumble in darkness and hunger. I turn from the window. I'm blind as a bat, sensing only from every direction the echo of my own thin cries.

I chanced on a wonderful book by Marius von Senden, called *Space and Sight*.[5] When Western surgeons discovered how to perform safe cataract

---

3. I.e., in the Palomar Observatory, on Palomar Mountain, in San Diego County, California.
4. Galileo Galilei (1564–1642), Italian astromer and physicist.

5. Written by the 20th-century German physi-cian and published in German in 1932 (English translation, 1960).

operations, they ranged across Europe and America operating on dozens of men and women of all ages who had been blinded by cataracts since birth. Von Senden collected accounts of such cases; the histories are fascinating. Many doctors had tested their patients' sense perceptions and ideas of space both before and after the operations. The vast majority of patients, of both sexes and all ages, had, in von Senden's opinion, no idea of space whatsoever. Form, distance, and size were so many meaningless syllables. A patient "had no idea of depth, confusing it with roundness." Before the operation a doctor would give a blind patient a cube and a sphere; the patient would tongue it or feel it with his hands, and name it correctly. After the operation the doctor would show the same objects to the patient without letting him touch them; now he had no clue whatsoever what he was seeing. One patient called lemonade "square" because it pricked on his tongue as a square shape pricked on the touch of his hands. Of another postoperative patient, the doctor writes, "I have found in her no notion of size, for example, not even within the narrow limits which she might have encompassed with the aid of touch. Thus when I asked her to show me how big her mother was, she did not stretch out her hands, but set her two index-fingers a few inches apart." Other doctors reported their patients' own statements to similar effect. "The room he was in . . . he knew to be but part of the house, yet he could not conceive that the whole house could look bigger"; "Those who are blind from birth . . . have no real conception of height or distance. A house that is a mile away is thought of as nearby, but requiring the taking of a lot of steps. . . . The elevator that whizzes him up and down gives no more sense of vertical distance than does the train of horizontal."

For the newly sighted, vision is pure sensation unencumbered by meaning: "The girl went through the experience that we all go through and forget, the moment we are born. She saw, but it did not mean anything but a lot of different kinds of brightness." Again, "I asked the patient what he could see; he answered that he saw an extensive field of light, in which everything appeared dull, confused, and in motion. He could not distinguish objects." Another patient saw "nothing but a confusion of forms and colours." When a newly sighted girl saw photographs and paintings, she asked, "'Why do they put those dark marks all over them?' 'Those aren't dark marks,' her mother explained, 'those are shadows. That is one of the ways the eye knows that things have shape. If it were not for shadows many things would look flat.' 'Well, that's how things do look,' Joan answered. 'Everything looks flat with dark patches.'"

But it is the patients' concepts of space that are most revealing. One patient, according to his doctor, "practiced his vision in a strange fashion; thus he takes off one of his boots, throws it some way off in front of him, and then attempts to gauge the distance at which it lies; he takes a few steps towards the boot and tries to grasp it; on failing to reach it, he moves on a step or two and gropes for the boot until he finally gets hold of it." "But even at this stage, after three weeks' experience of seeing," von Senden goes on, "'space,' as he conceives it, ends with visual space, i.e. with colour-patches that happen to bound his view. He does not yet have the notion that a larger object (a chair) can mask a smaller one (a dog), or that the latter can still be present even though it is not directly seen."

In general the newly sighted see the world as a dazzle of color-patches. They are pleased by the sensation of color, and learn quickly to name the colors, but the rest of seeing is tormentingly difficult. Soon after his operation a patient "generally bumps into one of these colour-patches and observes them to be substantial, since they resist him as tactual objects do. In walking about it also strikes him—or can if he pays attention—that he is continually passing in between the colours he sees, that he can go past a visual object, that a part of it then steadily disappears from view; and that in spite of this, however he twists and turns—whether entering the room from the door, for example, or returning back to it—he always has a visual space in front of him. Thus he gradually comes to realize that there is also a space behind him, which he does not see."

The mental effort involved in these reasonings proves overwhelming for many patients. It oppresses them to realize, if they ever do at all, the tremendous size of the world, which they had previously conceived of as something touchingly manageable. It oppresses them to realize that they have been visible to people all along, perhaps unattractively so, without their knowledge or consent. A disheartening number of them refuse to use their new vision, continuing to go over objects with their tongues, and lapsing into apathy and despair. "The child can see, but will not make use of his sight. Only when pressed can he with difficulty be brought to look at objects in his neighbourhood; but more than a foot away it is impossible to bestir him to the necessary effort." Of a twenty-one-year-old girl, the doctor relates, "Her unfortunate father, who had hoped for so much from this operation, wrote that his daughter carefully shuts her eyes whenever she wishes to go about the house, especially when she comes to a staircase, and that she is never happier or more at ease than when, by closing her eyelids, she relapses into her former state of total blindness." A fifteen-year-old boy, who was also in love with a girl at the asylum for the blind, finally blurted out, "No, really, I can't stand it any more; I want to be sent back to the asylum again. If things aren't altered, I'll tear my eyes out."

Some do learn to see, especially the young ones. But it changes their lives. One doctor comments on "the rapid and complete loss of that striking and wonderful serenity which is characteristic only of those who have never yet seen." A blind man who learns to see is ashamed of his old habits. He dresses up, grooms himself, and tries to make a good impression. While he was blind he was indifferent to objects unless they were edible; now, "a sifting of values sets in . . . his thoughts and wishes are mightily stirred and some few of the patients are thereby led into dissimulation, envy, theft and fraud."

On the other hand, many newly sighted people speak well of the world, and teach us how dull is our own vision. To one patient, a human hand, unrecognized, is "something bright and then holes." Shown a bunch of grapes, a boy calls out, "It is dark, blue and shiny. . . . It isn't smooth, it has bumps and hollows." A little girl visits a garden. "She is greatly astonished, and can scarcely be persuaded to answer, stands speechless in front of the tree, which she only names on taking hold of it, and then as 'the tree with the lights in it.'" Some delight in their sight and give themselves over to the visual world. Of a patient just after her bandages were removed, her doctor writes, "The first things to attract her attention were her own hands; she looked at them very closely, moved them repeatedly to and fro, bent and stretched the fingers, and seemed greatly astonished at the sight." One girl was eager to tell her blind friend that "men do not really look like trees at all," and astounded to discover that her every visitor had an utterly different face. Finally, a twenty-two-old girl was dazzled by the world's brightness and kept her eyes shut for two weeks. When at the end of that time she opened her eyes again, she did not recognize any objects, but, "the more she now directed her gaze upon everything about her, the more it could be seen how an expression of gratification and astonishment overspread her features; she repeatedly exclaimed: 'Oh God! How beautiful!'"

I saw color-patches for weeks after I read this wonderful book. It was summer; the peaches were ripe in the valley orchards. When I woke in the morning, color-patches wrapped round my eyes, intricately, leaving not one unfilled spot. All day long I walked among shifting color-patches that parted before me like the Red Sea and closed again in silence, transfigured, wherever I looked back. Some patches swelled and loomed, while others vanished utterly, and dark marks flitted at random over the whole dazzling sweep. But I couldn't sustain the illusion of flatness. I've been around for too long. Form is condemned to an eternal danse macabre with meaning: I couldn't unpeach the peaches. Nor can I remember ever having seen without understanding; the color-patches of infancy are lost. My brain then must have been smooth as any balloon. I'm told I reached for the moon; many babies do. But the color-patches of infancy swelled as meaning filled them; they arrayed themselves in solemn ranks down distance which unrolled and stretched before me like a plain. The moon rocketed away. I live now in a world of shadows that shape and distance color, a world where space makes a kind of terrible sense. What gnosticism is this, and what physics? The fluttering patch I saw in my nursery window—silver and green and shape-shifting blue—is gone; a row of Lombardy poplars takes its place, mute, across the distant lawn. That humming oblong creature pale as light that stole along the walls of my room at night, stretching exhilaratingly around the corners, is gone, too, gone the night I ate of the bittersweet fruit, put two and two together and puckered forever my brain. Martin Buber[6] tells this tale: "Rabbi Mendel once boasted to his teacher Rabbi Elimelekh that evenings he saw the angel who rolls away the light before the darkness, and mornings the angel who rolls away the darkness before the light. 'Yes,' said Rabbi Elimelekh, 'in my youth I saw that too. Later on you don't see these things any more.'"

Why didn't someone hand those newly sighted people paints and brushes from the start, when they still didn't know what anything was? Then maybe we all could see color-patches too, the world unraveled from reason, Eden before Adam gave names. The scales would drop from my eyes; I'd see trees like men walking; I'd run down the road against all orders, hallooing and leaping.

Seeing is of course very much a matter of verbalization. Unless I call my attention to what passes before my eyes, I simply won't see it. It is, as

6. Austrian-born Jewish philosopher (1878–1965) active in Germany and Israel.

Ruskin[7] says, "not merely unnoticed, but in the full, clear sense of the word, unseen." My eyes alone can't solve analogy tests using figures, the ones which show, with increasing elaborations, a big square, then a small square in a big square, then a big triangle, and expect me to find a small triangle in a big triangle. I have to say the words, describe what I'm seeing. If Tinker Mountain erupted, I'd be likely to notice. But if I want to notice the lesser cataclysms of valley life, I have to maintain in my head a running description of the present. It's not that I'm observant; it's just that I talk too much. Otherwise, especially in a strange place, I'll never know what's happening. Like a blind man at the ball game, I need a radio.

When I see this way I analyze and pry. I hurl over logs and roll away stones; I study the bank a square foot at a time, probing and tilting my head. Some days when a mist covers the mountains, when the muskrats won't show and the microscope's mirror shatters, I want to climb up the blank blue dome as a man would storm the inside of a circus tent, wildly, dangling, and with a steel knife claw a rent in the top, peep, and, if I must, fall.

But there is another kind of seeing that involves a letting go. When I see this way I sway transfixed and emptied. The difference between the two ways of seeing is the difference between walking with and without a camera. When I walk with a camera I walk from shot to shot, reading the light on a calibrated meter. When I walk without a camera, my own shutter opens, and the moment's light prints on my own silver gut. When I see this second way I am above all an unscrupulous observer.

It was sunny one evening last summer at Tinker Creek; the sun was low in the sky, upstream. I was sitting on the sycamore log bridge with the sunset at my back, watching the shiners the size of minnows who were feeding over the muddy sand in skittery schools. Again and again, one fish, then another, turned for a split second across the current and flash! the sun shot out from its silver side. I couldn't watch for it. It was always just happening somewhere else, and it drew my vision just as it disappeared: flash, like a sudden dazzle of the thinnest blade, a sparking over a dun and olive ground at chance intervals from every direction. Then I noticed white specks, some sort of pale petals, small, floating from under my feet on the creek's surface, very slow and steady. So I blurred my eyes and gazed towards the brim of my hat and saw a new world. I saw the pale white circles roll up, roll up, like the world's turning, mute and perfect, and I saw the linear flashes, gleaming silver, like stars being born at random down a rolling scroll of time. Something broke and something opened. I filled up like a new wineskin. I breathed an air like light; I saw a light like water. I was the lip of a fountain the creek filled forever; I was ether, the leaf in the zephyr; I was flesh-flake, feather, bone.

When I see this way I see truly. As Thoreau says, I return to my senses. I am the man who watches the baseball game in silence in an empty stadium. I see the game purely; I'm abstracted and dazed. When it's all over and the white-suited players lope off the green field to their shadowed dugouts, I leap to my feet; I cheer and cheer.

7. John Ruskin (1819–1900), English art critic and social observer.

But I can't go out and try to see this way. I'll fail, I'll go mad. All I can do is try to gag the commentator, to hush the noise of useless interior babble that keeps me from seeing just as surely as a newspaper dangled before my eyes. The effort is really a discipline requiring a lifetime of dedicated struggle; it marks the literature of saints and monks of every order East and West, under every rule and no rule, discalced and shod. The world's spiritual geniuses seem to discover universally that the mind's muddy river, this ceaseless flow of trivia and trash, cannot be dammed, and that trying to dam it is a waste of effort that might lead to madness. Instead you must allow the muddy river to flow unheeded in the dim channels of consciousness; you raise your sights; you look along it, mildly, acknowledging its presence without interest and gazing beyond it into the realm of the real where subjects and objects act and rest purely, without utterance. "Launch into the deep," says Jacques Ellul,[8] "and you shall see."

The secret of seeing is, then, the pearl of great price. If I thought he could teach me to find it and keep it forever I would stagger barefoot across a hundred deserts after any lunatic at all. But although the pearl may be found, it may not be sought. The literature of illumination reveals this above all: although it comes to those who wait for it, it is always, even to the most practiced and adept, a gift and a total surprise. I return from one walk knowing where the killdeer nests in the field by the creek and the hour the laurel blooms. I return from the same walk a day later scarcely knowing my own name. Litanies hum in my ears; my tongue flaps in my mouth Ailinon, alleluia![9] I cannot cause light; the most I can do is try to put myself in the path of its beam. It is possible, in deep space, to sail on solar wind. Light, be it particle or wave, has force: you rig a giant sail and go. The secret of seeing is to sail on solar wind. Hone and spread your spirit till you yourself are a sail, whetted, translucent, broadside to the merest puff.

When her doctor took her bandages off and led her into the garden, the girl who was no longer blind saw "the tree with the lights in it." It was for this tree I searched through the peach orchards of summer, in the forests of fall and down winter and spring for years. Then one day I was walking along Tinker Creek thinking of nothing at all and I saw the tree with the lights in it. I saw the backyard cedar where the mourning doves roost charged and transfigured, each cell buzzing with flame. I stood on the grass with the lights in it, grass that was wholly fire, utterly focused and utterly dreamed. It was less like seeing than like being for the first time seen, knocked breathless by a powerful glance. The flood of fire abated, but I'm still spending the power. Gradually the lights went out in the cedar, the colors died, the cells unflamed and disappeared. I was still ringing. I had been my whole life a bell, and never knew it until at that moment I was lifted and struck. I have since only very rarely seen the tree with the lights in it. The vision comes and goes, mostly goes, but I live for it, for the moment when the mountains open and a new light roars in spate through the crack, and the mountains slam.

1974

8. French sociologist, theologian, historian, philosopher, and critic of technology (1912–1994).
9. In Greek a representation of a woeful, plaintive dirge.

LYDIA DAVIS
b. 1947

Sharp-eyed, funny, unforgiving, and intensely preoccupied with words, Lydia Davis writes about characters who see, and say, uncomfortable things about ordinary life. Her stories are renowned for their brevity, often just a paragraph or a few pages. Much of Davis's fiction is about a world containing brute objects and people who seem as inscrutable as objects to the stories' narrators—they have their own private thoughts that are impossible for the narrator to know. The mystery of what other people are thinking causes the typical Davis narrator to doubt and obsess, especially over relationships. Davis reflects that "the only mind you have complete access to is your own. That's the mind you can study and work with and enjoy." Her stories thus sometimes read like autobiography, but it would be more accurate to say that they take readers into the life of the modern mind. About feelings—such as happiness, or grief, or boredom—Davis is both curious and suspicious. Once they are put into words, can they still be felt? Do our words for emotions ever succeed in containing them, or honoring them? Plot and setting are pared away in Davis's stories so that the focus on mind and feeling can deepen, though something always "happens," even when no events occur. "We are more aware of the great precariousness and the possible brevity of our lives than we were in the past," Davis has said in explaining her preference for short forms. "Perhaps we express not only more despair but also more urgency in some of our literature now, this urgency also being expressed as brevity itself." Her stories can feel like poems, and her collections are sometimes shelved in the poetry sections of bookstores.

Davis's storytelling practice is rooted in the traditions of English and French literature. She has published ten story collections, one novel, five works of translation (from the French), and an extended essay on translation. Her versions of Marcel Proust's *Swann's Way* (2003) and Gustave Flaubert's *Madame Bovary* (2010) were published to critical acclaim and commercial success. Each of these great French novels centers on what characters think as they go through life experiencing love and tragedy. Though their formal scale is so much larger than Davis's very short stories, these works are powerful influences on her fiction. Translation has made Davis profoundly aware of words and of their provenance. "I value the fact that English has two parallel vocabularies—the Germanic vocabulary and the Latinate vocabulary," she explains. "For example, we have the word *undersea*, and then we have *submarine*. Or *underground* and *subterranean*, *all-powerful* and *omnipotent*. So we can shift registers. . . . In a passage of plain Anglo-Saxon, you can throw in one Latinate word, unexpectedly, to great effect."

Her attention to craft as a writer parallels her professional commitment to teaching. She has held appointments at Bard College and SUNY Albany and is currently Lillian Vernon Distinguished Writer-in-Residence at New York University. Her writing has won major literary prizes, including the 2013 Man Booker International Prize, and she has garnered prestigious fellowships—a Guggenheim and a MacArthur "genius grant" among them.

In "Break It Down," reprinted here, the narrator assesses the loss of a relationship by literally counting up its costs—in money. In this and the other selections included here, speakers try to pin down the large meaning of small things. "Letter to a Funeral Parlor" showcases Davis's laserlike attention to vocabulary and emotion. Flaubert dedicated himself to finding *le mot juste*—"the right word"—for everything he wanted to express. Davis's wit and humor, on display throughout her fiction, offer wry laughter and *le mot juste* as consolations in what she sees as an absurd and baffling existence.

Break It Down

He's sitting there staring at a piece of paper in front of him. He's trying to break it down. He says:

I'm breaking it all down. The ticket was $600 and then after that there was more for the hotel and food and so on, for just ten days. Say $80 a day, no, more like $100 a day. And we made love, say, once a day on the average. That's $100 a shot. And each time it lasted maybe two or three hours so that would be anywhere from $33 to $50 an hour, which is expensive.

Though of course that wasn't all that went on, because we were together almost all day long. She would keep looking at me and every time she looked at me it was worth something, and she smiled at me and didn't stop talking and singing, something I said, she would sail into it, a snatch, for me, she would be gone from me a little ways but smiling too, and tell me jokes, and I loved it but didn't exactly know what to do about it and just smiled back at her and felt slow next to her, just not quick enough. So she talked and touched me on the shoulder and the arm, she kept touching and stayed close to me. You're with each other all day long and it keeps happening, the touches and smiles, and it adds up, it builds up, and you know where you'll be that night, you're talking and every now and then you think about it, no, you don't think, you just feel it as a kind of destination, what's coming up after you leave wherever you are all evening, and you're happy about it and you're planning it all, not in your head, really, somewhere inside your body, or all through your body, it's all mounting up and coming together so that when you get in bed you can't help it, it's a real performance, it all pours out, but slowly, you go easy until you can't anymore, or you hold back the whole time, you hold back and touch the edges of everything, you edge around until you have to plunge in and finish it off, and when you're finished, you're too weak to stand but after a while you have to go to the bathroom and you stand, your legs are trembling, you hold on to the door frames, there's a little light coming in through the window, you can see your way in and out, but you can't really see the bed.

So it's not really $100 a shot because it goes on all day, from the start when you wake up and feel her body next to you, and you don't miss a thing, not a thing of what's next to you, her arm, her leg, her shoulder, her face, that good skin, I have felt other good skin, but this skin is just the edge of something else, and you're going to start going, and no matter how much you crawl all over each other it won't be enough, and when your hunger dies down a little then you think how much you love her and that starts you off again, and her face, you look over at her face and can't believe how you got there and how lucky and it's still all a surprise and it never stops, even after it's over, it never stops being a surprise.

It's more like you have a good sixteen or eighteen hours a day of this going on, even when you're not with her it's going on, it's good to be away because it's going to be so good to go back to her, so it's still here, and you can't go off and look at some old street or some old painting without still feeling it in your body and a few things that happened the day before that don't mean much by themselves or wouldn't mean much if you weren't having this thing together, but you can't forget and it's all inside you all the time, so that's more like, say, sixteen into a hundred would be $6 an hour, which isn't too much.

And then it really keeps going on while you're asleep, though you're probably dreaming about something else, a building, maybe, I kept dreaming, every night, almost, about this building, because I would spend a lot of every morning in this old stone building and when I closed my eyes I would see these cool spaces and have this peace inside me, I would see the bricks of the floor and the stone arches and the space, the emptiness between, like a kind of dark frame around what I could see beyond, a garden, and this space was like stone too because of the coolness of it and the gray shadow, that kind of luminous shade, that was glowing with the light of the sun falling beyond the arches, and there was also the great height of the ceiling, all this was in my mind all the time though I didn't know it until I closed my eyes, I'm asleep and I'm not dreaming about her but she's lying next to me and I wake up enough times in the night to remember she's there, and notice, say, once she was lying on her back but now she's curled around me, I look at her closed eyes, I want to kiss her eyelids, I want to feel that soft skin under my lips, but I don't want to disturb her, I don't want to see her frown as though in her sleep she has forgotten who I am and feels just that something is bothering her and so I just look at her and hold on to it all, these times when I'm watching over her sleep and she's next to me and isn't away from me the way she will be later, I want to stay awake all night just to go on feeling that, but I can't, I fall asleep again, though I'm sleeping lightly, still trying to hold on to it.

But it isn't over when it ends, it goes on after it's all over, she's still inside you like a sweet liquor, you are filled with her, everything about her has kind of bled into you, her smell, her voice, the way her body moves, it's all inside you, at least for a while after, then you begin to lose it, and I'm beginning to lose it, you're afraid of how weak you are, that you can't get her all back into you again and now the whole thing is going out of your body and it's more in your mind than your body, the pictures come to you one by one and you look at them, some of them last longer than others, you were together in a very white clean place, a coffeehouse, having breakfast together, and the place is so white that against it you can see her clearly, her blue eyes, her smile, the colors of her clothes, even the print of the newspaper she's reading when she's not looking up at you, the light brown and red and gold of her hair when she's got her head down reading, the brown coffee, the brown rolls, all against that white table and those white plates and silver urns and silver knives and spoons, and against that quiet of the sleepy people in that room sitting alone at their tables with just some chinking and clattering of spoons and cups in saucers and some hushed voices her voice now and then rising and falling. The pictures come to you and you have to hope they won't lose their life too fast and dry up though you know they will and that you'll also forget some of what happened, because already you're turning up little things that you nearly forgot.

We were in bed and she asked me, Do I seem fat to you? and I was surprised because she didn't seem to worry about herself at all in that way and I guess I was reading into it that she did worry about herself so I answered what I was thinking and said stupidly that she had a very beautiful body, that her body was perfect, and I really meant it as an answer, but she said kind of sharply, That's not what I asked, and so I had to try to answer her again, exactly what she had asked.

And once she lay over against me late in the night and she started talking, her breath in my ear, and she just went on and on, and talked faster and faster, she couldn't stop, and I loved it, I just felt that all that life in her was running into me too, I had so little life in me, her life, her fire, was coming into me, in that hot breath in my ear, and I just wanted her to go on talking forever right there next to me, and I would go on living, like that, I would be able to go on living, but without her I don't know.

Then you forget some of it all, maybe most of it all, almost all of it, in the end, and you work hard at remembering everything now so you won't ever forget, but you can kill it too even by thinking about it too much, though you can't help thinking about it nearly all the time.

And then when the pictures start to go you start asking some questions, just little questions, that sit in your mind without any answers, like why did she have the light on when you came in to bed one night, but it was off the next, but she had it on the night after that and she had it off the last night, why, and other questions, little questions that nag at you like that.

And finally the pictures go and these dry little questions just sit there without any answers and you're left with this large heavy pain in you that you try to numb by reading, or you try to ease it by getting out into public places where there will be people around you, but no matter how good you are at pushing that pain away, just when you think you're going to be all right for a while, that you're safe, you're kind of holding it off with all your strength and you're staying in some little bare numb spot of ground, then suddenly it will all come back, you'll hear a noise, maybe it's a cat crying or a baby, or something else like her cry, you hear it and make that connection in a part of you you have no control over and the pain comes back so hard that you're afraid, afraid of how you're falling back into it again and you wonder, no, you're terrified to ask how you're ever going to climb out of it.

And so it's not only every hour of the day while it's happening, but it's really for hours and hours every day after that, for weeks, though less and less, so that you could work out the ratio if you wanted, maybe after six weeks you're only thinking about it an hour or so in the day altogether, a few minutes here and there spread over, or a few minutes here and there and half an hour before you go to sleep, or sometimes it all comes back and you stay awake with it half the night.

So when you add up all that, you've only spent maybe $3 an hour on it.

If you have to figure in the bad times too, I don't know. There weren't any bad times with her, though maybe there was one bad time, when I told her I loved her. I couldn't help it, this was the first time this had happened with her, now I was half falling in love with her or maybe completely if she had let me but she couldn't or I couldn't completely because it was all going to be so short and other things too, and so I told her, and didn't know of any way to tell her first that she didn't have to feel this was a burden, the fact that I loved her, or that she didn't have to feel the same about me, or say the same back, that it was just that I had to tell her, that's all, because it was bursting inside me, and saying it wouldn't even begin to take care of what I was feeling, really I couldn't say anything of what I was feeling because there was so much, words couldn't handle it, and making love only made it worse because then I wanted words badly but they were no good, no good at all, but I told her anyway, I was lying on top of her and her hands were up by her head and my hands were on hers and our fingers were locked and there was a little light on her face from the window but I couldn't really see her and I was afraid to say it but I had to say it because I wanted her to know, it was the last night, I had to tell her then or I'd never have another chance, I just said, Before you go to sleep, I have to tell you before you go to sleep that I love you, and immediately, right away after, she said, I love you too, and it sounded to me as if she didn't mean it, a little flat, but then it usually sounds a little flat when someone says, I love you too, because they're just saying it back even if they do mean it, and the problem is that I'll never know if she meant it, or maybe someday she'll tell me whether she meant it or not, but there's no way to know now, and I'm sorry I did that, it was a trap I didn't mean to put her in, I can see it was a trap, because if she hadn't said anything at all I know that would have hurt too, as though she were taking something from me and just accepting it and not giving anything back, so she really had to, even just to be kind to me, she had to say it, and I don't really know now if she meant it.

Another bad time, or it wasn't exactly bad, but it wasn't easy either, was when I had to leave, the time was coming, and I was beginning to tremble and feel empty, nothing in the middle of me, nothing inside, and nothing to hold me up on my legs, and then it came, everything was ready, and I had to go, and so it was just a kiss, a quick one, as though we were afraid of what might happen after a kiss, and she was almost wild then, she reached up to a hook by the door and took an old shirt, a green and blue shirt from the hook, and put it in my arms, for me to take away, the soft cloth was full of her smell, and then we stood there close together looking at a piece of paper she had in her hand and I didn't lose any of it, I was holding it tight, that last minute or two, because this was it, we'd come to the end of it, things always change, so this was really it, over.

Maybe it works out all right, maybe you haven't lost for doing it, I don't know, no, really, sometimes when you think of it you feel like a prince really, you feel just like a king, and then other times you're afraid, you're afraid, not all the time but now and then, of what it's going to do to you, and it's hard to know what to do with it now.

Walking away I looked back once and the door was still open, I could see her standing far back in the dark of the room, I could only really see her white face still looking out at me, and her white arms.

I guess you get to a point where you look at that pain as if it were there in front of you three feet away lying in a box, an open box, in a window somewhere. It's hard and cold, like a bar of metal. You just look at it there and say, All right, I'll take it, I'll buy it. That's what it is. Because you know all about it before you even go into this thing. You know the pain is part of the whole thing. And it isn't that you can say afterwards the pleasure was greater than the pain and that's why you would do it again. That has nothing to do with it.

You can't measure it, because the pain comes after and it lasts longer. So the question really is, Why doesn't that pain make you say, I won't do it again? When the pain is so bad that you have to say that, but you don't.

So I'm just thinking about it, how you can go in with $600, more like $1,000, and how you can come out with an old shirt.

1986

The Outing

An outburst of anger near the road, a refusal to speak on the path, a silence in the pine woods, a silence across the old railroad bridge, an attempt to be friendly in the water, a refusal to end the argument on the flat stones, a cry of anger on the steep bank of dirt, a weeping among the bushes.

1995

Happiest Moment

If you ask her what is a favorite story she has written, she will hesitate for a long time and then say it may be this story that she read in a book once: an English-language teacher in China asked his Chinese student to say what was the happiest moment in his life. The student hesitated for a long time. At last he smiled with embarrassment and said that his wife had once gone to Beijing and eaten duck there, and she often told him about it, and he would have to say the happiest moment of his life was her trip, and the eating of the duck.

2001

Letter to a Funeral Parlor

Dear Sir,

I am writing to you to object to the word *cremains*, which was used by your representative when he met with my mother and me two days after my father's death.

We had no objection to your representative, personally, who was respectful and friendly and dealt with us in a sensitive way. He did not try to sell us an expensive urn, for instance.

What startled and disturbed us was the word *cremains*. You in the business must have invented this word and you are used to it. We the public do not hear it very often. We don't lose a close friend or a family member very many times in our life, and years pass in between, if we are lucky. Even less often do we have to discuss what is to be done with a family member or close friend after their death.

We noticed that before the death of my father you and your representative used the words *loved one* to refer to him. That was comfortable for us, even if the ways in which we loved him were complicated.

Then we were sitting there in our chairs in the living room trying not to weep in front of your representative, who was opposite us on the sofa, and we were very tired first from sitting up with my father, and then from worrying about whether he was comfortable as he was dying, and then from worrying about where he might be now that he was dead, and your representative referred to him as "the cremains."

At first we did not even know what he meant. Then, when we realized, we were frankly upset. *Cremains* sounds like something invented as a milk substitute in coffee, like Cremora, or Coffee-mate. Or it sounds like some kind of a chipped beef dish.

As one who works with words for a living, I must say that any invented word, like *Porta Potti* or *pooper-scooper*, has a cheerful or even jovial ring to it that I don't think you really intended when you invented the word *cremains*. In fact, my father himself, who was a professor of English and is now being called *the cremains*, would have pointed out to you the alliteration in *Porta Potti* and the rhyme in *pooper-scooper*. Then he would have told you that *cremains* falls into the same category as *brunch* and is known as a portmanteau word.[1]

There is nothing wrong with inventing words, especially in a business. But a grieving family is not prepared for this one. We are not even used to our loved one being gone. You could very well continue to employ the term *ashes*. We are used to it from the Bible, and are even comforted by it. We would not misunderstand. We would know that these ashes are not like the ashes in a fireplace.

Yours sincerely.

2001

---

1. A word blending the sounds and combining the meanings of two others.

ANN BEATTIE
b. 1947

If one writer has been held responsible for chronicling the fortunes of young people from the American 1960s as they grew up, got married and divorced, worked at different jobs, and went to the same parties, Ann Beattie, who graduated from high school in 1965, is that writer; indeed, she has picked up some of the mythical reputation that adheres to the film *The Big Chill* (1983) as somehow "representative" in its representation of late-sixties idealism and conviction gone flat or sour. Yet to stress Beattie's importance as portraitist of a generation may be to do her a disservice, since she is above all else a *fiction* writer, often a comic one, with an unrepresentative, even idiosyncratic, style. Her stories and novels should be taken not merely as vehicles for displaying social attitudes and manners, but as mannerist compositions that need to be both looked at and listened to. Her style is too pronounced, too carefully contrived, to be treated as a transparent medium through which "reality" is given us directly.

On its surface her life has been relatively uneventful, from growing up in a middle-class suburb of Washington, D.C. (she was "an artsy little thing . . . painting pictures, writing," as she put it), taking her undergraduate degree at American University, then going on to graduate study for a time at the University of Connecticut. She soon began to send stories to the *New Yorker* and after the usual spate of rejections had one accepted, then others. By her mid-twenties she was contributing regularly to that most sought-after magazine, and in 1976, on the verge of her thirtieth birthday, she brought out simultaneously a collection of her stories, *Distortions*, and her first novel, *Chilly Scenes of Winter*.

The stories—some of them more experimental in style than her more recent work—are about transient, usually unsatisfactory relationships between people, married and single, male and female. Her characters' work provides them with little pleasure or fulfillment; almost anything threatens to become "just a job." What these people do best, and incessantly, is talk to each other about themselves, how they feel about their lives. In fact such talk is the essential ingredient in her fiction. As one of her more severe critics, Joseph Epstein, has pointed out, Beattie strives for not "development of character, accounts of motivation or moral resolution" but rather "states of feeling." In stories from her second collection, *Secrets and Surprises* (1978), such as "A Reasonable Man," "Lawn Party," and "Weekend," feelings are talked around, hinted at, never quite said, but are the only "things" that happen in the story. In "Weekend" (printed here) the force of that happening is cumulative and disturbing.

Like many fiction writers, Beattie acknowledges the influence of Hemingway ("I sound like someone talking in *The Sun Also Rises*," says a character in "The Lawn Party"), but her kinship with him is especially strong in that each uses language, exchanges between characters, to suggest—by all that is left unsaid in the spare, often dull sentences, the platitudinous conversations—that something interesting lies behind those words, that conversation. Hemingway manages in his best stories to make us feel the presence of something powerful behind the conventional words. Beattie's characters, decades later, yearn for there to be something real or interesting behind their banal words, but her work's poignancy lies in the hint that, as the characters themselves half guess, there may be nothing much behind them at all. Something important got lost, back there in the sixties.

Of her novels the most ambitious is *Falling in Place* (1980), which spreads the usual urban and suburban anomie over the usual Beattie cast of dispirited seekers after a better-than-usual day. But the book comes to life when it focuses on a fifteen-year-old girl, whose favorite characterizing response to things is "Suck-O," and her younger brother, a compulsive eater who loves violent comics but little else. This twosome, who could give the most obnoxious of Flannery O'Connor's fictional children a run for their money, is observed with satiric verve, and the book includes a number of brilliant parts. Beattie is essentially a writer of scenes rather than a contriver of extended sequences, just as the people she writes about can deal with life only—and just barely—a moment at a time.

The following text is from *Secrets and Surprises* (1978).

Weekend

On Saturday morning Lenore is up before the others. She carries her baby into the living room and puts him in George's favorite chair, which tilts because its back legs are missing, and covers him with a blanket. Then she lights a fire in the fireplace, putting fresh logs on a few embers that are still glowing from the night before. She sits down on the floor beside the chair and checks the baby, who has already gone back to sleep—a good thing, because there are guests in the house. George, the man she lives with, is very hospitable and impetuous; he extends invitations whenever old friends call, urging them to come spend the weekend. Most of the callers are his former students—he used to be an English professor—and when they come it seems to make things much worse. It makes *him* much worse, because he falls into smoking too much and drinking and not eating, and then his ulcer bothers him. When the guests leave, when the weekend is over, she has to cook bland food: applesauce, oatmeal, puddings. And his drinking does not taper off easily anymore; in the past he would stop cold when the guests left, but lately he only tapers down from Scotch to wine, and drinks wine well into the week—a lot of wine, perhaps a whole bottle with his meal—until his stomach is much worse. He is hard to live with. Once when a former student, a woman named Ruth, visited them—a lover, she suspected—she overheard George talking to her in his study, where he had taken her to see a photograph of their house before he began repairing it. George had told Ruth that she, Lenore, stayed with him because she was simple. It hurt her badly, made her actually dizzy with surprise and shame, and since then, no matter who the guests are, she never feels quite at ease on the weekends. In the past she enjoyed some of the things she and George did with their guests, but since overhearing what he said to Ruth she feels that all their visitors have been secretly told the same thing about her. To her, though, George is usually kind. But she is sure that is the reason he has not married her, and when he recently remarked on their daughter's intelligence (she is five years old, a girl named Maria) she found that she could no longer respond with simple pride; now she feels spite as well, feels that Maria exists as proof of her own good genes. She has begun to expect perfection of the child. She knows this is wrong, and she has tried hard not to communicate her anxiety to Maria, who is already, as her kindergarten teacher says, "untypical."

At first Lenore loved George because he was untypical, although after she had moved in with him and lived with him for a while she began to see that he was not exceptional but a variation on a type. She is proud of observing that, and she harbors the discovery—her silent response to his low opinion of her. She does not know why he found her attractive—in the beginning he did—because she does not resemble the pretty, articulate young women he likes to invite, with their lovers or girl friends, to their house for the weekend. None of these young women have husbands; when they bring a man with them at all they bring a lover, and they seem happy not to be married. Lenore, too, is happy to be single—not out of conviction that marriage is wrong but because she knows that it would be wrong to be married to George if he thinks she is simple. She thought at first to confront him with what she had overheard, to demand an explanation. But he can weasel out of any corner. At best, she can mildly fluster him, and later he will only blame it on Scotch. Of course she might ask why he has all these women come to visit, why he devotes so little time to her or the children. To that he would say that it was the quality of the time they spent together that mattered, not the quantity. He has already said that, in fact, without being asked. He says things over and over so that she will accept them as truths. And eventually she does. She does not like to think long and hard, and when there is an answer—even his answer—it is usually easier to accept it and go on with things. She goes on with what she has always done: tending the house and the children and George, when he needs her. She likes to bake and she collects art postcards. She is proud of their house, which was bought cheaply and improved by George when he was still interested in that kind of work, and she is happy to have visitors come there, even if she does not admire them or even like them.

Except for teaching a night course in photography at a junior college once a week, George has not worked since he left the university two years ago, after he was denied tenure. She cannot really tell if he is unhappy working so little, because he keeps busy in other ways. He listens to classical music in the morning, slowly sipping herbal teas, and on fair afternoons he lies outdoors in the sun, no matter how cold the day. He takes photographs, and walks alone in the woods. He does errands for her if they need to be done. Sometimes at night he goes to the library or goes to visit friends; he tells her that these people often ask her to come too, but he says she would not like them. This is true—she would not like them. Recently he has done some late-night cooking. He has always kept a journal, and he is a great letter writer. An aunt left him most of her estate, ten thousand dollars, and said in her will that he was the only one who really cared, who took the time, again and again, to write. He had not seen his aunt for five years before she died, but he wrote regularly. Sometimes Lenore finds notes that he has left for her. Once, on the refrigerator, there was a long note suggesting clever Christmas presents for her family that he had thought of while she was out. Last week he scotch-taped a slip of paper to a casserole dish that contained leftover veal stew, saying "This was delicious." He does not compliment her verbally, but he likes to let her know that he is pleased.

A few nights ago—the same night they got a call from Julie and Sarah, saying they were coming for a visit—she told him that she wished he would talk more, that he would confide in her.

"Confide what?" he said.

"You always take that attitude," she said. "You pretend that you have no thoughts. Why does there have to be so much silence?"

"I'm not a professor anymore," he said. "I don't have to spend every minute *thinking*."

But he loves to talk to the young women. He will talk to them on the phone for as much as an hour; he walks with them through the woods for most of the day when they visit. The lovers the young women bring with them always seem to fall behind; they give up and return to the house to sit and talk to her, or to help with the preparation of the meal, or to play with the children. The young woman and George come back refreshed, ready for another round of conversation at dinner.

A few weeks ago one of the young men said to her, "Why do you let it go on?" They had been talking lightly before that—about the weather, the children—and then, in the kitchen, where he was sitting shelling peas, he put his head on the table and said, barely audibly, "Why do you let it go on?" He did not raise his head, and she stared at him, thinking that she must have imagined his speaking. She was surprised—surprised to have heard it, and surprised that he had said nothing after that, which made her doubt that he had spoken.

"Why do I let what go on?" she said.

There was a long silence. "Whatever this sick game is, I don't want to get involved in it," he said at last. "It was none of my business to ask. I understand that you don't want to talk about it."

"But it's really cold out there," she said. "What could happen when it's freezing out?"

He shook his head, the way George did, to indicate that she was beyond understanding. But she wasn't stupid, and she knew what might be going on. She had said the right thing, had been on the right track, but she had to say what she felt, which was that nothing very serious could be happening at that moment because they were walking in the woods. There wasn't even a barn on the property. She knew perfectly well that they were talking.

When George and the young woman had come back, he fixed hot apple juice, into which he trickled rum. Lenore was pleasant, because she was sure of what had not happened; the young man was not, because he did not think as she did. Still at the kitchen table, he ran his thumb across a pea pod as though it were a knife.

This weekend Sarah and Julie are visiting. They came on Friday evening. Sarah was one of George's students—the one who led the fight to have him rehired. She does not look like a troublemaker; she is pale and pretty, with freckles on her cheeks. She talks too much about the past, and this upsets him, disrupts the peace he has made with himself. She tells him that they fired him because he was "in touch" with everything, that they were afraid of him because he was so in touch. The more she tells him the more he remembers, and then it is necessary for Sarah to say the same things again and again; once she reminds him, he seems to need reassurance—needs to have her voice, to hear her bitterness against the members of the tenure committee. By evening they will both be drunk. Sarah will seem both agitating and consoling, Lenore and Julie and the children will be upstairs, in bed. Lenore suspects that she will not be the only one awake listening to them. She thinks that in spite of Julie's glazed look she is really very attentive. The night before, when they were all sitting around the fireplace talking, Sarah made a gesture and almost upset her wineglass, but Julie reached for it and stopped it from toppling over. George and Sarah were talking so energetically that they did not notice. Lenore's eyes met Julie's as Julie's hand shot out. Lenore feels that she is like Julie: Julie's face doesn't betray emotion, even when she is interested, even when she cares deeply. Being the same kind of person, Lenore can recognize this.

Before Sarah and Julie arrived Friday evening, Lenore asked George if Sarah was his lover.

"Don't be ridiculous," he said. "You think every student is my lover? Is Julie my lover?"

She said, "That wasn't what I said."

"Well, if you're going to be preposterous, go ahead and say that," he said. "If you think about it long enough, it would make a lot of sense, wouldn't it?"

He would not answer her question about Sarah. He kept throwing Julie's name into it. Some other woman might then think that he was protesting too strongly—that Julie really was his lover. She thought no such thing. She also stopped suspecting Sarah, because he wanted that, and it was her habit to oblige him.

He is twenty-one years older than Lenore. On his last birthday he was fifty-five. His daughter from his first marriage (his *only* marriage; she keeps reminding herself that they are not married, because it often seems that they might as well be) sent him an Irish country hat. The present made him irritable. He kept putting it on and pulling it down hard on his head. "She wants to make me a laughable old man," he said. "She wants me to put this on and go around like a fool." He wore the hat all morning, complaining about it, frightening the children. Eventually, to calm him, she said, "She intended *nothing*." She said it with finality, her tone so insistent that he listened to her. But having lost his reason for bitterness, he said, "Just because you don't think doesn't mean others don't think." Is he getting old? She does not want to think of him getting old. In spite of his ulcer, his body is hard. He is tall and handsome, with a thick mustache and a thin black goatee, and there is very little gray in his kinky black hair. He dresses in tight-fitting blue jeans and black turtleneck sweaters in the winter, and old white shirts with the sleeves rolled up in the summer. He pretends not to care about his looks, but he does. He shaves carefully, scraping slowly down each side of his goatee. He orders his soft leather shoes from a store in California. After taking one of his long walks—even if he does it twice a day—he invariably takes a shower. He always looks refreshed, and very rarely admits any insecurity. A few times, at night in bed, he has asked, "Am I still the man of your dreams?" And when she says yes he always laughs, turning it into a joke, as if he didn't care. She knows he does. He pretends to have no feeling for clothing, but actually he cares so strongly about his turtlenecks and shirts (a few are Italian silk) and shoes that he will have no others. She has noticed that the young women who visit are always vain. When Sarah arrived, she was wearing a beautiful silk scarf, pale as conch shells.

Sitting on the floor on Saturday morning, Lenore watches the fire she has just lit. The baby, tucked in George's chair, smiles in his sleep, and Lenore thinks what a good companion he would be if only he were an adult. She gets up and goes into the kitchen and tears open a package of yeast and dissolves it, with sugar and salt, in hot water, slushing her fingers through it and shivering because it is so cold in the kitchen. She will bake bread for dinner—there is always a big meal in the early evening when they have guests. But what will she do for the rest of the day? George told the girls the night before that on Saturday they would walk in the woods, but she does not really enjoy hiking, and George will be irritated because of the discussion the night before, and she does not want to aggravate him. "You are unwilling to challenge anyone," her brother wrote her in a letter that came a few days ago. He has written her for years—all the years she has been with George—asking when she is going to end the relationship. She rarely writes back because she knows that her answers sound too simple. She has a comfortable house. She cooks. She keeps busy and she loves her two children. "It seems unkind to say *but*," her brother writes, "but . . ." It is true; she likes simple things. Her brother, who is a lawyer in Cambridge, cannot understand that.

Lenore rubs her hand down the side of her face and says good morning to Julie and Sarah, who have come downstairs. Sarah does not want orange juice; she already looks refreshed and ready for the day. Lenore pours a glass for Julie. George calls from the hallway, "Ready to roll?" Lenore is surprised that he wants to leave so early. She goes into the living room. George is wearing a denim jacket, his hands in the pockets.

"Morning," he says to Lenore. "You're not up for a hike, are you?"

Lenore looks at him, but does not answer. As she stands there, Sarah walks around her and joins George in the hallway and he holds the door open for her. "Let's walk to the store and get Hershey bars to give us energy for a long hike," George says to Sarah. They are gone. Lenore finds Julie still in the kitchen, waiting for the water to boil. Julie says that she had a bad night and she is happy not to be going with George and Sarah. Lenore fixes tea for them. Maria sits next to her on the sofa, sipping orange juice. The baby likes company, but Maria is a very private child; she would rather that she and her mother were always alone. She has given up being possessive about her father. Now she gets out a cardboard box and takes out her mother's collection of postcards, which she arranges on the floor in careful groups. Whenever she looks up, Julie smiles nervously at her; Maria does not smile, and Lenore doesn't prod her. Lenore goes into the kitchen to punch down the bread, and Maria follows. Maria has recently gotten over chicken pox, and there is a small new scar in the center of her forehead. Instead of looking at Maria's blue eyes, Lenore lately has found herself focusing on the imperfection.

As Lenore is stretching the loaves onto the cornmeal-covered baking sheet, she hears the rain start. It hits hard on the garage roof.

After a few minutes Julie comes into the kitchen. "They're caught in this downpour," Julie says. "If Sarah had left the car keys, I could go get them."

"Take my car and pick them up," Lenore says, pointing with her elbow to the keys hanging on a nail near the door.

"But I don't know where the store is."

"You must have passed it driving to our house last night. Just go out of the driveway and turn right. It's along the main road."

Julie gets her purple sweater and takes the car keys. "I'll be right back," she says.

Lenore can sense that she is glad to escape from the house, that she is happy the rain began.

In the living room Lenore turns the pages of a magazine, and Maria mutters a refrain of "Blue, blue, dark blue, green blue," noticing the color every time it appears. Lenore sips her tea. She puts a Michael Hurley record on George's stereo. Michael Hurley is good rainy-day music. George has hundreds of records. His students used to love to paw through them. Cleverly, he has never made any attempt to keep up with what is currently popular. Everything is jazz or eclectic: Michael Hurley, Keith Jarrett, Ry Cooder.[1]

Julie comes back. "I couldn't find them," she says. She looks as if she expects to be punished.

Lenore is surprised. She is about to say something like "You certainly didn't look very hard, did you?" but she catches Julie's eye. She looks young and afraid, and perhaps even a little crazy.

---

1. Musical performers; respectively, folk, jazz, and roots rock.

"Well, we tried," Lenore says.

Julie stands in front of the fire, with her back to Lenore. Lenore knows she is thinking that she is dense—that she does not recognize the implications.

"They might have walked through the woods instead of along the road," Lenore says. "That's possible."

"But they would have gone out to the road to thumb when the rain began, wouldn't they?"

Perhaps she misunderstood what Julie was thinking. Perhaps it has never occurred to Julie until now what might be going on.

"Maybe they got lost," Julie says. "Maybe something happened to them."

"Nothing happened to them," Lenore says. Julie turns around and Lenore catches that small point of light in her eye again. "Maybe they took shelter under a tree," she says. "Maybe they're screwing. How should I know?"

It is not a word Lenore often uses. She usually tries not to think about that at all, but she can sense that Julie is very upset.

"Really?" Julie says. "Don't you care, Mrs. Anderson?"

Lenore is amused. There's a switch. All the students call her husband George and her Lenore; now one of them wants to think there's a real adult here to explain all this to her.

"What am I going to do?" Lenore says. She shrugs.

Julie does not answer.

"Would you like me to pour you tea?" Lenore asks.

"Yes," Julie says. "Please."

George and Sarah return in the middle of the afternoon. George says that they decided to go on a spree to the big city—it is really a small town he is talking about, but calling it the big city gives him an opportunity to speak ironically. They sat in a restaurant bar, waiting for the rain to stop, George says, and then they thumbed a ride home. "But I'm completely sober," George says, turning for the first time to Sarah. "What about you?" He is all smiles. Sarah lets him down. She looks embarrassed. Her eyes meet Lenore's quickly, and jump to Julie. The two girls stare at each other, and Lenore, left with only George to look at, looks at the fire and then gets up to pile on another log.

Gradually it becomes clear that they are trapped together by the rain. Maria undresses her paper doll and deliberately rips a feather off its hat. Then she takes the pieces to Lenore, almost in tears. The baby cries, and Lenore takes him off the sofa, where he has been sleeping under his yellow blanket, and props him in the space between her legs as she leans back on her elbows to watch the fire. It's her fire, and she has the excuse of presiding over it.

"How's my boy?" George says. The baby looks, and looks away.

It gets dark early, because of the rain. At four-thirty George uncorks a bottle of Beaujolais and brings it into the living room, with four glasses pressed against his chest with his free arm. Julie rises nervously to extract the glasses, thanking him too profusely for the wine. She gives a glass to Sarah without looking at her.

They sit in a semicircle in front of the fire and drink the wine. Julie leafs through magazines—*New Times, National Geographic*—and Sarah holds a small white dish painted with gray-green leaves that she has taken from the coffee table; the dish contains a few shells and some acorn caps, a polished stone or two, and Sarah lets these objects run through her fingers. There are several such dishes in the house, assembled by George. He and Lenore gathered the shells long ago, the first time they went away together, at a beach in North Carolina. But the acorn caps, the shiny turquoise and amethyst stones—those are there, she knows, because George likes the effect they have on visitors; it is an expected unconventionality, really. He has also acquired a few small framed pictures, which he points out to guests who are more important than worshipful students—tiny oil paintings of fruit, prints with small details from the unicorn tapestries. He pretends to like small, elegant things. Actually, when they visit museums in New York he goes first to El Grecos and big Mark Rothko canvases. She could never get him to admit that what he said or did was sometimes false. Once, long ago, when he asked if he was still the man of her dreams, she said, "We don't get along well anymore." "Don't talk about it," he said—no denial, no protest. At best, she could say things and get away with them; she could never get him to continue such a conversation.

At the dinner table, lit with white candles burning in empty wine bottles, they eat off his grandmother's small flowery plates. Lenore looks out a window and sees, very faintly in the dark, their huge oak tree. The rain has stopped. A few stars have come out, and there are glints on the wet branches. The oak tree grows very close to the window. George loved it when her brother once suggested that some of the bushes and trees should be pruned away from the house so it would not always be so dark inside; it gave him a chance to rave about the beauty of nature, to say that he would never tamper with it. "It's like a tomb in here all day," her brother had said. Since moving here, George has learned the names of almost all the things growing on the land: he can point out abelia bushes, spirea, laurels. He subscribes to *National Geographic* (although she rarely sees him looking at it). He is at last in touch, he says, being in the country puts him in touch. He is saying it now to Sarah, who has put down her ivory-handled fork to listen to him. He gets up to change the record. Side two of the Telemann[2] record begins softly.

Sarah is still very much on guard with Lenore; she makes polite conversation with her quickly when George is out of the room. "You people are so wonderful," she says. "I wish my parents could be like you."

"George would be pleased to hear that," Lenore says, lifting a small piece of pasta to her lips.

When George is seated again, Sarah, anxious to please, tells him, "If only my father could be like you."

"Your father," George says. "I won't have that analogy." He says it pleasantly, but barely disguises his dismay at the comparison.

"I mean, he cares about nothing but business," the girl stumbles on.

The music, in contrast, grows lovelier.

Lenore goes into the kitchen to get the salad and hears George say, "I simply won't let you girls leave. Nobody leaves on a Saturday."

---

2. Georg Philipp Telemann (1681–1767), German composer.

There are polite protests, there are compliments to Lenore on the meal—there is too much talk. Lenore has trouble caring about what's going on. The food is warm and delicious. She pours more wine and lets them talk.

"Godard, yes, I know . . . panning that row of honking cars *so* slowly, that long line of cars stretching on and on."[3]

She has picked up the end of George's conversation. His arm slowly waves out over the table, indicating the line of motionless cars in the movie.

"That's a lovely plant," Julie says to Lenore.

"It's Peruvian ivy," Lenore says. She smiles. She is supposed to smile. She will not offer to hack shoots off her plant for these girls.

Sarah asks for a Dylan record when the Telemann finishes playing. White wax drips onto the wood table. George waits for it to solidify slightly, then scrapes up the little circles and with thumb and index finger flicks them gently toward Sarah. He explains (although she asked for no particular Dylan record) that he has only Dylan before he went electric. And "Planet Waves"—"because it's so romantic. That's silly of me, but true."[4] Sarah smiles at him. Julie smiles at Lenore. Julie is being polite, taking her cues from Sarah, really not understanding what's going on. Lenore does not smile back. She has done enough to put them at ease. She is tired now, brought down by the music, a full stomach, and again the sounds of rain outside. For dessert there is homemade vanilla ice cream, made by George, with small black vanilla-bean flecks in it. He is still drinking wine, though; another bottle has been opened. He sips wine and then taps his spoon on his ice cream, looking at Sarah. Sarah smiles, letting them all see the smile, then sucks the ice cream off her spoon. Julie is missing more and more of what's going on. Lenore watches as Julie strokes her hand absently on her napkin. She is wearing a thin silver choker and—Lenore notices for the first time—a thin silver ring on the third finger of her hand.

"It's just terrible about Anna," George says, finishing his wine, his ice cream melting, looking at no one in particular, although Sarah was the one who brought up Anna the night before, when they had been in the house only a short time—Anna dead, hit by a car, hardly an accident at all. Anna was also a student of his. The driver of the car was drunk, but for some reason charges were not pressed. (Sarah and George have talked about this before, but Lenore blocks it out. What can she do about it? She met Anna once: a beautiful girl, with tiny, childlike hands, her hair thin and curly—wary, as beautiful people are wary.) Now the driver has been flipping out, Julie says, and calling Anna's parents, wanting to talk to them to find out why it has happened.

The baby begins to cry. Lenore goes upstairs, pulls up more covers, talks to him for a minute. He settles for this. She goes downstairs. The wine must have affected her more than she realizes; otherwise, why is she counting the number of steps?

3. A famous scene from Jean-Luc Godard's film *Weekend* (1969).
4. The American singer, musician, and com-

poser Bob Dylan (b. 1941) combined electric rock with acoustic folk in 1965. He released the *Planet Waves* album in 1974.

In the candlelit dining room, Julie sits alone at the table. The girl has been left alone again; George and Sarah took the umbrellas, decided to go for a walk in the rain.

It is eight o'clock. Since helping Lenore load the dishes into the dishwasher, when she said what a beautiful house Lenore had, Julie has said very little. Lenore is tired, and does not want to make conversation. They sit in the living room and drink wine.

"Sarah is my best friend," Julie says. She seems apologetic about it. "I was so out of it when I came back to college. I was in Italy, with my husband, and suddenly I was back in the States. I couldn't make friends. But Sarah wasn't like the other people. She cared enough to be nice to me."

"How long have you been friends?"

"For two years. She's really the best friend I've ever had. We understand things—we don't always have to talk about them."

"Like her relationship with George," Lenore says.

Too direct. Too unexpected. Julie has no answer.

"You act as if you're to blame," Lenore says.

"I feel strange because you're such a nice lady."

A nice lady! What an odd way to speak. Has she been reading Henry James? Lenore has never known what to think of herself, but she certainly thinks of herself as being more complicated than a "lady."

"Why do you look that way?" Julie asks. "You *are* nice. I think you've been very nice to us. You've given up your whole weekend."

"I always give up my weekends. Weekends are the only time we socialize, really. In a way, it's good to have something to do."

"But to have it turn out like this . . ." Julie says. "I think I feel so strange because when my own marriage broke up I didn't even suspect. I mean, I couldn't act the way you do, anyway, but I—"

"For all I know, nothing's going on," Lenore says. "For all I know, your friend is flattering herself, and George is trying to make me jealous." She puts two more logs on the fire. When these are gone, she will either have to walk to the woodshed or give up and go to bed. "Is there something . . . *major* going on?" she asks.

Julie is sitting on the rug, by the fire, twirling her hair with her finger. "I didn't know it when I came out here," she says. "Sarah's put me in a very awkward position."

"But do you know how far it has gone?" Lenore asks, genuinely curious now.

"No," Julie says.

No way to know if she's telling the truth. Would Julie speak the truth to a lady? Probably not.

"Anyway," Lenore says with a shrug, "I don't want to think about it all the time."

"I'd never have the courage to live with a man and not marry," Julie says. "I mean, I wish I had, that we hadn't gotten married, but I just don't have that kind of . . . I'm not secure enough."

"You have to live somewhere," Lenore says.

Julie is looking at her as if she does not believe that she is sincere. Am I? Lenore wonders. She has lived with George for six years, and sometimes she thinks she has caught his way of playing games, along with his colds, his bad moods.

"I'll show you something," Lenore says. She gets up, and Julie follows. Lenore puts on the light in George's study, and they walk through it to a bathroom he has converted to a darkroom. Under a table, in a box behind another box, there is a stack of pictures. Lenore takes them out and hands them to Julie. They are pictures that Lenore found in his darkroom last summer; they were left out by mistake, no doubt, and she found them when she went in with some contact prints he had left in their bedroom. They are high-contrast photographs of George's face. In all of them he looks very serious and very sad; in some of them his eyes seem to be narrowed in pain. In one, his mouth is open. It is an excellent photograph of a man in agony, a man about to scream.

"What are they?" Julie whispers.

"Pictures he took of himself," Lenore says. She shrugs. "So I stay," she says.

Julie nods. Lenore nods, taking the pictures back. Lenore has not thought until this minute that this may be why she stays. In fact, it is not the only reason. It is just a very demonstrable, impressive reason. When she first saw the pictures, her own face had become as distorted as George's. She had simply not known what to do. She had been frightened and ashamed. Finally she put them in an empty box, and put the box behind another box. She did not even want him to see the horrible pictures again. She does not know if he has ever found them, pushed back against the wall in that other box. As George says, there can be too much communication between people.

Later, Sarah and George come back to the house. It is still raining. It turns out that they took a bottle of brandy with them, and they are both drenched and drunk. He holds Sarah's finger with one of his. Sarah, seeing Lenore, lets his finger go. But then he turns—they have not even said hello yet—and grabs her up, spins her around, stumbling into the living room, and says, "I am in love."

Julie and Lenore watch them in silence.

"See no evil," George says, gesturing with the empty brandy bottle to Julie. "Hear no evil," George says, pointing to Lenore. He hugs Sarah closer. "I speak no evil. I speak the truth. I am in love!"

Sarah squirms away from him, runs from the room and up the stairs in the dark.

George looks blankly after her, then sinks to the floor and smiles. He is going to pass it off as a joke. Julie looks at him in horror, and from upstairs Sarah can be heard sobbing. Her crying awakens the baby.

"Excuse me," Lenore says. She climbs the stairs and goes into her son's room, and picks him up. She talks gently to him, soothing him with lies. He is too sleepy to be alarmed for long. In a few minutes he is asleep again, and she puts him back in his crib. In the next room Sarah is crying more quietly now. Her crying is so awful that Lenore almost joins in, but instead she pats her son. She stands in the dark by the crib and then at last goes out and down the hallway to her bedroom. She takes off her clothes and gets into the cold bed. She concentrates on breathing normally. With the door closed and Sarah's door closed, she can hardly hear her. Someone taps lightly on her door.

"Mrs. Anderson," Julie whispers. "Is this your room?"

"Yes," Lenore says. She does not ask her in.

"We're going to leave. I'm going to get Sarah and leave. I didn't want to just walk out without saying anything."

Lenore just cannot think how to respond. It was really very kind of Julie to say something. She is very close to tears, so she says nothing.

"Okay," Julie says, to reassure herself. "Good night. We're going."

There is no more crying. Footsteps. Miraculously, the baby does not wake up again, and Maria has slept through all of it. She has always slept well. Lenore herself sleeps worse and worse, and she knows that George walks much of the night, most nights. She hasn't said anything about it. If he thinks she's simple, what good would her simple wisdom do him?

The oak tree scrapes against the window in the wind and rain. Here on the second floor, under the roof, the tinny tapping is very loud. If Sarah and Julie say anything to George before they leave, she doesn't hear them. She hears the car start, then die out. It starts again—she is praying for the car to go—and after conking out once more it rolls slowly away, crunching gravel. The bed is no warmer; she shivers. She tries hard to fall asleep. The effort keeps her awake. She squints her eyes in concentration instead of closing them. The only sound in the house is the electric clock, humming by her bed. It is not even midnight.

She gets up, and without turning on the light, walks downstairs. George is still in the living room. The fire is nothing but ashes and glowing bits of wood. It is as cold there as it was in the bed.

"That damn bitch," George says. "I should have known she was a stupid little girl."

"You went too far," Lenore says. "I'm the only one you can go too far with."

"Damn it," he says and pokes the fire. A few sparks shoot up. "Damn it," he repeats under his breath.

His sweater is still wet. His shoes are muddy and ruined. Sitting on the floor by the fire, his hair matted down on his head, he looks ugly, older, unfamiliar.

She thinks of another time, when it was warm. They were walking on the beach together, shortly after they met, gathering shells. Little waves were rolling in. The sun went behind the clouds and there was a momentary illusion that the clouds were still and the sun was racing ahead of them. "Catch me," he said, breaking away from her. They had been talking quietly, gathering shells. She was so surprised at him for breaking away that she ran with all her energy and did catch him, putting her hand out and taking hold of the band of his swimming trunks as he veered into the water. If she hadn't stopped him, would he really have run far out into the water, until she couldn't follow anymore? He turned on her, just as abruptly as he had run away, and grabbed her and hugged her hard, lifted her high. She had clung to him, held him close. He had tried the same thing when he came back from the walk with Sarah, and it hadn't worked.

"I wouldn't care if their car went off the road," he says bitterly.

"Don't say that," she says.

They sit in silence, listening to the rain. She slides over closer to him, puts her hand on his shoulder and leans her head there, as if he could protect her from the awful things he has wished into being.

1978

DAVID MAMET
b. 1947

One of the American poet Wallace Stevens's more arresting titles for a poem is "Men Made Out of Words"; the most original American playwright to emerge in the 1970s, David Mamet, is so in large part because his plays and screenplays are insistently and wholly made of the words that men, and sometimes women, speak to—more often mutter or hurl at—each other. Consider the following exchange, from Mamet's 1982 play *Glengarry Glen Ross*, between two real-estate salesmen who are entertaining the notion of breaking into their firm's offices and stealing the list of leads—names of desirable sales prospects—to sell their dubious properties and further their careers. George Aaronow asks Dave Moss whether he has "talked to" a prospective buyer of the leads:

MOSS   No. What do you mean? Have I talked to him about *this?* [*Pause.*]
AARONOW   Yes. I mean are you actually *talking* about this, or are we just . . .
MOSS   No, we're just . . .
AARONOW   We're just "*talking*" about it.
MOSS   We're just *speaking* about it. [*Pause.*] As an *idea.*
AARONOW   As an idea.
MOSS   Yes.
AARONOW   We're not actually *talking* about it.
MOSS   No.
AARONOW   Talking about it as a . . .
MOSS   *No.*
AARONOW   As a *robbery.*
MOSS   As a "robbery"? No.

This example typifies the way Mamet's characters do and don't communicate. In a program note to *Glengarry Glen Ross*, the drama critic John Lahr referred to what he called the "hilarious brutal sludge of [Mamet's] characters' speech," and in this outrageous attempt by Moss and Aaronow to distinguish between *talking* and *speaking* we see the playwright expertly deploying such sludge. Another critic has directed attention to Mamet's notion of the unreliability of language as demonstrated through his characters' "intoxicating mixture of evasions, pleadings, browbeatings, stonewalling, and spiel." It is the reader's (viewer's, actor's) challenge to navigate this mixture, and the voyage is usually not easy.

Mamet grew up on the Jewish south side of Chicago; attended a private school; worked in several theatrical groups (he was a busboy at Chicago's Second City, an improvisational cabaret where, among others, the comedians Mike Nichols and Elaine May appeared); and attended Goddard College, an experimental college in

Vermont. At Goddard he wrote his first play and also took a break from his studies to attend New York City's Neighborhood Playhouse School of the Theatre. There, he was strongly influenced by the Stanislavsky method of acting and its exercises in concentration. The Method, as it is called, was important to him as a writer, he said later, for the way it showed him how "the language we use, its rhythm, actually determines the way we behave, more than the other way around"—an indication of where viewers and readers of his plays and screenplays should direct their primary attention. After graduating from Goddard in 1969, Mamet taught acting and writing at Marlboro College and at Goddard, then in 1972 moved back to Chicago and worked in a variety of nontheatrical environments such as the real-estate agency that provided the material for *Glengarry Glen Ross*. By this time his short plays *Lakeboat* and *The Duck Variations* had been performed at Marlboro and Goddard. Then in 1974 his *Sexual Perversity in Chicago*, a fast-paced, irreverent excursion into the sexual fantasies and behavior of four people, won an award for the best new Chicago play. Two years later it played in New York, along with *The Duck Variations*, and won an Obie award. When in 1977 his *American Buffalo* won the New York Drama Critics award, Mamet was an established figure.

American Buffalo is a two-act play with just three characters: Don, who runs a small-time resale junk store; Bobby, a one-time drug addict whom Don tries to take care of; and Teach, a friend of Don's, who together with the others attempts (incompetently) to steal a coin collection, one item of which is a presumably valuable buffalo nickel. Everything goes awry, and the play's curve is a rising verbal aggression, especially in the speeches of Teach, that culminates in real violence. But, to employ a phrase of Robert Frost's, Mamet's "organized violence upon language" holds us, often painfully, through the two acts. "Calm down," Don says at one point, to which Teach replies, "I am calm, I'm just upset"—a response that perfectly describes the uneasy combination of attempted verbal control and patent verbal and emotional disorder.

Critics have said that *American Buffalo*, like Mamet's work generally, critiques American society and that Mamet is deeply pessimistic about the dreadful state of economic, social, and human relationships in the late twentieth and early twenty-first centuries. This is to some extent true; Mamet has said that "what I write about is what I think is missing from our society. And that's communication on a basic level." Yet that missing communication is exactly what motivates our interest in the plays. We do not, that is, use the plays' language as a springboard into concern about America and what it lacks; rather we find exhilarating Mamet's skillful manipulation of the "sludge" of character speech, well seasoned with self-loathing and mutual mistrust, so as to produce vivid entertainment. To say, as the writer of a book on Mamet has said, that "in spite of their callousness and selfishness" his characters "engage and retain our sympathy" is to put it backward. For in fact the brilliant rendering of callousness and selfishness, of failed communication, manipulation, and the basic venality of people is precisely what makes his work so compelling. In its refusal to present characters with sympathetic inner lives, Mamet's art is, in one way, as callous as those characters. But the inventive and surprising dramatic actions (glimpsed latterly in *Oleanna*, his 1992 play about sexual harassment), woven out of an American idiom resourcefully employed, are sensitive indeed.

The following text is that published in 1984.

Glengarry Glen Ross

The Characters

WILLIAMSON, BAYLEN, ROMA, LINGK
Men in their early forties.

LEVENE, MOSS, AARONOW
Men in their fifties.

THE SCENE

The three scenes of Act One take place in a Chinese restaurant.
Act Two takes place in a real estate office.

ALWAYS BE CLOSING.
Practical Sales Maxim

Act 1

SCENE I

A booth at a Chinese restaurant, WILLIAMSON *and* LEVENE *are seated at the booth.*

LEVENE   John . . . John . . . John. Okay. John. John. Look: [*Pause.*] The Glengarry Highland's leads, you're sending Roma out. Fine. He's a good man. We know what he is. He's fine. All I'm saying, you look at the *board*, he's throwing . . . wait, wait, wait, he's throwing them *away*, he's throwing the leads away. All that I'm saying, that you're wasting leads. I don't want to tell you your *job*. All that I'm saying, things get *set*, I know they do, you get a certain *mindset*. . . . A guy gets a reputation. We know how this . . . all I'm saying, put a *closer* on the job. There's more than one man for the . . . Put a . . . wait a second, put a *proven man out* . . . and you watch, now *wait* a second—and you watch your *dollar* volumes. . . . You start closing them for *fifty* 'stead of *twenty-five* . . . you put a *closer* on the . . .

WILLIAMSON   Shelly, you blew the last . . .

LEVENE   No. John. No. Let's wait, let's back up here, I did . . . will you please? Wait a second. Please. I didn't "blow" them. No. I didn't "blow" them. No. One kicked *out*, one I closed . . .

WILLIAMSON   . . . you didn't close . . .

LEVENE   I, if you'd *listen* to me. Please. I *closed* the cocksucker. His *ex*, John, his *ex*, I didn't know he was married . . . he, the *judge* invalidated the . . .

WILLIAMSON   Shelly . . .

LEVENE   . . . and what is that, John? What? Bad *luck*. That's all it is. I pray in your *life* you will never find it runs in streaks. That's what it does, that's all it's doing. Streaks. I pray it misses you. That's all I want to say.

WILLIAMSON   [*Pause.*]   What about the other two?

LEVENE   What two?

WILLIAMSON   Four. You had four leads. One kicked out, one the *judge*, you say . . .

LEVENE   . . . you want to see the court records? John? Eh? You want to go down . . .

WILLIAMSON   . . . no . . .

LEVENE   . . . do you want to go down*town* . . . ?

WILLIAMSON   . . . no . . .

LEVENE   . . . then . . .   .

WILLIAMSON   . . . I only . . .

LEVENE   . . . then what is this "you *say*" shit, what is that? [*Pause.*] What is that . . . ?

WILLIAMSON   All that I'm saying . . .

LEVENE   What is this "you *say*"? A deal kicks out . . . I got to *eat*. *Shit*, Williamson, *shit*. You . . . Moss . . . Roma . . . look at the *sheets* . . . look at the *sheets*. Nineteen *eighty*, eighty-one . . . eighty-*two* . . . six months of eighty-two . . . who's there? Who's up there?

WILLIAMSON   Roma.

LEVENE   Under him?

WILLIAMSON   Moss.

LEVENE   Bull*shit*. John. Bull*shit*. April, September 1981. It's *me*. It isn't *fucking* Moss. Due respect, he's an *order* taker, John. He *talks*, he talks a good game, look at the *board, and it's me*, John, it's me . . .

WILLIAMSON   Not lately it isn't.

LEVENE   Lately kiss my ass lately. That isn't how you build an org . . . talk, talk to Murray. Talk to Mitch. When we were on Peterson, who paid for his fucking *car*? You talk to him. The *Seville* . . . ? He came in, "You bought that for me Shelly." Out of *what*? *Cold calling. Nothing.* Sixty-*five*, when we were there, with Glen *Ross* Farms? You call 'em downtown. What was that? *Luck*? That was "luck"? *Bull*shit, John. You're burning my ass, I can't get a fucking *lead* . . . you think that was luck. My stats for those years? Bull*shit* . . . over that period of time . . . ? Bull*shit*. It wasn't luck. It was *skill*. You want to throw that away, John . . . ? You want to throw that away?

WILLIAMSON   It isn't me . . .

LEVENE   . . . it isn't you . . . ? Who *is* it? Who is this I'm talking to? I need the *leads* . . .

WILLIAMSON   . . . after the thirtieth . . .

LEVENE   Bull*shit* the thirtieth, I don't get on the board the thirtieth, they're going to can my ass. I need the leads. I need them now. Or I'm gone, and you're going to miss me, John, I swear to you.

WILLIAMSON   Murray . . .

LEVENE   . . . you *talk* to Murray . . .

WILLIAMSON   I have. And my job is to marshal those leads . . .

LEVENE   Marshal the leads . . . marshal the leads? What the fuck, what bus did *you* get off of, we're here to fucking *sell*. *Fuck* marshaling the leads. What the fuck talk is that? What the fuck talk is that? Where did you learn that? In school? [*Pause.*] That's "talk," my friend, that's "talk." Our job is to *sell*. I'm the *man* to sell. I'm getting garbage. [*Pause.*] You're giving it to me, and what I'm saying is it's *fucked*.

WILLIAMSON   You're saying that I'm fucked.

LEVENE   Yes. [*Pause.*] I am. I'm sorry to antagonize you.

WILLIAMSON   Let me . . .

LEVENE   . . . and I'm going to get bounced and you're . . .

WILLIAMSON . . . let me . . . are you listening to me . . . ?

LEVENE Yes.

WILLIAMSON Let me tell you something, Shelly. I do what I'm hired to do. I'm . . . wait a second. I'm *hired* to watch the leads. I'm given . . . hold on, I'm given a *policy*. *My* job is to *do that*. What I'm *told*. That's it. You, wait a second, *anybody* falls below a certain mark I'm not *permitted* to give them the premium leads.

LEVENE Then how do they come up above that mark? With *dreck*[1] . . . ? That's *nonsense*. Explain this to me. 'Cause it's a waste, and it's a stupid waste. I want to tell you something . . .

WILLIAMSON You know what those leads cost?

LEVENE The premium leads. Yes. I know what they cost. John. Because I, *I* generated the dollar revenue sufficient to *buy* them. Nineteen senny-*nine*, you know what I made? Senny-*nine*? Ninety-six thousand dollars. John? For *Murray* . . . For *Mitch* . . . look at the sheets . . .

WILLIAMSON Murray said . . .

LEVENE *Fuck* him. *Fuck* Murray. John? You know? You tell him I said so. What does *he* fucking know? He's going to have a "sales" contest . . . you know what our sales contest used to be? *Money*. A *fortune*. Money lying on the ground. Murray? When was the last time *he* went out on a sit? Sales contest? It's *laughable*. It's cold out there now, John. It's tight. Money is *tight*. This ain't sixty-five. It ain't. It just ain't. See? See? Now, I'm a good *man*—but I need a . . .

WILLIAMSON Murray said . . .

LEVENE John. John . . .

WILLIAMSON Will you please wait a second. Shelly. Please. Murray told me: the hot leads . . .

LEVENE . . . ah, *fuck* this . . .

WILLIAMSON The . . . Shelly? [*Pause.*] The hot leads are assigned according to the board. During the contest. *Period.* Anyone who beats fifty per . . .

LEVENE That's fucked. That's fucked. You don't look at the fucking *percentage*. You look at the *gross*.

WILLIAMSON Either way. You're out.

LEVENE I'm out.

WILLIAMSON Yes.

LEVENE I'll tell you why I'm out. I'm *out*, you're giving me toilet paper. John. I've *seen* those leads. I saw them when I was at Homestead, we pitched those cocksuckers Rio Rancho nineteen sixty-*nine* they wouldn't buy. They couldn't buy a fucking *toaster*. They're *broke*, John. They're cold. They're deadbeats, you can't judge on that. Even so. Even so. Alright. Fine. Fine. Even so. I go in, FOUR FUCKING LEADS they got their money in a *sock*. They're fucking Polacks, John. Four leads. I close two. *Two*. Fifty per . . .

WILLIAMSON . . . they kicked out.

LEVENE They *all* kick out. You run in *streaks*, pal. *Streaks*. I'm . . . I'm . . . don't look at the *board*, look at *me*. Shelly Levene. *Anyone*. Ask them on

---

1. Shit (Yiddish).

Western. Ask Getz at Homestead. Go ask Jerry Graff. You know who I am . . . I NEED A SHOT. I got to get on the fucking board. Ask them. *Ask* them. Ask them who ever picked up a check I was flush. Moss, Jerry Graff, Mitch himself . . . Those guys *lived* on the business I brought in. They *lived* on it . . . and so did Murray, John. You were here you'd of benefited from it too. And now I'm saying this. Do I want charity? Do I want *pity*? I want *sits*. I want leads don't come right out of a *phone book*. Give me a lead hotter than that, I'll go in and close it. Give me a chance. That's all I want. I'm going to *get* up on that fucking board and all I want is a chance. It's a *streak* and I'm going to turn it around. [*Pause.*] I need your help. [*Pause.*]

WILLIAMSON   I can't do it, Shelly. [*Pause.*]

LEVENE   Why?

WILLIAMSON   The leads are assigned randomly . . .

LEVENE   *Bullshit, bullshit*, you assign them. . . . What are you *telling* me?

WILLIAMSON   . . . apart from the top men on the contest board.

LEVENE   Then put me on the board.

WILLIAMSON   You start closing again, you'll *be* on the board.

LEVENE   I can't close these leads, John. No one can. It's a joke. John, look, just give me a hot lead. Just give me two of the premium leads. As a "test," alright? As a "test" and I promise you . . .

WILLIAMSON   I can't do it, Shel. [*Pause.*]

LEVENE   I'll give you ten percent. [*Pause.*]

WILLIAMSON   Of what?

LEVENE   Of my end what I close.

WILLIAMSON   And what if you don't close.

LEVENE   I *will* close.

WILLIAMSON   What if you *don't* close . . . ?

LEVENE   I *will* close.

WILLIAMSON   What if you *don't*? Then I'm *fucked*. You see . . . ? Then it's *my* job. That's what I'm *telling* you.

LEVENE   I *will* close. John, John, ten percent. I can get hot. You *know* that . . .

WILLIAMSON   Not lately you can't . . .

LEVENE   Fuck that. That's defeatist. Fuck that. Fuck it. . . . Get on my side. *Go* with me. Let's *do* something. You want to run this office, *run* it.

WILLIAMSON   Twenty percent. [*Pause.*]

LEVENE   Alright.

WILLIAMSON   And fifty bucks a lead.

LEVENE   John. [*Pause.*] Listen. I want to talk to you. Permit me to do this a second. I'm older than you. A man acquires a reputation. On the street. What he does when he's *up*, what he does otherwise. . . . I said "ten," you said "no." You said "twenty." I said "fine," I'm not going to fuck with you, how can I beat that, you tell me? . . . Okay. Okay. We'll . . . Okay. Fine. We'll . . . Alright, twenty percent, and fifty bucks a lead. That's fine. For now. That's fine. A month or two we'll talk. A month from now. Next month. After the thirtieth. [*Pause.*] We'll talk.

WILLIAMSON   What are we going to say?

LEVENE   No. You're right. That's for later. We'll talk in a month. What have you got? I want two sits. Tonight.

WILLIAMSON   I'm not sure I have two.

LEVENE   I saw the board. You've got *four* . . .

WILLIAMSON [*Snaps*]   I've got *Roma*. Then I've got Moss . . .

LEVENE   *Bullshit.* They ain't been in the office yet. Give 'em some stiff. We have a deal or not? Eh? Two sits. The Des Plaines.[2] Both of 'em, six and ten, you can do it . . . six and ten . . . eight and eleven, I don't give a shit, you set 'em up? Alright? The two sits in Des Plaines.

WILLIAMSON   Alright.

LEVENE   Good. Now we're talking. [*Pause.*]

WILLIAMSON   A hundred bucks. [*Pause.*]

LEVENE   Now? [*Pause.*] *Now?*

WILLIAMSON   Now. [*Pause.*] *Yes* . . . *When?*

LEVENE   Ah, *shit*, John. [*Pause.*]

WILLIAMSON   I wish I could.

LEVENE   You fucking asshole. [*Pause.*] I haven't got it. [*Pause.*] I haven't got it, John. [*Pause.*] I'll pay you tomorrow. [*Pause.*] I'm coming in here with the sales, I'll pay you *tomorrow.* [*Pause.*] I haven't *got* it, when I pay, the *gas* . . . I get back the hotel, I'll bring it in tomorrow.

WILLIAMSON   Can't do it.

LEVENE   I'll give you thirty on them now, I'll bring the rest tomorrow. I've got it at the hotel. [*Pause.*] John? [*Pause.*] We do that, for chrissake?

WILLIAMSON   No.

LEVENE   I'm asking you. As a favor to me? [*Pause.*] John. [*Long pause.*] John: my *daughter* . . .

WILLIAMSON   I can't do it, Shelly.

LEVENE   Well, I want to tell you something, fella, wasn't long I could pick up the phone, call *Murray* and I'd have your job. You know that? Not too *long* ago. For what? For *nothing.* "Mur, this new kid burns my ass." "Shelly, he's out." You're gone before I'm back from lunch. I bought him a trip to Bermuda once . . .

WILLIAMSON   I have to go . . . [*Gets up.*]

LEVENE   Wait. Alright. Fine. [*Starts going in pocket for money.*] The one. Give me the lead. Give me the one lead. The best one you have.

WILLIAMSON   I can't split them. [*Pause.*]

LEVENE   Why?

WILLIAMSON   Because I say so.

LEVENE [*Pause.*]   Is that it? Is that *it?* You want to do business that way . . . ?

    [WILLIAMSON *gets up, leaves money on the table.*]

LEVENE   You want to do business that way . . . ? Alright. Alright. Alright. Alright. What is there on the other list . . . ?

WILLIAMSON   You want something off the B list?

LEVENE   *Yeah.* Yeah.

WILLIAMSON   Is that what you're saying?

LEVENE   That's what I'm saying. Yeah. [*Pause.*] I'd like something off the other list. Which, very least, that I'm entitled to. If I'm still *working* here, which for the moment I guess that I am. [*Pause.*] What? I'm sorry I spoke harshly to you.

---

2. A community to the immediate northwest of Chicago.

WILLIAMSON That's alright.
LEVENE The deal still stands, our other thing.
    [WILLIAMSON *shrugs. Starts out of the booth.*]
LEVENE Good. Mmm. I, you know, I left my wallet back at the hotel.

SCENE 2

A booth at the restaurant, MOSS *and* AARONOW *seated. After the meal.*

MOSS Polacks and deadbeats.
AARONOW . . . Polacks . . .
MOSS Deadbeats *all.*
AARONOW . . . they hold on to their money . . .
MOSS All of 'em. They, *hey*: it happens to us all.
AARONOW Where am I going to work?
MOSS You have to cheer up, George, you aren't out yet.
AARONOW I'm not?
MOSS You missed a fucking sale. Big deal. A deadbeat Polack. Big deal.
    How you going to sell 'em in the *first* place . . . ? Your mistake, you
    shoun'a took the lead.
AARONOW I had to.
MOSS You had to, yeah. Why?
AARONOW To get on the . . .
MOSS To get on the board. Yeah. How you goan'a get on the board sell'n
    a Polack? And I'll tell you, I'll tell you what *else.* You listening? I'll tell
    you what else: don't ever try to sell an Indian.
AARONOW I'd never try to sell an Indian.
MOSS You get those names come up, you ever get 'em, "Patel"?
AARONOW Mmm . . .
MOSS You ever get 'em?
AARONOW Well, I think I had one once.
MOSS You did?
AARONOW I . . . I don't know.
MOSS You had one you'd know it. *Patel.* They keep coming up. I don't
    know. They like to talk to salesmen. [*Pause.*] They're *lonely,* something.
    [*Pause.*] They like to feel *superior,* I don't know. Never bought a fucking
    thing. You're sitting down "The Rio Rancho *this,* the blah blah blah,"
    "The Mountain View—" "Oh yes. My brother told me that. . . ." They
    got a grapevine. Fuckin' Indians, George. Not my cup of tea. Speaking
    of which I want to tell you something: [*Pause*] I never got a cup of tea
    with them. You see them in the restaurants. A supercilious race. What
    is this *look* on their face all the time? I don't know. [*Pause.*] I don't know.
    Their broads all look like they just got fucked with a dead *cat, I* don't
    know. [*Pause.*] I don't know. I don't like it. Christ . . .
AARONOW What?
MOSS The whole fuckin' thing . . . The pressure's just too great. You're
    ab . . . you're absolu . . . they're too important. All of them. You go in
    the door. I . . . "I got to *close* this fucker, or I don't eat lunch," "or I don't
    win the *Cadillac.* . . ." We fuckin' work too hard. You work too hard. We
    all, I remember when we were at Platt . . . huh? Glen Ross Farms . . .
    didn't we sell a bunch of that . . . ?

AARONOW   They came in and they, you know . . .

MOSS   Well, they fucked it up.

AARONOW   They did.

MOSS   They killed the goose.

AARONOW   They did.

MOSS   And now . . .

AARONOW   We're stuck with *this* . . .

MOSS   We're stuck with *this* fucking shit . . .

AARONOW   . . . *this* shit . . .

MOSS   It's too . . .

AARONOW   It is.

MOSS   Eh?

AARONOW   It's too . . .

MOSS   You get a bad month, all of a . . .

AARONOW   You're on this . . .

MOSS   All of, they got you on this "board . . ."

AARONOW   I, I . . . I . . .

MOSS   Some *contest* board . . .

AARONOW   I . . .

MOSS   It's not right.

AARONOW   It's not.

MOSS   No. [*Pause.*]

AARONOW   And it's not right to the *customers*.

MOSS   I know it's not. I'll tell you, you got, you know, you got . . . what did I learn as a kid on Western? Don't sell a guy one car. Sell him *five* cars over fifteen years.

AARONOW   That's right?

MOSS   Eh . . . ?

AARONOW   That's right?

MOSS   Goddamn right, that's right. Guys come on: "Oh, the blah blah blah, *I* know what I'll do: I'll go in and rob everyone blind and go to Argentina cause nobody ever *thought* of this before."

AARONOW   . . . that's right . . .

MOSS   Eh?

AARONOW   No. That's absolutely right.

MOSS   And so they kill the goose. I, I, I'll . . . and a fuckin' *man*, worked all his *life* has got to . . .

AARONOW   . . . that's right . . .

MOSS   . . . cower in his boots . . .

AARONOW [*simultaneously with "boots"*]   Shoes, boots, yes . . .

MOSS   For some fuckin' "Sell ten thousand and you win the steak knives . . ."

AARONOW   For some *sales* pro . . .

MOSS   . . . sales promotion, "You *lose*, then we fire your . . ." No. It's *medieval* . . . it's wrong. "Or we're going to fire your ass." It's wrong.

AARONOW   Yes.

MOSS   Yes, it is. And you know who's responsible?

AARONOW   Who?

MOSS   You know who it is. It's Mitch. And Murray. 'Cause it doesn't have to be this way.

AARONOW   No.

MOSS   Look at Jerry Graff. He's *clean*, he's doing business for *himself*, he's got his, that *list* of his with the *nurses* . . . see? You see? That's *thinking*. Why take ten percent? A ten percent comm . . . why are we giving the rest away? What are we giving ninety per . . . for *nothing*. For some jerk sit in the office tell you "Get out there and close." "Go win the Cadillac." Graff. He goes out and *buys*. He pays top dollar for the . . . you see?

AARONOW   Yes.

MOSS   That's *thinking*. Now, he's got the leads, he goes in business for *himself*. He's . . . that's what I . . . that's *thinking*! "Who? Who's got a steady *job*, a couple bucks nobody's touched, who?"

AARONOW   Nurses.

MOSS   So Graff buys a fucking list of nurses, one grand—if he paid two I'll eat my hat—four, five thousand nurses, and he's going *wild* . . .

AARONOW   He is?

MOSS   He's doing *very* well.

AARONOW   I heard that they were running cold.

MOSS   The nurses?

AARONOW   Yes.

MOSS   You hear a *lot* of things. . . . He's doing very well. He's doing *very* well.

AARONOW   With River Oaks?

MOSS   River Oaks, Brook Farms. *All* of that shit. Somebody told me, you know what he's clearing *himself*? Fourteen, fifteen grand a *week*.

AARONOW   Himself?

MOSS   That's what I'm *saying*. Why? The *leads*. He's got the good leads . . . what are we, we're sitting in the shit here. Why? We have to go to *them* to *get* them. Huh. Ninety percent our sale, we're *paying* to the *office* for the *leads*.

AARONOW   The leads, the overhead, the telephones, there's *lots* of things.

MOSS   What do you need? A *telephone*, some broad to say "Good morning," nothing . . . nothing . . .

AARONOW   No, it's not that simple, Dave . . .

MOSS   *Yes*. It *is*. It *is* simple, and you know what the hard part is?

AARONOW   What?

MOSS   Starting up.

AARONOW   What hard part?

MOSS   Of doing the thing. The dif . . . the difference. Between me and Jerry Graff. Going to business for yourself. The hard part is . . . you know what it is?

AARONOW   What?

MOSS   Just the *act*.

AARONOW   What act?

MOSS   To say "I'm going on my own." 'Cause what you do, George, let me tell you what you do: you find yourself in *thrall* to someone else. And we *enslave* ourselves. To *please*. To win some fucking *toaster* . . . to . . . to . . . and the guy who got there first made *up* those . . .

AARONOW   That's right . . .

MOSS   He made *up* those rules, and we're working for *him*.

AARONOW   That's the truth . . .

MOSS   That's the *God's* truth. And it gets me depressed. I *swear* that it does. At MY AGE. To see a goddamn: "Somebody wins the Cadillac this month. P.S. Two guys get fucked."

AARONOW   *Huh.*

MOSS   You don't *ax* your sales force.

AARONOW   No.

MOSS   You . . .

AARONOW   You . . .

MOSS   You *build* it!

AARONOW   That's what I . . .

MOSS   You fucking *build* it! Men come . . .

AARONOW   Men come *work* for you . . .

MOSS   . . . you're absolutely right.

AARONOW   They . . .

MOSS   They have . . .

AARONOW   When they . . .

MOSS   Look look look look, when they *build* your business, then you can't fucking turn around, *enslave* them, treat them like *children*, fuck them up the ass, leave them to fend for themselves . . . no. [*Pause.*] No. [*Pause.*] You're absolutely right, and I want to tell you something.

AARONOW   What?

MOSS   I want to tell you what somebody should do.

AARONOW   What?

MOSS   Someone should stand up and strike *back.*

AARONOW   What do you mean?

MOSS   *Somebody* . . .

AARONOW   Yes . . . ?

MOSS   Should do something to *them.*

AARONOW   What?

MOSS   Something. To pay them back. [*Pause.*] Someone, someone should hurt them. Murray and Mitch.

AARONOW   Someone should hurt them.

MOSS   Yes.

AARONOW   [*Pause.*]   How?

MOSS   How? Do something to hurt them. Where they live.

AARONOW   What? [*Pause.*]

MOSS   Someone should rob the office.

AARONOW   Huh.

MOSS   That's what I'm *saying.* We were, if we were that kind of guys, to knock it off, and *trash* the joint, it looks like robbery, and *take* the fuckin' leads out of the files . . . go to Jerry Graff. [*Long pause.*]

AARONOW   What could somebody get for them?

MOSS   What could we *get* for them? I don't know. Buck a *throw* . . . buck-a-half a throw . . . I don't know. . . . Hey, who knows what they're worth, what do they *pay* for them? All told . . . must be, I'd . . . three bucks a throw . . . *I* don't know.

AARONOW   How many leads have we got?

MOSS   The *Glengarry* . . . the premium leads . . . ? I'd say we got five thousand. Five. Five thousand leads.

AARONOW And you're saying a fella could take and sell these leads to Jerry Graff.

MOSS Yes.

AARONOW How do you know he'd buy them?

MOSS Graff? Because I worked for him.

AARONOW You haven't talked to him.

MOSS No. What do you mean? Have I talked to him about *this*? [*Pause.*]

AARONOW Yes. I mean are you actually *talking* about this, or are we just . . .

MOSS No, we're just . . .

AARONOW We're just *"talking"* about it.

MOSS We're just *speaking* about it. [*Pause.*] As an *idea*.

AARONOW As an idea.

MOSS Yes.

AARONOW We're not actually *talking* about it.

MOSS No.

AARONOW Talking about it as a . . .

MOSS *No.*

AARONOW As a *robbery*.

MOSS As a "robbery"?! No.

AARONOW *Well.* Well . . .

MOSS *Hey.* [*Pause.*]

AARONOW So all this, um, you didn't, actually, you didn't actually go talk to Graff.

MOSS Not actually, no. [*Pause.*]

AARONOW You didn't?

MOSS No. Not actually.

AARONOW Did you?

MOSS What did I say?

AARONOW What did you say?

MOSS Yes. [*Pause.*] I said, "Not actually." The fuck *you* care, George? We're just *talking* . . .

AARONOW We are?

MOSS Yes. [*Pause.*]

AARONOW Because, because, you know, it's a *crime*.

MOSS That's right. It's a crime. It is a crime. It's also very safe.

AARONOW You're actually *talking* about this?

MOSS That's right. [*Pause.*]

AARONOW You're going to steal the leads?

MOSS Have I said that? [*Pause.*]

AARONOW Are you? [*Pause.*]

MOSS Did I say that?

AARONOW Did you talk to Graff?

MOSS Is that what I said?

AARONOW What did he say?

MOSS What did he say? He'd *buy* them. [*Pause.*]

AARONOW You're going to steal the leads and sell the leads to him? [*Pause.*]

MOSS Yes.

AARONOW What will he pay?

MOSS A buck a shot.

AARONOW For five thousand?

MOSS However they are, that's the deal. A buck a throw. Five thousand dollars. Split it half and half.

AARONOW You're saying "me."

MOSS Yes. [*Pause.*] Twenty-five hundred apiece. One night's work, and the job with Graff. Working the premium leads. [*Pause.*]

AARONOW A job with Graff.

MOSS Is that what I said?

AARONOW He'd give me a job.

MOSS He would take you on. Yes. [*Pause.*]

AARONOW Is that the truth?

MOSS Yes. It is, George. [*Pause.*] Yes. It's a big decision. [*Pause.*] And it's a big reward. [*Pause.*] It's a big reward. For one night's work. [*Pause.*] But it's got to be tonight.

AARONOW What?

MOSS What? What? The *leads*.

AARONOW You have to steal the leads tonight?

MOSS That's *right*, the guys are moving them downtown. After the thirtieth. Murray and Mitch. After the contest.

AARONOW You're, you're saying so you have to go in there tonight and . . .

MOSS *You* . . .

AARONOW I'm sorry?

MOSS *You.* [*Pause.*]

AARONOW Me?

MOSS *You* have to go in. [*Pause.*] *You* have to get the leads. [*Pause.*]

AARONOW I do?

MOSS Yes.

AARONOW I . . .

MOSS It's not something for nothing, George, I took you in on this, you have to go. That's your thing. I've made the deal with Graff. I can't go. I can't go in, I've spoken on this too much. I've got a big mouth. [*Pause.*] "The fucking leads" et cetera, blah blah blah ". . . the fucking tight ass company . . ."

AARONOW They'll know when you go over to Graff . . .

MOSS What will they know? That I stole the leads? I *didn't* steal the leads, I'm going to the *movies* tonight with a friend, and then I'm going to the Como Inn. Why did I go to Graff? I got a better deal. *Period.* Let 'em prove something. They can't prove anything that's not the case. [*Pause.*]

AARONOW *Dave.*

MOSS Yes.

AARONOW You want me to break into the office tonight and steal the leads?

MOSS Yes. [*Pause.*]

AARONOW No.

MOSS Oh, yes, George.

AARONOW What does that mean?

MOSS   Listen to this. I have an alibi, I'm going to the Como Inn, why? Why? The place gets robbed, they're going to come looking for *me*. Why? Because I probably did it. Are you going to turn me in? [*Pause.*] George? Are you going to turn me in?

AARONOW   What if you don't get caught?

MOSS   They come to you, you going to turn me in?

AARONOW   Why would they come to me?

MOSS   They're going to come to *everyone*.

AARONOW   Why would I *do* it?

MOSS   You wouldn't, George, that's why I'm talking to you. Answer me. They come to you. You going to turn me in?

AARONOW   No.

MOSS   Are you sure?

AARONOW   Yes. I'm sure.

MOSS   Then listen to this: I have to get those leads tonight. That's something I have to do. If I'm not at the *movies* . . . if I'm not eating over at the inn . . . If you don't do this, then *I* have to come in here . . .

AARONOW   . . . you don't have to come in . . .

MOSS   . . . and *rob* the place . . .

AARONOW   . . . I thought that we were only talking . . .

MOSS   . . . they *take* me, then. They're going to ask me who were my accomplices.

AARONOW   *Me?*

MOSS   Absolutely.

AARONOW   That's ridiculous.

MOSS   Well, to the law, you're an accessory. Before the fact.

AARONOW   I didn't ask to be.

MOSS   Then tough luck, George, because you are.

AARONOW   Why? *Why*, because you only *told* me about it?

MOSS   That's right.

AARONOW   Why are you doing this to me, Dave. Why are you talking this way to me? I don't understand. Why are you doing this at *all* . . . ?

MOSS   That's none of your fucking business . . .

AARONOW   Well, well, well, *talk* to me, we sat down to eat *dinner*, and here I'm a *criminal* . . .

MOSS   You *went* for it.

AARONOW   In the abstract . . .

MOSS   So I'm making it concrete.

AARONOW   Why?

MOSS   Why? Why *you* going to give me five grand?

AARONOW   Do you need five grand?

MOSS   Is that what I just said?

AARONOW   You need money? Is that the . . .

MOSS   Hey, hey, let's just keep it simple, what I need is not the . . . what do *you* need . . . ?

AARONOW   What is the five grand? [*Pause.*] What is the, you said that we were going to *split* five . . .

MOSS   I lied. [*Pause.*] Alright? My end is *my* business. Your end's twenty-five. In or out. You tell me, you're out you take the consequences.

AARONOW   I do?

MOSS   Yes. [*Pause.*]

AARONOW   And why is that?

MOSS   Because you listened.

SCENE 3

The restaurant. ROMA *is seated alone at the booth.* LINGK *is at the booth next to him.* ROMA *is talking to him.*

ROMA   . . . all train compartments smell vaguely of shit. It gets so you don't mind it. That's the worst thing that I can confess. You know how long it took me to get there? A long time. When you *die* you're going to regret the things you don't do. You think you're *queer* . . . ? I'm going to tell you something: we're *all* queer. You think that you're a *thief*? So *what*? You get befuddled by a middle-class morality . . . ? Get *shut* of it. Shut it out. You cheated on your wife . . . ? You *did* it, *live* with it. [*Pause.*] You fuck little girls, so *be* it. There's an absolute morality? May *be*. And *then* what? If you *think* there is, then *be* that thing. Bad people go to hell? I don't *think* so. If you think that, act that way. A hell exists on earth? Yes. I won't live in it. That's *me*. You ever take a dump made you feel you'd just slept for twelve hours . . . ?

LINGK   Did I . . . ?

ROMA   Yes.

LINGK   I don't know.

ROMA   Or a *piss* . . . ? A great meal fades in reflection. Everything else gains. You know why? 'Cause it's only food. This shit we eat, it keeps us going. But it's only food. The great fucks that you may have had. What do you remember about them?

LINGK   What do I . . . ?

ROMA   Yes.

LINGK   Mmmm . . .

ROMA   I don't know. For *me*, I'm saying, what it is, it's probably not the orgasm. Some broads, forearms on your neck, something her *eyes* did. There was a *sound* she made . . . or, me, lying, in the, I'll tell you: me lying in bed; the next day she brought me café au lait. She gives me a cigarette, my balls feel like concrete. Eh? What I'm saying, what is our life? [*Pause.*] It's looking forward or it's looking back. And that's our life. That's *it*. Where is the *moment*? [*Pause.*] And what is it that we're afraid of? Loss. What else? [*Pause.*] The *bank* closes. We get *sick*, my wife died on a plane, the stock market collapsed . . . the house burnt down . . . what of these happen . . . ? None of 'em. We worry anyway. What does this mean? I'm not *secure*. How can I be secure? [*Pause.*] Through amassing wealth beyond all measure? No. And what's beyond all measure? That's a sickness. That's a trap. There is no measure. Only greed. How can we act? The right way, we would say, to deal with this: "There is a one-in-a-million chance that so and so will happen. . . . *Fuck* it, it won't happen to *me*. . . ." No. We know that's not the right way I think. [*Pause.*] We say the *correct* way to deal with this is "There is a one-in-so-and-so chance this will happen . . . God *protect* me. I am powerless, let it not happen to me. . . ." But no to *that*. I say. There's something else. What is it? "If it happens, AS IT MAY for that is not within our powers,

I will *deal* with it, just as I do *today* with what draws my concern today." I say *this* is how we must act. I do those things which seem correct to me *today*. I trust myself. And if security concerns me, I do that which *today* I think will make me secure. And every day I *do* that, when that day *arrives* that I need a reserve, (a) odds are that I have it, and (b) the *true* reserve that I have is the strength that I have of *acting each day* without fear. [*Pause.*] According to the dictates of my mind. [*Pause.*] Stocks, bonds, objects of art, real estate. Now: what are they? [*Pause.*] An opportunity. To what? To make money? Perhaps. To *lose* money? Perhaps. To "indulge" and to "learn" about ourselves? Perhaps. *So fucking what?* What *isn't*? They're an *opportunity*. That's all. They're an *event*. A guy comes up to you, you make a call, you send in a brochure, it doesn't matter, "There're these *properties* I'd like for you to see." What does it mean? What you *want* it to mean. [*Pause.*] Money? [*Pause.*] If that's what it signifies to you. Security? [*Pause.*] Comfort? [*Pause.*] All it is is THINGS THAT HAPPEN TO YOU. [*Pause.*] That's all it is. How are they different? [*Pause.*] Some poor newly married guy gets run down by a cab. Some *busboy* wins the lottery. [*Pause.*] All it is, it's a carnival. What's special . . . what *draws* us? [*Pause.*] We're all different. [*Pause.*] We're not the same. [*Pause.*] We are not the same. [*Pause.*] Hmmm. [*Pause. Sighs.*] It's been a long day. [*Pause.*] What are you drinking?

LINGK   Gimlet.

ROMA   Well, let's have a couple more. My name is Richard Roma, what's yours?

LINGK   Lingk. James Lingk.

ROMA   James. I'm glad to meet you. [*They shake hands.*] I'm glad to meet you, James. [*Pause.*] I want to show you something. [*Pause.*] It might mean *nothing* to you . . . and it might not. I don't know. I don't know anymore. [*Pause. He takes out a small map and spreads it on a table.*] What is that? Florida. Glengarry Highlands. Florida. "Florida. *Bullshit.*" And maybe that's true; and that's what *I* said: but look *here*: what is this? This is a piece of land. Listen to what I'm going to tell you now.

Act 2

The real estate office. Ransacked. A broken plate-glass window boarded up, glass all over the floor. AARONOW *and* WILLIAMSON *standing around, smoking.*

[*Pause.*]

AARONOW   People used to say that there are numbers of such magnitude that multiplying them by two made no difference. [*Pause.*]

WILLIAMSON   Who used to say that?

AARONOW   In school. [*Pause.*]

[BAYLEN, *a detective, comes out of the inner office.*]

BAYLEN   Alright . . . ? [ROMA *enters from the street.*]

ROMA   *Williamson* . . . Williamson, they stole the *contracts* . . . ?

BAYLEN   Excuse me, sir . . .

ROMA   Did they get my contracts?

WILLIAMSON   They got . . .

BAYLEN   Excuse me, fella.

ROMA . . . did they . . .

BAYLEN Would you excuse us, please . . . ?

ROMA Don't *fuck* with me, fella. I'm talking about a fuckin' Cadillac car that you owe me . . .

WILLIAMSON They didn't get your contract. I filed it before I left.

ROMA They didn't get my contracts?

WILLIAMSON They—excuse me . . . [*He goes back into inner room with the* DETECTIVE.]

ROMA Oh, *fuck. Fuck.* [*He starts kicking the desk.*] FUCK FUCK FUCK! WILLIAMSON!!! WILLIAMSON!!! [*Goes to the door* WILLIAMSON *went into, tries the door; it's locked.*] OPEN THE FUCKING . . . WILLIAMSON . . .

BAYLEN [*coming out*] Who are you? [WILLIAMSON *comes out.*]

WILLIAMSON They didn't get the contracts.

ROMA Did they . . .

WILLIAMSON They got, listen to me . . .

ROMA Th . . .

WILLIAMSON Listen to me: They got *some* of them.

ROMA Some of them . . .

BAYLEN Who told you . . . ?

ROMA Who told me wh . . . ? You've got a fuckin', you've . . . a . . . who is this . . . ? You've got a board-up on the window. . . . *Moss* told me.

BAYLEN [*Looking back toward the inner office.*] Moss . . . Who told him?

ROMA How the fuck do *I* know? [*To* WILLIAMSON] *What . . . talk* to me.

WILLIAMSON They took *some* of the con . . .

ROMA . . . some of the contracts . . . Lingk. James Lingk. I closed . . .

WILLIAMSON You closed him yesterday.

ROMA *Yes.*

WILLIAMSON It went down. I filed it.

ROMA You did?

WILLIAMSON Yes.

ROMA Then I'm over the fucking top and you owe me a Cadillac.

WILLIAMSON I . . .

ROMA And I don't want any fucking shit and I don't give a shit, Lingk puts me over the top, you filed it, that's fine, any other shit kicks out *you* go back. You . . . *you* reclose it, 'cause I *closed* it and you . . . you owe me the car.

BAYLEN Would you excuse us, please.

AARONOW I, um, and may . . . maybe they're in . . . they're in . . . you should, John, if we're ins . . .

WILLIAMSON I'm sure that we're insured, George . . . [*Going back inside.*]

ROMA Fuck insured. You owe me a car.

BAYLEN [*Stepping back into the inner room*] Please don't leave. I'm going to talk to you. What's your name?

ROMA Are you talking to me? [*Pause.*]

BAYLEN Yes. [*Pause.*]

ROMA My name is Richard Roma.

[BAYLEN *goes back into the inner room.*]

AARONOW   I, you know, they should be insured.

ROMA   What do *you* care . . . ?

AARONOW   Then, you know, they wouldn't be so ups . . .

ROMA   Yeah. That's swell. Yes. You're right. [*Pause.*] How are you?

AARONOW   I'm fine. You mean the *board*? You mean the *board* . . . ?

ROMA   I don't . . . yes. Okay, the board.

AARONOW   I'm, I'm, I'm, I'm fucked on the board. *You.* You see how . . . I . . . [*Pause.*] I can't . . . my mind must be in other places. 'Cause I can't do any . . .

ROMA   *What?* You can't do any *what*? [*Pause.*]

AARONOW   I can't close 'em.

ROMA   Well, they're old. I saw the shit that they were giving you.

AARONOW   Yes.

ROMA   Huh?

AARONOW   Yes. They are old.

ROMA   They're ancient.

AARONOW   Clear . . .

ROMA   Clear Meadows. That shit's dead. [*Pause.*]

AARONOW   It *is* dead.

ROMA   It's a waste of time.

AARONOW   Yes. [*Long pause.*] I'm no fucking good.

ROMA   That's . . .

AARONOW   Everything I . . . *you* know . . .

ROMA   That's not . . . Fuck that shit, George. You're a, *hey*, you had a bad month. You're a good man, George.

AARONOW   I am?

ROMA   You hit a bad streak. We've all . . . look at this: fifteen units Mountain View, the fucking things get stole.

AARONOW   He said he filed . . .

ROMA   He filed half of them, he filed the *big* one. All the little ones, I have, I have to go back and . . . ah, *fuck*, I got to go out like a fucking schmuck hat in my hand and reclose the . . . [*Pause.*] I mean, talk about a bad streak. That would sap *anyone's* self confi . . . I got to go out and reclose all my . . . Where's the phones?

AARONOW   They stole . . .

ROMA   They stole the . . .

AARONOW   What. What kind of outfit are we running where . . . where anyone . . .

ROMA [*To himself*]   They stole the phones.

AARONOW   Where criminals can come in here . . . they take the . . .

ROMA   They stole the phones. They stole the leads. They're . . . *Christ.* [*Pause.*] What am I going to do this month? Oh, *shit* . . . [*Starts for the door.*]

AARONOW   You think they're going to catch . . . where are you going?

ROMA   Down the street.

WILLIAMSON [*Sticking his head out of the door*]   Where are you going?

ROMA   To the restaura . . . what do you fucking . . . ?

WILLIAMSON   Aren't you going out today?

ROMA   With what? [*Pause.*] With what, John, they took the leads . . .

WILLIAMSON   I have the stuff from last year's . . .

ROMA   Oh. Oh. Oh, your "nostalgia" file, that's fine. No. Swell. 'Cause I
    don't have to . . .
WILLIAMSON   . . . you want to go out today . . . ?
ROMA   'Cause I don't have to *eat* this month. No. Okay. *Give* 'em to me . . .
    [*To himself*] Fucking Mitch and Murray going to shit a br . . . what am I
    going to *do* all . . . [WILLIAMSON *starts back into the office. He is accosted*
    by AARONOW.]
AARONOW   Were the leads . . .
ROMA   . . . what am I going to *do* all month . . . ?
AARONOW   Were the leads insured?
WILLIAMSON   I don't know, George, why?
AARONOW   'Cause, you know, 'cause they weren't, I know that Mitch and
    Murray uh . . . [*Pause.*]
WILLIAMSON   What?
AARONOW   That they're going to be upset.
WILLIAMSON   That's right. [*Going back into his office. Pause. To* ROMA]
    You want to go out today . . . ?
        [*Pause.* WILLIAMSON *returns to his office.*]
AARONOW   He said we're all going to have to go talk to the guy.
ROMA   What?
AARONOW   He said we . . .
ROMA   To the cop?
AARONOW   Yeah.
ROMA   Yeah. That's swell. *Another* waste of time.
AARONOW   A waste of time? Why?
ROMA   *Why?* 'Cause they aren't going to find the guy.
AARONOW   The cops?
ROMA   Yes. The cops. No.
AARONOW   They aren't?
ROMA   No.
AARONOW   Why don't you think so?
ROMA   Why? Because they're *stupid.* "Where were you last night . . ."
AARONOW   Where were you?
ROMA   Where was *I*?
AARONOW   Yes.
ROMA   I was at home, where were *you*?
AARONOW   At home.
ROMA   *See* . . . ? Were you the guy who broke in?
AARONOW   Was I?
ROMA   Yes.
AARONOW   No.
ROMA   Then don't sweat it, George, you know why?
AARONOW   No.
ROMA   You have nothing to hide.
AARONOW   [*Pause.*]   When I talk to the police, I get nervous.
ROMA   Yeah. You know who doesn't?
AARONOW   No, who?
ROMA   Thieves.
AARONOW   Why?
ROMA   They're inured to it.

AARONOW You think so?

ROMA Yes. [*Pause.*]

AARONOW But what should I *tell* them?

ROMA The truth, George. Always tell the truth. It's the easiest thing to remember. [WILLIAMSON *comes out of the office with leads.* ROMA *takes one, reads it.*]

ROMA *Patel?* Ravidam *Patel?* How am I going to make a living on these deadbeat *wogs?* Where did you get this, from the *morgue?*

WILLIAMSON If you don't want it, give it back.

ROMA I don't "want" it, if you catch my drift.

WILLIAMSON I'm giving you *three* leads. You . . .

ROMA What's the fucking point in *any* case . . . ? What's the *point.* I got to argue with *you,* I got to knock heads with the *cops,* I'm busting my *balls,* sell your *dirt* to fucking *deadbeats* money in the *mattress,* I come back you can't even manage to keep the contracts safe, I have to go back and close them *again.* . . . What the fuck am I wasting my time, fuck this shit. I'm going out and reclose last week's . . .

WILLIAMSON The word from Murray is: leave them alone. If we need a new signature he'll go out himself, he'll be the *president,* just come *in,* from out of *town* . . .

ROMA Okay, okay, okay, gimme this shit. Fine. [*Takes the leads.*]

WILLIAMSON Now, I'm giving you three . . .

ROMA Three? I count *two.*

WILLIAMSON Three.

ROMA Patel? Fuck *you.* Fuckin' *Shiva* handed him a million dollars, told him "sign the deal," he wouldn't sign. And Vishnu, too. Into the bargain. Fuck *that,* John. You know your business, I know mine. Your business is being an *asshole,* and I find out whose fucking *cousin* you are, I'm going to go to him and figure out a way to have your *ass* . . . fuck you—I'll wait for the new leads. [SHELLY LEVENE *enters.*]

LEVENE Get the *chalk.* Get the *chalk* . . . get the *chalk!* I closed 'em! I *closed* the cocksucker. Get the chalk and put me on the *board.* I'm going to Hawaii! Put me on the Cadillac board, Williamson! Pick up the fuckin' chalk. Eight units. Mountain View . . .

ROMA You sold eight Mountain View?

LEVENE You bet your ass. Who wants to go to lunch? Who wants to go to lunch? I'm buying. [*Slaps contract down on* WILLIAMSON'*s desk.*] Eighty-two fucking grand. And twelve grand in commission. John. [*Pause.*] On fucking deadbeat magazine subscription leads.

WILLIAMSON Who?

LEVENE [*Pointing to contract.*] *Read* it. Bruce and Harriett Nyborg. [*Looking around.*] What happened here?

AARONOW Fuck. I had them on River Glen. [LEVENE *looks around.*]

LEVENE What happened?

WILLIAMSON Somebody broke in.

ROMA Eight units?

LEVENE That's right.

ROMA *Shelly* . . . !

LEVENE Hey, big fucking deal. Broke a bad streak . . .

AARONOW Shelly, the Machine, Levene.

LEVENE   You . . .

AARONOW   That's great.

LEVENE   Thank you, George. [BAYLEN *sticks his head out of the room; calls in, "Aaronow."* AARONOW *goes into the side room.*]

LEVENE   Williamson, get on the phone, call Mitch . . .

ROMA   They took the phones . . .

LEVENE   They . . .

BAYLEN   *Aaronow* . . .

ROMA   They took the typewriters, they took the leads, they took the *cash*, they took the *contracts* . . .

LEVENE   Wh . . . wh . . . Wha . . . ?

AARONOW   We had a robbery. [*Goes into the inner room.*]

LEVENE   [*Pause.*]   When?

ROMA   Last night, this morning. [*Pause.*]

LEVENE   They took the leads?

ROMA   Mmm. [MOSS *comes out of the interrogation.*]

MOSS   Fuckin' asshole.

ROMA   What, they beat you with a rubber bat?

MOSS   Cop couldn't find his dick two hands and a map. Anyone talks to this guy's an *asshole* . . .

ROMA   You going to turn State's?

MOSS   Fuck you, Ricky. I ain't going out today. I'm going home. I'm going home because nothing's *accomplished* here. . . . Anyone *talks to this guy is* . . .

ROMA   Guess what the Machine did?

MOSS   Fuck the Machine.

ROMA   Mountain View. Eight units.

MOSS   Fuckin' cop's got no right talk to me that way. I didn't rob the place . . .

ROMA   You hear what I said?

MOSS   Yeah. He closed a deal.

ROMA   Eight units. Mountain View.

MOSS   [*To* LEVENE]   You did that?

LEVENE   Yeah. [*Pause.*]

MOSS   Fuck you.

ROMA   Guess who?

MOSS   When . . .

LEVENE   Just now.

ROMA   Guess who?

MOSS   You just this morning . . .

ROMA   Harriet and blah blah Nyborg.

MOSS   You did that?

LEVENE   Eighty-two thousand dollars. [*Pause.*]

MOSS   Those fuckin' *deadbeats* . . .

LEVENE   My ass. I told 'em. [*To* ROMA] Listen to this: I said . . .

MOSS   Hey, I don't want to hear your fucking war stories . . .

ROMA   Fuck *you*, Dave . . .

LEVENE   "You have to believe in your*self*. . . . you"—look—"alright . . . ?"

MOSS   [*To* WILLIAMSON]   Give me some leads. I'm going out . . . I'm getting out of . . .

LEVENE ". . . you have to believe in your*self* . . ."

MOSS Na, fuck the leads, I'm going home.

LEVENE "Bruce, Harriett . . . Fuck *me*, believe in your*self* . . ."

ROMA We haven't got a lead . . .

MOSS Why not?

ROMA They took 'em . . .

MOSS Hey, they're fuckin' garbage any case. . . . This whole goddamn . . .

LEVENE ". . . You look around, you say, 'This one has so-and-so, and I have nothing . . .'"

MOSS *Shit.*

LEVENE "*'Why? Why don't I get the opportunities . . . ?'*"

MOSS And did they steal the contracts . . . ?

ROMA Fuck *you* care . . . ?

LEVENE "I want to tell you something, Harriett . . ."

MOSS . . . the fuck is *that* supposed to mean . . . ?

LEVENE Will you shut up, I'm telling you this . . . [AARONOW *sticks his head out.*]

AARONOW Can we get some coffee . . . ?

MOSS How ya doing? [*Pause.*]

AARONOW Fine.

MOSS Uh-huh.

AARONOW If anyone's going, I could use some coffee.

LEVENE "You *do* get the . . ." [*To* ROMA] Huh? Huh?

MOSS *Fuck* is that supposed to mean?

LEVENE "You *do* get the opportunity. . . . You *get* them. As *I* do, as *anyone* does . . ."

MOSS Ricky? . . . That I don't care they stole the contracts? [*Pause.*]

LEVENE I got 'em in the kitchen. I'm eating her crumb cake.

MOSS What does that mean?

ROMA It *means*, Dave, you haven't closed a good one in a month, none of my business, you want to push me to answer you. [*Pause.*] And so you haven't got a contract to get stolen or so forth.

MOSS You have a mean streak in you, Ricky, you know that . . . ?

LEVENE Rick. Let me tell you. Wait, we're in the . . .

MOSS Shut the fuck up. [*Pause.*] Ricky. You have a mean streak in you. . . . [*To* LEVENE] And what the fuck are *you* babbling about . . . ? [*To* ROMA] Bring that shit up. Of my volume. You were on a bad one and I brought it up to *you* you'd harbor it. [*Pause.*] You'd harbor it a long long while. And you'd be right.

ROMA Who said "Fuck the Machine"?

MOSS "*Fuck the Machine*"? "*Fuck the Machine*"? What is this. *Courtesy* class . . . ? You're *fucked*, Rick—are you fucking *nuts*? You're hot, so you think you're the *ruler* of this place . . . ?! You want to . . .

LEVENE Dave . . .

MOSS . . . Shut up. Decide who should be dealt with how? Is that the thing? I come into the fuckin' office today, I get humiliated by some jagoff cop. I get accused of . . . I get this *shit* thrown in my face by you, you genuine shit, because you're top name on the board . . .

ROMA Is that what I did? Dave? I humiliated you? My *God* . . . I'm *sorry* . . .

MOSS   Sittin' on top of the *world*, sittin' on top of the *world*, everything's fucking *peach*fuzz . . .

ROMA   Oh, and I don't get a moment to spare for a bust-out *humanitarian* down on his luck lately. Fuck *you*, Dave, you know you got a big *mouth*, and *you* make a close the whole *place* stinks with your *farts* for a week. "How much you just ingested," what a big *man* you are, "Hey, let me buy you a pack of gum. I'll show you how to *chew* it." Your *pal* closes, all that comes out of your mouth is *bile*, how fucked *up* you are . . .

MOSS   *Who's* my pal . . . ? And what are you, Ricky, huh, what are you, Bishop *Sheean*? Who the fuck are *you*, Mr. Slick . . . ? What are you, friend to the *workingman*? Big deal. Fuck *you*, you got the memory a fuckin *fly*. I never liked you.

ROMA   What is this, your farewell speech?

MOSS   I'm going home.

ROMA   Your farewell to the troops?

MOSS   I'm not going home. I'm going to Wis*con*sin.

ROMA   Have a good trip.

MOSS   [*Simultaneously with "trip"*]   And fuck *you*. Fuck the *lot* of you. Fuck you *all*. [MOSS *exits. Pause.*]

ROMA   [*To* LEVENE]   You were saying? [*Pause.*] Come on. Come on, you got them in the kitchen, you got the stats spread out, you're in your shirtsleeves, you can *smell* it. Huh? Snap out of it, you're eating her *crumb* cake. [*Pause.*]

LEVENE   I'm eating her *crumb* cake . . .

ROMA   How was it . . . ?

LEVENE   From the store.

ROMA   Fuck *her* . . .

LEVENE   "What we have to do is *admit* to ourself that we see that opportunity . . . and *take* it. [*Pause.*] And that's it." And we *sit* there. [*Pause.*] I got the pen out . . .

ROMA   "Always be closing . . ."

LEVENE   That's what I'm *saying*. The *old* ways. The *old* ways . . . convert the motherfucker . . . *sell* him . . . *sell* him . . . *make him sign the check.* [*Pause.*] The . . . Bruce, Harriett . . . the kitchen, blah: they got their money in *government* bonds. . . . I say *fuck* it, we're going to go the whole route. I plat it out eight units. Eighty-two grand. I tell them. "This is now. This is that *thing* that you've been dreaming of, you're going to find that suitcase on the train, the guy comes in the door, the bag that's full of money. This is it, *Harriett* . . ."

ROMA   [*Reflectively*]   Harriett . . .

LEVENE   *Bruce* . . . "I don't want to fuck *around* with you. I don't want to go *round* this, and *pussyfoot* around the thing, you have to look back on this. I do, too. I came here to do good for you and me. For *both* of us. Why take an interim position? *The only arrangement I'll accept* is full investment. Period. The whole eight units. I know that you're saying 'be safe,' I know what you're saying. I know if I left you to yourselves, you'd say 'come back tomorrow,' and when I walked out that door, you'd make a cup of *coffee* . . . you'd sit *down* . . . and you'd think 'let's be safe . . .' and not to disappoint me you'd go *one* unit or maybe two, because you'd become scared because you'd met possibility. But this won't do, and that's not the subject. . . ." Listen to this, I actually said this. "That's not the subject of our *evening* together." Now I handed them the pen. I held it in my hand. I turned the contract, eight units eighty-two grand. "Now I want you to sign." [*Pause.*] I sat there. Five minutes. Then, I sat there, Ricky, *twenty-two minutes* by the kitchen *clock.* [*Pause.*] Twenty-two minutes by the kitchen clock. Not a *word,* not a *motion.* What am I thinking? "My arm's getting tired?" No. I *did* it. I *did* it. Like in the *old* days, Ricky. Like I was taught . . . Like, like, like I *used* to do . . . I did it.

ROMA   Like you taught me . . .

LEVENE   Bullshit, you're . . . No. That's raw . . . well, if I *did,* then I'm *glad* I did. I, *well.* I locked on them. All on them, nothing on me. All my thoughts are on them. I'm holding the last thought that I spoke: "Now is the time." [*Pause.*] They signed, Ricky. It was *great.* It was fucking great. It was like they wilted all at once. No *gesture* . . . nothing. Like together. They, I swear to God, they both kind of *imperceptibly slumped.* And he reaches and takes the pen and signs, he passes it to her, she signs. It was so fucking solemn. I just let it sit. I nod like this. I nod again. I grasp his hands. I shake his hands. I grasp *her* hands. I nod at her like this. "Bruce . . . Harriett . . ." I'm beaming at them. I'm nodding like this. I point back in the living room, back to the sideboard. [*Pause.*] *I didn't fucking know there was a sideboard there!!* He goes back, he brings us a drink. Little shot glasses. A pattern in 'em. And we toast. In silence. [*Pause.*]

ROMA   That was a great sale, Shelly. [*Pause.*]

LEVENE   Ah, fuck. Leads! Leads! Williamson! [WILLIAMSON *sticks his head out of the office.*] Send me *out!* Send me *out!*

WILLIAMSON   The leads are coming.

LEVENE   *Get* 'em to me!

WILLIAMSON   I talked to Murray and Mitch an hour ago. They're coming in, you understand they're a bit *upset* over this morning's . . .

LEVENE   Did you tell 'em my sale?

WILLIAMSON   How could I tell 'em your sale? Eh? I don't have a tel . . . I'll tell 'em your sale when they bring in the leads. Alright? Shelly. Alright? We had a little . . . You closed a deal. You made a good sale. Fine.

LEVENE   It's better than a good sale. It's a . . .

WILLIAMSON   Look: I have a lot of things on my mind, they're coming in, alright, they're very upset, I'm trying to make some *sense* . . .

LEVENE   All that I'm *telling* you: that one thing you can tell them it's a remarkable sale.

WILLIAMSON   The only thing remarkable is who you made it to.

LEVENE   What does *that* fucking mean?

WILLIAMSON   That if the sale sticks, it will be a miracle.

LEVENE   Why should the sale not stick? Hey, *fuck* you. That's what I'm saying. You have no idea of your job. A man's his job and you're *fucked* at yours. You hear what I'm saying to you? Your "end of month board . . ." You can't run an office. I don't care. You don't know what it *is,* you don't have the *sense,* you don't have the *balls.* You ever been on a sit? *Ever?* Has this cocksucker ever been . . . you ever sit down with a cust . . .

WILLIAMSON   I were you, I'd calm down, Shelly.

LEVENE *Would* you? *Would* you . . . ? Or you're gonna *what*, fire me?

WILLIAMSON It's not impossible.

LEVENE On an eighty-thousand dollar *day*? And it ain't even *noon*.

ROMA You closed 'em today?

LEVENE Yes. I did. This *morning*. [*To* WILLIAMSON] What I'm *saying* to you: things can *change*. You *see*? *This is where you fuck up*, because this is something you don't *know*. You can't look down the *road*. And see what's *coming*. Might be someone *else*, John. It might be someone *new*, eh? Someone *new*. And you can't look *back*. 'Cause you don't know *history*. You ask them. When we were at Rio Rancho, who was top man? A month . . . ? Two months . . . ? Eight months in twelve for three years in a row. You know what that means? You know what that means? Is that *luck*? Is that some, some, some purloined leads? That's *skill*. That's *talent*, that's, that's . . .

ROMA . . . *yes* . . .

LEVENE . . . and you don't *remember*. 'Cause you weren't *around*. That's cold *calling*. Walk up to the door. I don't even know their *name*. I'm selling something they don't even *want*. You talk about soft sell . . . before we had a name for it . . . before we called it anything, we did it.

ROMA That's right, Shel.

LEVENE And, and, and, I *did* it. And I put a kid through *school*. She . . . and Cold *calling*, fella. Door to door. But you don't know. You don't know. You never heard of a *streak*. You never heard of "marshaling your sales force. . . ." What are you, you're a *secretary*, John. Fuck *you*. That's my message to you. Fuck you and kiss my ass. You don't like it, I'll go talk to Jerry Graff. Period. Fuck you. Put me on the board. And I want three worthwhile leads today and I don't want any bullshit about them and I want 'em close together 'cause I'm going to hit them all today. That's all I have to say to you.

ROMA He's right, Williamson. [WILLIAMSON *goes into a side office. Pause.*]

LEVENE It's not right. I'm sorry, and I'll tell you who's to blame is Mitch and Murray. [ROMA *sees something outside the window.*]

ROMA [*Sotto*] Oh, Christ.

LEVENE The hell with him. We'll go to lunch, the leads won't be up for . . .

ROMA You're a client. I just sold you five waterfront Glengarry Farms. I rub my head, throw me the cue "Kenilworth."[3]

LEVENE What is it?

ROMA Kenilw . . . [LINGK *enters the office.*]

ROMA [*To* LEVENE] *I* own the property, my *mother* owns the property, I put her *into* it. I'm going to show you on the plats. You look when you get home A–3 through A–14 and 26 through 30. You take your time and if you still feel.

LEVENE No, Mr. Roma. I don't need the time, I've made a lot of *investments* in the last . . .

LINGK I've got to talk to you.

---

3. A community just north of Chicago.

ROMA [*Looking up*] Jim! What are you doing here? Jim Lingk, D. Ray Morton . . .

LEVENE Glad to meet you.

ROMA I just put Jim into Black Creek . . . are you acquainted with . . .

LEVENE No . . . Black *Creek*. Yes. In *Florida?*

ROMA Yes.

LEVENE I wanted to *speak* with you about . . .

ROMA Well, we'll do that this weekend.

LEVENE My *wife* told me to look into . . .

ROMA *Beautiful.* Beautiful rolling land. I was telling Jim and Jinny, Ray, I want to tell you something. [*To* LEVENE] You, Jim, you eat in a lot of restaurants. I know you do. . . . [*To* LINGK] Mr. Morton's with American Express . . . he's . . . [*To* LEVENE] I can tell Jim what you do . . . ?

LEVENE Sure.

ROMA Ray is director of all European sales and services for American Ex . . . [*To* LEVENE] But I'm saying you haven't had a *meal* until you've tasted . . . I was at the Lingks' last . . . as a matter of fact, what was that service feature you were talking about . . . ?

LEVENE Which . . .

ROMA "Home Cooking" . . . what did you call it, you said it . . . it was a tag phrase that you had . . .

LEVENE Uh . . .

ROMA Home . . .

LEVENE Home cooking . . .

ROMA The monthly interview . . . ?

LEVENE Oh! For the *magazine* . . .

ROMA Yes. Is this something that I can talk ab . . .

LEVENE Well, it isn't coming *out* until the February iss . . . *sure*. Sure, go ahead, Ricky.

ROMA You're sure?

LEVENE [*nods*] Go ahead.

ROMA Well, Ray was eating at one of his company's men's home in France . . . the man's French, isn't he?

LEVENE No, his *wife* is.

ROMA Ah. Ah, his wife is. Ray: what *time* do you have . . . ?

LEVENE Twelve-fifteen.

ROMA Oh! My God . . . I've got to get you on the *plane!*

LEVENE Didn't I say I was taking the two o' . . .

ROMA No. You said the one. That's why you said we couldn't talk till Kenilworth.

LEVENE Oh, my God, you're right! I'm on the one. . . . [*Getting up.*] Well, let's *scoot* . . .

LINGK I've got to talk to you . . .

ROMA I've got to get Ray to O'Hare[4] . . . [*To* LEVENE] Come on, let's hustle. . . . [*Over his shoulder*] John! Call American Express in *Pittsburgh* for Mr. Morton, will you, tell them he's on the one o'clock. [*To* LINGK] I'll see you. . . . Christ, I'm sorry you came all the way in. . . . I'm running Ray

---

4. Chicago's major airport.

over to O'Hare. . . . You wait here, I'll . . . no. [*To* LEVENE] I'm meeting
your man at the bank. . . . [*To* LINGK] I wish you'd phoned. . . . I'll tell
you, wait: are you and Jinny going to be home tonight? [*Rubs forehead.*]

LINGK   I . . .

LEVENE   Rick.

ROMA   What?

LEVENE   *Kenilworth . . . ?*

ROMA   I'm sorry . . . ?

LEVENE   *Kenilworth.*

ROMA   Oh, God . . . Oh, God . . . [ROMA *takes* LINGK *aside, sotto*] Jim,
excuse me. . . . Ray, I told you, who he is is *the* senior vice-president
American Express. His family owns 32 per. . . . Over the past years I've
sold him . . . I can't tell you the dollar amount, but *quite* a lot of land. I
promised five *weeks* ago that I'd go to the wife's birthday party in
Kenilworth tonight. [*Sighs.*] I *have* to go. You understand. They treat me
like a member of the family, so I have to go. It's funny, you know, you
get a picture of the Corporation-Type Company Man, all business . . .
this man, *no.* We'll go out to his home sometime. Let's see. [*He checks
his datebook.*] Tomorrow. No. Tomorrow, I'm in L.A. . . . *Monday* . . . I'll
take you to lunch, where would you like to go?

LINGK   My wife . . . [ROMA *rubs his head.*]

LEVENE   [*Standing in the door.*]   Rick . . . ?

ROMA   I'm sorry, Jim. I can't talk now. I'll call you tonight . . . I'm sorry.
I'm coming, Ray. [*Starts for the door.*]

LINGK   My wife said I have to cancel the deal.

ROMA   It's a common reaction, Jim. I'll tell you what it is, and I know that
that's why you married her. One of the reasons is *prudence.* It's a sizable
investment. One thinks *twice* . . . it's also something *women* have. It's
just a reaction to the size of the investment. *Monday,* if you'd invite me
for dinner again . . . [*To* LEVENE] This woman can *cook* . . .

LEVENE   [*Simultaneously*]   I'm sure she can . . .

ROMA   [*To* LINGK]   We're going to talk. I'm going to *tell* you something.
Because [*Sotto*] there's something about your acreage I want you to
know. I can't talk about it now. I really shouldn't. And, in fact, by *law,*
I . . . [*Shrugs, resigned.*] The man next to you, he bought his lot at forty-
two, he phoned to say that he'd *already* had an offer . . . [ROMA *rubs his
head.*]

LEVENE   Rick . . . ?

ROMA   I'm coming, Ray . . . what a day! I'll call you this evening, Jim. I'm
sorry you had to come in . . . Monday, lunch.

LINGK   My wife . . .

LEVENE   Rick, we really have to go.

LINGK   My wife . . .

ROMA   Monday.

LINGK   She called the consumer . . . the attorney, I don't know. The attorney gen . . . they said we have three days . . .

ROMA   *Who* did she call?

LINGK   I don't know, the attorney gen . . . the . . . some consumer office,
umm . . .

ROMA   Why did she do *that*, Jim?

LINGK   I don't know. [*Pause.*] They said we have three days. [*Pause.*] They said we have three days.

ROMA   Three days.

LINGK   To . . . you know. [*Pause.*]

ROMA   No, I don't know. *Tell* me.

LINGK   To change our minds.

ROMA   Of *course* you have three days. [*Pause.*]

LINGK   So we can't talk *Monday*. [*Pause.*]

ROMA   Jim, Jim, you saw my book . . . I *can't*, *you* saw my book . . .

LINGK   But we have to *before* Monday. To get our money ba . . .

ROMA   Three *business* days. They mean three *business* days.

LINGK   Wednesday, Thursday, Friday.

ROMA   I don't understand.

LINGK   That's what they are. Three business . . . if I wait till Monday, my time limit runs out.

ROMA   You don't count Saturday.

LINGK   I'm not.

ROMA   No, I'm saying you don't include Saturday . . . in your three days. It's not a *business* day.

LINGK   But I'm not *counting* it. [*Pause.*] Wednesday. Thursday. Friday. So it would have elapsed.

ROMA   What would have elapsed?

LINGK   If we wait till Mon . . .

ROMA   When did you write the check?

LINGK   Yest . . .

ROMA   What was yesterday?

LINGK   Tuesday.

ROMA   And when was that check cashed?

LINGK   I don't know.

ROMA   What was the *earliest* it could have been cashed? [*Pause.*]

LINGK   I don't know.

ROMA   *Today.* [*Pause.*] *Today.* Which, in any case, it was not, as there were a couple of points on the agreement I wanted to go over with you in any case.

LINGK   The check wasn't cashed?

ROMA   I just called downtown, and it's on their desk.

LEVENE   Rick . . .

ROMA   One moment, I'll be right with you. [*To* LINGK] In fact, a . . . *one* point, which I spoke to you of which [*Looks around.*] I can't talk to you about here, [DETECTIVE *puts his head out of the doorway.*]

BAYLEN   Levene!!!

LINGK   I, I . . .

ROMA   Listen to me, the *statute* it's for your protection. I have no complaints with that, in fact, I was a member of the board when we *drafted* it, so quite the *opposite*. It *says* that you can change your mind three working days from the time the deal is closed.

BAYLEN   Levene!

ROMA   Which, wait a second, which is not until the check is cashed.

BAYLEN   Levene!! [AARONOW *comes out of the* DETECTIVE's *office.*]

AARONOW   I'm *through*, with *this* fucking meshugaas.[5] No one should talk to a man that way. How are you *talking* to me that . . . ?

BAYLEN   Levene! [WILLIAMSON *puts his head out of the office.*]

AARONOW   . . . how can you *talk* to me that . . . that . . .

LEVENE [*To* ROMA]   Rick, I'm going to flag a cab.

AARONOW   *I* didn't rob . . . [WILLIAMSON *sees* LEVENE.]

WILLIAMSON   Shelly: get in the office.

AARONOW   I didn't . . . why should *I* . . . "Where were you last . . ." Is anybody listening to me . . . ? Where's Moss . . . ? Where . . . ?

BAYLEN   Levene? [*To* WILLIAMSON] Is this Lev . . . [BAYLEN *accosts* LINGK.]

LEVENE [*Taking* BAYLEN *into the office*]   Ah. Ah. Perhaps I can advise you on that. . . . [*To* ROMA *and* LINGK, *as he exits*] Excuse us, will you . . . ?

AARONOW [*Simultaneous with* LEVENE's *speech above*] . . . Come in here . . . I *work* here, I don't come in here to be *mistreated* . . .

WILLIAMSON   Go to *lunch*, will you . . .

AARONOW   I want to *work* today, that's why I came . . .

WILLIAMSON   The leads come in, I'll let . . .

AARONOW   . . . that's why I came in. I thought I . . .

WILLIAMSON   Just go to lunch.

AARONOW   I don't *want* to go to lunch.

WILLIAMSON   Go to lunch, George.

AARONOW   Where does he get off to talk that way to a working man? It's not . . .

WILLIAMSON [*Buttonholes him*]   Will you take it outside, we have people trying to do *business* here . . .

AARONOW   That's what, that's what, that's what *I* was trying to do. [*Pause.*] That's why I came in . . . I meet *gestapo* tac . . .

WILLIAMSON [*Going back into his office*]   Excuse me . . .

AARONOW   I meet *gestapo* tactics . . . I meet *gestapo* tactics. . . . That's not right. . . . No man has the right to . . . "Call an attorney," that means you're guilt . . . you're under sus . . . "Co . . . ," he says, "cooperate" or we'll go downtown. *That's* not . . . as long as I've . . .

WILLIAMSON [*Bursting out of his office*]   Will you get out of here. Will you get *out* of here. Will you. I'm trying to run an *office* here. Will you go to lunch? Go to lunch. Will you go to lunch? [*Retreats into office.*]

ROMA [*To* AARONOW]   Will you excuse . . .

AARONOW   Where did Moss . . . ? I . . .

ROMA   Will you excuse us please?

AARONOW   Uh, uh, did he go to the restaurant? [*Pause.*] I . . . I . . . [*Exits.*]

ROMA   I'm *very* sorry, Jimmy. I apologize to you.

LINGK   It's not me, it's my wife.

ROMA [*Pause.*]   What is?

LINGK   I told you.

ROMA   Tell me again.

LINGK   What's going on here?

ROMA   Tell me again. Your wife.

LINGK   I told you.

5. Craziness (Yiddish).

ROMA   You tell me again.

LINGK   She wants her money back.

ROMA   We're going to speak to her.

LINGK   No. She told me "right now."

ROMA   We'll speak to her, Jim . . .

LINGK   She won't listen. [DETECTIVE *sticks his head out.*]

BAYLEN   *Roma.*

LINGK   She told me if not, I have to call the State's attorney.

ROMA   No, no. That's just something she "said." We don't have to do that.

LINGK   She told me I *have* to.

ROMA   No, Jim.

LINGK   I *do.* If I don't get my *money* back . . . [WILLIAMSON *points out* ROMA *to* BAYLEN.]

BAYLEN   Roma! [*To* ROMA] I'm talking to you . . .

ROMA   I've . . . look. [*Generally*] Will someone get this guy off my back.

BAYLEN   You have a problem?

ROMA   Yes, I have a problem. Yes, I *do,* my fr . . . It's not me that ripped the joint off, I'm doing *business.* I'll be with you in a *while.* You got it . . . ? [*Looks back.* LINGK *is heading for the door.*] Where are you going?

LINGK   I'm . . .

ROMA   Where are you going . . . ? This is *me.* . . . This is Ricky, Jim. Jim, anything you *want,* you *want* it, you *have* it. You understand? This is *me.* Something *upset* you. Sit down, now sit down. You tell me what it is. [*Pause.*] Am I going to help you fix it? You're goddamned right I am. Sit down. Tell you something . . . ? *Sometimes* we need someone from *out*-side. It's . . . no, sit down. . . . Now *talk* to me.

LINGK   I can't negotiate.

ROMA   What does that mean?

LINGK   That . . .

ROMA   . . . what, what, *say* it. Say it to me . . .

LINGK   I . . .

ROMA   What . . . ?

LINGK   I . . .

ROMA   What . . . ? Say the words.

LINGK   I don't have the *power.* [*Pause.*] I said it.

ROMA   What power?

LINGK   The power to negotiate.

ROMA   To negotiate what? [*Pause.*] To negotiate what?

LINGK   *This.*

ROMA   What, "this"? [*Pause.*]

LINGK   The deal.

ROMA   The "deal," *forget* the deal. *Forget* the deal, you've got something on your mind, Jim, what is it?

LINGK   [rising]   *I can't talk to you, you* met my wife, I . . . [*Pause.*]

ROMA   What? [*Pause.*] What? [*Pause.*] What, Jim: I tell you what, let's get out of here . . . let's go get a drink.

LINGK   She told me not to talk to you.

ROMA   Let's . . . no one's going to know, let's go around the *corner* and we'll get a drink.

LINGK   She told me I had to get back the check or call the State's att . . .

ROMA *Forget* the deal, Jimmy. [*Pause.*] *Forget* the deal . . . you know me. The deal's *dead.* Am I talking about the *deal?* That's *over.* Please. Let's talk about *you.* Come on. [*Pause.* ROMA *rises and starts walking toward the front door.*] Come on. [*Pause.*] Come on, Jim. [*Pause.*] I want to tell you something. Your life is your own. You have a contract with your wife. You have certain things you do *jointly,* you have a *bond* there . . . and there are *other* things. Those things are yours. You needn't feel *ashamed,* you needn't feel that you're being *untrue* . . . or that she would abandon you if you knew. This is your life. [*Pause.*] *Yes.* Now I want to *talk* to you because you're obviously upset and that *concerns* me. Now let's go. Right now. [LINGK *gets up and they start for the door.*]

BAYLEN [*Sticks his head out of the door*] Roma . . .

LINGK . . . and . . . and . . . [*Pause.*]

ROMA What?

LINGK And the check is . . .

ROMA What did I *tell* you? [*Pause.*] What did I say about the three days . . . ?

BAYLEN Roma, would you, I'd like to get some lunch . . .

ROMA I'm talking with Mr. Lingk. If you please, I'll be back in. [*Checks watch.*] I'll be back in a while. . . . I told you, check with Mr. Williamson.

BAYLEN The people downtown said . . .

ROMA You call them again. Mr. Williamson . . . !

WILLIAMSON Yes.

ROMA Mr. Lingk and I are going to . . .

WILLIAMSON Yes. Please. Please. [*To* LINGK] The police [*Shrugs.*] can be . . .

LINGK What are the police doing?

ROMA It's nothing.

LINGK What are the *police* doing here . . . ?

WILLIAMSON We had a slight burglary last night.

ROMA It was nothing . . . I was assuring Mr. Lingk . . .

WILLIAMSON Mr. Lingk. James Lingk. Your contract went out. Nothing to . . .

ROMA John . . .

WILLIAMSON Your contract went out to the bank.

LINGK You cashed the check?

WILLIAMSON We . . .

ROMA . . . Mr. Williamson . . .

WILLIAMSON Your check was cashed yesterday afternoon. And we're completely insured, as you know, in *any* case. [*Pause.*]

LINGK [*To* ROMA] You cashed the check?

ROMA Not to my knowledge, no . . .

WILLIAMSON I'm sure we can . . .

LINGK Oh, . . . [*Starts out the door.*] Don't follow me. . . . Oh, [*Pause. To* ROMA] I know I've let you down. I'm sorry. For . . . Forgive . . . for . . . I don't know anymore. [*Pause.*] Forgive me. [LINGK *exits. Pause.*]

ROMA [*To* WILLIAMSON] You stupid fucking cunt. *You,* Williamson . . . I'm talking to *you,* shithead . . . You just cost me *six thousand dollars.* [*Pause.*] Six thousand dollars. And one Cadillac. That's right. What are you going to do about it? What are you going to do about it, asshole. You fucking *shit*. Where did you learn your *trade*. You stupid fucking *cunt*. You *idiot*. Whoever told you you could work with *men*?

BAYLEN   Could I . . .

ROMA   I'm going to have your *job*, shithead. I'm going *downtown* and talk to Mitch and Murray, and I'm going to Lemkin. I don't care *whose* nephew you are, who you know, whose dick you're sucking on. You're going *out*, I swear to you, you're going . . .

BAYLEN   Hey, fella, let's get this done . . .

ROMA   Anyone in this office lives on their *wits* . . . [*To* BAYLEN] I'm going to be with you in a second. [*To* WILLIAMSON] What you're hired for is to *help* us—does that seem clear to you? To *help* us. *Not* to fuck us up . . . to help *men* who are going *out* there to try to earn a *living*. You *fairy*. You company man . . . I'll tell you something else. I hope you knocked the joint off, I can tell our friend here something might help him catch you. [*Starts into the room.*] You want to learn the first rule you'd know if you ever spent a day in your life . . . you never open your mouth till you know what the shot is. [*Pause.*] You fucking *child* . . . [ROMA *goes to the inner room.*]

LEVENE   You *are* a shithead, Williamson . . . [*Pause.*]

WILLIAMSON   Mmm.

LEVENE   You can't think on your feet you should keep your mouth closed. [*Pause.*] You hear me? I'm *talking* to you. Do you hear me . . . ?

WILLIAMSON   Yes. [*Pause.*] I hear you.

LEVENE   You can't learn that in an office. Eh? He's right. You have to learn it on the streets. You can't *buy* that. You have to *live* it.

WILLIAMSON   Mmm.

LEVENE   *Yes*. Mmm. *Yes*. Precisely. Precisely. 'Cause your partner *depends* on it. [*Pause.*] I'm *talking* to you, I'm trying to tell you something.

WILLIAMSON   You are?

LEVENE   Yes, I am.

WILLIAMSON   What are you trying to tell me?

LEVENE   What Roma's trying to tell you. What I told you yesterday. Why you don't belong in this business.

WILLIAMSON   Why I don't . . .

LEVENE   You listen to me, someday you might say, "Hey . . ." No, fuck that, you just listen what I'm going to say: your partner *depends* on you. Your partner . . . a man who's your "partner" *depends* on you . . . you have to go *with* him and *for* him . . . or you're shit, you're *shit, you can't exist alone* . . .

WILLIAMSON   [*Brushing past him*]   Excuse me . . .

LEVENE   . . . excuse you, *nothing*, you be as cold as you want, but you just fucked a good man out of six thousand dollars and his goddamn bonus 'cause you didn't know the *shot*, you can do that and you aren't man enough that it gets you, then I don't know what, if you can't take *something* from that . . . [*Blocking his way*] you're *scum*, you're fucking white-bread. You be as cold as you want. A *child* would know it, he's right. [*Pause.*] You're going to make something up, be sure it will *help* or keep your mouth closed. [*Pause.*]

WILLIAMSON   Mmm. [LEVENE *lifts up his arm.*]

LEVENE   Now I'm done with you. [*Pause.*]

WILLIAMSON   How do you know I made it up?

LEVENE [*Pause.*]   What?

WILLIAMSON   How do you know I made it up?

LEVENE   What are you talking about?

WILLIAMSON   You said, "You don't make something up unless it's for sure to help." [*Pause.*] How did you know that I made it up?

LEVENE   What are you talking about?

WILLIAMSON   I told the customer that his contracts had gone to the bank.

LEVENE   Well, hadn't it?

WILLIAMSON   No. [*Pause.*] It hadn't.

LEVENE   Don't *fuck* with me, John, don't *fuck* with me . . . what are you saying?

WILLIAMSON   Well, I'm saying this, Shel: usually I take the contracts to the bank. Last night I didn't. How did you know that? One night in a year I left a contract on my desk. Nobody knew that but *you*. Now how did you know that? [*Pause.*] You want to talk to me, you want to talk to someone *else* . . . because this is *my* job. This is my job on the line, and you are going to *talk* to me. Now how did you know that contract was on my desk?

LEVENE   You're so full of shit.

WILLIAMSON   You robbed the office.

LEVENE [*Laughs*]   Sure! I robbed the office. Sure.

WILLIAMSON   What'd you do with the leads? [*Pause. Points to the* DETECTIVE's *room.*] You want to go in there? I tell him what I know, he's going to dig up *something* . . . You got an alibi last night? You better have one. What did you do with the leads? If you tell me what you did with the leads, we can talk.

LEVENE   I don't know what you are saying.

WILLIAMSON   If you tell me where the leads are, I won't turn you in. If you *don't*, I am going to tell the cop you stole them, Mitch and Murray will see that you go to jail. Believe me they will. Now, what did you do with the leads? I'm walking in that door—you have five seconds to tell me: or you are going to jail.

LEVENE   I . . .

WILLIAMSON   I don't care. You understand? *Where are the leads?* [*Pause.*] Alright. [WILLIAMSON *goes to open the office door.*]

LEVENE   I sold them to Jerry Graff.

WILLIAMSON   How much did you get for them? [*Pause.*] How much did you get for them?

LEVENE   Five thousand. I kept half.

WILLIAMSON   Who kept the other half? [*Pause.*]

LEVENE   Do I have to tell you? [*Pause.* WILLIAMSON *starts to open the door.*] Moss.

WILLIAMSON   *That* was easy, *wasn't* it? [*Pause.*]

LEVENE   I . . . I'm sure he got more than the five, actually.

WILLIAMSON   Uh-huh?

LEVENE   He told me my share was twenty-five.

WILLIAMSON   Mmm.

LEVENE   Okay: I . . . look: I'm going to make it worth your while. I am. I turned this thing around. I closed the *old* stuff, I can do it again. *I'm* the one's going to close 'em. *I* am! *I* am! 'Cause I turned this thing a . . . I can do *that*, can do *anyth* . . . last night. I'm going to tell you, I was ready to Do the Dutch. Moss gets me, "Do this, we'll get well . . ." Why not. Big fuckin' deal. I'm halfway hoping to get caught. To put me out of my . . . [*Pause.*] But it *taught* me something. What it taught me, that you've got to get *out* there. Big deal. So I wasn't cut out to be a thief. I was cut out to be a salesman. And now I'm back, and I got my *balls* back . . . and, you know, John, you have the *advantage* on me now. Whatever it takes to make it right, we'll make it right. We're going to make it right.

WILLIAMSON   I want to tell you something, Shelly. You have a big mouth. [*Pause.*]

LEVENE   What?

WILLIAMSON   You've got a big mouth, and now I'm going to show you an even bigger one. [*Starts toward the* DETECTIVE's *door.*]

LEVENE   Where are you going, John? . . . you can't do that, you don't want to do that . . . hold, hold on . . . hold on . . . wait . . . wait . . . wait . . . [*Starts splitting money.*] Look, twelve, twenty, two, twen . . . twenty-five hundred, it's . . . take it. [*Pause.*] Take it all . . . [*Pause.*] Take it!

WILLIAMSON   No, I don't think so, Shel.

LEVENE   I . . .

WILLIAMSON   No, I think I don't want your money. I think you fucked up my office. And I think you're going away.

LEVENE   I . . . what? Are you, are you, that's why you, I'm going to . . . [*Thrusting money at him.*] Here, here, I'm going to *make* this office . . . I'm going to be back there Number One . . . Hey, hey, hey! This is only the beginning . . . List . . . list . . . listen. Listen. Just one moment. List . . . here's what . . . here's what we're going to do. Twenty percent. I'm going to give you twenty percent of my sales. . . . [*Pause.*] Twenty percent. [*Pause.*] For as long as I am with the firm. [*Pause.*] Fifty percent. [*Pause.*] You're going to be my partner. [*Pause.*] Fifty percent. Of all my sales.

WILLIAMSON   What sales?

LEVENE   What sales . . . ? I just *closed* eighty-two grand. . . . Are you fuckin' . . . I'm *back* . . . I'm *back*, this is only the beginning.

WILLIAMSON   Only the beginning . . .

LEVENE   Abso . . .

WILLIAMSON   Where have you been, Shelly? Bruce and Harriett Nyborg. Do you want to see the *memos* . . . ? They're nuts . . . they used to call in every week. When I was with Webb. And we were selling Arizona . . . they're nuts . . . did you see how they were *living*? How can you delude yours . . .

LEVENE   I've got the check . . .

WILLIAMSON   Forget it. Frame it. It's worthless. [*Pause.*]

LEVENE   The check's no good?

WILLIAMSON   You stick around I'll pull the memo for you. [*Starts for the door.*] I'm busy now . . .

LEVENE   Their check's no good. They're nuts . . . ?

WILLIAMSON   I called them when we had the lead . . . four months ago. [*Pause.*] The people are insane. They just like talking to salesmen. [WIL-LIAMSON *starts for the door.*]

LEVENE Don't.

WILLIAMSON I'm sorry.

LEVENE *Why?*

WILLIAMSON Because I don't like you.

LEVENE John: John: . . . my *daughter* . . .

WILLIAMSON Fuck you. [ROMA *comes out of the* DETECTIVE's *door.* WIL-
LIAMSON *goes in.*]

ROMA [*To* BAYLEN] Asshole . . . [*To* LEVENE] Guy couldn't find his fuckin'
couch the *living room* . . . Ah, . . . what a day, what a day . . . I haven't
even had a cup of *coffee* . . . Jagoff John opens his mouth he blows my
Cadillac. . . . [*Sighs.*] I swear . . . it's not a world of men . . . it's not a
world of men, Machine . . . it's a world of clock watchers, bureaucrats,
officeholders . . . what it is, it's a fucked-up world . . . there's no adventure *to* it. [*Pause.*] Dying breed. Yes it is. [*Pause.*] We are the members of
a dying breed. That's . . . that's . . . that's why we have to stick together.
Shel: I want to talk to you. I've wanted to talk to you for some time. For
a long time, actually. I said, "The Machine, there's a man I would work
with. There's a man . . ." You know? I never said a thing. I should have,
don't know why I didn't. And that shit you were slinging on my guy
today was *so* good . . . it . . . it was, and, excuse me, 'cause it isn't even
my place to say it. It was admirable . . . it was the old stuff. Hey, I've
been on a hot streak, so *what?* There's things that I could learn from
you. You eat today?

LEVENE Me.

ROMA Yeah.

LEVENE Mm.

ROMA Well, you want to swing by the Chinks, watch me eat, we'll talk?

LEVENE I think I'd better stay here for a while.

[BAYLEN *sticks his head out of the room*]

BAYLEN Mr. *Levene* . . . ?

ROMA You're done, come down and let's . . .

BAYLEN Would you come in here, please?

ROMA And let's put this together. Okay? Shel? Say okay. [*Pause.*]

LEVENE [*Softly, to himself*] Huh.

BAYLEN Mr. Levene, I think we have to talk.

ROMA I'm going to the Chinks. You're done, come down, we're going to
smoke a cigarette.

LEVENE I . . .

BAYLEN [*Comes over*]   . . . Get in the room.

ROMA Hey, hey, hey, *easy* friend, That's the "Machine." That is Shelly
"The Machine" Lev . . .

BAYLEN Get in the goddamn room, [BAYLEN *starts manhandling* LEVENE
into the room.]

LEVENE Ricky, I . . .

ROMA Okay, okay, I'll be at the resta . . .

LEVENE Ricky . . .

BAYLEN "Ricky" can't help you, pal.

LEVENE   . . . I only want to . . .

BAYLEN Yeah. What do you want? You want to *what?* [*He pushes* LEVENE
into the room, closes the door behind him. Pause.]

ROMA   Williamson: listen to me: when the *leads* come in . . . listen to me: when the *leads* come in I want my top two off the list. For *me*. My usual two. Anything you give *Levene* . . .

WILLIAMSON   . . . I wouldn't worry about it.

ROMA   Well I'm *going* to worry about it, and so are you, so shut up and listen. [*Pause.*] I GET HIS ACTION. My stuff is *mine*, whatever *he* gets for himself, I'm taking half. You put me in with him. [AARONOW *enters.*]

AARONOW   Did they . . . ?

ROMA   You understand?

AARONOW   Did they catch . . . ?

ROMA   Do you understand? My stuff is mine, his stuff is ours. I'm taking half of his commissions—now, *you* work it out.

WILLIAMSON   Mmm.

AARONOW   Did they find the guy who broke into the office yet?

ROMA   No. *I* don't know. [*Pause.*]

AARONOW   Did the leads come in yet?

ROMA   No.

AARONOW [*Settling into a desk chair*]   Oh, god, I hate this job.

ROMA [*Simultaneous with "job," exiting the office*]   I'll be at the restaurant.

1984

YUSEF KOMUNYAKAA
b. 1947

The excavation of lost names is one of the driving impulses of Yusef Komunyakaa's work. His poems recover and reanimate figures from history such as the African American elevator operator, Thomas McKeller, who appears in a stunning portrait by John Singer Sargent ("Nude Study"). In researching the portrait, Komunyakaa learned that it had been "unearthed in Sargent's studio after his death" and that "McKeller's image had been cannibalized to depict [the ancient Greek and Roman god] Apollo and a bas-relief of [the ancient Greek poet and musician] Arion—other heads and lines grafted onto his classical physique." Komunyakaa's work continually questions and revises both the cultural contradictions projected onto the black body and the erasure of black presence from history and culture. Significantly, he adopted the lost surname of a Trinidadian grandfather who came to the United States as a child, "smuggled in like a sack of papaya / On a banana boat." As the poet recounts in "Mismatched Shoes," his grandfather's "true name" disappeared in the process of assimilation. After his death his grandson "slipped into his skin" and took back the name "Komunyakaa," in what the poet calls "an affirmation of my heritage and its ambiguity."

Komunyakaa was born in Bogalusa, Louisiana, seventy miles northeast of New Orleans. Bogalusa means "Magic City" (a phrase that became the title of his 1992 collection of poems), and a lush, semitropical landscape informs many of his poems. But as the oldest of six children, and as the son of a carpenter who could write only his name, Komunyakaa grew up in an impoverished neighborhood and experienced a racial inequity that coexisted with natural beauty. At a young age, he has said, he decided that "imagination could serve as a choice of weapons."

Because the military seemed to offer a way into a larger world, Komunyakaa enlisted in the army and was sent to Vietnam, where he served as a war correspondent and editor of the military newspaper, writing accounts of what he witnessed in combat. For his work he was awarded the Bronze Star. While in Vietnam he carried with him several anthologies of poetry, but only after his military service ended did he begin to write poems, studying at the University of Colorado and then at the University of California at Irvine, where his teachers included Charles Wright and C. K. Williams. In 1984, fourteen years after his tour of duty ended, Komunyakaa began to write poems about his war experience. From his father he had learned to build and renovate houses; as he works, he has said, he keeps a pad of paper close by. While renovating a house in New Orleans he began to write down images and lines about Vietnam and so began the first in what became a series of poems about his Vietnam experience. These were collected in *Dien Cai Dau* (1988), whose title (meaning "crazy") is a Vietnamese phrase used to describe American soldiers. In one of these poems, "Facing It," he sees his own "clouded reflection" in the "black granite" of the Vietnam War Memorial designed by Maya Lin, an image of which appears in the color insert of this anthology.

To write about his surreal wartime experiences Komunyakaa drew on the work of surrealists like the French poet and critic André Breton. Komunyakaa shares with these writers and artists an emphasis on the image as linked to the unconscious, and his poems often work through a series of short lines whose quick, associative images bypass logic. A surrealist impulse to distort the familiar and juxtapose beauty and violence appears in Komunyakaa's Vietnam poems and in the racial and erotic tensions of poems like "Jasmine" (from *The Pleasure Dome*, 2001). An emphasis on the dreamlike, irrational, and fantastic was already apparent in his first two books, *Copacetic* (1984) and *I Apologize for the Eyes in My Head* (1986), both of which also reflect the musical influences of his native Louisiana.

Growing up so close to New Orleans brought Komunyakaa in early contact with jazz and the blues. The title of his first book, *Copacetic*, is a term adapted by jazz musicians from the African American tap dancer Bill "Bojangles" Robinson; in jazz it refers to especially pleasing and mellow music. Like Langston Hughes, Komunyakaa explores throughout his work the power of music—blues, jazz, and poetry—to address and, in part, to heal the pain of living in a racially divided society. The rapid energy of poems like "Facing It" and "Slam, Dunk, & Hook" belong to what the poet calls a "felt and lived syncopation," a rhythm of shifting beats that bears the influence of musicians like Charlie Parker, John Coltrane, and Miles Davis. Komunyakaa also works in tighter formal structures, whose exactness and precision suggest the careful measuring and fitting of carpentry. The quatrains of *Talking Dirty to the Gods* (2000) and the three-line stanzas of *Taboo* (2004) provide what the poet calls "an illusion of control" over volatile and complicated social and psychic material. They reflect Komunyakaa's preferred poetic strategy of "insinuation and nuance." Although his work often looks unflinchingly at what otherwise is hidden or denied, the social, racial, or erotic context of a poem often emerges in details or images, rather than in direct description. *Warhorses* (2008) continues this poet's ongoing investigation of war and violence.

Komunyakaa coedited with J. A. Sascha Feinstein a two-volume collection, *The Jazz Poetry Anthology* (1991) and *Second Set* (1996), and has also been extensively involved in collaborations with jazz musicians and vocalists. His poetry has received numerous awards, among them both the Pulitzer Prize and the Kingsley Tuft Poetry Award for *Neon Vernacular: New and Selected Poems 1977–1989* (1994). He is a professor in the Council of Humanities and Creative Writing Program at Princeton University.

Facing It

My black face fades,
hiding inside the black granite.
I said I wouldn't
dammit: No tears.
I'm stone. I'm flesh.   5
My clouded reflection eyes me
like a bird of prey, the profile of night
slanted against morning. I turn
this way—the stone lets me go.
I turn that way—I'm inside   10
the Vietnam Veterans Memorial[1]
again, depending on the light
to make a difference.
I go down the 58,022 names,
half-expecting to find   15
my own in letters like smoke.
I touch the name Andrew Johnson;
I see the booby trap's white flash.
Names shimmer on a woman's blouse
but when she walks away   20
the names stay on the wall.
Brushstrokes flash, a red bird's
wings cutting across my stare.
The sky. A plane in the sky.
A white vet's image floats   25
closer to me, then his pale eyes
look through mine. I'm a window.
He's lost his right arm
inside the stone. In the black mirror
a woman's trying to erase names: 30
No, she's brushing a boy's hair.

1988

My Father's Love Letters

On Fridays he'd open a can of Jax[1]
After coming home from the mill,
& ask me to write a letter to my mother
Who sent postcards of desert flowers
Taller than men. He would beg,   5
Promising to never beat her
Again. Somehow I was happy

---

1. An image of the Vietnam War Memorial in
Washington, D.C., designed by the architect
Maya Lin and dedicated in 1982, appears in the
color insert of this anthology.
1. A beer originally brewed in New Orleans,
Louisiana.

She had gone, & sometimes wanted
To slip in a reminder, how Mary Lou
Williams' "Polka Dots & Moonbeams"[2]   10
Never made the swelling go down.
His carpenter's apron always bulged
With old nails, a claw hammer
Looped at his side & extension cords
Coiled around his feet.   15
Words rolled from under the pressure
Of my ballpoint: Love,
Baby, Honey, Please.
We sat in the quiet brutality
Of voltage meters & pipe threaders,   20
Lost between sentences . . .
The gleam of a five-pound wedge
On the concrete floor
Pulled a sunset
Through the doorway of his toolshed.   25
I wondered if she laughed
& held them over a gas burner.
My father could only sign
His name, but he'd look at blueprints
& say how many bricks   30
Formed each wall. This man,
Who stole roses & hyacinth
For his yard, would stand there
With eyes closed & fists balled,
Laboring over a simple word, almost   35
Redeemed by what he tried to say.

1992

Slam, Dunk, & Hook

Fast breaks. Lay ups. With Mercury's
Insignia[1] on our sneakers,
We outmaneuvered to footwork
Of bad angels. Nothing but a hot
Swish of strings like silk   5
Ten feet out. In the roundhouse
Labyrinth our bodies
Created, we could almost
Last forever, poised in midair
Like storybook sea monsters.   10
A high note hung there

2. The American jazz pianist Mary Lou Williams (1910–1981) performed with and composed for many of the great jazz artists of the 1940s and 1950s. The song "Polka Dots and Moonbeams" (1940) was composed by Jimmy Van Heusen (1913–1990) and Johnny Burke (1908–1964).

1. Mercury, the messenger of the ancient Greek gods, is depicted wearing winged sandals.

A long second. Off
The rim. We'd corkscrew
Up & dunk balls that exploded
The skullcap of hope & good   15
Intention. Lanky, all hands
& feet . . . sprung rhythm.[2]
We were metaphysical when girls
Cheered on the sidelines.
Tangled up in a falling,   20
Muscles were a bright motor
Double-flashing to the metal hoop
Nailed to our oak.
When Sonny Boy's mama died
He played nonstop all day, so hard   25
Our backboard splintered.
Glistening with sweat,
We rolled the ball off
Our fingertips. Trouble
Was there slapping a blackjack[3]   30
Against an open palm.
Dribble, drive to the inside,
& glide like a sparrow hawk.[4]
Lay ups. Fast breaks.
We had moves we didn't know   35
We had. Our bodies spun
On swivels of bone & faith,
Through a lyric slipknot
Of joy, & we knew we were
Beautiful & dangerous.   40

1992

From Song for My Father

[*Sometimes you could be*]

Sometimes you could be
That man on a red bicycle,
With me on the handlebars,
Just rolling along a country road
On the edge of July, honeysuckle   5
Lit with mosquito hawks.[1]
We rode from under the shady
Overhang, back into sunlight.
The day bounced off car hoods

---

2. "Sprung rhythm" is a term used by the English poet Gerard Manley Hopkins (1844–1889) to describe a poetic meter with a variable rather than fixed number of syllables in each poetic foot.

3. A small leather-covered bludgeon.
4. One of the best-known, handsomest, and smallest North American hawks.
1. In the American South, a term for dragonflies, which eat mosquitos and other small insects.

As the heat & stinking exhaust   10
Brushed against us like a dragon's
Roar, nudging the bike with a tremor,
But you steered us through the flowering
Dogwood like a thread of blood.

1993

When Dusk Weighs Daybreak

I want Catullus[1]
In every line, a barb
The sun plays for good
Luck. I need to know if iron

Tastes like laudanum[2]   5
Or a woman. I already sense
What sleeps in the same flesh,
Ariadne & her half brother[3]

Caught in the other's dream.
I want each question to fit me   10
Like a shiny hook, a lure
In the gullet. What it is

To look & know how much muscle
It takes to lift a green slab.
I need a Son House blues[4]   15
To wear out my tongue.

2000

Jasmine

I sit beside two women, kitty-corner
to the stage, as Elvin's[1] sticks blur
the club into a blue fantasia.
I thought my body had forgotten the Deep
South, how I'd cross the street   5
if a woman like these two walked
towards me, as if a cat traversed

1. Gaius Valerius Catullus (c. 86–c. 54 B.C.E.), Roman poet who wittily expressed love and hate in some of the finest lyric poetry of his time.
2. An opium-based painkiller.
3. In Greek mythology Ariadne was the daughter of Pasiphaë and the Cretan king, Minos. She fell in love with the Athenian hero Theseus and helped him escape the Labyrinth after he slew her half-brother, the Minotaur, a beast half bull and half man.
4. Eddie James House Jr. (1902–1988), better known as "Son," American blues singer and guitarist regarded as an epitome of the Delta blues tradition.
1. Elvin Jones (1927–2004), American jazz drummer and bandleader.

my path beneath the evening star.
Which one is wearing jasmine?
If my grandmothers saw me now   10
they'd say, Boy, the devil never sleeps.
My mind is lost among November
cotton flowers, a soft rain on my face
as Richard Davis[2] plucks the fat notes
of chance on his upright   15
leaning into the future.
The blonde, the brunette—
which one is scented with jasmine?
I can hear Duke in the right hand
& Basie in the left[3]   20
as the young piano player
nudges us into the past.
The trumpet's almost kissed
by enough pain. Give him a few more years,
a few more ghosts to embrace—Clifford's[4]   25
shadow on the edge of the stage.
The sign says, *No Talking.*
Elvin's guardian angel lingers
at the top of the stairs,
counting each drop of sweat   30
paid in tribute. The blonde
has her eyes closed, & the brunette
is looking at me. Our bodies
sway to each riff, the jasmine
rising from a valley somewhere   35
in Egypt, a white moon
opening countless false mouths
of laughter. The midnight
gatherers are boys & girls
with the headlights of trucks   40
aimed at their backs, because
their small hands refuse to wound
the knowing scent hidden in each bloom.

                                                          2001

Nude Study[1]

Someone lightly brushed the penis
   alive. Belief is almost
   flesh. Wings beat,

---

2. American bassist (b. 1930) known for his jazz sessions in an all-star small group at New York City's Village Vanguard under the rubric "Jazz for a Sunday Afternoon."
3. Duke Ellington (1899–1974), American pianist and bandleader who was also one of the greatest jazz composers. Count Basie (1904–1984), American jazz pianist and bandleader.

4. Clifford Brown (1930–1956), American jazz trumpeter noted for his graceful technique.
1. *Nude Study of Thomas E. McKeller* (1917–20?), a portrait by the American painter John Singer Sargent (1856–1925), hangs in the Museum of Fine Arts, Boston. McKeller was an African American elevator operator. The portrait was found in Sargent's studio after his death.

dust trying to breathe, as if the figure
  might rise from the oils   5
  & flee the dead

artist's studio. For years
  this piece of work was there
  like a golden struggle

shadowing Thomas McKeller, a black   10
  elevator operator at the Boston
  Copley Plaza Hotel, a friend

of John Singer Sargent—hidden
  among sketches & drawings, a model
  for Apollo & a bas-relief   15

of Arion.[2] So much taken
  for granted & denied, only
  grace & mutability

can complete this face belonging
  to Greek bodies castrated   20
  with a veil of dust.

2004

2. Ancient Greek poet and musician. "Apollo": the sun god in ancient Greek and Roman mythology.

LESLIE MARMON SILKO
b. 1948

Born in Albuquerque, New Mexico, Leslie Marmon Silko was raised in Old Laguna, a village fifty miles west of Albuquerque. The Spaniards had founded a mission there early in the eighteenth century, but Old Laguna had been formed centuries earlier by cattle-keeping Pueblos who successfully repelled raids on them by the Navajos and the Apaches. Writing of the unchanging character of Pueblo religious practices over the centuries, the historian Joe S. Sando notes that "the tradition of religious beliefs permeates every aspect of the people's life; it determines man's relation with the natural world and with his fellow man. Its basic concern is continuity of a harmonious relationship with the world in which man lives."

Silko's work addresses such matters. Her own heritage is complicated in that her great-grandfather Robert Marmon was white, whereas her mother was a mixed-blood Plains Indian who kept her daughter on the traditional cradle board during her first year of infancy. (Her ancestry also includes some Mexican blood.) Silko has made this heritage a source of strength. She writes: "I suppose at the core of my writing is the attempt to identify what it is to be a half-breed or mixed-blooded person; what it is to grow up neither white nor fully traditional Indian." At the same time she insists that "what I know is Laguna. This place I am from is everything I am as a writer and human being." An active child, Silko had a horse of her own by age eight, and by thirteen she owned a rifle, with which she took part in deer hunts. Commuting to Albuquerque, she attended Catholic schools, earned a B.A. at the University of New Mexico, then began law school under a special program for Native Americans, though she soon gave it up to become a writer and teacher.

Her first published story, "The Man to Send Rain Clouds" (1969), came out of a writing assignment in college. She had heard, in Laguna, of an old man who died in a sheep camp and was given a traditional native burial—a fact resented by the Catholic priest who was not called in. The story she wrote about this situation, published in the *New Mexico Quarterly*, put her on the road to success as a writer. In 1974 a selection of her poems was published in the volume *Laguna Woman*, and in 1977 her novel *Ceremony* brought her recognition as a leading voice among Native American writers. *Ceremony* shows the dark aspects of modern American Indian life, focusing on a World War II veteran who is in acute physical and emotional straits as the novel begins, but who manages to survive by reestablishing contact with his native roots. Silko has insisted that the book is not just or even mainly about characters: "This novel is essentially about the powers inherent in the process of storytelling. . . . The chanting or telling of ancient stories to effect certain cures or protect from illness and harm has always been a part of the Pueblo's curing ceremonies." So this story of a family represents an attempt "to search for a ceremony to deal with despair"—the despair that has led to the "suicide, the alcoholism, and the violence which occur in so many Indian communities today."

Thus a strong moral connection exists between Silko's purely aesthetic delight in the writing of a story and the therapeutic, functional uses she hopes the story will play in the Native American community. In *Ceremony*, the aptly titled 1981 collection *Storyteller* (which also contains poems and photographs), and her epic 1991 novel, *Almanac of the Dead*, Silko's prose is an expressive, active presence, sympathetically creating landscape as well as animals and human beings. Plants assume narrative status in her third novel, *Gardens in the Dunes* (1999), which looks back to late-nineteenth-century events to underscore a basic theme: that myth and history do not coincide.

The following text is from *Storyteller* (1981).

Lullaby

The sun had gone down but the snow in the wind gave off its own light. It came in thick tufts like new wool—washed before the weaver spins it. Ayah reached out for it like her own babies had, and she smiled when she remembered how she had laughed at them. She was an old woman now, and her life had become memories. She sat down with her back against the wide cottonwood tree, feeling the rough bark on her back bones; she faced east and listened to the wind and snow sing a high-pitched Yeibechei[1] song. Out of the wind she felt warmer, and she could watch the wide fluffy snow fill in her tracks, steadily, until the direction she had come from was gone. By the light of the snow she could see the dark outline of the big arroyo[2] a few feet away. She was sitting on the edge of Cebolleta Creek, where in the springtime the thin cows would graze on grass already chewed flat to the ground.

---

1. Navajo dance.

2. Gully carved by water.

In the wide deep creek bed where only a trickle of water flowed in the summer, the skinny cows would wander, looking for new grass along winding paths splashed with manure.

Ayah pulled the old Army blanket over her head like a shawl. Jimmie's blanket—the one he had sent to her. That was a long time ago and the green wool was faded, and it was unraveling on the edges. She did not want to think about Jimmie. So she thought about the weaving and the way her mother had done it. On the wall wooden loom set into the sand under a tamarack tree for shade. She could see it clearly. She had been only a little girl when her grandma gave her the wooden combs to pull the twigs and burrs from the raw, freshly washed wool. And while she combed the wool, her grandma sat beside her, spinning a silvery strand of yarn around the smooth cedar spindle. Her mother worked at the loom with yarns dyed bright yellow and red and gold. She watched them dye the yarn in boiling black pots full of beeweed petals, juniper berries, and sage. The blankets her mother made were soft and woven so tight that rain rolled off them like birds' feathers. Ayah remembered sleeping warm on cold windy nights, wrapped in her mother's blankets on the hogan's[3] sandy floor.

The snow drifted now, with the northwest wind hurling it in gusts. It drifted up around her black overshoes—old ones with little metal buckles. She smiled at the snow which was trying to cover her little by little. She could remember when they had no black rubber overshoes; only the high buckskin leggings that they wrapped over their elkhide moccasins. If the snow was dry or frozen, a person could walk all day and not get wet; and in the evenings the beams of the ceiling would hang with lengths of pale buckskin leggings, drying out slowly.

She felt peaceful remembering. She didn't feel cold any more. Jimmie's blanket seemed warmer than it had ever been. And she could remember the morning he was born. She could remember whispering to her mother, who was sleeping on the other side of the hogan, to tell her it was time now. She did not want to wake the others. The second time she called to her, her mother stood up and pulled on her shoes; she knew. They walked to the old stone hogan together, Ayah walking a step behind her mother. She waited alone, learning the rhythms of the pains while her mother went to call the old woman to help them. The morning was already warm even before dawn and Ayah smelled the bee flowers blooming and the young willow growing at the springs. She could remember that so clearly, but his birth merged into the births of the other children and to her it became all the same birth. They named him for the summer morning and in English they called him Jimmie.

It wasn't like Jimmie died. He just never came back, and one day a dark blue sedan with white writing on its doors pulled up in front of the boxcar shack where the rancher let the Indians live. A man in a khaki uniform trimmed in gold gave them a yellow piece of paper and told them that Jimmie was dead. He said the Army would try to get the body back and then it would be shipped to them; but it wasn't likely because the helicopter had burned after it crashed. All of this was told to Chato because he could understand English. She stood inside the doorway holding the baby while

---

3. Navajo dwelling usually made of logs and mud.

Chato listened. Chato spoke English like a white man and he spoke Spanish too. He was taller than the white man and he stood straighter too. Chato didn't explain why; he just told the military man they could keep the body if they found it. The white man looked bewildered; he nodded his head and he left. Then Chato looked at her and shook his head, and then he told her, "Jimmie isn't coming home anymore," and when he spoke, he used the words to speak of the dead. She didn't cry then, but she hurt inside with anger. And she mourned him as the years passed, when a horse fell with Chato and broke his leg, and the white rancher told them he wouldn't pay Chato until he could work again. She mourned Jimmie because he would have worked for his father then; he would have saddled the big bay horse and ridden the fence lines each day, with wire cutters and heavy gloves, fixing the breaks in the barbed wire and putting the stray cattle back inside again.

She mourned him after the white doctors came to take Danny and Ella away. She was at the shack alone that day they came. It was back in the days before they hired Navajo women to go with them as interpreters. She recognized one of the doctors. She had seen him at the children's clinic at Cañoncito about a month ago. They were wearing khaki uniforms and they waved papers at her and a black ball-point pen, trying to make her understand their English words. She was frightened by the way they looked at the children, like the lizard watches the fly. Danny was swinging on the tire swing on the elm tree behind the rancher's house, and Ella was toddling around the front door, dragging the broomstick horse Chato made for her. Ayah could see they wanted her to sign the papers, and Chato had taught her to sign her name. It was something she was proud of. She only wanted them to go, and to take their eyes away from her children.

She took the pen from the man without looking at his face and she signed the papers in three different places he pointed to. She stared at the ground by their feet and waited for them to leave. But they stood there and began to point and gesture at the children. Danny stopped swinging. Ayah could see his fear. She moved suddenly and grabbed Ella into her arms; the child squirmed, trying to get back to her toys. Ayah ran with the baby toward Danny; she screamed for him to run and then she grabbed him around his chest and carried him too. She ran south into the foothills of juniper trees and black lava rock. Behind her she heard the doctors running, but they had been taken by surprise, and as the hills became steeper and the cholla cactus were thicker, they stopped. When she reached the top of the hill, she stopped to listen in case they were circling around her. But in a few minutes she heard a car engine start and they drove away. The children had been too surprised to cry while she ran with them. Danny was shaking and Ella's little fingers were gripping Ayah's blouse.

She stayed up in the hills for the rest of the day, sitting on a black lava boulder in the sunshine where she could see for miles all around her. The sky was light blue and cloudless, and it was warm for late April. The sun warmth relaxed her and took the fear and anger away. She lay back on the rock and watched the sky. It seemed to her that she could walk into the sky, stepping through clouds endlessly. Danny played with little pebbles and stones, pretending they were birds eggs and then little rabbits. Ella sat at her feet and dropped fistfuls of dirt into the breeze, watching the dust and particles of sand intently. Ayah watched a hawk soar high above them, dark wings gliding; hunting or only watching, she did not know. The hawk was patient and he circled all afternoon before he disappeared around the high volcanic peak the Mexicans called Guadalupe.

Late in the afternoon, Ayah looked down at the gray boxcar shack with the paint all peeled from the wood; the stove pipe on the roof was rusted and crooked. The fire she had built that morning in the oil drum stove had burned out. Ella was asleep in her lap now and Danny sat close to her, complaining that he was hungry; he asked when they would go to the house. "We will stay up here until your father comes," she told him, "because those white men were chasing us." The boy remembered then and he nodded at her silently.

If Jimmie had been there he could have read those papers and explained to her what they said. Ayah would have known then, never to sign them. The doctors came back the next day and they brought a BIA[4] policeman with them. They told Chato they had her signature and that was all they needed. Except for the kids. She listened to Chato sullenly; she hated him when he told her it was the old woman who died in the winter, spitting blood; it was her old grandma who had given the children this disease. "They don't spit blood," she said coldly. "The whites lie." She held Ella and Danny close to her, ready to run to the hills again. "I want a medicine man first," she said to Chato, not looking at him. He shook his head. "It's too late now. The policeman is with them. You signed the paper." His voice was gentle.

It was worse than if they had died: to lose the children and to know that somewhere, in a place called Colorado, in a place full of sick and dying strangers, her children were without her. There had been babies that died soon after they were born, and one that died before he could walk. She had carried them herself, up to the boulders and great pieces of the cliff that long ago crashed down from Long Mesa; she laid them in the crevices of sandstone and buried them in fine brown sand with round quartz pebbles that washed down the hills in the rain. She had endured it because they had been with her. But she could not bear this pain. She did not sleep for a long time after they took her children. She stayed on the hill where they had fled the first time, and she slept rolled up in the blanket Jimmie had sent her. She carried the pain in her belly and it was fed by everything she saw: the blue sky of their last day together and the dust and pebbles they played with; the swing in the elm tree and broomstick horse choked life from her. The pain filled her stomach and there was no room for food or for her lungs to fill with air. The air and the food would have been theirs.

She hated Chato, not because he let the policeman and doctors put the screaming children in the government car, but because he had taught her to sign her name. Because it was like the old ones always told her about learning their language or any of their ways: it endangered you. She slept alone on the hill until the middle of November when the first snows came. Then she made a bed for herself where the children had slept. She did not lie down beside Chato again until many years later, when he was sick and shivering and only her body could keep him warm. The illness came after the white rancher told Chato he was too old to work for him anymore, and Chato and his old woman should be out of the shack by the next afternoon

---

4. Bureau of Indian Affairs, an agency of the U.S. government charged with assisting the tribal authorities of reservations.

because the rancher had hired new people to work there. That had satisfied her. To see how the white man repaid Chato's years of loyalty and work. All of Chato's fine-sounding English talk didn't change things.

It snowed steadily and the luminous light from the snow gradually diminished into the darkness. Somewhere in Cebolleta a dog barked and other village dogs joined with it. Ayah looked in the direction she had come, from the bar where Chato was buying the wine. Sometimes he told her to go on ahead and wait; and then he never came. And when she finally went back looking for him, she would find him passed out at the bottom of the wooden steps to Azzie's Bar. All the wine would be gone and most of the money too, from the pale blue check that came to them once a month in a government envelope. It was then that she would look at his face and his hands, scarred by ropes and the barbed wire of all those years, and she would think, this man is a stranger; for forty years she had smiled at him and cooked his food, but he remained a stranger. She stood up again, with the snow almost to her knees, and she walked back to find Chato.

It was hard to walk in the deep snow and she felt the air burn in her lungs. She stopped a short distance from the bar to rest and readjust the blanket. But this time he wasn't waiting for her on the bottom step with his old Stetson hat pulled down and his shoulders hunched up in his long wool overcoat.

She was careful not to slip on the wooden steps. When she pushed the door open, warm air and cigarette smoke hit her face. She looked around slowly and deliberately, in every corner, in every dark place that the old man might find to sleep. The bar owner didn't like Indians in there, especially Navajos, but he let Chato come in because he could talk Spanish like he was one of them. The men at the bar stared at her, and the bartender saw that she left the door open wide. Snowflakes were flying inside like moths and melting into a puddle on the oiled wood floor. He motioned to her to close the door, but she did not see him. She held herself straight and walked across the room slowly, searching the room with every step. The snow in her hair melted and she could feel it on her forehead. At the far corner of the room, she saw red flames at the mica window of the old stove door; she looked behind the stove just to make sure. The bar got quiet except for the Spanish polka music playing on the jukebox. She stood by the stove and shook the snow from her blanket and held it near the stove to dry. The wet wool smell reminded her of new-born goats in early March, brought inside to warm near the fire. She felt calm.

In past years they would have told her to get out. But her hair was white now and her face was wrinkled. They looked at her like she was a spider crawling slowly across the room. They were afraid; she could feel the fear. She looked at their faces steadily. They reminded her of the first time the white people brought her children back to her that winter. Danny had been shy and hid behind the thin white woman who brought them. And the baby had not known her until Ayah took her into her arms, and then Ella had nuzzled close to her as she had when she was nursing. The blonde woman was nervous and kept looking at a dainty gold watch on her wrist. She sat on the bench near the small window and watched the dark snow clouds gather around the mountains; she was worrying about the unpaved road. She was frightened by what she saw inside too: the strips of venison drying on a rope across the ceiling and the children jabbering excitedly in a language she did not know. So they stayed for only a few hours. Ayah watched the government car disappear down the road and she knew they were already being weaned from these lava hills and from this sky. The last time they came was in early June, and Ella stared at her the way the men in the bar were now staring. Ayah did not try to pick her up; she smiled at her instead and spoke cheerfully to Danny. When he tried to answer her, he could not seem to remember and he spoke English words with the Navajo. But he gave her a scrap of paper that he had found somewhere and carried in his pocket; it was folded in half, and he shyly looked up at her and said it was a bird. She asked Chato if they were home for good this time. He spoke to the white woman and she shook her head. "How much longer?" he asked, and she said she didn't know; but Chato saw how she stared at the box-car shack. Ayah turned away then. She did not say good-bye.

She felt satisfied that the men in the bar feared her. Maybe it was her face and the way she held her mouth with teeth clenched tight, like there was nothing anyone could do to her now. She walked north down the road, searching for the old man. She did this because she had the blanket, and there would be no place for him except with her and the blanket in the old adobe barn near the arroyo. They always slept there when they came to Cebolleta. If the money and the wine were gone, she would be relieved because then they could go home again; back to the old hogan with a dirt roof and rock walls where she herself had been born. And the next day the old man could go back to the few sheep they still had, to follow along behind them, guiding them, into dry sandy arroyos where sparse grass grew. She knew he did not like walking behind old ewes when for so many years he rode big quarter horses and worked with cattle. But she wasn't sorry for him; he should have known all along what would happen.

There had not been enough rain for their garden in five years; and that was when Chato finally hitched a ride into the town and brought back brown boxes of rice and sugar and big tin cans of welfare peaches. After that, at the first of the month they went to Cebolleta to ask the postmaster for the check; and then Chato would go to the bar and cash it. They did this as they planted the garden every May, not because anything would survive the summer dust, but because it was time to do this. The journey passed the days that smelled silent and dry like the caves above the canyon with yellow painted buffaloes on their walls.

He was walking along the pavement when she found him. He did not stop or turn around when he heard her behind him. She walked beside him and she noticed how slowly he moved now. He smelled strongly of woodsmoke and urine. Lately he had been forgetting. Sometimes he called her by his sister's name and she had been gone for a long time. Once she had found him wandering on the road to the white man's ranch, and she asked him why he was going that way; he laughed at her and said, "You know they can't run that ranch without me," and he walked on determined, limping on the leg that had been crushed many years before. Now he looked at her curiously, as if for the first time, but he kept shuffling along, moving slowly along the side of the highway. His gray hair had grown long and spread out on the shoulders of the long overcoat. He wore the old felt hat pulled down over his ears. His boots were worn out at the toes and he had stuffed pieces of an old red shirt in the holes. The rags made his feet look like little animals up to their ears in snow. She laughed at his feet; the snow muffled the sound of her laugh. He stopped and looked at her again. The wind had quit blowing and the snow was falling straight down; the southeast sky was beginning to clear and Ayah could see a star.

"Let's rest awhile," she said to him. They walked away from the road and up the slope to the giant boulders that had tumbled down from the red sandrock mesa throughout the centuries of rainstorms and earth tremors. In a place where the boulders shut out the wind, they sat down with their backs against the rock. She offered half of the blanket to him and they sat wrapped together.

The storm passed swiftly. The clouds moved east. They were massive and full, crowding together across the sky. She watched them with the feeling of horses—steely blue-gray horses startled across the sky. The powerful haunches pushed into the distances and the tail hairs streamed white mist behind them. The sky cleared. Ayah saw that there was nothing between her and the stars. The light was crystalline. There was no shimmer, no distortion through earth haze. She breathed the clarity of the night sky; she smelled the purity of the half moon and the stars. He was lying on his side with his knees pulled up near his belly for warmth. His eyes were closed now, and in the light from the stars and the moon, he looked young again.

She could see it descend out of the night sky: an icy stillness from the edge of the thin moon. She recognized the freezing. It came gradually, sinking snowflake by snowflake until the crust was heavy and deep. It had the strength of the stars in Orion, and its journey was endless. Ayah knew that with the wine he would sleep. He would not feel it. She tucked the blanket around him, remembering how it was when Ella had been with her; and she felt the rush so big inside her heart for the babies. And she sang the only song she knew to sing for babies. She could not remember if she had ever sung it to her children, but she knew that her grandmother had sung it and her mother had sung it:

> The earth is your mother,
>   she holds you.
> The sky is your father,
>   he protects you.
> Sleep,
> sleep.
> Rainbow is your sister,
>   she loves you.
> The winds are your brothers,
>   they sing to you.
> Sleep,
> sleep.
> We are together always
> We are together always
> There never was a time
> when this
> was not so.

1981

ART SPIEGELMAN
b. 1948

Comic panels have existed since the end of the nineteenth century, beginning with Richard F. Outcault's *The Yellow Kid* in 1895. By the 1920s panels had evolved into strips—George Herriman's *Krazy Kat* was the most famous—and by the end of the 1930s these strips had grown into comic books, most successfully with the *Superman* series produced by Jerry Siegel and Joe Schuster. It would take the cultural transformations of the 1960s, however, for this trend of interweaving visual elements with an expanding sense of narrative to achieve literary form. As opposed to simple entertainment, literature involves, on a genuinely cultural level, both expression and reflection, comprising the beliefs and practices of a people. In the 1960s, as long-established beliefs and practices were challenged and to some extent changed, comic-book art found itself uniquely positioned as an underground form ready to disrupt a traditional, more conservative order.

How underground comics became graphic novels is apparent from Art Spiegelman's career. A college dropout, Spiegelman found his first work in the most elemental form of cartoon humor, the illustrations for cards and stickers packaged with bubblegum and marketed as Wacky Packages and Garbage Pail Kids, a basely satirical form of 1960s counterculture created in the New York design studios of Topps and other novelty companies. When in 1970 Spiegelman moved from New York to San Francisco, his work progressed from novelty to subversion—of the comic-strip form and of larger cultural themes. Cartoonist R. Crumb had recently developed *Zap Comix* as a way of replacing convention with creation, both in the way comics were drawn and in the subjects they treated. Spiegelman's affinity was with the second wave of this movement, including the Zippy comics drawn by Bill Griffin, in which sequential art pushed common limits to be boldly experimental. Here older practices were turned against themselves, with action breaking out of frames, narratives interrogating themselves, and characters challenging all standards of social acceptability.

Spiegelman's return to New York prompted the key development in his work and emergence as a graphic novelist. Married to the artist and designer Françoise Mouly in 1977 and beginning a family, Spiegelman paid new attention to his father's stories about the signal event in the elder Spiegelmans' lives, the Holocaust. As Polish Jews who had been persecuted and imprisoned at Auschwitz, where their first son died, the Spiegelmans had emigrated first to Sweden (where Art was born three years after the war's end) and then to the United States, settling in the Rego Park neighborhood of Queens, New York City, and becoming naturalized American citizens. His parents' cultural transformation was greater than any Spiegelman had experienced in the 1960s, and he sought the artistic tools to represent it. In 1978 Will Eisner had taken comic books to a new level of expression by arguing theological matters in *A Contract with God*—the type of work that could be sold in bookstores rather than just on newsstands. But by applying his cartoonist's serial-narrative skills to his father's experiences, Siegelman gave the graphic novel literary importance.

Maus I (1986) and *Maus II* (1991) are complex creations, enfolding not just the father's tale but also his act of telling it, both of which are measured by the son's reception. Their handling of the Holocaust, a subject of countless previous treatments and certain to endure as one of humanity's major stories, as a cartoon adds great imaginative dimension. Thanks to a suggestive set of references, with Jews as mice (victims of prey), Germans as cats (predators of mice), French as frogs (a reminder of the self-conscious vulgarity of older comic strips), and Poles as pigs (a dietary contrast with Jews, but also a calculated insult), graphic representation gives new facets to a familiar story. Cartooning by nature involves a great amount of artistic license. Parameters of taste are much more elastic than those for fiction, poetry, and all but the most performative of drama, while the form's roots in popular culture continue to show despite the bleachings of high taste.

Even in becoming a countercultural icon, Spiegelman has maintained a sense of humor about himself. No matter how serious his subject matter (including his 2004 treatment of the 9/11 attacks, *In the Shadow of No Towers*), the cartoonist is always the fall guy, enduring his father's occasional impatience and the terrors of life. In this sense Spiegelman's mature works echo the sentiments of his first publications, *The Complete Mr. Infinity* (1970) and *The Viper Vicar of Vice, Villany, and Vickedness* (1972), both expressive of the 1960s counterculture and older comic-book tradition that a new generation of readers would accept as illustrative of their own sensibilities.

The following text is from *Maus I and II* (1997).

From Maus

C H A P T E R S I X

I WALKED SLOW...

BEHIND ME ALSO WALKED SLOW.

IF I WALKED FAST...

BEHIND ME ALSO WALKED FAST.

WE WERE ALONE. HE SPOKE...

AMCHA?

IN HEBREW HE SAID TO ME, "OUR NATION?"

HAD I TO ANSWER HIM, OR NO?

A-AMCHA.

I THOUGHT YOU WERE A JEW.

... I'M JEWISH TOO! THERE ARE VERY FEW OF US LEFT...

..MY WIFE AND I HAVE BEEN HIDING IN SOSNOWIEC FOR OVER A YEAR.

I'M WITH MY WIFE TOO. WE'RE HUNGRY AND WE NEED A PLACE TO HIDE!

GO TO THE BLACK MARKET ON DE-KERTA STREET, NUMBER 8.

SO I LEFT HIM AND WENT RIGHT AWAY TO DEKERTA 8. THERE IT WAS A BIG COURTYARD...

?

ALL AROUND I LOOKED, BUT IT WAS NOBODY.

PSSST!

!

WANNA BUY SOME FOOD WITHOUT COUPONS, MISTER?

SHE SHOWED TO ME SAUSAGES, EGGS, CHEESE ...THINGS I ONLY WAS ABLE TO DREAM ABOUT.

I BOUGHT AND WENT QUICK BACK TO ANJA.

GOOD MORNING.

VLADEK! YOU WERE GONE SO LONG.

I HAD TO GET BREAKFAST!... WANT SOME SAUSAGES? ...OR EGGS?..OR WOULD YOU PREFER CHOCOLATE?

WHAT?

IT'S A *MIRACLE!* HOW DID YOU MANAGE IT?

I'M A MAGICIAN! HAVE SOME MILK.

I WENT AGAIN BACK TO DEKERTA. THERE I COULD CHANGE JEWELRY FOR MARKS–AND MARKS FOR FOOD, OR A PLACE TO STAY.

THIS TIME IT WAS MORE PEOPLE...THERE EVEN, I SAW SOME JEWISH BOYS I KNEW FROM BEFORE THE WAR.

VLADEK SPIEGELMAN?! I HARDLY RECOGNIZED YOU. SO YOU'RE STILL ALIVE, EH?

LEO? YES. I'M WITH ANJA.

WE NEED A HIDING PLACE..

HOW ABOUT MRS. KAWKA?

SHE HAS A SMALL FARM ON THE OUTSKIRTS OF TOWN...

SHE MIGHT TAKE YOU IN, IF YOU CAN PAY.

IT WAS NOT SO FAR TO GO TO KAWKA'S FARM...

ALRIGHT THEN, MR. SPIEGELMAN. YOU AND YOUR WIFE CAN STAY IN MY BARN.

WE'LL COME LATE TONIGHT.

BUT, REMEMBER–IF YOU'RE FOUND THERE, I DON'T KNOW YOU! ... YOU MUST SAY THAT THE BARN DOOR WAS OPEN AND YOU JUST SNEAKED IN.

DON'T WORRY...WE WON'T BETRAY YOU!

IT'S ALMOST DAWN - WHEN MRS KAWKA COMES TO MILK HER COW, SHE'LL BRING YOU SOME COFFEE.

WHERE ARE YOU GOING?

TO DEKERTA.

AND SO WE CAME THERE TO LIVE WITH KAWKA'S COW.

DON'T LEAVE ME ALONE AGAIN. I'M TERRIFIED WHILE YOU'RE GONE.

DON'T WORRY, ANJA. I'LL BE SAFE. IF I DIDN'T GO OUT WE WOULDN'T HAVE FOOD...WE WOULDN'T HAVE THIS PLACE!..

AND WE'VE GOT TO FIND A WARMER PLACE FOR THE WINTER...AWAY FROM SOSNOWIEC IF POSSIBLE...

I-I'LL BE OKAY. COME BACK QUICK.

I TRAVELED OFTEN WITH THE STREETCAR TO TOWN.

IT WAS TWO CARS. ONE WAS ONLY GERMANS AND OFFICIALS. THE SECOND, IT WAS ONLY THE POLES.

ALWAYS I WENT STRAIGHT IN THE OFFICIAL CAR...

HEIL HITLER.

THE GERMANS PAID NO ATTENTION OF ME... IN THE POLISH CAR THEY COULD SMELL IF A POLISH JEW CAME IN.

AT THE BLACK MARKET I SAW SEVERAL TIMES A NICE WOMAN, WHAT I MADE A LITTLE FRIENDS WITH HER...

GOOD MORNING, MR. SPIEGELMAN.

HOW DO YOU DO, MRS. MOTONOWA! WHAT DO YOU HAVE IN YOUR BASKET TODAY?

HOW ABOUT A LOAF OF FRESH BREAD?

FINE, FINE.

OH. I'M SORRY. I DON'T HAVE ANY CHANGE.

IT'S OKAY... KEEP IT FOR YOUR LITTLE BOY.

ARE YOU AND YOUR WIFE STILL LIVING IN A BARN?

WE HAVEN'T FOUND ANYTHING BETTER.

I'VE BEEN THINKING ABOUT IT... WHY DON'T YOU BOTH MOVE IN WITH MY SON AND ME?

WHAT ABOUT YOUR HUSBAND?

HE WORKS IN GERMANY, AND ONLY COMES HOME FOR 10 DAYS EVERY 3 MONTHS... I'LL KEEP YOU HIDDEN IN THE CELLAR WHEN HE'S AROUND.

IT SOUNDS GOOD TO ME, BUT IT'S OVER 20 KILOMETERS TO YOUR HOUSE IN SZOPIENICE. MY WIFE WILL BE AFRAID TO GO!

DON'T WORRY. I'LL ESCORT YOU!

THE NEXT EVENING SHE CAME WITH HER 7-YEARS-OLD BOY TO KAWKA'S FARMHOUSE...

I WALKED WITH MOTONOWA AS IF SHE WAS MY WIFE.

AND ANJA, LIKE A GOVERNESS, WENT WITH THE LITTLE BOY BEHIND. AND NOBODY EVEN LOOKED ON US.

WE HAD HERE A LITTLE COMFORTABLE...WE HAD WHERE TO SIT.

REMEMBER, LITTLE ONE—NEVER TELL **ANYBODY** THERE ARE JEWS HERE. THEY'LL SHOOT US ALL!

YES, AUNT ANJA.

THE LITTLE BOY WAS VERY SMART AND HE LOVED VERY MUCH ANJA.

YOU HAD TO **PAY** MRS. MOTO-NOWA TO KEEP YOU, RIGHT?

OF COURSE I PAID.... AND **WELL** I PAID.

...WHAT YOU THINK? SOMEONE WILL RISK THEIR LIFE FOR NOTHING?

...I PAID ALSO FOR THE *FOOD* WHAT SHE GAVE TO US FROM HER SMUGGLING BUSINESS.

BUT, ONE TIME I MISSED A FEW COINS TO THE BREAD...

I'LL PAY YOU THE REST TOMORROW, AFTER I GO OUT AND CASH SOME VALUABLES.

SORRY...I WASN'T ABLE TO **FIND** ANY BREAD TODAY.

ALWAYS SHE GOT BREAD, SO I DIDN'T BELIEVE.... BUT, STILL, SHE WAS A GOOD WOMAN.

IN HIS SCHOOL THE BOY WAS VERY BAD IN GERMAN. SO ANJA TUTORED TO HIM.

ICH BIN... DU BIST.. ER IST...

SHE KNEW GERMAN LIKE AN EXPERT.

AND SOON HE CAME OUT WITH **VERY** GOOD GRADES.

MY TEACHER ASKED ME HOW I IMPROVED SO MUCH...

SO I TOLD HIM MY **MOTHER** WAS HELPING ME.

WHEW

HE WAS REALLY A CLEVER BOY.

But it was a few things here not so good... her home was very small and it was on the ground floor...

Be sure to keep away from the window—you might be seen!

NOK NOK

One minute! (Quick-get in the closet!)

If somebody came, we had fast to hide,

A letter from your husband, Mrs. Motonowa.

Thanks.

But I had something allergic in the closet..

AAH·

Or maybe it was a cold-I can't remember...

-CHMF

But always I had to sneeze.

Still, everything here was fine, until one Saturday Motonowa ran very early back from her black market work...

This is terrible! The Gestapo just searched me-they took my goods!

They may come search here any minute! You've got to leave!

What?

But where can we go?

I don't know. But you must get out NOW!

Oh my god...this is the end!

Anja started to cry... but we had not a choice.

WE'LL WALK TOWARD SOS-NOWIEC - AT LEAST WE'LL KNOW OUR WAY AROUND.

ANJA WAS SO AFRAID SHE WAS SHAKING.

STAY CALM - WALK AS IF WE'RE JUST STROLLING ... AND SPEAK GERMAN.

FOR HOURS WE WALKED.

B-BESUCHEN WIR DOCH FRAU KAWKA.

GUTE IDEE.

VLADEK - WE'RE BEING FOLLOWED.

RELAX

BUT IF WE TURNED A COR-NER, THEY ALSO TURNED.

ES IST KALT.

JA. JA.

OF COURSE I WAS RIGHT — THEY DIDN'T MEAN ANYTHING ON US.

WOOSH

THEY JUST WERE WALKING.

STAYING ON THE STREET ALL NIGHT IS TOO DANGEROUS ... MAYBE WE CAN HIDE IN THAT CONSTRUCTION SITE.

GOOD — I'M EXHAUSTED.

HERE WAS A FOUNDATION MADE VERY DEEP DOWN IN THE GROUND..

BE CAREFUL!

I JUMPED FIRST IN, AND I PULLED OVER BRICKS FOR ANJA TO STEP DOWN.

AND HERE WE WAITED A COLD FEW HOURS FOR THE DAY.

IT STARTED TO BE LIGHT...

COME. WE WON'T BE NOTICED IF WE MIX WITH PEOPLE OUT ON THE STREET.

I'M SO TIRED AND COLD...

WE CAN REST NOW.

WE CAME FINALLY AGAIN TO THIS PLACE WITH THE COW AND WENT INSIDE.

LATER, KAWKA CAME IN...

W-WHO'S IN HERE?

THE SPIEGEL- MANS... WE HAD NOWHERE ELSE TO GO.

WELL... I GUESS YOU CAN STAY. BUT, REMEMBER: I DON'T KNOW YOU'RE HERE!

WHY, MRS. SPIEGELMAN, YOU'RE SHIVERING!

YOU CAN COME INTO MY HOUSE FOR AN HOUR OR SO, 'TIL YOU WARM UP.

SHE TOOK ANJA INSIDE AND BROUGHT TO ME SOME FOOD...IN THOSE DAYS I WAS SO STRONG I COULD SIT EVEN IN THE SNOW ALL NIGHT...

THINGS CAN'T BE THIS BAD EVERYWHERE! I'D GIVE ANYTHING TO GET OUT OF POLAND!

YOU KNOW, BEFORE I TOOK YOU IN, I HAD A YOUNG MAN AND HIS SON HERE...

TWO PEOPLE I KNOW SMUG- GLED THEM INTO HUNGARY. I HEARD HE AND HIS BOY WERE DOING WELL THERE.

HUNGARY! REALLY?! I'D LIKE TO MEET THOSE SMUGGLERS!

SHE TOLD ME THESE TWO ACQUAINTANCES VISITED OFTEN TO HER ON THURS- DAY EVENINGS... TODAY WAS MAYBE A MONDAY...

I DON'T GET IT... WASN'T HUNGARY AS DANGEROUS AS POLAND?

 NO. FOR A LONGER TIME IT WAS BETTER THERE IN HUNGARY FOR THE JEWS... BUT THEN, NEAR THE VERY FINISH OF THE WAR, THEY ALL GOT PUT ALSO TO AUSCHWITZ.

 I WAS THERE, AND I SAW IT. THOUSANDS-HUNDREDS OF THOUSANDS OF JEWS FROM HUNGARY...

 SO MANY, IT WASN'T EVEN ROOM ENOUGH TO BURY THEM ALL IN THE OVENS.

 BUT AT THAT TIME, WHEN I WAS THERE WITH KAWKA, WE COULDN'T KNOW THEN.

 SO... I WENT NEXT DAY TO DEKERTA STREET TO BUY FOOD...

OH GOD! OH GOD! MR. SPIEGELMAN, YOU'RE ALIVE! I'M SO GLAD TO SEE YOU!

MRS. MOTO- NOWA!

I WANTED TO FIND A NEW CONNECTION TO HIDE US. BUT REALLY I DIDN'T THINK TO FIND AGAIN HER.

 PRAISE MARY, YOU'RE SAFE! I COULDN'T SLEEP, I FELT SO GUILTY ABOUT CHASING YOU AND YOUR WIFE OUT.

 THE GESTAPO NEVER EVEN CAME TO MY HOUSE. I JUST PANICKED FOR NOTHING.

PLEASE COME BACK AGAIN.

 ANJA WAS GLAD OF GOING BACK. AND MOTONOWA ALSO...ALWAYS I PAID HER NICELY.

 AND THAT SAME NIGHT WE SAID GOODBYE TO KAWKA AND WENT AGAIN TO SZOPIENICE.

BUT, THEN, MOTONOWA STOPPED TO COME DOWN.

IT'S BEEN 3 DAYS SINCE SHE BROUGHT ANY FOOD.

HERE... HAVE ANOTHER CANDY...

I HAD STILL CANDIES I ORGANIZED ON DEKERTA. ONLY *THIS* WE HAD TO EAT.

ALSO, HERE WE HAD NO PLACE WHERE TO WASH, SO ANJA GOT ON ALL HER SKIN A TERRIBLE RASH.

I DON'T KNOW WHAT'S WORSE—THE HUNGER OR THE ITCHING.

DON'T SCRATCH! IT ONLY—SHH!

KLIK

THE DOOR.

I'M SORRY I COULDN'T GET DOWN BEFORE—MY HUSBAND IS GETTING SUSPICIOUS.

HE ASKED WHY I GO TO THE CELLAR SO OFTEN. HE EVEN ASKED IF I WAS HIDING JEWS HERE! ...HE WAS JOKING, BUT STILL...

ARE YOU ALL RIGHT HERE?

THERE ARE *RATS*, GIANT RATS! THEY'RE HORRIBLE!

WELL—YOU'RE BETTER OFF WITH THE RATS THAN WITH THE GESTAPO... AT LEAST THE RATS WON'T *KILL* YOU!

MMM...

AND SHE WAS RIGHT. WE WERE HAPPY EVEN TO HAVE *THESE* CONDITIONS.

AFTER THE TEN DAYS HER HUSBAND LEFT, AND SHE TOOK US BACK.

IT'S GOOD TO BE "HOME," EH, VLADEK?

IT'S A LOT NICER THAN THAT CELLAR.

BUT I DIDN'T FEEL SAFE HERE. IT WAS TOO MANY WAYS SOMEBODY COULD FIND US OUT. I WANTED TO GO BETTER TO HUNGARY.

SO, WHEN IT CAME THURSDAY, I WENT IN THE DIRECTION TO TAKE A STREETCAR TO SEE KAWKA IN SOSNOWIEC.

LOOK!

I HAD TO PASS WHERE SOME CHILDREN WERE PLAYING.

A JEW! A JEW!

THEY RAN SCREAMING HOME.

HELP! MOMMY! A JEW!!

A JEW!

QUICK, THE MOTHERS CAME OUTSIDE TO SEE WHAT WAS!

THE MOTHERS ALWAYS TOLD SO: "BE CAREFUL! A JEW WILL CATCH YOU TO A BAG AND EAT YOU!" ... SO THEY TAUGHT TO THEIR CHILDREN.

I APPROACHED OVER TO THEM...

HEIL HITLER.

IF I RAN AWAY THEY WOULD SEE: "YES, IT IS A JEW HERE."

DON'T BE AFRAID, LITTLE ONES. I'M NOT A JEW. I WON'T HURT YOU.

SORRY, MISTER. YOU KNOW HOW KIDS ARE... HEIL HITLER.

SO I CAME OUT WELL FROM THIS...

BUT THE EXPERIENCE COST ME REALLY A LOT OF HAIRS.

1986

JOY HARJO

b. 1951

Joy Harjo was born in Tulsa, Oklahoma, to a mother of mixed Cherokee, French, and Irish blood. She has described her father's family, members of the Creek (also known as Muscogee) tribe, as "rebels and speakers," among them a Baptist minister (Harjo's paternal grandfather), two painters (her grandmother and aunt), and a great-great-grandfather who in 1832 led a Creek rebellion against their forced removal from Alabama into Oklahoma. As the critic Laura Coltelli has pointed out, the work of many contemporary Native American writers (a large number of whom are of mixed blood) enacts a quest to reenvision identity by confronting the historical, cultural, and political realities that shape lives experienced between different worlds. Drawing on a family tradition of powerful speaking, Harjo participates in a search to reimagine and repair painful fractures in contemporary experience: between past and present, between person and landscape, and between parts of the self. Thus traveling is a mythic activity in her poems, enacting this search for community and historical connectedness. As in the work of James Welch, Simon J. Ortiz, and Leslie Marmon Silko, the theme of traveling in Harjo's poems resonates with the historical displacements and migrations of native peoples (especially the forced removal of the Creeks). She has called herself the wanderer in her family, and her poems often map her journeys, whether on foot, by car, or in a plane. Perhaps Harjo thinks of herself as the family wanderer because she left Oklahoma to attend high school at the Institute of American Indian Arts in Santa Fe, New Mexico ("in a way it saved my life," she has said). Since receiving a B.A. from the University of New Mexico in 1976 and an MFA from the University of Iowa, she has taught at the Institute of American Indian Arts, Arizona State University, the University of Colorado, the University of Arizona, and the University of New Mexico.

Harjo's vision of the interrelatedness of all things is common to Native American storytelling. The ethic that emerges from this worldview stresses reciprocity between people and various sources of power, including tradition and the natural world. Harjo's poems bring together mythic, feminist, and cultural perspectives and also unite contemporary urban experience with Native American myth and legend. In her collection *She Had Some Horses* (1983) this integration seeks to assuage the loneliness and desperation of those on the margin who populate much of the volume: a woman raising her mixed-blood children alone, a friend who threatens suicide, a woman who threatens to drop from a thirteenth-story window. The collection *In Mad Love and War* (1990) exhibits anger at the separations caused by dispossession and violence, as in an elegy for Anna Mae Pictou Aquash, a young Micmac woman shot dead on the Pine Ridge Reservation. Poems such as this recall the passion for social justice in the works of James Wright, Audre Lorde, and Leslie Marmon Silko; indeed, the spirit of Harjo's rebel great-great-grandfather is never far from her work.

Harjo has been a leading figure in the adaptation of oral traditions into written forms, consciously using the written word in her poems in a way that duplicates certain oral and ceremonial techniques. Her poems extensively and emphatically use repetition, of both words and units of thought, as mnemonic and structuring devices. For example, her poem "When the World As We Knew It Ended," written in response to the events of September 11, 2001, begins a series of stanzas with the repetition and variation of "We saw it," "We heard it," "We knew it. . . ." Reflecting the understanding that Native American tradition is not fixed but evolves and changes, Harjo has fearlessly experimented, adapting new musical and poetic forms to Native Ameri-can traditions. She has long drawn on reggae, rock, Creek Stomp Dance songs, coun-try, and African music and has integrated performance and dance into her poetry. A musician and songwriter, she has released several CD collections, including *Letter from the End of the Twentieth Century* (1997), *Native Joy for Real* (2005), and a musi-cal version of *She Had Some Horses* (2006). Harjo plays the saxophone, which is not a traditional Native American instrument, but, she has said, "Someday it may be."

Metamorphosis, common in Native American storytelling, is central to Harjo's vision, where the world is constituted by change and constancy. Her collection *The Woman Who Fell from the Sky* (1994) embodies metamorphosis in its structure—the retelling of contemporary experience through traditional myths—and metamorphosis recurs in its stories. Various Native American traditions tell the story of a sky woman who falls through the void of space and creates the human universe. In the title poem of this volume, a group of women ("angry at their inattentive husbands") run off with stars; one of these women dares to look back at Earth and falls from the sky. In Harjo's hands this myth becomes the story of two lovers who were children together at an Indian boarding school. Adrift in an urban landscape, they are reunited, their narra-tive characterized by fracture and repair. In the same collection, "Flood" renders a young girl's sexuality and imaginative power through the myth of the water monster. The prose poems that form much of this book remind us that Native American story-telling, an oral tradition, does not distinguish between poetry and prose. For all Har-jo's anguished sense of the warring factions in our world and our selves, her works consistently engage in a process of healing and regeneration, themes that continue in her collection *A Map to the Next World* (2000). Like the kitchen table in her poem "Perhaps the World Ends Here," Harjo's poems are a space where "we sing with joy, with sorrow. We pray of suffering and remorse. We give thanks."

Harjo has also written screenplays and the text for Stephen Strom's photographs of the Southwestern landscape, *Secrets from the Center of the World* (1989), and she has edited an anthology of tribal women's writings from around the world. A collection of interviews, *The Spiral of Memory* (1996), edited by Laura Coltelli, is a valuable accompaniment to her poems. *How We Became Human* (2003) presents a selection from Harjo's earlier work, including poems from hard-to-find chapbooks, as well as newer work. In 2013 she published a memoir, *Crazy Brave*.

Call It Fear

There is this edge where shadows
and bones of some of us walk
                    backwards.
Talk backwards. There is this edge
call it an ocean of fear of the dark. Or   5
name it with other songs. Under our ribs
our hearts are bloody stars. Shine on
shine on, and horses in their galloping flight
strike the curve of ribs.
                  Heartbeat   10
and breathe back sharply. Breathe
                    backwards.
There is this edge within me
              I saw it once
an August Sunday morning when the heat hadn't   15
left this earth. And Goodluck

sat sleeping next to me in the truck.
We had never broken through the edge of the
singing at four a.m.
                          We had only wanted to talk, to hear   20
any other voice to stay alive with.
                          And there was this edge—
not the drop of sandy rock cliff
bones of volcanic earth into
                          Albuquerque.   25
Not that,
          but a string of shadow horses kicking
and pulling me out of my belly,
          not into the Rio Grande[1] but into the music
barely coming through   30
                          Sunday church singing
from the radio. Battery worn-down but the voices
talking backwards.

                                                   1983

White Bear

She begins to board the flight
    to Albuquerque. Late night.
But stops in the corrugated tunnel,
    a space between leaving and staying,
where the night sky catches   5

            her whole life

she has felt like a woman
    balancing on a wooden nickle heart
approaching herself from here to
    there, Tulsa or New York   10
with knives or corn meal.

The last flight someone talked
    about how coming from Seattle
the pilot flew a circle
    over Mt. St. Helens,[1] she sat   15
quiet. (But had seen the eruption
    as the earth beginning
to come apart, as in birth
    out of violence.)

She watches the yellow lights   20
    of towns below the airplane flicker,
fade and fall backwards. Somewhere,

1. River flowing from southern Colorado through
New Mexico and then forming the boundary
between Texas and Mexico.

1. A volcanic peak in Washington State; it erupted
in 1980.

she dreamed, there is the white bear
moving down from the north, motioning her paws
    like a long arctic night, that kind   25
of circle and the whole world balanced in
    between carved of ebony and ice

        oh so hard

the clear black nights
    like her daughter's eyes, and the white   30
bear moon, cupped like an ivory rocking
cradle, tipping back it could go
either way
        all darkness
            is open to all light.   35

            1983

Summer Night

The moon is nearly full,
        the humid air sweet like melon.
Flowers that have cupped the sun all day
            dream of iridescent wings
under the long dark sleep.   5
        Children's invisible voices call out
in the glimmering moonlight.
        Their parents play worn-out records
of the cumbia.[1] Behind the screen door
        their soft laughter swells   10
into the rhythm of a smooth guitar.
        I watch the world shimmer
inside this globe of a summer night,
        listen to the wobble of her
spin and dive. It happens all the time, waiting for you   15
        to come home.
There is an ache that begins
        in the sound of an old blues song.
It becomes a house where all the lights have gone out
        but one.   20
And it burns and burns
        until there is only the blue smoke of dawn
and everyone is sleeping in someone's arms
        even the flowers
even the sound of a thousand silences.   25
        And the arms of night
in the arms of day.
        Everyone except me.

---

1. A Latin American dance.

But then the smell of damp honeysuckle twisted on the vine.
And the turn of the shoulder   30
                of the ordinary spirit who keeps watch
over this ordinary street.
              And there you are, the secret
of your own flower of light
            blooming in the miraculous dark.   35

1990

The Flood

It had been years since I'd seen the watermonster, the snake who lived
at the bottom of the lake. He had disappeared in the age of reason, as
a mystery that never happened.

For in the muggy lake was the girl I could have been at sixteen, wrested
from the torment of exaggerated fools, one version anyway, though the   5
story at the surface would say car accident, or drowning while drinking,
all of it eventually accidental.

This story is not an accident, nor is the existence of the watersnake in
the memory of the people as they carried the burden of the myth from
Alabama to Oklahoma.[1] Each reluctant step pounded memory into the   10
broken heart and no one will ever forget it.

When I walk the stairway of water into the abyss, I return as the wife
of the watermonster, in a blanket of time decorated with swatches of
cloth and feathers from our favorite clothes.

The stories of the battles of the watersnake are forever ongoing, and those   15
stories soaked into my blood since infancy like deer gravy, so how could
I resist the watersnake, who appeared as the most handsome man in the
tribe, or any band whose visits I'd been witness to since childhood?

This had been going on for centuries: the first time he appeared I carried
my baby sister on my back as I went to get water. She laughed at a wood-   20
pecker flitting like a small sun above us and before I could deter the
symbol we were in it.

My body was already on fire with the explosion of womanhood as if
I were flint, hot stone, and when he stepped out of the water he was the
first myth I had ever seen uncovered. I had surprised him in a human   25
moment. I looked aside but I could not discount what I had seen.

My baby sister's cry pinched reality, the woodpecker a warning of a
disjuncture in the brimming sky, and then a man who was not a man
but a myth.

---

1. In 1832 the Muscogee (also known as Creek) tribe was forcibly relocated by the United States government from Alabama to Oklahoma.

What I had seen there were no words for except in the sacred language   30
of the most holy recounting, so when I ran back to the village, drenched
in salt, how could I explain the water jar left empty by the river to my
mother who deciphered my burning lips as shame?

My imagination swallowed me like a mica sky, but I had seen the water
monster in the fight of lightning storms, breaking trees, stirring up kill-   35
ing winds, and had lost my favorite brother to a spear of the sacred
flame, so certainly I would know my beloved if he were hidden in the
blushing skin of the suddenly vulnerable.

I was taken with a fever and nothing cured it until I dreamed my fiery
body dipped in the river where it fed into the lake. My father carried me   40
as if I were newborn, as if he were presenting me once more to the
world, and when he dipped me I was quenched, pronounced healed.

My parents immediately made plans to marry me to an important man
who was years older but would provide me with everything I needed to
survive in this world, a world I could no longer perceive, as I had been   45
blinded with a ring of water when I was most in need of a drink by a
snake who was not a snake, and how did he know my absolute secrets,
those created at the brink of acquired language?

When I disappeared it was in a storm that destroyed the houses of my
relatives; my baby sister was found sucking on her hand in the crook of   50
an oak.

And though it may have appeared otherwise, I did not go willingly.
That night I had seen my face strung on the shell belt of my ancestors,
and I was standing next to a man who could not look me in the eye.

The oldest woman in the tribe wanted to remember me as a symbol in   55
the story of a girl who disobeyed, who gave in to her desires before
marriage and was destroyed by the monster disguised as the seductive
warrior.

Others saw the car I was driving as it drove into the lake early one morning, the time the carriers of tradition wake up, before the sun or the   60
approach of woodpeckers, and found the emptied six-pack on the sandy
shores of the lake.

The power of the victim is a power that will always be reckoned with,
one way or the other. When the proverbial sixteen-year-old woman
walked down to the lake within her were all sixteen-year-old women who   65
had questioned their power from time immemorial.

Her imagination was larger than the small frame house at the north
edge of town, with the broken cars surrounding it like a necklace of
futility, larger than the town itself leaning into the lake. Nothing could
stop it, just as no one could stop the bearing-down thunderheads as they   70
gathered overhead in the war of opposites.

Years later when she walked out of the lake and headed for town, no one
recognized her, or themselves, in the drench of fire and rain. The watersnake was a story no one told anymore. They'd entered a drought that no
one recognized as drought, the convenience store a signal of temporary   75
amnesia.

I had gone out to get bread, eggs and the newspaper before breakfast
and hurried the cashier for my change as the crazy woman walked in, for
I could not see myself as I had abandoned her some twenty years ago in
a blue windbreaker at the edge of the man-made lake as everyone dove   80
naked and drunk off the sheer cliff, as if we had nothing to live for, not
then or ever.

It was beginning to rain in Oklahoma, the rain that would flood the
world.[2]

1994

When the World As We Knew It Ended—

We were dreaming on an occupied island at the farthest edge
of a trembling nation when it went down.

Two towers rose up from the east island of commerce and touched
the sky. Men walked on the moon. Oil was sucked dry
by two brothers. Then it went down. Swallowed   5
by a fire dragon, by oil and fear.
Eaten whole.

It was coming.

We had been watching since the eve of the missionaries in their long and
solemn clothes, to see what would happen.   10

We saw it
from the kitchen window over the sink
as we made coffee, cooked rice and
potatoes, enough for an army.

We saw it all, as we changed diapers and fed   15
the babies. We saw it,
through the branches
of the knowledgeable tree

2. Embedded in Muscogee tribal memory is the
creature known as the tie snake, a huge monster
who lives in waterways and will do what he can to
take us with him. He represents the power of the
underworld. He is still present today in the lakes and rivers
of Oklahoma and Alabama, a force we reckon
with despite the proliferation of inventions that
keep us from ourselves [Harjo's note].

through the snags of stars, through
the sun and storms from our knees   20
as we bathed and washed
the floors.

The conference of the birds warned us, as they flew over
destroyers in the harbor, parked there since the first takeover.
It was by their song and talk we knew when to rise   25
when to look out the window
to the commotion going on—
the magnetic field thrown off by grief.

We heard it.
The racket in every corner of the world. As   30
the hunger for war rose up in those who would steal to be president
to be king or emperor, to own the trees, stones, and everything
else that moved about the earth, inside the earth
and above it.

We knew it was coming, tasted the winds who gathered intelligence   35
from each leaf and flower, from every mountain, sea
and desert, from every prayer and song all over this tiny universe
floating in the skies of infinite
being.

And then it was over, this world we had grown to love   40
for its sweet grasses, for the many-colored horses
and fishes, for the shimmering possibilities
while dreaming.

But then there were the seeds to plant and the babies
who needed milk and comforting, and someone   45
picked up a guitar or ukelele from the rubble
and began to sing about the light flutter
the kick beneath the skin of the earth
we felt there, beneath us

a warm animal   50
a song being born between the legs of her,
a poem.

2003

EDWARD P. JONES
b. 1951

Whole worlds thrive in the imagination of Edward P. Jones, worlds he has shared with readers in short stories, an epic novel, and the recurring themes and characters that connect all his writing into a coherent vision. At the end of his 2003 Pulitzer Prize–winning novel, *The Known World*, a former slave named Alice is revealed as an artist: her huge, three-dimensional tapestry of the plantation where she was in bondage reconstructs its entire world from above, with all human beings, living and dead, standing in their accustomed places. Jones's stories create such tapestries, many of them—including the story reprinted here—mapped onto the precise geography of Washington, D.C., where Jones was born in 1950 and where he has spent most of his life.

Jones's first short-story collection, *Lost in the City* (1992), brought the black community of Northwest D.C. into vivid relief. The stories introduce readers to characters who struggle to make a living and maintain love of all sorts against conditions of poverty and despair. Unflinching in his view of that environment, Jones projects profound compassion for his creations. Born into these conditions himself, to a mother who could not read or write and an alcoholic father who abandoned them, Jones and his family moved eighteen times by the time he turned eighteen, fleeing the threat of "set out"—eviction—notices for falling behind on rent. Jones was educated at local public schools and won a scholarship to the College of the Holy Cross in Worcester, Massachusetts, ultimately earning an MFA at the University of Virginia. *Lost in the City* won him the PEN/Hemingway Award and the Lannan Foundation award, launching his career on a high note.

But nothing prepared the literary world for the novel that appeared in 2003. Jones had been working during the preceding decade for a trade journal called *Tax Notes*, first as a proofreader and then as a writer. As he tells the story, during this time he had the idea of writing a novel about a black slaveowner. Intimidated by the demand for accuracy in historical fiction, he held off writing, checking out dozens of books on antebellum life from the library (few of which he read). All the while, he was composing the novel in his head. Jones's agent at the time reports that in meetings with his client during those seemingly fallow years it became clear that Jones had memorized whole swaths of prose.

Jones took a vacation from his job in 2001, wrote the first few pages of his novel, and then was laid off several months later. With this new free time, the rest of the words finally found their way to the page. He solved the problem of the many history books he had checked out (and ignored) by inventing the historical documents he needed, punctuating the novel's multiple narrative strands with seemingly real census reports, government documents, letters, and inventories. Three months after the writing began, his 400+page magnum opus, *The Known World*, was finished. Upon its provocative premise—that a black man can deceive himself into becoming a "benevolent" slaveowner—Jones builds dozens of characters, a sweeping fictional setting, and heartbreaking tragedies, experimentally mixing a godlike narrative presence that sees both past and future with lavish "factual" detail grounding the story in its moment.

A remarkable feature of Jones's work is that characters, their descendants, and the objects they make reappear across various stories. An elaborately carved walking stick, for instance, made by a talented free black craftsman named Augustus in *The Known World*, reappears in the hands of a character in a story set over a hundred years later, in the collection *All Aunt Hagar's Children* (2006). These woven details make the tapestry of Jones's work palpable to his devoted readers.

"The First Day" evokes the pain and hope of a young girl taking her first steps into school, a journey that pulls her away from her illiterate mother and echoes Jones's own life journey into reading, writing, and literature.

The First Day

In an otherwise unremarkable September morning, long before I learned to be ashamed of my mother, she takes my hand and we set off down New Jersey Avenue to begin my very first day of school. I am wearing a checkered-like blue-and-green cotton dress, and scattered about these colors are bits of yellow and white and brown. My mother has uncharacteristically spent nearly an hour on my hair that morning, plaiting and replaiting so that now my scalp tingles. Whenever I turn my head quickly, my nose fills with the faint smell of Dixie Peach hair grease. The smell is somehow a soothing one now and I will reach for it time and time again before the morning ends. All the plaits, each with a blue barrette near the tip and each twisted into an uncommon sturdiness, will last until I go to bed that night, something that has never happened before. My stomach is full of milk and oatmeal sweetened with brown sugar. Like everything else I have on, my pale green slip and underwear are new, the underwear having come three to a plastic package with a little girl on the front who appears to be dancing. Behind my ears, my mother, to stop my whining, has dabbed the stingiest bit of her gardenia perfume, the last present my father gave her before he disappeared into memory. Because I cannot smell it, I have only her word that the perfume is there. I am also wearing yellow socks trimmed with thin lines of black and white around the tops. My shoes are my greatest joy, black patent-leather miracles, and when one is nicked at the toe later that morning in class, my heart will break.

I am carrying a pencil, a pencil sharpener, and a small ten-cent tablet with a black-and-white speckled cover. My mother does not believe that a girl in kindergarten needs such things, so I am taking them only because of my insistent whining and because they are presents from our neighbors, Mary Keith and Blondelle Harris. Miss Mary and Miss Blondelle are watching my two younger sisters until my mother returns. The women are as precious to me as my mother and sisters. Out playing one day, I have overheard an older child, speaking to another child, call Miss Mary and Miss Blondelle a word that is brand-new to me. This is my mother: When I say the word in fun to one of my sisters, my mother slaps me across the mouth and the word is lost for years and years.

All the way down New Jersey Avenue, the sidewalks are teeming with children. In my neighborhood, I have many friends, but I see none of them as my mother and I walk. We cross New York Avenue, we cross Pierce Street, and we cross L and K, and still I see no one who knows my name. At I Street, between New Jersey Avenue and Third Street, we enter Seaton Elementary School, a timeworn, sad-faced building across the street from my mother's church, Mt. Carmel Baptist.

Just inside the front door, women out of the advertisements in *Ebony*[1] are greeting other parents and children. The woman who greets us has pearls thick as jumbo marbles that come down almost to her navel, and she acts as if she had known me all my life, touching my shoulder, cupping her hand under my chin. She is enveloped in a perfume that I only know is not gardenia. When, in answer to her question, my mother tells her that we live at 1227 New Jersey Avenue, the woman first seems to be picturing in her head where we live. Then she shakes her head and says that we are at the wrong school, that we should be at Walker-Jones.

My mother shakes her head vigorously. "I want her to go here," my mother says. "If I'da wanted her someplace else, I'da took her there." The woman continues to act as if she has known me all my life, but she tells my mother that we live beyond the area that Seaton serves. My mother is not convinced and for several more minutes she questions the woman about why I cannot attend Seaton. For as many Sundays as I can remember, perhaps even Sundays when I was in her womb, my mother has pointed across I Street to Seaton as we come and go to Mt. Carmel. "You gonna go there and learn about the whole world." But one of the guardians of that place is saying no, and no again. I am learning this about my mother: The higher up on the scale of respectability a person is—and teachers are rather high up in her eyes—the less she is liable to let them push her around. But finally, I see in her eyes the closing gate, and she takes my hand and we leave the building. On the steps, she stops as people move past us on either side.

"Mama, I can't go to school?"

She says nothing at first, then takes my hand again and we are down the steps quickly and nearing New Jersey Avenue before I can blink. This is my mother: She says, "One monkey don't stop no show."

Walker-Jones is a larger, newer school and I immediately like it because of that. But it is not across the street from my mother's church, her rock, one of her connections to God, and I sense her doubts as she absently rubs her thumb over the back of her hand. We find our way to the crowded auditorium where gray metal chairs are set up in the middle of the room. Along the wall to the left are tables and other chairs. Every chair seems occupied by a child or adult. Somewhere in the room a child is crying, a cry that rises above the buzz-talk of so many people. Strewn about the floor are dozens and dozens of pieces of white paper, and people are walking over them without any thought of picking them up. And seeing this lack of concern, I am all of a sudden afraid.

"Is this where they register for school?" my mother asks a woman at one of the tables.

The woman looks up slowly as if she has heard this question once too often. She nods. She is tiny, almost as small as the girl standing beside her.

---

1. General interest magazine founded in 1945, focusing on African American life and often featuring black elites in entertainment, business, and politics.

The woman's hair is set in a mass of curlers and all of those curlers are made of paper money, here a dollar bill, there a five-dollar bill. The girl's hair is arrayed in curls, but some of them are beginning to droop and this makes me happy. On the table beside the woman's pocketbook is a large notebook, worthy of someone in high school, and looking at me looking at the notebook, the girl places her hand possessively on it. In her other hand she holds several pencils with thick crowns of additional erasers.

"These the forms you gotta use?" my mother asks the woman, picking up a few pieces of the paper from the table. "Is this what you have to fill out?"

The woman tells her yes, but that she need fill out only one.

"I see," my mother says, looking about the room. Then: "Would you help me with this form? That is, if you don't mind."

The woman asks my mother what she means.

"This form. Would you mind helpin me fill it out?"

The woman still seems not to understand.

"I can't read it. I don't know how to read or write, and I'm askin you to help me." My mother looks at me, then looks away. I know almost all of her looks, but this one is brand-new to me. "Would you help me, then?"

The woman says Why sure, and suddenly she appears happier, so much more satisfied with everything. She finishes the form for her daughter and my mother and I step aside to wait for her. We find two chairs nearby and sit. My mother is now diseased, according to the girl's eyes, and until the moment her mother takes her and the form to the front of the auditorium, the girl never stops looking at my mother. I stare back at her. "Don't stare," my mother says to me. "You know better than that."

Another woman out of the *Ebony* ads takes the woman's child away. Now, the woman says upon returning, let's see what we can do for you two.

My mother answers the questions the woman reads off the form. They start with my last name, and then on to the first and middle names. This is school, I think. This is going to school. My mother slowly enunciates each word of my name. This is my mother: As the questions go on, she takes from her pocketbook document after document, as if they will support my right to attend school, as if she has been saving them up for just this moment. Indeed, she takes out more papers than I have ever seen her do in other places: my birth certificate, my baptismal record, a doctor's letter concerning my bout with chicken pox, rent receipts, records of immunization, a letter about our public assistance payments, even her marriage license—every single paper that has anything even remotely to do with my five-year-old life. Few of the papers are needed here, but it does not matter and my mother continues to pull out the documents with the purposefulness of a magician pulling out a long string of scarves. She has learned that money is the beginning and end of everything in this world, and when the woman finishes, my mother offers her fifty cents, and the woman accepts it without hesitation. My mother and I are just about the last parent and child in the room.

My mother presents the form to a woman sitting in front of the stage, and the woman looks at it and writes something on a white card, which she gives to my mother. Before long, the woman who has taken the girl with the drooping curls appears from behind us, speaks to the sitting woman, and introduces herself to my mother and me. She's to be my teacher, she tells my mother. My mother stares.

We go into the hall, where my mother kneels down to me. Her lips are quivering. "I'll be back to pick you up at twelve o'clock. I don't want you to go nowhere. You just wait right here. And listen to every word she say." I touch her lips and press them together. It is an old, old game between us. She puts my hand down at my side, which is not part of the game. She stands and looks a second at the teacher, then she turns and walks away. I see where she has darned one of her socks the night before. Her shoes make loud sounds in the hall. She passes through the doors and I can still hear the loud sounds of her shoes. And even when the teacher turns me toward the classrooms and I hear what must be the singing and talking of all the children in the world, I can still hear my mother's footsteps above it all.

1992

RITA DOVE
b. 1952

What she has called the "friction" between the beauty of a poetic form and a difficult or painful subject appeals to Rita Dove. Her own formal control and discipline create a beautiful design and a haunting music in "Parsley," a poem based on a murderous event: in 1957 the dictator of the Dominican Republic, Rafael Trujillo, ordered twenty thousand black Haitians killed because they could not pronounce the letter "r" in perejil, the Spanish word for parsley. What compels Dove in this poem is the way a "single, beautiful word" has the power of life and death. More astonishing is that she writes from the perspectives of both the Haitians in the cane fields and General Trujillo in his palace. When asked in an interview about her capacity to imagine Trujillo, Dove responded, "I frankly don't believe anyone who says they've never felt any evil, that they cannot understand that process of evil. It was important to me to try to understand that arbitrary quality of his cruelty. . . . Making us get into his head may shock us all into seeing what the human being is capable of, because if we can go that far into his head, we're halfway there ourselves." An ability to enter into different points of view in a single poem is characteristic of Dove's disinterested imagination. Her method is to avoid commentary, to let the imagined person or object, the suggestive detail, speak for itself. Often her work suggests what the English poet John Keats called "negative capability," the gift of the poet to become what he or she is not.

Born in Akron, Dove attended Miami University of Ohio and, after her graduation, studied modern European literature as a Fulbright/Hays fellow at the University of Tübingen in Germany. When she returned from Europe she earned an MFA at the University of Iowa (in 1977). Later she taught creative writing at Arizona State University before joining the University of Virginia, where she is now Commonwealth Professor of English. Since her Fulbright year she has repeatedly chosen to live abroad, in Ireland, Israel, France, and especially Germany. Her travel in Europe and elsewhere suggests part of the imperative she feels as a poet: to range widely through fields of experience, to cross boundaries of space as well as time. Her first book, *The Yellow House on the Corner* (1980), is notable for its intense poems about adolescence; her second book, *Museum* (1983), dramatically extends the range of her work. "When I started *Museum*," she has said, "I was in Europe, and I had a way of looking back on America and distancing myself from my experience." As well as for several fine poems about her father (a subject that may also have needed distance), the book is remarkable for the way distance allowed Dove to move out of her immediate experience, freed her to imagine widely different lives.

As if to show that it is also possible to travel widely while staying at home, Dove's *Thomas and Beulah* (1986) is an extended sequence based on her grandparents' lives. Her continuing fascination with imagining different perspectives on the same event is evident in this sequence. Dove has described the book's origins this way:

> My grandmother had told me a story that had happened to my grandfather when he was young, coming up on a riverboat to Akron, Ohio, my hometown. But that was all I had, basically. And the story so fascinated me that I tried to write about it. I started off writing stories about my grandfather and soon, because I ran out of real fact, in order to keep going, I made up facts for this character, Thomas. . . . Then this poem "Dusting" appeared, really out of nowhere. I didn't realize this was Thomas's wife saying, "I want to talk. And you can't do his side without my side. . . ."

This is the story, in part, of a marriage and of a black couple's life in the industrial Midwest in the period from 1900 to 1960. Thomas's point of view controls the poems of the book's first section, while the second part imagines his wife's. The larger framework of the sequence links family history to social history. Thomas's journey from the rural South to the industrial city of Akron (where he finds employment in the Goodyear Zeppelin factory until the Depression puts him out of work) is part of the larger social movement of African Americans from the South into Northern industrial cities in the first part of the twentieth century. The individual lyrics of Dove's sequence create and sustain the story through distinct and often ordinary moments in which each life is vividly portrayed. It is part of Dove's gift that she can render the apparently unimportant moments that inform a life and set them against a background of larger historical forces, as do Robert Hayden in *Elegies for Paradise Valley* and Robert Lowell in *Notebook*.

Many of the figures in Dove's poems are displaced, on the border between different worlds: for example, Thomas and Beulah, and the biracial violin prodigy, George Bridgetower (1780–1860), who is the focus of her volume *Sonata Mulattica* (2009). The experience of displacement, of what she has called living in "two different worlds, seeing things with double vision," consistently compels this poet's imagination. It takes both detachment and control to maintain (and to live with) such doubleness. This may be why Dove's rich sense of language and her love of sound are joined to a disciplined formal sense. The forms of her poems often hold in place difficult or ambiguous feelings and keep the expression of feeling understated. While restraint is one strength of Dove's poems, her work can sometimes seem austere. Such careful control recalls Elizabeth Bishop's early work, also highly controlled and even, at times, guarded. As Bishop grew to relax her restraints, to open into an extraordinary expressiveness, so Dove's career shows a similar growth. Her collections *Grace Notes* (1989), *Mother Love* (1995), and *American Smooth* (2004) suggest just such a relaxing of the poet's guard, while *On the Bus with Rosa Parks* (2000) demonstrates an ongoing ability to unite social conscience with a transformative sense of language and form. With each book she asks something more from herself, and she has now become one of our indispensable poets. Dove was poet laureate of the United States from 1993 to 1995.

Geometry

I prove a theorem and the house expands:
the windows jerk free to hover near the ceiling,
the ceiling floats away with a sigh.

As the walls clear themselves of everything
but transparency, the scent of carnations   5
leaves with them. I am out in the open

and above the windows have hinged into butterflies,
sunlight glinting where they've intersected.
They are going to some point true and unproven.

1980

Adolescence—I

In water-heavy nights behind grandmother's porch
We knelt in the tickling grasses and whispered:
Linda's face hung before us, pale as a pecan,
And it grew wise as she said:
  "A boy's lips are soft,   5
  As soft as baby's skin."
The air closed over her words.
A firefly whirred near my ear, and in the distance
I could hear streetlamps ping
Into miniature suns   10
Against a feathery sky.

1980

Adolescence—II

Although it is night, I sit in the bathroom, waiting.
Sweat prickles behind my knees, the baby-breasts are alert.
Venetian blinds slice up the moon; the tiles quiver in pale strips.

Then they come, the three seal men with eyes as round
As dinner plates and eyelashes like sharpened tines.   5
They bring the scent of licorice. One sits in the washbowl,

One on the bathtub edge; one leans against the door.
"Can you feel it yet?" they whisper.
I don't know what to say, again. They chuckle,

Patting their sleek bodies with their hands.   10
"Well, maybe next time." And they rise,
Glittering like pools of ink under moonlight,

And vanish. I clutch at the ragged holes
They leave behind, here at the edge of darkness.
Night rests like a ball of fur on my tongue.   15

                                                        1980

Adolescence—III

With Dad gone, Mom and I worked
The dusky rows of tomatoes.
As they glowed orange in sunlight
And rotted in shadow, I too
Grew orange and softer, swelling out   5
Starched cotton slips.

The texture of twilight made me think of
Lengths of Dotted Swiss. In my room
I wrapped scarred knees in dresses
That once went to big-band dances;   10
I baptized my earlobes with rosewater.
Along the window-sill, the lipstick stubs
Glittered in their steel shells.

Looking out at the rows of clay
And chicken manure, I dreamed how it would happen: 15
He would meet me by the blue spruce,
A carnation over his heart, saying,
"I have come for you, Madam;
I have loved you in my dreams."
At his touch, the scabs would fall away.   20
Over his shoulder, I see my father coming toward us:
He carries his tears in a bowl,
And blood hangs in the pine-soaked air.

                                                        1980

Parsley[1]

1. The Cane[2] Fields

There is a parrot imitating spring
in the palace, its feathers parsley green.
Out of the swamp the cane appears

to haunt us, and we cut it down. El General
searches for a word; he is all the world   5
there is. Like a parrot imitating spring,

we lie down screaming as rain punches through
and we come up green. We cannot speak an R—
out of the swamp, the cane appears

and then the mountain we call in whispers *Katalina*.[3]   10
The children gnaw their teeth to arrowheads.
There is a parrot imitating spring.

El General has found his word: *perejil*.
Who says it, lives. He laughs, teeth shining
out of the swamp. The cane appears   15

in our dreams, lashed by wind and streaming.
And we lie down. For every drop of blood
there is a parrot imitating spring.
Out of the swamp the cane appears.

2. The Palace

The word the general's chosen is parsley.   20
It is fall, when thoughts turn
to love and death; the general thinks
of his mother, how she died in the fall
and he planted her walking cane at the grave
and it flowered, each spring stolidly forming   25
four-star blossoms. The general

pulls on his boots, he stomps to
her room in the palace, the one without
curtains, the one with a parrot
in a brass ring. As he paces he wonders   30
Who can I kill today. And for a moment
the little knot of screams
is still. The parrot, who has traveled

1. On October 2, 1937, Rafael Trujillo (1891–1961), dictator of the Dominican Republic, ordered 20,000 blacks killed because they could not pronounce the letter "r" in *perejil*, the Spanish word for parsley [Dove's note].
2. I.e., sugar cane.
3. Katarina (because "we cannot speak an R").

all the way from Australia in an ivory
cage, is, coy as a widow, practising   35
spring. Ever since the morning
his mother collapsed in the kitchen
while baking skull-shaped candies
for the Day of the Dead,[4] the general
has hated sweets. He orders pastries   40
brought up for the bird; they arrive

dusted with sugar on a bed of lace.
The knot in his throat starts to twitch;
he sees his boots the first day in battle
splashed with mud and urine   45
as a soldier falls at his feet amazed—
how stupid he looked!—at the sound
of artillery. *I never thought it would sing*
the soldier said, and died. Now

the general sees the fields of sugar   50
cane, lashed by rain and streaming.
He sees his mother's smile, the teeth
gnawed to arrowheads. He hears
the Haitians sing without R's
as they swing the great machetes: 55
Katalina, they sing, *Katalina*,

mi madle, mi amol en muelte.[5] God knows
his mother was no stupid woman; she
could roll an R like a queen. Even
a parrot can roll an R! In the bare room   60
the bright feathers arch in a parody
of greenery, as the last pale crumbs
disappear under the blackened tongue. Someone

calls out his name in a voice
so like his mother's, a startled tear   65
splashes the tip of his right boot.
My mother, my love in death.
The general remembers the tiny green sprigs
men of his village wore in their capes
to honor the birth of a son. He will   70
order many, this time, to be killed

for a single, beautiful word.

1983

---

4. All Soul's Day, November 2. An Aztec festival
for the spirits of the dead that coincides with the
Catholic calendar. In Latin America and the
Caribbean, people move in processions to cemeteries, bearing candles, flowers, and food, all of
which may be shaped to resemble symbols of
death, such as skulls or coffins.
5. I.e., *mi madre, mi amor en muerte*—"my
mother, my love in death."

FROM THOMAS AND BEULAH[1]

The Event

Ever since they'd left the Tennessee ridge
with nothing to boast of
but good looks and a mandolin,

the two Negroes leaning
on the rail of a riverboat   5
were inseparable: Lem plucked

to Thomas' silver falsetto.
But the night was hot and they were drunk.
They spat where the wheel

churned mud and moonlight,   10
they called to the tarantulas
down among the bananas

to come out and dance.
You're so fine and mighty; let's see
what you can do, said Thomas, pointing   15

to a tree-capped island.
Lem stripped, spoke easy: *Them's chestnuts,*
I believe. Dove

quick as a gasp. Thomas, dry
on deck, saw the green crown shake   20
as the island slipped

under, dissolved
in the thickening stream.
At his feet

a stinking circle of rags,   25
the half-shell mandolin.
Where the wheel turned the water

gently shirred.[2]

1986

---

1. The story in this sequence of poems begins with Thomas as he makes his way north to Akron, Ohio. He loses his best friend, who, on a drunken dare from Thomas, drowns, leaving his mandolin behind. Thomas carries the mandolin with him and eventually hangs it on his parlor wall. He and Beulah marry when he is twenty-four and she is twenty; they have four daughters. Thomas works at the Goodyear Zeppelin factory (a zeppelin is a cylindrical airship kept aloft by hydrogen). The Depression puts him out of work, so he sweeps offices for a living until Goodyear rehires him at the advent of World War II. Beulah works in a dress shop and later makes hats. Thomas dies at sixty-three from his second heart attack; Beulah dies six years later.

2. Drawn together (like folds of cloth).

The Zeppelin Factory

The zeppelin factory
needed workers, all right—
but, standing in the cage
of the whale's belly, sparks
flying off the joints   5
and noise thundering,
Thomas wanted to sit
right down and cry.

That spring the third
largest airship was dubbed   10
the biggest joke
in town, though they all
turned out for the launch.
Wind caught,
"The Akron" floated   15
out of control,

three men in tow—
one dropped
to safety, one
hung on but the third,   20
muscles and adrenalin
failing, fell
clawing
six hundred feet.

Thomas at night   25
in the vacant lot:
        Here I am, intact
        and faint-hearted.

Thomas hiding
his heart with his hat   30
at the football game, eyeing
the Goodyear blimp overhead:
        Big boy I know
        you're in there.

1986

Dusting

Every day a wilderness—no
shade in sight. Beulah[1]

---

1. Hebrew for "married one" or "possessed." In the Bible it refers to the Promised Land.

patient among knicknacks,
the solarium a rage
of light, a grainstorm   5
as her gray cloth brings
dark wood to life.

Under her hand scrolls
and crests gleam
darker still. What   10
was his name, that
silly boy at the fair with
the rifle booth? And his kiss and
the clear bowl with one bright
fish, rippling   15
wound!

Not Michael—
something finer. Each dust
stroke a deep breath and
the canary in bloom.   20
Wavery memory: home
from a dance, the front door
blown open and the parlor
in snow, she rushed
the bowl to the stove, watched   25
as the locket of ice
dissolved and he
swam free.

That was years before
Father gave her up   30
with her name, years before
her name grew to mean
Promise, then
Desert-in-Peace.
Long before the shadow and   35
sun's accomplice, the tree.

Maurice.

                                                    1986

Poem in Which I Refuse Contemplation

A letter from my mother was waiting:
read in standing, one a.m.,
just arrived at my German mother-in-law

six hours from Paris by car.
Our daughter hops on Oma's bed,   5
happy to be back in a language

she knows. *Hello, all! Your postcard
came on the ninth*—familiar misspelled
words, exclamations. I wish my body

wouldn't cramp and leak; I want to—   10
as my daughter says, pretending to be
"Papa"—pull on boots and go for a long walk

alone. *Your cousin Ronnie in D.C.—
remember him?—he was the one
a few months younger than you—*   15

*was strangulated at some chili joint,
your Aunt May is beside herself!*
Mom slaps to the garden which is

*producing—onions, swiss chard,
lettuce, lettuce, lettuce, turnip greens and more lettuce*   20
so far! The roses are flurishing.

Haven't I always hated gardening? And German,
with its patient, grunting building blocks,
and for that matter, English, too,

Americanese's chewy twang? *Raccoons*   25
have taken up residence
we were ten *in the crawl space*

but I can't feel his hand *who knows*
anymore *how we'll get them out?*
I'm still standing. Bags to unpack.   30

That's all for now. Take care.

1989

Missing

I am the daughter who went out with the girls,
never checked back in and nothing marked my "last
known whereabouts," not a single glistening petal.

Horror is partial; it keeps you going. A lost
child is a fact hardening around its absence,   5
a knot in the breast purring *Touch, and I will*

come true. I was "returned," I watched her
watch as I babbled *It could have been worse. . . .*
Who can tell
what penetrates? Pity is the brutal   10

discipline. Now I understand she can never
die, just as nothing can bring me back—

I am the one who comes and goes;
I am the footfall that hovers.

1995

Rosa[1]

How she sat there,
the time right inside a place
so wrong it was ready.

That trim name with
its dream of a bench   5
to rest on. Her sensible coat.

Doing nothing was the doing:
the clean flame of her gaze
carved by a camera flash.

How she stood up   10
when they bent down to retrieve
her purse. That courtesy.

2000

Fox Trot Fridays

Thank the stars there's a day
each week to tuck in

the grief, lift your pearls, and
stride brush stride

quick-quick with a   5
heel-ball-toe. Smooth

as Nat King Cole's[1]
slow satin smile,

---

1. Rosa Parks (1913–2005). From a series of poems titled *On the Bus with Rosa Parks*. On December 1, 1955, in Montgomery, Alabama, Parks, an African American seamstress and secretary of the local National Association for the Advancement of Colored People (NAACP), was arrested and taken to jail for refusing to yield her seat on a bus to a white passenger. Her arrest prompted a boycott of the city bus system and inspired the civil rights movement in the late 1950s and the 1960s.

1. Popular African American jazz singer, songwriter, and pianist (1919–1965).

easy as taking
one day at a time: 10

one man and
one woman,

rib to rib,
with no heartbreak in sight—

just the sweep of Paradise   15
and the space of a song

to count all the wonders in it.

2004

AMY TAN
b. 1952

Born in Oakland, California, to parents who had only recently immigrated from China, Amy Tan emerged as a novelist just when American readers were focusing on multiculturalism, mother-daughter relations, and contrasts between old-country and new-world generations—three important factors in Tan's own experience. Her first novel, *The Joy Luck Club* (1989), addresses precisely these issues, drawing its energy from the transitional forces at work on its characters' multiple cultures. Four sets of mothers and daughters feature in the book, and each pair's story is a personal narrative that juxtaposes different perspectives and radically different values. The daughters find their mothers' values alien and threatening, for example, until they learn to understand what their mothers are saying and grasp how a new generation's life can draw meaning from that of the old. Hence the novel delivers a series of conversations, the dynamics of which express the vital nature of each person.

The historical events behind *The Joy Luck Club* inform the pasts of many Chinese families whose older members immigrated to the United States soon after World War II. From missionary activities going back to the nineteenth century to a wartime alliance with Chiang Kai-shek's Nationalist government (which was even then being challenged by the Communist forces of Mao Zedong), American interests were involved with China. In China Amy Tan's father, John, worked as a Chinese citizen for the United States Information Service, and in the turbulence leading up to Mao's victory in 1949 he left for a career with the Baptist ministry in the United States. Her mother's early life was less kind, fraught with atrocities involving concubinage (the fate of Amy's grandmother, who eventually killed herself), orphanhood, and an arranged marriage that ended in divorce. After emigrating from China to the United States, she met John Tan and began the marriage that produced two sons plus a daughter who resisted assimilation into the more superficial and materialistic aspects of American culture.

Amy Tan's American childhood took an international turn at age fifteen, when following her father's and older brother's deaths her mother moved the remainder of the family to Switzerland. After graduation Tan returned to the San Francisco Bay Area for college and graduate school, earning a B.A. in English and an M.A. in linguistics. Marriage followed, and some uncompleted doctoral studies led to work as a language-development specialist for disabled children and then as a medical writer. Wanting an outlet from the demands of her professional schedule, she began writing fiction, becoming an immediate success with stories that were later incorporated into *The Joy Luck Club*. In this novel and in a second, *The Kitchen God's Wife* (1991), Tan addressed the daughterly relationship that gave her not only material for fruitful complaint but also grounds for reconciliation, based on her better understanding of her mother's past, a story she had turned a deaf ear to as a rebellious teenager. Sections of this second novel, for example, move back and forth between the mother's narrative and the daughter's, each character fully endowed with a persuasive voice that defines the nature of her being, different as the two experiences are.

Tan has since published other novels and two works for children. She moved toward lighthearted satire in her 2005 novel, *Saving Fish from Drowning*, a chronicle of the adventures and misadventures of some second-generation Chinese Americans who have embarked on a trip to discover the art and culture of ancient China and ancient Burma.

"Two Kinds" first appeared as a short story in the *Atlantic Monthly*. The following text is from *The Joy Luck Club* (1989).

From The Joy Luck Club

Two Kinds

My mother believed you could be anything you wanted to be in America. You could open a restaurant. You could work for the government and get good retirement. You could buy a house with almost no money down. You could become rich. You could become instantly famous.

"Of course you can be prodigy, too," my mother told me when I was nine. "You can be best anything. What does Auntie Lindo know? Her daughter, she is only best tricky."

America was where all my mother's hopes lay. She had come here in 1949 after losing everything in China:[1] her mother and father, her family home, her first husband, and two daughters, twin baby girls. But she never looked back with regret. There were so many ways for things to get better.

We didn't immediately pick the right kind of prodigy. At first my mother thought I could be a Chinese Shirley Temple.[2] We'd watch Shirley's old movies on TV as though they were training films. My mother would poke my arm and say, "*Ni kan*"—You watch. And I would see Shirley tapping her feet, or singing a sailor song, or pursing her lips into a very round O while saying, "Oh my goodness."

"*Ni kan*," said my mother as Shirley's eyes flooded with tears. "You already know how. Don't need talent for crying!"

Soon after my mother got this idea about Shirley Temple, she took me to a beauty training school in the Mission district[3] and put me in the hands of a student who could barely hold the scissors without shaking. Instead of getting big fat curls, I emerged with an uneven mass of crinkly black fuzz. My mother dragged me off to the bathroom and tried to wet down my hair.

"You look like Negro Chinese," she lamented, as if I had done this on purpose.

The instructor of the beauty training school had to lop off these soggy clumps to make my hair even again. "Peter Pan[4] is very popular these days," the instructor assured my mother. I now had hair the length of a boy's, with straight-across bangs that hung at a slant two inches above my eyebrows. I liked the haircut and it made me actually look forward to my future fame.

In fact, in the beginning, I was just as excited as my mother, maybe even more so. I pictured this prodigy part of me as many different images, trying each one on for size. I was a dainty ballerina girl standing by the curtains, waiting to hear the right music that would send me floating on my tiptoes. I was like the Christ child lifted out of the straw manger, crying with holy indignity. I was Cinderella[5] stepping from her pumpkin carriage with sparkly cartoon music filling the air.

In all of my imaginings, I was filled with a sense that I would soon become *perfect*. My mother and father would adore me. I would be beyond reproach. I would never feel the need to sulk for anything.

But sometimes the prodigy in me became impatient. "If you don't hurry up and get me out of here, I'm disappearing for good," it warned. "And then you'll always be nothing."

Every night after dinner, my mother and I would sit at the Formica[6] kitchen table. She would present new tests, taking her examples from stories of amazing children she had read in *Ripley's Believe It or Not*, or *Good Housekeeping*, *Reader's Digest*,[7] and a dozen other magazines she kept in a pile in our bathroom. My mother got these magazines from people whose houses she cleaned. And since she cleaned many houses each week, we had a great assortment. She would look through them all, searching for stories about remarkable children.

The first night she brought out a story about a three-year-old boy who knew the capitals of all the states and even most of the European countries. A teacher was quoted as saying the little boy could also pronounce the names of the foreign cities correctly.

"What's the capital of Finland?" my mother asked me, looking at the magazine story.

All I knew was the capital of California, because Sacramento was the name of the street we lived on in Chinatown. "Nairobi!" I guessed, saying

---

3. Multicultural neighborhood in San Francisco.
4. Children's play (1904) by the Scottish playwright and novelist James M. Barrie (1860–1937), basis for a feature cartoon and Broadway musical in the 1950s, in which the protagonist (a boy) wears his hair in a pixielike cut soon favored by many American girls.

5. Stepsister-turned-princess in a Walt Disney animated musical (1950) based on a folktale dating from 16th-century Europe.
6. Trademark for a laminated-plastic kitchen-countertop covering popular in the 1950s.
7. Popular middle-class American magazines of the era.

the most foreign word I could think of. She checked to see if that was possibly one way to pronounce "Helsinki"[8] before showing me the answer.

The tests got harder—multiplying numbers in my head, finding the queen of hearts in a deck of cards, trying to stand on my head without using my hands, predicting the daily temperatures in Los Angeles, New York, and London.

One night I had to look at a page from the Bible for three minutes and then report everything I could remember. "Now Jehoshaphat had riches and honor in abundance and[9] . . . that's all I remember, Ma," I said.

And after seeing my mother's disappointed face once again, something inside of me began to die. I hated the tests, the raised hopes and failed expectations. Before going to bed that night, I looked in the mirror above the bathroom sink and when I saw only my face staring back—and that it would always be this ordinary face—I began to cry. Such a sad, ugly girl! I made high-pitched noises like a crazed animal, trying to scratch out the face in the mirror.

And then I saw what seemed to be the prodigy side of me—because I had never seen that face before. I looked at my reflection, blinking so I could see more clearly. The girl staring back at me was angry, powerful. This girl and I were the same. I had new thoughts, willful thoughts, or rather thoughts filled with lots of won'ts. I won't let her change me, I promised myself. I won't be what I'm not.

So now on nights when my mother presented her tests, I performed listlessly, my head propped on one arm. I pretended to be bored. And I was. I got so bored I started counting the bellows of the foghorns out on the bay[1] while my mother drilled me in other areas. The sound was comforting and reminded me of the cow jumping over the moon.[2] And the next day, I played a game with myself, seeing if my mother would give up on me before eight bellows. After a while I usually counted only one, maybe two bellows at most. At last she was beginning to give up hope.

Two or three months had gone by without any mention of my being a prodigy again. And then one day my mother was watching *The Ed Sullivan Show*[3] on TV. The TV was old and the sound kept shorting out. Every time my mother got halfway up from the sofa to adjust the set, the sound would go back on and Ed would be talking. As soon as she sat down, Ed would go silent again. She got up, the TV broke into loud piano music. She sat down. Silence. Up and down, back and forth, quiet and loud. It was like a stiff embraceless dance between her and the TV set. Finally she stood by the set with her hand on the sound dial.

She seemed entranced by the music, a little frenzied piano piece with this mesmerizing quality, sort of quick passages and then teasing lilting ones before it returned to the quick playful parts.

8. Capital of Finland, in northern Europe. "Chinatown": ethnic Chinese neighborhood in San Francisco. "Nairobi": capital of Kenya, in Africa.
9. 2 Chronicles 17.5: "Therefore the Lord established the kingdom in his hand, and all Judah brought tribute to Jehoshaphat; and he had great riches and honor."

1. San Francisco Bay.
2. A Mother Goose rhyme.
3. Longest-running variety series (1948–71) in American television history, hosted by New York newspaper society and entertainment columnist Ed Sullivan (1902–1974).

"*Ni kan*," my mother said, calling me over with hurried hand gestures, "Look here."

I could see why my mother was fascinated by the music. It was being pounded out by a little Chinese girl, about nine years old, with a Peter Pan haircut. The girl had the sauciness of a Shirley Temple. She was proudly modest like a proper Chinese child. And she also did this fancy sweep of a curtsy, so that the fluffy skirt of her white dress cascaded slowly to the floor like the petals of a large carnation.

In spite of these warning signs, I wasn't worried. Our family had no piano and we couldn't afford to buy one, let alone reams of sheet music and piano lessons. So I could be generous in my comments when my mother bad-mouthed the little girl on TV.

"Play note right, but doesn't sound good! No singing sound," complained my mother.

"What are you picking on her for?" I said carelessly. "She's pretty good. Maybe she's not the best, but she's trying hard." I knew almost immediately I would be sorry I said that.

"Just like you," she said. "Not the best. Because you not trying." She gave a little huff as she let go of the sound dial and sat down on the sofa.

The little Chinese girl sat down also to play an encore of "Anitra's Dance" by Grieg.[4] I remember the song, because later on I had to learn how to play it.

Three days after watching *The Ed Sullivan Show*, my mother told me what my schedule would be for piano lessons and piano practice. She had talked to Mr. Chong, who lived on the first floor of our apartment building. Mr. Chong was a retired piano teacher and my mother had traded housecleaning services for weekly lessons and a piano for me to practice on every day, two hours a day, from four until six.

When my mother told me this, I felt as though I had been sent to hell. I whined and then kicked my foot a little when I couldn't stand it anymore.

"Why don't you like me the way I am? I'm *not* a genius! I can't play the piano. And even if I could, I wouldn't go on TV if you paid me a million dollars!" I cried.

My mother slapped me. "Who ask you be genius?" she shouted. "Only ask you be your best. For you sake. You think I want you be genius? Hnnh! What for! Who ask you!"

"So ungrateful," I heard her mutter in Chinese. "If she had as much talent as she has temper, she would be famous now."

Mr. Chong, whom I secretly nicknamed Old Chong, was very strange, always tapping his fingers to the silent music of an invisible orchestra. He looked ancient in my eyes. He had lost most of the hair on top of his head and he wore thick glasses and had eyes that always looked tired and sleepy. But he must have been younger than I thought, since he lived with his mother and was not yet married.

I met Old Lady Chong once and that was enough. She had this peculiar smell like a baby that had done something in its pants. And her fingers felt like a dead person's, like an old peach I once found in the back of the refrigerator; the skin just slid off the meat when I picked it up.

---

4. From the *Peer Gynt Suite* (1874–75), by the Norwegian composer Edvard Grieg (1843–1907).

I soon found out why Old Chong had retired from teaching piano. He was deaf. "Like Beethoven!"[5] he shouted to me. "We're both listening only in our head!" And he would start to conduct his frantic silent sonatas.

Our lessons went like this. He would open the book and point to different things, explaining their purpose: "Key! Treble! Bass! No sharps or flats! So this is C major! Listen now and play after me!"

And then he would play the C scale a few times, a simple chord, and then, as if inspired by an old, unreachable itch, he gradually added more notes and running trills and a pounding bass until the music was really something quite grand.

I would play after him, the simple scale, the simple chord, and then I just played some nonsense that sounded like a cat running up and down on top of garbage cans. Old Chong smiled and applauded and then said, "Very good! But now you must learn to keep time!"

So that's how I discovered that Old Chong's eyes were too slow to keep up with the wrong notes I was playing. He went through the motions in half-time. To help me keep rhythm, he stood behind me, pushing down on my right shoulder for every beat. He balanced pennies on top of my wrists so I would keep them still as I slowly played scales and arpeggios. He had me curve my hand around an apple and keep that shape when playing chords. He marched stiffly to show me how to make each finger dance up and down, staccato like an obedient little soldier.

He taught me all these things, and that was how I also learned I could be lazy and get away with mistakes, lots of mistakes. If I hit the wrong notes because I hadn't practiced enough, I never corrected myself. I just kept playing in rhythm. And Old Chong kept conducting his own private reverie.

So maybe I never really gave myself a fair chance. I did pick up the basics pretty quickly, and I might have become a good pianist at that young age. But I was so determined not to try, not to be anybody different that I learned to play only the most ear-splitting preludes, the most discordant hymns.

Over the next year, I practiced like this, dutifully in my own way. And then one day I heard my mother and her friend Lindo Jong both talking in a loud bragging tone of voice so others could hear. It was after church, and I was leaning against the brick wall wearing a dress with stiff white petticoats. Auntie Lindo's daughter, Waverly, who was about my age, was standing farther down the wall about five feet away. We had grown up together and shared all the closeness of two sisters squabbling over crayons and dolls. In other words, for the most part, we hated each other. I thought she was snotty. Waverly Jong had gained a certain amount of fame as "Chinatown's Littlest Chinese Chess Champion."

"She bring home too many trophy," lamented Auntie Lindo that Sunday. "All day she play chess. All day I have no time do nothing but dust off her winnings." She threw a scolding look at Waverly, who pretended not to see her.

"You lucky you don't have this problem," said Auntie Lindo with a sigh to my mother.

---

5. Ludwig van Beethoven (1770–1827), German composer who began losing his hearing in 1801 and was totally deaf by 1817, yet who continued to compose monumental works.

And my mother squared her shoulders and bragged: "Our problem worser than yours. If we ask Jing-mei wash dish, she hear nothing but music. It's like you can't stop this natural talent."

And right then, I was determined to put a stop to her foolish pride.

A few weeks later, Old Chong and my mother conspired to have me play in a talent show which would be held in the church hall. By then, my parents had saved up enough to buy me a secondhand piano, a black Wurlitzer[6] spinet with a scarred bench. It was the showpiece of our living room.

For the talent show, I was to play a piece called "Pleading Child" from Schumann's *Scenes from Childhood*.[7] It was a simple, moody piece that sounded more difficult than it was. I was supposed to memorize the whole thing, playing the repeat parts twice to make the piece sound longer. But I dawdled over it, playing a few bars and then cheating, looking up to see what notes followed. I never really listened to what I was playing. I daydreamed about being somewhere else, about being someone else.

The part I liked to practice best was the fancy curtsy: right foot out, touch the rose on the carpet with a pointed foot, sweep to the side, left leg bends, look up and smile.

My parents invited all the couples from the Joy Luck Club[8] to witness my debut. Auntie Lindo and Uncle Tin were there. Waverly and her two older brothers had also come. The first two rows were filled with children both younger and older than I was. The littlest ones got to go first. They recited simple nursery rhymes, squawked out tunes on miniature violins, twirled Hula Hoops;[9] pranced in pink ballet tutus, and when they bowed or curtsied, the audience would sigh in unison, "Awww," and then clap enthusiastically.

When my turn came, I was very confident. I remember my childish excitement. It was as if I knew, without a doubt, that the prodigy side of me really did exist. I had no fear whatsoever, no nervousness. I remember thinking to myself, This is it! This is it! I looked out over the audience, at my mother's blank face, my father's yawn, Auntie Lindo's stiff-lipped smile, Waverly's sulky expression. I had on a white dress layered with sheets of lace, and a pink bow in my Peter Pan haircut. As I sat down I envisioned people jumping to their feet and Ed Sullivan rushing up to introduce me to everyone on TV.

And I started to play. It was so beautiful. I was so caught up in how lovely I looked that at first I didn't worry how I would sound. So it was a surprise to me when I hit the first wrong note and I realized something didn't sound quite right. And then I hit another and another followed that. A chill started at the top of my head and began to trickle down. Yet I couldn't stop playing, as though my hands were bewitched. I kept thinking my fingers would adjust themselves back, like a train switching to the right track. I played this strange jumble through two repeats, the sour notes staying with me all the way to the end.

6. The Wurlitzer Company, manufacturer of pianos, organs, and jukeboxes.
7. That is, *Kinderszenen* (1838), a set of piano pieces by the German composer Robert Alexander Schumann (1810–1856).
8. In Tan's novel, a four-member club formed to play mah-jongg (a table game popular in its present form since 1920) and continued as a social unit.
9. Exercise toy popular as a novelty item in the 1950s.

When I stood up, I discovered my legs were shaking. Maybe I had just been nervous and the audience, like Old Chong, had seen me go through the right motions and had not heard anything wrong at all. I swept my right foot out, went down on my knee, looked up and smiled. The room was quiet, except for Old Chong, who was beaming and shouting, "Bravo! Bravo! Well done!" But then I saw my mother's face, her stricken face. The audience clapped weakly, and as I walked back to my chair, with my whole face quivering as I tried not to cry, I heard a little boy whisper loudly to his mother, "That was awful," and the mother whispered back, "Well, she certainly tried."

And now I realized how many people were in the audience, the whole world it seemed. I was aware of eyes burning into my back. I felt the shame of my mother and father as they sat stiffly throughout the rest of the show.

We could have escaped during intermission. Pride and some strange sense of honor must have anchored my parents to their chairs. And so we watched it all: the eighteen-year-old boy with a fake mustache who did a magic show and juggled flaming hoops while riding a unicycle. The breasted girl with white makeup who sang from *Madama Butterfly*[1] and got honorable mention. And the eleven-year-old boy who won first prize playing a tricky violin song that sounded like a busy bee.

After the show, the Hsus, the Jongs, and the St. Clairs from the Joy Luck Club came up to my mother and father.

"Lots of talented kids," Auntie Lindo said vaguely, smiling broadly.

"That was somethin' else," said my father, and I wondered if he was referring to me in a humorous way, or whether he even remembered what I had done.

Waverly looked at me and shrugged her shoulders. "You aren't a genius like me," she said matter-of-factly. And if I hadn't felt so bad, I would have pulled her braids and punched her stomach.

But my mother's expression was what devastated me: a quiet, blank look that said she had lost everything. I felt the same way, and it seemed as if everybody were now coming up, like gawkers at the scene of an accident, to see what parts were actually missing. When we got on the bus to go home, my father was humming the busy-bee tune and my mother was silent. I kept thinking she wanted to wait until we got home before shouting at me. But when my father unlocked the door to our apartment, my mother walked in and then went to the back, into the bedroom. No accusations. No blame. And in a way, I felt disappointed. I had been waiting for her to start shouting, so I could shout back and cry and blame her for all my misery.

I assumed my talent-show fiasco meant I never had to play the piano again. But two days later, after school, my mother came out of the kitchen and saw me watching TV.

"Four clock," she reminded me as if it were any other day. I was stunned, as though she were asking me to go through the talent-show torture again. I wedged myself more tightly in front of the TV.

"Turn off TV," she called from the kitchen five minutes later.

---

1. Opera (1904), set in Japan, by the Italian composer Giacomo Puccini (1858–1924).

I didn't budge. And then I decided. I didn't have to do what my mother said anymore. I wasn't her slave. This wasn't China. I had listened to her before and look what happened. She was the stupid one.

She came out from the kitchen and stood in the arched entryway of the living room. "Four clock," she said once again, louder.

"I'm not going to play anymore," I said nonchalantly. "Why should I? I'm not a genius."

She walked over and stood in front of the TV. I saw her chest was heaving up and down in an angry way.

"No!" I said, and I now felt stronger, as if my true self had finally emerged. So this was what had been inside me all along.

"No! I won't!" I screamed.

She yanked me by the arm, pulled me off the floor, snapped off the TV. She was frighteningly strong, half pulling, half carrying me toward the piano as I kicked the throw rugs under my feet. She lifted me up and onto the hard bench. I was sobbing by now, looking at her bitterly. Her chest was heaving even more and her mouth was open, smiling crazily as if she were pleased I was crying.

"You want me to be someone that I'm not!" I sobbed. "I'll never be the kind of daughter you want me to be!"

"Only two kinds of daughters," she shouted in Chinese. "Those who are obedient and those who follow their own mind! Only one kind of daughter can live in this house. Obedient daughter!"

"Then I wish I wasn't your daughter. I wish you weren't my mother," I shouted. As I said these things I got scared. It felt like worms and toads and slimy things crawling out of my chest, but it also felt good, as if this awful side of me had surfaced, at last.

"Too late change this," said my mother shrilly.

And I could sense her anger rising to its breaking point. I wanted to see it spill over. And that's when I remembered the babies she had lost in China, the ones we never talked about. "Then I wish I'd never been born!" I shouted. "I wish I were dead! Like them."

It was as if I had said the magic words. Alakazam![2]—and her face went blank, her mouth closed, her arms went slack, and she backed out of the room, stunned, as if she were blowing away like a small brown leaf, thin, brittle, lifeless.

It was not the only disappointment my mother felt in me. In the years that followed, I failed her so many times, each time asserting my own will, my right to fall short of expectations. I didn't get straight As. I didn't become class president. I didn't get into Stanford. I dropped out of college.

For unlike my mother, I did not believe I could be anything I wanted to be. I could only be me.

And for all those years, we never talked about the disaster at the recital or my terrible accusations afterward at the piano bench. All that remained unchecked, like a betrayal that was now unspeakable. So I never found a way to ask her why she had hoped for something so large that failure was inevitable.

---

2. A magical incantation (slang).

And even worse, I never asked her what frightened me the most: Why had she given up hope?

For after our struggle at the piano, she never mentioned my playing again. The lessons stopped. The lid to the piano was closed, shutting out the dust, my misery, and her dreams.

So she surprised me. A few years ago, she offered to give me the piano, for my thirtieth birthday. I had not played in all those years. I saw the offer as a sign of forgiveness, a tremendous burden removed.

"Are you sure?" I asked shyly. "I mean, won't you and Dad miss it?"

"No, this your piano," she said firmly. "Always your piano. You only one can play."

"Well, I probably can't play anymore," I said. "It's been years."

"You pick up fast," said my mother, as if she knew this was certain. "You have natural talent. You could been genius if you want to."

"No I couldn't."

"You just not trying," said my mother. And she was neither angry nor sad. She said it as if to announce a fact that could never be disproved. "Take it," she said.

But I didn't at first. It was enough that she had offered it to me. And after that, every time I saw it in my parents' living room, standing in front of the bay windows, it made me feel proud, as if it were a shiny trophy I had won back.

Last week I sent a tuner over to my parents' apartment and had the piano reconditioned, for purely sentimental reasons. My mother had died a few months before and I had been getting things in order for my father, a little bit at a time. I put the jewelry in special silk pouches. The sweaters she had knitted in yellow, pink, bright orange—all the colors I hated—I put those in mothproof boxes. I found some old Chinese silk dresses, the kind with little slits up the sides. I rubbed the old silk against my skin, then wrapped them in tissue and decided to take them home with me.

After I had the piano tuned, I opened the lid and touched the keys. It sounded even richer than I remembered. Really, it was a very good piano. Inside the bench were the same exercise notes with handwritten scales, the same secondhand music books with their covers held together with yellow tape.

I opened up the Schumann book to the dark little piece I had played at the recital. It was on the left-hand side of the page, "Pleading Child." It looked more difficult than I remembered. I played a few bars, surprised at how easily the notes came back to me.

And for the first time, or so it seemed, I noticed the piece on the right-hand side. It was called "Perfectly Contented." I tried to play this one as well. It had a lighter melody but the same flowing rhythm and turned out to be quite easy. "Pleading Child" was shorter but slower; "Perfectly Contented" was longer, but faster. And after I played them both a few times, I realized they were two halves of the same song.

1989

SANDRA CISNEROS
b. 1954

Sandra Cisneros began writing at age ten, much like the young Chicana narrator of *The House on Mango Street* (1984), the volume of interrelated vignettes from a child's perspective that brought Cisneros her first major attention. In brief, sharply drawn segments, the narrator, Esperanza, conveys the ambience of growing up in Chicago's Mexican American community. The social bond of this neighborhood eases the contrast between Esperanza's nurturing family and the more hostile forces of poverty and racism. Cisneros cultivates a sense of warmth and naive humor for her protagonists, qualities that are evident in introductory parts to *Woman Hollering Creek* (1991), a short-story collection that also focuses on young women facing hostile forces. Without sentimentalizing or idealizing her narrator's perspective, Cisneros presents glimpses of a world full of adult challenges and multicultural complexities. Sex is a topic in all Cisneros's work, including her poetry collected as *My Wicked Wicked Ways* (1987) and *Loose Woman* (1994)—sometimes gentle and even silly, other times brutally assaultive. What remains constant is the author's view that by romanticizing sexual relations women cooperate with a male view that can be oppressive, even physically destructive. As has been said of the protagonist of her 2002 novel, *Caramelo*, Cisneros is "caught between here and there." Yet "here" and "there" are not as dichotomous as young versus old, female versus male, or Mexico versus the United States. Instead, the flow of experience between these poles yields her work's subject: people finding their own lifestyles in the space between fixed boundaries. Because this intervening space is so rich in creative potential, Cisneros can balance unhappiness with humor and find personal victories where others might see social defeat.

Born in Chicago, the child of a Mexican father and a Mexican American mother, Cisneros spent parts of her childhood in Texas and Mexico as well. Her Catholic-school background led to a B.A. degree from Chicago's Loyola University, after which she earned a graduate degree in creative writing from the University of Iowa's Writers Workshop. Teaching in San Antonio, Texas, she used her position as a writer and an educator to champion Chicana feminism, especially as this movement combines cultural issues with women's concerns. In raising controversy by having her house painted very brightly, she openly questioned monocultural "historical districts" and "community covenants." *Whose* history? Cisneros asked. *Which* community sets standards? (Through research she established that her decorating style was in accordance with her home's background and that the standards used to dispute her choice were arbitrary.) A dissatisfaction with the politics of publishing has made her an advocate of small-press dissemination. Most of all, as in the story reprinted here, she is eager to show the rich dynamics of characters existing in the blend of Mexican and American cultures that begins with speaking two languages and extends to almost every aspect of life. Spanish words, Mexican holidays, ethnic foods, and localized religious practices punctuate her narratives; her characters have a facility with cultural play that reflects the bilingual and bicultural life shared by millions of Mexican Americans.

The following text is from *Woman Hollering Creek* (1991).

Woman Hollering Creek

The day Don Serafín gave Juan Pedro Martínez Sánchez permission to take Cleófilas Enriqueta DeLeón Hernández as his bride, across her father's threshold, over several miles of dirt road and several miles of paved, over one border and beyond to a town *en el otro lado*—on the other side—already did he divine the morning his daughter would raise her hand over her eyes, look south, and dream of returning to the chores that never ended, six good-for-nothing brothers, and one old man's complaints.

He had said, after all, in the hubbub of parting: I am your father, I will never abandon you. He *had* said that, hadn't he, when he hugged and then let her go. But at the moment Cleófilas was busy looking for Chela, her maid of honor, to fulfill their bouquet conspiracy. She would not remember her father's parting words until later. *I am your father, I will never abandon you.*

Only now as a mother did she remember. Now, when she and Juan Pedrito sat by the creek's edge. How when a man and a woman love each other, sometimes that love sours. But a parent's love for a child, a child's for its parents, is another thing entirely.

This is what Cleófilas thought evenings when Juan Pedro did not come home, and she lay on her side of the bed listening to the hollow roar of the interstate, a distant dog barking, the pecan trees rustling like ladies in stiff petticoats—*shh-shh-shh, shh-shh-shh*—soothing her to sleep.

In the town where she grew up, there isn't very much to do except accompany the aunts and godmothers to the house of one or the other to play cards. Or walk to the cinema to see this week's film again, speckled and with one hair quivering annoyingly on the screen. Or to the center of town to order a milk shake that will appear in a day and a half as a pimple on her backside. Or to the girlfriend's house to watch the latest *telenovela*[1] episode and try to copy the way the women comb their hair, wear their makeup.

But what Cleófilas has been waiting for, has been whispering and sighing and giggling for, has been anticipating since she was old enough to lean against the window displays of gauze and butterflies and lace, is passion. Not the kind on the cover of the ¡*Alarma!*[2] magazines, mind you, where the lover is photographed with the bloody fork she used to salvage her good name. But passion in its purest crystalline essence. The kind the books and songs and *telenovelas* describe when one finds, finally, the great love of one's life, and does whatever one can, must do, at whatever the cost.

Tú o Nadie. "You or No One." The title of the current favorite *telenovela*. The beautiful Lucía Méndez having to put up with all kinds of hardships of the heart, separation and betrayal, and loving, always loving no matter what, because *that* is the most important thing, and did you see Lucía Méndez on the Bayer aspirin commercials—wasn't she lovely? Does she dye her hair do you think? Cleófilas is going to go to the *farmacía*[3] and buy a hair rinse; her girlfriend Chela will apply it—it's not that difficult at all.

---

1. Serialized TV melodrama (Spanish).
2. Graphic, sensationalistic Mexican magazine

published since 1963.
3. Pharmacy, drugstore (Spanish).

Because you didn't watch last night's episode when Lucía confessed she loved him more than anyone in her life. In her life! And she sings the song "You or No One" in the beginning and end of the show. *Tú o Nadie.* Somehow one ought to live one's life like that, don't you think? You or no one. Because to suffer for love is good. The pain all sweet somehow. In the end.

Seguín. She had liked the sound of it. Far away and lovely. Not like *Monclova. Coahuia.*[4] Ugly.

Seguín, Tejas. A nice sterling ring to it. The tinkle of money. She would get to wear outfits like the women on the *tele*, like Lucía Méndez. And have a lovely house, and wouldn't Chela be jealous.

And yes, they will drive all the way to Laredo[5] to get her wedding dress. That's what they say. Because Juan Pedro wants to get married right away, without a long engagement since he can't take off too much time from work. He has a very important position in Seguin with, with . . . a beer company, I think. Or was it tires? Yes, he has to be back. So they will get married in the spring when he can take off work, and then they will drive off in his new pickup—did you see it?—to their new home in Seguin. Well, not exactly new, but they're going to repaint the house. You know newlyweds. New paint and new furniture. Why not? He can afford it. And later on add maybe a room or two for the children. May they be blessed with many.

Well, you'll see. Cleófilas has always been so good with her sewing machine. A little *rrrr, rrrr, rrrr* of the machine and ¡zas! Miracles. She's always been so clever, that girl. Poor thing. And without even a mama to advise her on things like her wedding night. Well, may God help her. What with a father with a head like a burro, and those six clumsy brothers. Well, what do you think! Yes, I'm going to the wedding. Of course! The dress I want to wear just needs to be altered a teensy bit to bring it up to date. See, I saw a new style last night that I thought would suit me. Did you watch last night's episode of *The Rich Also Cry*?[6] Well, did you notice the dress the mother was wearing?

La Gritona.[7] Such a funny name for such a lovely *arroyo.*[8] But that's what they called the creek that ran behind the house. Though no one could say whether the woman had hollered from anger or pain. The natives only knew the *arroyo* one crossed on the way to San Antonio, and then once again on the way back, was called Woman Hollering, a name no one from these parts questioned, little less understood. *Pues, allá de los indios, quién sabe*[9]—who knows, the townspeople shrugged, because it was of no concern to their lives how this trickle of water received its curious name.

"What do you want to know for?" Trini the laundromat attendant asked in the same gruff Spanish she always used whenever she gave Cleófilas change or yelled at her for something. First for putting too much soap in the machines. Later, for sitting on a washer. And still later, after Juan Pedrito was born, for not understanding that in this country you cannot let your baby

---

4. Respectively a town and state in Mexico, the latter bordering Texas. "Seguín": city in Guadalupe County, south-central Texas.
5. City in southwestern Texas, on the Mexican border.
6. First global soap opera (production beginning in Mexico in 1979), exported to Russia, China, the United States, and other countries.
7. The Shouter, Yeller, Hollerer (Spanish).
8. Stream (Spanish).
9. Well, beyond the Indians, who knows (Spanish).

walk around with no diaper and his pee-pee hanging out, it wasn't nice, ¿entiendes? Pues.[1]

How could Cleófilas explain to a woman like this why the name Woman Hollering fascinated her. Well, there was no sense talking to Trini.

On the other hand there were the neighbor ladies, one on either side of the house they rented near the arroyo. The woman Soledad on the left, the woman Dolores on the right.

The neighbor lady Soledad liked to call herself a widow, though how she came to be one was a mystery. Her husband had either died, or run away with an ice-house[2] floozie, or simply gone out for cigarettes one afternoon and never came back. It was hard to say which since Soledad, as a rule, didn't mention him.

In the other house lived la señora[3] Dolores, kind and very sweet, but her house smelled too much of incense and candles from the altars that burned continuously in memory of two sons who had died in the last war and one husband who had died shortly after from grief. The neighbor lady Dolores divided her time between the memory of these men and her garden, famous for its sunflowers—so tall they had to be supported with broom handles and old boards; red red cockscombs, fringed and bleeding a thick menstrual color; and, especially, roses whose sad scent reminded Cleófilas of the dead. Each Sunday la señora Dolores clipped the most beautiful of these flowers and arranged them on three modest headstones at the Seguin cemetery.

The neighbor ladies, Soledad, Dolores, they might've known once the name of the arroyo before it turned English but they did not know now. They were too busy remembering the men who had left through either choice or circumstance and would never come back.

Pain or rage, Cleófilas wondered when she drove over the bridge the first time as a newlywed and Juan Pedro had pointed it out. La Gritona, he had said, and she had laughed. Such a funny name for a creek so pretty and full of happily ever after.

The first time she had been so surprised she didn't cry out or try to defend herself. She had always said she would strike back if a man, any man, were to strike her.

But when the moment came, and he slapped her once, and then again, and again; until the lip split and bled an orchid of blood, she didn't fight back, she didn't break into tears, she didn't run away as she imagined she might when she saw such things in the telenovelas.

In her own home her parents had never raised a hand to each other or to their children. Although she admitted she may have been brought up a little leniently as an only daughter—la consentida,[4] the princess—there were some things she would never tolerate. Ever.

Instead, when it happened the first time, when they were barely man and wife, she had been so stunned, it left her speechless, motionless, numb. She had done nothing but reach up to the heat on her mouth and stare at the blood on her hand as if even then she didn't understand.

---

1. Do you understand? Well (Spanish).
2. Tavern.

3. The lady (Spanish).
4. The spoiled one (Spanish).

She could think of nothing to say, said nothing. Just stroked the dark curls of the man who wept and would weep like a child, his tears of repentance and shame, this time and each.

The men at the ice house. From what she can tell, from the times during her first year when still a newlywed she is invited and accompanies her husband, sits mute beside their conversation, waits and sips a beer until it grows warm, twists a paper napkin into a knot, then another into a fan, one into a rose, nods her head, smiles, yawns, politely grins, laughs at the appropriate moments, leans against her husband's sleeve, tugs at his elbow, and finally becomes good at predicting where the talk will lead, from this Cleófilas concludes each is nightly trying to find the truth lying at the bottom of the bottle like a gold doubloon on the sea floor.

They want to tell each other what they want to tell themselves. But what is bumping like a helium balloon at the ceiling of the brain never finds its way out. It bubbles and rises, it gurgles in the throat, it rolls across the surface of the tongue, and erupts from the lips—a belch.

If they are lucky, there are tears at the end of the long night. At any given moment, the fists try to speak. They are dogs chasing their own tails before lying down to sleep, trying to find a way, a route, an out, and—finally—get some peace.

In the morning sometimes before he opens his eyes. Or after they have finished loving. Or at times when he is simply across from her at the table putting pieces of food into his mouth and chewing. Cleófilas thinks, This is the man I have waited my whole life for.

Not that he isn't a good man. She has to remind herself why she loves him when she changes the baby's Pampers, or when she mops the bathroom floor, or tries to make the curtains for the doorways without doors, or whiten the linen. Or wonder a little when he kicks the refrigerator and says he hates this shitty house and is going out where he won't be bothered with the baby's howling and her suspicious questions, and her requests to fix this and this and this because if she had any brains in her head she'd realize he's been up before the rooster earning his living to pay for the food in her belly and the roof over her head and would have to wake up again early the next day so why can't you just leave me in peace, woman.

He is not very tall, no, and he doesn't look like the men on the *telenovelas*. His face still scarred from acne. And he has a bit of a belly from all the beer he drinks. Well, he's always been husky.

This man who farts and belches and snores as well as laughs and kisses and holds her. Somehow this husband whose whiskers she finds each morning in the sink, whose shoes she must air each evening on the porch, this husband who cuts his fingernails in public, laughs loudly, curses like a man, and demands each course of dinner be served on a separate plate like at his mother's, as soon as he gets home, on time or late, and who doesn't care at all for music or *telenovelas* or romance or roses or the moon floating pearly over the *arroyo*, or through the bedroom window for that matter, shut the blinds and go back to sleep, this man, this father, this rival, this keeper, this lord, this master, this husband till kingdom come.

A doubt. Slender as a hair. A washed cup set back on the shelf wrong-side-up. Her lipstick, and body talc, and hairbrush all arranged in the bathroom a different way.

No. Her imagination. The house the same as always. Nothing.

Coming home from the hospital with her new son, her husband. Something comforting in discovering her house slippers beneath the bed, the faded housecoat where she left it on the bathroom hook. Her pillow. Their bed.

Sweet sweet homecoming. Sweet as the scent of face powder in the air, jasmine, sticky liquor.

Smudged fingerprint on the door. Crushed cigarette in a glass. Wrinkle in the brain crumpling to a crease.

Sometimes she thinks of her father's house. But how could she go back there? What a disgrace. What would the neighbors say? Coming home like that with one baby on her hip and one in the oven. Where's your husband?

The town of gossips. The town of dust and despair. Which she has traded for this town of gossips. This town of dust, despair. Houses farther apart perhaps, though no more privacy because of it. No leafy *zócalo*[5] in the center of the town, though the murmur of talk is clear enough all the same. No huddled whispering on the church steps each Sunday. Because here the whispering begins at sunset at the ice house instead.

This town with its silly pride for a bronze pecan the size of a baby carriage in front of the city hall. TV repair shop, drugstore, hardware, dry cleaner's, chiropractor's, liquor store, bail bonds, empty storefront, and nothing, nothing, nothing of interest. Nothing one could walk to, at any rate. Because the towns here are built so that you have to depend on husbands. Or you stay home. Or you drive. If you're rich enough to own, allowed to drive, your own car.

There is no place to go. Unless one counts the neighbor ladies. Soledad on one side, Dolores on the other. Or the creek.

Don't go out there after dark, *mi'jita*.[6] Stay near the house. *No es bueno para la salud.*[7] Mala suerte. Bad luck. *Mal aire.*[8] You'll get sick and the baby too. You'll catch a fright wandering about in the dark, and then you'll see how right we were.

The stream sometimes only a muddy puddle in the summer, though now in the springtime, because of the rains, a good-size alive thing, a thing with a voice all its own, all day and all night calling in its high, silver voice. Is it La Llorona,[9] the weeping woman? La Llorona, who drowned her own children. Perhaps La Llorona is the one they named the creek after, she thinks, remembering all the stories she learned as a child.

La Llorona calling to her. She is sure of it. Cleófilas sets the baby's Donald Duck blanket on the grass. Listens. The day sky turning to night. The baby pulling up fistfuls of grass and laughing. La Llorona. Wonders if something as quiet as this drives a woman to the darkness under the trees.

---

5. Town square (Spanish).
6. My daughter (Spanish).
7. It's not good for one's health (Spanish).
8. Bad air (Spanish).

9. The Woman Who Cries (Spanish), a spurned mistress of Mexican legend who drowned her children and was fated to eternally seek their recovery.

What she needs is . . . and made a gesture as if to yank a woman's buttocks to his groin. Maximiliano, the foul-smelling fool from across the road, said this and set the men laughing, but Cleófilas just muttered. *Grosera*,[1] and went on washing dishes.

She knew he said it not because it was true, but more because it was he who needed to sleep with a woman, instead of drinking each night at the ice house and stumbling home alone.

Maximiliano who was said to have killed his wife in an ice-house brawl when she came at him with a mop. I had to shoot, he had said—she was armed.

Their laughter outside the kitchen window. Her husband's, his friends'. Manolo, Beto, Efraín, el Perico.[2] Maximiliano.

Was Cleófilas just exaggerating as her husband always said? It seemed the newspapers were full of such stories. This woman found on the side of the interstate. This one pushed from a moving car. This one's cadaver, this one unconscious, this one beaten blue. Her ex-husband, her husband, her lover, her father, her brother, her uncle, her friend, her co-worker. Always. The same grisly news in the pages of the dailies. She dunked a glass under the soapy water for a moment—shivered.

He had thrown a book. Hers. From across the room. A hot welt across the cheek. She could forgive that. But what stung more was the fact it was *her* book, a love story by Corín Tellado,[3] what she loved most now that she lived in the U.S., without a television set, without the *telenovelas*.

Except now and again when her husband was away and she could manage it, the few episodes glimpsed at the neighbor lady Soledad's house because Dolores didn't care for that sort of thing, though Soledad was often kind enough to retell what had happened on what episode of *María de Nadie*,[4] the poor Argentine country girl who had the ill fortune of falling in love with the beautiful son of the Arrocha family, the very family she worked for, whose roof she slept under and whose floors she vacuumed, while in that same house, with the dust brooms and floor cleaners as witnesses, the square-jawed Juan Carlos Arrocha had uttered words of love, I love you, María, listen to me, *mi querida*,[5] but it was she who had to say No, no, we are not of the same class, and remind him it was not his place nor hers to fall in love, while all the while her heart was breaking, can you imagine.

Cleófilas thought her life would have to be like that, like a *telenovela*, only now the episodes got sadder and sadder. And there were no commercials in between for comic relief. And no happy ending in sight. She thought this when she sat with the baby out by the creek behind the house. Celófilas de . . . ? But somehow she would have to change her name to Topazio, or Yesenia, Cristal, Adriana, Stefania, Andrea, something more poetic than Cleófilas. Everything happened to women with names like jewels. But what happened to a Cleófilas? Nothing. But a crack in the face.

---

1. Vulgar, crude (Spanish).
2. The Parakeet (Spanish).
3. Pseudonym of María del Socorro Tellado López (1927–2009), Spanish novelist.

4. *María of No One* (Spanish), television series produced in Argentina.
5. My dear (Spanish).

Because the doctor has said so. She has to go. To make sure the new baby is all right, so there won't be any problems when he's born, and the appointment card says next Tuesday. Could he please take her. And that's all.

No, she won't mention it. She promises. If the doctor asks she can say she fell down the front steps or slipped when she was out in the backyard, slipped out back, she could tell him that. She has to go back next Tuesday, Juan Pedro, please, for the new baby. For their child.

She could write to her father and ask maybe for money, just a loan, for the new baby's medical expenses. Well then if he'd rather she didn't. All right, she won't. Please don't anymore. Please don't. She knows it's difficult saving money with all the bills they have, but how else are they going to get out of debt with the truck payments? And after the rent and the food and the electricity and the gas and the water and the who-knows-what, well, there's hardly anything left. But please, at least for the doctor visit. She won't ask for anything else. She has to. Why is she so anxious? Because.

Because she is going to make sure the baby is not turned around backward this time to split her down the center. Yes. Next Tuesday at five-thirty. I'll have Juan Pedrito dressed and ready. But those are the only shoes he has. I'll polish them, and we'll be ready. As soon as you come from work. We won't make you ashamed.

Felice? It's me, Graciela.

No, I can't talk louder. I'm at work.

Look, I need kind of a favor. There's a patient, a lady here who's got a problem.

Well, wait a minute. Are you listening to me or what?

I can't talk real loud 'cause her husband's in the next room.

Well, would you just listen?

I was going to do this sonogram on her—she's pregnant, right?—and she just starts crying on me. *Híjole,*[6] Felice! This poor lady's got black-and-blue marks all over. I'm not kidding.

From her husband. Who else? Another one of those brides from across the border. And her family's all in Mexico.

Shit. You think they're going to help her? Give me a break. This lady doesn't even speak English. She hasn't been allowed to call home or write or nothing. That's why I'm calling you.

She needs a ride.

Not to Mexico, you goof. Just to the Greyhound.[7] In San Anto.

No, just a ride. She's got her own money. All you'd have to do is drop her off in San Antonio on your way home. Come on, Felice. Please? If we don't help her, who will? I'd drive her myself, but she needs to be on that bus before her husband gets home from work. What do you say?

I don't know. Wait.

Right away, tomorrow even.

Well, if tomorrow's no good for you . . .

It's a date, Felice. Thursday. At the Cash N Carry[8] off I-10. Noon. She'll be ready.

Oh, and her name's Cleófilas.

---

6. Shoot! or Gee! (Spanish).
7. Long-distance bus line.
8. Retail store.

I don't know. One of those Mexican saints, I guess. A martyr or something.

Cleófilas. C-L-E-O-F-I-L-A-S. Cle. O. Fi. Las. Write it down.

Thanks, Felice. When her kid's born she'll have to name her after us, right?

Yeah, you got it. A regular soap opera sometimes. *Qué vida, comadre. Bueno*[9] bye.

All morning that flutter of half-fear, half-doubt. At any moment Juan Pedro might appear in the doorway. On the street. At the Cash N Carry. Like in the dreams she dreamed.

There was that to think about, yes, until the woman in the pickup drove up. Then there wasn't time to think about anything but the pickup pointed toward San Antonio. Put your bags in the back and get in.

But when they drove across the *arroyo*, the driver opened her mouth and let out a yell as loud as any mariachi. Which startled not only Cleófilas, but Juan Pedrito as well.

Pues,[1] look how cute. I scared you two, right? Sorry. Should've warned you. Every time I cross that bridge I do that. Because of the name, you know. Woman Hollering. *Pues*, I holler. She said this in a Spanish pocked with English and laughed. Did you ever notice, Felice continued, how nothing around here is named after a woman? Really. Unless she's the Virgin. I guess you're only famous if you're a virgin. She was laughing again.

That's why I like the name of that *arroyo*. Makes you want to holler like Tarzan, right?

Everything about this woman, this Felice, amazed Cleófilas. The fact that she drove a pickup. A pickup, mind you, but when Cleófilas asked if it was her husband's, she said she didn't have a husband. The pickup was hers. She herself had chosen it. She herself was paying for it.

I used to have a Pontiac Sunbird.[2] But those cars are for *viejas*.[3] Pussy cars. Now this here is a *real* car.

What kind of talk was that coming from a woman? Cleófilas thought. But then again, Felice was like no woman she'd ever met. Can you imagine, when we crossed the *arroyo* she just started yelling like a crazy, she would say later to her father and brothers. Just like that. Who would've thought?

Who would've? Pain or rage, perhaps, but not a hoot like the one Felice had just let go. Makes you want to holler like Tarzan, Felice had said.

Then Felice began laughing again, but it wasn't Felice laughing. It was gurgling out of her own throat, a long ribbon of laughter, like water.

1991

9. What a life, girlfriend, well (Spanish).
1. Well (Spanish).

2. Compact American automobile.
3. Old ladies (Spanish).

LOUISE ERDRICH
b. 1954

Louise Erdrich grew up in the small town of Wahpeton, North Dakota, on the Minnesota border. Her mother was French Chippewa, her maternal grandmother was tribal chairman on the Turtle Mountain Reservation, and both of her parents worked in the Bureau of Indian Affairs boarding school in Wahpeton. She wrote stories as a child, encouraged by her father, who paid her a nickel for each one, but Erdrich's growing up was not marked by a special awareness of her Chippewa background. She has said that she never thought about "what was Native American and what wasn't. . . . There wasn't a political climate at the time about Indian rights." The eldest of seven children, she "grew up just taking it all in as something that was part of me."

In 1972 she entered Dartmouth College, participating in a Native American studies program run by Michael Dorris—himself part American Indian and a writer—whom eventually she would marry (a relationship ending with their separation and his suicide in 1997). In her undergraduate years she won prizes for poetry and fiction and worked at a variety of jobs, such as teaching poetry in prisons, editing a Boston Indian Council newspaper, and flag-signaling on a construction site. After deciding on a career as a writer, she earned an MFA degree at Johns Hopkins, for which degree she submitted a number of poems—later to appear in her collection *Jacklight* (1984)—and part of a novel. There followed the usual sending out of poems and stories, the rejection slips, eventually the acceptances.

Her first novel, *Love Medicine*, which won the National Book Critics Circle award for 1984, began as a short story. Collaborating with her husband, she not only expanded the story but planned the resulting novel as the first of a tetralogy, ranging over different periods of time and focusing on the lives of two Chippewa families. Her interest in the interaction of quirky, passionate, complex individuals—Native American, mixed blood, German American, or Anglo—lies at the center of her fiction.

Successive chapters of *Love Medicine* jump from 1981 to 1934 to 1948, each chapter told through a particular character's point of view (sometimes we see the same event from succeeding points of view). But each individual chapter is more a discrete whole than is the case with a traditional novel, a technique Erdrich uses in many of her novels, including *Tracks* (1988), the second chapter of which was published as the story "Fleur" (printed here). Like many of Erdrich's narratives, *Tracks* draws context from High Plains Dakotas town life, where Anglo and Native American cultures meet (if not mix).

Erdrich's style is easy, offhand, quietly unostentatious, but her language often has an unpredictability and sense of surprise, as in the first paragraph of "The Red Convertible," whose protagonist, Lyman Lamartine, tells us:

> I was the first one to drive a convertible on my reservation. And of course, it was red, a red Olds. I owned that car along with my brother Henry Junior. We owned it together until his boots filled with water on a windy night and he bought out my share. Now Henry owns the whole car, and his younger brother (that's myself) Lyman walks everywhere he goes.

Such clarity and directness are only part of the story, however, since her style also calls upon lyric resources, notable in the following sentence from her second novel,

The Beet Queen: "After the miraculous sheets of black ice came the floods, stranding boards and snaky knots of debris high in the branches, leaving brown leeches to dry like raisins on the sidewalks when the water receded, and leaving the smell of river mud, a rotten sweetness, in the backyards and gutters."

Native American oral expression does not distinguish between prose and poetry, and like many Native American writers Erdrich works in several forms. "I began as a poet, writing poetry," she has said. "I began to tell stories in poems." The lyrical descriptions in her fiction resemble the language of her poems, and the characterizations and narratives in her poetry resemble those of her fiction. Her most recent poetry collection, *Original Fire* (2003), presents new poems together with work from two earlier collections, *Jacklight* and *Baptism of Fire* (1989). Among the previously published poems are "The Butcher's Wife," which has close affinities in setting and character to her novels, and "The Potchikoo Stories," a group of prose poems about the mythical Potchikoo's life and afterlife. "Grief," a new poem, suggests the traditions of imagist poetry. But in the end such generic distinctions run counter to Erdrich's fusion of storytelling modes.

Like her fiction, Erdrich's poetry sometimes offers realistic accounts of small-town life and sometimes retells mythical stories. "I was Sleeping Where the Black Oaks Move" exemplifies her lyrical description and her mythical imagination. Many of the poems also reflect Erdrich's awareness of the historical and ongoing devastations of Native American life, what she calls in the poem "Dear John Wayne" "the history that brought us all here." Whatever forms her storytelling takes, its linguistic resources and mixture of grief, humor, anger, and tenderness deepen our understanding of the complexities of experience.

Dear John Wayne[1]

August and the drive-in picture is packed.
We lounge on the hood of the Pontiac
surrounded by the slow-burning spirals they sell
at the window, to vanquish the hordes of mosquitoes.
Nothing works. They break through the smoke screen for blood.   5

Always the lookout spots the Indians first,
spread north to south, barring progress.
The Sioux or some other Plains bunch[2]
in spectacular columns, ICBM missiles,[3]
feathers bristling in the meaningful sunset.   10

The drum breaks. There will be no parlance.
Only the arrows whining, a death-cloud of nerves
swarming down on the settlers
who die beautifully, tumbling like dust weeds
into the history that brought us all here   15
together: this wide screen beneath the sign of the bear.

---

1. American movie actor (1907–1979) who embodied the image of the strong, taciturn cowboy or soldier, and who in many ways personified the dominant American values of his era. He died of cancer.

2. The Sioux (Lakota) are a North American Plains Indian people.
3. Intercontinental Ballistic Missiles, developed starting in 1971.

The sky fills, acres of blue squint and eye
that the crowd cheers. His face moves over us,
a thick cloud of vengeance, pitted
like the land that was once flesh. Each rut,   20
each scar makes a promise: *It is*
not over, this fight, not as long as you resist.

Everything we see belongs to us.

A few laughing Indians fall over the hood
slipping in the hot spilled butter.   25
The eye sees a lot, John, but the heart is so blind.
Death makes us owners of nothing.
He smiles, a horizon of teeth
the credits reel over, and then the white fields

again blowing in the true-to-life dark.   30
The dark films over everything.
We get into the car
scratching our mosquito bites, speechless and small
as people are when the movie is done.
We are back in our skins.   35

How can we help but keep hearing his voice,
the flip side of the sound track, still playing:
Come on, boys, we got them
where we want them, drunk, running.
They'll give us what we want, what we need.   40
Even his disease was the idea of taking everything.
Those cells, burning, doubling, splitting out of their skins.

                                                          1984

I Was Sleeping Where the Black Oaks Move

We watched from the house
as the river grew, helpless
and terrible in its unfamiliar body.
Wrestling everything into it,
the water wrapped around trees   5
until their life-hold was broken.
They went down, one by one,
and the river dragged off their covering.

Nests of the herons, roots washed to bones,
snags of soaked bark on the shoreline: 10
a whole forest pulled through the teeth
of the spillway. Trees surfacing
singly, where the river poured off
into arteries for fields below the reservation.

When at last it was over, the long removal,   15
they had all become the same dry wood.
We walked among them, the branches
whitening in the raw sun.
Above us drifted herons,
alone, hoarse-voiced, broken,   20
settling their beaks among the hollows.

Grandpa said, *These are the ghosts of the tree people,*
moving above us, unable to take their rest.

Sometimes now, we dream our way back to the heron dance.
Their long wings are bending the air   25
into circles through which they fall.
They rise again in shifting wheels.
How long must we live in the broken figures
their necks make, narrowing the sky.

                                                          1984

Grief

Sometimes you have to take your own hand
as though you were a lost child
and bring yourself stumbling
home over twisted ice.

Whiteness drifts over your house.   5
A page of warm light
falls steady from the open door.

Here is your bed, folded open.
Lie down, lie down, let the blue snow cover you.

                                                          2003

Fleur[1]

The first time she drowned in the cold and glassy waters of Lake Turcot,
Fleur Pillager was only a girl. Two men saw the boat tip, saw her struggle in
the waves. They rowed over to the place she went down, and jumped in.
When they dragged her over the gunwales, she was cold to the touch and
stiff, so they slapped her face, shook her by the heels, worked her arms back
and forth, and pounded her back until she coughed up lake water. She shivered all over like a dog, then took a breath. But it wasn't long afterward that

---

1. First published in *Esquire* magazine, August 1986.

those two men disappeared. The first wandered off and the other, Jean Hat, got himself run over by a cart.

It went to show, my grandma said. It figured to her, all right. By saving Fleur Pillager, those two men had lost themselves.

The next time she fell in the lake, Fleur Pillager was twenty years old and no one touched her. She washed onshore, her skin a dull dead gray, but when George Many Women bent to look closer, he saw her chest move. Then her eyes spun open, sharp black riprock, and she looked at him. "You'll take my place," she hissed. Everybody scattered and left her there, so no one knows how she dragged herself home. Soon after that we noticed Many Women changed, grew afraid, wouldn't leave his house, and would not be forced to go near water. For his caution, he lived until the day that his sons brought him a new tin bathtub. Then the first time he used the tub he slipped, got knocked out, and breathed water while his wife stood in the other room frying breakfast.

Men stayed clear of Fleur Pillager after the second drowning. Even though she was good-looking, nobody dared to court her because it was clear that Misshepeshu, the waterman, the monster, wanted her for himself. He's a devil, that one, love-hungry with desire and maddened for the touch of young girls, the strong and daring especially, the ones like Fleur.

Our mothers warn us that we'll think he's handsome, for he appears with green eyes, copper skin, a mouth tender as a child's. But if you fall into his arms, he sprouts horns, fangs, claws, fins. His feet are joined as one and his skin, brass scales, rings to the touch. You're fascinated, cannot move. He casts a shell necklace at your feet, weeps gleaming chips that harden into mica on your breasts. He holds you under. Then he takes the body of a lion or a fat brown worm. He's made of gold. He's made of beach moss. He's a thing of dry foam, a thing of death by drowning, the death a Chippewa cannot survive.

Unless you are Fleur Pillager. We all knew she couldn't swim. After the first time, we thought she'd never go back to Lake Turcot. We thought she'd keep to herself, live quiet, stop killing men off by drowning in the lake. After the first time, we thought she'd keep the good ways. But then, after the second drowning, we knew that we were dealing with something much more serious. She was haywire, out of control. She messed with evil, laughed at the old women's advice, and dressed like a man. She got herself into some half-forgotten medicine, studied ways we shouldn't talk about. Some say she kept the finger of a child in her pocket and a powder of unborn rabbits in a leather thong around her neck. She laid the heart of an owl on her tongue so she could see at night, and went out, hunting, not even in her own body. We know for sure because the next morning, in the snow or dust, we followed the tracks of her bare feet and saw where they changed, where the claws sprang out, the pad broadened and pressed into the dirt. By night we heard her chuffing cough, the bear cough. By day her silence and the wide grin she threw to bring down our guard made us frightened. Some thought that Fleur Pillager should be driven off the reservation, but not a single person who spoke like this had the nerve. And finally, when people were just about to get together and throw her out, she left on her own and didn't come back all summer. That's what this story is about.

During that summer, when she lived a few miles south in Argus, things happened. She almost destroyed that town.

When she got down to Argus in the year of 1920, it was just a small grid of six streets on either side of the railroad depot. There were two elevators, one central, the other a few miles west. Two stores competed for the trade of the three hundred citizens, and three churches quarreled with one another for their souls. There was a frame building for Lutherans, a heavy brick one for Episcopalians, and a long narrow shingled Catholic church. This last had a tall slender steeple, twice as high as any building or tree.

No doubt, across the low, flat wheat, watching from the road as she came near Argus on foot, Fleur saw that steeple rise, a shadow thin as a needle. Maybe in that raw space it drew her the way a lone tree draws lightning. Maybe, in the end, the Catholics are to blame. For if she hadn't seen that sign of pride, that slim prayer, that marker, maybe she would have kept walking.

But Fleur Pillager turned, and the first place she went once she came into town was to the back door of the priest's residence attached to the landmark church. She didn't go there for a handout, although she got that, but to ask for work. She got that too, or the town got her. It's hard to tell which came out worse, her or the men or the town, although the upshot of it all was that Fleur lived.

The four men who worked at the butcher's had carved up about a thousand carcasses between them, maybe half of that steers and the other half pigs, sheep, and game animals like deer, elk, and bear. That's not even mentioning the chickens, which were beyond counting. Pete Kozka owned the place, and employed Lily Veddar, Tor Grunewald, and my stepfather, Dutch James, who had brought my mother down from the reservation the year before she disappointed him by dying. Dutch took me out of school to take her place. I kept house half the time and worked the other in the butcher shop, sweeping floors, putting sawdust down, running a hambone across the street to a customer's bean pot or a package of sausage to the corner. I was a good one to have around because until they needed me, I was invisible. I blended into the stained brown walls, a skinny, big-nosed girl with staring eyes. Because I could fade into a corner or squeeze beneath a shelf, I knew everything, what the men said when no one was around, and what they did to Fleur.

Kozka's Meats served farmers for a fifty-mile area, both to slaughter, for it had a stock pen and chute, and to cure the meat by smoking it or spicing it in sausage. The storage locker was a marvel, made of many thicknesses of brick, earth insulation, and Minnesota timber, lined inside with sawdust and vast blocks of ice cut from Lake Turcot, hauled down from home each winter by horse and sledge.

A ramshackle board building, part slaughterhouse, part store, was fixed to the low, thick square of the lockers. That's where Fleur worked. Kozka hired her for her strength. She could lift a haunch or carry a pole of sausages without stumbling, and she soon learned cutting from Pete's wife, a string-thin blonde who chain-smoked and handled the razor-edged knives with nerveless precision, slicing close to her stained fingers. Fleur and Fritzie Kozka worked afternoons, wrapping their cuts in paper, and Fleur hauled the packages to the lockers. The meat was left outside the heavy oak doors that were only opened at 5:00 each afternoon, before the men ate supper.

Sometimes Dutch, Tor, and Lily stayed at the lockers, and when they did I stayed too, cleaned floors, restoked the fires in the front smokehouses, while the men sat around the squat cast-iron stove spearing slats of herring onto hardtack bread. They played long games of poker or cribbage on a board made from the planed end of a salt crate. They talked and I listened, although there wasn't much to hear since almost nothing ever happened in Argus. Tor was married, Dutch had lost my mother, and Lily read circulars. They mainly discussed about the auctions to come, equipment, or women.

Every so often, Pete Kozka came out front to make a whist, leaving Fritzie to smoke cigarettes and fry raised doughnuts in the back room. He sat and played a few rounds but kept his thoughts to himself. Fritzie did not tolerate him talking behind her back, and the one book he read was the New Testament. If he said something, it concerned weather or a surplus of sheep stomachs, a ham that smoked green or the markets for corn and wheat. He had a good-luck talisman, the opal-white lens of a cow's eye. Playing cards, he rubbed it between his fingers. That soft sound and the slap of cards was about the only conversation.

Fleur finally gave them a subject.

Her cheeks were wide and flat, her hands large, chapped, muscular. Fleur's shoulders were broad as beams, her hips fishlike, slippery, narrow. An old green dress clung to her waist, worn thin where she sat. Her braids were thick like the tails of animals, and swung against her when she moved, deliberately, slowly in her work, held in and half-tamed, but only half. I could tell, but the others never saw. They never looked into her sly brown eyes or noticed her teeth, strong and sharp and very white. Her legs were bare, and since she padded in beadworked moccasins they never saw that her fifth toes were missing. They never knew she'd drowned. They were blinded, they were stupid, they only saw her in the flesh.

And yet it wasn't just that she was a Chippewa, or even that she was a woman, it wasn't that she was good-looking or even that she was alone that made their brains hum. It was how she played cards.

Women didn't usually play with men, so the evening that Fleur drew a chair to the men's table without being so much as asked, there was a shock of surprise.

"What's this," said Lily. He was fat, with a snake's cold pale eyes and precious skin, smooth and lily-white, which is how he got his name. Lily had a dog, a stumpy mean little bull of a thing with a belly drum-tight from eating pork rinds. The dog liked to play cards just like Lily, and straddled his barrel thighs through games of stud, rum poker, vingt-un.[2] The dog snapped at Fleur's arm that first night, but cringed back, its snarl frozen, when she took her place.

"I thought," she said, her voice soft and stroking, "you might deal me in."

There was a space between the heavy bin of spiced flour and the wall where I just fit. I hunkered down there, kept my eyes open, saw her black hair swing over the chair, her feet solid on the wood floor. I couldn't see up on the

---

2. Twenty-one (French); a card game.

table where the cards slapped down, so after they were deep in their game I raised myself up in the shadows, and crouched on a sill of wood.

I watched Fleur's hands stack and ruffle, divide the cards, spill them to each player in a blur, rake them up and shuffle again. Tor, short and scrappy, shut one eye and squinted the other at Fleur. Dutch screwed his lips around a wet cigar.

"Gotta see a man," he mumbled, getting up to go out back to the privy. The others broke, put their cards down, and Fleur sat alone in the lamplight that glowed in a sheen across the push of her breasts. I watched her closely, then she paid me a beam of notice for the first time. She turned, looked straight at me, and grinned the white wolf grin a Pillager turns on its victims, except that she wasn't after me.

"Pauline there," she said. "How much money you got?"

We had all been paid for the week that day. Eight cents was in my pocket.

"Stake me," she said, holding out her long fingers. I put the coins in her palm and then I melted back to nothing, part of the walls and tables. It was a long time before I understood that the men would not have seen me no matter what I did, how I moved. I wasn't anything like Fleur. My dress hung loose and my back was already curved, an old woman's. Work had roughened me, reading made my eyes sore, caring for my mother before she died had hardened my face. I was not much to look at, so they never saw me.

When the men came back and sat around the table, they had drawn together. They shot each other small glances, stuck their tongues in their cheeks, burst out laughing at odd moments, to rattle Fleur. But she never minded. They played their vingt-un, staying even as Fleur slowly gained. Those pennies I had given her drew nickels and attracted dimes until there was a small pile in front of her.

Then she hooked them with five card draw, nothing wild. She dealt, discarded, drew, and then she sighed and her cards gave a little shiver. Tor's eye gleamed, and Dutch straightened in his seat.

"I'll pay to see that hand," said Lily Veddar.

Fleur showed, and she had nothing there, nothing at all.

Tor's thin smile cracked open, and he threw his hand in too.

"Well, we know one thing," he said, leaning back in his chair, "the squaw can't bluff."

With that I lowered myself into a mound of swept sawdust and slept. I woke up during the night, but none of them had moved yet, so I couldn't either. Still later, the men must have gone out again, or Fritzie come out to break the game, because I was lifted, soothed, cradled in a woman's arms and rocked so quiet that I kept my eyes shut while Fleur rolled me into a closet of grimy ledgers, oiled paper, balls of string, and thick files that fit beneath me like a mattress.

The game went on after work the next evening. I got my eight cents back five times over, and Fleur kept the rest of the dollar she'd won for a stake. This time they didn't play so late, but they played regular, and then kept going at it night after night. They played poker now, or variations, for one week straight, and each time Fleur won exactly one dollar, no more and no less, too consistent for luck.

By this time, Lily and the other men were so lit with suspense that they got Pete to join the game with them. They concentrated, the fat dog sitting tense in Lily Veddar's lap, Tor suspicious, Dutch stroking his huge square brow, Pete steady. It wasn't that Fleur won that hooked them in so, because she lost hands too. It was rather that she never had a freak hand or even anything above a straight. She only took on her low cards, which didn't sit right. By chance, Fleur should have gotten a full or a flush by now. The irritating thing was she beat with pairs and never bluffed, because she couldn't, and still she ended each night with exactly one dollar. Lily couldn't believe, first of all, that a woman could be smart enough to play cards, but even if she was, that she would then be stupid enough to cheat for a dollar a night. By day I watched him turn the problem over, his hard white face dull, small fingers probing at his knuckles, until he finally thought he had Fleur figured as a bit-time player, caution her game. Raising the stakes would throw her.

More than anything now, he wanted Fleur to come away with something but a dollar. Two bits less or ten more, the sum didn't matter, just so he broke her streak.

Night after night she played, won her dollar, and left to stay in a place that just Fritzie and I knew about. Fleur bathed in the slaughtering tub, then slept in the unused brick smokehouse behind the lockers, a windowless place tarred on the inside with scorched fats. When I brushed against her skin I noticed that she smelled of the walls, rich and woody, slightly burnt. Since that night she put me in the closet I was no longer afraid of her, but followed her close, stayed with her, became her moving shadow that the men never noticed, the shadow that could have saved her.

August, the month that bears fruit, closed around the shop, and Pete and Fritzie left for Minnesota to escape the heat. Night by night, running, Fleur had won thirty dollars, and only Pete's presence had kept Lily at bay. But Pete was gone now, and one payday, with the heat so bad no one could move but Fleur, the men sat and played and waited while she finished work. The cards sweat, limp in their fingers, the table was slick with grease, and even the walls were warm to the touch. The air was motionless. Fleur was in the next room boiling heads.

Her green dress, drenched, wrapped her like a transparent sheet. A skin of lakeweed. Black snarls of veining clung to her arms. Her braids were loose, half unraveled, tied behind her neck in a thick loop. She stood in steam, turning skulls through a vat with a wooden paddle. When scraps boiled to the surface, she bent with a round tin sieve and scooped them out. She'd filled two dishpans.

"Ain't that enough now?" called Lily. "We're waiting." The stump of a dog trembled in his lap, alive with rage. It never smelled me or noticed me above Fleur's smoky skin. The air was heavy in my corner, and pressed me down. Fleur sat with them.

"Now what do you say?" Lily asked the dog. It barked. That was the signal for the real game to start.

"Let's up the ante," said Lily, who had been stalking this night all month. He had a roll of money in his pocket. Fleur had five bills in her dress. The men had each saved their full pay.

"Ante a dollar then," said Fleur, and pitched hers in. She lost, but they let her scrape along, cent by cent. And then she won some. She played unevenly, as if chance were all she had. She reeled them in. The game went on. The dog was stiff now, poised on Lily's knees, a ball of vicious muscle with its yellow eyes slit in concentration. It gave advice, seemed to sniff the lay of Fleur's cards, twitched and nudged. Fleur was up, then down, saved by a scratch. Tor dealt seven cards, three down. The pot grew, round by round, until it held all the money. Nobody folded. Then it all rode on one last card and they went silent. Fleur picked hers up and drew a long breath. The heat lowered like a bell. Her card shook, but she stayed in.

Lily smiled and took the dog's head tenderly between his palms.

"Say Fatso," he said, crooning the words. "You reckon that girl's bluffing?"

The dog whined and Lily laughed. "Me too," he said, "let's show." He swept his bills and coins into the pot and then they turned their cards over.

Lily looked once, looked again, then he squeezed the dog like a fist of dough and slammed it on the table.

Fleur threw out her arms and drew the money over, grinning that same wolf grin that she'd used on me, the grin that had them. She jammed the bills in her dress, scooped the coins up in waxed white paper that she tied with string.

"Let's go another round," said Lily, his voice choked with burrs. But Fleur opened her mouth and yawned, then walked out back to gather slops for the one big hog that was waiting in the stock pen to be killed.

The men sat still as rocks, their hands spread on the oiled wood table. Dutch had chewed his cigar to damp shreds, Tor's eye was dull. Lily's gaze was the only one to follow Fleur. I didn't move. I felt them gathering, saw my stepfather's veins, the ones in his forehead that stood out in anger. The dog rolled off the table and curled in a knot below the counter, where none of the men could touch it.

Lily rose and stepped out back to the closet of ledgers where Pete kept his private stock. He brought back a bottle, uncorked and tipped it between his fingers. The lump in his throat moved, then he passed it on. They drank, quickly felt the whiskey's fire, and planned with their eyes things they couldn't say aloud.

When they left, I followed. I hid out back in the clutter of broken boards and chicken crates beside the stock pen, where they waited. Fleur could not be seen at first, and then the moon broke and showed her, slipping cautiously along the rough board chute with a bucket in her hand. Her hair fell, wild and coarse, to her waist, and her dress was a floating patch in the dark. She made a pig-calling sound, rang the tin pail lightly against the wood, froze suspiciously. But too late. In the sound of the ring Lily moved, fat and nimble, stepped right behind Fleur and put out his creamy hands. At his first touch, she whirled and doused him with the bucket of sour slops. He pushed her against the big fence and the package of coins split, went clinking and jumping, winked against the wood. Fleur rolled over once and vanished into the yard.

The moon fell behind a curtain of ragged clouds, and Lily followed into the dark muck. But he tripped, pitched over the huge flank of the pig, who lay mired to the snout, heavily snoring. I sprang out of the weeds and climbed the side of the pen, stuck like glue. I saw the sow rise to her neat, knobby knees, gain her balance and sway, curious, as Lily stumbled forward. Fleur had backed into the angle of rough wood just beyond, and when Lily tried to jostle past, the sow tipped up on her hind legs and struck, quick and hard as a snake. She plunged her head into Lily's thick side and snatched a mouthful of his shirt. She lunged again, caught him lower, so that he grunted in pained surprise. He seemed to ponder, breathing deep. Then he launched his huge body in a swimmer's dive.

The sow screamed as his body smacked over hers. She rolled, striking out with her knife-sharp hooves, and Lily gathered himself upon her, took her foot-long face by the ears and scraped her snout and cheeks against the trestles of the pen. He hurled the sow's tight skull against an iron post, but instead of knocking her dead, he merely woke her from her dream.

She reared, shrieked, drew him with her so that they posed standing upright. They bowed jerkily to each other, as if to begin. Then his arms swung and flailed. She sank her black fangs into his shoulder, clasping him, dancing him forward and backward through the pen. Their steps picked up pace, went wild. The two dipped as one, box-stepped, tripped one another. She ran her split foot through his hair. He grabbed her kinked tail. They went down and came up, the same shape and then the same color until the men couldn't tell one from the other in that light and Fleur was able to launch herself over the gates, swing down, hit gravel.

The men saw, yelled, and chased her at a dead run to the smokehouse. And Lily too, once the sow gave up in disgust and freed him. That is where I should have gone to Fleur, saved her, thrown myself on Dutch. But I went stiff with fear and couldn't unlatch myself from the trestles or move at all. I closed my eyes and put my head in my arms, tried to hide, so there is nothing to describe but what I couldn't block out, Fleur's hoarse breath, so loud it filled me, her cry in the old language, and my name repeated over and over among the words.

The heat was still dense the next morning when I came back to work. Fleur was gone but the men were there, slack-faced, hung over. Lily was paler and softer than ever, as if his flesh had steamed on his bones. They smoked, took pulls off a bottle. It wasn't noon yet. I worked awhile, waiting shop and sharpening steel. But I was sick, I was smothered, I was sweating so hard that my hands slipped on the knives, and I wiped my fingers clean of the greasy touch of the customers' coins. Lily opened his mouth and roared once, not in anger. There was no meaning to the sound. His boxer dog, sprawled limp beside his foot, never lifted its head. Nor did the other men.

They didn't notice when I stepped outside, hoping for a clear breath. And then I forgot them because I knew that we were all balanced, ready to tip, to fly, to be crushed as soon as the weather broke. The sky was so low that I felt the weight of it like a yoke. Clouds hung down, witch teats, a tornado's green-brown cones, and as I watched one flicked out and became a delicate probing thumb. Even as I picked up my heels and ran back inside, the wind blew suddenly, cold, and then came rain.

Inside, the men had disappeared already and the whole place was trembling as if a huge hand was pinched at the rafters, shaking it. I ran straight through, screaming for Dutch or for any of them, and then I stopped at the heavy doors of the lockers, where they had surely taken shelter. I stood there a moment. Everything went still. Then I heard a cry building in the wind, faint at first, a whistle and then a shrill scream that tore through the walls and gathered around me, spoke plain so I understood that I should move, put my arms out, and slam down the great iron bar that fit across the hasp and lock.

Outside, the wind was stronger, like a hand held against me. I struggled forward. The bushes tossed, the awnings flapped off storefronts, the rails of porches rattled. The odd cloud became a fat snout that nosed along the earth and sniffled, jabbed, picked at things, sucked them up, blew them apart, rooted around as if it was following a certain scent, then stopped behind me at the butcher shop and bored down like a drill.

I went flying, landed somewhere in a ball. When I opened my eyes and looked, stranger things were happening.

A herd of cattle flew through the air like giant birds, dropping dung, their mouths opened in stunned bellows. A candle, still lighted, blew past, and tables, napkins, garden tools, a whole school of drifting eyeglasses, jackets on hangers, hams, a checkerboard, a lampshade, and at last the sow from behind the lockers, on the run, her hooves a blur, set free, swooping, diving, screaming as everything in Argus fell apart and got turned upside down, smashed, and thoroughly wrecked.

Days passed before the town went looking for the men. They were bachelors, after all, except for Tor, whose wife had suffered a blow to the head that made her forgetful. Everyone was occupied with digging out, in high relief because even though the Catholic steeple had been torn off like a peaked cap and sent across five fields, those huddled in the cellar were unhurt. Walls had fallen, windows were demolished, but the stores were intact and so were the bankers and shop owners who had taken refuge in their safes or beneath their cash registers. It was a fair-minded disaster, no one could be said to have suffered much more than the next, at least not until Pete and Fritzie came home.

Of all the businesses in Argus, Kozka's Meats had suffered worst. The boards of the front building had been split to kindling, piled in a huge pyramid, and the shop equipment was blasted far and wide. Pete paced off the distance the iron bathtub had been flung—a hundred feet. The glass candy case went fifty, and landed without so much as a cracked pane. There were other surprises as well, for the back rooms where Fritzie and Pete lived were undisturbed. Fritzie said the dust still coated her china figures, and upon her kitchen table, in the ashtray, perched the last cigarette she'd put out in haste. She lit and finished it, looking through the window. From there, she could see that the old smokehouse Fleur had slept in was crushed to a reddish sand and the stockpens were completely torn apart, the rails stacked helter-skelter. Fritzie asked for Fleur. People shrugged. Then she asked about the others and, suddenly, the town understood that three men were missing.

There was a rally of help, a gathering of shovels and volunteers. We passed boards from hand to hand, stacked them, uncovered what lay beneath the pile of jagged splinters. The lockers, full of meat that was Pete and Fritzie's investment, slowly came into sight, still intact. When enough room was made for a man to stand on the roof, there were calls, a general urge to hack through and see what lay below. But Fritzie shouted that she wouldn't allow it because the meat would spoil. And so the work continued, board by board, until at last the heavy oak doors of the freezer were revealed and people pressed to the entry. Everyone wanted to be the first, but since it was my stepfather lost, I was let go in when Pete and Fritzie wedged through into the sudden icy air.

Pete scraped a match on his boot, lit the lamp Fritzie held, and then the three of us stood still in its circle. Light glared off the skinned and hanging carcasses, the crates of wrapped sausages, the bright and cloudy blocks of lake ice, pure as winter. The cold bit into us, pleasant at first, then numbing. We must have stood there a couple of minutes before we saw the men, or more rightly, the humps of fur, the iced and shaggy hides they wore, the bearskins they had taken down and wrapped about themselves. We stepped closer and Fritzie tilted the lantern beneath the flaps of fur into their faces. The dog was there, perched among them, heavy as a doorstop. The three had hunched around a barrel where the game was still laid out, and a dead lantern and an empty bottle too. But they had thrown down their last hands and hunkered tight, clutching one another, knuckles raw from beating at the door they had also attacked with hooks. Frost stars gleamed off their eyelashes and the stubble of their beards. Their faces were set in concentration, mouths open as if to speak some careful thought, some agreement they'd come to in each other's arms.

Power travels in the bloodlines, handed out before birth. It comes down through the hands, which in the Pillagers were strong and knotted, big, spidery, and rough, with sensitive fingertips good at dealing cards. It comes through the eyes, too, belligerent, darkest brown, the eyes of those in the bear clan, impolite as they gaze directly at a person.

In my dreams, I look straight back at Fleur, at the men. I am no longer the watcher on the dark sill, the skinny girl.

The blood draws us back, as if it runs through a vein of earth. I've come home and, except for talking to my cousins, live a quiet life. Fleur lives quiet too, down on Lake Turcot with her boat. Some say she's married to the waterman, Misshepeshu, or that she's living in shame with white men or windigos, or that she's killed them all. I'm about the only one here who ever goes to visit her. Last winter, I went to help out in her cabin when she bore the child, whose green eyes and skin the color of an old penny made more talk, as no one could decide if the child was mixed blood or what, fathered in a smokehouse, or by a man with brass scales, or by the lake. The girl is bold, smiling in her sleep, as if she knows what people wonder, as if she hears the old men talk, turning the story over. It comes up different every time and has no ending, no beginning. They get the middle wrong too. They only know they don't know anything.

1988

LI-YOUNG LEE

b. 1957

I n his poem "Persimmons" Li-Young Lee remembers his father saying, "Some things never leave a person." Many of the poems in Lee's books—*Rose* (1986), *The City in Which I Love You* (1990), *Book of My Nights* (2001), and *Behind My Eyes* (2008)—testify to a sense of the past, especially his father's past, that never leaves Lee. The father in Lee's poems is personal and mythic; he instructs the poet-son in "the art of memory." Lee's father, born in China, served as a personal physician to Mao Zedong. He later was jailed for nineteen months, a political prisoner of the Indonesian dictator Sukarno. Lee was born in Jakarta, Indonesia. In 1959 the family fled Indonesia and traveled to Hong Kong, Macao, and Japan, finally arriving in America, where Lee's father became a Presbyterian minister in a small town in western Pennsylvania. Many of Lee's poems seek to remember and understand his father's life and to come to terms with Lee's differences from that powerful figure.

Lee's work reminds us about the ancient connections between memory and poetry. In his work memory is often sweet; it draws the poet to the past even when, as in "Eating Alone," that sweetness is as dizzying as the juice of a rotten pear in which a hornet spins. But memory can also be a burden, and its pull is countered in Lee's work by a sensuous apprehension of the present. As in his poem "This Room and Everything in It," the erotic immediacy of the moment can disrupt any effort to fix that moment in the orders of memory. Everywhere in Lee's work is the evidence of hearing, taste, smell, and touch as well as sight. If the poet's bodily presence in the world recalls his great American precursor Walt Whitman, Lee's fluid motion between the physical world and the domain of memory, dream, or vision also carries out Whitman's visionary strain and links Lee to the work of Theodore Roethke, James Wright, and Denise Levertov, among others. The intensity of Lee's poems, however, is often leavened by a subtle and winning humor and playfulness; such qualities are especially valuable in a poet at times too easily seduced by beauty.

Lee studied at the University of Pittsburgh (where one of his teachers was the poet Gerald Stern), the University of Arizona, and the State University of New York College at Brockport. He has since taught at various universities. In 1995 he published a prose memoir, *The Winged Seed: A Remembrance*. His prose, like his poetry, is characterized by his deep sense of connection between an individual life and a powerful past, mediated by his ability to move between plain speech and a lushness evocative of biblical language.

The Gift

To pull the metal splinter from my palm
my father recited a story in a low voice.
I watched his lovely face and not the blade.
Before the story ended, he'd removed
the iron sliver I thought I'd die from.   5

I can't remember the tale,
but hear his voice still, a well

of dark water, a prayer.
And I recall his hands,
two measures of tenderness   10
he laid against my face,
the flames of discipline
he raised above my head.

Had you entered that afternoon
you would have thought you saw a man   15
planting something in a boy's palm,
a silver tear, a tiny flame.
Had you followed that boy
you would have arrived here,
where I bend over my wife's right hand.   20

Look how I shave her thumbnail down
so carefully she feels no pain.
Watch as I lift the splinter out.
I was seven when my father
took my hand like this,   25
and I did not hold that shard
between my fingers and think,
Metal that will bury me,
christen it Little Assassin,
Ore Going Deep for My Heart.   30
And I did not lift up my wound and cry,
Death visited here!
I did what a child does
when he's given something to keep.
I kissed my father.   35

1986

Persimmons

In sixth grade Mrs. Walker
slapped the back of my head
and made me stand in the corner
for not knowing the difference
between *persimmon* and *precision*.   5
How to choose

persimmons. This is precision.
Ripe ones are soft and brown-spotted.
Sniff the bottoms. The sweet one
will be fragrant. How to eat: 10
put the knife away, lay down newspaper.
Peel the skin tenderly, not to tear the meat.
Chew the skin, suck it,
and swallow. Now, eat
the meat of the fruit,   15

so sweet,
all of it, to the heart.

Donna undresses, her stomach is white.
In the yard, dewy and shivering
with crickets, we lie naked, 20
face-up, face-down.
I teach her Chinese.
Crickets: *chiu chiu.* Dew: I've forgotten.
Naked: I've forgotten.
Ni, wo: you and me. 25
I part her legs,
remember to tell her
she is beautiful as the moon.

Other words
that got me into trouble were 30
fight and *fright, wren* and *yarn.*
Fight was what I did when I was frightened,
fright was what I felt when I was fighting.
Wrens are small, plain birds,
yarn is what one knits with. 35
Wrens are soft as yarn.
My mother made birds out of yarn.
I loved to watch her tie the stuff;
a bird, a rabbit, a wee man.

Mrs. Walker brought a persimmon to class 40
and cut it up
so everyone could taste
a *Chinese apple.* Knowing
it wasn't ripe or sweet, I didn't eat
but I watched the other faces. 45

My mother said every persimmon has a sun
inside, something golden, glowing,
warm as my face.

Once, in the cellar, I found two wrapped in newspaper,
forgotten and not yet ripe. 50
I took them and set both on my bedroom windowsill,
where each morning a cardinal
sang, *The sun, the sun.*

Finally understanding
he was going blind, 55
my father sat up all one night
waiting for a song, a ghost.
I gave him the persimmons,
swelled, heavy as sadness,
and sweet as love. 60

This year, in the muddy lighting
of my parents' cellar, I rummage, looking
for something I lost.
My father sits on the tired, wooden stairs,
black cane between his knees,   65
hand over hand, gripping the handle.

He's so happy that I've come home.
I ask how his eyes are, a stupid question.
All gone, he answers.

Under some blankets, I find a box.   70
Inside the box I find three scrolls.
I sit beside him and untie
three paintings by my father:
Hibiscus leaf and a white flower.
Two cats preening.   75
Two persimmons, so full they want to drop from the cloth.

He raises both hands to touch the cloth,
asks, *Which is this?*

This is persimmons, Father.

Oh, the feel of the wolftail on the silk,   80
the strength, the tense
precision in the wrist.
I painted them hundreds of times
eyes closed. These I painted blind.
Some things never leave a person: 85
scent of the hair of one you love,
the texture of persimmons,
in your palm, the ripe weight.

                                                                        1986

Eating Alone

I've pulled the last of the year's young onions.
The garden is bare now. The ground is cold,
brown and old. What is left of the day flames
in the maples at the corner of my
eye. I turn, a cardinal vanishes.   5
By the cellar door, I wash the onions,
then drink from the icy metal spigot.

Once, years back, I walked beside my father
among the windfall pears. I can't recall
our words. We may have strolled in silence. But   10
I still see him bend, that way—left hand braced
on knee, creaky—to lift and hold to my

eye a rotten pear. In it, a hornet
spun crazily, glazed in slow, glistening juice.

It was my father I saw this morning   15
waving to me from the trees. I almost
called to him, until I came close enough
to see the shovel, leaning where I had
left it, in the flickering, deep green shade.

White rice steaming, almost done. Sweet green peas   20
fried in onions. Shrimp braised in sesame
oil and garlic. And my own loneliness.
What more could I, a young man, want.

1986

Eating Together

In the steamer is the trout
seasoned with slivers of ginger,
two sprigs of green onion, and sesame oil.
We shall eat it with rice for lunch,
brothers, sister, my mother who will   5
taste the sweetest meat of the head,
holding it between her fingers
deftly, the way my father did
weeks ago. Then he lay down
to sleep like a snow-covered road   10
winding through pines older than him,
without any travelers, and lonely for no one.

1986

This Room and Everything in It

Lie still now
while I prepare For my future,
certain hard days ahead,
when I'll need what I know so clearly this moment.

I am making use   5
of the one thing I learned
of all the things my father tried to teach me:
the art of memory.

I am letting this room
and everything in it   10
stand for my ideas about love
and its difficulties.

I'll let your love-cries,
those spacious notes
of a moment ago,   15
stand for distance.

Your scent,
that scent
of spice and a wound,
I'll let stand for mystery.   20

Your sunken belly
is the daily cup
of milk I drank
as a boy before morning prayer.

The sun on the face   25
of the wall
is God, the face
I can't see, my soul,

and so on, each thing
standing for a separate idea,   30
and those ideas forming the constellation
of my greater idea.
And one day, when I need
to tell myself something intelligent
about love,   35

I'll close my eyes
and recall this room and everything in it:
My body is estrangement.
This desire, perfection.
Your closed eyes my extinction.   40
Now I've forgotten my
idea. The book
on the windowsill, riffled by wind . . .
the even-numbered pages are
the past, the odd-   45
numbered pages, the future.
The sun is
God, your body is milk . . .

useless, useless . . .
your cries are song, my body's not me . . .   50
no good . . . my idea
has evaporated . . . your hair is time, your thighs are song . . .
it had something to do
with death . . . it had something
to do with love.   55

1990

Nativity

In the dark, a child might ask, *What is the world?*
just to hear his sister
promise, *An unfinished wing of heaven,*
just to hear his brother say,
A house inside a house,   5
but most of all to bear his mother answer,
One more song, then you go to sleep.

How could anyone in that bed guess
the question finds its beginning
in the answer long growing   10
inside the one who asked, that restless boy,
the night's darling?

Later, a man lying awake,
he might ask it again,
just to hear the silence   15
charge him, *This night*
arching over your sleepless wondering,

this night, the near ground
every reaching-out-to overreaches,

just to remind himself   20
out of what little earth and duration,
out of what immense good-bye,

each must make a safe place of his heart,
before so strange and wild a guest
as God approaches.   25

2001

Creative Nonfiction

I n what is known today as "creative nonfiction," writers report on the world without the pretense of journalistic objectivity or the imperatives of timeliness associated with traditional "news." The novelist David Foster Wallace described his own forays into the genre as a process of "peeling back my skull. You know, welcome to my mind for twenty pages, see through my eyes." "Creative nonfiction" is a relatively new term—it first appeared officially in 1983 as a category for creative writing fellowships in the National Endowment of the Arts—but examples of the form appear much earlier in American literature. If Thoreau and Emerson were publishing their essays today, much of their work would probably be called creative nonfiction. Indeed, travel and nature writing have long been a part of American literature. The term is fluid, suggesting a hybrid that involves facts, research, and information while using the forms and strategies of fiction, poetry, film, drama, biography, autobiography, and even philosophy.

The term is closely allied with what was, in the 1970s, called "the New Journalism" (the writer Tom Wolfe published a combined manifesto and anthology with that title in 1973), in which, instead of simply reporting an event, the writer reports on himself or herself within the event, either as a participant or as an observer (or both). Examples of the "the New Journalism" include Wolfe's *The Kandy-Kolored Tangerine-Flake Streamline Baby* (1965), Truman Capote's *In Cold Blood* (1966), Norman Mailer's *Armies of the Night* (1968), Joan Didion's *Slouching Towards Bethlehem* (1968), Hunter S. Thompson's *Fear and Loathing in Las Vegas* (1972), and Michael Herr's *Dispatches* (1977). The New Journalism was intended by its practitioners to reflect critically on both the novel and journalism. Wolfe, for instance, insisted (as had others since the early twentieth century) that the novel was a dead end. Disconnected from reality, it did not have the relevance that nonfiction might have. The novelist Philip Roth echoed that thought in fiction: in *The Ghost Writer* (1979) he has his protagonist, a writer alter-ego named Nathan Zuckerman, lament, "If only I could invent as presumptuously as real life! If one day I could just *approach* the originality and excitement of what actually goes on!" For many writers, the upheavals of the 1960s—including the civil rights movement, the hippie counterculture, the Cold War, and the war in Vietnam—seemed to exceed what any individual could imagine and demanded an expressive mode that could match the "originality and excitement" of history itself. Wolfe turned to the language of the Beat writers, which he brought to his descriptions of the counterculture. Didion looked to the spare prose of Hemingway, certain that "the seemingly insignificant things that most of us spend our days noticing are really significant, have meaning, and tell us something."

For Capote and Mailer, the novel remained a force to be reckoned with, and they plundered its resources to narrate real dramas. In *Armies of the Night*, which was subtitled "History as a Novel / The Novel as History," Mailer begins by invoking a traditional journalistic account of the 1967 anti–Vietnam War march on the Pentagon, but soon dismisses it: "Now we may leave *Time* in order to find out what happened," he declares. The "novel" that follows presents Mailer as a character, alongside the poets Robert Lowell and Mitchell Goodman, radical activist Jerry Rubin, and other literary and political celebrities, whose escapades make reportage into absurdist modern comedy. Capote, too, found the novel a better tool for telling the story of a quadruple murder in *In Cold Blood*. Novels have always been able to present complex characters and mixed motives, and to show characters evolving over time. Capote's epic account of a real crime draws on that tradition in representing an incident of spectacular violence as well as the psychological and cultural vortex from which it was born.

The New Journalism called into question the traditional objectivity of reporting, addressing—and reveling in—what the physicist Werner Heisenberg called "the uncertainty principle" (a theory the novelist Thomas Pynchon frequently invokes in his work), which asserts that the observer's presence alters the phenomenon being observed. Like all movements, the one that rode under this banner came to an end. By 1975 writers were already asking, in print, "Whatever Happened to the New Journalism?" and by 1981 the writer Joe Nocera declared it dead—its credibility killed, he argued, by Hunter S. Thompson. And in the surest sign of the movement's end, its name has lately been resurrected, in Robert S. Boynton's anthology, as *The New New Journalism* (2005). What remained of the New Journalism, once "creative nonfiction" arose to replace it in the early 1980s, was the focus on narrative drive, inventive language, distinctive voice, and personal observation. Creative nonfiction is open in its aim of merging literary technique with fidelity to fact.

As with all hybrids, the distinctions between it and other forms are slippery. Among the selections here, Thompson and Didion represent the New Journalism, demonstrating how style shapes copious concrete detail into forms that ask readers to reflect on the significance of facts. Today, most memoirs, personal essays, long-form features, and environmental writing are considered to be creative nonfiction, but the writers in this cluster provide especially innovative examples of these forms. Edwidge Danticat mingles autobiography, political analysis, and biography. The environmental writings of Edward Abbey and Barry Lopez combine carefully observed, factual description of landscapes and natural creatures with an equal focus on the writer's feelings and reflections. Wallace's essay on the Maine Lobster Festival grounds itself in entertaining, feature-style magazine reportage but ends with rigorous intellectual inquiry more common to philosophy or science. It is easy to understand why many examples of the form slip back and forth between a variety of categories: among the selections here, Jamaica Kincaid's "Girl" appeared in a book collection advertised as "Stories," and it was featured under the rubric of "Fiction" when it was first published in the *New Yorker*; but many critics and reviewers have since called the work a prose poem or an autobiography.

The term "Creative Nonfiction" is fully at ease with such slippage and happily embraces work that mixes elements of many different genres; whatever the mixture, it's the quality of writing and the use of various techniques that establish the work as "creative." In the twenty-first century, hybridity is a significant cultural modality, and much of contemporary writing is self-consciously hybrid. Mixing poetry and essay, personal reflection and journalism, reportage and critique, nature writing and myth, or inventing other combinations, some of the most vital American writing is now, and always has been, creative nonfiction.

EDWARD ABBEY

A prolific writer, Edward Abbey (1927–1989) was the author of many novels but he is most famous for his personal essays, which have become classics of environmental writing. Born and raised in Pennsylvania, he went west in his teens, and late in the 1950s he worked at Arches National Monument (now Arches National Park) near Moab in eastern Utah, as a seasonal ranger. In the spirit of Thoreau's residence at Walden Pond and Gary Snyder's summers as a fire lookout in Washington State's

North Cascades, Abbey said he sought solitude in an effort to "confront, immediately and directly if possible, the bare bones of existence." His most famous book, *Desert Solitaire* (1968), came out of his journals from this period; the book is a compilation of description, natural history, tall tales, and polemical environmentalism.

One of the most gripping chapters in *Desert Solitaire* focuses on Abbey's time in Havasu, at the base of the Grand Canyon. As he tells it, during a stop at the Grand Canyon with friends en route to Los Angeles he decided on the spur of the moment to descend to the canyon floor ("fourteen miles by trail") to take a look at Havasu Canyon in Arizona, the homeland of the Havasupai Native people. Five weeks later, he emerged to find that his friends had sensibly gone on without him. During the weeks he spent there, Abbey camped and explored the surrounding landscape alone. The selection here focuses on one such day of exploration, when, looking for a short-cut back to his camp, he made a series of potentially fatal decisions.

Havasu

Most of my wandering in the desert I've done alone. Not so much from choice as from necessity—I generally prefer to go into places where no one else wants to go. I find that in contemplating the natural world my pleasure is greater if there are not too many others contemplating it with me, at the same time. However, there are special hazards in traveling alone. Your chances of dying, in case of sickness or accident, are much improved, simply because there is no one around to go for help.

Exploring a side canyon off Havasu Canyon[1] one day, I was unable to resist the temptation to climb up out of it onto what corresponds in that region to the Tonto Bench.[2] Late in the afternoon I realized that I would not have enough time to get back to my camp before dark, unless I could find a much shorter route than the one by which I had come. I looked for a shortcut.

Nearby was another little side canyon which appeared to lead down into Havasu Canyon. It was a steep, shadowy, extremely narrow defile with the usual meandering course and overhanging walls; from where I stood, near its head, I could not tell if the route was feasible all the way down to the floor of the main canyon. I had no rope with me—only my walking stick. But I was hungry and thirsty, as always. I started down.

For a while everything went well. The floor of the little canyon began as a bed of dry sand, scattered with rocks. Farther down a few boulders were wedged between the walls; I climbed over and under them. Then the canyon took on the slickrock[3] character—smooth, sheer, slippery sandstone carved by erosion into a series of scoops and potholes which got bigger as I descended. In some of these basins there was a little water left over from the last flood, warm and fetid water under an oily-looking scum, condensed by prolonged evaporation to a sort of broth, rich in dead and dying organisms. My canteen was empty and I was very thirsty but I felt that I could wait.

1. A canyon with waterfall, forming a side branch of the Grand Canyon, that was once the home of a prehistoric people and has been occupied by the Havasupai, "people of the blue-green waters," for the last 800 years.
2. The long, narrow strip of relatively level land

located in the Grand Canyon, separating the inner gorge from the upper canyon and following the course of the Colorado River.
3. A term used in the Southwest to refer to smooth, consolidated, and hardened sand dunes.

I came to a lip on the canyon floor which overhung by twelve feet the largest so far of these stagnant pools. On each side rose the canyon walls, roughly perpendicular. There was no way to continue except by dropping into the pool. I hesitated. Beyond this point there could hardly be any returning, yet the main canyon was still not visible below. Obviously the only sensible thing to do was to turn back. I edged over the lip of stone and dropped feet first into the water.

Deeper than I expected. The warm, thick fluid came up and closed over my head as my feet touched the muck at the bottom. I had to swim to the farther side. And here I found myself on the verge of another drop-off, with one more huge bowl of green soup below.

This drop-off was about the same height as the one before, but not over-hanging. It resembled a children's playground slide, concave and S-curved, only steeper, wider, with a vertical pitch in the middle. It did not lead directly into the water but ended in a series of steplike ledges above the pool. Beyond the pool lay another edge, another drop-off into an unknown depth. Again I paused, and for a much longer time. But I no longer had the option of turning around and going back. I eased myself into the chute[4] and let go of everything—except my faithful stick.

I hit rock bottom hard, but without any physical injury. I swam the stinking pond dog-paddle[5] style, pushing the heavy scum away from my face, and crawled out on the far side to see what my fate was going to be.

Fatal. Death by starvation, slow and tedious. For I was looking straight down an overhanging cliff to a rubble pile of broken rocks eighty feet below.

After the first wave of utter panic had passed I began to try to think. First of all I was not going to die immediately, unless another flash flood came down the gorge; there was the pond of stagnant water on hand to save me from thirst and a man can live, they say, for thirty days or more without food. My sun-bleached bones, dramatically sprawled at the bottom of the chasm, would provide the diversion of the picturesque for future wanderers—if any man ever came this way again.

My second thought was to scream for help, although I knew very well there could be no other human being within miles. I even tried it but the sound of that anxious shout, cut short in the dead air within the canyon walls, was so inhuman, so detached as it seemed from myself, that it terrified me and I didn't attempt it again.

I thought of tearing my clothes into strips and plaiting a rope. But what was I wearing?—boots, socks, a pair of old and ragged blue jeans, a flimsy T-shirt, an ancient and rotten sombrero[6] of straw. Not a chance of weaving such a wardrobe into a rope eighty feet long, or even twenty feet long.

How about a signal fire? There was nothing to burn but my clothes; not a tree, not a shrub, not even a weed grew in this stony cul-de-sac. Even if I burned my clothing the chances of the smoke being seen by some Hualapai Indian[7] high on the south rim were very small; and if he did see the smoke, what then? He'd shrug his shoulders, sigh, and take another pull from his

---

4. A waterfall or steep descent in a river.
5. A simple swimming style, often used by children.
6. A broad-brimmed hat common in Spain and

Spanish America.
7. "People of the tall pine," the Hualapai are a Native American people living along the pine-clad southern side of the Grand Canyon.

Tokay[8] bottle. Furthermore, without clothes, the sun would soon bake me to death.

There was only one thing I could do. I had a tiny notebook in my hip pocket and a stub of pencil. When these dried out I could at least record my final thoughts. I would have plenty of time to write not only my epitaph but my own elegy.[9]

But not yet.

There were a few loose stones scattered about the edge of the pool. Taking the biggest first, I swam with it back to the foot of the slickrock chute and placed it there. One by one I brought the others and made a shaky little pile about two feet high leaning against the chute. Hopeless, of course, but there was nothing else to do. I stood on the top of the pile and stretched upward, straining my arms to their utmost limit and groped with fingers and fingernails for a hold on something firm. There was nothing. I crept back down. I began to cry. It was easy. All alone, I didn't have to be brave.

Through the tears I noticed my old walking stick lying nearby. I took it and stood it on the most solid stone in the pile, behind the two topmost stones. I took off my boots, tied them together and hung them around my neck, on my back. I got up on the little pile again and lifted one leg and set my big toe on the top of the stick. This could never work. Slowly and painfully, leaning as much of my weight as I could against the sandstone slide, I applied more and more pressure to the stick, pushing my body upward until I was again stretched out full length above it. Again I felt about for a fingerhold. There was none. The chute was smooth as polished marble.

No, not quite that smooth. This was sandstone, soft and porous, not marble, and between it and my wet body and wet clothing a certain friction was created. In addition, the stick had enabled me to reach a higher section of the S-curved chute, where the angle was more favorable. I discovered that I could move upward, inch by inch, through adhesion and with the help of the leveling tendency of the curve. I gave an extra little push with my big toe—the stones collapsed below, the stick clattered down—and crawled rather like a snail or slug, oozing slime, up over the rounded summit of the slide.

The next obstacle, the overhanging spout twelve feet above a deep plunge pool, looked impossible. It *was* impossible, but with the blind faith of despair I slogged into the water and swam underneath the drop-off and floundered around for a while, scrabbling at the slippery rock until my nerves and tiring muscles convinced my numbed brain that *this was not the way.* I swam back to solid ground and lay down to rest and die in comfort.

Far above I could see the sky, an irregular strip of blue between the dark, hard-edged canyon walls that seemed to lean toward each other as they towered above me. Across that narrow opening a small white cloud was passing, so lovely and precious and delicate and forever inaccessible that it broke the heart and made me weep like a woman, like a child. In all my life I had never seen anything so beautiful.

The walls that rose on either side of the drop-off were literally perpendicular. Eroded by weathering, however, and not by the corrasion[1] of rush-

---

8. Tokay is a sweet wine, often cheaply available.
9. An epitaph is a short text inscribed on a tombstone, honoring a deceased person; an elegy is a mournful poem, especially a funeral song or a lament for the dead.
1. The wearing away of rock by the constant flow of water.

ing floodwater, they had a rough surface, chipped, broken, cracked. Where the walls joined the face of the overhang they formed almost a square corner, with a number of minute crevices and inch-wide shelves on either side. It might, after all, be possible. What did I have to lose?

When I had regained some measure of nerve and steadiness I got up off my back and tried the wall beside the pond, clinging to the rock with bare toes and fingertips and inching my way crabwise toward the corner. The watersoaked, heavy boots dangling from my neck, swinging back and forth with my every movement, threw me off balance and I fell into the pool. I swam out to the bank, unslung the boots and threw them up over the drop-off, out of sight. They'd be there if I ever needed them again. Once more I attached myself to the wall, tenderly, sensitively, like a limpet,[2] and very slowly, very cautiously, worked my way into the corner. Here I was able to climb upward, a few centimeters at a time, by bracing myself against the opposite sides and finding sufficient niches for fingers and toes. As I neared the top and the overhang became noticeable I prepared for a slip, planning to push myself away from the rock so as to fall into the center of the pool where the water was deepest. But it wasn't necessary. Somehow, with a skill and tenacity I could never have found in myself under ordinary circumstances, I managed to creep straight up that gloomy cliff and over the brink of the drop-off and into the flower of safety. My boots were floating under the surface of the little puddle above. As I poured the stinking water out of them and pulled them on and laced them up I discovered myself bawling again for the third time in three hours, the hot delicious tears of victory. And up above the clouds replied—thunder.

I emerged from that treacherous little canyon at sundown, with an enormous fire in the western sky and lightning overhead. Through sweet twilight and the sudden dazzling flare of lightning a I hiked back along the Tonto Bench, bellowing the Ode to Joy.[3] Long before I reached the place where I could descend safely to the main canyon and my camp, however, darkness set in, the clouds opened their bays and the rain poured down. I took shelter under a ledge in a shallow cave about three feet high—hardly room to sit up in. Others had been here before: the dusty floor of the little hole was littered with the droppings of birds, rats, jackrabbits, and coyotes. There were also a few long gray pieces of scat with a curious twist at one tip—cougar? I didn't care. I had some matches with me, sealed in paraffin (the prudent explorer); I scraped together the handiest twigs and animal droppings and built a little fire and waited for the rain to stop.

It didn't stop. The rain came down for hours in alternate waves of storm and drizzle and I very soon had burnt up all the fuel within reach. No matter. I stretched out in the coyote den, pillowed my head on my arm and suffered through the long long night, wet, cold, aching, hungry, wretched, dreaming claustrophobic nightmares. It was one of the happiest nights of my life.

1968

2. Common name for numerous kinds of salt-water and freshwater snails.
3. A famous theme in the final movement of German composer and pianist Ludwig van Beethoven's (1770–1827) Ninth Symphony (1824), based on a text by the German poet Friedrich Schiller (1759–1805).

BARRY LOPEZ

B arry Lopez's "The Raven" is a difficult piece of writing to categorize. In its specific attention to details of the desert landscape and creatures, it belongs to the genre of nature writing for which Lopez (b. 1945) is so well known (for example, his award-winning books *Arctic Dreams*, 1986, and *Of Wolves and Men*, 2004). But like much of Lopez's writing, "The Raven" is clearly not a simple factual description of ravens. Embedded in the piece are what we might call "raven tales"—fables or stories about the life and behaviors of a bird whose symbolic importance in indigenous cultures is widespread. And, in fact, the book in which this piece first appeared, *Desert Notes: Reflections in the Eye of a Raven* (1976), bore the subtitle "Short Stories." But as Lopez himself has pointed out, "the distinction between fiction and nonfiction, though logical and even useful, is not as important as the distinction between an authentic and inauthentic story." "The Raven" is an authentic story about the desert landscape and its inhabitants and, equally important, a story that creates in the writer and the reader an authentic sense of wonder. In its presentation of a natural world deeply connected to myth and storytelling there are clear affinities between this piece and the work of Native American writers like Louise Erdrich and Sherman Alexie.

Lopez is an intimate observer of the landscape he writes about in "The Raven." He grew up in rural Southern California and as a child spent time in the Mojave Desert. His interest in the relationships between landscapes and human culture has taken him on travels to both remote and populated parts of the world.

The Raven

I am going to have to start at the other end by telling you this: there are no crows in the desert. What appear to be crows are ravens. You must examine the crow, however, before you can understand the raven. To forget the crow completely, as some have tried to do, would be like trying to understand the one who stayed without talking to the one who left. It is important to make note of who has left the desert.

To begin with, the crow does nothing alone. He cannot abide silence and he is prone to stealing things, twigs and bits of straw, from the nests of his neighbors. It is a game with him. He enjoys tricks. If he cannot make up his mind the crow will take two or three wives, but this is not a game. The crow is very accommodating and he admires compulsiveness.

Crows will live in street trees in the residential areas of great cities. They will walk at night on the roofs of parked cars and peck at the grit; they will scrape the pinpoints of their talons across the steel and, with their necks outthrust, watch for frightened children listening in their beds.

Put all this to the raven: he will open his mouth as if to say something. Then he will look the other way and say nothing. Later, when you have forgotten, he will tell you he admires the crow.

The raven is larger than the crow and has a beard of black feathers at his throat. He is careful to kill only what he needs. Crows, on the other hand, will search out the great horned owl, kick and punch him awake, and then, for roosting too close to their nests, they will kill him. They will come out of the sky on a fat, hot afternoon and slam into the head of a dozing rabbit and go away laughing. They will tear out a whole row of planted corn and eat only a few kernels. They will defecate on scarecrows and go home and sleep with 200,000 of their friends in an atmosphere of congratulation. Again, it is only a game; this should not be taken to mean that they are evil.

There is however this: when too many crows come together on a roost there is a lot of shoving and noise and a white film begins to descend over the crows' eyes and they go blind. They fall from their perches and lie on the ground and starve to death. When confronted with this information, crows will look past you and warn you vacantly that it is easy to be misled.

The crow flies like a pigeon. The raven flies like a hawk He is seen only at a great distance and then not very clearly. This is true of the crow too, but if you are very clever you can trap the crow. The only way to be sure what you have seen is a raven is to follow him until he dies of old age, and then examine the body.

Once there were many crows in the desert. I am told it was like this: you could sit back in the rocks and watch a pack of crows working over the carcass of a coyote. Some would eat, the others would try to squeeze out the vultures. The raven would never be seen. He would be at a distance, alone, perhaps eating a scorpion.

There was, at this time, a small alkaline water hole at the desert's edge. Its waters were bitter. No one but crows would drink there, although they drank sparingly, just one or two sips at a time. One day a raven warned someone about the dangers of drinking the bitter water and was overheard by a crow. When word of this passed among the crows they felt insulted. They jeered and raised insulting gestures to the ravens. They bullied each other into drinking the alkaline water until they had drunk the hole dry and gone blind.

The crows flew into canyon walls and dove straight into the ground at forty miles an hour and broke their necks. The worst of it was their cartwheeling across the desert floor, stiff wings outstretched, beaks agape, white eyes ballooning, surprising rattlesnakes hidden under sage bushes out of the noonday sun. The snakes awoke, struck and held. The wheeling birds strew them across the desert like sprung traps.

When all the crows were finally dead, the desert bacteria and fungi bored into them, burrowed through bone and muscle, through aqueous humor[1] and feathers until they had reduced the stiff limbs of soft black to blue dust.

After that, there were no more crows in the desert. The few who watched from a distance took it as a sign and moved away.

Finally there is this: one morning four ravens sat at the edge of the desert waiting for the sun to rise. They had been there all night and the dew was like beads of quicksilver on their wings. Their eyes were closed and they were as still as the cracks in the desert floor.

The wind came off the snow-capped peaks to the north and ruffled their breath feathers. Their talons arched in the white earth and they smoothed

---

1. The thick watery substance filling the space in the eyeball between the lens and the cornea.

their wings with sleek, dark bills. At first light their bodies swelled and their eyes flashed purple. When the dew dried on their wings they lifted off from the desert floor and flew away in four directions. Crows would never have had the patience for this.

If you want to know more about the raven: bury yourself in the desert so that you have a commanding view of the high basalt[2] cliffs where he lives. Let only your eyes protrude. Do not blink—the movement will alert the raven to your continued presence. Wait until a generation of ravens has passed away. Of the new generation there will be at least one bird who will find you. He will see your eyes staring up out of the desert floor. The raven is cautious, but he is thorough. He will sense your peaceful intentions. Let him have the first word. Be careful: he will tell you he knows nothing.

If you do not have the time for this, scour the weathered desert shacks for some sign of the raven's body. Look under old mattresses and beneath loose floorboards. Look behind the walls. Sooner or later you will find a severed foot. It will be his and it will be well preserved.

Take it out in the sunlight and examine it closely. Notice that there are three fingers that face forward, and a fourth, the longest and like a thumb, that faces to the rear. The instrument will be black but no longer shiny, the back of it sheathed in armor plate and the underside padded like a wolf's foot.

At the end of each digit you will find a black, curved talon. You will see that the talons are not as sharp as you might have suspected. They are made to grasp and hold fast, not to puncture. They are more like the jaws of a trap than a fistful of ice picks. The subtle difference serves the raven well in the desert. He can weather a storm on a barren juniper limb; he can pick up and examine the crow's eye without breaking it.

1976

2. A common volcanic rock, usually fine-grained due to the rapid cooling of lava.

JAMAICA KINCAID

Jamaica Kincaid was born on the island of Antigua in the West Indies in 1949; at seventeen she felt she had to "rescue herself" from an oppressive cultural and family situation and came to New York as an *au pair* (she calls herself "a servant"). Writing, she has said, was for her "a matter of saving my life." In 1973 she changed her birth name of Elaine Cynthia Potter Richardson to Jamaica Kincaid, because, she said, her family disapproved of her writing. After she left Antigua she did not see her mother again for twenty years. When she began a career as a writer she became a regular contributor to the *New Yorker* magazine. Her first book, *Annie John* (1983), is an autobiographical coming-of-age novel, as is *Lucy* (1990), a fictional version of her coming to New York. Her other work includes a book about Antigua (*A Small Place*, 1988), a memoir (*My Brother*, 1998), two books on gardening (one of her passions), and the stylistically innovative novel *See Now Then* (2013).

"Girl," which first appeared in the *New Yorker* in 1978, is one all-but-uninterrupted sentence in which a West Indian mother instructs her daughter on how to be the "proper" young woman she is certain her daughter is not. Although the daughter twice tries to interject, she's unable to change what is essentially monologue into dialogue. Kincaid has said that the voice in the story is "my mother's voice exactly over many years" and that, as a child, "a powerless person," she spoke infrequently. Like the other pieces collected in *At the Bottom of the River* (1983), "Girl" resists classification. Its implicit narrative makes it story; its strong rhythm and vivid images make it poetry. Simultaneously, like an essay it documents issues of gender and power. And, like much of this writer's work, it is rooted in autobiography. "I am so happy to write that I don't care what you call it," she has said. The mother/daughter relationship in "Girl" is one of Kincaid's earliest explorations of her ongoing and self-proclaimed "obsessive theme" as a writer: "the relationship between the powerful and the powerless."

Girl

Wash the white clothes on Monday and put them on the stone heap; wash the color clothes on Tuesday and put them on the clothesline to dry; don't walk barehead in the hot sun; cook pumpkin fritters[1] in very hot sweet oil; soak your little cloths right after you take them off; when buying cotton to make yourself a nice blouse, be sure that it doesn't have gum[2] on it, because that way it won't hold up well after a wash; soak salt fish[3] overnight before you cook it; is it true that you sing benna[4] in Sunday school?; always eat your food in such a way that it won't turn someone else's stomach; on Sundays try to walk like a lady and not like the slut you are so bent on becoming; don't sing benna in Sunday school; you mustn't speak to wharf-rat[5] boys, not even to give directions; don't eat fruits on the street—flies will follow you; *but I don't sing benna on Sundays at all and never in Sunday school*; this is how to sew on a button; this is how to make a buttonhole for the button you have just sewed on; this is how to hem a dress when you see the hem coming down and so to prevent yourself from looking like the slut I know you are so bent on becoming; this is how you iron your father's khaki shirt so that it doesn't have a crease; this is how you iron your father's khaki pants so that they don't have a crease; this is how you grow okra[6]—far from the house, because okra tree harbors red ants; when you are growing dasheen,[7] make sure it gets plenty of water or else it makes your throat itch when you are eating it; this is how you sweep a corner; this is how you sweep a whole house; this is how you sweep a yard; this is how you smile to someone you don't like too much; this is how you smile to someone you don't like at all; this is how you smile to someone you like completely; this is how you set a table for tea; this is how you set a table for dinner; this is how you set a table for dinner with an important guest; this is how you set a table for lunch; this is how you set a table for

1. A Caribbean dish made from fried calabaza, or West Indian pumpkin.
2. A naturally occurring, viscous resin found in the woody parts of plants.
3. A popular West Indian dish of dried and salted codfish sautéed with spices.
4. A calypso-like music characterized by a call-and-response format; it was used as a form of folk communication to spread gossip and other local news across the islands of the British West Indies in the early 20th century.
5. Regarding an individual who lives by stealing from ships or warehouses near wharves.
6. Vegetable thought to be of African origin, grown in tropical and warm temperate climates, often cooked in soups and stews or served raw.
7. The edible, starchy, tuberous root of taro, a tropical plant.

breakfast; this is how to behave in the presence of men who don't know you very well, and this way they won't recognize immediately the slut I have warned you against becoming; be sure to wash every day, even if it is with your own spit; don't squat down to play marbles—you are not a boy, you know; don't pick people's flowers—you might catch something; don't throw stones at blackbirds; because it might not be a blackbird at all; this is how to make a bread pudding;[8] this is how to make doukona;[9] this is how to make pepper pot;[1] this is how to make a good medicine for a cold; this is how to make a good medicine to throw away a child before it even becomes a child; this is how to catch a fish; this is how to throw back a fish you don't like, and that way something bad won't fall on you; this is how to bully a man; this is how a man bullies you; this is how to love a man, and if this doesn't work there are other ways, and if they don't work don't feel too bad about giving up; this is how to spit up in the air if you feel like it, and this is how to move quick so that it doesn't fall on you; this is how to make ends meet; always squeeze bread to make sure it's fresh; *but what if the baker won't let me feel the bread?*; you mean to say that after all you are really going to be the kind of woman who the baker won't let near the bread?

1978, 1983

8. A dessert made from leftover bread.
9. A Caribbean pudding made from plantain and wrapped in a plantain leaf.

1. A Caribbean meat stew, strongly flavored with cinnamon, hot peppers, and cassareep, a special sauce made from the cassava root.

HUNTER S. THOMPSON

Hunter Stockton Thompson (1937–2005) was born in Louisville, Kentucky. He was a gifted student in literature, but misbehavior at the end of his senior year of high school earned him thirty days in juvenile detention, which prevented his graduation. Joining the air force as a way of getting out of town led to more trouble but also introduced him to the pleasures of life in the Caribbean, where he found work as a newspaper reporter. From there he moved on to feature journalism for such new countercultural magazines as *Scanlan's*, *Ramparts*, and *Rolling Stone*. Early attempts at fiction proved unpublishable until much later in his career, which he fashioned as an extreme style of literary journalism, his method focusing more on the observer's reaction to events than on events themselves (and using the techniques of fiction, such as characterization, imagery, and symbolism, to express those reactions). His most famous books remain his earliest ones: *Hell's Angels* (1967), covering a year he spent riding with this motorcycle gang; *Fear and Loathing in Las Vegas* (1971), an account of his failure to cover a dirt-bike race and a narcotics-law-enforcement convention; and *Fear and Loathing on the Campaign Trail '72* (1973), collecting his presidential campaign reporting as a correspondent for *Rolling Stone*. A self-styled Doctor of Gonzo Journalism, Thompson continued to publish personal reporting about the excesses of American culture until his death from a self-inflicted gunshot.

From Fear and Loathing in Las Vegas

The Circus-Circus[1] is what the whole hep world would be doing on Saturday night if the Nazis had won the war. This is the Sixth Reich.[2] The ground floor is full of gambling tables, like all the other casinos . . . but the place is about four stories high, in the style of a circus tent, and all manner of strange County-Fair/Polish Carnival madness is going on up in this space. Right above the gambling tables the Forty Flying Carazito Brothers are doing a high-wire trapeze act, along with four muzzled Wolverines and the Six Nymphet Sisters from San Diego . . . so you're down on the main floor playing blackjack, and the stakes are getting high when suddenly you chance to look up, and there, right smack above your head is a half-naked fourteen-year-old girl being chased through the air by a snarling wolverine, which is suddenly locked in a death battle with two silver-painted Polacks who come swinging down from opposite balconies and meet in mid-air on the wolverine's neck . . . both Polacks seize the animal as they fall straight down towards the crap tables—but they bounce off the net; they separate and spring back up towards the roof in three different directions, and just as they're about to fall again they are grabbed out of the air by three Korean Kittens and trapezed off to one of the balconies.

This madness goes on and on, but nobody seems to notice. The gambling action runs twenty-four hours a day on the main floor, and the circus never ends. Meanwhile, on all the upstairs balconies, the customers are being hustled by every conceivable kind of bizarre shuck. All kinds of funhouse-type booths. Shoot the pasties off the nipples of a ten-foot bull-dyke and win a cotton-candy goat. Stand in front of this fantastic machine, my friend, and for just 99¢ your likeness will appear, two hundred feet tall, on a screen above downtown Las Vegas. Ninety-nine cents more for a voice message. "Say whatever you want, fella. They'll hear you, don't worry about that. Remember you'll be two hundred feet tall."

Jesus Christ. I could see myself lying in bed in the Mint Hotel, half-asleep and staring idly out the window, when suddenly a vicious nazi drunkard appears two hundred feet tall in the midnight sky, screaming gibberish at the world: *"Woodstock Über Alles!"*[3]

We will close the drapes tonight. A thing like that could send a drug person careening around the room like a ping-pong ball. Hallucinations are bad enough. But after a while you learn to cope with things like seeing your dead grandmother crawling up your leg with a knife in her teeth. Most acid fanciers can handle this sort of thing.

But *nobody* can handle that other trip—the possibility that any freak with $1.98 can walk into the Circus-Circus and suddenly appear in the sky over downtown Las Vegas twelve times the size of God, howling anything that

---

1. Casino and entertainment center that opened in Las Vegas, Nevada, in 1968.
2. The Nazi government in Germany (1933–45) declared itself the Third Reich ("Empire"); there were no Fourth and Fifth Reichs.
3. Woodstock Above All (German); a play on the German National Anthem ("*Das Lied der Deutschen*," popularly known as "*Deutschland, Deutschland, Über Alles*"), with a reference to Woodstock, the rock festival held August 15–17, 1969, outside Bethel, an area southwest of Woodstock, New York, an event considered the high point of 1960s counterculture.

comes into his head. No, this is not a good town for psychedelic drugs. Reality itself is too twisted.

1971

JOAN DIDION

Joan Didion's collection of essays on the 1960s counterculture, *Slouching Towards Bethlehem* (1968), made her famous and established her as a practitioner of "the New Journalism." Her second essay collection, *The White Album* (1979), mixes autobiography with analyses of cultural events in Los Angeles in the 1960s (the book's title refers to the Beatles' 1968 double album which had no graphics or text on the cover other than the band's name). These widely influential books confirmed Didion's reputation as a shrewd and edgy cultural observer and literary stylist. She has also published several novels, including *Play It As It Lays* (1970) and *Democracy* (1984).

A native Californian, Didion (b. 1934) moved to New York as a young woman, where she worked for *Vogue* magazine and, in 1964, married the novelist John Gregory Dunne. In the mid-1960s they moved to Los Angeles, where they spent the next twenty years. Didion and Dunne collaborated on several screenplays and became a glamorous couple whose talents were sought after in Hollywood. In the 1980s they moved back to New York, where Didion continued her work as a screenwriter, novelist, and nonfiction author. *The Year of Magical Thinking* (2005) is Didion's account of the year following her husband's sudden death from cardiac arrest. Two months before its publication, the couple's daughter, Quintana Roo, whom they adopted in 1966, also died. In the memoir, Didion turned her steely-eyed gaze on herself, using all the tools at her disposal to offer an unsparing description of grief. "We tell stories in order to live," *The White Album* begins; over a quarter century later, Didion remained true to those words.

In this excerpt from the title essay of *Slouching Towards Bethlehem*, Didion presents the chaotic scene of "happenings" in 1960s San Francisco—spontaneous public performances meant to provoke thought and reaction. She penetrates the lives of those who drift through the transient crowds near Golden Gate Park. Coolly noting such details as blackface performers and little children taking LSD, Didion plays journalistic neutrality against what she views as the excesses of the counterculture.

From Slouching Towards Bethlehem

Janis Joplin is singing with Big Brother in the Panhandle and almost everybody is high and it is a pretty nice Sunday afternoon between three and six o'clock, which the activists say are the three hours of the week when something is most likely to happen in the Haight-Ashbury, and who turns up but Peter Berg.[1] He is with his wife and six or seven other people, along with

1. American actor, playwright, and activist (1937–2011), cofounder of the Diggers, a radical community action and street theater group operating in San Francisco from 1967 until 1968, and a member of the San Francisco Mime Troupe, a street theater group founded in 1959. "Janis Joplin": rock star (1943–1970) and lead singer of Big Brother and the Holding Company,

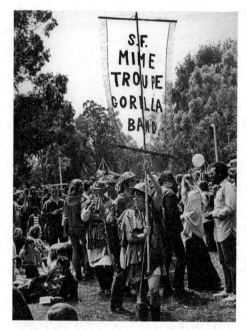

San Francisco Mime Troupe performing in Golden Gate Park.

Chester Anderson's associate The Connection,[2] and the first peculiar thing is, they're in blackface.

I mention to Max and Sharon[3] that some members of the Mime Troupe seem to be in blackface.

"It's street theater," Sharon assures me. "It's supposed to be really groovy."

The Mime Troupers get a little closer, and there are some other peculiar things about them. For one thing they are tapping people on the head with dime-store plastic nightsticks, and for another they are wearing signs on their backs. "HOW MANY TIMES YOU BEEN RAPED, YOU LOVE FREAKS?" and "WHO STOLE CHUCK BERRY'S[4] MUSIC?," things like that. Then they are distributing communication company fliers which say:

& this summer thousands of un-white un-suburban boppers are going to want to know why you've given up what they can't get & how you get away with it & how come you not a faggot[5] with hair so long & they want haight street one way or the other. IF YOU DON'T KNOW, BY AUGUST HAIGHT STREET WILL BE A CEMETERY.

Max reads the flier and stands up. "I'm getting bad vibes," he says, and he and Sharon leave.

I have to stay around because I'm looking for Otto so I walk over to where the Mime Troupers have formed a circle around a Negro. Peter Berg is saying if anybody asks that this is street theater, and I figure the curtain is up because what they are doing right now is jabbing the Negro with the nightsticks. They jab, and they bare their teeth, and they rock on the balls of their feet and they wait.

---

a band formed in San Francisco in 1965; "Panhandle": park in San Francisco adjacent to Golden Gate Park; "Haight-Ashbury": San Francisco neighborhood where hippies and thousands of others attracted to the counterculture movement gathered during the 1967 "Summer of Love."

2. Nickname for Claude Hayward, who along with writer and editor Chester Anderson (1932–1991), cofounded the Communications Company (ComCo), which made mimeographed posters for the Diggers, the San Francisco Mime

Troupe, and others.

3. Max, Sharon, Otto, Susan, Don, Sue Ann, and others mentioned by first name are people Didion met in San Francisco as she reported on the counterculture.

4. Charles Edward Anderson "Chuck" Berry (b. 1926), African American singer, guitarist, and songwriter who pioneered rock and roll in the mid-twentieth century.

5. Derogatory term for homosexual. "Boppers": slang for fans or players of bebop-style jazz.

"I'm beginning to get annoyed here," the Negro says. "I'm gonna get mad."

By now there are several Negroes around, reading the signs and watching.

"Just beginning to get annoyed, are you?" one of the Mime Troupers says. "Don't you think it's about time?"

"Nobody *stole* Chuck Berry's music, man," says another Negro who has been studying the signs. "Chuck Berry's music belongs to *every*body."

"Yeh?" a girl in blackface says. "Everybody *who?*"

"Why," he says, confused. "Everybody. In America."

"In *America*," the blackface girl shrieks. "Listen to him talk about *America*."

"Listen," he says helplessly. "Listen here."

"What'd *America* ever do for you?" the girl in blackface jeers. "White kids here, they can sit in the Park all summer long, listening to the music they stole, because their bigshot parents keep sending them money. Who ever sends you money?"

"Listen," the Negro says, his voice rising. "You're gonna start something here, this isn't right—".

"You tell us what's right, black boy," the girl says.

The youngest member of the blackface group, an earnest tall kid about nineteen, twenty, is hanging back at the edge of the scene. I offer him an apple and ask what is going on. "Well," he says, "I'm new at this, I'm just beginning to study it, but you see the capitalists are taking over the District, and that's what Peter—well, ask Peter."

I did not ask Peter. It went on for a while. But on that particular Sunday between three and six o'clock everyone was too high and the weather was too good and the Hunter's Point[6] gangs who usually come in between three and six on Sunday afternoon had come in on Saturday instead, and nothing started. While I waited for Otto I asked a little girl I knew slightly what she had thought of it. "It's something groovy they call street theater," she said. I said I had wondered if it might not have political overtones. She was seventeen years old and she worked it around in her mind awhile and finally she remembered a couple of words from somewhere. "Maybe it's some John Birch[7] thing," she said.

When I finally find Otto he says "I got something at my place that'll blow your mind," and when we get there I see a child on the living-room floor, wearing a reefer coat,[8] reading a comic book. She keeps licking her lips in concentration and the only off thing about her is that she's wearing white lipstick.

"Five years old," Otto says. "On acid."[9]

The five-year-old's name is Susan, and she tells me she is in High Kindergarten. She lives with her mother and some other people, just got over the measles, wants a bicycle for Christmas, and particularly likes Coca-Cola,

---

6. African American neighborhood in southeast San Francisco.
7. Anticommunist activist group that opposed the civil rights movement.

8. Short, double-breasted jacket, typically worn by sailors in the navy.
9. Lysergic acid diethylamide (LSD), a powerful hallucinogenic drug.

ice cream, Marty in the Jefferson Airplane, Bob in the Grateful Dead,[1] and the beach. She remembers going to the beach once a long time ago, and wishes she had taken a bucket. For a year now her mother has given her both acid and peyote.[2] Susan describes it as getting stoned.

I start to ask if any of the other children in High Kindergarten get stoned, but I falter at the key words.

"She means do the other kids in your class turn on, *get stoned*," says the friend of her mother's who brought her to Otto's.

"Only Sally and Anne," Susan says.

"What about Lia?" her mother's friend prompts.

"Lia," Susan says, "is not in High Kindergarten."

Sue Ann's three-year-old Michael started a fire this morning before anyone was up, but Don got it out before much damage was done. Michael burned his arm though, which is probably why Sue Ann was so jumpy when she happened to see him chewing on an electric cord. "You'll fry like rice," she screamed. The only people around were Don and one of Sue Ann's macrobiotic friends and somebody who was on his way to a commune in the Santa Lucias, and they didn't notice Sue Ann screaming at Michael because they were in the kitchen trying to retrieve some very good Moroccan hash[3] which had dropped down through a floorboard damaged in the fire.

1967

---

1. Bob Weir (b. 1947), guitarist for the Grateful Dead, rock band. "Marty": Martin Balin (b. 1942), founder and co–lead singer of the rock band Jefferson Airplane. Both bands were formed in San Francisco in 1965.
2. Small cactus used as a drug for its psychoactive properties. Historically used by Native Americans for spiritual purposes.
3. Abbreviated term for hashish, a drug in the cannabis family. "Macrobiotic": following a diet of unprocessed foods based on Taoist principles of balancing life forces of yin and yang. "Santa Lucias": mountain range along the central coast of California.

DAVID FOSTER WALLACE

Known both for his fiction—particularly his epic novels *Infinite Jest* (1996) and the posthumously published *The Pale King* (2011)—and for his exuberant nonfiction, Wallace represents a maximal style in both genres. Wallace was the son of Midwestern academics, his father a philosophy professor and his mother an English teacher. He grew up in Illinois and was educated at Amherst College, where he majored in philosophy and English, and where he started to study creative writing. He graduated from the MFA program in fiction at the University of Arizona in 1987; eleven years later *Infinite Jest* earned him a MacArthur Foundation "genius grant," which freed him from teaching for a time.

Wallace's intense approach to writing was distinguished by extended research projects—notably on the pornography industry for the essay "Adult World" and on the Internal Revenue Service for *The Pale King*—and a style that was by turns sincere and satirical, self-conscious and arrogant, intellectual and lowbrow. Plagued by manic depression and addiction throughout his adult life, Wallace committed suicide in 2008, inspiring an outpouring of regret and appreciation, as well as a serious biography and a posthumously assembled version of *The Pale King*, which he had been working on when he died. In his nonfiction, Wallace took up a wide array of subjects, from television to politics to tennis, with a verve and curiosity that made a mark on this swiftly evolving genre.

Wallace's appetite for arcane facts and attraction to American kitsch combine with his inward-looking attention to consciousness in this selection from one of his most widely admired essays, "Consider the Lobster." His assignment for *Gourmet* magazine was to report on the 2004 Maine Lobster Festival. Always fascinated by the experience of psychic pain and the ethics of inflicting pain on others, Wallace adopts a relentlessly questioning style that bars readers from simply consuming his description of the lobster's anatomy and passively accepting the ways cooks kill them.

From Consider the Lobster

There happen to be two main criteria that most ethicists agree on for determining whether a living creature has the capacity to suffer and so has genuine interests that it may or may not be our moral duty to consider.[1] One is how much of the neurological hardware required for pain-experience the animal comes equipped with—nociceptors, prostaglandins, neuronal opioid receptors, etc. The other criterion is whether the animal demonstrates behavior associated with pain. And it takes a lot of intellectual gymnastics and behaviorist[2] hairsplitting not to see struggling, thrashing, and lid-clattering as just such pain-behavior. According to marine zoologists, it usually takes lobsters between 35 and 45 seconds to die in boiling water. (No source I could find talks about how long it takes them to die in superheated steam; one rather hopes it's faster.)

There are, of course, other ways to kill your lobster on-site and so achieve maximum freshness. Some cooks' practice is to drive a sharp heavy knife point-first into a spot just above the midpoint between the lobster's eyestalks (more or less where the Third Eye[3] is in human foreheads). This is alleged either to kill the lobster instantly or to render it insensate, and is said at least to eliminate some of the cowardice involved in throwing a creature into boiling water and then fleeing the room. As far as I can tell from talking to proponents of the knife-in-head method, the idea is that it's more violent but ultimately more merciful, plus that a willingness to exert personal agency and accept responsibility for stabbing the lobster's head honors the lobster somehow and entitles one to eat it (there's often a vague sort

---

1. "Interests" basically means strong and legitimate preferences, which obviously require some degree of consciousness, responsiveness to stimuli, etc. See, for instance, the utilitarian philosopher Peter Singer, whose 1974 *Animal Liberation* is more or less the bible of the modern animal-rights movement:

> It would be nonsense to say that it was not in the interests of a stone to be kicked along the road by a schoolboy. A stone does not have interests because it cannot suffer. Nothing that we can do to it could possibly make any

difference to its welfare. A mouse, on the other hand, does have an interest in not being kicked along the road, because it will suffer if it is [Wallace's note].

2. Adherent of the theory that psychology is best understood by studying the external behavior of individuals.

3. The spiritual inner eye associated with Hindu tradition, represented as an eye or triangle set between the brows, in the middle of the forehead.

of Native American spirituality-of-the-hunt flavor to pro-knife arguments). But the problem with the knife method is basic biology: Lobsters' nervous systems operate off not one but several ganglia, a.k.a. nerve bundles, which are sort of wired in series and distributed all along the lobster's underside, from stem to stern. And disabling only the frontal ganglion does not normally result in quick death or unconsciousness.

Another alternative is to put the lobster in cold saltwater and then very slowly bring it up to a full boil. Cooks who advocate this method are going on the analogy to a frog, which can supposedly be kept from jumping out of a boiling pot by heating the water incrementally. In order to save a lot of research-summarizing, I'll simply assure you that the analogy between frogs and lobsters turns out not to hold—plus, if the kettle's water isn't aerated seawater, the immersed lobster suffers from slow suffocation, although usually not decisive enough suffocation to keep it from still thrashing and clattering when the water gets hot enough to kill it. In fact, lobsters boiled incrementally often display a whole bonus set of gruesome, convulsionlike reactions that you don't see in regular boiling.

Ultimately, the only certain virtues of the home-lobotomy[4] and slow-heating methods are comparative, because there are even worse/crueler ways people prepare lobster. Time-thrifty cooks sometimes microwave them alive (usually after poking several vent-holes in the carapace, which is a precaution most shellfish-microwavers learn about the hard way). Live dismemberment, on the other hand, is big in Europe—some chefs cut the lobster in half before cooking; others like to tear off the claws and tail and toss only these parts into the pot.

And there's more unhappy news respecting suffering-criterion number one. Lobsters don't have much in the way of eyesight or hearing, but they do have an exquisite tactile sense, one facilitated by hundreds of thousands of tiny hairs that protrude through their carapace. "Thus it is," in the words of T. M. Prudden's industry classic *About Lobster*, "that although encased in what seems a solid, impenetrable armor, the lobster can receive stimuli and impressions from without as readily as if it possessed a soft and delicate skin." And lobsters do have nociceptors,[5] as well as invertebrate versions of the prostaglandins and major neurotransmitters via which our own brains register pain.

Lobsters do not, on the other hand, appear to have the equipment for making or absorbing natural opioids like endorphins and enkephalins, which are what more advanced nervous systems use to try to handle intense pain. From this fact, though, one could conclude either that lobsters are maybe even *more* vulnerable to pain, since they lack mammalian nervous systems' built-in analgesia,[6] or, instead, that the absence of natural opioids implies an absence of the really intense pain-sensations that natural opioids are designed to mitigate. I for one can detect a marked upswing in mood as I contemplate this latter possibility. It could be that their lack of endorphin/enkephalin hardware means that lobsters' raw subjective experience of pain is so radically different from mammals' that it may not even

4. Surgery to sever nerves in the prefrontal lobe of the brain.
5. This is the neurological term for special pain-receptors that are "sensitive to potentially damaging extremes of temperature, to mechanical forces, and to chemical substances which are released when body tissues are damaged" [Wallace's note].
6. Ability to block pain.

deserve the term "pain." Perhaps lobsters are more like those frontal-lobotomy patients one reads about who report experiencing pain in a totally different way than you and I. These patients evidently do feel physical pain, neurologically speaking, but don't dislike it—though neither do they like it; it's more that they feel it but don't feel anything *about* it—the point being that the pain is not distressing to them or something they want to get away from. Maybe lobsters, who are also without frontal lobes, are detached from the neurological-registration-of-injury-or-hazard we call pain in just the same way. There is, after all, a difference between (1) pain as a purely neurological event, and (2) actual suffering, which seems crucially to involve an emotional component, an awareness of pain as unpleasant, as something to fear/dislike/want to avoid.

Still, after all the abstract intellection, there remain the facts of the frantically clanking lid, the pathetic clinging to the edge of the pot. Standing at the stove, it is hard to deny in any meaningful way that this is a living creature experiencing pain and wishing to avoid/escape the painful experience. To my lay mind, the lobster's behavior in the kettle appears to be the expression of a *preference*, and it may well be that an ability to form preferences is the decisive criterion for real suffering.[7] The logic of this (preference → suffering) relation may be easiest to see in the negative case. If you cut certain kinds of worms in half, the halves will often keep crawling around and going about their vermiform[8] business as if nothing had happened. When we assert, based on their post-op behavior, that these worms appear not to be suffering, what we're really saying is that there's no sign the worms know anything bad has happened or would *prefer* not to have gotten cut in half.

Lobsters, though, are known to exhibit preferences. Experiments have shown that they can detect changes of only a degree or two in water temperature; one reason for their complex migratory cycles (which can often cover 100-plus miles a year) is to pursue the temperatures they like best.[9] And, as mentioned, they're bottom-dwellers and do not like bright light—if a tank of food-lobsters is out in the sunlight or a store's fluorescence, the lobsters will always congregate in whatever part is darkest. Fairly solitary in the ocean, they also clearly dislike the crowding that's part of their captivity in

7. "Preference" is maybe roughly synonymous with "interests," but it is a better term for our purposes because it's less abstractly philosophical—"preference" seems more personal, and it's the whole idea of a living creature's personal experience that's at issue [Wallace's note].

8. Having the form of a worm.

9. Of course, the most common sort of counterargument here would begin by objecting that "like best" is really just a metaphor, and a misleadingly anthropomorphic one at that. The counterarguer would posit that the lobster seeks to maintain a certain optimal ambient temperature out of nothing but unconscious instinct (with a similar explanation for the low-light affinities upcoming in the main text). The thrust of such a counterargument will be that the lobster's thrashings and clankings in the kettle express not unpreferred pain but involuntary reflexes, like your leg shooting out when the doctor hits your knee. Be advised that there are professional scientists, including many researchers who use animals in experiments, who hold to the view that nonhuman creatures have no real feelings at all, merely "behaviors." Be further advised that this view has a long history that goes all the way back to Descartes, although its modern support comes mostly from behaviorist psychology.

To these what-looks-like-pain-is-really-just-reflexes counterarguments, however, there happen to be all sorts of scientific and pro-animal rights counter-counterarguments. And then further attempted rebuttals and redirects, and so on. Suffice it to say that both the scientific and the philosophical arguments on either side of the animal-suffering issue are involved, abstruse, technical, often informed by self-interest or ideology, and in the end so totally inconclusive that as a practical matter, in the kitchen or restaurant, it all still seems to come down to individual conscience, going with (no pun) your gut [Wallace's note].

tanks, since (as also mentioned) one reason why lobsters' claws are banded on capture is to keep them from attacking one another under the stress of close-quarter storage.

In any event, at the MLF,[1] standing by the bubbling tanks outside the World's Largest Lobster Cooker, watching the fresh-caught lobsters pile over one another, wave their hobbled claws impotently, huddle in the rear corners, or scrabble frantically back from the glass as you approach, it is difficult not to sense that they're unhappy, or frightened, even if it's some rudimentary version of these feelings . . . and, again, why does rudimentariness even enter into it? Why is a primitive, inarticulate form of suffering less urgent or uncomfortable for the person who's helping to inflict it by paying for the food it results in? I'm not trying to give you a PETA-like screed here—at least I don't think so. I'm trying, rather, to work out and articulate some of the troubling questions that arise amid all the laughter and saltation[2] and community pride of the Maine Lobster Festival. The truth is that if you, the festival attendee, permit yourself to think that lobsters can suffer and would rather not, the MLF begins to take on the aspect of something like a Roman circus or medieval torture-fest.

Does that comparison seem a bit much? If so, exactly why? Or what about this one: Is it possible that future generations will regard our present agribusiness and eating practices in much the same way we now view Nero's entertainments or Mengele's[3] experiments? My own initial reaction is that such a comparison is hysterical, extreme—and yet the reason it seems extreme to me appears to be that I believe animals are less morally important than human beings;[4] and when it comes to defending such a belief, even to myself, I have to acknowledge that (a) I have an obvious selfish interest in this belief, since I like to eat certain kinds of animals and want to be able to keep doing it, and (b) I haven't succeeded in working out any sort of personal ethical system in which the belief is truly defensible instead of just selfishly convenient.

Given this article's venue and my own lack of culinary sophistication, I'm curious about whether the reader can identify with any of these reactions and acknowledgments and discomforts. I'm also concerned not to come off as shrill or preachy when what I really am is more like confused. For those *Gourmet* readers who enjoy well-prepared and -presented meals involving beef, veal, lamb, pork, chicken, lobster, etc.: Do you think much about the (possible) moral status and (probable) suffering of the animals involved? If you do, what ethical convictions have you worked out that permit you not just to eat but to savor and enjoy flesh-based viands (since of course refined *enjoyment*, rather than mere ingestion, is the whole point of gastronomy[5])?

---

1. Maine Lobster Festival.

2. The two relevant meanings are dancing, and spurting forth of blood, both obsolete. "PETA": People for the Ethical Treatment of Animals, an animal-rights activist group.

3. Josef Mengele (1911–1979), German Shutzstaffel (SS) officer and physician who conducted medical experiments on prisoners in the Auschwitz concentration camp in Poland during World War II. "Nero": famously violent Roman emperor (37–68 C.E.), ruling from 54 to 68 C.E.

4. Meaning *a lot* less important, apparently, since the moral comparison here is not the value of one human's life vs. the value of one animal's life, but rather the value of one animal's life vs. the value of one human's taste for a particular kind of protein. Even the most diehard carniphile will acknowledge that it's possible to live and eat well without consuming animals [Wallace's note].

5. The art of choosing, preparing, and eating fine food.

If, on the other hand, you'll have no truck with confusions or convictions and regard stuff like the previous paragraph as just so much fatuous navel-gazing, what makes it feel truly okay, inside, to just dismiss the whole thing out of hand? That is, is your refusal to think about any of this the product of actual thought, or is it just that you don't want to think about it? And if the latter, then why not? Do you ever think, even idly, about the possible reasons for your reluctance to think about it? I am not trying to bait anyone here—I'm genuinely curious. After all, isn't being extra aware and attentive and thoughtful about one's food and its overall context part of what distinguishes a real gourmet? Or is all the gourmet's extra attention and sensibility just supposed to be sensuous? Is it really all just a matter of taste and presentation?

These last few queries, though, while sincere, obviously involve much larger and more abstract questions about the connections (if any) between aesthetics and morality—about what the adjective in a phrase like "The Magazine of Good Living"[6] is really supposed to mean—and these questions lead straightaway into such deep and treacherous waters that it's probably best to stop the public discussion right here. There are limits to what even interested persons can ask of each other.

2004

6. *Gourmet* magazine's slogan.

EDWIDGE DANTICAT

Edwidge Danticat was born in Port-au-Prince, the capital of Haiti, in 1969. Her novels *Breath, Eyes, Memory* (1994) and *The Farming of Bones* (1998), as well as her collection of stories, *Krik? Krak!* (1995—the title comes from a Haitian chant), draw on her experiences as a Haitian American. Danticat was two years old when her father left Haiti to make a better life for the family in the United States; two years later, her mother left to join him. For the next eight years Danticat and her brother remained in Haiti under the care of their uncle Joseph, a Baptist minister who founded his own church and school in Port-au-Prince. She then emigrated to the United States to be reunited with her parents. In 2004, after violence destroyed her uncle's church and put his life in jeopardy, Joseph entered the United States asking for temporary asylum but was detained in Miami by Department of Homeland Security officials suspicious of his plea. During questioning, Joseph collapsed but was refused treatment at the time. The next day he was taken to a Florida hospital where he died. In October 2007 Danticat testified on this issue before the House Judiciary Subcommittee on Immigration, Citizenship Refuges, Border Security, and International Law. Like many creative nonfiction writers, Danticat uses personal narrative to illuminate larger issues: the political and economic situation in Haiti, the challenges facing immigrants to the United States, and the need to reform the practices of immigration detainee medical care.

Brother, I'm Dying is a memoir partly of the writer's childhood in Haiti and, more particularly, of the interconnected lives of her uncle and father, who, after leaving Haiti, ran a car-service business in New York and died from pulmonary fibrosis soon after his brother's death. When the adult Danticat, now pregnant with her first child, listens to her gravely ill father respond to the question "Have you enjoyed your life?" by speaking of his children and family, she recalls living as a child with her uncle when the family would regularly receive letters from her father in the United States. This selection captures Danticat's exploration of what words can and cannot say, a question at the heart of this writer's work.

From Brother, I'm Dying

Listening to my father, I remembered a time when I used to dream of smuggling him words. I was eight years old and Bob and I were living in Haiti with his oldest brother, my uncle Joseph, and his wife. And since they didn't have a telephone at home—few Haitian families did then—and access to the call centers was costly, we had no choice but to write letters. Every other month, my father would mail a half-page, three-paragraph missive addressed to my uncle. Scribbled in his minuscule scrawl, sometimes on plain white paper, other times on lined, hole-punched notebook pages still showing bits of fringe from the spiral binding, my father's letters were composed in stilted French,[1] with the first paragraph offering news of his and my mother's health, the second detailing how to spend the money they had wired for food, lodging, and school expenses for Bob and myself, the third section concluding abruptly after reassuring us that we'd be hearing from him again before long.

Later I would discover in a first-year college composition class that his letters had been written in a diamond sequence, the Aristotelian *Poetics*[2] correspondence, requiring an opening greeting, a middle detail or request, and a brief farewell at the end. The letter-writing process had been such an agonizing chore for my father, one that he'd hurried through while assembling our survival money, that this specific epistolary formula, which he followed unconsciously, had offered him a comforting way of disciplining his emotions.

"I was no writer," he later told me. "What I wanted to tell you and your brother was too big for any piece of paper and a small envelope."

Whatever restraint my father showed in his letters was easily compensated for by Uncle Joseph's reactions to them. First there was the public reading in my uncle's sparsely furnished pink living room, in front of Tante[3] Denise, Bob and me. This was done so there would be no misunderstanding as to how the money my parents sent for me and my brother would be spent. Usually my uncle would read the letters out loud, pausing now and then to ask my help with my father's penmanship, a kindness, I thought, a way to include me a step further. It soon became obvious, however, that my father's handwriting was as clear to me as my own, so I eventually acquired the job of deciphering his letters.

Along with this task came a few minutes of preparation for the reading and thus a few intimate moments with my father's letters, not only the words and phrases, which did not vary greatly from month to month, but the vow-

1. That is, the formal French taught in Haitian schools, rather than the vernacular Creole of everyday life.
2. The earliest surviving work of dramatic and literary theory, written by Aristotle (384–322 B.C.E.), which analyzes poetry in terms of its essential elements.
3. Aunt (French).

els and syllables, their tilts and slants, which did. Because he wrote so little, I would try to guess his thoughts and moods from the dotting of his *i*'s and the crossing of his *t*'s, from whether there were actual periods at the ends of his sentences or just faint dots where the tip of his pen had simply landed. Did commas split his streamlined phrases, or were they staccato,[4] like someone speaking too rapidly, out of breath?

For the family readings, I recited my father's letters in a monotone, honoring what I interpreted as a secret between us, that the impersonal style of his letters was due as much to his lack of faith in words and their ability to accurately reproduce his emotions as to his caution with Bob's and my feelings, avoiding too-happy news that might add to the anguish of separation, too-sad news that might worry us, and any hint of judgment or disapproval for my aunt and uncle, which they could have interpreted as suggestions that they were mistreating us. The dispassionate letters were his way of avoiding a minefield, one he could have set off from a distance without being able to comfort the victims.

Given all this anxiety, I'm amazed my father wrote at all. The regularity, the consistency of his correspondence now feels like an act of valor. In contrast, my replies, though less routine—Uncle Joseph did most of the writing—were both painstakingly upbeat and suppliant. In my letters, I bragged about my good grades and requested, as a reward for them, an American doll at Christmas, a typewriter or sewing machine for my birthday, a pair of "real" gold earrings for Easter. But the things I truly wanted I was afraid to ask for, like when I would finally see him and my mother again. However, since my uncle read and corrected all my letters for faulty grammar and spelling, I wrote for his eyes more than my father's, hoping that even after the vigorous editing, my father would still decode the longing in my childish cursive slopes and arches, which were so much like his own.

The words that both my father and I wanted to exchange we never did. These letters were not approved, in his case by him, in my case by my uncle. No matter what the reason, we have always been equally paralyzed by the fear of breaking each other's heart. This is why I could never ask the question Bob did. I also could never tell my father that I'd learned from the doctor that he was dying. Even when they mattered less, there were things he and I were too afraid to say.

2007

---

4. A form of musical articulation, signifying unconnected notes, short and detached.

GEORGE SAUNDERS
b. 1958

F ew writers in the second half of the twentieth century have probed the commercial culture of America with the insight and wit of George Saunders. Saunders's ear tunes to the jargon of business management, the platitudes of marketing, the clichés of popular psychology, and the euphemisms that blind people to violence of all kinds. Within the distilled form of the short story, Saunders creates characters partially trapped in these ways of speaking—and thinking—who struggle to bend their language to more moral or soulful human ends.

Saunders's early life was suffused with the varieties of language so often on display in the stories. His father was in the Air Force, stationed in Amarillo, Texas, when Saunders was born in 1958. The family later moved to Chicago, where his father worked in the insurance and coal businesses, then bought a Chicken Unlimited franchise where the young Saunders worked in high school alongside his mother and sisters. Saunders tells how his father "would bring home books like Machiavelli's *The Prince* or Michael Harrington's *The Other Side of America* or *The Jungle* by Upton Sinclair, and he would just leave them on my bed, saying, 'I think you should take a look at this.'"

Saunders became a writer relatively late in life. He graduated from the Chicago School of Mines and worked in the Sumatran oil fields after college. Stationed at a remote jungle camp, he started reading seriously. After falling sick from swimming in a polluted river, he returned to the United States and took a variety of odd jobs, including, as he says, "doorman, roofer, convenience store clerk" and "knuckle-puller" in a slaughterhouse. Quoting the British Marxist critic Terry Eagleton, Saunders says he came to understand "capitalism as a benign-looking thing that . . . 'plunders the sensuality of the body.'" The sense that modern labor renders people less than human pervades Saunders's work, though he is also a comic writer.

Comic writing, for Saunders, does not always mean funny writing. He has said that "comic, for me, means that there is always a shortfall between what we think of ourselves and what we are. . . . Maybe the most clearly we ever see reality is when it boots us in the ass." He cites the work of Steve Martin, Monty Python, the Marx Brothers, and Dr. Seuss (alongside many literary sources) as influences on his writing. He became a student, and, less than a decade later, in 1996, a professor at the MFA program at Syracuse University. In 2006, he was awarded both Guggenheim and MacArthur Fellowships—the latter known as the "genius grant." He has published four short-story collections, a book of essays titled *The Braindead Megaphone* (2007), an illustrated fable, a children's book, and nonfiction articles for *GQ*, the *New Yorker*, and other publications on topics ranging from the "Minute Men" on the Mexican border to theme hotels in Dubai to a homeless tent city in Fresno, California, where he lived for a time while doing research.

In the story reprinted here, one of his most admired, Saunders meditates on the issues of racism and war in American history, as the Civil War is repackaged as contemporary entertainment but becomes, finally and inescapably, real. His weak hero struggles to find both words and actions to match the persistent nudge of human compassion that prompts him to resist these American legacies.

CivilWarLand in Bad Decline

Whenever a potential big investor comes for the tour the first thing I do is take him to the transplanted Erie Canal Lock.[1] We've got a good ninety feet of actual Canal out there and a well-researched dioramic of a coolie[2] campsite. Were our faces ever red when we found out it was actually the Irish who built the Canal. We've got no budget to correct, so every fifteen minutes or so a device in the bunkhouse gives off the approximate aroma of an Oriental meal.

Today my possible Historical Reconstruction Associate is Mr. Haberstrom, founder of Burn'n' Learn. Burn'n' Learn is national. Their gimmick is a fully stocked library on the premises and as you tan you call out the name of any book you want to these high-school girls on roller skates. As we walk up the trail he's wearing a sweatsuit and smoking a cigar and I tell him I admire his acumen. I tell him some men are dreamers and others are doers. He asks which am I and I say let's face it, I'm basically the guy who leads the dreamers up the trail to view the Canal Segment. He likes that. He says I have a good head on my shoulders. He touches my arm and says he's hot to spend some reflective moments at the Canal because his great-grandfather was a barge guider way back when who got killed by a donkey. When we reach the clearing he gets all emotional and bolts off through the gambling plaster Chinese. Not to be crass but I sense an impending sizable contribution.

When I come up behind him however I see that once again the gangs have been at it with their spray cans, all over my Lock. Haberstrom takes a nice long look. Then he pokes me with the spitty end of his cigar and says not with his money I don't, and storms back down the trail.

I stand there alone a few minutes. The last thing I need is some fat guy's spit on my tie. I think about quitting. Then I think about my last degrading batch of résumés. Two hundred send-outs and no nibbles. My feeling is that prospective employers are put off by the fact that I was a lowly Verisimilitude Inspector for nine years with no promotions. I think of my car payment. I think of how much Marcus and Howie love the little playhouse I'm still paying off. Once again I decide to eat my pride and sit tight.

So I wipe off my tie with a leaf and start down to break the Haberstrom news to Mr. Alsuga.

Mr. A's another self-made man. He cashed in on his love of history by conceptualizing CivilWarLand in his spare time. He started out with just a settler's shack and one Union costume and now has considerable influence in Rotary.[3]

His office is in City Hall. He agrees that the gangs are getting out of hand. Last month they wounded three Visitors and killed a dray horse.[4] Several of them encircled and made fun of Mrs. Dugan in her settler outfit

1. Completed in 1825, the Erie Canal runs from the Hudson River in the east to Lake Erie in the west; 35 locks manage water flow between stretches of water at different elevations, allowing two-way traffic.
2. Derogatory term for Asian laborers who came to the United States in the nineteenth century.
3. Founded in 1905, Rotary International is a service organization and social club operating in communities in the United States and around the world.
4. Horse bred to pull heavy loads.

as she was taking her fresh-baked bread over to the simulated Towne Meeting. No way they're paying admission, so they're either tunneling in or coming in over the retaining wall.

Mr. Alsuga believes the solution to the gang problem is Teen Groups. I tell him that's basically what a gang is, a Teen Group. But he says how can it be a Teen Group without an adult mentor with a special skill, like whittling? Mr. Alsuga whittles. Once he gave an Old Tyme Skills Seminar on it in the Blacksmith Shoppe. It was poorly attended. All he got was two widowers and a chess-club type no gang would have wanted anyway. And myself. I attended. Evelyn called me a bootlicker, but I attended. She called me a bootlicker, and I told her she'd better bear in mind which side of the bread her butter was on. She said whichever side it was on it wasn't enough to shake a stick at. She's always denigrating my paystub. I came home from the Seminar with this kind of whittled duck. She threw it away the next day because she said she thought it was an acorn. It looked nothing like an acorn. As far as I'm concerned she threw it away out of spite. It made me livid and twice that night I had to step into a closet and perform my Hatred Abatement Breathing.

But that's neither here nor there.

Mr. Alsuga pulls out the summer stats. We're in the worst attendance decline in ten years. If it gets any worse, staff is going to be let go in droves. He gives me a meaningful look. I know full well I'm not one of his key players. Then he asks who we have that might be willing to fight fire with fire.

I say: I could research it.
He says: Why don't you research it?
So I go research it.

Sylvia Loomis is the queen of info. It's in her personality. She enjoys digging up dirt on people. She calls herself an S&M buff in training. She's still too meek to go whole hog, so when she parties at the Make Me Club on Airport Road she limits herself to walking around talking mean while wearing kiddie handcuffs. But she's good at what she does, which is Security. It was Sylvia who identified the part-timer systematically crapping in the planters in the Gift Acquisition Center and Sylvia who figured out it was Phil in Grounds leaving obscene messages for the Teen Belles on Message-Minder. She has access to all records. I ask can she identify current employees with a history of violence. She says she can if I buy her lunch.

We decide to eat in-Park. We go over to Nate's Saloon. Sylvia says don't spread it around but two of the nine cancan girls are knocked up. Then she pulls out her folder and says that according to her review of the data, we have a pretty tame bunch on our hands. The best she can do is Ned Quinn. His records indicate that while in high school he once burned down a storage shed. I almost die laughing. Quinn's an Adjunct Thespian and a world-class worry-wart. I can't count the times I've come upon him in Costuming, dwelling on the gory details of his Dread Disease Rider.[5] He's a failed actor who won't stop trying. He says this is the only job he could find that would allow him to continue to develop his craft. Because he's ugly as sin he spe-

5. A clause added to a contract or agreement.

cializes in roles that require masks, such as Humpty-Dumpty during Mother Goose Days.

I report back to Mr. Alsuga and he says Quinn may not be much but he's all we've got. Quinn's dirt-poor with six kids and Mr. A says that's a plus, as we'll need someone between a rock and a hard place. What he suggests we do is equip the Desperate Patrol with live ammo and put Quinn in charge. The Desperate Patrol limps along under floodlights as the night's crowning event. We've costumed them to resemble troops who've been in the field too long. We used actual Gettysburg[6] photos. The climax of the Patrol is a re-enacted partial rebellion, quelled by a rousing speech. After the speech the boys take off their hats and put their arms around each other and sing "I Was Born Under a Wandering Star."[7] Then there's fireworks and the Parade of Old-Fashioned Conveyance. Then we clear the place out and go home.

"Why not confab with Quinn?" Mr. A says. "Get his input and feelings."

"I was going to say that," I say.

I look up the Thespian Center's SpeedDial extension and a few minutes later Quinn's bounding up the steps in the Wounded Grizzly suit.

"Desperate Patrol?" Mr. A says as Quinn sits down. "Any interest on your part?"

"Love it," Quinn says. "Excellent." He's been trying to get on Desperate Patrol for years. It's considered the pinnacle by the Thespians because of the wealth of speaking parts. He's so excited he's shifting around in his seat and getting some of his paw blood on Mr. A's nice cane chair.

"The gangs in our park are a damn blight," Mr. A says. "I'm talking about meeting force with force. Something in it for you? Oh yes."

"I'd like to see Quinn give the rousing speech myself," I say.

"Societal order," Mr. A says. "Sustaining the lifeblood of this goddamned park we've all put so much of our hearts into."

"He's not just free-associating," I say.

"I'm not sure I get it," Quinn says.

"What I'm suggesting is live ammo in your weapon only," Mr. A says. "Fire at your discretion. You see an unsavory intruder, you shoot at his feet. Just give him a scare. Nobody gets hurt. An additional two bills a week is what I'm talking."

"I'm an actor," Quinn says.

"Quinn's got kids," I say. "He knows the value of a buck."

"This is acting of the highest stripe," Mr. A says. "Act like a mercenary."

"Go for it on a trial basis," I say.

"I'm not sure I get it," Quinn says. "But jeez, that's good money."

"Superfantastic," says Mr. A.

Next evening Mr. A and I go over the Verisimilitude Irregularities List. We've been having some heated discussions about our bird-species percentages. Mr. Grayson, Staff Ornithologist, has recently recalculated and estimates that to accurately approximate the 1865 bird population we'll need to eliminate a couple hundred orioles or so. He suggests using air guns or

6. The Battle of Gettysburg (July 1–3, 1863), fought between the Union and Confederate armies, caused the highest casualties of any battle in the Civil War.

7. Song by Alan J. Lerner and Frederick Loewe from the musical comedy *Paint Your Wagon*, which premiered on Broadway in 1951.

poison. Mr. A says that, in his eyes, in fiscally troubled times, an ornithologist is a luxury, and this may be the perfect time to send Grayson packing. I like Grayson. He went way overboard on Howie's baseball candy. But I've got me and mine to think of. So I call Grayson in. Mr. A says did you botch the initial calculation or were you privy to new info. Mr. Grayson admits it was a botch. Mr. A sends him out into the hall and we confab.

"You'll do the telling," Mr. A says. "I'm getting too old for cruelty."

He takes his walking stick and beeper and says he'll be in the Great Forest if I need him.

I call Grayson back in and let him go, and hand him Kleenexes and fend off a few blows and almost before I know it he's reeling out the door and I go grab a pita.

Is this the life I envisioned for myself? My God no. I wanted to be a high jumper. But I have two of the sweetest children ever born. I go in at night and look at them in their fairly expensive sleepers and think: There are a couple of kids who don't need to worry about freezing to death or being cast out to the wolves. You should see their little eyes light up when I bring home a treat. They may not know the value of a dollar, but it's my intention to see that they never need to.

I'm filling out Grayson's Employee Retrospective when I hear gunshots from the perimeter. I run out and there's Quinn and a few of his men tied to the cannon. The gang guys took Quinn's pants and put some tiny notches in his penis with their knives. I free Quinn and tell him to get over to the Infirmary to guard against infection. He's absolutely shaking and can hardly walk, so I wrap him up in a Confederate flag and call over a hay cart and load him in a Confederate flag and call over a hay cart and load him in.

When I tell Mr. A he says: Garbage in, garbage out, and that we were idiots for expecting a milquetoast[8] to save our rears.

We decide to leave the police out of it because of the possible bad PR. So we give Quinn the rest of the week off and promise to let him play Grant now and then, and that's that.

When Visitors first come in there's this cornball part where they sit in this kind of spaceship and supposedly get blasted into space and travel faster than the speed of light and end up in 1865. The unit's dated. The helmets we distribute look like bowls and all the paint's peeling off. I've argued and argued that we need to update. But in the midst of a budget crunch one can't necessarily hang the moon. When the tape of space sounds is over and the walls stop shaking, we pass out the period costumes. We try not to offend anyone, liability law being what it is. We distribute the slave and Native American roles equitably among racial groups. Anyone is free to request a different identity at any time. In spite of our precautions, there's a Herlicher in every crowd. He's the guy who sued us last fall for making him hangman. He claimed that for weeks afterwards he had nightmares and because he wasn't getting enough sleep botched a big contract by sending an important government buyer a load of torn pool liners. Big deal, is my feeling. But he's suing us for fifty grand for emotional stress because the buyer ridiculed him

---

8. Weak and timid person.

in front of his co-workers. Whenever he comes in we make him sheriff but he won't back down an inch.

Mr. A calls me into his office and says he's got bad news and bad news, and which do I want first. I say the bad news. First off, he says, the gangs have spraypainted a picture of Quinn's notched penis on the side of the Everly Mansion. Second, last Friday's simulated frontier hunt has got us in hot water, because apparently some of the beef we toughen up to resemble buffalo meat was tainted, and the story's going in the Sunday supplement. And finally, the verdict's come in on the Herlicher case and we owe that goofball a hundred grand instead of fifty because the pinko[9] judge empathized.

I wait for him to say I'm fired but instead he breaks down in tears. I pat his back and mix him a drink. He says why don't I join him. So I join him.

"It doesn't look good," he says, "for men like you and I."

"No it doesn't," I say.

"All I wanted to do," he says, "was to give the public a meaningful perspective on a historical niche I've always found personally fascinating."

"I know what you mean," I say.

At eleven the phone rings. It's Maurer in Refuse Control calling to say that the gangs have set fire to the Anglican Church. That structure cost upwards of ninety thousand to transport from Clydesville and refurbish. We can see the flames from Mr. A's window.

"Oh Christ!" Mr. A says. "If I could kill those kids I would kill those kids. One shouldn't desecrate the dream of another individual in the fashion in which they have mine."

"I know it," I say.

We drink and drink and finally he falls asleep on his office couch.

On the way to my car I keep an eye out for the ghostly McKinnon family. Back in the actual 1860s all this land was theirs. Their homestead's long gone but our records indicate that it was located near present-day Information Hoedown. They probably never saw this many buildings in their entire lives. They don't realize we're chronically slumming, they just think the valley's prospering. Something bad must have happened to them because their spirits are always wandering around at night looking dismayed.

Tonight I find the Mrs. doing wash by the creek. She sees me coming and asks if she can buy my boots. Machine stitching amazes her. I ask how are the girls. She says Maribeth has been sad because no appropriate boy ever died in the valley so she's doomed to loneliness forever. Maribeth is a homely sincere girl who glides around mooning and pining and reading bad poetry chapbooks. Whenever we keep the Park open late for high-school parties, she's in her glory. There was one kid who was able to see her and even got a crush on her, but when he finally tried to kiss her near Hostelry[1] and found out she was spectral it just about killed him. I slipped him a fifty and told him to keep it under wraps. As far as I know he's still in therapy. I realize I should have come forward but they probably would have nut-hutted me, and then where would my family be?

9. Slang for a communist sympathizer.   1. Inn.

The Mrs. says what Maribeth needs is choir practice followed by a nice quilting bee. In better times I would have taken the quilting-bee idea and run with it. But now there's no budget. That's basically how I finally moved up from Verisimilitude Inspector to Special Assistant, by lifting ideas from the McKinnons. The Mrs. likes me because after she taught me a few obscure 1800s ballads and I parlayed them into Individual Achievement Awards, I bought her a Rubik's Cube. To her, colored plastic is like something from Venus. The Mr. has kind of warned me away from her a couple of times. He doesn't trust me. He thinks the Rubik's Cube is the devil's work. I've brought him lighters and *Playboys* and once I even dragged out Howie's little synth[2] and the mobile battery pak. I set the synth for carillon and played it from behind a bush. I could tell he was tickled, but he stonewalled. It's too bad I can't make an inroad because he was at Antietam[3] and could be a gold mine of war info. He came back from the war and a year later died in his cornfield, which is now Parking. So he spends most of his time out there calling the cars Beelzebubs[4] and kicking their tires.

Tonight he's walking silently up and down the rows. I get out to my KCar[5] and think oh jeez, I've locked the keys in. The Mr. sits down at the base of the A3 lightpole and asks did I see the fire and do I realize it was divine retribution for my slovenly moral state. I say thank you very much. No way I'm telling him about the gangs. He can barely handle the concept of women wearing trousers. Finally I give up on prying the window down and go call Evelyn for the spare set. While I wait for her I sit on the hood and watch the stars. The Mr. watches them too. He says there are fewer than when he was a boy. He says that even the heavens have fallen into disrepair. I think about explaining smog to him but then Evelyn pulls up.

She's wearing her bathrobe and as soon as she gets out starts with the lip. Howie and Marcus are asleep in the back. The Mr. says it's part and parcel of my fallen state that I allow a woman to speak to me in such a tone. He suggests I throttle her and lock her in the woodshed. Meanwhile she's going on and on so much about my irresponsibility that the kids are waking up. I want to get out before the gangs come swooping down on us. The Parking Area's easy pickings. She calls me a thoughtless oaf and sticks me in the gut with the car keys.

Marcus wakes up all groggy and says: Hey, our daddy.

Evelyn says: Yes, unfortunately he is.

Just after lunch next day a guy shows up at Personnel looking so completely Civil War they immediately hire him and send him out to sit on the porch of the old Kriegal place with a butter churn. His name's Samuel and he doesn't say a word going through Costuming and at the end of the day leaves on a bike. I do the normal clandestine New Employee Observation

---

2. Synthesizer; electronic keyboard. *"Playboy"*: popular adult magazine founded in 1953. "Rubik's Cube": puzzle toy made popular in the 1980s.
3. The Battle of Antietam, in Maryland (September 17, 1862) ended the first Confederate invasion into the North. This was the bloodiest

one-day battle in American history; the Union victory led to Abraham Lincoln's preliminary issuance of the Emancipation Proclamation.
4. Devils.
5. Inexpensive sedan manufactured by the Chrysler Corporation, 1981–95.

from the O'Toole gazebo and I like what I see. He seems to have a passable knowledge of how to pretend to churn butter. At one point he makes the mistake of departing from the list of Then-Current Events to discuss the World Series with a Visitor, but my feeling is, we can work with that. All in all he presents a positive and convincing appearance, and I say so in my review.

Sylvia runs her routine check on him and calls me at home that night and says boy do we have a hot prospect on our hands if fucking with the gangs is still on our agenda. She talks like that. I've got her on speakerphone in the rec room and Marcus starts running around the room saying fuck. Evelyn stands there with her arms crossed, giving me a drop-dead look. I wave her off and she flips me the bird.

Sylvia's federal sources indicate that Samuel got kicked out of Vietnam[6] for participating in a bloodbath. Sylvia claims this is oxymoronic. She sounds excited. She suggests I take a nice long look at his marksmanship scores. She says his special combat course listing goes on for pages.

I call Mr. A and he says it sounds like Sam's our man. I express reservations at arming an alleged war criminal and giving him free rein in a family-oriented facility. Mr. A says if we don't get our act together there won't be any family-oriented facility left in a month. Revenues have hit rock bottom and his investors are frothing at the mouth. There's talk of outright closure and liquidation of assets.

He says: Now get off your indefensible high horse and give me Sam's home phone.

So I get off my indefensible high horse and give him Sam's home phone.

Thursday after we've armed Samuel and sent him and the Patrol out, I stop by the Worship Center to check on the Foley baptism. Baptisms are an excellent revenue source. We charge three hundred dollars to rent the Center, which is the former lodge of the Siala utopian free-love community. We trucked it in from downstate, a redbrick building with a nice gold dome. In the old days if one of the Sialians was overeating to the exclusion of others or excessively masturbating, he or she would be publicly dressed down for hours on end in the lodge. Now we put up white draperies and pipe in Stephen Foster[7] and provide at no charge a list of preachers of various denominations.

The Foleys are an overweight crew. The room's full of crying sincere large people wishing the best for a baby. It makes me remember our own sweet beaners in their little frocks. I sit down near the wood-burning heater in the Invalid area and see that Justin in Prep has forgotten to remove the mannequin elderly couple clutching rosaries. Hopefully the Foleys won't notice and withhold payment.

The priest dips the baby's head into the fake marble basin and the door flies open and in comes a racially mixed gang. They stroll up the aisle tousling hair and requisition a Foley niece, a cute redhead of about sixteen.

6. That is, the American phase of the war in Vietnam (1955–75).
7. Stephen Collins Foster (1826–1864), American songwriter, famous for patriotic standards such as "My Old Kentucky Home" and "Oh! Susanna" as well as songs used in black-face minstrel shows.

Her dad stands up and gets a blackjack in the head. One of the gang guys pushes her down the aisle with his hands on her breasts. As she passes she looks right at me. The gang guy spits on my shoe and I make my face neutral so he won't get hacked off and drag me into it.

The door slams and the Foleys sit there stunned. Then the baby starts crying and everyone runs shouting outside in time to see the gang dragging the niece into the woods. I panic. I try to think of where the nearest pay phone is. I'm weighing the efficiency of running to Administration and making the call from my cubicle when six fast shots come from the woods. Several of the oldest Foleys assume the worst and drop weeping to their knees in the churchyard.

I don't know the first thing about counseling survivors, so I run for Mr. A.

He's drinking and watching his bigscreen. I tell him what happened and he jumps up and calls the police. Then he says let's go do whatever little we can for these poor people who entrusted us with their sacred family occasion only to have us drop the ball by failing to adequately protect them.

When we get back to the churchyard the Foleys are kicking and upbraiding six gang corpses. Samuel's having a glass of punch with the niece. The niece's dad is hanging all over Sam trying to confirm his daughter's virginity. Sam says it wasn't even close and goes on and on about the precision of his scope.

Then we hear sirens.

Sam says: I'm going into the woods.

Mr. A says: We never saw you, big guy.

The niece's dad says: Bless you, sir.

Sam says: Adios.

Mr. A stands on the hitching post and makes a little speech, the gist of which is, let's blame another gang for killing these dirtbags so Sam can get on with his important work.

The Foleys agree.

The police arrive and we all lie like rugs.

The word spreads on Sam and the gangs leave us alone. For two months the Park is quiet and revenues start upscaling. Then some high-school kid pulls a butter knife on Fred Moore and steals a handful of penny candy from the General Store. As per specs, Fred alerts Mr. A of a Revenue-Impacting Event. Mr. A calls Security and we perform Exit Sealage. We look everywhere, but the kid's gone. Mr. A says what the hell, Unseal, it's just candy, profit loss is minimal. Sam hears the Unseal Tone on the PA and comes out of the woods all mad with his face painted and says that once the word gets out we've gone soft the gangs will be back in a heartbeat. I ask since when do gangs use butter knives. Sam says a properly trained individual can kill a wild boar with a butter knife. Mr. A gives me a look and says why don't we let Sam run this aspect of the operation since he possesses the necessary expertise. Then Mr. A offers to buy him lunch and Sam says no, he'll eat raw weeds and berries as usual.

I go back to my Verisimilitude Evaluation on the Cimarron Brothel. Everything looks super. As per my recommendations they've replaced the young attractive simulated whores with uglier women with a little less on the ball. We were able to move the ex–simulated whores over to the Sweete

Shoppe, so everybody's happy, especially the new simulated whores, who were for the most part middle-aged women we lured away from fast-food places via superior wages.

When I've finished the Evaluation I go back to my office for lunch. I step inside and turn on the fake oil lamp and there's a damn human hand on my chair, holding a note. All around the hand there's penny candy. The note says: Sir, another pig disciplined who won't mess with us anymore and also I need more ammo. It's signed: Samuel the Rectifier.

I call Mr. A and he says Jesus. Then he tells me to bury the hand in the marsh behind Refreshments. I say shouldn't we call the police. He says we let it pass when it was six dead kids, why should we start getting moralistic now over one stinking hand?

I say: But sir, he killed a high-schooler for stealing candy.

He says: That so-called high-schooler threatened Fred Moore, a valued old friend of mine, with a knife.

A butter knife, I say.

He asks if I've seen the droves of unemployed huddled in front of Personnel every morning.

I ask if that's a threat and he says no, it's a reasonable future prognostication.

"What's done is done," he says. "We're in this together. If I take the fall on this, you'll eat the wienie as well. Let's just put this sordid ugliness behind us and get on with the business of providing an enjoyable living for those we love."

I hang up and sit looking at the hand. There's a class ring on it.

Finally I knock it into a garbage sack with my phone and go out to the marsh.

As I'm digging, Mr. McKinnon glides up. He gets down on his knees and starts sniffing the sack. He starts talking about bloody wagon wheels and a boy he once saw sitting in a creek slapping the water with his own severed arm. He tells how the dead looked with rain on their faces and of hearing lunatic singing from all corners of the field of battle and of king-sized rodents gorging themselves on the entrails of his friends.

It occurs to me that the Mr.'s a loon.

I dig down a couple feet and drop the hand in. Then I backfill and get out of there fast. I look over my shoulder and he's rocking back and forth over the hole mumbling to himself.

As I pass a sewer cover the Mrs. rises out of it. Seeing the Mr. enthralled by blood she starts shrieking and howling to beat the band. When she finally calms down she comes to rest in a tree branch. Tears run down her see-through cheeks. She says there's been a horrid violent seed in him since he came home from the war. She says she can see they're going to have to go away. Then she blasts over my head elongate and glowing and full of grief and my hat gets sucked off.

All night I have bad dreams about severed hands. In one I'm eating chili and a hand comes out of my bowl and gives me the thumbs-down. I wake up with a tingling wrist. Evelyn says if I insist on sleeping uneasily would I mind doing it on the couch, since she has a family to care for during the day and this requires a certain amount of rest. I think about confessing to her but then I realize if I do she'll nail me.

The nights when she'd fall asleep with her cheek on my thigh are certainly long past.

I lie there awhile watching her make angry faces in her sleep. Then I go for a walk. As usual Mr. Ebershom's practicing figure-skating moves in his foyer. I sit down by our subdivision's fake creek and think. First of all, burying a hand isn't murder. It doesn't say anywhere thou shalt not bury some guy's hand. By the time I got involved the kid was dead. Where his hand ended up is inconsequential.

Then I think: What am I saying? I did a horrible thing. Even as I sit here I'm an accomplice and an obstructor of justice.

But then I see myself in the penitentiary and the boys waking up scared in the night without me, and right then and there with my feet in the creek I decide to stay clammed up forever and take my lumps in the afterlife.

Halloween's special in the Park. Our brochure says: Lose Yourself in Eerie Autumnal Splendor. We spray cobwebs around the Structures and dress up Staff in ghoul costumes and hand out period-authentic treats. We hide holograph generators in the woods and project images of famous Americans as ghosts. It's always a confusing time for the McKinnons. Last year the Mr. got in a head-to-head with the image of Jefferson Davis.[8] He stood there in the woods yelling at it for hours while the Mrs. and the girls begged him to come away. Finally I had to cut power to the unit.

I drive home at lunch and pick the boys up for trick-or-treating. Marcus is a rancher and Howie's an accountant. He's wearing thick fake lips and carrying a ledger. The Park's the only safe place to trick-or-treat anymore. Last year some wacko in a complex near our house laced his Snickers with a virus. I drove by the school and they were CPRing this little girl in a canary suit. So forget it.

I take them around to the various Structures and they pick up their share of saltwater taffy and hard tasteless frontier candy and wooden whistles and toy soldiers made of soap.

Then just as we start across the Timeless Green a mob of teens bursts out of the Feinstein Memorial Conifer Grove.

"Gangs!" I yell to the boys. "Get down!"

I hear a shot and look up and there's Samuel standing on a stump at tree line. Thank God, I think. He lets loose another round and one of the teens drops. Marcus is down beside me whimpering with his nose in my armpit. Howie's always been the slow one. He stands there with his mouth open, one hand in his plastic pumpkin. A second teen drops. Then Howie drops and his pumpkin goes flying.

I crawl over and beg him to be okay. He says there's no pain. I check him over and check him over and all that's wrong is his ledger's been shot. I'm so relieved I kiss him on the mouth and he yells at me to quit.

Samuel drops a third teen, then runs yipping into the woods.

The ambulance shows up and the paramedics load up the wounded teens. They're all still alive and one's saying a rosary. I take the boys to City Hall and confront Mr. A. I tell him I'm turning Sam in. He asks if I've gone daft

---

8. Davis (1808–1889) was president of the Confederate States of America during the Civil War.

and suggests I try putting food on the table from a jail cell while convicts stand in line waiting to have their way with my rear.

At this point I send the boys out to the foyer.

"He shot Howie," I say. "I want him put away."

"He shot Howie's ledger," Mr. A says. "He shot Howie's ledger in the process of saving Howie's life. But whatever. Let's not mince hairs. If Sam gets put away, we get put away. Does that sound to you like a desirable experience?"

"No," I say.

"What I'm primarily saying," he says, "is that this is a time for knowledge assimilation, not backstabbing. We learned a lesson, you and I. We personally grew. Gratitude for this growth is an appropriate response. Gratitude, and being careful never to make the same mistake twice."

He gets out a Bible and says let's swear on it that we'll never hire a crazed maniac to perform an important security function again. Then the phone rings. Sylvia's cross-referenced today's Admissions data and found that the teens weren't a gang at all but a bird-watching group who made the mistake of being male and adolescent and wandering too far off the trail.

"Ouch," Mr. A says. "This could be a serious negative."

In the foyer the kids are trying to get the loaches in the corporate tank to eat bits of Styrofoam. I phone Evelyn and tell her what happened and she calls me a butcher. She wants to know how on earth I could bring the boys to the Park knowing what I knew. She says she doesn't see how I'm going to live with myself in light of how much they trusted and loved me and how badly I let them down by leaving their fates to chance.

I say I'm sorry and she seems to be thinking. Then she tells me just get them home without putting them in further jeopardy, assuming that's within the scope of my mental powers.

At home she puts them in the tub and sends me out for pizza. I opt for Melvin's Pasta Lair. Melvin's a religious zealot who during the Depression worked five jobs at once. Sometimes I tell him my troubles and he says I should stop whining and count my blessings. Tonight I tell him I feel I should take some responsibility for eliminating the Samuel problem but I'm hesitant because of the discrepancy in our relative experience in violence. He says you mean you're scared. I say not scared, just aware of the likelihood of the possibility of failure. He gives me a look. I say it must have been great to grow up when men were men. He says men have always been what they are now, namely incapable of coping with life without the intervention of God the Almighty. Then in the oven behind him my pizza starts smoking and he says case in point.

He makes me another and urges me to get in touch with my Lord personally. I tell him I will. I always tell him I will.

When I get home they're gone.

Evelyn's note says: I could never forgive you for putting our sons at risk. Goodbye forever, you passive flake. Don't try to find us. I've told the kids you sent us away in order to marry a floozy.

Like an idiot I run out to the street. Mrs. Schmidt is prodding her automatic sprinkler system with a rake, trying to detect leaks in advance. She asks how I am and I tell her not now. I sit on the lawn. The stars are very near. The phone rings. I run inside prepared to grovel, but it's only Mr. A. He says come down to the Park immediately because he's got big horrific news.

When I get there he's sitting in his office half-crocked. He tells me we're unemployed. The investors have gotten wind of the bird-watcher shootings and withdrawn all support. The Park is no more. I tell him about Evelyn and the kids. He says that's the least of his worries because he's got crushing debt. He asks if I have any savings he could have. I say no. He says that just for the record and my own personal development, he's always found me dull and has kept me around primarily for my yes-man capabilities and because sometimes I'm so cautious I'm a hoot.

Then he says: Look, get your ass out, I'm torching this shithole for insurance purposes.

I want to hit or at least insult him, but I need this week's pay to find my kids. So I jog off through the Park. In front of Information Hoedown I see the McKinnons cavorting. I get closer and see that they're not cavorting at all, they've inadvertently wandered too close to their actual death site and are being compelled to act out again and again the last minutes of their lives. The girls are lying side by side on the ground and the Mr. is whacking at them with an invisible scythe. The Mrs. is belly-up with one arm flailing in what must have been the parlor. The shrieking is mind-boggling. When he's killed everyone the Mr. walks out to his former field and mimes blowing out his brains. Then he gets up and starts over. It goes on and on, through five cycles. Finally he sits down in the dirt and starts weeping. The Mrs. and the girls backpedal away. He gets up and follows them, pitifully trying to explain.

Behind us the Visitor Center erupts in flames.

The McKinnons go off down the hill, passing through bushes and trees. He's shouting for forgiveness. He's shouting that he's just a man. He's shouting that hatred and war made him nuts. I start running down the hill agreeing with him. The Mrs. gives me a look and puts her hands over Maribeth's ears. We're all running. The Mrs. starts screaming about the feel of the scythe as it opened her up. The girls bemoan their unborn kids. We make quite a group. Since I'm still alive I keep clipping trees with my shoulders and falling down.

At the bottom of the hill they pass through the retaining wall and I run into it. I wake up on my back in the culvert. Blood's running out of my ears and a transparent boy's kneeling over me. I can tell he's no McKinnon because he's wearing sweatpants.

"Get up now," he says in a gentle voice. "Fire's coming."

"No," I say. "I'm through. I'm done living."

"I don't think so," he says. "You've got amends to make."

"I screwed up," I say. "I did bad things."

"No joke," he says, and holds up his stump.

I roll over into the culvert muck and he grabs me by the collar and sits me up.

"I steal four jawbreakers and a Slim Jim and your friend kills and mutilates me?" he says.

"He wasn't my friend," I say.

"He wasn't your enemy," the kid says.

Then he cocks his head. Through his clear skull I see Sam coming out of the woods. The kid cowers behind me. Even dead he's scared of Sam. He's so scared he blasts straight up in the air shrieking and vanishes over the retaining wall.

Sam comes for me with a hunting knife.

"Don't take this too personal," he says, "but you've got to go. You know a few things I don't want broadcast."

I'm madly framing calming words in my head as he drives the knife in. I can't believe it. Never again to see my kids? Never again to sleep and wake to their liquid high voices and sweet breaths?

Sweet Evelyn, I think, I should have loved you better.

Possessing perfect knowledge I hover above him as he hacks me to bits. I see his rough childhood. I see his mother doing something horrid to him with a broomstick. I see the hate in his heart and the people he has yet to kill before pneumonia gets him at eighty-three. I see the dead kid's mom unable to sleep, pounding her fists against her face in grief at the moment I was burying her son's hand. I see the pain I've caused. I see the man I could have been, and the man I was, and then everything is bright and new and keen with love and I sweep through Sam's body, trying to change him, trying so hard, and feeling only hate and hate, solid as stone.

1996

SHERMAN ALEXIE
b. 1966

Except for one great-grandparent, Sherman Alexie's lineage is entirely Native American: Coeur d'Alene on his father's side; Colville, Flathead, and Spokane on his mother's. The cities of Coeur d'Alene (Idaho) and Spokane (Washington) mark the interior northwest corner of the contiguous forty-eight states, the place where Alexie's poetry, fiction, and cinematic work is sometimes set. Yet his interest in Native American culture ranges widely, to include other tribes such as the Navajo and regions throughout the West and Southwest. Raised on the Spokane reservation at Wellpinit, Washington, Alexie thrived in the cultural immersion that secondary education at Reardan High School, some distance from home, provided—especially the popular culture that would later infuse his work. Hence both words in the designation "Native American" figure prominently in how he sees himself as a writer.

Equal doses of trouble and humor characterize Alexie's work. Having survived hydrocephalus (a cerebrospinal abnormality) as a child and alcoholism as a young adult, he drew on his college experience as an undergraduate at Gonzaga University in Spokane and Washington State University in Pullman to find a literary voice, inspired by writers as diverse as John Steinbeck and the Native American poets included by Joseph Bruchac in the anthology *Songs from This Earth on Turtle's Back* (1983). In 1992 he published his own first work, *The Business of Fancydancing: Stories and Poems*, with one of America's most prominent small presses, Hanging Loose (Brooklyn, New York).

When *The Business of Fancydancing* was published, a review in the *New York Times* called Alexie "one of the major lyric voices of our time." "I was a twenty-five-year-old Spokane Indian guy working as a secretary at a high school exchange program," he has written. "I thought 'Great! Where do I go from here?'"

Alexie has continued telling stories through poetry, fiction, and screenwriting. *Reservation Blues* (1994) was his first novel, followed by *Indian Killer* in 1996. *Flight* (2007) shows the influence of Kurt Vonnegut, from its device of time travel to its reinvention of history from a comparative point of view. Presented broadly, even comically, his stories often draw on simple incidents, as in the story reprinted here. His storytelling offers a tragicomic vision of contemporary Native American life, notably in his National Book Award–winning novel *The Absolutely True Diary of a Part-Time Indian* (2007), in the stories of his several collections, and in his several volumes of poetry. College educated and street-smart ("I'm a rez kid who's gone urban"), irreverent and also dead serious, Alexie resembles the trickster figure of Crow in his poem "Crow Testament."

Alexie's poems have a furious energy. Although some of his work, like the villanelle "Sister Fire, Brother Smoke," takes traditional forms, most of his poems are open and improvisational, frequently and effectively using repetition and parallelism. The title of Alexie's 2000 collection, *One Stick Song*, offers an apt image for his work; it refers to a gambling game in which sticks function like chips. When down to one stick, he explains, "You're desperate," and a "One Stick Song" is "a desperate celebration, a desperate attempt to save yourself, putting everything you have into one song." The best of Alexie's poems, like "The Exaggeration of Despair," make facing up to grief and anger an act of survival. The intensity of this effort is especially evident when he reads from or recites his work. A brilliant performer, sliding between humor, anger, and pain, he makes a poetry reading a dynamic event. It is no wonder that his interest in performance has extended to stand-up comedy as well.

Popular audiences know Alexie from the 2002 film he wrote and directed, *The Business of Fancydancing*, and especially his 1998 film *Smoke Signals*, a major Hollywood production he scripted from material in his story collection *The Lone Ranger and Tonto Fistfight in Heaven* (1993). These stories and the movies drawn from them cover a broad range of contemporary Native American experience. As one of his characters says, Native Americans have "a way of surviving. But it's almost like Indians can easily survive the big stuff. Mass murder, loss of language and land rights. It's the small things that hurt the most. The white waitress who wouldn't take an order, Tonto, the Washington Redskins." "This Is What It Means to Say Phoenix, Arizona" (reprinted here) is typical of both the collection's and the movie's sometimes raucous blending of the sentimental and the ridiculous. Family structures have been set askew by the imposition of a Reservation system, a system all the more confining in the social conditions of current times. Can tribal structures ameliorate these problems? In this story and elsewhere, Alexie's answers vary from comic to tragic.

The text of the story is from *The Lone Ranger and Tonto Fistfight in Heaven* (1993).

At Navajo Monument Valley Tribal School

from the photograph
by Skeet McAuley

the football field rises
to meet the mesa. Indian boys
gallop across the grass, against

Navajo Monument Valley playing field, where "the football field rises / to meet the mesa." Photograph by Skeet McAuley.

the beginning of their body.
On those Saturday afternoons,   5
unbroken horses gather to watch

their sons growing larger
in the small parts of the world.
Everyone is the quarterback.

There is no thin man in a big hat   10
writing down all the names
in two columns: winners and losers.

This is the eternal football game,
Indians versus Indians. All the Skins
in the wooden bleachers fancydancing,   15

stomping red dust straight down
into nothing. Before the game is over,
the eighth-grade girls' track team

comes running, circling the field,
their thin and brown legs echoing   20
wild horses, wild horses, wild horses.

1992

Pawn Shop

I walk into the bar, after being gone for a while, and it's empty. The Bartender tells me all the Indians are gone, do I know where they went? I tell him I don't know, and I don't know, so he gives me a beer just for

being Indian, small favors, and I wonder where all the Skins disappeared
to, and after a while, I leave, searching the streets, searching storefronts,   5
until I walk into a pawn shop, find a single heart beating under glass, and
I know who it used to belong to, I know all of them.

                                                        1992

Sister Fire, Brother Smoke

Have I become an accomplished liar,
a man who believes in his inventions?
When I see my sister in every fire,

is it me who sets her in those pyres
and burns her repeatedly? Should I mention   5
I may have become an accomplished liar,

a man who was absent when his sister died,
but still feeds those flames in the present tense?
When I see my sister in every fire,

am I seeing the shadow that survived her   10
conflagration? Because of my obsession
have I become an accomplished liar,

who strikes a match, then creates a choir
of burning matches, with the intention
of seeing my sister in every fire?   15

Is she the whisper of ash floating high
above me? I offer these charred questions.
Have I become an accomplished liar
if I see my sister in every fire?

                                                        1996

From Tourists

3. Marilyn Monroe[1]

drives herself to the reservation. Tired and cold,
she asks the Indian women for help.
Marilyn cannot explain what she needs
but the Indian women notice the needle tracks
on her arms and lead her to the sweat lodge   5
where every woman, young and old, disrobes

---

1. American actress and sex symbol (1926–1962).

and leaves her clothes behind
when she enters the dark of the lodge.
Marilyn's prayers may or may not be answered here
but they are kept sacred by Indian women.   10
Cold water is splashed on hot rocks
and steam fills the lodge. There is no place like this.
At first, Marilyn is self-conscious, aware
of her body and face, the tremendous heat, her thirst,
and the brown bodies circled around her.   15
But the Indian women do not stare. It is dark
inside the lodge. The hot rocks glow red
and the songs begin. Marilyn has never heard
these songs before, but she soon sings along.
Marilyn is not Indian, Marilyn will never be Indian   20
but the Indian women sing about her courage.
The Indian women sing for her health.
The Indian women sing for Marilyn.
Finally, she is no more naked than anyone else.

1996

The Exaggeration of Despair

I open the door

(this Indian girl writes that her brother tried to hang himself
with a belt just two weeks after her other brother did hang himself

and this Indian man tells us that, back in boarding school,
five priests took him into a back room and raped him repeatedly   5

and this homeless Indian woman begs for quarters, and when I ask
her about her tribe, she says she's horny and bends over in front of me

and this homeless Indian man is the uncle of an Indian man
who writes for a large metropolitan newspaper, and so now I know them
    both

and this Indian child cries when he sits to eat at our table   10
because he had never known his own family to sit at the same table

and this Indian woman was born to an Indian woman
who sold her for a six-pack and a carton of cigarettes

and this Indian poet shivers beneath the freeway
and begs for enough quarters to buy pencil and paper   15

and this fancydancer passes out at the powwow
and wakes up naked, with no memory of the evening, all of his regalia
    gone)

I open the door

(and this is my sister, who waits years for a dead eagle from the Park
  Service, receives it
and stores it with our cousins, who then tell her it has disappeared   20

though the feathers reappear in the regalia of another cousin
who is dancing for the very first time

and this is my father, whose own father died on Okinawa,[1] shot
by a Japanese soldier who must have looked so much like him

and this is my father, whose mother died of tuberculosis   25
not long after he was born, and so my father must hear coughing ghosts

and this is my grandmother who saw, before the white men came,
three ravens with white necks, and knew our God was going to change)

I open the door
and invite the wind inside.   30

            1996

Crow Testament[1]

1

Cain lifts Crow, that heavy black bird
and strikes down Abel.[2]

Damn, says Crow, I guess
this is just the beginning.

2

The white man, disguised   5
as a falcon, swoops in
and yet again steals a salmon
from Crow's talons.

Damn, says Crow, if I could swim
I would have fled this country years ago.   10

---

1. Japanese island, site of a major battle during
World War II.
1. Crow, like Raven, is a trickster figure in many
Native American cultures.
2. In Genesis, Cain kills his brother, Abel. They
are the sons of Adam and Eve.

3

The Crow God as depicted
in all of the reliable Crow bibles
looks exactly like a Crow.

Damn, says Crow, this makes it
so much easier to worship myself.   15

4

Among the ashes of Jericho,[3]
Crow sacrifices his firstborn son.

Damn, says Crow, a million nests
are soaked with blood.

5

When Crows fight Crows   20
the sky fills with beaks and talons.

Damn, says Crow, it's raining feathers.

6

Crow flies around the reservation
and collects empty beer bottles

but they are so heavy   25
he can carry only one at a time.

So, one by one, he returns them
but gets only five cents a bottle.

Damn, says Crow, redemption
is not easy.   30

7

Crow rides a pale horse
into a crowded powwow
but none of the Indians panic.

Damn, says Crow, I guess
they already live near the end of the world.   35

2000

---

3. This biblical city, famous for its great walls, was the first town attacked by the Israelites under Joshua, after they crossed the Jordan River.

This Is What It Means to Say Phoenix, Arizona

Just after Victor lost his job at the BIA,[1] he also found out that his father had died of a heart attack in Phoenix, Arizona. Victor hadn't seen his father in a few years, only talked to him on the telephone once or twice, but there still was a genetic pain, which was soon to be pain as real and immediate as a broken bone.

Victor didn't have any money. Who does have money on a reservation, except the cigarette and fireworks salespeople? His father had a savings account waiting to be claimed, but Victor needed to find a way to get to Phoenix. Victor's mother was just as poor as he was, and the rest of his family didn't have any use at all for him. So Victor called the Tribal Council.

"Listen," Victor said. "My father just died. I need some money to get to Phoenix to make arrangements."

"Now, Victor," the council said. "You know we're having a difficult time financially."

"But I thought the council had special funds set aside for stuff like this."

"Now, Victor, we do have some money available for the proper return of tribal members' bodies. But I don't think we have enough to bring your father all the way back from Phoenix."

"Well," Victor said. "It ain't going to cost all that much. He had to be cremated. Things were kind of ugly. He died of a heart attack in his trailer and nobody found him for a week. It was really hot, too. You get the picture."

"Now, Victor, we're sorry for your loss and the circumstances. But we can really only afford to give you one hundred dollars."

"That's not even enough for a plane ticket."

"Well, you might consider driving down to Phoenix."

"I don't have a car. Besides, I was going to drive my father's pickup back up here."

"Now, Victor," the council said. "We're sure there is somebody who could drive you to Phoenix. Or is there somebody who could lend you the rest of the money?"

"You know there ain't nobody around with that kind of money."

"Well, we're sorry, Victor, but that's the best we can do."

Victor accepted the Tribal Council's offer. What else could he do? So he signed the proper papers, picked up his check, and walked over to the Trading Post to cash it.

While Victor stood in line, he watched Thomas Builds-the-Fire standing near the magazine rack, talking to himself. Like he always did. Thomas was a storyteller that nobody wanted to listen to. That's like being a dentist in a town where everybody has false teeth.

Victor and Thomas Builds-the-Fire were the same age, had grown up and played in the dirt together. Ever since Victor could remember, it was Thomas who always had something to say.

Once, when they were seven years old, when Victor's father still lived with the family, Thomas closed his eyes and told Victor this story: "Your father's

---

1. Bureau of Indian Affairs, an agency of the U.S. government that assists tribal officials in the administration of Indian reservations.

heart is weak. He is afraid of his own family. He is afraid of you. Late at night he sits in the dark. Watches the television until there's nothing but that white noise. Sometimes he feels like he wants to buy a motorcycle and ride away. He wants to run and hide. He doesn't want to be found."

Thomas Builds-the-Fire had known that Victor's father was going to leave, knew it before anyone. Now Victor stood in the Trading Post with a one-hundred-dollar check in his hand, wondering if Thomas knew that Victor's father was dead, if he knew what was going to happen next.

Just then Thomas looked at Victor, smiled, and walked over to him.

"Victor, I'm sorry about your father," Thomas said.

"How did you know about it?" Victor asked.

"I heard it on the wind. I heard it from the birds. I felt it in the sunlight. Also, your mother was just in here crying."

"Oh," Victor said and looked around the Trading Post. All the other Indians stared, surprised that Victor was even talking to Thomas. Nobody talked to Thomas anymore because he told the same damn stories over and over again. Victor was embarrassed, but he thought that Thomas might be able to help him. Victor felt a sudden need for tradition.

"I can lend you the money you need," Thomas said suddenly. "But you have to take me with you."

"I can't take your money," Victor said. "I mean, I haven't hardly talked to you in years. We're not really friends anymore."

"I didn't say we were friends. I said you had to take me with you."

"Let me think about it."

Victor went home with his one hundred dollars and sat at the kitchen table. He held his head in his hands and thought about Thomas Builds-the-Fire, remembered little details, tears and scars, the bicycle they shared for a summer, so many stories.

Thomas Builds-the-Fire sat on the bicycle, waited in Victor's yard. He was ten years old and skinny. His hair was dirty because it was the Fourth of July.

"Victor," Thomas yelled. "Hurry up. We're going to miss the fireworks."

After a few minutes, Victor ran out of his house, jumped the porch railing, and landed gracefully on the sidewalk.

"And the judges award him a 9.95, the highest score of the summer," Thomas said, clapped, laughed.

"That was perfect, cousin," Victor said. "And it's my turn to ride the bike."

Thomas gave up the bike and they headed for the fair grounds. It was nearly dark and the fireworks were about to start.

"You know," Thomas said. "It's strange how us Indians celebrate the Fourth of July. It ain't like it was *our* independence everybody was fighting for."

"You think about things too much," Victor said. "It's just supposed to be fun. Maybe Junior will be there."

"Which Junior? Everybody on this reservation is named Junior."

And they both laughed.

The fireworks were small, hardly more than a few bottle rockets and a fountain. But it was enough for two Indian boys. Years later, they would need much more.

Afterwards, sitting in the dark, fighting off mosquitoes, Victor turned to Thomas Builds-the-Fire.

"Hey," Victor said. "Tell me a story."

Thomas closed his eyes and told this story: "There were these two Indian boys who wanted to be warriors. But it was too late to be warriors in the old way. All the horses were gone. So the two Indian boys stole a car and drove to the city. They parked the stolen car in front of the police station and then hitchhiked back home to the reservation. When they got back, all their friends cheered and their parents' eyes shone with pride. *You were very brave,* everybody said to the two Indian boys. *Very brave.*"

"Ya-hey,"[2] Victor said. "That's a good one. I wish I could be a warrior."

"Me, too," Thomas said.

They went home together in the dark, Thomas on the bike now, Victor on foot. They walked through shadows and light from streetlamps.

"We've come a long ways," Thomas said. "We have outdoor lighting."

"All I need is the stars," Victor said. "And besides, you still think about things too much."

They separated then, each headed for home, both laughing all the way.

Victor sat at his kitchen table. He counted his one hundred dollars again and again. He knew he needed more to make it to Phoenix and back. He knew he needed Thomas Builds-the-Fire. So he put his money in his wallet and opened the front door to find Thomas on the porch.

"Ya-hey, Victor," Thomas said. "I knew you'd call me."

Thomas walked into the living room and sat down on Victor's favorite chair.

"I've got some money saved up," Thomas said. "It's enough to get us down there, but you have to get us back."

"I've got this hundred dollars," Victor said. "And my dad had a savings account I'm going to claim."

"How much in your dad's account?"

"Enough. A few hundred."

"Sounds good. When we leaving?"

When they were fifteen and had long since stopped being friends, Victor and Thomas got into a fistfight. That is, Victor was really drunk and beat Thomas up for no reason at all. All the other Indian boys stood around and watched it happen. Junior was there and so were Lester, Seymour, and a lot of others. The beating might have gone on until Thomas was dead if Norma Many Horses hadn't come along and stopped it.

"Hey, you boys," Norma yelled and jumped out of her car. "Leave him alone."

If it had been someone else, even another man, the Indian boys would've just ignored the warnings. But Norma was a warrior. She was powerful. She could have picked up any two of the boys and smashed their skulls together. But worse than that, she would have dragged them all over to some tipi and made them listen to some elder tell a dusty old story.

The Indian boys scattered, and Norma walked over to Thomas and picked him up.

---

2. Invented reservation slang for "yes" or "hello."

"Hey, little man, are you okay?" she asked.

Thomas gave her a thumbs up.

"Why they always picking on you?"

Thomas shook his head, closed his eyes, but no stories came to him, no words or music. He just wanted to go home, to lie in his bed and let his dreams tell his stories for him.

Thomas Builds-the-Fire and Victor sat next to each other in the airplane, coach section. A tiny white woman had the window seat. She was busy twisting her body into pretzels. She was flexible.

"I have to ask," Thomas said, and Victor closed his eyes in embarrassment.

"Don't," Victor said.

"Excuse me, miss," Thomas asked. "Are you a gymnast or something?"

"There's no something about it," she said. "I was first alternate on the 1980 Olympic team."

"Really?" Thomas asked.

"Really."

"I mean, you used to be a world-class athlete?" Thomas asked.

"My husband still thinks I am."

Thomas Builds-the-Fire smiled. She was a mental gymnast, too. She pulled her leg straight up against her body so that she could've kissed her kneecap.

"I wish I could do that," Thomas said.

Victor was ready to jump out of the plane. Thomas, that crazy Indian storyteller with ratty old braids and broken teeth, was flirting with a beautiful Olympic gymnast. Nobody back home on the reservation would ever believe it.

"Well," the gymnast said. "It's easy. Try it."

Thomas grabbed at his leg and tried to pull it up into the same position as the gymnast. He couldn't even come close, which made Victor and the gymnast laugh.

"Hey," she asked. "You two are Indian, right?"

"Full-blood," Victor said.

"Not me," Thomas said "I'm half magician on my mother's side and half clown on my father's."

They all laughed.

"What are your names?" she asked.

"Victor and Thomas."

"Mine is Cathy. Pleased to meet you all."

The three of them talked for the duration of the flight. Cathy the gymnast complained about the government, how they screwed the 1980 Olympic team by boycotting.[3]

"Sounds like you all got a lot in common with Indians," Thomas said.

Nobody laughed.

After the plane landed in Phoenix and they had all found their way to the terminal, Cathy the gymnast smiled and waved good-bye.

"She was really nice," Thomas said.

"Yeah, but everybody talks to everybody on airplanes," Victor said. "It's too bad we can't always be that way."

---

3. The United States boycotted the 1980 Summer Olympics, held in Moscow, to protest the Soviet Union's 1979 invasion of Afghanistan.

"You always used to tell me I think too much," Thomas said. "Now it sounds like you do."

"Maybe I caught it from you."

"Yeah."

Thomas and Victor rode in a taxi to the trailer where Victor's father died.

"Listen," Victor said as they stopped in front of the trailer. "I never told you I was sorry for beating you up that time."

"Oh, it was nothing. We were just kids and you were drunk."

"Yeah, but I'm still sorry."

"That's all right."

Victor paid for the taxi and the two of them stood in the hot Phoenix summer. They could smell the trailer.

"This ain't going to be nice," Victor said. "You don't have to go in."

"You're going to need help."

Victor walked to the front door and opened it. The stink rolled out and made them both gag. Victor's father had lain in that trailer for a week in hundred-degree temperatures before anyone found him. And the only reason anyone found him was because of the smell. They needed dental records to identify him. That's exactly what the coroner said. They needed dental records.

"Oh, man," Victor said. "I don't know if I can do this."

"Well, then don't."

"But there might be something valuable in there."

"I thought his money was in the bank."

"It is. I was talking about pictures and letters and stuff like that."

"Oh," Thomas said as he held his breath and followed Victor into the trailer.

When Victor was twelve, he stepped into an underground wasp nest. His foot was caught in the hole, and no matter how hard he struggled, Victor couldn't pull free. He might have died there, stung a thousand times, if Thomas Builds-the-Fire had not come by.

"Run," Thomas yelled and pulled Victor's foot from the hole. They ran then, hard as they ever had, faster than Billy Mills, faster than Jim Thorpe,[4] faster than the wasps could fly.

Victor and Thomas ran until they couldn't breathe, ran until it was cold and dark outside, ran until they were lost and it took hours to find their way home. All the way back, Victor counted his stings.

"Seven," Victor said. "My lucky number."

Victor didn't find much to keep in the trailer. Only a photo album and a stereo. Everything else had that smell stuck in it or was useless anyway.

"I guess this is all," Victor said. "It ain't much."

---

4. William Mervin "Billy" Mills (b. 1938), Native American (Ogalala Lakota) Gold Medalist for the United States at the 1964 Olympics, where he won the 10,000 meter run in a stunning upset of the favorite, Australian Ron Clarke, a feat celebrated in the 1984 film *Running Brave*. James Francis "Jim" Thorpe (1888–1953), American athlete of Native American, Irish, and French descent, Gold Medalist for the United States at the 1912 Olympics, where he won the decathalon and the penthalon, only to be stripped of his awards in 1913 because of his status as a professional (he had played semi-pro baseball); he subsequently played professional baseball and football, and at the time of his death was hailed as the greatest athlete of the first half of the twentieth century.

"Better than nothing," Thomas said.

"Yeah, and I do have the pickup."

"Yeah," Thomas said. "It's in good shape."

"Dad was good about that stuff."

"Yeah, I remember your dad."

"Really?" Victor asked. "What do you remember?"

Thomas Builds-the-Fire closed his eyes and told this story: "I remember when I had this dream that told me to go to Spokane, to stand by the Falls in the middle of the city and wait for a sign. I knew I had to go there but I didn't have a car. Didn't have a license. I was only thirteen. So I walked all the way, took me all day, and I finally made it to the Falls. I stood there for an hour waiting. Then your dad came walking up. *What the hell are you doing here?* he asked me. I said, *Waiting for a vision.* Then your father said, *All you're going to get here is mugged.* So he drove me over to Denny's, bought me dinner, and then drove me home to the reservation. For a long time I was mad because I thought my dreams had lied to me. But they didn't. Your dad was my vision. *Take care of each other* is what my dreams were saying. *Take care of each other.*"

Victor was quiet for a long time. He searched his mind for memories of his father, found the good ones, found a few bad ones, added it all up, and smiled.

"My father never told me about finding you in Spokane," Victor said.

"He said he wouldn't tell anybody. Didn't want me to get in trouble. But he said I had to watch out for you as part of the deal."

"Really?"

"Really. Your father said you would need the help. He was right."

"That's why you came down here with me, isn't it?" Victor asked.

"I came because of your father."

Victor and Thomas climbed into the pickup, drove over to the bank, and claimed the three hundred dollars in the savings account.

Thomas Builds-the-Fire could fly.

Once, he jumped off the roof of the tribal school and flapped his arms like a crazy eagle. And he flew. For a second, he hovered, suspended above all the other Indian boys who were too smart or too scared to jump.

"He's flying," Junior yelled, and Seymour was busy looking for the trick wires or mirrors. But it was real. As real as the dirt when Thomas lost altitude and crashed to the ground.

He broke his arm in two places.

"He broke his wing," Victor chanted, and the other Indian boys joined in, made it a tribal song.

"He broke his wing, he broke his wing, he broke his wing," all the Indian boys chanted as they ran off, flapping their wings, wishing they could fly, too. They hated Thomas for his courage, his brief moment as a bird. Everybody has dreams about flying. Thomas flew.

One of his dreams came true for just a second, just enough to make it real.

Victor's father, his ashes, fit in one wooden box with enough left over to fill a cardboard box.

"He always was a big man," Thomas said.

Victor carried part of his father and Thomas carried the rest out to the pickup. They set him down carefully behind the seats, put a cowboy hat on the wooden box and a Dodgers cap on the cardboard box. That's the way it was supposed to be.

"Ready to head back home," Victor asked.

"It's going to be a long drive."

"Yeah, take a couple days, maybe."

"We can take turns," Thomas said.

"Okay," Victor said, but they didn't take turns. Victor drove for sixteen hours straight north, made it halfway up Nevada toward home before he finally pulled over.

"Hey, Thomas," Victor said. "You got to drive for a while."

"Okay."

Thomas Builds-the-Fire slid behind the wheel and started off down the road. All through Nevada, Thomas and Victor had been amazed at the lack of animal life, at the absence of water, of movement.

"Where is everything?" Victor had asked more than once.

Now when Thomas was finally driving they saw the first animal, maybe the only animal in Nevada. It was a long-eared jackrabbit.

"Look," Victor yelled. "It's alive."

Thomas and Victor were busy congratulating themselves on their discovery when the jackrabbit darted out into the road and under the wheels of the pickup.

"Stop the goddamn car," Victor yelled, and Thomas did stop, backed the pickup to the dead jackrabbit.

"Oh, man, he's dead," Victor said as he looked at the squashed animal.

"Really dead."

"The only thing alive in this whole state and we just killed it."

"I don't know," Thomas said. "I think it was suicide."

Victor looked around the desert, sniffed the air, felt the emptiness and loneliness, and nodded his head.

"Yeah," Victor said. "It had to be suicide."

"I can't believe this," Thomas said. "You drive for a thousand miles and there ain't even any bugs smashed on the windshield. I drive for ten seconds and kill the only living thing in Nevada."

"Yeah," Victor said. "Maybe I should drive."

"Maybe you should."

Thomas Builds-the-Fire walked through the corridors of the tribal school by himself. Nobody wanted to be anywhere near him because of all those stories. Story after story.

Thomas closed his eyes and this story came to him: "We are all given one thing by which our lives are measured, one determination. Mine are the stories which can change or not change the world. It doesn't matter which as long as I continue to tell the stories. My father, he died on Okinawa[5] in World War II, died fighting for this country, which had tried to kill him for

---

5. Largest of Japan's Ryukyu Islands in the Western Pacific Ocean, site in 1945 of a crucial American victory near the end of World War II that had proceeded from the victory on Iwo Jima in the Japanese Volcano Islands chain, where Ira Hayes (1923–1955), a Native American (Pima) achieved fame among the Marines raising the U.S. flag atop Mount Suribachi on February 23, 1945; "The Ballad of Ira Hayes" (by Peter LaFarge) was popularized by Bob Dylan in the 1960s as a folk song.

years. My mother, she died giving birth to me, died while I was still inside her. She pushed me out into the world with her last breath. I have no brothers or sisters. I have only my stories which came to me before I even had the words to speak. I learned a thousand stories before I took my first thousand steps. They are all I have. It's all I can do."

Thomas Builds-the-Fire told his stories to all those who would stop and listen. He kept telling them long after people had stopped listening.

Victor and Thomas made it back to the reservation just as the sun was rising. It was the beginning of a new day on earth, but the same old shit on the reservation.

"Good morning," Thomas said.

"Good morning."

The tribe was waking up, ready for work, eating breakfast, reading the newspaper, just like everybody else does. Willene LeBret was out in her garden wearing a bathrobe. She waved when Thomas and Victor drove by.

"Crazy Indians made it," she said to herself and went back to her roses.

Victor stopped the pickup in front of Thomas Builds-the-Fire's HUD[6] house. They both yawned, stretched a little, shook dust from their bodies.

"I'm tired," Victor said.

"Of everything," Thomas added.

They both searched for words to end the journey. Victor needed to thank Thomas for his help, for the money, and make the promise to pay it all back.

"Don't worry about the money," Thomas said. "It don't make any difference anyhow."

"Probably not, enit?"[7]

"Nope."

Victor knew that Thomas would remain the crazy storyteller who talked to dogs and cars, who listened to the wind and pine trees. Victor knew that he couldn't really be friends with Thomas, even after all that had happened. It was cruel but it was real. As real as the ashes, as Victor's father, sitting behind the seats.

"I know how it is," Thomas said. "I know you ain't going to treat me any better than you did before. I know your friends would give you too much shit about it."

Victor was ashamed of himself. Whatever happened to the tribal ties, the sense of community? The only real thing he shared with anybody was a bottle and broken dreams. He owed Thomas something, anything.

"Listen," Victor said and handed Thomas the cardboard box which contained half of his father. "I want you to have this."

Thomas took the ashes and smiled, closed his eyes, and told this story: "I'm going to travel to Spokane Falls one last time and toss these ashes into the water. And your father will rise like a salmon, leap over the bridge, over me, and find his way home. It will be beautiful. His teeth will shine like silver, like a rainbow. He will rise, Victor, he will rise."

Victor smiled.

---

6. Department of Housing and Urban Development, part of the U.S. government.

7. That is, "isn't it?"

"I was planning on doing the same thing with my half," Victor said. "But I didn't imagine my father looking anything like a salmon. I thought it'd be like cleaning the attic or something. Like letting things go after they've stopped having any use."

"Nothing stops, cousin," Thomas said. "Nothing stops."

Thomas Builds-the-Fire got out of the pickup and walked up his driveway. Victor started the pickup and began the drive home.

"Wait," Thomas yelled suddenly from his porch. "I just got to ask one favor."

Victor stopped the pickup, leaned out the window, and shouted back. "What do you want?"

"Just one time when I'm telling a story somewhere, why don't you stop and listen?" Thomas asked.

"Just once?"

"Just once."

Victor waved his arms to let Thomas know that the deal was good. It was a fair trade, and that was all Victor had ever wanted from his whole life. So Victor drove his father's pickup toward home while Thomas went into his house, closed the door behind him, and heard a new story come to him in the silence afterwards.

1993

Survivorman

Here's a fact: Some people want to live more
Than others do. Some can withstand any horror

While others will easily surrender
To thirst, hunger, and extremes of weather.

In Utah, one man carried another   5
Man on his back like a conjoined brother

And crossed twenty-five miles of desert
To safety. Can you imagine the hurt?

Do you think you could be that good and strong?
Yes, yes, you think, but you're probably wrong.   10

2009

NATASHA TRETHEWEY
b. 1966

Natasha Trethewey has been a significant voice in American poetry since the 1990s. As a young poet she was part of the Dark Room Collective in the 1990s, a group of Boston-based poets of African descent that began meeting first to establish a reading series, later becoming a tightly knit group that toured, read, and shared work together. The group included the poet Kevin Young and several others who went on to have distinguished careers. Trethewey, for her part, won the Pulitzer Prize for her 2006 collection, *Native Guard*, a recognition that significantly broadened the audience for her work, and she was named poet laureate of the United States in 2012.

What new and loyal readers of Trethewey's work find, from collection to collection, is a poet exquisitely attuned to medium: not only the rich medium of poetic language that marries emotion, narrative, and sound, but also multiple visual media. Her 2002 collection, *Bellocq's Ophelia*, contained a series of poems meditating on the photographs of E. J. Bellocq, who made portraits of multiracial women—often called "octoroons" and "quadroons" in the nineteenth century—working in the brothels of New Orleans in 1912. *Thrall*, her 2012 collection, probes the so-called Casta paintings—eighteenth-century Spanish canvases focused on the representation of skin color. The paintings set out to catalog in aesthetic terms the racial mixtures of colonialism and the transatlantic slave trade—white-skinned Spanish fathers in silk and lace posing with African or Native women and the children of these unions. In lyrics scattered throughout her collections, Trethewey engages photographs and visual environments ranging from family snapshots to museum exhibits. Choosing images at once beautiful and ethically disturbing, Trethewey translates vision—which renders its objects just that, *objects*—into voice. We hear the voices of Bellocq's models, who tell their stories beyond the photograph's frame. We hear the voice of a thinking narrator, who has us see the sumptuous tableaux of mixed races for what they are: the output of a racist hierarchy of beauty, power, sex, and history. And we hear the voice of an autobiographical speaker, a biracial woman addressing, mourning, accusing, and questioning by turns her white father and her black mother.

In Natasha Trethewey's hands poetry is a live wire to the past. In *Native Guard*, she brings readers into the consciousness of a private in the Louisiana Native Guard, a corps of black Union soldiers who guarded Confederate prisoners and died in battle on Trethewey's home ground in southern Mississippi. Alongside that history, Trethewey places a series of elegies for her mother, who was murdered at the hands of an abusive lover when Trethewey was in her twenties. In the most heartbreaking of these elegies, "Graveyard Blues," the familiar themes and rhymes of the blues allow the speaker to remember the act of burying her mother. It is a searing memory somehow comforted by the blues, a form that embodies the pain of generations of Americans of African descent. In the poem we feel both the blues' general sadness and the specific sharp fact of this speaker's story. *Thrall*, too, crosses the personal with the historical: meditations on the speaker's own biracial heritage entwine with the poems about the Casta paintings. Trethewey's poetry has a purchase on American life that is formally flexible, rich in aesthetic resources, keyed to the flow of the continent's violent history. That historical perspective has informed Trethewey's prose writing as well. Moved in the aftermath of Hurricane

The poets of the Dark Room Collective (1996). From left: Natasha Trethewey, Kevin Young, Major Jackson, Nehassaiu deGannes, Thomas Sayers Ellis, Sharan Strange, Adisa Vera Beatty.

Katrina to return to her native town of Gulfport, Mississippi, she offers a complicated and very human understanding of natural disaster and its aftermath there, laying out the relationship between poverty, race, and landscape in Mississippi since the experience of Hurricane Camille in the late 1960s.

To date, Trethewey has written four collections of poetry and one book of prose. Since 2001 she has been based in Atlanta, where she was raised, and where she is the Robert W. Woodruff Professor of English and Creative Writing at Emory University. Her perch in academia is fitting, given her erudition, the evidence of which we see especially in her historical poetry. But she is still very much a poet of the people. As poet laureate, Trethewey reinstated the great but lapsed tradition of the poet laureate's "office hours"—time she set aside each week in the Library of Congress to talk about poetry with anyone who wished to come by. In her second year as laureate, her main project was to work with the Public Broadcasting Service (PBS) on a series of films about the meaning and role of poetry in our ordinary lives today.

In keeping with such priorities, readers will find her poetry accessible, humane, and democratic—but it is not therefore safe or easy. Trethewey shows how our practice of art and our conception of beauty have been complicit with racist violence. She shows us how the human body and voice are unmade—and perhaps, ultimately, remade—under the weight of history.

Vignette

—from a photograph
by E. J. Bellocq, circa 1912[1]

They pose the portrait outside
the brothel—Bellocq's black scrim,
a chair for her to sit on. She wears
white, a rhinestone choker, fur,
her dark crown of hair—an elegant image,   5
one she might send to her mother.
Perhaps the others crowd in behind
Bellocq, awaiting their turns, tremors
of laughter in their white throats.
Maybe Bellocq chats, just a little,   10
to put her at ease while he waits
for the right moment, a look on her face
to keep in a gilded frame, the ornate box
he'll put her in. Suppose he tells her
about a circus coming to town—monkeys   15
and organ music, the high trapeze—but then

she's no longer listening; she's forgotten
he's there. Instead she must be thinking
of her childhood wonder at seeing
the contortionist in a sideshow—how   20
he could make himself small, fit
into cramped spaces, his lungs
barely expanding with each tiny breath.
She thinks of her own shallow breath—
her back straining the stays of a bustier,   25
the weight of a body pressing her down.
Picture her face now as she realizes
that it must have been harder every year,
that the contortionist, too, must have ached
each night in his tent. This is how   30
Bellocq takes her, her brow furrowed
as she looks out to the left, past all of them.
Imagine her a moment later—after
the flash, blinded—stepping out
of the frame, wide-eyed, into her life.   35

2002

---

1. John Ernest Joseph Bellocq (1873–1949), American photographer.

Graveyard Blues

It rained the whole time we were laying her down;
Rained from church to grave when we put her down.
The suck of mud at our feet was a hollow sound.

When the preacher called out I held up my hand;
When he called for a witness I raised my hand   5
Death stops the body's work, the soul's a journeyman.

The sun came out when I turned to walk away,
Glared down on me as I turned and walked away—
My back to my mother, leaving her where she lay.

The road going home was pocked with holes,   10
That home-going road's always full of holes;
Though we slow down, time's wheel still rolls.

    I wander now among names of the dead:
    My mother's name, stone pillow for my head.

2006

Photograph: Ice Storm, 1971

Why the rough edge of beauty? Why
the tired face of a woman, suffering,
made luminous by the camera's eye?

Or the storm that drives us inside
for days, power lines down, food rotting   5
in the refrigerator, while outside

the landscape glistens beneath a glaze
of ice? Why remember anything
but the wonder of those few days,

the iced trees, each leaf in its glassy case?   10
The picture we took that first morning,
the front yard a beautiful, strange place—

why on the back has someone made a list
of our names, the date, the event: nothing
of what's inside—mother, stepfather's fist?   15

2006

Native Guard[1]

*If this war is to be forgotten, I ask in the name of all things
sacred what shall men remember?*
—FREDERICK DOUGLASS

November 1862

Truth be told, I do not want to forget
anything of my former life: the landscape's
song of bondage—dirge in the river's throat
where it churns into the Gulf, wind in trees
choked with vines. I thought to carry with me   5
want of freedom though I had been freed,
remembrance not constant recollection.
Yes: I was born a slave, at harvest time,
in the Parish of Ascension; I've reached
thirty-three with history of one younger   10
inscribed upon my back. I now use ink
to keep record, a closed book, not the lure
of memory—flawed, changeful—that dulls the lash
for the master, sharpens it for the slave.

December 1862

For the slave, having a master sharpens   15
the bend into work, the way the sergeant
moves us now to perfect battalion drill,
dress parade. Still, we're called supply units—
not infantry—and so we dig trenches,
haul burdens for the army no less heavy   20
than before. I heard the colonel call it
nigger work. Half rations make our work
familiar still. We take those things we need
from the Confederates' abandoned homes:
salt, sugar, even this journal, near full   25
with someone else's words, overlapped now,
crosshatched beneath mine. On every page,
his story intersecting with my own.

1. Epigraph from "Address at the Grave of the Unknown Dead" by Frederick Douglass, Arlington, Virginia, May 30, 1871; quoted in *Race and Reunion: The Civil War in American Memory* by David Blight. Cambridge, Mass.: Belknap Press, 2001.
    The first regiments of the Louisiana Native Guards were mustered into service in September, October, and November of 1862—the 1st Regiment thus becoming the first officially sanctioned regiment of black soldiers in the Union Army, and the 2nd and 3rd made up of men who had been slaves only months before enlisting. During the war, the fort at Ship Island, Mississippi, called Fort Massachusetts, was maintained as a prison for Confederate soldiers—military convicts and prisoners of war—manned by the 2nd Regiment. Among the 2nd Regiment's officers was Francis E. Dumas—the son of a white Creole father and a mulatto mother—who had inherited slaves when his father died. Although Louisiana law prohibited him from manumitting these slaves, when he joined the Union Army, Dumas freed them and encouraged those men of age to join the Native Guards. (From *The Louisiana Native Guards: The Black Military Experience During the Civil War* by James G. Hollandsworth. Baton Rouge: Louisiana State University Press, 1995.) [Trethewey's note.]

January 1863[2]

O how history intersects—my own
berth upon a ship called the *Northern Star*   30
and I'm delivered into a new life,
Fort Massachusetts: a great irony—
both path and destination of freedom
I'd not dared to travel. Here, now, I walk
ankle-deep in sand, fly-bitten, nearly   35
smothered by heat, and yet I can look out
upon the Gulf and see the surf breaking,
tossing the ships, the great gunboats bobbing
on the water. And are we not the same,
slaves in the hands of the master, destiny?   40
—night sky red with the promise of fortune,
dawn pink as new flesh: healing, unfettered.

January 1863

Today, dawn red as warning. Unfettered
supplies, stacked on the beach at our landing,
washed away in the storm that rose too fast,   45
caught us unprepared. Later, as we worked,
I joined in the low singing someone raised
to pace us, and felt a bond in labor
I had not known. It was then a dark man
removed his shirt, revealed the scars, crosshatched   50
like the lines in this journal, on his back.
It was he who remarked at how the ropes
cracked like whips on the sand, made us take note
of the wild dance of a tent loosed by wind.
We watched and learned. Like any shrewd master,   55
we know now to tie down what we will keep.

February 1863

We know it is our duty now to keep
white men as prisoners—rebel soldiers,
would-be masters. We're all bondsmen here, each
to the other. Freedom has gotten them   60
captivity. For us, a conscription
we have chosen—jailors to those who still
would have us slaves. They are cautious, dreading
the sight of us. Some neither read nor write,
are laid too low and have few words to send   65
but those I give them. Still, they are wary
of a negro writing, taking down letters.

---

2. The Union ship *Northern Star* transported seven companies of the 2nd Louisiana Native Guards to Fort Massachusetts, Ship Island, on January 12, 1863. The lines ". . . I can look out / upon the Gulf and see the surf breaking. / tossing the ships, the great gunboats bobbing / on the water. And are we not the same, / slaves in the hands of the master, destiny?" are borrowed, in slightly different form, from *Thank God My Regiment an African One: The Civil War Diary of Colonel Nathan W. Daniels*, edited by C. P. Weaver. Baton Rouge: Louisiana State University Press, 1998. [Trethewey's note.]

X binds them to the page[3]—a mute symbol
like the cross on a grave. I suspect they fear
I'll listen, put something else down in ink.   70

March 1863

I listen, put down in ink what I know
they labor to say between silences
too big for words: worry for beloveds—
My Dearest, how are you getting along—
what has become of their small plots of land   75
did you harvest enough food to put by?
They long for the comfort of former lives—
I see you as you were, waving goodbye.
Some send photographs—a likeness in case
the body can't return. Others dictate   80
harsh facts of this war: *The hot air carries*
the stench of limbs, rotten in the bone pit.
Flies swarm—a black cloud. We hunger, grow weak.
When men die, we eat their share of hardtack.[4]

April 1863[5]

When men die, we eat their share of hardtack   85
trying not to recall their hollow sockets,
the worm-stitch of their cheeks. Today we buried
the last of our dead from Pascagoula,
and those who died retreating to our ship—
white sailors in blue firing upon us   90
as if we were the enemy. I'd thought
the fighting over, then watched a man fall
beside me, knees-first as in prayer, then
another, his arms outstretched as if borne
upon the cross. Smoke that rose from each gun   95
seemed a soul departing. The Colonel said:
an unfortunate incident; said:
their names shall deck the page of history.

June 1863[6]

Some names shall deck the page of history
as it is written on stone. Some will not.   100

3. Illiterate prisoners would sign letters written on their behalf with an "X."
4. A durable cracker of flour, water, and salt.
5. On April 9, 1863, 180 black men and their officers went onto the mainland to meet Confederate troops near Pascagoula, Mississippi. After the skirmish, as the black troops were retreating (having been outnumbered by the Confederates), white Union troops on board the gunboat *Jackson* fired directly at them and not at oncoming Confederates. Several black soldiers were killed or wounded. The phrases *an unfortunate*

incident and *their names shall deck the page of history* are also from *Thank God My Regiment an African One: The Civil War Diary of Colonel Nathan W. Daniels.* [Trethewey's note.]
6. During the battle of Port Hudson in May 1863, General Nathaniel P. Banks requested a truce to locate the wounded Union soldiers and bury the dead. His troops, however, ignored the area where the Native Guards had fought, leaving those men unclaimed. When Colonel Shelby, a Confederate officer, asked permission to bury the putrefying bodies in front of his lines, Banks

Yesterday, word came of colored troops, dead
on the battlefield at Port Hudson; how
General Banks was heard to say *I have*
no dead there, and left them, unclaimed. Last night,
I dreamt their eyes still open—dim, clouded   105
as the eyes of fish washed ashore, yet fixed—
staring back at me. Still, more come today
eager to enlist. Their bodies—haggard
faces, gaunt limbs—bring news of the mainland.
Starved, they suffer like our prisoners. Dying,   110
they plead for what we do not have to give.
Death makes equals of us all: a fair master.

August 1864

Dumas was a fair master to us all.
He taught me to read and write: I was a man-
servant, if not a man. At my work,   115
I studied natural things—all manner
of plants, birds I draw now in my book: wren,
willet, egret, loon. Tending the gardens,
I thought only to study live things, thought
never to know so much about the dead.   120
Now I tend Ship Island graves, mounds like dunes
that shift and disappear. I record names,
send home simple notes, not much more than how
and when—an official duty. I'm told
it's best to spare most detail, but I know   125
there are things which must be accounted for.

1865[7]

These are things which must be accounted for:
slaughter under the white flag of surrender—
black massacre at Fort Pillow; our new name,
the Corps d'Afrique—words that take the *native*   130
from our claim; mossbacks[8] and freedmen—exiles
in their own homeland; the diseased, the maimed,
every lost limb, and what remains: phantom
ache, memory haunting an empty sleeve;
the hog-eaten at Gettysburg, unmarked   135
in their graves; all the dead letters, unanswered;

---

refused, saying that he had no dead in that area. (From *The Louisiana Native Guards: The Black Military Experience During the Civil War.*) [Trethewey's note.]

7. In April 1864, Confederate troops attacked Fort Pillow, a Union garrison fifty miles north of Memphis. One correspondent, in a dispatch to the *Mobile Advertiser and Register*, reported that, after gaining control of the fort, the Confederates disregarded several individual attempts by the black troops to surrender, and "an indiscrim-

inate slaughter followed" in which Colonel Nathan Bedford Forrest purportedly ordered the black troops "shot down like dogs." (From "The Fort Pillow Massacre: Assessing the Evidence," by John Cimprich, in *Black Soldiers in Blue: African-American Troops in the Civil War Era*, edited by John David Smith. Chapel Hill: University of North Carolina Press, 2002.) [Trethewey's note.]

8. Men who hid to avoid conscription into the Confederate army.

untold stories of those that time will render
mute. Beneath battlefields, green again,
the dead molder—a scaffolding of bone
we tread upon, forgetting. Truth be told.   140

2006

Miracle of the Black Leg

*Pictorial representations of the physician-saints Cosmas and
Damian and the myth of the miracle transplant—black donor,
white recipient—date back to the mid-fourteenth century,
appearing much later than written versions of the story.*

1.

Always, the dark body hewn asunder; always
    one man is healed, his sick limb replaced,
placed in the other man's grave: the white leg
    buried beside the corpse or attached as if
it were always there. If not for the dark appendage   5
    you might miss the story beneath this story—
what remains each time the myth changes: how,
    in one version, the doctors harvest the leg
from a man, four days dead, in his tomb at the church
    of a martyr, or—in another—desecrate a body   10
fresh in the graveyard at Saint Peter in Chains:[1]
    there was buried just today an Ethiopian.
Even now, it stays with us: when we mean to uncover
    the truth, we dig, say *unearth.*

2.

Emblematic in paint, a signifier of the body's lacuna,   15
    the black leg is at once a grafted narrative,
a redacted line of text, and in this scene a dark stocking
    pulled above the knee. Here the patient is sleeping,
his head at rest in his hand. Beatific, he looks as if
    he'll wake from a dream. On the floor   20
beside the bed, a dead *Moor*—hands crossed at the groin,
    the swapped limb white and rotting, fused in place.
And in the corner, a question: poised as if to speak
    the syntax of sloughing, a snake's curved form.
It emerges from the mouth of a boy like a tongue—slippery   25
    and rooted in the body as knowledge. For centuries
this is how the myth repeats: the miracle—in words
    or wood or paint—is a record of thought.

---

1. Roman Catholic church and basilica in Rome; among the relics preserved there are chains said to
have bound Saint Peter when he was held captive in Jerusalem.

3.

See how the story changes: in one painting
    the *Ethiop* is merely a body, featureless in a coffin,   30
so black he has no face. In another, the patient—
    at the top of the frame—seems to writhe in pain,
the black leg grafted to his thigh. Below him
    a mirror of suffering: the *blackamoor*—
his body a fragment—arched across the doctor's lap   35
    as if dying from his wound. If not immanence,
the soul's bright anchor—blood passed from one
    to the other—what knowledge haunts each body,
what history, what phantom ache? One man always
    low, in a grave or on the ground, the other   40
up high, closer to heaven; one man always diseased,
    the other a body in service, plundered.

4.

Both men are alive in Villoldo's carving.[2]
    In twinned relief, they hold the same posture,
the same pained face, each man reaching to touch   45
    his left leg. The black man, on the floor,
holds his stump. Above him, the doctor restrains
    the patient's arm as if to prevent him touching
the dark amendment of flesh. How not to see it—
    the men bound one to the other, symbiotic—   50
one man rendered expendable, the other worthy
    of this sacrifice? In version after version, even
when the *Ethiopian* isn't there, the leg is a stand-in,
    a black modifier against the white body,
a piece cut off—as in the origin of the word *comma*:   55
    caesura in a story that's still being written.

2012

2. "Miracle of the Black Leg" (1547), by Spanish sculptor Isidro de Villoldo (1500–1556).

JHUMPA LAHIRI
b. 1967

When Jhumpa Lahiri writes, her setting is quite literally the world—focused sometimes here and sometimes there, but always with global implications. This orientation is a factor of her times. Unlike children of earlier immigrant generations, Lahiri did not face the pressures of assimilating into an American society apart from and in some cases above other cultures. Instead, international trade, travel, and communications have made global culture a practical reality. In "Sexy," one of Lahiri's most wide-ranging yet intimate stories, her protagonist listens to a sad tale about a friend's "cousin's husband." The bad news, "a wife's worst nightmare," is being conveyed in Boston, where the friends live, but it involves a flight from Delhi to Montreal stopping at Heathrow Airport outside London. Four locations in two hemispheres an ocean and a continent apart indicate the world that people with family backgrounds in India share when they become Americans. Geographical barriers become much more easily manageable thanks to cell phones and e-mail. Education, employment, friendships, and romantic relationships span the world. Films from India are viewed with American pop songs in mind and Chinese cuisine in the stomach, all, flavorful as they are, seeming as natural as the lives being lived among such givens.

The flavor of Lahiri's fiction defies categorization, other than being dependent on no single national ingredient. A visit to Boston's Mapparium (a giant globe viewed from inside) or Museum of Fine Arts is less a field trip through region and history than a comfortable part of her characters' way of living, a reminder of the larger culture they share.

The author's Bengali parents parted from their large extended family when they moved from Kolkata to London, where Lahiri was born. Following a normal progression in the former British Commonwealth, Lahiri's parents then relocated to the United States, where they worked as educators in Rhode Island while she studied at Barnard College and Boston University, concentrating on literature and creative writing and ending with a Ph.D. Her first stories reflect how much of her family's past had to be conveyed to her via storytelling, such as in "When Mr. Pirzada Came to Dine," where a ten-year-old in America learns about political troubles in India from a visiting family friend. To the youngster, it sounds exotic, but no more so than the situation experienced by a pair of Indian newlyweds, in "This Blessed House," who are alternately intrigued and mystified by fundamentalist Christian curios left behind by the previous tenants of their new home. Much of Lahiri's short fiction, first collected in *Interpreter of Maladies* (1999) and extended in *Unaccustomed Earth* (2008), involves discoveries of this nature, in which she is particularly adept at portraying the learning process of someone acting without monocultural constraint. The curiosity of children or young adults is a hallmark of her style.

In 2003, having married, become a mother, and settled in the Park Slope area of Brooklyn, New York, a neighborhood popular with writers, Lahiri published her novel *The Namesake*. Like her earlier work, it contrasts cultural assimilation with curiosity about the values, beliefs, and practices of a preceding generation. But here a certain amount of anger and confusion come into play, as the protagonist, Gogol Ganguli, is uncomfortable with how the private first name his parents have used for him at home has become his public name as well, all without his understanding its personal (much less literary) significance. Lahiri had been saddled with "Jhumpa" as a first name by her teachers, who found it easier to pronounce than her other two given names, either of which would have been more appropriate for formal use. But while Lahiri's enforced assimilation didn't bother her, Ganguli's does, although much of his discomfort is comic, such as when he assumes that a sociologist's anagrammatical reference to "ABCDs" means not "multiculturals" but "American-born confused deshi" (India countrymen). In fact, Ganguli doesn't even know what "deshi" properly means, just that his parents customarily refer to India as "desh." He "never thinks of India as desh. He thinks of it as Americans do, as India." Other contrasts, such as arranged marriages versus modern ones, are handled with more gravity in this novel, and two fraught marriages structure Lahiri's ambitious 2013 novel, *The Lowland*.

The following text is from *Interpreter of Maladies* (1999).

Sexy

It was a wife's worst nightmare. After nine years of marriage, Laxmi told Miranda, her cousin's husband had fallen in love with another woman. He sat next to her on a plane, on a flight from Delhi to Montreal, and instead of flying home to his wife and son, he got off with the woman at Heathrow.[1] He called his wife, and told her he'd had a conversation that had changed his life, and that he needed time to figure things out. Laxmi's cousin had taken to her bed.

"Not that I blame her," Laxmi said. She reached for the Hot Mix she munched throughout the day, which looked to Miranda like dusty orange cereal. "Imagine. An English girl, half his age." Laxmi was only a few years older than Miranda, but she was already married, and kept a photo of herself and her husband, seated on a white stone bench in front of the Taj Mahal,[2] tacked to the inside of her cubicle, which was next to Miranda's. Laxmi had been on the phone for at least an hour, trying to calm her cousin down. No one noticed; they worked for a public radio station,[3] in the fundraising department, and were surrounded by people who spent all day on the phone, soliciting pledges.

"I feel worst for the boy," Laxmi added. "He's been at home for days. My cousin said she can't even take him to school."

"It sounds awful," Miranda said. Normally Laxmi's phone conversations—mainly to her husband, about what to cook for dinner—distracted Miranda as she typed letters, asking members of the radio station to increase their annual pledge in exchange for a tote bag or an umbrella. She could hear Laxmi clearly, her sentences peppered every now and then with an Indian word, through the laminated wall between their desks. But that afternoon Miranda hadn't been listening. She'd been on the phone herself, with Dev, deciding where to meet later that evening.

"Then again, a few days at home won't hurt him." Laxmi ate some more Hot Mix, then put it away in a drawer. "He's something of a genius. He has a Punjabi mother and a Bengali[4] father, and because he learns French and English at school he already speaks four languages. I think he skipped two grades."

Dev was Bengali, too. At first Miranda thought it was a religion. But then he pointed it out to her, a place in India called Bengal, in a map printed in an issue of *The Economist*.[5] He had brought the magazine specially to her apartment, for she did not own an atlas, or any other books with maps in them. He'd pointed to the city where he'd been born, and another city where his father had been born. One of the cities had a box around it, intended to attract the reader's eye. When Miranda asked what the box indicated, Dev rolled up the magazine, and said, "Nothing you'll ever need to worry about," and he tapped her playfully on the head.

Before leaving her apartment he'd tossed the magazine in the garbage, along with the ends of the three cigarettes he always smoked in the course of his visits. But after she watched his car disappear down Commonwealth Avenue,[6] back to his house in the suburbs, where he lived with his wife, Miranda

---

1. International airport near London.
2. Muslim mausoleum near Agra, India, built on a monumental scale in the mid-17th century by Emperor Shah Jahan for his favorite wife, Mumtaz Mahal.
3. Noncommercial, listener-supported, often oriented toward arts and culture in its broadcasting.

4. Punjab, state in northern India; Bengal, former province of India, now a region that includes Bengal State and East Bengal, the latter part of Bangladesh.
5. Weekly British magazine of news and commentary.
6. Major thoroughfare in Boston.

retrieved it, and brushed the ashes off the cover, and rolled it in the opposite direction to get it to lie flat. She got into bed, still rumpled from their love-making, and studied the borders of Bengal. There was a bay below and mountains above. The map was connected to an article about something called the Gramin Bank.[7] She turned the page, hoping for a photograph of the city where Dev was born, but all she found were graphs and grids. Still, she stared at them, thinking the whole while about Dev, about how only fifteen minutes ago he'd propped her feet on top of his shoulders, and pressed her knees to her chest, and told her that he couldn't get enough of her.

She'd met him a week ago, at Filene's.[8] She was there on her lunch break, buying discounted pantyhose in the Basement. Afterward she took the escalator to the main part of the store, to the cosmetics department, where soaps and creams were displayed like jewels, and eye shadows and powders shimmered like butterflies pinned behind protective glass. Though Miranda had never bought anything other than a lipstick, she liked walking through the cramped, confined maze, which was familiar to her in a way the rest of Boston still was not. She liked negotiating her way past the women planted at every turn, who sprayed cards with perfume and waved them in the air; sometimes she would find a card days afterward, folded in her coat pocket, and the rich aroma, still faintly preserved, would warm her as she waited on cold mornings for the T.[9]

That day, stopping to smell one of the more pleasing cards, Miranda noticed a man standing at one of the counters. He held a slip of paper covered in a precise, feminine hand. A saleswoman took one look at the paper and began to open drawers. She produced an oblong cake of soap in a black case, a hydrating mask, a vial of cell renewal drops, and two tubes of face cream. The man was tanned, with black hair that was visible on his knuckles. He wore a flamingo pink shirt, a navy blue suit, a camel overcoat with gleaming leather buttons. In order to pay he had taken off pigskin gloves. Crisp bills emerged from a burgundy wallet. He didn't wear a wedding ring.

"What can I get you, honey?" the saleswoman asked Miranda. She looked over the tops of her tortoiseshell glasses, assessing Miranda's complexion.

Miranda didn't know what she wanted. All she knew was that she didn't want the man to walk away. He seemed to be lingering, waiting, along with the saleswoman, for her to say something. She stared at some bottles, some short, others tall, arranged on an oval tray, like a family posing for a photograph.

"A cream," Miranda said eventually.

"How old are you?"

"Twenty-two."

The saleswoman nodded, opening a frosted bottle. "This may seem a bit heavier than what you're used to, but I'd start now. All your wrinkles are going to form by twenty-five. After that they just start showing."

While the saleswoman dabbed the cream on Miranda's face, the man stood and watched. While Miranda was told the proper way to apply it, in swift upward strokes beginning at the base of her throat, he spun the

---

7. Properly the Grameen Bank, which provides credit to the poorest classes in rural Bangladesh as a means of fighting poverty and promoting social economic development.

8. A department store. Filene's Basement, downstairs, was a renowned discount store.

9. Metropolitan Transit Authority (MTA), Boston's subway system.

lipstick carousel. He pressed a pump that dispensed cellulite gel and massaged it into the back of his ungloved hand. He opened a jar, leaned over, and drew so close that a drop of cream flecked his nose.

Miranda smiled, but her mouth was obscured by a large brush that the saleswoman was sweeping over her face. "This is blusher Number Two," the woman said. "Gives you some color."

Miranda nodded, glancing at her reflection in one of the angled mirrors that lined the counter. She had silver eyes and skin as pale as paper, and the contrast with her hair, as dark and glossy as an espresso bean, caused people to describe her as striking, if not pretty. She had a narrow, egg-shaped head that rose to a prominent point. Her features, too, were narrow, with nostrils so slim that they appeared to have been pinched with a clothespin. Now her face glowed, rosy at the cheeks, smoky below the brow bone. Her lips glistened.

The man was glancing in a mirror, too, quickly wiping the cream from his nose. Miranda wondered where he was from. She thought he might be Spanish, or Lebanese. When he opened another jar, and said, to no one in particular, "This one smells like pineapple," she detected only the hint of an accent.

"Anything else for you today?" the saleswoman asked, accepting Miranda's credit card.

"No thanks."

The woman wrapped the cream in several layers of red tissue. "You'll be very happy with this product." Miranda's hand was unsteady as she signed the receipt. The man hadn't budged.

"I threw in a sample of our new eye gel," the saleswoman added, handing Miranda a small shopping bag. She looked at Miranda's credit card before sliding it across the counter. "Bye-bye, Miranda."

Miranda began walking. At first she sped up. Then, noticing the doors that led to Downtown Crossing,[1] she slowed down.

"Part of your name is Indian," the man said, pacing his steps with hers.

She stopped, as did he, at a circular table piled with sweaters, flanked with pinecones and velvet bows. "Miranda?"

"Mira. I have an aunt named Mira."

His name was Dev. He worked in an investment bank back that way he said, tilting his head in the direction of South Station.[2] He was the first man with a mustache, Miranda decided, she found handsome.

They walked together toward Park Street station,[3] past the kiosks that sold cheap belts and handbags. A fierce January wind spoiled the part in her hair. As she fished for a token in her coat pocket, her eyes fell to his shopping bag. "And those are for her?"

"Who?"

"Your Aunt Mira."

"They're for my wife." He uttered the words slowly, holding Miranda's gaze. "She's going to India for a few weeks." He rolled his eyes. "She's addicted to this stuff."

Somehow, without the wife there, it didn't seem so wrong. At first Miranda and Dev spent every night together, almost. He explained that he couldn't

1. Major interchange of MTA subway lines.
2. MTA commuter hub for lines from the south
suburbs.
3. MTA stop in the business district.

spend the whole night at her place, because his wife called every day at six in the morning, from India, where it was four in the afternoon. And so he left her apartment at two, three, often as late as four in the morning, driving back to his house in the suburbs. During the day he called her every hour, it seemed, from work, or from his cell phone. Once he learned Miranda's schedule he left her a message each evening at five-thirty, when she was on the T coming back to her apartment, just so, he said, she could hear his voice as soon as she walked through the door. "I'm thinking about you," he'd say on the tape. "I can't wait to see you." He told her he liked spending time in her apartment, with its kitchen counter no wider than a breadbox, and scratchy floors that sloped, and a buzzer in the lobby that always made a slightly embarrassing sound when he pressed it. He said he admired her for moving to Boston, where she knew no one, instead of remaining in Michigan, where she'd grown up and gone to college. When Miranda told him it was nothing to admire, that she'd moved to Boston precisely for that reason, he shook his head. "I know what it's like to be lonely," he said, suddenly serious, and at that moment Miranda felt that he understood her—understood how she felt some nights on the T, after seeing a movie on her own, or going to a bookstore to read magazines, or having drinks with Laxmi, who always had to meet her husband at Alewife station[4] in an hour or two. In less serious moments Dev said he liked that her legs were longer than her torso, something he'd observed the first time she walked across a room naked. "You're the first," he told her, admiring her from the bed. "The first woman I've known with legs this long."

Dev was the first to tell her that. Unlike the boys she dated in college, who were simply taller, heavier versions of the ones she dated in high school, Dev was the first always to pay for things, and hold doors open, and reach across a table in a restaurant to kiss her hand. He was the first to bring her a bouquet of flowers so immense she'd had to split it up into all six of her drinking glasses, and the first to whisper her name again and again when they made love. Within days of meeting him, when she was at work, Miranda began to wish that there were a picture of her and Dev tacked to the inside of her cubicle, like the one of Laxmi and her husband in front of the Taj Mahal. She didn't tell Laxmi about Dev. She didn't tell anyone. Part of her wanted to tell Laxmi, if only because Laxmi was Indian, too. But Laxmi was always on the phone with her cousin these days, who was still in bed, whose husband was still in London, and whose son still wasn't going to school. "You must eat something," Laxmi would urge. "You mustn't lose your health." When she wasn't speaking to her cousin, she spoke to her husband, shorter conversations, in which she ended up arguing about whether to have chicken or lamb for dinner. "I'm sorry," Miranda heard her apologize at one point. "This whole thing just makes me a little paranoid."

Miranda and Dev didn't argue. They went to movies at the Nickelodeon and kissed the whole time. They ate pulled pork and cornbread in Davis Square,[5] a paper napkin tucked like a cravat into the collar of Dev's shirt. They sipped sangria at the bar of a Spanish restaurant, a grinning pig's head presiding over their conversation. They went to the MFA[6] and picked

---

4. MTA stop in Cambridge, Massachusetts, across the Charles River from Boston.
5. MTA stop near Tufts University in a formerly working-class, now upscale neighborhood.
6. Museum of Fine Arts (Boston).

out a poster of water lilies for her bedroom. One Saturday, following an afternoon concert at Symphony Hall, he showed her his favorite place in the city, the Mapparium[7] at the Christian Science center, where they stood inside a room made of glowing stained-glass panels, which was shaped like the inside of a globe, but looked like the outside of one. In the middle of the room was a transparent bridge, so that they felt as if they were standing in the center of the world. Dev pointed to India, which was red, and far more detailed than the map in *The Economist*. He explained that many of the countries, like Siam and Italian Somaliland,[8] no longer existed in the same way; the names had changed by now. The ocean, as blue as a peacock's breast, appeared in two shades, depending on the depth of the water. He showed her the deepest spot on earth, seven miles deep, above the Mariana Islands.[9] They peered over the bridge and saw the Antarctic archipelago[1] at their feet, craned their necks and saw a giant metal star overhead. As Dev spoke, his voice bounced wildly off the glass, sometimes loud, sometimes soft, sometimes seeming to land in Miranda's chest, sometimes eluding her ear altogether. When a group of tourists walked onto the bridge, she could hear them clearing their throats, as if through microphones. Dev explained that it was because of the acoustics.

Miranda found London, where Laxmi's cousin's husband was, with the woman he'd met on the plane. She wondered which of the cities in India Dev's wife was in. The farthest Miranda had ever been was to the Bahamas once when she was a child. She searched but couldn't find it on the glass panels. When the tourists left and she and Dev were alone again, he told her to stand at one end of the bridge. Even though they were thirty feet apart, Dev said, they'd be able to hear each other whisper.

"I don't believe you," Miranda said. It was the first time she'd spoken since they'd entered. She felt as if speakers were embedded in her ears.

"Go ahead," he urged, walking backward to his end of the bridge. His voice dropped to a whisper. "Say something." She watched his lips forming the words; at the same time she heard them so clearly that she felt them under her skin, under her winter coat, so near and full of warmth that she felt herself go hot.

"Hi," she whispered, unsure of what else to say.

"You're sexy," he whispered back.

At work the following week, Laxmi told Miranda that it wasn't the first time her cousin's husband had had an affair. "She's decided to let him come to his senses," Laxmi said one evening as they were getting ready to leave the office. "She says it's for the boy. She's willing to forgive him for the boy." Miranda waited as Laxmi shut off her computer. "He'll come crawling back, and she'll let him," Laxmi said, shaking her head. "Not me. If my husband so much as looked at another woman I'd change the locks." She studied the picture tacked to her cubicle. Laxmi's husband had his arm draped over her shoulder, his knees leaning in toward her on the bench. She turned to Miranda. "Wouldn't you?"

---

7. Large walk-through globe that maps the earth as stars and planets would be seen in a planetarium.
8. Presently Thailand and Somalia.

9. Island chain in the western Pacific Ocean.
1. Group of islands northwest of the Antarctic Peninsula.

She nodded. Dev's wife was coming back from India the next day. That afternoon he'd called Miranda at work, to say he had to go to the airport to pick her up. He promised he'd call as soon as he could.

"What's the Taj Mahal like?" she asked Laxmi.

"The most romantic spot on earth." Laxmi's face brightened at the memory. "An everlasting monument to love."

While Dev was at the airport, Miranda went to Filene's Basement to buy herself things she thought a mistress should have. She found a pair of black high heels with buckles smaller than a baby's teeth. She found a satin slip with scalloped edges and a knee-length silk robe. Instead of the pantyhose she normally wore to work, she found sheer stockings with a seam. She searched through piles and wandered through racks, pressing back hanger after hanger, until she found a cocktail dress made of a slinky silvery material that matched her eyes, with little chains for straps. As she shopped she thought about Dev, and about what he'd told her in the Mapparium. It was the first time a man had called her sexy, and when she closed her eyes she could still feel his whisper drifting through her body, under her skin. In the fitting room, which was just one big room with mirrors on the walls, she found a spot next to an older woman with a shiny face and coarse frosted hair. The woman stood barefoot in her underwear, pulling the black net of a body stocking taut between her fingers.

"Always check for snags," the woman advised.

Miranda pulled out the satin slip with scalloped edges. She held it to her chest.

The woman nodded with approval. "Oh yes."

"And this?" She held up the silver cocktail dress.

"Absolutely," the woman said. "He'll want to rip it right off you."

Miranda pictured the two of them at a restaurant in the South End[2] they'd been to, where Dev had ordered foie gras and a soup made with champagne and raspberries. She pictured herself in the cocktail dress, and Dev in one of his suits, kissing her hand across the table. Only the next time Dev came to visit her, on a Sunday afternoon several days since the last time they'd seen each other, he was in gym clothes. After his wife came back, that was his excuse: on Sundays he drove into Boston and went running along the Charles. The first Sunday she opened the door in the knee-length robe, but Dev didn't even notice it; he carried her over to the bed, wearing sweatpants and sneakers, and entered her without a word. Later, she slipped on the robe when she walked across the room to get him a saucer for his cigarette ashes, but he complained that she was depriving him of the sight of her long legs, and demanded that she remove it. So the next Sunday she didn't bother. She wore jeans. She kept the lingerie at the back of a drawer, behind her socks and everyday underwear. The silver cocktail dress hung in her closet, the tag dangling from the seam. Often, in the morning, the dress would be in a heap on the floor; the chain straps always slipped off the metal hanger.

Still, Miranda looked forward to Sundays. In the mornings she went to a deli and bought a baguette and little containers of things Dev liked to eat,

2. Trendy Boston neighborhood.

like pickled herring, and potato salad, and tortes of pesto and mascarpone cheese. They ate in bed, picking up the herring with their fingers and ripping the baguette with their hands. Dev told her stories about his childhood, when he would come home from school and drink mango juice served to him on a tray, and then play cricket by a lake, dressed all in white. He told her about how, at eighteen, he'd been sent to a college in upstate New York during something called the Emergency,[3] and about how it took him years to be able to follow American accents in movies, in spite of the fact that he'd had an English-medium education. As he talked he smoked three cigarettes, crushing them in a saucer by the side of her bed. Sometimes he asked her questions, like how many lovers she'd had (three) and how old she'd been the first time (nineteen). After lunch they made love, on sheets covered with crumbs, and then Dev took a nap for twelve minutes. Miranda had never known an adult who took naps, but Dev said it was something he'd grown up doing in India, where it was so hot that people didn't leave their homes until the sun went down. "Plus it allows us to sleep together," he murmured mischievously, curving his arm like a big bracelet around her body.

Only Miranda never slept. She watched the clock on her bedside table, or pressed her face against Dev's fingers, intertwined with hers, each with its half-dozen hairs at the knuckle. After six minutes she turned to face him, sighing and stretching, to test if he was really sleeping. He always was. His ribs were visible through his skin as he breathed, and yet he was beginning to develop a paunch. He complained about the hair on his shoulders, but Miranda thought him perfect, and refused to imagine him any other way.

At the end of twelve minutes Dev would open his eyes as if he'd been awake all along, smiling at her, full of a contentment she wished she felt herself. "The best twelve minutes of the week." He'd sigh, running a hand along the backs of her calves. Then he'd spring out of bed, pulling on his sweatpants and lacing up his sneakers. He would go to the bathroom and brush his teeth with his index finger, something he told her all Indians knew how to do, to get rid of the smoke in his mouth. When she kissed him good-bye she smelled herself sometimes in his hair. But she knew that his excuse, that he'd spent the afternoon jogging, allowed him to take a shower when he got home, first thing.

Apart from Laxmi and Dev, the only Indians whom Miranda had known were a family in the neighborhood where she'd grown up, named the Dixits. Much to the amusement of the neighborhood children, including Miranda, but not including the Dixit children, Mr. Dixit would jog each evening along the flat winding streets of their development in his everyday shirt and trousers, his only concession to athletic apparel a pair of cheap Keds. Every weekend, the family—mother, father, two boys, and a girl—piled into their car and went away, to where nobody knew. The fathers complained that Mr. Dixit did not fertilize his lawn properly, did not rake his leaves on time, and agreed that the Dixits' house, the only one with vinyl siding, detracted from the neighborhood's charm. The mothers never invited Mrs. Dixit to join them around the Armstrongs' swimming pool. Waiting for the school bus

---

3. State of internal emergency declared in 1975 by Indira Gandhi (1917–1984), prime minister of India, that allowed her to rule by decree until 1977, when she was defeated in an election.

with the Dixit children standing to one side, the other children would say "The Dixits dig shit," under their breath, and then burst into laughter.

One year, all the neighborhood children were invited to the birthday party of the Dixit girl. Miranda remembered a heavy aroma of incense and onions in the house, and a pile of shoes heaped by the front door. But most of all she remembered a piece of fabric, about the size of a pillowcase, which hung from a wooden dowel at the bottom of the stairs. It was a painting of a naked woman with a red face shaped like a knight's shield. She had enormous white eyes that tilted toward her temples, and mere dots for pupils. Two circles, with the same dots at their centers, indicated her breasts. In one hand she brandished a dagger. With one foot she crushed a struggling man on the ground. Around her body was a necklace composed of bleeding heads, strung together like a popcorn chain. She stuck her tongue out at Miranda.

"It is the goddess Kali,"[4] Mrs. Dixit explained brightly, shifting the dowel slightly in order to straighten the image. Mrs. Dixit's hands were painted with henna, an intricate pattern of zigzags and stars. "Come please, time for cake."

Miranda, then nine years old, had been too frightened to eat the cake. For months afterward she'd been too frightened even to walk on the same side of the street as the Dixits' house, which she had to pass twice daily, once to get to the bus stop, and once again to come home. For a while she even held her breath until she reached the next lawn, just as she did when the school bus passed a cemetery.

It shamed her now. Now, when she and Dev made love, Miranda closed her eyes and saw deserts and elephants, and marble pavilions floating on lakes beneath a full moon. One Saturday, having nothing else to do, she walked all the way to Central Square,[5] to an Indian restaurant, and ordered a plate of tandoori chicken. As she ate she tried to memorize phrases printed at the bottom of the menu, for things like "delicious" and "water" and "check, please." The phrases didn't stick in her mind, and so she began to stop from time to time in the foreign-language section of a bookstore in Kenmore Square,[6] where she studied the Bengali alphabet in the Teach Yourself series. Once she went so far as to try to transcribe the Indian part of her name, "Mira," into her Filofax,[7] her hand moving in unfamiliar directions, stopping and turning and picking up her pen when she least expected to. Following the arrows in the book, she drew a bar from left to right from which the letters hung; one looked more like a number than a letter, another looked like a triangle on its side. It had taken her several tries to get the letters of her name to resemble the sample letters in the book, and even then she wasn't sure if she'd written Mira or Mara. It was a scribble to her, but somewhere in the world, she realized with a shock, it meant something.

During the week it wasn't so bad. Work kept her busy, and she and Laxmi had begun having lunch together at a new Indian restaurant around the corner, during which Laxmi reported the latest status of her cousin's marriage. Sometimes Miranda tried to change the topic; it made her feel the way

---

4. Hindu goddess of destruction.
5. In Cambridge.
6. In Boston.

7. Loose-leaf personal organizer, manufactured by the Filofax Company in England.

she once felt in college, when she and her boyfriend at the time had walked away from a crowded house of pancakes without paying for their food, just to see if they could get away with it. But Laxmi spoke of nothing else. "If I were her I'd fly straight to London and shoot them both," she announced one day. She snapped a papadum in half and dipped it into chutney.[8] "I don't know how she can just wait this way."

Miranda knew how to wait. In the evenings she sat at her dining table and coated her nails with clear nail polish, and ate salad straight from the salad bowl, and watched television, and waited for Sunday. Saturdays were the worst because by Saturday it seemed that Sunday would never come. One Saturday when Dev called, late at night, she heard people laughing and talking in the background, so many that she asked him if he was at a concert hall. But he was only calling from his house in the suburbs. "I can't hear you that well," he said. "We have guests. Miss me?" She looked at the television screen, a sitcom that she'd muted with the remote control when the phone rang. She pictured him whispering into his cell phone, in a room upstairs, a hand on the doorknob, the hallway filled with guests. "Miranda, do you miss me?" he asked again. She told him that she did.

The next day, when Dev came to visit, Miranda asked him what his wife looked like. She was nervous to ask, waiting until he'd smoked the last of his cigarettes, crushing it with a firm twist into the saucer. She wondered if they'd quarrel. But Dev wasn't surprised by the question. He told her, spreading some smoked whitefish on a cracker, that his wife resembled an actress in Bombay named Madhuri Dixit.[9]

For an instant Miranda's heart stopped. But no, the Dixit girl had been named something else, something that began with P. Still, she wondered if the actress and the Dixit girl were related. She'd been plain, wearing her hair in two braids all through high school.

A few days later Miranda went to an Indian grocery in Central Square which also rented videos. The door opened to a complicated tinkling of bells. It was dinnertime, and she was the only customer. A video was playing on a television hooked up in a corner of the store: a row of young women in harem pants were thrusting their hips in synchrony on a beach.

"Can I help you?" the man standing at the cash register asked. He was eating a samosa,[1] dipping it into some dark brown sauce on a paper plate. Below the glass counter at his waist were trays of more plump samosas, and what looked like pale, diamond-shaped pieces of fudge covered with foil, and some bright orange pastries floating in syrup. "You like some video?"

Miranda opened up her Filofax, where she had written "Mottery Dixit." She looked up at the videos on the shelves behind the counter. She saw women wearing skirts that sat low on the hips and tops that tied like bandannas between their breasts. Some leaned back against a stone wall, or a tree. They were beautiful, the way the women dancing on the beach were beautiful, with kohl-rimmed eyes and long black hair. She knew then that Madhuri Dixit was beautiful, too.

8. Thick, sweet, spicy sauce used as a condiment. "Papadum": crisp lentil wafer.
9. Indian film actress (b. 1967) renowned for her beauty.
1. Deep-fried turnover filled with vegetables or ground meat.

"We have subtitled versions, miss," the man continued. He wiped his fingertips quickly on his shirt and pulled out three titles.

"No," Miranda said. "Thank you, no." She wandered through the store, studying shelves lined with unlabeled packets and tins. The freezer case was stuffed with bags of pita bread and vegetables she didn't recognize. The only thing she recognized was a rack lined with bags and bags of the Hot Mix that Laxmi was always eating. She thought about buying some for Laxmi, then hesitated, wondering how to explain what she'd been doing in an Indian grocery.

"Very spicy," the man said, shaking his head, his eyes traveling across Miranda's body. "Too spicy for you."

By February, Laxmi's cousin's husband still hadn't come to his senses. He had returned to Montreal, argued bitterly with his wife for two weeks, packed two suitcases, and flown back to London. He wanted a divorce.

Miranda sat in her cubicle and listened as Laxmi kept telling her cousin that there were better men in the world, just waiting to come out of the woodwork. The next day the cousin said she and her son were going to her parents' house in California, to try to recuperate. Laxmi convinced her to arrange a weekend layover in Boston. "A quick change of place will do you good," Laxmi insisted gently, "besides which, I haven't seen you in years."

Miranda stared at her own phone, wishing Dev would call. It had been four days since their last conversation. She heard Laxmi dialing directory assistance, asking for the number of a beauty salon. "Something soothing," Laxmi requested. She scheduled massages, facials, manicures, and pedicures. Then she reserved a table for lunch at the Four Seasons. In her determination to cheer up her cousin, Laxmi had forgotten about the boy. She rapped her knuckles on the laminated wall.

"Are you busy Saturday?"

The boy was thin. He wore a yellow knapsack strapped across his back, gray herringbone trousers, a red V-necked sweater, and black leather shoes. His hair was cut in a thick fringe over his eyes, which had dark circles under them. They were the first thing Miranda noticed. They made him look haggard, as if he smoked a great deal and slept very little, in spite of the fact that he was only seven years old. He clasped a large sketch pad with a spiral binding. His name was Rohin.

"Ask me a capital," he said, staring up at Miranda.

She stared back at him. It was eight-thirty on a Saturday morning. She took a sip of coffee. "A what?"

"It's a game he's been playing," Laxmi's cousin explained. She was thin like her son, with a long face and the same dark circles under her eyes. A rust-colored coat hung heavy on her shoulders. Her black hair, with a few strands of gray at the temples, was pulled back like a ballerina's. "You ask him a country and he tells you the capital."

"You should have heard him in the car," Laxmi said. "He's already memorized all of Europe."

"It's not a game," Rohin said. "I'm having a competition with a boy at school. We're competing to memorize all the capitals. I'm going to beat him."

Miranda nodded. "Okay. What's the capital of India?"

"That's no good." He marched away, his arms swinging like a toy soldier. Then he marched back to Laxmi's cousin and tugged at a pocket of her overcoat. "Ask me a hard one."

"Senegal," she said.

"Dakar!" Rohin exclaimed triumphantly, and began running in larger and larger circles. Eventually he ran into the kitchen. Miranda could hear him opening and closing the fridge.

"Rohin, don't touch without asking," Laxmi's cousin called out wearily. She managed a smile for Miranda. "Don't worry, he'll fall asleep in a few hours. And thanks for watching him."

"Back at three," Laxmi said, disappearing with her cousin down the hallway. "We're double-parked."

Miranda fastened the chain on the door. She went to the kitchen to find Rohin, but he was now in the living room, at the dining table, kneeling on one of the director's chairs. He unzipped his knapsack, pushed Miranda's basket of manicure supplies to one side of the table, and spread his crayons over the surface. Miranda stood over his shoulder. She watched as he gripped a blue crayon and drew the outline of an airplane.

"It's lovely," she said. When he didn't reply, she went to the kitchen to pour herself more coffee.

"Some for me, please," Rohin called out.

She returned to the living room. "Some what?"

"Some coffee. There's enough in the pot. I saw."

She walked over to the table and sat opposite him. At times he nearly stood up to reach for a new crayon. He barely made a dent in the director's chair.

"You're too young for coffee."

Rohin leaned over the sketch pad, so that his tiny chest and shoulders almost touched it, his head tilted to one side. "The stewardess let me have coffee," he said. "She made it with milk and lots of sugar." He straightened, revealing a woman's face beside the plane, with long wavy hair and eyes like asterisks. "Her hair was more shiny," he decided, adding, "My father met a pretty woman on a plane, too." He looked at Miranda. His face darkened as he watched her sip. "Can't I have just a little coffee? Please?"

She wondered, in spite of his composed, brooding expression, if he were the type to throw a tantrum. She imagined his kicking her with his leather shoes, screaming for coffee, screaming and crying until his mother and Laxmi came back to fetch him. She went to the kitchen and prepared a cup for him as he'd requested. She selected a mug she didn't care for, in case he dropped it.

"Thank you," he said when she put it on the table. He took short sips, holding the mug securely with both hands.

Miranda sat with him while he drew, but when she attempted to put a coat of clear polish on her nails he protested. Instead he pulled out a paperback world almanac from his knapsack and asked her to quiz him. The countries were arranged by continent, six to a page, with the capitals in boldface, followed by a short entry on the population, government, and other statistics. Miranda turned to a page in the Africa section and went down the list.

"Mali," she asked him.

"Bamako," he replied instantly.

"Malawi."

"Lilongwe."

She remembered looking at Africa in the Mapparium. She remembered the fat part of it was green.

"Go on," Rohin said.

"Mauritania."

"Nouakchott."

"Mauritius."

He paused, squeezed his eyes shut, then opened them, defeated. "I can't remember."

"Port Louis," she told him.

"Port Louis." He began to say it again and again, like a chant under his breath.

When they reached the last of the countries in Africa, Rohin said he wanted to watch cartoons, telling Miranda to watch them with him. When the cartoons ended, he followed her to the kitchen, and stood by her side as she made more coffee. He didn't follow her when she went to the bathroom a few minutes later, but when she opened the door she was startled to find him standing outside.

"Do you need to go?"

He shook his head but walked into the bathroom anyway. He put the cover of the toilet down, climbed on top of it, and surveyed the narrow glass shelf over the sink which held Miranda's toothbrush and makeup.

"What's this for?" he asked, picking up the sample of eye gel she'd gotten the day she met Dev.

"Puffiness."

"What's puffiness?"

"Here," she explained, pointing.

"After you've been crying?"

"I guess so."

Rohin opened the tube and smelled it. He squeezed a drop of it onto a finger, then rubbed it on his hand. "It stings." He inspected the back of his hand closely, as if expecting it to change color. "My mother has puffiness. She says it's a cold, but really she cries, sometimes for hours. Sometimes straight through dinner. Sometimes she cries so hard her eyes puff up like bullfrogs."

Miranda wondered if she ought to feed him. In the kitchen she discovered a bag of rice cakes and some lettuce. She offered to go out, to buy something from the deli, but Rohin said he wasn't very hungry, and accepted one of the rice cakes. "You eat one too," he said. They sat at the table, the rice cakes between them. He turned to a fresh page in his sketch pad. "You draw."

She selected a blue crayon. "What should I draw?"

He thought for a moment. "I know," he said. He asked her to draw things in the living room: the sofa, the director's chairs, the television, the telephone. "This way I can memorize it."

"Memorize what?"

"Our day together." He reached for another rice cake.

"Why do you want to memorize it?"

"Because we're never going to see each other, ever again."

The precision of the phrase startled her. She looked at him, feeling slightly depressed. Rohin didn't look depressed. He tapped the page. "Go on."

And so she drew the items as best as she could—the sofa, the director's chairs, the television, the telephone. He sidled up to her, so close that it was sometimes difficult to see what she was doing. He put his small brown hand over hers. "Now me."

She handed him the crayon.

He shook his head. "No, now draw me."

"I can't," she said. "It won't look like you."

The brooding look began to spread across Rohin's face again, just as it had when she'd refused him coffee. "Please?"

She drew his face, outlining his head and the thick fringe of hair. He sat perfectly still, with a formal, melancholy expression, his gaze fixed to one side. Miranda wished she could draw a good likeness. Her hand moved in conjunction with her eyes, in unknown ways, just as it had that day in the bookstore when she'd transcribed her name in Bengali letters. It looked nothing like him. She was in the middle of drawing his nose when he wriggled away from the table.

"I'm bored," he announced, heading toward her bedroom. She heard him opening the door, opening the drawers of her bureau and closing them.

When she joined him he was inside the closet. After a moment he emerged, his hair disheveled, holding the silver cocktail dress. "This was on the floor."

"It falls off the hanger."

Rohin looked at the dress and then at Miranda's body. "Put it on."

"Excuse me?"

"Put it on."

There was no reason to put it on. Apart from in the fitting room at Filene's she had never worn it, and as long as she was with Dev she knew she never would. She knew they would never go to restaurants, where he would reach across a table and kiss her hand. They would meet in her apartment, on Sundays, he in his sweatpants, she in her jeans. She took the dress from Rohin and shook it out, even though the slinky fabric never wrinkled. She reached into the closet for a free hanger.

"Please put it on," Rohin asked, suddenly standing behind her. He pressed his face against her, clasping her waist with both his thin arms. "Please?"

"All right," she said, surprised by the strength of his grip.

He smiled, satisfied, and sat on the edge of her bed.

"You have to wait out there," she said, pointing to the door. "I'll come out when I'm ready."

"But my mother always takes her clothes off in front of me."

"She does?"

Rohin nodded. "She doesn't even pick them up afterward. She leaves them all on the floor by the bed, all tangled.

"One day she slept in my room," he continued. "She said it felt better than her bed, now that my father's gone."

"I'm not your mother," Miranda said, lifting him by the armpits off her bed. When he refused to stand, she picked him up. He was heavier than she expected, and he clung to her, his legs wrapped firmly around her hips, his head resting against her chest. She set him down in the hallway and shut the door. As an extra precaution she fastened the latch. She changed into the dress, glancing into the full-length mirror nailed to the back of the door. Her ankle socks looked silly, and so she opened a drawer and found the stockings. She searched through the back of the closet and slipped on the high heels with the tiny buckles. The chain straps of the dress were as light as paper clips against her collarbone. It was a bit loose on her. She could not zip it herself.

Rohin began knocking. "May I come in now?"

She opened the door. Rohin was holding his almanac in his hands, muttering something under his breath. His eyes opened wide at the sight of her. "I need help with the zipper," she said. She sat on the edge of the bed.

Rohin fastened the zipper to the top, and then Miranda stood up and twirled. Rohin put down the almanac. "You're sexy," he declared.

"What did you say?"

"You're sexy."

Miranda sat down again. Though she knew it meant nothing, her heart skipped a beat. Rohin probably referred to all women as sexy. He'd probably heard the word on television, or seen it on the cover of a magazine. She remembered the day in the Mapparium, standing across the bridge from Dev. At the time she thought she knew what his words meant. At the time they'd made sense.

Miranda folded her arms across her chest and looked Rohin in the eyes. "Tell me something."

He was silent.

"What does it mean?"

"What?"

"That word. 'Sexy.' What does it mean?"

He looked down, suddenly shy. "I can't tell you."

"Why not?"

"It's a secret." He pressed his lips together, so hard that a bit of them went white.

"Tell me the secret. I want to know."

Rohin sat on the bed beside Miranda and began to kick the edge of the mattress with the backs of his shoes. He giggled nervously, his thin body flinching as if it were being tickled.

"Tell me," Miranda demanded. She leaned over and gripped his ankles, holding his feet still.

Rohin looked at her, his eyes like slits. He struggled to kick the mattress again, but Miranda pressed against him. He fell back on the bed, his back straight as a board. He cupped his hands around his mouth, and then he whispered, "It means loving someone you don't know."

Miranda felt Rohin's words under her skin, the same way she'd felt Dev's. But instead of going hot she felt numb. It reminded her of the way she'd felt at the Indian grocery, the moment she knew, without even looking at a picture, that Madhuri Dixit, whom Dev's wife resembled, was beautiful.

"That's what my father did," Rohin continued. "He sat next to someone he didn't know, someone sexy, and now he loves her instead of my mother."

He took off his shoes and placed them side by side on the floor. Then he peeled back the comforter and crawled into Miranda's bed with the almanac. A minute later the book dropped from his hands, and he closed his eyes. Miranda watched him sleep, the comforter rising and falling as he breathed. He didn't wake up after twelve minutes like Dev, or even twenty. He didn't open his eyes as she stepped out of the silver cocktail dress and back into her jeans, and put the high-heeled shoes in the back of the closet, and rolled up the stockings and put them back in her drawer.

When she had put everything away she sat on the bed. She leaned toward him, close enough to see some white powder from the rice cakes stuck to the corners of his mouth, and picked up the almanac. As she turned the pages she imagined the quarrels Rohin had overheard in his house in Montreal. "Is she pretty?" his mother would have asked his father, wearing the same bathrobe she'd worn for weeks, her own pretty face turning spiteful. "Is she sexy?" His father would deny it at first, try to change the subject. "Tell me," Rohin's mother would shriek, "tell me if she's sexy." In the end his father would admit that she was, and his mother would cry and cry, in a bed surrounded by a tangle of clothes, her eyes puffing up like bullfrogs. "How could you," she'd ask, sobbing, "how could you love a woman you don't even know?"

As Miranda imagined the scene she began to cry a little herself. In the Mapparium that day, all the countries had seemed close enough to touch, and Dev's voice had bounced wildly off the glass. From across the bridge, thirty feet away, his words had reached her ears, so near and full of warmth that they'd drifted for days under her skin. Miranda cried harder, unable to stop. But Rohin still slept. She guessed that he was used to it now, to the sound of a woman crying.

On Sunday, Dev called to tell Miranda he was on his way. "I'm almost ready. I'll be there at two."

She was watching a cooking show on television. A woman pointed to a row of apples, explaining which were best for baking. "You shouldn't come today."

"Why not?"

"I have a cold," she lied. It wasn't far from the truth; crying had left her congested. "I've been in bed all morning."

"You do sound stuffed up." There was a pause. "Do you need anything?"

"I'm all set."

"Drink lots of fluids."

"Dev?"

"Yes, Miranda?"

"Do you remember that day we went to the Mapparium?"

"Of course."

"Do you remember how we whispered to each other?"

"I remember," Dev whispered playfully.

"Do you remember what you said?"

There was a pause. "'Let's go back to your place.'" He laughed quietly. "Next Sunday, then?"

The day before, as she'd cried, Miranda had believed she would never forget anything—not even the way her name looked written in Bengali. She'd fallen asleep beside Rohin and when she woke up he was drawing an airplane on the copy of *The Economist* she'd saved, hidden under the bed. "Who's Devajit Mitra?" he had asked, looking at the address label.

Miranda pictured Dev, in his sweatpants and sneakers, laughing into the phone. In a moment he'd join his wife downstairs, and tell her he wasn't going jogging. He'd pulled a muscle while stretching, he'd say, settling down to read the paper. In spite of herself, she longed for him. She would see him one more Sunday, she decided, perhaps two. Then she would tell him the things she had known all along: that it wasn't fair to her, or to his wife, that they both deserved better, that there was no point in it dragging on.

But the next Sunday it snowed, so much so that Dev couldn't tell his wife he was going running along the Charles. The Sunday after that, the snow had melted, but Miranda made plans to go to the movies with Laxmi, and when she told Dev this over the phone, he didn't ask her to cancel them. The third Sunday she got up early and went out for a walk. It was cold but sunny, and so she walked all the way down Commonwealth Avenue, past the restaurants where Dev had kissed her, and then she walked all the way to the Christian Science center. The Mapparium was closed, but she bought a cup of coffee nearby and sat on one of the benches in the plaza outside the church, gazing at its giant pillars and its massive dome, and at the clear-blue sky spread over the city.

1999

JUNOT DÍAZ
b. 1968

The people of two neighborhoods inspire most of Junot Díaz's fiction: those living in Villa Juana, a district of Santo Domingo in the Dominican Republic, and others residing in the London Terrace area of Palin, New Jersey. Born on the last day of 1968, Díaz lived in Villa Juana for his first five years, a time when his father was away working in the United States. Just before his fifth birthday he joined his father in New Jersey. Becoming an American did not mark a division in his life, nor would it as a source for his writing. Instead, Díaz appreciates the rich duality of any immigrant's experience. Narratives set in the Dominican Republic show characters ever mindful of what is happening among their relations on the North American mainland, and the young people in his New Jersey stories speak an English heavily laced with Dominican slang and live in a manner still marked by their Caribbean heritage. Not so much people of two worlds, Díaz's characters are creatures of a new world fashioned by fluid migrations and ultimately shaped by their own ingenuity.

The stories collected in *Drown* (1996) show the influence of two authors whose work Díaz read in college, Sandra Cisneros and Toni Morrison. Majoring in English at Kean College and Rutgers University, Díaz profited from a "living-and-learning" residence hall program that provided an immersion in both creative writing and literary studies. From Cisneros's fiction he learned how a neighborhood, such as the one she depicted in *The House on Mango Street* (1984), can be as vital and vibrant a creation as any character—how the neighborhood itself can be a character in the writer's imagination, a technique Díaz would later develop in his own manner. Morrison's novels popular during Díaz's undergraduate years (1988–92) are especially strong in privileging the novelist as creator of an otherwise unwritten minority history, a theme the younger writer would extend to the immigrant's experience of living in two worlds, neither of which conform to dominant cultural models. At the same time Díaz was paying for his education by working numerous part-time jobs that he recalls as roles customarily reserved for adult Latinos recently arrived in the United States, such as in the service industries (washing dishes, delivering pool tables) and in a steel plant. An MFA in creative writing from Cornell University followed in 1995, by which time Díaz had published many of the stories collected in *Drown*, including several in such prestigious venues as the *New Yorker* and the *Paris Review*. Díaz lives in New York City, where he remains active in the Dominican community; at the Massachusetts Institute of Technology he teaches creative writing in the Program in Writing and Humanistic Studies.

The fact that Díaz's novel, *The Brief Wondrous Life of Oscar Wao* (2007), appeared eleven years after *Drown* is indicative of his painstaking writing method. A winner of both the 2008 Pulitzer Prize for fiction and the National Book Critics Circle Award for the best novel of 2007, *The Brief Wondrous Life of Oscar Wao* presents a character who fulfills Díaz's professed goal of challenging "the type of protagonist that many of the young male Latino writers I knew were writing," as the author told Meghan O'Rourke of *Slate* in the wake of his awards. In a similar discussion with Jaime Perales Contreras of the bilingual *Literal* magazine, Díaz explained that his title character's name was prompted by a young Mexican literature student's pronunciation of Oscar Wilde's name. "Spanglish" is the slang term for such colorful mixtures of Spanish and English, and as a poetry of sorts it contributes to the texture and rhythm of Díaz's narration. As O'Rourke puts it, his fiction "is propelled by its attention to the energetic hybridity of American life," stretching from the questions of identity and inclusion dealt with in the stories of *Drown* to the complexities of a multicultural boyhood depicted in the novel. Throughout Díaz's work "authority" is an ever-present concern, from the memories of Oscar Wao's family suffering under the Trujillo dictatorship in the Dominican Republic to the contested nature of various narrative accounts with which young Oscar struggles in his American high school.

The following text is the title story from the 1996 collection *Drown*.

Drown

My mother tells me Beto's home, waits for me to say something, but I keep watching the TV. Only when she's in bed do I put on my jacket and swing through the neighborhood to see. He's a pato[1] now but two years ago we were friends and he would walk into the apartment without knocking, his heavy voice rousing my mother from the Spanish of her room and drawing me up from the basement, a voice that crackled and made you think of uncles or grandfathers.

We were raging then, crazy the way we stole, broke windows, the way we pissed on people's steps and then challenged them to come out and stop us. Beto was leaving for college at the end of the summer and was delirious from the thought of it—he hated everything about the neighborhood, the break-apart buildings, the little strips of grass, the piles of garbage around the cans, and the dump, especially the dump.

I don't know how you can do it, he said to me. I would just find me a job anywhere and go.

Yeah, I said. I wasn't like him. I had another year to go in high school, no promises elsewhere.

---

1. Dominican slang (pejorative) for a gay man (literally, "duck" in Spanish).

Days we spent in the mall or out in the parking lot playing stickball, but nights were what we waited for. The heat in the apartments was like something heavy that had come inside to die. Families arranged on their porches, the glow from their TVs washing blue against the brick. From my family apartment you could smell the pear trees that had been planted years ago, four to a court, probably to save us all from asphyxiation. Nothing moved fast, even the daylight was slow to fade, but as soon as night settled Beto and I headed down to the community center and sprang the fence into the pool. We were never alone, every kid with legs was there. We lunged from the boards and swam out of the deep end, wrestling and farting around. At around midnight abuelas,[2] with their night hair swirled around spiky rollers, shouted at us from their apartment windows. ¡Sinvergüenzas![3] Go home!

I pass his apartment but the windows are dark; I put my ear to the busted-up door and hear only the familiar hum of the air conditioner. I haven't decided yet if I'll talk to him. I can go back to my dinner and two years will become three.

Even from four blocks off I can hear the racket from the pool—radios too—and wonder if we were ever that loud. Little has changed, not the stink of chlorine, not the bottles exploding against the lifeguard station. I hook my fingers through the plastic-coated hurricane fence. Something tells me that he will be here; I hop the fence, feeling stupid when I sprawl on the dandelions and the grass.

Nice one, somebody calls out.

Fuck me, I say. I'm not the oldest motherfucker in the place, but it's close. I take off my shirt and my shoes and then knife in. Many of the kids here are younger brothers of the people I used to go to school with. Two of them swim past, black and Latino, and they pause when they see me, recognizing the guy who sells them their shitty dope. The crackheads have their own man, Lucero, and some other guy who drives in from Paterson,[4] the only full-time commuter in the area.

The water feels good. Starting at the deep end I glide over the slick-tiled bottom without kicking up a spume or making a splash. Sometimes another swimmer churns past me, more a disturbance of water than a body. I can still go far without coming up. While everything above is loud and bright, everything below is whispers. And always the risk of coming up to find the cops stabbing their searchlights out across the water. And then everyone running, wet feet slapping against the concrete, yelling, Fuck you, officers, you puto sucios,[5] fuck you.

When I'm tired I wade through to the shallow end, past some kid who's kissing his girlfriend, watching me as though I'm going to try to cut in, and I sit near the sign that runs the pool during the day. *No Horseplay, No Running, No Defecating, No Urinating, No Expectorating.* At the bottom someone has scrawled in *No Whites, No Fat Chiks* and someone else has provided the missing *c.* I laugh. Beto hadn't known what expectorating meant though he was the one leaving for college. I told him, spitting a greener by the side of the pool.

Shit, he said. Where did you learn that?

2. Grandmothers (Spanish).
3. Shameless, brazen ones (Spanish).
4. City in northern New Jersey.
5. Dirty whores (Spanish).

I shrugged.

Tell me. He hated when I knew something he didn't. He put his hands on my shoulders and pushed me under. He was wearing a cross and cutoff jeans. He was stronger than me and held me down until water flooded my nose and throat. Even then I didn't tell him; he thought I didn't read, not even dictionaries.

We live alone. My mother has enough for the rent and groceries and I cover the phone bill, sometimes the cable. She's so quiet that most of the time I'm startled to find her in the apartment. I'll enter a room and she'll stir, detaching herself from the cracking plaster walls, from the stained cabinets, and fright will pass through me like a wire. She has discovered the secret to silence: pouring café without a splash, walking between rooms as if gliding on a cushion of felt, crying without a sound. You have traveled to the East and learned many secret things, I've told her. You're like a shadow warrior.

And you're like a crazy, she says. Like a big crazy.

When I come in she's still awake, her hands picking clots of lint from her skirt. I put a towel down on the sofa and we watch television together. We settle on the Spanish-language news: drama for her, violence for me. Today a child has survived a seven-story fall, busting nothing but his diaper. The hysterical baby-sitter, about three hundred pounds of her, is head-butting the microphone.

It's a goddamn miraclevilla,[6] she cries.

My mother asks me if I found Beto. I tell her that I didn't look.

That's too bad. He was telling me that he might be starting at a school for business.

So what?

She's never understood why we don't speak anymore. I've tried to explain, all wise-like, that everything changes, but she thinks that sort of saying is only around so you can prove it wrong.

He asked me what you were doing.

What did you say?

I told him you were fine.

You should have told him I moved.

And what if he ran into you?

I'm not allowed to visit my mother?

She notices the tightening of my arms. You should be more like me and your father.

Can't you see I'm watching television?

I was angry at him, wasn't I? But now we can talk to each other.

Am I watching television here or what?

Saturdays she asks me to take her to the mall. As a son I feel I owe her that much, even though neither of us has a car and we have to walk two miles through redneck territory to catch the M15.[7]

Before we head out she drags us through the apartment to make sure the windows are locked. She can't reach the latches so she has me test them.

<hr>

6. Slang term for "miraculous" in "Spanglish," an amalgamation of Spanish and English as spoken in some Hispanic communities.

7. Bus route in the New Brunswick area of New Jersey.

With the air conditioner on we never open windows but I go through the routine anyway. Putting my hand on the latch is not enough—she wants to hear it rattle. This place just isn't safe, she tells me. Lorena got lazy and look what they did to her. They punched her and kept her locked up in her place. Those morenos[8] ate all her food and even made phone calls. Phone calls!

That's why we don't have long-distance, I tell her but she shakes her head. That's not funny, she says.

She doesn't go out much, so when she does it's a big deal. She dresses up, even puts on makeup. Which is why I don't give her lip about taking her to the mall even though I usually make a fortune on Saturdays, selling to those kids going down to Belmar or out to Spruce Run.

I recognize like half the kids on the bus. I keep my head buried in my cap, praying that nobody tries to score. She watches the traffic, her hands somewhere inside her purse, doesn't say a word.

When we arrive at the mall I give her fifty dollars. Buy something, I say, hating the image I have of her, picking through the sale bins, wrinkling everything. Back in the day, my father would give her a hundred dollars at the end of each summer for my new clothes and she would take nearly a week to spend it, even though it never amounted to more than a couple of t-shirts and two pairs of jeans. She folds the bills into a square. I'll see you at three, she says.

I wander through the stores, staying in sight of the cashiers so they won't have reason to follow me. The circuit I make has not changed since my looting days. Bookstore, record store, comic-book shop, Macy's. Me and Beto used to steal like mad from these places, two, three hundred dollars of shit in an outing. Our system was simple—we walked into a store with a shopping bag and came out loaded. Back then security wasn't tight. The only trick was in the exit. We stopped right at the entrance of the store and checked out some worthless piece of junk to stop people from getting suspicious. What do you think? we asked each other. Would she like it? Both of us had seen bad shoplifters at work. All grab and run, nothing smooth about them. Not us. We idled out of the stores slow, like a fat seventies car. At this, Beto was the best. He even talked to mall security, asked them for directions, his bag all loaded up, and me, standing ten feet away, shitting my pants. When he finished he smiled, swinging his shopping bag up to hit me.

You got to stop that messing around, I told him. I'm not going to jail for bullshit like that.

You don't go to jail for shoplifting. They just turn you over to your old man.

I don't know about you, but my pops hits like a motherfucker.

He laughed. You know my dad. He flexed his hands. The nigger's got arthritis.

My mother never suspected, even when my clothes couldn't all fit in my closet, but my father wasn't that easy. He knew what things cost and knew that I didn't have a regular job.

You're going to get caught, he told me one day. Just you wait. When you do I'll show them everything you've taken and then they'll throw your stupid ass away like a bad piece of meat.

---

8. Dark-skinned persons (Spanish).

He was a charmer, my pop, a real asshole, but he was right. Nobody can stay smooth forever, especially kids like us. One day at the bookstore, we didn't even hide the drops. Four issues of the same *Playboy* for kicks, enough audio books to start our own library. No last-minute juke either. The lady who stepped in front of us didn't look old, even with her white hair. Her silk shirt was half unbuttoned and a silver horn necklace sat on the freckled top of her chest. I'm sorry fellows, but I have to check your bag, she said. I kept moving, and looked back all annoyed, like she was asking us for a quarter or something. Beto got polite and stopped. No problem, he said, slamming the heavy bag into her face. She hit the cold tile with a squawk, her palms slapping the ground. There you go, Beto said.

Security found us across from the bus stop, under a Jeep Cherokee. A bus had come and gone, both of us too scared to take it, imagining a plainclothes waiting to clap the cuffs on. I remember that when the rent-a-cop tapped his nightstick against the fender and said, You little shits better come out here real slow, I started to cry. Beto didn't say a word, his face stretched out and gray, his hand squeezing mine, the bones in our fingers pressing together.

Nights I drink with Alex and Danny. The Malibou Bar is no good, just washouts and the sucias[9] we can con into joining us. We drink too much, roar at each other and make the skinny bartender move closer to the phone. On the wall hangs a cork dartboard and a Brunswick Gold Crown[1] blocks the bathroom, its bumpers squashed, the felt pulled like old skin.

When the bar begins to shake back and forth like a rumba, I call it a night and go home, through the fields that surround the apartments. In the distance you can see the Raritan,[2] as shiny as an earthworm, the same river my homeboy goes to school on. The dump has long since shut down, and grass has spread over it like a sickly fuzz, and from where I stand, my right hand directing a colorless stream of piss downward, the landfill might be the top of a blond head, square and old.

In the mornings I run. My mother is already up, dressing for her housecleaning job. She says nothing to me, would rather point to the mangu[3] she has prepared than speak.

I run three miles easily, could have pushed a fourth if I were in the mood. I keep an eye out for the recruiter who prowls around our neighborhood in his dark K-car.[4] We've spoken before. He was out of uniform and called me over, jovial, and I thought I was helping some white dude with directions. Would you mind if I asked you a question?

No.

Do you have a job?

Not right now.

Would you like one? A real career, more than you'll get around here?

I remember stepping back. Depends on what it is, I said.

Son, I know somebody who's hiring. It's the United States government.

Well. Sorry, but I ain't Army material.

---

9. Sluts (Spanish).
1. Pool table.
2. River in New Jersey.
3. Dominican dish made from plantains with butter, salt, pepper, and water.
4. A Chrysler Corporation automobile popular as a fleet vehicle.

That's exactly what I used to think, he said, his ten piggy fingers buried in his carpeted steering wheel. But now I have a house, a car, a gun and a wife. Discipline. Loyalty. Can you say that you have those things? Even one?

He's a southerner, red-haired, his drawl so out of place that the people around here laugh just hearing him. I take to the bushes when I see his car on the road. These days my guts feel loose and cold and I want to be away from here. He won't have to show me his Desert Eagle[5] or flash the photos of the skinny Filipino girls sucking dick. He'll only have to smile and name the places and I'll listen.

When I reach the apartment, I lean against my door, waiting for my heart to slow, for the pain to lose its edge. I hear my mother's voice, a whisper from the kitchen. She sounds hurt or nervous, maybe both. At first I'm terrified that Beto's inside with her but then I look and see the phone cord, swinging lazily. She's talking to my father, something she knows I disapprove of. He's in Florida now, a sad guy who calls her and begs for money. He swears that if she moves down there he'll leave the woman he's living with. These are lies, I've told her, but she still calls him. His words coil inside of her, wrecking her sleep for days. She opens the refrigerator door slightly so that the whir of the compressor masks their conversation. I walk in on her and hang up the phone. That's enough, I say.

She's startled, her hand squeezing the loose folds of her neck. That was him, she says quietly.

On school days Beto and I chilled at the stop together but as soon as that bus came over the Parkwood hill I got to thinking about how I was failing gym and screwing up math and how I hated every single living teacher on the planet.

I'll see *you* in the p.m., I said.

He was already standing on line. I just stood back and grinned, my hands in my pockets. With our bus drivers you didn't have to hide. Two of them didn't give a rat fuck and the third one, the Brazilian preacher, was too busy talking Bible to notice anything but the traffic in front of him.

Being truant without a car was no easy job but I managed. I watched a lot of TV and when it got boring I trooped down to the mall or the Sayreville library, where you could watch old documentaries for free. I always came back to the neighborhood late, so the bus wouldn't pass me on Ernston and nobody could yell Asshole! out the windows. Beto would usually be home or down by the swings, but other times he wouldn't be around at all. Out visiting other neighborhoods. He knew a lot of folks I didn't—a messed-up black kid from Madison Park, two brothers who were into that N.Y. club scene, who spent money on platform shoes and leather backpacks. I'd leave a message with his parents and then watch some more TV. The next day he'd be out at the bus stop, too busy smoking a cigarette to say much about the day before.

You need to learn how to walk the world, he told me. There's a lot out there.

---

5. A semi-automatic military pistol.

Some nights me and the boys drive to New Brunswick. A nice city, the Raritan so low and silty that you don't have to be Jesus to walk over it. We hit the Melody and the Roxy, stare at the college girls. We drink a lot and then spin out onto the dance floor. None of the chicas[6] ever dance with us, but a glance or a touch can keep us talking shit for hours.

Once the clubs close we go to the Franklin Diner, gorge ourselves on pancakes, and then, after we've smoked our pack, head home. Danny passes out in the back seat and Alex cranks the window down to keep the wind in his eyes. He's fallen asleep in the past, wrecked two cars before this one. The streets have been picked clean of students and townies and we blow through every light, red or green. At the Old Bridge Turnpike we pass the fag bar, which never seems to close. Patos are all over the parking lot, drinking and talking.

Sometimes Alex will stop by the side of the road and say, Excuse me. When somebody comes over from the bar he'll point his plastic pistol at them, just to see if they'll run or shit their pants. Tonight he just puts his head out the window. Fuck you! he shouts and then settles back in his seat, laughing.

That's original, I say.

He puts his head out the window again. Eat me, then!

Yeah, Danny mumbles from the back. Eat me.

Twice. That's it.

The first time was at the end of that summer. We had just come back from the pool and were watching a porn video at his parents' apartment. His father was a nut for these tapes, ordering them from wholesalers in California and Grand Rapids. Beto used to tell me how his pop would watch them in the middle of the day, not caring a lick about his moms, who spent the time in the kitchen, taking hours to cook a pot of rice and gandules.[7] Beto would sit down with his pop and neither of them would say a word, except to laugh when somebody caught it in the eye or the face.

We were an hour into the new movie, some vaina[8] that looked like it had been filmed in the apartment next door, when he reached into my shorts. What the fuck are you doing? I asked, but he didn't stop. His hand was dry. I kept my eyes on the television, too scared to watch. I came right away, smearing the plastic sofa covers. My legs started shaking and suddenly I wanted out. He didn't say anything to me as I left, just sat there watching the screen.

The next day he called and when I heard his voice I was cool but I wouldn't go to the mall or anywhere else. My mother sensed that something was wrong and pestered me about it, but I told her to leave me the fuck alone, and my pops, who was home on a visit, stirred himself from the couch to slap me down. Mostly I stayed in the basement, terrified that I would end up abnormal, a fucking pato, but he was my best friend and back then that mattered to me more than anything. This alone got me out of the apartment and over to the pool that night. He was already there, his body pale and flabby under the water. Hey, he said. I was beginning to worry about you.

Nothing to worry about, I said.

---

6. Girls (Spanish).
7. Pigeon peas (Spanish).

8. Dominican slang for "stuff" (Spanish).

We swam and didn't talk much and later we watched a Skytop crew pull a bikini top from a girl stupid enough to hang out alone. Give it, she said, covering herself, but these kids howled, holding it up over her head, the shiny laces flopping just out of reach. When they began to pluck at her arms, she walked away, leaving them to try the top on over their flat pecs.

He put his hand on my shoulder, my pulse a code under his palm. Let's go, he said. Unless of course you're not feeling good.

I'm feeling fine, I said.

Since his parents worked nights we pretty much owned the place until six the next morning. We sat in front of his television, in our towels, his hands bracing against my abdomen and thighs. I'll stop if you want, he said and I didn't respond. After I was done, he laid his head in my lap. I wasn't asleep or awake, but caught somewhere in between, rocked slowly back and forth the way surf holds junk against the shore, rolling it over and over. In three weeks he was leaving. Nobody can touch me, he kept saying. We'd visited the school and I'd seen how beautiful the campus was, with all the students drifting from dorm to class. I thought of how in high school our teachers loved to crowd us into their lounge every time a space shuttle took off from Florida. One teacher, whose family had two grammar schools named after it, compared us to the shuttles. A few of you are going to make it. Those are the orbiters. But the majority of you are just going to burn out. Going nowhere. He dropped his hand onto his desk. I could already see myself losing altitude, fading, the earth spread out beneath me, hard and bright.

I had my eyes closed and the television was on and when the hallway door crashed open, he jumped up and I nearly cut my dick off struggling with my shorts. It's just the neighbor, he said, laughing. He was laughing, but I was saying, Fuck this, and getting my clothes on.

I believe I see him in his father's bottomed-out Cadillac, heading towards the turnpike, but I can't be sure. He's probably back in school already. I deal close to home, trooping up and down the same dead-end street where the kids drink and smoke. These punks joke with me, pat me down for taps, sometimes too hard. Now that strip malls line Route 9, a lot of folks have part-time jobs; the kids stand around smoking in their aprons, name tags dangling heavily from pockets.

When I get home, my sneakers are filthy so I take an old toothbrush to their soles, scraping the crap into the tub. My mother has thrown open the windows and propped open the door. It's cool enough, she explains. She has prepared dinner—rice and beans, fried cheese, tostones.[9] Look what I bought, she says, showing me two blue t-shirts. They were two for one so I bought you one. Try it on.

It fits tight but I don't mind. She cranks up the television. A movie dubbed into Spanish, a classic, one that everyone knows. The actors throw themselves around, passionate, but their words are plain and deliberate. It's hard to imagine anybody going through life this way. I pull out the plug of bills from my pockets. She takes it from me, her fingers soothing the creases. A man who treats his plata[1] like this doesn't deserve to spend it, she says.

---

9. Flattened fried plantains, a side dish in the Dominican Republic.
1. Slang term for money (literally, "silver" in Spanish).

We watch the movie and the two hours together makes us friendly. She puts her hand on mine. Near the end of the film, just as our heroes are about to fall apart under a hail of bullets, she takes off her glasses and kneads her temples, the light of the television flickering across her face. She watches another minute and then her chin lists to her chest. Almost immediately her eyelashes begin to tremble, a quiet semaphore. She is dreaming, dreaming of Boca Raton, of strolling under the jacarandas[2] with my father. You can't be anywhere forever, was what Beto used to say, what he said to me the day I went to see him off. He handed me a gift, a book, and after he was gone I threw it away, didn't even bother to open it and read what he'd written.

I let her sleep until the end of the movie and when I wake her she shakes her head, grimacing. You better check those windows, she says. I promise her I will.

1996

2. Flowering trees native to the tropics.

TRACY K. SMITH
b. 1972

Tracy K. Smith's poetry is marked by wonder and joy. Smith was born in 1972, the daughter of an engineer (her father) who worked on the Hubble Space Telescope, which was launched in 1990 and is able to look at the universe from a position outside the distortions of Earth's atmosphere. This connection inspires her Pulitzer Prize–winning volume, *Life on Mars* (2011), her third book of poetry. Alive with the idea of a universe suddenly visible in all its star-strewn glory, the poems weave together the perspectives of child, teenager, daughter, and adult poet, embracing the multiple ways humans have looked towards space, from David Bowie's Ziggy Stardust songs to popular science-fiction films to the Hubble's massive mirrors. The question "what do you believe in?" guides Smith's poetry here and throughout her oeuvre. *Life on Mars* was written in the aftermath of her father's death and during her first pregnancy. Raised by a beloved and devoutly Christian mother, Smith has said that the proximity of birth and death made questions about God and the afterlife especially urgent in this collection.

Even when they are reflecting on cosmic questions, Smith's poems often ground themselves in the body—dancing, loving, eating, singing, and traveling. Her first book, *The Body's Question* (2003), contains a cluster of poems that question and celebrate human physicality. The title poem is partly an elegy for Smith's mother, Kathryn. The third section, "Joy," recounts the last days of her mother's life and the first days afterward. "I know you are deciding," Smith writes, apostrophizing her mother, "That the body's a question." In the title poem of Smith's second collection, *Duende* (2007)—the word *duende* can be roughly translated as a compelling artistic power or charm—the speaker watches dancers whose art staves off want. Longing to join them, the speaker hesitates: "I hate to do it here. / To set myself heavily beside them / Not now that they've proven / The body a myth, a parable / for what not even language / moves quickly enough to name."

Smith has said that, next to her parents, her education has most profoundly shaped her poetic vision and practice. A student of Irish poet Seamus Heaney at Harvard, and of American poet Lucie Brock-Broido at Harvard and at Columbia University's MFA program, Smith says that in their poetry workshops "the world began to make a different kind of sense." While at Harvard, Smith also interned at the Dark Room Collective, which ran a reading series for African American writers in Boston (members of the Collective have included Natasha Trethewey, also in this volume). Smith's memoir, *Ordinary Light* (2015), recounts the longer story of her formation as a writer, from her childhood in Northern California through her mother's death just after Smith finished college.

In addition to poems from *Life on Mars*, the selections here include two inspired by a trip to Mexico when Smith was experiencing writer's block. She has said that her immersion in Spanish language and Mexican culture "sent me back into English with a new sense of what to listen for, and a new sense of my own capacity as an expressive being." The "Gospel" poems are based on Smith's realization that the Gospels in the Bible are different ways of telling the same story about Jesus; Smith's "gospels" tell multiple versions of a story about suffering and migration. The appeal of Smith's poetry rests in her ability to revisit ancient stories—about the universe and human existence—in a voice that brings with it her generation's experiences and cultural touchstones.

Thirst

The old man they called Bagre[1]
Who welcomed us with food
And rice-paper cigarettes
At the table outside his cabin
Was the one who told the soldiers   5
To sit down. They were drunk.
They'd seen the plates on our car
From the road and came to where
You and I and Bagre and his son
Sat laughing. I must have been   10
Drunk myself to laugh so hard
At what I didn't understand.

It was night by then. We smoked
To keep off the mosquitoes.
There was fish to eat—nothing but fish   15
Bagre and the other men caught.
The two little girls I'd played with
Were asleep in their hammocks.
Even Genny and Manuel,
Who rode with us and waited   20
While we hurried out of our clothes
And into those waves the color
Of atmosphere.

Before the soldiers sat down,
They stood there, chests ballooned.   25

---

1. Spanish for "catfish."

When we showed them our papers,
They wanted something else.
One of them touched the back of my leg.
With your eyes, you told me
To come beside you. There were guns   30
Slung over their shoulders
Like tall sticks. They stroked them
Absently with their fingers.

Their leader was called Jorge.
I addressed him in the familiar.[2]   35
I gave him a half-empty bottle
Of what we were drinking.
When it was empty, I offered to fill it
With water from the cooler.
He took a sip, spat it out   40
And called you by your name.
I didn't want to see you
Climb onto that jeep of theirs—so tall
And broad it seemed they'd ridden in
On elephants yoked shoulder to shoulder,   45
Flank to flank.

Maybe this is a story
About the old man they called Bagre.
The one with the crooked legs
That refused to run.   50
Maybe this is a story about being too old
To be afraid, and too young not to fear
Authority, and abuse it, and call it
By its name, and call it a liar.
Or maybe it's a story about the fish.   55
The ones hanging on branches
To dry, and the ones swimming
With eyes that would not shut
In water that entered them
And became them   60
And kept them from thirst.

                                                    2003

Gospel: Juan

We crossed the border
Hours before dawn
Through a hole
Dug under a fence.

---

2. Grammatical mode of informal address in Spanish.

We crossed   5
Dressed as soldiers,
Faces painted
Mud green.

The *coyotes*[1]
That promised   10
We'd make it, gave us
A straw broom

To drag behind,
Erasing our tracks.
They gave us meat   15
Drugged for the dogs.

Farther off,
There were engines,
Voices, a light
That swept the ground.   20

We crossed
On our bellies.
I wonder
If we'll ever stand up.

2003

Gospel: Jesús

I'd like to smash a goblet in my fist.
Instead, I watch my hands baptize each piece,
making piles of the things I have watched myself
make new.
I watch my hands   5
until I am watching out from my hands—
now in air, now water, each element
a shadow of the other.

2003

From "My God, It's Full of Stars"[1]

3

Perhaps the great error is believing we're alone,
That the others have come and gone—a momentary blip—

1. Smugglers who take people across borders illegally for a fee.
1. From the novel *2001: A Space Odyssey*, by Arthur C. Clark: the protagonist's final words as he enters a gateway to a new part of the universe.
The novel was adapted in Stanley Kubrick's 1968 film of the same title; the quotation was used to open the 1984 sequel *2010: The Year We Made Contact* (directed by Peter Hyams).

When all along, space might be choc-full of traffic,
Bursting at the seams with energy we neither feel
Nor see, flush against us, living, dying, deciding,   5
Setting solid feet down on planets everywhere,
Bowing to the great stars that command, pitching stones
At whatever are their moons. They live wondering
If they are the only ones, knowing only the wish to know,
And the great black distance they—we—flicker in.   10

Maybe the dead know, their eyes widening at last,
Seeing the high beams of a million galaxies flick on
At twilight. Hearing the engines flare, the horns
Not letting up, the frenzy of being. I want it to be
One notch below bedlam, like a radio without a dial.   15
Wide open, so everything floods in at once.
And sealed tight, so nothing escapes. Not even time,
Which should curl in on itself and loop around like smoke.
So that I might be sitting now beside my father
As he raises a lit match to the bowl of his pipe   20
For the first time in the winter of 1959.

2011

The Universe: Original Motion Picture Soundtrack

The first track still almost swings. High hat and snare, even
A few bars of sax the stratosphere will singe-out soon enough.

Synthesized strings. Then something like cellophane
Breaking in as if snagged to a shoe. Crinkle and drag. White noise,

Black noise. What must be voices bob up, then drop, like metal shavings   5
In molasses. So much for us. So much for the flags we bored

Into planets dry as chalk, for the tin cans[1] we filled with fire.
And rode like cowboys into all we tried to tame. Listen:

The dark we've only ever imagined now audible, thrumming,
Marbled with static like gristly meat. A chorus of engines churns.   10

Silence taunts: a dare. Everything that disappears
Disappears as if returning somewhere.

2011

---

1. "Tin can": reference to the rock musician David Bowie's 1969 song "Space Oddity": "Here am I floating in my tin can, far above the moon."

Selected Bibliographies

Reference Works and Histories

Jennifer Ashton's *Cambridge Companion to American Poetry since 1945* (2013) and John Duvall's *Cambridge Companion to American Fiction after 1945* (2011) collect general essays well suited to introducing students and teachers to the broad contours of the period. Excellent treatment of the period up to the end of the twentieth century can be found in vol. 7 ("Prose Writing, 1940–1990"; 1999) and 8 ("Poetry and Criticism, 1940–1995"; 1996) of *The Cambridge History of American Literature* (Sacvan Bercovitch, general editor). The vast *Dictionary of Literary Biography*, under the supervision of Matthew J. Bruccoli, the Scribners *American Writers* series, edited by Jay Parini, and vol. 2 of David Perkins's *History of Modern Poetry* (1976) offer wide coverage of specific authors. A more general history appears in Robert von Hallberg's *American Poetry and Culture 1945–1980* (1985). An indispensable reference guide for poetry is *Contemporary Poets*, 7th ed. (2000), edited by Thomas Riggs. Specific areas are treated by editors Darryl Dickson-Carr's *The Columbia Guide to Contemporary African American Fiction* (2005), editor Eric Cheyfitz's *The Columbia Guide to American Indian Literatures of the United States since 1945* (2006), and José F. Aranda Jr.'s *When We Arrive: A New Literary History of Mexican America* (2003). Gershun Avilez's chapter on the Black Arts movement and other essays in *The Cambridge Companion to American Civil Rights Literature* (2015) are especially useful for contextualizing American writing in the 1950s and '60s; Steven Conner's *The Cambridge Companion to Postmodernism* (2004) provides a guide to other cultural and aesthetic contexts of the period. Lawrence Jackson's *The Indignant Generation* (2011) gives the best fine-grained literary and social history of black writing between 1940 and 1960. Histories of specific movements in poetry are explored in Michael Palmer's *The San Francisco Renaissance* (1991) and David Lehmann's *The Last Avant-Garde: The Making of the New York School of Poets* (1998). Useful introductory series are the Modern Language Association's *Approaches to Teaching . . .* series, the University of South Carolina Press's *Understanding . . .* volumes, the University Press of Mississippi's *Conversations with . . .* , the *Critical Essays* books from G. K. Hall Publishers, the Greenwood Press *Critical Response* series, the *Cambridge Companion* series, and the *Modern Critical Views* collections edited by Harold Bloom. The University of Michigan's Poets on Poetry series offers volumes in which poets comment on their own and others' work.

Criticism

Criticism on the fiction, poetry, and drama of the second half of the twentieth century has reached a critical mass such that few critics or particular works can be said to dominate the discussion. Rather, excellent criticism— both monographs and articles—can be found on a range of topics and writers, much of which is flagged in bibliographies for the individual authors below. That said, a few works stand out for their broad arguments taking in a crowd of writers and artists working the period, representing a strong reading of what American literary production in the second half of the twentieth century, and in the opening decade of the twenty-first century, has accomplished artistically and culturally.

The study of poetics has remained important throughout the last several decades, and can generate a broad perspective through which to read and teach the poetry in this volume. Influential studies of contemporary poetics by Marjorie Perloff include *The Poetics of Indeterminacy* (1981), *Radical Artifice: Writing in the Age of Media* (1991), and *21st-Century Modernism: The New Poetics* (2001). Jennifer Ashton's *From Modernism to Postmodernism: American Poetry and Theory in the Twentieth Century* (2006), and Charles Altieri's *The Art of Twentieth-Century American Poetry: Modernism and After* (2006) share Perloff's theoretically sophisticated understanding of the period's writing. Anthony Reed's highly theoretical *Freedom Time: The Poetics and Politics of Black Experimental Writing* (2014) discusses contemporary poetics and experiment in relation to the distinct position of black and Caribbean writers; while his focus is not on writers included in this volume, his way of reading black poetics is essential alongside arguments such as Perloff's and Altieri's. (His prose, like theirs, is suited to the theoretically intrepid reader.) Timothy Yu's edited volume, *Nests and Strangers: On Asian American Women Poets* (2015) and Yu's monograph, *Race and the Avant-Garde: Experimental and Asian American Poetry since 1965* (2009) effectively bring together theoretical and cultural-studies approaches. Gillian White's *Lyric Shame: The 'Lyric' Subject of Contemporary American Poetry* (2014) joins a more recent body of criticism about lyric as a genre, a turn best captured in Virginia Jackson's and Yopie Prins's edited volume, *The Lyric Theory Reader: A Critical Anthology* (2014). Jahan Ramazani's monographs on poetry's transnational context and on poetry's relationship to prayer, song, news, and other genres open up fruitful new ways of connecting poetry of the twentieth and twenty-first centuries with the large context of human expression, even though his work is not exclusively about contemporary or American poetry.

The tradition of the poet-critic lives on in American letters today, and several works in this vein are particularly worthy of mention. In *Close Calls with Nonsense: Reading New Poetry* (2009), Stephen Burt opens difficult contemporary poetry (including Ashbery, Ammons, Berryman, Bidart,

Gunn, and others) to readers. The poet and critic Elizabeth Alexander writes about black poets of the late twentieth century in *Power and Possibility: Essays, Reviews, and Interviews* (2007); poet Kevin Young reflects on black poetics more generally in *The Grey Album: On the Blackness of Blackness* (2012). On lyric, the poet Allen Grossman and Mark Halliday's *The Sighted Singer: Two Works on Poetry for Readers and Writers* (1992) is more theoretical but generative and accessible nevertheless. The history of thinking about poetry may also be traced through statements on poetics by both poets and critics: *Poetics of the New American Poetry* (1973), edited by Donald Allen, was groundbreaking, and *Twentieth-Century American Poetry* (2004), edited by Dana Gioia, David Mason, and Meg Schoerke, gathers statements on poetics from throughout the period.

Among the vibrant criticism on American fiction, Mark McGurl's *The Program Era* (2009) has been widely influential, documenting the rise and significance of the writing program since the 1930s. The book examines a host of writers in its capacious arguments about craft, multiculturalism, the university, and middlebrow reading. Mark Greif's *The Age of the Crisis of Man: Thought and Fiction in America, 1933–1973* (2015) sets a wide array of midcentury American writers and critics in the philosophical and political context of a mid-century sense of cultural "crisis." Min Hyoung Song's *The Children of 1965: On Writing, and Not Writing, as an Asian American* sets discussions of fiction by many American writers of East Asian or South Asian decent in a broad context of Asian American writing in the late twentieth century. His appendix, "Contemporary Asian American Literature 101," is indispensible as a resource, listing over a hundred works of contemporary literature by Asian American authors across genres of fiction, poetry, life writing, comics, and creative nonfiction. Loren Glass's *Counterculture Colophon: Grove Press, the Evergreen Review, and the Incorporation of the Avant-Garde* (2013) gives a detailed history of the literary environment of experiment and resistance to censorship in the 1960s through the story of Grove Press, influential publisher of many of the avant-garde American and European writers of the day. Dean Rader, in *Engaged Resistance: American Indian Art, Literature, and Film from Alcatraz to the NMAI* (2011), reads literature, film and visual art that puts Native authors such as Harjo, Silko, Erdrich, and Alexie in a broader aesthetic context. George Cotkin's *Feast of Excess: A Cultural History of the New Sensibility* (2016) documents the literary counterculture across genres in chronologically arranged chapters on an array of writers and artists from the early fifties through the early seventies, including short chapters on six authors in this volume. Broad overviews of drama in the period can be found in Sanford Sternlich's *A Reader's Guide to Modern American Drama* (2002), Thomas S. Hischak's *American Theatre: A Chronicle of Comedy and Drama, 1969–2000* (2001), Christopher Bigsby's *Contemporary American Playwrights* (1999), and Herbert Blau's *The Dubious Spectacle: Extremities of the Theater, 1976–2000* (2002).

American literary studies in the last decade has attempted to see American literature in a global and transnational context. This trend can be felt in many of the more recent critical works mentioned here, but a fine introduction to the central issues can be found in the collection *Globalizing*

American Studies (2010), edited by Brian T. Edwards and Dilip Parameshwar Gaonkar. A more reflective treatment about the contemporary situation of American literature among global readers can be found in Caroline Levander's thought-provoking *Where Is American Literature?* (2013).

While teachers and students of literature naturally focus on the written word, the period covered by this volume inspires many to consider the broader media landscape of the late twentieth and early twenty-first centuries as they seek to understand the literature of the time. A quartet of books provides a fine overview of the issues addressed by media studies, including insights from the rejuvenated field of the history of the book. These critical works do not refer to specific writers in this volume, but they abound in big, interesting ideas that will enliven consideration of the anthology's texts for teachers and students so inclined. See Lisa Nakamura, *Digitizing Race: Visual Cultures of the Internet* (2008), Matthew Kirschenbaum, *Mechanisms: New Media and the Forensic Imagination* (2008), Robert Darnton, *The Case for Books: Past, Present and Future* (2010), and Alan Liu, *The Laws of Cool: Knowledge Work and the Culture of Information* (2004). Liu and Darnton, widely admired critics of Romantic poetry and eighteenth-century French literature, respectively, are particularly helpful in thinking about literature's relationship to new forms of media. David Shields's provocative book, *Reality Hunger* (2010), offers a version of a manifesto for a wide range of work by creative nonfiction writers.

Many studies of American literature since 1945 have been motivated by the social and identity movements of the period and seek to document these in and through the history of American writing. Two important studies from a feminist perspective are Nancy J. Peterson's *Against Amnesia: Contemporary Women Writers and the Crisis of Historical Memory* (2001) and Linda S. Kauffman's *Bad Girls and Sick Boys: Fantasies in Contemporary Art and Culture* (1998). A feminist approach to the study of poetry can be found in *Gendered Modernisms: American Women Poets and Their Readers* (1996), edited by Margaret Dickie and Thomas Travisano. Multiculturalism concerns Martha J. Cutter in *Lost and Found in Translation: Contemporary Ethnic American Writing and the Politics of Language Diversity* (2005), Paula M. L. Moya in *Learning from Experience: Minority Identities, Multicultural Struggles* (2002), Robert Jackson in *Seeking the Region in American Literature and Culture* (2005). Multiculturalism in poetry is the subject of Satya Mohanty's *Literary Theory and the Claims of History: Postmodernism, Objectivity, and Multicultural Politics* (1997). African American writing is the focus in Bernard W. Bell's *The Contemporary African American Novel: Its Folk Roots and Modern Literary Branches* (2004), Cheryl A. Wall's *Worrying the Line: Black Women Writers, Lineage, and Literary Tradition* (2005), Suzanne W. Jones's *Race Mixing: Southern Fiction since the Sixties* (2004). *African American Theater: A Cultural Companion* (2008) by Gloria Dickerson covers its subject in a narrative manner. African American poetry is examined in Joanne Gabbin's *The Furious Flowering of African American Poetry* (1999) and Alden Lynn Nielsen's *Black Chant: Languages of African-American Postmodernism* (1992). Chicano/a work is treated by Charles M. Tatum in *Chicano Popular Culture* (2001), Mary Pat Brady in *Extinct Lands, Temporal Geographies: Chicana Literature and the Urgency of Space* (2002), Elisabeth Mermann-Jozwiak in *Postmodern Vernaculars: Chicana Literature and Postmodern Rhetoric* (2005), Tey Diana Rebolledo in *The Chronicles of Panchita Villa and Other Guerrilleras* (2005), Ramon Saldívar in *Chicano Narrative* (1990), and Ellie D. Hernandez in *Postnationalism in Chicana/o Literature and Culture* (2009). Deborah L. Madsen's *Understanding Contemporary Chicana Literature* (2000) examines the work of women poets.

Transnational Asian American Literature: Sites and Transits (2006), edited by Shirley Geok-lin Lim et al., includes essays covering issues from immigration to feminism and globalism. Xiaojing Zhou studies Asian American poetry in *The Ethics and Poetics of Alterity in Asian American Poetry* (2006). Arnold Krupat's *Red Matters: Native American Studies* (2002) looks beyond nationalism, indigenism, and cosmopolitanism to gauge Native American literature's importance to the ethical and intellectual heritage of the West. Catherine Rainwater's *Dreams of Fiery Stars: The Transformation of Native American Fiction* (1999) offers strong artistic analysis. John Lloyd Purdy's *Writing Indian, Native Conversations* (2009) combines criticism and interviews. Kenneth Lincoln's *Sing with the Heart of a Bear: Fusions of Native and American Poetry, 1890–1999* (1999) stresses poetry's flexible and adaptable nature rather than its conformity to rigid ethnic and literary categories. Robin Riley First's *The Heart Is a Drum: Continuance and Resistance in American Indian Poetry* (2000) provides cultural and historical readings of a wide range of poems.

Especially useful for understanding how and why contemporary writers produce their work is the critical interview. Larry McCaffery, with various coeditors, has produced a series of extensive dialogues with important authors of the past four decades: *Anything Can Happen* (1983), *Alive and Writing* (1987), *Across the Wounded Galaxies* (1990), and *Some Other Frequency* (1996). Individual bibliographies below routinely mention interview sources one may consult.

An increasing amount of high-quality material can be found online, including websites that offer audio versions of writers reading from their work. The Academy of American Poets' poets.org; the Poetry Foundation's poetryfoundation.org; and Penn Sound's website (writing.upenn.edu/pennsound) are the best general sites for poetry and including poems, biography, and troves of recordings and other resources. Over the years the *Paris Review* has conducted a series of interviews under the rubrics "Writers at Work" and "The Art of Fiction"; these include some of the most important writers of this period and are now available in full, and without cost, on the *Paris Review* website. The Internet Public Library offers "Native American Authors" at www.ipl.org/div/natam/. Post45.org offers a small stream of free access, curated critical essays, reviews, and occasional writer interviews on American literature and culture in the period.

AMERICAN LITERATURE SINCE 1945

Edward Abbey

A prolific writer, Abbey published numerous nonfiction works of environmental writing as well as eight novels. His most significant works remain *Desert Solitaire: A Season in the Wilderness* (1968; nonfiction) and his novel *The Monkey Wrench Gang* (1975), which has become, for some environmentalists, a sort of handbook for protest tactics. An anthology, *The Best of Edward Abbey*, appeared in 1988. His poetry is collected in *Earth Apples: The Poetry of Edward Abbey* (1994). Two volumes with selections from Abbey's journals are *A Voice Crying in the Wilderness: Notes from a Secret Journal* (1989) and *Confessions of a Barbarian: Selections from the Journals of Edward Abbey, 1951–1989* (1995). His selected letters can be found in *Postcards from Ed: Dispatches and Salvos from an American Iconoclast* (2006). *Edward Abbey: A Voice in the Wilderness* (1993), produced and directed by Eric Temple, is a documentary film about Abbey's life.

Among the critical discussions of Abbey's work are Anne Ronald's *The New West of Edward Abbey* (1982), John Cooley's edited collection, *Earthly Words: Essays on Contemporary American Nature and Environmental Writers* (1994), James I. McClintock's *Nature's Kindred Spirits: Aldo Leopold, Joseph Wood Krutch, Edward Abbey, Annie Dillard, and Gary Snyder* (1994), Peter Quigley's *Coyote in the Maze: Tracking Edward Abbey in a World of Words* (1998), and John M. Cahalan's important biography, *Edward Abbey: A Life* (2001).

Sherman Alexie

Alexie's novels are *Reservation Blues* (1995), *Indian Killer* (1996), *Flight: A Novel* (2007) and, for young adult readers, *The Absolutely True Diary of a Part-Time Indian* (2007; his best-known book) and *Radioactive Love Song* (2009). *Blasphemy: New and Selected Stories* (2013) offers a selection of his best stories from several previous collections alongside new ones. The stories in *The Lone Ranger and Tonto Fistfight in Heaven* (1993) were adapted as a film script for *Smoke Signals* in 1998. He both wrote and directed the movie *The Business of Fancydancing* (2000). He has published eleven poetry collections to date, beginning with *The Business of Fancydancing* (1992); his most recent is *Face* (2009).

Daniel Grassian provides critical analysis in *Understanding Sherman Alexie* (2005); an array of critical perspectives on his major works can be found in *Sherman Alexie: A Collection of Critical Essays* (2012), edited by Jeff Berglund and Jan Roush.

A. R. Ammons

Collections of Ammons's poetry include *A. R. Ammons: Selected Poems* (2006), *Collected Poems 1951–1971* (reissued in 2001), *Really Short Poems of A. R. Ammons* (1991), and *Selected Longer Poems* (1980). A collection of Ammons's essays and interviews, *Set in Motion*, appeared in 1996. A selection of his unpublished poems appeared in a special Ammons issue of *Chicago Review* (Summer/Autumn, 2012), alongside critical essays, an interview, historical materials, and an exhaustive bibliography of his work.

Critical discussions of his work can also be found in Helen Vendler's *The Music of What Happens* (1988), Robert Kirschten's edited *Critical Essays on A. R. Ammons* (1997), Steven P. Schneider's edited *Complexities of Motion: New Essays on A. R. Ammons' Long Poems* (1999), and Roger Gilbert and David Borak's edited *Considering the Radiance: Essays on the Poetry of A. R. Ammons* (2005).

Rudolfo Anaya

Anaya's best-known work is the novel *Bless Me, Ultima* (1972), but he has written many novels, ranging from autobiographical narratives to detective fiction, all centering on the hybrid Anglo-Mexican-Native cultures of New Mexico. He has also written several volumes of poetry, short stories, and young adult fiction.

Margarite Fernández Olmos provides a comprehensive study in *Rudolfo A. Anaya: A Critical Companion* (1999). Cesar A. Gonzales has prepared *A Sense of Place: Rudolfo A. Anaya, An Annotated Bio-Bibliography* (1999). The author's crime novels are studied by Ralph C. Rodriguez in *Brown Gumshoes: Detective Fiction and the Search for Chicano Identity* (2005).

Gloria Anzaldúa

Borderlands/La Frontera (1987), excerpted in this volume, includes memoir, historical analysis, and narrative poetry. Anzaldúa wrote in multiple genres throughout her career, authoring several novels for adults and for young readers, essays both autobiographical and theoretical, and short fiction. An influential cultural critic and feminist thinker, she edited *Making Face, Making Soul / Haciendo Caras: Creative and Critical Perspectives by Feminists of Color* (1990), and (with Cherríe Moraga) coedited the landmark collection *This Bridge Called My Back: Writings by adical Women of Color* (1981). In 2002 she coedited, with AnaLouise Keating, *This Bridge We Call Home: Radical Visions for*

Transformation. After Anzaldúa's death, AnaLouise Keating edited *The Gloria Anzaldúa Reader* (2009), which includes previously unpublished writing and offers a well-chosen selection of the author's work across the several genres in which she wrote.

Anzaldúa's ouvre is studied by Deborah L. Madsen in *Understanding Contemporary Chicana Literature* (2000), Sonia Sandivár-Hull in *Feminism on the Border: Chicana Politics and Literature* (2000), Paula M. L. Moya in *Learning from Experience: Minority Identities, Multicultural Struggles* (2002), Catrióna Rueda Esquibel in *With Her Machete in Her Hand: Reading Chicana Lesbians* (2006), and AnaLouise Keating in *Extremundos / Between Worlds* (2008).

John Ashbery

Ashbery's most discussed collections are *Some Trees* (1956; his first) and *Self-Portrait in a Convex Mirror* (1975). *Notes From the Air* (2007) is a selection of his later poems, and Ashbery is now represented in the Library of America series by *John Ashbery: Collected Poems 1956–87* (2008). Ashbery's Charles Eliot Norton Lectures on Poetry appear in *Other Traditions* (2000), and he has also published *Selected Prose* (2004).

Among useful critical essays are David Kalstone's *Five Temperaments* (1977) and John Shoptaw's book-length study of Ashbery's poetry, *On the Outside Looking Out* (1994). David K. Kermani's *John Ashbery: A Comprehensive Bibliography* (1975) is indispensable and amusing. See also *Beyond Amazement: New Essays on John Ashbery* (1980), edited by David Lehman, Charles Altieri's *Postmodernisms Now* (1998), John Emil Vincent's *John Ashbery and You: His Later Books* (2007). Ben Hickman's *John Ashbery and English Poetry* (2012) revises the critical tendency to read Ashbery as exclusively an American or a postmodern poet, showing his work's connections to canonical English poets such as Donne, Marvell, Clare, Wordsworth, and Auden Jesse Zuba's chapter on *Some Trees* in *The First Book: Twentieth-Century Poetic Careers in America* (2016) examines how Ashbery's poetry first found its audience. Michael Clune's brilliant essay on Ashbery, "'Whatever Charms Is Alien': John Ashbery's Everything" (*Criticism*, summer 2008) offers a way to think about the difficulty of reading Ashbery by relating it to science fiction.

James Baldwin

Baldwin published novels, short stories, essays, and plays throughout his career, but is best known for the early novel *Go Tell It on the Mountain* (1953) and for his politically charged essays, especially *The Fire Next Time* (1963). His literary critical essay on Stowe's *Uncle Tom's Cabin*, "Everybody's Protest Novel" (1949) is widely taught. His prose has been gathered in three Library of America volumes: *Early Novels and Stories* (1998), *Later Novels* (2015), and *Collected Essays* (1998, edited by Toni Morrison). Baldwin's nonfiction has been also been gathered as *Collected Essays* (1998) and *The Cross of Redemption* (2010).

Critical and popular interest in Baldwin has blossomed since the turn of the century. The first biography, James Campbell's *Talking at the Gates: A Life of James Baldwin* (1991), is now supplemented by Magdalena J. Zaborowska's *James Baldwin's Turkish Decade: Erotics of Exile* (2009); by Herb Boyd's *Baldwin's Harlem: A Biography of James Baldwin* (2008), which tells the story of Baldwin's life through his relationships with other Harlem writers of his time, including Langston Hughes, Malcolm X, and Countee Cullen; by Hilton Als's exceptional essay about Baldwin for the *New Yorker*, "The Enemy Within: The Making and Unmaking of James Baldwin" (February 16, 1998); and by stand-alone biographical essays included in the many recent collections of critical essays on his work. Criticism has embraced various topics in Baldwin's work, including his religious themes, gay life and queer sexuality, transnational contexts, and his interest in performance and drama. Selected criticism would inclue: Lynn Orilla Scott's *James Baldwin's Later Fiction: Witness to the Journey* (2002), Clarence E. Hardy III's *James Baldwin's God: Sex, Hope and Crisis in Black Holiness Culture* (2003), D. Quentin Miller's edited collection of essays, *Reviewing James Baldwin: Things Not Seen* (2000), D. Quentin Miller, *"A Criminal Power": James Baldwin and the Law* (2012); *James Baldwin: America and Beyond* (2012), edited by Cora Kaplan and Bill Schwarz (an exceptional collection of essays by major writers and critics), and *James Baldwin Now* (1999), edited by Dwight McBride. Several works on Baldwin by critic Douglas Field include *A Historical Guide to James Baldwin* (2010), edited by Field, which lays out the state of what might be called "Baldwin Studies"; Field's introduction to Baldwin, *James Baldwin* (2011); and his recent analytical and historical essays on Baldwin in *All Those Strangers: The Art and Lives of James Baldwin* (2015). Consuela Francis, *The Critical Reception of James Baldwin, 1963–2010* (2014) reveals the changing understanding of Baldwin's work over the course of his career and beyond. The most recent overview of the field, useful for teaching, is *The Cambridge Companion to James Baldwin* (2015).

Toni Cade Bambara

Bambara's novel *The Salt Eaters* was published in 1980 and won the American Book award as well as other prizes and remains her best-known work. Bambara wrote two collections of short stories, and, in the 1970s and 1980s, numerous screenplays, including an adaption of Toni Morrison's *The Tar Baby* (1984) and a treatment of writer Zora Neale Hurston, *Zora* (1971). She edited the anthologies *The Black Woman* (1970), *Tales and Stories for Black Folks* (1971, for children), and (with Leah Wise) *Southern Black Utterances Today* (1975). *Deep Sightings and Rescue Missions: Fiction, Essays, and Conversations* (1996) is a posthumous collection of Bambara's later work, edited by Toni Morrison. Thabiti Lewis's edited collection of interviews, *Conversations with Toni Cade Bambara* (2012) gives a comprehensive sense of her connections to other writers from the late 1960s onward, and an overview of her perspectives on literary history, writers of color, feminism, and politics (she was an unapologetic Marxist).

A *Joyous Revolt* (2014), by Linda Janet Holmes, is the first comprehensive biography, complemented by Holmes and Cheryl A. Wall's edited collection on Bambara's legacy and influence, *Savoring the Salt* (2007), which includes essays by poets, scholars, writers, activists, and filmmakers to whom her work was important. Critical analyses of Bambara's work are found in Philip Page's *Reclaiming Community in Contemporary African American Fiction* (1999), Elliott Butler-Evans's *Race, Gender, and Desire: Narrative Strategies in the Fiction of Toni Cade Bambara, Toni Morrison, and Alice Walker* (1989), and Robert H. Cataliotti's *The Songs Became the Stories: The Music in African American Fiction 1970–2005* (2007).

Amiri Baraka (LeRoi Jones)

In addition to his poetry and plays, Baraka authored four books on music: *Blues People* (1963), *Black Music* (1968), and *The Music: Reflections on Jazz and Blues* (1987), and *Digging: The Afro-American Soul of American Classical Music* (2009). His essays are collected in *Home* (1966), *Raise Race Rays Raze* (1971), and *Selected Plays and Prose of Amiri Baraka / LeRoi Jones* (1979). Baraka edited three important anthologies: *The Moderns* (1963), *Black Fire* (1968, with Larry Neal), and *Confirmation: An Anthology of African American Women* (1983), with Amina Baraka. In 1984 he published *The Autobiography of LeRoi Jones / Amiri Baraka*.

Early but still useful studies are *Baraka: The Renegade and the Mask* (1976) by Kimberly W. Benston and *Amiri Baraka / LeRoi Jones: The Quest for a "Populist Modernism"* (1978) by Werner Sollors. William J. Harris has written *The Poetry and Poetics of Amiri Baraka: The Jazz Aesthetic* (1985) and edited *The LeRoi Jones / Amiri Baraka Reader* (1991), supplying introductory literary history and a bibliography. Ross Posnock's *Color and Culture* (1998) locates the author's thought in the context of other writers and thinkers of color. On the relationship between Baraka's art and politics, see Jerry Gafio Watt's *Amiri Baraka: The Politics and Art of a Black Intellectual* (2001), Komozi Woodard's *A Nation Within a Nation: Amiri Baraka (LeRoi Jones) and Black Power Politics*, and Harry J. Elam's *Taking It to the Streets: The Social Protest Theater of Luis Valdez and Amiri Baraka* (1997). *Amiri Baraka and Edward Dorn: The Collected Letters* (2013) documents the extraordinary interracial epistolary friendship between these two avant-garde poets from the end of the 1950s to the middle of the 1960s. In the wake of Baraka's death in January of 2014, the journal *Callaloo* (Summer, 2014) published a cluster of essays on Baraka's legacy, as did the journal *Transition* (no. 114, 2014). Biography can be gleaned from these sources and his autobiography, and may be complemented by the memoir from Baraka's first wife, Hettie Cohen, *How I Became Hettie Jones* (1990).

Donald Barthelme

While best known as a writer of short stories, Barthelme wrote four novels, a children's book, and *Sam's Bar* (1987), which provides a narrative for adult cartoons by Seymour Chwast. Kim Hertingzer edited *The Teachings of Don B.: Satires, Parodies, Fables, Illustrated Stories, and Plays of Donald Barthelme* (1992), many of which were omitted from Barthelme's own collections, and *Not Knowing: The Essays and Interviews of Donald Barthelme* (1997).

Stanley Trachtenberg's *Understanding Donald Barthelme* (1990) is a sound introduction, while Maurice Couturier and Régis Durand's *Donald Barthelme* (1982) offers a superb explication of Barthelme's literary theory. Jerome Klinkowitz examines the author's entire canon in *Donald Barthelme: An Exhibition* (1991) and provides a primary and secondary bibliography. *Critical Essays on Donald Barthelme* (1992), edited by Richard Patteson, offers a variety of readings of his work. Tracey Daugherty's *Hiding Man: A Biography of Donald Barthelme* (2009) is historically comprehensive and critically acute.

Ann Beattie

Beattie's novels and story collections are supplemented by her writing on the visual arts. She wrote a critical study of the painter Alex Katz (1987) and collaborated with the photographer Bob Adelman on *Americana* (1992). Her *Spectacles* (1985) is for children. Barbara Ann Schapiro studies Beattie's fiction in the company of work by John Updike and Toni Morrison in *Literature and the Representational Self* (1994). A broad sampling of critical opinion distinguishes Jaye Berman Montressor's *The Critical Reaction to Ann Beattie* (1993). Beattie's interviews are collected in *Conversations with Ann Beattie* (2007), edited by Dawn Trouard.

Saul Bellow
Bellow was the author of fourteen novels and novellas starting with *Dangling Man* (1944), ending with *Ravelstein* (2000). His short stories appear in three collections; these are joined by an additional story in the comprehensive *Collected Stories* (2001). A play, *The Last Analysis*, was produced in New York in 1964 and published the following year. *To Jerusalem and Back* (1976) is a personal account of his activities in Israel. *It All Adds Up* (1994) draws on Bellow's essays dating back to 1948. In 2010 Bellow's *Letters* appeared, edited by Benjamin Taylor. Selected interviews from 1953 to 1991 are collected in *Conversations with Saul Bellow* (1995; edited by Gloria Cronin and Ben Siegel).

James Atlas's *Bellow: A Biography* (2000) is exhaustive yet critically focused. Malcolm Bradbury provides the best concise introduction to this author's major work in *Saul Bellow* (1982), while in *Saul Bellow: Drumlin Woodchuck* (1980) fellow writer Mark Harris offers an insightful portrait of Bellow as a professional figure. John J. Clayton's *Saul Bellow: In Defense of Man* (1979) celebrates the author's stressfully tested humanism, while Ellen Pifer's *Saul Bellow: Against the Grain* (1990) argues for his culturally atypical belief in the transcendent soul, as does M. A. Quayum's *Saul Bellow and American Transcendentalism* (2004). Gender is Gloria L. Cronin's focus in *A Room of His Own: In Search of the Feminine in the Novels of Saul Bellow* (2001). In *Saul Bellow: Vision and Revision* (1984) Daniel Fuchs examines manuscripts and letters to establish Bellow's Dostoyevskian engagement with issues of character. Julia Eichelberger sums up his work in *Prophets of Recognition* (1999). The essays in *A Political Companion to Saul Bellow* (2013; edited by Gloria Cronin and Lee Trepanier) consider political themes in Bellow's work and present Bellow as a political thinker as he evolved from Troskyism to neoconservatism over the decades of his career. Bellow figures importantly in Mark Greif's *The Age of the Crisis of Man: Thought and Fiction in America, 1933–1973* (2015), as a writer focused on "the crisis of man" and as

the one-time housemate of Ralph Ellison.

John Berryman
Berryman's *Collected Poems: 1937–1971* appeared in 1991; *John Berryman: Selected Poems*, in 2004. Berryman's critical biography, *Stephen Crane*, appeared in 1950, and a collection of his short fiction and literary essays was issued under the title *The Freedom of the Poet* (1976). Berryman's unfinished novel about his alcoholism, *Recovery*, appeared in 1973. *Berryman's Shakespeare: Essays, Letters, and Other Writings by John Berryman* (2001, edited by John Haffenden) presents a substantial selection of work from Berryman's unfinished critical and biographical project on Shakespeare.

Valuable critical introductions to Berryman's poetry can be found in Helen Vendler's *The Given and the Made* (1995) and Thomas Travisano's *Midcentury Quartet* (1999). Paul Mariani's *Dream Song: The Life of John Berryman* (1996) and Eileen Simpson's *Poets in Their Youth* (1982) are useful biographical studies. Tom Rogers's *God of Rescue: John Berryman and Christianity* (2010) documents Berryman's lifelong engagement with religion.

Frank Bidart
Frank Bidart has published nine volumes of poetry; the first three are collected in *In the Western Night: Collected Poems, 1965–1990* (1990). Criticism of Bidart's work does not abound: the only collection of critical essays available to date is *On Frank Bidart: Fastening the Voice to the Page* (2007) edited by Liam Rector and Tree Swenson. Two stand-alone articles are worth finding: Langdon Hammer's "Frank Bidart and the Tone of Contemporary Poetry" in *Southwest Review* 87.1 (2002), and Dan Chiasson's "Presence: Frank Bidart" in *Raritan* 20.4 (2001). Useful interviews with the poet include "Frank Bidart—An Interview (with Mark Halliday)," *Ploughshares* 9.1 (1983), and "An Interview with Frank Bidart," Andrew Rathmann, Danielle Allen, and Frank Bidart, *Chicago Review* 47.3 (Fall 2001).

Elizabeth Bishop
Bishop's poems are available in *The Complete Poems 1927–1979* (1983). *The Collected Prose* (1984) includes memoirs and stories, especially the memory-based story "In the Village," invaluable for a reading of her poems. A remarkable selection of Bishop's correspondence, *One Art* (1994), was edited by her friend and publisher, Robert Giroux, and *Words in the Air: The Complete Correspondence between Elizabeth Bishop and Robert Lowell* (2008), edited by Thomas Travisano and Saskia Hamilton, documents one of the

great literary friendships in twentieth-century poetry. Her correspondence with editors at the *New Yorker*, offering a glimpse into the contemporary publishing world, is collected in *Elizabeth Bishop and* The New Yorker (2011). Reproductions of Bishop's watercolor paintings appear in *Exchanging Hats* (1996). Alice Quinn edited *Edgar Allan Poe & The Juke-Box: Uncollected Poems, Drafts, and Fragments* (2006). Bishop also translated from the Portuguese *The Diary of Helena Morley* (1957, 1977, 1991), an enchanting memoir of provincial life in Brazil.

Critical study of Bishop has been steady and robust in the last twenty years, showing no sign of abatement. Useful critical essays on Bishop appear in Seamus Heaney's *The Redress of Poetry* (1995), Lorrie Glodensohn's *Elizabeth Bishop: The Biography of a Poetry* (1992), and David Kalstone's *Becoming a Poet* (1989). *Elizabeth Bishop and Her Art*, edited by Lloyd Schwartz and Sybil P. Estess (1983), includes two interviews as well as essays. A provocative essay on Bishop appears in Adrienne Rich's *Blood, Bread, and Poetry* (1986). The novelist Colm Tóibín offers a personal view of Bishop's writing and its meaning for his own life and work in *On Elizabeth Bishop* (2015). Among the most valuable of the many critical studies are Brett C. Miller's important biography, *Elizabeth Bishop: Life and the Memory of It* (1993); *Elizabeth Bishop: The Geography of Gender* (1993), a collection of essays edited by Marilyn Lombardi; *Conversations with Elizabeth Bishop* (1996), edited by George Monteiro; and Thomas Travisano's *Midcentury Quartet* (1999). Candace MacMahon's *Elizabeth Bishop: A Bibliography* (1980) is indispensable. A dual biography of Bishop and the Brazilian architect Lota de Macedo Soares, Bishop's romantic partner from 1951 to 1967, can be found in Carmen Oliviera's *Rare and Commonplace Flowers: The Story of Elizabeth Bishop and Lota de Macedo Soares* (2003); the book was a best seller in Brazil, where the couple met and made their home, and it offers invaluable Brazilian context for the poems Bishop wrote during these years. Peggy Samuels's *Deep Skin: Elizabeth Bishop and Visual Art* (2010) documents the relationship between Bishop's poetry and her involvement with the museum world of the 1930s and '40s. *The Cambridge Companion to Elizabeth Bishop* (2014), edited by Angus Cleghorn and Jonathan Ellis, gives a fine overview of critical issues and resources. *Elizabeth Bishop in the Twenty-First Century: Reading the New Editions* (2012), edited by Angus Cleghorn, Bethany Hicok, and Thomas Travisano, collects critical essays that take into account recent developments in archival studies of Bishop's work. These developments

are reflected in the 2011 editions of her poetry and prose published by Farrar, Straus and Giroux, in celebration of the centenary of her birth.

Gwendolyn Brooks

Brooks wrote twelve stand-alone collections of poetry, starting with *A Street in Bronzeville* in 1945. Many of these poems are collected in *Selected Poems* (1999), *The Essential Gwendolyn Brooks* (2005), and the *Gwendolyn Brooks CD Poetry Collection* (2005). She also wrote two prose autobiographies, *Report from Part One* (1972) and *Report from Part Two* (1996).

Other useful biographical material appears in *A Life Distilled*, edited by M. K. Mootry and others, and George E. Kent's *A Life of Gwendolyn Brooks* (1990). Valuable discussions of Brooks's poetry appear in *Black Women Writers (1950–1980)*, edited by Mari Evans (1984). Stephen Wright's *On Gwendolyn Brooks: Reliant Contemplation* (1996), Harold Bloom's *Gwendolyn Brooks* (2000), and Martha E. Rhynes's *Gwendolyn Brooks: Poet from Chicago* (2003) are recent critical studies. An interview with Brooks appears in Janet Mullaney's *Truthtellers of the Times: Interviews with Contemporary Women Poets* (1998). Brooks and Gloria Jean Wade Gayles published *Conversations with Gwendolyn Brooks* (2002). Passages on Brooks in Lawrence Jackson's magisterial account of African American literary culture at midcentury, *The Indignant Generation: A Narrative History of African American Writers and Critics, 1934–1960*, place Brooks in the context of her times.

Raymond Carver

Principal collections of Carver's extensive short fiction are *Put Yourself in My Shoes* (1974), *Will You Please Be Quiet, Please?* (1976), *Furious Seasons* (1977), *What We Talk About When We Talk About Love* (1981), *The Pheasant* (1982), *Cathedral* (1983), and *Where I'm Calling From* (1988). *Fires* (1983) is a sampling of essays, poems, and narratives. Carver's uncollected work has been edited by William L. Stull as *No Heroics, Please* (1991), expanded as *Call If You Need Me* (2000). The Library of America's *Collected Stories* (2009), edited by William L. Stull and Maureen P. Carroll, includes drafts of stories before changes were introduced by his long-time editor, Gordon Lish. A fine introduction to the controversies surrounding Lish's extensive editing of Carver's fiction can be found in "Rough Crossings: The Cutting of Raymond Carver," the *New Yorker*, December 24, 2007, by Simon Armitage, available online through the *New Yorker*'s web archives. Throughout his career Carver published poetry as well, the bulk of which appears in several volumes from *Near Klamath* (1968) to *A New Path to the Waterfall* (1989); *All of Us* (1998) collects all his poems.

Arthur M. Saltzman's *Understanding Raymond Carver* (1988) looks beyond the author's apparent realism, as does Randolph Runyon's *Reading Raymond Carver* (1992). Carver's return to traditionalism is celebrated by Kirk Nesset in *The Stories of Raymond Carver* (1995). Editors Sandra Lee Kleppe and Robert Miltner present a wide variety of critical commentaries in *New Paths to Raymond Carver* (2008). Sam Halpert sifts through comments by Carver's associates in *Raymond Carver: An Oral Biography* (1995). The standard biography is *Raymond Carver: A Writer's Life* (2009) by Carol Sklenicka. Important interviews with Carver are collected in *Conversations with Raymond Carver* (1990), edited by Marshall Bruce Genry and William L. Stull.

John Cheever

Cheever's seven volumes of short stories, which appeared between 1943 and 1973, are assembled in *The Stories of John Cheever* (1978); *The Uncollected Stories of John Cheever* appeared posthumously in 1988. Two Library of America volumes of his work, both edited by Blake Bailey, collect the complete novels and "collected stories and other writings." *The Letters of John Cheever*, edited by his son, Benjamin Cheever, was published in 1988. *The Journals of John Cheever* (1991) was edited by Robert Gottlieb.

Biographies include Scott Donaldson's *John Cheever* (1988) and Blake Bailey's well-researched and engaging *Cheever: A Life* (2009). *Home before Dark* (1984), by his daughter, Susan Cheever, is a personal memoir. Francis J. Bosha has edited *The Critical Response to John Cheever* (1994). Samuel Chase Coale provides an overview in *John Cheever* (1977), while George W. Hunt explores religious dimensions in *John Cheever: The Hobgoblin Company of Love* (1983). The stories are given close study by James Eugene O'Hara in *John Cheever: A Study of the Short Fiction* (1989) and in *John Cheever* (2004), Harold Bloom's edited collection of criticism in the Chelsea House series "Bloom's Major Short Story Writers."

Sandra Cisneros

The House on Mango Street (1984) has been described as both interrelated short stories and a novel, whereas *Woman Hollering Creek* (1991) collects more evidently independent short stories. *Caramello* (2002) is an epic novel telling a multigenerational family story that entwines with major developments of twentieth-century American history. Cisneros has published two major collections of poetry, *My Wicked Wicked Ways* (1987) and *Loose Woman* (1994). Her *Hairs/Pelitos* (1994), written in English and accompanied by a Spanish text translated by Liliana Valenzuela, and *Have You Seen Marie?* (2012), illustrated by Ester Hernández, are narratives for children.

Recent studies on late-twentieth-century fiction show Cisneros's importance to creative writing programs and the later evolution of the Chicano literature movements; see sections on Cisneros in Mark McGurl, *The Program Era* (2009) and John Alba Cutler, *Ends of Assimilation: The Formation of Chicano Literature* (2015). Jean Wyatt's *Risking Difference* (2004) focuses on *Women Hollering Creek*, as do the essays edited by Cecilia Donahue in *Sandra Cisneros's Women Hollering Creek* (2010). Ramón Saldívar discusses Cisneros's fiction in *Chicano Narrative* (1990), as do Tey Diana Rebolledo in *Women Singing in the Snow* (1995) and Sonia Saldívar-Hull in *Feminism on the Border* (2000). *Class Definitions: On the Lives and Writings of Maxine Hong Kingston, Sandra Cisneros, and Dorothy Allison* (2008), by Michelle M. Tokarczyk, provides a comparative perspective. *Border Crossings and Beyond: The Life and Works of Sandra Cisneros* by Carmen Hydée Rivera (2009) combines critical and biographical approaches. An extensive dialogue with her appears in *Interviews with Writers of the Post-Colonial World* (1992), edited by Feroza Jussawalla and Reed Way Dasenbrock.

Lucille Clifton

Clifton's poetry is now gathered in *The Collected Poems of Lucille Clifton, 1965–2010* (2012), edited by Kevin Young and Michael S. Glaser. Her memoir, *Generations* (1976), provides a valuable context for her work. Clifton published over twenty books for children during the course of her career. Critical discussions of her work include Hilary Holiday's *Wild Blessings: The Poetry of Lucille Clifton* (2004). Mary Jane Lupton has published *Lucille Clifton: Her Life and Letters* (2006).

Billy Collins

Among the many collections of Collins's poetry it is useful to begin with his two volumes of selected poems: *Sailing Alone Around the World: New and Selected Poems* (2001), and *Aimless Love: New and Selected Poems* (2013). *The Best Cigarette* (1997), an audiobook, provides a chance to hear Collins reading thirty-three of his poems. He selected and introduced the anthologies *Poetry 180: A*

Turning Back to Poetry (2003) and *180 More: Extraordinary Poems for Everyday Life* (2005). One can find more occasional prose by Collins (anthology introductions, forewords, etc.) and interviews than criticism of his work, attesting to his popularity among a wide audience of readers and, perhaps, the relative simplicity of his poetry, which seems not to cry out for explication. Nevertheless, some critical discussion of Collins's work can be found in David Baker's *Heresy and the Ideal: On Contemporary Poetry* (2000).

Edwidge Danticat

Danticat has published both fiction and nonfiction. Her nonfiction works include *After the Dance: A Walk Through Carnival in Jacmel, Haiti* (2002) and *Brother, I'm Dying* (2007). She also edited *The Butterfly's Way: Voices from the Haitian Dyaspora in the United States* (2003). Her fiction includes *Krik? Krak!* (1996), *The Farming of Bones* (1998), and *The Dew Breaker* (1994), as well as the young adult novels *Breath, Eyes, Memory* (1994), *Behind the Mountains* (2002), and *Anacaona: Golden Flower, Haiti, 1490* (2005). A video, audio, and print transcript of her 2011 interview on Democracy Now, "The Immigrant Artist at Work," can be found on the program's website www.democracynow.org.

Critical discussion of Danticat's work can be found in Meredith M. Gadsby's *Sucking Salt: Caribbean Women Writers, Migration, and Survival* (2006). *Edwidge Danticat: A Reader's Guide* (2010), edited by Martin Munro, offers an appreciative collection of analytic, biographical, contextual, and reflective essays (these last by writers who know or have been influenced by Danticat), and includes interview materials.

Lydia Davis

Davis's story collections through 2009 are compiled in *The Collected Stories of Lydia Davis* (2009); she has published additional collections since. Her translations include Maurice Blanchot *The Gaze of Orpheus and Other Literary Essays* (1981); Michel Leiris, *The Rules of the Game: Scratches* (1997); Marcel Proust, *Swann's Way* (2004); Vivant Denon, *No Tomorrow* (2009); and Gustave Flaubert, *Madame Bovary* (2010). Davis's stand-alone essay on translation was written for the Center for Writers and Translators: *Proust, Blanchot, and a Women in Red* (2007).

A useful critical introduction can be found in Kasia Boddy, "Lydia Davis" in *The Columbia Companion to the Twentieth-Century American Short Story* (2004), edited by Blanche H. Gelfant and Lawrence Graver. Marjorie Perloff discusses Davis's experimentalism in "Fiction as Language Game: The Hermeneutic Parables of Lydia Davis and Maxine Chernoff" in *Breaking the Sequence: Women's Experimental Fiction* (2014). James Wood's essay on the occasion of the publication of the *Collected Stories* gives an excellent introduction to the author and an overview of Davis's work to that point: "Songs of Myself," the *New Yorker* (October 19, 2009).

Don DeLillo

In addition to his many novels, DeLillo has written several plays and occasional essays. Of particular interest among the latter is "In the Ruins of the Future, Reflections on Terror, Loss, and Time in the Shadow of September 11," published in *Harper's*, December 2001. DeLillo's interviews are gathered in *Conversations with Don DeLillo*, edited by Thomas DePietro (2005).

Overviews useful for teaching *White Noise* include *The Cambridge Companion to Don DeLillo* (2007; edited by John N. Duvall); the short reader's guide, *White Noise* (2003) by Leonard Orr; *Approaches to Teaching DeLillo's White Noise* (2007), edited by John Duvall and Tim Engles; *New Essays on White Noise* (1991), edited by Frank Lentricchia; and *White Noise: Text and Criticism* (1998), edited by Mark Osteen. Significant monograph studies on DeLillo include Mark Osteen's *American Magic and Dread: Don DeLillo's Dialogue with Culture* (2000); David Cowart's *DeLillo's Physics of Language* (revised edition, 2003); and Peter Boxall's *Don DeLillo: The Possibility of Fiction* (2004). Religion has been a dominant topic of critical interest: see Jesse Kavadlo, *Don DeLillo: Balance at the Edge of Belief* (2004); John McClure's *Partial Faiths: Postsecular Fiction in the Age of Pynchon and Morrison* (2010); Amy Hungerford's *Postmodern Belief: American Literature and Religion since 1960* (2010), which discusses DeLillo's Catholicism; Mark C. Taylor, *Rewiring the Real: In Conversation with William Gaddis, Richard Powers, Mark Danielewski, and Don DeLillo* (2013) two excellent and well-maintained free websites offer updated bibliographies and myriad other materials; see "DeLillo's America" and the website of the Don DeLillo Society.

Junot Díaz

Drown (1996) collects Díaz's short stories; his two novels to date are *The Brief Wondrous Life of Oscar Wao* (2007) and *This Is How You Lose Her* (2012).

Jacquelyn Loss studies Díaz's fiction in *Latino and Latina Writers* (2003), edited by Alan West-Durán, as do Raphael Dalleo and Elena Machado Sáez in *The Latino/a Canon and the Emergence of a Post-Sixties Literature*

(2007). Díaz's cultural context is examined by Lucia Suarez in *The Tears of Hispaniola: Haitian and Dominican Diaspora Memory* (2006). Díaz is an exceptionally sharp critic himself, and has granted many interviews; these are essential reading alongside his fiction. Online searches will easily turn up material suitable for teaching. Of particular interest are his interviews with Edwidge Danticat, available online and also print in *BOMB: The Author Interviews* (2014), edited by Betsy Sussler, and with Taryne Jade Taylor in *Paradoxa 26* ("A Singular Dislocation: An Interview with Junot Díaz," "SF Now").

Philip K. Dick
Dick is the author of dozens of novels and over a hundred short stories. His most widely read novel is *Do Androids Dream of Electric Sheep* (1968).

The definitive biography is Lawrence Sutin's *Divine Invasions: A Life of Philip K. Dick* (2005). Eric Link's *Understanding Philip K. Dick* (2010) gives a critical overview; a focused in-depth study can be found in Umberto Rossi, *The Twisted Worlds of Philip K. Dick: A Reading of Ontologically Uncertain Novels* (2011). Useful essays that set Dick's work in a larger context include N. Katherine Hayles's chapter on Dick in *How We Became Posthuman: Virtual Bodies in Cybernetics, Literature, and Informatics* (1999); Frederic Jameson's two essays on Dick in *Archaeologies of the Future: The Desire Called Utopia and Other Science Fictions* (2005); and Erik Davis's discussion of Dick in *TechGnosis: Myth, Magic, and Mysticism in the Age of Information* (2015).

James Dickey
Dickey's poetry is available in individual collections, in several volumes of selected poems, and, recently, in *The Complete Poems of James Dickey* (2013), edited by Ward Briggs, with a foreword by Richard Howard. Dickey's literary criticism and autobiographical collections include *The Suspect in Poetry* (1964), *Babel to Byzantium* (1968), *Self-Interviews* (1970), *Sorties: Journals and New Essays* (1971), and *The Poet Turns on Himself* (1982). *A James Dickey Reader*, edited by Henry Hart, appeared in 1999, offering a curated collection of these materials. His novels *Deliverance* and *Alnilam* were published in 1970 and 1987, respectively.

Gordon Van Ness edited *The One Voice of James Dickey: His Letters and Life, 1942–1969* (2003). *Elements: Novels of James Dickey* (2002), by Casey Clabough, traces the evolution of Dickey's novels, including an examination of unpublished screenplays, manuscript materials, and notes. *The Imagination as Glory* (1984), edited by Bruce Weigl and T. R.

Hummer, Robert Kirschten's *Struggling for Wings: The Art of James Dickey* (1997), and Henry Hart's *James Dickey: The World as Lie* (2000) offer critical perspectives on his work. *Reading, Learning, Teaching James Dickey* (2008), by William B. Thesing, Dickey's long-time colleague at the University of South Carolina, is a helpful guide to Dickey's life and the themes of his poetry, aimed at classroom use. Thesing has also edited, with Theda Wrede, *The Way We Read James Dickey: Critical Approaches for the Twenty-First Century* (2011). *The Ecological Poetics of James Dickey* (2013) explores Dickey's interest in landscape and nature through the lenses of philosophy, psychology and religion.

Joan Didion
Didion's long and varied career as a writer includes works of both fiction and nonfiction as well as multiple screenplays. Among her nonfiction volumes it is helpful to start with *We Tell Ourselves Stories in Order to Live: Collected Nonfiction* (2006) and and *Vintage Didion* (2004). Her creative nonfiction memoir, *The Year of Magical Thinking*, appeared in 2005. Two interviews with Didion have appeared in the *Paris Review*, one in 1978; a second, "The Art of Nonfiction" (2006), is available online at www.parisreview.org.

Critical discussion of Didion's work can be found in James N. Still's "The Minimal Self: Joan Didion's Journalism of Survival" in *Literary Selves: Autobiography and Contemporary American Nonfiction* (1993), Doug Underwood's *Journalism and the Novel: Truth and Fiction, 1700–2000* (2008), and Steven Belletto and Daniel Grausam's edited collection, *American Literature in an Age of Cold War: A Critical Reassessment* (2012). A general introduction to her work can be found in *Reading Joan Didion* (2009), by Lynn Marie Houston and William Lombardi. *The Last Love Song* (2015), by Tracy Daugherty, is the first full-length biography of Didion.

Annie Dillard
Dillard's nonfiction ranges from autobiography and meditations on nature and philosophy to literary criticism and essays about writing and writers.

Nancy C. Parrish provides a critical biography in *Lee Smith, Annie Dillard, and the Hollins Group* (1998), setting Dillard in the institutional context of Hollins, a southern women's college, among a distinguished group of women writers who emerge from the college in the mid-sixties. Dillard figures importantly in Lawrence Buell's field-defining book, *The Environmental Imagination: Thoreau, Nature Writing, and the Formation of American Culture* (1996), and in most subsequent surveys of American eco-critical writing. Still useful for its insights on Dillard's first major books is Sandra Humble Johnson's *The Space Between: Literary Epiphany in the Works of Annie Dillard* (1982). Dillard's position in literary history is assessed by Sue Yore in *The Mystic Way in Postmodernity* (2009). Colleen Warren argues for a theological understanding of Dillard's work in *Annie Dillard and the Word Made Flesh: An Incarnational Theory of Language* (2010); in general, essays on Dillard's connection to religion and mysticism have established a trend in recent treatments of her work.

Rita Dove

Dove has published eight volumes of poetry; a collection of fiction, *Fifth Sunday* (1985); a novel, *Through the Ivory Gate* (1992); plays; and a valuable collection of essays, *The Poet's World* (1995). *Conversations with Rita Dove*, edited by Earl G. Ingersol, appeared in 2003.

Therese Steffen's critical study *Crossing Color: Transcultural Space and Place in Rita Dove's Poetry, Fiction, and Drama* appeared in 2001; Malin Pereira's *Rita Dove's Cosmopolitanism*, in 2003, places Dove in the context of the aftermath of the Black Arts movement; and Pat Righelato's *Understanding Rita Dove* (2006) offers an overview of her whole body of work.

Ralph Ellison

In his lifetime Ellison published three books: a novel, *Invisible Man* (1952), and two volumes of essays, *Shadow and Act* (1964) and *Going to the Territory* (1986). The latter materials are combined with other nonfiction in *The Collected Essays of Ralph Ellison* (1995), edited by John F. Callahan with a preface by Saul Bellow. Fragments of his novel in progress are noted in the bibliography to Mark Busby's *Ralph Ellison* (1991) in the Twayne United States Authors series; *Flying Home and Other Stories* (1997) gathers thirteen short stories written between 1937 and 1954, six of which were previously unpublished. In 1999 Callahan, as Ellison's literary executor, drew on manuscripts to assemble *Juneteenth* as a posthumous novel, a fuller version of which is presented by Callahan and editor Adam Bradley as *Three Days Before the Shooting . . .* (2010). Robert G. O'Meally edited *Living with Music: Ralph Ellison's Jazz Writings* (2001). *Trading Twelves: The Selected Letters of Ralph Ellison and Albert Murray*, edited by Murray and Callahan, appeared in 2000.

In the last decade several major critics have turned their attention to Ellison. Tracking their footnotes will provide readers with citations for earlier works of criticism. Ross Posnock's edited volume, *The Cambridge Companion to Ralph Ellison* (2006), provides an overview of the texts and the scholarship. Arnold Rampersand's *Ralph Ellison* (2007) is a comprehensive biography. The author's lifelong growth is measured by Adam Bradley in *Ralph Ellison in Progress* (2010). Timothy Parrish's *Ralph Ellison and the Genius of America* (2012) argues against the version of Ellison Rampersad presents, recasting Ellison as an intellectual whose thinking drove the civil rights movement and intersected with that of figures such as Philip Roth; the historian of slavery, C. Vann Woodward; Martin Luther King Jr.; and novelist and poet, Robert Penn Warren. Lawrence Jackson's *Ralph Ellison: The Emergence of Genius* (2002) is a biography that emphasizes Ellison's connection to the political Left in the 1930s and '40s; Kenneth Warren's *So Black and So Blue: Ralph Ellison and the Occasion of Criticism* (2003) reads Ellison as a writer of his times.

Political interests shape Barbara Foley's *Wrestling with the Left: The Making of Ralph Ellison's Invisible Man* (2010) and the critical essays collected by Lucas E. Morel in *Ralph Ellison and the Raft of Hope* (2004); music focuses Horace A. Porter's *Jazz Country: Ralph Ellison in America* (2001). *Ulysses in Black* (2008) by Patrice D. Rankin considers Ellison's debts to the classics. Lena Hill's *Visualizing Blackness and the Creation of the African American Literary Tradition* (2014), based on extensive archival and biographical research, argues for the centrality of Ellison's interest in and practice of the visual arts.

Louise Erdrich

Erdrich is best known for her novels but she has also published several poetry collections, short stories, children's books, and two memoirs, *The Blue Jay's Dance: A Birth Year* (1995), her account of becoming a mother, and *Birds and Islands in Ojibwe Country* (2003).

Approaches to Teaching the Works of Louise Erdrich (2004), edited by Greg Sarris, Connie A. Jacobs, and James R. Giles, provides a fine pedagogical overview. Erdrich's fiction is set more extensively in the Native American tradition by Louis Owens in *Other Destinies: Understanding the American Indian Novel* (1992), in the essays edited by Allan Chavkin in *The Chippewa Landscape of Louise Erdrich* (1999), and in *Studies in the Literary Achievement of Louise Erdrich, Native American Writer: Fifteen Critical Essays* (2008), edited by Brajesh Sawhney. Interview material can be found in *Conversations with Louise Erdrich and Michael Dorris* (1994), edited by Allan Chavkin and Nancy Feyl Chavkin. Peter G. Beidler and Gay Barton provide a general overview in *A Reader's Guide to the Novels of Louise Erdrich* (2006).

Allen Ginsberg

Ginsberg's poetry is gathered in *Collected Poems, 1947–1980* (1984), *White Shroud: Poems, 1980–1985* (1986), and *Death and Fame: Poems 1993–1997* (1999). His individual volumes, with the exception of *Empty Mirror* (1961), have been issued in the now unmistakable City Lights paperbacks. *Deliberate Prose: Selected Essays, 1952–1995* (2000) is a useful complement to the poetry, as are the many published selections from his journals and letters. Particularly helpful are his lively interviews: *Composed on the Tongue: Literary Conversations 1967–1977* (1980), edited by Donald Allen, and *Spontaneous Mind: Selected Interviews, 1958–1996* (2001), edited by David Carter. Notable among the published letters are *Jack Kerouac and Allen Ginsberg: The Letters* (2011), which includes both sides of this very early correspondence, brilliantly edited by Bill Morgan and David Stanford; and *The Selected Letters of Allen Ginsberg and Gary Snyder* (2008), edited by Bill Morgan. Ginsberg's photography can be found in *Photographs: Allen Ginsberg* (1991), among other collections.

Jane Kramer's *Allen Ginsberg in America* (1969) is a brilliant documentary piece on Ginsberg in the 1960s. Biographies include Michael Schumacher's *Dharma Lion: A Critical Biography of Allen Ginsberg* (1997); Graham Caveney's *Screaming with Joy* (2001); and Bill Morgan's *I Celebrate Myself: The Somewhat Private Life of Allen Ginsberg* (2007). Connections to religion are explored in Amy Hungerford's *Postmodern Belief* (2011), John Lardas's *The Bop Apocalypse* (2001) and in Tony Trigillio's *Allen Ginsberg's Buddhist Poetics* (2007). On Ginsberg and race, see the first chapter of Timothy Yu's *Race and the Avant-Garde: Experimental and Asian American Poetry Since 1965* (2009). On *Howl* and its aftermath, see *The Poem That Changed America: Howl Fifty Years Later* (2006), edited by Jason Shinder.

Louise Glück

Poems 1962–2012 (2013) is the best omnibus edition of Glück's work, compiling the poetry collections in the original order they appeared. Glück's collection of essays, *Proofs and Theories* (1994), is an indispensable companion to her work, both for its discussions of poetic vocation and for its description of the autobiographical contexts of specific poems.

Critical discussion of Glück's poetry can be found in Upton Lee's *The Muse of Abandonment* (1998), Joanne Diehl's edited volume, *On Louise Glück: Change What You See* (2005), and Daniel Morris's *The Poetry of Louise Glück: A Thematic Introduction* (2006). Helen Vendler's collection of essays on poetry, *Soul Says* (1995), includes commentary-reviews of Glück's work. Elizabeth Dodd's *The Veiled Mirror and The Woman Poet: H. D., Louise Bogan, Elizabeth Bishop, and Louise Glück* (1992) contains a chapter on Glück. Jesse Zuba's chapter on Glück's poetry in *The First Book: Twentieth-Century Poetic Careers in America* (2016) examines how the idea of the poet's first book informs her poetics throughout her career.

Joy Harjo

Harjo's selected poems, *How We Became Human: New and Selected Poems 1975–2001* (2002), is a good introduction to her large body of work. In *Secrets from the Center of the World* (1989), she wrote the text to accompany Steven Strom's photographs of the southwestern landscape. Her memoir is *Crazy Brave: A Memoir* (2013). She has also edited an anthology of Native American women's writing, *Reinventing the Enemy's Language: Contemporary Native Women's Writing of North America* (1997). Two collections of interviews are especially helpful: *Soul Talk, Song Language: Conversations with Joy Harjo* (2011), edited by Tanaya Winder; and Laura Coltelli's edited collection, *The Spiral of Memory* (1990). Commentary on the contexts of Harjo's work appears in Paula Gunn Allen's *The Sacred Hoop: Recovering the Feminine in American Indian Traditions* (1986), Norma Wilson's *The Nature of Native American Poetry* (2001), and Dean Rader's *Engaged Resistance: American Indian Art, Literature, and Film from Alcatraz to the NMAI* (2011).

Michael S. Harper

Harper's poetry collections have been gathered in *Songlines in Michaeltree: New and Collected Poems* (2001) and selected in the much slimmer volume *Selected Poems* (2005), which may serve as a good introduction to his work. With Anthony Walton, Harper edited *Every Shut Eye Ain't Asleep: An Anthology of Poetry by African Americans Since 1945* (1994) and *The Vintage Book of African American Poetry* (2000); with Robert Stepto, he edited a collection of African American literature, art, and scholarship, *Chants of Saints* (1976).

A conversation about Harper's work can be found in Joanne Gabbin's edited *The Furious Flowering of African American Poetry* (1999). The *Worcester Review* (35.1/2) published a special issue on Harper's work, titled "Michael Harper: Sacred Geometries" (2014).

Robert Hayden

Hayden's *Collected Poems* appeared in 1985; his *Collected Prose* appeared the previous year. Both were edited by Frederick Glaysher. Fred M. Fetrow's *Robert Hayden* (1984) is a critical study of Hayden's work. Essays on Hayden's work appear in *Robert Hayden: Essays on the Poetry* (2003), edited by Robert Chrisman and Laurence Goldstein; and in Harold Bloom's edited volume *Robert Hayden* (2005).

Patricia Highsmith

Highsmith wrote twenty-two novels, and published nine collections of short stories. Readers may begin with *Patricia Highsmith: Selected Novels and Short Stories* (2010) *and Uncollected Short Stories* (2002). She discusses craft in *Plotting and Writing Suspense Fiction* (1966).

There are two Highsmith biographies: *Beautiful Shadow: A Life of Patricia Highsmith* (2004), by Andrew Wilson, and *The Talented Miss Highsmith: The Secret Life and Serious Art of Patricia Highsmith* (2009), by Joan Schenkar. A useful reader's guide is Russell Harrison, *Patricia Highsmith* (1997). Fiona Peters give a psychoanalytic reading in *Anxiety and Evil in the Work of Patricia Highsmith* (2011). Readers can find an open-access cluster of essays in the online journal *Post45*, "On Patricia Highsmith" (2012) edited by Tom Perrin and Mary Esteve, with contributions from Mark Seltzer, Mary Esteve, and Michael Trask. The following critics place Highsmith in a larger context: Michael Trask, in *Camp Sites* (2013); Leonard Cassuto, in *Hard-Boiled Sentimentality* (2009); Marco Abel, in *Violent Affect: Cinema, Literature, and Critique* (2007); and George Haggerty, in *Queer Gothic* (2006).

Randall Jarrell

Jarrell's *Complete Poems* was published in 1969, and a *Selected Poems* appeared in 1991. A selection of Jarrell's brilliant critical essays is available in *No Other Book* (1999), edited by Brad Leithauser. His novel satirizing American academic life, *Pictures from an Institution*, appeared in 1954. *Randall Jarrell's Book of Stories*, an anthology of Jarrell's favorite stories and narrative poems, was published in 1958 with a substantial introductory essay by Jarrell, and republished by the *New York Review of Books* in 2002. Steven Burt and Hannah Brooks-Motl edited Jarrell's writings and lectures on the poet W. H. Auden in *Randall Jarrell on W. H. Auden* (2005), which includes worthwhile essays by the writer Adam Gopnick and by Burt that frame the history and significance of Jarrell's engagement with Auden.

Some of the most valuable commentary on Jarrell's life and work is to be found in a memorial volume of essays edited by Robert Lowell, Peter Taylor, and Robert Penn Warren, *Randall Jarrell, 1914–1965* (1967). William Pritchard's fine *Randall Jarrell: A Literary Life* (1990) illumines Jarrell's life and work, as does Mary Randall's *Remembering Randall* (1999). Critical discussion of Jarrell's work appears in Thomas Travisano's *Midcentury Quartet* (1999). Stephen Burt's *Randall Jarrell and His Age* (2002) examines the poet's entire oeuvre, including previously undiscovered essays and poems.

Jack Kerouac

Kerouac published numerous novels, poetry collections, and works of nonfiction; his most famous novel is *On the Road* (1957). Kerouac also recorded his poetry for a number of LPs many of which have been re-released in newer media and are widely available. In 2004, Douglas Brinkley edited *Windblown World: The Journals of Jack Kerouac, 1947–1954,* and in 2007, Howard Cunnell restored and edited an important first draft of *On the Road, On the Road: The Original Scroll* (2007).

John Tytell's *Naked Angels: The Lives and Literature of the Beat Generation* (1983) situates Kerouac in his historical and critical context, as do Raj Chandarlapaty's *The Beat Generation and Counterculture* (2009) and Ann Charters and Samuel Charters's *Brother-Souls* (2010). Stylistic analyses of Kerouac are undertaken in Regina Weinrich's *The Spontaneous Prose of Jack Kerouac* (1987), Michael Hrebeniak's *Action Writing: Jack Kerouac's Wild Form* (2006), and Tim Hunt's *The Textuality of Soulwork* (2014). Kerouac's friend Carolyn Cassady has written a memoir, *Off the Road* (1990), as has Edie Kerouac-Parker, *You'll Be Okay: My Life with Jack Kerouac* (2007). Among many biographies, the best include Barry Gifford and Lawrence Lee's excellent *Jack's Book: Jack Kerouac in the Lives and Words of His Friends* (1978), Tom Clark's *Jack Kerouac* (1984), Gerald Nicosia's *Memory Babe* (1983), Ann Charters's *Jack Kerouac* (1987), and Jorge García-Robles's *At the End of the Road: Jack Kerouac in Mexico* (2014). Kerouac's papers are housed in the Berg Collection of the New York Public Library.

Edward P. Jones

Jones has published two short-story collections and one epic novel, *The Known World*. His work has been discussed in a couple of dozen critical articles available through major library search engines. His interviews provide the best companion to the fiction: see Maryemma Graham, "An Interview with Edward P.

Jones," in *African American Review* 42.3/4 (2008); Lawrence P. Jackson, "An Interview with Edward P. Jones," *African American Review* 34.1 (2000); Angela Elam, "To Make a Story: An Interview with Edward P. Jones," in *New Letters* 74.1 (2007/8). His excellent interview with Terry Gross of National Public Radio's "Fresh Air" (November 11, 2003) can be found online.

Maxine Hong Kingston

Beginning with *The Woman Warrior* (1976) and as recently as *Fifth Book of Peace* (2003), Maxine Hong Kingston has blended together elements of memoir and fiction. Her early works were first received as autobiography, though Kingston scholars now recognize important fictive elements. *Tripmaster Monkey: His Fake Book* (1989) is her most obvious novel. Essays Kingston wrote in 1978 appear as *Hawai'i One Summer* (1999). *I Love a Broad Margin to My Life* (2011) is an autobiography that uses poetry to address the author's concerns about aging. Shirley Geok-lin Lim edited *Approaches to Teaching Kingston's "The Woman Warrior"* (1991); also helpful is Sidonie Smith's *A Poetics of Women's Autobiography: Marginality and the Fictions of Self-Representation* (1987). More cognizant of fiction's role in Kingston's writing is *Articulate Silences: Hisaye Yamamoto, Maxine Hong Kingston, and Joy Kogawa* (1993) by King-Kok Cheung and *Writing Tricksters* (1997) by Jeanne Rosier Smith. Kingston is discussed in Christopher Lee's *The Semblance of Identity: Aesthetic Mediation in Asian-American Literature* (2012).

Jamaica Kincaid

Kincaid is the author of five novels, a collection of short stories, *At the Bottom of the River* (1983), and many works of autobiographical nonfiction and reportage, much of which was originally published in the *New Yorker*. Her essay "On Seeing England for the First Time" (originally published in *Transition* magazine in 1991) was selected by Susan Sontag for *The Best American Essays* (1992).

Critical discussion of Kincaid's work includes Moira Ferguson's *Jamaica Kincaid: Where the Land Meets the Body* (1994), Lisa Paravisini-Gebert's *Jamaica Kincaid: A Critical Companion* (1999), Justin D. Edwards's *Understanding Jamaica Kincaid* (2007), and Mary Ellen Snodgrass's *Jamaica Kincaid: A Literary Companion* (2008). *My Brother* (1997), Kincaid's nonfictional account of her brother's AIDS diagnosis and death, plays a significant role in Katherine Stanton's *Cosmopolitan Fictions: Ethics, Politics, and Global Change in the Works of Kazuo Ishiguro, Michael Ondaatje, Jamaica Kincaid, and J. M. Coetzee.*

Galway Kinnell

Kinnell wrote more than twenty books of poetry, from *What a Kingdom Was* (1960) to *Strong Is Your Hold* (2006). His book-length poem *The Book of Nightmares* (1971) is rarely anthologized but marks a significant contribution to poetry of the Vietnam era. Kinnell's *Selected Poems* (1980) won both a Pulitzer Prize and a National Book Award; *New Selected Poems* (2001) focuses on Kinnell's poetry of the 1960s and '70s. Selections from interviews with Kinnell were published in *Walking Down the Stairs* (1978).

Critical works on Kinnell include Lee Zimmerman's *Intricate and Simple Things: The Poetry of Galway Kinnell* (1987); *On the Poetry of Galway Kinnell: The Wages of Dying* (1987), edited by Howard Nelson; *Critical Essays on Galway Kinnell* (1996), edited by Nancy Tuten; and Katarzyna Malecka's *Death in the Works of Galway Kinnell* (2008).

Yusef Komunyakaa

Komunyakaa's first poetry collection was *Dedications and Other Dark Horses* (1977); his most recent is *The Emperor of Water Clocks* (2015). With Martha Collins he has translated Nguyen Quang Thieu's *The Insomnia of Fire* (1992). With Sascha Feinstein he has edited two volumes of jazz poetry. In 2000 he published *Blue Notes: Essays, Interviews, and Commentaries*. He wrote a verse play of *Gilgamesh* (2006), which he produced as a stage adaptation with Chad Garcia.

Critical discussions of his work include Angela M. Salas's *Flashback Through the Heart: The Poetry of Yusef Komunyakaa* (2004). His work is set into a broader context by Wai Chee Dimock, "Gilgamesh's Planetary Turns" in *The Planetary Turn: Relationality and Geoaesthetics in the Twenty-First Century*, edited by Amy J. Elias and Christian Moraru (2015) and by Stephen Burt, "2001: 'Comrades, Be Not in Mourning': Twenty-First-Century Free Verse," in *New Literary History of America*, edited by Greil Marcus and Werner Sollors (2009).

Jhumpa Lahiri

Lahiri's collections of stories are *Interpreter of Maladies* (1999) and *Unaccustomed Earth* (2008); her novels are *The Namesake* (2003) and *The Lowland* (2013). *In Other Words*, a collection of her autobiographical essays, originally written in Italian and translated by Ann Goldstein, appeared in 2016.

Criticism of her fiction is found in *Transnational Asian American Literature: Sites and Transits* (2006), edited by Shirley Geok-lin Lim et al., and in *Literary Gestures: The Aesthetic in Asian American Writers* (2007), edited by Rocío G. Davis and Sue-Im Lee. In the context of theoretical arguments about neoliberalism and cosmopolitanism, Susan Koshy has published two articles about Lahiri: "Neoliberal Family Matters," *American Literary History* 25.2 (2013): 36, and "Minority Cosmopolitanism," *PMLA* 126.3 (2011): 592–609. Min Song sets Lahiri's work in the context of a generation of Asian American writers born after 1965 in *The Children of 1965: On Writing, and Not Writing, as an Asian American* (2013).

Li-Young Lee

Lee is the author of four books of poetry and a memoir, *The Winged Seed: A Remembrance* (1995). Gerald Stern's foreword to the collection *Rose* (1986) provides useful biographical material on Lee. *Breaking the Alabaster Jar: Conversations with Li-Young Lee* (2006) is a collection of interviews, edited by Earl G. Ingersoll. Other interviews with Lee appear in *Words Matter: Conversations with Asian American Writers* (2000), edited by King-Kok Cheung and *Poetry in Person: Twenty-Five Years of Conversation with America's Poets* (2010), edited by Alexander Neubauer.

Critical studies of Lee's verse can be found in Steven G. Yao's *Foreign Accents: Chinese American Verse from Exclusion to Postethnicity* (2010) and Dorothy J. Wang's *Thinking Its Presence: Form, Race, and Subjectivity in Contemporary Asian American Poetry* (2014).

Ursula K. Le Guin

Le Guin is the author of twenty-two novels, beginning with *Rocannon's World* (1966) and ending with *Lavinia* (2008). Her short stories appear in eleven collections; these are joined by *Tales from Earthsea* (2001), which presents a novella and new short stories. She has also authored fifteen books for children, ten poetry collections, two plays, four works of translation, and several volumes of nonfiction, including *The Language of Night: Essays on Fantasy and Science Fiction* (1979, 1989) and *Cheek by Jowl: Talks and Essays on How Fantasy Matters* (2009). *Understanding Ursula K. Le Guin* (1990) by Elizabeth Cummins Cogell is a good introduction; more critically sophisticated are James Bittner's *Approaches to the Fiction of Ursula K. Le Guin* (1984) and Bernard Selinger's *Le Guin and Identity in Contemporary Fiction* (1988). Two recent essays on Le Guin can be found in *Green Planets: Ecology and Science Fiction* (2014), edited by Gerry Canavan and Kim Stanley Robinson.

Denise Levertov

Levertov was a prolific poet, with more than twenty volumes of poetry from *Double Image* (1946) to *The Great Unknowing: Last Poems* (1999). *Making Peace* (2005) is a posthumous collection of Levertov's poems, edited by Peggy Rosenthal, and *The Collected Poems of Denise Levertov* was published in 2013. *The Poet in the World* (1973), *Light Up the Cave* (1981), and *Tesserae: Memories and Suppositions* (1995) include essays on Levertov's own work, autobiographical fragments, reviews of other poets, and some theoretical essays. Levertov's *New and Selected Essays* appeared in 1992. *The Letters of Denise Levertov and William Carlos Williams* (1998), *The Letters of Robert Duncan and Denise Levertov* (2004), and *Conversations with Denise Levertov*, a 1998 collection of interviews, mark important contributions to the study of Levertov's life and work.

The most authoritative biography of Levertov is Donna Krolik Hollenberg's *A Poet's Revolution: The Life of Denise Levertov* (2013), and critical studies include *Critical Essays on Denise Levertov* (1991), edited by Linda Wagner-Martin, Audrey T. Rogers' *Denise Levertov: The Poetry of Engagement* (1993), Linda Arbaugh's *Poetics of the Feminine* (1994) and *Denise Levertov: New Perspectives* (2000), edited by Anne Little and Susie Paul.

Philip Levine

Levine's *New Selected Poems* (1991) gathers work from many of his volumes of poetry. A memoir, *The Bread to Time: Toward an Autobiography*, appeared in 1994. His translations from the Spanish are available in *Tarumba: The Selected Poems of Jaime Sabines* (with Ernest Trejo, 1979) and *Off the Map: Selected Writings of Gloria Fuertes* (with Ada Long, 1984). A collection of Levine's interviews, *Don't Ask*, appeared in 1981. Another collection of essays and interviews, *So Ask*, appeared in 2002.

Christopher Buckley's *On the Poetry of Philip Levine* appeared in 1991, and Edward Hirsch's "The Visionary Poetics of Philip Levine and Charles Wright" appears in *The Columbia History of American Poetry* (1993). David St. John's *Where Angels Come Toward Us* (1995) contains discussion of Levine's work. *Coming Close: Forty Essays on Philip Levine* (2013), edited by Mari L'Esperance and Tomas Q. Morin, is a collection of tributes from Levine's students and fellow writers.

Barry Lopez

Lopez is a prolific writer and has published numerous works of fiction and nonfiction; as is the case with many creative nonfiction writers, his work often combines these genres. Teachers might well begin with Lopez's interviews, many of which can be found in William Tydeman's *Conversations with Barry Lopez: Walking the Path of Imagination* (2013), and Mike Newell's *No Bottom: In Conversation with Barry Lopez* (2008).

Critical discussions of Lopez can also be found in turn-of-the-twenty-first-century "ecocriticism"; he is discussed in the context of a whole body of environmental writing in many of the essays in *The Ecocriticism Reader: Landmarks in Literary Ecology*, edited by Cheryll Glotfelty and Harold Fromm (1996) and in Lawrence Buell's important book, *Writing for an Endangered World: Literature, Culture, and the Environment in the U. S. and Beyond* (2001). See also Scot Slovic's *Seeking Awareness in American Nature Writing: Henry Thoreau, Annie Dillard, Edward Abbey, Wendell Berry, and Barry Lopez* (1992) and Willliam H. Rueckert's essay, "Barry Lopez and the Search for a Dignified and Honorable Relationship with Nature," in *Earthly Words: Essays on Contemporary American Nature and Environmental Writers*, edited by John Cooley (1994).

Audre Lorde
The Collected Poems of Audre Lorde (2000) brings together Lorde's poetry, while a collection of Lorde's essays and speeches, *Sister Outsider* (1984), provides a powerful context for reading her work. Her autobiographical writing includes *The Cancer Journals* (1980) and *Zami: A New Spelling of My Name* (1982). A useful interview with Lorde appears in *Women Writers at Work* (1998), edited by George Plimpton.

Critical studies of Lorde's work appear in Mari Evans's edited *Black Women Writers* (1984) and Cassie Steele's *We Heal From Memory: Sexton, Lorde, Anzaldúa, and the Poetry of Witness* (2000). Cheryl Clark's *"After Mecca": Women Poets and the Black Arts Movement* (2005) and Kelly Lynch Reames's *Women and Race in Contemporary U.S. Writing: From Faulkner to Morrison* (2009) situate Lorde within American literary history, while Catherine A. John's *Clear Word and Third Sight* (2003) considers Lorde within the context of diasporic writing.

Robert Lowell
Lowell published numerous books of verse, and he adapted works by Aeschylus, Racine, Hawthorne, and Melville for the stage. His *Collected Prose* (1987) is an indispensable companion to the poetry and contains valuable essays on the work of other writers. An edition of Lowell's letters, edited by Saskia Hamilton, appeared in 2005, and *Words in the Air: The Complete Correspondence Between Elizabeth Bishop and Robert Lowell* (2008), edited by Saskia Hamilton and Thomas Travisano, documents one of the great literary friendships in twentieth-century poetry.

Useful early critical works on Lowell are Stephen Yenser's *Circle to Circle* (1975) and Steven Axelrod's *Robert Lowell: Life and Art*

(1978). *Robert Lowell: A Collection of Critical Essays* (1968), edited by Thomas Parkinson, includes an important interview with the poet, and *The Critical Response to Robert Lowell* (1999), edited by Steven Axelrod, provides an overview of criticism on the work. Thomas Travisano's *Midcentury Quartet* (1999), Nick Halpern's *Everyday and Prophetic* (2003), and Helen Vendler's *Last Looks, Last Books* (2010) all contain chapters on Lowell that situate him in the midcentury American poetic tradition. Paula Hayes studies Lowell's style in *Robert Lowell and the Confessional Voice* (2013). Ian Hamilton's biography, *Robert Lowell*, appeared in 1982.

Bernard Malamud
Malamud published eight novels and four short-story collections. Robert Giroux has also edited Malamud's unfinished novel and a number of short fictions in *The People and Uncollected Stories* (1990), together with *The Complete Stories* (1997). Alan Cheuse and Nicholas Delbanco edited his essays in *Talking Horse: Bernard Malamud on Life and Work* (1996).

A comprehensive overview of Malamud's works and their place in the American tradition is provided by Edward A. Abramson in *Bernard Malamud Revisited* (1993). Sanford Pinsker's *Jewish-American Fiction, 1917–1987* (1992) examines the author's specifically Jewish-American contribution. Critical essays are collected in Leslie A. Field and Joyce W. Field's edited *Bernard Malamud* (1975), Joel Salzberg's edited *Critical Essays on Bernard Malamud* (1987), and Evelyn Avery's edited *The Magic Worlds of Bernard Malamud* (2001). Janice Malamud has written *My Father Is a Book: A Memoir of Bernard Malamud* (2006), and Philip Davis has authored a comprehensive biography, *Bernard Malamud: A Writer's Life* (2007). Rita N. Kosofsky has compiled *Bernard Malamud: A Descriptive Bibliography* (1991).

David Mamet
Mamet has written numerous plays and screenplays and has directed multiple films. He has also written nonfiction prose, including political critique and Torah commentary, and novels and novellas as well. In 1998 Mamet published *Three Uses of the Knife: On the Nature and Purpose of Drama*.

C. W. E. Bigsby's *David Mamet* (1985) is an excellent introduction. Critical studies of Mamet's style include Michael Stephens's *The Dramaturgy of Style* (1986), which considers Mamet's use of voice, and Bruce Barton's *Imagination in Transition* (2005), which considers Mamet's move to film. Criticism, bibliographies, and interviews about *Glengarry Glen*

Ross are available in Leslie Kane's edited *David Mamet's Glengarry Glen Ross: Text and Performance* (1996), and Kane gives a biographical reading of Mamet in *Weasels and Wisemen: Education, Ethics, and Ethnicity in David Mamet* (1999). Ira Nadel provides a biography in *David Mamet: A Life in the Theatre* (2008).

James Merrill

An edition of Merrill's *Collected Poems* (2001), edited by J. D. McClatchy and Stephen Yenser, gathers the collected poems, with the exception of his book-length epic *The Changing Light at Sandover* (1982). *Collected Novels and Plays* (2002) and *Collected Prose* (2004) present Merrill's fiction, drama, and nonfiction. Langdon Hammer's *James Merrill: Life and Art* (2015) is the major biography. Useful critical essays on Merrill appear in David Kalstone's *Five Temperaments* (1977), David Lehman and Charles Berger's edited *James Merrill: Essays in Criticism* (1983), and Guy Rotella's edited *Critical Essays on James Merrill* (1996). Stephen Yenser's book-length study of Merrill's work, *The Consuming Myth* (1987), remains invaluable. Recent critical work includes Timothy Materer's *James Merrill's Apocalypse* (2000), Reena Sastri's *James Merrill: Knowing Innocence* (2007), and Helen Vendler's *Last Looks, Last Books* (2010).

W. S. Merwin

Merwin's *Collected Poems* appeared in a two-volume Library of America edition in 2013, while *The Miner's Pale Children* (1970) is an important example of Merwin's prose. Merwin has also published the autobiographical prose collections *Unframed Original* (1982) and *Summer Doorways* (2005), while *Regions of Memory* (1987) combines memoir and commentary on the work of poetry. In addition, Merwin has published numerous translations from a variety of languages, many of which can be found in his *Selected Translations 1948–2010* (2013). *Conversations with W. S. Merwin*, a collection of interviews edited by Michael Wutz and Hal Crimmel, appeared in 2015.

Critical essays on Merwin's work are gathered in *W. S. Merwin: Essays on the Poetry* (1987), edited by Cary Nelson and Ed Folsom. Book-length studies of Merwin's poetry include Edward J. Brunner's *Poetry as Labor and as Privilege* (1991) and H. L. Hicks's *W. S. Merwin* (1997). Jane Frazier's *From Origin to Ecology: Nature and the Poetry of W. S. Merwin* (1999) and Leonard M. Scigaj's *Sustainable Poetry* (1999) examine Merwin's nature poetry.

Arthur Miller

Miller's early plays are brought together in *Arthur Miller's Collected Plays* (1957), which also includes a lengthy and useful introduction by Miller. Later dramas are available in *Collected Plays, 1957–1981* (1981), *Collected Plays 1944–1961* (2006), and individual volumes. Miller also wrote many nonfiction pieces, as well as radio plays, screenplays, short stories, and the novel *Focus* (1945). *Echoes Down the Corridor: Collected Essays, 1944–2000* appeared in 2000. Miller published *Salesman in Beijing*, an account of the production of *Death of a Salesman* in China, in 1984, and an autobiography, *Timebends: A Life*, in 1987.

Martin Gottfried's *Arthur Miller: His Life and Work* (2003) is the major biography, while Enoch Brater's biography *Arthur Miller: A Playwright's Life and Works* (2004) provides useful performance histories for Miller's plays. The best recent analysis of Miller's work is found in Christopher Bigsby's *Arthur Miller, 1915–1962* (2010), supplemented by Bigsby's *Arthur Miller: A Critical Study* (2005) and his edited *The Cambridge Companion to Arthur Miller* (1997). Also helpful are the essays in Steven R. Centola's edited *The Achievement of Arthur Miller: New Essays* (1995). *Death of a Salesman* is analyzed in-depth in Brenda Murphy's *Miller: Death of a Salesman* (1995), Matthew C. Rodané's *Approaches to Teaching Miller's Death of a Salesman* (1995), Eric J. Sterling's edited *Arthur Miller's Death of a Salesman* (2008), and Peter L. Hays's *Arthur Miller's Death of a Salesman* (2008). Jeffrey D. Mason treats Miller in the context of American political history in *Stone Tower: The Political Theater of Arthur Miller* (2008).

N. Scott Momaday

Momaday has published a number of novels, including the Pulitzer Prize–winning *House Made of Dawn* (1968), numerous memoirs and essay collections, and multiple volumes of poetry. *Three Plays: The Indolent Boys, Children of the Sun, and The Moon in Two Windows* appeared in 2007. Momaday has also written books for children, edited editions of other writers, and written the commentary for photographer David Muench's *Colorado: Summer, Fall, Winter, Spring* (1973).

Kenneth Lincoln's *Native American Renaissance* (1985) locates Momaday at the beginning of a renaissance in Native American literature, while book-length studies of Momaday include Matthias Schubnell's *N. Scott Momaday: The Cultural and Literary Background* (1985) and Jim Charles's *Reading, Learning, and Teaching N. Scott Momaday* (2007). Valuable interviews with Momaday include Joseph Bruchac's "The Magic of Words: An Interview with N. Scott Momaday" in Bruchac's edited *Survival This Way: Interviews with American Indian Poets* (1987) and Louis Owens's "N. Scott Momaday" in *This Is about Vision: Interviews with Southwestern Writers* (1990), edited by William Balassi, John F. Crawford, and Annie O. Eysturoy. Arnold Krupat's *The Voice in the Margin: Native American Literature and the Canon* (1989) compares Momaday's autobiographical writing with Leslie Marmon Silko's, while Sean Kicummah Teuton's *Red Land, Red Power: Grounding Knowledge in the Native American Novel* (2008) explores place and embodiment in Momaday's work. *House Made of Dawn* is analyzed in depth in Susan Scarberry-Garcia's *Landmarks of Healing: A Study of "House Made of Dawn"* (1990), Louis Owens's *Other Destinies: Understanding the American Indian Novel* (1992), and Scott B. Vickers's *Native American Identities* (1998). Phyllis S. Morgan's *N. Scott Momaday: An Annotated Bio-Bibliography* (2010) provides a biography of Momaday and a comprehensive bibliography of critical works about Momaday.

Toni Morrison

Morrison has published eleven novels, from *The Bluest Eye* (1970) to *God Help the Child* (2015), and three books for children. Her plays are *Dreaming Emmett* (1986), *Desdemona* (2011), and a libretto, *Margaret Garner* (2005). Morrison has written and edited a number of critical works, including the seminal *Playing in the Dark: Whiteness and the Literary Imagination* (1992) and *Race-ing Justice, En-gendering Power: Essays on Anita Hill, Clarence Thomas, and the Construction of Social Reality* (editor, 1992). Her *Nobel Lecture in Literature* was published in 1994.

General book-length studies include Trudier Harris's *Fictions and Folklore: The Novels of Toni Morrison* (1991), John N. Duvall's *The Identifying Fictions of Toni Morrison* (2000), and Linda Wagner-Martin's *Toni Morrison: A Literary Life* (2015), which covers Morrison's first ten novels and emphasizes her role as a public intellectual. Henry Louis Gates Jr. and K. A. Appiah have edited the useful *Toni Morrison: Critical Perspectives Past and Present* (1993). Victoria Burrows's *Whiteness and Trauma* (2004) and Evelyn Jaffe Schreiber's *Race, Trauma, and Home in the Novels of Toni Morrison* (2010) address trauma and race in Morrison's work, while La Vinia Delois Jenning's *Toni Morrison and the Idea of Africa* (2008) and K. Zauditu-Salassie's *African Spiritual Traditions in the Novels of Toni Morrison* (2009) examine the Africanist presence in Morrison's novels. Gender in Morrison's fiction is analyzed in Andrea Reilly's *Toni Morrison and Motherhood* (2004) and Susan Neal Mayberry's *Can't Love What I Criticize: The Masculine and Morrison* (2007), while religion in Morrison's fiction is

treated in John A. McClure's *Partial Faiths: Postsecular Fiction in the Age of Pynchon and Morrison* (2007) and Amy Hungerford's *Postmodern Belief: American Literature and Religion since 1960* (2010).

Flannery O'Connor

O'Connor's novels and stories are collected in a volume in the Library of America series edited by Sally Fitzgerald (1988), while her letters are collected in *The Habit of Being: The Letters of Flannery O'Connor* (1979). *The Presence of Grace, and Other Book Reviews* (1983) collects some of her critical prose, as does *Mystery and Manners* (1969), edited by Sally Fitzgerald and Robert Fitzgerald. A *Prayer Journal* (2013), edited by W.A. Sessions, reproduces O'Connor's journal from 1946 to 1947.

Jean W. Cash provides a biography in *Flannery O'Connor: A Life* (2003), as does Brad Gooch in *Flannery* (2009). Critical overviews include Richard Giannone's *Flannery O'Connor, Hermit Novelist* (2000), Sarah Gordon's *Flannery O'Connor: The Obedient Imagination* (2000), and *Flannery O'Connor's Radical Reality* (2006), edited by Jan Nordby Grettund and Karl-Heinz Westarp. Studies of religion in O'Connor's fiction include Lorine M. Gertz's *Flannery O'Connor, Literary Theologian* (2000), Susan Srigley's *Flannery O'Connor's Sacramental Art* (2004), and Jordan Cofer's *The Gospel According to Flannery O'Connor* (2014). Donald E. Hardy explores embodiment in *The Body in Flannery O'Connor's Fiction* (2007), while Jon Lance Bacon situates O'Connor in American history in *Flannery O'Connor and Cold War Culture* (1993). *Flannery O'Connor: A Descriptive Bibliography* (1981) was compiled by David Farmer, and *Flannery O'Connor: The Contemporary Reviews* (2009), edited by R. Neil Scott, Irwin H. Streight, and M. Thomas Inge, collects contemporaneous reviews of O'Connor's fiction. A chapter in Mark McGurl's *The Program Era* (2009) reads some of her early stories and discusses the importance of her time at the Iowa Writer's Workshop.

Frank O'Hara

Frank O'Hara was the author of seven books of poetry, the most influential of which were *Meditations in an Emergency* (1957) and *Lunch Poems* (1964). *The Collected Poems of Frank O'Hara* was first published in 1971, and his art criticism can be found in *Art Chronicles 1954–1966* (1975) and *In Memory of My Feelings: Frank O'Hara on American Art* (1999). O'Hara also wrote autobiographical fragments, literary manifestos, and plays, some of which are collected in *Selected Poems* (2008), edited by Mark Ford.

Brad Gooch's *City Poet: The Life and Times of Frank O'Hara* (1993) remains the definitive biography of the poet. David Lehman's *The Last Avant-Garde: The Making of the New York School of Poets* (1998) provides valuable contexts for O'Hara's work. An informative critical study is Marjorie Perloff's *Frank O'Hara: Poet among Painters* (1977), and noteworthy readings of O'Hara's personal poems can be found in Michael W. Clune's *American Literature and the Free Market, 1945–2000* (2010) and Oren Izenberg's *Being Numerous: Poetry and the Ground of Social Life* (2011).

Sharon Olds
Olds's recent poetry collections are *One Secret Thing* (2008) and *Stag's Leap* (2012), while *Strike Sparks: Selected Poems 1980–2002* (2004) brings together work from her previous volumes. Her Judith Stonach Memorial Lecture on the Teaching of Poetry, *What Does an Elegy Do?*, was published in book form in 2010. Informative interviews with Olds appear in the online journal *Salon* (1999), in Alan Fox's edited *Rattle Conversations: Interviews with Contemporary American Poets* (2008), and in Betsy Sussler's edited *BOMB: The Author Interviews* (2014). Alicia Ostriker discusses Olds's erotic discourse in *Dancing at the Devil's Party: Essays on Poetry, Politics, and the Erotic* (2000).

Mary Oliver
Volumes 1 (2004) and 2 (2005) of *New and Selected Poems* contain selections from Oliver's volumes of poetry between 1963 and 2005, and Oliver has published a number of poetry collections since. Oliver has written two guides to poetry, *A Poetry Handbook* (1994) and *Rules for the Dance* (1998), and a collection of mixed nonfiction and poetry, *Long Life: Essays and Other Writings* (2004). J. Scott Bryson's edited *Ecopoetry: A Critical Introduction* (2002) and Bryson and Roger Thompson's edited *Twentieth-Century American Nature Poets* (2008) each contain a chapter on Oliver's nature poetry.

Simon J. Ortiz
Ortiz has published numerous volumes of poetry and short stories, and he has also edited two collections, *These Hearts, These Poems* (1984) and *Speaking for the Generations: Native Writers on Writing* (1998).

A discussion of Ortiz's poetry appears in Kenneth Lincoln's seminal *Native American Renaissance* (1983) and in Lucy Maddox's "Native American Poetry" in *The Columbia History of American Poetry* (1993), while David King Dunaway and Sara Spurgeon's edited *Writing the Southwest* (2003) contains a biography of Ortiz. Jace Weaver, Craig S. Womack, and Robert Warrior use Ortiz as their launching point in *American Indian Literary Nationalism* (2006), to which Ortiz contributed the Forward. Susan Berry Brill de Ramírez and Evelina Zuni Lucero's edited *Simon J. Ortiz: A Poetic Legacy of Indigenous Continuance* (2009) collects recent critical essays on Ortiz.

Grace Paley
The Collected Stories (1994) draw on Paley's three major volumes of short fiction. Other stories and poems appear (with paintings by Vera B. Williams) in *Long Walks and Intimate Talks* (1991). *Begin Again: Collected Poems* (2000) brings together the work from two early volumes of Paley's poetry. *Just As I Thought* (1998) collects Paley's essays. With Robert Nichols she published *Here and Somewhere Else: Stories and Poems* (2007). *Fidelity* (2008) was her last volume of poetry. *Conversations with Grace Paley* (2007) collects Paley's interviews.

The three major studies of Paley's fiction are *Grace Paley's Life Stories: A Literary Biography* (1993) by Judith Arcana, *Grace Paley: A Study of the Short Fiction* (1990) by Neil D. Isaacs, and *Grace Paley: Illuminating the Dark Lives* (1990) by Jacqueline Taylor.

Robert Pinsky
Pinsky's *The Figured Wheel: New and Collected Poems 1966–1996* (1996) gathers work from four collections, as well as presenting new poems and selections from his translations. He has published two book-length translations, the prize-winning *The Inferno of Dante: A New Verse Translation* (1994) and, together with Robert Hass, a translation of the Polish poet Czeslaw Milosz's *The Separate Notebook* (1984). He retells the story of King David from the Bible in *The Life of David* (2005). Pinsky's two volumes of criticism, *The Situation of Poetry: Contemporary Poetry and Its Traditions* (1975) and *Poetry and the World* (1988), illuminate his work as well as that of the writers he discusses. He is also the author of *The Sounds of Poetry* (1998), *Democracy, Culture, and the Voice of Poetry* (2002), and *Singing School: Learning to Write (and Read) Poetry by Studying with the Masters* (2013). Pinsky edited the collection *America's Favorite Poems* (1999).

Discussion of Pinsky's work can also be found in Robert Archambeau's *Laureates and Heretics: Six Careers in American Poetry: Yvor Winters, Robert Pinsky, James McMichael, Robert Hass, John Matthias, John Peck* (2010).

Sylvia Plath

Plath's books of poetry have been gathered in *Plath's Collected Poems*, edited by Ted Hughes (1983). Plath's novel, *The Bell Jar*, was first published in England in 1963; her short fiction and other prose writing was collected posthumously by Hughes in *Johnny Panic and the Bible of Dreams* (1977). Plath's mother, Aurelia Schober Plath, edited the useful *Letters Home: Correspondence 1950–63* (1975). Karen Kukil edited *The Unabridged Journals of Sylvia Plath, 1950–1962* (2000).

Among the biographical and critical studies of Plath's work are Judith Kroll's *Chapters in a Mythology* (1976), Anne Stevenson's *Bitter Fame: The Undiscovered Life of Sylvia Plath* (1988), Jacqueline Rose's *The Haunting of Sylvia Plath* (1993), and Heather Clark's *The Grief of Influence: Sylvia Plath and Ted Hughes* (2011). Amy Hungerford's *The Holocaust of Texts: Genocide, Literature, and Personification* (2003) discusses the meaning of and responses to Plath's Holocaust imagery. In *The Art of Cruelty: A Reckoning* (2011), Maggie Nelson situates Plath's poetry in a lineage of violent and transgressive art in the twentieth century, emphasizing the ethical core of her work. *The Cambridge Companion to Sylvia Plath*, edited by Jo Gill, appeared in 2006.

Thomas Pynchon

Pynchon has published nine novels, from *V.* (1963) to *Bleeding Edge* (2013). *Slow Learner* (1984) collects early stories.

Book-length studies of Pynchon's early novels are Thomas H. Schaub's *Pynchon, The Voice of Ambiguity* (1981), David Seed's *The Fictional Labyrinths of Thomas Pynchon* (1988), and Alan N. Brownlie's *Thomas Pynchon's Narratives: Subjectivity and the Problems of Knowing* (2000). Newer critical essays are collected by Niran Abbas in *Thomas Pynchon: Reading from The Margins* (2003) and Ian D. Copestake in *American Postmodernity: Essays on the Recent Fiction of Thomas Pynchon* (2003). David Cowart's *Thomas Pynchon and the Dark Passages of History* (2012) and Joanna Freer's *Thomas Pynchon and American Counterculture* (2014) situate Pynchon in postwar history. The fiction's relationship to contemporary religious thought is explored by John A. McClure in *Partial Faiths: Postmodern Fiction in the Age of Pynchon and Morrison* (2007); C. Namwali Serpell considers Pynchon's ambiguity in *Seven Modes of Uncertainty* (2014); and Mark Greif sets his work among mid-twentieth-century writers considering the "crisis of man" in *The Age of the Crisis of Man: Thought and Fiction in America, 1933–1973* (2015).

Ishmael Reed

Reed has published ten novels, from *The Free-Lance Pallbearers* (1967) to *Juice!* (2011), and six collections of poetry, including *New and Collected Poems* (2006). Reed's plays are collected in *Ishmael Reed, The Plays* (2009). Reed has published ten essay collections, a libretto called *Gethsemane Park* (1998), and two travelogues. He has edited numerous anthologies, including *The Before Columbus Foundation Fiction and Poetry Anthology* (1991).

Jay Boyer's booklet *Ishmael Reed* (1993) is a good introduction, while Patrick McGee's *Ishmael Reed and the Ends of Race* (1997) focuses on gender and race. Jerome Klinkowitz studies Reed's polemics in *Literary Subversions* (1985), while Reginald Martin takes a more theoretical approach in *Ishmael Reed and the New Black Aesthetic Critics* (1987). Pierre-Damien Mvuyekure explores Reed's spiritualism and innovations in *The "Dark Heathenism" of the American Novelist Ismael Reed: African Voodoo as American Literary HooDoo* (2007), as does Glenda Carpio in *Laughing Fit to Kill: Black Humor in the Fictions of Slavery* (2008). Elizabeth A. Settle and Thomas A. Settle have compiled *Ishmael Reed: A Primary and Secondary Bibliography* (1982), useful for locating the early critical response.

Adrienne Rich

The Fact of a Doorframe: Poems 1950–2001 (2002) collects five decades of Rich's poetry. Her last volume of poetry was *Tonight No Poetry Will Serve: Poems 2007–2010* (2010). Several valuable collections gather Rich's essays, lectures, and speeches: *On Lies, Secrets, and Silence* (1979), *Blood, Bread, and Poetry* (1986), *What Is Found There?: Notebooks on Poetry and Politics* (1993), *Arts of the Possible* (2001), *Poetry and Commitment: An Essay* (2007), and *A Human Eye: Essays on Art in Society* (2009). Rich is also the author of an important study, *Of Woman Born: Motherhood as Experience and Institution* (1976).

Valuable critical essays and an interview appear in *Adrienne Rich's Poetry* (1975), edited by Barbara Charlesworth Gelpi and Albert Gelpi. Other studies are *Reading Adrienne Rich* (1984), edited by Jane Roberta Cooper; Paula Bennett's *My Life, a Loaded Gun: Female Creativity and Feminist Poetics* (1986); Margaret Dickie's *Stein, Bishop, & Rich: Lyrics of Love, War, & Place* (1997); Molly McQuade's *By Herself: Women Reclaim Poetry* (2000); *"Catch If You Can Your Country's Moment": Recovery and Regeneration in the Poetry of Adrienne Rich* (2007), edited by William S. Waddell; and Sylvia Henneberg's *The*

Creative Crone: Aging and the Poetry of May Sarton and Adrienne Rich (2010).

Theodore Roethke

The Collected Poems of Theodore Roethke was published in 1966. *Dirty Dinkey and Other Creatures: Poems for Children*, edited by B. Roethke and Stephen Lushington, appeared in 1973. Useful comments on poetic tradition and his own poetic practice are to be found in several collections of Roethke's prose: *On the Poet and His Craft: Selected Prose of Theodore Roethke* (1965), edited by Ralph J. Mills Jr.; *Straw for the Fire: From the Notebooks of Theodore Roethke, 1948–63* (1972), edited by David Wagoner; and *The Selected Letters of Theodore Roethke* (1970), edited by Mills.

Among the useful studies of Roethke's work are *Theodore Roethke: Essays on the Poetry* (1965), edited by Arnold Stein, and Laurence Lieberman's *Beyond the Muse of Memory: Essays on Contemporary Poets* (1995). Allan Seager's *The Glass House* (1968) contains useful biographical material.

Philip Roth

Roth is the author of twenty-seven novels and novellas, beginning with *Goodbye, Columbus* (1959) and concluding with *Nemesis* (2010). *The Facts: A Novelist's Autobiography* (1988) and *Patrimony* (1991) are Roth's memoirs. *Reading Myself and Others* (1975) and *Shop Talk* (2001) collect essays and interviews.

Philip Roth (1982) by Hermione Lee is an excellent introduction, as is *Understanding Philip Roth* (1990) by Murray Baumgarten and Barbara Gottfried. *Philip Roth and the Jews* (1996) by Alan Cooper considers religious and cultural dimensions of the author's work. The broad sweep of Roth's career is covered by Mark Shechner in *Up Society's Ass, Copper: Reading Philip Roth* (2003), Deborah Shostak in *Philip Roth—Countertexts, Counterlives* (2004), and David Brauner in *Philip Roth* (2007). Elaine B. Safer's *Mocking the Age: The Later Novels of Philip Roth* (2006) discusses his experiments in narrative, while Ross Posnock handles controversy in *Philip Roth's Rude Truth* (2005). David Gooblar's *The Major Phases of Philip Roth* (2011) and Patrick Hayes's *Philip Roth: Fiction and Power* (2014) evaluate the full scope of Roth's career. Claudia Roth Pierpont's biography *A Writer and His Books* (2013) situates Roth's fiction in his personal history.

George Saunders

In addition to his several short-story collections, Saunders has published an illustrated fable, *The Brief and Frightening Reign of Phil* (2005), and a book for children, *The Very Persistent Gappers of Frip* (2006). His essays are an excellent accompaniment to the fiction; see the collection *The Braindead Megaphone* (2007). Readers may also be interested in his published commencement speech: *Congratulations, by the way: Some Thoughts on Kindness* (2014). He has collaborated on two stage adaptations of stories, "Jon" and "CommComm," with playwright Seth Bockley.

Very little criticism exists to date; two articles in mainstream academic journals are David Rando, "George Saunders and the Postmodern Working Class," in *Contemporary Literature* 53.3 (2012); and Sarah Pogell, "'The Verisimilitude Inspector': George Saunders as the New Baudrillard?" *Critique: Studies in Contemporary Fiction* 52.4 (2011).

Anne Sexton

Sexton authored eight volumes of poetry starting with *To Bedlam and Part Way Back* (1960) and ending with *The Awful Rowing toward God* (1975). *Complete Poems* appeared in 1981. Diane Wood Middlebrook's biography, *Anne Sexton* (1991), and Sexton's *A Self-Portrait in Letters* (1977) give useful biographical material. Important interviews and critical essays are to be found in J. D. McClatchy's *Anne Sexton: The Artist and Her Critics* (1978) and Diane Hume George's *Sexton: Selected Criticism* (1988). An interview with Sexton appears in *Women Writers at Work* (1998), edited by George Plimpton.

Sam Shepard

Shepard is the author of thirty-eight plays, starting with *Cowboys* (1964) and ending with *Ages of the Moon* (2009). His short stories and other nondramatic writings appear in five collections.

The aesthetics of Shepard's playwriting and its surrealist influences are analyzed by Emma Creedon in *Sam Shepard and the Aesthetics of Performance* (2015). James A. Crank conducts a wide-ranging study of Shepard's theatrical work in *Understanding Sam Shepard* (2012). Shepard's place in theatrical history is assessed by Robert J. Andreach in *Creating the Self in the Contemporary American Theatre* (1998). Also helpful are Doris Auerbach's *Sam Shepard, Arthur Kopit, and the Off Broadway Theater* (1982), Stephen J. Bottoms's *The Theatre of Sam Shepard: States of Crisis* (1998), Laura Graham's *Sam Shepard: Theme, Image, and the Director* (1995), Lynda Hart's *Sam Shepard's Metaphorical Stages* (1987), and Ron Mottram's *Inner Landscapes: The Theater of Sam Shepard* (1984).

Leslie Marmon Silko

Silko has written three novels, six collections of stories and poetry, and a Kindle Singles novella called *Oceanstory* (2011). *Yellow*

Woman and a Beauty of the Spirit (1996) collects Silko's essays on contemporary Native American life. *The Turquoise Ledge* (2010) is Silko's memoir. *Lullaby*, coauthored with Frank Chin, was dramatically adapted and produced in San Francisco in 1976. *Delicacy and Strength of Lace*, a collection of letters between Silko and the poet James Wright, edited by Anne Wright, was published in 1985, while Ellen L. Arnold edited *Conversations with Leslie Marmon Silko* in 2000. Silko's work also appeared in *Yellow Woman* (1993), edited by Melody Graulich.

Introductions to Silko's work are Per Seyersted's *Leslie Marmon Silko* (1980), Melody Graulich's edited *'Yellow Woman': Leslie Marmon Silko* (1993), and Louise K. Barnett and James L. Thorson's edited *Leslie Marmon Silko* (1999). Catherine Rainwater's *Dreams of Fiery Stars* (1999), Sean Kicummah Teuton's *Red Land, Red Power: Grounding Knowledge in the American Indian Novel* (2008), and Mishuana Goeman's *Mark My Words: Native Women Mapping Our Nations* (2013) situate Silko within Native American literary culture. Rosemary A. King's *Border Influences from the Mexican War to the Present* (2001) and Claudia Sadowsky-Smith's *Border Fictions* (2008) locate Silko in the history of America's borderlands.

Charles Simic
New and Selected Poems: 1962–2012 (2013) gathers much of the work from Simic's numerous collections of poetry. He has also published several volumes of essays and memoirs and is a prolific translator of Serbian poetry into English.

Critical discussions of Simic's poetry can be found in Bruce Weigl's *Charles Simic: Essays on the Poetry* (1996), Peter Stitt's *Uncertainty and Plentitude: Five Contemporary Poets* (1997), and Anthony Hecht's *Melodies Unheard* (2003).

Tracy K. Smith
In addition to her three collections of poetry, Smith has published *Ordinary Light: A Memoir* (2015). Her interview with Charles Henry Rowell, "'Something We Need': An Interview with Tracy K. Smith," was published in *Callaloo* 27.4 (2004).

Gary Snyder
Snyder's many volumes of poetry have been published by several different presses, often with duplication of poems. *Riprap*, originally published in 1959, is most easily obtained in *Riprap and Cold Mountain Poems* (1965, 1991). Snyder has also published important prose collections dealing with ecology, such as *Earth House Hold* (1969) and *A Place in*

Space: Ethics, Aesthetics, and Watersheds (1995). A useful gathering of Snyder's prose and poetry appears in *The Gary Snyder Reader* (1999). *The Real Work: Interviews and Talks 1964–1979*, edited by William Scott McLean, appeared in 1980. Another essay collection, *Back on Fire*, appeared in 2007.

Helpful critical discussion of Snyder's work can be found in Patrick Murphy's *A Place for Wayfaring: The Poetry and Prose of Gary Snyder* (2000); Timothy Gray's *Gary Snyder and the Pacific Rim: Creating Countercultural Community* (2006); Paige Tovey's *Transatlantic Eco-Romanticism of Gary Snyder* (2013); and *Sense of the Whole: Reading Gary Snyder's Mountains and Rivers without End* (2015), edited by Mark Gonnerman.

Art Spiegelman
Spiegelman's most important books include the two parts of *Maus, a Survivor's Tale*, published in 1986 and 1991, and *In the Shadow of No Towers* (2004). *Be a Nose* (2009) excerpts Spiegelman's sketchbooks, while *MetaMaus* (2011) contains background material about *Maus*. *Breakdowns* (2008) and *Co-Mix* (2013) anthologize Spiegelman's shorter works. *MetaMaus* (2011) provides source materials, interview, and background about the making of *Maus*.

Joseph Witek locates Spiegelman's importance in the evolution of underground comics and the graphic novel in *Comic Books as History: The Narrative Art of Jack Jackson, Art Spiegelman, and Harvey Pekar* (1989), as do Charles Hatfield in *Alternative Comics: An Emerging Literature* (2005) and Hillary Chute in *Disaster Drawn* (2016). Amy Hungerford's chapter on *Maus*, "Surviving Rego Park," in *The Holocaust of Texts: Genocide, Literature, and Personification* (2003) discusses the relationship between history and identity in Spiegelman's work. Alan Rosen analyzes *Maus* in *Sounds of Defiance: The Holocaust, Multilingualism, and the Problem of English* (2005), as do contributors to Jeet Heer and Kent Worcester's *A Comic Studies Reader* (2009). Kristiaan Versluys analyzes Spiegelman's response to 9/11 in *Out of the Blue: September 11 and the Novel* (2009), while Nicole Stamant considers Spiegelman as an American memoirist in *Serial Memoir: Archiving American Lives* (2014).

Amy Tan
Tan has published six novels, from *The Joy Luck Club* (1989) to *The Valley of Amazement* (2013), and two children's books, *The Moon Lady* (1992) and *Sagwa, the Chinese Siamese Cat* (1994). *The Opposite of Fate: A Book of Musings* (2003) is nonfiction. Critical

overviews of Tan and her work are found in E. D. Huntley's *Amy Tan: A Critical Companion* (1998) and Amy Ling's *Between Worlds: Women Writers of Chinese Ancestry* (1990). James Nagel studies *The Joy Luck Club* in *The Contemporary American Short-Story Cycle* (2001), as does Magali Cornier Michael in *New Visions of Community in Contemporary American Fiction* (2006). Mary Jane Hurst locates Tan within American quests for identity in *Language, Gender, and Community in Late-Twentieth-Century Fiction* (2011).

Natasha Trethewey

In addition to her several poetry collections, Trethewey has published a book of nonfiction, *Beyond Katrina: A Meditation on the Mississippi Gulf Coast* (2010). *Conversations with Natasha Trethewey* (2013), edited by Joan Wylie, gathers useful interviews. Two of Trethewey's essays, "On Whitman, Civil War Memory, and My South," in Ivy Wilson's edited collection *Whitman Noir: Black America and the Good Gray Poet* (2014), and "Why I Write," in *South Central Review* 31.1 (2014) may be of special interest to teachers. *The Southern Quarterly* 54.4 (2013), collects critical essays in a special issue on Trethewey's work in honor of her naming as U.S. poet laureate.

John Updike

Updike authored twenty-three novels including the popular *Rabbit* tetralogy: *Rabbit, Run* (1960), *Rabbit Redux* (1971), *Rabbit Is Rich* (1981), and *Rabbit at Rest* (1990). His two-volume *Collected Stories* was published in 2013. Updike's early poems are gathered in *Collected Poems 1953–1993* (1993), while *Americana: and Other Poems* (2001) and *Endpoint and Other Poems* (2009) are later works. Fourteen collections of criticism and four children's books round out his oeuvre.

Donald J. Greiner's thorough examination of the early canon appears in his *John Updike's Novels* (1984) and *The Other John Updike: Poems/Short Stories/Prose/Plays* (1981). Longer views are taken by James A. Schiff in *John Updike Revisited* (1998) and by William Pritchard in *Updike: America's Man of Letters* (2000). *Conversations with John Updike* (1993), edited by James Plath, collects thirty-two interviews with the writer between 1959 and 1993. Jack De Bellis has prepared *The John Updike Encyclopedia* (2007) and, with Michael Broomfield, *John Updike: A Bibliography* (2007). In 2006, Stacey Olster edited *The Cambridge Companion to John Updike*, and Adam Begley provides a compendious chronicle of the author's life in *Updike* (2014). Updike's papers have been deposited in the Houghton Library at Harvard University.

Kurt Vonnegut

Vonnegut was the author of fourteen novels. His short stories are collected in *Canary in a Cat House* (1961), *Welcome to the Monkey House* (1968), and *Bagombo Snuff Box* (1999). His essays fill four volumes: *Wampeters, Foma & Granfalloons* (1974), *Palm Sunday* (1981), *Fates Worse Than Death* (1991), and *A Man Without a Country* (2005). *Happy Birthday, Wanda June* (1971) is a play, while *Between Time and Timbuktu* (1972) is a television script, prefaced by Vonnegut, drawing on his fiction. *Sun/Moon/Star* (1980), with illustrations by Ivan Chermayeff, is a book for children. *God Bless You, Dr. Kevorkian* (1999) collects Vonnegut's radio satires; *Like Shaking Hands with God* (1999) is his dialogue with social activist Lee Stringer. Noncanonical rejected stories from the early 1950s have been published posthumously as *Armageddon in Retrospect* (2008), *Look at the Birdie* (2009), and *While Mortals Sleep* (2010).

Jerome Klinkowitz surveys Vonnegut's career in *The Vonnegut Effect* (2004), studies his essays in *Vonnegut in Fact* (1998), and undertakes cultural analysis in *Kurt Vonnegut's America* (2009). Specific theses are argued by Leonard Mustazza in *Forever Pursuing Genesis: The Myth of Eden in the Novels of Kurt Vonnegut* (1990), Leonard Broer in *Sanity Plea: Schizophrenia in the Novels of Kurt Vonnegut* (1989, revised 1994), and Todd Davis in *Kurt Vonnegut's Crusade* (2006), Lawrence R. Broer in *Vonnegut and Hemingway: Writers at War* (2011), and Robert T. Talley in *Kurt Vonnegut and the American Novel: A Postmodern Iconography* (2011). Broad samples of criticism are made by editor David Simmons in *New Critical Essays on Kurt Vonnegut* (2009) and by editor Leonard Mustazza in *The Critical Response to Kurt Vonnegut* (1994), while Vonnegut's later work (including his public spokesmanship) are examined in *The Vonnegut Chronicles* (1996), edited by Peter J. Reed and Marc Leeds. Loree Rackstraw's *Love As Always, Kurt* (2009) is a memoir. Asa B. Pieratt Jr., Julie Huffman-Klinkowitz, and Jerome Klinkowitz have compiled *Kurt Vonnegut: A Comprehensive Bibliography* (1987).

Alice Walker

Walker has published seven novels, including *The Color Purple* (1982), three short-story collections, and eight collections of poetry. Her *Collected Poems* appeared in 2005. Walker's literary essays are collected in *In Search of Our Mothers' Gardens* (1983), *Living by the Word* (1988), and *Anything We Love Can Be Saved* (2000). She has also written *Warrior Marks: Female Genital Mutilation and the Sexual Blinding of Women* (1987, with Pratibha Parmar), *We Are the Ones We Have Been Waiting*

For (2006), and *Overcoming Speechlessness: A Poet Encounters the Horror in Rwanda, Eastern Congo, and Palestine/Israel* (2010). Her children's books include an illustrated *To Hell with Dying* (1988), *Finding the Green Stone* (1991), and a biography, *Langston Hughes, American Poet* (1974). Rudolph P. Byrd has edited a collection of interviews, *The World Has Changed: Conversations with Alice Walker* (2010).

Evelyn C. White's *Alice Walker: A Life* (2004) is a comprehensive biography. Good samplings of scholarship on Walker are offered by Henry Louis Gates Jr. and K. Anthony Appiah's edited *Alice Walker: Critical Perspectives Past and Present* (1993) and Lillie P. Howard's edited *Alice Walker and Zora Neale Hurston: The Common Bond* (1993). *Alice Walker* (2011) is Maria Lauret's book-length study, while Melanie L. Harris's *Gifts of Virtue, Alice Walker, and Womanist Ethics* (2010) analyzes Walker's politics of "womanism."

Robert Penn Warren

Warren wrote numerous books of poetry, fiction, and criticism. An edition of Warren's *Collected Poems*, edited by John Burt, appeared in 1998, and Burt has also edited a volume of Warren's *Selected Poems* (2001). Warren's best-known novels are *All the King's Men* (1946) and *World Enough and Time* (1950). His Thomas Jefferson Lectures, *Democracy and Poetry*, appeared in 1975. Also available is a collection of interviews, *Robert Penn Warren Talking* (1980), edited by Floyd Watkins and John Tiers.

Early critical studies of Warren's poetry are Victor Strandberg's *The Poetic Vision of Robert Penn Warren* (1977), Calvin Bedient's *In the Heart's Last Kingdom* (1986), and James H. Justus's *The Achievement of Robert Penn Warren* (1981). More recent critical studies include Lesa Carnes Corrigan's *Poem of Pure Imagination: Robert Penn Warren and the Romantic Tradition* (1999), David Madden's edited *The Legacy of Robert Penn Warren* (2000), and James A. Grimshaw Jr.'s *Understanding Robert Penn Warren* (2001). Warren's literary criticism is treated in Michael Kreyling's *Inventing Southern Literature* (1998) and Charlotte H. Beck's *Robert Penn Warren: Critic* (2006).

Eudora Welty

Welty was the author of five novels, including the Pulitzer Prize–winning *The Optimist's Daughter* (1972), and one novella, *The Robber Bridegroom* (1942). The *Collected Stories of Eudora Welty* (1980) was followed by two more collections of short stories and one collection of autobiographical essays, *One Writer's Beginnings* (1984). Among Welty's many volumes of nonfiction prose are *The Eye of the Story: Selected Essays and Reviews* (1978), *and A Writer's Eye: Collected Book Reviews* (1994).

Biographies of Welty include Ann Waldron's *Eudora: A Writer's Life* (1998) and Suzanne Marrs's *Eudora Welty: A Biography* (2005). Critical introductions to Welty's fiction are available in Marrs's *One Writer's Imagination: The Fiction of Eudora Welty* (2002), Gail Mortimer's *Daughter of the Swan: Love and Knowledge in Eudora Welty's Fiction* (1994), Jan Nordby Gretlund's *Eudora Welty's Aesthetics of Place* (1994), and Ruth D. Weston's *Gothic Traditions and Narrative Techniques in the Fiction of Eudora Welty* (1994). The collection of essays *Eudora Welty and Politics: Did the Writer Crusade?* (2001), edited by Suzanne Marrs and Harriet Pollack, seeks to revise the critical consensus that Welty avoided political and historical engagement in her writing and photography.

Richard Wilbur

Wilbur's recent poetry collections are *Anterooms* (2010) and *The Nutcracker* (2012), while *Collected Poems 1943–2004* (2004) gathers work from his earlier volumes. He has also published the prose collections *Responses* (1976) and *The Catbird's Song* (1997), and he has translated Molière, Corneille, and Racine from the French. A collection of interviews, *Conversations with Richard Wilbur*, edited by William Butts, appeared in 1990.

Critical discussion of Wilbur's work can be found in Wendy Salinger's edited *Richard Wilbur's Creation* (1983), John B. Hougen's *Ecstasy Within Discipline: The Poetry of Richard Wilbur* (1995), and Anthony Hecht's *Melodies Unheard* (2003). Scott Knickerbocker discusses Wilbur's nature poetry in *Ecopoetics: The Language of Nature, and Nature of Language* (2012).

Tennessee Williams

Most of Williams's plays are collected in the seven-volume *The Theatre of Tennessee Williams* (1971–81). Some later dramas are available in separate editions; a few others are still to be published. Other writings include a novel, *The Roman Spring of Mrs. Stone* (1950); his short-story collections are brought together in *Collected Stories* (1986), edited by Gore Vidal; a volume of screenplays, *Stopped Rocking* (1984); and poems collected as *In the Winter of Cities* (1964) and *Androgyne, Mon Amour* (1977). *Where I Live: Selected Essays*, edited by Christine R. Day and Bob Woods, appeared in 1978. *The Selected Letters of Tennessee Williams, Volume I, 1920–1945* (2000) was edited by Albert J. Devlin and Nancy M. Tischler. Margaret Bradham Thornton has edited Williams's *Notebooks* (2007).

John Lahr's *Tennessee Williams: Mad Pilgrimage of the Flesh* (2014) is the best biographical account. Williams's own *Memoirs* (1975) is interestingly revelatory but is not a reliable biographical guide. Judith J. Thompson provides a Jungian analysis of the plays and identifies structural patterns in *Tennessee Williams' Plays: Memory, Myth, and Symbol* (1987, rev. 2002). Time relationships are explored by Patricia Schroeder in *The Presence of the Past in Modern American Drama* (1989). Williams's homosexuality functions in a complex way in his writing, as demonstrated by Michael Paller's *Gentlemen Callers: Tennessee Williams; Homosexuality, and Mid-Twentieth Century Drama* (2005) and Michael S. D. Hopper's *Sexual Politics in the Work of Tennessee Williams* (2012). The difficult aesthetics of Williams's late plays are examined by Annette Saddik in *Tennessee Williams's Theatre of Excess: The Strange, the Crazed, The Queer* (2015). Williams's female characters are analyzed by James Grissom in *Follies of God: Tennessee Williams and the Women of the Fog* (2015). Brenda Murphy edited *Tennessee Williams: Critical Insights* (2010); Philip G. Kolin edited *Tennessee Williams: A Guide to Research and Performance* (1998); Matthew C. Rodané prepared The *Cambridge Companion to Tennessee Williams*.

August Wilson

Wilson is the author of ten plays, starting with *Ma Rainey's Black Bottom* (1985) and ending with *Radio Golf* (2005). *Ma Rainey's Black Bottom* (1985), *Fences* (1985), *Joe Turner's Come and Gone* (1986) have been collected with a preface by Wilson (*Three Plays*, 1991).

Temporality is examined by Harry J. Elam Jr. in *Past as Present in the Drama of August Wilson* (2006). Christopher Bigsby edited *The Cambridge Companion to August Wilson* (2007). Alan Nadel edited *August Wilson: Completing the Twentieth-Century Cycle* (2010). Mary Bogumil's *Understanding August Wilson* (2011) is a wide-ranging study of his work.

James Wright

Above the River: The Complete Poems (1992) collects the work in Wright's individual volumes of poetry, while an edition of his *Collected Prose*, edited by Anne Wright, was published in 1983. His letters appear in *A Wild Perfection: The Selected Letters of James Wright* (2008) and *The Delicacy and Strength of Lace: Letters Between Leslie Marmon Silko and James Wright* (2009), both edited by Anne Wright. Some of Wright's translations from the Spanish and German are available in *Twenty Poems of Georg Trakl* (1963), *Twenty Poems of Cesar Vallejo* (1964), and *Twenty Poems of Pablo Neruda* (with Robert Bly, 1968).

Dave Smith's edited *The Pure Clear Word: Essays on the Poetry of James Wright* (1982) and Peter Stitt and Frank Graziano's edited *James Wright: The Heart of the Light* (1990) collect critical essays on Wright. Laurence Lieberman's *Beyond the Muse of Memory* (1995) contains a good critical discussion of Wright.

PERMISSIONS ACKNOWLEDGMENTS

IMAGE CREDITS

P. 2: Roy Lichtenstein, *Blam*, Yale University Art Gallery, Gift of Richard Brown Baker, BA. 1935, (1995.32.9) © Estate of Roy Lichtenstein; p. 5: National Archives & Records Administration; p. 6: Keystone-France/Gamma-Keystone/Getty Images; p. 8: Courtesy of and copyright The Gordon Parks Foundation; p. 9: Bernard Gotfryd/Getty Images; p. 10 (left): Tony Linck/The LIFE Picture Collection/Getty Images; p. 10 (right): Margaret Bourke-White/The LIFE Picture Collection/Getty Images; p. 14: Courtesy of the California History Room, California State Library, Sacramento, California; p. 18 (left): Beinecke Rare Book and Manuscript Library, Yale University; p. 18 (right): Beinecke Rare Book and Manuscript Library, Yale University; p. 20: Grace Paley at Sarah Lawrence College. Photograph by Gary Gladstone. Courtesy of the Sarah Lawrence College Archives; p. 75: AP Photo; p. 158: Lisa Larsen/Time Life Pictures/Getty Images; p. 220: W. Eugene Smith/Time Life Pictures/Getty Images; p. 333: Henry W. and Albert A. Berg Collection of English and American Literature, The New York Public Library, Astor, Lenox and Tilden Foundations; p. 343 (left): Richard Petersen/Getty Image; p. 343 (right): Popperfoto/Getty Images; p. 486: Jack Manning/The New York Times/Redux; p. 733: © Roy Harte Jazz Archives/CTSIMAGES; p. 828: © Mosaic Records; p. 1142: © Robert Altman/The Image Works; p. 1167: Skeet McAuley; p. 1182: Kwaku Alston Photography, Inc.

COLOR INSERT CREDITS

C1 (top): Jackson Pollock, *Autumn Rhythm (Number 30)*, The Metropolitan Museum of Art, George A. Hearn Fund, 1957 (57.92), Photograph © 1998 The Metropolitan Museum of Art, © 2016 The Pollock-Krasner Foundation for the Visual Arts, Inc./Artists Rights Society (ARS), New York; C1 (bottom): Carl Van Vechten, used by permission of The Van Vechten Trust; C2: Roy Lichtenstein, *Blam*, Yale University Art Gallery, Gift of Richard Brown Baker, BA. 1935 (1995.32.9), © Estate of Roy Lichtenstein; p. C3 (top): Robert Rauschenberg, *Estate*, 1963 (oil & screen-printed inks on canvas), Robert Rauschenberg (1925–2008)/Philadelphia Museum of Art, Pennsylvania, PA, USA/Gift of the Friends of the Philadelphia Museum of Art, 1967/Bridgeman Images/Licensed by VAGA, New York, NY; C3 (bottom): Andy Warhol, *Campbell's Soup I (Tomato)* 1968, © 2016 The Andy Warhol Foundation for the Visual Arts, Inc./Artists Rights Society (ARS), New York/Photo: Digital Image © 2016 Museum Associates/LACMA/Licensed by Art Resource, NY; C4 (top): Corbis via Getty Images; C4 (bottom): Fritz Scholder, *The American Indian*, 1970, Indian Arts and Crafts Board Collection, Department of the Interior, Smithsonian National Museum of the American Indian, Washington, DC., Photo by Walter Larrimore; C5 (top): *Untitled*, 1981 (colour coupler print), Cindy Sherman (b. 1954)/Private Collection/Bridgeman Images; C5 (bottom): © James P. Blair/Corbis via Getty Images/VCG; C6: Faith Ringgold © 1986; C7: Jeff Wall, *After 'Invisible Man' by Ralph Ellison, the Prologue*, 1999–2001. Transparency in lightbox, 174.0 x 250.5 cm. Courtesy of the artist; C8 (top): Peter Morgan/Reuters/Newscom; C8 (bottom): Courtesy of Sudden Oak.

TEXT CREDITS

Edward Abbey: From "Havasu" from DESERT SOLITAIRE is reprinted by permission of Don Congdon Associates, Inc. Copyright © 1968 by Edward Abbey, renewed 1996 by Clarke Abbey.

Sherman Alexie: "Crow Testament" from ONE STICK SONG, copyright © 2000 by Sherman Alexie. "Sister Fire, Brother Smoke," # 3 from "Tourists," and "The Exaggeration of Despair" from THE SUMMER OF BLACK WIDOWS, copyright © 1996 by Sherman Alexie. "At Navajo Monument Valley Tribal School" and "Pawn Shop" from THE BUSINESS OF FANCY, copyright © 1992 by Sherman Alexie. Used by permission of Hanging Loose Press. "This Is What It Means to Say Phoenix, Arizona" from THE LONE RANGER AND TONTO FISTFIGHT IN HEAVEN, copyright © 1993, 2005 by Sherman Alexie. Used by permission of Grove/Atlantic, Inc. and the author. Any third party use of this material, outside of this publication, is prohibited. "Survivorman," copyright © 2009 by Sherman Alexie. Used by permission of the author. All rights reserved.

A. R. Ammons: "Corsons Inlet," copyright © 1963 by A. R. Ammons, "Easter Morning," copyright © 1979 by A. R. Ammons, "Singling and Doubling Together," copyright © 1983 by A. R. Ammons and "So I Said I am Ezra," copyright © 1955 by A.R. Ammons from THE SELECTED POEMS, EXPANDED EDITION by A. R. Ammons. "Part 2" from GARBAGE by A. R. Ammons. Copyright © 1993 by A. R. Ammons. Used by permission of W. W. Norton & Company, Inc. From "A Poem Is a Walk" by A. R. Ammons, first published in *Epoch*, vol. 18, Fall 1968. All rights reserved. Reprinted by permission of the Estate of A. R. Ammons c/o Writers Representatives LLC, New York, NY 10011. www.writersreps. com/permissions. All rights reserved.

Rudolfo Anaya: From BLESS ME, ULTIMA. Copyright © 1974 by Rudolfo Anaya. Published in hardcover, paperback, and ebook by Warner Books, an imprint of Hachette Book Group, in 1994; originally published by TQS Publications. Reprinted by permission of Susan Bergholz Literary Services, New York, NY and Lamy, NM. All rights reserved.

Gloria Anzaldúa: "La conciencia de la mestiza/Towards a New Consciousness," "How to Tame a Wild Tongue" and "El sonavabitche" from BORDERLAND/LA FRONTERA: THE NEW MESTIZA. Copyright © 1987, 1999, 2007, 2012 by Gloria Anazldúa. Reprinted by permission of Aunt Lute Books.

John Ashbery: "Illustration," from SOME TREES. Copyright © 1956, 1978 by John Ashbery. "Myrtle" from AND THE STARS WERE SHINING. Copyright © 1994 by John Ashbery. "Soonest Mended" from THE DOUBLE DREAM OF SPRING. Copyright © 1966, 1970 by John Ashbery. Reprinted by permission of Georges Borchardt, Inc., on behalf of the author and Carcanet Press Limited. Collected in COLLECTED POEMS: 1956–1987. "Self-Portrait in a Convex Mirror" from SELF-PORTRAIT IN A CONVEX MIRROR. Copyright © 1974 by John Ashbery. Used by permission of Viking Books, an imprint of Penguin Publishing Group, a division of Penguin Random House LLC and Carcanet Press Limited.

Index

American Literature since 1945

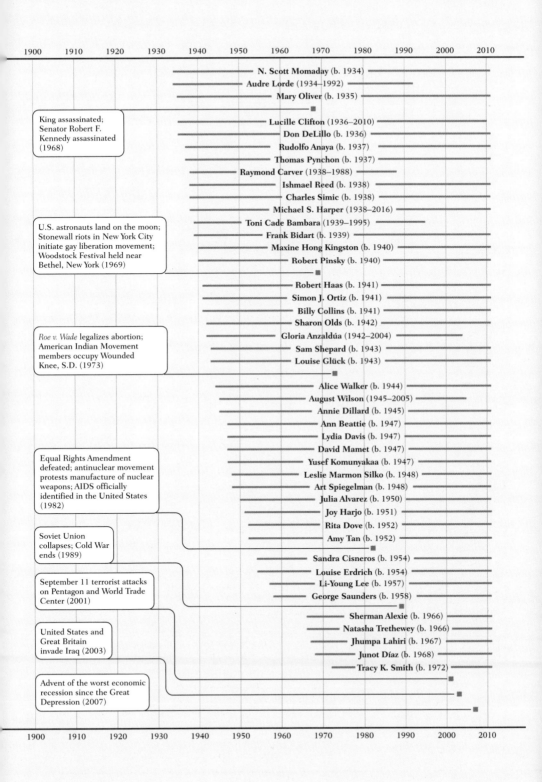

1900   1910   1920   1930   1940   1950   1960   1970   1980   1990   2000   2010

N. Scott Momaday (b. 1934)
Audre Lorde (1934–1992)
Mary Oliver (b. 1935)

King assassinated;
Senator Robert F.
Kennedy assassinated
(1968)

Lucille Clifton (1936–2010)
Don DeLillo (b. 1936)
Rudolfo Anaya (b. 1937)
Thomas Pynchon (b. 1937)
Raymond Carver (1938–1988)
Ishmael Reed (b. 1938)
Charles Simic (b. 1938)
Michael S. Harper (1938–2016)
Toni Cade Bambara (1939–1995)
Frank Bidart (b. 1939)
Maxine Hong Kingston (b. 1940)
Robert Pinsky (b. 1940)

U.S. astronauts land on the moon;
Stonewall riots in New York City
initiate gay liberation movement;
Woodstock Festival held near
Bethel, New York (1969)

Robert Haas (b. 1941)
Simon J. Ortiz (b. 1941)
Billy Collins (b. 1941)
Sharon Olds (b. 1942)
Gloria Anzaldúa (1942–2004)
Sam Shepard (b. 1943)
Louise Glück (b. 1943)

Roe v. Wade legalizes abortion;
American Indian Movement
members occupy Wounded
Knee, S.D. (1973)

Alice Walker (b. 1944)
August Wilson (1945–2005)
Annie Dillard (b. 1945)
Ann Beattie (b. 1947)
Lydia Davis (b. 1947)
David Mamet (b. 1947)
Yusef Komunyakaa (b. 1947)
Leslie Marmon Silko (b. 1948)
Art Spiegelman (b. 1948)
Julia Alvarez (b. 1950)
Joy Harjo (b. 1951)
Rita Dove (b. 1952)
Amy Tan (b. 1952)

Equal Rights Amendment
defeated; antinuclear movement
protests manufacture of nuclear
weapons; AIDS officially
identified in the United States
(1982)

Soviet Union
collapses; Cold War
ends (1989)

Sandra Cisneros (b. 1954)
Louise Erdrich (b. 1954)
Li-Young Lee (b. 1957)
George Saunders (b. 1958)

September 11 terrorist attacks
on Pentagon and World Trade
Center (2001)

Sherman Alexie (b. 1966)
Natasha Trethewey (b. 1966)
Jhumpa Lahiri (b. 1967)
Junot Díaz (b. 1968)
Tracy K. Smith (b. 1972)

United States and
Great Britain
invade Iraq (2003)

Advent of the worst economic
recession since the Great
Depression (2007)

1900   1910   1920   1930   1940   1950   1960   1970   1980   1990   2000   2010